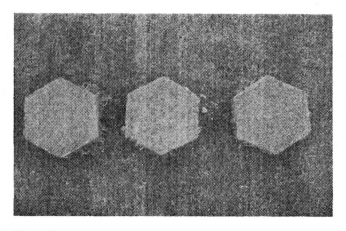

PLATE 1–1 Improved bermudagrasses such as Champion (left) and TifEagle (right) compared to the previous standard, Tifdwarf bermudagrass (middle), provide desirable putting surfaces under close mowing heights.

PLATE 1–2 Bentgrass is a popular putting green grass since it tolerates close mowing heights, has fine leaf texture, and provides a smooth playing surface.

PLATE 1–3 Kentucky bluegrass golf course fairway.

PLATE 2–1 Salinity effects on plants include leaves becoming thin, stiff, and dark green in color.

PLATE 2–2 Spotty stands of grass often develop when exposed to high salinity levels. This is most acute in poorly drained, low lying areas.

PLATE 2–3 Salinity damage to ryegrass.

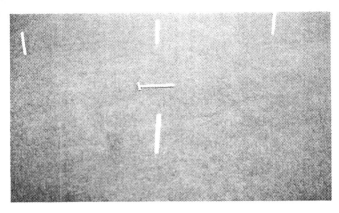

PLATE 10–1 Dark, blue-green colored turf from phosphorus deficiency (right) compared to normal bentgrass (left). Inadequate phosphorus inhibits normal carbohydrate utilization causing sugars to accumulate, leading to purple anthocyanin accumulation.

PLATE 10–4 Iron chlorosis often occurs in spring when turf shoots temporarily use more iron than the slowed turf roots can absorb from cold soils. High soil pH and/or excessive phosphorus levels also can contribute to iron chlorosis.

PLATE 10–2 Red fescue rooting under normal fertilization (left), minus nitrogen (middle), and minus phosphorus (right). Although topgrowth and color were reduced with the minus nitrogen treatments, root length and density increased.

PLATE 10–3 Healthy bermudagrass growth (left) compared to potassium-insufficient bermudagrass (right). Potassium deficiency in plants can be difficult to diagnose but typically involves poor growth, inadequate turf color retention, thin turf density, and leaf tips and margins that wither and die.

Best Golf Course Management Practices

Construction, Watering, Fertilizing, Cultural Practices, and Pest Management Strategies to Maintain Golf Course Turf with Minimal Environmental Impact

Second Edition

L.B. (Bert) McCarty

Department of Horticulture
Clemson University
Clemson, SC

PEARSON

Prentice
Hall

Upper Saddle River, New Jersey 07458

Library of Congress Cataloging-in-Publication Data

McCarty, L. B. (Lambert Blanchard), 1958-
   Best golf course management practices: construction, watering, fertilizing, cultural
practices, and pest management strategies to maintain golf course turf with minimal
environmental impact / L.B. (Bert) McCarty.—2nd ed.
      p. cm.
   Includes bibliographical references (p.) and index.
   ISBN 0-13-139793-1
   1. Golf courses—Management. 2. Turf management. I. Title.

GV975.5.M33 2004
796.352'06'9—dc22

2003064788

Editor-in-Chief: Stephen Helba
Executive Editor: Debbie Yarnell
Associate Editor: Kimberly Yehle
Managing Editor: Mary Carnis
Production Editor: Melissa Scott, Carlisle Publishers Services
Production Liaison: Janice Stangel
Director of Manufacturing and Production: Bruce Johnson
Manufacturing Buyer: Cathleen Petersen
Creative Director: Cheryl Asherman
Cover Design Coordinator: Christopher Weigand
Cover Designer: Christopher Weigand
Marketing Manager: Jimmy Stephens
Cover Image: Wade Hampton Golf Club located in Cashiers, NC. This Tom Fazio design is a creeping bertgrass facility located at an
elevation of 3,200 ft (960 m).

Pearson Prentice Hall™ is a trademark of Pearson Education, Inc.
Pearson® is a registered trademark of Pearson plc
Prentice Hall® is a registered trademark of Pearson Education, Inc.

Pearson Education LTD.
Pearson Education Australia PTY, Limited
Pearson Education Singapore, Pte. Ltd.
Pearson Education North Asia Ltd.
Pearson Education Canada, Ltd.
Pearson Educación de Mexico, S.A. de C.V.
Pearson Education—Japan
Pearson Education Malaysia, Pte. Ltd.

10 9 8 7 6 5 4 3 2 1
ISBN 0-13-139793-1

To those golf course superintendents who grow and maintain the best playing conditions in the world and to the students who should relentlessly pursue knowledge in turf management, personnel skills, and human relationships.

To my parents, family, students, and colleagues who have provided vast opportunities for me to learn and work.

To T. E. (Ed) Freeman, my mentor, my colleague, and my friend—you are dearly missed.

BRIEF CONTENTS

CONTENTS

CHAPTER 22 *Turfgrass Diseases* 545

CHAPTER 28   *Best Golf Course Environmental Protection Strategies*   743

PREFACE

Golf courses are continually increasing in number, as well as sophistication in terms of design, management, and increased scrutiny from the general public and regulatory agencies. Golf course management quality and intensity range from very low-maintained facilities to exquisite, highly maintained touring courses. Many resort courses rely on the tourist industry; however, on other courses, membership and daily fees are major sources of play. In these cases, the year-round conditions become very important.

This book is intended as a reference guide for golf course superintendents, assistants, club managers, green's committee members, students, and regulatory agencies in their efforts to grow and maintain some of the world's most prestigious courses. Authors with expertise in specific areas of turfgrass and environmental science have contributed to this book, making the information as complete and up-to-date as possible. However, management and pesticide recommendations are constantly being updated. New products, grasses, and management techniques continue to evolve, while older ones often disappear. Contact your State University Turf Specialist, County Cooperative Extension Service office, and attend the various Turfgrass Field Days and Turfgrass Association's Annual Conference and Trade Show for the latest recommendations.

The use of trade names in this publication is solely for the purpose of providing specific information. It is not a guarantee or warranty of the products named, and does not signify they are approved to the exclusion of others of suitable composition.

The pesticide recommendations presented in this publication were current with state and Federal regulations at the time of publication. The user is responsible for determining that the intended pesticide use is consistent with the directions on the product label being used. Use pesticides safely. Read and follow label directions.

ACKNOWLEDGMENTS

Any project of such magnitude is definitely the result of the efforts of many competent, dedicated professionals. The editor wishes to express gratitude to the following reviewers: First edition: Ed Freeman, Professor *Emeritus,* University of Florida; and golf course superintendents Fred Biggers, Don Garrett, Chuck Green, Will Holroyd, and David Lowe, second edition: Michael Ventola, Sandhills College; John Wildmon, Lake City Community College; J. Phillip Thomas, Kirkwood Community College; Bob Emmons, State University of New York at Cobleskill. Hopefully no one has been omitted, from this list; if so, we apologize for the oversight.

CONTRIBUTING AUTHORS

Bellinger, Bob, Clemson University, Clemson, South Carolina.
Bigelow, Cale A., Purdue University, West LaFayette, Indiana.
Boyd, John, University of Arkansas, Little Rock.
Bowman, Daniel C., North Carolina State University, Raleigh.
Camberato, Jim, Clemson University, Florence, South Carolina.
Gorsuch, Clyde, Clemson University, Clemson, South Carolina.
Guertal, E. A., Auburn University, Auburn, Alabama.
Hale, Trent C., Clemson University, Florence, South Carolina.
Higgins, Jeffery M., Purcell Technologies, Inc., Sylacauga, Alabama.

Hubbard, L. Ray, Jr., Professional Engineer, Clemson University, Clemson, South Carolina.
Klaine, Stephen J., Clemson University, Clemson, South Carolina.
Landry, Gil, Jr., University of Georgia, Griffin.
Martin, S. Bruce, Clemson University, Florence, South Carolina.
McCarty, L. B. (Bert), Clemson University, Clemson, South Carolina.
McLaughlin, Rich, North Carolina State University, Raleigh.
Miller, Grady, University of Florida, Gainesville.
Murphy, Tim R., University of Georgia, Griffin.
Skipper, Horace, Clemson University, Clemson, South Carolina.
Waltz, F. Clint, Jr., University of Georgia, Griffin.
Wells, Christina E., Clemson University, Clemson, South Carolina.
Whitwell, Ted, Clemson University, Clemson, South Carolina.
Williams, David, University of Kentucky, Lexington.
Yelverton, Fred H., North Carolina State University, Raleigh.

ABOUT THE AUTHOR

Bert McCarty is a Professor of Horticulture specializing in turfgrass science and management at Clemson University in Clemson, South Carolina. A native of Batesburg, South Carolina, McCarty received a BS degree from Clemson University in Agronomy and Soils, an MS from North Carolina State University in Crop Science, and a PhD from Clemson University in Plant Physiology and Plant Pathology. Dr. McCarty spent nine years as a turfgrass specialist at the University of Florida in Gainesville. While at the University of Florida, he oversaw the design and construction of a state-of-the-art research and education turfgrass facility named "The Envirotron." He also was author or co-author of the books *Best Management Practices for Florida Golf Courses, Weeds of Southern Turfgrasses,* and *Florida Lawn Handbook.* In 1996, he moved to Clemson University, where he is currently involved in research, extension, and teaching activities. He has published over 500 articles dealing with all phases of turfgrass management and has given over 700 presentations. He is currently co-author of the books *Color Atlas of Turfgrass Weeds, Southern Lawns, Managing Bermudagrass Turf,* and *Fundamentals of Turfgrass and Agricultural Chemistry.* He is also a co-author for the GCSAA seminars *Weed Control* and *Advanced Weed Management,* and is active in a number of professional societies.

INTERNET RESOURCES

Agriculture Supersite

This site is a free on-line resource center for both students and instructors in the Agricultural field. Located at http://www.prenhall.com/agsite, students will find additional study questions, job search links, photo galleries, PowerPoints, *The New York Times* eThemes archive, and other agricultural-related links.

Instructors will find a complete listing of Prentice Hall's agriculture titles, as well as instructor supplements supporting Prentice Hall Agriculture textbooks available for immediate download. Please contact your Prentice Hall sales representative for password information.

The New York Times eThemes of the Times for Agriculture and *The New York Times* eThemes of the Times for Agribusiness

Taken directly from the pages of *The New York Times,* these carefully edited collections of articles offer students insight into the hottest issues facing the industry today. These free supplements can be accessed by logging onto the Agriculture Supersite at: http://www.prenhall.com/agsite.

Agribooks: A Custom Publishing Program for Agriculture

Just can't find the textbook that fits *your* class? Here is your chance to create your own ideal book by mixing and matching chapters from Prentice Hall's agriculture textbooks. Up to 20% of your custom book can be your own writing or come from outside sources. Visit us at: http://www.prenhall.com/agribooks.

SECTION

I

BEST TURFGRASSES FOR GOLF COURSES

CHAPTER
1

Turfgrasses

INTRODUCTION

The game of golf originated back in mid-14th century Scotland. However, it was not until 1522, during the reign of Mary Queen of Scots, that St. Andrews, the first golf course, came into existence. St. Andrews is a links land golf course with no artificial characteristics. Receding seas left sandy waste areas with ridges and furrows, while natural plateaus became greens and tees. Burrowing animals, along with wind and rain, formed the bunkers.

In the United States, golf began as a formal sport in 1888 thanks to a transplanted Scot, John Reid. In Yonkers, New York, he and four others formed St. Andrews, the first permanent U.S. golf club.

Currently, there are over 17,000 golf courses in the United States, with 73 percent of these being public and 27 percent private. The annual increase in this number is over 300 courses. The average size of each 18-hole course 6,000 yards in length ranges between 120 to 180 acres, with an average of 133 acres for 18-hole facilities and 62 acres for 9-hole courses. If water, buildings, parking lots, and so on, are added, total acreages increase to almost 200 acres for 18-holes (Table 1–1). This totals to over 2.3 million acres of golf courses in the United States. Greens and tees account

TABLE 1–1 *Typical size for an 18- and 9-hole golf course, with the 18-hole course being 6,000 yards in length.*

Area	18-holes		9-holes	
	Size, acres (ha)	Percentage of size	Size, acres (ha)	Percentage of size
Rough/out-of-play/water/woods	147 (60)	76	45 (18.2)	60
Fairways	35 (14)	18	25 (10)	33
Buildings/parking lots	5 (2)	2.6	3 (1.2)	4
Greens/greens surround	3 (1.2)	1.6	1.5 (0.61)	2
Tees	3 (1.2)	1.5	1 (0.4)	1
Total	193 (78)	100	70 to 80 (28 to 32)	100

for approximately 6 percent of this total, and on a typical 18-hole facility greens occupy between 2.1 and 3.3 acres. Green surrounds (collar, bunkers, and grassy surrounds) compose between 2.5 to 5.0 acres, tees 0.4 to 3.0 acres, fairways 30 to 60 acres, and roughs 35 to 90 acres. The wooded area for an 18-hole course averages 35 acres, while 20 acres is average for a 9-hole course. These figures depend on if the courses are regulation, executive, or par-3 in size.

Golf courses in the United States provide the economy with an estimated $20 billion each year. More importantly, turfgrasses provide soil erosion control, dust stabilization, heat dissipation, noise abatement, air pollution control, wildlife habitat, safety to competitive athletic participants, increased property values, and are an integral component of the landscape. Turfgrasses provide many of these benefits due to their high number of plant shoots and roots—49 to 85 billion shoots per acre (123 to 213 billion per hectare), with up to 163 billion shoots per acre (408 billion per hectare) for putting greens and a combined root weight of up to 14,363 pounds per acre for a lawn. Due to this high shoot and root mass, turfgrasses are often used as filter strips for mining operations, animal production facilities, and agricultural croplands. Research also demonstrates bare ground loses almost 200 pounds of soil per acre (224 kg/ha) during a 3-inch (7.6 cm) rainstorm while turfgrass-covered ground loses between 9 and 54 pounds of soil per acre, or 10 to 60 kg/ha (Gross et al., 1991).

Golf Course Rating

Golf courses are rated to develop a handicap system which is equitable everywhere. This rating includes the length (yardage) of the course and measurement of difficulty to formulate a handicap system. A Course Rating Team reviews numerous variables of a course to rate its relative difficulty for all levels of golfers. The standards of yardage for par are defined in the USGA *Rules of Golf* (Table 1–2).

Grass Taxonomy

Grasses are the most important agricultural plants in the world. In addition to providing a wide variety of food, they help stabilize various environments; provide the major plants used as turf in lawns, parks, sports fields, and golf courses; and furnish a large group of ornamental grasses for horticultural uses (Figure 1–1).

Living organisms are classified based on shared characteristics and natural relationships. The grass family, *Poaceae* (formerly known as *Gramineae*), includes six subfamilies and about 600 genera with more than 7,500 species. Within some species, there are further subdivisions called subspecies, varieties, or cultivars. Of the six subfamilies, three of them contain turfgrasses—the cool-season grasses fall into the *Festucoideae*, while the warm-season grasses belong in the *Panicoideae* and *Eragrostoideae* (Table 1–3).

About 150 grass genera and 1,500 species are found growing in the United States; however, less than 25 species are important as turfgrasses. By having such a wide diversity of habitats, grasses show a considerable measure of ecological adaptation.

Living organisms are identified by a Latin binomial classification system. The first name is the Latin description for the genus while the second name represents the species. The taxonomic authority may be added to the Latin binomial following the species designation to indicate who

TABLE 1–2 *Yardage guidelines for par ratings of golf courses and playing lengths for normal and championship play (USGA).*

Par	Yardage (meter) minimum and maximum	
	Men	Women
3	≤250 (228.5)	≤210 (192)
4	251 to 470 (229 to 429.6)	211 to 400 (192.8 to 365.6)
5	≥471 (430.5)	401 to 575 (366.5 to 525.9)
6	—	≥576 (526.8)
Normal play	6,200 to 6,600 (5,667 to 6,032)	5,000 to 5,600 (4,520 to 5,118)
Championship play	6,600 to 7,200 (6,032 to 6,580)	5,800 to 6,400 (5,301 to 5,850)

FIGURE 1-1 Turfgrasses have transformed barren and unproductive land sites such as quarries (shown), landfills, and strip mines into aesthetically pleasing and economical stimulating community assets such as golf courses, ballparks, and playgrounds.

TABLE 1-3 *Turfgrass family taxonomy is subdivided into subfamilies, tribes, genera, and species.*

Family	Subfamily	Tribe	Genera
Poaceae (also called Gramineae)	Festucoideae	Aveneae	Bentgrass (*Agrostis*)
		Festuceae	Bluegrasses (*Poa*)
			Fescues (*Festuca*)
			Ryegrasses (*Lolium*)
	Eragrostoideae	Chlorideae	Bermudagrass (*Cynodon*)
			Buffalograss (*Buchloe*)
		Zoysia	Zoysiagrass (*Zoysia*)
	Panicoideae	Andropogoneae	Centipedegrass (*Eremochloa*)
		Paniceae	Carpetgrass (*Axonopus*)
			Paspalums (*Paspalum*)
			Kikuyugrass (*Pennisetum*)
			St. Augustinegrass (*Stenotaphrum*)

first identified the species. For example, perennial ryegrass has the Latin binomial (also called the scientific name) of *Lolium perenne* L., with the L. serving as an abbreviation representing Carl Linnaeus, a botanist who first described this species.

Other variations of the describing authors occur. For example, bermudagrass has the Latin binomial of *Cynodon dactylon* [L.] Pers., which indicates Linnaeus (or L.) first described the species but in a different genus or as a separate species or at a different rank. Later, another author, Christiaan Persoon (abbreviated as Pers.), moved it to the *Cynodon* genus and is considered the primary author while Linnaeus, in brackets, is the secondary author.

Other rules apply with multiple authorities. For example, with the Latin name of mascarenegrass, (*Zoysia tenuifolia* Willd. ex Trin.), the term "ex" represents Carl Ludwig Willdenow (abbreviated Willd.) first proposed the name but Carl Bernhard von Trinius (abbreviated Trin.) later provided the recognized valid description. Further subdivisions are necessary when important differences exist within a species but not to the extent to warrant separation into a different species. **Cultivars,** a contrived word meaning CULTIvated VARiety (abbreviated as cv.), represent a subdivision of cultivated plants and subspecies (ssp.). Variety (var.) and form (f.) describe further subdivisions in wild populations of plants. For example, the Latin designation for the Rebel cultivar of tall fescue is *Festuca arundinacea* Schreb. cv. Rebel or *Festuca arundinacea* Schreb. "Rebel," while the subdivision of the perennial (creeping) biotype of the wild population of annual bluegrass is *Poa annua* L. ssp. *reptans* or *Poa annual* L. var. *reptans.*

Interspecific hybrids are designated by the names of the two parent species included in the Latin name separated by an X. For example, Emerald zoysiagrass is referred to as *Zoysia japonica* X *Z. tenuifolia* since it is a selected hybrid between *Zoysia japonica* and *Zoysia tenuifolia.*

Turf Quality

The overall quality of a turf stand is determined by its (1) visual and (2) functional quality components. Areas such as lawns are judged more on the visual quality of the turf while sites such as roadsides are judged more on the functional quality of the grass stand. Golf course turf quality is judged based on the combination of looks and playability; thus, they require excellent visual and functional qualities.

The most visible components of turf quality include density, color, growth habit, texture, smoothness, and uniformity. **Density** is a measure of the number of aerial shoots per unit area. **Texture** is a measure of the leaf blade width, with most golf course turf in the medium-to-fine texture range. Density and texture most often combine to determine the smoothness of a turf surface. **Uniformity** refers to the even appearance of the turf with regards to variation in turfgrass shoots and the presence of weeds. **Smoothness** is a surface feature of the turf affecting visual quality and playability; an example might be a poor surface formed from using a dull mower which shreds or frays turf plants. **Growth habit** describes the type of shoot growth, such as bunch-type, rhizomatous, and stoloniferous. **Color** is a measure of the light reflected by a turfgrass. Color ranges from light to very dark green and is often a useful indicator of the general condition of the plants. Unfortunately, color alone is often the visible component most used by golfers to judge turf quality.

In addition to color and the other listed components of turfgrass quality, golf course turf is often rated by its rooting, recuperative ability, leaf growth rate, grain, resiliency, and putting speed.

PLANT CHARACTERISTICS

Flowering plants, (also called **angiosperms**) are divided into two subclasses, named for the number of **cotyledons,** or food storage organs, possessed by their seed embryo (Table 1–4). **Dicotyledons,** also known as **dicots,** have two storage organs, while **monocotyledons,** also known as **monocots,** have one. Other important differences also occur between the two groups. Monocots typically have long, two-ranked, thin leaves with parallel veins and scattered bundles of vascular tissue (Figure 1–2). Their floral parts (sepals, petals, and sex organs) are arranged in threes. Dicots, however, have leaves of various shapes, often wider than long, with a vein network (Figure 1–3). They often have showy flowers, as well as a continuous cylinder of vascular tissue

TABLE 1–4 *Distinguishing characteristics of monocots compared to dicots.*

Characteristic	Monocot	Dicot
Seed cotyledons	one	two
Leaf vernation	parallel	netted
Ligules	present, rarely absent	absent
Vascular bundles	scattered	distinct
Vascular tissue growth	primary	secondary
Meristems	basal	terminal
Root system	fibrous without cambium layer	tap root with a cambium layer
Flowers	not showy	showy
Flower parts	group of threes	group of fours or fives
Members	grasses, sedges, and rushes	most broadleaf plants

FIGURE 1–2 The primary structures of a grass plant.

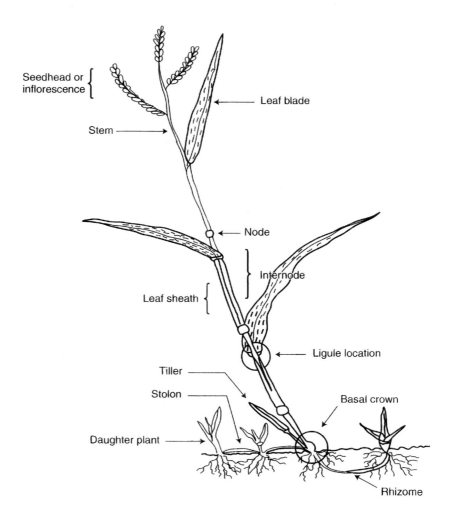

Seedhead or inflorescence

Leaf blade

Stem

Node

Internode

Leaf sheath

Ligule location

Tiller

Stolon

Basal crown

Daughter plant

Rhizome

FIGURE 1–3 Germinating dicotyledons, also known as *dicots* (right), compared to monocotyledons, also known as *monocots* (left). Dicots have two storage organs while monocots have one. Monocots typically have long, two-ranked, thin leaves with parallel veins while dicots have leaves of various shapes, often wider than long, with a vein network. They often have showy flowers (not shown). Monocots' leaves are usually attached directly to the stem while dicot leaves usually have short stalks called petioles.

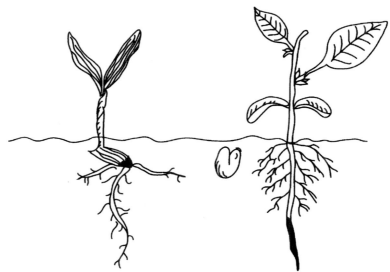

in the stem. Vascular tissue of the stem is also arranged in a ring of bundles surrounding a central pith. Their flowers are mostly arranged in fours or fives. Perennial dicots also produce bark through secondary thickening of cambium cells. Monocot leaves are usually attached directly to the stem while dicot leaves usually have short stalks called **petioles.** Monocot plants also lack a cambium, and thus cannot develop secondary thickening like dicot plants can. As a result, monocot plants do not grow as tall or strong as dicot plants such as trees (palm trees are notable monocot exceptions). All turfgrasses are monocots while most broadleaf weeds are dicots.

Cells are the small units that make up all organisms and their parts. Cells that are grouped and perform the same functions are **tissues.** These various tissues are the components of the plant's systems of structures. Cells are able to divide or enlarge in meristematic regions which increase the size of the plant.

The vascular system in plants consists of **xylem** and **phloem.** These are tubelike tissues which connect the belowground with the aboveground plant structures and serve as a pipeline through which water, nutrients, and food move to various portions of the plant. Xylem carries water and nutrients absorbed by the roots and plant growth regulators (hormones) produced in roots to the stems and leaves. The driving force for this movement is **transpiration,** the loss of water to the atmosphere through **evaporation** at the leaf surface. This water loss creates a tension which "pulls" the water and dissolved nutrients in the xylem upward into the plant. Food and plant growth regulators manufactured by photosynthesis in leaves travels down in the plant via the phloem system. Monocot xylem and phloem tissue are **primary,** meaning when they form during the stem's initial development, they never increase or are ever replaced.

Seed

Grasses are either **annuals** (live one year or less) or **perennials** (live more than two years). Turf-grasses are most often grown as perennials, meaning the plant lives and continually replaces all of its components during the course of two or more years. Turf management involves ensuring this replacement growth occurs at the rate needed by losses due to natural senescence, injury, or disease.

Most grasses are **herbaceous** (or non-woody) plants. The seed of a grass is actually a fruit known as a **caryopsis.** The caryopsis contains the true seed, which typically has a relatively elaborate embryo situated at one end next to its food source, the **endosperm.** The embryonic shoot and root axes are found at the center of the **scutellum.** When germination begins, the caryopsis absorbs water and swells. If the seed dries following this, viability is significantly lowered. The first indication of growth is the appearance of the primary root, the **radicle,** which pushes through its protective organ, the **coleorhiza.** The developing shoot then expands within a protective modified leaf, the **coleoptile,** which splits through the caryopsis. The first leaf then elongates through a pore at the apex of the coleoptile (Figure 1–3). After entering light, new leaf initials develop from the apical meristem. **Chlorophyll** is then synthesized and **photosynthesis** begins.

The primary root lives only one to two months and is not the main absorbing system of grass plants. Water and nutrient absorption is performed by **adventitious roots,** which arise from the lowermost nodes of the first shoot and tillers. In bunchgrasses, adventitious roots usually originate from basal nodes of the main stem or from **tillers** near the ground level. In sod-forming grasses, adventitious roots also may develop from nodes of **stolons** or **rhizomes** (Figure 1–2).

Requirements for germination vary between grasses, but all require water, favorable temperatures, and oxygen. Light is essential for certain grass seed (e.g., goosegrass, crabgrass, and bluegrass). Optimum germination of cool-season grasses occurs when air temperatures are between 60 and 80°F (16 and 27°C) while warm-season grasses require 70 to 95°F (21 to 35°C). Seed viability and longevity increase when stored in cool (<80°F, 27°C), dry (<20 percent relative humidity) conditions. Bermudagrass seed is generally short-lived (≤1 year), fescue and ryegrass seed are intermediate, and bentgrass and buffalograss seed are considered long-lived (>2 years).

Certain grass seeds have a hard, impermeable coat or bur for survival purposes. Germination generally increases if this coat is removed or **scarified** before planting, as seen in bermudagrass, buffalograss, zoysiagrass, and bahiagrass.

Crowns

Crowns are, arguably, the most important organ in grasses. The crown is the primary **meristematic tissue** or growth zone for cell division and enlargement of established plants and is located at the base of the plant near the soil surface where leaves, roots, and stems join (Figure 1–2). All new leaf, root, and stem growth originates at the crown. Crowns consist of a **stem apex, unelongated** (or highly compacted) **internodes, axillary buds,** and **nodes** and are generally very short (1/8 inch, 3.2 mm) in length. Adventitious roots initiate from the lower nodes of crowns while lateral shoots and leaves initiate from the upper portion where the **apical meristem** is located. The crown is the primary meristematic tissue and as long as it is not damaged, the plant can recover from environmental stresses, dormancy, excessive defoliation, and pest damage. Healthy crowns are white and turgid (filled with water) while damaged crowns turn brown and dry out.

Grasses are well-adapted to mowing since leaf formation continues after each defoliation. This occurs because the primary growing point, the crowns, are located at the base of the plant, close to the soil surface and below mower blades. Also, grass internodes do not normally elongate, except when flowering. Keeping crown tissue alive is a key to growing plants.

Leaves

The organs of grasses are the shoots (stems plus leaves, referred to as **primary shoot**) and roots. As the plant develops from germinating seed, the shoot (or **culm**) becomes apparent. At this stage, the shoot consists of a series of concentric leaves, with the oldest on the outside and younger ones forming in the center, pushing upwards until they emerge.

As seedlings develop, emerging leaves show variations in structure which become important for species identification. Leaf width, shape, hairs, vernation, collars, leaf tips, and so on, all aid in the identification of turfgrasses.

Leaves consist of a sheath, blade, and ligule. The **sheath** is the lower portion of the leaf which is wrapped around the shoot above the node and from which the leaf bud emerges (Figure 1–2). **Blades** (also called **lamina**) are parallel veined and typically flat, long, and narrow. Leaves on mature plants are borne on the **stem,** alternately in two rows, one at each node. A large vein, the **midrib,** extends through the middle of the blade and lesser veins run parallel on each side of it. In some grasses, the edge of the blade feels rough when rubbed. The blade may have hairs on either the upper or lower surface or both.

Vernation is the arrangement of the youngest leaf protruding from the sheath of an older leaf in the bud shoot and is either **rolled** or **folded** (Figure 1–4). Turfgrasses with rolled vernation include annual ryegrass, buffalograss, creeping bentgrass, and zoysiagrass. Bermudagrass, perennial ryegrass, bluegrass, and St. Augustinegrass have folded vernation.

Leaf tip shapes also aid in separating and identifying certain turfgrasses. **Pointed** leaf tips are the most common for turfgrasses (Figure 1–5). Examples include bahiagrass, ryegrass, fescue, zoysiagrass, and bermudagrass. **Blunted** or **rounded** leaf tips are associated with carpetgrass, centipedegrass, and St. Augustinegrass. **Boat-shaped** leaf tips are associated with the bluegrasses and centipedegrass.

The intervals between the leaf junctions are **internodes.** As leaves mature and die, they are replaced by new ones developing within the sheath of the next oldest leaf. A specialized **intercalary meristem** is located between two previously differentiated tissues of certain organs such as between the leaf blade and sheath or between a node and an internode. Intercalary (which means separated) meristematic tissue called **leaf primordia** located at the leaf base is the site of new leaf initiation. Consequently, new growth occurs at the base of the sheath just above the

FIGURE 1–4 Ligule types and vernation of grasses.

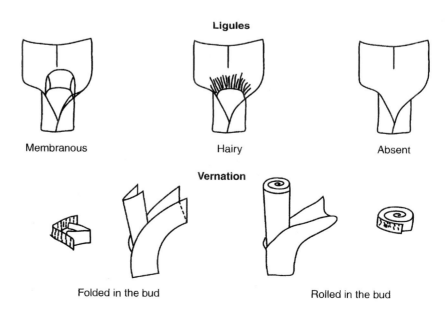

FIGURE I–5 Three
common leaf blade tips
associated with turfgrasses.

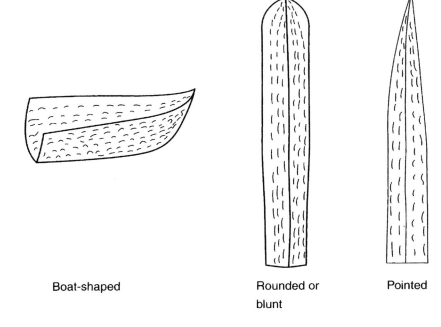

Boat-shaped   Rounded or   Pointed
                     blunt

ligule, and is the youngest portion of the leaf, while the oldest portion of the leaf is at the tip of the blade. Since the leaf tip is physiologically more mature, it is the first part to senesce when the leaf dies. The new leaf emerges at the top of the plant.

The collar region is where the leaf blade and sheath join, and contains the **collar, auricles, and ligule.** The ligule, one of the most important diagnostic features of grasses, is a projection or extension from the top of the leaf sheath where the leaf sheath and blade join. It can vary considerably in its texture, size, and shape (Figure 1–4). Most commonly, the ligule is either a membranous structure, a fringe of hairs, or is absent. Auricles are appendages extending from the edge of the leaf where the blade and sheath meet. Auricles are claw-like, short, or absent. The development of these appendages mark the end of elongation growth, at which point the leaf has reached its final length. Meanwhile, the next leaf is moving up inside the previous leaf's sheath.

Photosynthesis, or food production, occurs in leaf cells with the presence of chlorophyll. The outer layer of cells in leaves is the **epidermis** and often is coated with a thin waterproof wax covering called the **cuticle** (Chapter 2). The cuticle serves, in part, as a sealant to prevent excess water loss from the leaf. Openings in the leaf epidermis, called **stomata,** allow gas exchange in the plant. Most commonly, carbon dioxide is absorbed during photosynthesis, oxygen is exchanged during respiration, and water vapor is lost during transpiration. Stomata close at night since photosynthesis is not occurring.

During periods of drought, stomata close to prevent water vapor loss. This closure also stops photosynthesis since the necessary gases for this process cannot be absorbed.

The **mesophyll** consists of cells between the upper and lower epidermal layers. Except for veins, mesophyll cells contain chlorophyll. Typically, mesophyll cells located at the top are tall and cylindrical, forming the **palisade** layer. Cells below the palisade layer are irregular in shape and have large spaces between them. They form a spongy layer in which carbon dioxide and oxygen move.

Leaf number, size, and emergence rate are governed by numerous factors including the plant's genetic makeup and exposure to certain environmental parameters. Turfgrass leaf life expectancy is approximately one to two months. Turf managers, therefore, need to stimulate new leaf development to replace the older brown-colored (or **necrotic**) dying ones.

Temperature and light are the environmental factors with the greatest influence on leaf appearance, assuming other parameters such as soil moisture, soil oxygen, and rootzone area are not limiting. Generally, warmer temperatures, higher light intensities, and longer daylengths promote leaf emergence, especially with warm-season grasses. If either becomes limiting (e.g., too high or low; too long or short), the corresponding leaf appearance rate is influenced. Nitrogen is the nutrient with the greatest influence on leaf growth rate. Nitrogen application stimulates new, darker-green leaves and not the greening of older leaves; normally there is a lag period between fertilization and the green color and growth response. Increasing nitrogen fertilization also tends to increase leaf area.

Leaf size is also influenced by the environment. Again, temperature, light intensity, and nutrient supply are the most important factors. In general, leaves tend to be shorter and wider during cool temperatures, but longer and narrower when it is warm.

Reduced light intensity (e.g., shade) usually causes grass leaves to become wider and longer. Leaf thickness and corresponding weight decline; thus, under shade, grass leaves stretch and widen, but are low in weight. The leaf under low light conditions develops this larger surface area in an attempt to capture as much filtered sunlight as possible.

Stems

Stems are the basic structural feature from which turfgrasses develop and are the connecting structures between leaves and roots. Stems consist of internodes spaced between nodes with attached leaves. Grasses are composed of three different types of stems: crowns, **flowering culm** (or **seedhead**), and **lateral stems** (rhizomes, stolons, and tillers). Most grasses have soft, succulent growth and are referred to as herbaceous (or non-woody). The jointed stem of a grass is distinctly divided into a series of nodes and internodes and is terminated by an **apical bud.** Internodes are usually cylindrical and hollow, while nodes are solid. Successive leaves are initiated by the swollen meristematic stem apex at the node, which in most species remains short during vegetative development so leaves arise close together. Since they originate from the same point, the number of nodes and internodes equals the number of leaves.

Most species delay extended stem development until shortly before flowering. When stem development does occur, the structure is fairly long and narrow with elongated internodes separated by solid nodes. Nodes generally appear as slight swellings of the stem. Stems are either solid or hollow, but typically are hollow in turfgrasses. In solid stems, the central **parenchyma** provides storage for carbohydrates, which may be used later during plant development. Hollow stems have vascular bundles arranged in one or two concentric rings. Modified stems and leaves make up the inflorescence and fruits.

Alternately appearing on either side of the crown is a series of axillary buds which give rise to lateral stems, such as tillers, rhizomes, and stolons. Tillers, or primary lateral shoots, develop when lateral stems grow up within the leaf lying under the node. As the leaf sheath develops from the crown, it appears to wrap completely around the crown, including the axillary buds. Therefore, developing axillary buds either must grow through or within the leaf sheath. When these are retained within the surrounding leaf sheath and grow upright, tillering is referred to as **intravaginal,** and produces a tufted or bunch-type (non-creeping) growth habit. Ryegrass and fescue have bunch-type growth habits, spread very slowly, and tend to grow in clumps or bunches.

Extravaginal tillering (or shoot development) occurs where the lateral stem elongates and penetrates through the side of the surrounding leaf sheath to produce a spreading or creeping growth habit. Extravaginal tillers form either rhizomes (belowground stems) or stolons (aboveground stems which possess fully developed leaves) and are referred to as **secondary lateral shoots.** Being stems, rhizomes and stolons possess nodes, internodes, and an apical bud. Both can root and produce new shoots at the nodes, permitting a single plant to spread over a wide region. Rhizomes and stolons serve as major storage areas for reserve carbohydrates and provide sod strength and recuperative ability. Creeping red fescue and Kentucky bluegrass are examples of rhizomatous turfgrasses.

Unlike roots, which grow by adding cells at their tips, rhizomes grow by intercalary meristematic activity in the vicinity of stem nodes. The resulting elongation of stem internodes is partly responsible for pushing the rhizome tip through soil. Rhizomes grow faster under long days, high light, and low nitrogen levels.

Stolons resemble rhizomes in that they have definite nodes, internodes, and nodal meristems from which secondary structures arise. They are more stemlike than rhizomes since they creep above ground and their leaves develop and function normally. St. Augustinegrass, creeping bentgrass, centipedegrass, and *Poa trivialis* are examples of stoloniferous turfgrasses. Some turfgrasses, such as bermudagrass and zoysiagrass, produce both rhizomes and stolons.

Tillering is favored by high light intensity, frequent mowing, and moderate nitrogen levels, and is generally greatest for cool-season grasses in the spring and fall (Table 1–5). Conversely, as light is reduced from 100 percent intensity, tiller production also declines. Shade, therefore, discourages tiller formation.

TABLE I–5 *Parameters influencing tillering in turfgrasses.*

Parameter	Tillering response
Temperature	Optimum when temperatures are 50 to 60°F (10 to 16°C) for cool-season grasses and 80 to 90°F (27 to 32°C) for warm-season turfgrasses.
Light intensity	As light intensity is reduced (or shade increases), tillering is also reduced.
Nitrogen	Moderate nitrogen levels encourage tillering while high levels may favor shoot growth over tillering and root growth.
Mowing	Proper mowing height and frequency remove the tillering-inhibiting hormone, auxin; thus, tillering is promoted.
Daylength	Longer days encourage tillering.
Moisture	Tillering decreases as soil moisture dries from field capacity.

Temperatures also must be favorable for optimum tiller production. Cool-season grasses require cool (50 to 60°F, 10 to 16°C) temperatures while warm-season grasses require higher (80 to 90°F, 27 to 32°C) temperatures for optimum tiller production.

Tiller production also is influenced by mowing height and frequency. Physiological control of tillering is influenced by the concentration of the internal growth hormone, **auxin.** When sufficient concentrations of auxin are produced in the apical meristem and expanding leaves, tillering is inhibited. Tillering is stimulated when the auxin in shoot tips is removed by mowing. Thus, frequently mowing hybrid bermudagrasses at ≤1.0 inch (2.5 cm), for example, encourages tiller production. However, if mowed less frequently above this height, auxin accumulates at the leaf tips, tillering is suppressed, and the plant uses its carbohydrate reserves to form new leaves at the expense of tiller production.

Roots

Roots anchor plants to soil and take up water and nutrients. Roots also function in food storage, and are the primary source of certain plant growth regulators, such as gibberellins and cytokinins.

Turfgrasses have fibrous, branched root systems, mostly located in the upper foot of soil. The **primary** (also called **seminal**) grass roots arise from the root tissues of seed embryo and generally persist for only a short time (one to two months) after germination. The primary root is the first structure to emerge from the embryo. The **secondary** (also called adventitious) roots arise two to three weeks after germination at the lower nodes just below the internodal intercalary meristem of young stems and comprise the major part of the permanent root system. The root system is progressively replaced by adventitious roots which arise at nodes of creeping stems (stolons), lower plant crowns, and from older roots.

The tip of roots, the **root cap,** is a thimble-shaped group of protective cells for the meristematic region located just behind it. The cap minimizes damage to this meristematic region as the root grows (or pushes) through soil. The meristematic region behind the root cap is the site of active cell growth. Here cells divide and elongate, pushing the root through soil. Root hairs are tiny projections on the outer surface of roots that increase the surface area of the root system. Plant water and nutrient uptake occur here. Unlike leaves, roots have a growing point at their tips which is capable of branching into soil air spaces at every opportunity. However, grass roots lack a cambium for secondary thickening.

The life expectancy for most turfgrass roots is less than one year. Roots of cool-season grasses grow prolifically in fall and winter months when soil temperatures are about 55°F (13°C), but begin to decline in the spring when flowering occurs and eventually die or are severely restricted during periods of summer heat and drought (Table 1–6). Creeping bentgrass, for example, ceases root initiation when soil temperatures exceed 75°F (24°C). Roots of cool-season grasses are smaller in diameter and grow shallower than warm-season grasses. When maintained as turf, cool-season grasses such as bentgrass, *Poa trivialis,* and ryegrass rarely have roots greater than one foot deep; most often, they are much less.

Roots of warm-season grasses begin growing in spring when soil temperatures at four inches (10 cm) reach 64°F (18°C). Tillers, from nodes of stolons and rhizomes, break dormancy and begin growth. Carbohydrate reserves are converted to soluble sugars and new leaves begin to appear.

TABLE 1-6 *Primary parameters influencing turfgrass rooting.*

Parameter	Rooting response
Soil temperature	Optimum soil temperature range for cool-season grasses is 50 to 65°F (10 to 16°C) and 75 to 85°F (24 to 29°C) for warm-season grasses.
Soil pH	Soil pH outside the range of 5.0 to 8.0 may limit root growth.
Plant age	Young plants generally produce the most roots.
Moisture	Moisture extremes (too dry or wet) discourage rooting.
Soil compaction/soil oxygen levels	Rooting is reduced due to physical impedance from soil compaction and from the resulting low soil oxygen levels. Anaerobic conditions (such as with severe soil compaction or excessively wet soils) may lead to toxic sulfide, carbon dioxide, and methane buildup.
Mowing height	Higher mowing heights usually promote deeper, more extensive rooting systems. Cool-season grasses are much more sensitive to mowing heights than warm-season grasses and tend to be severely restricted as mowing height is decreased.
Nutrient availability	Rooting is promoted with moderate nitrogen levels and adequate levels of potassium, phosphorus, iron, and calcium. High nitrogen levels decrease root growth, especially with cool-season grasses.
Light intensity	Shade (reduced light levels) discourages deeper rooting.

Roots of warm-season grasses begin a major flush of growth in late spring, summer, and early fall months when soil temperatures reach about 80°F (27°C). Roots tend to store little energy reserves during summer due to their repeated use for regrowth following mowing. During late fall, plant-soluble sugars are converted to starch granules and stored in roots, stolons, and rhizomes during winter months. In early spring, when warm-season turfgrasses are greening-up from winter dormancy, these starch energy reserves are converted to soluble sugars for growth, and are depleted. Root systems may experience severe die-back with the appearance of new leaves. This die-back, called "spring root decline," lasts one to three weeks, during which time plants are susceptible to environmental and chemical stresses or from competition from overseeded cool-season grasses.

Low soil temperature will adversely affect bermudagrass rooting even if air temperatures are high. These conditions often exist in early spring and fall months. Similar rooting decreases occur if light levels are reduced, presumably due to less carbohydrate assimilation with lower photosynthesis. Complete green-up requires two to six weeks, depending on the temperature (faster green-up occurs with warmer temperatures).

If temperatures remain favorable for shoot growth during the spring transition period, normal green-up and recovery can proceed. If these favorable growth conditions, however, are interrupted by a late freeze, the young, tender green leaves may be killed and new leaves then must be regrown. If several intermittent freezes occur, an enormous drain is placed on the root energy reserves, often resulting in thin turf stands.

Age also influences root growth patterns. Young plants produce maximum root growth. Young plant roots are generally white, small in diameter, fibrous, and multi-branched. As plants mature, their roots change in color from white to brown, become larger in diameter, and become less efficient in nutrient and water absorption. Environmental and biotic extremes negatively impacting turf rooting are temperatures outside the optimum range, soil compaction, low soil oxygen, drought, and excessive moisture. Cultural practices restricting rooting include improper mowing practices (height and frequency), excessive nitrogen and thatch levels, phosphorus and potassium deficiencies, and improper herbicide use. In general, the combination of continuous high soil moisture (frequent, light irrigation), close mowing, and high nitrogen fertility discourages the rooting of most turfgrasses.

Growth also is interrelated between roots and shoots. Roots depend on the shoots (leaves and stems) for the carbohydrates produced during photosynthesis. Meanwhile, shoots depend on roots for water and nutrients. Turf managers normally strive to have a high **root to shoot ratio.** Shoot growth is favored over rooting when (1) soil temperatures are above the optimum for root growth; (2) the turf is mowed at close mowing heights; (3) excessive nitrogen is applied; and (4) conditions of low light intensities exist which reduce plant photosynthesis, therefore limiting the carbohydrates available for root development.

Inflorescence

The seedhead or **inflorescence** of a turfgrass is the reproductive organ where seeds are formed. Unlike other organs, inflorescences are not present throughout the life of the plant. They originate when a grass plant enters the reproductive stage and an elongated stem from the apical meristem of the crown is produced. Flowers and seed appear at the top of this elongated stem, called the flowering culm. The unit of the grass inflorescence is composed of a group of subunits called **spikelets** (Figure 1–6). Spikelets are composed of two **bracts** or leaves called **glumes,** which enclose one or more **florets.** Florets consist of a **lemma, palea,** and the enclosed flower. Mature florets harvested from the inflorescence of flowering grass plants are commonly referred to as grass seed. The axis or branch of the spikelet is referred to as the **rachilla.** The spikelets usually are in groups or clusters, which constitute the inflorescence.

Several spikelet cluster types exist, including **raceme, spike,** and **panicle** (Figure 1–7). The simplest is the raceme where spikelets are borne on individual stalks (or **pedicels**) on an unbranched main axis. St. Augustinegrass, bahiagrass, zoysiagrass, and centipedegrass have raceme inflorescences. The spike differs from the raceme, since spike has sessiled (without a stalk or pedicel) spikelets on the main axis while racemes have simple stalked spikelets. Wheatgrass and ryegrass have the spike form of inflorescence (Tables 1–7 and 1–8).

FIGURE 1–6 Spikelet, floret, and flower structures of the turfgrass inflorescence.

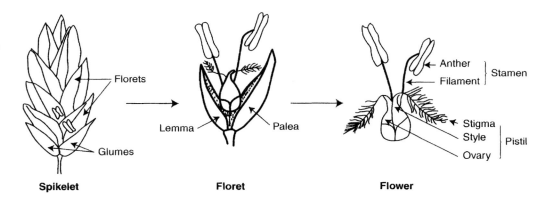

FIGURE 1–7 Three types of seedheads for turfgrasses based on the arrangement of the spikelets include panicle (left), raceme (center), and spike (right).

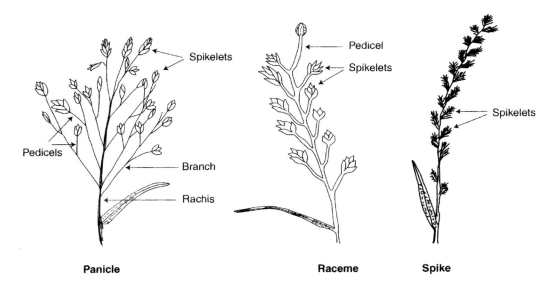

TABLE 1-7 Distinguishing morphological characteristics of warm-season (or C_4) turfgrasses.

Turfgrass	Leaf texture (width, mm)	Lateral shoot type	Leaf vernation	Ligule type (length, mm)	Auricles	Leaf blade tip	Inflorescence	Additional characteristic(s)
Bahiagrass *Paspalum notatum* Flugge.	coarse (4–8)	very short stolons, rhizomes	folded or rolled	membrane (1)	absent	pointed	branched spikelike racemes (two, rarely three branched racemes)	Tall, two- to three-spiked, V-shaped seedheads. Wide leaf blade with hairy margins. Reddish-purple stem base. Tough, drought and nematode resistant, low maintenance.
Bermudagrass *Cynodon dactylon* (L.) Pers.	fine to coarse (1–3)	stolons, rhizomes	folded	hair (1–3)	absent	pointed	four or five digitate spikelike racemes	Turf types have fine leaf texture and dense stand density. Some hairs are on the leaf surface. Widely used for sports and golf turf. Very poor shade tolerance.
Blue Grama *Bouteloua gracilis* (HBK) Lag. ex Steud.	fine to medium (1–2)	rhizomes	rolled	hair (0.1–0.5)	absent	pointed	spike, spreading at maturity	Has blue-green color from hairy leaves. Adapted to warmer regions of the arid transition zone. Forms a low-maintenance turf.
Buffalograss *Buchloe dactyloides* (Nutt.) Engelm	fine to medium (1–3)	stolons	rolled	hair (0.5–1)	absent	pointed	separate male and female flowers	Collars hairy. Blue-gray color due to leaf pubescence. Drought resistant but has very poor shade tolerance. Male flowers appear as curved branches at the main stem top while female flowers are hard burs just above the leaf sheath.
Carpetgrass *Axonopus affinis* Chase	medium to coarse (4–8)	stolons	folded	hair (1)	absent	rounded (blunt)	raceme (usually three)	Similar to St. Augustinegrass except for its lighter-green color leaves, and have "waves" along their margins. Seedheads resembling "crabgrass seedheads" with two to five spikes at their apex. Tolerates wet conditions.
Centipedegrass *Eremochloa ophiuroides* (Monro.) Hack	medium (3–5)	stolons	folded	membrane (0.5)	absent	rounded (blunt)	single spikelike solitary racemes	Has a natural yellow-green color medium with textured leaves with hairs along their edges. Used as a low-maintenance grass. Grows best at slightly acidic (5.0 to 6.0) soil pH.
Kikuyugrass *Pennisetum clandestinum* Hochst ex. Chiov.	medium (4–5)	rhizomes and stolons	folded	hair (2)	absent	pointed	two to four spikelets	Very tough grass with hairy leaves. Has poor shade tolerance. Usually considered a weed. Very difficult to eradicate once established. Use cautiously.
Seashore Paspalum *Paspalum vaginatum* Swartz	medium to coarse (3–8)	stolons, rhizomes	folded or rolled	membrane (0.8–1.2)	absent	pointed	spikelike racemes	Good salt tolerance, but poor cold tolerance. Has blue-green color. Good for brackish water areas. Breeding efforts are improving selections for golf courses.
St. Augustinegrass *Stenotaphrum secundatum* (Walt.) Kuntze.	coarse (4–10)	stolons	folded	hair (0.3)	absent	rounded, boat-shaped	single spikelike racemes	Has long, thick stolons and wide leaf blades. Cold tolerance is poor to fair. Good shade and salt tolerance.
Zoysiagrass: Manilagrass *Zoysia matrella* (L.) Merr.	fine (2–3) to coarse (4–6)	stolons, rhizomes	rolled	hair (0.2)	absent	pointed	spikelike terminal racemes	Stiff to the touch. Collar covered with long hairs; hairy on leaf surface. Fine leaf texture, dark green, dense turf. Has good shade tolerance (cultivar dependent).
Meyer *Z. japonica* Steud.								
Mascarenegrass *Z. matrella* (L.) Merr. var. *tenuifolia* (Willd. ex Thiele) Sasaki								

15

TABLE 1-8 *Distinguishing morphological characteristics of cool-season (or C_3) turfgrasses.*

Turfgrass	Leaf texture (width, mm)	Lateral shoot type	Leaf vernation	Ligule type (length, mm)	Auricles	Leaf Blade tip	Inflorescence	Additional characteristic(s)
Annual bluegrass *Poa annua* L.	fine (0.5–2.2)	tillers (annual biotype), short stolons (perennial biotype)	folded	membrane (1.5–2)	absent	boat-shaped	panicle	Pale-green color; dull on underleaf; profile seedhead producer under all mowing heights. Transparent, parallel "light" lines on either side of the midrib. Often a major weed. Perennial biotypes (*P. annua* ssp. *reptans*) are being evaluated for golf greens.
Annual ryegrass *Lolium multiflorum* Lam.	medium to coarse (3–7)	tillers	rolled	membrane (1–2)	long, narrow, claw-like	pointed	spike	Glossy on underleaf; red stem base. Lighter-green color and coarser leaf texture than perennial ryegrass. Seed (spikelets) awned.
Colonial bentgrass *Agrostis tenuis* Sibth.	fine (1–3)	tillers, short stolons	rolled	membrane (0.4–1.2)	absent	pointed	panicle	Has a tufted (patch-like) growth habit. Rhizomes and stolons are either absent or short.
Creeping bentgrass *Agrostis palustris* subsp. *stolonifera* L.	fine (1–3)	stolons	rolled	membrane (1–3)	absent	pointed	panicle	Leaf blades rough along the edges.
Crested wheatgrass *Agropyron cristatum* (L.) Gaertn.	medium (2–5)	tillers	rolled	membrane (0.5–1.5)	claw-like	pointed	spike	Prominent veins above and midrib below. Has natural blue-green color. Adapted to cooler regions of arid transition zone.
Fine fescue: Red fescue *Festuca rubra* L. Chewings fescue *F. rubra* ssp. *communtata* Gaud.	fine (0.5–2)	rhizomes, tillers	folded	membrane (0.2–0.5)	absent	pointed	panicle	Very fine, needlelike, leaf texture. Red fescue produces rhizomes while chewings fescue does not. Sheep, creeping, meadow, and hard fescues are additional fine fescues.
Kentucky bluegrass *Poa pratensis* L.	medium (2–4)	rhizomes, tillers	folded	membrane (0.5–2)	absent	boat-shaped	panicle	Transparent, parallel "light" lines on either side of the midrib.
Orchardgrass *Dactylis glomerata* L.	coarse (2–10)	tillers	folded	membrane (3.5–7)	absent	pointed	panicle	Coarse leaf texture; pale blue-green color. Prominent leaf midrib. Often a seed contaminant in tall fescue.
Perennial ryegrass *Lolium perenne* L.	medium (2–5)	tillers	folded	membrane (0.5–1.5)	short, non-clasping	pointed	spike	Prominent veins and leaf midrib. Very glossy on the back of leaves; red stem base. Seed (spikelets) unawned.
Roughstalk bluegrass *Poa trivialis* L.	fine (1–6)	short stolons	folded	membrane (2–6)	absent	boat-shaped	panicle	Short creeping stolons. Light-green leaf color; glossy on underleaf. "Boat-shaped" leaf tips. Leaf margins rough.
Tall fescue *Festuca arundinacea* Schreb.	coarse (5–10)	tillers, short rhizomes	rolled	membrane (0.2–0.8)	rudimentary to absent	pointed	panicle	Leaf blade rough along the edges, bunch-type growth, prominent midrib and veins; red stem base.
Velvet bentgrass *Agrostis canina* L.	fine (<1)	short stolons	rolled	membrane (0.4–0.8)	absent	pointed	panicle	Leaf blades rough along the edges.

FIGURE 1–8 Seedhead formation often disrupts the uniformity and desired function of a turf stand. Shown are *Poa annua* seedheads in creeping bentgrass.

The panicle is the most common type of grass inflorescence. In this case, the spikelets are similar to the raceme because they are attached to the main axis (or rachis) but are in a branched inflorescence. Racemes have simple stalked spikelets. Some panicles are tightly branched while some are multi-branched, resembling the limbs and leaves of trees. Most turfgrass inflorescence have the panicle arrangement including bluegrass, creeping bentgrass, and tall fescue.

Seedhead formation in most turf situations is undesirable because it disrupts the uniformity of the turf stand (Figure 1–8) and becomes a visibility hazard, such as with bahiagrass or tall fescue seedhead formations along roadsides. In addition, seedhead formation occurs at the expense of vegetative growth since the plant uses its food and energy to form seedheads instead of producing leaves and roots. Therefore, flowering inhibits tiller production and occurs by using carbohydrate reserves located in roots.

Seedheads develop during the spring or summer, depending on the turfgrass species. For cool-season grasses, inflorescence development occurs predominantly in spring, while warm-season species develop in the summer. Daylength and temperature are the two major environmental factors which regulate the timing of flowering for most turfgrass species. **Long-day plants** are those triggered to flower when a critical minimum daylength is exceeded. They tend to flower in late spring through early summer when days are longest. Under shorter daylengths, long-day plants remain in the vegetative state. **Short-day plants** flower only when the daylength is shorter than a critical maximum period. They tend to flower during the shorter days of late summer and fall. These plants remain in the vegetative state and do not flower when daylength is long. Warm-season grasses tend to be short-day plants (bahiagrass being a notable exception) and flower when days are of less than a critical length.

As mentioned, most cool-season grasses are long-day plants and flower only when the photoperiod exceeds a certain critical length. However, the effect of daylength is highly modified by temperature. Cool-season grasses tend to have floral induction in fall in response to cooler (e.g., 32 to 50°F, 0 to 10°C) temperatures. Higher night temperatures (approx. 54 to 64°F, 12 to 18°C), however, tend to delay or inhibit flower initiation in cool-season grasses. Conversely, short-day grasses (most warm-season grasses) often require night temperatures above 54 to 61°F (12 to 16°C) for floral initiation. Frequent mowing, adequate soil moisture, and increased nitrogen levels also discourage seedhead formation. Once seedheads have been mowed off, the turf has a stemmy appearance which reduces its quality until sufficient new tillers emerge from vegetative stems.

Day-neutral plants do not flower in response to daylength and can flower as soon as they are mature. Annual bluegrass, and arguably, common bermudagrass, for example, are day-neutral plants and are insensitive to, or only weakly influenced by, photoperiod and produce seedheads over a wide range of photoperiods. Turfgrasses also aggressively develop seedheads when under environmental stress such as drought.

ADAPTATION

Climate

Climate (or environment) is the primary factor determining the region of adaptation of turf-grasses (Figure 1–9). Temperature and moisture are the major components of climate influencing adaptation. Light and wind are two additional climatic parameters influencing adaptation. Grasses evolve in nature through natural selection or naturalization in order to adapt to specific regions. This naturalization may involve mutations (rapid genetic changes), physiological adjustments over long periods, or most likely some combination of numerous change processes.

Turfgrasses are divided into two groups based on their temperature requirements. Cool-season (or C_3) grasses, such as bentgrass, fine fescue, tall fescue, rough bluegrass (or *Poa trivialis*), and Kentucky bluegrass, are adapted and grown in cooler temperatures and subarctic regions of the world, with optimum growth at temperatures between 60 and 75°F (15.5 and 24°C). Their peak growth periods occur in spring and fall. Conversely, their growth is slow during summer and winter. During hot periods, cool-season grasses slow in growth, become dormant, and can eventually die if management practices are not manipulated to better favor their growth and survival.

Warm-season (or C_4) grasses grow best at air temperatures between 80 and 95°F (26 and 35°C) and night temperatures in the high 60°Fs (15.6°Cs) to low 70°Fs (21°Cs). Warm-season grasses such as bahiagrass, bermudagrass, carpetgrass, centipedegrass, St. Augustinegrass, and zoysiagrass are better adapted in the southern (tropical and subtropical) regions but can grow further north into the transition zone. The main flush of growth of warm-season grasses occurs during summer and will continue even at 55 to 60°F (12.8 to 15.6°C) but go dormant at temperatures less than 50°F (10°C). In spring when temperatures rise above 50°F (10°C), warm-season turf-grasses resume growth. The greatest stress period for warm-season grasses is winter due to potential low-temperature damage.

Cool Humid Zone

The cool humid zone consists of two areas: (1) a larger area in the north central to northeastern part of the continental United States, and (2) a smaller region along the Pacific coast extending from Washington State through Oregon into northern California (Figure 1–9). It is characterized by cold winters and mild to hot summers. Annual rainfall in the eastern and central regions range from 20 to 45 inches (51 to 114 cm), while the Pacific coast region ranges from 16 to 150 inches (41 to 381 cm).

The primary turfgrasses in the cool humid area are the bentgrasses, bluegrasses, fescues, and ryegrasses. In the southern portion of the cool humid area, tall fescue, zoysiagrass, and cold hardy bermudagrasses are sometimes used.

FIGURE 1–9 Climatic zones in the mainland United States.

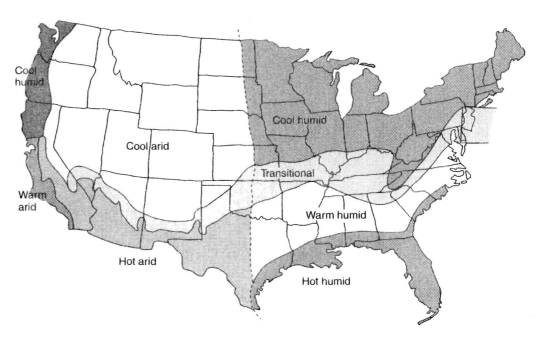

Cool Arid Zone

The cool arid zone consists of two areas: (1) the Northern Great Plains to the east, and (2) the Intermountain Region (Rockies) to the west (Figure 1–9). Elevations in this zone vary from 1,000 feet (305 m) in the plains to more than 14,000 feet (4,267 m) in the western mountain sections. This zone experiences hot summers and cold winters, depending on the elevation. As altitude increases, temperature decreases. Typically a 1°F (~0.6°C) temperature change occurs with every 300 foot (91 m) altitude differential. Annual rainfall ranges from less than 10 inches (25 cm) in the intermountain plateaus to about 25 inches (64 cm) along the eastern side of the zone. The majority of this precipitation falls during spring and summer. Snow accumulations can be substantial, especially at higher elevations.

The turfgrasses used most often in the cool arid zone include Kentucky bluegrass, bentgrass, and the fine fescues. In many areas, quality turf is achieved only with irrigation. In the plains area without irrigation, native species are commonly grown. These include buffalograss, gramagrass, bluestem, and various wheatgrasses. Low temperatures throughout most of this region limit the use of most warm-season grasses. However, along the southern border of Kansas and Oklahoma and the northern border of Texas, bermudagrass and zoysiagrass are used to a limited extent.

Hot Arid Zone

The hot arid zone is a semi-arid to arid region extending in a wide belt from central Texas to California (Figure 1–9). Rainfall is less than five inches (13 cm) in desert parts of Arizona and California to about 20 inches (51 cm) in western Texas. Relative humidity tends to be low and, along with mostly clear skies, the region generally experiences cool nights and hot days.

Bermudagrass is the primary turfgrass used for golf courses in the hot arid zone. It is often overseeded with ryegrass for winter color. Zoysiagrass is also used to a limited extent. Golf greens are either bermudagrass or bentgrass. Other grasses used on low-maintenance (non-irrigated) fairways and roughs include buffalograss, crested wheatgrass, gramagrass, and sometimes lovegrass. Kikuyugrass is sometimes used in California but generally does not produce a high-quality playing surface unless intensively managed. Without irrigation, high-quality turfgrass is difficult to achieve in the hot arid zone. Due to high evaporative rates and limited rainfall, salinity problems also are typical in this area.

Warm Humid and Hot Humid Zones

The warm humid zone runs from southern Virginia through the Carolinas to central Texas. It extends northward into southern Illinois and Oklahoma (Figure 1–9). The hot humid zone includes the coastal areas of the southern-Atlantic states, all of Florida, and the Gulf coastal regions to the southern tip of Texas. Many of these parts are considered subtropical. Humidity is usually high during summer months with rainfall ranges from a low of 20 inches (51 cm) in central Texas and western Oklahoma to a high of about 70 inches (178 cm) along the Gulf coast and about 80 inches in the southern western portion of the Appalachian mountains.

The primary turfgrasses grown in these two regions include bermudagrass, zoysiagrass, bahiagrass, St. Augustinegrass, carpetgrass, and centipedegrass. Ryegrass is used for temporary winter overseeding. Kentucky bluegrass and tall fescue are used along the northern edge of the warm humid zone. Creeping bentgrass is often used on golf greens in the northern portions of the warm humid zone and on fairways at higher (e.g., >2,000 ft, 610 m) elevations. Seashore paspalum is also used along coastal areas in the hot humid zone, especially where poorer quality irrigation water is used.

Transition Zone

An imaginary line passing east to west at 37° north latitude separates the temperate and subtropical zones in the eastern United States (Figure 1–9). This line marks the center of a 200-mile-wide (322 km) belt, called the **transition zone,** where cool-season and warm-season turfgrasses encounter the limits of their southern and northern adaptation, respectively. Many warm- and cool-season turfgrasses can be found growing together in the transition zone.

Turfgrasses often grown in the transition zone include bermudagrass, zoysiagrass, tall fescue, bentgrass, and Kentucky bluegrass. Some shade is generally needed in the transition zone to support permanent tall fescue and Kentucky bluegrass while full sunny conditions are needed for bermudagrass. It is typically too cold for most cultivars of St. Augustinegrass, carpetgrass, centipedegrass, and bahiagrass and too hot for the fine fescues and perennial ryegrasses as a permanent turf cover, unless grown at higher (e.g., >2,000 ft, 610 m) elevations.

CULTIVARS AND THEIR CHARACTERISTICS

Warm-Season Grasses

Bermudagrass

Bermudagrass is a long-lived perennial grass originating under subhumid, open, closely grazed rangelands characterized by hot, dry summers around the Indian ocean ranging from Eastern Africa to the East Indies. Bermudagrass grows almost continuously across all continents and islands between the latitudes of 45°N and 45°S. It is believed to have been introduced to the United States from Africa in 1751 or earlier. The *Cynodon* genus is comprised of nine species with chromosomal numbers ranging from 18 to 54. The four main turf-type bermudagrasses are (1) Common bermudagrass (*Cynodon dactylon* (L.) Pers. var. *dactylon*), a tetraploid with 36 (predominately) chromosomal numbers; (2) African bermudagrass (*C. transvaalensis* Burtt-Davy), a diploid with chromosome numbers of 18 (predominately); (3) their interspecific hybrid Magennis bermudagrass [*Cynodon* X *magennisii* Hurcombe (= *C. dactylon* X *C. transvaalensis*)], a naturally occurring triploid with 27 (predominately) somatic chromosomes; and (4) Bradley bermudagrass (*C. incompletus* var. *hirautus*), an aneuploid with 18 somatic chromosomes. Hexaploid *Cynodons,* with 54 chromosomes, also exist but are rarely used.

Advantages

Bermudagrass produces a vigorous, deep rooted, light to dark green, dense turf well-adapted to most soils and climatic regions in the southern United States (Figure 1–10). Bermudagrass has excellent wear, drought, and salt tolerance and is a good choice for ocean front property. It establishes rapidly, produces lateral stems, is competitive against weeds and, depending on the variety, is available as seed, sod, or sprigs (Figure 1–11). Bermudagrass has inherently few pest problems, especially relating to diseases.

Disadvantages

Bermudagrass has several cultural and pest problems which may restrict its use in certain situations. In most temperate areas, bermudagrasses become dormant (turn brown) in cold weather. Overseeding in fall with ryegrass is a common practice to maintain year-round green color.

FIGURE 1–10
Approximate range of bermudagrass use for golf greens in the mainland United States (**Note:** overlapping ranges often occur).

Transitional use

FIGURE 1-11 When properly maintained, bermudagrass produces a desirable dark-green, dense turf that withstands traffic and many pests.

FIGURE 1-12 Bermudagrass inherently has very poor shade tolerance, requiring eight hours of full sunlight daily when grown under short mowing conditions, such as in golf greens and tees.

Bermudagrasses are susceptible to several nematode, insect, and disease problems. Bermudagrasses also have very poor shade tolerance and should not be grown underneath tree canopies or building overhangs (Figure 1-12). It spreads very rapidly by both aboveground (stolons) and below (rhizomes) ground runners which are very difficult to control along flower beds, walks, and borders. Due to its rapid growth, thatch buildup can become a problem in bermudagrass. A reel mower should also be used to produce the highest possible quality turf stand. Bermudagrass also periodically "winter-kills" when grown in the upper transitional zone in the United States where temperatures periodically drop below 10°F (−12°C).

Bermudagrass Cultivars

Prior to the mid-1940s, golf courses used common bermudagrass from tee to green. Common bermudagrass provided a course-textured, uneven, and thin putting surface. Many golf courses still had sand greens where a roller was used to smooth the ball line toward the cup and heavy oils or diesel fuel was used to pack the sand. Common bermudagrass seed was not certified until 1963 in an attempt to rid seed from a tall, rapid growing Giant bermudagrass (*Cynodon dactylon* var.

aridus). This common bermudagrass was also called Arizona common since the production fields were in Arizona. The first recognized turf-type bermudagrass cultivar in the United States was "St. Lucie," a fine-textured dwarf plant used in Florida lawns.

In 1947, the first recorded release of an improved vegetatively established bermudagrass occurred when "U-3" bermudagrass was provided by the USGA in cooperation with the United States Department of Agriculture (USDA). It survived as far north as Cleveland, Ohio, and central Pennsylvania (40°north). "Ormond" and "Texturf 10" were released after "U-3." During the 1950s and 1960s, Dr. Glen W. Burton of the USDA in Tifton, Georgia, released several interspecific hybrids, including "Tiflawn," "Tifgreen," "Tifway," and "Tifdwarf," which are still widely used. These are from various crosses of common bermudagrass (2n=36) with African bermudagrass (2n=18) to produce sterile triploid hybrid bermudagrass (2n=27).

The first improved seeded bermudagrass was "Guymon," released for its improved cold tolerance, darker-green color, and lower seedhead counts compared to common in 1982 by the Oklahoma Agriculture Experiment Station. Until then, "Arizona common" or simply "common" was the only seeded bermudagrass (2n=36) sold. "NuMex Sahara," the next improved seeded common bermudagrass, was released in 1987. Today, there are numerous bermudagrass cultivars used for turf (Table 1–9). Currently, improved seeded bermudagrass varieties are being aggressively developed. Most seed is available with the hull removed (**hulled**) or with the hull remaining (**unhulled**). Hulled seed germinates faster but costs more; unhulled seed lasts longer during unfavorable weather before germinating. Only some cultivars are commercially available from sod producers. If your situation requires the use of bermudagrass, check with your county Cooperative Extension Service office for the best cultivar for your location and use.

Fairways and Roughs

Tifway (or Tifton 419)

Tifway is a dark-green bermudagrass released in 1960 with medium texture and high shoot density. It is the current standard used in warm-season areas for quality fairways, most roughs, sports fields, and lawns. It produces few seedheads, and those produced are very elongated and thin. It tends to green-up quicker in spring compared to common (Figure 1–13) and forms a much denser, finer textured stand. It must be vegetatively established by sprigs, plugs, stolons, or sod and is prone to spring dead spot disease when overmanaged. Various off-types, mutants, and/or contaminants have plagued the industry in recent years.

TABLE 1–9 *Characteristics of popular improved bermudagrass varieties.*

Greens Grade Varieties

These are used for golf greens, collars, approaches, and high-maintenance tees. They all are vegetatively propagated with no available seed.

Aussie Green, Champion, Classic Dwarf, FloraDwarf, Jensen, Mini Verde, MS Supreme, Pee Dee 102, Reesegrass, Tifdwarf, TifEagle, Tifgreen (328), Tifgreen II.

Vegetative Propagated Varieties for Fairways, Roughs, and Tees.

Baby Bermuda, Bulls-Eye (MS Choice), Cardinal, Celebration, FloraTeX, GN-1, Guymon, Midfield*, Midiron*, Midlawn*, Midway*, MS Express, MS Pride, Ormond, Patriot*, Plateau, Quickstand*, Santa Ana, Shanghai, Sunturf, Texturf 10 (T 47), Tiflawn (57), TifSport, Tifton 10, Tifway (419), Tifway II, Transcontinental, Windsor Green, Wintergreen.

Seeded Varieties for Fairways, Roughs, and Tees.

Blackjack, Blue-Muda, Bradley, Burning Tree, Cheyenne, Common, DelSol, Guymon, Jackpot, LaPaloma, LaPrima (a blend of certified bermudagrasses), Majestic, Mercury, Mirage, Mohawk, NuMex Sahara, Panama, Paradise, Primavera, Primo, Princess 77, Pyramid, Riviera (OKS 95-1)*, Sahara, Savannah, Shangri-La, Soleil, Sonesta, Southern Star, SR 9554, Sultan, Sundance II, Sundevil II, SunStar, Sultan, Sydney, U-3, Yukon (OKS 91-11)*, Yuma.

*Noted for cold tolerance.

FIGURE 1–13 Spring
green-up differences between
Tifway (419) bermudagrass
(right) and common
bermudagrass (left).

Tifway II

Tifway II is an induced mutant of Tifway released in 1984 for its improved frost and nematode tolerance. It has a similar appearance to Tifway with increased shoot density and seedheads. Tifway II can be used in moderate maintenance situations. Tifway and Tifway II make beautiful turf if adequate time, machine, and labor resources are dedicated to their establishment and upkeep.

Midway, Midiron, Midlawn, Midfield

These selections were predominantly released by the Kansas Agricultural Experiment Station for their cold tolerance. These are presumed hybrids between cold tolerant *C. dactylon* and *C. transvaalensis*. These are medium-textured grasses which produce few seedheads and are used for lawns, fairways, and roughs where winter kill is a common problem.

TifSport (Tift - 94)

This 1997 bermudagrass release from the USDA and the University of Georgia is an induced gamma irradiated mutant from Midiron bermudagrass with desirable turf texture and density. Tested as Tift MI40, this grass has a texture and color similar to Tifway and Tifway II and should be used in similar sites such as fairways and tees. It has shown good winter hardiness in Georgia, Kentucky, Tennessee, and Oklahoma. It produces no seed; therefore, it is vegetatively propagated.

Common

This is the bermudagrass (*C. dactylon*) traditionally available for establishment by seed. However, it produces a more open turfgrass with a coarse texture, low shoot density, and light-green color, and for these reasons is less desirable than other available cultivars (Figure 1–14). Common is often planted in seed mixes with bahiagrass for roadsides or reclamation sites and its seed is sometimes contaminated with Giant bermudagrass.

Improved Seeded Common Bermudagrasses

These are "improved" common type seeded varieties and are darker-green, deeper rooted, medium-textured and moderately denser compared to common bermudagrass (Table 1–9). They are general-purpose, turf-type bermudagrasses used for golf course roughs and fairways, lawns, parks, roadsides, and sports turf. These should be used in areas where improved characteristics are desired when compared to common but quality and level of maintenance are lower than the sterile hybrid varieties. Cold tolerance the first year after seeding also is a concern with seeded varieties. Yukon (OKS91-11) and Riviera (OKS 95-1) are seeded varieties from Oklahoma State University noted for their cold tolerance, excellent quality color, density, texture, and resistance to spring dead spot disease. Riviera has higher quality and faster establishment and recover rates than Yukon but requires more intensive management. Most of today's world bermudagrass seed is produced in western Arizona, the Imperial Valley of California, and Oklahoma.

GN-I

GN-1 is an introduction by Greg Norman evaluated as CT-2. It is a hybrid bermudagrass with darker-green color than Tifway bermudagrass and similar leaf density but with a slightly wider leaf texture. It is vegetatively established as seed is unavailable. It has an aggressive lateral growth habit; thus, it recovers quickly from damage and also "stripes" better from mowing during summer than most other bermudagrass selections.

Quickstand (or Quicksand)

Quickstand is a selection from Kentucky released in 1993. It is a common bermudagrass which is extremely winter hardy and is an aggressive growing and spreading grass. It is not as fine textured nor as dense as hybrid bermudagrasses, but is a suitable alternative in areas which experience periodical "winter kill."

Tifgreen II

Tifgreen II, an induced mutant of Tifgreen released in 1983, is a light-green bermudagrass with vigorous, dense growth used most often for tees. Tifgreen II has better cold and nematode tolerance than Tifgreen. Excessive seedhead production and poor density at low mowing heights are problems with Tifgreen II.

Patriot

Patriot bermudagrass (OKC 18-4) was developed and released by the Oklahoma Agricultural Experiment Station. It is a hybrid between Tifton 10 and *C. transvaalensis*. It has more freeze tolerance than Tifway (419) and has fine texture and dark-green color (Figure 1–15). Patriot recovers well from physical injury with turf quality equal to Tifway during the early and middle parts of the growing season. However, it often does not hold turf quality as well as Tifway at the end of the growing season. No serious pest problems have been associated with Patriot. It is suitable for high-quality, intensively managed fairways/tee boxes and surrounds.

Greens

Tifgreen (or Tifton 328)

Tifgreen was released in 1956 and is a hybrid between a fine-textured *C. dactylon* and *C. transvaalensis*. It is a medium dark-green bermudagrass with high shoot density, fine texture, and low growth habit. It has soft leaves and tolerates close, frequent mowing. Tifgreen produces few seedheads at putting green height. This cultivar is the most commonly planted bermudagrass on golf greens around the world. It requires a high level of maintenance in terms of irrigation, fertilizing, dethatching, close mowing, and edging frequencies. Tifgreen is also popular for golf course tees,

FIGURE 1–15 Low-temperature tolerance of Patriot bermudagrass (bottom) compared to other cultivars (top).

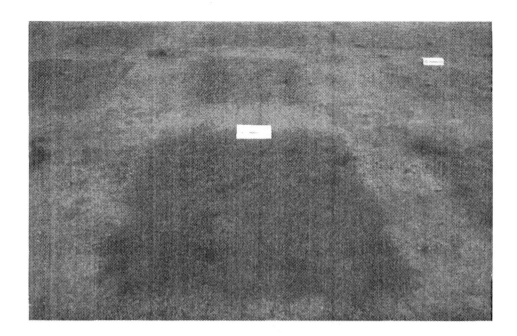

baseball and softball fields, tennis courts, and lawn bowling activities. It does not tolerate a long-term mowing height less than 3/16 inch (4.8 mm) and is susceptible to sting nematodes and spring dead spot.

Tifdwarf

This cultivar is believed to be a natural mutant from Tifgreen and was released in 1965. Tifdwarf resembles Tifgreen except for its shorter leaves and internodes. It is a high-maintenance grass used primarily on golf greens where a very low cutting height is desired for fast putting conditions. It develops a very dark-green turf with high shoot density and a low, slow growth habit. Tifdwarf has few seedheads, but it is susceptible to caterpillar and mole cricket damage. Tifdwarf turns a purple color when chilled (50°F, 10°C) and normally requires overseeding on golf greens in the winter. Problems with off-types or contaminants in recent years also have led to impure stands.

Pee Dee 102

Like Tifdwarf, Pee Dee 102 was selected from previously planted Tifgreen bermudagrass. It is dark green, very fine-textured, and fast spreading, compared to Tifdwarf. Pee Dee 102 was released in 1968 by the South Carolina Agricultural Experiment Station, Clemson, and is used predominantly on golf greens.

FloraDwarf

FloraDwarf bermudagrass, released from the University of Florida in 1995, was selected from a previously planted Tifgreen bermudagrass golf green located in Hawaii but is genetically different from Tifgreen and Tifdwarf. FloraDwarf growth characteristics appear similar to Tifdwarf except for its much finer leaf blade, denser stand, shorter internodal spacing, and extremely low growth habit. If left unmowed, it grows only to about 1/2 inch (1.3 cm) high. FloraDwarf produces no viable seeds, but does turn the characteristic purple color in cold weather and is thatch prone. FloraDwarf should be considered on golf greens, tennis courts, and bowling alleys.

Champion, Classic, Florida Dwarf, Jensen, Mini Verde, MS Supreme, Reese-grass, TifEagle, and other "Dwarf" Bermudagrasses

These low-growing grasses for closely mowed areas such as putting greens and lawn bowling (**Plate 1–1**) are believed to be somatic mutations from Tifdwarf or Tifgreen, possess a low growth habit, and are frequently maintained at a 1/8-inch (3.2-mm) mowing height. They have good density with cold tolerance similar to Tifdwarf. However, the greater shoot density of these grasses increase resistance to ball roll; thus, to obtain faster putting speeds, aggressive management practices, such as double cutting and/or rolling of the greens, are often necessary. They require relatively high fertility to maintain their appearance and vigor. As these are triploid hybrids, they

In recent years, considerable attention has been made toward the occurrence of mutants or off-types of grasses in previously pure bermudagrass stands (Figure 1–16). In addition to different color, texture, and density, off-types often have differential susceptibility to environmental stresses such as high temperature, humidity, and reduced sunlight intensity. Additional stresses such as low mowing height or verticutting often delay recovery. When 30 to 40 percent of the total surface has become contaminated, it becomes difficult to provide consistent, acceptable playing conditions, especially during periods of stressful weather. When over 50 percent of the surface becomes contaminated, it is almost impossible to provide a quality playing surface.

FIGURE 1–16 Patches of "off-type" bermudagrasses disrupt the uniformity and color of a playing surface.

It is believed off-types have arisen from the chance mutation of the parent material or possibly contamination through mechanical means or encroachment from collars. Mutations are abrupt inheritable changes brought about by alterations in a gene or a chromosome or by an increase in chromosome number. The rate of mutation occurrence can be increased artificially, but the results cannot be controlled. As they are usually recessive, mutations may be unexpressed for generations.

Mutations are produced by internal disorders, such as inaccurate gene duplication, and by natural external forces, such as severe temperature changes and sunlight radiation. They are induced experimentally by use of atomic radiation, X-rays, chemicals, and sudden temperature changes. Natural mutations appear very infrequently while artificial ones occur quicker. Tifway II, Tifgreen II, and TifEagle are induced mutations of original grasses created by exposing parent material to artificially high levels of radiation. Tifdwarf, FloraDwarf, and Pee Dee 102 bermudagrasses are believed to be natural mutants from Tifgreen bermudagrass.

Since Tifdwarf is a probable vegetative mutant from Tifgreen bermudagrass, a possibility exists that an original planting of Tifdwarf can undergo another mutation to produce a different grass. Champion, Mini Verde, MS Supreme, and others are believed mutations of Tifdwarf bermudagrass. Mutations offer breeders new ways of introducing genetic variability into breeding lines but also may cause existing materials to be somewhat unstable; thus, they may produce undesirable off-types after several years of growth.

produce no viable seed and must be vegetatively propagated. Due to tight density, these grasses are thatch prone; thus, they require periodic vertical mowing, grooming, and topdressing. They tend to be slower growing and develop a purplish color during cool (50°Fs, 10°Cs) temperatures similar to Tifdwarf. TifEagle (TW-72) is a 1997 release developed as an induced mutant by cobalt radiation from Tifway II bermudagrass. It resembles other "dwarfs" in its extremely fine leaf texture and excellent density.

Zoysiagrasses

Zoysiagrasses, named after Karl von Zois, an 18th-century Austrian botanist, are warm-season grasses (2n=40) native to the hot, humid Southeast Asia region including China, Korea, and Japan. They are becoming more important as golf course grasses due to their excellent wear tolerance, slow growth rate, improved winter hardiness (Figure 1–17), salt tolerance, unique green color during the summer, and golden color during winter months (Figure 1–18). Zoysiagrasses also have better shade tolerance than bermudagrass and lower fertility requirements. Zoysiagrasses are well-adapted for use on golf course fairways, tees, bunker faces (Figure 1–19), and collars.

Zoysiagrasses as a whole, however, are very slow-growing grasses; thus, they have slow recuperative potential. This slow lateral growth, however, is often an advantage as zoysiagrasses are often planted on the perimeter of sand traps and golf greens to greatly reduce or slow off-site lateral growth. They tend to develop thatch over time, and are susceptible to several diseases, most notably rusts and brown patch. Most improved zoysias have to be propagated vegetatively and are

FIGURE I–17
Approximate zoysiagrass
(*Zoysia japonica*) use range
in the mainland United
States.

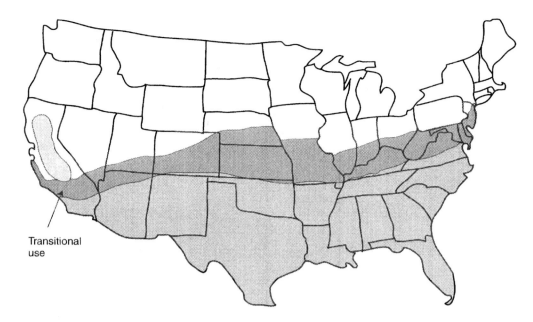

Transitional
use

FIGURE I–18 Zoysiagrass
is used on golf courses due to
its slow lateral growth, tight
density, cold-temperature
tolerance, and unique
summer and winter
appearance. Shown is
"Meyer" zoysiagrass.

extremely slow in becoming established. Other disadvantages include slow recovery from damage; poor growth on acid and compacted soils; higher water requirements than most bermudagrasses; susceptibility to bermudagrass invasion; and possible severe damage by nematodes, hunting billbugs, and several diseases. Zoysiagrass, being native to areas which naturally receive heavy yearly precipitation, also tends to be shallower rooting and is weakened when grown in soils low in potassium levels. For maximum beauty, a reel mower should be used for cutting.

There are several species and varieties of zoysiagrasses which can be used for golf courses (Table 1–10). These varieties vary widely in color, texture, and establishment rate. Only the more common varieties will be discussed.

Zoysia japonica Steud

This species, commonly called Japanese, Chinese, or Korean Common lawngrass, was introduced into the United States as seed in 1930 from Kokai, North Korea. It has a very coarse texture; hairy, light-green leaves; a faster growth rate; and the best cold tolerance of the zoysias. Although cold tolerant, it quickly loses color with slight frost. The hunting billbug and nematodes cause considerable damage to this lawngrass. *Zoysia japonica* is the only zoysia for which seed is commercially available. It can be used for lawns or general turf areas where convenience of

FIGURE 1-19
Zoysiagrass is often used around high-maintenance areas such as bunkers due to its slower lateral growth rate; thus, there is a less frequent need to trim.

TABLE 1-10 *Zoysiagrasses used for fine turf purposes.*

Zoysiagrass (common names)	Propagation method	
	Vegetative	Seeded
Zoysia japonica (Japanese, Chinese, or Korean Common)	Belaire, Crowne, El Toro, Empire, Empress, Meyer, Palisades	Cathay, Companion, Compatibility, J-36 & 37, Ming, SR 9150 & 9200, Sunrise, Sunstar, Traveler, W3-2, Zen 100-300, Zenith, Zoysia japonica
Zoysia matrella (Manilagrass)	Cashmere, Cavalier, Diamond	—
Zoysia japonica x *Z. matrella*	Z-3	—
Zoysia tenuifolia (Mascarenegrass, Templegrass, or Korean Velvetgrass)	—	—
Z. japonica x *Z. tenuifolia*	Emerald	—
Z. japonica x (*Z. matrella* x *Z. tenuifolia*)	DeAnza, Victoria	—
Z. sinica	J-14	Zoysia sinica
Other cultivars (these are mostly selections from *Z. japonica*)	GN 2, JaMur, Links, Marion Miyako, Omni, Royal, Serene, VJ, Zeon, Zoy-Boy, Zorro (9601)	—

establishment by seed is more important than quality. The optimum soil temperature range for seed germination is 70 to 95°F (21 to 35°C), with slowest germination occurring at the lower range. Current seeded cultivars include Cathay, Companion, Compatibility, J-36 & 37, Ming, SR 9150 & 9200, Sunrise, Sunstar, Traveler, W3-2, Zen 100-300, Zenith, and Zoysia japonica. Important vegetatively established cultivars of Z. *japonica* include the following.

Meyer
Meyer zoysia, also called Z-52 or Amazoy, is an improved selection of *Zoysia japonica* released in 1951 and named after Frank N. Meyer, who was one of the first plant explorers to collect zoysiagrass seed in Korea in 1905. Meyer has a deep-green color and medium-leaf texture. It spreads faster than many other varieties although it produces few rhizomes. Meyer makes an excellent fairway once established. Meyer is less shade tolerant than Emerald but is the most cold-tolerant

zoysiagrass. Hunting billbugs, brown patch, nematodes, and particularly mole crickets are potential problems with Meyer. Meyer is the zoysiagrass often advertised as the "miracle" or "wonder" grass in newspapers and magazines.

Belaire
Belaire, a *Zoysia japonica* developed in Maryland and released in 1985, is noted for its excellent cold tolerance and medium-green color. Compared to Meyer, Belaire has a more open growth habit, coarser leaf texture, and faster establishment rate.

El Toro
El Toro is another improved *Zoysia japonica* released in 1986 from California. It resembles Meyer but has a coarser leaf texture, quicker establishment rate, improved cool-season color, and less thatch buildup. El Toro is also reported to have early spring green-up and improved resistance to rust disease. El Toro has the quickest recuperative potential of the zoysiagrasses, has good shade tolerance, and uses less water than Meyer and Emerald. El Toro, however, does have a medium-coarse leaf texture. It also is easily mowed with a rotary mower.

Crowne
Crowne (DALZ8512) is a medium-coarse textured (3 to 4 mm leaf width), vegetatively propagated clone of *Zoysia japonica*. It is noted for drought tolerance, cold hardiness, rapid recuperative ability, and intermediate resistance to zoysiagrass mite. It is suitable for golf course roughs, lawns, industrial parks, and highway right-of-ways.

Palisades
Palisades (DALZ8514) is a medium-coarse textured (average width of 3.4 mm) vegetatively propagated clone of *Zoysia japonica* noted for shade tolerance, cold hardiness, rapid recuperative potential, moderate salinity tolerance, and low water use need. It is used for golf course fairways and roughs, lawns, and industrial parks.

Empire and **Empress** are two *Z. japonica* selections from Brazil released in the United States by a private vendor. Empire is a coarse-textured (6 to 8 mm leaf width), blue-green colored turfgrass with an open growth habit (32 shoots per sq.dm.) noted for rapid coverage and tolerance to rotary mowers. Empress is a small, fine-bladed (1 to 2 mm leaf width) *Z. japonica* similar to Emerald that possesses a blue-green color, has rapid coverage compared to Emerald, but has poor cold tolerance.

Zoysia matrella (L.) Merr
Also called Manilagrass since it was introduced from Manila, the Philippines, in 1912, this species produces a finer and denser lawn than *Zoysia japonica* but is less winter hardy. Its leaf blades are thin, sharply pointed, and wiry. Manilagrass resembles bermudagrass in texture, color, and quality and is recommended for a high-quality, high-maintenance turf where a slow rate of establishment is not a disadvantage. *Zoysia matrella* appears to be highly susceptible to damage by nematodes. Cultivars include the following.

Diamond
Diamond (DALZ8502) is a fine-textured (1 to 1.3 mm wide), highly rhizomatous, vegetatively propagated *Zoysia matrella* selection from Texas. Diamond is distinguished from other varieties of zoysiagrass by the combination of characters of shade tolerance, salinity tolerance, and turf quality. "Diamond" is closest in appearance to Emerald. "Diamond" generally lacks winter hardiness and is recommended for use south of the Red River (Texas-Oklahoma) and in the coastal plain states. It is suitable for golf course fairways, tees, and collars.

Cavalier
Cavalier (DALZ8507) is another *Zoysia matrella* selection from Texas and is distinguished from other zoysiagrass by its fine-textured, long-narrow leaf (1.3 mm to 1.7 mm width), with low rhizome but high stolon production. It has good-to-excellent salt tolerance and good shade tolerance. Cavalier is resistant to the fall armyworm and the tropical sod webworm. It is intermediate in its growth and recovery rate, has good-to-excellent winter hardiness, and will persist in regions north to Kansas, Missouri, and Southern Illinois. Cavalier is suitable for golf course fairways, tees, and home lawns.

Cashmere

Cashmere is a *Zoysia matrella* selection from the Florida Keys and is a 1988 release from Pursley Turf Farms located in Palmetto, Florida. It resembles Emerald zoysiagrass in color, fine-leaf texture, and density, but does not exhibit the stiff, bristle-like feel Emerald does. Its shade tolerance is not fully known but lacks cold hardiness; thus, it is best adapted to the lower southern region. It is recommended to be grown in soil containing clay, shell, rock, marl, or sand.

Zoysia japonica x *Z. matrella*

The only reported cultivar of this cross is Z-3 in Hawaii. It is medium-textured, apple-green in color, and forms a tight mat. It develops less thatch than "Emerald" but somewhat more than "El Toro."

Zoysia tenuifolia Willd. ex Trin

Also called Mascarenegrass and Korean velvetgrass, this species is the finest textured, most dense, least winter hardy zoysiagrass available. It is native to the Far East and was introduced from the Mascarene Islands. It has good wear tolerance but is extremely slow to spread and develops excessive thatch, giving it a puffy appearance (Figure 1–20). Since it also is the least cold hardy zoysiagrass, *Zoysia tenuifolia* is best adapted only to tropical and subtropical climates.

Zoysia japonica x *Z. tenuifolia*

Emerald

Emerald zoysia is a selected hybrid between *Zoysia japonica* and *Z. tenuifolia* released in 1955, although recent DNA fingerprinting suggests it is possibly a cross between *Z. matrella* and *Z. pacifica*. This hybrid combines the winter hardiness, color, and faster growth rate of *Z. japonica* with the fine texture and density of *Z. tenuifolia*. Emerald resembles Manilagrass in color, texture, and density, but is faster-spreading and has wider adaptation. Emerald zoysia is highly recommended for quality turf where time and money allow for an adequate maintenance program. Emerald may be the most beautiful of the zoysiagrasses, but it also is subject to thatch buildup, puffiness, and is susceptible to dollar and leaf spot and brown patch disease. Seed of Emerald zoysiagrass is very expensive and does not reproduce true to the variety.

Zoysia japonica x *(Z. matrella* x *Z. tenuifolia)*

Two cultivars released in 1993 from the University of California are **DeAnza** and **Victoria.** These hybrids include El Toro and other experimental lines as parents, which provide them with faster lateral growth than most traditional cultivars. Both also have a finer leaf texture, although not as fine as Emerald zoysiagrass. Both are mowed between 1/2 and 1 1/2 inch (1.3 to 3.8 cm) and both appear to have good shade and cold tolerance. Victoria tends to respond or green-up earlier in spring while DeAnza tends to hold its color later into the fall with both having better cool-season

FIGURE 1–20 Puffy, uneven appearance resulting from excessive thatch in zoysiagrass.

color than El Toro. Victoria and DeAnza should be used under medium-to-high maintenance situations and can become stemmy during certain growing seasons. Victoria produces flowers which are white to yellow in color while DeAnza has maroon-colored flowers. DeAnza also has slightly more blue tint to its color compared to Victoria while Victoria has a softer leaf blade touch than DeAnza.

Additional Zoysiagrass Cultivars

Much research is currently being conducted on breeding and selecting additional zoysiagrass cultivars for the turfgrass sector. SR 9000 is a two-clone synthetic which produces a moderately dense, medium textured, aggressive turf. It has excellent cold tolerance and should be used as a low-maintenance turf. SR 9100 zoysiagrass has a moderately fine texture and good disease and drought tolerance. Other vegetative zoysiagrasses being developed and evaluated include JaMur, Links, Marion, Miyako, Omni, Royal, Serene, VJ, Zeon, Zorro (9601), Zoy-Boy, and several numbered entries. A new turf-type seeded zoysia (Z. sinica Hance) also is being investigated for turfgrass potential, especially in low-to-moderate maintenance saline areas. J-14 is a commercial variety of Z. sinica. Other zoysia species being investigated for turf use include Z. macrostaycha Franch. et Sav. and Z. korenia, supposedly the most salt-tolerant zoysia species.

Management of Zoysiagrass Fairways

As with any turfgrass, once the species and variety of grass has been selected and established, success or failure of the grass is determined by its level of care. Successful management of any turfgrass requires the turf manager to know its biological limitations and manage these limitations. The primary limitations of zoysiagrass are shallow rooting, susceptibility to brown patch, bermudagrass encroachment, and slow recovery from damage, particularly scalping. The severity of these limitations is dependent upon the species and cultivar, as well as the environment and management.

Once zoysiagrass turf is established, the most important practice a turf manager can implement is the reduction of nitrogen fertilization. By reducing the amount of applied nitrogen, less vegetative growth and thatching occur. Excessive thatch restricts movement of water, fertilizer, and pesticides in the soil profile. This leads to weak, thin turf more susceptible to diseases, insects, and weed invasion. Shallow rooting turf is unable to survive periods of drought and severe winter temperatures, and delays recovery from damage. In general, zoysiagrasses should not be fertilized with more than three pounds of nitrogen per 1,000 square feet (15 kg/100 m^2) per growing season in most areas. Regions with longer growing seasons may require more nitrogen and regions with shorter growing seasons may require less. In addition, heavy traffic areas such as tee boxes may require more nitrogen. Applications of fertilizers high in phosphorus may lead to chlorosis early in spring, since phosphorus can bind certain micronutrients essential to early spring greening. In alkaline soils, a timely application of sulfur may provide adequate availability of these micronutrients. Iron in the form of ferrous sulfate or a chelated source may also provide color enhancement.

A unique problem occurs when a broad-leafed zoysiagrass (*japonica* type) is on the collars of bentgrass or bermudagrass greens. Most greens are fertilized with nitrogen at higher rates than recommended for the zoysiagrass collar. Fertilizer applied to the collar area at the same rates as the putting green can cause severe thatching. Collar areas require frequent, close mowing, which can result in severe scalping. For this reason, fertilizers should be applied to greens with a drop spreader or a boom sprayer. This solution is not always practical, but helps provide the needed result. Every effort should be made to reduce the amount of misapplied fertilizer to the collar. The application of plant-growth regulators may also alleviate scalping of collars. Some research has shown mowing zoysiagrasses with groomers can also reduce scalping. Grooming twice per week during the growing season has enhanced the performance of zoysiagrasses while reducing scalping.

Zoysiagrasses are known for their excellent traffic tolerance and resist tissue damage due to a high lignin and silica content within their leaves. Unfortunately, zoysiagrasses are also known for their lack of tolerance to compacted soils. For this reason, a good aerification and verticutting program must be developed and implemented after the turf is established. The soil profile must allow for good root moisture, drainage, and gas exchange for zoysiagrasses to perform at their peak. A routine aerification and heavy verticutting program will also help reduce any existing thatch. Core removal is recommended as well as a timely application of a labeled preemergence herbicide. Areas receiving excessive wear or high traffic, such as tee boxes, will require frequent aerification, and fertilizer rates and irrigation should be adjusted to encourage recovery. Additionally, care should be taken to keep bermudagrass from encroaching into zoysiagrass, as it is very difficult to control once established.

Bahiagrass

Bahiagrass (*Paspalum notatum* Flugge.) is a very coarse-textured species originally from rangelands and forest fringes in Argentina and Brazil in South America. It was introduced into the United States in 1914 and forms a low to fairly dense turf. It has very tough leaves and spreads vegetatively by short stout rhizomes and stolons. Its inflorescence bears two racemes as opposed to three to five for dallisgrass (*P. dilatatum*) or seven to nine for vaseygrass (*P. urvillei*). It is best adapted to the warm humid and hot humid zones. Bahiagrass has excellent drought tolerance, due in part to an extensive root system. It has fair shade and good wear tolerance, does particularly well on infertile, droughty sands, and seems affected little by nematodes. Fertility requirements are minimum. A major drawback about bahiagrass, however, is the constant production of tall (2 to 4 feet, 0.6 to 1.2 m), V-shaped seedheads continuously throughout the summer months. Salt tolerance is poor and a high mowing height (2 to 3 inches, 5 to 7.6 cm) is required to maintain an acceptable stand. Bahiagrass also often expresses iron chlorosis in spring and fall months. Often used as a roadside grass because of its toughness, bahiagrass frequently escapes into bermudagrass fairways and roughs. However, as water resources become more restrictive, fertilizer rates become reduced, and effective nematicides are lost, bahiagrass use may increase. Cultivars include Argentine, Common, Paraguay, Pensacola, RCP, Riba, and Wilmington.

Carpetgrass

Common carpetgrass (*Axonopus affinis* Beauv.) and tropical carpetgrass (*A. compressus* [Swarty] Beauv.) originated from the eastern regions of the hot, humid, poorly drained soils of South Central American continents including the West Indies. These are coarse-textured species which form a fairly dense turf. Carpetgrass spreads by stolons and appears similar to St. Augustinegrass and centipedegrass except for its lighter-green color and wavy leaf margin. It has limited cold, drought, and wear tolerance with only fair shade tolerance. Carpetgrass produces tall, unsightly crabgrass-like seedheads throughout the summer, giving the turf a ragged, unmowed appearance. Leaf tips also easily discolor with cool weather. Carpetgrass is also susceptible to brown patch disease. Like centipedegrass, carpetgrass grows best on acidic (pH 5 to 6) soils. It does tolerate wet, poorly drained soils very well, and often becomes established in these locations before escaping into other sites. Chase is an improved cultivar.

Centipedegrass

Centipedegrass [*Eremochloa ophiuroides* (Munro.) Hack.] is originally from hot, humid, high-rainfall areas of China and forms a relatively dense turf. Seeds of centipedegrass were found in the baggage of Frank N. Meyer, USDA plant explorer, who disappeared on his fourth trip to China in 1916. It spreads vegetatively by slow-growing stolons and is a diploid (2n = 18). It has medium leaf texture and a natural light-green (crab apple-green) color. The stems may be red, yellow, or green. Centipedegrass is more cold tolerant than St. Augustinegrass and carpetgrass but less so than bermudagrasses and most zoysiagrasses. Due to exposed stolons and a shallow root system, centipedegrass has limited cold and drought tolerance. Shade tolerance is fair. Maintenance requirements in terms of fertility and mowing frequency are low.

Centipedegrass grows on a variety of soils but is best adapted to slightly acid (pH 5 to 6) soils. It has poor salt tolerance and is susceptible to ring nematode damage. It also often experiences iron chlorosis during spring months. It is sometimes planted as golf course roughs due to its unique, lighter-green color and coarser texture. However, invariably, centipedegrass in this situation receives excessive amounts of fertilizer and water, is mowed too short, and is often accidently treated with sensitive herbicides. The results are often disappointing. Centipedegrass, however, does fairly well in shady areas which receive minimum play and maintenance. Cultivars include AU Centennial, Centi-Seed (common), Common, Oaklawn, TennTurf (formerly Tennessee Hardy), and TifBlair. The improved cultivars have better cold tolerance than common. AU Centennial is only vegetatively propagated.

Kikuyugrass

Kikuyugrass (*Pennisetum clandestinum* Hochst ex. Chiov.) is a coarse-to-medium-textured, lime-green, dioecious species originating from heavily grazed pastures in the hot, arid regions of the Kenyan highlands in eastern Africa. The common name is derived from a native tribe. It spreads by thick, leafy rhizomes, stolons, and seed, and has a very rapid growth rate under warm, moist environments. It is found primarily in California, certain islands of Hawaii, Australia, New Zealand, South Africa, Colombia, Mexico, South America, Spain, and other tropical areas of the world, where it is considered a weed as well as a turfgrass. It has a very aggressive growth habit, often invading and overtaking areas with more desirable species, and was initially used in California for erosion control.

Kikuyugrass forms a dense, tough sod when mowed close, although the production of white filaments often gives it a silvery cast. Its leaf width ranges from 1/8 to 1/4 inch (3.2 to 6.4 mm), similar to Japonica zoysiagrasses and St. Augustinegrass. Due to its similar texture, growth habit, and thick stolons, kikuyugrass is often confused with St. Augustinegrass. It has good drought and wear tolerance but poor cold and limited shade tolerance. Compared to bermudagrass, kikuyugrass grows better under low light conditions and is not as prone to dormancy in cool (50 to 60°F, 10 to 15.6°C) weather. It usually outcompetes bermudagrass where climates are mild, hazy, and subtropical. Kikuyugrass tolerates light frosts better than most warm-season grasses without a loss of color. Kikuyugrass can escape and become very problematic. Hosaka is a cultivar established mostly by sprigs. Whittet is a forage-type cultivar from which AZ-1 (or Arizona-1) was selected. AZ-1 has a less-invasive, turf-type cultivar with good traffic tolerance.

When mowed high (>1.5 inch, 3.8 cm), kikuyugrass forms an open growth habit due to the fleshy stolons and relatively wide leaf blade. When mowed at lower heights, stand density generally improves. Due to its rapid growth rate, kikuyugrass is thatch prone. Greens and tee encroachment can be problematic and, when left unmowed in roughs, the grass is very difficult to hit out of. Best growth often occurs in medium-to-heavy-textured soils with a neutral-to-alkaline pH. Advantages and disadvantages of kikuyugrass include (modified from Gross, 2003):

Advantages	Disadvantages
Excellent tolerance to traffic	Medium to coarse texture
Rapid recovery from injury	Rapid thatch accumulation
Good heat, drought, and salinity tolerance	Natural lime-green color
Tough, competitive grass for hitting golf shots	Often has a silvery cast appearance from production of white filaments above the turf canopy
Good growth and color retention at temperatures from 50 to 60°F (10 to 15.6°C)	Potential for mower scalping
Tolerant of a wide range of soil and water environments	Frequent mowing, verticutting, and aerification to minimize scalping and to control rapid growth
Good pest resistance	Damaged by many postemergence herbicides
Low nutrient requirements, e.g., two to three pounds N/1,000 sq.ft. (10 to 15 kg N/100 m^2) yearly	Other pests and their control are largely unknown

Management Practices

For successful kikuyugrass management, proper mechanical, growth regulator, moisture, and fertility components must be integrated. By being integrated, these components help maintain a dense, less-coarse, and less-thatchy stand of kikuyugrass. Insufficient moisture restricts rooting, causing the grass to become puffy and more prone to scalping.

Mowing, Vertical Mowing, and Aerification

Mowing heights for kikuyugrass range from 0.25 inch (6.4 mm) on tees and collars to more than two inches (5 cm) in roughs. Fairways are typically mowed from 1/2 to 5/8 inch (1.3 to 1.6 cm) three to five times weekly during active growth to minimize scalping. Unlike other fairway grasses, heavier, motor-driven reel mowing units are preferred with kikuyugrass to push reels into the turf canopy for a higher-quality cut. Roughs are maintained between 1.5 and 2 inches (3.8 to 5 cm) and require twice-weekly mowing to prevent scalping. Due to the tough shoots of kikuyugrass, added wear on mowing equipment generally reduces their life expectancy by 10 percent or more.

Vertical mowing helps minimize thatch development and prevents formation of long, coarse, poorly rooted stolons. Thatch and long stolons increase scalping and excessive turf removal by mowing. Verticutting three times a year [e.g., April, July, and September at approximately 0.5 inch (1.3 cm)] seems necessary to achieve this standard for kikuyugrass fairways. Alternatively, light (e.g., 0.25 inch, 0.64 cm), monthly vertical mowings during periods of active growth help avoid the heavy debris generated by less-frequent, heavier vertical mowings.

Vertical mowing is incorporated with deep tine aerification which promotes deeper rooting by alleviating compaction. At least one deep-tine (e.g., 6 to 10 inches, 15 to 25 cm) aerification in spring followed by light verticutting in spring and two additional regular aerifications in summer help "tighten" the stand of kikuyugrass. The use of plant-growth regulators are also incorporated in this mechanical management. Gibberellic acid-inhibiting PGRs, such as trinexapac-ethyl (e.g., Primo), applied every three to four weeks, have dramatically improved kikuyugrass stands by reducing scalping and clipping production. These PGRs cause a shorter, more compact growth habit, with finer leaf texture and denser stands. Treated plants also have a darker color. When combined with verticutting and aerification, PGRs allow mowing heights of 0.5 inch (1.3 cm) or less without scalping, excessive clipping production, or exposure of brown, senescing leaves underneath. Bermudagrass encroachment may also be discouraged at higher PGR rates. Chelated iron should be tank-mixed with the PGRs, especially with the first seasonal application, as temporary discoloration often occurs then.

Fertility

Fertility rates also should be closely regulated so as not to be too heavy to encourage thatch or scalping of the kikuyugrass or underfertilized grass which discourages aggressive growth. Use two to three pounds of nitrogen per 1,000 square feet (98 to 147 kg N/ha) in late spring as a slow-release source or as 1 lb N/1,000 sq.ft. applications (4.9 kg N/100 m^2) in April, June, and August. Additional light (1/8 to 1/4 lbs N/1,000 sq.ft., 6 to 12 kg N/ha) nitrogen applications seem to promote good, but not too aggressive, kikuyugrass growth. Supplemental chelated iron and manganese also promote green color without promoting excessive growth. Phosphorus, potassium, and other nutrient needs should be based on annual soil and tissue tests.

Pest Problems

Being a relatively new turfgrass to the United States, the full potential of pest problems on kikuyugrass probably has not been experienced. It is sensitive to most postemergence herbicides, especially MSMA, quinclorac, and triclopyr. Three-way mixtures of 2,4-D, MCPP, and dicamba can be used but only at one-half to one-fourth of their normal recommended label rates. Clopyralid appears safe on kikuyugrass.

Brown patch and take-all patch are other known pest problems. Manganese sulfate at one pound product per 1,000 square feet (4.9 kg/100 m^2) helps control take-all patch without the use of fungicides. As the use range of kikuyugrass expands, additional pest problems will probably occur.

Seashore Paspalum

Seashore paspalum (*Paspalum vaginatum* Swartz.) is a sexually reproducing, diploid ($2n=20$), dense, variable-textured species of relatively dark-green color, originally from South Africa and secondarily from Argentina north into Brazil, where it is often found growing along seashores (hence, its common name) and in brackish water (Figure 1–21). In the United States, it grows in coastal areas of the Southeast to Texas (Figure 1–22) and southward into Mexico and Argentina. Due to self-incompatibility, seed production is inhibited; thus, seashore paspalum is mostly propagated vegetatively. Traditional selections include Excaliber (formerly Adalayd) and Futurf. New releases include AP-10, Boardwalk, FWY-1, Neptune Salam (fairways), Seadwarf (greens), Sea-Green (greens), Sea Isle I (tees and fairways), Sea Isle 2001 (greens), SeaSpray (seeded), and Sea-Way (fairways).

FIGURE 1–21 Seashore paspalum has excellent salt tolerance and grows best in saline or brackish locations.

FIGURE 1–22
Approximate anticipated use range of seashore paspalum in the mainland United States.

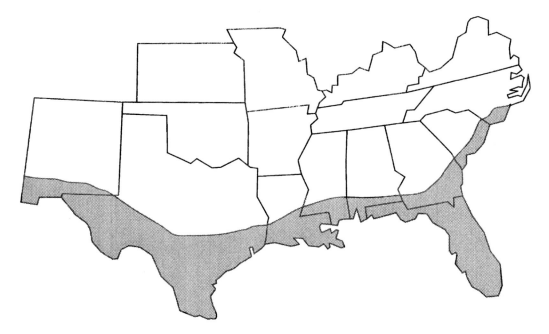

Advantages of seashore paspalum include:

- It has the highest salinity tolerance of all warm-season grasses—withstanding short irrigation duration with seawater (~35,000 ppm salts). However, the turf must be fully grown-in to withstand this and have excellent soil drainage available. With diligence and the right growing conditions, water with ~5,000 ppm salts can routinely be used.
- Compared to bermudagrass, seashore paspalum has better low-light and cool-temperature tolerance from shorter winter days, or cloudy, rainy, foggy, or smoggy conditions.
- Due to its good water logging or low oxygen tolerance, seashore paspalum can be inundated for short intervals with minimal detrimental effects.
- Requires between 30 to 50 percent less nitrogen than bermudagrass. If fertilized similar to bermudagrass, seashore paspalum tends to thatch and then severely scalps.
- Minimal seedhead production with certain cultivars and does not readily produce viable seed. However, when stressed, seashore paspalum, like most grasses, produces a flush of seedheads.
- Seashore paspalum has a shiny, glassy dark-green hue, similar to Kentucky bluegrass or perennial ryegrass, with similar striping capabilities.

Limitations of seashore paspalum include:

- Poor shade tolerance, requiring about six to eight hours of full sunlight daily for acceptable performance, similar to bermudagrass.

- Limited cold-tolerance, thus, appears limited in geographic range: tropical areas, or coastal areas in subtropical zones.
- Although it has superior salt tolerance when established, seashore paspalum cannot be effectively and rapidly established with irrigation water high in salinity (>5,000 ppm total salts) due to suppression of root growth. Fresh water will be necessary during grow-in or extended time will be necessary to achieve this. Fresh water also is needed periodically during prolonged droughts. Salinity tolerance, however, substantially increases as the turf matures. Leaf tip burn can also occur following irrigation of high-salt containing water.
- **Although salt tolerant, having a sandy profile with high percolation rates is virtually mandatory for proper salt management of seashore paspalum. Areas with poor-draining silty or clay soils, or severely compacted soils, will find it extremely difficult to maintain any grass, including seashore paspalum.** Many rivers and salt-laden estuaries used to irrigate contain high levels of silt and clay, and with prolonged use may reduce the infiltration rates of soils.
- Irrigation heads have to be monitored constantly to ensure each sprinkler is operating properly. Additional heads are often needed to improve application uniformity. Granular calcium applications such as gypsum ($CaSO_4$), calcium nitrate, or possibly liquid potash are needed to displace the excess sodium (Na) in the soil. The sodium then is leached down below the turf root system; hence, the need for a soil profile with high percolation capabilities. Soil compaction, thus, needs to be avoided. An aggressive deep-tine aerification program will be needed in poorly draining soils. Other nutrients such as phosphorus, potassium, magnesium, and manganese also are critical for good turf performance, requiring constant tissue and soil testing and regular spoon feeding.
- Seashore paspalum appears very thatch prone; thus, it may require more grooming, verticutting, and topdressing to control this. Also, due to paspalum's tougher leaves, mower bed-knives and reels dull quicker and need replacing more frequently.
- Few pesticides are labeled specifically for seashore paspalum.
- Bermudagrass and other grassy weeds can be very problematic. Currently, no selective herbicides are labeled to control grassy weeds in seashore paspalum. Weed control, especially bermudagrass suppression, involves using less nitrogen to discourage the bermudagrass, using saline irrigation to slow bermudagrass more than the paspalum, and applying rock salt to infested areas. All planting stock should be certified bermudagrass free.
- Other sporadic pests include billbugs, armyworms, webworms, leaf spots, dollarspot, and patch diseases.
- Excess nitrogen leads to succulent growth and enhanced scalping, predisposing the grass to pathogen attack.
- Seedheads may persist with some cultivars during certain months of the growing season (Figure 1–23).

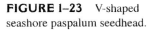

FIGURE 1–23 V-shaped seashore paspalum seedhead.

- Most agronomic practices and long-term problems are still largely unknown or unproven for seashore paspalum; thus, only limited information is available on this.

With these in mind, seashore paspalum is best grown in high-draining sand content environments where salinity or poor water quality is an issue and inadequate quality water is available. If agronomic conditions of the site will support bermudagrass, it is advised to do so.

St. Augustinegrass

St. Augustinegrass [*Stenotaphrum secundatum* (Walt.) Kuntze] is believed to be native to open-to-lightly shaded, high rainfall, and humid regions of coastal South and Central America including the West Indies. It spreads by thick, long stolons and forms a very coarse-textured turf of medium density. Due to the lack of cold tolerance, St. Augustinegrass use is restricted to coastal areas of the lower Atlantic states, the gulf coast regions, all of Florida, and parts of southwest and southern California. Its drought tolerance is fair to good but often develops chlorosis (yellowing) when grown on alkaline soils. Certain cultivars have good shade and salt tolerance. Chinch bugs, gray leaf spot disease, St. Augustinegrass Decline (SAD) virus, and brown patch disease are problems. The mowing height ranges from 1.5 to 3 inches (3.8 to 7.6 cm). Its use on most golf courses is limited to shade areas or lower-quality roughs. Cultivars include Amerishade (80-10), Bitterblue, Delmar, Emerald Blue, Floralawn, Floratam, Floratine, FX-10, FX-33, Gulf Star, Island, Jade, Levi, Mercedes, Palmetto, Raleigh, Raleigh-S, Sapphire, Seville, Sunclipse, Texas Common, Winchester, Woerner Classic, and 80-10.

Blue Couch

Blue couch, Queensland blue couch, or serangoon (*Digitaria dactyloides*) is a fine-leaved, warm-season, blue-green colored grass used for lawns and golf greens in tropical regions of Australia. It grows as far north as southern Malaysia and Asia, where it is called serangoon. Blue couch possesses a rolled vernation, an entire membranous ligule up to two millimeters long. Auricles are absent. Leaf blades are soft, becoming hairless as they taper to a pointed leaf tip. It has stolons which root at the nodes and a slender panicle with two to four spike-like branches for an inflorescence. Blue couch produces a dense, soft turf subject to thatching. Its use on golf greens is being replaced by the hybrid bermudagrasses.

Cool-Season Grasses

Bentgrasses

Bentgrass (*Agrostis* sp.) is native to the cool, moist climate of central Europe and is adapted to cool, humid environments from the Northeast to the Northwest in the United States (Figure 1–24). Bentgrasses, however, are used outside this climatic region predominantly only on small, highly maintained areas such as golf greens. It provides a year-round green surface, not requiring yearly overseeding and transition in spring as bermudagrass does (Figure 1–25). Hot (temperatures >90°F, 32°C), humid summer conditions are unfavorable for its growth and development. Under such conditions it often becomes very shallow rooted due to the depletion of carbohydrate reserves and is very susceptible to stresses such as drought, traffic, and diseases. The microclimate surrounding the bentgrass grown in these areas is often altered to better favor its survival. This includes soil preparation, irrigation, surface and subsurface air circulation, shade, and other parameters. Bentgrass, due to its aggressive stoloniferous growth, can become a serious weed in other cool-season turfgrasses such as fescue and Kentucky bluegrass.

Varieties

The genus *Agrostis*, which bentgrass belongs to, has approximately 125 species which evolved from Europe and are adapted to the cooler regions of the world. Turf-type bentgrasses currently include Creeping (*Agrostis palustris* subsp. *stolonifera* L.), Colonial (*A. tenuis* Sibth., also listed as *A. capillaris* L.), Redtop (*A. alba* L.), and Velvet bentgrass (*A. canina* L.) (Plate 1–2). Various bentgrass varieties produce a broad range of colors, from greenish-yellow to dark green and dark blue-green.

FIGURE 1–24
Approximate bentgrass use range for golf courses in the mainland United States (**Note:** overlapping ranges often occur).

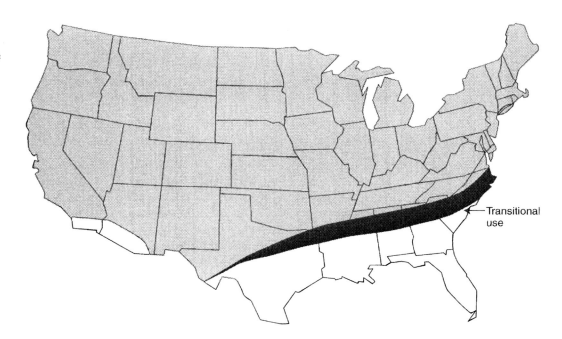

FIGURE 1–25 Creeping bentgrass provides a closely mowed, desirable fairway, approach, and putting green playing surface which noticeably stripes when mowed.

Creeping and colonial bentgrass are the two most widely used species for golf course purposes (Table 1–11). Creeping bentgrass is a fine-textured, cool-season perennial with excellent cold tolerance and is stoloniferous; hence, the name "creeping." It has less wear tolerance than may other turfgrass species, poor soil compaction tolerance, and slow recuperative ability following damage or environmental stress. Creeping bentgrass also is a heavy thatch producer which must be controlled. It is the primary bentgrass used for cool-season golf greens in the temperate and transition zones of the United States. The most widely used creeping bentgrass varieties for putting greens have been "Arlington," "Cohansey," "Toronto," and "Congressional." However, beginning in the 1950s, "Penncross," "Pennlinks," "Penneagle," "Seaside," and "Emerald" began to dominate. Currently, "Crenshaw," "SR 1019/1020," Penn "A" and "G" series, and L-93 rapidly are being used in place of the old industry standard, Penncross. The newer cultivars should be mowed lower (5/32 to 1/8 inch, 4 to 3 mm), aerated, and topdressed more as they tend to be more aggressive in their growth habit. Small (3/16 to 1/4 inch, 4.8 to 6.4 mm) tines are used to aerify more often along with frequent brushing and light topdressing to manage thatch and soil

TABLE 1-11 *Bentgrass cultivars used for golf course purposes.*

Creeping Bentgrass (*Agrostis palustris* subsp. *stolonifera* L.)

Penn A & G Series (A-1; A-4; G-1; G-2; G-4; G-6), Backspin, Barifera, Bengal, Brighton, Carman, Cato, Century, CEO, Cobra, Crenshaw, Dominant (SR 1019 + SR 1020), Dominant Plus/Xtreme, Emerald, Grand Prix, 18th Green, Imperial, Independence, Inverness, L-93, Lopez, LS-44, Mariner, National, Penncross, Penneagle, Pennlinks, PLS, Princeville, ProCup, Prominent, Providence (SR 1019), Putter, Regent (Normark 101), Seaside II, Southshore, SR 1020, 1119, 1120, T1, T2, Tendenz, Trueline, Viper.

Comments. Penncross, released in 1954, is currently the most widely used creeping bentgrass variety. It is a polysynthetic variety between the accession numbers 10(37)4 (or Pennlu creeping bentgrass), 9(38)5, and 11(38)4. However, it lacks resistance to *Pythium* and *Rhizoctonia* diseases, has a shallow rooting system, becomes grainy, and tends to segregate into various patches in the fall (Figure 1–26). Improved varieties have better putting and color characteristics but still lack specific disease resistance, especially to dollar spot, and have limited heat tolerance. Blends (e.g., Cato + Crenshaw) show potential for overcoming some of these limitations. Improvements are being made on heat tolerance, putting quality (density and fine leaf blades), and summer rooting. Seaside and Mariner (a selection from Seaside) are noted for their salt tolerance.

This list is very dynamic as new varieties are continually being released and others are discontinued. Check with your state turfgrass extension specialist and seed supplier for the latest available and recommended cultivars for your specific area and needs.

Arlington (C-1), Cohansey (C-7), Collins, Congressional (C-19), Emerald (seeded), Evansville, Metropolitan (C-51), Norbeck (C-36), Old Orchard (C-52), Pennlu (10[37]4), Pennpar, Toronto (C-15), Washington (C-50).

Comments. These older varieties either have excessive stripe smut or bacterial wilt disease problems and/or are not competitive enough on golf greens to recover from traffic damage, ball marks, and stress damage, or cannot aggressively compete with annual bluegrass (*Poa annua*). Their use, therefore, is becoming less important.

Colonial Bentgrass (*A. tenuis* Sibthorp)

Alister, Allure, Astoria, Bardot, Barostis, Boral, Egmont, Glory, Heriot, Holfior, SR 7000/7100/7150, Tendenz, Tiger I-II, Tracenta.

Comments. These are bunchgrasses which tend to grow more upright and require less water and fertility than creeping bentgrass. They generally do not tolerate close mowing like creeping bentgrass. They have been used mostly as a component of mixtures for fairways and general turfgrass areas in coastal areas of the Pacific Northwest, Northeast, and northern Europe (summer temperatures less than 85°F, 29°C). Newer cultivars may prove better adapted to other regions and other uses.

Velvet Bentgrass (*A. canina* subsp. *canina* L.), Dryland or Highland Bentgrass (*A. castellana*), Browntop (*A. capillaris*), Redtop (*A. alba* L.)

Acme (velvet), Barracuda (redtop), Bavaria (velvet), BR 1518 (dryland), Egmont (browntop), Exeter (dryland), Greenwich (velvet), Highland (dryland), Kernwood (velvet), Kingston (velvet), Piper (velvet), Raritan (velvet), Reten (redtop), Rudiger (redtop), Sefton (browntop), SR 7200 (velvet), Streaker (redtop), Vesper (velvet).

Comments. These produce some of the finest textured turfgrasses used for putting surfaces due to upright growth habit and density. However, due to lack of heat, disease, and traffic tolerance, they are used mostly in upper New England and the Pacific Northwest, New Zealand, Australia, and in other places as a part of blends. Velvet bentgrass is also noted for its shade tolerance. Redtop establishes the quickest of the *Agrostis* species and performs well on wet, poorly drained sites.

Idaho Bentgrass (*Agrostis idahoensis* Nash)

GolfStar

Comments. A new turf species, Idaho bentgrass has a fine texture, upright leaves, dark-green color, and non-creeping (bunch-type) growth habit. It is useful for winter overseeding or as a low-maintenance permanent turf in fairways or roughs.

---

compaction. However, the fine-textured, aggressive-growing newer varieties are more susceptible to thatch buildup, scalping, and "puffiness"; thus, they need more aggressive management.

Colonial bentgrass, by contrast, has minimal creeping tendencies. Colonial bentgrass is currently being used in the maritime regions of Canada and the Northeast, Great Lakes, and Northwestern areas of the United States. They are being genetically improved for fairway use. Under close mowing, creeping bentgrass tends to form a fine-textured, dense, and low-growing turf, while colonial bentgrass forms an upright turf with more resistance to dollar spot disease and less nitrogen requirements. It is often mixed with fine fescues. Other bentgrass species currently being investigated for use on golf courses include Dryland (*Agrostis castellana*), Idaho (*A. idahoensis*), and Browntop (*A. capillaris*).

For tees and fairways, blends are often used to broaden the genetic base, thereby reducing disease occurrence. Two- and three-way blends containing Cato, Cobra, L-93, Penneagle, Pennlinks, Providence, or Seashore are currently popular.

Two popular grasses used for golf greens, bermudagrass and bentgrass, originated from separate continents. The point of origin of creeping bentgrass is Eurasia (Germany), while colonial bentgrass come from the arid conditions of Spain. Bermudagrass, however, originated in South Africa around the Indian Ocean. The points of origin and the areas of bentgrass use in the United States have similar but not the same climatic conditions. Germany's latitude is 52° north, whereas the latitude for the main area of use in the United States is near 42° north. The annual average temperatures in January and July in Germany are 30°F and 52°F (−1.1° and 11°C), respectively. The annual average rainfall in Germany is 25 inches (64 cm) versus 35 inches (89 cm) in the United States. Bentgrass, therefore, is being grown outside its normal adaptation range in the United States (see Figure 1–24). Many states can have annual temperatures 20 to 40 degrees higher than the optimum temperature for bentgrass. Also, the average rainfall can be 20 to 30 inches (51 to 76 cm) higher than the region of bentgrass origin.

Other areas with warm temperatures but low relative humidities can grow bentgrass with less effort than those with higher relative humidities. This probably is because, under low humidity conditions, evaporation is enhanced, which cools the surface of the plant and reduces photorespiration. In addition, temperatures cool down significantly at night. Low humidity areas also tend to have greater day/night temperature fluctuations. Although day temperatures are hot in these areas, the lack of humidity results in

night temperatures dropping substantially low compared to higher humidity regions. Plants grown under high temperatures and humidities have air moisture capacity nearer saturation; therefore, evaporation rates are reduced. With these conditions, man must alter the micro-climate surrounding bentgrass greens grown in areas outside their natural adaptation or they will perform poorly; therefore, optimum conditions for diseases are provided. Bentgrass management is discussed in more detail in Chapter 19.

Bermudagrass, however, has acclimated to varying elevations and temperatures from the areas in which it originated (see Figure 1–10). The latitude of South Africa is 25° south with an annual average rainfall of 30 inches (76 cm). Bermudagrass grows best in the United States near 33° north with an annual average rainfall of 50 inches (127 cm). The average temperature in January and July in South Africa is 85°F and 80°F, respectively (29° and 27°C), whereas in the United States it is 48°F and 80°F, respectively (9° and 27°C). The genus *Cynodon* consists of nine species, with *C. dactylon* being the most widespread. Today, most of the bermudagrasses used for turf are hybrids of two different *Cynodon* species: *C. dactylon* and *C. transvaalensis*. *Cynodon dactylon* is a highly fertile tetraploid with a broad genetic variability; thus, it is widely distributed in the United States. *Cynodon transvaalensis*, however, is a diploid; thus, it has a narrower adaptation region and also rarely produces viable seed. It is often used as part of the breeding stock of fine-leaf bermudagrasses such as Tifway, Tifdwarf, and Tifgreen.

FIGURE 1–26
"Penncross" creeping bentgrass often segregates into distinct patches several years after establishment. Neither a disease nor environmental stress is involved.

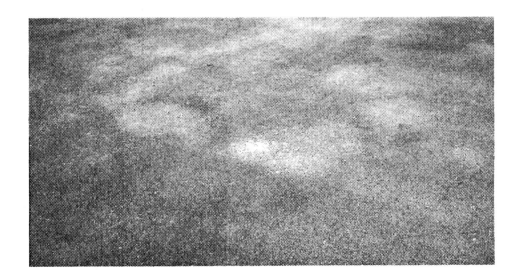

Kentucky Bluegrass

Kentucky bluegrass (*Poa pratensis* L.) is the most widely used cool-season turfgrass (Plate 1–3) and became popular due to its ability to survive summer drought through dormancy. It is native to cool, open areas in Europe and was introduced during the 1600s. It possesses a vigorous rhizome system which forms a very dense cover, allowing it to recover from divots and traffic damage, and has fair-to-good drought tolerance. During extended heat and drought stress without

TABLE 1–12 *Kentucky bluegrass cultivars (**Note:** check with your seed supplier and state turfgrass specialist for the latest recommended cultivar(s) for your particular area and needs).*

Improved, high-maintenance cultivars	Lower maintenance cultivars	Improved shade tolerance cultivars
Aaron, 4-Aces, Abbey, Able 1, Adams, Adelphi, Admiral, Alene, Alexa, Alpine, Amazon, America, Apart, Apex, Apollo, Arcadia, Arron, Ascot, Aspen, Asset, Award, Awesome, Banff, Banjo, Barcelona, Bariris, Baritone, Barmax, Baron, Baronette, Baronie, Barrister, Barsweet, Bartitia, Baruzo, Barzan, Bayside, Bedazzle, Bensun (A-34), Beyond, Blacksburg I-II, Blackstone, Blaze, Blue Chip, Blue Jay, Blue Knight, Blue Moon, Blue Note, Blueprint, Bluestar, Bodacious, Bonnieblue, Boomerang, Bordeaux, Boutique, Brilliant, Bristol, Broadway, Bronco, Brooklawn, Buckingham, Cabernet, Caliber, Cannon, Canterbury, Challenger, Champagne, Charlotte, Chateau, Cheri, Chicago I-II, Classic, Cobalt, Cocktail, Columbia, Confidence Blend, Coventry, Crest, Cynthia, Dawn, Deepblue, Dellwood, Denin, Destiny, Dormie, Dragon, Eagleton, Emmundi, Enoble, Envicta, Escort, Estate, Excursion, Explorer, Fairfax, Famous, Fortuna, Freedom I-III, Georgetown, Geronimo, Glacier, Glade, Gnome, Goldrush, Haga, Hallmark, Holiday, Huntington, Huntsville, Ikone, Impact, Indigo, Jefferson, Julia, Julius, Kelly, Langara, Liberator, Liberty, Limousine, Livingston, Majestic, Marquis, Mercury, Merion, Merit, Midnight I-II, Midnight Star, Minstrel, Misty, Mona, Moonlight, Moon Shadow, Mystic, Nassau, Nimbus, North Star, Nottingham, NuBlue, NuDestiny, Nugget, NuStar, Odyssey, Opal, Opti-Green, P-105, Penn Pro, Perfection, Platini, Preakness, Princeton 105, Quantum Leap, Ram 1, Rambo, Raven, Rita, Ronde, Royale, Rugby I-II, S-21, Serene, Shamrock, Shasta, Showcase, Sodnet, Sonoma SR 2000-2100, 2284, Suffolk, Sydsport, Tendos, Tiger, Total Eclipse, Touchdown, Trenton, Troy, True Blue, Tsunami, Unique, Viva, Voyager, Washington, Wellington, Wildwood.	Advocate, Argyle, Barblue, Baritone, Belmont, Blue Ridge, Cabernet, Cache, Delta, Fylking, Harmony, HB 129, Kenblue, Kimono, Lakeshore, Mallard, Markham, Mesa, Monopoly, Monte Carlo, Newport, Parade, Park, Parkland, Piedmont, Plush, Sonoma, South Dakota Certified, Vantage, Vanessa, Victa, Wabash. *Comment:* These are best suited for low-maintenance areas since they have a more upright growth habit and should be mowed at the higher end of the recommended range. They also have early spring green-up and good tolerance to environmental stresses and their seed tends to be less expensive. They tend, however, to be more disease susceptible than the improved cultivars. These often are found in low-cost, general-purpose mixtures used for non-irrigated situations such as parks, school grounds, cemeteries, and so on.	Absolute, America, Bensun, Blue Moon, Bristol, Eclipse, Equator, Glade, Glenmont, Impact, Marquis, Merit, Midnight, Nugget, NuGlade, Ram 1, Royale', Sebring. *Comment:* Although these cultivars have improved shade tolerance, they will not tolerate heavily shaded conditions.

Comment: Improved cultivars have a lower, more prostrate growth habit, better disease resistance, and overall higher quality. They require, however, a higher level of maintenance than the common non-improved cultivars and can become thatchy. These are best suited for higher maintained, irrigated sites such as roughs. Some are dwarf growing and able to be mowed between 0.5 and 1 inch (1.3 to 2.5 cm).

irrigation, it will enter dormancy where the aboveground tissue ceases growth and can turn brown. With favorable growing conditions, new shoots are initiated from rhizomes and crowns. Kentucky bluegrass also has greater cold temperature tolerance than grasses such as perennial ryegrass or tall fescue. Overall, shade tolerance is only poor to fair, but breeding efforts are improving shade and low mowing height (<1 inch, 2.5 cm) tolerance. Under a high-maintenance program, thatch and diseases (e.g., summer patch, rust, powdery mildew, leaf spot) can be serious problems.

Kentucky bluegrass seed, compared to ryegrass, can be slow to germinate and become established. At warmer soil temperatures (>60°F, 15.6°C), germination occurs in about 10 days. Cooler temperatures (<55°F, 12.8°C) extends germination to 14 to 21 days. For good quality, density, and beauty, Kentucky bluegrass requires a moderate-to-high fertility (e.g., 3 to 4 lbs yearly N/1,000 sq.ft., 146 to 195 kg N/ha). "Merion" was the first improved Kentucky bluegrass developed, primarily for its resistance to leaf spot disease. Over 200 cultivars currently exist; Table 1–12 lists some of these.

FIGURE 1–27 Tall fescue has a somewhat coarse-textured, bunch-type growth habit.

Tall Fescue

Tall fescue (*Festuca arundinacea* Schreb.) is a coarse-textured, bunch-type species originally from southern Europe where summers are warmer and drier than in other European regions (Figure 1–27). Tall fescue forms a low-density turf with wider leaves than other cool-season turfgrasses. Although improvements have been made toward developing a rhizomatous cultivar, tall fescue has an overall bunch-type growth habit. Due to its clumping growth habit, tall fescue often requires reseeding every two to three years to maintain desirable turf density. Grande, Labrinth, and Tulsa II are initial releases with rhizomatous growth habit while Pure Gold and Tomahawk RT are early members of a new generation of glyphosate (Roundup)-tolerant cultivars.

Tall fescue has very poor low-temperature hardiness, thereby limiting its use for those areas which experience severe winter temperatures. However, it has the best heat tolerance of the cool-season turfgrasses and is commonly grown in the transition zone, mid-Atlantic region, and the upper portion of the warm-humid zone. It also survives in arid climates when irrigated. Due to its extensive root system, tall fescue also has excellent drought tolerance and disease and insect resistance. Shade tolerance is fair but will tolerate infertile, saline, alkaline, wet, and dry soil conditions.

When overirrigated and/or fertilized, tall fescue often becomes susceptible to leaf spot and brown patch diseases, as well as white grub damage. Due to its coarse leaf texture, low shoot density, and clumpy growth habit, tall fescue can be considered a serious weed in finer-textured monostand turfs such as Kentucky bluegrass. When seeded with Kentucky bluegrass, the seed mix on a weight basis should be at least 70 percent tall fescue. "Rebel" was the first introduced turf-type tall fescue and provided improved leaf width, stand density, color, and disease resistance. Table 1–13 lists some of the more than 150 available cultivars.

Perennial Ryegrass

Perennial ryegrass (*Lolium perenne* L.) is a short-lived perennial with a medium leaf texture and good shoot density originating from open to fringed forest regions of southern Europe and western Asia to northern Africa. It has a non-spreading, bunch-type growth habit which makes it slow to recover from divots, good wear resistance, good soil compaction tolerance, good drought tolerance, fast establishment rate, and bright-green color. Perennial ryegrass tolerates lower mowing heights than Kentucky bluegrass or tall fescue. It does not tolerate low or high temperature extremes and has limited shade tolerance. Perennial ryegrass is primarily used as a component in seed mixtures with other cool-season turfgrasses such as Kentucky bluegrass to broaden the resistance to various diseases and other pests. It is often used for overseeding purposes in bermudagrass and zoysiagrass for winter color. Table 1–14 lists some of the more than 200 cultivars available.

TABLE 1–13 *Tall fescue cultivars (****Note:*** *check with your seed supplier and state turfgrass specialist for the latest recommended cultivar(s) for your particular area). The "E" or "E+" designation associated with certain cultivars indicates endophyte enhancement.*

Turf-types (or fine-leafed)	Medium to coarse-leafed types
Admiral, Adobe, Adventure I-II, Alamo, Alamo E+, Amigo, Anthem I-II, Apache I-II, Aquara, Arabia, Arid I-III, Arriva, ASP 400 & 410, Astro 2000, Avalon, Avanti, Austin, Aztec I-II, Barlexas, Barnone I-II, Barrera, Barrington, Benton, Biltmore, Bingo, Black Beauty, Black Magic, Bonanza II, Bonsai, Bonsai Plus, Bonsai 2000, Brandy, Bravo, Brookston, Bulldawg, Bullet, Carefree, Cayenne, Chieftain I-II, Cimarron, Cochise I-II, Cody, Colorado Gold, Confederate Blend, Coronada, Coronada Gold, Cortez, Coyote, Crew Cut I-II, Crossfire I-II, DaVinci, Daytona, Debutante, Defiance, Denim, Dixie Green, Dodge City, Dominion, Duke, Durana, Durango, Duster, Dynasty, Earthsave, Ebony, Eldorado, Emperor, Empress, Endeavor, Endure, Equinox, Era, Excalibur, Exeda, Falcon II-III, Finelawn 5GL & 88, Finelawn Petite, Finesse II, Focus, Forte, Gala, Galway, Gazelle, Genesis II, Grande I-II*, GQ, Guardian, Heritage, Houndog, Houndog V, Hubbard 87, Inferno, J 101 Proseeds, Jaguar I-III, Jubilee, Justice, Kittyhawk, Labrinth*, Lancer, Laramie, Leprechaun, Lexus, Lion, Magellan, Matador, Marathon, Marksman, Masterpiece, Maverick I-II, Mesa, Micro, Millennium, Mini-Mustang, Mirage, Mohawk, Mojva, Monarch, Montauk, Morgan, MowLess Blend, Murietta, Mustang II-III, MVP Blend, Nashville, Ninja, Oasis, Obsidian, Olympic I-II, Olympic Gold, OnCue, Onyx, Pacer, Padre, Palisades II, Phoenix, Picasso, Pixie E+, Plantation, Pride, Prospect, Pure Gold, Pyramid, Quest, Rebel I-II, Rebel Exeda, Rebel Jr., Rebel Sentry, Rebel 3D, Rebel 2000, Regiment I-II, Rembrandt, Rendition, Renegade, Reserve, Richmond, Safari, Santa Fe, Sapphire, Scorpion, Second Millennium, Shenandoah I-II, Shortstop I-II, Signia, Silverado, Silver Star, Simplote, Slo-Mow, Southern Choice, Southern Comfort, SR 8200-8600, Starfire, Starlett, Stetson, Sundance II, Sunpro, Survivor, Talisman, Taos, Tar Heel, Taurus, Tempest, Tempo, TF-66, Thunderbird, Titan I-II, Tomahawk-E, Tomahawk RT, Tombstone, Tomcat, Tracer, Tradition, Trailblazer I-II, Triathalawn, Tranquility, Tribute, Trophy, Tulsa II*, Turf Gem Blends, Tuscany, Twilight I-II, Vegas, Velocity, Venus, Veranda, Virtue, War, Watchdog, Wildfire, Willamette, Winchester, Wolfpack, Wolverine, Wrangler I-II, Wyatt.	Alta, Festival, Goar, Greystone, Kenhy, Kentucky 31, Kenwell, Magellan, Prospect, Siesta, Southeast, Stonewall, Tenacity. *Comment:* These are characterized by having very wide leaf blades, light-green color, and low shoot density. Kentucky 31 is still the most popular and widely used cultivar due to its good heat tolerance, disease resistance, deep rooting, cheaper price, and good drought tolerance.

Comment: Over 150 turf-type tall fescue cultivars are available. These have finer, softer leaves, greater shoot density, darker-green color, and a slightly lower growth habit which permits closer mowing than the coarse-leafed types. Turf-type tall fescues also tend to have better shade tolerance.

*Cultivars with rhizomatous growth characteristic.

Fine Fescue

Fine fescue is a general term used for several fine-leafed *Festuca* spp. Originally from the cool, forested European Alps, fine fescues have delicate and wiry leaves which are usually less than 0.5 mm wide and have a clumping, bristle-like appearance. These normally are maintained at 2 to 3 inches (5 to 7.6 cm) in height and should receive two pounds or less of nitrogen per 1,000 square feet (98 kg N/ha) annually. Traffic and mowing should be withheld during heat or drought stress as turf injury or death often occurs. Red fescue (*F. rubra* L.) and Spreading fescue (*F. pratensis* Huds.) have slow spreading rhizomes while Chewings fescue (*F. rubra* ssp. *commutata* Gaud.), Sheep fescue (*F. ovina* L.), Blue fescue (*F. ovina* ssp. *glauca*), and Hard fescue (*F. longifolia* auct. non Thuill.) have a bunch-type growth habit.

Hard fescue tends to have a deep-green color, whereas sheep fescues are bluish-green. Creeping red fescue performs in shady conditions in humid regions whereas chewings, hard, and sheep fescues grow well in full-sun or partial shade, especially in the drier regions of the midwest. These often are planted in shaded, low-traffic areas or in secondary roughs or out-of-play areas. If left unmowed, their leaf growth and seedheads often provide a low-maintenance, natural appearing area.

As a group, the fine fescues are noted for shade tolerance, winter hardiness, and adaptability to infertile and dry soil conditions. They do not tolerate wet, poorly drained soils well, but are particularly adapted to dry, shady conditions as well as to low-maintenance situations. Fine fescues

TABLE 1–14 *Perennial ryegrass cultivars* (**Note:** *check with your seed supplier and state turfgrass specialist for the latest recommended cultivar(s) for your particular area and needs*).

Turf-type perennial ryegrass cultivars

A+, Accent, Achiever, Admire, Advantage, Advent, Affinity, Affirmed, Allaire II, Allegro, Alliance Brand, All Sport, All Star I-II, Amazing, APM, Applaud, Aquarius I-III, Archer, Aron, Arrival, ASAP 400 & 410, Ascend, Assure, Atlantis, Avon, Barlenium, Barclay, Barrage, Barredo, Barry, Bayou, Belle, Birdie I-II, Blackhawk, Blazer I-IV, Boardwalk, Brightstar I-II, Bullet, Caddieshack, Caliente, Calypso II, Capri, Catalina I-II, Cathedral II, 2CB, CBS II Blend, Celebration Blends, Champion GQ, Chaparral I-II, Charger I-III, Charismatic, Chatham, Churchill, Cinderella, Citation I-III, Citation Fore, Commander, Competitor, Covet, Cowboy, Cutless, Cutter, Dandy, Danaro, Darkstar I-II, Dasher I-II, Delray, Derby, Dimension, Diplomat, Divine, Duet, Easy Livin, Ecologic, Edge, Elegance, Elf, Elfkin, Elka, Enchanted, Envy, Equal, Esquire, Essence, Evening Shade, Exacta, Excel, Express, Extreme, Fiesta I-III, Finelawn, Gauery, Gator II-III, Gettysburg, Goalie, GoalKeeper, Greenland, Greenville, Hawkeye, Head Start, Highlife, Ice, Icon, IG2, Imagine, Inspire, Integra, Jet, Jiffie, Jockey, Keystone, Legacy II, Lindsay, Line Drive, Linn, Laredo, Loretta, Low Grow, Mach 1, Magic II, Majesty, Malham, Manhattan III-IV, Mardi Gras, MB-45, Morning Star, Monterey II, Mulligan, Navajo, Nobility, Nomad II, Omega I-III, Omni, Ovation, Pace, Pacesetter, Palmer I-III, Panther, Paragon, Partner II, Passport, Patriot III, PDQ, Peak, Pearl, Pebble Beach, Pegasus, Pennant II, Pennfine, Penguin, Phantom, PhD, Pinnacle II, Pirouette, Pizzazz, Playmate, Pleasure XL, Precision, Prelude I-III, Premier I-III, Preston, Prism, Prizm, Promise, Pronto II, ProSport, Prowler, Quest, Quickstart, Quick Trans, R2, Racer, Radiant, Rebound, Regal, Renaissance, Repell I-III, Riviera, Roadrunner, Rodeo II-III, Salinas, Saturn II, Secretariat, Select, Seville I-II, Sherwood, Shining Star, Skipton, Solitaire, Sommerville, Sonata, Splendid, Splendor, SR 4000-5000, Stallion, Stallir, Stardance, Summerset, Sunrye (246), Sunshine, Superfly, Supreme, Surprise, Symphony, Tara, Target, TopGun, Top Hat I-II, Toronto, Transist, Transist 2200, Triple Play, Troubadour, Vail, Vantage, Vibrant, VIP II, Vixen, Williamsburg, Wilmington, Wind Dance, Wind Star, Wizard, WPXXX, Yorkshire Dales, Yorktown I-III.

Comment: More than 200 cultivars of perennial ryegrass are available and this list is very dynamic. When used for overseeding, newer cultivars have better heat and disease tolerance; therefore, they may remain longer into the summer season than desired.

TABLE 1–15 *Fine fescue cultivars* (**Note:** *check with your seed supplier and state turfgrass specialist for the latest recommended cultivar(s) for your particular area and needs*).

Red fescue	Chewings fescue	Hard fescue	Sheep fescue	Others
Aberdeen, Arctared, Aruba, Audubon, Badger, Barcrown, Bargena I-III, Boreal, Camilla, Celestial, Cindy, Cindy Lou, Dawson Red, Edgewood, Ensylva, Eugene, Florentine, Flyer, Franklin, Hector, Herald, Illahee, Inverness, Jasper II and E, Logro, Medallion, Miramar, Pathfinder, Pennlawn, Player, Rainier, Reptans, Revere, Ruby, Salem, Shademark, Shademaster I-II, SR 5200E/5210, Sylvester, Treasure, Valda, Vista.	Agram, Ambassador, Atlanta, Banner, Banner II, Bargreen, Barnica, Bridgeport, Brittany, Camaro, Carmen, Cascade, Center, Checker, Culumbra, Darwin, Disnity, Dover, Eco, Enjoy, Highlight, Hood, Intrigue, Jamestown I & II, K2, Koket, Lifalla, Longfellow I-II, Mary, Molinda, Nimrod, Polaris, Sandpiper, Scarlet, Shadow II and E, Southport, SR 5000, 5100, 5200E, Tiffany, Trophy, Victory I-II, Waldorf, Wintergreen.	Anvil, Attila, Aurora I-II, Aurora Gold, Barcrown, Bardur, Barreppo, Berkshire, Biljart, Bonny Dunes blend, Brigade, Defiant, Discovery, Durar, EcoStar, Eureka I-II, Gladiator, Hardtop, Harpoon, Moxie, Nordic, Osprey, Oxford, Reliant, Reliant II, Rescue, Rescue 911, Ridu, Scaldis, Silvana, Spartan, SR 3000 & 3100, Stonehenge, Valda, Vernon, Waldina, Warwick.	Azay, Azay Blue, Azure, Barok, Bighorn, Little Bighorn, MX-86AE, Quatro.	Arcta (Slender), Bighorn (Blue), Cindy Lou (Strong), Diego, Fenway, Gordon, Marker (Slender), Minotaur (Blue), Perville, Raisa, Rose, Seabreeze (Slender), Shademark, Silhouette, SR 3200 (Blue), Sunset, Trapeze, Weston, Wilma, Wrigley.

rarely are used alone but are usually mixed with other cool-season grasses such as Kentucky bluegrass, perennial ryegrass, and colonial bentgrass. They tend to eventually dominate the stand when grown in shady conditions. They are also used in blends for winter overseeding of warm-season turfgrasses. Seeds tend to germinate in 7 to 10 days under good environmental conditions. Aurora Gold is a glyphosate (Roundup)-tolerant hard fescue cultivar. Table 1–15 lists some of the currently available fine fescue cultivars.

Annual Bluegrass

Annual bluegrass (*Poa annua* L.) originated from Europe and traditionally has been a very troublesome bunchgrass weed in most turfgrass situations. This is due to its prolific seed production which disrupts the appearance and uniformity of the turf stand, its competitive growth habit, and poor heat and disease tolerance which often leaves bare or thin areas in the turf. Selective herbicide control has also been marginal at best. However, perennial or "creeping" biotypes (*P. annua* ssp. *reptans*) have recently been identified which have a more desirable putting characteristic. *Poa annua* (2n=28) is believed to have derived from hybridization of two *Poa* ancestors, *P. supina* and *P. infirma*. *Poa annua* biotypes adapted to turf areas restrict their flowering and seed production instead of favoring more vegetative growth. Breeding efforts are underway to identify potential permanent selections for golf greens. Peterson and True Putt creeping bluegrasses are improved perennial biotype bluegrasses for putting greens.

Canada Bluegrass

Canada bluegrass (*Poa compressa* L.) is a bluish-green, weakly rhizomatous grass originally from Europe which forms a low-density turf of inferior quality. It does tolerate droughty and infertile soils, low temperatures, and shady conditions in the cooler, humid areas of the United States and Canada better than Kentucky bluegrass. It is most used in colder climates where it is too dry to grow Kentucky bluegrass without irrigation. Its overall low quality is best suited for minimum-use or low-maintenance situations in cool temperate and subarctic climates. Improved cultivars include Canon, Reubens, and Talon.

Supina Bluegrass

Supina bluegrass (*Poa supina*), a naturally apple-green grass native to the European Alps, can tolerate extreme shade (80 to 90 percent) and heavy traffic. It can be undesirable due to its light-green color, though darker-green ecotypes are being developed. It has high seed cost and a shallow root system. It is a common grass type used on golf courses in Europe and in the cooler regions of the United States. It displays good disease resistance but is susceptible to *Microdochium* patch (Pink snow mold). Commercial varieties include Supra and Supranova.

Other Cool-Season Turfgrasses

Numerous additional cool-season turfgrasses are available, with most having only a very small role on golf courses. Many are used as blends with other cool-season grasses, especially for overseeding purposes or for very low-maintenance, non-irrigated, out-of-play areas. Several also can become very weedy species. Refer to the Native Grasses section of this chapter and the Overseeding chapter for more information on these.

Selecting a Fairway/Rough Grass

In cool humid and arid regions and northern portions of the warm humid region, golf courses typically use cool-season grasses alone or blended with other cultivars or species for year-round color in fairways, roughs, and out-of-play areas. Kentucky bluegrass, perennial ryegrass, and/or the fescues (tall and fine fescues) are often used alone or as blends to reduce disease, insect, and summer stress problems. Bentgrass also is used for fairways but typically as a monoculture and mostly at higher-budgeted courses. In much of the northern United States and Canada, Kentucky bluegrass, bentgrass, and fine fescues are widely used. Tall fescue and perennial ryegrass are less winter hardy; thus, they are used more in the mid-central regions of the United States including the transition zone. Tables 1–16 and 1–17 list general characteristics of these turfgrasses, while Table 1–18 lists the advantages and disadvantages of each. Cool-season grass cultivars constantly change as new selections are introduced and older ones become less important. Contact your state turfgrass specialist for the latest releases recommended in your area.

Current trends in cooler regions use predominantly pure perennial ryegrass stands in the upper transition zone and the cool semiarid zone, especially if the mowing height is maintained at or below one inch (2.5 cm) (Table 1–19). With pure ryegrass, however, the disease grey leaf spot and winter kill periodically thin or weaken the stand. Courses try to overcome this by adding a

TABLE 1-16 *General characteristics of cool-season turfgrasses used for golf course fairways (cultivar differences may occur).*

Characteristic	Annual bluegrass	Kentucky bluegrass	Browntop	Colonial bentgrass	Creeping bentgrass	Perennial ryegrass	Red fescue	Chewings fescue	Tall fescue	Crested wheatgrass
Establishment										
Method	seed	seed/vegetative	seed/vegetative	seed/vegetative	seed/vegetative	seed	seed	seed	seed/vegetative	seed
Rate	very fast	slow	medium	medium	slow	very fast	medium	very slow	medium	slow
Days to germination	—	8 to 21	7 to 14	7 to 14	7 to 14	5 to 12	10 to 21	10 to 21	10 to 14	—
Growth rate	fast	fast	fast	fast	fast	fast	slow - medium	slow - medium	fast	slow
Density	excellent	good	excellent	excellent	excellent	very good	excellent	very good	good	fair
Leaf texture	fine	medium	fine	fine	very fine	medium	very fine	very fine	medium-coarse	medium
Polystand compatibility	low	good	medium	medium	medium	medium	good	medium	medium	low
Cultural Requirements										
Intensity	high	medium	medium	medium	high	medium	low	low	medium	low
Fairway mowing height, in. (cm)	0.3 to 1.0 (0.8 to 2.5)	1.5 to 2.5 (3.8 to 6.4)	0.5 to 1.0 (1.3 to 2.5)	0.5 to 1.0 (1.3 to 2.5)	0.25 to 0.5 (0.6 to 1.3)	0.75 to 2.5 (1.9 to 6.4)	1.5 to 2.5 (3.8 to 6.4)	1.5 to 2.5 (3.8 to 6.4)	1.5 to 3 (3.8 to 7.6)	1.5 to 2.5 (3.8 to 6.4)
Mowing frequency (days)	1 to 3	5 to 7	3	1 to 3	1 to 3	5 to 7	7	7	7 to 14	7 to 14
Irrigation needs	high	medium	medium	medium	high	medium	low	medium	medium	low
Evapotranspiration (ET) (mm/day)	>10	>10	na	na	>10	8.5 to 10	7 to 8.5	7 to 8.5	>10	na
Nitrogen needs (lbs/1,000 sq.ft./growing month)	0.5 to 1.0	0.4 to 1.0	0.5 to 1.0	0.5 to 1.0	0.5 to 1.4	0.4 to 1.0	0.2 to 0.5	0 to 0.5	0.3 to 0.75	0 to 0.2
Performance										
Heat tolerance	low	fair	medium	poor to fair	fair to good	poor to fair	fair	fair	good	fair
Cold tolerance	poor	very good	good	good	good	fair	good	good	good	good
Killing temperature (°F)	na	na	na	na	na	na	na	na	na	na
Winter performance	fair	fair	very good	good	fair	excellent	very good	very good	good	fair
Drought tolerance	poor	good	poor	poor	poor	good	very good	excellent	excellent	excellent
Shade tolerance	poor	poor to fair	fair to good	fair to good	fair to good	fair	excellent	excellent	good	fair
Wear tolerance	poor	good	fair	fair	fair	excellent	good	fair	good	poor
Recuperative potential	poor	good	medium	medium	good	poor	medium	poor	good	poor
Low mow tolerance	excellent	poor	excellent	excellent	excellent	very good	very good	good	medium	good
Salt tolerance	poor	poor	good	fair	poor to excellent	good	good	good	good	good
Soil pH range	5.5 to 6.5	6.0 to 7.0	5.0 to 6.0	5.5 to 6.7	5.5 to 6.5	6.0 to 7.0	5.5 to 6.5	5.5 to 6.5	4.7 to 8.5	6.0 to 8.0
Acid soil tolerance (below pH 5.5)	good	poor	excellent	excellent	excellent	very good	very good	very good	very good	poor
Thatch tendency	medium	medium	high	high	high	low	medium	medium	low	low
Disease tendency	high	medium	high	high	high	medium to high	medium	medium	low	low
Submersion tolerance	fair	medium	na	na	na	fair	fair	na	na	na

TABLE 1-17 *General characteristics of warm-season turfgrasses used for golf course fairways (cultivar differences may occur).*

Characteristic	Bahiagrass	Bermudagrass	Buffalograss	Centipedegrass	Kikuyugrass	Seashore Paspalum	St. Augustinegrass	Zoysiagrass
Establishment								
Method	seed/vegetative	seed/vegetative	seed/vegetative	seed/vegetative	vegetative	vegetative	vegetative	seed/vegetative
Rate	poor to intermediate	excellent (fast)	medium	poor	good	poor	good	poor
Days to germination	21 to 35	14 to 21	14 to 21	35 to 40	na	na	na	21 to 28
Growth rate	slow	good-fast	good-fast	slow-poor	fast	slow-good	medium fast	slow
Density	fair	excellent	fair	good	fair	good	excellent	excellent
Leaf texture	coarse	fine to medium	fine to medium	medium	medium	medium to coarse	coarse	fine to medium
Polystand compatibility	medium	medium	poor	poor	poor	poor	poor	poor
Cultural Requirements								
Intensity	very low	high	low	low	medium	medium	medium	medium
Mowing height in. (cm.)	1.5 to 2.5 (3.8 to 6.4)	0.1 to 3.0 (0.3 to 7.6)	0.5 to 3.0 (1.3 to 7.6)	1.0 to 2.0 (2.5 to 5)	0.5 (1.3)	0.1 to 2.0 (0.3 to 5)	1.5 to 4.0 (3.8 to 10)	0.2 to 2.5 (0.5 to 6.4)
Mowing frequency (days)	7 to 28	1 to 4	3 to 14	10 to 14	2 to 4	1 to 7	7 to 14	1 to 14
Irrigation needs	low	low	low	medium	low	high	high	low to medium
Evapotranspiration (ET) (mm/day)	2.5 to 8.5	6 to 7	<6	6 to 7	—	2.5 to 8.5	7 to 8.5	6 to 7
Nitrogen needs (lbs/1,000 sq.ft./growing month)	0.1 to 0.4	0.3 to 1.3	0.1 to 0.4	0.1 to 0.3	0.2 to 0.5	0.3 to 1.0	0.5 to 1.0	0.2 to 1.0
Performance								
Heat tolerance	excellent	excellent	excellent	excellent	excellent	excellent	excellent	excellent
Cold tolerance	fair	good	fair to medium	fair	poor	poor	poor to fair	good to very poor
Killing temperature, °F (°C)	~23 (~5)	~19 (~7.2)	—	~11 (~11.7)	—	~19 (~7.2)	~23 (~5)	~6 (~14.4)
Drought tolerance	excellent	excellent	excellent	poor	good	excellent	fair	moderate
Shade tolerance	good	poor	poor	fair to good	poor	fair to good	excellent	fair to good
Wear tolerance	good	excellent	medium	poor	good	good	medium	excellent
Recuperative potential	slow	excellent	good	poor	good	good	good	excellent
Low mow tolerance	poor	excellent	fair	fair	good	good	poor	excellent to good
Salt tolerance	poor	good	fair	poor	excellent	excellent	fair	good
Soil pH range	4.5 to 8.0	5.5 to 7.5	6.0 to 7.5	4.5 to 6.0	na	5.5 to 7.5	5.0 to 8.0	5.0 to 7.0
Acid soil tolerance (below pH 5.5)	good	good	poor	excellent	na	good	good	good
Thatch tendency	low	high	low	medium	high	medium	high	high
Disease tendency	low	low	low	low	low	low	medium	medium
Submersion tolerance	medium	excellent	excellent	poor	good	good	excellent	excellent

TABLE 1–18 Region of adaptation, advantages, and disadvantages of various turfgrasses used for golf course fairways.

Turfgrass	Region of adaptation	Advantages	Disadvantages
Bentgrass (*Agrostis* spp.)	Most cool-region zones (temperate regions) if irrigation is available	Tolerates close (≤0.5 in., 1.3 cm) mowing Produces dense stands from stolons, has excellent recuperative ability, and doesn't require yearly interseeding Stripes easily, good color contrast with darker-colored bluegrass roughs Provides excellent playing surface	Generally intolerant of heat and drought Maintenance expense due to susceptibility to diseases such as *Pythium*, dollar spot, and brown patch Must control thatch Susceptible to winter dessication *Poa annua* infestations require lightweight mowers, clipping removal, extra aerification, and continued herbicide/PGR use
Bermudagrass (*Cynodon* spp.)	Tropical to subtropical regions into lower half of the transition zone, southern Illinois, Missouri, and Kansas	Adapted to poor soils, harsh (hot) climates Efficient water users Excellent wear tolerance Good pesticide options Rapid and cost effective to establish Low-cost option for fairways	High nitrogen requirements Aggressive growth habit Shade intolerant Nematode susceptible Cold sensitive in northern locations Has dark tan/brown winter color which may need overseeding with ryegrass Poor spring playability Poor spring transition when overseeded
Buffalograss (*Buchloe dactyloides*)	Drier regions of the Midwest such as Kansas and Nebraska	Low maintenance in terms of water and nutrient requirements Tolerates hot, dry conditions	Poor shade tolerance Produces unsightly seedheads (burs) Produces a coarse-rough texture and somewhat thin density Disease susceptible in high humidity areas
Fine fescue (*Festuca* spp.)	Shady areas in upper transition zone and northward	Withstands very low maintenance in terms of nutrient and water requirements Has slow vertical growth rate, requiring about half the mowings of taller-grown grasses Alternative to Kentucky bluegrass in unirrigated, infrequently mowed roughs	Goes dormant with warm summer temperatures All are bunch grasses except the rhizomatous creeping red fescue Slow recuperative rates Dollar spot and red thread susceptible
Kentucky bluegrass (*Poa pratensis*)	Irrigated regions in the cool zones, midwest throughout Canada into Alaska	Excellent color, texture, and density Affordable seed Good recuperative ability from rhizomes Excellent cold tolerance	Slow establishment from seed Shallow root system, thus, poor water use Poor shade tolerance Poor tolerance to low (<1.5 in.) mowing heights Susceptible to diseases (e.g., summer patch)
Perennial ryegrass (*Lolium perenne*)	Lower temperate (cool, humid zone) into upper transition zone, also southern portions of Midwest	Inexpensive seed which establish rapidly Has bright-green color which stripes well Compatible with Kentucky bluegrass Good wear and drought tolerance Good tolerance to low mowing Good tolerance to ethofumesate and other products for *Poa annua* control Good playability	Requires more frequent mowing than fine fescue or Kentucky bluegrass Thins out and turns stemmy at lower fertility levels High disease susceptible to *Pythium*, red thread, and grey leaf spot Slow to spread, slow recovery from divots Usually requires yearly interseeding Rapid spring and early summer growth Only fair cold tolerance, susceptible to ice damage in shaded, low-lying areas

Species	Region/Adaptation	Positive Characteristics	Limitations
Tall fescue (*Festuca arundinacea*)	Irrigated and non-irrigated lower maintenance courses throughout the temperate region	Good heat drought tolerance; Easily established by seeding; Compatible with Kentucky bluegrass and perennial ryegrass	Clumpy growth habit requires reseeding to maintain density; Intolerant to close (<2 in., 5 cm) mowing; Slow to recover from damage; Requires more-frequent mowing than other cool-season grasses; Brown patch susceptible
Weeping Alkaligrass (*Puccinella distans*)	High sodium regions of the Midwest	Excellent salt tolerance; Good cold tolerance, fair heat tolerance; Low maintenance in terms of nutrient and water requirements	Produces open, coarse stands; Has gray-green, tufted bunch-growth habit; Requires overseeding to maintain a uniform, dense stand
Wheatgrasses (*Agropyron* and *Pascopyrum* spp.)	Drier regions of the Midwest and intermountain region of the western United States	Provides an alternative to Kentucky bluegrass in non-irrigated regions	Forms coarse-textured, low-density turf stands
Zoysiagrass (*Zoysia* spp.)	Tropical and subtropical areas into the upper transition zone	Can be low maintenance after establishment; Produces dense, weed-resistant turf, with good playability; Best winter hardy warm-season grass; Has light, attractive tan color when dormant	Expensive and slow to establish from sprigs or seed, slow to recover from divots; Traffic restrictions when dormant; Eventually becomes thatchy; Winter damage in low areas holding water; Bermudagrass invasion and brown patch susceptible

TABLE 1-19 Common seed mixtures for cool-season grasses within three major climatic zones.

Climatic zone (Figure 1-10)	Fairways			Roughs		Grass bunkers	Low maintenance areas
	Sunny, with higher fertility levels		Shaded, non-irrigated with low fertility levels	Sun	Shade		
	Irrigated	Non-irrigated					
Upper portion of the cool humid transition zone and cool semiarid (upper great plains) areas	**Mowing height >1 inch, 2.5 cm:** 70 to 80% Kentucky bluegrass blend + 20 to 30% perennial ryegrass **Mowing height <1 inch, 2.5 cm, irrigated:** 100% perennial ryegrass blend or 100% creeping bentgrass for higher budgets	100% tall fescue or buffalograss or alkaligrass in salty environments	**Mowing height >1 inch, 2.5 cm:** 20 to 40% Kentucky bluegrass blend + 60 to 80% fine fescue blend or 60% Kentucky bluegrass blend + 40% perennial ryegrass	60% Kentucky bluegrass blend + 20% chewings fescue + 20% perennial ryegrass or 90% tall fescue + 10% Kentucky bluegrass	40% Kentucky bluegrass + 40% chewings fescue + 20% perennial ryegrass or 90% tall fescue + 10% Kentucky bluegrass	Fine fescue blend such as 80% hard fescue + 20% chewings fescue	In cool, humid areas—Fine fescue blend such as 80% hard fescue + 20% chewings fescue In cool, arid areas—40% buffalograss + 40% blue grama + 20% hard fescue
Lower portion of the cool humid transition zone and cool semiarid (lower great plains) areas	**Mowing height >1 inch, 2.5 cm:** 10 to 30% Kentucky bluegrass blend + 70 to 90% perennial ryegrass or 90% tall fescue **Mowing height <1 inch, 2.5 cm, irrigated:** 100% perennial ryegrass blend or 100% creeping bentgrass **In grey leaf spot infested areas:** 100% bentgrass	100% buffalograss or tall fescue or alkaligrass in salty environments	**Mowing height >1 inch, 2.5 cm:** 10 to 20% Kentucky bluegrass blend + 40 to 60% perennial ryegrass + 30 to 40% fine fescue	90% tall fescue + 10% Kentucky bluegrass or 60% Kentucky bluegrass + 20% perennial ryegrass + 20% chewings fescue	90% tall fescue + 10% Kentucky bluegrass or 65% chewings fescue + Kentucky bluegrass + 15% perennial ryegrass	100% tall fescue blend or 80% hard fescue + 20% chewings fescue	100% tall fescue blend or 80% hard fescue + 20% chewings fescue
Cool humid Pacific coast zone	**Mowing height >1 inch, 2.5 cm:** 10 to 30% Kentucky bluegrass blend + 70 to 90% perennial ryegrass or tall fescue **Mowing height <1 inch, 2.5 cm, irrigated:** 100% perennial ryegrass blend. **In grey leaf spot infested areas:** 100% bentgrass	100% tall fescue	**Mowing height >1 inch, 2.5 cm:** 60 to 80% fine fescue + 20 to 40% colonial bentgrass or 60% Kentucky bluegrass + 40% perennial ryegrass	60% Kentucky bluegrass blend + 20% chewings fescue + 20% perennial ryegrass	40% Kentucky bluegrass + 40% chewings fescue + 20% perennial ryegrass	Fine fescue blend such as 80% hard fescue + 20% chewings fescue	Fine fescue blend such as 80% hard fescue + 20% chewings fescue or 35% hard fescue + 20% red fescue + 20% perennial ryegrass

small amount (e.g., 20 to 30 percent) of Kentucky bluegrass since it has better recuperative ability due to rhizomatous growth or by switching to bentgrass or zoysiagrass in more southern areas. However, if Kentucky bluegrass is used, the mowing height should be maintained above one inch (2.5 cm). In non-irrigated areas of the Midwest, low-maintenance grasses such as buffalograss or weeping alkalinegrass may be considered. These, however, should be viewed as low-maintenance grasses which do not provide the color, density, and texture of irrigated Kentucky bluegrass, bentgrass, or ryegrass.

In the southern United States, bermudagrass is used almost exclusively for fairways and roughs. Irrigated fairways use a hybrid bermudagrass while non-irrigated ones use an improved common bermudagrass. Zoysiagrass is used sparingly when cold temperature damage is an issue with bermudagrass. Some golf course architectures use other grasses such as centipedegrass or bahiagrass roughs with bermudagrass fairways to provide contrasting color and textural differences. However, in most cases, this is a maintenance mistake as many of the pesticides, especially herbicides, used on bermudagrass invariably are sprayed on these other turfgrasses, causing damage. Also, the higher nitrogen and watering requirements of bermudagrass usually weaken these other grasses.

In the upper areas of cool regions, winter kill periodically occurs to ryegrass and tall fescue; thus, Kentucky bluegrass is often used alone. However, the bluegrass should be mowed above one inch (2.5 cm) in these situations for best turf growth and hardiness. In addition, a blend of two or more bluegrass cultivars should be used to help in pest resistance. Fine fescues are used, especially in shady areas or areas without irrigation, but these tend to establish slowly and are susceptible to several diseases.

Native Grasses

It has become popular to use native American grasses in an attempt to reduce inputs such as water, fertilizer, and pesticides to grow grass. Most native grasses provide loosely knitted, blue-green colored turf stands when grown naturally. When placed under higher maintenance such as periodic irrigation and fertilizing, many of these become weakened and thin, become disease susceptible, and face invasion from other grasses and weeds. If used, native grasses should be maintained as close to their natural adaptation as possible; mow these high (>2 inches, 5 cm), fertilize only lightly (0 to 2 lbs N/1,000 sq.ft. annually, 0 to 98 kg N/ha), and only seldom water. Native grasses from the United States currently being used include buffalograss, wheatgrass, and grama grass. Breeding efforts are being made to make these more turf-type in appearance and maintenance.

Buffalograss

Buffalograss [*Buchloe dactyloides* (Nutt.) Engelm.] is a low-maintenance, perennial warm-season species native to the grazed arid and semiarid regions of the North American western great plains from southern Canada to the highlands of Central Mexico receiving low rainfall (10 to 25 inches yearly, 25 to 64 cm) (Figure 1–28). It is named from the American buffalo (bison) for which it served as primary grazing. It spreads by stolons and seed and forms a medium- to fine-textured, relatively thin turf with a soft blue-green color which resembles common bermudagrass (Figure 1–29). The grayish-green color is due to the fine hairs covering the leaves. Curling of the leaf blades also is a distinctive feature. Ecotypes are adapted to either southern or northern areas; thus, the origin of improved cultivars should be considered before selecting it for turf purposes. Buffalograss is adapted for use on unirrigated lawns, parks, golf course roughs, and roadsides in the warm zones of the arid and semiarid regions.

Buffalograss is a **dioecious** species, meaning it produces separate male and female flowers and plants. The female flower is a short spike where the glumes, lemma, and palea form a bur-like enclosure for the seed. The male flower is more prominent as its seed stalk extends above the turf canopy.

Advantages

Buffalograss spreads vegetatively by numerous stolons which branch profusely to form a tight sod. It has excellent hardiness to high temperature and tolerates fairly low temperatures in comparison to most warm-season turfgrasses. It is adapted to a wide range of soil types with the possible exception of deep sands. It also appears to tolerate a wide range of soil pH. The spring green-up rate and low-temperature color retention are intermediate to fair. The excellent drought

FIGURE 1–28 Present
adaptation and projected
adaptation of improved
buffalograss cultivars
(adapted from Riordan, T.
1991. *Grounds
Maintenance*, 26:2).

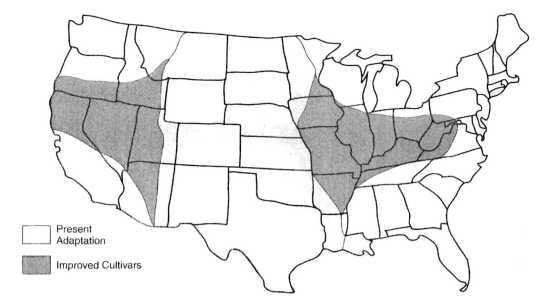

Present
Adaptation

Improved Cultivars

FIGURE 1–29
Buffalograss provides an
open growing, low-
maintenance turf often valued
for its low water and fertility
requirements.

resistance of buffalograss is one of its most outstanding characteristics. It has the ability to go dormant with the advent of severe drought and to initiate new growth after prolonged periods of moisture stress. Advantages of buffalograss include:

- Seed (burs) are available.
- It requires low maintenance in terms of fertilizer and water requirements.
- It possesses drought and heat tolerance.
- It is deep rooted.
- It tolerates a wide range of soil textures and soil pH, although it prefers heavy, alkaline soils.
- It displays salt tolerance.

Disadvantages

Several disadvantages are noted with buffalograss. It is naturally adapted to areas low in annual rainfall (10 to 25 inches per year, 25 to 64 cm). Bermudagrass and weeds are very competitive with buffalograss in higher rainfall (>25 inches, 64 cm) areas. Diseases such as brown patch, dollar spot, and leaf spot also become a problem when grown in such areas and when overfertilized

(Figure 1–30). During extended dry spells, buffalograss will turn brown, which is a natural survival mechanism. Buffalograss also has very poor shade and traffic tolerance. Buffalograss generally has poor tolerance to most postemergence herbicides; therefore, if used, herbicides must be applied before weeds emerge. As with most low-maintenance grasses, buffalograss will not provide a dark-green, dense, aesthetically pleasing turf. Its appearance resembles a light-green colored, thin, coarse common bermudagrass planting. It will not provide the quality higher-maintained grasses such as hybrid bermudagrass, zoysiagrass, or St. Augustinegrass will.

Disadvantages of buffalograss include:

- Excessive rainfall/watering (>25 inches/year, 64 cm, total) weakens it.
- It is disease prone when grown under excessive watering or humidity.
- It turns brown (dormant) during extended drought.
- It has very poor shade tolerance.
- It has very poor traffic tolerance.
- Due to its thin, open growth habit, weeds often invade.
- It has poor herbicide tolerance.
- It has overall inferior stand density, color, and appearance.

Establishment

Propagation may be done vegetatively or by seed (burs) (Figure 1–31). Vegetative propagation by sodding has been the main method of establishment primarily because of a seed shortage. If vegetatively propagated, female plants are generally used since male plants produce unsightly seedstalks. When viable seed (or burs) are available, seeding rates range from one to five pounds per 1,000 square feet (48 to 245 kg/ha). The higher rate is needed if seeds are broadcasted and/or if irrigation is not available, or if a quicker establishment rate is desired. Lower rates (e.g., 10 to 20 pounds per acre, 11 to 22 kg/ha) may be used if the seeds are drilled in rows.

Plugs ≥2 inches (5 cm) also may be used for establishment. These are spaced from six inches (15 cm) to two feet (0.6 m) apart, depending on the desired establishment rate. Soil should be well-watered before and after planting for several weeks to aid survival. The establishment rate using seed or plugs is generally slower than most other warm-season grasses.

Maintenance

Buffalograss is somewhat pest-free in its native habitat but problems occur when grown under warmer, more humid, and wetter areas. Some authors even suggest the quickest way to thin a buffalograss stand is to start fertilizing and watering it. Therefore, only minimum maintenance practices should be used to keep a buffalograss stand. For golf course fairways, a cutting height between

FIGURE 1-31 Seedhead burs associated with buffalograss.

0.75 to 2 inches (1.9 to 5 cm) is preferred. For golf course rough areas, buffalograss is mowed between two and three inches (5 to 7.6 cm) and only as needed. The mowing interval is generally infrequent due to a slow vertical shoot growth rate. A dense stand requires minimum water, mowing, and weed control. Nitrogen requirements range from 0 to 1 pound of nitrogen/1,000 square feet per year (0 to 48 kg N/ha). Higher fertilizer rates encourage bermudagrass encroachment.

Supplemental watering normally is not advisable since overwatering can produce undesirable effects. If watered, apply only in deep (e.g., 3/4 inch, 1.9 cm), infrequent (weekly or longer) cycles.

Available Varieties

Vegetative varieties include Bonnie Brae, Buffalawn, Buffalo (609), Density, Legacy, Midget, Oasis, Plains, Prairie, Scout (118), Sharps Improved, Stampede, TopGun, UC Verde, 378, and 86-61. They have better density, are lower growing, and have more competitive turf-type characteristics compared to older varieties. These were mostly bred and perform quite well in the arid Southwestern United States, but have shown varying potential to withstand humid conditions elsewhere. However, as newer cultivars are developed, a wider use range of buffalograss may occur. Seeded varieties include BAM-1000, Bison, Cody, Comanche, Tatanka, and Texoka.

In general, those cultivars which are diploids (have 20 chromosomes) and most tetraploids (40 chromosomes) lack cold tolerance and are better adapted to southern growing areas. Most intermediate (or pentaploid) types with 50 chromosomes and hexaploids (60 chromosomes) have better cold tolerance. However, the intermediate types tend to have a dwarf growth habit and less vigor. Tetraploid types are a lighter apple-green color, are more vigorous, and have more sod tensile strength than most diploids or hexaploids.

Other Native Grasses

Several other grasses native to the arid great plains regions of North America are occasionally used as a turfgrass. Most of these originated as pasture grasses, forage, or for roadside soil stabilization. They are occasionally used for low-maintenance roughs and out-of-play areas on golf courses due to their distinct characteristics such as seedhead height or plant color (Figure 1–32). These help provide distinct differences from the playing surface. Blends are often planted. However, if regularly watered, these grasses tend to lose their competitiveness and often become invaded by weeds and diseases. Weed control prior to planting, and for the first two years thereafter, is essential for success. Examples include the warm-season grasses gramagrass, switchgrass, bluestems, Indiangrass, and lovegrass (Table 1–20) and the cool-season grasses wheatgrass and alkaligrass. Most of these have a blue-green color and should be mowed relatively high, two to three inches (5 to 7.6 cm), only fertilized sparingly, e.g., 0 to 2 pounds of nitrogen/1,000 square

FIGURE 1-32 Low-maintenance grasses such as bluegrass, bluestem, broomsedge, fescue (shown), Indiangrass, switchgrass, and lovegrass are often used in roughs or non-play areas due to their distinct color, seedhead, and textural characteristics.

TABLE 1-20 *Native warm-season grasses used for low-maintenance sites.*

Common name	Latin name	Growing height, ft (m)	Soil conditions	Moisture needs	Sunlight requirements
Big bluestem	*Andropogon gerardi*	5 to 8 (1.5 to 2.4)	Clay, loam, sand	Dry to moist	Full sun to light shade
Switchgrass	*Panicum virgatum*	6 (1.8)	Clay, loam, sand	Dry to moist	Full sun to light shade
Indiangrass	*Sorghastrum nutans*	5 to 8 (1.5 to 2.4)	Clay, loam, sand	Dry to moist	Full sun to light shade
Prairie cordgrass	*Spartina pectinata*	5 to 8 (1.5 to 2.4)	Clay, loam, sand	Moist to wet	Full sun
Broomsedge	*Andropogon virginicus*	1 to 3 (0.3 to 0.9)	Clay, loam	Dry to moist	Full sun
Side oats grama	*Bouteloua curtipendula*	1 to 3 (0.3 to 0.9)	Loam, sand	Dry to medium moist	Full sun
Little bluestem	*Andropogon scoparius*	1 to 3 (0.3 to 0.9)	Loam, sand	Dry to medium moist	Full sun
Prairie dropseed	*Sporobolus heterolepsis*	1 to 3 (0.3 to 0.9)	Loam, sand	Dry to medium moist	Full sun

feet yearly (0 to 98 kg N/ha), and watered only during establishment. These are adapted to arid regions.

Warm-Season Grasses

Bluestems

Big bluestem (*Andropogon gerardii* Vitman) grows up to six feet (1.8 m) high at maturity. It has strong deep roots and short rhizomes. Seeds are planted in mid-spring at 5 to 20 pounds/acre (5.6 to 22 kg/ha) of pure live seed. Seeds mature in late summer. Big bluestem will not tolerate continued close mowing. It is good as a strong accent plant and as a backdrop for shorter plants, and turns bright red in fall. "The Blue" is an available cultivar.

Little bluestem (*Andropogon scoparius* Michx.) reaches a mature height of about four feet. It is more drought resistant than big bluestem and should be used in sandy sites. It produces a noticeable crimson fall color and is planted in mid-spring at 8 to 12 pounds per acre (9 to 13 kg/ha).

Prairie cordgrass (*Spartina pectinata* Link.) is a relatively tall-growing (4 to 6 ft, 1.2 to 1.8 m) grass grown for its long, graceful leaves and ability to grow in relatively moist sites where it is often used to stabilize streambanks, shorelines, and other wet soil sites. "Aureo-marginata" is an improved cultivar.

Broomsedge (*Andropogon virginicus* L.) is sometimes a weed species, and is a bunchgrass which grows on low-fertility acid (pH 4.0) soils. In contrast to the other bluestems, broomsedge has a shallow root system, the seedheads are partially enclosed in the sheath, and the mature plants have a distinct brownish-orange color, although some variants are silver. Seedheads may reach four feet (1.2 m) tall. It is planted in mid-spring at 8 to 12 pounds per acre (9 to 13 kg/ha). "Silver Beauty" is a cultivar. Other bluestems include Sand bluestem (*Andropogon hallii* Hack.), Yellow bluestem (*Bothriochloa ischaemum* Keng.), and Old World or Caucasian bluestem (*Bothriochloa caucasica* C. E. Hubb.).

Prairie dropseed (*Sporobulus heterolepis* A. Gray) is a short grass one to three feet tall (0.3 to 0.9 m). It is an elegant growing grass with fountain-like emerald green leaves originating from a tight clump. It is seeded in fall or early spring at 8 to 12 pounds per acre (9 to 13 kg/ha).

Grama Grasses

Sideoats grama (*Bouteloua curtipendula* Michx.Torr.) is a perennial, warm-season, bunch-forming plant native to the North American Great Plains, which rarely exceeds three feet (0.9 m). It has a rolled vernation and long flower stalks with short, dangling purplish spikes. Seeds mature in late summer. Due to its relatively tall growth habit, sideoats grama is better suited to infrequently mowed sites. It is used for regrassing dry sites such as rangelands, erosion control along highways, and in roughs and out-of-play areas on golf courses. Seeding rates range from 8 to 12 pounds per acre (9 to 13 kg/ha) in mid-spring. It is often planted with other prairie grasses such as buffalograss and blue grama.

Blue grama (*Bouteloua gracilis* (HBK) Lag. ex Steud.) has a relatively fine leaf texture, weak rhizomatous growth habit, good heat tolerance, and low fertility and irrigation needs. Wear tolerance is poor, however. The fine, curling basal leaves have a distinctive grayish-green color and a folded vernation. It is adapted to higher pH soils (6.5 to 8.5) of warmer arid to semiarid plains regions and has few pests. It is best suited to low-maintenance, non-use sites such as out-of-play areas and roadsides; it is often planted with buffalograss. Cultivars include Alma, Hachita, and Lovington.

Lovegrass

The lovegrasses are distinct bunchgrasses noted chiefly for their ability to grow on low-fertility, low pH, sandy or rocky soils. They are best suited to the southern transition zone of the United States and similar climates in the world. Seeding rates are 1 (roadsides) to 10 (golf courses) pounds per acre (1.1 to 11 kg/ha) timed in late spring. These reach a height of 1 to 1.5 feet (0.3 to 0.5 m). These perennial grasses have an extensive but shallow fibrous root system and eventually form a bunch about two feet (0.6 m) in diameter. Examples include Weeping lovegrass [*Eragrostis curvula* (Schrad.) Nees.], "Consol," "Ermelo," "Moysa"; Sand lovegrass [*Eragrostis trichodes* (Nutt.) Wood], "Bend," "Mason," "Neb. 27"; Boer lovegrass (*Eragrostis chloromelas* Steud.), "Catalina," "OTA-S"; and Lehmann lovegrass (*Eragrostis lehmanniana* Nees.), "A-68," "Kuivato," "Puhuima." Boer lovegrass is a long-lived perennial bunchgrass, less winter hardy but more drought tolerant than weeping lovegrass. Lehmann lovegrass has prostrate stems which root and produce new plants at the nodes; thus, it creeps. It is the least winter hardy of the lovegrasses. Sand lovegrass tolerates sandy, droughty soils.

Switchgrass

Switchgrass (*Panicum virgatum* L.) is a perennial sod-forming grass native to the Great Plains and most of the eastern United States which reaches four to six feet (1.2 to 1.8 m) in height. It is a coarse-stemmed plant spreading slowly by short rhizomes which form dense bunches or colonies. It is seeded at 5 to 20 pounds per acre (5.6 to 22 kg/ha) pure live seed in spring. Cultivars include "Campfire," "Cloud Nine," "Dallas Blues," "Heavy Metal," "Northwind," and "Shenandoah."

Indiangrass

Indiangrass [*Sorghastrum nutans* (L.) Nash] is another native grass from the prairies of the eastern Great Plains and eastern United States. It is a perennial bunchgrass which spreads by long rhizomes. It is deep rooted and grows tall, three to six feet (0.9 to 1.8 m). It produces distinct yellow panicles (plumes) which are particularly showy in fall. It is planted in spring at 6 to 10 pounds per acre (6.7 to 11 kg/ha) pure live seed. "Sioux Blue" is a commercial cultivar.

Cool-Season Grasses

Crested wheatgrass (*Agropyron cristatum* (L.) Gaertn.), also called fairway wheatgrass, is best adapted to cooler areas of the semiarid to arid regions. It is also a low-maintenance species requiring little supplemental irrigation and fertilization. It has a medium-to-coarse (2 to 8 mm) leaf texture, dark- to bright-green color, a bunch-type growth habit, rolled vernation, membranous ligule, pubescent leaf, and slow recuperative potential. Crested wheatgrass begins vigorous growth in early spring, often goes dormant during summer drought, and resumes growth in the fall with precipitation. It is used on unirrigated lawns, fairways, and roadsides. Cultivars include "Hycrest," "Parkway," and "Ruff." Western wheatgrass (*Pascopyrum smithii*) is similar except for its short rhizomes.

Alkaligrass (*Puccinella distans* [L.] Parl.) or "Weeping Alkaligrass" is a bunch-type cool-season perennial grass with exceptional tolerance to high sodium and high pH (7 to 8) soils. It possesses a gray-green color, has a membranous ligule, rolled vernation, boat-shaped leaf tips, and parallel light lines to the blade's midrib resembling a bluegrass (*Poa*) species. It grows best in the cool-arid regions and along roads which have been treated with salt for snow and ice removal. Alkaligrass is often found growing in low, salt-laden areas where sodium tends to accumulate. Plants are leafy and leaves are narrow with a natural dark-green color. Seeding rates are one to three pounds/1,000 square feet (49 to 146 kg/ha) and down to 10 pounds/acre (11 kg/ha) when used in soil conservation mixtures. Seed germination requires 14 to 21 days, and is often blended with fine fescue and bluegrasses in higher maintained turf situations. It is often crowded out by tall fescue, smooth bromegrass, or Kentucky bluegrass on neutral to acid soils. Cultivars available include "Fults" (or Fultz), "Chaplin," and "Salty."

Miscellaneous Grasses

Several other miscellaneous low-maintenance cool-season grasses include Rough hairgrass (*Agrostis scabra*); Crested dogtail (*Cynosurus cristatus*), "Shade Star"; Orchardgrass (*Dactylis glomerata* L.); Timothy (*Phleum pratense* L.), "Barvanti"; Tufted hairgrass (*Deschampsia caespitosa* (L.) Beauv.), "SR 6000," "Shade Champ"; Junegrass (*Koeleria gracilis* (L.) Pers.); Crested hairgrass or Prairie junegrass (*Koeleria macrantha*), "Barleria," and "Barkoel"; Alphine fescue (*Festuca ovina* var. *brachyphylla*); Meadow fescue (*Festuca elatior* L. or *F. pratensis* Huds.); and Sheep fescue (*Festuca ovina* L.). Numerous Poa species are also being screened and bred for fine turfgrass purposes and include Alpine bluegrass (*Poa alpina* L.); Bulbous bluegrass (*P. bublosa* L.); Creeping bluegrass (*P. reptans*); Fowl bluegrass (*Poa palustris*); Texas bluegrass (*P. arachnifera* Torr.); Wood bluegrass (*P. nemoralis* L.); and Canby bluegrass (*P. canbyi* (Scribn.) Piper), as well as interspecific hybrids among different Poa species such as "Reveille," and "AmeriBlue," crosses between Kentucky bluegrass and Texas bluegrass.

Sand Dune Grasses

Northern ocean-side courses usually stabilize sand dunes with the cool-season grass American beachgrass (*Ammophila breviligulata* Fernald), while southern ocean-side courses often use the warm-season grass Sea-Oats (*Uniola paniculata* L.). Saltgrass (*Distichlis* spp.) is a warm-season, rhizomatous, sod-forming dioecious grass adapted to high salt laden soils and brackish marshes. Its use as a low-maintenance turf may increase as the use of poorer (salty) irrigation sources also increase.

CHAPTER
2

Turfgrass Physiology and Environmental Stress

INTRODUCTION

Good turfgrass management decisions are based on a scientific understanding of how plants grow, develop, and acquire resources throughout the year. The study of these processes is called **plant physiology.** Plants are products of their genetic information modified by their environment; each part or organ of a plant is further modified by its internal environment. Turfgrass managers who become familiar with the concepts of plant physiology are better able to select products and practices which improve turfgrass performance and prevent plant stress.

In this chapter, the plant physiological processes—photosynthesis, respiration, biosynthesis, water and nutrient uptake, and transpiration—are reviewed. Seasonal patterns of below and aboveground turfgrass growth are described, as well as the important plant hormones governing these patterns. Finally, the physiology of environmental stress and suggested steps managers can take to prevent, diagnose, and alleviate turfgrass stress are covered.

All plant physiological processes are interconnected, as illustrated in Figure 2–1. The process of photosynthesis supplies plants with energy and biomass. During photosynthesis, leaves capture energy from the sunlight and store this energy in the chemical bonds of newly synthesized **sugar** molecules. Photosynthesis requires **carbon dioxide (CO_2)** from the atmosphere and **water (H_2O)** from the soil; the process eventually releases **oxygen (O_2).**

Overall Chemical Reaction of Photosynthesis

$$6CO_2 + 6H_2O \xrightarrow{\lambda(light)} 6O_2 + C_6H_{12}O_6$$

carbon dioxide   water   photosynthesis   oxygen   carbohydrate

Sugars (carbohydrates) formed in photosynthesis are transported throughout the plant, bringing carbon and energy to sites where they are needed. During **respiration,** the reversal of photosynthesis occurs where the energy contained in the photosynthetically produced sugars is transferred to adenosine triphosphate (ATP), a cellular "energy currency" which fuels many chemical reactions, including those involved in **biosynthesis** and **mineral nutrient uptake.** Sugars and

FIGURE 2–1 Energy and metabolite flow through the plant. Plants convert energy from light to chemical energy as ATP and NADPH through the formation of sugars. The functions of water in this process include: (1) an electron donor in photosynthesis; (2) a solvent in which cellular reactions occur; (3) a means to transport sugars and mineral nutrients within the plant body; (4) a method to cool the leaf through transpiration; and (5) a way to maintain cell turgor or shape.

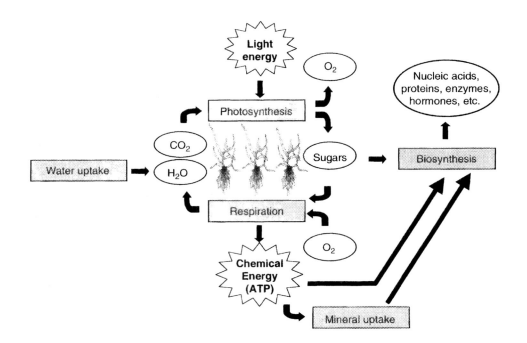

mineral nutrients form the raw materials from which proteins, enzymes, nucleic acids, hormones, and all other chemical components of the plant are synthesized.

All physiological processes require adequate water. In addition to its specific role of providing electrons during photosynthesis, water serves many additional functions in the plant (Figure 2–1). Water is the solvent in which most biochemical reactions occur; proteins, enzymes, DNA, and other macromolecules require the presence of water to maintain proper shape and function. Nutrient ions dissolve readily in water and are carried throughout the plant body dissolved in xylem sap. Water can absorb a great deal of heat without changing temperature; thus, it buffers the plant tissues against rapid temperature fluctuations. When water evaporates from the leaf (termed transpiration), it absorbs large quantities of heat and cools the leaf surface, reducing leaf temperatures under hot conditions. Movement of water into individual plant cells also produces the positive hydrostatic pressure which gives plants their rigidity, or turgor. Given water's central role in plant physiology, it is not surprising many plant stresses are related to inadequate water supply.

Oxygen (O_2) is also crucial to plant physiological processes. It is well-known plants produce oxygen during photosynthesis, but plants also consume oxygen during respiration. Without the ability to respire, most plant cells would lose their function and eventually die. Adequate oxygen supply, particularly in the root zone, is therefore crucial for turfgrass health.

PHOTOSYNTHESIS

The reason why some plants, such as bentgrass, "prefer" cooler climates while others, such as bermudagrass, "prefer" warm climates was not fully understood until the 1950s and 1960s. During this time, researchers discovered the existence of two distinct photosynthetic pathways. One, the **Calvin-Benson** or **C_3 cycle,** operates primarily in cool-season turfgrasses such as bentgrass, while the other, the **Hatch-Slack** or **C_4 cycle,** operates primarily in warm-season turfgrasses such as bermudagrass and zoysiagrass.

Understanding how these two photosynthetic pathways differ in physiology and stress response allows superintendents to manipulate environmental conditions which allow turfgrass species to grow in areas where they do not naturally occur.

The chemical reactions of photosynthesis can be divided into two phases. In the first phase, called the **light reactions,** the sun's light energy is captured and stored in the chemical bonds of two "energy transfer" molecules, ATP and NADPH. During this process, water is consumed and oxygen is released (Figure 2–1). The light reactions are identical in C_3 and C_4 turfgrasses. In the

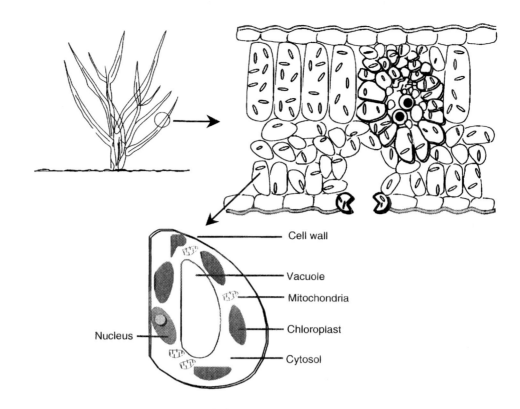

FIGURE 2–2 Cross-section of a grass leaf indicating where chloroplasts, the site of photosynthesis, are located.

Cell wall

Vacuole

Mitochondria

Chloroplast

Cytosol

Nucleus

second phase, called the **dark** or **carbon reactions,** carbon from atmospheric CO_2 and energy from ATP and NADPH produced in the light reactions are used to form triose phosphates, the chemical precursors of simple sugars. The dark reactions proceed differently in C_3 and C_4 turfgrasses. Before examining this difference in detail, leaf anatomy and photosynthesis common to all turfgrasses will be covered.

Leaf and Chloroplast Anatomy

An examination of turfgrass leaf anatomy reveals several specialized cell layers, all of which play specific roles in maintaining optimal conditions for photosynthesis (Figure 2–2). The cuticle, a waxy layer protecting the leaf from uncontrolled evaporative water loss, covers the upper and lower surfaces of the leaf. Beneath the upper and lower cuticles are the **upper epidermis** and **lower epidermis.** The epidermis is a layer of cells, usually one cell thick, which secretes cuticular waxes and protects the deeper cell layers of the leaf.

The cuticle and epidermal layers seal the inner atmosphere of the leaf from the outside atmosphere of the bulk air. Movement of CO_2, H_2O, and O_2 between the leaf and the air is then controlled by the stomates, specialized points of entry located within the epidermal cell layers (Figure 2–3). Stomates are microscopic pores in the epidermis which open or close in response to the movement of two specialized cells (**guard cells**) surrounding each pore. The guard cells respond rapidly to hormonal signals and environmental conditions; for example, in response to drought or very low humidity, the guard cells close the stomates to prevent excessive water loss. This system of cuticle, epidermis, and stomates provides the leaf with some control over its internal environment; however, this control is not absolute. Even with all stomates completely closed, water can slowly diffuse across the cuticle boundary, ultimately dehydrating the leaf under prolonged drought.

Below the upper epidermal cell layer are several layers of mesophyll cells, where most photosynthesis occurs. The mesophyll cells are in direct contact with the inner gaseous environment of the leaf through a network of interconnected air spaces. Within the mesophyll cells are the **chloroplasts,** membrane-bound subcellular compartments (organelles) where the reactions of photosynthesis take place. Chlorophyll and other pigments involved in photosynthesis are found in the chloroplasts.

The internal structure of the chloroplast is dominated by a complex array of flattened, sac-like membranes called the **thylakoids** (Figure 2–4). Embedded within the thylakoids are the pigments

FIGURE 2–3 Close-up of a cross-section of a leaf indicating where the major components are located.

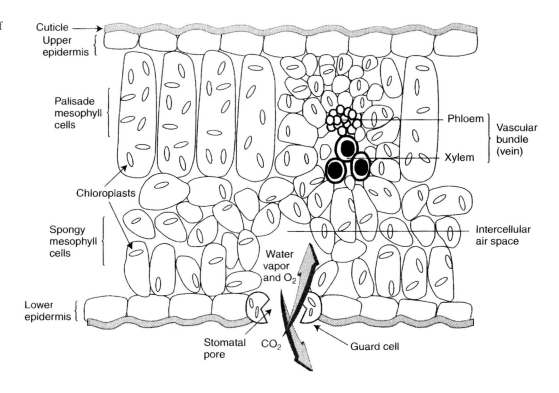

FIGURE 2–4 The structure of plant chloroplasts with flattened, stacked sac-like structures called thylakoids interspersed in a fine granular matrix termed stroma. Light-absorbing pigments and the machinery for harvesting light energy are located in the thylakoid membranes. Reactions converting CO_2 to carbohydrates occur in the stroma. As electrons pass through this transport chain, protons (H^+) are transported into the inner thylakoid space (called lumen).

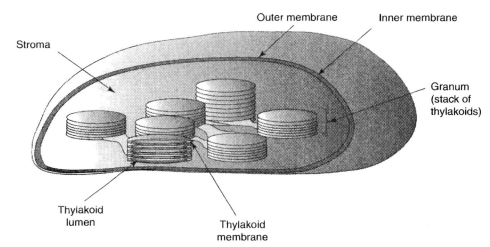

and electron carriers of the photosynthetic light reactions. Light-absorbing pigments and the machinery for harvesting light energy are located in the thylakoid membranes. The thylakoids are suspended in a fine granular matrix called the **stroma,** which contains the enzymes of the photosynthetic dark reactions where reactions converting CO_2 to carbohydrates occur. The thylakoids enclose another fluid-filled space, the **lumen,** in which protons (H^+) accumulate during the light reactions and are used to drive ATP synthesis from ADP and phosphate (H_2PO_4). This accumulation creates a proton gradient where the inside of the thylakoid membrane is acidic and the outside (or stroma) is alkaline. This proton gradient is the energy source needed to create ATP from ADP and phosphate (H_2PO_4). The end products of thylakoid reactions are the high-energy compounds ATP and NADPH, which are used for the synthesis of sugars. The thylakoids are arranged in stacks, called **grana,** which are connected by unstacked, bridge-like regions called **stromal lamellae.**

 Vascular bundles, running in distinct strands through the mesophyll layers, are parallel to the long axis of the leaf. Vascular bundles consist of xylem vessels which transport water and nutrients from the roots, and phloem cells which transport sugars from the mesophyll cells of mature leaves to other parts of the plant. The xylem and phloem are surrounded by several layers of densely packed cells called the **bundle sheath;** these cells play an important role in the dark reactions of C_4 turfgrasses. Above and below the vascular bundles are strands of thick, lignified **schlerenchyma** cells which provide support and rigidity to the leaf.

All features of basic leaf anatomy contribute to the process of photosynthesis. Photosynthetic reactions occur in the mesophyll cells and, in C_4 turfgrasses, also in the bundle sheath cells. Water and mineral nutrients required for photosynthesis are supplied to these cells by the xylem. Products of photosynthesis are transported in the phloem. The cuticle and epidermis protect the photosynthesizing cells, while the opening and closing of stomates regulate the internal levels of CO_2, H_2O, and O_2.

Basic Reaction of Photosynthesis

The simple reaction of photosynthesis shown earlier disguises the complex nature of the photosynthetic process, which involves numerous electron transfers, enzymatic reactions, and cellular compartments. On the left-hand side of the equation are the raw materials of photosynthesis: CO_2 and H_2O. On the right-hand side are the products: O_2 and a six-carbon sugar molecule such as glucose or fructose. The equilibrium constant for this equation is approximately 10^{-500}, meaning this reaction is impossible without a large input of energy. Light provides this energy.

Nature of Light

Light is a form of electromagnetic radiation with the qualities of both a particle and a wave. One light particle is called a **photon,** and each photon contains a discrete quantity of energy called a **quantum.** The magnitude of a photon's energy is related to its **wavelength,** or the distance between adjacent wave peaks. The higher the wavelength of light, the less energy contained in its photons. The energy of blue light (430 nm) is "high," about 70 kcal/einstein, whereas the energy of red light (680 nm) is "low," about 40 kcal/einstein. Thus, X-rays, whose wavelengths are on the order of 0.1 nm, have a great deal of energy, while infrared light waves, whose wavelengths are on the order of 10^{12} nm, have relatively low energy (Figure 2–5).

The human eye can perceive light within the wavelength range of 400 nm (violet) to 700 nm (red). Photosynthesis uses light within the same range. For this reason, light between 400 and 700 nm is often referred to as **photosynthetically active radiation,** or **PAR.** Leaves can also absorb light at wavelengths above and below PAR, but this cannot be used for photosynthesis. High-energy, short-wavelength ultraviolet (UV) light can damage DNA, membranes, and other cellular components. Genetic mutations in turfgrass are, at least partially, from sunlight. They have led to "off-types," which are oftentimes aesthetically undesirable but also provide new genetic material for breeding purposes. Low-energy, long-wavelength infrared light is experienced by the plant as heat.

FIGURE 2–5 White light from the sun is actually a mixture of different colored light and is only a small portion of a vast electromagnetic spectrum. The visible range of wavelengths of radiation to humans extends from about 380 nm (violet) to about 750 nm (red). Short-wavelength has a high energy content while long-wavelength has a low energy content.

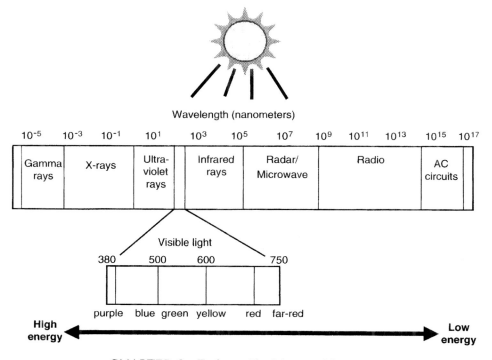

Pigment Composition

Light energy is captured by pigment molecules embedded in the thylakoid membranes; these include chlorophyll (chlorophyll a and b) and **carotenoids.** These pigment molecules absorb light in the 400 to 700 nm wavelength range in sufficient amounts to support photosynthesis. Chlorophyll molecules are green-colored pigments; carotenoids are light yellow to orange in color. Two kinds of carotenoids exist, red to orange **carotenes** and deeply yellow **xanthophylls.** Plants also contain other pigments such as the **anthocyanins** (red to blue). These additional pigments contribute to light harvesting in photosynthesis; the various colors of flowers, fruits, and other plant parts; and possibly to plant defense mechanisms.

While the specific chemical structures of these pigments differ, all exhibit a large number of carbon-carbon double bonds (e.g., $-CH=CH-$) where electrons are shared among several adjacent carbon nuclei (Figure 2–6). These shared, or "delocalized," electrons can absorb energy in the form of a photon and move from their ground state to a higher energy state where they are farther from the nucleus. Absorption of light energy by a pigment is referred to as "excitation," and the higher energy state of the delocalized electron is called the "excited state." An electron in the excited state can be compared to water at the top of a mountain. Just as water flows downhill, an excited electron gives up its extra energy and drops back down to its ground state. And just as flowing water can be used to turn a mill wheel, the energy of the excited electron can also be used to do work. In the case of photosynthesis, this work is the formation of ATP and NADPH.

Each type of pigment in the thylakoid membrane absorbs a specific wavelength of light. Chlorophylls a and b absorb blue (430 nm) and red (680 nm) light and appear green in color. Their structure includes a tetrapyrrole ring (contains four pyrroles joined; see Figure 2–6) consisting of nitrogen, carbon, hydrogen, and oxygen and contains conjugated unsaturated bonds with a magnesium ion in the center and a long phytol tail. Carotenoids, including carotenes and xanthophylls, absorb light in the 400 to 500 nm range and appear yellow or orange in color. Their structure contains carbon, oxygen, and hydrogen and includes a long chain of conjugated carbon double bonds cyclized on either end. These unsaturated bonds allow the plant pigment molecules to capture and transfer light energy to chlorophyll without damage to the plant's cellular structure.

Besides capturing light energy, carotenoids also help in the dissipation of excess light energy at very high light intensities. By absorbing excess photons and dissipating their energy harmlessly as heat, carotenoids protect the rest of the cell from photo-oxidative damage.

FIGURE 2–6 Structures of chlorophyll and carotene, the primary light-absorbing pigments involved in photosynthesis.

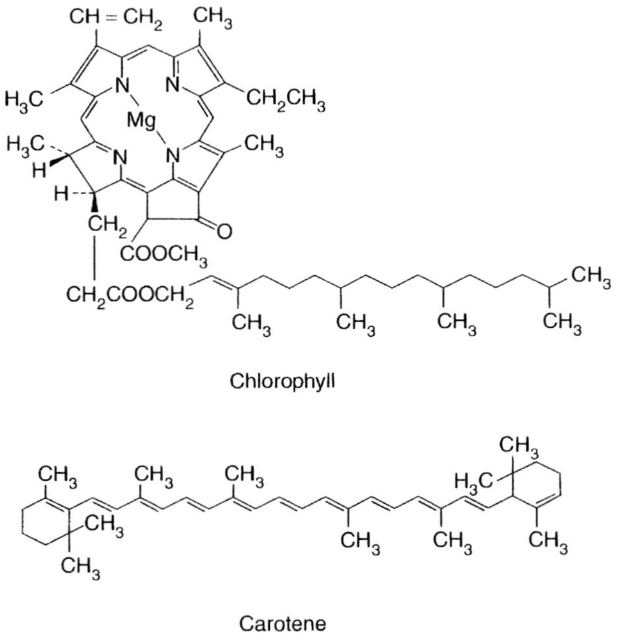

Chlorophyll

Carotene

The Light Reactions

Photosynthesis is actually a combination of two separate but related processes—a light reaction and a dark or carbon reaction. Light is absorbed by pigments and its energy is converted into usable chemical energy (**ATP** and **NADPH**). In the dark or carbon reaction, products of the light reaction are used to fix atmospheric CO_2 into carbohydrate (sugars). The use of energy derived from the absorption of light is possible because of a series of oxidation/reduction reactions carried out by chemicals arranged in two parts of what is termed the "light reaction."

Components of the light reactions (also called the **electron transport system** or **"Z" scheme;** Figure 2–7) are designated **photosystem I (PSI)** and **photosystem II (PSII).** These photo systems can be considered as light-driven electron pumps which work in two different, but overlapping, areas. PSII absorbs light in the red region (around 680 nm), while PSI absorbs light in the far-red region (around 700 nm). The PSII contains a different chlorophyll designated P_{680}, chl a antenna and carotenoids. The PSI complex contains the following pigments: a special chl a or P_{700} in the reaction center; chl a antenna; and the carotenoids, b-carotene and xanthophyll. Photosystem II and PSI are arranged sequentially in the electron transport chain to transfer energy from H_2O to $NADP^+$ (Figure 2–7). Electron transport involves several carrier molecules connecting the two photosystems. The electrons are finally passed to **ferredoxin (Fd),** a water-soluble iron-sulfur protein found on the stromal side of the thylakoid membrane. Fd donates the electron to NADP+, reducing it to NADPH.

While this scheme for electron transport may seem very complex, it accomplishes the transfer of electrons from H_2O to $NADP^+$ to form NADPH with the evolution of O_2 and the production of ATP as previously discussed. NADPH is vital for the reduction of CO_2, and ATP is an energy carrying molecule used in many energy-requiring processes including various synthesis reactions (e.g., the synthesis of proteins). The formation of ATP is referred to as **photophosphorylation.**

Practical Implications of the Light Reactions

Passing high-energy electrons through a series of electron carriers is not without risk. Cold temperatures, high light levels, and insufficient water may all cause more light energy to be absorbed than can be processed in photosynthesis. Under these conditions, the majority of the photosynthetic

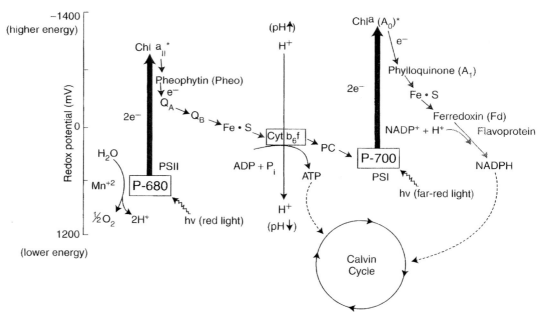

FIGURE 2–7 Simplified diagram of electron (e^-) transport in the chloroplasts of higher plants (also known as the Z-scheme). Individual components are positioned according to their redox potential (electron donating or accepting properties). As electrons are excited from sunlight energy, redox potential goes from an oxidized (low energy) to a reduced (high energy) state. The antennae chlorophyll molecules feed energy from sunlight (hv) into chlorophylls (Chl $a_{II \text{ and } I}$) associated with PSII and PSI. The cyclic electron flow in photosystem II (PSII) allows electrons to be recycled through pheophytin, plastoquinone (Q_A and Q_B), iron-sulfur protein (Fe·S), cytochrome b_6f complex (Cyt b_6f), plastocyanin (PC), and ferredoxin (Fd) under special conditions. In photosystem I (PSI), electrons flow from chlorophyll a (chl a) to phylloquinone (A_1), iron-sulfur protein (Fe·S) to ferredoxin (Fd). The end products of the electron transport system, ATP and NADPH, are shuttled to the Calvin cycle to provide energy for the reduction of carbon dioxide into sugars.

electron carriers become reduced and are unable to accept more electrons. Excited electrons may then be captured by oxygen (O_2), converting it to one of several highly damaging forms, or a **reactive oxygen species,** which indiscriminately attack proteins, enzymes, membranes, and other cellular components.

This vulnerability of the light reactions is exploited by many herbicides. About half of all commercial herbicides directly target carriers of the photosynthetic electron transport chain, deliberately blocking electron flow and/or diverting electrons to oxygen. Some herbicides, like atrazine, block electron flow between Q_a and Q_b in PSII. Others, like diquat, prevent the flow of electrons to ferredoxin. Still others compete with plastoquinone for binding to cytochrome b_6f.

Carbon Reactions

The biosynthesis of carbohydrates is, with respect to the amounts produced, the most important biochemical process in the chloroplast. While the overall photosynthesis reaction was previously shown, it does not show the involvement of ATP and NADPH which have been generated from the light reaction. The following reaction shows the involvement of the products of the light reaction to convert atmospheric CO_2 to plant-usable carbohydrates.

Carbon (or Dark) Chemical Reaction

$$CO_2 + 3ATP + 2NADPH + 2H^+ \rightarrow [CH_2O] + H_2O + 3ADP + 3P + 2NADP^+$$

These reactions were thought to be independent of light; therefore, they were previously referred to as dark reactions. However, since these reactions depend on products of light-regulation processes, they are now referred to as the carbon reactions of photosynthesis.

Carbon dioxide is absorbed through leaf **stomates.** In addition to providing an entry of atmospheric CO_2 into the leaf, stomates release water vapor during transpiration. Normally, stomates are open during the day or in the light and closed during the night or dark in an attempt to conserve H_2O. The carbon in CO_2 is in a highly oxidized state, whereas carbon in a carbohydrate such as sucrose is in a highly reduced state. The electrons which have been transported to $NADP^+$, forming NADPH in the light reaction, are used to reduce the oxidation level of carbon during the dark reaction.

C$_3$ Plants

The first product formed from CO_2 fixation is a three-carbon sugar, **3-phosphoglycerate (3-PGA; Figure 2–8),** which gives rise to the designation of C_3 or Calvin cycle (also the designation of C_3 plants). As shown in Figure 2–8, CO_2 is added to a receptor molecule, **ribulose-bisphosphate (RuBP),** a five-carbon sugar, producing two molecules of 3-PGA via the enzyme ribulose 1,5-bisphosphate carboxylase/oxygenase (designated as **RuBP carboxylase** or **Rubisco**). The Calvin cycle involves a number of other intermediate compounds (sugars). The result of this cycle is the production of a pool of triose phosphates. These three carbon compounds are the precursors to six carbon sugars including glucose and fructose. The net reaction consumes $6CO_2$, yielding a six-carbon sugar through the energy provided in the light reactions. These basic six-carbon sugars are later used to synthesize larger carbohydrate molecules such as sucrose, starch, cellulose, and many others. A summary reaction is as follows.

Calvin Cycle Chemical Reaction

$$6CO_2 + 12NADPH + 12H^+ + 18ATP + 6H_2O \rightarrow C_6H_{12}O_6 + 17Pi + 18ADP + 12NADP^+$$

The sugar-phosphates are used in plant growth and development while the ADP and $NADP^+$ are cycled back to the light reaction to form additional ATP and NADPH. The reactions of the Calvin cycle are common to all photosynthetic plants and are the only known series of reactions which produce a net gain in carbohydrates.

Cool-season turfgrass species such as fescues, bentgrass, bluegrass, and ryegrass all are C_3 plants; thus, they are genetically adapted to cooler regions. As temperatures increase, the concentration of CO_2 to O_2 decreases. As a result, photorespiration increases relative to photosynthesis. When grown in high-temperature environment regions, C_3 plants weaken. Their microenvironments must be manipulated to relieve heat stress or they may eventually die.

FIGURE 2–8 Simplified diagram of the photosynthetic steps associated with the Calvin or C_3 cycle in cool-season grasses. ATP and NADPH from the electron transport process located in the thylakoid membrane provide the chemical energy to drive this cycle. The end products in the triose-phosphate pool contain the primary precursors to six carbon carbohydrates, starches, and sugars.

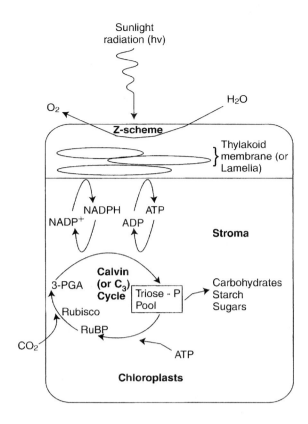

Sucrose and Starch

When photosynthesis exceeds the capacity of chloroplasts to export triose phosphate sugars, glucose is formed and polymerized to form starch which temporarily accumulates in the chloroplasts. When light dims and photosynthesis slows, as in the fall, this starch is hydrolyzed to glucose, synthesized to sucrose, and transported to storage sink organs—leaf sheaths, crowns, rhizomes, and stolons. Sucrose is the principal transport sugar in the phloem of grasses. In warm-season grasses, sucrose is then re-synthesized to starch and stored in plastids (amyloplasts) for use when needed. In cool-season grasses, sucrose is synthesized into various fructose polymers (fructans) in vacuoles and stored temporarily in leaves or for longer periods in crowns, rhizomes, and stolons. Unlike starch, fructans are water soluble and help cool-season grasses tolerate freezing temperatures.

C_4 Plants

Until 1965, scientists thought the Calvin cycle was the only pathway of carbon fixation in higher plants. It was discovered in sugarcane that instead of a three-carbon compound, 3-PGA, being the first product of carbon fixation, a four-carbon compound, **oxaloacetic acid (OAA),** was the first product formed, hence the name C_4. This gave rise to the designation of the **C_4 cycle** or **C_4 plants** and allows these plants a more efficient method of fixing CO_2. C_4 turfgrasses eliminate photorespiration, but at the cost of additional ATP required for carbon fixation. Under high light, this trade-off benefits the plant: photosynthetic rates in C_4 species increase with temperature without a loss in efficiency. However, under low light conditions, the additional ATP cost for C_4 carbon fixation can slow growth.

Most (but not all) C_4 plants are monocots and presumably evolved from the tropics since high temperatures and light intensities are needed for their optimum performance. All warm-season turf species (bahiagrass, bermudagrass, buffalograss, carpetgrass, centipedegrass, kikuyugrass, seashore paspalum, St. Augustinegrass, and zoysiagrass) are C_4 plants; thus, they are adapted to warmer temperatures and higher light intensities (Table 2–1). Other C_4 grasses include dallisgrass, crabgrass, and goosegrass, all of which are common weeds in turf. These weeds, when present in C_3 turfgrasses such as fescue, ryegrass, or bluegrass, have the distinct physiological growth edge during warm summer months since they grow faster during warm temperatures.

TABLE 2–1 *Distinguishing characteristics between C$_3$ (cool-season) and C$_4$ (warm-season) grasses.*

Characteristics	C$_3$ (cool-season)	C$_4$ (warm-season)
Leafy anatomy	Laminar mesophyll which allows large air spaces and less concentrated CO$_2$ levels.	Mesophyll arranged radially around bundle sheaths called Kranz- or halo-type anatomy. This close association allows C$_4$ plants to concentrate CO$_2$ in bundle sheath cells.
CO$_2$-compensation concentration	30 to 70 ppm	<10 ppm
Primary CO$_2$ receptor molecule	RuBP	PEP
First product of photosynthesis	C$_3$ acids (PGA)	C$_4$ acids (oxaloacetate)
Photosynthesis depressed by O$_2$	yes	no
CO$_2$ released in light (photorespiration)	yes	no
Light levels required for photosynthesis	one-fourth to one-half full sunlight	full sunlight
Net photosynthetic capacity	slight to high	high to very high
Dry-matter production	medium	high
Food storage	simple sugars (fructosan)	starch
Optimum temperatures for photosynthesis	60 to 77°F (15.6 to 25°C)	85 to 117°F (29 to 47°C)
Optimum temperatures for root growth	50 to 65°F (10 to 18°C)	75 to 95°F (24 to 35°C)

FIGURE 2–9 Simplified diagram of the photosynthetic steps in C$_4$ or warm-season grasses. C$_4$ grasses can concentrate CO$_2$ in the bundle sheath by transporting malate or aspartate from the mesophyll cell into the bundle-sheath cell. This establishes a very efficient conversion of CO$_2$ to carbohydrates.

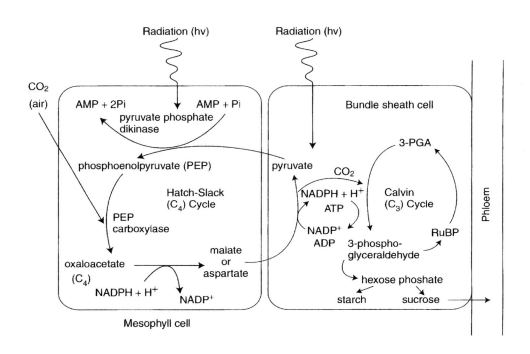

Carbon dioxide (CO$_2$) fixation in C$_4$ plants begins in the mesophyll cells (Figure 2–9) where it is combined with phosphoenolpyruvate (PEP) to produce oxaloacetate (OAA). The carboxylation enzyme is phosphoenolpyruvate carboxylase (PEP carboxylase). The OAA is quickly converted into either malate or aspartate (both four-carbon compounds), which are then transported to cells surrounding the vascular bundles of the leaf, or bundle sheath cells. In the bundle sheath cells CO$_2$ is cleaved from the four-carbon acids and combined with ribulose bisphosphate, producing 3-PGA and triose phosphates via the Calvin cycle. In C$_4$ plants, the four-carbon acid acts to shuttle and concentrate CO$_2$ in the bundle sheath cells. Identical to C$_3$ plants, NADPH and ATP from the light reaction are required for CO$_2$ fixation and functioning of the pathway. Thus, in C$_4$ plants CO$_2$ fixation involves a combination of two CO$_2$ fixation pathways and seems much too complex to be efficient. However, consideration of this mechanism combined with a distinct leaf anatomy, described later, will illustrate a unique evolutionary development.

Kranz Anatomy

It is important to note that the internal structural anatomy of a C_4 leaf is different from a C_3 plant. In C_4 plants, vascular tissues (phloem) are surrounded by bundle sheath cells, which are the site of the second CO_2 fixation via the Calvin cycle. These are surrounded by mesophyll cells which largely fill the leaf; thus, there is little air space. Mesophyll cells are the site of the first CO_2 fixation and responsible for the transport of the four-carbon acid to the bundle sheath cells. The decarboxylation reaction in the bundle sheath creates a very high concentration of CO_2, referred to as **Kranz anatomy** (German for "wreath"). In contrast, C_3 plants do not contain chloroplasts in their bundle sheath cells; therefore, they are not able to concentrate CO_2 for maximum Rubisco activity. Rather, in C_3 plants there are large air spaces since the parenchyma cells are arranged into two distinct tissues, the palisade layer and the **spongy parenchyma.** Thus, in the C_4 leaf the distance for CO_2 diffusion to the carboxylation sites is shorter compared to C_3 plants. The distance between the mesophyll cells and the bundle sheath cells is also shorter; intercellular transport of malic and aspartic acids is also short. Thus, the distinct anatomy of C_4 plants enables a warm-season grass to concentrate CO_2 in the bundle sheath cells at about a 12-fold increase compared to C_3 plants and demonstrate a more efficient CO_2 fixation. A C_3 grass such as bentgrass is not as efficient at utilizing CO_2 but has an advantage under lower light intensities and cooler temperatures.

Photorespiration

The enzyme responsible for CO_2 fixation in the Calvin cycle (C_3) is Rubisco (short for RuBP carboxylase/oxygenase). Rubisco can react with O_2 as well as with CO_2. High levels of O_2 favor the oxygenase activity whereas high levels of CO_2 favor the carboxylase activity. The oxygenase activity converts RuBP to 2-phosphoglycolate and 3-phosphoglycerate (3-PGA), rather than the two molecules of 3-PGA produced during carboxylase activity (the normal carboxylase activity of RuBP carboxylase/oxygenase). This oxygenase activity is termed **photorespiration** (Figure 2–10). It is not true respiration as in Glycolysis or the Krebs cycle where carbon compounds are converted to CO_2, ATP, and carbon compounds with consumption of O_2. Photorespiration, therefore, in C_3 plants is considered wasteful and reduces photosynthetic efficiency and plant productivity. Although photosynthetically inefficient, photorespiration maintains the flow of energy (NADPH and ATP) from the light reactions to the dark reactions to prevent damage to the photosynthetic apparatus of the light reactions in high light environments. In C_4 plants, PEP carboxylase is not affected by O_2 as Rubisco is in C_3 plants; thus, in C_4 plants, photorespiration is not significant.

For every two glycolates passing through the photorespiration cycle, 3 O_2 are consumed, 1 CO_2 is released, 1 ATP is consumed, and 1 PGA is made. Three times more O_2 is used in photorespiration than CO_2 released.

FIGURE 2–10
Photorespiration pathway in C_3 plants where normal carbon dioxide (CO_2) levels are depleted due to closed stomates, which reduce transpiration during heat stress. This favors oxygen (O_2) uptake and utilization. It also favors seemingly wasteful carbon dioxide loss through sugar and carbohydrate utilization with neither ATP or NADH production as with regular respiration. Photorespiration is a key reason C_3 grasses grow poorly outside their naturally adapted cooler regions.

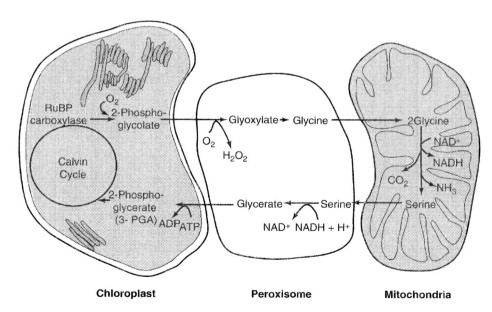

Chloroplast   Peroxisome   Mitochondria

Environmental parameters favoring photorespiration are bright, hot, dry days. Under these conditions, C_3 plants try to reduce transpiration water loss by closing their stomates. In turn, CO_2 intake levels are reduced and O_2 levels begin to build up in the leaf from photosynthesis. Higher O_2 levels reduce the efficiency of CO_2 fixation by RuBP carboxylase/oxygenase. Increasing temperatures increase photorespiration in C_3 plants, but since this process does not occur in C_4 plants, increasing temperatures normally only increase growth. As the temperature rises, C_3 plants gradually have decreased efficiencies due to faster CO_2 loss by photorespiration and may be up to 50 percent less efficient in carbon fixation compared to C_4 plants.

Since C_3 plants cannot concentrate CO_2 as C_4 plants do, their stomates must stay open longer to capture the necessary CO_2 levels to incorporate into carbohydrates. However, the more stomates stay open, the larger amount of water lost via transpiration. Thus, C_4 plants lose less water per unit of CO_2 fixed compared to C_3 plants and are more efficient at utilizing water and in photosynthesis. Cool-season turfgrass species such as fescues, bentgrass, bluegrass, and ryegrass all are C_3 plants; thus, they are genetically adapted to cooler regions. As temperatures increase, the concentration of CO_2 to O_2 decreases. As a result, photorespiration increases relative to photosynthesis. When grown in high-temperature environment regions, C_3 plants weaken. Their microenvironments must be manipulated to resemble cooler areas or they may eventually die. Photorespiration and prolonged transpiration during summer months typically weaken C_3 plants.

Given the apparent wastefulness of photorespiration, one wonders why the oxygenase activity of Rubisco has been retained in C_3 turfgrasses. It has been suggested photorespiration plays a legitimate physiological role in stress protection. When light levels are high and stomates are closed, the light reactions can outpace the dark reactions, causing accumulation of ATP and NADPH and the over-reduction of electron carriers in the thylakoid membranes. These conditions favor the formation of reactive oxygen species which cause significant photo-oxidative damage. However, photorespiratory metabolism of 2-phosphoglycolate and the production of 3-PGA keep the C_3 cycle running and replenish the supply of ADP and $NADP^+$ for the light reactions, thereby preventing photo-oxidative damage in high light.

Overall, energy in the form of ATP required to fix CO_2 into carbohydrates is initially higher in C_4 plants. Five molecules of ATP are required per CO_2 fixed in C_4 plants while only three molecules of ATP per CO_2 fixed are required in C_3 plants. However, additional ATPs are consumed in photorespiration in C_3 plants.

C_4 Plants Compared to C_3 Plants

In addition to differences in carbon fixation efficiency, leaf anatomy, water usage, and energetics of photosynthesis, there are other differences between C_4 plants and C_3 plants. These physiological differences affect plant response to various environmental conditions and growth or productivity.

Nitrogen Use

Not only are C_4 plants more efficient at utilizing CO_2 and water compared to C_3 plants, but they also utilize nitrogen more efficiently. A two-fold greater dry matter production per unit of leaf nitrogen and nearly a two-fold greater rate of photosynthesis often occurs with C_4 plants compared with C_3 plants. The efficient utilization of nitrogen can be attributed to the "CO_2 trap" found within C_4 plants. C_4 plants possess an active isozyme of PEP carboxylase, thus allowing only 10 to 25 percent of the leaf nitrogen to be used in RuBP carboxylase. C_3 plants do not have a "CO_2 trap"; therefore, they invest 40 to 60 percent of their leaf nitrogen in RuBP carboxylase.

Temperature Tolerance

In addition to greater efficiencies, C_4 plants have an ability to withstand certain other environmental pressures which C_3 plants cannot. The primary stress C_4 plants are better adapted to are high temperatures. Mentioned earlier, C_3 plants do not photosynthesize as well as C_4 plants in warmer temperatures because of photorespiration. As the temperature becomes warmer, the reaction of RuBP carboxylase with O_2 occurs faster and the growth of C_3 plants is slowed. Eventually, heat stress in cool-season grasses occurs by damaging cell membranes, especially by denaturing proteins. However, as the temperature gets cooler, C_4 plants do not photosynthesize as well as C_3 plants. This is perhaps related to the cold sensitivity of pyruvate phosphate dikinase.

This enzyme is needed to regenerate PEP from pyruvate, and its cold sensitivity would stop photosynthesis in C_4 plants.

Light

Another factor influencing plant growth is light. C_4 plants exhibit a nonsaturating growth curve at light intensities found in nature, meaning they require full sunlight for optimum photosynthesis. C_3 plants, however, are fully saturated at one-half full sunlight. At conditions beyond one-half full sunlight, photosynthesis decreases in C_3 plants because of photorespiration. Therefore, C_4 plants require full sunlight for maximum growth while cool-season grasses in general can photosynthesize at much less (or lower) light intensities.

Light intensities also greatly influence turfgrass growth. C_4 plants (such as bermudagrass) grow best when exposed to full sunlight. At lower light intensities (<70 percent full sunlight), C_4 plants respond by developing narrow, elongated leaves, thin upright stems, elongated internodes, and weak rhizomes and stolons. Consequently, most C_4 plants, such as bermudagrass, develop very sparse turf when grown under shady conditions. When mowed excessively low, such as in a golf green, it is frequently invaded by other pests such as algae. This higher light intensity requirement is why most C_4 grasses have relatively poor shade tolerance compared to C_3 grasses.

In the field, only a small fraction of the light striking the upper leaves of a turf stand filters through to leaves below. The second layer of leaves receives about 10 percent of the light striking the top layer, and only 1 percent strikes the lower third layer. The arrangement and angle of the leaves also help determine how much light will pass to lower leaf layers. The more upright the leaves, the more sunlight can reach the lower layers and the more efficient the plants can utilize full sunlight. This explains why during shorter light duration days, like those found in late summer and fall, C_4 plants such as bermudagrass become "stemmy." This is an attempt by the plant to allow lower leaves to capture as much sunlight as possible to make the plant as efficient in photosynthesis as possible to store carbohydrates for winter months. During longer days, like those found during late spring and early summer, bermudagrass has more of a **prostrate** (or **decumbent**) growth habit. Lower leaves are not as important to the plant during these times since the longer days allow enough sunlight absorption by the upper leaves to adequately sustain growth.

Daylength and temperature also have been shown to be the most important environmental parameters influencing bermudagrass growth. Growth declines exponentially when daylength hours are decreased. Optimum growth of warm-season grasses occurs when daily solar radiation daylength is greater than 13 hours. When solar radiation daylength is reduced below 13 hours, growth is slowed regardless if adequate irrigation or nitrogen fertilizer is available. The opposite effect occurs with some cool-season grasses. For example, shorter daylength periods, like those experienced in spring and fall, promote the greatest tillering of perennial ryegrass and annual bluegrass.

When full sunlight hours are reduced below eight hours, bermudagrass, especially in shorter mowed areas such as greens, will gradually thin. Taller mowed bermudagrass, such as fairways and approaches, can withstand less sunlight due to their higher mowing heights; thus, they provide more leaf surface area to capture available light. Golf greens, meanwhile, due to their shorter mowing heights, have less leaf surface area and cannot maintain a strong stand at reduced daylength or light quality condition. Bermudagrass golf greens, therefore, require eight hours minimum of full sunlight, year-round.

In the natural environment, trees and grasses rarely are found growing together—the major exception being the oak savannas of the eastern fringes of the tall grass prairies. However, on golf courses, trees and other shade sources often occur together. Tall trees obviously intercept light first, leaving grasses only speckled flecks and filtered light to live on.

Conifer (e.g., pines) and shade-intolerant trees tend to have more open growth habits, allowing more sunlight to penetrate through. In some instances, conifer trees, such as pines, planted far enough apart will allow enough light through to support a somewhat thin stand of grass. Shade-tolerant trees, such as oaks, sycamores, and maples, however, have denser canopies of foliage, allowing little sunlight to penetrate through. Deciduous trees also tend to selectively filter out the photosynthetically active wavelengths (blue-violet and orange-red wavelengths) necessary for grass to grow. This further adds to the problem of trying to grow grass underneath shade-tolerant deciduous trees.

As mentioned, a minimum of six to eight hours of full sunlight is needed to reach the grass through shade sources year-round. In winter, when days are shortest and the sun is lowest on the horizon, excessive shade from trees 30 to 50 feet away from the greens often occurs. This is especially true for trees on the south to southeastern direction of the greens. As these trees mature and grow larger, golf courses must maintain an ongoing aggressive selective limb pruning and possible tree removal program.

In addition to reducing light, shaded areas generally have (1) increased competition to the turf for nutrients and water by trees and shrubs; (2) increased humidity; (3) reduced or restricted air movement; (4) longer periods of dew and frost occurring during the morning before "burning-off"; and (5) lower temperatures.

Greens experiencing other stresses, such as being push-up construction type, diseases, excessive soil compaction, poor drainage, and salinity stress, are especially sunlight-deficient sensitive. The results are a gradual thinning of the grass, increased occurrence of algae, increased diseases, poor surface drainage, and slow recovery time from surface damage. Optimum growth of C_3 plants also appears related to having good morning sunlight. By afternoon, during summer in many places, cloud and haze build up to naturally reduce the quality and quantity of sunlight reaching the earth's surface. Therefore, reducing morning shade sources, thereby allowing the earliest sunlight, appears best for most grasses. Early sunlight also reduces the time needed for dew evaporation and frost melting. The opposite is true for C_4 plants where afternoon sun is most important since sunlight intensity is greatest then.

Although C_3 plants, such as bentgrass, theoretically require less sunlight to grow than C_4 plants such as bermudagrass, the best bentgrass greens occur when grown in wide-open, shade-free areas. Other factors, such as reduced air movement, thus higher humidities, and longer drying periods created by shade sources, often promote other life-threatening conditions, such as diseases, on bentgrass.

RESPIRATION

Respiration is essentially the reversal of photosynthesis where the sugars and starches (carbohydrates or food) synthesized during photosynthesis are utilized to provide energy and metabolites for plant growth and maintenance. All cells in plants and animals must respire to live. Plant respiration, an oxidation process, uses oxygen as a final electron acceptor through the processes of **Glycolysis** (an anaerobic process located in the cytosol) and the **Citric Acid cycle** (also called the **Krebs cycle** or **electron transport chain**), which is an aerobic or oxygen-requiring process located in the mitochondria where CO_2 and water are the final byproducts, as well as energy in the form of ATP (Figure 2–11). Oxygen released from photosynthesis can be used directly in respiration while CO_2 released from respiration can be used in photosynthesis.

Carbohydrates, such as glucose, are relatively stable under cellular conditions, and will not break down at any appreciable rate. However, in the process of Glycolysis, carbohydrates are activated, can undergo energy-releasing reactions, and are eventually converted to pyruvate. The net gain for each glucose molecule consumed in Glycolysis is 2 ATP, 2 NADH molecules, and two molecules of pyruvate.

Glycolysis is essentially an inefficient process if considered as a free-standing oxidative pathway. Its end product, pyruvate, contains only slightly less energy than the starting carbohydrate material. Under aerobic conditions, the pyruvate from Glycolysis is channeled to the mitochondria where it is oxidized to form the NADH, $FADH_2$, ATP, and carbon intermediates which are used in other metabolic reactions such as the synthesis of amino acids necessary for protein synthesis. Such a process is referred to as the Citric Acid cycle, the **Tricarboxylic Acid cycle (TCA cycle),** or the Krebs cycle (named after Hans Krebs, the discoverer). Pyruvate is converted into acetyl-CoA, which is combined with a four-carbon compound (OAA) to form citric acid or citrate (hence, the other designated name). By the end of two cycle turns, acetyl-CoA is completely oxidized into CO_2 and H_2O, producing NADH and $FADH_2$. The high-energy compounds from the Krebs cycle (NADH and $FADH_2$) are converted to ATP through a series of O_2-dependent electron transfers. This mitochondrial process is the ATP-producing electron transport chain. Glucose oxidation via Glycolysis and the Krebs cycle in combination with mitochondrial activities yields a net sum of 36 molecules of ATP compared to only two through Glycolysis alone.

FIGURE 2–11 Simplified illustration of plant respiration which involves three major processes in the mitochondria: Glycolysis, Krebs (or Citric Acid or TCA) cycle, and the electron transport chain. The production of important plant compounds and metabolites from the products of the three major processes of respiration (carbohydrate metabolism) are also shown. The ultimate end result is a release of stored energy from glucose, starch (fatty acids), and other carbohydrates for plant use in the form of ATP and the formation of water (H_2O).

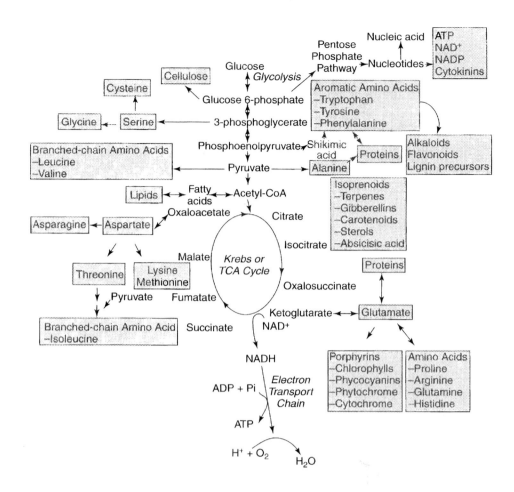

In light, photosynthesis and respiration occur simultaneously. However, the photosynthetic rate usually occurs more rapidly, resulting in an accumulation of carbohydrates and a net positive release of O_2 by the plant. In darkness, plants release CO_2 from respiratory oxidation reactions.

ENVIRONMENTAL STRESSES

Temperature Stress

Turfgrasses exhibit optimum growth within a certain range of temperatures (Table 2–2). Cool-season turfgrasses exhibit optimum growth when ambient temperatures range between 50 and 75°F (10 and 24°C), whereas warm-season turfgrasses exhibit optimum growth between 75 and 100°F (24 and 38°C). Temperature stress can occur to both cool- and warm-season turfgrasses. Extremely warm or hot temperatures during spring and/or summer can cause stress to cool-season turfgrasses, while cold temperatures during winter and/or spring months can cause stress to warm-season turfgrasses. It is often difficult to identify any one single factor which predisposes turfgrasses to temperature stress. More commonly, it is a combination of parameters influencing their susceptibility. Injury from temperature stress often is a reflection of the accumulation of various stresses over an entire growing season which ultimately lead to less-hardy turfgrass plants.

Low Temperature Stress on Warm-Season Turfgrasses

Winter turfgrass injury due to low temperature stress on warm-season turfgrasses is commonly referred to as "winter kill." The term "winter kill," in the simplest of terms, refers to the loss of turfgrass during the winter or early spring season (Figure 2–12). The vivid memories of periodic winters resulting in severe losses of warm-season turfgrasses in the southern areas of the United States should keep superintendents concerned about management practices to minimize future losses and the steps in diagnosing and correcting turfgrass damage.

TABLE 2–2 *Air and soil temperatures (°F) affecting turfgrass growth and development.*

| Turfgrass response | Cool-season (C₃) turfgrasses | | Warm-season (C₄) turfgrasses | |
	Air temp., °F (°C)	Soil temp., °F (°C)*	Air temp., °F (°C)	Soil temp. °F (°C)*
Heat kill	131 (55)	-	>140 (>60)	-
Maximum for shoot growth	90 (32)	-	120 (49)	-
Maximum for root growth	-	70 to 75 (21 to 24)	-	-
Suggested for planting	75 to 80 (24 to 27)	60 to 70 (15.6 to 21)	80 to 90 (27 to 32)	70 to 80 (21 to 27)
Optimum for shoot growth	59 to 75 (15 to 24)	-	85 to 100 (29 to 38)	-
Optimum for root growth	-	50 to 65 (10 to 18)	-	75 to 80 (24 to 27)
Minimum for shoot growth	40 (4.4)	-	55 (13)	-
Minimum for root growth	-	33 (0.6)	-	35 to 50 (1.7 to 10)
Possible low-temperature kill	-	20 (-6.7)	-	25 (-4)
Possible chilling injury	-	-	50 (10)	-
Trigger spring root decline	-	-	-	64 (18)
50% Stand Kill:				
Alkaligrass	-	-6 to -17 (-21 to -27)	-	-
Perennial ryegrass	-	5 to 23 (-15 to -5)	-	-
Fine fescue	-	-6 to -11 (-21 to -24)	-	-
Kentucky bluegrass	-	-6 to -22 (-21 to -30)	-	-
Bentgrass	-	-31 (-35)	-	-
Bermudagrass	-	-	-	18 to 23 (-8 to -5)
Centipedegrass	-	-	-	19 to 21 (-7.2 to -6)
Zoysiagrass	-	-	-	12 (-11)

*Soil temperatures at a four (4) inch (10 cm) depth.

The growth of warm-season turfgrasses slows significantly when the average daytime temperatures decrease to below 60°F (15.5°C) and leaf discoloration (onset of dormancy) begins when temperatures drop below 50°F (10°C). However, warm-season turfgrasses can continue to slowly grow with nighttime temperatures as low as 34°F (1.1°C) as long as daytime temperatures increase to near 70°F (21°C). Permanent turfgrass injury to warm-season turfgrasses often occurs if ambient temperatures drop rapidly to below 23°F (−5°C) or drop gradually to below 10°F (−12.2°C).

Each spring, golf course superintendents patiently wait to see how well their warm-season turfgrasses survived the winter. Then, sometimes what appears to be healthy turfgrass in early spring ends up declining significantly. This is largely due to low-temperature injury occurring after the warm-season turfgrasses begin to grow in spring. Therefore, winter injury to warm-season turfgrasses may not be related to winter at all, but to the early spring season. Evidence of this occurred during the spring of 1994 and 1996, when significant amounts of warm-season turfgrasses were lost across the southern parts of the United States during the spring transition period due to unexpected low temperatures.

During the spring transition period, warm-season turfgrasses are very vulnerable to "**low temperature injury,**" due to the biological and physiological growth conditions of turfgrasses during this time. Lateral buds at the nodes of turfgrass stolons and rhizomes begin breaking dormancy, and food reserves are converted to usable energy sources for the production and growth of new leaves and roots. The ability of turfgrasses to withstand low temperatures, along with competing with winter grasses and weeds, and being able to tolerate herbicide applications is greatly reduced during the spring transition. Consequently, the major contributing factor to low-temperature injury is the one golf course superintendents have little control over; however, several turfgrass management practices can help minimize this susceptibility of warm-season turfgrasses.

FIGURE 2–12 "Winter kill" or low-temperature stress on a bermudagrass fairway. Proper mowing height, fall fertilization, drainage, and crown desiccation prevention help prevent this.

One should develop a greater understanding of turfgrass biology and growth, types of low-temperature damage, and some of the conditions promoting low-temperature injury. Early diagnosis of low-temperature injury is essential to alleviating turfgrass damage.

Turf managers begin to prepare for winter hardiness the previous growing season by promoting maximum energy production from photosynthesis. Stored energy from photosynthesis is needed for the respiration of plants when they are dormant. If this energy storage is insufficient, plants become more susceptible to stresses and pests.

Warm-season turfgrasses begin their growth in the spring (green-up) when ambient temperatures exceed 60°F (15.6°C). At this time, lateral buds at the nodes of rhizomes and stolons begin to break dormancy, the stored carbohydrate or food reserves are converted to soluble sugars, and the growth or greening process begins. Simultaneously, there is a rapid die-back of old roots just prior to the production of new roots. This phase of turfgrass growth is a very susceptible stage to low-temperature stress or injury. Also, areas planted (seeded, sprigged, or sodded) late the previous year are typically more susceptible to low temperatures since the growing time for adequate establishment and root development is insufficient.

Low temperature or cold weather damage to plants is a collective term used to describe any form of injury related to low temperatures with several forms of injury. It is important to distinguish between these forms of low-temperature injury and have an understanding of the conditions promoting the specific types of injury. In general, the major types of low-temperature injury are caused by the following:

1. Hydration
2. Direct low temperature exposure
3. Desiccation
4. Traffic effects
5. Ice cover
6. Frost heaving
7. Diseases

Crown Hydration

One of the most common types of low-temperature injury is **crown hydration,** where turfgrass plants remain in or under constant moisture following a thaw. Consequently, these plants absorb high levels of water. If temperatures then decrease below freezing, ice crystals form within the plant cell walls (or intracellularly), rupturing them and, thereby, killing tissues (Figure 2–13). Ice crystals can also form "extracellularly," or in intercellular spaces between protoplasts and the cell wall. As ice crystals form, the vapor pressure becomes lower than in the protoplasts; thus, water

is drawn from within the cells. The protoplasts then shrink in size and the concentration of dissolved substances, such as salt ions and organic acids, increase and become toxic via osmotic damage. Plants surviving winter are more successfully able to tolerate ice formation between cells (extracellularly). Plants are able to tolerate extracellular ice formation by having increased cell membrane fluidity (flexibility) that can tolerate freezing. Plants increase this fluidity by increasing the ratio of short chain unsaturated fatty acids (those containing double bonds) to saturated ones (those containing single bonds). Having higher ratios of unsaturated fatty acids prevents membranes from gelling and freezing, allowing the protein components of membranes to alter their shape or change position during freezing without permanent damage.

Direct Low-Temperature Exposure

Another common type of low-temperature injury is **direct low-temperature exposure.** Basically, two types of injury are associated with direct low-temperature exposure: (1) lethal, and (2) nonlethal. When turfgrass plants are exposed directly to a rapid decrease in temperature below 23°F (5°C), the injury can be lethal, resulting in significant stand loss. Turfgrass leaves initially appear water soaked, turn whitish-brown in color, and then turn dark brown. Low-temperature exposure causes plants to lose control of membrane function, resulting in solute leakage and, eventually, a water-soaked appearance. Damaged turfgrass tends to mat over the soil surface and emit a distinct putrid (rotten) odor. Normal fall turf dormancy begins similarly except direct exposure occurs when temperatures only fall to approximately 50°F (10°C) during periods of high light intensity. This type of injury, referred to as **"chilling" injury,** only results in the normal discoloration (browning) of turfgrass leaves without lethal injury to the plants.

Insufficiently hardened turfgrass plants have lush growth (high moisture content) and are more susceptible to direct low-temperature injury. Turfgrass plants become "hardened" by being exposed to gradual decreases in temperature and frosts prior to a drastic, sudden drop in temperature or a hard freeze. This hardening process involves an environmentally induced 10 to 25 percent reduction in plant tissue water content and an accumulation of carbohydrate reserves. Three to five light frosts prior to a sudden, hard freeze help increase carbohydrate reserves, membrane structure, and protein constitutes in turfgrass plants. This enables crown tissue to withstand low temperatures without severe protoplasmic membrane disruption. Turfgrasses not exposed to these preconditioning frosts have succulent crown tissues which are highly susceptible to freeze damage.

Maximum low-temperature tolerance for warm-season turfgrasses is reached in November to January. Plant damage occurs most often in late winter or early spring, just prior to or during spring greening (green-up). This is associated with widely fluctuating temperatures during this time in which plants lose their earlier cold hardening effects. Wide temperature swings also may interrupt spring greening as warm temperatures favor turfgrass growth and occasional freezes kill the new leaves. Thus, new leaves must be reproduced, delaying the complete greening process in spring while placing a greater demand on carbohydrate reserves in the roots, rhizomes, and stolons. This repeated "die-back" and regeneration of new leaves depletes energy reserves, reduces rooting, and makes the plant more susceptible to direct low-temperature injury.

An initial low mowing height (scalping height) in spring after the last expected frost date will help remove the brown and/or dead overlying turfgrass plant material damaged from low temperatures. By removing this turfgrass material, sunlight can reach the soil surface more effectively and warm the soil, thereby producing quicker green-up of the turfgrass.

Desiccation

Another very common form of low-temperature turfgrass injury is **desiccation,** caused by high winds in combination with low relative humidity. This desiccation or "drying out" occurs on turfgrass plants that are unprotected from wind and have limited soil moisture due to either drought conditions or low temperatures (frozen soil moisture) (Figure 2–14). When temperatures rise above 32°F (0°C), turfgrass leaves lose water to the atmosphere due to pressure gradient. Consequently, turfgrass crown, nodes, and roots dry out, causing desiccation of these plant tissues and important plant proteins. Turfgrass injury from desiccation can result in significant losses of turfgrass. It is important to maintain adequate soil moisture during these conditions, especially in spring when turfgrass roots are developing, to prevent desiccation from occurring. If the area is not continuously covered by snow or ice, artificial covers are often placed to help protect the turf from desiccation.

Traffic

Traffic can play a significant role in low-temperature turfgrass injury, caused by vehicular and/or foot traffic that occurs on frozen or slush-covered turfgrass (Figure 2–15). The most common type of low-temperature injury due to traffic is from frost damage where traffic causes mechanical injury that ruptures plant cells in the early morning before frost melts. Frozen turfgrass crowns are easily damaged from traffic. Traffic should be minimized or diverted from frozen turfgrass until the soil and turfgrass plants have completely thawed. Lightly syringing frozen turfgrass areas prior to allowing traffic will aid in reducing traffic injury. Highly trafficked areas are also prone to high soil compaction. Generally, compacted soils reduce turfgrass rooting and overall plant health, resulting in weak turf that is more susceptible to low-temperature injury. Such areas should be heavily cultivated during summer months to improve soil physical properties.

FIGURE 2–14
Bermudagrass winter kill on a hill exposed to windy conditions and excessive desiccation.

FIGURE 2–15 Turfgrass winter kill from vehicular traffic when plant crowns were frozen.

FIGURE 2–16 Extended coverage of a golf green by ice eventually leads to turf damage from lack of soil oxygen and toxic gas buildup.

Ice Cover

Low-temperature injury from **ice cover** (Figure 2–16) results from turfgrass plants being covered by ice for extended periods of time (greater than 50 days). Injury occurs from oxygen suffocation and toxic gas buildup. *Poa annua* greens, for example, can withstand approximately 50 to 60 days under ice while creeping bentgrass and Kentucky bluegrass may survive 150 days of coverage.

A key to alleviating turf damage from extended ice cover is physically disrupting or breaking the ice. This allows toxic gases to escape. A darkening agent such as compost, charcoal, or natural organic fertilizer may be used to absorb heat and create pores in the ice to allow for gas exchange. The melted ice must drain away or the turf remains susceptible to refreezing during the next cold snap.

Frost Heaving

Another uncommon type of low-temperature turfgrass injury is **frost heaving,** caused by the freezing and thawing cycles on wet soils where the soil surface moves due to ice formation. Heaving pushes turfgrass crowns and roots out of the soil, where they are exposed. Frost heaving mainly occurs on newly germinated seedlings.

Diseases

The interaction of diseases and low temperatures can combine to cause more winter kill than either parameter alone. Presumably, the disease organism somehow predisposes the grass to winter kill by reducing internal moisture supplies, altering cell wall components, elevating plant nitrogen levels, or producing or disrupting normal plant products, such as growth hormone production, which influence low-temperature tolerance.

An example of a disease/low-temperature interaction is spring dead spot of bermudagrass (Figure 2–17). Several organisms are associated with this disease including various closely related species of *Gaeumannomyces*, *Leptosphaeria*, and *Ophiosphaerella*. The disease is characterized by roughly circular dead spots formed during spring green-up of the bermudagrass or zoysiagrass. Roots and stolons of affected turf are severely rotted. Affected spots often remain greener in late fall going into winter as if extra nitrogen had been applied to them. It is believed the disease predisposes the grass to low-temperature kill as spring dead spot is not normally found where extreme freezes do not occur. This, therefore, suggests low temperatures as well as the disease organisms are both necessary for symptom development.

Parameters Influencing Turfgrass Susceptibility to Low-Temperature Stress

There are several parameters influencing the susceptibility of warm-season turfgrasses to low-temperature stress; however, only a few are controllable by turfgrass managers. Temperature, freeze and thaw frequency, and freeze and thaw rate are factors outside a turfgrass manager's control. Conversely, several parameters within the control of turfgrass managers include (1) degree of shading, (2) drainage, (3) fertility, (4) irrigation, (5) mowing, (6) pest control, (7) soil cultivation, (8) thatch level, (9) traffic, and (10) turfgrass selection.

Shade

Exposure of turfgrass plants to sunlight is critical for several reasons, such as food production (photosynthesis) and hardening. Prolonged shade reduces carbohydrate levels in turfgrass plants, produces weaker plants, and suppresses soil temperatures (Figure 2–18). Shaded areas also remain colder for prolonged periods due to minimal sunlight exposure. In addition, competition from tree roots for nutrients and water also weakens turfgrass plants. Bright sunlight exposure

FIGURE 2–17 Spring dead spot of bermudagrass is believed to occur from a disease organism predisposing the turf to low-temperature damage.

FIGURE 2–18 Shade weakens bermudagrass, often increasing its susceptibility to low-temperature kill.

also signals plants to harden off during fall. Turfgrass plants are 'hardened' by being exposed to light frosts prior to a heavy freeze. Northern or northeastern facing slopes receive less (or little) direct sunlight in the winter months and are more susceptible to low-temperature stress. Interestingly, due to tree root respiration that increases soil temperatures, shade can moderate light frost or freezes, especially on cool-season turfgrasses.

One method to determine and document the degree of shading on each golf hole is using time-lapsed photography. This can be performed by setting up a camera on a tripod either at the teeing area or the putting green area and taking time-lapsed photographs at one-hour intervals for the entire day to document a representative degree of shading for each hole. These photographs can be invaluable if and when a severe loss of turfgrass stand occurs due to low-temperature stress and/or data is needed to selectively remove some trees.

Drainage

Poor surface and/or subsurface drainage can result in direct low-temperature damage or injury to the crowns of turfgrass plants. The level of water or moisture content within turfgrass crowns is positively correlated to the degree of low-temperature injury. The higher the moisture content of turfgrass crowns, the higher the susceptibility of low-temperature damage. Turfgrass plants growing in areas with poor drainage (surface or subsurface), high compaction, or excessive irrigation are at a greater risk of low-temperature injury.

Fertility

Research indicates excessive late-season nitrogen fertilization can decrease the low-temperature tolerance of some turfgrasses. Late fall nitrogen fertilization promotes succulent or "lush" turfgrass growth and reduced root carbohydrate formation by forcing shoot growth over root or rhizome growth. Turfgrass susceptibility to low-temperature stress can be reduced by applying a late summer application of a 4-1-2 or 3-1-2 ratio of N-P-K fertilizer. Adequate levels of potassium (K) have been shown to improve low-temperature stress tolerance. Potassium plays a regulatory role in plant water relations, which is important in low-temperature tolerance. Soil test results should indicate medium-to-high levels of potassium while leaf tissue analysis should be at least 1.5 percent potassium. However, excessive levels of potassium have not been shown to increase winter hardiness, and the high salt content from these may cause crown dessication.

Irrigation

Water is the primary requirement for turfgrass growth and survival. Irrigation should be utilized to "condition" the turfgrass. Several methods exist on scheduling irrigation; however, irrigation should be managed according to the exact amount of water needed at any given time or any given condition. Just as excessive moisture may increase low-temperature damage or injury, the lack of moisture can be equally damaging. A certain amount of water or moisture is needed for crown tissues to survive low-temperature stress. If a moisture deficiency occurs, crown tissues become desiccated; thus, they are severely weakened and more susceptible to low-temperature stress and injury. Maintaining soil moisture at or slightly below field capacity and preventing standing water helps keep crown tissue properly hydrated.

Mowing

Mowing is the most basic, yet most important, cultural turf management practice. Improper mowing decreases root and rhizome growth and depletes food reserves needed for the regeneration of shoot growth. If turfgrass plants are mowed too low in late summer, rooting will be discouraged and the accumulation of carbohydrates reduced, which can contribute to a greater susceptibility to low-temperature stress. The one-third (1/3) rule of mowing height should be utilized to schedule mowing frequency. If mowing height is increased in late summer or early fall, the leaf area of the turfgrass is increased; therefore, photosynthesis and carbohydrate production are increased. In addition, by increasing the mowing height, turfgrass crowns and growing points are better insulated from low-temperature exposure.

Pests

Pests damaging to turfgrass roots, such as mole crickets, nematodes, spring dead spot, root rot diseases (*Pythium* species), patch diseases (*Rhizoctonia, Gauemannomyces,* and *Leptosphaeria* species), and white grubs may decrease the tolerance of turfgrasses to low-temperature stress. In addition, improper application timing of certain pesticides which affect root growth (certain pre-emergence herbicides) may contribute to low-temperature stress damage or injury.

Soil Cultivation

Soil cultivation is accomplished by several means, such as aerification, spiking, and vertical mowing. These operations help relieve soil compaction, improve surface drainage, allow for deeper and faster root and water penetration, and reduce thatch accumulation (Figure 2–19). Applying topdressing after soil cultivation operations also improves soil structure.

Thatch Level

Thatch is the accumulation of organic material (turfgrass leaves, stems, stolons, clippings, etc.) within the top layer of the turfgrass biosphere. As thatch accumulates, the crowns, rhizomes, and stolons of the turfgrass tend to grow and develop within this thatch layer. These growing points then become elevated above the more insulating soil zone, and therefore are more exposed. Frequent soil cultivation and topdressing are the most effective means of controlling and/or reducing thatch levels.

Traffic

Traffic (either vehicular or foot) can be very damaging to frozen turfgrass crowns, leading to the eventual death of plants. In addition, traffic leads to soil compaction that reduces soil oxygen levels (porosity) and water infiltration and percolation rates. Compacted soils may not drain excessive water; as a result, they often remain wet and saturated, thereby increasing the risk of low-temperature stress and injury. Most often these problems are observed on teeing areas, approach areas to tees and putting greens, and in golf cart traffic areas onto and in the fairways. Reducing, diverting, or withholding traffic can aid in relieving soil compaction and decreasing the chances of low-temperature stress and injury.

FIGURE 2-19 Turfgrass low-temperature damage from soil compaction on an approach to a green.

TABLE 2-3 *Relative rankings of low-temperature tolerance of turfgrasses (cultivars within a species can vary).*

Low-temperature tolerance	Warm-season species	Cool-season species
Most tolerant of low temperatures	Zoysiagrass	Roughstalk bluegrass
	Buffalograss	Creeping bentgrass
	Common bermudagrass	Kentucky bluegrass
	Hybrid bermudagrass	Canada bluegrass
	Centipedegrass	Colonial bentgrass
	Bahiagrass	Annual bluegrass
	Carpetgrass	Fine fescues
	St. Augustinegrass	Tall fescue
	Seashore paspalum	Perennial ryegrass
Least tolerant of low temperatures		Annual ryegrass

Turfgrass Selection

Turfgrass species and varieties or cultivars within a particular species have varying degrees of low-temperature tolerance (Tables 2–3 and 2–4). Generally, turfgrass cultivars possessing greater low-temperature tolerance tend to exhibit a deeper growing, more dense rhizome network. Deeper growing roots and rhizomes are more insulated by being deeper in the soil profile; therefore, they are less exposed to low-temperature damage or injury. Extensive research and turfgrass breeding efforts are ongoing for improved low-temperature tolerance (Figure 2–20).

Turf Covers

Turf covers may help protect turfgrass crowns from direct low winter temperatures and desiccation. Snow is probably the best insulator and should remain as long as possible. Artificial covers which use an air layer to insulate the turf from extreme moisture and temperatures are next best. However, covers should not be used to prematurely green-up plants if temperatures are still likely to suddenly drop.

TABLE 2–4 *Relative rankings of low-temperature tolerance of selective warm-season turfgrass cultivars.*

Relative tolerance	Bahiagrass	Bermudagrass	Centipedegrass	St. Augustinegrass	Zoysiagrass
Best Cold Tolerance ↑					Z. japonica
		Quickstand			
		Vamont			
		Midiron			
		Midlawn			
		Midway			Z. japonica X
		Patriot			Z. tenuifolia
		Yukon			
		Riviera			
		Tifway			Z. matrella
		Tifsport			
		Tiflawn	Tenn Turf		
			Oaklawn	Raleigh	
	Wilmington	Common	AU Centennial	Palmetto	
	Pensacola	Tifeagle	Common		
	Argentine	Tifgreen		Bitterblue	
	Common	Tifdwarf		Delmar, Jade	Z. tenuifolia
		Ormond			
Least Cold Tolerance ↓		Pee Dee		Floratam	
				Common	

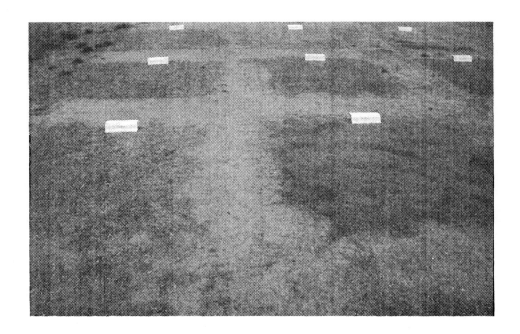

FIGURE 2–20 Good low-temperature tolerance by Midlawn bermudagrass (right) compared to other less-tolerant cultivars.

Diagnosing Low-Temperature Injury

Each year, prior to normal turfgrass green-up in spring, diagnostic measures should be taken by superintendents suspecting possible cold weather injury to determine the extent of the damage.

Superintendents should anticipate certain areas of turfgrass which may be more susceptible to low-temperature injury than other areas. Cultural factors contributing to low-temperature injury and increased susceptibility include poor drainage (soil compaction), excessive thatch, reduced light intensity (shade), north or northeastern facing slopes, excessive fall nitrogen fertilization, and low mowing heights. Any areas exhibiting one or more of these may be more susceptible to low-temperature injury.

If any of the aforementioned conditions are present, or have occurred, and low-temperature injury is suspected, utilize one of the following methods to determine the severity of the potential damage.

Method One

1. Remove the individual turfgrass plant crown near the soil surface.
2. Cut a slice through it with a sharp razor blade or knife.
3. Examine the crown under a 10X magnifying lens. If the crown tissue is firm and white in color with turgid cells, it should be healthy and has survived the low-temperature stress. Crowns exhibiting dark-colored or brownish color with a "mush" or soft appearance have been injured from low-temperature exposure.

Method Two

1. Use a cup cutter to remove samples from the suspected damaged areas.
2. Label the samples appropriately.
3. Remove soil from turfgrass samples by washing with water.
4. Remove the "old" dormant top growth from the turfgrass samples.
5. Expose the crown, rhizomes, and stolons by pulling the sample apart.
6. Place the turfgrass sample in a clear, plastic ziploc bag along with a wet paper towel.
7. Place the bags under a grow light or in a south facing window to create summer-like growing conditions.
8. Rewet the paper towel in the bag as needed to prevent the sample from drying out.
9. If healthy, greening of the surviving samples should occur within five to seven days.

Method Three

1. Collect turfgrass plugs using a cup cutter from suspected low-temperature damage areas.
2. Place or plant these plugs in a suitable container of native soil with drainage holes, properly labeling them.
3. Place the containers in a greenhouse, or in a room beneath a heat lamp or grow light, or as a last resort, in a southern facing window.
4. Keep the turfgrass plugs adequately watered.
5. Note that turfgrass should initiate growth and greening within 7 to 10 days.
6. Assess the amount of greening after plugs have been grown for two to three weeks. Suspected areas with less than 50 percent greening should be considered extensively damaged from low-temperature exposure and will probably require renovation. Lesser damaged areas may recover with proper management practices and extra attention.
7. Repeat the above sampling procedure on a 14- to 21-day interval through the periods of potential cold weather injury.

Turfgrass samples should be taken during January, February, and March to assay low-temperature damage. Samples exhibiting less than 50 percent greening represent areas with extensive damage and will probably require renovation.

If initial green-up in spring indicates only small areas of turfgrass damage (<6 inch, 15 cm, diameter), then surrounding plants should be aggressively encouraged to grow or fill in these damaged areas. Small damaged turfgrass areas on putting greens can be easily repaired by plugging them with healthy turfgrass taken with a cup cutter.

For those areas with widespread damage, renovation may be the best, and possibly the only, alternative. Options for renovation include seeding, plugging, sprigging (hand, broadcast, row planting), and sodding. For fairways and roughs, row planting or row sprigging may be the least expensive and best method of renovation. However, approximately six (6) weeks will be required before an adequate stand of bermudagrass will develop. In many instances, turfgrass damage from low-temperature stress is most severe on the shoots (leaves and stolons) of plants while the deeper rooted rhizomes are often healthy and unaffected by the low-temperature stress. When soil temperatures reach 75°F (24°C) for several consecutive days, these rhizomes will "sprout" new growth and, over time, will eventually fill in damaged areas. Therefore, it may sometimes be worthwhile to wait until soil temperatures warm sufficiently, allowing the growth and development of these deeper rhizomes to occur. In either case, it will be necessary to intensify the management practices and apply additional nitrogen, conduct some form of soil cultivation(s), and irrigate to encourage regrowth and/or establishment to occur.

Renovation Steps

If renovation is required, some steps to consider include the following:

- Communicate with the membership and/or golf customers that some turfgrass areas will be under renovation in spring to improve playing conditions due to turfgrass injury from low-temperature stress.
- Determine which variety of turfgrass to establish during the renovation process.
- Contract with your preferred turfgrass supplier for a quantity of grass to complete the renovation process, visit the turfgrass farm, and select and/or approve the turfgrass selected.
- Ascertain the equipment and financial requirements needed to complete the renovation process and budget accordingly.
- Strategically plan your fertilization and herbicide programs to promote optimum grow-in conditions for the renovated turfgrass. Fertility should be based on soil sample recommendations to provide a well-balanced growth response between turfgrass roots and leaves. DO NOT apply a root-inhibiting preemergence herbicide until the renovation process is completed. In addition, selective postemergence herbicides may be needed for weed control in the renovated turfgrass to promote optimum shoot growth without impeding root growth.

Best Management Practices Minimizing Low-Temperature Stress

There are few means of preventing low-temperature stress from causing damage or injury to turfgrasses; however, there are several management practices which help minimize the probabilities of damage or injury.

Documentation

Documentation or record keeping is probably one of the most overlooked aspects of turfgrass management and one of the most important. Historical documentation of parameters such as shade patterns, wind movement, and drainage problems can be directly correlated to the risks associated with low-temperature stress and turfgrass damage or injury. These parameters should be documented for each golf hole and a proactive management plan initiated to improve problem areas. Other maintenance practices should be documented as well, such as irrigation amounts, mowing heights, mowing patterns, rainfall amounts, minimum and maximum temperatures, frost occurrences, length of frost, fertilizer applications, and pesticide applications (Figure 2–21). All of these and other parameters should be documented in detail and retained for later use, if needed.

Frequent Soil Sampling

Soil samples should be taken on a frequent basis until a baseline for certain parameters is completely documented. Soil samples should be taken and utilized to determine chemical analysis (fertility levels), disease pathogens, nematodes, and physical property analysis (particle size, bulk density, porosity, water infiltration rates). All of the information garnered from these samples could be correlated to low-temperature stress tolerance or lack thereof.

There are several other management practices which decrease the risk of turfgrass damage or injury as a result of temperature stresses. Mowing heights should be increased in the fall on warm-season turfgrasses prior to the onset of cold weather and in the summer on cool-season turfgrasses to enhance rooting, rhizome growth, and carbohydrate accumulation. Thatch levels

FIGURE 2–21 Snow and ice cover everywhere except underneath trees due to elevated soil temperatures from root and microbial respiration which create heat.

should be monitored and managed with an aggressive soil cultivation and topdressing program. Turfgrass should be scouted on a daily basis for pests and/or other potential problems which may develop. Fertility programs should be based on soil test results for the specific turfgrass species and/or cultivars present. Herbicide usage should be limited in fall and summer to not add any additional stress to the turfgrasses prior to the onset of temperature stress periods.

Heat Stress on Cool-Season Turfgrasses

In many areas, high temperature/humidity stress is a concern for superintendents with cool-season turfgrasses present on the golf course. Generally, high-temperature stress is closely associated with water stress. A cool-season turfgrass may turn brown and enter a dormancy phase if rainfall or irrigation is not available during high-temperature stress periods of summer. This phase of dormancy occurs with cool-season turfgrasses as a means of survival during severe high temperature and/or water stress. These dormant turfgrass plants will initiate growth from basal crowns and lateral stems when the stress is relieved.

The growth of cool-season turfgrasses slows significantly when the average daytime temperatures increase above 90°F (32°C). This is especially acute if night temperatures remain in the high 60°Fs (15.5°Cs) or above and if the relative humidity of air remains near saturation. However, cool-season turfgrasses will continue to grow with temperatures above 90°F (32°C) as long as nighttime temperatures fall below approximately 65°F (18°C) and adequate but not saturated soil moisture is available. Low nighttime temperatures provide turfgrass with a recovery time to mobilize stored carbohydrate reserves for energy production. Permanent turfgrass injury to cool-season turfgrasses often occurs if ambient temperatures reach 130°F (54°C).

In general, there are three basic types of high-temperature stress to cool-season turfgrasses: (1) heat exposure, (2) scalding, and (3) desiccation. As mentioned, each of these stresses has an association with water stress.

Heat Exposure

Heat exposure can be lethal to cool-season turfgrasses when temperatures exceed the range for plant growth processes. As temperatures rise above optimum levels, plant photosynthesis decreases while respiration increases. Direct kill of the turfgrass can occur if the temperatures are well in excess of 100°F (38°C) and the exposure causes plant cells to be disrupted and cell protoplasm precipitates (or leaks). Heat exposure can cause indirect stress to cool-season turfgrass plants by slowing the growth of roots and shoots when soil temperatures exceed 75°F (24°C). Indirect stresses occur with decreased photosynthesis including the interruption of electron transport in photosystem II, reduction in RuBP carboxylase activity, decreased chlorophyll content, and leaf senescence from decreased cytokinin activity. This indirect stress may also lead to plant death if the stress is not relieved.

Photosynthesis produces carbohydrates that are consequently used in respiration to produce ATP for energy. When ambient temperatures rise above a specific level, C_3 plants cannot produce enough carbohydrates to fulfill the demand for respiration. This is especially important for low mowed turf which removes large amounts of leaf area used for photosynthesis while respiration continues. This temperature is referred to as the **temperature compensation point.** At this temperature, the amount of CO_2 fixed by the dark reactions of photosynthesis is equal to the amount of CO_2 released by mitochondrial respiration. Prolonged exposure of temperatures in excess of the temperature compensation point will result in continuous depletion of carbohydrate reserves and eventual weakening of the turf. For creeping bentgrass golf greens, this temperature is 86°F or 30°C. Reducing the soil temperature to 84°F (29°C) allows resumed bentgrass growth, with the optimum soil temperature being around 75°F (24°C). Even with an air temperature of 95°F (35°C), lowering the soil temperature to 90°F (32°C) improves bentgrass turf quality and shoot and root growth.

Scalding

Scalding occurs when turfgrasses are in standing pools of water and intense sunlight creates a rise in the water's temperature. Consequently, the plants are "scorched" or scalded from the water temperature.

Desiccation

Desiccation of turfgrass shoots can occur due to an imbalance in water relations between the plant and the atmosphere (Figure 2–22). Shoots can be desiccated even if soil moisture is adequate. This type of desiccation occurs when the rate of transpiration (loss of water to the atmosphere) of shoots exceeds the rate of water absorption from soil by roots. Warm, low humidity days are a typical scenario for turf desiccation. Although soil moisture is adequate, it cannot provide the water necessary for the transpiration demand due to low atmospheric humidity levels. Desiccation can also occur if soil moisture levels are inadequate to provide roots with enough moisture to sustain the transpiration rates.

Best Management Practices for Reducing Heat Stress of Cool-Season Turfgrasses

High-temperature stress to cool-season turfgrasses can be minimized by using cultural practices which promote maximum rooting. Root development is directly correlated to water absorption and uptake from the soil. If adequate soil moisture is available and plants can access

FIGURE 2–22 Damage to creeping bentgrass due to desiccation and heat stress.

this moisture, then the plant can maintain its ability to "cool" itself via transpiration. This is acutely important with cool-season turfgrasses associated with putting greens due to the low mowing heights. Root development is also associated with mowing height or shoot height. Turfgrasses mowed at a lower mowing height have a shorter or shallower root system. Therefore, it is most important to manage these closely mowed areas more intensely to promote maximum root growth and development. Five (5) basic management practices help plants survive severe high-temperature stress and/or water stress:

1. Irrigation
2. Mowing
3. Soil cultivation
4. Fertilization
5. Pest control

Irrigation

Irrigation is a very important management practice affecting turfgrass survival against heat and moisture stress (Figure 2–23). In spring, when root growth rates are rapid, cool-season turfgrasses should be irrigated sparingly to encourage plants to root deeper in "search" of moisture. If plants are overwatered in spring, they develop short root systems, creating a "lazy" root system that is not required to grow and develop in order to search for deeper moisture. However, during heat stress periods, it is important to maintain adequate soil moisture to prevent any loss of turfgrass roots and also provide the necessary moisture to allow transpiration cooling necessary for survival. Deep, infrequent watering practices should be used to minimize continuous saturated soil water conditions. In addition to causing a poor soil atmosphere with limited soil O_2, saturated soils have a high heat capacity, not allowing rootzone temperature cooling during nighttime hours compared to drier soils.

Mowing

Mowing height can make a significant difference in cool-season turfgrass survival during high-temperature stress, especially on cool-season turfgrass putting greens. A reduction in mowing height on a bentgrass putting green during high-temperature stress is often detrimental. The mowing heights of cool-season turfgrasses on putting greens should be increased during these stress periods to enhance root survival and transpiration rates.

FIGURE 2–23 Reducing heat stress on bentgrass by hand misting in front of fans.

Soil Cultivation

Soil cultivation or aerification is considered to be a key management practice to the survival of cool-season turfgrasses in high temperatures. Soil cultivation is critical to the management of poor drainage, soil compaction, soil oxygen and carbon dioxide levels, and turfgrass growth. It is important to aerify cool-season turfgrasses in the fall and early in spring during their optimum growth period to stimulate shoot and root growth as much as possible. Cool-season turfgrasses need as deep a root system as possible going into the summer when high-temperature stress is expected. In addition, adequate drainage during these high-temperature periods is important to minimize disease pressure.

Fertilization

Proper fertilization is also important to minimize high-temperature stress. During early summer, prior to the onset of high temperatures, reducing the amount of nitrogen fertilization and increasing the amount of potassium fertilization on cool-season turfgrasses is generally recommended. This will promote more root growth versus shoot growth and improve stress tolerance. Heavy summer nitrogen (N) fertility will allocate sugars and energy into shoot production, decreasing root carbohydrate reserves and growth. A fertilizer with an N-K ratio of 1:1 is often utilized prior to the onset of high temperatures. Slow release nitrogen sources should be used cautiously to avoid excess nitrogen release under high temperatures. On putting greens, liquid applications are used to control nitrogen availability to plants during this time.

Pest Control

Pest control is of paramount importance during high-temperature stress periods on turfgrasses. Disease pressures such as patch diseases, crown rot, and *Pythium* can all be detrimental during summer. Preventive fungicide applications should be utilized where possible to minimize disease potential. In addition, any pesticide which may negatively affect root development, such as some herbicides, should be avoided during these stress periods.

SALINITY

Saline water can cause stress and injury to plants by several means. Direct salt injury occurs with the accumulation of salts such as sodium, chloride, boron, and other ions in soil as well as ion accumulation in plants. Salts, however, reduce plant growth, mostly by their osmotic effect. The more salt in its rootzone, the harder plants must work to take up water. This direct osmotic stress causes water to move from the plant into the soil because of a salt concentration gradient. Salt stress is similar to drought stress in appearance (Plate 2–1), except the soil can still be moist. The initial response of turfgrass to salinity stress is reduced shoot growth. Leaf blades become narrower and stiff, and can become darker green, or even blue-green, in color as the plant cannot take up enough water, resulting in a lack of soil moisture (Plate 2–2). There also is a tendency for turf to wilt faster than normal as a result of osmotic stress. Root growth initially increases, but over time, root growth is reduced, presumably as a response to reduced shoot growth. Shoot and root growths are reduced at high salt levels through both direct and indirect salt injury. Leaf tipburn and a general thinning of turf occurs at higher salinity levels. Due to mowing, leaf tips containing high levels of sodium are removed in turf. However, on golf greens, such a small amount of leaf blade is removed during mowing that sodium accumulation may be more problematic. A common symptom of turf damaged by high salinity soils is spotty stands of grass (Plate 2–3). Young plants are more sensitive to salinity stress than mature ones. Salinity also reduces the number of seeds which germinate, delays the rate of seed germination, and establishes sprigs.

Plant nutrient deficiencies may also occur in saline soils due to the typically high levels of sodium and calcium which reduce uptake of other nutrients by competition. The most common example of this is the antagonistic effects of sodium on plant uptake of calcium, potassium, magnesium, and ammonium nitrate. As excess sodium displaces calcium in root cell walls and membranes, these cells start to leak out their contents, especially potassium.

Plant tolerance to salt stress varies greatly. Some plants avoid salt stress by either excluding salt absorption, extruding excess salts, sequestering (capturing) Na^+ and Cl^- in vacuoles of root cells, or diluting absorbed salts. Other plants tolerate salt stress by adjusting their metabolism to withstand direct or indirect injury. Others regulate their internal osmotic potential of tissue fluid to compensate for increases in substrate osmotic potentials, often using internal supplies of calcium to displace the sodium. In most cases the mechanism of salt tolerance in plants is a combination of several methods. As a compensatory adaptive mechanism to nutrients and water stress under saline conditions, plants often increase root biomass to enlarge their water and nutrient absorbing area. Highest root weights occur at intermediate salt levels but decline at high levels. Ornamental plants tend to be much more sodium, chlorine, and boron sensitive than turfgrasses.

Turfgrass Salt Tolerance

Turfgrass species have been classified according to salt tolerance (Table 2–5). Most turfgrass comparisons are based on the salt levels which cause a 50 percent reduction in top or root growth. Only a few species grow well under saline conditions. Zoysiagrass, seashore paspalum, bermudagrass, and St. Augustinegrass are the best warm-season turf species to grow if irrigation is limited to saline water; while alkaligrass, tall fescue, and perennial ryegrass are the best cool-season turfgrasses. Creeping bentgrass/*Poa annua* mixed green becomes difficult to maintain when ECw

TABLE 2–5 *Approximate salt tolerance of turfgrass species grown in solution (modified from Harivandi, et al., 1992; Kopec, 1996).*

Salt tolerance	Species (listed alphabetically)	ECw [or dS/m]	ppm
Excellent	Alkaligrass	>10	6,500
	Seashore paspalum		
Good	Bermudagrass	6–10	4,000–6,500
	Buffalograss		
	Kikuyugrass		
	St. Augustinegrass		
	Western wheatgrass		
	Zoysiagrass		
Fair	Annual ryegrass	3–6	2,000–4,000
	Bluegrama		
	Chewings fescue		
	Creeping bentgrass cv. Seaside, Mariner		
	Orchardgrass		
	Perennial ryegrass		
	Smooth brome		
	Tall fescue		
Poor	Bahiagrass	<3	<2,000
	Centipedegrass		
	Colonial bentgrass		
	Creeping bentgrass		
	Creeping red fescue		
	Kentucky bluegrass		
	Meadow fescue		
	Poa annua		
	Poa trivialis		
Very poor	Bentgrass/*Poa annua* golf greens	1.5 to 2.0	960–1,280

TABLE 2–6 *Salt tolerance of various bermudagrass and bentgrass cultivars.*

Salt tolerance	Bermudagrass	Bentgrass
Most ↑	Tifdwarf	Seaside creeping
	Tifgreen	Kingstown velvet
	Tifway	Streaker red top
	Tiflawn	Colonial
	Arizona common	Pennlinks creeping
↓	Ormond	Penncross creeping
Least		Penneagle creeping

nears 1.5 to 2.0 dS/m (soil ECe >3.0 dS/m) while bermudagrass greens show stress at a higher ECw of 4 to 15 (soil ECe 6 to 20 dS/m). Certain cultivars of creeping bentgrass, such as Seaside, Seaside II, and Mariner, can tolerate an ECw up to 6.0 dS/m but are limited by heat stress. Under these conditions, grasses require good draining soils and moist soil conditions to produce good quality turf; adequate leaching (whether it is from rainfall or excess saline irrigation); specific management techniques, such as the use of gypsum or acidified water; and skilled turf managers.

Salinity values and the species rankings listed in Table 2–5 are relative to each other, meaning these can often shift in real agronomic conditions. For example, as moisture stress and temperatures increase, and soil infiltration/percolation rates and atmospheric relative humidity decrease, salinity tolerance levels by all turfgrasses also decrease. This is compounded by surface compaction, reduced air movement, and high water pH and bicarbonate levels.

Cultivars within a species often show a wide range of salt tolerance (Table 2–6). Sometimes cultivar differences are greater than species differences. Of those reported, Tifdwarf and Tifgreen are the most salt-tolerant bermudagrass cultivars available while Seaside creeping is the most tolerant bentgrass cultivar.

GROWTH HORMONES

Unlike mammals, plants lack a nervous system and sensory organs that allow them, among other things, to respond to various environmental stimuli. Plants, however, substitute a nervous system with various growth hormones that are produced in one part of the plant, translocated to other parts, and in low concentrations can cause various growth responses. A plant hormone is defined as a chemical messenger involved in the regulation of plant metabolism, growth, and morphogenesis. Due to their low concentrations found in plants, discovery and understanding of most plant growth hormones has been delayed until the advent of highly sensitive scientific equipment. Growth-promoting hormones include auxins, gibberellins, and cytokinins. Growth-inhibiting hormones include ethylene and abscisic acid.

Growth Promoters

Auxins

The discovery of auxin can be traced to the observations of Darwin (around 1880) who was investigating the phototropic curvature of grass seedlings' coleoptiles. Went later (1926) found evidence which led to the physiological proof of auxin as a plant growth substance. It is produced in meristematic or other actively growing tissue, moves throughout the plant, and is capable, in minute concentrations, of affecting elongation in cells below this meristem or site of production. **Indole-3-acetic acid (IAA; Figure 2–24)** is the primary auxin found in plants. Other auxin-like compounds include **phenylacetic acid, naphthalene acetic acid (NAA),** and **2,4-dichlorophenoxy acetic acid (2,4-D).**

The primary influence of auxin is stimulation of cellular elongation (Table 2–7). **Phototropism** (light-induced bending) of stems is induced by a differential distribution of IAA within the shoot. Auxins also stimulate **cell division** and **cell differentiation** (e.g., into xylem and phloem tissue). Auxin also is known to influence **apical dominance** by inhibiting lateral bud

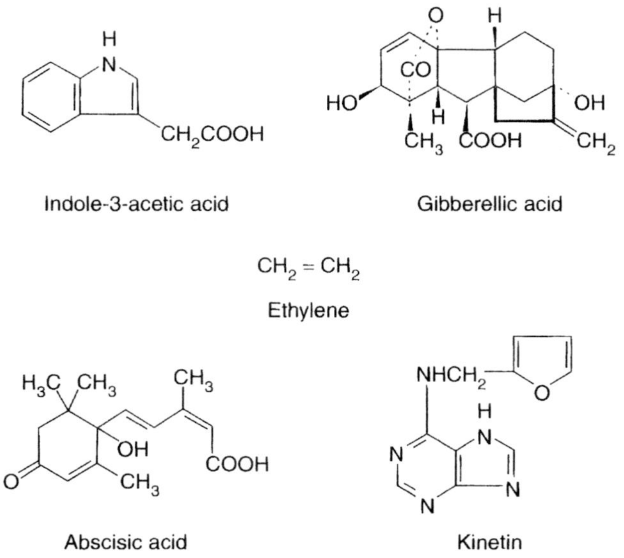

FIGURE 2–24 Chemical structures of the endogenous hormones found in higher plants; IAA or indole-3-acetic acid, gibberellic acid (GA₁), ethylene, abscisic acid, and kinetin. Kinetin is not a naturally occurring cytokinin, but is commonly used in plant growth and development work.

Indole-3-acetic acid

Gibberellic acid

Ethylene

Abscisic acid

Kinetin

TABLE 2–7 *Growth hormones influencing plant growth and development.*

Hormone	Examples	Site of production	Major growth influence
Growth promoters			
Auxin	indole-3-acetic acid (IAA), phenylacetic acid, naphthalene acetic acid (NAA), dichlorophenoxy acetic acid (2,4-D)	meristematic tissue	Stimulates cell elongation, cell division, and cell differentiation. Its presence promotes apical dominance, which inhibits lateral bud development and delays leaf senescence and fruit ripening.
Gibberellins	GA₁, GA₃, GA₄, GA₇, and many others	meristematic tissue in young leaves, developing roots and seeds	Promotes cell division and cellular elongation.
Cytokinins	kinetin and other derivatives of adenine.	root tips	Stimulates cytokinesis or cell division. Delays plant aging and leaf senescence by delaying chlorophyll and protein degradation. May help plants overcome external stresses.
Growth inhibitors			
Ethylene	ethylene gas (C₂H₄)	shoots	Promotes plant aging, and senescence. Inhibits root growth, lateral bud development, and cell elongation.
Abscisic acid	ABA	green tissue (chloroplasts)	Inhibits coleoptile growth and promotes senescence, and abscission. ABA levels increase when plants are exposed to stresses such as drought, flooding, starvation, injury, and salinity.

development and delaying leaf senescence and fruit ripening, but promoting flowering and fruit set. Low concentrations of auxin also promote root growth.

Excessive auxin levels can inhibit growth, depending on the tissue involved. For example, the amount of auxin needed to stimulate plant growth in a stem, making it bend toward light, will stop growth in a root, bending it away from light. Stolon shoot tip removal by mowing or slicing removes the auxin; thus, apical dominance is eliminated and additional stolon production is promoted from axillary buds. Excessive auxin levels may even kill the plant, as evident by the auxin-like herbicide, 2,4-D.

Gibberellins

Gibberellins were first discovered when rice plants were noticed to grow excessively tall when infected by the fungus, *Gibberella fujikuroi*, which produced certain gibberellins. Japanese scientists isolated the substance, and in 1954–1955 the structure of the biologically active gibberellin, GA_1 (Figure 2–24), was established from culture filtrates. Approximately 125 gibberellins have been identified and most plants contain complex mixtures of several gibberellins. The most important gibberellins in agriculture are GA_1 and GA_3 and, to a lesser degree, GA_4 and GA_7 (Table 2–7). Gibberellins basically stimulate internodal elongation in intact plants. They are synthesized in young leaves (as is auxin) and in developing roots and seeds via a branch of the terpenoid pathway. They promote both cell division and cellular elongation, and are also known to stimulate flowering by overcoming cold temperature requirements needed by certain plants to flower (referred to as **vernalization**). In addition, Gibberellins stimulate the need for long days of some plants; cause juvenile growth patterns in plants to mature; reverses dwarfism in certain plants; stimulates the release of certain hydrolytic enzymes in some seeds; and can cause **parenthogenesis,** which is seed production in some plants without pollination. RyzUp or ProGibb are commercial formulations of gibberellic acids used to aid bermudagrass color recovery after a mild cold stress period or light frost.

Several plant-growth regulators retard shoot growth through the interference of gibberellin biosynthesis. Cell division and seedhead formation are not greatly influenced, but cell elongation is retarded. The results from using these growth retardants are miniature plants. Examples of gibberellin-inhibiting growth retardants include trinexapac-ethyl, paclobutrazol, flurprimidol, and fenarimol.

Cytokinins

Cytokinins are compounds which stimulate **cytokinesis,** or cell division (Table 2–7). Most cytokinins are derivatives of **adenine** (a purine), one of the key bases found in nucleic acids. All naturally occurring cytokinins are derivatives of adenine. An important adenine-derived cytokinin is **kinetin** (Figure 2–24), which does not naturally occur but rather is formed when DNA is broken down. Zeatin is the naturally occurring cytokinin in plants.

Currently, it is believed the primary sites of cytokinin synthesis in plants are root tips. They are then translocated to shoots through the vascular system. They are also synthesized in tissues with high meristematic activity; (e.g., cambium, vegetative apices, and young leaves). Cytokinins are known to promote cell division and cell enlargement; delay plant aging and leaf senescence by delaying the rate of chlorophyll disappearance and protein degradation; replace the light requirements for certain processes such as seed germination, pigment synthesis, and chloroplast development; stimulate lateral shoot (branch) development in some plants; and inhibit branch formation in roots.

Growth Inhibitors

Ethylene

Ethylene is a gas discovered when oranges and bananas were shipped together and the bananas prematurely ripened. This was due to a gaseous substance, ethylene (Figure 2–24), emitted by the oranges. Around 1960, when it became possible to reliably measure small amounts of ethylene, it was demonstrated to have important physiological roles in plant growth and development. In addition to simulating ripening of fleshy fruits, ethylene is known to induce aging (senescence) in many plants; for example, leaf abscission and abscission of floral parts (Table 2–7).

Ethylene also is known to inhibit root growth, inhibit lateral bud development, increase membrane permeability, and cause epinastic (curvature downward) responses of leaves. Ethylene also tends to inhibit cell elongation, but enhances a cellular increase in width. The results are shorter but broader stems and petioles. Ethylene production by plants is high wherever auxin concentration is high. Thus, shoots produce ethylene, whereas roots produce little. Ethylene gas is produced when the sulfur-containing amino acid, methionine, is degraded and is very mobile in plants by diffusion. Ethephon is a commercial PGR which causes ethylene production in plants.

Abscisic Acid (ABA)

ABA was discovered around 1960 by two groups whose research was based on two different physiological functions: "abscisin," causing the abscission of cotton fruits; and "dormin," inducing the dormancy of buds in birch trees. In 1965 these substances were found to be the same compound and the term "abscisic acid" was adopted (Figure 2–24). ABA is present in all vascular plants and inhibits coleoptile growth and promotes senescence and abscission by blocking DNA and certain protein synthesis (Table 2–7).

An increase in endogenous plant ABA levels occurs when plants are exposed to a variety of stress conditions such as flooding, drought, salinity, injury, and starvation. This is especially acute when plants wilt from drought stress. ABA is believed to be a signaling messenger for stomatal closure in response to drought or water stress. The role ABA and ethylene play in turfgrass growth and development is still poorly understood.

Biostimulants

Biostimulants are materials which promote plant growth when applied in small quantities. Research indicates biostimulants may increase photosynthesis rates, reduce turfgrass senescence, enhance seed germination and root growth, help sod establish faster, and increase salt tolerance and drought resistance after application. They often contain cytokinin as their principal ingredient and tend to help plants withstand harsh environments through enhanced cytokinesis (Table 2–7). They also exhibit other growth-regulating actions as found from auxins, gibberellin, and abscisic acid. **Seaweed extract** (or seaweed kelp), most commonly from the sea kelp species *Ascophyllum nodosum*, is a common commercial cytokinin-containing growth material used in turf. A commercially available synthetically produced cytokinin is **benzyladenine** (or **BA**).

Products with cytokinin-like properties also are available such as the triazole systemic fungicides—propiconazole, triadimefon, and others. These fungicides inhibit **sterol biosynthesis,** cause an increase in ABA synthesis, and inhibit gibberellin synthesis. Sterols are part of cell membranes and help protect plants and promote growth. When sterol and gibberellin biosynthesis are inhibited, plant ABA levels rise which favor plant stomatal closure, thereby creating an increase in plant water content. Cytokinin levels also tend to decrease when drought stress begins and ABA level increases, resulting in closed stomata. Further evidence suggests these triazole fungicides translocate to shoot tips and cause growth reduction of the foliage but not the roots. Therefore, enhanced root development occurs with reduced shoot growth and increased plant water content. Additionally, research shows triazol-treated plants not only inhibit reduced transpiration, but increased yields are observed when plants are under moisture stress, senescence is delayed, and chlorophyll levels as well as carbohydrate levels are increased. These compounds also have protected plants from chilling temperatures, heat stress, and ozone exposure.

The levels of cytokinin in plants regulate, to an extent, the growth response. For example, large applications of cytokinin have been shown to inhibit root formation, but it is known that a small amount of cytokinin is necessary for the formation of rooting. Root growth, therefore, appears to require a certain cytokinin level and a favorable auxin-to-cytokinin ratio.

One of the greatest benefits turfgrass receives from biostimulant application is when the turf is being grown under a physiological stress. These stresses include cold (or chilling) temperatures, low soil nutrient levels (especially potassium and/or phosphorus), low mowing height stress, and periods of rapid growth where these and other resources become limiting. Other possible stresses that may be partially overcome by biostimulant applications include salinity and nematode exposure. Newly planted turfgrasses also may benefit from biostimulant use. Replicated field research of biostimulants on turfgrasses is limited; thus, caution should be used when trying such materials.

SECTION

II

BEST SOIL MANAGEMENT PRACTICES

CHAPTER 3

Soil Chemical Properties

INTRODUCTION

Soil, the covering of the earth, consists of mineral particles, organic matter, water, air, and organisms that support plant life. Soils are formed over long periods of time through the weathering of rock minerals (in the case of mineral soils) and by the deposition of vegetative matter (in the case of organic soils). Soils vary widely in properties and in their suitability for various types of land use. The type of soil that forms is dependent on the parent material (type of rock minerals or sediments), the climate (particularly rainfall and temperature), vegetation, landscape position or topography (consisting of elevation, slope, and aspect), and the time in which these factors have been acting.

An ideal soil for plant growth is well-aerated so as not to limit rooting nor the activity of soil organisms. Its pH is slightly acid to neutral to limit the availability of toxic elements and to promote the availability of essential nutrients. A productive soil also contains an ample supply of plant-available water. The properties of pH and nutrient availability are important components of soil fertility.

Every golf course superintendent should have an understanding and appreciation of soil chemical properties influencing their turf. These include soil organic matter, soil pH, soil salinity, and available soil nutrients. These properties not only directly influence the turfgrass stand but also indirectly influence other soil characteristics such as nutrient and pesticide leaching, disease activity, and availability of native and applied nutrients. The following discussion is an overview of important chemical reactions influencing soil nutrient levels and their interactions with respect to turf growth and management.

Horizons

Soil chemical and physical characteristics often change dramatically with soil depth. Distinct changes result in layers of soil being formed, which are referred to as **horizons;** the totality of these is called the **soil profile.** The properties of a soil are dependent both on characteristics of the surface and subsurface horizons.

The **A horizon** is the uppermost layer of soil, typically several inches to nearly a foot thick, and is characterized by an accumulation of organic matter. Organic matter gives this "**topsoil**" its brown to black color and high amount of biological activity (fungi, bacteria, earthworms, insects, etc.). Most of a turfgrass root system resides in the A horizon. Although mostly desirable, organic matter levels are not always a reliable indicator of soil fertility; thus, not all dark, high organic matter A horizons have high soil fertility.

Horizons below the A level are referred to as **subsoil,** and contain declining biological activity with increasing depth into the profile. The **B horizon** is defined as the zone of clay accumulation and it occurs below the A horizon. The **C horizon** is found below the B horizon. Although chemically weathered from parent material, little biological activity occurs in the C horizon. Plant rooting can occur in the B and C horizons dependent on the suitability of their chemical and physical properties and their distance from the soil surface. In some soils, the A horizon is immediately underlain by the **E horizon,** a highly weathered horizon with little accumulation of organic matter in comparison to the A horizon and depleted in clay in comparison to the B horizon which lies below it. The E horizon is absent in some soils, but when present, it can range in thickness from only a few inches to several feet. Although rooting may occur in the E horizon, it is generally not as suitable a rooting media as the A horizon.

CATION EXCHANGE

Many soil nutrients occur naturally as complex, insoluble compounds that may not be readily available for plant use. Over time, as weathering occurs, these elements slowly enter the soil solution and become plant-available. Organic matter also may be degraded by the soil microbial population, releasing its nutrient constituents for possible plant uptake.

Organic matter is the resulting residue from the decay of plant material, mainly by bacteria and fungi. Organic matter material mostly has a positive effect on soil quality.

The two properties accounting for soil reactivity are surface area and surface charge. Surface area and charge are largely a direct result of particle size and shape and are mostly influenced by soil organic matter content and clay-sized particles.

As soils are formed during the weathering processes, some minerals and organic matter are broken down to extremely small particles called **colloids.** Colloids have tremendous amounts of surface area; therefore, they have more impact on soil properties than its weight. As a result, colloids are primarily responsible for the chemical reactivity of soils. Colloids from clay and organic matter sources typically have a net negative ($-$) charge, developed during the formation process. These, therefore, can attract and hold (a process called **ionic bonding**) positively ($+$) charged particles, called **cations** (including many nutrients), similar to opposite poles of a magnet attracting each other.

One of the most important parameters affecting cationic nutrient supply to the turfgrass root is **cation exchange capacity (CEC).** Cation exchange capacity refers to the quantity of negative charges in soil existing on the surfaces of clay and organic matter. The negative charges attract cations; hence, the name "cation exchange capacity." Many essential plant nutrients exist in the soil as cations and are accumulated by the grass plant in this form. Potassium (K^+), calcium (Ca^{+2}), and magnesium (Mg^{+2}) can be found in relative abundance on the CEC. Iron (Fe^{+2}), zinc (Zn^{+2}), copper (Cu^{+2}), manganese (Mn^{+2}), and ammonium (NH_4^+) occur to a lesser extent. Sodium (Na^+), which may cause severe problems in soils irrigated with poor quality irrigation water, also occurs as a cation. Hydrogen (H^+) and aluminum (Al^{+3}) are the other predominant cations occupying the CEC in soils. These two cations are responsible for the detrimental effects on turfgrass health which occur in extremely acid soils. The number accompanying the superscript ($^+$) indicates how many positive charges the cation carries. The major ions influencing plants are listed in Table 3–1.

Cation exchange involves the reversible process where cations in solution are exchanged (or replaced) with another cation on the soil's negatively charged solid phase, such as clay minerals or organic matter. Exchangeable cations are not readily leached unless they are replaced (or exchanged). Ions more strongly attracted to the cation exchange sites can replace the existing ones. For example, calcium can be exchanged for potassium or hydrogen, or vice versa. Also, this exchange may occur when the soil solution concentration is altered and is not in equilibrium with cations on the exchange sites. Only a small percentage of the essential plant nutrient cations (K^+, Ca^{+2}, Mg^{+2}, and NH_4^+) will be "loose" in the soil water and thus available for plant uptake. Therefore, the CEC is important because it provides a reservoir of nutrients to replenish those removed from the soil water by plant uptake. Similarly, cations in soil water which are leached below the

TABLE 3–1 *The major ions influencing plant growth, shown as their most common states in soil solutions (modified from Bohn et al., 2001).*

Major exchangeable cations	Comments
Ca^{+2}, Mg^{+2}, Na^+, K^+, NH_4^+, Al^{+3}, H^+	Occur mostly as exchangeable cations in soils; readily manipulated by liming, acidification, or irrigation; H^+ concentrations determine active soil pH while Al^{+3} is a portion of reserve soil acidity; Na^+ ions can disrupt soil physical characteristics by causing deflocculation. Productive soils typically contain abundant exchangeable Ca^{+2}.
Major anions	
NO_3^-, SO_4^{-2}, Cl^-, HCO_3^-, CO_3^{-2}, SeO_4^{-2}, Br^-, I^-	These anions are repelled to weakly retained in soils. Normally, these are in much lower concentrations than the major cations. SO_4^{-2} and NO_3^- are important plant nutrients; SO_4^{-2}, Cl^-, and HCO_3^- salts accumulate in saline soils; CO_3^{-2} ions occur mostly when soil pH is >9.0.
Weakly soluble anions	
$H_2PO_4^-$, HPO_4^{-2}, H_3BO_3, $H_2BO_3^-$, $Si(OH)_4$, MoO_4^{-2}, H_2S, HS^-, F^-, $H_2AsO_4^-$, CrO_4^{-2}	These are moderately to strongly retained by soils. Soil pH greatly influences the retention of these: MoO_4^{-2} and $Si(OH)_4$ are more soluble at high pH; phosphate is more soluble at slightly acid pH. Borates are the most soluble of this group.
Transition metals and aluminum	
Al^{+3}, $AlOH^{+2}$, $Al(OH)_2^{-1}$, $Fe(OH)_2^{+1}$, Fe^{+2}, Mn^{+2}	These are insoluble hydroxides which accumulate as silica and other weathered ions.
Cu^{+2}, Zn^{+2}	Copper and zinc are more soluble and are increasingly available with increasing soil acidity; strongly complexed by organic matter.
Toxic ions	
Al^{+3}, Cd^{+2}, Pb^{+2}, Hg^{+2}, Hg	Al^{+3} is a hazard to plants while the others are more of a concern with animals.
Active in oxidation-reduction (redox) reactions	
organic $C \rightarrow HCO_3^-$ $-NH_2 \rightarrow NO_3^-$ $-SH \rightarrow SO_4^{-2}$ $Fe^{+2} \rightarrow FeOOH$ $Mn^{+2} \rightarrow MnO_2$ organic $Se \rightarrow SeO_4^{-2}$ organic $Hg \rightarrow Hg^{+2}$	Changes in the oxidation state of soil carbon, nitrogen, and sulfur compounds are key components of soil biochemistry, with oxygen being the main electron acceptor; Fe(III), Mn(III-IV), nitrate, and sulfate are electron acceptors when soil oxygen levels are low, leading to anaerobic conditions and possible "black layer" formation.

rootzone by excess rainfall or irrigation water are replaced by cations formerly bound to the CEC. Low CEC soils require more frequent additions of the cationic nutrients to remain sufficient.

Cations are attracted to the CEC in different strengths. This determines which cations are more easily lost from the soil by leaching. Usually, a cation with a high charge of 2 or 3 (e.g., Ca^{+2}, or Al^{+3}) is preferentially held over cations with a lesser charge (e.g., K^+). Also, smaller ions have greater affinity than larger ones. Cations also are adsorbed and exchanged on a chemically equivalent basis. For example, one K^+ can replace one Na^+, while two K^+ are required to replace (or exchange) for one Ca^{+2}. The bonding strength and presence of exchangeable cations in fertile soils most often occur in the following sequence:

General Order of Bonding Strength of Exchangeable Cations

$$Al^{+3} > H^+ > Ca^{+2} > Mg^{+2} > NH_4^+ > K^+ = Na^+$$

Calcium (Ca^{+2}) is the most tightly held nutrient cation. Heavy applications of Ca^{+2} may induce deficiencies of magnesium (Mg^{+2}) and potassium (K^+), in part due to enhanced leaching of these cations. The strong bonding of Ca^{+2} is also the reason gypsum (calcium sulfate) applications are frequently used to displace (or exchange) sodium (Na^+) from salt-affected soils.

The major CEC source in soil is from clay minerals and organic matter. Soils low in CEC retain cationic nutrients poorly, so they may be readily leached through the soil profile. This leaching results in inefficient use of applied nutrients and possibly a negative environmental impact on underlying water sources. In general, soils with high CECs are more fertile than soils with low CEC, because high-CEC soils retain more exchangeable plant nutrients. A high Ca^{+2} level is desirable as well, because it reflects low concentrations of other potentially troublesome cations—Al^{+3} and H^+ in acidic soils and Na^+ in sodic (saline) soils. Liming a soil with a calcium-containing product is a cation exchange reaction where most of the exchangeable Al^{+3} and H^+ are replaced by the Ca^{+2} and neutralized by the basic component of the liming material (usually a carbonate).

Cation exchange capacity is calculated by summing the exchangeable cations (CEC = H^+ + Al^{+3} + Ca^{+2} + Mg^{+2} + K^+ + Na^+) and is expressed in units of milliequivalents per 100 grams of soil (meq/100 g) or centimoles of charge per kilogram of soil ($cmol_c$/kg). Numerically, meq/100 g and $cmol_c$/kg are the same. One milliequivalent of negative charge on a clay particle is neutralized by one milliequivalent of cation, but the weight of cation may differ dependent on the atomic weight of the cation.

Soil Type

The CEC of a soil can be estimated from its texture, due to the direct relationship between soil texture and clay mineral content and the indirect relationship of texture and soil organic matter (generally the sandier the soil, the lower its organic matter content). The CEC of soil organic matter ranges from 150–350 meq/100 g. Clay minerals may range from as low as 4 meq/100 g to as high as 150 meq/100 g (Table 3–2).

Organic matter, or humus, and certain clays have large CEC values and surface areas. Organic matter surfaces are negatively charged due to the following reaction with hydroxyl ions as soil pH is increased:

Cation Exchange Capacity of Organic Matter Greatly Increases as Soil pH Increases

COOH	+ OH⁻ $\longrightarrow$	COO⁻	+ H_2O
(organic matter carboxyl group)	(hydroxyl ion; ↑pH)	cation-exchange site	water

Sands

Sandy soils generally have low CEC values due to their relatively small surface areas, resulting in less-exposed negative charges to attract or hold cations (Figure 3–1). Sandy soils also contain relatively little organic matter or clay which may increase soil CEC. Nutrients in low-CEC soils are more easily leached. This results in soils of low CEC, which are relatively infertile and have low water-retention potential. Most of the essential plant nutrients must, therefore, be applied via the turf nutrient-maintenance program. These soils generally profit from additions of clay or organic matter to increase their CEC values. The primary factor affecting the amount of variable charge in the soil is pH. Increasing pH increases CEC. For example, increasing pH from 5.5 to 6.5 may double the CEC of a typical sandy soil when most of the CEC arises from organic mat-

TABLE 3–2 *Cation exchange capacity (CEC) examples of various soils.*

Soil texture	CEC (meq/100 g)	Relative level
Sand	0 to 6	Very low
Sandy loam	6 to 12	Low
Loam	12 to 30	Medium
Silt loam	10 to 50	Medium
Clay loams	4 to 30	Medium
Clays	18 to 150	High
Organic matter/humus	150 to 350	Very high

FIGURE 3–1 Sandy soils drain well but often have low cation exchange capacities (CECs) due to a lack of organic matter, silt, or clay and from sand having relatively small surface areas; thus, less-exposed negative charges attract and hold positively charged cations.

FIGURE 3–2 Clay soils generally hold nutrients well but may drain poorly. Soils high in montmorillonite clay have high surface areas due to their characteristic shrink-swell capabilities.

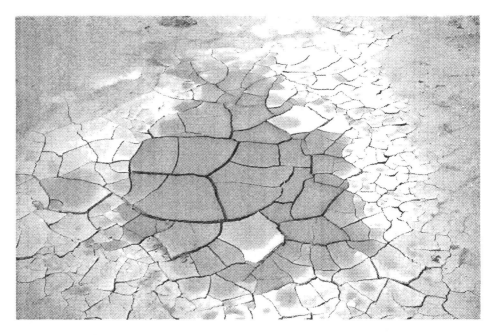

ter. A pH of 6.5 is generally the highest pH recommended for most grasses. Maintaining soil pH near this level provides near-optimum CEC and phosphorus availability while providing acceptable conditions for micronutrient availability.

Clays

If clay is present, its type is important. The surface charge and expandability of clays are important in resulting CEC values. Due to their small size, clay particles expose a large external surface. In addition, certain clay particles (e.g., montmorillonite) have relatively extensive internal surfaces due to their plate-like crystal units which compose each particle. Clays that swell in the presence of water (Figure 3–2) increase their surface area and allow the replacement of cations in the internal surface. Much of the charge in montmorillonite and vermiculite is permanent and is located within the structure of the clay particle. This charge arises by a process called **isomorphous substitution** during the formation of the clay. Negative charges are created when cations of lesser charge are substituted for cations of higher charge. For example, aluminum ions can

TABLE 3–3 *Typical characteristics and cation exchange capacities (CEC) of various clay minerals and humus.*

Material	Structural type	Permanent charge	Expands in water	Surface area	CEC at pH 7 (meq/100 g)
Kaolinite	1:1	very low	no	extremely low	4 to 6
Chlorite	2:1:1 (2:2)	medium	no	low	20 to 30
Mica (Illite)	2:1	high	slightly	low	20 to 40
Montmorillonite (Smectite)	2:1	medium	yes	high	60 to 100
Vermiculite	2:1	high	limited	medium	100 to 150
Humic acid	organic	high	slightly	high	150 to 350

replace silicon ions within clay sheets when they expand while Mg^{+2} and $Fe^{+2 \text{ or } +3}$ can substitute for Al^{+3} ions. This regulates the permanent charge of most soils and is influenced little by the soil solution. The lower charge but similar-sized replacement cations result in a net negative charge which attracts other cations; thus, it increases its CEC value. Montmorillonite and vermiculite clays, with high CEC and surface area, are more effective than non-expandable, lower-CEC clay such as kaolinite, chlorite, or illite (Table 3–3). In fact, due to its low expandability, kaolinite is often used to make tile, pottery, and other fired-clay items.

Example:

A fairway soil contains 40 percent clay and 5 percent humus. Determine the CEC of the soil, assuming the clay is kaolinite. Kaolinte clay has a CEC range of 4 to 6 meq/100 g and humus 150 to 350 meq/100 g.

Step 1: Determine the CEC contribution of the kaolinite clay. With a range of 4 to 6 meq/100 g, an average of 5 meq/100 g is used. The CEC of the clay contribution is determined by multiplying the percent clay (40 percent) by the CEC of pure kaolinite (5 meq/100 g) to obtain 2 meq/100 g.

CEC contribution of the clay = 0.4 × 5 meq/100 g = 2 meq/100 g

Step 2: Determine the CEC contribution of the humus. Humus has a CEC range of 150 to 350 meq/100 g; thus, an average of 250 meq/100 g is used. The CEC of the humus contribution is determined by multiplying the percent humus (5 percent) by the CEC of pure humus (250 meq/100 g) to obtain 12.5 meq/100 g.

CEC contribution of the humus = 0.05 × 250 meq/100 g = 12.5 meq/100 g

Step 3: To determine the CEC of the fairway soil, sum the contribution of each component. CEC of fairway soil = 2 meq/100 g (from clay) + 12.5 meq/100 g (from humus) = 14.5 meq/100 g

Increasing Soil CEC

Increasing CEC by adding clay or organic matter to soil is difficult due to the large amount of material needed. For example, to increase the CEC of a soil 1 meq/100 g, it is necessary to increase the soil content of clay or organic matter by 10 tons per acre (22,460 kg/ha) of soil (assuming a CEC of 100 meq/100 g for the clay or organic matter and incorporation six inches, 15 cm, deep). Adding this much material would increase the clay or organic matter content of the soil 1 percent. In general, organic matter has a greater potential to increase CEC than clay. For example, a 5 percent content of organic matter by weight equals the CEC provided by a 30 percent content of an illitic clay (Figure 3–3). Although additions of clay and organic matter may increase the CEC of sandy soils, excessive increases in these materials may adversely affect the soils' physical properties such as infiltration and percolation rate.

Conversely, reducing organic matter by core aerification and replacement with topdressing sand will obviously decrease CEC. Generally, aerification decisions are based on reducing compaction and increasing water and air movement through the rootzone, although some CEC may be sacrificed.

FIGURE 3–3 Organic matter sources, such as peat (shown), are often added to sand soils used on golf courses to increase nutrient and water-holding capacities.

TABLE 3–4 *Desired cation exchange capacity (CEC) and percent base saturation ranges and ratios in soils.*

Cation	Percent CEC	Percent base saturation
Ca^{+2}	60 to 70	50 to 80
Mg^{+2}	10 to 20	18 to 22
K^+	5 to 10	3 to 6
Na^+	0 to 1[*]	0 to 1
H^+	0 to 10[*]	0
Ca:Mg	—	<6.5:1
Ca:K	—	<13:1
Mg:K	—	<2:1

*A Na^+ or H^+ percentage above 15 percent may indicate a nutrient imbalance or potential toxic level.

Base Saturation of the Cation Exchange Capacity or Percentage Cation Saturation

The CEC of the soil exchange complex (organic matter and clay) generally increases as the soil pH increases due to the dissociation of hydrogen ions from surface sites, as previously illustrated for COOH. The degree to which the exchange sites are saturated with cations such as calcium, magnesium, sodium, and potassium, as opposed to acid cations hydrogen (H^+) and aluminum (Al^{+3}), is referred to as the **base saturation** of a soil (Table 3–4). In general, the pH and fertility of a soil increase as the percentage base saturation increases. Higher base saturation generally increases the ease with which cations are absorbed by plants because a higher concentration of cations are maintained in the soil solution. The greatest availability of most nutrients to plants is in the soil pH range of 6 to 7. In acidic soils (pH<5.5), exchangeable Al^{+3} may be present and, along with Mg^{+2} and/or H^+ ions, can suppress plant uptake of Ca^{-2} or K^+. However, toxic aluminum becomes less prevalent, and therefore less detrimental to the plant, as the base saturation increases. Maintaining soil pH between 5.8 and 7.0 is a much better way to avoid Al^{+3} and H^+ toxicity than trying to attain 100 percent base saturation. In order to achieve 100 percent base saturation in many soils, the pH must exceed 7.0, which in turn results in micronutrient deficiencies.

Cation saturation is also a useful measurement to manage soil sodium (Na^+) and can also be utilized to determine soil magnesium (Mg^{+2}) availability. When Na^+ exceeds 15 percent of the

CEC, water and air infiltration into the soil may be reduced and poor growing conditions may result. To overcome this problem, calcium (Ca^{+2}) is added to replace the Na^+ from the CEC, most often from calcium sulfate ($CaSO_4$ or gypsum). Sodium in the soil water is then leached out of the rootzone by excess irrigation or rainfall. The amount of Ca^{+2} needed to replace the Na^+ is based on the amount of exchangeable Na^+ as well as Na^+ saturation. Similarly, Mg^{+2} availability is based on both the total amount of Mg^{-2} and the Mg^{+2} saturation. As a general rule of thumb on sandy soils, Mg^{+2} saturation greater than 10 percent at soil Mg^{+2} between 60 and 120 pounds per acre (67 to 134 kg/ha) is sufficient. If Mg^{+2} saturation is less than 10 percent Mg and soil Mg^{+2} is between 60 and 120 pounds per acre (67 to 134 kg/ha), then additional Mg^{+2} is needed to provide sufficient Mg^{+2} availability. If soil Mg^{-2} is below 60 pounds per acre (67 kg/ha), additional Mg^{+2} is needed irrespective of Mg^{+2} saturation. No additional Mg^{+2} is needed if soil Mg^{+2} exceeds 120 pounds per acre (134 kg/ha) in most situations.

Example:

From the following soil test report data, calculate the percent base saturation: $Ca^{+2} = 20$, $Mg^{+2} = 7.0$, $K^+ = 0.2$, $Na^+ = 0.3$, $Al^{+3} = 7.0$, and $H^+ = 4.0$ meq/100 g:

Step 1: CEC, the total of all cations present, is determined.

$$20 + 7.0 + 0.2 + 0.3 + 7.0 + 4.0 = 38.5 \text{ meq/100 g}$$

Step 2: Next, the base saturation is the sum of the basic cation Ca^{+2}, Mg^{+2}, K^+, and Na^+. Therefore, the calculation is the sum of the basic cations divided by the CEC and then multiplied by 100.

$$\text{Percent base saturation} = \frac{20.0 + 7.0 + 0.2 + 0.3}{38.5} \times 100 = 71.4\%$$

Measuring Soil CEC

Cation exchange capacity can be estimated or measured by several different methods. Since the direct measurement of CEC is costly and time-consuming, most soil testing laboratories routinely estimate CEC by measuring the predominant extractable cations (Ca^{+2}, Mg^{+2}, K^+, Na^+) and estimating extractable acidity (H^+ and Al^{+3}) from soil pH and buffer pH.

Estimates will be erroneously high in two commonly occurring situations. First, CEC will be overestimated if a soil is sampled shortly after a heavy fertilizer or gypsum application. This error arises as the cations in the soil solution are misrepresented as exchangeable. These conditions may be found on a sand-based green with recent fertilization. Second, extraction of high pH soils containing calcium carbonate (limestone) with an acid extracting agent will also provide inflated CEC estimates. The acid extractant dissolves a portion of the limestone and considers the Ca^{-2} removed as exchangeable.

Direct measurements of CEC may be obtained from some soil testing laboratories. Methods utilized vary primarily in the pH at which CEC is measured. Soil pH has a large effect on CEC measurement in soils where the CEC originates mostly from organic matter and low-CEC clay minerals. The method that determines soil CEC at a pH closest to the pH of the soil is the most useful method. Soil CEC measured by different methods or estimated by different methods are not directly comparable.

Equivalent Weight

Cations are adsorbed and exchanged on a chemically equivalent weight (eq) basis. An **equivalent weight** (also called **moles of ion charge**) is the amount (or weight) of an ion needed to equal the amount (or weight) of another ion. Equivalent weights are calculated by dividing the atomic weight of a cation by its valence, regardless of the sign. For example, one equivalent of Ca^{+2} is calculated by dividing the atomic weight of calcium (40 g/mole) by the valence of calcium (+2) to obtain 20 grams. Likewise, one equivalent of K^+ is calculated by dividing the atomic weight of potassium (39 g/mole) by the valence of potassium (+1) to obtain 39 grams. Therefore, for one equivalent of Ca^{+2} to equal one equivalent of K^+, it requires only 20 grams of calcium compared to 39 grams of potassium. Calculating milliequivalent weight (meq) is the same, only the amounts are in mil-

TABLE 3–5 *Equivalent and milliequivalent weights of common soil cations.*

Cation	Molecular weight	Valence	Equivalent weight (g)	Milliequivalent weight (mg)
Hydrogen (H$^+$)	1	1	1	1
Aluminum (Al^{+3})	27	3	9	9
Calcium (Ca^{+2})	40	2	20	20
Magnesium (Mg^{+2})	24	2	12	12
Potassium (K$^-$)	39	1	39	39
Sodium (Na$^+$)	23	1	23	23

ligrams (mg) instead of grams (g). For a further demonstration of equivalents, see the following example. Also, Table 3–5 lists equivalent and milliequivalent weights of common cations.

Example:

How many milliequivalents (meq) of K$^+$ are in 78 milligrams of K$^+$?

Step 1: Determine the mass of K$^+$ in one meq of K$^+$. The periodic table shows potassium has an atomic mass of 39 mg/mmol (millimole). The single positive sign on the cation (K$^+$) indicates potassium has a valence of one. With this information, meq can be calculated by dividing the atomic mass by the valence. For potassium, one meq of K$^+$ weighs 39 milligrams.

$$1 \text{ meq K}^+ = \frac{39 \text{ mg/mmol}}{1} = 39 \text{ mg}$$

Step 2: To determine the number of meq K$^-$ in 78 milligrams of K$^+$, it is easiest to set up a ratio. One meq K$^+$ is 39 milligrams; therefore, 78 milligrams must equal two meq K$^+$.

$$\frac{1 \text{ meq K}^+}{39 \text{ mg}} = \frac{X \text{ meq K}^+}{78 \text{ mg}}$$

$$X \text{ meq K}^+ = \frac{78 \text{ mg}}{39 \text{ mg}} = 2$$

The concept of cation exchange is based on moles of charge. One **mole** of an element is the quantity of it having a mass in grams equal to the atomic weight. For example, the atomic weight of sodium is 23, so one mole of sodium weighs 23 grams. One mole of an element contains Avogadro's number (6.022×10^{23}) of atoms of the element. Therefore, one mole of charge is 6.022×10^{23} charges. So, if sodium exists as a cation (Na$^+$), then a solution containing one mole of sodium would contain 6.022×10^{23} positive charges and weigh 23 grams. In the case of a divalent cation (having two positive charges per mole) like Ca^{+2}, only half of its mass would be needed to equal the same amount of charge as a monovalent cation. Trivalent cations (e.g., Al^{+3}) would require a third as much. The next example determines the CEC of a given soil.

Example:

Calculate the CEC of a soil using the following information:

Cation	Atomic weight (g/mole)	Amount on exchange sites (ppm or mg/kg)
Calcium (Ca^{+2})	40	4,000
Magnesium (Mg^{+2})	24	840
Potassium (K$^+$)	39	78
Sodium (Na$^+$)	23	69
Aluminum (Al^{+3})	27	630
Hydrogen (H$^+$)	1	40

Step 1: Since CEC is generally expressed in milliequivalents (meq)/100 g soil, convert mg/kg soil by multiplying by 0.1 (100 g divided by 1,000 g/kg).

Cation	Atomic weight (g/mole)	Amount on exchange sites (mg/kg)	Amount on exchange sites (mg/100 g)
Calcium (Ca^{+2})	40	4,000	400
Magnesium (Mg^{+2})	24	840	84
Potassium (K^+)	39	78	7.8
Sodium (Na^+)	23	69	6.9
Aluminum (Al^{+3})	27	630	63
Hydrogen (H^+)	1	40	4

Step 2: Now calculate the mass of meq for each cation. Recall, meq are equal to the atomic weight divided by the valence (e.g., Ca^{+2} has a valence of two while K^+ has a valence of one). Therefore, one meq of Ca^{+2} is equal to the atomic weight (40 g/mole) divided by the valence (2), and thus one meq of Ca^{+2} has a mass of 20 milligrams.

Cation	Atomic weight (g/mole)	Amount on exchange sites (mg/100 g)	Mass of one meq of cation (mg)
Calcium (Ca^{+2})	40	400	20
Magnesium (Mg^{+2})	24	84	12
Potassium (K^+)	39	7.8	39
Sodium (Na^+)	23	6.9	23
Aluminum (Al^{+3})	27	63	9
Hydrogen (H^+)	1	4	1

Step 3: To calculate the meq of cation on the exchange site, divide the amount on the exchange site by the mass of one meq of the cation (e.g., for Ca^{+2}, divide 400 mg/100 g soil by 20 mg to find 20.0 meq Ca^{+2} 100/g soil).

Cation	Atomic weight (g/mole)	Amount on exchange sites (mg/100 g)	Mass of one meq of cation (mg)	Amount on exchange sites (meq/100 g)
Calcium (Ca^{+2})	40	400	20	20.0
Magnesium (Mg^{+2})	24	84	12	7.0
Potassium (K^+)	39	7.8	39	0.2
Sodium (Na^+)	23	6.9	23	0.3
Aluminum (Al^{+3})	27	63	9	7.0
Hydrogen (H^+)	1	4	1	4.0

Step 4: To calculate the CEC, sum the amount of cations on the exchange site in meq/100 g soil [e.g., CEC = Ca^{+2} (20.0) + Mg^{+2} (7.0) + K^+ (0.2) + Na^+ (0.3) + Al^{+3} (7.0) + H^+ (4.0) = 38.5 meq/100 g].

Cation	Atomic weight (g/mole)	Amount on exchange sites (mg/100 g)	Mass of one meq of cation (mg)	Amount on exchange sites (meq/100 g)
Calcium (Ca^{+2})	40	400	20	20.0
Magnesium (Mg^{+2})	24	84	12	7.0
Potassium (K^+)	39	7.8	39	0.2
Sodium (Na^+)	23	6.9	23	0.3
Aluminum (Al^{+3})	27	63	9	7.0
Hydrogen (H^+)	1	4	1	4.0
CEC				**38.5**

Example:

A sample from an 85:15 (sand:sphagnum peat by volume) putting green mix is oxidized (burned) and determined to have 1 percent organic matter by weight. Calculate a CEC for the mixture; assume the CEC of the peat alone is 125 meq/100 g.

Due to the relatively low surface area and lack of surface negative charges to retain cations, the CEC contribution of the sand in the mix can be considered negligible. Therefore, the peat will be responsible for nutrient retention and thus the calculation is simple. CEC is determined by multiplying the amount, by weight, of organic matter (1 percent) by the CEC of the organic matter (125 meq/100 g).

$$\text{CEC of 85:15 green's mix} = 0.01 \times 125 \text{ meq/100 g} = 1.25 \text{ meq/100 g}$$

Thus, the CEC of the 85:15 mix is 1.25 meq/100 g.

Anion Exchange Capacity

Several nutrients are present in the soil, and absorbed by the plant, as **anions** (negatively charged ions), not as cations (Table 3–1). These include nitrate (NO_3^-), phosphate ($H_2PO_4^-$), sulfate (SO_4^{-2}), and chloride (Cl^-). Carbonate (CO_3^{-2}) and bicarbonate (HCO_3^-) may also be found in soil as a result of liming or the use of irrigation water high in these anions. **Anion exchange capacity (AEC)** is the sum of exchangeable anions a soil can adsorb, expressed as centimoles of charge per kilogram of soil (cmol$_c$/kg or meq/100 g). AEC reflects the amount of positive charge on the surface of organic matter and clay colloids. Anion exchange capacity only occurs to any appreciable extent when soil pH is below 5. Since surface soil pH is usually maintained at higher pH levels, little anion exchange occurs in the rootzone of soils used for turf. However, anion exchange may occur in the subsoil of some turf soils. The Cl^-, SO_4^{-2}, and NO_3^- anions are the ones commonly exhibiting net anion repulsion; thus, they are retained less in soils.

Turf managers should remember the form of nitrogen available to plants in warm soils is primarily nitrate (NO_3^-). Turfgrasses also can utilize ammonium nitrogen (NH_4^+) but, due to typically high soil temperatures, ammonium nitrogen is readily converted by microorganisms to nitrate nitrogen in many soils. Since little anion exchange capacity exists in soils, nitrate (NO_3^-) is not retained and instead leaches through the rootzone. Nitrate that has moved below the rootzone will leach to lower depths or will be denitrified. Other forms of nitrogen in the soil are generally held as insoluble organic matter compounds. Relatively small, frequent nitrogen applications are, therefore, generally more efficient for plant use compared to heavy, infrequent applications. Slow-release nitrogen sources also help to reduce the amount of nitrogen leached, because of the more gradual release of nutrients into the soil solution.

Phosphate and sulfate anions are retained in soils by mechanisms other than anion exchange. Retention of these ions is favored by high iron and aluminum oxide content and low pH. The strength of the bonding between these anions and the soil, particularly in the case of phosphate, may be quite strong with little of each nutrient remaining plant available. In addition, little downward movement of phosphate occurs in most soils, except in extremely sandy soils and with high application rates of phosphate. Sulfate is retained much more weakly than phosphate;

therefore, retention of sulfate does not occur in the presence of phosphate. Leaching of sulfate from soil layers containing high levels of phosphorus readily occurs. Retention of sulfate, however, will occur when the leaching sulfate encounters layers of low phosphorus soil.

In summary, the type of cation bound to exchange sites on soil colloids is important in determining the fertility and pH of a soil. The greater the quantity of Ca^{+2}, K^+, Mg^+, Fe^{+2}, and other secondary plant minerals, the more fertile the soil. Also, the more Al^{+3} and H^+ held by the soil, the more acidic it is.

Example:

A soil analysis report indicates the following cations are present per 100 g soil:

Ca^{+2}	5 meq	H^+	1 meq
K^+	6 meq	NO_3^-	4 meq
Mg^{+2}	2 meq	Na^+	0 meq
Al^{+3}	4 meq		

What is the CEC, the percent base saturation, and percent exchangeable acidity of this soil?

$$CEC = Ca^{+2} + Al^{+3} + K^+ + H^+ + Mg^{+2} = (5 + 4 + 6 + 1 + 2) = 18 \text{ meq/100 g soil}$$

$$\%BS = \frac{Ca^{+2} + K^+ + Mg^{+2} + Na^+}{CEC} \times 100 = \frac{(5 + 6 + 2 + 0)}{18} \times 100 = 72\%$$

$$\%EA = \frac{H^+ + Al^{+3}}{CEC} \times 100 = \frac{1 + 4}{18} \times 100 = 28\%$$

Flocculation and Dispersion

Cations can also influence the interactions of soil colloids and soil structure. The term **flocculation** describes the attraction of soil colloids to one another (Figure 3–4). Clay particles have an electronegative charge on their surface; therefore, they have the ability to attract cations. When cations swarm to these negative charges, they provide a bridging for clays to form structure. Cations, such as Ca^{+2}, Fe^{+2}, and Al^{+3}, with a high charge density and/or a small hydrated radius, promote flocculation or clay structure. These cations suppress the negative charge of the clays allowing them to attract one another, thereby improving soil structure.

Some cations disperse, rather than attract, clay particles. This process is referred to as **dispersion** or **deflocculation.** Dispersion is common in arid and semiarid regions where sodium (Na^+) accumulates in soils because of low rainfall. Sodium (Na^+) is responsible for dispersion since the large hydrated radius of a sodium ion does not allow it to get close enough to the clay particle to completely neutralize the electronegative charge (Figure 3–4). Sodium is also monovalent (only reacts with one exchange site), thereby failing to create a bridge for clay attraction. The lack of colloid attraction degrades soil structure. Soils with poor structure fail to sustain plant growth effectively by reducing drainage and oxygenation. Dispersed soils can be amended with applications of gypsum, also known as calcium sulfate ($CaSO_4$). Gypsum improves flocculation by replacing the Na^+ ion with Ca^{+2}. Soil dispersion is generally not a problem in sand-based golf greens because of the absence of electrochemical charges on sand particles. However, sodium can cause other problems in sand-based soils, as discussed in the water quality chapter.

SOIL ACIDITY AND LIMING

Soil pH is an important chemical property of soils with a substantial effect on plant nutrient availability, root function and health, pesticide effectiveness, and microbial activity. Soil pH is defined as the negative logarithm of the H^+ activity.

$$pH = \frac{1}{\log[H^+]} = -\log[H^+]$$

where hydrogen ion activity $[H^+]$ is in moles per liter.

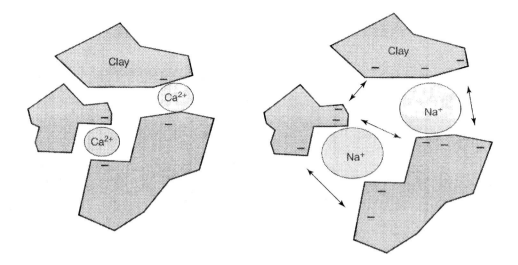

FIGURE 3–4 Flocculated and dispersed soil clay particles are shown. Calcium with the high charge density and small hydrated radius is able to attract soil colloids. Sodium has a larger radius and low charge density that does not satisfy the electronegativity of clays, causing repulsion of colloids and reducing soil structure.

A relationship exists between hydrogen and hydroxyl ion concentrations, where in water at 25°C:

Relationship between Hydrogen and Hydroxyl Ion Concentrations

$$[H^+] \quad \times \quad [OH^-] \quad = \quad 10^{-14}$$

hydrogen ion   hydroxyl ion

For example, if the H^+ activity is 0.0001 mole per liter (1×10^{-4} mole per liter), then the negative log of this activity is 4. At a pH of 6 the H^+ activity is 0.000001 and at a pH of 8 the H^+ activity is 0.00000001.

Hydroxyl ion (OH^-) is termed base and counteracts the acid. In the soil water, H^+ and OH^- are inversely related (when one increases, the other decreases).

When H^+ and OH^- are equal, the pH is 7 and the solution is termed neutral, neither acidic nor basic. When H^+ exceeds OH^- the pH is less than 7 and the solution is acidic. The lower the pH, the greater the acidity. Conversely, when H^+ is less than OH^-, the solution is basic and the pH is greater than 7. The higher the pH, the less acidic the solution. The pH of several common substances is listed in Table 3–6.

An **acid** is a substance that releases (or donates) hydrogen ions (also called protons) to another substance. The extent to which an acid dissociates (converts to a hydrogen ion and an accompanying anion) determines its strength. When saturated with hydrogen, a soil behaves as a weak acid.

An Acid's Strength Is Determined by the Extent it Dissociates or Releases H^+ Ions

AH	H_2O	A^-	+	H^+
[potential acid, exchangeable acid, or buffer capacity]	$\longleftrightarrow$ (dissociation or anion ionization)	[————Active acidity————]		hydrogen ion

Hydrochloric, sulfuric, and nitric acid are "strong" acids, because they dissociate completely, meaning they readily release all of their hydrogen ions into solution, thus dramatically reducing the solution pH. Weak acids, such as carbonic, boric, and acetic acids, dissociate only partially when placed in solution; therefore, they do not reduce the pH as much as strong acids. Neutralization of an acid occurs when it reacts with a base (a source of hydroxyl or OH^- ions) to form a salt and water. In turf, acid neutralization is usually achieved by using lime as the base:

Using Lime to Neutralize an Acid

AH	+	BOH	$\rightarrow$	BA	+	H_2O
potential acid		base (e.g., lime)		salt		water

For example:

2HCl	+	$Ca(OH)_2$	$\rightarrow$	$CaCl_2$	+	$2H_2O$
hydrochloric acid		calcium hydroxide		calcium chloride		water

TABLE 3–6 *Range of pH values for several common substances.*

Substance	pH	Description
Lye (bleach)	13.0	Strong alkaline
Soap	9.3	↑
Antacid tablets	9.4	
Baking soda	8.0	
Seawater	7.9	↓
Human blood	7.3	Weak alkaline
Pure water	7.0	Neutral
Fresh milk	6.7	Weak acid
Natural rainfall	5.6	↑
Sour milk	4.7	
Beer	4.4	
Coffee	4.2	
Orange juice	3.7	
Vinegar	2.9	
Lemon juice	2.4	↓
Battery acid	0.5	Strong acid

Active and Exchangeable Acidity

Soil pH reported by soil test laboratories is a measurement of the dissociated H^+. This is referred to as **active acidity.** The H^+ remaining on the exchange complex along with exchangeable soil Al^{+3} are referred to as **exchangeable acidity, potential acidity,** or the **buffer capacity.** There is much more exchangeable acidity in soils than there is active acidity. Soil test laboratories often list the measure of exchangeable acidity as buffer pH on soil test reports. Soils containing appreciable amounts of clay, organic matter, and humus (have high CEC values) tend to have high potential acidities. They resist pH changes when limed, and are said to be well-buffered. Another example involves comparing two soil types, a clay loam soil and a sandy soil. It would require more lime to raise the pH of the clay loam soil than raise the pH of the sandy soil. Thus, the clay soil has a higher buffering capacity than the sandy soil.

By definition, exchangeable acidity represents the portion of hydrogen and aluminum ions that can be displaced from exchange sites by a concentrated salt solution. Hydrogen ion (H^+) is the primary source of exchangeable acidity in organic soils. In mineral soils, most of the exchangeable acidity is due to aluminum (Al^{+3}). Aluminum is the third most abundant element in the earth's crust, with many clay minerals being alumina silicates.

Aluminum Hydrolysis under Very Acid Soil Conditions (pH<5.0)

$$Al^{+3} \quad + \quad H_2O \quad \rightarrow \quad Al(OH)^{+2} \quad + \quad H^+$$
aluminum   water   hydroxy-Al   hydrogen ($\rightarrow$ pH)

The hydrogen ions liberated from exchange sites and the hydrogen produced by hydrolysis of liberated aluminum ions lower soil pH to a range of about 4.5 to 5. Application of a liming material, however, produces hydroxyl ions (OH^-) which react with (neutralize) the liberated H^+ to produce water. The hydroxyl-Al ($Al(OH^{+2})$) polymer formed is irreversibly sorbed to the surface of inorganic soil colloids and, as a result, decreases CEC and a pH of about 5 to 6.5.

As soil pH increases, aluminum ions eventually precipitate, leaving negative charges that allow other available cations, such as calcium, to be retained until they can be absorbed by plants. With this decrease in the degree of Al^{+3} and H^+ saturation of the exchange complex, the degree of saturation with exchangeable bases increases. This occurs at a pH of about 6.5 to 8.5. Exchangeable bases such as calcium and magnesium then dominate, while the aluminum ions form insoluble gibbsite and the hydrogen ions react with hydroxyl ions (OH^-) to form water:

Aluminum and Hydrogen Ion Conversion as Soil pH Is Increased

$$Al(OH)_2^+ \quad + \quad OH^- \quad \rightarrow \quad Al(OH)_3$$
hydroxy-Al (soluble) $\qquad$ hydroxyl ion $\qquad\qquad$ gibbsite (insoluble)

$$H^+ \qquad\qquad + \quad Ca(OH)_2 \quad \rightarrow \quad Ca^{+2} \qquad + \qquad H_2O$$
hydrogen ion $\qquad\qquad$ or $\qquad\qquad\qquad$ or Mg^{+2} $\qquad\qquad$ water
$\qquad\qquad\qquad\qquad\qquad Mg(OH)_2$

Origin of Acidity

A number of processes decrease soil pH. Gradual changes occur due to the leaching of bases from excess rainfall and organic matter decomposition. More substantial and rapid decreases in pH occur through the microbial oxidation of nitrogen and sulfur.

Leaching and Plant Removal of Cations

Exchangeable aluminum (Al^{+3}) and hydrogen (H^+) and soil acidity increase when leaching and plant removal reduce the exchangeable bases calcium (Ca^{+2}), magnesium (Mg^{+2}), potassium (K^+), and sodium (Na^+). Leaching of bases downward in the soil profile occurs when rainfall and irrigation exceed water use by the plant. The excess water containing cations and anions percolates down through the soil. Cations formerly held on the exchange complex replace those removed from the soil water, and Al^{+3} and H^+ replace the cations on the exchange. In arid regions (areas receiving less than 20 inches of rain annually), soils tend to have a high pH because rainfall does not exceed water use and leaching of the basic cations does not occur. The accumulation of cations by the turfgrass plant, accompanied by the removal of clippings, acidifies the soil in the same manner as leaching. Plants may also acidify the rootzone when accumulating most of their nitrogen in the NH_4^+ form by the release of H^+ to maintain cation/anion balance.

Atmospheric Deposition and Organic Matter Decomposition

Rainfall contributes some acidity directly to soils as well as being the primary agent of leaching. Carbon dioxide reacts with the rainfall to produce carbonic acid (H_2CO_3), a weak acid. Long-term exposure to carbonic acid in rainfall produces sinkholes and caves in predominantly limerock-based soils. More abrupt decreases in pH may occur with rainfall contaminated with industrial pollutants, such as oxides of sulfur and nitrogen.

The decomposition of organic matter also produces H^+, as illustrated.

Reducing Soil pH as Organic Matter Is Decomposed

Step 1

$$C_2H_4ONS \quad + \quad 5O_2 \quad + \quad H_2O \quad \rightarrow \quad H_2CO_3 \quad + \quad RCOOH \quad + \quad H_2SO_4 + HNO_3$$
organic matter $\qquad\qquad\qquad\qquad\qquad\qquad\qquad$ carbonic $\qquad$ strong organic $\qquad$ strong inorganic
$\qquad\qquad\qquad\qquad\qquad\qquad\qquad\qquad\qquad$ acid $\qquad$ acid from humus $\qquad\qquad$ acids

Step 2

$$RCOOH \qquad\qquad\qquad \rightarrow \quad RCOO^- \quad + \quad H^+ \quad \& \quad ROH \quad \rightarrow \quad RO^- \quad + \quad H^+$$
carboxyl group $\qquad\qquad\qquad\qquad\qquad\qquad\qquad (\downarrow pH) \qquad$ hydroxyl $\qquad\qquad\qquad\qquad (\downarrow pH)$
of humus (organic matter) $\qquad\qquad\qquad\qquad\qquad\qquad\qquad$ group

Nitrification and Sulfur Oxidation

Microbial degradation of ammonium (NH_4^+) containing fertilizers such as urea, ammonium nitrate, ammonium sulfate, and many organic nitrogen sources also produce H^+ through a process called **nitrification.**

Nitrification Reaction

$$NH_4^+ \qquad + \quad 2O_2 \quad \xrightarrow{\text{proper temperature, aeration,}} \quad NO_3^- \quad + \quad 2H^+ \quad + \quad H_2O$$
ammonium ion $\qquad$ oxygen $\quad$ soil water & microorganisms $\quad$ nitrate $\qquad (\downarrow pH) \qquad$ water

Less acidity is generated from ammonium nitrate per unit of applied nitrogen than from ammonium sulfate, as only half of the nitrogen in ammonium nitrate can be further oxidized. Industrial byproducts, such as sulfur dioxide and nitric acid, also reduce soil pH, and when released in the atmosphere they combine with rainfall and eventually enter the soil.

Bacteria also oxidize sulfur and sulfur-containing compounds to produce sulfate (SO_4^{-2}) and hydrogen ions (H^+).

Sulfur Oxidation

$$2S + 3O_2 + 2H_2O \longrightarrow 2SO_4^{-2} + 4H^+$$

2S	+	3O$_2$	+	2H$_2$O	⟶	2SO$_4^{-2}$	+	4H$^+$
sulfur		oxygen		water		sulfate		($\downarrow$ pH)

Soil Acidity

Acidity results when the number of hydrogen ions (H^+) outnumber hydroxyl ions (OH^-). Neutrality occurs when the hydrogen and hydroxyl ion concentrations are equal. The relative concentrations of these two ions drastically affect soil nutrient availability as well as plant growth.

Soil pH generally is between 5 and 7 for humid-region soils, 7 to 9 for arid-region soils, below 5 for acidic peat soils, and above 9 for sodic soils. When using this logarithmic scale, a one point change in pH equals a tenfold change in hydrogen ion concentration. For example, a pH of 4.0 is 10 times more acidic as a pH of 5.0. This means the amount of lime needed increases dramatically as pH drops.

Active acidity reflects the hydrogen concentration in the soil solution and can be measured with an indicator solution or a pH meter. Exchangeable hydrogen and aluminum ions on soil colloids represent potential or exchangeable acidity. When bases like lime are added to neutralize active acidity, potential acidity is released from the exchange sites to maintain an equilibrium between the two forms of acidity.

A common method of determining the amount of lime needed is based on the pH change of a buffered solution compared to the pH as a soil-water suspension. An acid soil will lower the pH of the buffer. By calibrating pH changes in the buffered solution (most often pH of 8) which accompany the addition of known amounts of acid, the amount of lime required to bring a soil to a particular pH can be determined. This is the soil's **buffer pH.**

Soil pH also impacts nutrient availability (Figure 3–5). Phosphorus availability is reduced at both high and low soil pH. The availability of copper, zinc, manganese, and boron are optimized at low pH, whereas molybdenum availability is decreased by low pH.

Soils dominated by hydrogen ions (e.g., low pH) are generally those that have experienced leaching of exchangeable bases due to excessive precipitation or irrigation. Soils containing high organic matter, such as peat and muck, also contain reactive carboxylic and phenolic groups that can dissociate, releasing hydrogen ions. The cations of fertilizers can also react with soils to displace adsorbed aluminum, causing a temporary reduction in pH.

Soil pH Effects on Plants

The soil pH range for optimum turf growth is 5.5 to 6.5. Soil pH below and above this range may impact plants in several ways. First, and likely most important, is the abundance of toxic elements aluminum, hydrogen, and manganese in the soil solution. Aluminum becomes more prevalent in soils when pH is below 5.8; however, aluminum toxicity to turfgrass roots generally does not occur until pH falls below 5.5 and, more typically, not until around pH 5.0. Hydrogen ion damage of root systems typically does not occur until soil pH approaches 4.0. Root systems become short, thickened, and brown with damage from aluminum and/or hydrogen. The uptake of nutrients, particularly phosphorus and calcium, and water is usually reduced by these toxicities. A decreased tolerance to environmental stresses, such as drought and heat, results, as does a decrease in the turf's recuperative potential. Manganese toxicity which affects the aboveground portion of the plant can occur at soil pH below 5.5, but is not common in turfgrasses.

Thatch accumulation and algae problems also tend to be associated with low soil pH (below 5). Naturally present bacteria that decompose thatch are less prevalent and less effective at low soil pH. Bacterial activity is also important for the release of nitrogen from organic and some slow-release fertilizers. Low pH slows the release of nitrogen from these materials.

FIGURE 3–5 Effects of soil pH on the availability of soil nutrients to plants and the population of soil organisms. The width of the bar indicates the relative availability of each element with a change in soil reaction (pH).

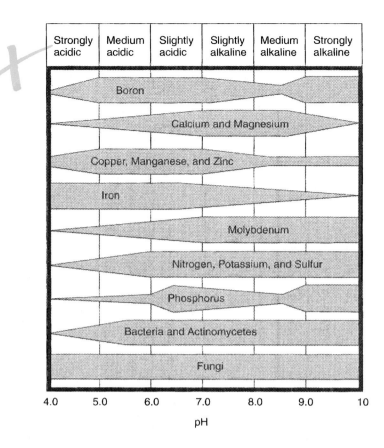

Liming Materials

A liming material by definition contains calcium (Ca) and neutralizes acidity. All liming material, whether it is the oxide (CaO), hydroxide [Ca(OH)$_2$], or carbonate (CaCO$_3$) form of calcium, react with carbon dioxide and water to yield the bicarbonate form [Ca(HCO$_3$)$_2$] when applied to an acid soil. The calcium (or magnesium) of the liming material displaces H$^+$ and Al^{+3} ions from the soil exchange complex and places them in solution with a resulting increase in the base saturation. In addition to raising the pH of acidic soils, liming materials can contribute to the plant nutrients calcium and/or magnesium, make phosphorus more available, improve microbial activity, and make potassium more efficient in plant nutrition. The general reaction of a liming material such as calcium carbonate (CaCO$_3$) being added to the soil can be written as:

Two-Step Process When Soil Is Limed with Calcium Carbonate

Step 1

$$Al^{+3} + CaCO_3 + OH^- \rightarrow Ca^{+2} + Al(OH)_3 + OH^- + CO_2\uparrow$$

aluminum   lime   calcium   aluminum hydroxide   carbon
(acid)   (calcium carbonate)   (precipitates out)   dioxide

Step 2

$$H^+ + OH^- \rightarrow H_2O$$

hydrogen ion   hydroxyl ion   ($\uparrow$pH)

As shown in the second reaction, hydrogen ions in the soil solution then combine with the hydroxyl ions (OH$^-$) to form water. This neutralization of the hydrogen ions results in an increased (or higher) soil pH. Other reactions of liming materials with acid soils are generalized as follows:

Generalized Process When Soil Is Limed with Calcium Hydroxide or Calcium Bicarbonate

$$Al^{+3}, H^+ + 2Ca(OH)_2 \rightarrow Ca^{+2} + Al(OH)_3 + H_2O$$

calcium hydroxide

$$Al^{+3}, H^+ + 2Ca(HCO_3)_2 \rightarrow Ca^{+2} + Al(OH)_3 + H_2O + 4CO_2\uparrow$$

calcium bicarbonate

Liming materials most commonly consist of calcium and calcium-magnesium carbonates (including ground, pelletized, and flowable limestone), calcium hydroxide, calcium oxide, marl, and slags (Table 3–7). Ground limestone is the most inexpensive source but is dusty and not as easily spread as the pelletized form.

Flowable limestone is available as a liquid. It is dust-free and can uniformly be applied with a spray unit, but only small amounts can be applied at one time and the spray suspension may be abrasive to sprayer parts. The liming material has a fineness of <60-mesh (or <250 μm).

Pelletized limestone is ground limestone (either calcitic or dolomitic) which is aggregated into larger particles to aid in spreading and reduce dust. These pellets disintegrate quickly when they become wet.

In addition, localized sources of other materials containing calcium and/or magnesium are used as liming agents, including fly ash from coal-burning electrical power plants, ash from hardwoods, sludge from water-treatment plants, pulp mill lime, flue dust from cement manufacturing, and carbide lime. The relative purity or neutralizing value (also referred to as the calcium carbonate equivalent) is shown in Table 3–8. Application rates are adjusted according to the source used, as impurities such as clay often lower the neutralizing values of many limestone sources. A good lime source should have a neutralizing value of 70 or higher.

TABLE 3–7 *Characteristics of commonly used liming materials.*

Source	Alternative name(s)	Chemical symbol	Characteristics
Calcium carbonates	calcite calcitic limestone aglime marl chalk	$CaCO_3$	Contains approximately 40 percent calcium when pure. Often used when magnesium is not needed. Marl is lime from deposits in the bottom of small freshwater ponds while chalk is soft limestone deposits in oceans.
Calcium-magnesium carbonates	dolomite	$CaMg(CO_3)_2$	Generally has about 50 percent calcium carbonate, 35 percent magnesium carbonate, and 15 percent soil and other impurities. Used when magnesium is needed. Often pelletized to increase ease of application.
	dolomitic limestone	$CaMg(CO_3)_2$	Has unequal proportions of calcium and magnesium carbonate with 21 to 30 percent calcium and 6 to 11 percent magnesium. Used when magnesium is needed.
Calcium oxide and/or magnesium oxide	unslaked lime burned lime quicklime	CaO or $CaO + MgO$	White powdery substance which is the most effective and quickest reacting liming material. However, these have high burn potential, are caustic to handle, and difficult to soil mix.
Calcium hydroxide	slaked lime hydrated lime builder's lime	$Ca(OH)_2$	White powdery substance similar to calcium oxide except moisture has been added. Second most effective and quickest reacting material; however, like calcium oxide, calcium hydroxide has a high burn potential, is caustic to handle, and is difficult to soil mix. Also used to make mortar.
Slags	blast-furnace slag basic slag electric-furnace slags	mostly by calcium silicate $(CaSiO_3)$	Byproduct of iron manufacturing which is ground and screened. Effective if locally available and economically priced. Basic slag also often contains phosphorus (2 to 17 percent), magnesium (about 3 percent), and iron.

TABLE 3–8 *Relative neutralizing values of common liming materials compared to calcium carbonate.*

Material	Relative neutralizing value
Calcium carbonate (CaCO$_3$)	100
Dolomitic lime (CaMg(CO$_3$)$_2$)	95 to 108
Calcitic lime (CaCO$_3$ + impurities)	85 to 100
Baked oyster shells (CaCO$_3$ + impurities)	80 to 90
Burned oyster shells (CaCO$_3$ + impurities)	90 to 110
Marl (CaCO$_3$ + impurities)	50 to 90
Burned lime (calcium oxide, CaO)	150 to 175
Hydrated lime (calcium hydroxide, slake lime, builder's lime, Ca(OH)$_2$)	120 to 135
Basic slag (calcium oxide, CaO + impurities, or CaSiO$_3$)	50 to 70
Gypsum (calcium sulfate, CaSO$_4$)	0

The higher the neutralizing value, the less lime is required to change pH. For example, if burned lime had a neutralizing value of 160, 63 pounds of this material would produce the same effect on pH as 100 pounds of calcium carbonate. Table 3–9 lists various conversion factors for calcium and magnesium sources used for liming.

Calcium and Calcium-Magnesium Carbonates

Calcium and calcium-magnesium carbonates are commonly referred to as calcitic and dolomitic limestone. Various forms of calcium and calcium-magnesium carbonates occur, including:

calcite or calcitic limestone (also known as calcium carbonate or CaCO$_3$) —composed primarily of crystalline calcium carbonate, containing approximately 40 percent calcium when pure and only trace amounts of magnesium. Also called aglime.
dolomite [CaMg(CO$_3$)$_2$] —has equal molecular proportions of calcium (CaCO$_3$) and magnesium carbonate (MgCO$_3$).
dolomitic limestone —has unequal proportions of calcium and magnesium carbonate, with calcium dominant, from 21 to 30 percent, and normally magnesium of 6 to 11 percent.

Limestone is most often obtained by open-pit mining. The neutralizing capability of most agricultural limestones containing calcium and calcium-magnesium carbonates is commonly between 90 and 98 percent because of associated impurities such as clay. Dolomitic lime is recommended for acidic soils low in magnesium, and for sandy soils of low nutrient-retention capacity.

Calcium Oxide and/or Magnesium Oxide (CaO, or CaO plus MgO)

This source is also known as ***unslaked lime, burned lime,*** or ***quicklime.*** Calcium oxide is produced by roasting calcitic or dolomitic limestone (CaCO$_3$ or CaCO$_3$ and MgCO$_3$) in an oven, driving off carbon dioxide, resulting in a white powder (CaO, or CaO and MgO) which is caustic and difficult to handle. It is the most effective and most quickly reacting of all liming materials. It has a neutralizing value of up to 179 percent compared with calcium carbonate (calcite). However, it has a high potential to injure (burn) plants, an increased cost, and is difficult to thoroughly mix with the soil without almost immediately caking. Calcium oxide is not widely used or recommended in turf management. It is often used in the building industry for various brick-laying mortars.

Calcium Hydroxide (Ca(OH)$_2$)

This source is also known as ***slaked lime, hydrated lime,*** or ***builder's lime,*** since it also is used in making mortar. It is produced by hydrating (adding water to) calcium oxide (CaO), and is the second most effective and quickly reacting of liming materials, with a neutralizing value of up to 136 percent. Like calcium oxide, calcium hydroxide is a white, powdery substance, which is difficult and unpleasant to handle, and has a high degree of burn potential to plants.

TABLE 3–9 *Conversion factors for various calcium and magnesium sources used for liming.*

$CaCO_3$	×	0.56	=	CaO	$MgCO_3$	×	0.48	=	MgO
$CaCO_3$	×	0.40	=	Ca	$MgCO_3$	×	0.29	=	Mg
CaO	×	0.71	=	Ca	MgO	×	0.60	=	Mg
CaO	×	1.78	=	$CaCO_3$	MgO	×	2.09	=	$MgCO_3$
Ca	×	1.40	=	CaO	Mg	×	1.66	=	MgO
Ca	×	2.50	=	$CaCO_3$	Mg	×	3.48	=	$MgCO_3$
$CaCO_3$	×	0.84	=	$MgCO_3$	$MgCO_3$	×	1.19	=	$CaCO_3$
$CaMg(CO_3)_2$	×	0.43	=	Ca					
$CaMg(CO_3)_2$	×	0.63	=	CaO					
$CaMg(CO_3)_2$	×	1.09	=	$CaCO_3$					

Ammonia gas, which may injure grass, also can form if calcium hydroxide and ammonia-based nitrogen fertilizers are applied close (e.g., within two weeks) to each other.

Marl

Marl, also known as **bog lime,** is mined from shallow, natural deposits of soft calcium carbonates, often being quite moist and impure. **Shell marl** is bog lime or marl that contains numerous shells. When present, marl may become mixed with surface organic soils or peat. These normally acidic organic soils thus become neutral or even alkaline due to the liming action of the marl. Many of the peat or muck sod farms in south Florida, for example, are on soils with marl intermixing. These soils are almost always low in magnesium as well as potassium, phosphorus, copper, and zinc. Marl, when mined for liming purposes, has a neutralizing value between 50 and 90 percent, depending on the amount of impurities (clay and organic matter) it contains. Oyster shells and other seashells are composed mostly of calcium carbonate, and can also make acceptable liming materials when properly pulverized. **Chalk** is from soft calcic limestone deposits in oceans.

Slags

Slags are the byproduct of smelting operations and contain mostly calcium silicate ($CaSiO_3$). The calcium and magnesium are present as silicates and not as carbonates or oxides as in limestone or quicklime. A slag is formed when metal is made. The slag is then ground, screened, and shipped for use as a liming material. Three important slags include blast-furnace slag, basic slag, and electric-furnace slag. Their neutralizing values range from 65 to 90 percent, and each has been shown to be effective liming material if locally available and economically priced. They often contain significant levels of phosphorus (2 to 17 percent), magnesium (about 3 percent), and iron as well.

Liquid Lime Materials

Liquid lime materials are available which consist of finely ground limestone (50 percent), water (47 percent), clay (2 percent), and a dispersing agent (1 percent). Since the particle size of the limestone is extremely small, the reaction rate is as rapid as a finely ground limestone. The advantage of using a liquid lime over a finely ground dry limestone is the liquid lime can be applied more uniformly and with less mess. Liquid lime materials are generally more costly than dry limestone, but their ease in utilization may justify the increased cost in some situations. Due to potential plant phytotoxicity, only small amounts of liquid lime can be applied at one time and the spray suspension may be abrasive to sprayer parts.

Pelletized Limestone

This form of limestone consists of small particles compressed to form a granule. Upon application and wetting, the pellet is dispersed into smaller particles. The advantage of pelletized lime over standard limestone materials is minimum dust and ease of application. Complete dispersion of the individual particles is necessary for a pelletized lime to be as effective as standard finely ground limestone.

Fineness and Purity of Liming Material

The fineness of a liming material will determine how fast it reacts with a soil to neutralize acidity. The finer the limestone, the more soil surface it contacts and the more quickly it reacts. However, the cost of limestone increases with its fineness. Powder-like limestone also is difficult to handle and to uniformly apply. Although faster acting, the effects of fine limestone are not as long-lasting as for coarser materials since coarser materials dissolve slower. Therefore, most agricultural limestone contains both coarse and fine materials. In general, a pulverized limestone, which will pass a 10-mesh screen (at least 50 percent passing a 100-mesh screen), should provide desirable results, and yet be economical. Particles unable to pass an 8-mesh screen have almost no effect on soil pH.

Incorporation and Mixing

Since limestone is relatively insoluble (only one pound will dissolve in 500 gallons of water), the extent of contact between the soil and the limestone is important in determining how fast the limestone will react and increase soil pH. The best time to adjust soil pH is during construction. Uniformly mixed limestone maximizes the neutralization of soil acidity, whereas clumps of limestone react slowly. Limestone should be thoroughly mixed into the upper six to eight inches (15 to 20 cm) of soil based on soil analysis of the same soil depth.

Once the turf is established, lime application rates should be based on the soil analysis of the upper four inches (10 cm) of soil, and limestone applications are applied to the soil surface. Surface-applied limestone is in contact with very little soil; therefore, it reacts extremely slowly and the downward movement of neutralization is minimal. With established turf, soil pH should be monitored and adjusted (if necessary) annually, since correction with lime will be slow. Liming after core aerification is a way to more uniformly mix limestone into the soil on established turfgrass and increase the amount of neutralization occurring beyond the upper inch (2.5 cm) of soil.

It should be noted that limestone crushed for road construction is generally too coarse to be effective in lowering soil pH. Even if this material is applied in excessive amounts, it is usually inferior to a finer ground source in raising soil pH.

Selecting a Liming Material

When choosing a liming material, the degree of fineness, neutralizing value, magnesium content, plant-tissue burn potential, and moisture content should each be considered. In most areas, materials with the least cost per unit of neutralizing value should be considered, assuming the same degree exists for fineness of all materials. However, many soils are deficient in magnesium; thus, dolomitic lime is often used. Turf managers also must carefully consider the burn potential of available materials, especially when irrigation is not readily available and/or temperatures are hot. In these cases, a more slowly reacting dolomitic limestone may still be the best choice.

Most lime sources contain a certain degree of moisture to minimize dust. In many states, a maximum moisture content of 10 percent is allowed to prevent consumers from paying for more moisture than needed to reduce dust.

Most commercially available limestone sources contain impurities, reducing their overall effectiveness and ability to be active in the soil. Limestone quality is determined by two factors: (1) fineness and (2) purity or calcium carbonate equivalent (CCE). These two factors combine to produce the **effective calcium carbonate (ECC)** rating.

ECC	=	**CCE**	×	**Fineness factor**
(effective calcium carbonate)		(calcium carbonate equivalent)		

The **fineness factor** determines the activity and speed of reaction to neutralize acidity. Most states have laws requiring percentages of lime that must pass through a 20-mesh sieve (0.84 mm opening). Activity factor of limestone sizes is based on the fraction of the material effective over a two- to three-year period. Activity factors can be found in Table 3–10.

TABLE 3–10 *Determining limestone activity over a two- to three-year period based on its particle size.*

Sieve size	Particle size (mm)	Activity factor
Coarser than 8-mesh	> 2.36	0
8- to 40-mesh	0.425 to 2.36	25
40- to 60-mesh	0.250 to 0.425	60
Finer than 60-mesh	< 0.250	100

According to this table, 60 percent of limestone passing through a 40-mesh sieve but not through a 60-mesh would be active in increasing pH over two to three years.

Calcium carbonate equivalent (CCE) measures the ability to neutralize acid relative to an identical weight of pure $CaCO_3$. In most cases, natural limestone has CCE values less than 100 percent because of impurities. CCE is determined in laboratories by combining $CaCO_3$ with hydrochloric acid (HCl). The solution is then titrated with a base, sodium hydroxide (NaOH), to determine the CCE. Liming materials can have CCE ranging from 50 to 150. A liming material with a CCE of 50 percent would have only one-half (0.5) of the neutralizing value of pure $CaCO_3$. In contrast, a liming material with a CCE of 150 percent would have 1.5 times the neutralizing value of pure $CaCO_3$.

Example:

A 100 gram sample of limestone was shaken through a set of sieves. Five grams were retained on the 8-mesh sieve, 15 grams were retained on the 40-mesh, 40 grams were retained on the 60-mesh, and 20 grams passed the 60-mesh. The limestone has a CCE of 95 percent. Find the effective calcium carbonate (ECC) and lime required to satisfy a recommendation of 5,000 pounds lime/A.

Step 1: Determine the fineness factor:

Sieve size	Retained (g)	×Activity factor	= Percent available for reaction
Coarser than 8-mesh	5 g	0	0
8- to 40-mesh	5 g	0.25	1.25
40- to 60-mesh	20 g	0.60	12
Finer than 60-mesh	70 g	1.00	70
			Sum = 83.25

In two to three years, approximately 83 percent of the liming material will be active.

Step 2: Find ECC

Since the CCE was given, multiply the CCE and fineness factor to determine the ECC.

%CCE	×	%Fineness factor	=	ECC
95	×	83.25	=	79.1

Step 3: Limestone recommendation

The ECC was found to be 79.1 percent; therefore, 79 percent of the applied limestone will be active in neutralizing acidity. The limestone recommendation was 5,000 pounds/A of pure $CaCO_3$.

$$\frac{5,000 \text{ lbs}}{\text{acre}} \times \frac{1}{79\%} = 6,329 \text{ lbs/acre } (7,089 \text{ kg/ha})$$

You would need to apply 6,329 pounds/A (7,089 kg/ha) of the tested limestone to equivalently apply 5,000 pounds (5,600 kg/ha) of pure $CaCO_3$.

TABLE 3–11 *Examples of rates of dolomitic limestone or calcium carbonate required to raise pH of sand, loam, clay, or muck soil to 6.5.*

	Pounds required per 1,000 square feet*		
Current pH	Sand	Loam	Clay or muck
6.0	20	35	50
5.5	45	75	100
5.0	65	110	150
4.5	80	150	200
4.0	100	175	230

*Multiply values by 48.83 to obtain kg/ha.

Rates

Rates of lime required to neutralize excessive acidity vary with the degree of soil weathering and soil texture (Table 3–11). Lime rate requirements depend on: (1) the change of soil pH desired, (2) the buffering capacity of the soil, and (3) the chemical composition and fineness of the liming material to be used. Soils with high cation exchange capacities, such as clay or muck soils, may require up to double the amount needed for soils of low CEC, such as sands. Sand soils, however, often require more frequent applications than clay soils.

Intensively weathered soils generally are highly aluminum dominated with low calcium and magnesium. To replace (or exchange) this aluminum, the amount of lime needed is commonly considered to be 1.5 times the amount of exchangeable aluminum listed on the soil test report.

Recommended rates should be determined by a soil testing lab, and generally do not exceed 50 to 100 pounds per 1,000 square feet (2,442 to 4,883 kg/ha). If hydrated or burned lime is used, rates over 25 pounds per 1,000 square feet (1,221 kg/ha) should be avoided in one application. Rates exceeding this, or applications during periods of hot temperatures, can injure (e.g., burn) the turfgrass. The turf should be dry at the time of application and should be immediately irrigated to wash all lime off the leaves and into the soil. If over 100 pounds per 1,000 square feet (4,883 kg/ha) are needed, splitting applications several months apart will improve the efficacy of lime use. Soil analysis will usually indicate the specific amount and type of lime needed to raise the pH of a specific soil type. Aerifying prior to lime application aids in placing the material into the rootzone.

The buffer capacity of a soil is determined in the laboratory by mixing soil with a buffer solution. The buffer solution alone has a high pH (usually around 8.0). The decrease in pH of the buffer/soil mix is an indication of the soil's buffer capacity. If the soil's buffer capacity is low, the pH of the buffer/soil mix will be close to the original pH of the buffer. If the buffer capacity of the soil is high, then the pH of the buffer/soil mix will be much lower than the initial pH of the buffer. Methods employed differ among soil test laboratories so comparisons of buffer pH readings among laboratories may not be valid, unless they use the same method to measure buffer capacity.

The purpose for applying the lime will also influence the application rate used. As noted, relatively large amounts are needed if the desire is to increase soil pH. One ton or more may be needed per acre for this purpose. If the purpose of liming is to supply calcium or magnesium to the soil as a nutrient, the amount applied is greatly reduced. If the desire is to supply these nutrients and not raise soil pH, then another source of calcium or magnesium should be used. For example, gypsum and magnesium sulfate supply calcium and magnesium, respectively, without affecting soil pH.

Example:

1. A soil test report indicates acidity of 1 meq/100 g of H^+ and 3 meq/100 g of Al^{+3}. How many pounds of $CaCO_3$ are needed per acre to totally replace these? Molecular weights: Ca = 40, C = 12, O = 16, H = 1, Al = 27. It is assumed an acre six-inches deep weighs 2,000,000 pounds.

Step 1: The equivalent weights of Ca^{+2}, Al^{+3}, and H^+ need to be determined:

equivalent weights = molecular weights ÷ valence charge:

$$Ca^{+2} \qquad = 40 \text{ g} \div 2(+2 \text{ valence charge for } Ca^{+2}) = 20 \text{ g}$$

$$Al^{+3} \qquad = 27 \text{ g} \div 3 = 9 \text{ g}$$

$$H^{+1} \qquad = 1 \text{ g} \div 1 = 1 \text{ g}$$

Step 2: Determine the total acidity of the soil composed of H^+ and Al^{+3} ions from the soil test report:

$$3 \text{ meq } Al^{+3}/100 \text{ g soil} \quad + \quad 1 \text{ meq } H^+/100 \text{ g soil} \quad = \quad 4 \text{ meq acid}/100 \text{ g soil}$$

Step 3: Determine the total amount of $CaCO_3$ needed to neutralize 4 meq acid/100 g soil and convert to a per acre basis. Two calculations can be performed to achieve these:

a. $\dfrac{4 \text{ meq}}{100 \text{ g soil}} \times \dfrac{1 \text{ eq}}{1,000 \text{ meq}} \times \dfrac{20 \text{ Ca}^{+2}}{\text{eq Ca}^{+2}} \times \dfrac{2,000,000 \text{ lbs soil}}{\text{acre}} \times \dfrac{1 \text{ lb CaCO}_3}{40\% \text{ ai}} = \dfrac{4,000 \text{ lbs}}{\text{acre}}$

b. $\dfrac{4 \text{ meq}}{100 \text{ g soil}} \times \dfrac{1 \text{ eq}}{1,000 \text{ meq}} \times \dfrac{9 \text{ g Al}^{+3}}{\text{eq Al}^{+3}} \times \dfrac{20 \text{ lbs Ca}^{+2}}{9 \text{ lbs Al}^{+3}} \times \dfrac{2,000,000 \text{ lbs soil}}{\text{acre}} \times \dfrac{1 \text{ lb CaCO}_3}{40\% \text{ ai}} = \dfrac{4,000 \text{ lbs}}{\text{acre}}$

2. You have the option to completely replace 5 meq/100 g of Al^{+3} with either $MgCO_3$ or $CaCO_3$. Which would you choose if the least amount of product was desired? 1 acre = 2,000,000 pounds soil, and equivalent weights of Ca^{+2} = 20 grams and Mg^{+2} = 12 grams.

Step 1: Determine how much $CaCO_3$ is needed to replace 5 meq/100 g Al^{+3}:

$$\dfrac{5 \text{ meq Al}^{+3}}{100 \text{ g soil}} \times \dfrac{1 \text{ eq}}{1,000 \text{ meq}} \times \dfrac{20 \text{ Ca}^{+2}}{\text{eq Ca}^{+2}} \times \dfrac{2,000,000 \text{ lbs soil}}{\text{acre}} \times \dfrac{1 \text{ lb CaCO}_3}{40\% \text{ ai}} = \dfrac{5,000 \text{ lbs CaCO}_3}{\text{acre}}$$

Step 2: Determine how much $MgCO_3$ is needed to replace 5 meq/100 g Al^{+3}:

$$\dfrac{5 \text{ meq Al}^{+3}}{100 \text{ g soil}} \times \dfrac{1 \text{ eq}}{1,000 \text{ meq}} \times \dfrac{12 \text{ Mg}^{+2}}{\text{eq Mg}^{+2}} \times \dfrac{2,000,000 \text{ lbs soil}}{\text{acre}} \times \dfrac{1 \text{ lb MgCO}_3}{28.6\% \text{ ai}} = \dfrac{4,196 \text{ lbs MgCO}_3}{\text{acre}}$$

Therefore, 4,196 pounds per acre of $MgCO_3$ is needed to neutralize 5 meq Al^{+3} per 100 grams soil compared to 5,000 pounds $CaCO_3$.

Acidic Irrigation Water

With the increase in acid rain and acidic lakes, problems with excessively low (<5.6) pH irrigation water have also increased. This is most notable around heavy industrial areas, presumably due to industrial air and water pollution problems. Acidic irrigation water not only may create problems for plants, but it also causes considerable corrosion to irrigation pumping and piping systems. A quality, powered carbonate containing material such as dolomitic lime is the material most often injected into an irrigation system to raise the pH of the irrigation water.

SOIL ALKALINITY

Soil alkalinity occurs when an excess of calcium, magnesium, or sodium ions occurs. Moderate alkalinity occurs in the pH range of 7.5 to 8.5, with excessive alkalinity above these figures. A 2 to 3 percent by weight calcium carbonate content usually results in a soil pH range between 7.5 and 8.5. In the United States, soil alkalinity is generally of greatest concern in arid (dry) or semi-arid western regions, where rainfall is minimal. Leaching of calcium, magnesium, and sodium ions does not readily occur in these areas. However, due to deposits of calcium carbonates in the form of shell marl and/or underlying limestone, or to overliming or irrigation with water from limestone aquifers, other selected areas, such as coastal regions, also can have excessive soil pH values.

Deficiencies of several micronutrients necessary for plant growth may occur as a result of excessive soil alkalinity. Iron, manganese, zinc, boron, and copper all tend to be less available to plants under these conditions. Chlorotic, unhealthy-appearing plants, often resembling nitrogen deficiency, may result (Figure 3–5). Superintendents not experienced in managing grass grown under alkaline conditions may be confused by these symptoms. The pathogenicity of several diseases is also promoted by excessively high soil pH.

Reducing Soil pH

Reducing soil alkalinity often is a never-ending chore, especially if high pH water is used for irrigation. Turf managers must constantly regulate and adjust their management programs to compensate for alkalinity. The best materials for acidifying soil are elemental sulfur and aluminum sulfate (Table 3–12). Elemental sulfur (S) is usually the most efficient and practical of these sources. The granular elemental sulfur source (90 percent powdered sulfur plus 10 percent bentonite clay) is preferred for spreading with conventional fertilizer spreaders. Oxidation of elemental sulfur produces acidity, in the form of sulfuric acid, to reduce soil pH. Sulfur-coated ureas and acid-forming fertilizers such as ammonium sulfate also are sometimes used to reduce soil pH due to the limited hydrogen ions produced via nitrification, but they do not generally contain enough sulfur or supply enough hydrogen to quickly correct the alkalinity. They can, however, gradually reduce or regulate pH if used long term. Sulfuric acid or sulfur dioxide can be injected into irrigation water to reduce its pH. Sulfuric acid, however, is very corrosive to metal and is dangerous to handle. Materials such as calcium sulfate (gypsum or $CaSO_4$), copper sulfate ($CuSO_4$), potassium sulfate (K_2SO_4), and magnesium sulfate (Epsom salt or $MgSO_4$) are neutral salts and have little acidity effect.

Table 3–13 indicates the amount of calcium carbonate neutralized by 100 pounds of various amendments and how to calculate the pounds of these amendments equivalent to pounds of sulfur.

For example, 100 pounds ammonium sulfate are needed to neutralize approximately 45 pounds of calcium carbonate while 6.9 pounds of the ammonium sulfate is required to equal the acidifying effects of one pound of elemental sulfur.

Elemental Sulfur

Elemental (or granular) sulfur ranges from 99 to 20 percent purity, or less, with the lower contents in low-grade deposits containing clay and other materials. It is a yellow, inert, water-insoluble crystalline solid. Applied elemental sulfur is oxidized by soil microorganisms, the prominent group being various *Thiobacillus* species, into sulfuric acid:

TABLE 3–12 *Sulfur-containing compounds that produce an acidifying effect* (Source: *The Sulphur Insutute*).

Material	Sulfur (%)	Sulfur content (lb/ton)	Nitrogen (%)	Other (%)
Aluminum sulfate	14	288	0	11(Al)
Ammonia-sulfur solution	10	200	74	
Ammonium bisulfite solution	17	340	9	
Ammonium polysulfide solution	40	800	20	
Ammonium sulfate	24	484	21	
Ammonium thiosulfate solution	26	520	12	
Aqua-sulfur solution	5	100	20	
Lime sulfur (dry)	57	1,140	0	43(Ca)
Lime sulfur (solution)	23 to 24	480	0	9(Ca)
Sulfuric acid (100%)	33	654	0	
Sulfuric acid (66° Be = 93%)	30	608	0	
Sulfur (Elemental)	100	2,000	0	
Sulfur dioxide	50	1,000	0	

TABLE 3–13 *Pounds of calcium carbonate ($CaCO_3$) neutralized by 100 pounds of amendment and factor needed to calculate pounds of amendment equivalent to pounds of sulfur.*

Amendment	Pounds of $CaCO_3$ neutralized by 100 pounds of amendment	Factor to calculate pounds amendment equivalent to pounds sulfur
Aluminum sulfate	45	6.9
Ammonium nitrate	59	5.3
Ammonium sulfate	110	2.8
Diammonium phosphate	70	4.5
Monoammonium phosphate	65	4.8
Sulfuric acid	100	3.1
Sulfur	312	1.0
Sulfur coated urea	118	2.6
Urea	84	3.7
Ureaformaldehyde	68	4.6

Conversion of Elemental Sulfur to Sulfuric Acid by Soil Microorganisms

$$S + \tfrac{3}{2}O_2 + H_2O \xrightarrow[\text{(\textit{Thiobacillus} spp.)}]{\text{microorganisms}} H_2SO_4$$

elemental sulfur   oxygen   water   (*Thiobacillus* spp.)   sulfuric acid

Sulfuric acid is considered a "strong" acid since it readily dissociates, releasing its hydrogen ions that lower soil pH. The conversion of elemental sulfur to sulfuric acid, because it is a biological reaction involving microorganisms, increases with increasing temperature. This conversion does not occur readily when soil temperatures are below 40°F (4.4°C). A steady increase in oxidation occurs above 40°F (4.4°C); however, a *sharp* increase occurs at temperatures above 70°F. Smaller particle-sized material also reacts faster than larger particles.

Oxidation also is optimum when soil moisture is near field capacity. Excessive soil moisture, however, reduces the degree of soil aeration needed for oxidation; thus, sulfur conversion is reduced.

Approximately one-third the quantity of sulfur is required to reduce soil pH by one unit as the amount of lime needed to raise it the same amount (Table 3–14). It would be difficult to decrease the pH of soils containing sufficient free calcium carbonate (e.g., > 8 percent) without adding excessive, and most often impractical, sulfur amounts.

After application, elemental sulfur should be thoroughly mixed into the top six to eight inches (15 to 20 cm) of soil. Best and fastest results follow thorough mixing either by a power rotor-tiller or by running a disk in several directions across the treated area. Adequate soil moisture (though not saturation) is necessary for this conversion to occur. Irrigation should therefore begin immediately after sulfur incorporation and should be continued at regular intervals to maintain moisture levels near field capacity, as long as oxidation is desired. This process may take several months, especially if initial soil pH is high or if soil temperatures are cool.

Established Turf

Once the turf is established, significantly reducing soil pH becomes much more difficult because of the plant-tissue burn that can occur when using high rates of acidifying materials. Since elemental sulfur is sparingly soluble, it also does not readily move down the soil profile, and tends to reduce soil pH (by an amount greater than desired) only in a thin zone near the application surface. This results in little benefit to the roots from the acidifying effect. Care must be taken not to create too toxic a surface acidic layer near the turf-plant crown surface. To minimize the injury potential, and to facilitate sulfur's acidifying effects in the turfgrass rootzone, it is suggested elemental sulfur application be in conjunction with turf coring or aerification.

TABLE 3–14 *Approximate amounts of elemental sulfur (99 percent purity) per 1,000 square feet to lower soil pH to 6.5 in the top seven inches (17.8 cm) of soils before planting. To determine application rates of other amendments, use the conversion factors in the last column of Table 3–13.*

Current pH	Pounds per 1,000 square feet*		
	Sandy	Loam	Clay or muck
8.5	35 to 50	50 to 60	60 to 70
8.0	25 to 30	30 to 35	40 to 50
7.5	10 to 15	15 to 20	20 to 25
7.0	2 to 3	3 to 5	5 to 8

*Multiply by 43.5 to convert rates to pounds per acre or 48.83 to obtain kg/ha.

If a soil is inherently alkaline, the turf manager basically has two methods of reducing pH once the site has been established in grass. One is to use ammonia-based fertilizers, such as ammonium nitrate or ammonium sulfate. Hydrogen ions produced during nitrification (the conversion of the ammonium to nitrite and nitrate) will help reduce soil pH.

Nitrification of Ammonium-Based Fertilizer to Reduce Soil pH

$$NH_4^+ \quad + \quad 2O_2 \quad \rightarrow \quad 2H^+ \quad + \quad NO_3^- \quad + \quad H_2O$$

ammonium $\quad\quad$ oxygen $\quad\quad\quad\quad$ ($\downarrow$pH) $\quad\quad$ nitrate $\quad\quad$ water

The other procedure is to add small, frequent applications of sulfur to the turf. Only elemental sulfur or sulfur compounds oxidized to sulfate ion produce the desired acidification (Table 3–12). Up to five pounds of elemental sulfur may be applied per 1,000 square feet (25 kg/100 m^2) on taller maintained grasses, such as fairways or roughs. Applications to putting greens should be no greater than one-half pound per 1,000 square feet (2.4 kg/100 m^2). Applications should be spaced at least three to four weeks apart. Application during hot weather also should be avoided, as should application to wet leaf surfaces, and each application should be followed by irrigation. Total application of elemental sulfur should not exceed 10 pounds per 1,000 square feet yearly (49 kg/100 m^2). Excessive amounts of sulfur and/or excessive watering (e.g., lack of soil oxygen) can result in hydrogen sulfide (H_2S) formation, which reacts with trace metal ions and precipitates in soils as compounds such as FeS_2, instead of escaping as a gas. The formation of a "black-layer" one to two inches (2.5 to 5 cm) below the putting green surface is evidence of this. Other toxic components associated with soils of low oxygen content include carbon dioxide (CO_2) and methane (CH_4). Proper aerification and irrigation management minimize the chance of such conditions occurring. Applications during winter may not produce the desired results until spring when temperatures are warm enough to drive the reaction. Excessive application therefore may occur since immediate results are not seen and additional materials are applied in an attempt to speed up the reaction. Oftentimes in spring, following this scenario, the added sulfur begins to oxidize at the same time and the pH in the top inch (2.5 cm) of soil dramatically drops.

Acid-Injection

If the soil pH is raised by bicarbonate levels in the irrigation source, then a sulfur-injection system may be used to maintain or lower water pH. Reducing soil pH also helps dissolve insoluble carbonates (salts) into much more soluble bicarbonates to help flush and remove various salts from the soil surface.

Reducing Soil pH by Dissolving Carbonates into Soluble Bicarbonate

$$CaCO_3 \quad + \quad H^+ \quad\quad\quad\quad\quad \leftrightarrow \quad Ca^{+2} \quad\quad + \quad HCO_3^-$$

insoluble calcium $\quad$ hydrogen ions from acid $\quad$ soluble calcium$\downarrow$ $\quad$ soluble bicarbonate$\downarrow$
carbonate $\quad\quad\quad\quad$ injection

Elemental sulfur, in its pure form, is insoluble and therefore cannot be applied alone with the irrigation water. However, a slurry of finely graded sulfur with about 2 percent clay results in a

FIGURE 3-6 Pelletized form (chips or flakes) of sulfur used to reduce the pH of irrigation water. The chips are melted before being incorporated into the irrigation line.

suspension containing 40 to 60 percent sulfur, and can generally be successfully used with the irrigation water. Recently, pelletized forms (chips) of sulfur have been introduced that must be heated prior to irrigation injection (Figure 3-6).

Sulfuric acid also is sometimes added to the irrigation water. Sulfuric acid is a heavy, corrosive liquid that is dangerous to handle and is corrosive to most metals, concrete pipes, and culverts. However, its reaction time is much faster than elemental sulfur, it does not require a bacterial oxidation process like elemental sulfur, and it reacts with calcium in the soil to form gypsum in place. Sulfuric acid is combined with the water before it enters the pump station. The sulfuric acid is first diluted and then mixed with a large volume of water in a wet well, avoiding pressure injection that may be unsafe. Courses without a wet well may be restricted to an acidic fertilizer injection system using fertigation techniques. All equipment used to handle and apply sulfuric acid should be constructed of stainless steel or other noncorrosive materials. Workers also must be extremely careful when handling or applying this material, and should always wear protective clothing.

Another product often used as an acidifying solution is monocarbamide dihydrogensulfate, which is formed from the reaction of urea and sulfuric acid. The acidic fertilizer or monocarbamide dihydrogensulfate should be injected into a plastic pipe rather than an iron irrigation line to minimize corrosion. The operator also should keep good records as dual application of an acidic fertilizer with a urea nitrogen source in this fertigation set-up may lower the soil pH more than desired.

Phosphoric acid also is used for acidification of irrigation water. Although useful, at pH above 6.0, phosphoric acid may react with calcium and magnesium ions in the water to form insoluble calcium or magnesium phosphate which may clog or significantly interfere with irrigation head operation.

Benefits of Sulfur

In addition to lowering soil pH, several additional benefits are associated with sulfur applications. Sulfur is required as one of the 16 essential elements for plant growth, and is necessary for root growth, chlorophyll production, protein synthesis, and tissue development. Turfgrasses require almost as much sulfur, for example, as they do phosphorus. For nutritional purposes, turfgrasses require approximately one pound of sulfur per 1,000 square feet per year (4.9 kg/100 m^2).

Sulfur also sometimes reduces the incidence of several plant diseases, especially "patch" diseases, and annual bluegrass (*Poa annua*) levels. Research indicates one-half pound of elemental sulfur per 1,000 square feet (2.4 kg/100 m^2) on golf greens, and two pounds per 1,000 square feet (9.8 kg/100 m^2) on higher-cut turfgrass, reduces several patch diseases. Rates of 3 1/2 pounds per

1,000 square feet per year (17 kg/100 m^2) also has gradually reduced annual bluegrass stands. Superintendents should regularly test the soil to ensure soil pH is not drastically reduced after sulfur application in a short period of time.

Sampling Soils for Nutrient Recommendations

There are many different soil types and soil fertility conditions on a golf course. This arises from natural variation in soils in the landscape, as well as from soil disturbance and movement during construction, and from construction of artificial soils such as those used for putting greens. If topsoil is moved during construction, subsoil may become exposed. Topsoil and subsoils in most cases have very different soil fertility levels. In addition, the previous use of the soil will also alter its nutrient and pH status. Land previously cropped will likely have much higher fertility and pH levels than forested land. Once the golf course is established, differences in fertilization, liming, irrigation, and removal of clippings will be practiced dependent on the playing surface in question. Soil samples should be taken to represent differences in soil type, prior land use, and current management practices because all these factors can dramatically alter soil fertility levels.

Soil cores should be taken in a random pattern throughout the area to be sampled. Fifteen to twenty soil cores (about 0.75 inches, 1.9 cm, in diameter) should be obtained from each area. Soil samples should be taken with a soil probe, auger, or other implement that can make a relatively straight hole into the ground to a depth of six inches (15 cm). Soil cores should be placed in a clean plastic bucket, thoroughly mixed, and approximately one pint of soil should be removed for analysis. Paper or cardboard are preferred over plastic because the porous media allows the samples to dry out, preventing changes in the levels of some soil nutrients and facilitating analysis. Once the samples arrive in the laboratory they will be dried, ground, and then partitioned (by weighing or scooping, dependent on the lab) for the various analyses.

The recommended depth of soil sampling is greater before, rather than after, turf establishment because the best opportunity to correct low levels of soil pH and phosphorus happens prior to turf establishment. Prior to establishment, therefore, soil samples should be taken to a depth of six inches (15 cm), which is a reasonable depth for the incorporation and mixing of lime and fertilizer. After establishment, the sampling depth should be adjusted for the depth of turfgrass rooting. Generally, this ranges from two to four inches (5 to 10 cm) for turfgrasses mowed frequently at fairway height or lower.

Soil samples should be taken at least annually on a well-maintained golf course. Ideally, samples should be taken prior to the period of maximum fertilization—in spring for warm-season grasses and in fall for cool-season grasses. Soils different in color, texture, drainage, and composition should be sampled separately. Greens and tees also should be sampled separately, as should most fairways and roughs. Soil pH measurements and subsequent lime applications (if needed) can be performed in winter since lime is relatively slow to react.

Foliar tissue testing should be performed periodically to compare those levels actually in the plant compared to those levels in the soil and to discover any hidden nutrient deficiencies. About one cup, or enough to fill a sandwich-size ziplock-bag, of fresh clippings should be collected. Use a plastic bag, as paper bags may have boron residues. The person taking samples also should be a non-smoker, since cigarettes may leave a nitrogen residue and minerals on fingers. In order not to distort the results with residues, do not collect clippings within 10 days of applying lime, fertilizer (granular or liquid), or pesticides.

CHAPTER
4

Soil Mineral Properties and Drainage Characteristics

INTRODUCTION

Soil is a mixture of mineral matter and organic sources. Mineral soils consist of minerals (approximately 50 percent by volume), water (approximately 25 percent), and air (approximately 25 percent). Some soils also contain a small amount (<5 percent) of organic matter (Figure 4–1). The type, size, and relative proportions of the mineral components and the amount and nature of the organic fraction affect the soil's physical and chemical properties. These properties in turn determine the soil's ability to hold water, its nutrient availability, its susceptibility to compaction, its potential for pesticide leaching, its disease and nematode levels, and other characteristics. Important soil physical properties include: (1) depth of soils, (2) soil texture, (3) bulk density, (4) soil porosity, (5) infiltration rates, (6) hydraulic conductivity, and (7) water-holding capacity.

FIGURE 4–1 "Ideal" soils are composed of approximately 50 percent solids (minerals), 25 percent each of water and air (pores), and possibly a small (≤5 percent) fraction of organic matter.

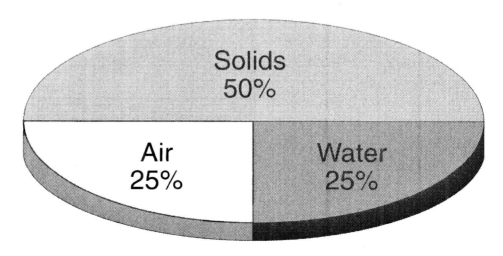

SOIL PHYSICAL PROPERTIES

Soil Particle Analysis

Many of a soil's physical properties are influenced by the size distribution of its particles. For the purposes of quantifying and describing soil texture, soil mineral particle sizes are subdivided into three fractions based on the average diameter of the particle: sand, silt, and clay. The relative proportion of these fractions in a soil determine its texture.

According to the **U.S. Department of Agriculture (USDA) classification system,** particle sizes greater than two millimeters are classified as gravel. Sand particles are between 0.05 to 2.0 millimeters, silt 0.002 to 0.05 millimeters, and clay < 0.002 millimeters (Table 4–1). Subdivisions within the sand fraction are very coarse, coarse, medium, fine, and very fine. The United States Golf Association (USGA) utilizes the USDA system with a slight modification in the classification of very fine sand (USGA, 0.05 to 0.15 mm versus USDA, 0.05 to 0.10 mm) and fine sand (USGA, 0.15 to 0.25 mm versus USDA, 0.10 to 0.25 mm).

Particle-size analysis provides a general description of physical and textural soil properties and is the basis for assigning the soil's textural class name (e.g., sand, sandy loam, clay, etc.). Once the percentages of sand, silt, and clay in a soil have been identified, the soil's textural class can be determined by using the USDA textural triangle (Figure 4–2). Twelve soil textural classes make up the USDA textural triangle. Some familiar soil textural names are loamy sand, sandy loam, loam, and silt loam. To determine soil textural class from sieve and sedimentation analysis, first find the percent of sand along the base of the triangle and follow the corresponding diagonal line up and to the left. Then find the percent of clay on the left leg of the triangle and draw a horizontal line toward the right leg of the triangle. The intersection of the sand and clay percentage lines indicates the textural class of the soil. For example, if the particle-size distribution of a soil is 40 percent sand, 40 percent silt, and 20 percent clay, the 40 percent sand and 20 percent clay lines intersect at the center of the loam textural classification.

To facilitate the understanding of soil texture and its relation to other soil properties and turf practices such as fertilization, liming, irrigation, and drainage, soil texture has general classes and detailed subclasses. These include:

1. **Clays**—clay, silty clay, and sandy clay
2. **Clay loams**—clay loam, silty clay loam, and sandy clay loam
3. **Loams**—loam, silt loam, sandy loam, and loamy sand
4. **Others**—silt and sand

The term "loam" implies the soil possesses properties of all three particle fractions (sand, silt, and clay), but none to a dominant degree. If one particular particle size sufficiently alters the proper-

TABLE 4–1 *Particle-size classifications as determined by the United States Department of Agriculture.*

Textural name		Particle-size range (mm)	U.S. standard (sieve number)	Sieve opening (mm)	Number of particles per gram	Typical settling velocity
Gravel	Gravel	> 4.76	4	4.76	< 2	20 cm/sec
	Fine gravel	2.00 to 4.76	10	2.00	11	3 cm/sec
Sand	Very coarse sand	1.00 to 2.00	18	1.00	90	1 cm/sec
	Coarse sand	0.50 to 1.00	35	0.50	720	13 cm/min
	Medium sand	0.25 to 0.50	60	0.25	5,700	3 cm/min
	Fine sand	0.10 to 0.25	140	0.10	46,000	31 cm/hr
	Very fine sand	0.05 to 0.10	270	0.05	722,000	6 cm/hr
Silt	—	0.002 to 0.05	—	—	5,776,000	1.3 mm/hr
Clay	—	< 0.002	—	—	90,260,853,000	<1.3 mm/hr

FIGURE 4–2 The United States Department of Agriculture's textural triangle is used to determine the textural class based on sand, silt, and clay content.

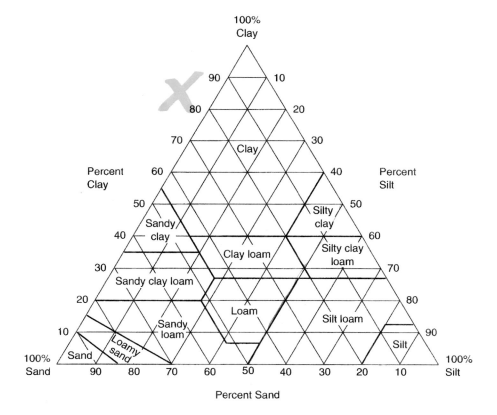

ties of the soil, then a modifying term is used (e.g., clay loam, silt loam, or sandy loam). Loam-textured soils are generally considered to possess the best overall physical properties for plant growth.

General descriptions for soil classification include:

1. A "sand" soil is high (85 to 100 percent) in sand content and contains small amounts (0 to 15 percent) each of silt and clay.
2. As the silt or clay content increases, the soil becomes either "loamy sand" or "sandy loam." A "loamy sand" is 70 to 90 percent sand, 0 to 30 percent silt, and 10 to 30 percent clay. A "sandy loam" is 45 to 85 percent sand, 0 to 50 percent silt, and 15 to 55 percent clay. A "loam" soil contains 40 percent sand, 40 percent silt, and 20 percent clay.
3. A "clay" soil is mostly (~60 percent) clay, with approximately 20 percent each sand and silt.

The sand fraction consists mostly of primary minerals such as quartz, feldspars, micas, and other weather-resistant minerals. Silts are basically weathered sands and primary minerals plus additional minerals susceptible to weathering. Silt particles feel smooth like powder. Clay particles tend to be plate-like rather than spherical like many sand particles, and consist mostly of secondary or clay minerals like kaolinite, montmorillonite, vermiculite, illite, and sesquioxides (iron and aluminum oxides). Surface areas of clay particles are many times greater than those of sand or silt; thus, they adsorb much more water. Conversely, when certain clay soils are dried, very hard soil clods often form due to the enormous area of contact between the plate-shaped clay particles.

Some sand companies provide particle-size distribution information, but in many cases the analysis is based on engineering criteria rather than the USDA sieve sizes. The construction industry often defines sand broadly by particle-size distribution as follows:

Concrete sand is typically composed of a broad distribution of sand-sized particles and some fine gravel-sized particles.

Mason's sand is similar to concrete sand but without the fine gravel.

Dune sand is wind- or water-deposited; thus, it has a narrow particle-size range.

River sand is from river bottom deposits and can vary in particle-size uniformity from very uniform to highly variable, and often contains silt and clay.

Determining Particle Size

Particle-size analysis is based on **sieving** and **sedimentation methods.** To determine particle size, a sample of soil is broken up and particles larger than silt (e.g., gravel and sand) are separated into their various size groups, as outlined in Table 4–1, by the use of sieves. The weight of each group is found to determine a percentage of total sample weight. Silt and clay percentages are determined based on the rate of settling of these two separates in a suspension. This method involves the proportionality of clay and silt settling rates to their size (particle diameter). The larger the particle (e.g., sand or gravel), the quicker it will settle in a suspension (e.g., water) solution. Conversely, the smaller the particles (e.g., silt and clay), the slower settling occurs. This is referred to as **Stokes' law** (Appendix A). Sand generally takes only several minutes or less to settle, while silt takes several hours and clay requires up to several days.

Another method of measuring particle-size distribution in suspension is based on the rate of settling by monitoring changes in the specific gravity of the suspension. A **hydrometer** is a device used to measure suspension density at various times, thus reflecting the amount of particles that remain in suspension after a certain settling time. A hydrometer with a Bouyoucos scale in grams per liter (g/L) is used to determine the amount of soil in suspension. The greater the density of a suspension, the greater the buoyant force on the hydrometer and the higher the reading. As particles settle out of the suspension, density decreases and a lower reading is obtained. Since temperature influences the settling rate, a temperature correction must be made if the suspension temperature differs from the temperature at which the hydrometer is calibrated.

Particle Shape and Soil Structure

Particle shape may also influence whether a particular soil is acceptable for the construction of golf greens and sports fields. Nearly round sand particles can result in excessive percolation rates and less-stable soil surfaces. Particles too angular may provide excessive bulk density that leads to unacceptable soil compaction. **Soil structure** is the grouping of individual soil particles into aggregates, which are formed when soil particles adhere to each other and behave as a single soil unit. Aeration, hydraulic conductivity, bulk density, and porosity are soil properties highly influenced by structure. Soil structure, like texture, may vary with depth in the soil, as well as across the landscape. However, unlike texture, soil structure may be altered. Destruction of soil structure is generally detrimental and may occur rapidly with misuse. By comparison, improving soil structure is a slow and difficult process.

Soils where structure is absent are often referred to as "structureless." This term denotes a condition where individual soil particles are not arranged into aggregates. Sand-textured soils with low organic matter contents are often essentially structureless. Some subsoil horizons may also be structureless.

Particle Density and Bulk Density

Two important weight measurements of soils include **particle density** and **bulk density.** Particle density is the average density of soil particles and is defined as mass (weight) of dry soil per unit volume of soil solids, not including pore volumes occupied by air or water. Generally, mineral soils (sands, silts, clays) have higher particle densities than organic matter. Particle density can vary considerably, but for most mineral soils this range has a narrow limit of 2.60 to 2.75 g/cm^3 (or g/cc) while organic matter has a lower particle density of 1.1 to 1.4 g/cm^3. An average mineral soil (minerals and organic matter) has a particle density of 2.65 g/cm^3. For comparison, water, steel, and lead have densities of 1.0, 7.7, and 11.3 g/cm^3, respectively.

Bulk density is a measure of soil compaction (or density) and is defined as the mass (weight) of dry soil per given unit volume, including both solids and pores occupied by air and water.

$$\text{bulk density} = \frac{\text{weight of dry soil (g)}}{\text{total soil volume (cm}^3)}$$

Bulk density, unlike particle density, is an indicator of pore space volume in addition to soil solids. Since most soils are about half solids and half pore space by volume, bulk densities tend

TABLE 4–2 *Typical bulk density and total porosity values for various soil textural classes.*

Soil textural class	Bulk density, g/cm^3 (lb/ft^3)	Porosity, %
Sands or compact clay	1.4 to 1.8 (87 to 112)	35 to 45 (low)
Loam	1.2 to 1.6 (75 to 100)	45 to 50 (medium)
Loose silt loams or clay	1.0 to 1.4 (62 to 87)	55 to 60 (high)
Organic soils	0.2 to 1.0 (12 to 62)	60 to 70 (very high)

FIGURE 4–3 Compacted soils (left) have higher bulk densities (number of particles in a given volume); thus, they have slower water infiltration and percolation compared to noncompacted soils (right).

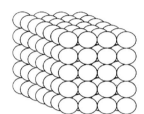
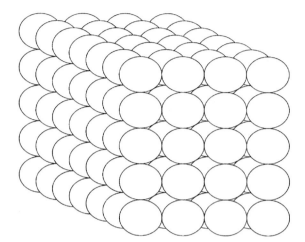

to be about half of the particle density. A typical acre of soil six inches deep weighs approximately 2,000,000 pounds, assuming an average bulk density of 1.5 g/cm^3.

$$6 \text{ inch} \times \frac{1 \text{ ft deep}}{12 \text{ inches}} \times \frac{43{,}560 \text{ ft}^2}{\text{acre}} \times \frac{1.5 \text{ g}}{\text{cm}^3} \times \frac{1 \text{ lb}}{454 \text{ g}} \times \frac{28{,}320 \text{ cm}^3}{\text{ft}^3} = \frac{2{,}037{,}917 \text{ lbs}}{\text{acre}}$$

Finer-textured soils, such as silt loams, clays, and clay loams, are generally more compact and have less large pore space (and thus, higher bulk densities) than sandy soils that have a higher proportion of pore space to solids. Bulk densities of soils generally range from 1.0 to 1.9 g/cm^3 (Table 4–2). Clay, clay loam, and silt loam soils normally range from 1.0 to 1.6 g/cm^3, while sands and sandy loams normally range between 1.2 and 1.8 g/cm^3. Organic soils have extremely low bulk densities (0.2 to 0.8 g/cm^3) due to low particle densities and large amounts of pore space. Highly compacted soils may have bulk densities as high as 2.0 g/cm^3 or more. Compacted soils have less large pore space and thus have higher bulk densities (Figure 4–3). This results in slower infiltration and percolation. Noncompacted sandy soils have lower bulk densities and can have infiltration and percolation rates as high as four feet (1.3 m) per hour while compacted clay loams have significantly lower rates, often <one inch (2.5 cm) per hour, and higher bulk densities. Modern golf green and sports field designs integrate compaction-resistant soil mixes of predominantly medium- and fine-sized sands with organic matter and other materials. These mixes withstand compaction while retaining enough moisture to maintain plant survival. The bulk density range for golf greens is between 1.25 to 1.55 g/cm^3, with an optimum level of 1.40 g/cm^3.

Soil Porosity

Soil porosity, pore space, or **void space** is the percentage of total soil volume not occupied by solid particles, or the percentage of total soil volume occupied by air and water. In dry soils, pores are mostly filled with air. In moist soils, pore spaces contain both air and water. The arrangement and size of solid particles in soil largely determines pore space. If solid particles lie close together, as in many fine sands or compacted subsoils, porosity is low. If they are arranged in porous aggregates, as often found in medium-textured soils high in organic matter, pore space per unit volume will be high. Organic matter increases soil porosity by promoting soil particle aggregation and improving soil structure. Porosity can be determined from bulk density by the equation (Appendix B):

$$\text{Porosity (\%)} = 100 - [(\text{bulk density/particle density}) \times 100]$$

Generally, particle density is usually assumed to be 2.65 g/cm^3 and bulk density is determined on an undisturbed soil core. "Ideal" soil contains 50 percent solids (approximately 45 percent mineral matter + 5 percent organic matter) and 50 percent pore space, with this pore space equally divided into 25 percent water and 25 percent air (Figure 4–1). Sandy soils generally have a total pore space between 35 and 45 percent, while finer-textured soils vary in total pore space from 45 to 60 percent (Table 4–2).

Small pores, called **capillary** or **micropores,** hold water against the pull of gravity and are responsible for the soil's water-holding capacity. Larger **noncapillary** or **macropores** drain rapidly and are typically air-filled. The relative proportion of macro- and microporosity is primarily determined by soil texture and structure. Sandy soils typically have a high proportion of macropores because sand particles, often spherical as well as large, cannot pack closely together. Thus, the pore sizes tend to be large. Clay and silt particles, however, pack together tightly because these particles are very small and platelike (flat).

The suggested porosity range for golf greens is 35 to 55 percent total pore space with an optimum range of 40 to 55 percent by volume. Capillary porosity is usually between 15 and 25 percent and noncapillary porosity between 15 and 35 percent. Ideally, capillary and noncapillary pore space should be equal at 25 percent of the total soil volume. Minimum air-filled porosity at which soils will support good turfgrass growth is between 10 and 15 percent. Lower porosity values indicate a clay soil and/or excessive soil compaction. These porosity ranges are for a rootzone mix that has been compacted, allowed to percolate water for 24 hours, and then exposed to a 40-centimeter tension (or suction). A method of calculating total pore space is outlined in Appendix B.

Water-retention capacity at 40 centimeters for oven-dry soils typically ranges from 12 to 25 percent by weight, with 18 percent (1.5 mm water held per 10 mm soil) being optimum. Table 4–3 lists plant-available moisture for various textural classes. Table 4–3 also presents typical values of available moisture for various soil types. This may be estimated in the field by applying a known amount of water to the soil when the profile water content is near the permanent wilting point, observing the volume of soil wetted, and calculating the volume of water stored per unit volume of soil.

TABLE 4–3 *Plant-available moisture range for various textural classes and at field capacity (one-third bars) and permanent wilting point (15 bars).*

Textural class	Available moisture		Percent moisture content by volume at	
	Percent by volume	Inches water/foot of soil	One-third bars	15 bars
Sand	< 5	< 0.6	7	3
Loamy sand	5 to 10	0.6 to 1.2	11	4
Sand loam	10 to 15	1.2 to 1.8	22	9
Loam	—	—	28	15
Sandy clay loam	—	—	27	17
Clay loam	—	—	33	21
Silty clay	—	—	39	27
Clay	—	—	40	29
Silt loam	15 to 20	1.8 to 2.4	32	14
Silty clay loam	—	—	27	17
Silt	20 to 25	2.4 to 3.0	31	10
Organic soils	17 to 25	2.0 to 3.0	—	—

SOIL-WATER RELATIONSHIPS

Describing Soil Moisture

Several values are used to describe soil moisture, including saturation, field capacity, and permanent wilting point. Soil is completely **saturated** when all the pores are filled with water, such as during or right after a heavy rain. Water then occupies about 50 percent of the total soil volume. The addition of more water results in surface runoff and puddling.

After drainage has removed water from the macropores and the two forces of gravity and capillary tension become equalized, the soil is at **field capacity** (which is equivalent to **water-holding capacity**), with water normally occupying 20 to 35 percent of the total volume (Figure 4–4). Any water in excess of field capacity will drain due to gravitational pull. Since saturated soil for an extended period is undesirable, the primary function of drainage is removal of this excess gravitational water from soil.

In constructed greens, field capacity is determined by applying a force of 30 or 40 centimeters (cm) of tension to the soil to simulate the gravitational force on a rootzone 12 to 16 inches (30 to 40 cm) thick. In native soils, field capacity is usually determined at 0.33 bars [33 kilopascals (kPa)]. The higher the clay and organic matter content of the soil, the greater the water content at field capacity. Sand-textured soils may have as little as 7 percent moisture at field capacity, whereas clay soils may have as much as 40 percent moisture (Table 4–3).

Soil does not stay at field capacity very long. Evaporation of water from the soil surface and soil water absorption by plant roots deplete water from the larger of the micropores, and

FIGURE 4–4 The relationships between the various classifications of soil water showing the mathematical relationship between soil water tension (expressed as bars) and available and unavailable soil moisture.

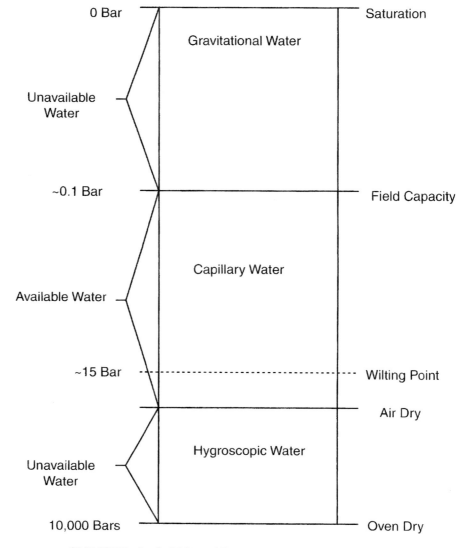

soil begins to dry out. Forces of soil adsorption and capillarity pull at water molecules and hold them. As particle and pore size decrease, these combined forces strengthen. At some point, roots can no longer take up water from the smallest pores as it is held too tightly, and the plant starts to wilt. A soil is considered to be at the **permanent wilting point** when a severely wilted plant is unable to recover, even after irrigation. This usually occurs when soil moisture is around 10 to 15 percent of the total volume. Water held at a tension of 15 bars (1,500 kPa) is often considered the lower limit of available water. In sandy soils the amount held is small in proportion to the total, but in clayey soils it can be a large percentage of the total soil water content (Table 4–3). These values are estimates, and actual values depend on the soil texture, structure, and the type of plant growing in the soil.

Volumetric water content is the most common measure used to express the quantity of water in a soil. Volumetric water content is defined as the volume of water per unit volume of soil. This value is usually expressed in inches of water per inch of soil (Table 4–3). For example, a volumetric water content of 10 percent refers to one inch of water in 10 inches of soil or 1.2 inches of water in one foot (9 cm per meter) of soil. The units of depth may be used to describe volumetric measurements since cross-sectional area is the same for both water volume and total soil volume. This is a convenient unit because rainfall, irrigation, and turf water use are expressed in the same units.

Soil scientists measure the amount of water left in the soil at various tensions (or pressures) to create a **moisture release** (or **retention**) **curve.** Different soils have different-shaped moisture release curves with different heights of perched water tables. The shape and characteristics of this curve reflect the particle-size distribution of a soil and degree of soil compaction. Moisture release curves indicate water movement and amounts at various tensions, allowing soil scientists to predict soil water behavior at various depths and drying points.

Plant-Available Water

The amount of water held in the soil between field capacity and the permanent wilt point is termed **plant-available water** (Table 4–3). Soils with a high percentage of silt have the greatest plant-available water content, as much as 25 percent or three inches per foot of soil (23 cm per meter). Sand-textured soils have less available water than silt-textured soils because the total amount of water they hold is less. The plant-available water content of clay-textured soils is also less than silty soils because much of the water in a clay soil is held too tightly to be used by plants.

If the available water content of the soil and the depth of turfgrass rooting are known, then the amount of water the plant has access to can be estimated by the following:

$$\text{Total water available} = \frac{\text{rooting depth} \times \text{percent available water by volume}}{100}$$

Example:

If a bentgrass green has an average rooting depth of two inches, and the soil it is grown on has a field capacity of 21.4 percent and a permanent wilting point of 14.6 percent, how much water is available to the grass from the soil?

$$\text{Total water available} = \frac{\text{rooting depth} \times \text{percent available water by volume}}{100}$$

$$= \frac{\text{rooting depth} \times (\text{field capacity} - \text{permanent wilting point})}{100}$$

$$= \frac{2 \text{ inches} \times (21.4 - 14.6)}{100}$$

$$= 0.136 \text{ inch}$$

Therefore, 0.136 inch of water is available to the grass from the soil. If water use by the turf is 0.10 inch per day, then daily irrigation is needed so moisture stress of the plant does not occur.

Infiltration and Percolation Rates

Infiltration rate is the speed at which water enters the soil surface. **Percolation rate** is the speed at which water moves downward through the soil profile. Infiltration determines whether applied water enters soil, runs off (if sloped), or ponds. The rate at which water enters soil is in part dependent on soil texture and structure and the impact of these factors on soil porosity. Soils having a high proportion of noncapillary (large) pores have high infiltration rates. Coarse sandy soils have high infiltration rates because the large sand particles result in an abundance of noncapillary pores. Finer-textured soils (having more silt and/or clay) may also have high infiltration rates if good structure results in the presence of large pores between structural aggregates. More often, however, fine-textured soils have slow infiltration rates because most of the pores are small and accept water slowly. The infiltration rate of a soil is also highest when it is dry. As a soil becomes wetter, infiltration rates decrease.

On an established turfgrass site, an infiltrometer is often used to determine the soil's hydraulic conductivity (Figure 4–5). Water is added to the single- or double-ring infiltrometer and, after a period of time, the depth of water absorbed is measured. Hydraulic conductivity of established turf sites can also be determined by extracting intact soil cores, taking them to the laboratory, subjecting them to a hydraulic head, and using **Darcy's Law** (Appendix A).

The infiltration rate of golf greens is critical as this determines playability after rainfall. Although relatively high initial percolation rates can be achieved on sand-based greens, percolation rate usually decreases over time. The macropores may be blocked by silt, and clay may be inadvertently added in soil amendments and irrigation water, or by wind-blown soil and dust. Sand-sized particles from sandstone are not stable and may break down with traffic. Excessive accumulation of soil organic matter in sand-based greens also decreases macroporosity and the percolation rate. However, because a rapid percolation rate is generally correlated with a low water-holding capacity, a balance between percolation and water-holding capacity is needed.

In fairways, roughs, and tees, infiltration rates not only determine playability after rainfall, but also dictate the rate at which irrigation can be supplied. The precipitation rate of irrigation sprinklers must be less than the soil's infiltration rate so irrigation water does not run off.

Water Movement in Soil

Soil water movement is largely dependent on (1) water being pulled downward by **gravity** (or **hydraulic gradient**), (2) water sticking to itself due to hydrogen bonding (called **surface tension** or **cohesion**), and (3) water sticking to other surfaces, such as soil particles (referred to as **adhesion, adsorption,** or **hygroscopic moisture**). This relationship is described by Darcy's Law (Appendix A).

FIGURE 4–5 A double-ring infiltrometer used to measure hydraulic conductivity (internal drainage) of an established turf site.

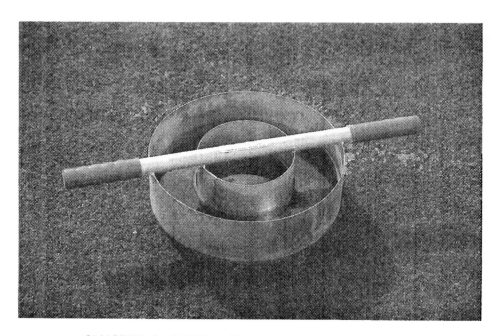

Gravity (or Hydraulic Gradient)

Gravity is the constant downward-pulling force that moves water through soil. As the soil profile depth increases, so does the height (elevation) of the water column being pulled down and the weight (or pressure) of water. Gravity limits the height water can rise by capillary tension, and limits the thickness of water film held by tension around each soil particle.

Surface Tension (or Cohesion)

Due to their hydrogen-bonding characteristic, water molecules are attracted to each other in all directions and are attracted much more to each other than to adjacent air molecules. Surface tension is created when water meets air, causing water molecules to become round and bead up. The smaller the drop of water, the stronger the surface tension becomes, and the more difficult it becomes to break this tension. The surface of water can be bent slightly by gently touching it. However, if the force applied is too great, the surface will break. Wet soils have less tension than dry soils.

Water Adhesion (or Adsorption) to Soil Particles

As soil particle (pore) size decreases, an increase in attraction (or adhesion) occurs between soil particles and soil water. In most instances, water adheres to soil particles very strongly, much more so than to other water molecules. This adhesive force "pulls" water against the force of gravity. It can, in fact, pull water in all directions away from a water source in soil, independent of gravity (Figure 4–6). If a dry column of soil is placed in contact with free water, moisture will rise into the soil. However, capillary water movement is generally limited (rarely more than 4 in., 100 mm) from its source and is very slow. Furthermore, the smaller the soil pore spaces, the slower water will move laterally (sideways) and the more tightly the water is held. Soil with a larger pore size (e.g., coarse-textured sand) holds less moisture at a given potential than soil held with a smaller pore size (e.g., silt or clay).

Capillarity

Capillary tension is the combined forces of surface tension and adhesion that retains water in small soil pores against the pull of gravity. This retained water held in the soil against gravity is collectively referred to as **capillary water.** It includes the film of water left around soil particles and water in capillary soil pores after gravity water has drained. Once water molecules wet a par-

FIGURE 4–6 Forces influencing water movement in a soil with drainage. These forces include gravity, adhesion, capillary tension, evaporation, and capillary film.

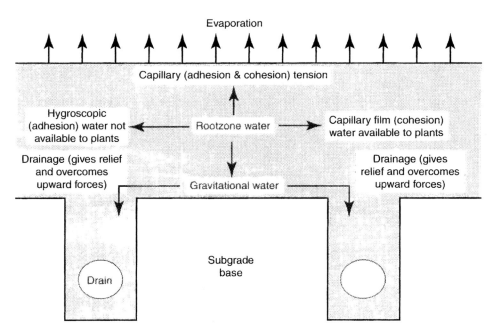

ticle, they seek another dry surface on which to cling. As water moves, it pulls additional water along with it. This pulling action produces a negative pressure or vacuum.

A similar reaction can be seen with a sponge and water. When dry, contact with water (capillary tension) causes a sponge to wet-up both downward and sideways. Likewise, if the sponge is highly saturated, some water will initially drip out of it, but a certain amount will be held. Capillarity and adsorption forces cause the sponge to hold water in a way very similar to soils. The extent to which capillary action works depends on the size of spaces or channels formed when soil particles pack together. The smaller the channels (e.g., more compacted or finer textured the soil), the greater the capillary action.

Surface tension is weaker than adhesion and is the first force to break under the pull of gravity. Therefore, surface tension is the limiting factor in the amount of water a pore can hold. Water held by adhesive forces requires greater gravitational forces to remove it. This is seen when a soil becomes saturated. All the pore spaces are filled with water, additional water has nowhere to go, and gravity is then easily able to pull water downward, after which the soil begins to drain. The larger pores eventually empty out and drainage stops. Water in the small (or capillary) pores is retained by capillary forces, allowing it to be used by plants.

Saturated and Unsaturated Hydraulic Conductivity

The rate of moisture movement through the soil under saturated conditions is reported as percolation rate, **permeability**, or as **saturated hydraulic conductivity** (indicated as K_{sat}), as determined by Darcy's Law (Appendix A).

Saturated hydraulic conductivity is defined as the proportional relationship of water flow through a saturated soil in response to a given difference in head (pressure). Large pores allow for high saturated hydraulic conductivities. Sandy soils, therefore, generally have much higher saturated hydraulic conductivities than clay-type soils. However, clay soils with strong structure may have substantial macroporosity and saturated hydraulic conductivities. Hydraulic conductivity for rootzone mixes can be determined in the laboratory. Combinations of sand, soil, and/or organic material (usually peat) can be mixed in various ratios for testing purposes. The USGA guidelines for rootzone mixes recommend a saturated hydraulic conductivity between 6 and 24 inches (15 and 61 cm) per hour. The saturated hydraulic conductivity of rootzone mixes will decrease over time due to compaction and organic matter accumulation. Laboratory measurements of hydraulic conductivity can also be determined on soil cores taken from established soils using specialized equipment and extreme care. Hydraulic conductivity is then determined by Darcy's Law (Appendix A).

Unsaturated hydraulic conductivity is the proportional relationship of water flow through an unsaturated soil in response to a given difference in head. Water rising in the profile from a perched water table or being drawn out of a sand-based green by a native soil collar are examples of unsaturated flow. Small pores allow high unsaturated hydraulic conductivities because movement is by matric potential or capillary action. The smaller the pore, the faster the movement. Overall, water movement in unsaturated soils is much slower than in saturated soils.

Water is attracted to dry soil particles and forms a moisture film around them. As this film gets thicker, the particle's attractive forces are reduced and approach zero. Water then flows through the capillary (small) micropores to adjacent particles having thin moisture films and higher attractive forces. Since capillary action is stronger in fine soils having smaller capillary passages, more lateral movement occurs in finer-textured soils than in coarser soils or sand.

Water Potential

In order for water to move in soil, work must be done on the water by the previously discussed forces. To predict the movement of water in soil, the energy potential of water is considered. Water always moves from a point of high total potential to a point of lower total potential. Total water potential (Ψw) is the sum of gravitational potential (Ψg), pressure (or turgor, or matric) potential (Ψp), and osmotic (or solute) potential (Ψo).

$$\Psi w \ = \ \Psi g \ + \ \Psi p \ + \ \Psi o$$

Gravitational potential (Ψg) of soil water at a point is determined by the elevation of the point relative to an arbitrary reference level. Water above the reference elevation has positive ($+$)

gravitational potential. Water below the reference elevation has negative ($-$) gravitational potential. Gravitational potential is independent of the chemical and pressure conditions of water. It depends solely on relative elevation.

Pressure potential (Ψp) of soil water is determined by the comparison to water at atmospheric pressure (e.g., at a free-water surface). Soil water at a hydrostatic pressure greater than atmospheric has a positive pressure potential. For example, water under a free-water surface (such as a groundwater table) has a positive pressure potential. Water at the free-water surface has zero pressure potential. At hydrostatic pressure less than atmospheric (in other words, under *suction* or *tension*), a negative pressure potential occurs. Negative pressure potential is often termed **capillary** or **matric potential.** Water above the free-water surface is held by capillary and adsorptive forces. This water has a negative pressure (or matric) potential.

Osmotic (or solute) potential (Ψo) is created by the presence of solutes (or salts) in the water solution. The more solutes present, the more their molecules (or ions) are attracted to water. Due to solute presence, a greater amount of tension or suction (or work) is required by plant roots to extract water from soil. Soil salts and fertilizer (such as nitrogen or potassium) are common sources of these solute salts.

Pore Size

The rate of water movement down through a soil is strongly affected by the pore size through which it must move. This rate is approximately proportional to the square of the pore diameter. As the soil water content decreases due to drainage (gravity pull), the rate of drainage decreases at an exponential rate since the remaining water is held in the smaller, often narrower, pores. Once the soil is no longer saturated, water is prevented from moving downward at the rate of saturated hydraulic conductivity. This occurs even though large pores exist in the soil below the draining front. Water is prevented from filling these larger pores because it is held in the smaller pores above by adhesion, and by the surface tension at the ends of the smaller pores. If the soil becomes saturated, water will quickly enter and fill these large pores and move downward, again at the rate of saturated hydraulic conductivity.

Perched Water Table

A **perched water table** (or **zone of free water**) is a zone of saturated soil just above the interface of a finer-textured soil over a coarser-textured soil. This is often a desirable condition, created by design for golf greens and sports fields, where finer sand is placed over a coarser aggregate layer such as gravel (Figure 4–7). Water will not drain from the upper finer-textured soil until a sufficient zone of saturation develops above the coarser soil. At that point, the weight of the water cannot be contained by the capillary retention forces, and water starts flowing. This saturated zone will extend from the top of the coarser layer up to the air entry point.

FIGURE 4–7 Desirable flat perched water table formed when an appropriately sized rootzone sand is placed over a gravel layer, such as in USGA specification golf greens.

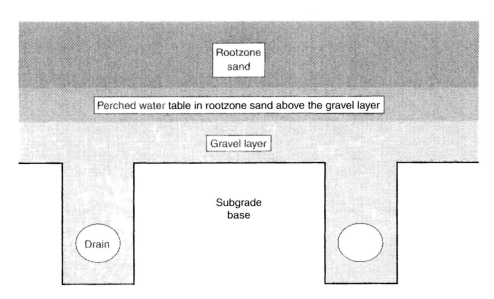

Rootzone sand

Perched water table in rootzone sand above the gravel layer

Gravel layer

Subgrade base

Drain

This saturated zone develops as the adhesive force of the finer-diameter soil particles on water is greater than the drainage force due to gravity. The finer textured and/or more compacted a soil becomes, or the greater the difference in particle-size distribution between the soils, the harder it is for water to cross over from one surface to another, and the higher the perched water table. Conversely, a coarser soil will have a shallower perched water table. If the topsoil depth is not greater than the depth of the perched water table, the whole soil profile remains saturated and will not drain.

The upper portion of this saturated zone of free water is known as the **capillary fringe.** If a hole is dug down to the capillary fringe, water will not enter the hole even though the soil in the capillary fringe is saturated. If the hole is dug slightly deeper, down into the zone of free water below the capillary fringe, the hole will fill with water up to the level of the perched water table.

By creating an adequate perched water table, fast-draining, low-compacted sand can be used as a rootzone. When the correct depth of top sands are placed over the correctly sized gravel layer, the perched water table provides a reservoir of water for the grass to use, but the complete profile still drains sufficiently. Drainage flow will continue from the sand into the gravel due to the combined forces of gravity and the adhesive forces at the contact points between the sand and gravel particles. This "flow" continues until the surface tension in the pores of sand and the adhesive forces of sand particles in contact with the gravel equal those forces (gravity and adhesion) pulling the water down.

At this point, equilibrium is reached and a saturated perched water table exists above the sand/gravel interface. Unless additional water is added to the system above, no further water moves downward out of the perched water table.

Choosing Sands for Golf Greens

Several factors should be considered when choosing a sand for golf green construction, including the climate (especially rainfall amount and intensity), local available sand, the type of turfgrass being grown, irrigation water quality, the amount of play, and golfer expectations. These considerations help determine an acceptable range of saturated hydraulic conductivity and water-holding capacity for the rootzone mix. Unfortunately, it is impossible to optimize both hydraulic conductivity and water-holding capacity because as one increases the other decreases. A rootzone mix with a high hydraulic conductivity will drain rapidly after heavy rains, allowing play to resume quickly, and will provide a firm playing surface. However, moisture holding capacity will be low, necessitating frequent irrigation. Low hydraulic conductivity mixes will hold more moisture and fertilizer, but playing conditions after a heavy rain may be delayed compared with those having a high hydraulic conductivity.

Rootzone mix characteristics can be altered by adjusting the sizing of the sands or the amount of soil amendment such as peat. For example, two sands of differing particle size distribution were separately mixed with peat in different proportions and their physical properties determined (Table 4–4). Sand A is a relatively coarse sand, composed of 37 percent coarse-size sand and 41 percent medium-size sand. Sand B is composed of a similar amount of medium-size sand (38 percent), but only 2 percent coarse sand. Sand B has 59 percent fine-size sand in comparison to 15 percent for Sand A. The differences in particle size between Sands A and B are reflected in their physical properties. Sand A has lower total porosity than Sand B, 44 percent versus 48 percent (unamended with peat), respectively. Most of the difference in porosity is in the capillary pores, those responsible for water-holding capacity. Sand A has only 15 percent capillary pores whereas Sand B has 24 percent capillary pores. Thus, water-holding capacity is lower for Sand A than for Sand B, 10 percent versus 17 percent. Noncapillary pores are greater in Sand A than Sand B, 29 percent compared to 26 percent. As a result, Sand A has a higher saturated hydraulic conductivity (26 inches/hour, 66 cm) than Sand B (17 inches/hour, 43 cm).

Increasing the proportion of peat in the rootzone mix has similar effects on the soil's physical properties as choosing a sand with a greater proportion of fine-size sand particles. Increasing peat from 0 to 20 percent in combination with Sand A decreased noncapillary porosity from 29 to 26 percent and saturated hydraulic porosity from 26 to 10 inches per hour. Capillary porosity was increased from 15 to 22 percent, which increased water-holding capacity from 10 to 16 percent.

A detailed particle size and physical property analysis such as in Table 4–4 is the preferred way to choose a rootzone mix. Considerable additional information on choosing the appropriate rootzone mix for golf greens is in Chapter 8.

TABLE 4-4 *An example of altered rootzone mix physical properties from changing particle size distribution and percentage of peat.*

Sand	Very coarse 2.0 to 1.0 mm	Coarse 1.0 to 0.5 mm	Medium 0.5 to 0.25 mm	Fine 0.25 to 0.15 mm	Very fine 0.15 to 0.05 mm	Total sand 2.0 to 0.05 mm	Silt 0.05 to 0.002 mm	Clay <0.002 mm
				Particle-size distribution (%)				
A	7	37	41	12	39	99	0.7	0.3
B	0.0	2.1	38	48	10	98	0.8	0.4

Sand	Sand	Peat	Saturated hydraulic conductivity	Porosity (%)			Bulk density	Water-holding capacity
	percent by volume		inches/hour (cm/hr)	Noncapillary	Capillary	Total	g/cm^3	percent
A	100	0	26 (66)	29	15	44	1.47	10
	90	10	20 (51)	27	20	47	1.41	14
	85	15	15 (38)	27	21	48	1.38	15
	80	20	10 (25)	26	22	49	1.35	16
B	100	0	17 (43)	26	24	48	1.37	17
	90	10	13 (33)	23	28	51	1.30	21
	85	15	10 (25)	22	29	52	1.27	23
	80	20	6 (15)	21	31	53	1.24	25

SOIL DRAINAGE CHARACTERISTICS

Introduction

Water management is the primary key to success for most commercial turfgrass facilities. Soil serves as the storehouse for water used for plant growth that must be readily available to satisfy the demand created by transpiration. Being able to apply water when needed (irrigation) and being able to expediently remove excess water (drainage) ensures good turfgrass growth and prevents prolonged play delay. Improper or inadequate drainage is the most common agronomic problem cited by golf course superintendents and sports field managers. As with many topics in turfgrass management, drainage is a subject widely misunderstood, full of myths, nonscientifically-based practices, and unproven materials.

Many of the terms and techniques needed to determine which types of soil mixtures are needed on golf greens were introduced earlier in this chapter. These concepts will now be used to explain and then determine, scientifically, the best drainage strategies for different turfgrass installations. All too often, the concepts, machines, and technology used to design and construct roads are used to build turf facilities like golf courses or sports fields. In most cases this is a serious mistake, as the exacting requirements and internal drainage needs for turf sites are much different and more precise than for roads.

Drainage Methods

Two primary forms of drainage are utilized in turfgrass facilities—surface and subsurface.

1. In surface drainage, land surfaces are reshaped, sloped, and smoothed as needed to eliminate ponding and to induce gravitational flow overland to an outlet. Diverting and excluding water from an area often involves diversion ditches, swales, and floodways.
2. With subsurface drainage, soils may be modified to induce surface water infiltration and percolation through the rootzone to buried drains that collect and transport excess soil water to an outlet. The drop in pressure (or water potential) due to outlet discharge induces excess soil water flow into the drains. Subsurface drainage may also involve interceptor drains oriented perpendicular to the direction of groundwater flow.

FIGURE 4–8
Uncontrolled flooding can
cause extensive turfgrass
damage and course closing,
resulting in unexpected
revenue loss.

A combination of surface and subsurface drainage is often required to quickly remove water from the soil surface to minimize delays in play, avoid excessive compaction, and allow maintenance practices to continue (Figure 4–8). First, soil water movement and the factors influencing this movement will be discussed.

Surface Drainage

Surface drainage is often a missing component in the design of modern fairways and sports fields. Soccer fields, for example, have almost totally gone to "flat" surfaces, as have many football fields. Some of the major problems of poor playability and performance of these facilities are caused by insufficient surface drainage, especially when the rootzone has poor internal drainage properties. Almost all long-term successful turfgrass facilities have adequate surface slope (grade) to remove excess surface water. Surface drainage uses the potential energy existing due to elevation change to provide a hydraulic gradient. The surface drainage system creates a water-free surface by moving surface water to an outlet at a lower elevation.

Runoff occurs when the rate of precipitation or irrigation exceeds the soil infiltration rate (the rate water can enter a soil). The infiltration rate is dependent on two parameters. The first parameter affecting infiltration is soil structure. Infiltration into heavier soils, such as clay, will be slower than infiltration into sandy soil. The second parameter is the soil moisture status at the time of rainfall or irrigation. Drier soils have higher infiltration rates that continue until the point of saturation is reached. The rate of water entry then begins to slow.

As water enters the soil, pores (large and small) near the soil surface fill first. When pores become full, gravity begins to pull water downward. Water on the soil surface will puddle (or pond) if the water application rate exceeds the amount that gravity can pull further down the profile. Once soil saturation is reached in shallow golf green or sports field profiles, the rate of water entering the soil is dependent on the rate the subsoil can remove it. If water sits or ponds on the surface for more than a couple of hours, the whole topsoil is saturated. This is most common in surface depressions and on flat surfaces. If play commences while soil is saturated, the moisture acts like a lubricant allowing the soil particles to compress, causing compaction. Turf plants and roots are easily damaged when soils are saturated. In addition, saturated soils contain less oxygen, thus encouraging anaerobic conditions that lead to root loss and possible buildup of toxic gases such as carbon dioxide and methane, as well as substances such as iron and aluminum oxides, the chief causes of black layer.

A major advantage of good surface drainage is the capability to remove large volumes of water. This capability is especially important during heavy rainfall events. For example, a one-inch rainfall across one acre equals 27,154 gallons (25 mm over 0.40 ha equals 102,870 L).

Slopes

The slope at which a particular surface should be constructed is determined by several variables. Slopes up to 3 percent (1:33) are acceptable for soils with poor infiltration rates. In competitive sports, players and coaches often feel slopes greater than 3 percent affect ball roll and play. A minimum of 1 percent slope (1:100) is almost always necessary, except with extensively modified rootzones and subsurface drainage such as USGA or California-style constructed greens. For most nonmodified soils, a 1.5 percent (1:65) to 2.5 percent (1:40) slope is usually adequate.

The following equation calculates the velocity of water across a bare surface as influenced by the slope and depth of ponded water or rainfall:

$$V = 0.35 \times D^{0.67} \times S^{0.5}$$

where: V = velocity, in./sec
D = water depth (in.)
S = slope

Example:

1. A one-inch rainfall onto saturated soil with a 1 percent slope would yield:

$$V = 0.35 \times 1^{0.67} \times 0.01^{0.5}$$

$$= 0.035 \text{ inches } (0.9 \text{ cm}) \text{ of water movement over a bare surface per second}$$

2. A similar rainfall on a 2 percent slope would yield:

$$V = 0.35 \times 1^{0.67} \times 0.02^{0.5}$$

$$= 0.05 \text{ in./sec } (1.3 \text{ mm})$$

3. On a 3 percent slope, velocity increases to:

$$V = 0.35 \times 1^{0.67} \times 0.03^{0.5}$$

$$= 0.06 \text{ in./sec } (1.5 \text{ mm})$$

These examples demonstrate the large amount of water surface drained by properly designed and constructed slopes. Insufficient slope means water must be drained through soil infiltration, which can be insufficiently slow.

The length of slope becomes important as areas at the bottoms of long slopes remain wet for longer periods than areas further up the slope; thus, they become subject to compaction. Wet areas often appear toward the end of long slopes, usually in excess of about 75 yards (69 m). High traffic areas at the ends of such long slopes are prime target areas for compaction damage. Such areas are often found at the intercept of surface drainage from the fairway and front of golf greens. This also occurs often in front of soccer and football goals. Golf course fairways should be designed so surface drainage is toward the outside of the fairway, rather than down the slope toward the green (Figure 4–9).

Interceptor Drains

Surface drainage from areas adjacent to golf course fairways, such as parking lots, hills, or adjacent fairways, often becomes problematic. Usually this water is easily collected by installing surface cutoff (or **interceptor**) drains to collect the water at the bottom (or "toe") of slopes, prior to entering the playing surface, or by diversion using surface terraces (or swales) (Figure 4–10).

Sloping water tables are found in slightly rolling, hilly, or mountainous areas. The free groundwater in these areas will flow in the direction of the slope, usually along an underlying impervious soil layer. Precipitation on the soil surface percolates downward until it encounters this impervious layer and then flows laterally over this layer. At the bottom of the hill, this free water

FIGURE 4–9 Various slopes on fairways used to deflect surface drainage (redrawn from McIntyre & Jakobsen, 2000).

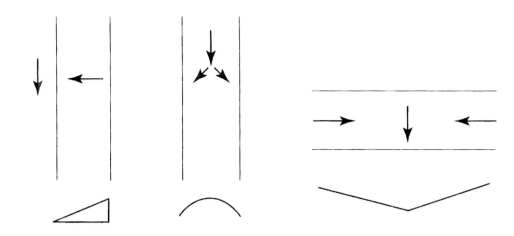

FIGURE 4–10 A sloping water table on hills allows free groundwater to flow in the direction of the slope along an impervious layer. An intercepting drain is placed at the junction of this slope with a flat area (e.g., golf green) to intercept and remove this free groundwater, thereby helping to prevent a wet area (seep).

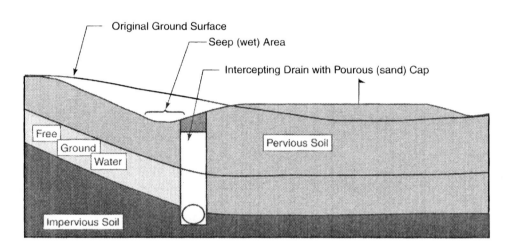

can create a wet area (**seep**), or even reach the surface. The most likely place for a water table to appear at the soil surface is near the intersection of a steep slope and a flatter slope. This is a common problem on golf courses, such as when an elevated green meets the surrounding land area. Wet seep areas are also common on approaches where the fairway slopes downhill toward the green, which is slightly elevated. Here the approach may be wet from irrigation water being retained in the green base material, and a seep may be caused in the same approach area from a surfacing water table on the fairway side. Interceptor drains are placed in these situations where the free groundwater of the hill meets the flat area.

Determining placement of an interceptor drain can best be performed by digging test holes or miniature wells (called **piezometers**) when most of the area is dry enough to use, but the seep area is still wet. Piezometers are small-diameter pipes driven into the subsoil so no leakage occurs around the pipes and water entrance is only from the open bottom. This indicates hydrostatic pressure of groundwater at the specific point in the soil. By observing the water level in the piezometer holes 24 hours after being dug, the depth to the water table or water flowing over the impervious layer in the ground can be determined. The drain line should be installed where the water table is one to two feet (0.3 to 0.6 m) below the soil surface. The trench should be dug to approximately 2.5 feet (0.75 m) deep to extend below the water table. To facilitate drainage, the trench should be backfilled to the depth of the water table with coarse stone. If the water table intersects the soil surface, additional drains may be necessary. If not, additional interceptor drains may be needed further down the slope.

The bottom of drain trenches should be uniform in slope to prevent depressions and should have a minimum slope of 2 percent (1:50). This allows quick removal of surface water, and helps prevent ponding, wheel depressions, and trash accumulation. Fairway drains should be spaced no more than about 45 to 50 yards (41 to 46 m) apart. Mowable drains or graded drains are ideal to minimize maintenance requirements and to facilitate play.

Existing Surface Depressions

Once depressions form, several means of correction are used. Small (shallow) depressions can gradually be brought up to grade by frequent, light topdressing (adding sand). Topdressing should never be so heavy as to smother the grass and should only be performed when the grass is actively growing and not under any environmental or agronomic stresses. However, topdressing and turf-grass repairs can cause dissimilar layering or stratification problems if finer soil is used as a top-dressing material. A one-eighth-inch (3.2-mm) layer of fine soil (such as silt or clay) is enough to disrupt normal water flow in an otherwise ideal soil profile. Successive layering further slows drainage to the point that it may stop.

For deeper depressions, topdressing may take too long or may require excessive amounts of fill to bring the area up to grade (Figure 4–11). The existing turf should then be cut (lifted), the area brought up to grade with soil, and the turf should be relaid. Additional topdressing will probably be needed thereafter to help smooth the surface and fill in any seams between sod pieces.

Subsurface Drainage

Subsurface drainage involves water movement through a soil profile and often includes the installation of subsurface drains to remove excess water that can create undesirable (e.g., saturated) growing conditions. Water available to plants is held in soil by capillarity, while excess water flows by gravity into drains. This lowers the groundwater level below the rootzone of plants. The movement of water into drains for turf facilities is influenced primarily by:

1. **Soil permeability**—This includes soil horizontal and vertical water permeability.
2. **Drain spacing**
3. **Depth of drain**—Drain depth and spacing are interrelated. As the depth of the drain increases, generally so does the optimum spacing distance between drain lines.
4. **Drain size**—More correctly, the ability of the drain to lower the water potential sufficiently to promote water movement to and out of the drain.

Soil Modification to Improve Permeability

Soil modification to enhance internal soil moisture percolation is a common practice in the turf-grass industry. However, several misconceptions exist regarding soil modification to improve permeability. One such misconception is manifested in the practice of applying a two- to six-inch (5- to 15-cm) layer of sand over a native soil with little or no surface slope provided and no

FIGURE 4–11 Puddling at the bottom of a green's slope that is lower than the collar area, thereby preventing surface drainage.

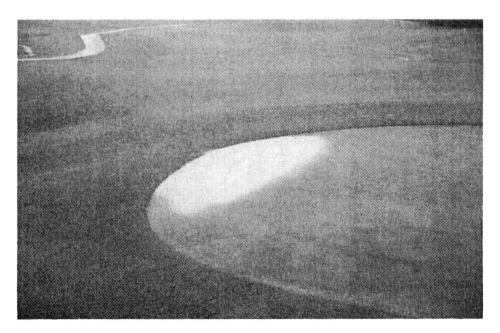

subsurface drain lines installed. This is often referred to as the "bathtub" effect where the finer-textured native soil will not adequately drain and the area holds water like a bathtub. Heavy rainfall then causes saturation of the added sand layer and surface water accumulates, causing poor playing conditions. This is why most heavy use turf areas need 10 to 12 inches (25 to 31 cm) of modified topsoil and properly spaced drain lines to lower this excess surface moisture further down in the soil profile. The drains act similar to a drain in a bathtub, providing a means of water removal.

Another misconception is that an inch or so of a coarse sand, such as a river bottom sand, can be tilled into the top three to six inches (7.6 to 15 cm) of native soil to enhance internal percolation. Unfortunately, this practice is rarely successful. First, a uniform, medium to medium-course sand should be used that has consistent particle size. River bottom sand often has a wide range of particle sizes. This variety in particle size allows smaller silt particles to become dispersed among the larger sand particles, effectively reducing the pore space for water to percolate. Similarly, adding sand to native soil, which often has a high degree of silt and/or clay, often "clogs" these larger internal sand pores, again reducing internal percolation (Figure 4–12). Lastly, trying to uniformly "mix" the surface applied sand with the underlying soil is virtually impossible with a tractor-mounted roto-tiller. These machines will not provide the blended soil mix desired. Proper mixing requires "off-site" machine blending.

Table 4–5 demonstrates the results of blending high-quality (USGA specified) sand into a native Cecil clay soil. The sand:clay blend was performed "off-site" in a laboratory, providing a very uniform distribution of sand and soil in the various ratios. As shown in Table 4–5, adding just 10 percent clay soil to this sand reduced its hydraulic conductivity by almost 85 percent (from 58 in./hr to 9 in./hr, 148 to 23 cm/hr). Conductivity values quickly dropped as the clay soil content increased; for example, with a 50:50 blend, the hydraulic conductivity was less than 0.2 in./hr (0.5 cm/hr), totally unacceptable by today's standards. Furthermore, adding 20 percent sand to the soil reduced drainage more than 50 percent compared to straight (100 percent) soil. This again represents small soil particles "clogging" the larger pores between sand particles.

The following equation provides a guideline for using a suitable sand with a soil of known mechanical composition to create a rootzone with the desired drainage rate:

$$A = \frac{[R - B]}{[C - R]} \times 100$$

where A = weight of sand to add to 100 weight units of the original soil
B = percent of original soil in the desired particle-size range (e.g., 0.125 to 0.5 mm)
C = percent of desired particle-size range (e.g., 0.125 to 0.5 mm) in the sand used as an amendment
R = percent of desired particle-size range (e.g., 0.125 to 0.5 mm) sand in the final mix

FIGURE 4–12 Soil A represents a predominant medium/medium-coarse sand mixture containing large macropores producing a high hydraulic conductivity and good soil aeration. Soil mixture B is the same sand modified with a native soil high in silt and clay. Smaller textured particles (silts and clays) mixed with sands create a non-uniform particle-size distribution resulting in a reduced hydraulic conductivity and potential drainage problems.

Soil A
Uniform sand

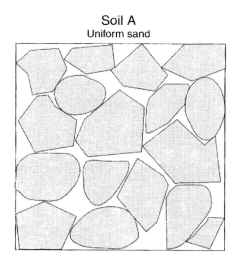

Soil B
Non-uniform sand/soil mix

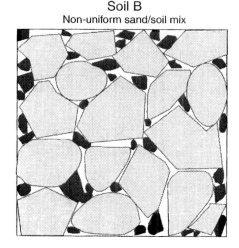

TABLE 4–5 *Hydraulic conductivity of a USGA medium sand and a Cecil clay, alone and in various combinations.*

Sand:Soil ratio	Hydraulic conductivity (K_{sat})	
	(in./hr)	(cm/hr)
0:100	0.07	0.18
10:90	0.05	0.13
20:80	0.03	0.06
30:70	0.09	0.22
40:60	0.13	0.33
50:50	0.15	0.39
60:40	0.19	0.47
70:30	1.89	4.80
80:20	3.24	8.23
90:10	9.01	22.89
100:0	58.1	147.6

Example:

Assume the following particle-size distribution (%) and bulk density values are found in the sand and soil sources in Table 4–6.

Soil type	Particle-size distribution (mm)							Bulk density
	2 to 1	1 to 0.5	0.5 to 0.25	0.25 to 0.125	0.125 to 0.05	0.05 to 0.002	<0.002	(g/cm^3)
				%				
Sand	3	32	44	21	0	0	0	1.65
Soil	3	17	15	20	5	29	11	1.35

TABLE 4–6 *Calculated values of various v/v ratios of sand to soil from known particle-size distribution and bulk density values.*

Soil type	Percent particle-size distribution (mm)							Bulk density
	2 to 1	1 to 0.5	0.5 to 0.25	0.25 to 0.125	0.125 to 0.05	0.05 to 0.002	<0.002	(g/cm^3)
Known values								
Sand	3	32	44	21	0	0	0	1.65
Soil	3	17	15	20	5	29	11	1.35
Calculated values of various sand:soil ratios								
1:1	3	24.5	29.5	20.5	2.5	14.5	5.5	1.50
2:1	3	27	34	21	1.7	9.7	3.7	1.55
3:1	3	28	37	21	1.3	7.3	2.8	1.58
9:1	3	30.5	41	21	0.5	2.9	1.1	1.62

If a nine inch/hour (23 cm/hr) percolation rate is desired for this sand:soil rootzone, the R value would be 90 percent as determined from Table 4–5 in the desired particle-size range of 0.125 to 0.5 millimeters.

$$A = \frac{(90 - 35)}{(65 - 90)} \times 100 = 220$$

Therefore, 220 tons of sand per 100 tons of soil would be required to raise the percentage of soil particles between 0.125 and 0.5 millimeters to 90 percent in the final mix.

Note: Values generated are absolute values regardless of their positive or negative signs, as the actual calculation value in the previous example is −220.

If mixed on a volume basis (such as with off-site blending) instead of a weight basis, one must find the volumetric ratio of sand to soil using the equation: volume = mass/density. The bulk density of sand in this example is 1.65 g/cm^3 and soil is 1.35 g/cm^3, giving:

$$\text{volume (ratio)} = \frac{V_{\text{sand}}}{V_{\text{soil}}} = \frac{220/1.65}{100/1.35} = \frac{220 \times 1.35}{100 \times 1.65} = 1.8$$

Therefore, 1.8 unit volumes of this particular sand are needed per one unit volume of this soil to achieve the desired ratio of 220 tons of sand per 100 tons of soil.

Calculating Volume to Volume (V/V) Ratios

If one wishes to determine the outcome of mixing sand with topsoil on a volume to volume (v/v) ratio basis, the following calculations can be performed for a sand to soil ratio mix.

$$\text{New percent particle size} = \frac{[\text{sand fraction\% } \times \text{ ratio sand}] + [\text{soil fraction\% } \times \text{ ratio soil}]}{\text{total sand } + \text{ soil ratio}}$$

Example:

Calculate the new percent particle size in the 0.5 to 0.25 millimeter range from the sand/soil ratio listed in Table 4–6 in a 3:1 ratio.

$$\text{New percent particle size} = \frac{[\text{sand fraction\% } \times \text{ ratio sand}] + [\text{soil fraction\% } \times \text{ ratio soil}]}{\text{total sand } + \text{ soil ratio}}$$

$$= \frac{(44 \times 3) + (15 \times 1)}{3 + 1} = 37$$

The following example demonstrates how to determine the new particle-size distribution obtained by tilling a known volume of sand into native soil.

Example:

1,500 tons (1,814 metric tons) of sand with a bulk density of 1.65 g/cm^3 is tilled into the top five inches (13 cm) of native soil 1.7 acres (0.7 ha) in area. Calculate the predicted new particle-size distribution percentages and bulk densities.

First, determine the depth of 1,500 tons of sand over the 1.7 acres:

$$\frac{1{,}500 \text{ tons}}{1.7 \text{ acre}} \times \frac{2{,}000 \text{ lbs}}{\text{ton}} \times \frac{454 \text{ g}}{\text{lb}} \times \frac{1 \text{ cm}^3}{1.65 \text{ g}} \times \frac{1 \text{ acre}}{43{,}460 \text{ ft}^2} \times \frac{1 \text{ ft}^2}{929 \text{ cm}^2} \times \frac{1 \text{ in.}}{2.54 \text{ cm}} = 4.7 \text{ inches deep}$$

Since 4.7 inches (12 cm) of sand in depth is to be tilled into the top five inches (13 cm) of soil, this can be approximated using a 1:1 ratio as presented in Table 4–6.

Although this equation helps predict projected particle-size distribution and bulk density values of two known sand/soil sources, it cannot be reliably used to predict percolation rates. For example, with the same sand and soil from the previous example in a 1:1 ratio, the following calculations could be performed to predict a percolation rate for the mix

$$\text{predicted percolation rate} = \frac{[\text{perc. rate sand} \times \text{ratio sand}] + [\text{perc. rate soil} \times \text{ratio soil}]}{\text{total and} + \text{soil ratio}}$$

$$= \frac{[58 \times 1] + [0.07 \times 1]}{2} = 29 \text{ in./hr (74 cm)}$$

However, when actual samples are mixed in a 1:1 ratio, the percolation rate is only 0.15 inches/hour (0.4 cm/hr) (Table 4–7). The small amount of fine-textured clay in the soil mix is sufficient to "clog" the pores in the sand, thus reducing the actual percolation. This demonstrates the importance of actually measuring particle-size distribution, bulk density, and hydraulic conductivity (percolation rate) of the various soil/sand mix being considered as well as the ratios of each.

Table 4–7 reflects the percent (by volume) change when a known amount of amendment is mixed into a soil. For example, if a contractor places two inches (5 cm) of an amendment on the existing soil surface and roto-tills this six inches (15 cm) deep, the theoretical percent volume this added amendment occupies is 25 percent.

Lateral Soil Water Movement

Lateral (sideways) water movement in a soil is influenced or restricted by three factors:

1. Depth (hydraulic head) of the saturated free-water zone in the topsoil
2. Hydraulic conductivity of the rootzone soil
3. Slope of the subgrade or base

As a soil absorbs more water, a saturated zone eventually develops and reaches the subsoil base. Until this saturated zone reaches the subsoil base and a buildup of "free water" occurs, little water will move laterally (sideways). This saturated zone of free water is the only water moved sideways by gravity. The smaller the soil pore space, the slower water will move laterally.

At the top of this saturated section of the profile, a zone (called the capillary fringe) exists where water is held in the pores and will not move laterally out of this zone into a drain or a hole.

TABLE 4–7 *Amount (inches) of surface-applied amendment converted into percent volume.*

Amount (in.) amendment mixed into the upper	inches of soil =	percent by volume
0.5	2	20
0.5	3	14
0.5	4	11
0.5	6	8
1	2	33
1	3	25
1	4	20
1	6	14
1.5	2	43
1.5	3	33
1.5	4	27
1.5	6	20
2	2	50
2	3	40
2	4	33
2	6	25

Water will not enter a hole dug into this capillary fringe zone even though the surrounding soil is saturated, since the surface tension and adhesive forces of soil particles in the capillary fringe zone are greater than the saturated soil. If a hole is dug that penetrates below the capillary fringe, it will fill with water, but only to the level of the top of the free-water zone. This miniature drainage occurs as there is a sufficient "head" of water above it "pushing" the water out of the pores. This helps illustrate the principle that the shallower the topsoil (rootzone mix), the closer drains need to be spaced, since only water from the free-water zone will move into subsoil drains. Water from the capillary fringe will not move laterally toward the drainage pipe even though this zone is saturated. Drain pipes lower the depth of free-water and the capillary fringe moves down at the same rate. As water drains into the drain pipes, the height of the free-water zones diminishes, as does the gradient from the drain to the top of the free-water zone at the midpoint between the drains. As this gradient diminishes, so does the rate of water movement into the drains. This occurs because the component of gravity that pulls water laterally decreases as the height of the free-water zone decreases.

Lateral water movement ceases when the free-water zone is removed. This occurs even if the capillary fringe is still saturated. Hooghoudt's equation (discussed later) is used to calculate the rate at which the saturated free-water zone of the topsoil will drain at the midpoint between two drains (the slowest draining point).

Gravel Size and Shape

In USGA specification profiles, the height of the perched water table is also determined by the number of gravel particles in the gravel layer in contact with the sand above. As the gravel size becomes smaller or contains many fine particles, there is more contact with the sand above, a shallower perched water table develops, and more water flows downward across these contacts. In addition, if the gravel particle shape becomes flatter and narrower, it is able to pack closer together, lie more horizontally, and thus create a large surface area in contact with the sand. Gravel that is more round in shape will have only a small point of contact with the sand and less water will flow downward across these contacts, creating a higher (or deeper) perched water table.

In the laboratory, the correct gravel size in relation to the average size of sand particles that the gravel will contact can be determined. The properties used in specifying materials used in construction include: D-value, coefficient of uniformity (also called the gradation index), and percentage of particles within a desirable size range. The D_x value is the sieve mesh size through which x percent of particles in a sample pass. Two D-values are commonly used, with the larger value indicating the general coarseness of the sample while the lower D-value often reflects the largest makeup of particles in a sand-based rootzone mix.

D_{85} is defined as the particle diameter below which 85 percent of soil particles (by weight) are smaller. D_{15} is the particle diameter below which 15 percent of soil particles (by weight) are smaller. In turfgrass soil mixes, the largest 15 percent diameter of the sand "bridges" with the smallest 15 percent of the gravel particles. This bridging is caused by the irregular shape of particles, friction between particles, and the weight of the material above, all working to "lock" the smaller particles into voids in the gravel. Once the particles have locked together and "bridged" above the voids, this prevents any further particle movement, while maintaining adequate permeability. For bridging to occur, the USGA recommends the gravel D_{15} be *less than or equal to* five times the sand rootzone D_{85}. To maintain sufficient permeability across this gravel/rootzone interface, the gravel D_{15} should be *greater than or equal to* five times the sand rootzone D_{15}. Research, however, indicates a gravel D_{15} up to eight times the rootzone D_{85} is acceptable if the root zone mix is moist (Baker & Binns, 2001).

The uniformity coefficient describes the uniformity of the distribution of particle sizes, helping indicate the potential for interpacking. Interpacking of sands with a large gradation index reduces total pore space and reduces hydraulic conductivity. The gravel should have a uniformity coefficient (Gravel D_{90}/Gravel D_{15}) *less than or equal to* 2.5. Lastly, gravel should totally pass through a 0.5-inch (12-mm) sieve, with less than 10 percent passing a 0.08-inch (2-mm) sieve (No. 10) and *greater than* 5 percent passing a 0.04-inch (1-mm) sieve (No. 18) (Table 4–8).

Sand meeting the USGA specs will have a D_{85} between 0.4 and 0.7 millimeters (0.016- and 0.03-in.); in other words, 15 percent of the sand particles will be larger than this size. Using the bridging factor, gravel D_{15} (smallest 15 percent diameter of the gravel) should not be larger than five times sand D_{85} (0.4 to 0.7 mm), or 2 to 3.5 millimeters (five times 0.4 to 0.7 mm). If the

TABLE 4–8 *Size recommendations by the USGA for gravel when an intermediate sand ("choker") layer is not used in golf green construction.*

Performance factors	Recommendation[*]
Bridging factor	D_{15} of gravel $\leq$ five times the D_{85} of the rootzone.
Permeability factor	D_{15} of the gravel $\geq$ five times the D_{15} of the rootzone.
Uniformity factor	D_{90}/D_{15} ratio of gravel $\leq$ 2.5.
	No particles of the gravel >12 mm.
	Not more than 10 percent of gravel diameter <2 mm.
	Not more than 5 percent of gravel diameter <1 mm.

[*]D_{15}, gravel = the particle diameter below which 15 percent of gravel particles (by weight) are smaller.
D_{85}, rootzone = the particle diameter below which 85 percent of rootzone particles (by weight) are smaller.

gravel is too coarse, the bridging factor will be too high, and if the sand is very dry, it may migrate into the gravel. When sand and gravel are matched to bridge, sand will not migrate into the gravel voids, even though many of these gravel voids are larger than 0.4 to 0.7 millimeters.

Lateral water movement in soil is generally limited in distance and time. However, gravity is able to "pull" water down a sloped base (subgrade). The steeper the subgrade slope, the greater the effect of gravity. Generally, water will move laterally (sideways) along the subgrade's surface in direct proportion to the subgrade's slope. For example, if the slope is 2 percent (1:50), water will move laterally 2 percent (or one-fiftieth) as fast as it will move downward based on its hydraulic conductivity. If the hydraulic conductivity of a soil is 15 inch/hour (381 mm), the maximum rate at which water would move laterally due to gravity would be 2 percent $\times$ 15 = 0.3 inch (7.6 mm) per hour.

In addition, for water to continuously drain (move) down the subgrade, water must be removed from the end or low point of the subgrade with drains or ditches. If this water is not removed, an equilibrium will be reached, often resulting in ponding of water on the surface and excessively wet conditions at the end of a slope or against an impermeable obstruction such as a wall. Such conditions frequently occur when water drains down banks or hills onto a flatter playing surface. In this case, disposal of water from the bottom of the slope can be achieved by: (1) installing a cutoff surface drain at the top of the hill to collect water before it reaches the hill; (2) constructing a terrace to move the water gently across or around the perimeter of the hill; or (3) most commonly, by placing an interceptor drain at the bottom of the hill (discussed earlier).

Drain Lines

Two parameters largely determine the rate water is removed by a drain; namely, (1) depth and (2) spacing of drain lines. In addition, slopes of drain lines in the trenches also affect drainage capacity. Generally, the deeper the drain lines and closer their spacing, the quicker and more effectively soil moisture is removed. Optimum depth and spacing are directly related to the permeability of the soil. Since golf greens have a relatively shallow rootzone (~1 foot, 30 cm) of highly permeable soil (sand), and need to quickly and completely remove surface water so play can resume, their optimum drain spacings are much narrower (closer) than most unmodified soil situations.

Example:

The following information was determined on a potential rootzone mix and gravel sample. Can this rootzone mix meet the bridging criteria to prevent migration into the gravel?

1. For bridging to occur: D_{15} (gravel) $\leq 5 \times D_{85}$ (rootzone).
   From the data in the table, a regression equation is developed to fit the line or curve to determine D_{15} and D_{85}. For sands, this curve is often sigmoidal-shaped while it is linear or quadratic in nature for gravel. For D_{15} (gravel), this is 2.95 millimeters while for the D_{85} (rootzone), it is 0.84 millimeters. Therefore, $5 \times 0.84 = 4.20$ millimeters and 2.95 millimeters ≤ 4.20 millimeters. Bridging of the coarsest 15 percent rootzone particles

	Particle diameter (%)								
Sample	6.3 mm	4.75 mm	3.35 mm	2.0 mm	1.0 mm	0.50 mm	0.25 mm	0.15 mm	0.05mm
Gravel									
% Retained (>D)	33.2	21.9	26.1	14.8	3.2	0.8	0.0	0.0	0.0
% Passed (<D)	66.8	44.9	18.8	4.0	0.8	0.0	0.0	0.0	0.0
Rootzone mix									
% Retained (>D)	0.0	0.0	0.0	0.3	5.5	36.2	38.9	12.7	3.3
% Passed (<D)	0.0	0.0	0.0	99.7	94.2	58.0	19.1	6.4	3.1

should occur with the finest 15 percent gravel particles. This gravel is considered compatible for bridging with the sand.

An alternative method to determine D_{15} and D_{85} would be by interpolation. For example, to determine D_{15} by interpolation between $D_{18.8}$ of 3.35 millimeters and $D_{4.0}$ of 2.0 millimeters for the gravel percent passed (<D), the difference in D values is proportional to the difference in particle diameters; therefore:

$$\frac{\Delta \text{ particle size}}{18.8\% - 15.0\%} = \frac{3.35 \text{ mm} - 2.0 \text{ mm}}{18.8\% - 4.0\%}$$

$$\Delta \text{ particle size} = 0.35 \text{ mm}$$

Therefore $D_{15} = 3.35 \text{ mm} - 0.35 \text{ mm} = 3.00$ millimeters is close to the 2.95 millimeters value determined using linear regression

For adequate permeability: D_{15} (gravel) $\geq 5 \times D_{15}$ (rootzone).

Again, a regression equation or interpolation is needed to determine D_{15} for the rootzone, which is 0.22 millimeters. From this, the D_{15} (gravel) is $\geq 5 \times D_{15}$ (rootzone), which is $5 \times 0.22 = 1.10$ millimeters. Therefore, adequate permeability should occur with this gravel and rootzone sand.

2. For uniformity coefficient of gravel: D_{90} (gravel)/D_{15} (gravel) ≤ 2.5.

From the regression equation, D_{90} (gravel) = 7.30 millimeters and D_{15} (gravel) = 2.95 millimeters. Therefore, D_{90} (gravel)/D_{15} (gravel) = 7.30/2.95 = 2.47, which is less than 2.5. Thus, the uniformity of coefficient of this gravel passes the criteria in Table 4–8.

As mentioned, the closer drains are together, the faster a profile will drain. Also, as the free-water depth in the soil profile decreases, so too does the gravitational gradient. A deeper topsoil has a greater storage space in the profile for the free-water zone. Therefore, in shallower soils, the rate of drainage and soil water storage capacity decrease and drains need to be spaced closer together. Golf green drainage lines should be spaced so water will not have to travel more than 10 feet to reach any individual line. If the golf course is situated on an area with a high water table, it may be necessary to place larger drainage lines deeper into the subgrade to lower the water table and handle the increased internal flow of water.

Calculating drainage line spacing can be done with a modification of **Hooghoudt's equation.** In Hooghoudt's equation, the drain discharge is assumed to equal the incoming rainfall or irrigation, and the water table midway between drains is maintained at a steady height above the drain level. Water enters the soil more rapidly over the drains than midway between them. The equation takes into account both horizontal flow and radial flow caused by the convergence of flow lines over the drains (Figure 4–13). In shallow topsoil, widely spaced drains only remove water from a very small area immediately adjacent to the drains and do not adequately drain the topsoil between them.

Hooghoudt's Equation

$$S = \sqrt{\frac{4Kh^2}{\nu}}$$

CHAPTER 4 *Soil Mineral Properties and Drainage Characteristics* **151**

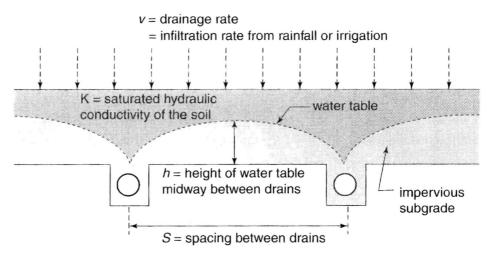

FIGURE 4–13 An uneven, elliptically shaped perched water table between two subsoil drains resulting from a sand overlaying a finer, more compacted, slow-draining subgrade base. Hooghoudt's equation can be used to determine the drain tile spacing or hydraulic conductivity needed for a particular drain spacing design. S is the distance between drain line spacing, v is the amount of rainfall or irrigation applied, and h is the height or depth of the saturated zone with free water, also known as the water table. Hydraulic conductivity of the soil is another variable needed to calculate drain tile spacing. Hooghoudt's equation calculates drainage at the slowest draining point over the total soil surface in consideration.

where: S = Drain line spacing (inches); the units used for h must be the same as those used for S.

K = Saturated hydraulic conductivity (in./hr) of the soil in question.

h = Height of the free-water zone, also known as the water table, midway between the two drains (inches). Two calculations are suggested; one involves the assumption of a worse-case scenario where the free-water zone extends to the surface or the total depth of the topsoil resulting on ponding. The other calculation is performed with the free-water zone lowered by two or three inches. This gives an indication of how quickly water can be removed from the top of the profile. Often this removal is slow if drains alone are being relied on.

v = Drain discharge rate, assumed to equal irrigation or rainfall rate (in./hr). Normally, the anticipated maximum rainfall or irrigation event amount is used here.

Since S and h are squared in Hooghoudt's equation, varying them will change the drainage rate by the square of the magnitude of drainage in distance apart or height, respectively. In other words, if drain spacing (S) is halved, or depth of the saturated zone (h) is doubled, the effectiveness of drains increase fourfold. Conversely, shallower topsoil and wider-spaced drains decrease soil water drainage exponentially.

Several points are illustrated by Hooghoudt's equation:

1. As the free water (water table) depth decreases (e.g., the shallower the topsoil), the gravitational gradient decreases, resulting in decreased drainage, and the closer drain lines need to be spaced. Conversely, the deeper the topsoil, the greater the storage space in the profile for the free-water zone, and the further apart drain lines may be spaced.
2. The closer the drains, the faster a profile will drain.

Note: The Hooghoudt's equation becomes inaccurate when drain spacing (S) approaches the same value as the height of the saturated free-water zone (h). However, this does not occur often in turfgrass facilities since relatively shallow topsoils are used. Hooghoudt's equation cannot be used in a two-tier soil profile with a sand rootzone over a gravel bed (USGA specified green). The gravel bed allows rapid rootzone drainage and movement to the drain pipes, and soil water movement is most influenced by the saturated hydraulic conductivity of the rootzone. For Hooghoudt's equation to be accurate, the soil must be uniform in hydraulic conductivity and must have an impervious layer located below the soil and the drain.

Example:

If the hydraulic conductivity of a loam soil is 12 inches/hour, the height from the drain line to the soil surface is 18 inches, and the typical rainfall event is one inch per hour, determine the proposed drain line spacing required to prevent ponding.

$$S = \sqrt{\frac{4Kh^2}{v}} = \sqrt{\frac{4(12\ inches/hr)(18\ inches)^2}{1\ inch/hr}} = 124\ inches\ (10.3\ feet)$$

Calculating Necessary Soil Hydraulic Conductivity

Hooghoudt's equation also can be rearranged to calculate the desired hydraulic conductivity (percolation) for a given drain line spacing:

$$K = \frac{S^2 v}{4h^2}$$

Example:

1. If an area has a proposed drain spacing of 10 feet (120 in., 305 cm) between drain lines, a 10-inch (25.4-cm) deep rootzone, a one inch/hour (2.54 cm/hr) anticipated rainfall rate, and the free-water zone extends to the surface, as might occur after prolonged rain, determine the necessary hydraulic conductivity (in./hr) of the soil.

$$K = \frac{S^2 v}{4h^2} = \frac{(120\ in.)^2(1\ in./hr)}{4(10\ in.)^2} = \frac{14{,}400\ in.^3/hr}{400\ in.^2} = 36\ in./hr\ (91\ cm/hr)$$

2. If the same area had a 12-inch (or 1-ft) deep rootzone instead of 10 inches as in the example above, what would be the necessary hydraulic conductivity of the soil?

$$K = \frac{S^2 v}{4h^2} = \frac{(120)^2(1)}{4(12)^2} = \frac{14{,}000}{576} = 24\ in./hr\ (61\ cm/hr)$$

3. If the same 10-inch rootzone area had an anticipated maximum rainfall of 0.5 inch/hour instead of 1 inch/hour, what would be the necessary hydraulic conductivity of the soil?

$$K = \frac{S^2 v}{4h^2} = \frac{(120)^2(0.5)}{4(10)^2} = \frac{7{,}000}{400} = 18\ in./hr\ (46\ cm/hr)$$

Calculating Drainage Rates

Hooghoudt's equation can also be rearranged to calculate the drainage rate between subsoil drains.

$$v = \frac{4Kh^2}{S^2}$$

where: v = drainage rate (in./hr) of the saturated free-water zone at the midpoint between drains.

Example:

1. A soil has a hydraulic conductivity rate of two inches/hour, a saturated depth midway between the drains of 10 inches (or 0.83 ft), and drains spaced 10 feet (3 m) apart. Determine the drainage rate at the midpoint between the drain lines.

$$v = \frac{4Kh^2}{S^2} = \frac{4 \times 2\ in./hr \times (0.83\ ft)^2}{(10\ ft)^2} = 0.055\ in./hr\ (1.4\ mm/hr)$$

2. If the soil's depth in the above example is increased to 12 inches (1 foot), determine the new drainage rate at the midpoint between the drain tiles.

$$v = \frac{4Kh^2}{S^2} = \frac{4 \times 2\ in./hr \times (1\ ft)^2}{(10\ ft)^2} = 0.08\ in./hr\ (2\ mm/hr)$$

3. If the same soil has 15 feet (4.5 m) of drain tile spacing instead of 10 feet, what will be the resulting drainage rate?

$$v = \frac{4Kh^2}{S^2} = \frac{4 \times 2 \text{ in./hr} \times (1 \text{ ft})^2}{(15 \text{ ft})^2} = 0.036 \text{ in./hr } (0.9 \text{ mm/hr})$$

Increasing tile spacing from 10 to 15 feet (3 to 4.5 m) decreases the drainage rate from 0.08 to 0.036 inches/hour (2 to 0.9 mm/hr).

4. Now determine the drainage rate for the above example if tile lines are spaced five feet (1.5 m) apart.

$$v = \frac{4Kh^2}{S^2} = \frac{4 \times 2 \text{ in./hr} \times (1 \text{ ft})^2}{(5 \text{ ft})^2} = 0.32 \text{ in./hr } (8 \text{ mm/hr})$$

Decreasing tile spacing from 10 to 5 feet (3 to 1.5 m) increases the drainage rate from 0.08 to 0.32 inches/hour (2 to 8 mm/hr).

These examples illustrate that, the closer the drain tiles or deeper the saturated rootzone, the faster a profile will drain. Specifically, if the drain spacings are halved, drainage increases fourfold. Similarly, as soil depth is doubled, drainage increases fourfold.

Determining Drain Line Discharge Rates

If the length of the drain line is known, then the total amount of water expected to drain from a particular area following a known amount of rainfall or irrigation can be determined from the following equation modified from Darcy's and Hooghoudt's equations:

$$Q = \frac{2Kh^2w}{S}$$

where: Q = discharge rate of water through a drain
w = length of the drain line (Figure 4–14)

Example:

Determine the volume of water flowing from an area with a drain spacing of 10 feet (3 m), drain lines of 12.5 feet (3.8 m) long, in a one-inch (2.54-cm) rainfall event, a rootzone hydraulic conductivity of 16 inches/hour (41 cm/hr) and a 10-inch (2-cm) rootzone depth (water has a volume of 0.00434 gal per cubic inch, 1 ml/cm³).

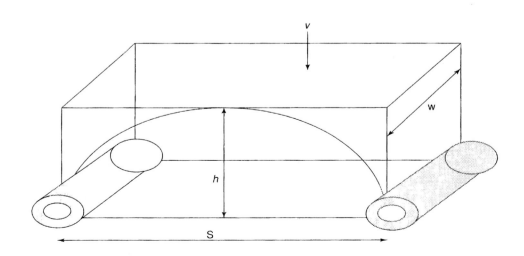

FIGURE 4–14 Variables used in the modified Hooghoudt's equation and Darcy's Law for determining the total volume (area) of a section of drained soil. S is the distance between drain lines, v is the amount of rainfall or irrigation applied, and h is the height or depth of the saturated zone of free water, also known as the water table; w is the width (length) of the drain line.

$$Q = \frac{2Kh^2w}{S} = \frac{2(16 \text{ in./hr})\,(10 \text{ in.})^2\,(150 \text{ in.})}{120 \text{ in.}}$$

$$= 4{,}000 \text{ in.}^3/\text{hr} \times 0.00434 \text{ gal/in.}^3$$

$$= 17.4 \text{ gal/hr}$$

Therefore, drain lines should be selected that can remove at least 18 gallons/hour (6 L/hr).

Multiple Layered Systems

In USGA-designed turf systems, two- or three-layer (or tier) systems are used to allow turf managers to take advantage of a perched water table. When determining drain spacing for such designs, two methods are used by soil scientists. The first and simplest is used when an intermediate (choker) layer is not present by inserting the height and percolation values of the gravel layer in Hooghoudt's equation in place of the topsoil mix (Figure 4–15).

The second method is used when multiple layers are present and takes into account the depth and hydraulic conductivity of the rootzone and intermediate (choker) layer. This method determines the drainage rate as regulated by the saturated hydraulic conductivity of the rootzone and the intermediate (choker) layer. The downward permeability is calculated using Luthin's equation (Figure 4–15):

$$\text{apparent permeability} = \frac{(h_1 + h_2 + \ldots h_n)}{[h_1/K_1 + h_2/K_2 + \ldots h_n/K_n]}$$

where: n = the total number of layers
h_1 = depth of layer 1
h_2 = depth of layer 2
h_n = depth of layer n
K_1 = saturated hydraulic conductivity of layer 1
K_2 = saturated hydraulic conductivity of layer 2
K_n = saturated hydraulic conductivity of layer n

The generated apparent permeability value is incorporated into Hooghoudt's equation as the overall K value. Each method assumes the topsoil mix has an infiltration and percolation rate greater than any anticipated rainfall event.

Example:

If a 12-inch (30-cm) topsoil has a percolation rate of 13 inches/hour (33 cm/hr), a two-inch (5-cm) intermediate (choker) layer has a percolation rate of 20 inches/hour (51 cm/hr), a four-inch (10-cm) underlying gravel layer has a percolation rate of 500 inches/hour (1,270 cm/hr), and an anticipated rainfall maximum of two inches/hour (5 cm/hr), what drain line spacing should be used according to each of the above methods?

FIGURE 4–15 Variables used in Hooghoudt's equation when a gravel layer is present (left) and variables used in Luthin's equation when multiple-tiered (layered) systems, including an intermediate ("choker") layer, are used (right).

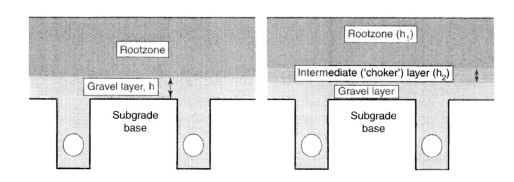

When the intermediate layer is not installed, the gravel values are used in Hooghoudt's equation, as follows:

$$S = \sqrt{\frac{4Kh^2}{v}} = \sqrt{\frac{4(500 \; inches/hr)(4 \; inches)^2}{2 \; inches/hr}} = 126 \; inches \; (10.5 \; feet)$$

In this example, sufficiently sized drain lines should be spaced 10.5 feet (3 m) apart.

If an intermediate ("choker") layer is used, a permeability value is first generated from both the rootzone and intermediate (choker) layer values using Luthin's equation. This apparent permeability value is then used in Hooghoudt's equation.

$$\text{apparent permeability} = \frac{(h_1 + h_2)}{[h_1/K_1 + h_2/K_2]}$$

$$= (12 \; in. + 2 \; in.)/[12 \; in. \div 13 \; in./hr + 4 \; in. \div 20 \; in./hr]$$

$$= 14/[0.92 + 0.2]$$

$$= 12.5 \; in./hr$$

Therefore, water flowing at a maximum rate of 12.5 inches/hour (32 cm/hr) could enter a gravel layer typically four-inches (10-cm) deep with an elevated percolation rate (>241 in./hr, 615 cm/hr). The 12.5 inches/hour value and 14-inch total is then inserted into Hooghoudt's equation as follows:

$$S = \sqrt{\frac{4Kh^2}{v}} = \sqrt{\frac{4(12.5 \; inches/hr)(14 \; inches)^2}{2 \; inches/hr}} = 70 \; inches \; (6 \; feet)$$

As demonstrated, Luthin's equation is usually more conservative in terms of drain line spacing recommendations. This further demonstrates the economic savings of using properly sized rootzone and gravel layers, rather than an intermediate (choker) layer. Not only are there savings from deleting the intermediate layer, but wider drain line spacings are typically allowed.

Determining Drain Size and Length

Sizing drain pipe for a particular area requires a considerable amount of information, including proposed drain depth, slope, width, length, and spacing; average rainfall event (inflow rates); soil type; area to be drained; and surface slope. First, the amount of water to drain following a rainfall event needs to be determined.

Example:

Calculate the volume of water to be drained following a design rainfall event of two inches/hour (50 mm/hr), using a two-inch (50-mm) pipe with 1 percent slope and a drain spacing of 10 feet (3 m) (one cubic foot (0.028 m^3) equals 7.5 gal (28 L)). Every foot (0.3 m) of trench should collect:

10 ft × 1 ft × 2 in./hr × 1ft/12 in. = 1.7 ft^3/hr × 7.5 gal/ft^3 = ~13 gal/hr or 0.21 gal/min (0.79 L/min)

The next question is how long of a run can this two-inch pipe handle. Each linear foot of pipe should collect 0.21 gallons/minute (0.79 L/min) and the maximum drainage rate the pipe can handle is 7.9 gallons/minute (30 L/min) (this is from the manufacturer's specification for two-inch (50-mm) pipe with 1 percent slope). Therefore, the two-inch pipe's effective length is 7.9 gallons/minute ÷ 0.21 gallons/minute = 38 feet (11.4 m). A collector (lateral) drain would be needed after a maximum two-inch (5-cm) pipe run of 38 feet (11.4 m).

In a similar scenario, a four-inch (10-cm) diameter drain pipe is used instead of two-inch (5-cm) pipe. Per the manufacturer's specifications, the four-inch pipe has a maximum flow rate on a 1 percent slope of 0.85 gallons/second (or 51 gal/min). Therefore, the four-inch pipe's effective length would be 51 gallons/minute ÷ 0.21 gallons/minute = 242 feet (72.6 m) compared to 38 feet (11.4 m) for the two-inch (5-cm) diameter pipe. A four-inch (10-cm) drain pipe is the current standard for most golf greens. These are more than sufficient to handle most rainfall events. Lateral lines are typically increased to six inches in diameter to handle the total output of a draining green.

Drain Line Types

A wide array of drain line types, sizes, and configurations are available. A common misconception is that all of these work equally well. Unless the drainage line provides lower water potential than the surrounding soil and the pipe is laid on grade in the bottom of the trench, water will not efficiently enter it nor move down it. A suitable outlet is also needed to remove drained water.

Corrugated Pipe

In the past, drainage lines were built from agricultural clay tile, concrete, or flexible corrugated plastic. Today, four-inch (10-cm) diameter corrugated high-density polyethylene (HDPE) pipe with perforations (slits or holes) is the industry standard, due to its ease of installation and relatively low cost (Figure 4–16). The perforations in HDPE pipe are laid facing downward on a bed of gravel to prevent clogging by downward-migrating soil particles. Drain lines with smooth inner walls provide more efficient water removal than lines with corrugated inner walls.

Water enters the bottom of the pipe(s) through slits or holes fabricated by the manufacturer (Figure 4–17). Water moves down through the medium and stops at the bottom of the trench. As the water level rises in the trench, it moves into the pipe through the holes and then moves down the pipe. An alternative to corrugated HDPE pipe is rigid PVC pipe with two rows of holes drilled

FIGURE 4–16 Corrugated tile pipe is widely used for golf course drainage. A smooth inner-walled pipe should be considered for increased drainage efficiency.

FIGURE 4–17 Water enters drain lines from the bottom of trenches, as this is the point of lowest water potential.

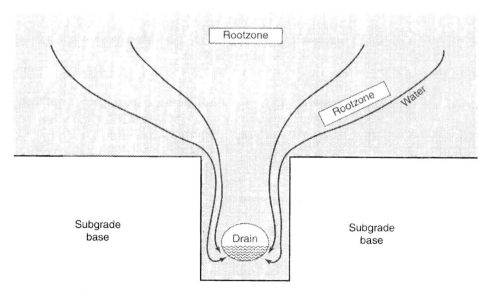

FIGURE 4–18 Strip drains involve a narrow trench of sand with pipes embedded to remove surface water. This figure shows a composite drain consisting of several stacked smaller diameter drains.

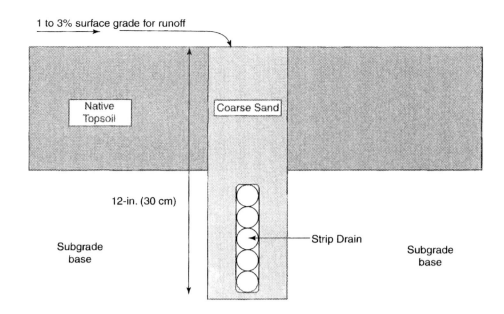

adjacent to each other over the length of the pipe for drainage water to enter. PVC pipe is generally more expensive but is able to withstand heavier traffic pressure than flexible HDPE pipe.

Strip Drains

Strip drains exist where a narrow (2- to 4-in. wide, 5- to 10-cm) trench is dug, a one-inch (2.5-cm) wide perforated drain (or "strip") sleeve is installed, and trenches are backfilled with sand (Figure 4–18). The drain types used include one-inch (2.5-cm) wide cloth-wrapped waffle- or honeycomb-shaped drain sleeves, vertically stacked small diameter pipes (composite drains), or other similar narrow sleeved material. Drains are placed at the bottom of the trench and extend about halfway to the soil surface. Water will enter the lowest pipe of a composite drain first. Once this pipe is filled, water will enter and flow through the next lowest, and so on. Narrower trenches are used for this stacked pipe, reducing the costs of trenching and fill material. However, the smaller diameter pipe means greater surface area contacting the water; thus, there is more friction loss and lower water-carrying capacity. This makes stacked pipe less efficient for water removal and more prone to clogging than single larger tile lines.

Strip drains allow an increase in water infiltration rates into the soil surface without complete renovation of the native soil profile. However, in many cases the trenches filled with gravel and sand on grade actually work as "dry wells" where they lower the water table, removing surface water. The drain lines are not directly involved in this water removal. Drain lines must be installed deep enough to avoid disruption or displacement by heavy equipment.

A secondary tier of sand-only slit drains may also be installed at 0.5 to 1 foot (0.15 to 0.3 m) spacing at right angles to the mini-pipe slit drains to provide a more intensive means for water interception. In this system, the sand-filled trenches drain away some surface water without it having to traverse across the field.

Slit Drains

A modification of subsurface drainage lines is the **slit drain,** also called sand injection, sand banding, sand placement, or surface grooming (Figures 4–19 and 4–20). Slit drains are constructed by digging a drainage trench and then backfilling with either gravel and/or coarse sand. The top two to four inches (5 to 10 cm) of the slit drain trench are filled with coarse sand to serve as a growing medium for the turfgrass. This sand should be compacted prior to installing sod to decrease the amount of settling occurring over time. If sod is installed, its soil should be removed by washing prior to installation to minimize any negative impact from introducing dissimilar soil from the sod onto the sand medium. Slit drains have the advantage of being easily installed at a fraction of the cost of pipe drains. Slit drains act as "dry wells," removing surface water, but when the trench completely fills, the soil around it becomes soggy. Also, in heavy native soils, the tops of slit drains often remain excessively dry, causing turf desiccation (Figure 4–21).

FIGURE 4–19 Slit drains (also called "cell system") may have a narrow trench backfilled with sand to remove excess surface moisture.

FIGURE 4–20 A one- to two-inch diameter (2.5- to 5-cm) pipe may be placed at the bottom of the trench to facilitate water removal.

A modification of the slit drain is a **French drain,** which involves a trench four to eight inches (10 to 20 cm) wide dug on a 1 to 3 percent slope, with a drainage pipe laid at its bottom and backfilled with sand (Figure 4–22). This drainage system provides a wider trench than slit drains, which extends its life expectancy and potentially drains a larger area. Additional fill material is necessary for this system and more surface area disruption occurs. However, many facilities readily have access to the trenching equipment and the wider trench is usually easier to work with. In heavy soils, the wider trench filled with sand easily desiccates, shows nutrient deficiencies, and may become more susceptible to low-temperature damage (Figure 4–23).

The advantages of slit and strip drains include installation with minimal surface disturbance and the need for less labor, as these steps are largely mechanized. They also provide drainage to poorly designed and constructed facilities at an attractive cost compared to complete soil profile renovation. However, due to the complex design of the drains, personnel turnover in management often leads to eventual disturbances of the drain's integrity. Sufficient surface slopes must be present for lateral water movement to these drains. Gravel and possibly small pipe in the bottom of the slits also are needed to expedite water removal from the site. Traffic from play, soil migration, erosion, and aerification can also cause glazing of silt and/or clay over the sand, reducing water

FIGURE 4–21 Turf desiccation and/or nutrient deficiency at the surface of slit drains composed of sand that are prone to drying and leaching. Cool-season grasses grown in heavy soils during warm, dry weather are especially susceptible.

FIGURE 4–22 Installation of slit drains (also called French drains) in a fairway where a four- to eight-inch (10- to 20-cm) wide trench is backfilled with sand. A drain tile may also be placed at the bottom of these to facilitate water removal.

infiltration. Topdressing with finer sand or soil used to fill the trench can also clog pore spaces and disrupt water infiltration. Heavy equipment can crush or disturb the integrity of the drain. The smaller diameter (1-in., 2.5-cm) pipe used in the strip drains are also prone to eventual clogging by downward-migrating soil particles. These drains typically require closer spacings than traditional lateral drains; thus, more pipe junctions are needed.

Due to these inherent limitations, strip or slit drains should be viewed as a technique for removing the symptoms of waterlogging rather than as a technique for curing the problem. They also have a finite life span and often are a means of providing a temporary fix that will have to be performed repeatedly to succeed continually. They generally are not viewed as a substitute for sound surface and subsurface drainage planning and installation, which should occur prior to construction.

Filter Cloth

Nylon-netted filter drainage sleeves are also available, which are wrapped around perforated pipe to prevent soil particles from impeding water flow into drainage lines (Figure 4–24). There is much debate over the probability of these nets/sleeves clogging over time from soil particle movement toward the drain. If excessive (>5 to 10 percent) silt and clay are present in the topsoil, these

FIGURE 4–23 Turf damage above slit drains that dried excessively and became more susceptible to low-temperature kill.

FIGURE 4–24 Nylon-netted filter sleeves wrapped around perforated drain pipe to prevent soil particles from impeding water flow into the drain tile.

drainage sleeves may clog. In this situation, filter cloth should be considered to line the drainage ditch but should not be physically wrapped around the individual drain lines.

Drainage Line Patterns

Typically, a gridiron or herringbone pattern is used for drainage line arrangement. The drainage pattern should be designed so drain lines are placed nearly perpendicular to the slope and rotated downhill as required to drain. However, any pattern is acceptable as long as each line has a continuous downward slope and water in golf greens does not have to travel more than 10 feet (3 m) to a drainage line.

Drainage Line Trenches

Trenches in which golf green drainage lines are to be laid should be cut a minimum of six to eight inches (15 to 20 cm) in depth into the subgrade and five to six inches (12.7 to 15 cm) in width. In native soil, three- to four-foot (0.9- to 1.2-m) deep drain lines are sufficient. Lines less than two feet (0.6 m) deep become subject to damage or disruption by heavy machinery or excessive traffic.

The bottom of the trench should be a minimum of two inches (5 cm) wider than the outside diameter of the pipe. Trenches up to 12 inches (30.5 cm) wide have been utilized. However, more gravel is needed to fill the wider trenches, which increases cost. Normally, a drainage line trench should be no more than twice the width of the drain pipe. A five- to six-inch (12.7- to 15-cm) wide "U"-shaped trench will allow for a 0.5- to 1-inch (12.7- to 25.4-mm) bed of gravel to be placed around (below, above, and on either side of) a four-inch (10-cm) diameter drain line to reduce washing of subgrade soil into the drain line. The soil displaced by digging the trench should be removed or placed between drainage lines to provide a slight slope toward the trench and then compacted.

Prior to digging trenches, the area should be surveyed. Proposed trench lines should be staked and labeled with the desired depth of cut. Drain lines should not be placed any deeper than necessary to obtain the desired slope. Trenches should have a minimum downward slope of 0.5 percent (1 foot of drop for every 200 feet, 0.3 m per 60 m) and a maximum slope of 4 percent (1 foot of drop for every 25 feet, 0.3 m per 7.5 m). Slopes of 1 to 2 percent (1 foot of drop for every 100 feet, 0.3 m per 30 m, to 1 foot of drop for every 50 feet, 0.3 m per 15 m, respectively) are ideal. Drain lines with slopes of 0.5 percent or less are difficult to properly grade, install, and maintain due to the slight elevation changes and slow flow rates. Drain lines with slopes greater than 4 percent will lose lateral drainage capability. Steeper slopes also require greater elevation changes within the drain line and a lower outlet point.

When establishing the subgrade of a drain system, it is best to start at the outlet and establish the grade of the main collector line. After establishing this main line grade, the grade of each lateral can be determined. Care must be taken to ensure the drainage trench and drain lines always slope downward to avoid any entrapment or collection of water along the drainage lines. If a section of pipe is lower than the section closer to the outlet, water will pond in the lower section. This causes any sediment in the water to settle and collect in the bottom of the pipe, eventually clogging (slowing) drainage. Grades of all main and lateral drainage lines should be checked with a level prior to backfilling.

Drain line ends and joints should be covered with asphalt paper, fiberglass composition, or plastic spacers or caps to prevent gravel and/or soil from entering the drain lines. It is common for the main drain lines into which the lateral feeder lines flow to have their upper end extended to the soil surface and properly capped. If these lines become clogged or contaminated from gravel, soil, or some other material, the cap can then be removed and the lines flushed. This can greatly extend the useful life of the drainage system without the need of disturbing the playing surfaces to clean individual lines. After the drain line is laid, trenches should be backfilled with gravel and care taken not to displace the slope or joint covers of the drain tiles. An alternative design element is to have the main lateral line daylight into a catch basin. This allows for periodic flushing of the line and also allows air entry into the line for more efficient drainage.

CHAPTER

5

Soil Oxygen and Temperature Properties

INTRODUCTION

Adequate soil oxygen (O_2) is an essential part of encouraging desirable turf rooting, which in turn helps maintain healthy plants. Table 5–1 lists the composition of clean, dry air near sea level. However, soil air differs from atmospheric air as carbon dioxide (CO_2) levels are higher, ranging from 0.03 to 21 percent; O_2 content is slightly lower, ranging from 0 to 21 percent; and water vapor content is much higher, often 80 to almost 100 percent. Soil oxygen is utilized by plant root and microbial respiration, producing CO_2, as shown:

Carbon dioxide formation from oxygen utilization by microorganisms

$$\begin{array}{ccccc} C & + & O_2 & \rightarrow & CO_2 \\ \text{carbon} & & \text{oxygen} & & \text{carbon dioxide} \end{array}$$

The composition of soil air is dependent on the amount of respiration and air exchange between the soil and atmosphere. As O_2 is consumed by this respiratory process, the concentration of CO_2 proportionally increases. This process accelerates as temperatures increase.

Ideally, soils should consist of roughly 25 percent pore space filled with gases (mostly, O_2). When this percentage drops to below about 10 percent due to either higher bulk densities or increased soil moisture, the soil becomes **anaerobic** (without oxygen), and a gradual decline in turfgrass vigor and quality will follow. Plant root growth is restricted through soil compaction by reducing root water utilization, restricting nutrient uptake, lack of O_2, accumulation of CO_2 and other toxic gases such as methane and sulfides, and physically restricting root penetration. Accompanying this decline in plant growth (especially root growth) is the reduction of nutrient and water absorption and the formation of certain inorganic compounds toxic to plant growth, including organic gases such as methane (CH_4) and ethylene (C_2H_4); nitrogenous gases such as dinitrogen (N_2), nitrous oxide (N_2O), nitric oxide (NO), and ammonia (NH_3); and sulfur gases such as hydrogen sulfide (H_2S). As mentioned, through the processes of plant respiration and the decomposition by microorganisms of organic residues, oxygen is utilized and carbon dioxide is produced. As a result, soil air commonly contains 10 to 100 times more carbon dioxide and slightly less oxygen than the atmosphere (nitrogen remains roughly the same).

TABLE 5–1 *Composition of clean, dry air near sea level (Bremner & Blackmer, 1982).*

Component	Volume content	
	------ percent ------	----- ppm -----
Nitrogen (N₂)	78.09	780,900
Oxygen (O₂)	20.94	209,400
Argon (Ar)	0.93	9,300
Carbon dioxide (CO₂)	0.0332	332
Neon (Ne)	0.0018	18
Helium (He)	0.00052	5.2
Methane (CH₄)	0.00015	1.5
Krypton (Kr)	0.0001	1
Hydrogen (H₂)	0.00005	0.5
Nitrous oxide (N₂O)	0.000033	0.33
Carbon monoxide (CO)	0.00001	0.1
Xenon (Xe)	0.000008	0.08
Ozone (O₃)	0.000002	0.02
Ammonia (NH₃)	0.000001	0.01
Nitrogen dioxide (NO₂)	0.0000001	0.001
Sulfur dioxide (SO₂)	0.00000002	0.0002

The rate in which soil oxygen exchanges with atmospheric oxygen is the **oxygen diffusion rate** (or **ODR**). The ODR through a soil typically represents oxygen utilization by plant roots instead of the actual soil oxygen concentration level. Oxygen must diffuse through large soil pores and through the water layer surrounding roots before it reaches the root. Moist soils have a lower ODR than drier soils. When soils are saturated, ODR is limited to the solubility at a given temperature. Increasing soil organic matter provides an energy source for soil microorganisms, resulting in increased soil carbon dioxide as oxygen is consumed. Increased surface winds also increase soil oxygen exchange, as a pressure gradient is produced at the soil surface.

No one single value exists as being the critical value of soil oxygen for all plants in all situations. The critical soil ODR for root growth of many plants is approximately 20×10^{-8} g cm^{-2} min^{-1} (or 0.20 μg cm^{-2} min^{-1}) but may be less for some grasses such as creeping bentgrass (5×10^{-8} g cm^{-2} min^{-1}), Kentucky bluegrass (5 to 9×10^{-8} g cm^{-2} min^{-1}), or common bermudagrass (15 to 20×10^{-8} g cm^{-2} min^{-1}). Values less than this often are seen following irrigation or rainfall, especially on compacted soils (Carrow & Petrovic, 1992). Soils composed of large pores allow more rapid ODR than soils composed of smaller pores. For example, clay soils with small pores often have a slow ODR, essentially reducing the depth roots will penetrate. Kavanagh and Jelley (1981) reported carbon dioxide levels at 130 millimeters depth in golf greens as ranging from 0.5 to 2.2 percent for sandy soil greens and 3.2 to 4.7 percent in clay loam soil greens. They also noted traffic and irrigation or rainfall events significantly influenced these values. Oxygen diffuses 10,000 times quicker through air than water; thus, a minimum continuity of air-filled porosity is required for roots and aerobic microorganisms to respire. Compaction and excessive soil moisture often limit diffusion, leaving the highest ODR near the soil surface and decreasing values with increasing soil depth.

If no mechanism exists to replenish oxygen and permit the escape of carbon dioxide, plant growth will be reduced. Plants attempt to adapt to low soil oxygen levels by increasing surface rooting compared to deeper rooting. Some plants also have special tissues in their stems and roots that conduct oxygen to the roots. Soil aeration is the mechanism of gas exchange in soils that prevents oxygen deficiency and carbon dioxide toxicity (Figure 5–1).

Reduced Soil Oxygen Levels

ATP Production

Oxygen utilization by plant roots and soil microorganisms drastically increases with higher temperatures, and these can totally deplete soil oxygen within 24 hours. When soil oxygen is depleted, the Krebs (or TCA) cycle stops and ATP can be produced only by fermenting pyruvate (from Glycolysis) to lactate. Fermentation is very inefficient in ATP production, with only two moles produced per mole of hexose sugar respired, compared with 36 moles of ATP produced per mole of hexose in aerobic respiration. Thus, initial root injury by oxygen-deficient soils is from a lack of ATP for other metabolic processes. Without adequate ATP, cellular pH levels are not maintained, causing membrane deterioration.

Oxidation-Reduction Reactions

Another important chemical characteristic of soils related to soil aeration is the **oxidation** and **reduction** (also called **redox**) states of the chemical elements in these soils. If a soil is well-aerated (or oxidized), oxidized states such as ferric iron, manganic manganese, nitrate, and sulfate dominate. Soils with red, yellow, and reddish-brown colors usually indicate well-oxidized conditions. In poorly drained and poorly aerated soils, the reduced forms of such elements are found; for example, ferrous iron [pyrite (FeS_2) and ferrous sulfide (FeS)], manganous, ammonium, and sulfides. Reduction occurs when oxygen is removed by organisms that can extract the oxygen component of oxidized elements, hydrogen is gained, or an electron is gained in a solution. The presence of these reduced forms is an indication of restricted drainage and poor aeration. Iron in its reduced ferrous form causes a grey-green color formation (gleying) of mineral soils. If present, iron can quickly react with and neutralize sulfide ions to form ferrous (or iron) sulfide. Ferrous sulfide gives the characteristic black color (e.g., "black layer") of many anaerobic soils. Subdued shades such as grays and blues also indicate insufficient soil oxygen.

When wetland-type soils are drained or aerified, the ferrous sulfide and elemental sulfur in them are oxidized, ultimately forming sulfuric acid, causing soil pH to dramatically drop. Enormous amounts of lime are then required to neutralize this acidity.

Reduced soil pH when ferrous sulfide and elemental sulfur are oxidized

$$4FeS + 9O_2 + 4H_2O \rightarrow 2Fe_2O_3 + 4H_2SO_4$$

ferrous sulfide   oxygen   water   ferric oxide   sulfuric acid

$$2S + 3O_2 + 2H_2O \rightarrow 4H_2SO_4$$

elemental sulfur   oxygen   water   sulfuric acid

TABLE 5–2 *Oxidized and reduced forms of inorganic redox components under low soil oxygen levels.*

Element	Normal form in oxidized soils	Form in reduced (anaerobic) soils	Approximate redox values for change of forms (mv)	Bacteria type and conditions present
Oxygen	O_2	H_2O (water)	350	Aerobic bacteria and conditions
Nitrogen	NO_3^- (nitrate)	NH_4^+ (ammonium) N_2O (nitrous oxide) N_2 (nitrogen gas)	250	Facultative anaerobic bacteria and conditions
Manganese	Mn^{+4} or MnO_2 (manganic oxides)	Mn^{+2} (manganous oxides)	225	
Iron*	Fe^{+3} or Fe_2O_3 (ferric oxides)	Fe^{+2} (ferrous oxides)	120	
Sulfur	SO_4^{-2} (sulfate)	S^{-2} (sulfide) H_2S (hydrogen sulfide)	-75 to -150	Obligate anaerobic bacteria
Carbon	CO_2 (carbon dioxide)	CH_4 (methane)	-250 to -350	

*The reduction reaction for iron is $Fe^{+3} \xrightarrow{\text{te}^-} Fe^{+2}$ (or more specifically, $FeOOH + e^- + 3H^+ \rightarrow Fe^{+2} + 2H_2O$).

Table 5-2 lists the oxidized and reduced forms of several important elements.

The range of redox potentials or oxidation-reduction values encountered in waterlogged soils and aerated soils are shown as follows:

Oxidation-reduction values in waterlogged (reduced) and aerated (oxidized) soils.

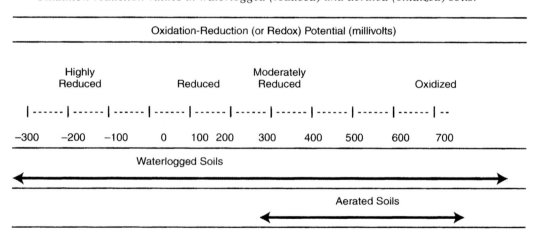

This figure shows the approximate range of redox potential values where soils are either oxidized or reduced, and if reduced, the relative ranking of this reduction. The lower the redox potential value, the less soil oxygen available. Oxidation-reduction (or redox potential) provides a measure of the tendency of a system to reduce or oxidize chemicals and is usually measured in volts or millivolts. If it is positive and high, strong oxidizing conditions exist. If it is low and even negative, elements are found in reduced forms indicating oxygen is less available to plants.

In a well-drained or aerated soil, the redox potential is in the 400 to 700 millivolt range. As aeration is reduced, the redox potential declines to a level of about 300 to 350 millivolts. At lower redox potentials, oxygen dissolved in soil water is used by soil microbes, and finally combined oxygen in nitrates, sulfates, and ferric oxides is utilized for microbial metabolism, and these nutrients are changed into reduced forms as listed in Table 5–2. Under drastic waterlogged conditions, the redox potential value may be lowered to an extreme of -400 millivolts. Toxic compounds such as hydrogen sulfide and elemental sulfur then develop since anaerobic bacteria use the oxygen molecule in sulfate, leaving a reduced form of sulfide. The rotten egg smell of anaerobic soils results when sulfides are formed. These sulfides are highly toxic to plants. Other toxic substances may also form when compounds are reduced under waterlogged soils. For example, sulfide and methane may be produced from soil sugars found in decaying plants.

Soil Sulfide and methane production from decaying plants

$$SO_4^{-2} \quad + \quad 8e^- \quad + \quad 9H^+ \quad \rightarrow \quad HS^- \quad + \quad 4H_2O$$

sulfate electrons sulfides water

$$CO_2 \quad + \quad 8e^- \quad + \quad 8H^+ \quad \rightarrow \quad CH_4 \quad + \quad 2H_2O$$

carbon dioxide methane

The presence of the reduced forms of these and other compounds can be in such quantities as to be toxic. This is especially true in anaerobic soils that are acid. Acid soils, thus, intensify the adverse effects of poor aeration on several of these reduced forms of compounds such as iron and manganese.

SOIL TEMPERATURES

Soil temperature, along with water, influence the biological and chemical activity of a soil and the adaptability of plants that will grow in it. As soils cool, their chemical and biological rates are proportionally slowed, often limiting the availability of necessary nutrients and slowing plant processes such as seed germination and root growth.

The sun's radiation is the primary heat source for most soils. Much of the heat energy from solar radiation can be transferred from one environmental feature to another by various processes, including evaporation, radiation, conduction, convection, and advection (Figure 5–2). Soil temperature at any given point depends on the ratio of energy being absorbed to that being lost. Heat lost by the earth (known as far-infrared radiation) is replaced by energy from the sun (in the form of incoming shortwave solar radiation). The equation demonstrating net energy (R_N) of incoming shortwave solar radiation (R_S) minus heat lost by the earth as reflected shortwave radiation (R_R) and longwave infrared radiation (R_L) is:

$$R_N \quad = \quad R_s \quad - \quad R_R \quad - \quad R_L$$

net energy   shortwave radiation   reflected shortwave radiation   longwave infrared radiation

Atmospheric temperature, like the soil, is greatly influenced by its moisture content. Evaporation of water absorbs relatively large amounts of heat (580 calories are absorbed to evaporate each gram of liquid water), leaving a cooler surface. Condensation of moisture, likewise, releases large amounts of heat back to the system (580 calories per gram of water). Conversely, when water is frozen, heat is given off as 60 calories per gram of water. When ice melts, 60 calories of heat is absorbed per gram of water.

FIGURE 5–2 Heat (or net energy, R_N) received by the earth involves absorbed shortwave solar radiation (R_S) less that lost by reflected shortwave radiation (R_R), longwave infrared radiation (R_L), evaporation, conduction, and convection.

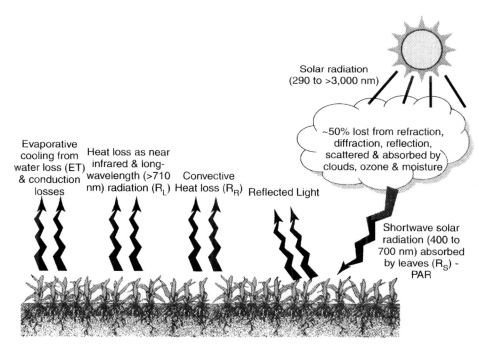

FIGURE 5-3 This air unit
attaches to drain lines to help
regulate soil moisture and
gases.

Heat retention by a soil is primarily determined by its composition and color, moisture content, and cover. If soil moisture content is high, more heat is needed for temperature increases because the heat retention capacity of water is three to five times greater than for soil minerals. For example, only 0.2 calories of heat energy is required to increase the temperature of one gram of dry soil by 1°C; compared to one calorie of heat energy required for each degree increase per gram of water. Conversely, the higher the soil moisture content, the more heat held by the soil. For superintendents, this is an important consideration. During summer stress periods on bentgrass greens, for example, a goal is to reduce the heat load in soil. Superintendents, therefore, should provide only enough soil moisture to prevent wilt, allowing evaporative cooling to reduce this heat load. Excessive moisture also promotes other problems such as algae and diseases. New tools, such as subsurface air units, provide better control of potentially harmful excessive soil moisture and gases (Figure 5-3).

Darker soils (e.g., high organic matter soils) absorb more heat than lighter color soils (e.g., sands). However, this increase in heat retention by certain soils may be offset by their higher moisture holding capacities. Compacted soils also tend to hold more heat than loosened soil, but due to the compaction, these soils have more material to heat per volume and tend to be delayed in heat gain and loss compared to coarser materials.

Typically, due to heat flow being slower in soil than in the atmosphere, a lag occurs between maximum air temperatures and soil temperatures. In addition to those parameters previously discussed, this lag is influenced by soil depth and time of day. The deeper the soil, the longer a temperature change takes to reach it; thus, a lag occurs in maximum daily temperature and soil temperature and the temperature fluctuates less over time. Soil depths below about 12 inches (0.3 m) are seldom affected by daily temperature fluctuations. On cool nights, deeper soil layers do not cool as quick as surface soil due to the insulating effect of the overlying soil.

Microenvironments also influence soil temperatures. For example, relatively flat soils will absorb less heat when the sun is low in the southern sky, such as during winter. However, south and southwestern facing slopes during winter will absorb more energy from the sun since these are at a more acute angle with the sun.

EXAMPLE: Calculating the Heat Capacity of Soils.

Soil moisture content influences changes in soil temperatures through its impact on the heat capacity (or specific heat) of a soil. For example, consider two similar golf green soils, $Soil_1$ is wet with 35 grams of water per 100 grams of soil, while $Soil_2$ is a drier soil with only 15 grams of water per 100 grams of soil. The following equation is used to calculate the weighted average heat capacity of a mixture of substances:

$$\text{heat capacity (or } C) = \frac{C_1 M_1 + C_2 M_2}{M_1 + M_2}$$

where C_1 and M_2 are the heat capacity and mass of substance 1 (soil in this case), and C_2 and M_2 are the heat capacity and mass of substance 2 (water in this case).

C_1 = heat capacity of soil, 0.2 calorie/gram of soil
M_1 = mass of soil, in this case, one gram of soil
C_2 = heat capacity of water, 1.0 calorie/gram of water
M_2 = mass of water or number of calories needed to raise the temperature of the water by 1°C. The amount of water present (grams) is multiplied by 1.0 calorie/gram. For example, for $Soil_1$, 35 grams of water/100 grams of soil (or 0.35 g) occurs. This is multiplied by 1.0 calorie/gram, which is the number of calories needed to raise the temperature of 0.1 gram of water by 1°C to achieve 0.35.

$$Soil_1 = \frac{C_1 M_1 + C_2 M_2}{M_1 + M_2}$$

$$= \frac{(0.2 \text{ cal/g} \times 1 \text{ g}) + (1 \text{ cal/g} \times 0.35 \text{ g})}{1.0 \text{ g} + 0.35 \text{ g}}$$

$$= 0.407 \text{ cal/g}$$

$$Soil_2 = \frac{C_1 M_1 + C_2 M_2}{M_1 + M_2}$$

$$= \frac{(0.2 \text{ cal/g} \times 1 \text{ g}) + (1 \text{ cal/g} \times 0.15 \text{ g})}{1.0 \text{ g} + 0.15 \text{ g}}$$

$$= 0.304 \text{ cal/g}$$

The wetter $Soil_1$ has a heat capacity of 0.407 calories/gram, where the drier $Soil_2$ has a heat capacity of 0.304 calories/gram. The wet soil, therefore, needs an additional 0.103 calories (0.407–0.304) of solar radiation for every degree of temperature rise of the dry soil and will warm up and cool down slower than the dry soil.

CHAPTER
6

Soil Organisms

INTRODUCTION

In addition to the mineral and organic composition of soils, a wide array of organisms also inhabit soils. They range in size from microscopic (bacteria, nematodes, algae, actinomycetes, and fungi) to groups visible to the naked eye (earthworms, insect larvae, mole crickets). Soil organisms make up less than 1 percent of the soil by volume, but are necessary to sustain plant life. Without a healthy and balanced complement of these organisms, many of the essential processes involved in plant growth could not be accomplished. Soil organisms also contribute, through their death, to soil nutrient levels. For example, 100 pounds (45 kg) of dead microbes provide 10 pounds (4.5 kg) of nitrogen, 2 pounds (0.9 kg) of phosphorus, and 1 1/2 pounds (0.7 kg) of potassium. Soil organisms also fix atmospheric nitrogen, make many elements available, and recycle nutrients.

Biologists divide the living world into two groups of organisms based on the types of living cells each organism is composed of. **Eukaryotes** are composed of cells with a membrane-bound nucleus; these cells divide through mitosis. This includes higher animals and plants. **Prokaryotes** have cells with no nucleus. Instead, they have a single, circular DNA molecule (chromosome) not bound by a membrane. Their cells also divide by binary division instead of mitosis. Bacteria and mycoplasmas are important prokaryotes.

Organisms may also be further classified according to their carbon, oxygen, and energy requirements. **Autotrophs** are organisms that obtain atmospheric carbon from carbon dioxide (CO_2) and methane (CH_4), inorganic nutrients from the soil solution, and their energy from the sun through photosynthesis to synthesize cellular components for growth, survival, and reproduction. Higher plants and algae are autotrophic. Some bacteria are also autotrophic since they use carbon dioxide and inorganic nutrients similar to the higher plants. However, these bacteria obtain energy from the oxidation of inorganic elements such as nitrogen (N) or sulfur (S). These autotrophic, nitrifying bacteria (*Nitrosomonas* spp. and *Nitrobacter* spp.) are essential to produce nitrate (NO_3^-) for the growth of turfgrasses. Other autotrophic bacteria (*Thiobacillus* spp.) convert elemental sulfur (S) to sulfuric acid (H_2SO_4), which lowers the soil pH.

Heterotrophs are consuming organisms, meaning they obtain carbon and energy by ingesting carbohydrates and other organic substances from organic materials in the soil such as humus, thatch, roots, and even other organisms. They may be subdivided as primary consumers that feed on dead organic matter and secondary consumers that are predators and parasites. **Aerobes** are organisms that require free oxygen in the air to perform respiration. **Anaerobes** can use the combined oxygen from various compounds such as nitrate or sulfate. Examples of heterotrophs include certain bacteria, fungi, protozoa, and animals.

Bacteria

Bacteria are the most abundant of the soil organisms. Most soil **bacteria** are very small (< 1/1,000,000-in., $<2.5 \times 10^{-5}$ mm), single-cell microorganisms without a nucleus or chlorophyll. These exist as mats, clumps, and filaments on and around soil particles and roots. Their shape ranges from spheres (cocci), ovals (spirals), or rods (bacilli) to branching filaments (actinomycetes). They are responsible for many key biochemical reactions necessary to support higher plants including nitrification, nitrogen fixation, and sulfur oxidation, which provides these nutrients to plants. Due to the abundance of roots and organic matter, bacteria are found in the highest numbers in grasslands. Heterotrophic bacteria decompose organic materials, as their primary function in ecosystems is to release nutrients for recycling to higher plants. Bacteria populations, like most soil organisms, fluctuate with the season. Numbers are generally highest in temperate regions in early summer and in fall. Bacteria are rapid multipliers, doubling in population in as fast as 20 minutes. Cyanobacteria, also known as blue-green algae, contain chlorophyll and fixed limited amounts of nitrogen under damp, wet conditions.

Bacteria can be divided into three basic groups based on differences in their cell walls. **Mycoplasmas** and **phytoplasmas** have no cell walls and are not normally found living freely in soil. The other two groups are separated based on the composition of their cell wall, which is determined by a test called the **Gram stain. Gram-positive bacteria** retains an applied purple dye, and therefore have a purple color; whereas **gram-negative bacteria** do not retain this dye and remain red in color.

Over 200 major types of bacteria are found in soils. Soil aeration largely determines the type of bacteria in soil. Where gaseous oxygen is available (e.g., aerated, oxidized soils), aerobic bacteria exist and use oxygen to oxidize or decompose organic matter. Bacteria also help decompose turf thatch by breaking down simple organic compounds such as plant exudates and other compounds. In the absence of gaseous oxygen, anaerobic *Thiobacillus* bacteria take over, utilizing compounds such as nitrates, sulfates, and iron (ferric) oxides in metabolism. As mentioned, the reduced forms of some elements, such as iron and manganese, may be present in sufficiently high quantities to be toxic to higher plants. When sulfate is used rather than oxygen, hydrogen sulfide (H_2S) is produced that can be toxic and stinks like rotten eggs, possibly leading to "black layer" formation.

Great interest exists in some bacteria as possible biological control agents. These include *Bacillus popillae* and *B. thuringensis* for control of certain insects, and *Beauvaria* and *Pasteuria* species for biological control of certain nematodes and possibly soil insects. The only known bacterial disease of turfgrass is "C-5 decline" of "Toronto" creeping bentgrass.

Research on the use of bacteria as a possible biological control agent is growing. A biopesticide identifying a specific weed, insect, disease, or nematode pest it can control must be registered as a biopesticide. Such materials are usually a very specific bacteria or fungus, and will be registered with the U.S. Environmental Protection Agency as to their specific pesticidal activity. Information about biopesticides is available on the EPA's web site at: www.epa.gov/pesticides/biopesticides/.

Biological control agents differ from "bioproducts" or biostimulants, which are general mixes containing a wide variety of growth-enhancing compounds including fertilizer nutrients, bacteria, fungi, vitamins, or hormones. Such products cannot claim a specific pesticidal activity, and instead will have vague claims, such as "improves turf health."

Fungi

Soil **fungi** are multicellular organisms without chlorophyll, and are aerobic and heterotrophic in their nutritional requirements. Examples of fungi include single-celled yeasts, multicellular filamentous mildews, molds, rusts, smuts, and larger mushrooms. Although fungi can sometimes be pathogenic to cultivated plants, most present in the soil are actually beneficial due to their ability to decompose complex organic residues (cellulose, starch, gums, lignin, proteins, and sugars), help control other microbes such as nematodes and bacteria, and physically build soil particles. This leads to the formation of desirable humus and aggregate stabilization. Soil fungi, called

mycorrhizae, also are involved in an important symbiotic association with roots of higher plants to aid in improved plant nutrition and exchange, especially phosphorus. Endophytic fungi also are beneficial in turf for their ability to discourage certain insects.

Actinomycetes

Developmentally, soil **actinomycetes** are a special type of primitive bacteria with some featured characteristics of fungi. Actinomycetes are single celled without chlorophyll, have branched mycelia, and are aerobic and heterotrophic in nature. They occur second, only to bacteria, in abundance in soils. They are of great importance in the decomposition of soil organic matter and the liberation of nutrients from this material. As with fungi, they are also able to degrade the more complex-resistant compounds such as cellulose, lignin, chitin, and phospholipids. The presence of actinomycetes in abundance in soils is an indication of their capacity to attack complex compounds. Actinomycetes, particularly *Streptomyces* sp., produce antibiotics and volatile substances that give good soil a rich, sweet smell. They, as well as most soil organisms, prefer a pH of 5 or above, with most activity occurring between 6.5 and 8. If the pH is above 5.5, bacteria and actinomycetes are favored, while fungi grow well over a wide range of soil pH but have less competition from bacteria and actinomycetes when pH is <5.5. Fungi most often dominate low pH soils.

Algae

Algae are multicellular organisms with chlorophyll and are aerobic and autotrophic in their nutritional requirements. They thrive on or near the soil surface since most have photosynthesis capability; thus, they require sunlight to produce food. The predominant types of algae are cyanobacteria or blue-green algae (some which also fix nitrogen), green algae, and diatoms. Green algae are evident when soil pH is low (<5.0), while blue-green algae prefer a soil pH between 7 to 8.5 and seldom are found when soil pH drops below 5.0.

Protozoa

Protozoa are the most simple form of animal life in soil and are the most abundant of soil invertebrates. They are primitive, unicellular organisms and are generally found in the upper six inches (15 cm) of soil. Protozoa include organisms such as amoeba and paramecium. Their life cycle consists of an active stage and a resting (or cyst) stage that allows them to resist adverse environmental conditions and survive for many years.

Protozoa feed on organic matter and other microbes, and some are cannibalistic. Some amoeba and other ciliates can divide several times daily and may consume several thousand bacteria per division. Despite the fact they are very abundant and common in soil, little is known regarding the function of protozoa. They are thought to be primarily involved in regulating bacterial and algal populations.

Other Soil Organisms

Larger **soil animals** and **insects** inhabiting soils include nematodes, earthworms, grubs, slugs, protozoa, mole crickets, and mites. Most of these feed primarily on other soil animals, bacteria, fungi, actinomycetes, and plant debris; thus, they add to organic residue decomposition. Certain ones (e.g., nematodes, grubs, and mole crickets), however, feed directly on plant roots and can reduce the vigor of turfgrasses. Others, such as ants and termites, can substantially alter soil structure and till the soil, but also become a nuisance when in direct contact with humans or wooden structures. Large burrowing animals such as armadillos, moles, gophers, skunks, raccoons, and prairie dogs eat vegetation and soil insects; thus, they disrupt the turf surface through their digging activities.

Abundance of Soil Organisms

A nonsterilized biologically active soil can contain as many as 45 quadrillion microorganisms per 1,000 square feet of turfgrass rootzone. Normal populations, however, can be deficient in sand-based rootzones like golf greens, especially those that have been sterilized. Three to five years may be required for such systems to obtain a stable microbial population, presumably due to the time necessary for organic matter to buildup from root and shoot turnover. Amendments, such as organic matter, added to sand-based rootzones shorten the time needed to stabilize the soil organism population. Until a stable population of organisms occurs, the lack of microbial activity to help minimize environmental extremes and soil pathogens may explain certain problems when growing-in new greens.

BENEFITS OF SOIL ORGANISMS

As mentioned, soil organisms are very important in the breakdown and recycling of plant and animal residues with a corresponding release of water, heat, carbon dioxide, and nutrients such as nitrogen, phosphorus, and sulfur. One year after adding plant residues to soil, 60 to 80 percent of its carbon is typically converted to carbon dioxide by soil organisms. Approximately 5 percent remains as either live soil organisms (or biomass); 5 percent as nonhumic compounds such as acids, polysaccharides, and polyuronides; with the remaining 10 to 30 percent as humic substances. Soil organisms also function in the formation of beneficial humus, improve soil physical properties such as improved aeration and better tilth, break down certain pesticides and a variety of environmental pollutants, and provide antagonistic reactions against plant root pathogens.

The amount of available nitrogen often controls this rate of organic matter decomposition as it is needed to build proteins in new bacterial and fungal colonies. The **carbon:nitrogen ratio** (or **C:N ratio**) indicates the nitrogen content in the microorganisms and in organic matter. A material low in nitrogen content is indicated by a wide C:N ratio. A carbon:nitrogen ratio of 10 to 1 is normally optimum for these organisms. Soil amendments with higher ratios than this (e.g., 74 to 1 for rice hulls, 80 to 1 for straw, 142 to 1 for fir bark, and 400 to 1 for sawdust) need supplemental nitrogen applications to support and encourage microbial activity and to provide nitrogen for higher plants; otherwise, the bacteria will consume the nitrogen, the higher plants will show nitrogen deficiency, and the high carbon containing materials will slowly decompose. Conditions favoring most soil organisms include moisture near field capacity, near neutral pH, adequate nutrient content, and warm temperatures (approximately 85°F, 29°C).

Soil organisms account for many of the biochemical reactions and changes, ranging from physical disintegration of large plant residues by insects and earthworms to the eventual complete decomposition of these residues by smaller organisms such as bacteria, fungi, and actinomycetes. The most abundant plant substrates for soil microorganisms are cellulose, hemicellulose, lignin, and humus. Accompanying these decaying processes is the release of several nutrient elements including nitrogen, phosphorus, and sulfur from organic combination.

Cellulose is a long-chain polymer of glucose molecules. Breakdown of soil cellulose is slow and is most often performed by fungi, bacteria, protozoa, and actinomycetes.

Hemicellulose is broken down faster than cellulose and can be performed by a wider range of microorganisms. Hemicellulose are water-insoluble polysaccharides mostly made of hexose and pentose sugars not structurally related to cellulose.

Lignin is a complex polymer of subunits of a C_6-C_3 resinous material that impregnates cell walls as plants age. Lignin normally is found mixed with cellulose; thus, it is difficult to extract alone. As the plant lignin content rises, decomposition rates decrease. High lignin content in turfgrasses, such as zoysiagrass and bluegrass, tend to develop heavy thatch layers due to the relative inability of most soil microorganisms to break lignin down. Fungi in the basidiomycete family (e.g., mushrooms) are the main lignin decomposers since they are best suited for decomposition of hard, woody substrates (like tree bark).

Humus is the final product of organic matter decomposition in soils and consists of numerous chemical substances such as water-soluble sugars and amino acids, and water-insoluble *fulvic acid, humic acid,* and *humin.* Humus is the relatively stable, dark-colored colloidal organic matter in soils. It is very important in improving soil nutrient exchange, soil tilth, and soil water-holding capacity. It is a product of microbial biosynthesis from organic residues; therefore, its susceptibility to further microbial decomposition is very low, and because of the advanced stage of decomposition, humus does not greatly stimulate increased microbial activity.

Organic substance	Decomposition rate
Carbohydrates, proteins, starches, sugars	fast
Hemicellulose	fast
Cellulose	moderate
Fats, waxes	slow
Lignins, lipids, humus	very slow

Carbohydrates, proteins, sugars, and organic acids are easily broken down by these organisms while lignaceous materials, lipids, and soil humus are more resistant, and therefore slower to degrade. Numerous heterotrophic bacteria, including those called **ammonifiers,** help in the breakdown and conversion of organic nitrogen from organic matter to ammonium (NH_4^+). Autotrophic bacteria called nitrifiers then convert ammonium into nitrite (NO_2^-) and nitrate nitrogen (NO_3^-). Nitrite nitrogen is toxic to higher plants, whereas ammonium and nitrate nitrogen are forms used by plants. *Nitrosomonas* spp. convert ammonium to nitrite while *Nitrobacter* spp. convert nitrite to nitrate (Figure 6–1). These bacteria are extremely difficult to purify and to enrich. Therefore, it is highly unlikely these will be found in various microbial products.

The biological fixing of nitrogen requires a considerable amount of energy. Sixteen ATPs are needed to make two molecules of ammonia from one dinitrogen. Therefore, sufficient carbon is necessary to supply this massive amount of energy. Sufficient oxygen and nitrogen levels are also needed for these bacteria to convert nitrogen.

Many soil organisms produce substances that are toxic, or antagonistic, to the growth of other soil organisms. An example involves certain soil fungi and bacteria that parasitize and kill nematodes. The antagonistic relationships help control or reduce plant root parasites. Other organisms compete very strongly for nutrients with pathogenic bacteria and fungi to inhibit their growth and so reduce their damage to higher plants. Hyphae from mycorrhizal fungi can also compensate for the loss of roots to nematodes and diseases.

Potential Harmful Effects of Certain Soil Organisms

In the absence of oxygen, many microorganisms utilize oxidized forms of soil nutrients to conduct respiration rather than oxygen. The resulting reduced forms of these nutrients [e.g., hydrogen sulfide (H_2S) and methane (CH_4)] may buildup to toxic levels in plant roots if oxygen is not reintroduced into the root profile. This is one of the important reasons to aerify soils that tend to compact, such as heavy traffic areas like golf greens and athletic fields.

FIGURE 6–1 The major portions of the turfgrass nitrogen cycle showing soil nitrogen changes, additions, and losses.

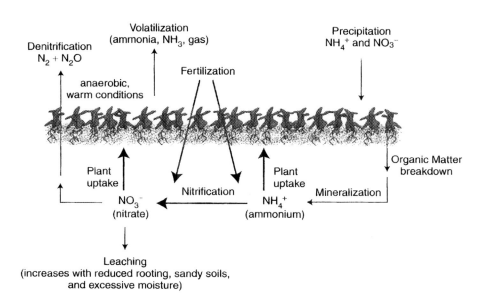

Under wet conditions, microorganisms convert nitrate-N to gaseous products in a process known as **denitrification.** While this may prevent leaching of excess nitrate-N to groundwater, it is an economical loss of nitrogen and could result in nitrogen-deficiency for plants. Sulfur may also be lost as gaseous H_2S under wet conditions.

During the nitrification process, soil acidity is generated through the production of H^+ ions, and **lime** must be periodically applied to maintain the proper soil pH for the growth of turfgrasses.

Pesticide Failure

In an effort to control harmful organisms in turfgrasses, repeated applications of certain pesticides may be used. With this continuous use, soil microorganisms begin to use certain pesticides rapidly as sources of energy and carbon to the extent the efficacy of the pesticide is lost. This process is known as **enhanced biodegradation** and can result in performance failure in certain insecticides, fungicides, herbicides, and nematicides. **Biodegradation** is a normally slow transformation of complex organic chemicals by microorganisms into simple end products such as carbon dioxide (CO_2) and water (H_2O), while enhanced biodegradation is a rapid breakdown or detoxification of a pesticide faster than normal by a biological agent in the soil. For example, when a golf course superintendent notices a pesticide such as fenamiphos (Nemacur) does not control nematodes as expected, enhanced biodegradation could be a possibility. Figure 6–2 illustrates this, as the normal half-life (50 percent of the pesticide remains) of the pesticide is 25 days in the nonproblem soil. In problem soil, however, the half-life (or $t_{1/2}$) is only eight days. In a similar manner, after repeated applications the half-life is reduced from 20 days with the first application to 10 days with the second application, and subsequently to five days with the third application of a specific pesticide. Thus, the microorganisms detoxify the pesticide before the chemical can control the pest.

Enhanced biodegradation of pesticides is responsible for the loss of efficacy and ultimately for the performance failures of certain pesticides in certain regions of the United States. For example, in limited studies, fenamiphos has been shown to degrade more rapidly when repeat applications were made compared to golf courses that never used the product. Not using the product for two to three years and/or rotating to a product in another chemical class are potential solutions to this problem.

INOCULATING SOIL WITH ORGANISMS AND OTHER PRODUCTS

The turf industry is famous for its spectacular claims of unproven products. These magical growth additives usually have colorful descriptive terms like "root biostimulants," "all-natural," "organic," "conditioner," "biologicals," "super," "hormones," and "secret" to describe them. Although some of these prove partially beneficial, caution should be heeded before treating a whole golf course. Ask the sales representative for research data/results from your state land grant university. If some product is tried, treat a small area first, such as the practice or nursery green or driving area, before treating large areas.

FIGURE 6–2 A graphic illustration of pesticide half-lives in a problem and nonproblem soil.

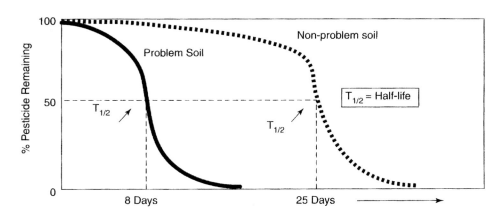

Biostimulants

Biostimulants are used to encompass non-nutritional growth-promoting substances such as microbes, plant-growth hormones, soil conditioners, and microbe energy sources (Nelson, 1998). Although not marketed as fertilizers or pesticides, these products are often touted to improve turfgrass health, vigor, and overall quality, especially turf under environmental or cultural stress. Rarely does a biostimulant elicit a noticeable growth response in healthy turf. In some instances, biostimulants will provide an erratic growth response but usually only if the plant is exposed to a stressful environment such as cold weather, heat stress, nematodes, dollar spot disease, moisture extremes, or with young seedlings growing in sand-based (e.g., low nitrogen and carbon-containing) rootzones.

Biostimulants are believed, at least in part, to promote the plant production of **antioxidants.** Antioxidants react with toxic oxygen radicals that form when plants are under stress. Toxic oxygen radicles are often referred to as free radicals and include the superoxide (O_2^{-}), singlet oxygen ($^1O_2$), hydrogen peroxide (H_2O_2), and the hydroxyl ($OH^{\cdot}$) radical. If they remain unchanged, oxygen radicals cause pigment breakdown (or bleaching), causing damage to plant cell walls, mitochondria, and chloroplasts, leading to inefficient photosynthesis, eventual cell death, and finally plant death.

The benefits of most biostimulants are difficult to measure as a wide array of ingredients, from "seaweed" to "cultural living microorganisms" to various "natural" or "organic" compounds, are shown on the label (Table 6–1). Manufacturers, in an attempt to produce a more consistent growth response, often fortify biostimulants with various nutrients such as nitrogen, iron, and sulfur. This then becomes very confusing to the turf manager trying to determine whether the biostimulant or nutrient component of the mixture produces the growth response.

Most biostimulants contain at least one growth hormone, often cytokinin (for rooting) or gibberellic acid (for shoot growth). However, if an anti-gibberellic acid plant growth retardant is being regularly used (such as trinexapac-ethyl, flurprimidol, or paclobutrazol), adding a biostimulant containing gibberellic acid may negate or diminish the desired effects of the PGRs.

TABLE 6–1 *Common ingredients listed in the labels of common biostimulants (modified from Karnock, 2000).*

Activated nutrients	Gibberellic acid	PGRs
Active humic acid	Growth stimulators	Plant extracts
Amides	Humic substances	Plant hormones
Amino acids	Humic/fulvic acids	Plant nutrients
Antioxidants	Hydrated organic proteins	Polysaccharides
Bacteria	Intermediate metabolites	Proteins
B-12 vitamins	Invert sugars	Scientifically balanced formulation
Carbohydrates	Kelp extract	Sea kelp
Carbon-rich organics	Lignin	Seaweed
Cellulose fiber	Manure extract	Secondary nutrients
Chelated micronutrients	Metabolites	Simple sugars
Chelates	Micronutrients	Soil conditioners
Chemical activators	Minerals	Sugar acid chelates
Complex sugars	Monosaccharides	Vitamins
Cultured living microorganisms	Mycorrhizae	Wetting agents
Cyanobacteria	Natural wetting agents	Yeast
Cytokinin	N-fixing bacteria	Yucca extract wetting agent
Disaccharides	Non-ionic wetting agents	
Enzymes	Nutrient broth	
Fermentation materials	Organic chelates	
Fungi	Peptides	

Hormones are well-known to promote certain plant responses. However, an overabundance or imbalance of hormones also have the potential to inhibit the same growth responses. Typically, certain environmental and cultural stresses can limit the plant's ability to produce the specific hormones it needs for normal growth and development. However, little is known on when and what stressful conditions require specific hormones, and their balance for maximum benefit. For example, scientists postulate when plants are under stress, they produce greater levels of the hormone ethylene, which signals the initiation of leaf senescence and conservation of energy reserves. Plants stop growing and the levels of growth hormones, cytokinins and auxin, drop. Biostimulants may change this hormonal balance to favor cytokinins and auxin over ethylene enough so antioxidant production can continue and the plant can "protect" itself during periods of stress when it normally begins to shut down.

Most times, this is a hit or miss proposition. Turf managers, therefore, should test these products on a small scale before using them indiscriminately. Always leave an untreated area in these tests so side-by-side comparisons can be made, and also apply an area with just the fertilizer component in the biostimulant to indicate if it is just a turfgrass fertility response or a true biostimulant reaction.

Other biostimulants are available such as various carbohydrate fertilizers and sucrose sources such as syrup, honey, and sugar. These are touted to increase microbial activity, but little research or consistent positive observations are available.

Microbial Inoculants

In an attempt to boost soil microbial populations, various inoculants are available to apply to turf stands. These are applied frequently, often nightly, many times through irrigation systems. Keeping the inoculum alive and stable is a major manufacturing, distribution, and storage challenge, as these organisms are alive, need constant nutrition and moisture, and have natural fluctuations in consistency and populations. Dehydration is one method to overcome some of these problems, but this technology has not been perfected for all organisms.

If applied during daylight, many of the microbes are sensitive to ultraviolet light and to drying conditions. Furthermore, applied inoculants become exposed to existing, adapted organisms; thus, they must be competitive, and therefore are often applied daily to try to produce a stable population. Trying to determine which organisms are actually beneficial to the turfgrass biosphere also is highly debatable and largely unknown. If unknown inoculants are added, these could actually compete with the naturally occurring beneficial microbes present; therefore, they may be more harmful than beneficial.

A question often asked involves the benefits of inoculating (adding) soil organisms (mostly bacteria) on golf greens. These are typically sprayed, added through various compost materials, or injected into the irrigation system. Benefits of inoculating soils with alien bacteria are basically unknown. They are, however, prone to several potentially lethal environments when added. Indigenous (organisms already present and, presumably, best adapted) may outcompete the added organisms. The existing soil biosphere (moisture, pH, organic matter content, etc.) may not be conducive for growth of the newly added ones. Surface applications expose these organisms to a wide array of potentially unfavorable environmental conditions, such as heat, drought stress, and exposure to harmful ultraviolet light. Pesticide applications also may adversely effect these.

Without direct contact with soil particles, especially organic matter, most bacterium will quickly die. Continual applications of these organisms probably have a much better chance of surviving and providing beneficial results compared to a one-time application. If perceived benefits are seen, ascertain whether or not these are a result of the additive or if it is from a change to favorable weather, nutrients added to the mix, or other management practices. Be sure to save untreated areas for a comparison, preferably three or four sites with and without the additive. These should be monitored for a substantial period of time to achieve consistent results.

Soil microbiology is a relatively new and unexplored science in turfgrass management. Much is to be learned on what organisms are present, their particular roles, their interactions with other organisms, and various turf responses to added inoculants. Much of the data published so far has been positive; however, negative data is seldom published. Furthermore, much of the research has been on field crops where yield and not aesthetics is the measure of success. With so much uncertainty, use these products with care and objectively to determine if and to what extent they may be beneficial to your particular operation.

SECTION

III

BEST GOLF COURSE CONSTRUCTION AND ESTABLISHMENT PRACTICES

CHAPTER
7

Golf Course Construction and Renovation

INTRODUCTION

The construction or renovation of a golf course is a tremendous undertaking, requiring the expenditure of significant time and capital. Over the years, however, far greater sums will be spent on the upkeep and maintenance of the golf course, especially those initially designed and/or constructed poorly. It is best to do the job correctly initially to ensure the course will not close in the future for renovation(s) to correct earlier mistakes.

Certain construction practices are expensive and necessary; however, others are not needed and inevitably drive up the total cost. The difference between an average and a good golf course is often not as much a question of money as it is a question of time dedication and attention to detail in the design and construction phases.

Regardless of how the golf course construction or renovation is initiated, the overall objective remains the same—construct features (e.g., greens, tees, bunkers) that will distinguish the golf course, make it a challenging yet enjoyable experience to play, and allow it to be maintained in proper playing conditions at a competitive price that is consistent with the expected return on the investment.

GOLF COURSE CONSTRUCTION

Good golf courses are the result of: (1) careful, detailed, and organized design and planning; (2) good communication among all parties; and (3) attention to construction details and management. Good golf course construction occurs from detailed contracts and specifications.

For those undertaking new construction, it is important to have an overall understanding of the steps and processes required to build a golf course. Construction is not a simple series of distinctive steps, but instead is a combination of overlapping steps performed on each successive golf hole (Table 7–1).

The procedures outlined in Table 7–1 are followed on each golf hole, but the holes are not normally constructed individually nor numerically. The most effective construction operation maximizes the management and overlapping of these steps, creating the most efficient use of

TABLE 7–1 *A general outline of steps involved in constructing a golf course.*

1. Verify the need for a golf course, select a property, assess the suitability of the site, and establish project goals
   - Secure funding/financing
2. Assemble a team of professionals to do a thorough site analysis and address planning, design, and construction issues
3. Prepare the architectural design (golf course, clubhouse, irrigation)
4. Initiate permitting and engineering, especially concerning environmental issues, land use, and construction regulations
5. Meet with appropriate regulatory agencies, environmental groups, and concerned citizens to review and receive input on the initial design and construction plan. The overall design is then adjusted based on these inputs and submitted for approval
6. Hire a qualified superintendent to help administer construction bidding and site inspection
7. Prepare the site
   - Surveying and staking (centerline, perimeters)
   - Erosion control, stormwater management, and environmental protection
   - Identify and develop utility sources
   - Land clearing
   - Trees and shrubs, indicating those to remain
   - Grubbing, or removal of roots and stumps
   - Rocks and stones
   - Rough grading
   - Soil cultivation
8. Establish drainage systems
   - Water or drainage retention facilities (dams, spillways)
   - Surface storm drainage (catch basins, ditches)
   - Subsurface storm drainage (including corrugated metal pipe and polyethylene tile)
9. Construction and shape features (greens, tees, bunkers)
10. Install the irrigation system, wells, and pump station
11. Prepare the seedbed
    - Redistribution of topsoil
    - Rootzone soil modifications (amendments, greens mix)
    - Soil pH and fertility adjustments (based on soil tests)
    - Fumigation of rootzone mix (pest control for greens, tees)
    - Final grading
12. Establish turfgrass including planting and mulching (if necessary)
13. Install sand trap including design, grading, and drainage
14. Complete accessibility, bridge, and cart path construction
    - Shelter construction and drinking fountains
15. Develop turfgrass "grow-in" and maintenance
    - irrigation
    - fertilization
    - mowing

equipment and other resources. The length of time to complete these steps typically ranges from 150 days to two years.

Scheduling of the construction process is very important, with steps 9, construction and shaping of features, and 12, turfgrass establishment, ideally based on the optimum date for establishing the turfgrasses in a given climate. It is very important to recognize that it may require a month or longer to "grass" all 18 golf holes; therefore, the target date for planting turfgrasses should consider this. In addition, sufficient time should be allowed for delays due to inclement weather conditions, especially if the golf course is being built on poorly drained soil or potentially highly erodible soil sites.

Property Selection

A critical consideration influencing all elements of construction is property selection. Instead of being liabilities, golf courses have transformed barren and unproductive land sites such as reclaimed strip mines, quarries, and sanitary landfills into community assets (Figure 7–1). Many

FIGURE 7–1 Golf courses have transformed barren and unproductive land sites such as quarries (shown), landfills, and strip mines into productive, aesthetically pleasing community assets.

of today's golf courses are the principal part of residential or resort developments with their own priorities for property selection. This is not just a problem of recent occurrence, as Garden G. Smith stated in *The World of Golf* in 1898: "It is quite certain that, had the ground on which ordinary inland golf is played today been the only available ground for the purpose, the game would never have been invented at all."

There are several principal considerations in determining if a piece of property can be utilized for a golf course site: (1) economics, (2) acreage, (3) topography, (4) soil, (5) vegetation, (6) environment, (7) water, and (8) utilities.

Economics

In simplest terms, supply and demand should dictate if a particular site is economically feasible for a golf course. Market information to verify the need of a golf course, including such things as demographics, potential golfing demand, and existing golf accessibility, should all be considered during this evaluation process. In addition, costs associated with land purchase and construction must be considered and entered into the economic equation to determine if a piece of property will provide an adequate return on the investment.

Acreage

Generally speaking, the more property available for a course, the better. An 18-hole golf course and practice facility generally requires a minimum of 150 acres (61 ha) (refer to Chapter 1). Additional land is needed if extensive wetlands or steep topography precludes these areas from being utilized in the scheme of the golf course. The configuration of the property also is important for the routing of the golf course and siting the practice facilities, clubhouse, parking lot, maintenance facility, and possibly swimming and tennis facilities. Given less property to work with, the golf course architect will have to "force" the golf holes on the acreage.

Housing development also is a reality surrounding many courses, and a balance on land allocation between the course and development is necessary. Many courses were built with housing development as the primary consideration. However, residents soon discover that corners cut during design and development prove to be great liabilities on maintaining their courses.

Topography

Topography is a very integral part of property selection for a golf course site. Topography gives the golf course its character by determining traffic routing (flow) and the layouts of holes. It also

FIGURE 7–2 Flat topography, as often found near coastal areas, often requires considerable earth moving to add character to a golf hole.

contributes to the construction costs as large scale earth moving is expensive and should be held to a minimum (Figure 7–2). If a golf course has more elevation change than 150 feet (45 m) between the highest and lowest point, it will be very difficult to walk. In addition, maximum visibility should be provided from the tee to the landing area, and from the landing area to the green, to ensure player safety as well as speed of play.

Soil

Soil and the related aspect of drainage are the next most important factors associated with property selection. Coarser-textured soils (loam and sandy soils) are preferred for a golf course site over finer-textured soils (clay). Fine-textured soils have inherent problems, making it difficult to maintain high-quality turfgrass. These soils are very prone to soil compaction, especially under intense traffic, and soil compaction restricts and/or impedes water infiltration and internal drainage. Poor drainage delays golfers from playing following rain; thus, it reduces cash flow. Finer-textured soils are also slow to thaw after being frozen, thus increasing the chances of low-temperature stress and injury, and again, delaying play.

Generally, as soils compact and drain poorly, there is an increased need for cart paths. These slow play, and therefore reduce cash flow.

A sandy loam soil is the ideal soil type for a golf course since it retains enough moisture to support healthy turfgrass growth, but drains well enough to allow the course to remain playable following rain. For the same reasons, a sandy loam soil reduces construction costs by minimizing delays due to wet weather conditions. It is not surprising many "world class" golf courses are constructed on coarser-textured soils. However, on a parcel of 150 acres (61 ha) or more, one expects to encounter a variety of soil types that create either problems or opportunities for the golf course architect and superintendent.

Vegetation

Native vegetation adds immensely to the beauty, character, and playability of a golf course. Generally, some select trees and shrubs have to be removed during construction. This can be an expensive undertaking depending on the density of the trees and shrubs. Clearing through dense woods can cost as much as $3,000 per acre ($1,214/ha). Laws in most regions of the United States require an environmental impact study to be conducted and approved prior to any large scale tree removal. After approval, trees may be removed and sold to help offset the clearing costs, or burned where allowed.

FIGURE 7–3 Wetlands, both natural and man-made, provide habitat to a wide array of wildlife and help minimize run-off. Their occurrence, however, often restricts the use of the property.

Environment

In today's regulated world, even if all of the property criteria previously listed were ideal, it still may be impossible to build a golf course due to environmental restrictions. The most common environmental considerations or restrictions are the presence of wetland areas, flood plains, or endangered plants or animals (Figure 7–3). By definition, many wetlands may not be detectable to the untrained eye. A wetland is often defined as any area where the water table rises to within six inches (15 cm) of the surface for more than two weeks per year. Wetlands include natural bodies of water as well as marshes, bogs, and seasonally flooded lands. Wetlands must accurately be located by a specialist to ensure the golf course site can be utilized.

In the United States, such areas are subject to the jurisdiction of the Army Corps of Engineers. Wetlands cannot be filled under present statutes, although in some states fills may be allowed if new wetlands are created elsewhere.

Just as restrictions on the filling of wetlands have been imposed because of their ecological impact in the recharging of the groundwater supplies, other ecological and biological considerations may restrict the site as a golf course. Flood plains cannot be graded unless the work is determined not to increase the downstream flow of water. This means a golf course site located on a flood plain is subject to flood damage. Property considered a wildlife habitat also may have restrictions placed on its use by environmental agencies, especially those areas with "endangered" species. Property deemed to have archaeological or historical significance can also be deemed sensitive. Anti-growth factions frequently use environmental issues to defend the use of a piece of property for a golf course.

Water

Water is a key component of turfgrass growth and maintenance, and its accessibility and quality are critical in the property selection for a golf course site. A typical 18-hole golf course requires between 4,000 and 10,000 gallons per acre (37,000 to 93,500 L/ha) of turfgrass per day during summer. Sources include streams, creeks, rivers, ponds, lakes, drainage canals, wells, municipalities, utility companies, or a combination of these. Water quality biologists advise no more than 5 percent of the low-water flow be removed, or damage to fish and plants may result. Therefore, it usually is necessary to locate an underground supply of clean, salt-free water to supply irrigation. The use of effluent water (treated wastewater) from development and/or municipality sources is becoming increasingly common. If effluent water is considered, ensure an adequate supply is available and note if the course is required to use (or store) a certain amount on a daily basis.

Utilities

Electrical and fuel requirements are substantial for the construction and maintenance of a golf course. The availability of and/or distance to these sources should be determined for a particular piece of property. The costs associated with connecting electrical lines can be substantial, especially if these costs cannot be offset by a surrounding development.

Architectural Design

The selection of a golf course architect is one of the most important aspects in the successful construction of a golf course. The golf course architect's primary task is to route the golf holes to take greatest advantage of a given piece of property's assets and blend them with the natural surroundings. One, therefore, should spend considerable time in evaluating and selecting a golf course architect and not make hasty decisions. A team of qualified professionals led by the architect should be assembled to perform a thorough site analysis to address any complex planning, design, or construction issues.

Golf Course Design

The architectural plan usually revolves around using the natural topography to make interesting golf holes. The first step in this process is to look on topographical maps for suitable putting green sites and fairway landing areas. When evaluating a site, the architect emphasizes contour lines of the topographic map to optimize the land's natural features. For instance, if the site is relatively flat, the architect focuses on areas where contour lines are close together to maximize as many of the limited natural features as possible. In contrast, if the property is hilly and/or steep, the architect looks for widely spaced contour lines that indicate flatter areas for possible landing sites. A slope of more than 5 percent on a putting green or 10 percent in a fairway is considered excessively steep, and it is extremely difficult to blend landing areas in with adjacent slopes through grade leveling. Putting green sites generally are located on natural plateaus, at a natural saddle in the ground, at the crest of a knoll, in a punch bowl or valley, or carved out of a slope. Once a green site is discovered, a "natural" golf hole may be possible by tracing back along a visible line of approach to a suitable point for either the tees on a shorter hole or a landing area of a longer hole. Obviously, not every hole will feature a natural green site or natural landing area. The idea is to discover as many "natural" holes as possible with at least one natural feature to distinguish it apart from the others. Usually, however, the "natural" golf holes are disjointed and occur randomly across a piece of property. The key is to connect the golf holes into suitable loops of either 9 or 18 holes.

Clubhouse Site Selection

Once the golf holes have been looped together, the architect must select an appropriate clubhouse location site. Several factors should be considered in this site selection: (1) access to the golf course; (2) room for facility expansion, if needed; and (3) the ability to accommodate at least two starting golf holes, two finishing holes, a practice range, a parking lot, an entrance road, and access to fuel and power supplies. Most often the best clubhouse sites are near the middle or eastern half of the property due to golfer problems associated with the rising and setting sun.

Irrigation Design

Another aspect of golf course design requiring special attention is irrigation. An irrigation system must provide sufficient water to sustain turfgrass during periods of drought. In temperate climates, the design may be as simple as a single irrigation line running down the middle of each fairway with regularly spaced sprinkler heads. However, in steeper terrain or more sophisticated golf course layouts, proper irrigation design is essential to ensure the golf course is evenly and accurately watered. In arid or subtropical climates, the irrigation design must allow all turfgrass areas to receive adequate coverage.

Irrigation design, as well as sprinkler head selection and location, depend on a number of local parameters. Undulating terrain, varying soil types, prevailing wind patterns, tree or building location, and south-facing slopes are all-important microenvironment considerations influencing irrigation systems. A typical fairway irrigation system is designed with two rows of heads spaced approximately 65 feet (20 m) apart to form an equilateral triangle that provides head-to-head coverage. Swing joints are used under each irrigation head. Isolation values also should be strategically placed throughout the golf course to allow one section of the course to be turned off while repairs or additions are made on another section. Other valves needed on some golf courses are drain valves and pressure reduction valves. Drain valves are installed on low spots of the course to purge the water system during freezing temperatures. In areas of extreme topographical elevation change, pressure reduction valves may be necessary to counter the added line pressure caused by gravity.

Modern irrigation systems also integrate radio controllers, lightning protection, and computers to allow maximum watering efficiency, pump power, and system longevity. Satellite controllers that control a "zone" or group of sprinklers are often connected to these main computers to allow micro-control of irrigation needs. Other water-saving techniques include integrating soil moisture sensors and weather stations into the design. These monitor moisture levels, wind speeds, rainfall, and evapotranspiration rates to closely match turf water needs in relation to soil moisture levels and weather conditions. Low-volume, low-pressure heads that use about one-half the pressure and water volume of larger heads are being implemented. With the ever-increasing technology and sophistication of products, it is wise to hire an irrigation designer that specializes in this field.

Permitting and Engineering

Permitting and engineering for a golf course construction project can require considerable time, frustration, and expense. Permits should be obtained as soon as possible prior to the initiation of the detailed design. Approvals will be needed before the architect spends considerable time designing the golf course, assuming there is accessibility to the entire site. Wetlands and flood plains must be identified and approval sought for their use in the golf course layout. Other possible needed permits include damming of rivers or streams where water flow may be interrupted, land clearing, vegetation burning, proposed water use source, and use of electricity or other power sources.

Meeting with Local Groups

Either before or immediately after the permitting and engineering phase, the project team should meet with all regulatory agencies, environmental groups, and interested citizens to review and modify the design, if needed, based on their input. Inputs and concerns by these groups should be implemented whenever possible to minimize future criticism and to project a neighborhood-friendly image.

Site Preparation

There are several steps needed in preparing a site as a golf course, including (1) surveying and staking, (2) identifying and developing the power and water sources, (3) land clearing, (4) rough grading, (5) soil cultivation, and (6) shaping of features such as greens, tees, and bunkers. It is recommended that a qualified superintendent be hired prior to major construction to help administer and manage the project.

Surveying and Staking

The first step of site preparation involves property surveying and staking including identifying sensitive areas such as wetlands and flood plains and not disturbing them during construction. Other reference points such as fence rows, large trees, trails, and streams also are incorporated into the initial base map. From the base map, the final routing and general size and location of greens, tees, fairways, natural hazards, and site characteristics are initially identified. Additional drawing sheets are developed to identify the anticipated clearing, thinning, grubbing, and disposal operations.

The next base sheet identifies the overall grading design including existing and proposed contours and subsurface drainage. Additional base sheets are developed to indicate irrigation, trees, utilities, shelters, planting areas, cart paths, roadways, and so on.

Based on the architect's staking plan, a "centerline" is cleared and staked off down the middle of each golf hole. Stakes along the centerline are usually placed on 100 feet (30 m) intervals from the back of the rear tee, through the center of each fairway, to the center of the putting green. Other stakes may be placed to mark property lines and other features such as traps, ponds, and so on. Once the centerline has been staked for each hole and agreed upon by all concerned parties, the surveyor establishes a permanent bench mark (or elevation point) to serve as a reference for all subsequent elevations and elevation changes.

As stated, the bench mark usually is located in the center of the golf course construction site; however, uneven terrain and/or unavoidable obstacles may necessitate several permanent bench marks across the site. Once these are established and identified, the perimeter of each hole is staked at 25 to 100 foot (7.5 to 30 m) intervals using the centerline stakes plus any elevation differences from the bench mark. These perimeter stakes identify and outline the shape of the fairway to indicate the initial ground surface contours according to the architect's plans. All stakes should be appropriately marked (tees, greens, perimeters, etc.) to preclude errors during the land clearing operations, especially if the rough grading plan requires extensive earth moving.

Erosion Control and Environmental Protection

Most jurisdictions have regulations to minimize soil erosion and siltation on a construction site. The project's civil engineer usually prepares plans that include control devices such as sediment basins, silt fences, hay bales, and other structures conforming with current guidelines and regulations (Figure 7–4). These control and/or protection measures are installed before the clearing and grading operations begin.

Identify and Develop Utility Sources

Power and water accessibility to the construction site is imperative in developing, building, and maintaining a golf course. The irrigation pumping station will require a power source such as electricity or fuel. If the power source is a considerable distance from the site, then connection costs will substantially increase.

The same is true for an available water source on site. Water is essential to the establishment and maintenance of turfgrass. The preferred water source is one located within the confines of the golf course site. Sources for irrigation water include: (1) subsurface water such as wells and springs; (2) surface water such as ponds, lakes, or streams; and (3) processed water such as gray water (or effluent), municipal sources, or possibly desalinized water. In recent years, effluent wastewater use as an irrigation source has increased, especially in arid climates where water is

FIGURE 7–4 Soil erosion into a green due to the absence of sediment basins, sod, erosion control mats, silt fences, and/or hay bales on the construction site.

extremely limited. Golf courses are ideal candidates for effluent water use as irrigation and will play an increasing role in recycling, conservation, and treatment of this most vital natural resource. Often, holding ponds are needed if several wells are drilled or if a certain amount of effluent water must be accepted by the course, regardless of need. Refer to the chapter on irrigation for more details on water sources, quality, and turf requirements. Time must be allowed for the proper permitting of needed utilities, especially if well drilling, pond construction, or access to a river or streams is required.

Land Clearing

Before initiating land clearing, the golf course architect and the developer/owner should agree on the overall golf course design and layout. During surveying and staking, particular attention should be given to "specimen" trees and vegetation that add to the natural beauty of the site and environment. These specimen trees and vegetation should be identified and incorporated when possible into the strategic layout of the golf course as the construction process continues. The land-clearing operation should be conducted in various phases or stages to prevent any irreparable damage to the site during clearing.

The first stage of land clearing involves tree removal along each hole's centerline stakes. Final tree selection and thinning is then completed. Grass requires light for optimum growth, yet tree selection is very important in the overall golf design of a hole. The architect should mark all trees to be preserved, removing all that are not needed to help speed play and to readily allow movement of construction equipment and, later on, tractor-pulled turf-maintenance equipment. Pruning lower limbs of remaining trees also should be considered to further facilitate equipment movement, play speed, sunlight penetration, and air circulation. Although owners and members plant large trees near greens and tees, shade and turfgrasses do not mix. Grass on greens and tees require a minimum of eight hours of full sunlight year-round. Shade is most pronounced during late fall and winter months when days are shorter and the sun is lower on the horizon. Shade patterns during these times should be closely considered when deciding on tree removal. If usable timber exists from this tree removal, the owner may wish to salvage and sell it.

Generally, the contractor is provided a clearing plan from the architect that outlines the clearing width. This width varies from 20 to 50 feet (6 to 15 m) on each side of the centerline depending on the hole's length and shape. The resulting vegetation is stockpiled in the center of each hole, typically windrowed, and burned or removed from the construction site (Figure 7–5).

After the initial clearing, the architect walks each golf hole, and visualizes how each fits in with the terrain, and estimates how it will play. The architect then initiates the second stage of

FIGURE 7–5 When clearing new land, the vegetation is usually stockpiled as a windrow, then burned or removed.

land clearing by specifically marking the boundary lines for each golf hole. This stage of land clearing is intended to open up each golf hole enough so the architect can further visualize the playing characteristics of each hole (Figure 7–6). Architects are typically conservative during this second stage of clearing so as not to remove too many trees that may strategically affect the way the hole plays. The remaining trees should be fenced-off to prevent soil compaction and accidental hitting by construction equipment. Whenever possible, leave trees and underbrush in out-of-play areas undisturbed to provide wildlife habitat.

The final stage of land clearing involves the removal of stumps, roots, rocks, and stones. The objective of this final stage is to leave the site free of rocks and organic debris to a depth of 12 to 15 inches (30 to 38 cm), thereby preventing interference with subsequent construction activities. This process is sometimes referred to as **grubbing.** This very important operation should not bury any tree stumps, branches, or other vegetation, as these will decompose over time and possibly leave depressions that may collect water and produce uneven playing or riding surfaces. From this decomposition process, soil microorganisms may also initiate fairy ring disease development, which disrupts the turfgrass surface uniformity later. Stumps are removed with a large hydraulic backhoe or with a bulldozer and a clearing blade to push out the biggest material. Large debris removal is followed by a bulldozer with a root rake and finished with a tractor-pulled rake or a large root disk. Depending on the site, it may be necessary to excavate a non-play area to bury these stumps and roots, especially if burn permits are unavailable. Small rocks in the upper two inches (5 cm) are removed with rock-picking machines. Every effort should be made to remove or dispose of debris and to save the topsoil.

Rough Grading

Rough grading is the site preparation stage where all major contours and features of the golf course subgrade are set to shape the future final product within six inches (15 cm) of the final grade. Rough grading is sometimes referred to as **heavy earth moving** since it involves bulldozers, pans, power shovels, dredges, sand pumps, and other large equipment to reposition soil around the golf course site. During this phase of construction, the sculptural aspects of the design begin to take shape. The proposed subgrade contour is finalized, and it is common to have the land forms shaped several times to achieve the exact look the architect desires. Some architects provide detailed grading plans while others prefer to "work on site" with specialized equipment operators (or shapers) that contour the subgrade as the golf course is constructed. Shapers often make or break an architect's design and are key personnel when bringing out the final beauty and playability of a hole.

While forming the subgrade, topsoil is often removed or stripped from high areas of the subgrade and stockpiled for later use during construction. This topsoil is then respread over depressed or low areas of the fairways and roughs as needed to maintain the proper elevations. In the past, grading stakes and strings were utilized to aid in achieving the proper grade levels; however, laser grading has largely replaced these.

Initial shaping of the subgrade contours involves the placement of fixed grading stakes referenced to the centerline and permanent bench mark(s) elevations. The bulldozer and/or pan operators then follow these routes of elevation to their indicated depths as outlined by the architect's plans. In areas where topsoil has been excavated and removed, the subgrade should be established at an appropriate level below the finished grade level to compensate for adding topsoil back to the grade. These stakes remain in place until major grading is completed and topsoil is placed.

It is also quite common to encounter rocks during the rough grading process. Loose rocks and large stones should be excavated and/or removed (Figure 7–7). Rocks and stones can be sold to local landscapers, disposed of by burying them in non-play areas, or possibly utilized in the construction process for stabilizing banks, ditches, or streams.

The seedbed preparation begins with the successful completion of the subgrade during the rough grading operation. Ideally, in order to form a uniform rootzone depth throughout the golf course site, contours of the subgrade should closely match those needed for the finished surface grade. Slopes should be 1 to 2 percent with a minimum of 0.5 percent. Once the initial contours have been made, they should be resurveyed and checked against the centerline and permanent bench mark stakes to ensure the settled subgrade elevations are as originally specified. The architect then carefully inspects the subgrade and contours against the plan specifications and makes any needed modifications to ensure the conditions are appropriate for play as well as establishing and maintaining turfgrass. The rough grading is completed when all the topsoil has been properly placed and positioned on the golf course (Figure 7–8). The rough grading process is successful when all areas of the subgrade are left with slopes that provide positive surface water drainage.

Rough grading and the installation of major drainage overlap somewhat during the construction process and usually are simultaneously completed.

Soil Cultivation

Construction sites often become highly compacted due to traffic from heavy construction equipment, their operation, site deliveries, and/or site cleanup operations. Soil cultivation may be necessary on these areas to alleviate any soil compaction problems prior to "grassing" the golf course. Soil cultivation can be accomplished utilizing several different types of equipment, including chisel plows, subsoilers, disks, harrows, or plows.

FIGURE 7–7 Windrowing rocks to be removed during rough grading.

FIGURE 7–8 Rough grade of a new golf course where major rocks, stumps, and other debris have been removed and a specific outline of the golf hole is recognizable.

FIGURE 7–9 Flooding not only damages the playing surface and irrigation systems, but it significantly delays reopening the facility, thereby reducing cash flow.

Drainage

It has been stated that successful golf course architecture is nothing more than making drainage features appear pleasing to the human eye! Good drainage is essential to the health of the grass and its ability to tolerate concentrated traffic from play and maintenance equipment use. If drainage is not sufficient, it will be difficult to maintain the turfgrass without causing physical damage, and a finely groomed playing surface will be elusive to achieve, regardless of budget. As previously stated, without good drainage, golfers are delayed from playing; thus, potential revenue is lost (Figure 7–9).

The stormwater drainage system must be designed to conform with local regulations regarding upstream and downstream watersheds. Nonconformance to these plans without written review and approval can result in civil and criminal actions against all parties involved with the project. Golf courses, especially around residential or resort developments, should pay close attention to drainage and drainage requirements since the amount of surface run-off is increased with storms (Figure 7–10). Ponds, grass swales, and wetlands are incorporated into this water management

FIGURE 7–10 Installing large-diameter pipe for diverting surface and subsurface stormwater drainage.

FIGURE 7–11 Ponds, swales, wetlands, and catch basins are used for stormwater drainage and for providing water for irrigation.

plan to reduce run-off, create natural habitats, and help filter sediments and nutrients from the water. One-hundred-year rainfall maximums also should be anticipated because, invariably, they will occur within several years of opening. The stormwater drainage system should account for these. Chapter 4 contains considerably more information on drainage.

Water or Drainage Retention Facilities

Lakes, ponds, dams, spillways, wetlands, and other water-retention facilities are often integral parts of the stormwater management system and an irrigation source for the course (Figure 7–11). A civil engineer prepares construction drawings that are in conformance with the regulatory standards for dams, overflow structures, and inlet and outlet structures. Water-retention facilities should be shaped and graded concurrently with other rough grading operations. Retention structures are normally created at the low end of the golf course or throughout the course to collect the surface run-off water during a storm and is then released at a naturally occurring rate prior to construction. These water-retention facilities are usually lined with some type of impervious material such as polyethylene, clay soil, or bentonite, according to design specifications.

Surface Storm Drainage

Surface drainage is probably the most important component of the stormwater drainage system since it is the most rapid and easiest means of removing excess water from the golf course. Surface drainage can be accomplished by providing contours to fairways and primary roughs to divert the surface run-off water away from the golf course. Run-off should be directed away from features such as greens and bunkers where it will cause immense maintenance problems (Figure 7–12). Any surface with less than 1 percent slope is likely to shed water too slowly; 2 or 3 percent is ideal. Surface stormwater drainage work could include grading and shaping drainage swales, establishing drainage ditches, stabilizing stream banks, and constructing overflow and drainage structures connecting water-retention facilities. Water in active play areas generally should not be allowed to drain more than 150 feet (45 m) before intercepting a drain or it is out of play. Shaping is performed skillfully to direct this water and to hide catch basins or drop inlets.

Once rough grading and surface drainage are completed, any specialized construction, such as stone or wood walls, is installed. These walls not only stabilize banks and slopes that otherwise would collapse, but they add a distinct look to many facilities.

Subsurface Storm Drainage

Subsurface drainage is merely the management of stormwater infiltration, percolation, and movement through the soil profile. Subsurface drainage is needed where natural low areas occur, or where water is slow in drainage. Subsurface drainage is imperative where the subgrade is a clay soil or if the soil has an impermeable layer (e.g., hardpan); otherwise, the area could remain excessively wet for several days after heavy rainfall.

The most common means of subsurface drainage involves surface catch basins connected to a network of underlying drainage lines (tile or plastic pipe) (Figure 7–13). The drainage lines intercept the water as it moves through the soil profile and then route it to an outlet located several feet lower than the existing grade. Subsurface drainage is commonly used in greens, bunkers, some tees, and low lying fairways.

The vertical elevations of stormwater drainage lines are expressed as **invert elevations** (or vertical elevation measured at the bottom of the interior of the drainage pipe or drainage structure) and directly relate to the final elevations of the playing surfaces. Any unaccounted changes to the invert elevations could seriously hamper the golf course's playability and maintenance. Depending on the location, underground piping may be performed before major earthmoving is performed.

Subsurface Drainage Outlet

The first phase of installing subsurface stormwater drainage involves locating an adequate outlet for the drainage water. Typically, drainage lines are routed into nearby water-retention facilities such as ditches, ponds, larger drainage lines, catch basins, French drains, or other sources. The discharge lines should be nonperforated (pipe or tile) and should not be laid straight down a steep slope, but instead have a gradual slope to reduce the flow rate of the drainage water from the area. In some cases, a suitable discharge source may not be readily available. If this is the case, a sump and pump may be required.

Sump and Pump Drainage

A sump is considered a pit or reservoir serving as a drain receptacle for liquids (water). This sump is commonly in the form of a tank or several concrete rings placed on top of each other and enclosed with a cover. A low-lift pump (or sump pump) is then installed inside the sump at the lowest point with a float-activated switch so the water level may be controlled within specified limits. Once a predetermined amount of water is allowed to drain into the sump, the discharge water is then pumped up to an appropriate discharge area. Sumps should be located away from the fairway and in areas receiving little to no traffic. Covering the main drainage line outlet of the sump with a mesh wire screen is also advisable to prevent animals from entering and possibly causing damage.

Subsurface Drainage Line Spacing

Drainage lines should be spaced so water will not have to travel more than 10 feet to reach any individual line. If the golf course is situated on an area with a high water table, it may be necessary to place larger drainage lines deeper into the subgrade to lower the water table and handle the increased internal flow of water. Calculating the precise drainage line spacing needed can be done with a modification of Hooghoudt's equation (see Chapter 4).

Drainage Line Types

In the past, drainage lines consisted of agricultural clay tile, concrete, or flexible corrugated plastic. Today, two- to four-inch (5- to 10-cm) diameter flexible corrugated pipe with perforations (slits) is utilized due to their ease of installation and relatively low cost (Figure 7–14). The perforations in the plastic pipe should be laid facing downward on a bed of gravel to prevent them from clogging by downward-migrating soil particles. Nylon-netted filter drainage sleeves are also available that can be wrapped around the perforated pipe to prevent soil particles from impeding water flow into the drainage lines.

Drainage Line Patterns

Typically, a gridiron or herringbone design pattern is used for drainage line arrangement. The drainage pattern is placed diagonally to the grade. However, any pattern is acceptable as long as each line has a continuous downward slope and water does not have to travel more than 10 feet (3 m) to a drainage line.

Drainage Line Trenches

Trenches in which the drainage lines are to be laid should be a minimum of six to eight inches (15 to 20 cm) in depth into the subgrade and five to six inches (13 to 15 cm) in width. Trenches up to 12 inches (30.5 cm) wide have been utilized; however, the wider the trench the greater the amount of gravel needed to fill the trench, which elevates costs. Normally, a drainage line trench should be no more than twice the size of the drainage line. A five- to six-inch (13- to 15-cm) wide "U"-shaped trench will allow for a 0.5 to 1 inch (1.3 to 2.5 cm) bed of gravel to be placed around (below, above, and on either side) a four-inch (10-cm) diameter drainage line. The soil created from digging the trench should be either removed or placed between drainage lines to provide a slight contour before being compacted.

Prior to digging trenches, the area should be surveyed and staked with proper labeling for the desired depth of cut. Drainage lines should not be placed any deeper than necessary to obtain the desired amount of slope. Grade stakes should be placed in order to achieve a minimum downward slope of 0.5 percent (1 foot of drop for every 200 feet, 0.3 m in 60 m). Ideally, a slope of 1 to 2 percent (1 foot of drop for every 100 feet, 0.3 m in 30 m, and 1 foot of drop for every 50 feet, 0.3 m in 15 m, respectively) would be preferred, with a maximum slope of 4 percent (1 foot of drop for every 25 feet, 0.3 m in 7.5 m). Drainage lines with 0.5 percent slope or less are difficult to properly grade, install, and maintain due to the slight elevation changes and slow flow rate. Slopes with greater than 4 percent will lose lateral drainage capability and also require greater elevation changes within the drainage line and a lower outlet point.

Care must be taken to ensure the drainage trench and drainage lines are always sloping downward to preclude any entrapment or collection of water along the drainage lines. Drainage lines should be placed diagonally to the slope and not at right angles. All main and lateral drainage lines should be checked with a level prior to backfilling to ensure the grade provides adequate drainage. Drainage line ends or joints should be covered with asphalt paper, fiberglass composition, and plastic spacers or caps to prevent gravel and/or soil from entering the drainage lines. It is recommended the main drainage line(s) into which the lateral feeder lines flow have their upper end extended to the soil surface and properly capped. In the future, if these lines become clogged or contaminated from gravel, soil, or some other material(s), the cap can then be removed and the line(s) flushed. This will greatly extend the useful life of the drainage system without the need of disturbing the playing surfaces to clean individual lines.

French Drains

A modification of subsurface drainage lines is French or slit drains. French drains involve digging a drainage trench and then backfilling with either gravel and/or coarse sand. The top two to four inches (5 to 10 cm) of the French drain trench should be filled with coarse sand to serve as a growing medium for the turfgrass. This sand should be compacted prior to installing sod to decrease the amount of settling that will occur over time. If sod is installed, its soil should be removed by washing prior to installation to minimize any negative impact from introducing dissimilar soil from the sod onto the sand medium. French drains have the advantage of being easily installed at a fraction of the cost of tile lines.

Construction and Shaping of Features (Greens, Tees, and Bunkers)

Detailing of the features, such as greens, tees, and bunkers, are the cornerstones of the golf course architecture's art. Interestingly, the putting greens and tees account for less than 5 percent of the total golf course area, yet play a role in 75 percent of all golf strokes.

Putting Greens

After rough shaping of greens has been completed, the drainage trenches are "cut" into the subgrade. This is typically performed by a trencher or small backhoe. The drainage lines are typically laid out in a herringbone pattern with a discharge to nearby water-retention facilities (Figure 7–15). Perforated drainage pipe is placed in the trenches and surrounded by clean gravel, with a four-inch (10-cm) layer of the same gravel placed over the entire green subgrade, carefully following the established contours. Gravel must be clean and free of any native soils that could block drainage lines. If small "pea" (e.g., 1/4 to 3/8 inch, 6.4 to 9.5 mm) gravel is unavailable, a two-inch (5-cm) layer of coarse sand ("choker" layer) is added and spread carefully, following the established contours of the green. A 12- to 14-inch (30.5- to 35.6-cm) layer of greensmix or rootzone mix is then added on top of this coarse sand. The greensmix or rootzone mix is shaped, compacted, and prepared for the planting of turfgrass (refer to Chapter 8 for more information).

FIGURE 7–15 Typical herringbone (or fishbone) design for drain tile in a golf green so subsurface drainage will not have to travel in excess of 10 feet (3 m) before encountering a drain line.

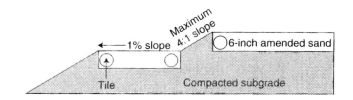

FIGURE 7–16 Side view for a typical tee, which needs either a slight (e.g., 1 percent) slope and/or an amendment with sand and tile for drainage.

FIGURE 7–17 Teeing areas of a golf course should be sufficiently sized to allow play rotation, and both surface and subsurface drainage should be provided so play can be expedited following rain.

Teeing Areas

Due to concentrated use, tees receive more abuse per square area than any other part of most golf courses. Tees should be well-drained, nearly flat, with a 1 percent slope away from the golfer's entrance side and a 1 percent slope to its back, and free of any depressions that could hold water (Figure 7–16). Teeing areas are often constructed like the putting greens, with the same kind of drainage system, layers of the subgrade, and greensmix or rootzone mix for the surface. If not, use at least six inches (15 cm) of an amended sand with drain tile installed at junctions between tees or on exceptionally large tees (Figure 7–17). After the tee is rough graded, tile should be installed, especially when tees are constructed at various elevations and connected.

Courses cannot have enough tee area, especially on par-3 holes. Tee surface area should be one to two times larger than the green surface area for a particular hole. Another specific method to determine tee size is to allow 100 square feet (9.3 m^2) of usable tee footage for every 1,000 rounds of golf played yearly. On par-3 holes and the first and tenth holes, where irons or mulligans are used, doubling the size to 200 square feet (18.6 m^2) of usable tee footage for every 1,000 rounds played yearly is suggested.

Another common mistake when designing tees and greens is allowing trees to remain, especially those located to the east, south or southwestern side. Shade from these growing trees increases over time, often ruining even the best-constructed turf area.

Bunkers

Bunkers are the most common hazards incorporated into golf courses to force strategic play (Figure 7–18). Proper bunker construction is important to avoid costly maintenance and/or unsightly problems later. Sand used in bunkers should drain and play well. The sand selected should be determined based on the size of the particles, purity, shape, composition, and color.

During bunker construction, particular attention should be made to the overall topography around them. Failure to direct surface run-off water away or around sand bunkers will lead to extensive erosion problems, along with the possible contamination of the bunkers with unsightly

FIGURE 7–18 Bunkers have become an important component in the game of golf. These are considered hazards, and players are potentially penalized by hitting into them. Bunkers should not be designed to drastically increase maintenance, such as having sides too steep.

FIGURE 7–19 Bunker erosion is a constant maintenance problem, especially after thunderstorms.

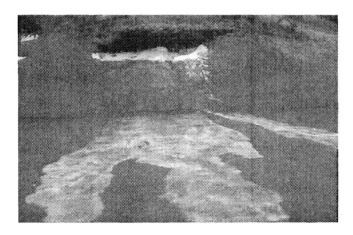

clay or other native soils (Figure 7–19). Bunker erosion and soil contamination require costly maintenance and/or replacement measures and invariably occur just prior to important tournaments and other events.

Excessive surface run-off flow onto or over bunkers should be addressed during construction. Small diversion trenches or swells and/or drainage lines should be installed at the interface of the bunker lip (or edge) on the higher grade. These should be extended (or "wrapped") around the bunker's edge, preventing higher ground surface run-off from reaching the sand.

Bunker interiors should have between 2 and 3 percent slope to ensure drainage. Drainage lines should be placed in larger bunkers and typically require a herringbone arrangement like putting greens (Figure 7–20). A perimeter (also called "smile") drain should be placed at the interface between steep slopes and inside the bunker to intercept the increased water drainage from the slope. Drainage lines are connected to an adequate outlet. A two-inch (5-cm) gravel blanket is placed over the bunker floor. Washed pea gravel or crushed stone 1/4- to 3/8-inch (6.4- to 9.5-mm) deep is best. In some instances, bunker liners have been incorporated into the construction process to aid in weed control and to prevent "bleeding" of sand color from the underlying native soil (Figure 7–21). Liners can be perforated polyethylene, plastic, rubber, filter cloth, or synthetic fabric and/or net. Liners should be placed in the bottom of sand bunkers over the gravel blanket prior to the addition of four to six inches (10 to 15 cm) of compacted sand. Bunker liners can become damaged from the use of powered sand rakes if the sand depth is not adequate. Therefore, if a bunker liner is used, it should be of heavy strength and have an adequate depth of sand placed

FIGURE 7–20 Swells, trenches, and/or drainage lines surrounding the bunker should divert water away from it, and drainage lines in the bunker should be considered to prevent standing water.

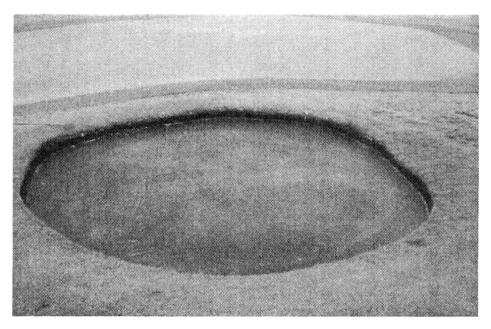

FIGURE 7–21 Liners are often used in the bottom of bunkers to minimize erosion, prevent weeds, and reduce "bleeding" of bunker sand with underlying soil.

on top of it to ensure it will not be damaged during routine raking and maintenance. These are secured to the bunker floor with metal staples.

The bunker sand should be inspected and approved for cleanliness and freedom of weeds at its origin. Subsequently, each truckload of sand should also be checked upon arrival before being placed into the bunkers. The sand is then introduced or placed into the bunkers and spread by various means. A small tractor plus box blade, small bulldozer, mechanical rakes, or raking by hand are all acceptable means of spreading the sand. The use of a "gunite" machine has also been utilized to spread the sand. This machine is capable of receiving bulk sand and, under high pressure, delivers the sand into the bunker with sufficient force so the sand is compacted and efficiently spread evenly at the same time.

Installation of Irrigation System

An irrigation system provides sufficient water to sustain turfgrass growth during drought periods and is the most important component in maintaining proper turfgrass conditions for optimum play (Figure 7–22). In certain climates, this may require only a simple irrigation design with a single irrigation line running down the middle of each fairway. However, in most climates, the irrigation system is more sophisticated so as to cover all areas intended for turfgrass. On modern golf courses, the irrigation system can cost as much as one-fourth of the total construction budget. In addition, many golf courses today are utilizing a variety of turfgrass species for greens, tees, fairways, and roughs. Therefore, a carefully designed irrigation system is required to allow an ade-

quate supply of water for each of these turfgrasses according to their needs and to be able to efficiently and accurately distribute the water to these areas.

The installation of the irrigation system normally begins after the shaping of features within a few inches of design-finish grade and installation of major drainage have been completed, often done as a set of two to three golf holes together. To maximize efficiency and workmanship, irrigation installation usually begins at a logical starting point such as the pumping station and radiates outward, or starts at the furthest point and works back toward the pump station. The system must be in place and operational before planting or establishing turfgrass begins. The irrigation system can also be used to settle the greensmix or rootzone mix prior to planting, and to settle backfilled areas during the construction process.

A quality irrigation system is dependent on accurate design plans and specifications. The first step in installation involves the designer laying out or staking the complete irrigation system. Staking should be accurately established for the entire irrigation system including the main lines, sprinkler heads, valves, satellite controllers, and other key features. This staking should be done exactly by following the design specifications to ensure sprinkler head spacing and coverage are adequate. Individual sprinkler head staking is needed to ensure the design specifications accurately fit the actual topography. If conditions dictate, this is the time to make modifications to the irrigation design and system by adding either lines and/or sprinkler heads to ensure adequate coverage and performance. The stakes also serve as a guide or map for the trenching operation.

The trenching route should follow the design layout as marked by the staking operation. The depth and width of the trenches should be determined by the pipe size, soil depth needed to prevent freezing, and slope needed to provide adequate drainage. The completed trenches should be smooth, free of rocks, and on the specified grade level.

After trenching, irrigation lines or pipe are installed. Installation of irrigation pipe normally begins at the water source with the main line(s) installed first. The control, drain, and gate valves are then installed in coordination with the lateral irrigation lines. Next, the control lines are placed in the trenches. The trenches are then partially backfilled with either sand or other fine-textured soil free of rocks and/or stones. It is generally advised that joints and fittings associated with the main line(s) not be backfilled initially so they can be checked for leakage and easily repaired during the initial startup of the irrigation system.

After the irrigation pipe has been installed, the system is connected to the water source (pumping station) and backfilled with sufficient soil to prevent movement. The pump station is the heart of an irrigation system and is generally delivered preassembled, placed on the pump pad, and wired-up (Figure 7–23). The system should then be activated and "flushed" by passing sufficient

FIGURE 7–23 Modern golf course irrigation pumps are typically designed and assembled prior to installation. Two or more turbine pumps are usually needed for satisfactory water pressure on large courses or courses with significant elevation changes.

FIGURE 7–24 Swing joints are used to connect irrigation heads to main lines, allowing vertical head movement to prevent traffic damage and ease of adjustment of the head height.

water through all pipe, fittings, valves, and sprinkler head risers to ensure no soil, pipe chips, or other debris is present in the lines.

After the system has been completely flushed, sprinkler heads are installed, sometimes during the flushing operation. Sprinkler heads are normally installed several inches above the projected rough grade level through the use of "swing" joints and are left to operate in this position until after the turfgrass has become established (Figure 7–24). Sprinkler heads are then lowered to the permanent finished grade after the soil has settled and the turfgrass has become established. The system is then pressure tested to ensure it can operate above the normal operating pressure. The system is also checked for any leakage at joints at this time prior to backfilling. This is most often done by pressurizing the system to about 120 psi (827 kPa) and allowing it to sit for 24 hours. If the pressure drops more than several pounds, leaks are likely and must be detected and fixed, followed by another 24-hour pressure test until the pressure stabilizes.

After successful pressure testing, irrigation lines are then backfilled to a level slightly above the original soil level to compensate for settling and compaction over the irrigation trenches. The irrigation system is then ready to be properly adjusted for achieving the accurate pressure setting and water distribution. A final "as built" site-plan for the irrigation system is recommended for future reference by the golf course superintendent to maintain, winterize, repair, or make modifications.

Seedbed Preparation

Redistribution of Topsoil

Whether the area is to be established by sprigging, sodding, or seeding, soil preparation for each is the same. After final subgrade shaping, features construction, and irrigation installation, the stockpiled topsoil can then be respread. Due to the potential damage created from equipment operation, this phase is sometimes completed before irrigation is installed. Particular attention is needed in preserving the final shaping contours and grade when redepositing topsoil.

The topsoil is spread evenly over all prepared subgrade areas except the greens, tees, and bunkers. The generally accepted standard requires a minimum of six inches (15 cm) of topsoil over all fairways, tee slopes, and green surroundings, and a minimum of four inches (10 cm) over the roughs. If the topsoil is imported, the golf course architect must specify its structure. Once the topsoil has been evenly spread, seedbed preparation begins by disking or harrowing the soil to a depth of six inches (15 cm). The soil is then raked to a depth of four inches (10 cm) to remove any rocks and/or stones larger than 0.5 inch (1.3 cm) in diameter. The upper few inches of soil is then ready for any necessary amendments or modifications.

Rootzone Soil Modifications

Sometimes the soil(s) must be modified to ensure adequate and uniform soil moisture, drainage, and nutrient exchange. Due to economic reasons, the modification of fairway soils is performed much less frequently than on greens or tees. Determining which type of soil amendment and how much to add is crucial, since the use of an improper soil amendment can forever diminish the quality of the turfgrass site.

Sand Soil Types

In coarse-textured sandy soils, adding the proper soil amendment(s) is recommended to increase the soil's water and nutrient holding capacities. In these coarse-textured soils, drainage is normally not a problem, but adequately holding soil moisture and nutrients potentially is. In addition, sandy soil modified with an amendment discourages pests such as nematodes. In sandy soils, the addition of a good topsoil generally provides the desired results at the most economical price. However, the topsoil source must be acceptable to prevent later drainage problems resulting from excessive silt, clay, or pests.

Other soil amendments used in sandy soils include peat sources, rotted sawdust, rice hulls, calcined clays, and colloidal phosphate. These amendments improve soil aeration, increase nutrient and water-holding capacity, and encourage microbial activity. Peat sources are generally added at a rate of 45 to 90 cubic yards per acre (85 to 170 cubic meters per hectare).

Other soil amendments are added according to the type of material used and the degree of soil modification required. These amendments are often incorporated at a rate of 10 to 15 percent by volume in the top four to six inches (10 to 15 cm) of the seedbed. Table 7–2 lists the volumes of soil amendments (cubic yards to add to 1 cubic yard of soil) to provide the desired percentages of various treatment or incorporation depths. Refer to the section on "soils" for additional information regarding soil amendments and their characteristics. For example, from Table 7–2, to modify a soil six inches (15 cm) deep with 15 percent amendment by volume, 2.78 cubic yards (2.1 m³) of soil amendment is needed per one cubic yard (0.76 m³) of soil.

Clay Soil Types

Fine-textured, native clay soils also may be modified to facilitate internal drainage. The modification of fine-textured, heavy soils such as clay can be both an agronomic and financial challenge. These fine-textured soils are prone to compaction and generally require substantial amounts of soil amendment for any significant improvement to be observed. A properly sized sand source is generally the most popular and recommended amendment for improving clay-type soils. However, as discussed in Chapter 4, not all sands are created equal. Some types are better suited for making concrete while others are better for soil modification. Do not use any

TABLE 7–2 *Soil amendment volumes (cubic yards) for modifying existing depths (McNeely & Morgan, 1968b).*

Desired percent of amended soil	Modification depth (inches)*								
	4	5	6	7	8	9	10	11	12
	cubic yards**								
5	0.61	0.77	0.93	1.08	1.23	1.39	1.55	1.71	1.86
10	1.23	1.54	1.85	2.16	2.47	2.78	3.09	3.40	3.71
15	1.85	2.32	2.78	3.24	3.70	4.17	4.63	5.09	5.55
20	2.47	3.09	3.71	4.32	4.94	5.55	6.17	6.79	7.40
25	3.08	3.86	4.63	5.40	6.17	6.95	7.72	8.49	9.27
30	3.70	4.64	5.56	6.48	7.41	8.33	9.26	11.18	12.10
35	4.32	5.40	6.48	7.57	8.64	9.72	10.80	11.87	12.95
40	4.94	6.18	7.41	8.64	9.88	11.13	12.34	13.61	14.81
45	5.55	6.95	8.33	9.72	11.10	12.52	13.88	15.17	16.67
50	6.17	7.72	9.26	10.80	12.34	13.88	15.42	16.96	18.50
55	6.78	8.49	10.19	11.88	13.58	15.28	16.98	18.67	20.37
60	7.41	9.26	11.11	12.86	14.81	16.67	18.52	20.37	22.22
70	8.64	10.80	12.96	15.11	17.28	19.44	21.60	23.77	25.92
80	9.88	12.35	14.81	17.28	19.76	22.22	24.69	27.16	29.63

*Multiply inches by 2.54 to obtain centimeters.
**Multiply cubic yards by 0.7645 to obtain cubic meters (m^3).

sand without careful investigation into its usefulness for this application. It is advisable to consult a competent soil-testing laboratory well in advance before the soil modification step.

For most amended soils, it is desirable to end up with 75 to 90 percent by weight of the final amended mix in the desired 0.1 to 0.5 millimeter particle-size range. The following equation can determine the amount of a specific sand required to be mixed with a soil of known composition to create a "free" draining rootzone material:

$$A = \frac{(R - B)}{(C - R)} \times 100$$

where: A = weight of sand needed to add to 100 weight units of the original soil
B = percent of original soil in the desired (e.g., 0.1 to 0.5 mm) size range
C = percent of sand added in the desired particle-size range
R = the desired percentage (typically 75 to 90 percent) amended sand in the final mix

If these amendments are mixed "off site," it would be better to mix the two on a volume basis instead of on a weight basis.

Example:

If a clay loam soil is to be amended but has only 25 percent of its particles in the 0.1 to 0.5 millimeter size range, how much sand (with 80 percent of its particles in the 0.1 to 0.5 millimeter size range) is needed to provide a 75 percent amended mix?

$$A = \frac{(R - B)}{(C - R)} \times 100 = \frac{75 - 25}{80 - 75} \times 100 = 1,000$$

Therefore, in this example, 1,000 units (in weight) of this sand source would be needed per 100 units (in weight) of the original clay loam soil to provide a 75 percent amended mix in the desired 0.1 to 0.5 millimeter size range.

As the previous example illustrates, large amounts of sand are generally required to significantly alter or improve the internal drainage of fine-textured soils. As another example, 450 tons (cubic yards), or 408 metric tons, of sand are typically required per acre to amend a soil five inches (13 cm) deep consisting of considerable silt and clay. Additional amounts of sand may be required if a soil contains a higher percentage of clay. A physical analysis of soil should be conducted by a competent soil testing laboratory to determine the amount of sand to add.

Modification Depth

The soil should be modified or amended to a minimum depth of six inches (15 cm), with 10 to 12 inches (25 to 30.5 cm) being the ideal depth. "On site" mixing of the soil amendment will require extensive harrowing, disking, and roto-tilling to ensure as uniform an incorporation of the amendment as possible. These areas should be mixed or incorporated a minimum of four times (passes) in different directions. Pockets of "pure" soil amendment or soil should be avoided to prevent poor draining areas or excessive drying.

Greens Mix

In the past, golf courses were often constructed on sites where the putting greens were formed by merely "pushing up" native soil into the desired greens shape or, worse, using soil from excavated ponds or lakes. This type of greens construction necessitated choosing green sites where a coarse-textured soil type was present. However, this type of construction and use of native soil as a green root mix is currently not normally recommended. Rootzone mixtures currently consist of a specially prepared soil mix to ensure greens will withstand the intense traffic from play as well as provide rapid drainage. Mixes consist mostly of a coarse-textured sand that is less prone to soil compaction and has high water infiltration and percolation rates. In contrast, these mixes have minimal water retention and limited nutrient holding capacity; thus, there are increased needs for both.

The amount of soil, sand, and organic matter utilized for green mixes depends on the physical and chemical characteristics of each individual component. These should be submitted to a physical soil testing laboratory for quantitative analysis to determine the best combination of each to achieve the optimum rootzone mix for a golf green. The soil testing laboratory should conduct physical analysis of these components to determine the water infiltration rate (hydraulic conductivity), particle size, porosity (pore space), water-retention capacity, bulk density, aggregation, and cation exchange capacity. Results will then serve as the recipe for blending a mixture of these components that would best serve as the greens mix.

The greens mix should also be chemically analyzed to determine soil pH, levels of nutrients and micronutrients, and soluble salts.

Soil pH and Fertility Adjustments

Soil test results provide the basis for soil pH and fertility adjustments prior to turfgrass establishment. These adjustments can be made during the rootzone modification stage while mixing the soil amendments, or afterwards by incorporating the necessary soil pH or fertility products. A better distribution of these materials normally can be accomplished by incorporating these during the soil modification stage.

As a general rule, the soil pH should be between 5.5 and 7.0. Agricultural limestone (calcium carbonate) or dolomitic limestone is applied to soils with a low soil pH. Sulfur is utilized to adjust soils with a high soil pH. Gypsum is sometimes applied to compensate for high salt soils. The exact amount of these materials must be determined by a soil test. Refer to Chapter 3 for additional information.

The addition of starter fertilizer into the soil is required in almost all golf course sites. The specific nutrient application rate should be based on soil test recommendations. The fertilizer is normally applied for broadcast just prior to turfgrass planting or establishment and incorporated into the top four inches (10 cm) of the soil rootzone. Research studies indicate a fertilizer with a 1-2-2 ratio of nitrogen, phosphorous, and potassium is most beneficial during the turfgrass establishment phase. However, the specific recommendations for adjusting soil pH and soil fertility levels should be based on the type(s) of turfgrass to be established and their specific requirements.

FIGURE 7–25

Fumigation controls most
weeds, diseases, nematodes,
and insects. Fumigation is
also highly recommended if
the site was previously
planted or infested with
difficult-to-control weeds
such as common
bermudagrass, kikuyugrass,
quackgrass, or torpedograss.

Fumigation of Rootzone Mix

Fumigating the rootzone soil mix for greens, and sometimes tees, is recommended just prior to the final grading to control disease organisms, insects, nematodes, weed seeds, and perennial weeds (Figure 7–25). The more common fumigant materials include methyl bromide, metam-sodium, or dazomet. Fumigation requires special application equipment and is very toxic to humans; therefore, it should only be applied by properly certified and trained professionals. Fumigation treatments normally require about 48 hours of exposure to achieve adequate results. Another 48 hours or so is normally needed to allow the rootzone mix to "air out" after this gas treatment has been applied and the plastic covers are removed.

Fairways should be periodically tilled before establishment to reduce weeds or else sprayed with a nonselective herbicide prior to planting. A minimum of three applications of a nonselective herbicide will be necessary to control existing perennial grassy weeds such as common bermudagrass, kikuyugrass, quackgrass, or torpedograss.

Final Grading

Final grading of the areas to be planted with turfgrass consists of smoothing the seedbed to remove any depressions or rough areas, breaking up large clods of dirt, removing rocks larger than two inches (5 cm), removing roots and stems, smoothing low and high spots, and conditioning the seedbed for planting (Figure 7–26). For small areas, such as tees and greens, and for working and smoothing around all sprinkler heads, hand or mechanical raking is utilized (Figure 7–27). Larger areas such as fairways require grading and fitting tools such as box blades, wire mats, boarded mats, plank drags, and other specialized harrows and/or equipment. This consists of disking the soil to break up the clods and float up any rocks, removing rocks with a rock rake, using a landscape rake to windrow this debris, which will be picked up by a pan or front-end loader, and finally smoothing the surface with a land leveler, box scraper, or finishing rake. These operations should be performed when the soil is moist (not wet). A vibratory roller or similar roller normally provides the firming needed to settle an area before turfgrass establishment. It is key to remember this final grading process is the last chance to smooth and firm the seedbed prior to turfgrass establishment. Once the turfgrass is established, any undulations create an uneven playing surface and will remain until corrective measures are implemented. The final grading process or finished grade and last 24-hour irrigation check should be approved by the golf course architect before "grassing" begins as this is the last chance to make major modifications or repairs before planting.

FIGURE 7–26 Final grading should smooth the seedbed for planting, eliminate small swales and depressions, remove small rocks and limbs, and allow soil conditioners and fertilizers to be added.

FIGURE 7–27 Hand smoothing a golf green's surface prior to sodding. Successfully sodding greens is difficult due to the precision required for providing a smooth, flat surface that does not scalp when mowed.

Turfgrass Establishment

The specification of different turfgrasses for use on the golf course is the golf course architect's last responsibility, but one not to be taken lightly considering the amount of money to be spent in the future to maintain these. The threat of erosion during establishment also must be considered or much money, time, and delays can occur from even one severe thunderstorm.

Once the final grading process is complete, the area must be planted as quickly as possible before rain, wind, traffic, or other conditions damage the prepared seedbed. If the seedbed becomes damaged, the surface must be carefully reshaped and the seedbed again prepared for "grassing."

The surface soil condition in terms of firmness is also important. If too compacted, seeds will have a difficult time germinating and becoming established; thus, the soil requires additional cultivation. If the soil is too wet, it could rut during planting and mowing, causing a very uneven and bumpy playing and maintenance surface. If it's too dry and powdery, obtaining a proper finishing grade is again difficult and planting will be delayed until a more favorable soil moisture level is achieved.

The type of turfgrass specified will largely determine the method of planting or establishment. Turfgrasses are established by either seeding or by vegetative propagation (refer to Chapter 9 for more specific information).

Vegetative propagation involves planting a vegetative portion of the turfgrass plant (rhizome, stolon) and relying on its growth to form a turfgrass mat. This process of vegetative propagation is referred to as sprigging, stolonizing, and plugging. When planted at the right time and maintained properly, vegetative propagation normally produces an acceptable turfgrass playing surface faster than by seeding the same turfgrass species. Likewise, vegetative propagation can provide an acceptable playing surface as fast as or faster than sodding in most instances. Each nine holes requires about 30 days to plant, either with sprigs or seed.

Sodding provides "instant greening" and excellent soil erosion control; however, supply and labor costs to install sod often make it prohibitive. During sodding, the possibility of introducing different soil types from the sod into the rootzone also exists. "Washed" sod is a recent development where soil is removed from sod to reduce the previously mentioned problems. However, sod should be laid for areas prone to soil erosion, such as steep slopes and areas surrounding bunkers, tees, and greens (Figure 7–28). Drainage basins also should be sodded or protected with straw bales or erosion control nets at this time.

Turfgrass species commonly established vegetatively by sprigging or plugging include centipedegrass, older creeping bentgrass cultivars, hybrid bermudagrasses, St. Augustinegrass, velvet bentgrass, and zoysiagrass. There are seeded varieties of both cool- and warm-season turfgrasses. Almost all cool-season turfgrasses, such as creeping bentgrass, bluegrass, ryegrass, and fescues, are established by seeding. Only a limited number of warm-season turfgrasses can be established by seeding. Buffalograss, centipedegrass, common bermudagrass, and common zoysiagrass can be established by seeding; however, the time required to achieve an acceptable playing surface is much longer when compared to vegetative propagation of these species.

Planting Sequence

Golf greens, collars, and slope areas just within the throw of the greens sprinklers are normally the first areas planted. After planting by hand sprigging, seeding, or sodding, these areas are lightly rolled to smooth the surface and to ensure good soil contact.

Tees, bunker edges and outslopes, catch basins, pond and ditch banks, and other areas prone to severe erosion also are planted early in the sequence. Often, these areas are sodded to reduce erosion. Fairways are planted next, followed lastly by the rough area. These are planted mechanically by seeding or sprigging, with close attention given to minimizing rutting.

FIGURE 7–28 Sod strips or other erosion control measures should be provided in erodible areas such as the perimeter of greens, bunkers, tees, ditches, and catch basins.

FIGURE 7–29 Seeded areas should be mulched to minimize erosion, conserve moisture, and minimize stand establishment time. A hydroseeding operation is shown, where seed is mixed with water and a shredded paper-like mulch material and then blown onto the hillside.

Seeded areas are then mulched to minimize wind and water erosion and to help conserve soil moisture. Mulching materials include straw, wood, or paper fiber or a synthetic plastic coating. A tacking material such as an asphalt binder is often used to prevent wind and water movement of the seed and mulching material (Figure 7–29).

Accessibility, Bridge, and Cart Path Construction

Construction of access roads, service roads, bridges, and cart paths normally commences during or immediately after the turfgrass has been planted. Their initial construction steps, such as grading and subgrade preparation, are coordinated with these corresponding construction phases of the golf course. The installation of a gravel layer over the compacted subgrade for these accessories is sometimes completed during the final course grading process and then surface graded either immediately or after turfgrass planting.

Cart path, when properly designed, installed, and maintained, provides traffic flow, prevents damage to the turf from excessive traffic, allows rapid transport for maintenance personnel and equipment, and produces a professional-appearing facility without worn, bare areas from unrestricted cart traffic (Figure 7–30). In areas where vehicular traffic should be restricted to the cart paths, a low-face curbing, fence, rope, or other means should be installed to prevent unbounded access (Figure 7–31). Cart paths should be a minimum six-feet (1.8-m) wide, and preferably eight feet (2.4 m). This provides sufficient width for two carts to pass without leaving the path and allows the access of larger maintenance equipment to the course (Figure 7–32).

Turfgrass "Grow-In" and Maintenance

Immediately after "grassing" or turfgrass establishment, a critical period of specialized maintenance occurs to ensure the golf course's survival and healthy growth. This "grow-in" phase is the most overlooked expense of any golf course construction project. The "grow-in" period can be characterized as the time between when the golf course is grassed until the time it opens for play and should be supervised by a competent, experienced golf course superintendent or grow-in specialist. It can vary from three months to as long as 18 months, depending on the location and climate of the golf course. A minimum of 10 weeks of *ideal* growing conditions is needed before play can begin. It is important to recognize the cost of "grow-in" cannot be offset by income since the golf course is not open for play (refer to Chapter 9 for additional information). Normal "grow-in" requires aggressive irrigation, fertilization, and mowing.

FIGURE 7–30 Golf course cart paths should be at least six feet (1.8 m) wide, and preferably eight feet (2.4 m), to allow dual cart passage and access by maintenance equipment.

FIGURE 7–31 Edges of cart paths should have curbing, ropes, fences, or other such devices to restrict access in high traffic areas.

Irrigation

Proper water management is critical for the first several weeks after turfgrass establishment. Where the turfgrass was seeded, the seedbed should be maintained continuously moist with irrigation of light amounts several times daily (four to eight times per day). Avoid excessive water, as this can cause the planted seed to wash and move. Sprigs are watered two to four times daily, while sod is watered once daily. As seed germinate and seedlings emerge and begin to spread, the frequency of watering should be decreased and the amount of irrigation water applied should be increased.

Vehicle accessibility to the golf course during grow-in should be limited to essential traffic only as this equipment can cause excessive rutting, getting stuck, delaying opening, and adding unforeseen expenses.

Fertilization

The new seedlings should be fertilized approximately two to four weeks after planting or seeding, or as a general rule, after the second mowing. A complete (N-P-K) fertilizer designed specifically

FIGURE 7–32
Insufficient cart path width
dramatically increases
maintenance and reduces
aesthetics.

for use on turfgrass should be applied at an equivalent rate of one pound of nitrogen per 1,000 square feet (4.9 kg N/100 m^2) of turfgrass. Preferably, a slow release nitrogen source should be a component of the fertilizer. Turfgrasses established by vegetative means should be fertilized with an equivalent rate of one pound of water-soluble nitrogen per 1,000 square feet (4.9 kg N/100 m^2) of turfgrass every two weeks. A 1-2-2 ratio fertilizer should be applied to these vegetatively established turfgrasses during alternative weeks at an equivalent rate of one pound of nitrogen per 1,000 square feet (4.9 kg N/100 m^2) of turfgrass. Once the turfgrasses have become fully established, the fertilizer program should then be converted to a less-aggressive program (refer to Chapter 11).

Mowing

Mowing of newly established turfgrasses should begin as soon as the turfgrass reaches 130 to 150 percent of the desired mowing height. It is imperative to use a mower with sharp blades to prevent turfgrass seedlings from being torn or pulled from the soil during mowing. It is advisable to use walking reel mowers on greens and tees until complete coverage of turfgrass is achieved. Do not mow when the turfgrass is wet, and remove the turfgrass clippings if the moisture level of the clippings promotes clumping and subsequent shading of the newly established turfgrass. At this point, refer to Chapter 9 for additional information on these topics.

GOLF COURSE RENOVATION

Over time, due to increased play, competition, tree growth, players' demands, and better grasses and maintenance equipment, many golf courses face a critical financial decision whether to renovate. Also, many older courses were not built using today's standards or materials, which are designed to handle heavy traffic or play. Improved golf equipment and better-conditioned players have forced many older and shorter courses to renovate. Older courses also typically had 8,000 to 10,000 rounds of golf played yearly compared to 30,000 to 40,000 rounds currently played on many courses. These older courses often fall prey to excessive compaction and steadily decline, especially on greens and tees. Older tees also are often inadequately sized and need enlarging.

Webster defines **renovation** as ". . . a restoration to an earlier condition or to impart new vigor to; to revive." In some instances, renovation projects can be compared to plastic surgery where dramatic results and improvements are obvious; in others, however, it can resemble malpractice! In reality, renovation projects are in fact like plastic surgery because the renovation process, like surgery, leaves some scars to the golf course that will require time to heal (mature). Therefore, one cannot appreciate the importance of communication before and during any renovation project. Not only do the positive aspects of the project need to be communicated, but also the negatives and risks associated with the renovation. Computer-generated three-dimensional images of the proposed renovations are also available and are often used to convince membership of the proposed changes.

There are three different types of golf course renovations: (1) restoration to the original design and form, (2) renovation or improvement of the design to update and/or enlarge areas more like a modern golf course, and (3) complete redesign.

Restoration

There are very few golf course managers and/or members who would admit they have deliberately or by neglect allowed their golf course to change for the worse. Restoration projects usually are focused on the perseverance of a "classic" design such as the work of golf course architects like Donald Ross, Alister Mackenzie, Willie Park, Charles Blair McDonald, A. W. Tillinghast, or Harry Colt. It is imperative to select a golf course architect with an appreciation of the original golf course architect's work and who understands the design principles.

Renovation

Many of the older golf courses were constructed without standards or were not designed for the level or talent of play they receive today. The rationale for renovating a golf course arises from many reasons ranging from speed of play to the need for additional golf holes. Some of the reasons for considering renovation include (1) lengthening the golf course or improving the strategy of play; (2) expanding the number of golf holes; (3) correcting poor construction and/or drainage; (4) expanding the size of the tees and/or greens; (5) speeding or facilitating play by installing new cart paths; (6) alleviating soil compaction problems on tees and/or greens; (7) upgrading or changing the turfgrass species and/or variety (Figure 7–33); (8) reestablishing turfgrass due to loss from some form or combination of stresses (e.g., winter kill); (9) converting from a mixture of turfgrass species with contaminants and/or "off-types" to a monoculture or pure stand of a turfgrass species; (10) rebuilding bunkers with proper sand and drainage; and (11) removing or replanting of mature trees that unfairly restrict play or limit turfgrass growth. Renovation can extend from a single tee or green to an entire golf course. One should consider the comparative economics of the renovation and the long-term implications before making a decision. Golf courses that have undergone properly planned renovations rarely regret the money or time invested.

When renovating, a qualified golf course architect should be hired to review and make suggestions on course changes. A master plan will then be developed by the architect outlining these

FIGURE 7–33 Sod clumps from tilling a fairway when renovating an older golf course.

potential changes and upgrades which is presented to the green's committee, board, and then finally, to the general membership. This master plan allows a course to make renovation changes in phases, as funds become available (Figure 7–34).

Redesign

Many golf courses could be dramatically improved for the enjoyment of its members through a redesign of the course. However, if a golf course is committed to redesign, the focus should be on the improvement of the golf course's strategic interest and not merely on its appearance.

It is important to note that with any form of golf course renovation, careful attention should be given to the existing facilities, such as water lines, power lines, sewer lines, easements, and drainage outlets (refer to Chapter 9 for more specific information on renovation methods).

CHAPTER
8

Putting Green Construction

INTRODUCTION

Golf greens typically experience heavy use throughout the year. Many public courses receive as many as 400 rounds of golf per day, or over 100,000 rounds of golf per year. Although putting greens represent approximately 2 percent of the total course area, 50 percent of the game is actually played on them. This concentrated traffic combined with daily mowing almost guarantees a problem with soil compaction, especially if the greens are poorly constructed.

Years ago, turf was usually grown on native soils, but as traffic and maintenance intensities increased, soil structure began to deteriorate (Figure 8–1). A golf green must rapidly accept and drain away excess water and yet retain enough moisture to avoid excessive, frequent irrigation. Rootzones constructed from the native soil frequently turn into mudbaths. The objective of this

FIGURE 8–1 Native soil high in silt and clay should not be used for golf greens due to its susceptibility to compaction and inability to drain satisfactorily.

chapter is to discuss the proper sequence of decision-making and construction processes needed to create a high-quality putting green.

INITIAL PLANNING

The most important phase of green construction is the initial planning. As the saying goes, "plan your work, then work your plan." A golf course planning committee should include the club president, greens committee chairperson, golf course architect, club pro, building contractor, and most importantly, golf course superintendent. Communication is the key to success. Several key topics requiring early priority include the following.

Location

Locating a green is almost as much an art as a science. Non-agronomic considerations provide the aesthetic background and challenge for the golfer. Natural features, such as water, topography, scenic views, and natural hazards, such as trees, are incorporated into the location, shape, and size of a green. Agronomic inputs, such as type of soil, proximity to irrigation, and competition from trees, should also be part of this decision. Even the best-designed hole will be limited by parameters affecting the health of the turf.

Drainage

Being able to control soil moisture is a key parameter in the success or failure of a golf green (Figure 8–2). Greens, bunkers, and surrounding mounds should be located and shaped so surface water from heavy rains will drain quickly away from, rather than onto, the green. Locating greens in consistently wet areas, such as along river beds, flood plains, or marshes, must also be carefully planned to allow for adequate subsurface drainage. A current trend in the industry is to build greens elevated above the fairway. Elevation encourages surface drainage, helps prevent run-off from adjacent slopes onto the green's surface, and adds character to the hole.

Greens generally require extensive drainage systems, with drain lines placed every 10 to 20 feet across the entire green. Greens with a 2- to 3-percent slope often have a greater proportion of excess water draining to the front of the green. In such cases, most drainage will occur from those lines located at the front of the green, with little or no drainage from lines higher up on the slope, except during heavy rainfall. An extra drain line (often referred to as a "smile" line) along the

FIGURE 8–2 Thin, undesirable turf is due to excessive traffic on greens constructed with poor soil and internal drainage.

front edge of the green should be installed to handle the large volumes of water collecting at this traditional low spot.

Shade

Shade affects turfgrass quality and health by reducing the amount of carbohydrates produced through photosynthesis. Without adequate carbohydrate reserves, the turfgrass plant is more susceptible to stress and considerably less able to recover from frequent mowing. Sunlight also helps dry greens after a heavy dew or rain, and discourages algae and moss buildup.

As discussed in Chapter 2, bermudagrass has relatively poor shade tolerance. This is especially true for bermudagrass maintained under putting green conditions since close mowing reduces the leaf surface responsible for photosynthesis (Figure 8–3). Bermudagrass maintained at putting green height requires full sunlight for a minimum of eight hours per day, year-round. To ensure this light penetration, it may be necessary to remove all sources of moderate to heavy shade surrounding the putting surface. Although golf courses are often noted for their beautiful landscaping, dense shade trees and healthy golf greens do not mix.

Bentgrass is somewhat more shade tolerant than bermudagrass. However, shade decreases evapotranspiration (ET) and generally restricts air movement. Low-growing ornamental shrubs also restrict air movement and should be carefully planned. Lack of air movement can increase humidity, heat stress, and disease pressure for bentgrass/Poa greens.

Planning should consider that the sun is lowest on the horizon during fall and winter months. Trees to the east, south and southwest of greens will cast longer shadows during cooler months and may cause shade problems even though trees may be some distance from the green. Shade also may increase the potential for cold damage to grasses, since shade-covered greens stay colder longer than greens in full sunlight. It is suggested during the planning stage that summer (June) and winter (December) shade patterns for proposed golf green sites be sketched every two hours starting at 8:00 A.M. until dark. These sketches will indicate which trees may need to be removed; or, if trees cannot be removed, whether the putting green may need to be relocated. If tree removal is not possible, light can be increased by pruning, and air movement improved with fans.

Adjacent Holes, Houses, and Roads

Another location consideration is a green's relationship to adjacent golf holes, housing developments, highways, and other high-population areas. Many times a green can be strategically placed to guide players away from these areas. However, tree barriers, shrub lines, and nets are sometimes required to protect nearby personnel and property.

Size and Slope

The size of a golf green should be large enough to allow for adequate selection of pin placement but not so large as to become a burden. Smaller-sized greens will readily show the effects from traffic concentration, while larger ones increase maintenance costs. In general, golf greens range from 5,000 to more than 7,500 square feet (465 to 697 m²), averaging about 6,000 square feet (557 m²). Greens on par-3 holes are usually larger, whereas longer holes have smaller putting surfaces, therefore requiring a more accurate shot.

In order to provide challenge and interest to players, a good putting green design should incorporate unique characteristics in size, shape, contour, and location of bunkers or other hazards. The placement of bunkers and shaping of contours surrounding a green should prevent concentrated traffic in any one area, and also allow adequate room for efficient turfgrass maintenance practices. The outline of the green should avoid any sharp turns, as the resulting pressure exerted by mowers will cause compacted, worn areas. Severe contours or mounds also are not necessary to produce a good test of putting. Instead, they limit cup placement and produce doughty, easily scalped areas.

The newer "ultradwarf" grasses on greens allow closer mowing heights than older cultivars. Sharp contours or ridge lines are easily scalped or gouged by low-mowing machines. In addition, surface slopes in excess of 2.5 to 3 percent in combination with these "ultradwarf" grasses reduce the usable hole locations and provide more penal play characteristics.

Profile

The modern putting green consists of two to four distinct components, including (from top to bottom) the rootzone medium, choker sand layer, gravel layer, and drain lines. The rootzone medium is the finest textured, the choker layer is intermediate-textured, and the gravel layer is the coarsest-textured component. This profile creates a **perched water table** in the finer-textured layer, since water will not move (or percolate) readily from the small pores of the finer-textured layer into the large pores of the coarser layer unless the finer layer is saturated with water to some depth. An example of this principle involves placing a saturated sponge on top of a bed of gravel, coarse sand, or another material. The water will stay in the sponge due to the differential particle size between it and the coarser material (called **granular discontinuity**). However, if additional water is added to the sponge, its weight will eventually break the tension between the two materials and water will start flowing. There are several successful putting green construction systems, each using some or all of these components.

USGA Specifications

The best known and most widely used system is a tiered or layered system used by the United States Golf Association (USGA) (Figure 8–4). In this system, 12 to 14 inches (30.5 to 35.6 cm) of rootzone medium overlay a two- to four-inch (5- to 10-cm) coarse sand layer (choker), which

FIGURE 8–4 Cross-section of a USGA-adopted golf green profile showing drainage tile, four inches of "pea" gravel, and a two-to four-inch "choker" layer, topped with 12 to 14 inches of proper root soil medium. Although successful, the construction profile is generally costly and difficult to install due to the two-to four-inch coarse sand layer.

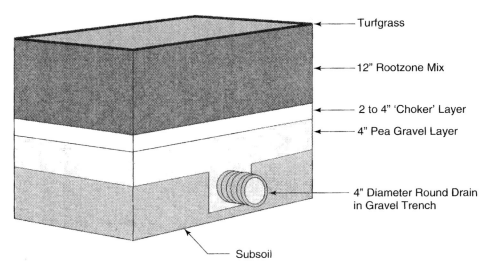

- Turfgrass
- 12" Rootzone Mix
- 2 to 4" 'Choker' Layer
- 4" Pea Gravel Layer
- 4" Diameter Round Drain in Gravel Trench
- Subsoil

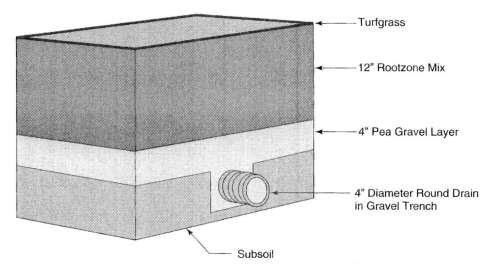

FIGURE 8–5 Cross section of a revised golf green profile showing proper sized "pea" gravel without the two- to four-inch "choker" layer. **Note:** For this profile to be successful, strict adherence to specific particle-size restrictions are needed for the rootzone mixture and the gravel layer. If appropriate materials and construction procedures are used, this type of green profile provides the best construction option for the cost. This configuration is highly recommended, especially for bentgrass greens grown in environmentally stressful areas.

in turn covers a four-inch (10-cm) layer of gravel. Drainage is provided by drain lines embedded in the gravel at 15- to 20-foot (4.5- to 6-m) spacings. The gravel blanket helps move water rapidly to the drainage lines and out of the green. The physical textural difference between the gravel and rootzone mix creates a capillary break, where water will not move freely into the gravel unless the rootzone mix above it is saturated.

A modification to the USGA system allows the intermediate choker layer to be eliminated (Figure 8–5). This deletion depends on if very specific criteria, as determined by laboratory analyses, are met by the rootzone medium and the gravel (see Chapter 4). USGA greens, if constructed properly, have a history of providing many years of satisfactory service. However, appropriate sands and gravel may be difficult and expensive to obtain, and the expertise and care required in construction are demanding.

Hybrid Greens

For golf courses with limited financial resources, other types of rootzone have been used successfully. Figure 8–5 depicts a two-tier design consisting of a 12- to 14-inch (30- to 36-cm) rootzone profile over a four-inch (10-cm) gravel layer with drain lines embedded in the gravel. This profile is similar to the USGA profile minus the choker sand layer, except more stringent criteria are placed on gravel and rootzone media selection. If the gravel is too coarse or the rootzone medium too fine, problems may arise when sand from the rootzone migrates into and clogs the coarse gravel layer. Sometimes the four-inch (10-cm) gravel layer is deleted. Slower drainage usually results as the water must transverse to the drain tile to be removed instead of simply dropping from the soil mix into the gravel drainage bed.

Sand Greens

Figure 8–6 offers a one-tier profile with the minimum construction standards for pure sand golf greens (often referred to as the "California Method"). It consists simply of 12 to 14 inches (30.5 to 35.6 cm) of an approved rootzone sand overlaying the native soil. Drain lines are trenched into the subgrade and backfilled with gravel. Unlike the previous two profiles, the four-inch (10-cm) gravel layer is deleted, as is the two- to four-inch (5- to 10-cm) choker layer. This type of green is simple and relatively inexpensive to construct. It can perform quite well if the native soil underlying the rootzone is either impermeable, or a layer of plastic (e.g., six-mil) is placed on the subsoil before adding the rootzone mix to prevent the downward movement of water. However, if the native soil readily drains, moisture will be literally sucked out of the rootzone medium and the green will be extremely droughty and difficult to manage. Research also indicates for sand greens to drain as fast as two-tier greens, sand greens must percolate at least 20 inches/hour (51 cm/hr) greater than sand percolation rates in two-tier greens. Sand greens are most difficult to grow-in as they tend to remain droughty and lack nutrient holding capabilities. Drainage line spacing also should be based on the permeability of the rootzone sand, average rainfall rate, and

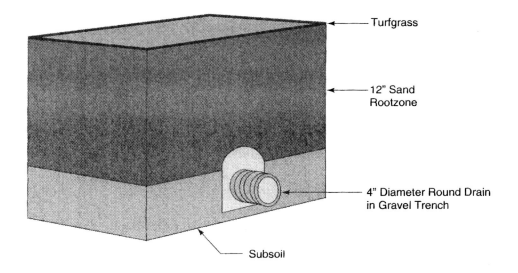

FIGURE 8–6 Profile of an alternative method of green construction which eliminates the four-inch pea gravel layer and two- to four-inch coarse sand (e.g., choker) layer. **Note:** Pea gravel is used to fill drainage line trenches and a plastic barrier may be necessary between the rootzone mix and the subsoil. If pure sand is used as the rootzone, this is referred to as the "California Method." Although less costly to construct, the California Method requires additional water and fertilize to grow-in.

Turfgrass

12" Sand Rootzone

4" Diameter Round Drain in Gravel Trench

Subsoil

the amount of water to be removed or retained. This drain spacing is much more critical for water removal than in a two-tier profile; a qualified laboratory should be consulted to make this determination. The planning committee should consider all three green profiles and weigh the benefits of each against their negative points. Generally, better results can be expected from those greens depicted in Figures 8–4 and 8–5; however, under financial restraints, Figure 8–6 may be a suitable alternative.

Native Soil Greens

Despite the advances of putting green construction, a high interest remains in building native topsoil-containing greens, mainly for financial reasons. In temperate areas, for example, where play only occurs two to four months annually, it is hard to justify the considerably increased funds for a modified soil profile green. If native soil is used, however, one must recognize these will not drain as well internally; thus, sufficient (e.g., 1 to 3 percent) surface drainage must be included in the design. Also, soil compaction is the other major culprit of using most native soils. Compaction is minimized during construction by keeping large, heavy machines off the greens. Also, compaction may require additional coring (aerification) and topdressing once the greens are established to help combat drainage problems. The advantages of native soil greens include (1) they are cheaper to build, (2) they hold water and nutrients much more efficiently than sand-based soils, and (3) they are less likely to have drastic changes in soil chemical properties (e.g., soil pH). However, be prepared to accept some risk of failure with these since these greens vary from a proven standard. Visit similar examples of the type of construction and materials being considered. No substitute for proper materials and construction methods exists.

Tax Depreciation

The Internal Revenue Service (IRS) in the United States has ruled the cost of building or rebuilding "modern" golf greens is depreciable over 15 years (20 years under ADS). However, "push-up" or native soil greens without internal tile drainage systems, along with the cost of general earthmoving, grading, or initial shaping of all golf greens, are nondepreciable. "Push-up" greens are considered undistinguishable from land, have an unlimited useful life, and therefore are not depreciable. "Modern" greens typically have lost drainage effectiveness after 20 years and their tile systems are replaced; thus, they have a determinable useful life.

CONSTRUCTION

Green construction is a time-consuming and costly procedure when building a golf course because of the extensive excavation and restructuring of the area and the expensive materials used. After the design of the greens has been agreed upon, construction steps involve:

1. professional surveying and staking of the green area
2. shaping and compacting the subgrade and grading the surrounding area
3. installing subsurface drainage
4. placing the gravel layer, if used
5. installing the choker layer, if used
6. off-site mixing of rootzone mix and its subsequent placement
7. installing the irrigation system
8. sterilizing the soil (sometimes, optional)
9. settling and finishing grading prior to planting

Shortcuts usually result in long-term dissatisfaction by the golfers and increased maintenance for the superintendent.

Surveying and Initial Staking

The architect provides a plan drawn to scale detailing the slope and shape of the intended green. A competent, licensed surveyor is then responsible for ensuring this plan is transferred to the field. A permanent bench mark (permanent elevation point) must first be established from which all subsequent elevations are made. Bench marks are usually centered in the golf course construction site, but uneven terrain or unavoidable obstacles may necessitate the use of several bench marks throughout the course. Once the bench mark is established, the perimeter of the putting green is staked at intervals of every 15 to 25 feet (4.5 to 7.5 m) or at every change in direction or elevation. The purpose of the perimeter stakes are to identify the outline of the green and provide initial surface contours according to the architect's drawings. These stakes should be properly coded (e.g., colored) to minimize errors.

The Subgrade

Contours

Final subgrade contours should closely reflect the contours of the surface. Consequently, successful green construction starts with a properly planned and constructed subgrade. Internal drainage follows the contours of the subgrade. Under normal circumstances, subgrade contours should not be sloped exclusively toward the front of the green since this will cause the front edge to be extremely wet. A soggy turf exposed to concentrated foot traffic quickly becomes worn and thin. It is better to have the green's slopes draining away from high traffic areas and also from any side facing the cart path's entrance and exit.

Depending on the green design and elevation of the site, the subgrade will be built into the existing grade or cut into the subsoil. If the grade is to be cut into the subsoil, the stripped topsoil may be stockpiled for future construction, such as mounds adjacent to the green, or distributed over the fairway and rough. Usually, greens built into the existing grade are elevated, requiring outside fill material for the subgrade. Heavier soils, such as clays, are desirable for the subgrade since these are easily compacted to form a firm base that does not readily shift or settle. In either case, the subgrade must be compacted to prevent future settling that might create depressions or pockets of poor drainage or, in the event of a higher grade, droughty areas. The best device to accomplish this is a power-driven vertical compactor (modified jackhammer) or, as a second choice, a water-filled mechanical roller operated in several directions across the subgrade.

The subgrade is constructed 18 inches (46 cm) below the planned surface, and should look like the finished green, but at a lower elevation. Contours of the subgrade should match those of the surface to within a tolerance of one inch (2.5 cm). The gravel layer must conform to the finished surface grade even if the subgrade does not. Initial shaping of subgrade contours involves placement of fixed grade stakes that are referenced to the permanent bench mark. The bulldozer operator then follows these pre-marked stakes to the depths indicated. Once the initial grade is established, it should be re-surveyed and then inspected by the architect to ensure the settled contour elevations match original specifications (Figure 8–7).

This uniform subgrade, or uniform depth of green, is critical since soil and water physics that dictate the amount of water retained in a soil profile are inversely proportional to its depth. Practically, this means greens with uneven soil profile depths will have areas that re-

FIGURE 8–7 Golf green subgrade should be compacted; smooth; free of pockets, rocks, or tire tracks; and should closely match the intended contour of the final green surface. If subgrade contouring is insufficient, internal drainage will be slow.

main excessively dry while others will remain soggy. This greatly increases costs later as the superintendent struggles to maintain uniform soil moisture, usually by using extensive hand watering.

The finished subgrade should be smooth, free of any pockets, rocks, or tire tracks, and firm enough to support construction equipment to prevent settling later. Any plants growing in the subgrade should be removed or killed before applying gravel or sand layers.

Drainage Installation

Putting green rootzones are formulated to drain quickly and allow play to be resumed shortly after heavy rain or irrigation. However, installation of a well-designed drainage system is critical for water removal from the subgrade, especially if the native soil is a clay or has an impermeable layer. Without drainage, the green could remain excessively wet and unplayable for several days after heavy rain.

Outlet Location

The first task in drainage installation is locating an adequate-sized outlet area for the water. Typically, drain lines are routed into nearby ditches, ponds, retention areas, larger drain lines, existing French drains in the fairways, or nearby out-of-play grass areas. Discharge lines are normally non-perforated pipe and should be laid across, rather than down, a steep slope to reduce the flow rate from the green. In some cases, a suitable discharge area may not be readily available and a sump and pump may be required. The sump may be formed with several concrete rings placed on top of each other and enclosed with a lid. A low-lift pump is installed inside the sump with float-activated switching so the water level may be controlled within specified limits. Once a predetermined level of water is drained into the sump, the water is then pumped up to an appropriate discharge area. Sumps should be located away from the green and in areas receiving little traffic. Avoid directing the main drain line from the green into adjacent sandtraps, as washouts will be common. It is also a good idea to cover the main drain line outlet with a screen to prevent animals from entering the line.

Spacing

Drain lines should be spaced 10 to 20 feet (3 to 6 m) apart. If the golf green is in an area with a high water table, it may be necessary to place larger drain lines deeper into the subgrade to lower the water table and handle the increased drainage.

Design

Typically, drainage lines are installed diagonally to the grade in a gridiron or herringbone pattern (Figure 8–8). However, any arrangement is acceptable as long as each line has a continuous down-

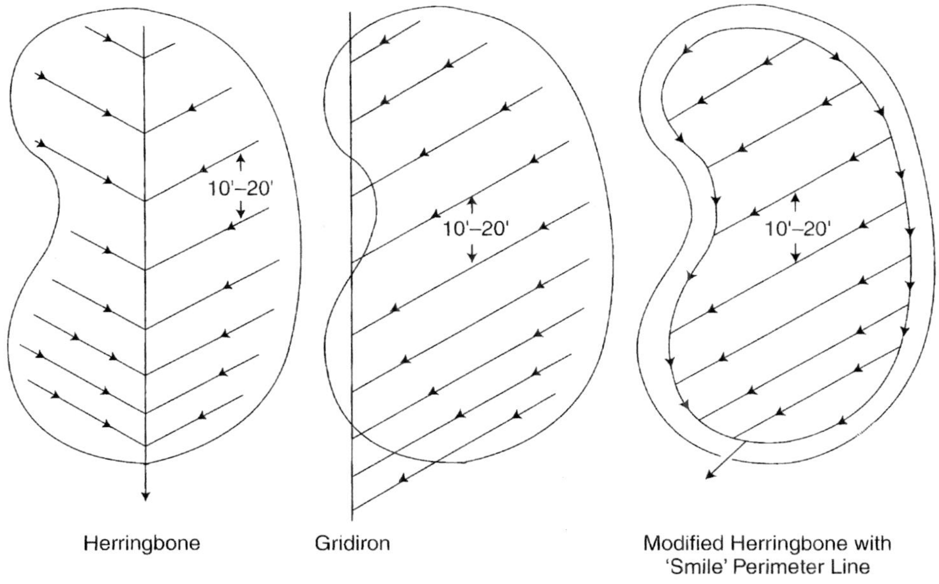

FIGURE 8–8 Typical drainage tile pattern used in golf greens so water will not have to travel in excess of 10 feet to intercept a drain line. In the middle is a gridiron tile pattern. On the left is a herringbone tile design where lateral drain pipe branches off simultaneously (as shown) or alternately at an angle of approximately 30 degrees. On the right is a modified herringbone tile design that "rings" the green with drainage line when slopes are greater than 2 percent or surface water run-off from higher surrounding ground occurs across the green's surface. Semi-circle drainage rings (also called "smiles") are used in front (lower end) of poorly drained greens instead of ringing the whole green.

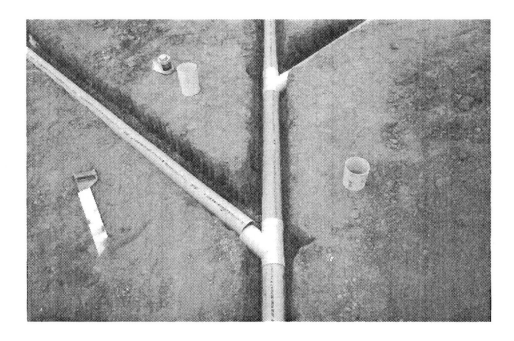

Herringbone   Gridiron   Modified Herringbone with
                                        'Smile' Perimeter Line

FIGURE 8–9 The herringbone design is used most often for drainage line installation for golf greens. With this design, lateral pipes are placed at 45 degrees from the center drain.

ward slope and water does not have to travel more than 10 feet (3 m) to a drain line. Greens with slopes greater than 2 percent or having surface water run-off from higher surroundings should have an interceptor drain line that rings the perimeter of the green, especially in the front or lowest areas (Figure 8–8).

Herringbone designs are generally the most popular, and are well-suited for irregularly shaped or relatively large turf areas due to the numerous lateral drain lines (Figure 8–9). However, herringbone systems are complicated to install and the pipes may be difficult to locate once installed. If slit drainage is needed later, cutting the slits at 90° angles to the lateral lines becomes difficult.

Type

In the past, drain lines were fashioned of agricultural clay tile or concrete. Today, two- to four-inch (5- to 10-cm) diameter corrugated, flexible, plastic pipe with slits is widely used because it is easy to install and inexpensive. Always place the slits of the plastic pipe face-down on the gravel bed to prevent clogging of drain lines with soil migrating downward from the rootzone. Nylon drain sleeves that wrap around the line are available (Figure 8–10). However, if silt and clay exist in the rootzone, these may plug the filters and ultimately restrict drainage. Other pipe or tile

FIGURE 8–10 Plastic
corrugated tile is widely used
for providing internal golf
green drainage. Fabric
sleeves or "socks" are often
used to reduce soil movement
(contamination) of the pipe.

FIGURE 8–11 Flat panel
tile has recently been used for
golf green drainage. The tile
is laid directly on the green's
subgrade, eliminating the
difficult and laborious task of
digging trenches for
traditionally used round pipe.

designs are also available; however, little research exists on the total benefits of these. Refer to Chapter 4 for additional information on determining if other tile types may be successfully used.

An alternative design involves using flat drainage pipe instead of the traditional round pipe (Figure 8–11). The flat pipe is laid directly on the subgrade base and is not cut into the subgrade as with round pipe. Pea gravel is then placed around the flat pipe (Figure 8–12). The flat pipe still must be on a downward grade to facilitate drainage. This technique is cheaper as drainage ditches are not needed and less gravel is required to surround the flat pipe. Limited research suggests this pipe design is beneficial; however, being such a new technique, this construction design has not been proven for all situations and environmental conditions.

Installation

Drain lines are laid in trenches dug into the subgrade six to eight inches (15 to 20 cm) deep and six to eight inches (15 to 20 cm) wide. Wider trenches are sometimes used, but this means more

FIGURE 8–12 Alternative golf green drainage design where a flat panel drain is laid on the subgrade and pea gravel or coarse sand is placed around it. A downward slope of 1 to 3 percent is still required to remove drained water from the green.

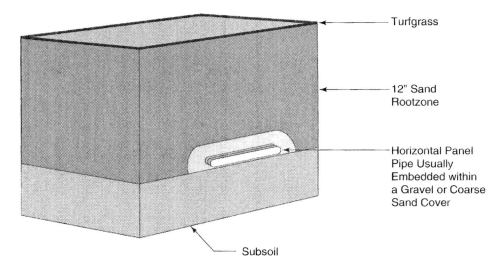

Turfgrass

12" Sand Rootzone

Horizontal Panel Pipe Usually Embedded within a Gravel or Coarse Sand Cover

Subsoil

FIGURE 8–I3 Once drain tile is installed, their trenches are filled to grade with gravel. Small (1/4- to 3/8-inch) "pea" gravel is ideally used in golf green construction.

gravel and higher costs are required to fill the trench. Normally, the trench width and depth should be no greater than twice the diameter of the drain line. Soil (or spoil) dug from the trenches should be removed or spread between the drain lines and then compacted to provide a slight crown. A one-inch (2.5-cm) bed of pea gravel should be placed in the bottom of the trenches before the drain line is laid. Once drain tile is installed, the trenches should be filled with gravel (Figure 8–13). Care should be taken not to contaminate the gravel with surrounding native soil or drainage may be sacrificed (Figure 8–14).

Slopes

Before excavation, the trenches should be surveyed and staked with the desired depth of cut clearly marked. Drains should be placed only as deep as necessary to obtain the desired slope. Stakes should be marked to give drain lines a minimum downward slope of one-half percent (or 1 ft/200 ft., 0.3 m/60 m), an ideal slope of 1 to 2 percent (or 1 ft/100 ft to 1 ft/50 ft, 0.3 m/30 to 15 m), and a maximum slope of 3 to 4 percent (or 1 ft/33 ft to 1 ft/25 ft, 0.3 m/9.9 to 7.5 m). Care must be taken to ensure the trench and drain line are always sloping downward so pockets of standing water do not develop. These lines should be placed diagonally to the slope of the green and not at right angles. All main and lateral lines should be double checked with a level prior to backfilling to ensure the grade provides the desired drainage. Joints connecting drain lines should be covered with tape, asphalt paper, fiberglass composition, plastic spacers, or covers to prevent gravel and sand from entering the line.

FIGURE 8–14 Care
should be taken to prevent
contamination of drain lines
with native soil or the
drainage characteristic of the
drain line may be lost.

FIGURE 8–15 An
extension of the main tile to
the soil surface allows future
flushing if clogging occurs.

It is recommended that the main drain line have its upper end extended to the soil surface and capped (Figure 8–15). If this line becomes clogged with soil in the future, the cap can be removed and the line periodically flushed. This greatly extends the useful life of the drainage system and reduces the need to disturb the playing surface to clean the lines.

Grade Stakes

After the drain lines are installed, the surveyor should place grade stakes into the subgrade (Figure 8–16). With allowance for the depth needed to drive the stakes into the ground, each stake should be marked at four inches (10 cm), six to eight inches (15 to 20 cm), and 18 to 20 inches (46 to 51 cm) above the subgrade, respectively (Figure 8–17). These markings correspond to the intended depth of the gravel, coarse sand layer (if used), and rootzone layer required in the green profile. Stakes should be placed at frequent spacing throughout the putting green site to indicate any changes in elevation or contouring of the surface.

FIGURE 8–16 Grade stakes are placed into the subgrade to mark the intended depth of the green's gravel and rootzone layers.

FIGURE 8–17 Grade stakes are marked at various levels for the corresponding depths of the green profile.

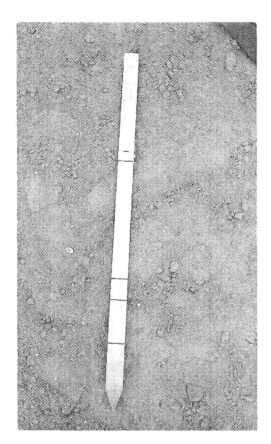

Gravel and Coarse Sand Layers

After the drains are installed, the packed subgrade should be covered with four inches (10 cm) of "pea" (1/4 to 2/5-inch diameter, 6.4 to 10 mm) gravel (Figure 8–18). The gravel layer serves several purposes:

1. It is very porous and allows water to rapidly move laterally to the drain lines.
2. It separates the subgrade from the rootzone and prevents the subgrade soil from extracting water from the rootzone.

FIGURE 8–18 Golf green showing the four-inch (10-cm) layer of gravel installed.

FIGURE 8–19 Placing plastic on the bottom of a new green's subgrade and extending it between the green and collar prevents undesirable moisture movement from the coarser green's sand and the surrounding heavier soil. Plastic prevents soil contamination into the green as well.

3. It impedes salt movement from the subsoil into the rootzone. Near coastal areas, where the water table may be contaminated by seawater intrusion, salts can move to the soil surface during periods of hot, dry weather.
4. It helps prevent an excessively wet rootzone due to a rising water table.
5. The interface between the gravel and the sand or rootzone mix above temporarily creates the perched water table which increases the water-holding capacity of the rootzone mix.

Successful greens have been constructed without the four-inch (10-cm) pea gravel layer. However, it is critical that drainage trenches are backfilled with some gravel. If this strategy is chosen, the parent subgrade soil must be compacted and/or a six-mil plastic layer used to separate the rootzone medium from the subsoil and from the collar (Figure 8–19). It is recommended courses with adequate financial resources not eliminate the gravel layer since it increases the probability of success.

Gravel Size

The physical properties of the rootzone mix will determine the size of gravel to be used. In theory, the diameter of the gravel should be five to seven times the diameter of the sand used to construct the rootzone. This will permit stable "bridging" between the sand and gravel and prevent migration of smaller particles from the rootzone into the gravel. For example, if the sand used to construct the rootzone is approximately one millimeter (1/24 inch) in diameter, then six-millimeter (1/4-inch) pea gravel is used (Figure 8–20).

If the proper-sized "pea" gravel is not available, then a two- to four-inch (5 to 10 cm) layer of coarse sand (1 to 4 millimeter) is placed on top of the gravel layer. This coarse sand layer is commonly referred to as the "choker" layer (Figure 8–4), which acts as a barrier to prevent soil particles from the rootzone from migrating downward into the gravel. It also creates a perched water table. It is best to install the coarse sand layer manually to prevent mixing with or into the gravel bed. Sand should be delivered and dumped on the outside perimeter of the green and moved into place in wheelbarrows on a plywood board path. If one-fourth to two-fifths inch (6.4 to 10 mm) of pea gravel is available and the rootzone particle size conforms to those limits previously discussed, then the choker layer may not be necessary (Figure 8–5). Normally, it is cheaper and easier to use properly sized pea gravel alone compared to using coarser-sized gravel plus a choker layer since the choker layer must be evenly spread by hand instead of using a machine (Figure 8–21). The operator of a tractor or bulldozer will have difficulty spreading the choker layer uniformly and a chance exists the heavy equipment may crush the underlying drain lines.

FIGURE 8–20 Granite "pea" (1/4 to 3/8 in., 6.4 to 9.5 mm diameter) gravel is often used for golf green construction.

FIGURE 8–21 The use of a coarse sand "choker" layer has been reduced due to the difficulty of evenly spreading it and the amount of labor necessary to properly install it.

Stone Type

Superintendents should carefully choose their gravel. Several types of stone are sold for use in drainage—crushed limestone, crushed granite, and river rock or gravel (mainly quartz). Other local sources of stone may be available. Granite and quartz gravels are best since they are strong and less likely to be crushed. Softer gravels, such as limestone (calcium carbonate), may break down over time due to the weight of the overlying soil and to chemical reactions with acidic water. Gravel suspected of being soft should be tested by a soils laboratory using the LA Abrasion Test (ASTM procedure C-131) and values should exceed 40. Gravel sources other than granite and quartz should also be analyzed to determine weathering stability using the Sulfate Soundness Test (ASTM procedure C-88). Weight loss should be less than 12 percent.

Alternatives to the Choker Layer

A topic currently under debate is whether it is possible to substitute a nonbiodegradable woven filter (geotextile) fabric for the coarse-sand choker layer to prevent the downward migration of fine particles. Earlier versions of these fabrics commonly clogged within a year or two of installation. As newer and improved materials are developed, this clogging problem may be eliminated. Recent research suggests a benefit of using or substituting geotextile fabric for the coarse-sand choker layer. An appropriate selected material should maintain acceptable water infiltration and percolation rates, and not clog.

Rootzone Mix Selection

In earlier times, the most common rootzone material for green construction was simply native soil. A bulldozer operator would "push up" the surrounding soil to a final grade, followed by grass planting. These greens performed adequately as long as traffic was light and the soil was not excessively wet.

As golf became more popular and courses received additional play, many of these greens declined or failed. They became seriously compacted, drained poorly, became algae infested, and were more susceptible to damaging outbreaks of disease, particularly *Pythium* (Figure 8–2). An extensive survey of "push-up" greens revealed the poorest turf was associated with heavier loams and clay soils, while the healthiest turf was usually growing on sands or sandy soils. Today this seems obvious, since it is well-known sands resist compaction, maintain good drainage, and promote deep rooting, but at the time it was a revelation. This insight led to recommendations that putting greens should be constructed using sands or sandy soils as the primary ingredient.

Numerous refinements have been made to the sand-based rootzone over the past several decades, and modern recommendations for rootzone materials are considerably more specific and detailed. Because the success or failure of a putting green often hinges on the performance of the turfgrass root system, experts agree that choosing the rootzone mix is the most important decision when constructing golf greens.

Sand Sources

Particle Size

The successful use of sand for green construction depends primarily on three factors: (1) average particle size, (2) uniformity of particles, and (3) correct mixing of the sand with amendments. All sands are not created equal. Highly uniform sands are well-suited for constructing golf greens while less-uniform sands are better for making concrete or providing a stable road bed.

Uniform sands are characterized as having most of the individual particles similar in size, which is termed a **narrow particle-size distribution.** This is important, since like-sized particles do not interpack, and result in good and stable porosity in the soil (Figure 8–22). By contrast, non-uniform sands have particles ranging from very coarse to very fine in size, and these can interpack. Intermediate particles fill the spaces (pores) between the largest particles, smaller particles fill the spaces between the intermediate particles, and silt and clay can fill any remaining spaces. The net result is a dense sand with reduced pore space, smaller average pores, and a tendency to compact.

Soil physical properties are controlled or influenced by the size distribution of its particles. **In general, standard builder's sand used in construction or for concrete mixing has a broad**

FIGURE 8–22 Using sand with a uniform diameter provides the necessary pore space for aeration and drainage (bottom). Blending sand into native soil or using non-uniform diameter sand causes pore spaces to "clog," essentially stopping drainage and increasing compaction (top).

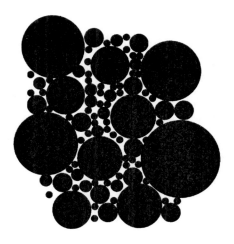

particle-size distribution and is not suitable for golf green construction. Such sands are either too coarse, and remain droughty, or have a broad particle-size distribution, making the sand dense, hard, and impermeable. Builder's sands often contain small percentages of silt and clay, which will cause these sands to have poor infiltration and become very compacted. In fact, small amounts of silt and clay can affect the performance of even the most uniform sands. For example, the addition of only 4 percent silt and clay to a uniform fine sand reduces the infiltration rate from 27 to 6 inches (69 to 15 cm) per hour (Davis et al., 1990).

Chapter 4 lists the United States Department of Agriculture (USDA) particle-size classification for those materials of general interest for building the rootzone of desirable putting greens. Some sand companies provide particle-size distribution, but in many cases the analysis is based on engineering criteria, not the USDA sieve sizes.

Soil Testing

Materials being considered for rootzone construction should be submitted to a soil laboratory for testing. Only a reputable, reliable soil testing facility should be used to determine the best rootzone mixture for a particular location. Before choosing a soil testing laboratory, consider the experience and reputation of the laboratory and the sample turnover rate they can provide. Most soil labs can run samples, but only a few have the necessary training and field experience in turfgrass soils. If the laboratory personnel do not have turf experience, then they probably do not understand the specific goals of putting green construction.

Laboratory testing of rootzone materials is important to help formulate the final mix, and also for quality control once a mix has been chosen. Although they may look identical, sands can change dramatically depending on where a supplier happens to be digging. Sometimes particle size varies with the depth in the pit, or between adjacent pits. It is the superintendent's responsibility to make sure all materials delivered for green construction meet the original specifications. Random samples of the rootzone components and proposed mixes should be taken and submitted to the soils laboratory to ensure the physical properties do not change. This is where quick turnaround of the samples by the laboratory becomes important.

Soil-testing laboratories usually need a minimum of two gallons (7.6 L) of sand and one gallon (3.8 L) each of organic matter, soil, and gravel. Once the samples are received, the lab will analyze the physical characteristics of each component to determine the best proportions for the rootzone mix. Included in the analyses are saturated hydraulic conductivity (infiltration and percolation rate), particle-size distribution, total pore space, moisture retention, bulk density, and mineral derivation.

Shape

Sand shape varies with weathering, chemical properties, and geographic location. The four basic shapes are round, angular, sub-angular, and crushed. Crushed, sharp sand particles tend to damage turf roots and the particles do not pack properly. Very round sand acts like ball bearings and will shift under foot or machine traffic. They also tend to be somewhat droughty. Angular or sub-angular sands are preferred because they form a more stable matrix, are more resistant to compaction, and provide desirable capillary pore space for drainage and root growth.

Composition

Quartz silica sand is preferred for every golf course use (bunkers, greens, tees, and fairways) because it is very resistant to breakdown and retains its original shape. The chosen sand should contain 95 percent or greater quartz silica. Manufactured sands generally have poor quality and undesirable chemical content, while calcareous sands are soft, unstable, and have a high pH, which can reduce the availability of some micronutrients (e.g., Mg) to grass.

Particle and Bulk Density

Particle density is defined as the mass (or weight) of dry soil per unit volume of the soil solids (excluding pores). An average value of 2.65 g/cm^3 has been found for most mineral soils, and is the standard value used by soil scientists in calculating other soil properties.

Bulk density, defined as the mass (or weight) of dry soil per actual volume of the soil, is the more important parameter for golf course superintendents. Bulk density, unlike particle density, includes the pore space volume as well as the volume of soil solids. Since most soils are about half solids and half pore space, bulk densities tend to be about half the particle density. The bulk density range for golf greens is between 1.25 and 1.55 g/cm^3, with a lower limit of 1.20 g/cm^3, an upper limit of 1.60 g/cm^3, and an optimum level of 1.40 g/cm^3. Incorporating organic matter, such as peat, is one means of reducing the bulk density of a golf green rootzone.

Soil Porosity

Soil porosity or **total pore space** is the fraction of soil volume not occupied by solid particles. Porosity is important, since it is the pores between solid particles that hold both air and water. The arrangement and size of particles largely determines pore space. Optimum porosity for golf greens ranges from 40 to 55 percent by volume, evenly divided between smaller capillary (water filled) and larger noncapillary (air filled) pore space (Table 8–1).

TABLE 8–1 *Recommended porosity of golf green soils by selected references.*

| Reference | Porosity (cm^3/100 cm^3 or percent by volume) | | |
	Capillary	Noncapillary (Aeration porosity)	Total
USGA (or two-tier) Greens (Anonymous, 1993c)	15 to 25	15 to 30	35 to 55
Bloodworth et al., 1993	22 (min. 15)	25	40 to 55
California (sand or one-tier) Greens (Hummel, 1998)	10 to 20	15 to 30	35 to 55

Smaller capillary pores largely determine the amount of water held by soil, while larger noncapillary pores determine air content. Noncapillary pores also control how quickly water and air move through a soil. If capillary pores predominate, moisture holding capacity of the soil will be high, but water and air movement may be inhibited. If noncapillary pores predominate, excessive drainage and high aeration result at the expense of adequate moisture holding capacity. Golf greens should have a capillary porosity between 15 and 25 percent by volume, and noncapillary pore space between 15 and 35 percent, with an ideal value between 18 and 25 percent (Table 8–1). These values are based on laboratory analyses where rootzone samples have been compacted, then saturated, and allowed to drain for 24 hours. The *minimum* noncapillary air-filled porosity that will support good turfgrass growth is between 10 and 15 percent. Moisture content following drainage should fall between 12 and 25 percent by volume, with 18 percent being ideal.

Particle-Size Analysis

The mineral fraction of soil is composed of sand, silt, and clay. The relative proportion of these in a soil determines its texture. A particle-size analysis provides a general description of physical soil properties to soil scientists, and is the basis for assigning the textural class name, such as sand, sandy loam, clay, and so on, to the soil sample. Once the percentage of sand, silt, and clay has been determined, the specific textural class of the soil can be determined from the U.S. Department of Agriculture's textural triangle (Chapter 4). Native soils used for push-up type golf greens should fall in the sand or loamy sand textural classes. If a modern sand rootzone is being constructed, a pure sand free of silt and clay should be used.

Sand specification

The particle-size distribution should be determined for all sands being considered for the rootzone. Values from the analyses can then be compared to the specifications listed in Table 8–2, which summarizes recommendations from several different sources. Although experts may disagree on precisely which sands are best suited for golf greens, three general recommendations should be met:

1. The sand should be free of silt and clay. If present, silt should not exceed 5 percent and clay 3 percent by volume. Larger amounts of silt and clay will reduce infiltration and percolation (Figure 8–22). Riverbed sands or other sedimentary type soil or peat are often unacceptable due to their high clay or silt content. Sometimes these sands are washed to remove the silt and clay, but all materials being considered should be tested before use.
2. The sand should also be free of very coarse sand and gravel. If present, very coarse sand should not exceed 7 percent and gravel 3 percent by volume. If these limits are exceeded:
   a. Large particles may cut or bruise the stolons/rhizomes of the turfgrass.
   b. Large particles tend to accumulate at the soil surface, resulting in hard greens.
   c. Large particles at the surface may dull mower blades.
   d. Large particles make cup-setting and core aerification difficult.
   e. The soil may not hold adequate water or nutrients.
3. The sand should have a narrow particle-size distribution with the majority (>80 percent) of the particles falling in the fine, medium, and coarse sand (0.1 to 1.0 millimeter) fractions. Within this range, the medium-sized particles (0.25 to 0.5 mm) should comprise at least 50 to 70 percent.

Infiltration and Percolation Rates

Even though the particle-size distribution of a sand falls within the ranges listed in Table 8–2, the sand could have unacceptable infiltration or water-retention values. Therefore, it is essential that the soils lab perform a compacted infiltration test (hydraulic conductivity) on all sands before use. This will help eliminate questionable sands that might create problems later. Refer to Chapter 4 for details on this procedure.

For most putting greens, the initial percolation rate should be 10 to 15 inches (25 to 38 cm) per hour. This rate will decline over time by approximately 33 percent, but it should still be well

TABLE 8–2 *Suggested specifications for sandy soils used for turfgrass rootzones by various references.*

Textural name	Particle size (mm)	Approximate saturated hydraulic conductivity (in./hr)	United States Golf Association (USGA) %	University of California (sand only) %	Australian Turfgrass Research Institute %
Clay	<0.002	—	≤3	} 0 to 8	} 5 to 10 } <30
Silt	0.002 to 0.05	<5	≤5 } ≤10		
Very fine sand	0.05 to 0.1	5	<5		—
Fine sand	0.1 to 0.25	18	≤20	} 82 to 100	} 60 to 70
Medium sand	0.25 to 0.5	59	>35 (75 ideal) } ≥60		
Coarse sand	0.5 to 1.0	217	<45	} 0 to 10	10 to 30
Very coarse sand	1.0 to 2.0	>217	<7 } ≤10		<5
Gravel	>2	—	<3		0

above the minimum of four inches (10 cm) per hour. Bermudagrass greens with adequate surface slope can have slightly lower percolation rates of 6 to 10 inches (15 to 38 cm) per hour. High or "accelerated" percolation rates of 12 to 14 inches/hour, 30 to 36 centimeters/hour, may be appropriate for bentgrass/Poa courses at some locations to handle heavy rains or if irrigation water quality is poor or cool-season turfgrasses are being grown outside their range of adaptation. In this case, the sand should contain a minimum of 65 percent coarse-(0.5 mm) and medium-(0.25 mm) sized particles. Even more desirable would be a sand having 75 percent in the medium-sized, and the majority of the remaining 25 percent in coarse-sand, classes. Alternatively, a minimum amount of organic matter, or even none at all, should be added to the rootzone mix.

However, accelerated (e.g., >16 in./hr, 41 cm/hr) draining rootzones often require a longer period of time for full maturity due to excessive moisture applied and lower cation (nutrient) exchange capacity. These also tend to remain firm longer after grow-in and are more difficult to manage due to their low water and nutrient holding capacities. Sand (or California-style or one-tier system) greens also require a rootzone permeability about 20 inches/hour (51 cm/hr) greater than a two-tier (USGA) green to provide a similar drainage rate.

For other courses desiring a slower infiltration rate, the particle distribution should include 75 percent medium and up to 15 percent fine (0.10 mm) sand. Even slower infiltration rates can be achieved by selecting a sand with a minimum of 65 percent in the fine and medium sand classes. Why would a golf course select slower-draining rootzones? Generally, the faster draining the rootzone, the lower the water and nutrient holding capacity. A slower-draining rootzone should hold more water, be less prone to drought and localized dry spots, and perhaps require less fertilizer.

The values just discussed are meant as guidelines. Depending on location, it may be difficult to obtain sands that meet these rigid specifications. In these cases, look for a sand containing at least 80 percent of the particles in the fine, medium, and coarse classes, combined. Avoid sands containing large amounts of very coarse sand and gravel, since they will drain too quickly and have excessively low water and nutrient holding capacity. However, rootzone mixes dominated by smaller-sized particles (fine sand, very fine sand, silt, and clay) will hold too much water, have poor aeration, and be conducive to algae, moss, and soil diseases. These are sometimes referred to as "dirty" sands. Sometimes a sand pit can wash a "dirty" sand over a number 140 or 200 screen to remove the very fine sand, silt, and clay.

Soil Amendments

Organic Matter

The addition of well-decomposed organic matter enhances soil structure by improving soil aggregation, nutrient retention, and the water-holding capacity of sands. These are typically inexpensive and somewhat short-lived. However, there are differing opinions regarding the use of organic amendments for golf greens.

A trend in the 1970s and 1980s was to use pure sand with no additional amendments (Figure 8–23). This strategy is known as the UC system or the California system, since it was based on research conducted at the University of California, Davis. Organic amendments were specifically excluded because over time they decomposed and tended to plug up, or "constipate," a green, plus they added to the cost of construction. Roots and soil microorganisms die and decompose, which quickly establishes a satisfactory level of soil organic matter in most pure sands.

More recently, concerns about pure sand greens and environmental contamination have many courses reconsidering whether to use organic amendments in their rootzone mix. Nitrate, a contaminant of surface and groundwaters, leaches more readily from a pure sand green than from a green constructed with sand plus organic amendment, but only during the first year of establishment. In subsequent years similar leaching characteristics between the pure sand green and the sand plus organic matter green occur.

Other problems have been associated with the use of pure sands:

1. Poor or non-uniform germination and establishment of a seeded green.
2. Difficulty in controlling rootzone moisture. High spots tend to dry out while low areas stay too wet (Figure 8–24). This may indicate a poor choice of sand.

FIGURE 8–23 Using pure sand (with no added soil amendments such as peat) to construct a green often provides poor or sporadic germination of seed due to poor water and nutrient holding capacities.

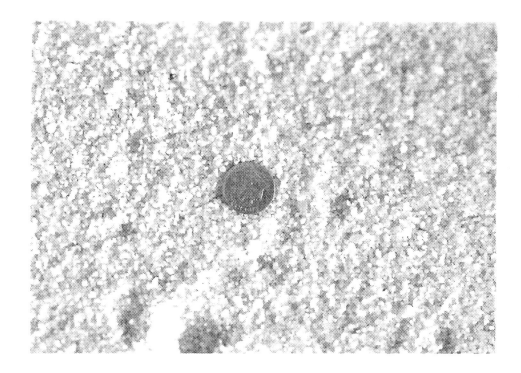

FIGURE 8–24 Excessive drying three years after constructing a bentgrass green using pure sand (no amendments) (right) compared to using an 85:15 ratio of sand to peat (left).

3. Difficulty in maintaining adequate nutrition. Nitrogen, potassium, and sulfur deficiencies may be more common on pure sands, at least during establishment.
4. Difficulty in maintaining a stable surface until the turf matures. This may indicate a very round, rather than angular, sand was used.
5. Reduced microorganism activity, especially during grow-in.

All but the first problem are usually reduced or eliminated after the green matures, due to the natural accumulation of organic matter from dying roots and microorganisms. Germination and establishment can be challenging in a pure sand green, requiring careful irrigation and nutrient management. Organic amendments, such as those listed in Table 8–3, will improve germination and establishment by increasing moisture and nutrient holding capacity.

TABLE 8–3 *Qualitative comparison of soil organic amendments used to modify golf green rootzones.*

Soil amendment	pH	Cation exchange capacity	Water-holding capacity	Durability (years)
Peat humus	acid	good	good	5+
Reed-sedge peat	acid	good	good	4 to 5
Peat moss	acid	fair	excellent	1 to 3
Rice hulls	acid	fair	poor	1 to 3
Ground fir bark	acid	fair	fair	5
Lignified wood waste	acid	poor–fair	good	8+
Sawdust	acid	fair–good	fair–good	1+
Sphagnum moss peat	acid	good	excellent	1 to 3

Characteristics of Organic Matter

Percent Organic Matter

Percent organic matter is determined by a loss on ignition. A peat should have a minimum organic matter content of 85 percent. Compost, by nature, has a lower organic matter content than peat. A 60 percent organic matter content for compost should be a minimum.

Fiber Content

Fibrous peats act like sponges that hold water and are characteristic of younger peats such as sphagnum moss peat. Older peats are less fibrous as they decompose; thus, they have less water-holding capacity.

Density

Density is the weight of peat per unit volume. Density is influenced by the age, texture, and moisture content of the peat. A lightweight (low density) peat requires more peat on a volume basis to produce desirable physical soil properties in a mix.

Carbon:Nitrogen Ratio

Soil microorganisms use the carbon in organic matter as a food (or energy) source. However, as these soil organisms multiply, insufficient nitrogen may be in the organic matter source to support them. The organisms then use soil nitrogen sources for this food source that otherwise would be used by the turfgrass plant. Additional amounts of nitrogen can typically be added to the rootzone mix to compensate for this loss and will be mandatory if a sawdust organic matter source is used.

Ash Content

Ash is what remains after the organic carbon of organic matter content is burned off. Lower ash content reflects a purer organic matter content composition of the material.

Moisture content

Dry peats often are hydrophobic (water hating); thus, they are difficult to re-wet once they have dried out. Wet peats, meanwhile, tend to be lumpy. A moisture content between 35 and 55 percent is characteristic of most high-quality peats.

Peat

Peat is a generic term for partially decomposed plant material formed in bogs under cool and moist conditions (Figure 8–25). It is also the most commonly used organic amendment for putting green soil mixes. Most commercial peats are mined in Canada, North Dakota, Minnesota, and Europe, and since they are derived from different plant materials decomposing under different environmental conditions, these products vary considerably in pH, water retention, organic content, ash and fiber content, and level of decomposition. Peats are broadly classified into moss peat, reed-sedge peat, and peat humus. Moss peats are composed of sphagnum, hypnum, and other mosses. Reed-sedge peat is formed from reeds, sedges, cattails, marsh grasses, and other

FIGURE 8–25 Peat is the most commonly added organic soil amendment for golf green sands to increase water and nutrient holding capacities.

plants. Peat humus is decomposed to the point where the original plant materials are not recognizable. Fibrous peats are preferred over sedimentary and woody-type peats. Peats used to modify sands should be high in organic content and low in ash. Amounts of peat used range from 5 to 20 percent by volume. Table 8–4 lists specific characteristics of some commonly used peats for modifying rootzone mixtures.

Humus

Humus is the relatively stable, dark-colored colloidal organic matter in soils that contains no recognizable plant parts. It is very important in improving soil nutrient exchange, soil tilth, and soil moisture holding capacity. Chemically, humus is a very complex and diverse group of molecules in the final stage of decomposition, including water-soluble sugars, amino acids, and water-insoluble **humic acids** (Figure 8–26). **Humate** (or **humin**) is partially decomposed humus, or soil organic matter, and is defined as the salts of the humic acids and has cation exchange sites that bind protons (H^+), calcium, sodium, iron, potassium, copper, aluminum, and magnesium. Under acid soil conditions, most of the humate exchange sites will be occupied by protons. To take advantage of the extremely high cation exchange potential of humate, the pH of the soil must be raised to remove protons from the exchange sites and replace them with nutrient cations.

Humic acid is commercially produced by adding a dilute (approximately 2 percent) alkali, usually sodium hydroxide, to a humus-bearing material, usually leonardite or possibly coal, lignite, or well-composed peat. Leonardite is a lignitic-organic material related to coal. The sodium hydroxide separates the humus from the alkali-insoluble plant residues present in the leonardite. Acid is added to this humus extraction that produces lignin, humic acid, and fulvic acid. About 50 percent of the leachate is insoluble precipitate of lignin, which is the difficult to decompose portion of plants. The half-life of humic acid can be centuries, while for fulvic acid, it may be 10 to 50 years.

The other 50 percent of the leachate is the water-soluble portion—40 percent of this being humic acid and the other 10 percent **fulvic acid.** The exchange sites of humic acid are filled predominately with protons (H^+ ions), hence, the name; while fulvic acid contains much of the biostimulant-like materials. These acids have a minimum effect on soil pH because the acids are insoluble in water.

In high sodium (or sodic) soils, humic acid dissolves to form a black organic crust called black alkali on the soil surface, restricting infiltration. Algae also often forms on this black alkali to further restrict water infiltration.

TABLE 8–4 *Characteristics of commonly used peats for soil modification.*

Type	Composition	Color	Level of decomposition	Remarks
Peat humus (cultivated peat, black peat)	nonfibrous fine-textured	dark brown to black	advanced	Very stable, longest durability of peats (approximately five years); low to intermediate water-holding capacity (three to six times their weight). The C:N ratio is low. Often used in topdressing mixes. Have a moist density of 30 to 40 pounds per cubic foot and 15 to 20 pounds organic matter per cubic foot.
Reed-sedge peat (lowmoor peat)	semi-fibrous fine-textured	reddish brown to dark brown	partially to substantially	These originate from reeds and sedges with good (85 to 95 percent) organic matter. They are older, and therefore more stable; finer in texture (denser), and therefore they are used often for topdressing. Have good water-holding capacity (four to seven times their weight). Intermediate in durability; usually high in exchangeable Ca. C:N ratio is somewhat low (23). Have a moist density of 15 to 18 pounds per cubic foot and six to nine pounds organic matter per cubic foot. CEC is 118 meq/100 g; pH of 6.6.
Hypnum moss peat (peat moss, sphagnum peat, highmoor peat)	fibrous	tan to brown	partially	Difficult to mix into soil; usually quite acid and low in Ca; high in water-holding capacity and intermediate in durability.
Sphagnum moss peat (top moss)	fluffy, fibrous young residue of moss	yellow to tan	fresh	These are from surfaces of bogs; contain six to nine pounds per cubic foot moist density and three to five pounds organic matter per cubic foot. Also contains high organic (e.g., >95 percent) matter and are fibrous. The C:N ratio is high (65). Have high water-holding capacity (10 to 14 times their weight). CEC is 75 meq/100 g and has pH of 4.3. Difficult to mix into soil; decomposes faster than peats; used more as a surface cover and for packing boxes.
Sedimentary peat	nonfibrous	brown to black	—	Contains silt and ash; typically hard and lumpy; low water-holding capacity; least desirable of the peats; use with caution.

As mentioned earlier, when the predominant exchange sites contain other cations than hydrogen, such as calcium, sodium, iron, potassium, copper, aluminum, and magnesium, the material is called humate. Humates vary widely depending on the source, and commercial sources often contain fulvic and humic acids, but are still referred to as humates. The general rule of thumb is the higher the organic matter and humic acid content, the stronger the soil reaction and, therefore, the better the humate. Granular humates have been used to increase the microbial population of soil, provide a slow release of humic substances, and sustain fertility. Liquid products may affect the plant directly, perhaps by enhancing rapid foliar uptake of liquid fertilizers and micronutrients.

Determining which source of humate to buy, or whether to buy at all, is somewhat confusing. When considering granular sources, use the humate with the highest content of humic acids, the highest organic matter content, and the highest carbon and lowest ash content. Also consider whether the humate matrix is sand or clay, since clay is undesirable on putting greens.

Liquid humic acid consists of short chain organic acids, ash, and various micronutrients. The dry humic acids percentage combined with the ash content reveals the product's true organic content. Products should contain substantial true humic acid, with the remainder as short chain organic acids.

FIGURE 8–26 A schematic showing the soil organic matter transformation from humus to humic and fulvic acids based on their extraction with alkali and acid (redrawn and modified from Brady & Weil, 1999). Sand and root coating with fulvic acids are believed to cause water repellency that leads to localized dry spots in turf.

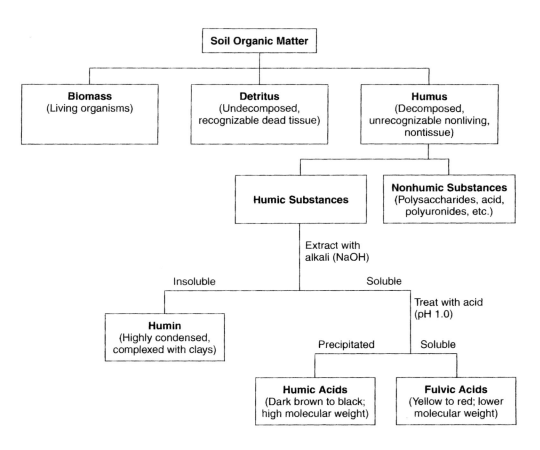

Pure humic acid content generally varies from 0.5 to 8 percent by dry weight. If the ash content is significant (>5 percent), one needs to check to see if it will clog sprayer tips (the higher the ash content, the less active the product). Humate materials may have differing concentrations of micronutrients. Determine which product contains those micronutrients most needed by the turfgrass. Liquid sources may be fortified with nutrients such as potassium and phosphorus. Seaweed is a source of chelated micronutrients and other complexed organic compounds, as well as surfactants and urea.

Humates have been reported to temporarily increase root growth, improve seed germination, and increase microbial activity. This is thought to occur by humic acids providing polyphenols that catalyze plant respiration. Increased plant respiration may temporarily enhance those enzyme systems needed in root growth. Due to the high cation and anion exchange capacity, humic acids also provide a high buffering capacity and increased water and nutrient retention. These materials also are important in soil structure and aggregate stability.

However, as with many things in life, a small quantity of humates may be beneficial, especially in sand-dominated greens low in organic matter, but excessive amounts may inhibit growth. Always follow the manufacturer's rate and timing recommendations and ask to see detailed analysis of the product and independent test results.

Sawdust

Sawdust is sometimes used as an organic amendment. Fresh sawdust, however, can have adverse effects by causing severe nitrogen deficiencies. The carbon:nitrogen ratio (C:N) of sawdust can be as high as 400. Carbon:nitrogen ratios above approximately 20 cause a nutrient imbalance that results in soil microorganisms rapidly using up most or all of the available nitrogen. Some sawdusts also contain excessive salts. If used, sawdust should be well-composted, free of toxic materials, and have some nitrogen fertilizer added for plant use.

Muck Soil

Muck soils are available in certain areas and appear similar to peat in their dark color. However, muck soils are usually a silt loam soil with only 20 to 60 percent organic matter compared to 60 to 95 percent organic matter for peats. Due to their silty loam nature, muck soils should not normally be used in golf greens due to their tendency to compact and reduce drainage.

Composts

The use of composts for sand-based rootzone mixes has become popular as regional composting facilities are built. Composts used in sand-based rootzone mixes should be of the highest quality, preferably aerobically composted in a closed vessel system to ensure complete digestion. Compost should then be ground and screened through a one-fourth (preferably) to one-half-inch (6.4- to 13-mm) screens. Composts are often nitrogen and phosphorus rich, resulting in rapid and relatively easier grow-in. They also display suppression of certain diseases such as *Pythium* root rot, brown patch, and dollar spot. Carbon:nitrogen ratios vary but tend to be low in composts. Their pH values also vary but tend to be high. Composts being considered should have an excellent record of being used as a plant-growing medium. If not, a bioassay should be performed to ensure they do not contain any toxins.

Other Sources

Other organic materials have been used as components of a rootzone mix. These include rice hulls, composted bark, and various animal and vegetable byproducts. However, availability and product consistency may vary by location. When considering organic sources, ensure the product is (1) finely shredded (e.g., screened to one-fourth- to one-half-inch, 6.4 to 13 mm) to achieve the best possible mixing; (2) very low in silt, clay, and salt; (3) well-decomposed; and (4) free of toxic chemicals.

Organic amendments should persist in the soil for at least two years. Due to poor drainage and the introduction of pests, organic materials such as animal manure and mushroom compost generally are not acceptable amendments for golf green soil mixes.

Inorganic Soil Amendments

A number of inorganic amendments (Table 8–5) are marketed as rootzone amendments, and may merit consideration if they are readily available, meet the infiltration and percolation specifications, and are affordable. Inorganic soil amendments do not promote microbial growth the way organic materials do, but may improve either water-holding capacity or aeration of the sand. Since they do not decompose, inorganic amendments usually persist. Also, inorganic soil amendments tend to displace sand on a 1:1 basis while organic amendments do not. Less total material is needed when using inorganic amendments compared to organic. For example, if a 90:10 sand to amendment ratio is desired, 100 cubic yards (77 m^3) of organic amendment are necessary for each 1,000 cubic yards (765 m^3) of sand since organic amendments do not appreciably displace (add to the total volume or bulk of) the sand. Inorganic amendments, however, do displace the sand; thus, only 900 cubic yards (689 m^3) of sand are needed with the 100 cubic yards (77 m^3) of inorganic amendment to achieve a total volume of a 90:10 mixture.

Some unstable inorganic materials, however, may crush into finer particles when subjected to compaction. Inorganic amendments also may retain and release water tightly and retain nutrients less efficiently than organic amendments; they are more difficult to grow-in and are more costly than most organic amended sands.

TABLE 8–5 *Comparison of miscellaneous inorganic soil amendments used in golf green construction.*

Soil amendment	pH	Cation exchange capacity	Water-holding capacity	Durability (years)
Porous ceramics				
- Calcined clay	slightly acidic	moderate	high	10+
- Calcined diatomaceous earth	slightly acidic	moderate	high	10+
Clinoptilolite/zeolite	neutral	high	high	10+
Perlite	neutral	low	moderate	10+
Pumice	neutral	low	low	10+
Vermiculite	neutral	poor	low to fair	10+
Colloidal phosphate	neutral	good	good	10+

Calcined Clay (also called Porous Ceramics)

Calcined clay is formed when clays such as montmorillonite and attapulgite are fired to about 1,200°F (650°C), crushed, and then screened. By firing (heating) these materials, it increases air-filled porosity, permeability, cation exchange capacity (nutrient retention), and water-holding capacity. After firing, calcined clay particles become stable, maintaining their original shape and hardness, even when wet. Due to their porosity, calcined clays are also used as absorbents in cat litter and for grease and oil spills. However, cat litter and industrial absorbents are not manufactured to the same hardness specifications as agricultural products, and should not be used in root-zone mixes. Calcined clays have an average bulk density of 0.6 g/cm^3 and a wide range of particle sizes. Choose a particle size compatible with the sand to be used. Isolite, Profile, and Profile Fine are commercial examples of porous ceramic sources.

Calcined Diatomaceous Earth

Diatomaceous earth is a natural material composed of the microscopic silicon skeletons of diatoms. Diatoms are one-celled ocean organisms whose cell walls consist of interlocking parts and valves containing approximately 85 to 95 percent silica. The skeleton of diatoms have a high degree of internal pore structure and large water-holding capacities. Clay binders may or may not be used with diatomaceous earth. The products can be extruded or formed into pellets, and then fired to form rigid, highly porous particles compatible with many sands. These products have a bulk density ranging from approximately 0.5 to 0.9 g/cm^3, and have a moderate cation exchange capacity. Like calcined clays, these materials are used to increase air-filled porosity, permeability, cation exchange, and water-holding capacity. Commercial sources include PSA, a diatomaceous earth; Axis, a nonfired calcined diatomaceous earth composed of poorly crystalline silica (silicon dioxide); and Green's Choice, a crystalline silica source.

Perlite

Perlite is a light, expanded, porous material produced by heating volcanic rock. It is resistant to weathering but is fragile and may be easily broken by compaction, thus, is not normally recommended for greens. Bulk density ranges from 0.10 to 0.14 g/cm^3. Particle size will influence performance. Finer materials can increase porosity and available soil water. A coarser size will also increase porosity but reduces available water.

Pumice

Pumice is another volcanic rock product containing approximately 70 percent silica. Pumice, like perlite, is available in various grades and also may be unstable. Finer grades increase soil water availability while coarser grades increase porosity.

Zeolite/Clinoptilolite

Zeolites are natural minerals noted for their very high cation exchange capacity. They have found widespread use in industry to remove environmental pollutants, as filtering and purifying agents, and have recently been introduced to the turfgrass market. Zeolites are mixed with sand primarily to increase cation exchange capacity to improve nutrient retention, but in some cases may also improve aeration, drainage, and water-holding capacity. Due to their ability to bind cations (especially potassium), zeolite-based amendments may reduce nutrient leaching from porous sand rootzones. Additionally, they may be formulated to slowly release potassium and/or ammonium to the turf, and thereby help control nutrition levels. Commercial sources include Clinolite, Ecolite, EcoSand, EcoSand X, and ZeoPro.

Colloidal Phosphate

Colloidal phosphate is formed when hard-rock and land-pebble phosphates are washed in preparation for market. Soft phosphate, a byproduct of this process, is washed into holding ponds. This soft phosphate is recovered and marketed under the name colloidal phosphate and contains 18 to 23 percent P_2O_5 (7 to 9 percent P). Colloidal phosphate increases the cation exchange capacity of a sand and increases the small pore space. It also decreases hydraulic conductivity and improves the wettability of hydrophobic sands. Due to this decrease in hydraulic conductivity, colloidal phosphate should be used to amend topsoil and not golf green sand. A suggested mix with sand is 5 to 8 percent colloidal phosphate by volume. Order dry material.

Native Soil

Many areas have desirable local soil sources that, when used in small amounts, provide desirable water and cation exchange capacities. A 5 to 10 percent soil addition often provides these desirable characteristics at economic prices. Care, however, must be used when choosing a soil source since excessive silt and clay may be present. A loamy sand or sandy loam material is best. Representative soil samples along with the sand source should be analyzed by a reputable soil laboratory to determine their compatibility.

Research and experience show many of these inorganic soil amendments can increase porosity and water retention of sand mixtures as well as decrease bulk density. However, research also suggests too much of several of these may limit the amount of available water to plants. Another concern is the long-term stability of the material once traffic, compaction, and excessive rainfall are introduced on the amended turf. However, as a soil amendment and minor (5 to 20 percent) component of a sand-based greens mix, most of these will probably initially provide desirable characteristics normally provided by other amendments such as peat. Likewise, the addition of inorganic soil amendments to push-up greens through aerification and topdressing may improve its rootzone characteristics. Other amendments also provide similar results, but unfortunately, extensive and long-term research and experience are lacking on most all of these. Even though long-term studies are lacking, a soil testing laboratory should be consulted before using any soil amendment for golf green construction.

Once a suitable particle-size sand is determined, the laboratory will then run several trial mixes containing varying proportions of the sand with organic matter and soil being considered by the golf course. The synthetically composed samples will then be compacted and evaluated as previously discussed for hydraulic conductivity and pore space distribution. This process is repeated until a ratio is found that approaches the optimum standard for each component. Once this is determined, the laboratory can then make a recommendation to the volume of each component used in the rootzone mix. Acceptable ranges for many mixes often involve 80 to 90 percent sand, 0 to 10 percent soil, and/or 5 to 20 percent organic matter (e.g., peat) on a volume basis.

ROOTZONE INSTALLATION

Off-Site Mixing

After formulating a soil mix, the next step is to uniformly blend the components. All rootzone mixing should be completed off-site. The use of commercial blending equipment is strongly suggested (Figure 8–27). When mixed on-site (e.g., soil components placed on top of each other and roto-tilled in), the individual components are often poorly distributed, resulting in localized areas of wet or dry spots (Figure 8–28). Most roto-tillers only penetrate the top six to eight inches (15 to 20 cm) of soil, leaving the lower six inches unamended. For smaller jobs, mixing can be accomplished by tumbling the sand plus amendments in a concrete mixer or by spreading the measured quantities on a hard, smooth surface (such as pavement) and then moving the pile repeatedly and in several directions using a front-end loader or tractor.

Once the mixing operation is underway, random samples should be obtained and checked by the laboratory to ensure specifications are being met. Typically a small amount of mix (25 to 50 tons, 23 to 25 metric tons) should be initially blended by the machine and the mix tested for its suitability. Afterwards, the rootzone mix is typically blended in increments of 500 to 1,000 tons (450 to 900 metric tons) and tested to ensure quality control. Each sample is compared to the initial sample to check if the physical specifications are within preapproved tolerance levels. If this cannot be performed, then every truckload of each component utilized in the rootzone mix should be checked at delivery to ensure specifications are met.

Moisture

Sand should be periodically moistened during the mixing operation to facilitate uniform distribution. Adequate moisture also provides the desired "bridging" between the rootzone mixture and underlying gravel layer. Fibrous organic matter should also be moistened to prevent it from clinging to wet sand. Incorporate a starter fertilizer and/or lime as needed.

FIGURE 8–27
Commercial mixing of the
components of a golf green
rootzone "off-site" provides
the most consistent mixing of
the components used for a
golf green rootzone.

FIGURE 8–28   Uneven golf green soil mix (right) from on-site placement differs from roto-tilling of soil amendments (left).

Starter Fertilizer

Soil test results should be used as the basis for determining the amount of fertilizer or lime needed. Phosphorus and potassium are essential nutrients often low in high sand content greens. When soil test results are unavailable, a complete fertilizer such as 10-20-20 should be added at 2.5 to 3 pounds per cubic yard (1,485 to 1,782 g/m^3) of mix. An organic fertilizer such as processed sewage sludge should also be added to high sand content greens at one pound of a 6-2-0 or equivalent per cubic yard (594 g/m^3) of mix. These should be performed during off-site mixing to encourage uniform distribution throughout the soil profile. Some prefer to mix fertilizers to the surface and roto-till twice into the top six to eight inches (15 to 20 cm). In this case, 100 pounds of 10-20-20 or equivalent and 35 pounds of 6-2-0 or equivalent are added and roto-tilled twice per 1,000 square feet. A granular micronutrient package and a humate or carbohydrate soil conditioner also may be added according to label directions. These become especially important if sand-only (e.g., no peat) greens are constructed.

Settling and Sloping Greens

Once the four-inch (10-cm) gravel or two- to four-inch (5- to 10-cm) choker layer is evenly distributed, the rootzone mix is spread on top to a depth of 14 to 15 inches. This will settle to a final depth of approximately 12 inches (30 cm). Depending on the amount and type of organic amendment, approximately 20 percent settling of the original mix can be expected. Severely sloping greens typically have excessive wet conditions in low areas while dry conditions occur in elevated areas. Increasing the rootzone depth at the lower ends of sloping greens reduces (lowers) soil moisture while shallower depths of rootzone mix on elevated areas increases soil moisture in the upper layer.

Installation

The rootzone mix is transported to the edge of the green and then unloaded (Figure 8–29). To prevent disturbance and tire rutting, the soil at the edge of the green should be dry and firm, or plywood sheets should be placed on the soil surface to prevent compaction from the delivery trucks. This becomes critical if the soil surrounding the work site is wet or loose.

A small crawler tractor with a blade is used for pushing and positioning the rootzone mix to a rough grade (Figure 8–30). The tractor should always be operated with its weight on the distributed rootzone mix and not directly on top of the underlying gravel. This minimizes the possibility of crushing or displacing the underlying drain and gravel layer. Grade stakes placed at 10- to 15-foot (3- to 4.5-m) intervals should be used as a guide in spreading the rootzone mix to ensure the final contours are developed. Once the initial rough grading is completed, irrigation installation and soil sterilization should follow. After the irrigation system is installed, the entire green should be settled and firmed by thorough wetting. This wetting will also check the effectiveness of the drainage system.

Building Materials

To estimate costs, the USGA Green Section has tabulated the quantities of materials required per 1,000 square feet of putting surface (Table 8–6). In general, one ton of sand will cover approximately 20 square feet to a depth of 12 inches (refer to the calculation section at the end of this chapter). It is recommended an additional two-year supply of rootzone mix be purchased for future topdressing and minor repairs. If a sand dissimilar to that originally used for construction is applied as topdressing, the chance of introducing excessive amounts of very fine sand, silt, and clay is increased. Fine-textured materials could clog soil macropores, resulting in reduced infiltration and percolation and eventual failure of the green. Other costs involve comparing amendments such as organic versus inorganic materials, transportation costs, a 10 to 20 percent "waste" factor, laboratory testing, blending costs, and sales tax.

FIGURE 8–29 Rootzone mix is placed at the edge of a newly constructed green. Plywood is often placed around greens to prevent wheel marks and the collapse of the green's perimeter.

FIGURE 8–30 The rootzone mix is spread in a fan-shape direction across a green. The heavy machinery should stay on the rootzone pile and not on the subgrade, which may disturb the drainage capabilities of the subgrade and tile.

TABLE 8–6 *Estimated materials needed to build 1,000 square feet of putting green surface.*

Material	Depth, inches (cm)	Amount of material required per 1,000 square feet
Gravel	4 (10)	12 cubic yards (10 m^3/100 m^2)
Coarse sand (choker) layer	2 to 4 (5 to 10)	6 to 12 cubic yards (5 to 10 m^3/100 m^2)
Rootzone mixture	12 (30)	37 cubic yards (31 m^3/100 m^2)
Tile	—	approximately 100 linear feet (30 m)

Irrigation Installation

A green normally has an underground, automatic pop-up irrigation system installed at the perimeter of the collar. Individual greens usually require four to six irrigation heads with spacing determined by the size and shape of the green and the infiltration rate of the soil. Normal head spacing is approximately 60 feet, varying from 45 to 90 feet. Having operational control of each head is preferred over systems that provide total green or zone irrigation control. Individual head control increases irrigation flexibility by allowing for wind correction, watering localized dry spots, and other special local needs. One or two quick-coupler hose-end outlets should also be installed around each green to facilitate syringing, watering localized dry spots, and for hydro-aerifying or emergency irrigation. Irrigation line trenches are installed along the perimeter of the green, never across or through it.

Irrigation heads need to be strategically placed to minimize the amount of water applied to bunkers. Constant watering of bunkers results in erosion, soggy shots for the players, and algae and weed encroachment. Separate irrigation lines (or dual heads) should be provided for slopes and areas surrounding the greens. Normally, the grass used here is different than on the green; thus, it has different water requirements. The native soils in these areas also are often heavier and drain slower compared to the modified greens mix. Most native soils also hold more water and do not need to be irrigated as frequently as the well-drained green. Water from fairway irrigation also should just reach the perimeter of the green, but not be on it.

The irrigation pipe bed should be fully settled before planting to prevent future uneven surfaces around the green. Soil from the irrigation line should not be allowed to contaminate the green's soil profile. Swing joints, a system of fittings that permits irrigation head adjustment without raising or lowering the irrigation pipe, are used for each head to prevent irrigation head or line

damage from foot, vehicular, or maintenance traffic (Figure 8–31). Swing joints also readily allow for head adjustment once the turf is established and the soil settles. During establishment, sprinkler heads are often placed three to four inches (7.6 to 10 cm) above the finish grade for easy marking. These are lowered after turf is matured to the finish grade.

Soil Sterilization

Soil sterilization is the next step. Sterilization eliminates most weeds, insects, and nematodes in the rootzone mix. This is truly a case of an ounce of prevention being worth a pound of cure, since the cost of controlling pests in a nonsterilized green can be considerable. This is especially true when considering nematode and weed control.

The two most common soil fumigants are methyl bromide and metam sodium. Methyl bromide is the most effective soil sterilant. However, it is highly toxic, requires a polyethylene cover after application for optimum efficacy (Figure 8–32), and requires a special pesticide license for purchase and use. Metam sodium does not absolutely require a cover, but is more effective if one is used. Additionally, three weeks are generally required to air the metam sodium-treated soil before planting. It should be noted the production of methyl bromide is scheduled to stop in 2005, and its use phased out thereafter. Research is currently evaluating the use of methyl iodide and other alternative substitutes that are less persistent and less damaging to the environment. It is suggested superintendents unfamiliar with soil sterilants contract with a custom applicator.

Final Grading

Once fumigation is completed, the final grade should be rechecked using a level or transit to ensure it conforms to the original specifications. Any final grading should be performed manually using shovels, push boards, and/or laser-guided drags (Figure 8–33). Once the final grade is established, the green is ready for firming. A small crawler tractor, a mechanically powered one-ton roller, a vibratory settler, a drag with weight, or a tractor with wide tires is operated back and forth in all directions until the entire surface has been compacted (Figure 8–34). The profile can be encouraged to settle and become firm by irrigating deeply enough so water continuously flows out of the drain pipe. This usually requires up to one hour irrigation the first time. This heavy irrigation should also be repeated the day prior to planting to ensure sufficient soil moisture for seedlings or sprigs. The rootzone is deemed firm when foot or tire prints are less than 0.25 inch (6.4 millimeter) deep. If deeper than this, additional irrigation and rolling are needed.

Once a compacted rootzone is achieved, the surface should be smoothed by hand raking, although certain types of mechanical sand rakes are acceptable as long as the final grade is not

FIGURE 8–32 A polyethylene cover is used to obtain maximum efficiency from soil fumigation. Fumigation is highly recommended when weeds and pests such as nematodes are suspected.

FIGURE 8–33 Final grading of a golf green requires extensive hand labor, push boards, and various drags. A laser-guided tractor-drawn box scrape is shown that provides an exceptional final grade.

significantly disturbed. The area is now ready to be planted. Refer to Chapter 9 for an explanation of planting and maintenance for newly established turf sites.

Additional Information

Collars

The collar region should be constructed using the same techniques as the green, since they receive similar traffic. This should reduce problems and improve turfgrass quality. The same grass should be used for both the green and the collar. This helps minimize encroachment of coarser fairway grasses. An additional strip of a slow-growing grass, such as zoysiagrass, should be considered between the collar and fairway grasses to provide an additional buffer to minimize encroachment. Generally, since collars are mowed higher than the greens, their maintenance levels are somewhat less.

FIGURE 8–34 The process of settling or "firming" a green's surface prior to planting.

FIGURE 8–35 A properly constructed collar (top) with a 60 to 80 percent slope (minimum 3:1) prevents excessive soil compaction, dry spot development, and thin turf that usually develop from improper (bottom) construction with a thin layer of sand. The minimum width of the collar should be three feet, and ideally five feet.

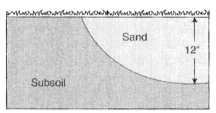

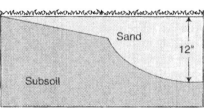

Excessive Drying

Collars sometimes have a problem with being droughty. This occurs from the adjacent native soil, which is usually finer in texture, having greater tension for water in the coarser rootzone mix of the collar. This can be prevented by ringing the collar with an impermeable barrier or by grading the collar's perimeter to a slope of 60 to 80 percent (minimum 3:1) (Figure 8–35). In the "ringing" process, a strip of polyethylene sheeting is inserted between the outer soil and the sandy rootzone mix to act as a vertical barrier, preventing lateral transfer of water into the adjacent soil (Figure 8–19). This polyethylene barrier should be positioned on the outside perimeter of the collar's modified rootzone mix before the mix is placed. Extending the polyethylene four to six inches (10 to 15 cm) above the soil during construction will minimize soil erosion into the green construction site. The width of the collar should be a minimum of three feet (0.9 m), and ideally five feet (1.5 m).

Bunker Sand

No "official" specifications exist dealing with a properly selected bunker sand. An initial set of specifications was provided by the USGA where 100 percent of the sand should fall in the range of 0.25 to 1.00 millimeters. This was later refined to suggest ≥75 percent of the sand particles should fall in the 0.25 to 0.50 meter range. However, other guidelines have been proposed (Golf Course Management, July, 1986 vol. 54:64-70) since sands with these specific USGA textures are very difficult to find and very costly to make (Tables 8–7 and 8–8). Greater than 65 percent of the

TABLE 8–7 *Sand particle-size recommendations for bunkers (Brown & Thomas, 1986).*

Size (mm)	Percent
0.05 to 0.1	<5
0.1 to 1.0	78 to 100
1.0 to 2.0	<15
>2.0	<2

TABLE 8–8 *Sand criteria for bunkers (Brown & Thomas, 1986).*

Test	Good	Fair	Poor
Silt and clay	<3%	3%	>3%
Ball penetration (MPa)	>0.24	0.18 to 0.24	<0.18
Crusting	none	slight	predominant
Set-up (thick crust formation or adherence)	none	slight	predominant
Shape	angular	sub-angular	round

bunker sand should fall in the coarse to medium sand range (1/2 to 1/4 mm). Sands in this range usually sift through the grass and down to the soil surface after being blasted out of the bunker. Smaller particles may create drainage problems when blasted onto greens while silt and clay (particles <0.05 mm) should be minimized in the sand to prevent surface crusting. Sand particles exceeding one millimeter tend to remain on the putting surface and interfere with mowing operations and putting.

If available, golfers seem to prefer white-colored sand. However, the decision on color should not supersede the size and drainage quality of the sand in question. Crusting of bunkers occur when poor quality sand is used. To prevent this, sands with excess (>3 percent) silt and clay particles, calcareous sand, and sands with less than 20 inches per hour hydraulic conductivity should be avoided. As calcareous sands weather (break down), calcium carbonates dissolve, acting as weak cementing agents, thereby forming a crusted restrictive drainage layer. A silica (quartz)-based sand is preferred.

Buried balls (fried-egg lie) occur when sand is too soft (Figure 8–36). To test this, the bunker sand is subjected to a penetrometer test. Bunker sand with a penetrometer reading <1.8 kg/cm^2 is too soft. Readings between 1.8 and 2.4 kg/cm^2 are acceptable with readings >2.4 kg/cm^2 being desirable. Sand particles may also be either angular, sub-angular, subrounded, or rounded in shape, depending upon the sharpness of the edges and corners of the particles. Desirable bunker sand shape is angular with a low degree of sphericity ("roundness"), or in other words, are flatter. Highly angular sands tend to pack tightly and may injure (abrade) turf roots. Highly rounded (spherical) sands usually do not adequately pack, remaining loose and unstable. Desirable sand with sharp angles resist movement under impact from a golf ball, and thus have fewer buried ("fried-egg") balls.

Regrassing Greens

If the original soil mix is acceptable and adequate subsurface drainage is present, courses wanting to switch putting surface grass often can strip the existing grass, refill the sand to bring the surface back to grade, fumigate, and replant. The steps include:

1. Cut the existing turf as deep as possible with a sod cutter and remove the grass by hand or by scraping it off with a front-end loader.
2. If an excessive thatch and organic matter layer is present, remove an additional two to four inches (2.5 to 5 cm) of rootzone material. If not removed, these layers disrupt proper drainage.
3. Bring the subsoil back to grade using suitable laboratory-tested sand.
4. To mix the new sand and existing subsoil, roto-till as deep as possible and in multiple directions. If not performed adequately, layers develop that disrupt proper drainage.

FIGURE 8–36 Buried golf ball ("fried-egg") on the right when the bunker sand is not firm. Desirable bunker sand is firm enough so golf balls do not sink excessively when hit into it (left).

5. Following roto-tilling, the surface is roughly shaped and packed using a water-filled roller making multiple passes.
6. Fumigate with a tarp to assure the original grass is eradicated and to kill nematodes and diseases. Once the grass is planted, if any original grass is not eradicated, contaminated surfaces eventually occur.
7. The area is then final-shaped, recompacted, and then planted.

This renovation method generally requires four to eight weeks to complete. Warm-season grasses should be planted in early summer (June/July) while planting cool-season grasses in late summer (August/September) allows maximum growth before seasonal stresses occur.

GOLF COURSE GREEN CALCULATIONS

Estimating Tons of Material for a Given Area

In order to estimate the necessary amount of material to cover a given area, the following assumption is made: one cubic yard of sand, choker sand, or pea gravel weighs approximately 2,600 pounds (or 1.3 tons).

cubic feet (ft) = area (ft^2) × desired depth (ft)
one cubic yard (yd^3) = 27 ft^3
number of tons = number of cubic yards (yd^3) × 1.3

Example:

To determine the tons of mix required for a 5,000 square foot green area one foot deep:

- Area of green (ft^2) × depth (1 foot) = cubic feet of mix, or 5,000 ft^2 × 1 ft = 5,000 ft^3,
- Cubic feet of mix ÷ 27 = cubic yards of mix needed, or 5,000 ft^3 ÷ 27 = 185 yd^3, and
- Cubic yards of mix × 1.3 = tons of mix, or 185 yd^3 × 1.3 = 240 tons

Estimating Volumes of Material for a Given Area

To estimate fill dirt or topsoil volumes needed to cover a given area, use the following (this assumes the units are the same for all variables and the thickness and shape of the layer is reasonably uniform):

$$\text{volume} = \text{surface area or cross-sectional area} \times \text{depth}$$

Example:

To determine topsoil amount (in yd^3) needed to spread a one-inch layer over an area of 9,500 square feet:

> convert all values to a common unit: 1 inch = 0.08333 ft
> compute the volume: $0.08333 \text{ ft} \times 9,500 \text{ ft}^2 = 791.6 \text{ ft}^3$
> convert to desired units (yd^3): $791.6 \text{ ft}^3 \div 27 = 29.3 \text{ yd}^3$

CHAPTER
9

Turfgrass Establishment and "Grow-In"

INTRODUCTION

The modern golfer demands and expects high-quality turfgrasses and near-perfect playing conditions. This level of quality, in turn, requires a higher intensity of turfgrass maintenance with sufficient personnel and budgets, and the demand for high quality typically starts before a course opens. Following golf course construction, everyone wants "instant" turfgrass so the golf course can open as soon as possible. Golfers are eager to play. Owners, developers, and/or financial partners want to start receiving a return on their investment. The general contractor worries about soil erosion from wind or water, hoping they will not have to reshape the golf course. These expectations place great pressure on the golf course superintendent and/or general contractor. Newly established turfgrass is very vulnerable to the elements and must receive adequate time to develop and sufficiently mature to withstand the wear and stresses associated with golf play.

Frequently, the question "How fast can it be done?" is asked rather than "How long will it take?" Neither can be answered with accuracy because of weather uncertainties and varying environmental conditions. However, turfgrass managers can plan ahead and optimize the timing of turfgrass establishment to improve the chances of providing a quality turfgrass playing surface as quickly as possible.

Turfgrass Selection

One of the most important golf course decisions in regard to establishment is the selection of turfgrass species and cultivars for a golf course. A basic understanding of the local environmental patterns, cultural requirements, and species adaptations are necessary to make these decisions. Other questions to address include the level of resources (e.g., time and money) allocated for the maintenance of the turfgrass. Refer to Chapter 1 to determine the options in selecting the appropriate turfgrass species or cultivar for your specific area and use.

Plant Material Quality

The components of turfgrass quality reflect its genetic makeup, environmental influences on the turfgrass plant, and the expressed characteristics from biochemical and physiological processes. The characteristics of turfgrass quality have traditionally been established by the personal preferences and needs of the end user. In addition, turfgrass quality characteristics vary with seeds versus vegetative materials.

Numerous varieties of a specific turfgrass species typically exist. According to the Plant Variety Protection Act of 1970, a variety must be new, distinct, uniform, and stable (DUS). However, a new variety does not necessarily have to be "better" or an improvement on an older one, even though this is largely understood. The label will indicate "PVP Number XYZ. Approved (or Pending), unauthorized propagation prohibited."

PVP is a form of patent on seed-propagated plants and provides seed companies a return on their investment. In the United States, PVP species since 1994 are protected for 20 years (18-year protection was offered prior to 1994). The distinguishing characteristic must be stable and observable for this 20-year period of protection.

In the application to the USDA-ARS PVP office, five exhibits (checklists) must be completed.

1. The origin and breeding history of the variety.
2. The statement of distinctness, showing how the variety differs from all other varieties in that species.
3. The objective description of the variety, describing crucial characteristics of the new variety as compared to a control or standard variety.
4. Additional data, such as tables, figures, photographs, molecular analysis, and so on, that are useful in describing and distinguishing the variety.
5. Description on how ownership of the variety was obtained.

Once a certificate of protection is issued, the protected variety can be sold or advertised for sale by variety name only by the owner of the certificate or with the owner's permission. The vegetative plants produced following planting are also protected and may not be increased without the owner's permission. Superintendents, however, can use the nursery green, for example, to repair regular greens but can not legally use the turf from the nursery to grass another course.

Turfgrass seed quality is determined by the seed production and processing practices. The two basic components analyzed for turfgrass seed quality are seed purity and seed germination. These can be analyzed by any reputable seed laboratory. **Seed purity** is the percentage of pure seed in a bag compared to other crop or weed seed and inert materials, while **seed germination** indicates the expected germination percentage. Turfgrass seed certification programs also exist to guarantee the "trueness to type" from a genetic perspective.

Ascertaining vegetative turfgrass plant material quality is more difficult due to the inherent variability of the type of turfgrass, time of the year, and personal evaluation criteria. Vegetative turfgrass quality characteristics to consider include turfgrass texture, color, density, uniformity, growth habit, mowing height, and smoothness.

To ensure quality, one should personally inspect all turfgrass materials (seed and vegetative) from which planting stock will be utilized. It is imperative to utilize the same source of turfgrass planting stock over time to avoid contamination of the initial planting stock with "off-types" or mutations. This not only includes material from the same grower, but also the same fields or blocks, as variations often occur between these. Most states have turfgrass certification programs providing a paper trail to ensure quality, but these are not standardized or monitored across state lines. Use reputable producers and sellers because, once the turf is established, it becomes very expensive, difficult, and time-consuming to convert grasses. Proceed with extreme caution on lowest-bid or lowest-cost sources.

METHODS OF ESTABLISHMENT

As discussed, turfgrasses can be established by two basic means: (1) seeding or (2) vegetative. These are influenced by having proper soil moisture, balanced nutrients, adequate light, and favorable temperatures.

Seeding

Seeding normally is cheaper compared to vegetative planting methods; however, the establishment time with seeding exceeds the time from vegetative means, and the area may be more prone to erosion. Seeded varieties exist for both cool- and warm-season turfgrasses. Most cool-season turfgrasses such as bluegrass, bentgrass, fescues, and ryegrasses can be established by seeding. However, only a limited number of warm-season golf course turfgrasses can be established by seeding. Bahiagrass, buffalograss, carpetgrass, centipedegrass, common bermudagrass, St. Augustinegrass, and zoysiagrass are warm-season grasses that can be established by seeding, but the time required to achieve an acceptable playing surface is much longer compared to vegetative propagation of these species. In addition, most varieties of St. Augustinegrass and zoysiagrass do not produce many viable seeds or seeds remaining "true to type" once they germinate; therefore, these turfgrasses are normally established by vegetative means.

Seed Labels

The Federal Seed Act and State Laws regulate the sale, transportation, and distribution of seed. Up to four paper trail steps exist when new seeds are being developed and produced for consumers. These steps help ensure the intended purity and identity of the plant is maintained and available.

The first step involves **breeder seed,** which is produced under the direct supervision of the breeder. In most cases, the same species must not have previously been grown in the same field for five years and must be separated from any other variety of this species by 900 feet (275 m). This helps ensure purity. From breeder seed, **foundation seed** is produced as a primary source of a genetically identified variety from which all subsequent increases are made. Foundation seed is developed and produced under supervision of the breeder, the foundation seed agency, a private association or co-operation of seed growers, private business, or the agricultural experiment station. As the field grows in, it is inspected by both the breeder and certification agency for any off-types or weeds. Foundation seed is then released for surveillance to other growers, whose subsequent second generation seeds are referred to as **registered seed.** Registered seed is the progeny of foundation seed used to maintain satisfactory genetic identity and purity, and has been approved and certified by the seed certification agency according to the rules defined by the Association of Official Seed Analysts. Registered seed goes to those farmers who grow seed for the retail market. This final product is checked by the certification agency, who certifies varietal characteristics. Such a seed can then be marketed as **certified seed,** seed that is genetically pure. The color of the certified seed tag is blue, the registered seed tag color is purple, and the breeder and foundation seed tag is normally white. Superintendents should always buy and plant certified seed as this is the only means of ensuring seed purity.

Steps to increase need and maintain purity

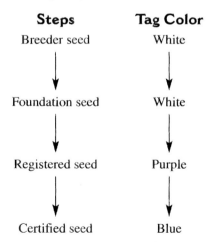

Steps	Tag Color
Breeder seed	White
Foundation seed	White
Registered seed	Purple
Certified seed	Blue

Normally, seed laws and regulations require the following to be indicated on the labels:

1. Species, variety, strain
2. Purity
3. Germination
4. Weeds, including noxious weeds

```
┌─────────────────────────────────────────────────────────────────┐
│                      Seed Tag Example                             │
│                                                                   │
│   Kind:                                Creeping bentgrass         │
│   Variety:                             T-93                       │
│   Lot Number:                          XYZ-3-111                  │
│   Pure Seed:                           99.31%                     │
│   Crop Seed:                           00.00%                     │
│   Inert Matter:                        00.69%                     │
│   Weed Seed:                           00.00%                     │
│   Noxious Weeds:                       None Found                 │
│   Origin:                              OR                         │
│   Germination:                         93%                        │
│   Test Date:                           12/05                      │
│   Net WT:                              25 lbs (11.4 kg)           │
│   Manufacturer's Code:                 ABC 123                    │
│                      Best Seed Company                            │
│                       1234 Seed Road                              │
│                     Anywhere, OR 12345                            │
└─────────────────────────────────────────────────────────────────┘
```

When seed is obtained, it will not be 100 percent pure nor have 100 percent germination. It will contain some inert matter (e.g., chaff, dirt, sand, broken seed, etc.), weed seed, and other crop seed. Its germination is also usually less than 100 percent. Therefore, one pound of seed will not result in one pound of pure, viable seed.

For seed to germinate, it requires moisture, suitable temperature, and air. The seed absorbs water and, if other conditions are suitable, the cells of the embryo become active. Cell division starts and seed germinates. Some seed may be viable but dormant. Dormancy, a resting stage of the seed, may be caused by a seedcoat impervious to water; therefore, the seed does not germinate. Soaking or scratching (also called scarifying) the seedcoat may be beneficial to promote germination. Other physiological and biochemical reasons also may exist for this dormancy. The seed may carry inhibitors that have to undergo chemical modification before the embryo is released to sprout. Seed testing laboratories grow seed under favorable conditions to measure germination and list this fact on the seed label.

Germination is the quality of seed most likely to change. Germination of seed stored in high moisture and high temperatures typically drops in a few weeks. The best storage conditions are cool and dry places that are free of rodents such as rats. Time also reduces germination. Seed older than one year generally loses a significant percentage of germination and should be replaced.

Other things being equal, the heavier the seed of a grass, the better the germination and more vigorous the young seedlings are. This weight is due to more food in the endosperm for the embryo to draw from. However, the larger the seed, the more seed is needed to achieve the same number of seedlings in a given area.

Pure Live Seed

Pure live seed (or **PLS**) is often used to express the quality of seed, although it is not normally shown on the label. Pure live seed is the percentage of pure seed that will germinate. This value is determined by multiplying the percentage of pure seed by the percentage of germination and dividing by 100. For example, if a label indicates the seed has 90 percent purity and 80 percent germination, the pure live seed would be:

$$\textbf{pure live seed} = \frac{\text{germination} \times \text{purity}}{100} = \frac{80 \times 90}{100} = 72 \text{ percent}$$

This means 72 percent of the package contents consist of pure seed that can germinate and produce plants.

Seed Number

When seeding to establish turf, the number of seedlings per unit area (such as per square inch) is an important indicator on the amount of seed actually required. Since seed size varies among turfgrass species, the exact number of seedlings per unit area varies with the species and the intent of the seeding. When establishing a new area, the ideal number of seedlings per square inch varies from about 8 to 18 (1.2 to 2.8 per cm^2), with 10 per square inch (or about 1,500 seedlings per square foot, 1.5 per cm^2) being a good medium range.

Example:

This example involves a mixture of bentgrass and *Poa trivialis* seed with the following information:

Grass	Percent purity	Percent germination	Seeds/pounds (seed/kg)
Creeping bentgrass	95	90	6,000,000 (2,724,000)
Poa trivialis	90	85	2,500,000 (1,135,000)

If a seeding mixture contains 60 percent creeping bentgrass and 40 percent *Poa trivialis* seed, what is the maximum seedling density per square inch resulting from a seeding rate of eight pounds of seed per 1,000 square feet?

Step 1: Determine the percentage of seed weight of each grass in the eight-pound seeding rate.

Bentgrass: eight pounds seed × 60 percent = 4.8 pounds of bentgrass in this eight-pound seeding rate

Poa trivialis: eight pounds seed × 40 percent = 3.2 pounds of *Poa trivialis* in this eight-pound seeding rate

Step 2: Find the total PLS for each grass:

PLS: percent purity × percent germination × seeds/pound × seeding rate
Bentgrass: 0.95 × 0.90 × 6,000,000 × 4.8 pounds = 24,624,000 PLS total
Poa trivialis: 0.90 × 0.85 × 2,500,000 × 3.2 pounds = 6,120,000 PLS total

Step 3: Convert this total seed-to-seedling density per square inch, remembering the initial seeding rate was based on 1,000 square feet:

$$\text{Bentgrass:} \frac{24,624,000 \text{ PLS}}{1,000 \text{ ft}^2} \times \frac{1 \text{ ft}^2}{144 \text{ in}^2} = 171 \text{ bentgrass seedlings per square inch}$$

$$\textit{Poa trivialis:} \frac{6,120,000 \text{ PLS}}{1,000 \text{ ft}^2} \times \frac{1 \text{ ft}^2}{144 \text{ in}^2} = 43 \textit{ Poa trivialis} \text{ seedlings per square inch}$$

Example:

How many pounds of common bermudagrass seed (2,000,000 seed/lb), 93 percent purity and 88 percent germination, would be needed to achieve 1,500 PLS per square foot over a 5,500 square foot area?

Step 1: Determine the total number of seedlings required:

$$\frac{1,500 \text{ seedlings}}{\text{ft}^2} \times 5,500 \text{ ft}^2 = 8,250,000 \text{ seedlings total over the whole area}$$

Step 2: Determine the PLS per pound of seed: percent germination × percent purity × seed no./pound

$$0.88 \times 0.93 \times 2,000,000 = 1,636,800 \text{ PLS per pound}$$

Step 3: Divide the total seedlings needed by the PLS per pound:

$$8,250,000 \div 1,636,800 = \text{five pounds of seed needed to provide 1,500 PLS/ft}^2$$
over a 5,500 ft^2 area.

Example:

An assistant superintendent calls his local seed supplier and requests a particular cultivar of perennial ryegrass for overseeding. The supplier says three lots are available, depending on age. Determine which of the following seed lots is considered the "best buy."

	Lot A	Lot B	Lot C
Germination	95%	75%	90%
Purity	65%	80%	95%
Cost (per lb)	$2.00	$1.75	$2.10

Step 1: Calculate PLS for each: $\dfrac{\text{percent germination} \times \text{percent purity}}{100}$

$$A = 62\%$$
$$B = 60\%$$
$$C = 86\%$$

Step 2: Calculate the cost per pound of PLS using the following: $\dfrac{\text{cost/lb}}{\text{PLS}} \times 100$

$$A = \$3.24$$
$$B = \$2.87$$
$$C = \$2.46$$

Although Lot C costs more per pound of seed, when this cost is considered per pound of PLS, it actually is the "best buy."

Seeding Rates

Turfgrass seeding rates are influenced by the seed size, seed costs, and growth habit. A general guide for seeding is to apply a sufficient number of pure live seed to develop from 1,000 to 2,000 seedlings per square foot (10,760 to 21,500 per m^2). In general, smaller-sized seed such as buffalograss, bentgrass, roughstalk bluegrass, and centipedegrass have lower seeding rates (based on weight) and are more expensive. Turfgrasses with a creeping growth habit also are normally seeded at lower rates since the developing stolons or rhizomes aid in establishment and coverage. Table 9–1 provides the seeding rates, approximate number of seeds per pound, and the optimum time of the year for seeding for most available turfgrasses. Table 9–2 lists similar planting information for native and prairie grasses and selected legumes.

Optimum Seeding Time

Since superintendents have no real means of warming soil, adjusting the planting time according to the proper season is the only means of influencing soil temperatures. The optimum time of year for seeding varies with the turfgrass species (Table 9–1). These recommended seeding times correspond with the optimum temperatures required for maximum germination and growth. The optimum seeding time for cool-season turfgrasses is in the fall when soil temperatures are between 60 and 70°F (15.6 to 21°C) at a depth of four inches (10 cm). Little or only sporadic seed germination will occur when soil temperatures are below 50°F (10°C). Seeding should cease approximately 30 days before the first expected killing frost. As a second choice, cool-season turfgrasses may be seeded in the early spring before soil temperatures increase above the required growth range. However, seeding these turfgrasses during spring usually results in immature seedlings during the summer heat stress and drought periods, which transcends into a higher susceptibility to diseases such as brown patch and leaf spot. Annual weeds can also be a problem if thin turfgrass occurs from the late seeding in spring.

TABLE 9–1 Seeding rates, approximate number of seed per pound, and optimum time of year for planting various turfgrasses for golf course fairways.

Turfgrass	Seeding rate lb/1,000 ft²	Seeding rate lb/A	Approximate number of seed/pound**	Optimum seeding time	Optimum germination temperatures °F***	Days to germination
Annual bluegrass	3 to 7	130 to 300	2,250,000	late summer into early fall	68 to 86	—
Annual ryegrass	5 to 9*	220 to 400	225,00	fall	59 to 77	3 to 7
Bahiagrass	3 to 8	130 to 350	170,000	spring	68 to 95	7 to 21
Bermudagrass						
- hulled	1 to 2	45 to 90	2,000,000	spring into early summer	68 to 95	10 to 20
- unhulled	4 to 8	175 to 350	2,000,000	spring into early summer	68 to 95	14 to 21
Blue grama	1 to 3	45 to 130	900,000	spring	68 to 86	14
Buffalograss						
- hulled	0.5 to 2	22 to 90	200,000	spring	68 to 95	1 to 7
- burs	1 to 2	45 to 90	50,000	spring	68 to 95	7 to 28
Carpetgrass	3 to 4	130 to 175	1,300,000	spring	68 to 95	—
Centipedegrass	0.25 to 1	11 to 45	400,000	spring	68 to 95	10 to 20
Colonial bentgrass	1 to 2*	45 to 90*	7,000,000	fall	50 to 86	6 to 12
Creeping bentgrass	0.5 to 1*	22 to 45*	6,000,000	fall	59 to 86	4 to 12
Crested wheatgrass	3 to 5	130 to 220	320,000	late summer into early fall	59 to 86	14
Fine fescue—hard	4 to 5	175 to 220	350,000	fall	59 to 77	10 to 20
Fine fescue—chewings/red	4 to 5	175 to 220	375,000	fall	59 to 77	5 to 10
Intermediate ryegrass	6 to 10	260 to 450	250,000	late summer into early fall	59 to 77	3 to 7
Kentucky bluegrass	2 to 3*	90 to 130	2,250,000	late summer into early fall	59 to 77	6 to 30
Kikuyugrass	0.5	25	na	spring	68 to 86	3 to 10
Lovegrass	0.25 to 0.5	11 to 22	1,500,000	spring	58 to 95	14
Perennial ryegrass	6 to 10*	260 to 450*	250,000	late summer through early fall	59 to 77	3 to 7
Redtop	0.5 to 1	22 to 45	5,000,000	fall	68 to 86	4 to 10
Roughstalk bluegrass (*Poa trivialis*)	1 to 2*	45 to 90	2,500,000	late summer through early fall	68 to 86	10 to 21
St. Augustinegrass						
-hulled	0.5 to 0.75	22 to 33	380,000	spring	—	—
-unhulled	0.5 to 0.75	22 to 33	450,000	spring	—	—
Tall fescue	5 to 8	220 to 350	250,000	late summer through early fall	59 to 86	6 to 12
Velvet bentgrass	0.5 to 1	22 to 45	8,000,000	fall	68 to 86	—
Zoysiagrass	0.5 to 3	22 to 130	1,000,000	spring	68 to 95	10 to 14

*Seeding rates for overseeding purposes are higher than listed.

**Seed counts per pound can vary significantly among cultivars of a species.

***Optimum germination temperatures are listed by the Association of Official Seed Analysts (1998). The lower value indicates a continuous 16-hour temperature exposure time while the higher value indicates a continuous eight-hour temperature exposure time needed for germination at that particular temperature.

TABLE 9–2 Seeding rates, approximate number of seed per pound, and optimum time of year for planting various native and prairie grasses and legumes for golf course roughs and out-of-play areas.

Plants	Seeding rate (lb/A)	Approximate number of seed/pound	Optimum seeding time	Minimum rainfall (in.)	Preplanting treatment	Days to germination
Warm-Season Grasses						
Little bluestem	5 to 40 PLS*	260,000	spring	16	—	14
Big bluestem	10 to 60 PLS	150,000	spring	20	—	—
Blue grama	2 to 20 PLS	900,000	spring	10	—	14
Sideoats grama	5 to 40 PLS	180,000	spring	17	—	14
Switchgrass	4 to 30 PLS	400,000	spring	16	—	14
Weeping lovegrass	4 to 40 PLS	1,500,000	spring	15	—	14
Japanese millet	20 to 30	115,000	spring	—	—	10
Browntop millet	10 to 20	142,000	spring	—	—	7
Cool-Season Grasses						
Smooth bromegrass	7 to 40 PLS	140,000	spring	16	—	14
Crested wheatgrass	10 to 30 PLS	320,000	fall or early spring	9	—	14
Western wheatgrass	10 to 40 PLS	110,000	spring	14	—	28
Indian ricegrass	7 to 30 PLS	140,000	fall	6	—	42
Reed canary grass	3 to 10 PLS	530,000	spring or fall	moist areas	—	21
Alkaligrass	20 to 80 PLS	1,900,000	spring or fall	—	—	28
Legumes						
Lespedeza sp.	25 to 60	90,000	spring or fall	—	innoculate	21
Crown vetch	20 to 25	110,000	spring or fall	—	scarify and innoculate	14
Birdsfoot trefoil	6 to 12	375,000	spring or fall	—	scarify and innoculate	12
Strawberry clover	5 to 10	300,000	spring or fall	—	scarify and innoculate	7
Crimson clover	15 to 30	140,000	spring or fall	—	scarify and innoculate	7
Red clover	6 to 12	275,000	spring or fall	—	scarify and innoculate	7
White clover	6 to 12	800,000	spring or fall	—	scarify and innoculate	7

*PLS = pure live seed = purity × germination.

Warm-season turfgrasses are normally seeded in late spring or early summer when soil temperatures are between 70 and 80°F (21 to 26.7°C). Early or premature seeding of warm-season turfgrasses will delay their germination until soil temperatures reach the required germination range and may lose some of their viability. Planting too late may not allow sufficient plant maturity before cooler fall temperatures and shorter daylight days slow growth.

Seeding Methods

Seeding

Turfgrass seeds are generally planted using either a mechanical seeder (also called a slit seeder), gravity flow drop seeder, rotary (or centrifugal) spreader, or hydroseeder. After planting, seeds are lightly incorporated into the top 0.25 inch (6.4 mm) of the seedbed and the seedbed is firmed with a roller.

Mechanical or slit seeders are used on relatively flat surfaces (4 to 1 slope is the maximum limit). These make a small furrow, drop seed into this furrow, cover the seed with approximately 0.25 inch (6.4 mm) of rootzone mix, and firm the seedbed by rolling (Figure 9–1). Many of these mechanical seeders are retrofitted with bins or hoppers to simultaneously apply starter fertilizers.

Drop or rotary spreaders are utilized to broadcast-apply seed over a large area. However, the degree of post-planting maintenance is more extensive to achieve optimum results from these types of seeders. To ensure adequate seed distribution and coverage when utilizing these methods, the quantity of seed to be applied should be halved and distributed in two different directions at right angles to each other. Seed are often mixed 50:50 with a granular product such as fine sand or organic fertilizer for easier and more even distribution. A drop spreader is often used to outline or highlight certain areas, thus minimizing cross-contamination of different turfgrass varieties. Once seeds have been broadcast or seeded, the area must be covered lightly with soil via topdressing to prevent them from desiccation or drying out. The area should then be lightly rolled to ensure adequate seed-to-soil contact for optimum germination. Alternatively, newly seeded areas are immediately pressed via tractor tires or sand trap machine tires running back and forth until complete coverage is achieved. This helps firm the seedbed surface besides providing excellent seed-to-soil contact. Extra attention on surface firming is often necessary for the two to three foot (0.6 to 0.9 meter) outside perimeter of a green where it is more difficult to reach by certain machines. Extra tracking or rolling now often saves time and work later when trying to smooth this transition from collar to putting green.

Hydroseeding and Mulching

Hydroseeding (hydraulic seeding) or hydromulching is used to seed areas that are severely sloping, susceptible to wind or water erosion, and/or relatively inaccessible (Figure 9–2). In some

FIGURE 9–1 Mechanical or slit seeders (shown) create small furrows (or slits), drop the seed into these, cover them with soil, and firm the seedbed by rolling. In the absence of a slit seeder, drop spreaders are often used that require adequate soil preparation before seeding and rolling afterwards to provide sufficient seed-to-soil contact.

FIGURE 9–2
Hydroseeding is often used to
plant severely sloping or
inaccessible areas or as a way
to seed greens. Seed is mixed
with mulch, fertilizer, and a
tacking agent such as asphalt
or a synthetic binder.

cases, hydroseeding can reduce the establishment time needed for a turf species. Also, if green mulch is used, a favorable illusion is created of a more finished look.

Hydroseeding uses water as a carrier source for the seed, where both are applied under pressure (hydraulic). Hydromulching mixes seed with mulch and fertilizer and is often mixed with asphalt spray or synthetic binder to reduce wind and water erosion. If a binder is not used, the mulch is often crimped or pressed into the soil by a specialized machine. Typically, a mulch such as hay, straw, wood, or fiber is applied to reduce soil erosion and help maintain good soil moisture. A rate of 1.5 to 2 tons of hay or straw mulch per acre (or 1 to 3 bales per 1,000 square feet) with 50 to 90 gallons of binder per acre, depending on the slope, is most often used with turfgrass seeding. Ideally, after mulching, equal proportions of soil and mulch should be visible as one looks directly down on the seeded surface. The mulch is left to rot when used on fairways and roughs but is removed on greens. A leaf rake is delicately used to remove about half the mulch on greens when seedlings reach two to three inches (5 to 7.6 cm).

Wood cellulose mulch is similarly applied as hydromulching and has less chance of weed seed contamination and no need for crimping or tacking to stabilize it. Application rate with wood cellulose mulch is between 1,500 and 3,000 pounds per acre (1,680 and 3,360 kg/ha) in 3,000 to 10,000 gallons (1.1×10^4 to 3.79×10^4 L) of water.

Cross-contamination of grass varieties is a potential problem with hydroseeding. Wind and equipment operator skills determine if this problem occurs. Currently, research is being conducted on using recycled green waste and compost materials as mulch sources for hydroseeding. In addition, work is being conducted to evaluate the addition of slow-release fertilizers to these mulches to enhance turfgrass seed germination and establishment. Such materials should be free of noxious weeds and, if grass straw is used, seed contamination of this mulch source is likely.

Seedbed Preparation

Proper seedbed preparation is essential for the successful establishment of turfgrasses. Refer to Chapter 7 for the proper procedures to prepare a seedbed for planting.

Vegetative Propagation

Vegetative propagation involves planting a portion of the turfgrass plant (rhizome, stolon) and relying on these to form a mat of turfgrass. When properly timed and maintained, vegetative propagation normally produces an acceptable turfgrass playing surface faster than if the same turfgrass species was seeded. Turfgrass species commonly established by vegetative means include bahiagrass, centipedegrass, creeping bentgrass, hybrid bermudagrasses, St. Augustinegrass, velvet bentgrass, and zoysiagrass.

FIGURE 9–3 Broadcast sprigging shows sprigs evenly spread over the area and then cut (or pressed) into the soil with a light disk, topdressed, and rolled.

There are four basic methods of vegetative turfgrass propagation:

1. sprigging
2. stolonizing
3. plugging
4. sodding

Sprigging and stolonizing are two means of vegetative propagation where the soil is not transferred. In contrast, plugging and sodding both transfer soil as part of the establishment unit, although "washed" sod is available without soil.

Sprigging

Sprigging utilizes both rhizomes and stolons as vegetative sources of turfgrass planting material. Sprigging is simply the process of broadcast-planting these rhizomes and stolons (sprigs) or planting them in narrow-spaced furrows (Figure 9–3). These rhizomes and stolons have little to no soil associated with them. Sprigging is considered to be the most economical means of vegetative turfgrass establishment.

Sprigs can be purchased by the bushel or sod can be cut and shredded apart into sprigs. Other harvesting methods include roto-tilling of sod into sprigs and then raking them up. Tall grown bermudagrass is sometimes verticut to remove the rhizomes and stolons. This method generally requires a higher planting or sprigging rate since the roots and crowns of the turfgrass are missing. Refer to Table 9–3 for the vegetative planting rates of sprigs and/or plugs for the various turfgrasses.

One inconsistency within the turfgrass industry is the definition of a **"bushel"** for determining the planting rate of turfgrass sprigs. A bushel of hybrid bermudagrass was originally determined by the amount of stolons and rhizomes required to plant a specific area. However, the introduction of lower-growing varieties such as "Tifdwarf" and "Tifgreen" necessitated a different planting rate than the taller-growing "Tifway" varieties. A bushel of turfgrass sprigs generally involves measuring the amount of sprigs harvested by vertically removing all plant parts (rhizomes, stolons, stems, and leaves) to a soil depth of two inches from an area of one square meter or from one square yard. A square yard of bermudagrass or zoysiagrass sod will yield 2,000 to 4,000 sprigs. One square yard of St. Augustinegrass and centipedegrass will only yield 500 to 1,000 sprigs, respectively. The approximate number of stolons per bushel for bermudagrass is 2,000, St. Augustinegrass is 500, and zoysiagrass is 3,000. One square yard of sod yields 1,296 one-inch square plugs, 324 two-inch square plugs, or 81 four-inch square plugs.

Other definitions of a bushel also exist. For example, a "Georgia bushel" is defined as the amount of rhizomes, stolons, stems, and leaves held within a 0.4-cubic foot container while a "Texas bushel" is what is within 1.24 cubic feet. Knowing the exact definition and expectation of

TABLE 9–3 *Vegetative planting rates for various grasses and uses.*

Area	Variety	Planting rate* (1 U.S. bushel is from 1 sq. yd. of sod or equals 1.24 ft³, 0.035 m³)
Putting Greens	Bermudagrass	15 to 30 bu/1,000 ft²
	Bentgrass	8 to 12 bu/1,000 ft²
	Seashore paspalum	8 to 15 bu/1,000 ft²
	Zoysiagrass	14 to 18 bu/1,000 ft²
Tees	Bermudagrass	10 to 20 bu/1,000 ft²
	Bentgrass	6 to 10 bu/1,000 ft²
	Kikuyugrass	8 to 14 bu/1,000 ft²
	Seashore paspalum	7 to 12 bu/1,000 ft²
	Zoysiagrass	9 to 16 bu/1,000 ft²
Fairways/primary rough	Bermudagrass	400 to 800 bu/acre
	Kikuyugrass	250 to 350 bu/acre
	Seashore paspalum	200 to 300 bu/acre
	St. Augustinegrass	175 to 3000 bu/acre
	Zoysiagrass	300 to 400 bu/acre
	Zoysiagrass	40 to 50 ft²/100 ft² of nursery sod. Plugs or sprigs placed two inches apart in six-inch rows/1,000 ft²
Roughs	Bermudagrass	200 to 400 bu/acre

*A Georgia bushel is only 0.4 cubic feet or 0.32 U.S. bushel.

FIGURE 9–4 Sprigging often results in brown, lifeless-appearing plants several days after planting. These soon begin to grow, producing roots and leaves, and eventually turn back to green.

a bushel should be made prior to signing a contract because the planting rate using Texas bushels is approximately one-third of a Georgia bushel.

Ideally, sprigs should average at least six inches (15 cm) in length, be planted with eight to 12 live sprigs per square foot (85 to 130 per square meter) and contain at least two vegetative nodes with only a few green leaves. If sprigs contain excessive leaves, they tend to dry out more rapidly, often within hours after their harvest, leaving an aesthetically displeasing brown turfgrass cover. Excessive leaves also increase transportation and storage problems associated with sprigs. Turfgrass sprigs often appear brown and lifeless to those unfamiliar with the sprigging process; however, these brown sprigs soon are rejuvenated and grow if properly planted and cared for (Figure 9–4).

Turfgrass sprigs need to be freshly harvested for best survival. If sprigs are allowed to dry out or overheat, their survival greatly diminishes. Best survival is by planting sprigs within 48 hours of harvest. Sprigs not planted within two days may experience more damage from respiration and appear moldy and smell musty. To increase survival, "turn" or rotate the sprigs if possible to allow air flow through them, keep them moist (not wet), and place them in shade to minimize heat buildup. Sprigs also can be covered with a wet tarp or cloth or placed under a mist system to extend their time of survival. Ideally, sprigs should be stored in a layer not more than eight inches (20 cm) in depth.

Two primary methods are used for sprigging: (1) broadcast sprigging, and (2) row planting. These methods are normally a single-pass, one-step operation, best suited for larger areas such as fairways since the equipment is large and bulky. Soil should be moist (not saturated) prior to planting to prevent root tip burn when contacting dry, hot soil. Sprigs should be watered immediately after planting, and watered several times daily for several weeks until the turfgrass establishes a root system. Do not sprig more area than can be immediately watered. Generally, turfgrass sprigs will cover and become established within 6 to 16 weeks after planting. The length of time for establishment depends on the sprigging rate, time of the year of planting, and maintenance practices implemented after planting. For example, 75 to 120 days are necessary for Tifdwarf bermudagrass to grow-in and develop an acceptable playing surface, while 50 to 80 days are needed with the ultradwarf cultivars.

Broadcast Sprigging

Broadcast sprigging involves spreading sprigs over the area (like mulch) either by hand or by specialized mechanical equipment. Sprigging rates for various turfgrasses are listed in Table 9–3. After spreading, sprigs are then cut (or pressed) into the soil with a light disk, covered with one-half inch (1.3 cm) of topdressing, and then rolled to firm the seedbed to ensure sprig-to-soil contact (Figure 9–5). Sprigs are then immediately watered. This method of sprigging provides very fast coverage and turfgrass establishment. However, since sprigs are planted at a shallow depth, they are susceptible to drying out. Light, frequent irrigation (four to six times daily) should be provided until the turfgrass roots become established (two to four weeks).

Row Planting

Row planting involves a one-step, one-machine operation that opens a furrow or slit in the seedbed, drops sprigs into these furrows, presses the furrow or slits together, and rolls to smooth the surface and ensure good sprig-to-soil contact. Row planting is generally performed on four- to six-inch (10- to 15-cm) centers for even distribution and faster establishment (Figure 9–6).

FIGURE 9–5 Cutting or pressing in new sprigs provides good soil-to-sprig contact for moisture utilization.

FIGURE 9–6 Furrows remain after mechanically sprigging a fairway. This machine cuts the furrows, drops sprigs onto the soil surface, presses (or cuts) them in, and rolls the surface for firmness in one step.

Little to no soil preparation is required for successful row planting, and in many cases golf play can resume immediately after planting.

Stolonizing

Stolonizing is similar to sprigging; however, only stolons are utilized as vegetative establishment units. Stolons are broadcast-spread across the prepared seedbed, covered lightly with soil and/or topdressing, and then rolled to firm the seedbed to ensure good stolon-to-soil contact. Stolonizing is most commonly practiced with creeping bentgrass and hybrid bermudagrasses. The planting rate for stolonizing is greater (≈ 10 percent) than with sprigging due to greater mortality of stolons and lack of other vegetative parts such as rhizomes to become established. Stolons can also be planted or applied via hydromulching equipment as previously described. Hydrostolonizing is utilized on more severely sloped areas and requires less labor and time. However, establishment success of hydrostolonizing is less than with more conventional stolonizing methods.

Plugging

Plugging involves vegetative propagation of turfgrasses with plugs or small pieces of sod. Plugging is utilized in establishment of less-aggressive turfgrass species such as centipedegrass, St. Augustinegrass, and zoysiagrass. Since soil accompanies plugging, it is safer than sprigging or stolonizing in terms of survival due to heat and drought stresses. Plugs are obtained from a nursery utilizing a specialized harvesting machine that cuts, divides, and separates sod plugs into either one- to four-inch (2.5- to 10-cm) diameter circular plugs or two- to four-inch (2.5- to 10-cm) square plugs. Plugs are then mechanically planted into the seedbed on 6- to 12-inch (15- to 30-cm) centers every 6 to 12 inches (15 to 30 cm) in a row (Figure 9–7). Obviously, the shorter the distance between two plugs, the faster the turfgrass is established. After plugging, the area should be rolled to firm the seedbed and irrigated for more favorable establishment conditions.

Sodding

Sodding provides "instant greening" and excellent soil erosion control (Table 9–4). Sodding, however, is initially more expensive, and has the possibility of introducing different soil types or pests, such as nematodes, weeds, or fire ants, from the harvested field into the rootzone. As a minimum specification, sodding should be utilized for areas prone to soil erosion, such as steep slopes and areas surrounding bunkers, tees, and greens (Figure 9–8).

Historically, turfgrass managers and general contractors have assumed sod costs were prohibitive. However, one should examine more than the initial cost in determining whether sodding is the most expensive means of establishment or not. A pallet of sod is initially more expensive than a bushel of sprigs or a bag of seed. However, the basic cost of the original turfgrass material is not the end of the expenses or associated costs. If the "real" costs such as a scheduled timing or opening date, the cost of "grow-in" (fertilizer, water, topdressing), and the length of time for generation of income and cash flow (profit) is considered, the bottom line may show sodding is an effective and affordable means of turfgrass establishment. Innovations in the sod production industry have made the use of

FIGURE 9–7 Plugging a new green is rarely used except on small areas due to labor requirements and extended time needed for coverage.

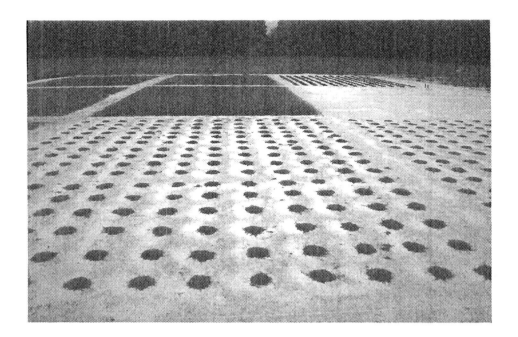

TABLE 9–4 *Soil loss, reduced runoff, and time to runoff initiation for various erosion-control materials (Krenisky et al., 1998).*[a]

Materials	Soil loss[b] (kg/ha)	Runoff loss (% of rain)	Time to runoff (seconds)
Tall fescue sod	100	28	341
Straw (4.5 kg/ha)	590	60	102
Fiber mat (coconut)	1,070	76	86
Wood shavings in nonwoven polyester netting	810	74	74
Woven mesh (jute)	410	68	62
Bare soil	6,650	83	34

[a]All plots (except sod) were seeded with Kentucky '31 tall fescue and covered with the materials listed.
[b]Soil loss from a single rain event at 96 millimeters/hour. Readings are means of two soils: a loamy sand with 8 percent slope and a sandy clay loam with 15 percent slope.

FIGURE 9–8 Sodding produces an "instant" green surface and helps control erosion. Sod, however, should be allowed to properly root, or "knit-down," before traffic or play is allowed.

sod more practical and affordable. Large rolls of sod reduce labor and installation time, as well as the number of seams on large areas such as fairways (Figure 9–9). Sod "washed" free of soil and/or grown on a custom growing medium (e.g., USGA-specified greens mix) also provides turfgrass managers with more options (Figure 9–10).

Before installing sod, the seedbed should be watered. Rooting rate and establishment will be significantly increased if the underlying soil is moist and cool, and therefore receptive for rooting to occur. The sod should be installed soon, preferably within 48 hours, after harvest. When sod remains stacked or rolled on pallets for longer periods, respiration of the turfgrass plants create heat that can dry out and injure the grass.

Start laying the sod along the straightest line possible. Edges of the sod should butt against each other tightly without stretching. Avoid gaps or overlaps by using machetes or sharp knives to trim around corners and edges. Joints between the sod should be staggered in a brick-like fashion so none of the edges of adjacent pieces of sod are parallel. It is important to handle the sod with care to avoid tearing or stretching. If sod is stretched, it will shrink as it dries out, leaving gaps between the edges. On slopes and bunker faces, place the sod across the slope and anchor the pieces with sod staples or wooden pegs until the roots have become established. To help avoid

FIGURE 9–9 Sodding entire golf courses is becoming more popular as this provides instant green for real estate purposes, reduces soil erosion, and possibly allows the facility to open sooner. This figure shows the laying of large (or big) rolls of sod that reduce labor, installation time, and the number of exposed seams.

FIGURE 9–10 Washed sod reduces soil nematodes and soil interface problems.

indentations or air pockets, refrain from walking on the newly laid sod. Sometimes, the sod is installed by using plywood boards to ensure it is evenly installed. This also ensures good sod-to-soil contact.

After installation, the sod should be rolled to ensure evenness and smoothness and immediately watered heavily to wet the entire depth of the sod and top portion of the rootzone. Topdressing should be implemented to fill-in creases and low pieces and to help conserve moisture. Although sodding produces an almost instant green-appearing turf, it should be allowed to knit-down (or root) before it is subject to traffic and play. Four weeks is generally the minimum time necessary for this during periods of active turfgrass growth, and longer when the turfgrass is not actively growing.

It is advisable to consider and utilize a combination of these establishment methods to achieve the most economical and efficient means of turfgrass establishment. Some of these establishment methods offer advantages over the others, but the specific method of establishment selected will depend on those factors discussed.

TURFGRASS "GROW-IN"

Immediately after seeding or vegetative propagation, turfgrass requires special attention and maintenance to ensure survival and healthy growth. This "grow-in" phase is the most overlooked expense of any golf course construction or renovation project. The "grow-in" period is the time between seeding or vegetative propagation (grassing) until the time the golf course opens for play. This phase can vary from a short time period such as three months to as long as 18 months depending on the location, turfgrass type, method of turfgrass planting, and climate of the golf course. Most courses should budget and plan for an average grow-in period of at least six months after planting starts. Labor is generally the greatest expense, but fertilizer is the largest material needed during this period. It is important to recognize the cost of "grow-in" cannot be offset by income since the golf course is not open for play.

Seeding Establishment

Successful seeding establishment of turfgrass involves seed germination, initiation of roots, and lateral shoot development into mature plants. This involves imbibition (or uptake) of water into the seed and, in turn, primary root and shoot growth are initiated from which plants develop. Temperature, oxygen, light exposure, and water are all essential environmental parameters required for successful germination. However, sometimes successful seed germination does not occur even with favorable environmental conditions for seed germination. Several parameters may influence successful germination of seed under favorable conditions such as (1) presence of inhibitors, (2) an impermeable seed coat, (3) seed planted too deeply, (4) damaged seed, (5) injury from fertilizers and/or pesticides, (6) damage by insects or diseases, or (7) crusted soil surfaces. Successful establishment from seed germination can be enhanced with some turfgrass types by using pregerminated seeds, especially if temperatures are cool. Seed can be pregerminated by placing them in a moist environment, such as a barrel of warm water, at favorable germination temperatures. These pregerminated seed must be planted immediately to prevent injury to the primary root and shoot system.

Irrigation

Proper water management is critical for the first several weeks after turfgrass planting. Irrigation or watering is essential to the germination process and survival of the turfgrass seedlings by preventing drought conditions and moisture stress. Irrigation or watering should be conducted during the predawn hours while moisture or dew is present. This prevents extended "free" water or moisture periods, which may enhance seedling diseases such as *Pythium* and *Fusarium*. The areas should be irrigated immediately after seeding with enough water to "moisten" the seed to ensure their germination. Seed must remain moist until they germinate and emerge (7 to 30 days). The seedbed should also remain moist with frequent, light irrigation several times daily (four to eight times per day). The first watering is commonly between 7 and 8 A.M. and the last between 6 and 7 P.M. The majority of watering is from 10 A.M. and 6. P.M. with no irrigation at night which might promote disease occurrence. Avoid excessive watering, as this can cause "puddling" of water or create soil erosion and "washes" that concentrate seed into areas or drifts. If this occurs, use a stiff bristled brush or broom to redistribute the seed. Irrigation heads should also be frequently inspected to ensure proper working order and complete coverage. As seeds germinate and seedlings emerge, the frequency of watering should be decreased and the amount of water applied should be increased.

Fertilization

Proper fertilization is essential for plant growth and development after seed germination. Prior to planting, a starter fertilizer with a 1-2-2 ratio of N-P-K or similar should be incorporated into the soil mix. The nitrogen source should be slow release and applied at the equivalent of 1 pound of nitrogen per 1,000 square feet (4.9 kg N/100 m^2). This should provide between 1.5 to 2 pounds of phosphorus per 1,000 square feet (7.3 to 9.8 kg P/100 m^2). A granular micronutrient package and a humate or carbohydrate soil conditioner also may be added according to label recommendations. Conditioners are especially beneficial if pure sand greens are used.

After planting, the new seedlings should be fertilized approximately two to four weeks after seeding, or as a general rule, after the second mowing. A complete fertilizer (one that contains N-P-K nutrients) designed specifically for use on turfgrass should be applied at an equivalent rate of one pound of nitrogen per 1,000 square feet (4.9 kg N/100 m^2) of turfgrass. Preferably, a slow-release nitrogen source should be a component of the N-P-K fertilizer. Cool-season grasses are fertilized weekly with one-half pound of nitrogen per 1,000 square feet (2.4 kg N/100 m^2) on greens and tees, while fairways and roughs are fertilized every two weeks until establishment with three-fourths to one pound of nitrogen per 1,000 square feet (3.7 to 4.9 kg N/100 m^2). A complete fertilizer is normally used for each of these fairway applications. For bermudagrass, one pound of nitrogen per 1,000 square feet (4.9 kg N/100 m^2) applied weekly provides the quickest establishment.

Potassium and phosphorus should be added with each alternate nitrogen application in a balanced ratio until establishment. If sulfur deficiencies are suspected, use potassium sulfate as the potassium source to supply the needed sulfur. Supplemental liquid potassium and iron (such as a 0-0-28 plus Fe) should be applied every two to three weeks if color wanes or growth slows. Once the turfgrasses have become fully established, the fertilizer program should then be converted to a less-aggressive program (refer to the chapter on "Fertility"). If cool-season grasses are seeded in spring, the aggressive fertilizer program should commence until normal summer temperatures are anticipated. At this time, summer color is best maintained with soluble fertilizer sources. Monthly summer application of a 0-0-28 or 0-0-50 at three-fourths pound of potassium per 1,000 square feet (3.7 kg N/100 m^2) will help harden grass for summer stress. Liquid iron and/or a micronutrient spray supplements the potassium as needed for summer color.

Soil Amendments and Conditioners

Other soil amendments such as lime, gypsum, or sulfur also are often needed in certain areas. Soil testing should be performed to determine these needs. Most of these should be incorporated before turf establishment. In acidic clay soils, for example, lime is often needed from one to three tons per acre (2.2 to 6.7 tons [metric] per ka). Commonly, 1.5 tons per acre (3.4 tons [metric] per ha) are initially applied and incorporated, followed by another ton per acre the following fall or early spring. Gypsum supplies calcium and helps dissociate sodic (sodium) soils. If needed, 300 to 400 pounds gypsum per acre (336 to 448 kg/ha) pre-plant are often suggested by soil testing. Sulfur helps promote grow-in and reduce soil pH in alkaline areas. High pH (≥ 8.0)-containing fairways may need 150 to 200 pounds per acre (168 to 224 kg/ha) of a granular dispersible sulfur, pre-plant. Greens also may need sulfur prior to planting and also frequently receive additional sulfur after planting via fertigation and/or with sulfur-containing (e.g., potassium sulfate) or coated fertilizer products.

Biostimulants are a class of plant growth regulators (enhancers) that help turf growth under certain conditions. Their benefits are most noticeable when turf is grown on very sandy soils, such as golf greens, although benefits are not always experienced. Biostimulants containing seaweed extracts are composed of a variety of cytokinins, humates, and other materials. Cytokinins benefit root growth and subtle positive results may be seen when used.

Mowing

Mowing is the most common turfgrass maintenance operation and is potentially one of the most damaging. A common mistake with mowing is waiting too long to mow the first time. Proper mowing promotes lateral growth and plant maturity. Mowing of the newly established turfgrasses should begin as soon as the turfgrass reaches 130 percent of the desired turfgrass mowing height. For sprigged bermudagrass greens, begin mowing when the grass reaches two-thirds to three-fourths inch (1.7 to 1.9 cm). Slowly lower this to one-half inch (1.3 cm) until complete coverage is achieved and then slowly lower it to the normal playing height. Mow fairways when the bermudagrass reaches 1.25 to 1.5 inch (3.2 to 3.8 cm) and bluegrass/ryegrass when they reach 1.5 to 2 inches (3.8 to 5 cm).

Bentgrass seedlings should be mowed within two to three weeks of germination, initially between 3/8 and 1/2 inch (9.5 to 12.7 mm). Lower the mowing height between 1/16 and 1/32 inch per week (1.6 to 0.8 mm) until the final desired cut is reached. It is imperative to use sharp blades to prevent turfgrass seedlings from being torn or "pulled up" during mowing. It is advisable to use walking reel mowers on greens and tees until complete coverage of turfgrass is achieved. Do not mow when the turfgrass is wet, and remove the clippings if their moisture levels promote clumping, thereby subsequently shading the newly established turfgrass. Solid front rollers should be used the first several months as grooved rollers are often too damaging and can dig into the exposed soil surface.

Pest Control

When establishing new turfgrass areas, pest problems such as diseases, insects, nematodes, and weeds must be minimized. This is best accomplished utilizing a preventive pest management strategy coupled with a routine pest monitoring or "scouting" schedule (Best Management Practices). Many pest problems can be alleviated by fumigating putting greens prior to planting to control pests and using clean soil, seed, sprigs, and sod.

As previously mentioned, irrigation or watering is required to achieve seed germination and turfgrass establishment; however, the amount and timing of its application can prevent or contribute to the development of pest problems. Most fungal disease pathogens require "free water" or very high humidity to initiate the disease infection process. Disease development is dependent on humidity and temperature. Irrigating in the evening before dew forms or in the morning after dew evaporates extends the dew or moisture period. Newly planted turfgrass seedlings, therefore, should be watered when dew or moisture is already present, such as in the predawn hours.

To reduce potential disease development to newly planted turfgrass seedlings, it is recommended to use seed treated with a fungicide. If untreated seed is used, then a fungicide should be broadcast-applied to the newly planted areas to minimize seedling diseases.

In addition to being unsightly, weeds compete with turfgrasses for light, soil nutrients, soil moisture, and space. Weeds can also play host to other pests such as diseases, insects, and nematodes; therefore, it is important to control these during turfgrass establishment.

Prior to planting, siduron (trade name Tupersan) is often applied to help control crabgrass. Six pounds active ingredient per acre is applied to newly seeded or seedling cool-season grasses or zoysiagrass sprigs for preemergent grassy weed control.

Postemergence control of grassy weeds is by CMA on cool-season turfgrasses and MSMA or DSMA on warm-season grasses. Normally, six to eight weeks are required after turf seed germination before these products can safely be used. Postemergence control of seedling broadleaf weeds is with light rates of 2,4-D alone or mixed with MCPP and dicamba.

Delay any herbicide applications as long as possible to allow the turfgrass to become well-established. Hand pulling or "roughing" should be conducted if only a few weeds are present; however, if many weeds emerge, the use of selective postemergence-applied herbicides may be required. These herbicides should be used judiciously only after careful herbicide selection.

For most new greens, the surface is not firm enough to support a self-propelled sprayer without ruts. For the first six to eight weeks after planting, a walk-type boom or back-pack sprayer system should be used.

Vegetative Propagation Establishment

Turfgrass establishment from vegetative propagation requires favorable environmental conditions similar to those used for seeding. Temperature, oxygen, light exposure, and water are essential to the successful growth and development of vegetative materials. Bermudagrass is ideally sprigged between early June through mid-July while cool-season grasses are stolonized in late summer. Proper cultural and turfgrass management practices also are needed to achieve successful establishment of a newly planted area. Under ideal growing conditions, sprigged areas require 6 to 10 weeks for complete establishment (Figure 9–11).

FIGURE 9–11   A green three weeks after sprigging (left) and seven weeks after sprigging (right).

Irrigation

Proper irrigation or watering is one of the most important steps in achieving successful turfgrass establishment. Turfgrass establishment from sprigging, stolonizing, or plugging requires constant moisture due to the lack of soil associated with these vegetative materials. In contrast, sod requires the least amount of water because soil associated with sod provides some moisture.

It is critical for newly sprigged, stolonized, or plugged turfgrasses to be irrigated or watered immediately after planting to avoid desiccation or drying out (Figure 9–12). Timing is not as critical with plugging due to some soil associated with the plugs. Plugging establishment is still best if irrigation occurs as soon as possible. Irrigation or watering should continue on a frequent basis to maintain a moist soil surface for the vegetative plantings. Frequent surface irrigation should be continued for a two- to three-week period or until establishment occurs.

Fertilization

Prior to planting, a starter fertilizer should be applied to the site to encourage good rooting and quicker turf cover. A starter fertilizer with a 1-2-2 ratio of N-P-K (such as 10-20-20) should be used with a slow-release nitrogen source. This ratio of fertilizer should be applied at the equivalent rate of one pound of nitrogen per 1,000 square feet (4.9 kg N/100 m^2). After planting, it is recommended to fertilize with an equivalent rate of one pound of water-soluble nitrogen per 1,000 square feet of turfgrass (4.9 kg N/100 m^2) every five to seven days for greens and tees and every 10 to 14 days on fairways or roughs. With bermudagrass, each application of a quick-release fertilizer such as ammonium sulfate (21-0-0) or ammonium nitrate (45-0-0) should be alternated with a 1-2-2 ratio fertilizer (such as 5-10-10, or equivalent) at an equivalent rate of three-fourths to one pound of nitrogen per 1,000 square feet (3.7 to 4.9 kg N/100 m^2). Potassium nitrate is often successful for bentgrass. Lighter rates, 0.3 to 0.6 pounds nitrogen per 1,000 square feet (1.5 to 3.0 kilograms nitrogen per 100 square meters), applied every five days are generally more successful than heavier nitrogen rates applied less frequently. If additional color is needed or if growth slows, supplement these fertilizations as needed with a liquid nitrogen application at a rate of one-fifth pound nitrogen per 1,000 square feet (1 kg N/100 m^2). Micronutrient sprays of iron, magnesium, and manganese are applied as needed to aid in turf grow-in. Each granular fertilization should be irrigated or watered-in immediately to avoid foliar turfgrass burn. In high sand containing greens, expect to need 8 to 12 pounds of nitrogen per 1,000 square feet (39 to 59 kilograms nitrogen per 100 square meters) during the grow-in process.

Mowing

Mowing should be initiated after stolons have reached a growing height or length between two and four inches (5 to 10 cm). Mowing is recommended during midday when the turfgrass is dry. Turfgrass clippings should be returned to the soil surface for the first couple of mowings to promote rooting of any stolons that may have been cut during mowing. The initial mowing height should be two inches (5 cm) or greater and then reduced over time as the turfgrass becomes established. Use only a sharpened mower blade as dull ones shred and pull sprigs from soil.

Pest Control

Vegetative planting operations disturb the soil, which can promote germination and establishment of weeds during grow-in. In addition, an ample supply of moisture and fertilizer provide optimum growing conditions for weeds as well. Preemergence control of annual grass weeds such as crabgrass and goosegrass without impeding new turfgrass growth can be obtained by applying a herbicide containing oxadiazon (e.g., Ronstar). Oxadiazon products should be applied immediately after vegetative planting at the recommended labeled use rate. The use of selective postemergence herbicides should be delayed for at least three weeks after vegetative planting.

Oxadiazon is often applied prior to sprigging on a starter fertilizer source such as a 5-10-20 or similar. Postemergence crabgrass control is with MSMA or DSMA while seedling broadleaf weeds are controlled with light rates of 2,4-D alone or combined with MCPP and dicamba. Caution should be used with postemergence applied herbicides to ensure the newly planted turfgrass is not injured nor growth reduced.

Topdressing

Frequent topdressing during turfgrass establishment from vegetative planting of putting greens is recommended to achieve a smooth playing surface and enhance turfgrass establishment (Figure 9–13). The topdressing amount and frequency is dependent upon the existing smoothness of the surface. A light rate of 0.5 to 0.7 cubic feet per 1,000 square feet is a good starting point for this. This should commence four to six weeks after seeding and three to four weeks after sprigging. Topdressing also serves as a "covering" for vegetatively planted sprigs, stolons, or plugs, thereby enhancing their establishment. Sodded areas should also be rolled throughout the grow-in period to push roots into the soil and to smooth the surface to prevent mower scalping. Weekly rolling should be performed until the eventual permanent mowing height is achieved.

Surface Firmness

When greens are planted and maintained at today's low mowing heights, it requires a certain period of time to develop enough organic matter or "pad" or "cushion" in the upper rootzone to provide surface resiliency. Complaints are often initially heard about hard greens that do not hold approach shots well. One to two full growing seasons are typically required to develop a mature surface. Aerification helps to "soften" greens and should commence and continue once the grass is sufficiently mature to withstand this process. The first several aerifications should be with 3/8-inch (9.5 millimeter) on two-inch (5 centimeters) centers. One-inch (2.5 cm) centers can be used thereafter as greens become firmer and have more surface stability.

FIGURE 9–13
Topdressing following
planting helps smooth the
surface and provides moisture
retention.

Budgeting

Budgeting during grow-in and for the first year after establishment is difficult depending on the time of year for planting, grasses grown, quality of course design and construction, unexpected weather phenomena, and so on. Other unexpected problems such as poor drainage sites, low areas, and additional tree removal/stump grinding are other examples. These and other problems should be expected, projected, and budgeted for so enough funds are available to finish a quality job and to meet the anticipated high expectations of new members and players. Funds often become limited at this time and corners are cut. However, most of these occurrences are only one-time events and will not be dealt with again except on a limited basis. The following list includes predominant situations often incurred during this period:

1. **Labor**—In addition to the needed full-time superintendent, assistant superintendent, mechanic, irrigation technician, spray technician, and normal full-time or part-time employees, additional temporary employees may be necessary to finish unexpected special projects without sacrificing routine maintenance needs.
2. **Fertilizer and soil amendments**—During grow-in, much higher than normal fertilizer and soil amendments are used to hasten establishment. Also during the first year, an additional 15 percent or so above normal maintenance needs will be necessary to finish establishment in difficult areas. Uneven coverage and color may occur if amendments or fertilizers are not uniformly applied (Figure 9–14).
3. **Tree removal and replacement**—Despite best efforts, some unexpected tree die-out can be anticipated during grow-in. This also includes stump removal. Additional trees restricting air movement or creating excessive shade not identified in construction or grow-in may need removal. Some of these trees may need to be replaced in accordance with the course's master plan.
4. **Low spots and poor drainage areas**—Low spots that drain poorly invariably happen as settling occurs in fairways, tees, and collars. In most cases, low spots can be corrected by additional sand topdressing. If it is too severe, sod in these areas should be removed, the areas brought up to grade with soil or sand, and then resodded. Also, despite the best drawings, additional drainage will be needed in certain areas as settling occurs or wet springs surface. Sand, gravel pipe, and outlets will be needed to correct these. Other needed items are a backhoe and trencher and hand labor to install this equipment. Equipment rental may be an option for this equipment.

FIGURE 9–14 Uneven turf color and coverage from nonuniform incorporation of soil amendments prior to planting.

FIGURE 9–15 Erosion control during planting is required in most areas. Many techniques and supplies are involved with this, including the use of mats (left) and sod around highly erodible and costly areas such as greens, bunkers, irrigation heads, culverts, and tees (right).

5. **Additional irrigation heads**—Due to poor or irregular pressure, shifting winds, or mounds that receive poor coverage, some additional irrigation heads may be necessary for complete course coverage, as are pipe and possibly control valves. Buy additional heads before the course is opened to have a stock on hand.

6. **Erosion control/sodding**—To comply with local and state regulations and to prevent washouts, erosion control materials should be available and used when necessary. This includes ryegrass seed for winter stabilization (200 lbs/acre on average), silt fencing, mulch, jute mat, hay bales, straw, soil, gravel, and sand (Figure 9–15). Additional sod should also be anticipated to help control erosion and to repair areas that die. Two to four loads often are needed for this.

Other miscellaneous items should also be anticipated during grow-in and first-year maintenance. These include extra gas and oil for equipment, soil testing, ornamentals for landscaping, bunker trim/spread, irrigation head leveling, and chemicals for weed control. If temporary greens are needed during renovation, using a larger golf cup such as a large coffee or soup cup can often keep players interested and satisfied until renovations are completed (Figure 9–16).

SEED CALCULATION PROBLEM EXAMPLES

1. What is the pure live seed content of a 50-pound bag of 55 percent Crenshaw bentgrass (93% germination/90% purity) and 45 percent Cato (96% germination/90% purity)? (answer: 42.4 lbs)
   a. How many pounds of each bentgrass cultivar are in the bag? (answer: Crenshaw: 27.5; Cato: 22.5)
   b. How many pounds of each bentgrass cultivar are PLS? (answer: Crenshaw 23.0; Cato: 19.4)

2. How many pounds of centipedegrass seed (400,000 seeds/lb) are needed to plant a 6,500 square foot area around the clubhouse with an average of five germinating seed per square inch? The seed source has 80 percent germination and 96 percent purity. (answer: 15.2 lbs)

3. If a creeping bentgrass (6,000,000 seed/lb) seed source had 90 percent purity and 95 percent germination, how many PLS per square inch would result from a planting rate of three pounds per 1,000 square feet? (answer: 107)

4. If the seeding specification called for 30 pounds PLS of ryegrass per 1,000 square feet, how many actual pounds of ryegrass must be planted to obtain this when the seed germination is 92 percent and 90 percent purity? (answer: 36)

SECTION

IV

BEST TURFGRASS FERTILIZATION PRACTICES

CHAPTER 12 *Fertilizer Calculations*

CHAPTER
10

Plant Nutrition and Turf Fertilizers

INTRODUCTION

Proper fertilization is essential for turfgrasses to sustain desirable color, growth density, and vigor; to better resist diseases, weeds, and insects; and to provide satisfactory golf course playability. Grasses may survive in some soils without added fertility, but it is unlikely the turf will be dense enough to support continued play or resist pest invasion. Turf plants need 16 elements that are divided into two categories: **macronutrients** and **micronutrients** (Table 10–1). Macronutrients typically are found at concentrations greater than 500 to 1,000 ppm in plant tissue while micronutrients are generally found at concentrations less than 100 ppm.

Macronutrients can further be subdivided into **primary nutrients** (nitrogen, phosphorus, and potassium) and **secondary nutrients** (calcium, magnesium, and sulfur). Carbon (C), hydrogen (H), and oxygen (O) are macronutrients obtained from air and water, and are the building blocks for the process of photosynthesis. These three nutrients, when combined in the presence of chlorophyll and light through the process of photosynthesis, form carbohydrates, the sugars used to provide plant growth. Plants, therefore, do not obtain their food through the soil; rather, they manufacture this via photosynthesis utilizing the raw materials—mineral nutrients—as components of this food.

Photosynthesis Reaction

$$\underset{\text{carbon dioxide}}{6CO_2} \quad + \quad \underset{\text{water}}{12H_2O} \quad \xrightarrow[\text{chlorophyll}]{\text{light}} \quad \underset{\substack{\text{carbohydrates} \\ \text{(or sugars)}}}{C_6H_{12}O_6} \quad + \quad \underset{\text{oxygen}}{6O_2} \quad + \quad \underset{\text{water}}{6H_2O}$$

Carbon dioxide is absorbed by plants through leaf stomata, and water is absorbed through roots. Therefore, fertilizer practices affecting root growth and function, as well as stomata opening and closing, indirectly influence a plant's ability to produce food by photosynthesis.

Simple carbohydrates produced from photosynthesis are used to generate more complex compounds such as starch and amino acids that require other elements in addition to carbon, oxygen, and hydrogen. These remaining essential elements are mainly absorbed into plants through roots. They are in the form of ions and are in the soil solution. Understanding how these processes interact and are influenced by soil chemical properties is important to turf managers who strive to optimize their fertilization programs.

TABLE 10-1 *Elements, their most common available forms for plant uptake, and primary functions in turfgrass growth.*

	Element (chemical symbol)	Most commonly used form(s)	Function in plant growth
Macronutrients			
Obtained from air and water	Oxygen (O) Carbon (C) Hydrogen (H)	CO_2 CO_2 H_2O	Through photosynthesis, these elements are converted to simple carbohydrates, and finally into amino acids, proteins, protoplasm, enzymes, and lipids.
Obtained primarily from fertilization	Nitrogen (N)	NO_3^- (nitrate) NH_4^+ (ammonium)	A mobile element within the plant used in the formation of amino acids, enzymes, proteins, nucleic acids, and chlorophyll. It generally increases color and shoot growth. Conversely, excessive nitrogen generally reduces heat, cold, and drought hardiness; disease and nematode resistance; wear tolerance; and root growth.
	Phosphorus (P)	$H_2PO_4^-$ HPO_4^{-2} (phosphates)	A mobile element that is a constituent of phospholipids and nucleic acids. They are involved in a carbohydrate transport system that moves energy to all parts of the plant for vital growth processes. This function in root development is most vital. Phosphorus also hastens plant maturity, and is needed for glycolysis, amino acid metabolism, fat metabolism, sulfur metabolism, biological oxidation, and photosynthesis. In addition, phosphorus influences maturation, establishment, and seed production.
	Potassium (K)	K	A mobile element used by plants in large quantities, second only to nitrogen, potassium is essential for the control and regulation of various minerals; adjustment of stomatal movements and water relation; promotion of meristematic tissue and rooting; activation of various enzymes; synthesis of proteins; and carbohydrate metabolism. Potassium helps increase heat, cold, and drought hardiness; wear tolerance; and increases disease and nematode resistance.
Secondary Nutrients			
Present in some fertilizer formulations; available in most soils, and/or as part of conditioners such as lime, dolomitic lime, and gypsum.	Calcium (Ca)	Ca^{+2}	An immobile element required for cell division (mitosis); important in cell membrane permeability; activates certain enzymes; provides chromosome stability and structure; enhances carbohydrate translocation and formation, and increases protein content of mitochondria. It influences absorption of other plant nutrients, and also strongly influences soil pH and can improve soil structure, water retention, and infiltration by displacing sodium ions.
	Magnesium (Mg)	Mg^{+2}	A mobile element which is a component of chlorophyll; assists in the stabilization of ribosome particles, and activates several plant enzyme systems such as carbohydrate and phosphate metabolism and cell respiration. It serves as a specific activator for a number of enzymes.
	Sulfur (S)	SO_4^{-2}	A partially mobile element required for the synthesis of sulfur-containing amino acids—cystine, cysteine, and methionine; required for protein synthesis and activation of certain enzymes and hormone constituents.

Element (chemical symbol)	Most commonly used form(s)	Function in plant growth
Micronutrients		
Most premium fertilizers contain these. Iron (Fe)	Fe^{+2} (ferrous) Fe^{+3} (ferric) $Fe(OH)_2^+$	An immobile element necessary for chlorophyll, heme, and cytochrome production, and in ferredoxin, which participates in cellular respiratory (oxidation-reduction or electron transfer reactions) mechanism; an essential component of iron enzymes and carriers. Generally it increases color, shoot, and root growth.
Manganese (Mn)	Mn^{+2}, organic salts	An immobile element that activates Mangano-enzyme; needed in photosystem II of photosynthesis; connected with carbohydrate (nitrogen) metabolism, chlorophyll synthesis, oxidation-reduction process, enzyme activation, phosphorylation reaction, and the citric acid (or TCA) cycle.
Copper (Cu)	Cu^{+2} (cupric) Cu^+ (cuprous)	An immobile element connected with the light reaction during photosynthesis as a constituent of oxidation-reduction or electron transfer enzymes; found in cytochrome oxidase that is essential for plant (carbohydrate) metabolism, and is used for production of the enzyme polyphenol oxidase; used as catalysts in plant metabolism.
Chlorine (Cl)	Cl^- (chloride)	An immobile element possibly required for photosynthesis of isolated chloroplasts and as a bromide substitute. It is believed to influence osmotic pressure and balance cell cationic charges. It also affects root growth.
Zinc (Zn)	Zn^{+2} $Zn(OH)^+$	A mobile elemental component of the enzyme dehydrogenase, which is needed for RNA and cytoplasmic ribosomes in cells, proteinases, peptidases, and IAA (auxin) synthesis. It is involved in the conversion of ammonium to amino nitrogen and is necessary for chlorophyll production and promoting seed maturation and production.
Boron (B)	H_3BO_3 (boric acid) HBO_3^{-2} $B_4O_7^{-2}$ BO_3^{-3}	An immobile element that facilitates sugar transport through membranes; involved in auxin metabolism in root elongation, protein, and phosphate utilization; influences cell division (growth) by control of polysaccharide formation. Boron is a nonmetal and is one of two nonmetallic micronutrients call deficiencies slowly affect moistems of roots and shoots. Boron is a nonmetal and is one of two nonmetallic micronutrients called **metalloids.**
Molybdenum (Mo)	MoO_4^{-2} (molybdate)	An element required for the assimilation and reduction processes in nitrogen fixation to produce amino acids and proteins.
Sodium (Na)	Na^-	An element that regulates stomatal opening and nitrate reductase. Toxic levels are generally more of a concern than deficiencies.

NUTRIENT UPTAKE

Large amounts of the nutrient anions are stored in soil organic matter. As the organic matter decomposes, these nutrients are released. Up to 80 percent of the soil sulfur, 95 percent of the soil nitrogen, and over 50 percent of the total soil phosphorus are stored in soil organic matter. Other anions, such as boron, molybdenum, and iron and aluminum oxide reserves, are also held in organic matter.

Roots are the principal means where nutrients and water enter plants. The root system is usually very large and extensive, allowing the plant to make contact with a tremendous volume of soil. Root hairs greatly increase the surface area of roots and are the principal site of nutrient and water uptake.

The absorption (transfer from the soil solution into the root cells) of a nutrient element is primarily an "active" process and, as a result of a metabolic process, roots take in the nutrient element. For the element to be absorbed by plant roots, it must be dissolved in soil water.

The nutrient elements exist as either anions (negatively charged) or cations (positively charged) in the soil solution. As the root makes contact with moist soil, the anions and cations move by diffusion from the soil water into the outer free cellular space of the root. Many nutrients are not readily soluble in soil water. Therefore, before uptake by the plant occurs, these nutrients must be dissolved. This occurs by roots creating an acid environment around the roots through carbonic acid formed from released carbon dioxide by the plant and water from the soil solution. Carbonic acid lowers soil pH which, in turn, releases hydrogen ions that can be "exchanged" with various soil clays and organic matter for cations, such as potassium, calcium, and magnesium.

Although active absorption accounts for most of the elements found in plants, a small portion diffuse into the plant and move about in the free space in plants. This is a "passive" process where the plant plays no active role in this absorption mechanism.

Since active absorption is the primary mechanism for element uptake by plants, roots must be growing in an aerobic medium—that is, oxygen must be present. If oxygen is not present, respiration will cease and element absorption will not occur. Under these conditions, plants may develop nutrient deficiency symptoms. If the anaerobic conditions continue, the plant will eventually die. Any soil condition that affects soil aeration, such as compaction or continuous saturation, will negatively influence root growth and nutrient uptake.

Temperature also influences nutrient uptake. Higher temperatures usually mean increased root growth; therefore, the plant encounters more soil nutrients. Warmer temperatures also increase leaf transpiration which provides the "pull" for water (and dissolved nutrient) uptake.

If water levels are inadequate, nutrient absorption decreases since water mass flow decreases. Inadequate water around soil particles, combined with plant transpiration, may "pump dry," breaking the columns of water from the root surfaces to the surrounding soil area.

Adequate soil nutrient levels also are needed for uptake by plants. The amount of an element in the soil solution is affected by the total concentration of the element in the soil, the soil pH, the concentration of other elements in the soil and soil solution, the extent of biological activity, and soil temperature. The composition of soil solution can be altered by liming, fertilizing, draining, irrigating, and mechanically manipulating a soil.

Mineral Mobility and Deficiencies

Nutrients are **mobile** if the plant can transport it from one tissue to another, and these tend to show deficiency symptoms in older tissue first as plants will withdraw these to support new growth. Mobile elements include nitrogen, phosphorus, potassium, magnesium, and zinc, while sulfur has limited mobility. **Immobile** elements show deficiencies in new growth as they are not transferred from older growth if external supplies are inadequate. Immobile elements include calcium, iron, boron, manganese, and copper.

Plant deficiencies in nutrients often occur due to external conditions that prevent their uptake rather than actually being lacking in soil. Soil and tissue testing, therefore, should be used to ascertain if sufficient supplies are in the soil and if plant tissue are able to obtain them. Restricted root and tissue growth from improper soil pH, inadequate or excessive moisture, or temperatures outside the optimum growth range are several common reasons nutrient deficiency symptoms in plant tissue may occur, although tests indicate adequate soil levels.

PRIMARY NUTRIENTS AND FERTILIZERS

Nitrogen, phosphorus, and potassium receive a great amount of attention because they are typically deficient in soils and must be regularly applied. These elements are required in the greatest amounts, and are therefore referred to as the primary (or essential) nutrients or elements. The numerical designation on a fertilizer bag refers to the percentage of nitrogen, phosphate (expressed as P_2O_5), and potash (expressed as K_2O). Thus, a bag of 10-10-10 would contain 10 percent nitrogen, 10 percent available phosphate, and 10 percent potash.

Secondary elements consist of calcium, magnesium, and sulfur. Dolomitic limestone provides calcium and magnesium to deficient soils while sulfur is added by sulfur-containing fertilizers. Sulfur is also provided by acidifying materials to lower soil pH, such as elemental sulfur; by desalinization materials such as gypsum; by rainwater containing the air pollutant sulfur dioxide; or from salts of nitrogen, magnesium, potassium, and various micronutrients. The influence of increasing levels of five essential nutrients on turfgrasses are listed in Table 10–2.

Micronutrients are essential elements but are only required in small amounts by plants. Sandy soils, for example, may not contain ample micronutrients to sustain optimum plant growth. Due to the high sand content of many golf greens and extremes in soil pH (Chapter 3), micronutrient management becomes somewhat more important for superintendents. Deficiencies in iron and manganese often occur under high pH (>7.0) conditions and are sometimes mistaken for nitrogen deficiency. A number of turfgrass specialty fertilizers contain some, or all, of these micronutrients.

Nitrogen

Nitrogen (designated as N) is the key element due to its influence on color, growth rate, density, pest occurrence, and stress tolerance. Turfgrasses consist of between 20 and 60 grams of nitrogen per kilogram of plant tissue (or 2 to 6 percent of the total dry matter) while soil organic matter typically contains about 5 percent nitrogen. In plants, nitrogen is used primarily for chlorophyll production, plant proteins, and nucleic acids. It is the most applied element and is required in larger quantities than any other element except carbon, hydrogen, and oxygen. Problems, however, may develop if excessive nitrogen is used (Table 10–2). Excessive nitrogen increases shoot growth and selective diseases, as well as lowers stress tolerance to heat, cold, drought, and traffic. Most importantly, root and lateral shoot growth also are reduced.

High nitrogen levels encourage thin plant cell walls and an unusually high content of water. Thin cells tend to be easily invaded by certain fungi, insects, and other pests. A plant containing excessive water also requires additional irrigation to maintain this level and becomes more sensitive to heat and drought stress. Root growth suppression lowers turf tolerance to heat and drought and increases susceptibility to nematode damage. Additionally, excessive nitrogen fertilization

TABLE 10–2 *Influence of increasing levels of primary and secondary nutrients on several turfgrass plant responses.*

Turf plant response	Increasing levels of						
	Nitrogen	Phosphorus	Potassium	Iron	Sulfur	Calcium	Magnesium
Turf color	↑		↑	↑	↑		↑
Shoot growth and density	↑↓			↑	↑		↑
Rooting	↓	↑	↑	↑	↑	↑	
Carbohydrate formation	↓↑			↑	↑	↑	
Recuperative ability	↓↑						
Heat-, cold-, and drought-tolerance	↓	↑	↑	↑			
Wear tolerance	↓		↑				
Nematode tolerance	↓		↑				
Disease tolerance	↓↑		↑		↑	↑	

↑-Ample supply of the nutrient usually increases the specific turf plant response.
↓-Excessive nutrient level usually decreases the specific turf plant response.
↓↑-Adequate nutrient levels increase the specific turf plant response while excessive amounts decrease the response.

FIGURE 10–1 Adequate nitrogen is needed for desirable turfgrass density, texture, and color (right). Excessive amounts, however, can encourage excessive growth, increase disease and nematode susceptibility, and decrease rooting while insufficient amounts reduce turf color, stress hardiness, and recuperative ability.

may adversely affect the environment through possible groundwater contamination. Nitrogen deficiency causes plants to grow poorly, be spindly, lose color, and be stunted (Figure 10–1).

Origins and Losses

Turfgrasses may obtain nitrogen from organic matter decomposition and, to a small degree, from air oxidized by lightning and dispersed by rainfall.

$$N_2 \quad + \quad 2\tfrac{1}{2}O_2 \quad + \quad H_2O \quad \xrightarrow{\text{energy}} \quad 2HNO_3$$

$$\text{gaseous nitrogen} \qquad \text{oxygen} \qquad \text{water} \qquad\qquad \text{nitric acid}$$

In soil, ammonium (NH_4^+), nitrate (NO_3^-), and nitrite (NO_2^-) forms are the most important compounds and originate either from aerobic decomposition of organic matter or from the addition of commercial fertilizers. Ammonium and nitrate forms of nitrogen are the only ones used by turf plants. No matter the nitrogen source applied (e.g., manure, crop residues, organic matter, or commercial fertilizer), it must be changed to one of these two forms for plant use.

Mineralization is the overall process where organic matter, organic fertilizers, and some slow-release fertilizers are broken down or transformed by soil microorganisms to provide available ammonium and nitrate forms for plants. Mineralization is a three-step process involving **aminization, ammonification,** and **nitrification.** Aminization and ammonification are steps of mineralization in which proteins, amines, and amino acids (usually from organic matter or humus) are converted to ammonium, a nitrogen source utilized by plants.

Mineralization (Aminization and Ammonification)

$$R\text{-}NH_2 \quad + \quad H_2O \quad \xrightarrow{\text{microorganisms}} \quad NH_4^+ \quad + \quad R\text{-}OH \quad + \quad 275\text{ kJ}$$

$$\text{organic nitrogen} \quad \text{water} \qquad\qquad \text{ammonium} \quad \text{hydroxyl group} \quad \text{energy}$$
$$\text{nitrogen}$$

Ammonium nitrogen (NH_4^+) is then absorbed by plants or is further transformed to nitrate (NO_3^-). Ammonium nitrogen is the preferred nitrogen source since extra energy is required to transform nitrate into usable forms by plants and because of its smaller likelihood of losses by leaching and denitrification. The ammonium nitrogen transformation to nitrate nitrogen is referred to as nitrification.

Nitrification

$$NH_4^+ + 1\tfrac{1}{2}O_2 \xrightarrow[\substack{\text{warm} \\ \text{temperatures}}]{\substack{\text{Nitrosomonas} \\ \text{bacteria}}} NO_2^- + 2H^+ + H_2O \xrightarrow[+\tfrac{1}{2}O_2]{\text{Nitrobacteria}} NO_3^- + H_2O + 76\,kJ$$

ammonium		nitrite		nitrate	energy
nitrogen		nitrogen		nitrogen	

Nitrification is dependent on environmental conditions favoring soil microbiological activity. Warm temperatures, adequate soil moisture, and soil oxygen are necessary for this activity. However, nitrification does not readily occur under extreme temperatures (e.g., below freezing or above 105°F, 40.6°C), in saturated or poorly aerated soil, in excessively dry soil, or in low pH (<4.8) soil. Under these unfavorable conditions, microorganisms do not perform nitrification, and ammonium may accumulate. Ammonium nitrogen also may become toxic to turfgrasses when grown under cool, low light conditions since nitrification is minimized.

Nitrate nitrogen is readily soluble in water and may be repelled by negatively charged exchange sites of the soil components. Therefore, unless grasses rapidly utilize this form, it may be lost through leaching if excessive moisture is applied. This may be especially true during winter months when grass is not actively growing. In addition to nitrate and water, hydrogen ions (H^+) also are produced during nitrification, and a reduction in soil pH may be observed. This reduction is especially acute when a high rate of nitrogen is applied on sandy soils low in calcium. These soils are poorly buffered against pH changes induced through the acidifying effect of nitrification.

Besides leaching and clipping removal, additional avenues of nitrogen loss are through **denitrification** and **volatilization**. Denitrification is the conversion of nitrate nitrogen under anaerobic conditions to gaseous nitrogen that can result in atmospheric losses. Certain anaerobic soil organisms can obtain oxygen from nitrates. They also can obtain oxygen from nitrites in waterlogged soils with a subsequent release of nitrous oxide and nitrogen gas. Low soil oxygen levels and/or high soil moisture, alkaline (high pH) soils, and high temperatures favor denitrification. Applied nitrogen can be lost at the rate of 10 to 30 percent by denitrification in soils that are compacted, waterlogged, and which have an especially high pH (>7.5).

Denitrification (numbers in parenthesis represent valence state)

$$2NO_3^- \xrightarrow{\uparrow O_2} 2NO_2^- \xrightarrow{\uparrow O_2} 2NO \xrightarrow{\uparrow O} N_2O\uparrow \xrightarrow{\uparrow O} N_2\uparrow$$

nitrate nitrogen	nitrite nitrogen	nitric oxide	nitrous oxide	gaseous nitrogen
(+5)	(+3)	(+2)	(+1)	(0)

Volatilization is the conversion of ammonium nitrogen (NH_4^+) to ammonia gas (NH_3^-) that escapes to the atmosphere. If ammonium nitrogen comes in direct contact with free calcium carbonate in the soil, ammonium bicarbonate will be formed. This generally is of practical significance if the pH is >7 and the fertilizer is applied to bare soil. Ammonium bicarbonate is a relatively unstable compound. Upon exposure to the sun, it decomposes into ammonia, carbon dioxide, and water.

Nitrogen Volatilization

$$NH_4^+ + CaCO_3 \longrightarrow NH_3^-\uparrow + HCO_3^- + Ca^{+2}$$

ammonium nitrogen	calcium carbonate	ammonia gas	bicarbonate	calcium
(surface application)	(lime)			

Volatilization of ammonia nitrogen can usually be avoided by incorporating an ammonium nitrogen fertilizer source into soil. Ammonium nitrogen fertilizer also should not be applied immediately after lime application. In addition, surface application of an ammonium nitrogen fertilizer source to a sandy soil, free of lime or calcium carbonate, does not result in volatile loss of ammonia nitrogen. Furthermore, irrigating with approximately one-fourth to one-half inch (0.6 to 1.3 cm) water after fertilizer application will serve to eliminate this potential nitrogen loss.

Nitrogen Effects on Turfgrass

Nitrogen is the most important element turf managers apply to turfgrass. In addition to affecting turf color and growth rate, nitrogen influences thatch accumulation, disease and insect incidence, cold tolerance, heat and drought stress, nematode tolerance, lime requirements, and most importantly to the golfer, putting speed. Turf managers often measure nitrogen needs based on turf color, density, and/or clipping amount. However, the effects of nitrogen on other aspects of turf management often influence the success or failure of a superintendent.

Turf Color, Growth, and Density

When plants are deficient in nitrogen, leaf color is initially an overall pale yellow-green color from **chlorosis.** Chlorosis reflects a reduction in chlorophyll production. Nitrogen is a part of the chlorophyll molecule, so it is essential in its manufacture. Since nitrogen is a mobile element, chlorosis usually appears first on the lower (older) leaves before eventually changing to yellow as the deficiency symptoms progress to the base of the plant (often called "firing" for yellowing and senescence). In addition, plant growth rate and density may decrease, resulting in weak turf that has difficulty recovering from damage.

Other parameters also contribute, or possibly cause, symptoms similar to nitrogen deficiency. Deficiency in other nutrients such as iron, sulfur, or manganese resemble nitrogen deficiency. Sandy soils, including many that are alkaline, often are deficient in these elements. Compounding this problem are high populations of nematodes and poor water-holding capacity soils that can reduce rooting and increase water stress. Therefore, turf managers should determine the cause of chlorosis and turf thinning before indiscriminately applying nitrogen or micronutrient fertilizer.

In general, nitrogen has a direct relationship with turf growth and recovery from injury such as divots or ball marks. However, turf growth in terms of clipping matter produced is a poor judge of nitrogen needs. If adequate color and density are present, do not universally use clipping matter or weight as a gauge to judge nitrogen needs. However, if turf begins to thin, or excessive damage occurs, turf growth and density may become relatively good indicators of nitrogen needs.

Improper nitrogen fertilization can have an undesirable effect on grass rooting. Turfgrasses, in general, use carbohydrates stored in their roots to support shoot growth. These carbohydrates are replenished by products from photosynthesis. If heavy amounts of nitrogen are used, excessive shoot growth occurs at the expense of roots. These roots, therefore, may not have enough recovery time to replenish their carbohydrates before being forced to support excessive shoot growth when nitrogen is re-applied. Grass maintained at low nitrogen levels has up to twice as much root growth as plants maintained at high nitrogen levels.

In addition to forcing excessive shoot growth at the expense of root growth, physiological changes such as cell wall thinning, succulent tissue growth, and reduced root carbohydrate levels can also occur with excessive nitrogen use. Accordingly, increased stress susceptibility makes the plant less hardy.

Nitrogen Carriers

Turfgrass fertilizer carriers are available in an array of forms such as granules, pellets, liquids, powders, and suspensions. Granules are the most popular and range in size from coarse (1 to 3 mm in diameter) to fine, green's grade (<1 mm).

Over 90 percent of all nitrogen fertilizers are initially produced synthetically by reacting atmospheric nitrogen (N_2) and hydrogen gas (H_2) to form ammonia (called the **Haber process**). Large amounts of energy are required in the form of temperature and pressure for this process.

Ammonia Production Reaction

$$N_2 + 3H_2 \xrightarrow[\text{pressure}]{\text{heat}} 2NH_3^-$$

gaseous nitrogen   hydrogen gas   ammonia nitrogen

Gaseous ammonia nitrogen, also called anhydrous ammonia, is colorless and lighter than air but becomes a liquid when compressed and cooled. It contains 82 percent nitrogen by weight. From the basic ammonia compound, many different nitrogen-containing fertilizer compounds are manufactured. It may be liquefied to form anhydrous ammonia, dissolved in water to form nitrogen solution (NH_4OH), or formulated into other inorganic fertilizers (Figure 10–2).

FIGURE 10–2 A diagram showing the manufacture of various fertilizer derivatives from ammonia by adding various chemicals.

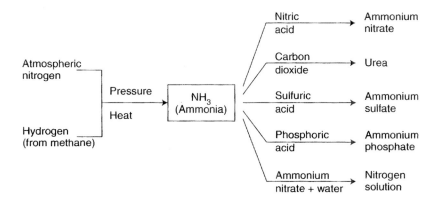

Chemically, nitrogen sources are classified as either (1) **quick release** (also called **soluble** source) forms that are water soluble and available as liquids or granules, or (2) **slow release** (also called **water-insoluble**) forms, which are either coated products or control-release reacted products, available as granules, powders, or suspensions. Table 10–3 lists the most widely used nitrogen-containing turf fertilizers and their characteristics.

Nitrogen release (or availability) to plants from a particular carrier is facilitated by one of several mechanisms. The two most common release mechanisms include hydrolysis (dissolving of fertilizer with water) or microbial (Table 10–4). Microbial release is very environmental dependent; this must be favorable for soil microorganisms to function. Extreme weather conditions (too hot, cold, or dry) may reduce or delay nitrogen release from microbial degradation.

Turf response from nitrogen sources is influenced by application rate, particle size, solubility, and coating alterations. Response time, therefore, can be adjusted from a few weeks to several months in duration by manipulating these parameters. Table 10–5 lists the release means of major turfgrass fertilizers.

Soluble Sources

Soluble or quickly available nitrogen sources result in an expedient response in terms of shoot growth and greening. This occurs approximately two days after application, peaking in seven to ten days, and tapering off to original levels in three to six weeks, depending on the application rate and subsequent amount of water applied. These are exemplified by urea and synthetic organics such as ammonium nitrate, ammonium sulfate, potassium nitrate, and calcium nitrate.

The nitrogen in soluble sources is in either the ammonium or nitrate form. The ammonium nitrogen form is prone to volatilization but less prone to leaching. The nitrate nitrogen form is more prone to leaching.

Soluble (liquid) nitrogen sources have salt-like characteristics. They dissolve readily in water to form cations and anions. The greater availability of these ions corresponds with a greater burn potential of the fertilizer. Burn potential can be lowered by making applications only to dry turf surfaces and when air temperatures are <80°F (27°C). Watering-in soluble nitrogen immediately following application further reduces the chance of burning plant tissue. Other disadvantages of using soluble nitrogen sources can be minimized by frequently applying small amounts. Rates at or below one-half pound of nitrogen per 1,000 square feet (2.4 kg N/100 m²) will minimize these problems but will increase application frequency and treatment costs. Table 10–6 lists major advantages and disadvantages of using soluble nitrogen sources.

Urea

Urea is one of today's most widely used nitrogen sources due to its relatively low cost and completely soluble nature. It is formed by reacting atmospheric nitrogen with methane to produce ammonia gas and carbon dioxide. The ammonium is then subjected to high temperature and pressure and reacted with the carbon dioxide to form urea containing about 45 percent nitrogen. Urea is unavailable to plants until it is converted to ammonium. Once applied, urea is broken down into ammonium carbonate by the enzyme *urease* that is present on plant tissue and organic matter. Ammonium is a cation (positively charged) and is attracted to negatively charged clay particles, root hairs, and organic matter. Direct applications of urea to the turf surface can result in conversion of

TABLE 10–3 *Primary nutrient sources and characteristics used in turf fertilizers.*

Nutrient source [formula]	Approximate nutrient percentage				Salt index (foliar burn potential)		Acidifying effect	Comment
	Nitrogen (N)	Phosphate (P_2O_5)	Potash (K_2O)	Water-insoluble nitrogen	Per nutrient unit[a]	Relative to sodium nitrate (100)		
Synthetic inorganic								
Ammonium nitrate [NH_4NO_3]	33	0	0	0	3.0 (high)	105	Medium	Water soluble; half nitrogen is ammonium form, the other half is the nitrate form; high burn potential; potential fire and explosive hazard; very hygroscopic (water loving) unless coated.
Ammonium sulfate [$(NH_4)_2SO_4$]	21	0	0	0	3.3 (high)	69	High	Water soluble; contains 24 percent sulfur; has greatest acidifying effect of listed sources; often used in flooded soils;
Calcium nitrate [$Ca(NO_3)_2$]	16	0	0	0	4.1 (v. high)	53	Basic	Very hygroscopic unless in airtight containers; contains 19 percent calcium and 1.5 percent magnesium; fast acting with high burn potential; nitrogen release is not temperature dependent; used on sodic soils to displace sodium.
Potassium nitrate [KNO_3]	13	0	44	0	1.6 (high)	74	Basic	Also known as saltpeter or nitre. Water-soluble potassium source with supplemental nitrogen; low salt concentration, low chloride, fire hazard; has alkalinity effect.
Nitrate of soda (sodium nitrate) [$NaNO_3$]	16	0	0	0	6.1 (v. high)	100	Basic	Water soluble; has highest burn potential of all materials; has alkalinity effect.
Synthetic organics								
Urea [$CO(NH_2)_2$]	45	0	0	0	1.6 (high)	75	Medium	Water soluble; rapid release; may volatilize if surface applied, especially under alkaline conditions; may leach rapidly if rainfall occurs immediately after application.
Urea formaldehyde (or UF) [$CO(NH_2)_2 \, CH_2]_n CO(NH_2)_2$]	18 to 40 (38)	0	0	12 to 35 (27)	0.3 (low)	6.1	Low	Slowly soluble; nitrogen release rate is temperature and formulation dependent; ureaform contains 38-0-0 (27 percent water-insoluble), methylene ureas are 40-0-0 (~15 percent water-insoluble).
Isobutylidene Diurea (or IBDU) [$CO(NH_2)_2]_2C_4H_8$]	31	0	0	27	0.2 (low)	5.0	Low	Slowly soluble; nitrogen release rate is not temperature dependent but depends on moisture availability and particle size; fine particle sizes contain 26 percent water-insoluble nitrogen while coarse particles contain 28 percent water-insoluble nitrogen.

Source								Comments
Sulfur-coated urea (or SCU) [CO(NH$_2$)$_2$ + S]	15 to 45 (32)	0	—		0.7 (low)	25	Medium	Slowly soluble; contains 10 to 20 percent sulfur; nitrogen release rate is temperature and coating thickness dependent; has minor acidifying effect.
Plastic or poly resin-coated urea	10 to 44	0	—		0.6 (low)	25	Low	Slowly soluble: nitrogen release rate is temperature and coating thickness dependent.
Natural organics								
Milorganite	6	4	0	5.5	0.007 (low)	0.04	Low	Activated sewage sludge; nitrogen release rate increases with higher temperatures; contains micronutrients, especially iron.
Ringer Turf, Nature Safe, Red Rooster, Sustane, Actinite, Hynite, + others	5 to 18	1 to 6	5 to 6	—	varies (low)	~3.5	Low	Nitrogen is from urea, methylene ureas, ammoniacal sources, water and hydrolyzed poultry feather meal, bone meal, leather tankage, fish meal, and blood.

ᵃBased on 20 pounds of plant nutrients. Generally, the higher the salt index/unit of nutrient, the higher burn potential of the particular fertilizer material.

TABLE 10–4 *Nitrogen release mechanisms for various granular fertilizers.*

Release mechanism	Comments
Water soluble (rapid hydrolysis)	Water is required to dissolve the particle (hydrolysis).
Slow dissolution (slow hydrolysis)	Primarily particle-size dependent; also influenced by soil moisture level, temperature, and sometimes pH.
Osmosis across a barrier or layer	Primarily particle-coating thickness dependent; also influenced by chemical nature, integrity, particle size, soil moisture, and microbial breakdown of any wax coating.
Microbial degradation	Primarily soil-temperature dependent; release is limited by cool temperatures, large particle size, low pH, and low soil oxygen. Simple organic sources release nitrogen before complex ones.

TABLE 10–5 *Release means for the major turfgrass fertilizers.*

Nitrogen source	Hydrolysis (moisture)	Microbial Dependent[a]
Isobutylidene diurea (IBDU)	yes	—
Organic sources	—	yes
Milorganite	—	yes
Urea formaldehyde (UF)	—	yes
Poly (or resin)-coated urea (PCU)	yes	—
Methylene urea (MU)	—	yes
Sulfur-coated urea (SCU)	yes	yes
Ammonium nitrate/sulfate	yes	—
Urea	yes	—
Mono- or diammonium phosphate	yes	—
Calcium nitrate	yes	—

[a]Microbial nitrogen release generally increases with increasing temperatures, soil moisture, oxygen levels, and near-neutral soil pH.

the ammonium carbonate to ammonia and carbon dioxide, resulting in excess loss as shown below. This loss can be avoided by irrigating after application to incorporate the nitrogen.

Urea Volatilization

$$(NH_2)_2CO \xrightarrow[\text{H}_2\text{O}]{\text{urease}} (NH_4)_2CO_3 \longrightarrow NH_3^- \uparrow + CO_2$$

urea H_2O ammonia bicarbonate   ammonia   carbon dioxide

Urea has a quick initial release rate of short duration and a high foliar burn potential. Nitrogen from urea is also prone to leaching and volatilization losses. Urea-based fertilizer programs should therefore involve light applications (½ lb N per 1,000 sq.ft., 2.4 kg N/100 m^2) made frequently (e.g., every two to four weeks) to reduce these potential losses.

Ammonium Sulfate/Nitrate

Ammonium sulfate/nitrate, ammonium phosphate, potassium nitrate, and calcium nitrate are other commonly used water-soluble nitrogen sources collectively referred to as inorganic salts. Once these fertilizers solubilize in soil, ammonium ions can be adsorbed by negatively charged clay or organic matter. As with urea, soil nitrobacteria convert this ammonium to nitrate, which is the main form available to plants. Unlike ammonium sulfate and phosphate, potassium nitrate and calcium nitrate fertilizers do not need to undergo conversion by nitrobacteria since their nitrogen source is already in nitrate forms.

TABLE 10–6 *Advantages and disadvantages of various nitrogen fertilizer sources.*

Advantages	Disadvantages
Soluble (liquid), quick-release sources	
• Rapid initial color and growth response	• High potential for foliar burn, especially at higher application rates and temperatures
• High in total nitrogen	
• Odorless	• Potential undesirable growth surge
• Maintain satisfactory nitrogen levels if applied frequently in small amounts	• Relatively short residual plant response; therefore, frequent applications are needed, increasing labor costs
• Minimum temperature dependence for availability	• Greater nitrogen loss potential to volatility, leaching, and run-off
• Low cost per unit of nitrogen	• Often difficult to handle
• Versatile in terms of being applied as a granular or as a liquid	
Synthetic slow-release sources	
• Slow-release liquid sources available	• High cost per unit of nitrogen
• High in total nitrogen	• Release rates can be confusing, depending on temperature, moisture, and soil microorganisms
• Low potential for foliar burn	
• Potential slow-release rates over extended time; product dependent	
Organic slow-release sources	
• Controlled release rates extending color response	• Often have inconsistent release rates
• Low potential for foliar burn	• May have unpleasant odor
• Other nutrients (e.g., P, K, and micronutrients) often included	• High cost per unit of nitrogen
• Viewed as a more "environmentally friendly" source	• May contain high salt or metal content (e.g., chicken manure)
• Dark color may help warm soils	

FIGURE 10–3 A diagram showing the manufacture of various slowly available nitrogen fertilizers from urea by reacting different chemicals.

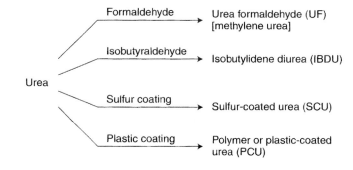

Slow-Release Nitrogen Sources

In an attempt to overcome some of the disadvantages of soluble nitrogen sources, fertilizer manufacturers have developed an array of slow or control-released nitrogen sources where the nitrogen is either slowly soluble, slowly released, or held in a natural organic form (Figure 10–3). Slow-release sources are placed in one of three broad categories:

1. Organic nitrogen
2. Coated nitrate, urea, or ammonium
3. Chemically reacted urea to make it more slowly available

These sources generally provide a more uniform growth response and longer residual plant response. They also have less potential for nitrogen loss, and allow a higher application rate than readily soluble sources. In addition, their burn potentials are lower because of their low salt index

TABLE 10–7 *General characteristics of several slow-release nitrogen sources.*

	Sulfur-coated urea (SCU)	Polymer-coated urea (PCU)	Urea formaldehyde (UF)	Methylene urea (MU)	Isobutylidene diurea (IBDU)	Natural organic
Percent nitrogen	39% N	41 to 43% N	38% N	40% N	31% N	2 to 10% N
Immediately available nitrogen	3.9% N	0% N	11% N	26% N	3.1% N	10% N
Release time	6 to 16 weeks	8 to 16 weeks	2 years	8 to 12 weeks	12 to 16 weeks	8 to 52 weeks
Release mechanism	coating breakdown	osmosis	microbial	microbial	hydrolysis	microbial
Release requirements	moisture	moisture	moisture & soil temperature	moisture & soil temperature	moisture	moisture & soil temperature
Best response season	all seasons	summer	summer	summer	spring & fall	summer
Initial response	medium	slow	medium-slow	medium	medium-slow	slow
Residual effect	extended	extended	extended	extended	extended	extended
Water solubility	low	low	medium-low	medium	medium-low	low
Foliar burn potential	low	low	low	low	low	low
Soil temperature release dependence	low	medium	high	medium	low	high

values. The application rate at which these sources release nitrogen may vary with fertilizer timing, source, temperature, moisture, pH, and particle size.

Drawbacks of slow-release nitrogen sources include high per-unit cost and slow initial plant response. Some sources also are not adaptable to liquid application systems. General characteristics of several slow-release nitrogen sources are listed in Table 10–7.

Coated, Slow-Release Nitrogen Sources

Coated nitrogen fertilizers consist of urea or other soluble sources being coated with a semipermeable barrier. The nitrogen-release rate is slow since the coating prevents wetting of the soluble nitrogen source. Release rates are dependent on coating degradation or by the physical integrity of the coating. Synthetic-controlled release fertilizers account for approximately 30 percent of all fertilizers supplied to golf courses in the United States while controlled-release nitrogen represents almost 70 percent of total nitrogen in fertilizers.

Sulfur-Coated Urea (SCU)

Sulfur-coated ureas are particles of urea coated with a layer of sulfur and usually a sealant. Sulfur is used since it is relatively cost effective and is needed by plants. Sulfur-coated ureas are formulated by moving granulated or prilled preheated urea pellets through a stream of molten sulfur using a rotating drum. It is then coated (sealed) with a microcrystalline wax to protect the surface from microbial degradation, to strengthen the sulfur shell, and to decrease the initial rate of urea release. The product is then cooled and a diatomaceous earth or vermiculite clay conditioner is applied to further reduce cracking and to promote sealant stickiness. Urea is released by gradually diffusing through this coating through cracks, pinholes, and imperfections naturally occurring in the surface as the particles cool.

Because of non-uniformity and lack of integrity in the coating process, urea granules crack at differing times; thus, they exhibit variable nitrogen release rates. These granules also are large in size; thus, they become subjected to damage during transportation, blending, and application, or by weight from mower reels, rollers, or wheels. Therefore, handling SCU should be kept to a minimum and drop spreaders avoided when applying it. Microprill technology has reduced these problems.

Rate of urea diffusion from SCU depends on microorganism activity, particle size, and as previously discussed, coating thickness and integrity. As the coating breaks down, water enters and dissolves the urea. Nitrogen release from SCU increases with warm temperatures, moist soils, and neutral soil pH. These favor soil microorganism activity, as does a thinner wax coating. Heavy sulfur coatings form larger fertilizer granules that release the nitrogen slower. Problems with mower crushing or pick-up may occur with these larger granules. To minimize this, a fine microprilled or miniprilled product is produced for greens application that has a very uniform nitrogen release rate.

The slow-release pattern is therefore from averaging the release of individual granules, some releasing immediately, others with release somewhat delayed, and the remainder releasing only after considerable delay.

SCU applied during winter months may produce a mottled turfgrass appearance. The intensity of this mottled appearance is correlated with coating thickness and granule size. It normally dissipates two to four weeks after appearing, depending on the nitrogen application rate and weather conditions.

Sulfur-coated urea has little effect on soil salinity but can reduce soil pH slightly due to the sulfur coating. The sulfur coating also is a sulfur source for plants. Sulfur-coated urea tends to be a lower-cost, slow-release nitrogen source when compared to other coated materials. Leaching and volatilization losses generally are low, assuming excessive moisture is not applied. The nitrogen content of SCU ranges from 32 to 38 percent depending upon the thickness of the sulfur coating, and 10 to 22 percent sulfur.

Polymer-Coated Urea or Plastic/Resin-Coated Urea

A relatively new but similar technology to SCU is a resin-coating (or polymer-coating) process involving coating a soluble nitrogen source, such as urea, nitrate, or ammonium, with resin or a plastic. Resin-coated fertilizers rely on osmosis rather than coating imperfections to release nitrogen. Once inside the coated granules, water dissolves some of the solid fertilizer. This creates a highly concentrated solution which then diffuses back through the plastic barrier and out into the soil. As the fertilizer particle swells, internal pressure either causes the pellet to crack open, releasing the urea, or the urea is forced out through the pores. This continues until all the fertilizer has dissolved and diffused out. Nutrient release, therefore, is due to controlled diffusion through the coating, is fairly constant over time, and essentially all the fertilizer is released from the coated granules.

Since the coating is semipermeable, nitrogen is time-released. As a result, resin-coated products have a more predictable controlled-release characteristic than sulfur-coated products, which provides a higher degree of control over nitrogen availability. Release rates generally vary from 70 to 270 days depending on the thickness of the coating and dissolution of water into the prill. Higher temperatures also increase release rate and decrease longevity.

The major disadvantage of poly-coating is the increased cost when compared to other slow-release fertilizers. *Osmocote* was the first significant commercial fertilizer to utilize a polymer coat. Others include *Agriform* and *Escote*.

Multiple-coating (called polymer-coated sulfur-coated, PSCF, or Multicote) of urea is a recent development. Urea is first coated with sulfur to form one layer and then coated with a polymer that further protects the nutrients, and, in combination with the sulfur layer, determines the rate of release. Unlike SCU, these particles are not coated with wax. Diffusion and capillary action are the release mechanisms of the nitrogen and can be regulated by varying the levels of each of the coating components. An advantage, in addition to the control release rate, is better resistance to abrasion than SCU. Dust problems when handling the material are also minimal, as are leaching potentials. *Poly-S* is one of the first commercially available dual-coated fertilizer sources using this technology. *Sulfur Kote II* is a multiple-coating fertilizer.

A similar technology to *Poly-S,* marketed under the trade name *Poly-N,* is called **reactive layer coating** and involves two coats of resin, instead of one coat plus one coat of a sulfur like *Poly-S.* The first resin coating reacts with the urea and the second coating reacts with the first coating to form an even-harder coating that does not break easily during handling. The coatings are very thin but effective. The thickness of the coating can be controlled to produce varying release rates. Dissolution of water into the prill also controls the nitrogen release rate, while temperature does not appear to have an effect. Other polymer-coated, sulfur-coated urea sources include *Poly-X, NS-52, GoldCote,* and *Poly Plus.*

The newest coating process involves applying diisocyanide first to urea (or other nitrogen substrate) followed by a polyol layering, forming polyurethane. Longevity of release is governed by coating thickness. The nitrogen is released by diffusion directly through the coating. Temperature, coating thickness, and solubility of the nitrogen substrate determine the nitrogen release rate.

Longevity of release can be controlled by coating thickness. *Poly-On* and *Tricote Poly-SCU* are polyurethane (or plastic)-coated fertilizer sources. *ESN* and *UHS* are other coated products. The *Signature Blue* line of fertilizer has an additional coating of *Prospect Plus,* a fertilizer coating.

Controlled-Release Urea Reaction Synthetic Nitrogen Sources (noncoated)

The noncoated urea reaction fertilizers are made by reacting urea with either formaldehyde or isobutyraldehyde (Figure 10–3). Ureaform (UF) and methylene urea (MU) are fertilizers produced by reacting urea with formaldehyde. Isobutylidene diurea (IBDU) is produced from reacting urea with isobutyraldehyde.

Isobutylidene Diurea (IBDU)

IBDU is formed by reacting isobutyraldehyde with urea in an acid solution to form a material composed of a single molecule containing 31 percent nitrogen, 90 percent of which is water insoluble. In the presence of water, IBDU hydrolyzes back to urea and butyric acid. IBDU's nitrogen-release rate is predominantly affected by soil moisture and particle size and is not as dependent on temperature. IBDU, therefore, releases quicker in cool weather compared to slowly available nitrogen fertilizers dependent on the temperature activity of microbes. Higher soil moisture and smaller particle size result in a faster release rate. Higher temperatures also increase nitrogen-release rate where it is two to three times higher at 75°F (24°C) than at 50°F (10°C). Conversely, organic nitrogen sources and urea-formaldehyde may exhibit a tenfold increase in release rate between similar temperatures.

With IBDU, an optimum pH range for nitrogen release is between 5 and 8, with a significant rate reduction occurring outside these ranges. Although nitrogen release is independent of microbial activity, and therefore more readily available during cool weather, this is somewhat dependent on its particle size, with finer particles providing a greater surface area and faster rate of hydrolysis (nitrogen-release mechanism). Usually a range of particle sizes between 8 and 24 mesh are used to increase nitrogen-release rates over a longer period of time. Particles greater than two millimeters in diameter are slow to hydrolyze and are subject to excessive mower pick-up.

The influence of IBDU on soil salinity and pH is minimum. However, at excessive rates (e.g., 6 lbs N per 1,000 sq.ft., 29 kg N/100 m^2), ammonia gas may be absorbed by the turf, resulting in temporary chlorosis. IBDU's reliance on water for nitrogen release may be absent or stimulated at a time when it is least desired. IBDU is a Japanese product under the trade name *Par Ex.*

Ureaformaldehyde (UF)

Ureaformaldehyde is a generic designation for several methylene urea (**MU**) polymers made from reacting urea with formaldehyde to first form monomethylol urea and then form soluble methylene urea and ureaform. Ureaformaldehyde was first produced in 1936 and commercialized in 1955. These products have varying lengths of polymers of methylene urea depending on the proportion of ureas and formaldehyde in the initial reaction. These vary from water-soluble molecules to highly water-insoluble molecules to provide controlled nitrogen release. Chain length determines solubility and how rapidly nitrogen is released to plants. Nitrogen in ureaformaldehyde nitrogen sources are classified as:

1. **Cold water soluble nitrogen** (or **CWSN**)—This is readily available to plants and can appear as liquid formulations. These are made up of "free" urea or short polymer chains.
2. **Water insoluble nitrogen** (or **WIN**)—These are slowly available to plants.
   a. **Cold water insoluble nitrogen** (or **CWIN** at 68 to 77°F, 20 to 25°C)—Plant availability is over several weeks by microbial degradation.
   b. **Hot water insoluble nitrogen** (or **HWIN** at 208 to 212°F, 98 to 100°C)—Plant availability is over many months by slow microbial degradation.

The overall nitrogen availability is described by an *activity index,* which compares the proportion of hot water insoluble nitrogen with cold water insoluble nitrogen. By altering the proportion of urea and formaldehyde in the initial reaction, activity indexes are produced to meet the needs of turfgrass species at different geographical locations. The smaller the ratio of urea to formaldehyde, the longer the chain of polymers formed and the longer the residual time for nitrogen availability. These increase in length from methylene diurea (most soluble), dimethylene triurea, trimethylene tetraurea, and tetramethylene pentaurea to pentamethylene hexaurea (least soluble). As polymer lengths and the number of longer polymers increase, solubility decreases, resulting in nitrogen being released more slowly. For example, a methylene urea having a 1.9 urea to 1 formaldehyde ratio is two-thirds water soluble and one-third water insoluble. Ureaform fertilizers contain 38 percent nitrogen with at least 60 percent of the total nitrogen as CWIN, and less than 15 percent of the total nitrogen CWSN, and are commercially available as *Nitroform, Organiform, Granuform, Ureaform, MethEx 38,* and *Blue-Chip.* These sources are for soil applications only and not as liquids, except *Powder Blue,* which can be applied as a suspension. They are more costly than soluble nitrogen fertilizers. A recent line of shorter-chain UF fertilizers is *Triaform.*

A combination methylene diurea/dimethylene triurea (abbreviated MDU/DMTU) product containing two- and three-urea chain materials, respectively, is available as *Contec.* This is a granular product containing at least 40 percent nitrogen with less than 25 percent CWIN.

All UF products depend on microbial breakdown for nitrogen availability. Therefore, environmental conditions favoring microbial activity (e.g., warm temperatures (>55°F, 13°C), neutral soil pH, and adequate soil moisture and oxygen) promote nitrogen release. Conversely, low temperatures, acid soils, and low soil oxygen inhibit nitrogen release from UF. Ureaform fertilizers containing appreciable amounts of water-insoluble nitrogen polymers will not perform well during cooler weather. Quickly available sources are usually applied alone or in combination with ureaform fertilizers during cool periods.

Shorter-chained water-soluble polymers are readily digestible by soil microorganisms and release nitrogen to the soil in the form of ammonium in a relatively short time. Longer-chained polymers contain water-insoluble nitrogen, which is more slowly digested by soil bacteria. Unlike IBDU and SCU, where nitrogen goes back to the soil as urea, nitrogen from methylene urea and ureaform is gradually converted directly back to the ammonium form throughout the growing season via mineralization. A lag in nitrogen availability may occur when using UF. A buildup of "residual" nitrogen may take several seasons, resulting in a more uniform response. During this lag phase, higher rates of UF can be applied or supplemental soluble nitrogen sources can be used to produce adequate shoot color.

As with any nitrogen source, UF losses by mower pick-up can be significant, especially immediately after application. To avoid this problem, the grass should be allowed to dry before mowing for several days after application. Alternatively, grass catcher boxes can be removed to allow clippings and fertilizer granulars to return to the soil surface.

Losses of nitrogen by leaching and volatilization are less for UF than for readily available nitrogen sources. Over time, UF sources are about equal to soluble sources in terms of nitrogen use efficiency. Under conditions favoring leaching and volatilization, however, UF sources often are more efficient. Labor costs for applying fertilizer numbers also must be weighed, since UF applications are less frequent. Soil pH or salinity are little affected by UF, and its burn potential is low.

A similar product to UF is *Nutralene,* a soluble methylene urea product containing approximately 40 percent nitrogen. It is more readily available than UF because of its short-chained methylation. Its mechanism of nitrogen release depends on both microbial activity and hydrolysis. Its nitrogen release rate, therefore, is faster than for UF products, but its long-term fertilizer effects on the turf are shortened. Nutralene performs better during cooler temperatures than many fertilizers due to its quicker release during these conditions. Other methylene urea products include *Country Club Greens Keeper, MethEx 40,* and *Pro Turf.* An aminourea-formaldehyde product, *Novex,* is another line of controlled-release MU/UF fertilizer.

Another flowable UF source, *FLUF,* contains 18 percent nitrogen, of which 20 to 25 percent of the total nitrogen is water insoluble. The initial response of FLUF is generally slower than urea. FLUF also has less foliar burning potential than urea. *Slo-Release* is another liquid UF source.

Other Slow-Release Sources

Other slow-release nitrogen sources being developed include Oxamide, Triazines, and Triazones. *Oxamide* is a diamine of oxalic acid produced in Japan for rice production. It is a double urea product containing approximately 31 percent nitrogen and is approximately twice as soluble as IBDU. The release rate is directly related to its particle size, hardness, and water present. Following dissolution, hydrolysis primarily occurs by microbial cleavage of the carbon bonds, in the presence of the enzyme *amidase,* resulting in the formation of ammonium carbonate. Powdered and fine particles of oxamide nitrify faster than ammonium sulfate and at a rate similar to urea in acid soils. Their residual effects, however, are not as long lasting as coarser grades. When used on turf, it imparts a dark bluish-green color. Currently, costs are prohibitive.

A pure form of triazine that contains 66 percent nitrogen includes the commercial products *Melamine* and *Nitrazine*. Commercial formulations usually contain a mixture of triazine and urea containing 40 to 60 percent nitrogen. Nitrogen release is microbial dependent and generally slow due to the product containing double carbon bonds that are difficult to cleave (break). Four- to six-month response times occur. A soluble nitrogen source, such as urea, should be used initially with Melamine to provide initial color and to encourage breakdown of the product.

Triazones are similar to triazines except their ring structure does not contain double bonds. Triazones contain approximately 40 percent nitrogen and can be formulated in a clear, stable, water-soluble form. Nitrogen release is governed by microbial action. *N-Sure* is a liquid source containing 28 percent nitrogen, but exhibits slower nitrogen release (8 to 12 weeks).

Natural Organic Nitrogen Sources

Natural organic nitrogen sources usually involve various levels of composted or waste (either human or animal) materials. Manure, sludges, bone meal, humates, and composted plant residues are traditionally used natural organic nitrogen sources (Table 10–8). Nutrient contents are typically low—1 to 8 percent nitrogen; 0.2 to 1 percent phosphorus; and 0.5 to 3 percent potassium. All organic nitrogen forms are converted first to the ammonium form (NH_4) and then to the nitrate (NO_3) form by soil microorganisms. Advantages of these include low burn potential due to

TABLE 10–8 *Approximate amounts of macronutrients often found in common organic fertilizer sources.*

Nutrient source	Nitrogen (N)	Phosphate (P_2O_5)	Potash (K_2O)
	---------------------- % -----------------		
Animal byproducts			
Dried blood	13	2	1
Bone meal, steamed	3	25	0
Dried fish meal	10	7	0
Tankage, animal	7	10	1
Excreta			
Guano, bat	8.5	5	1.5
Cattle manure	2 to 5	1.5	2
Horse manure	2 to 8	1 to 3	2 to 7
Poultry manure	5 to 15	3	1.5
Sewage sludge, dried	2	2	—
Sewage sludge, activated	6	3	0.5
Swine manure	7	4	6
Plant residues			
Cottonseed meal	7	3	2
Garbage tankage	2.5	3	1
Linseed meal	5.5	2	1.5
Rapeseed meal	5.5	2.5	1.5
Soybean meal	7	1.5	2.5
Tobacco stems	2	0.5	6

limited water-insoluble nitrogen, little effect on pH, and low leaching losses. Other advantages include a variety of nutrients included in addition to nitrogen, and certain organic sources that may possibly improve the physical condition of soils, especially sandy ones. In addition, depending on the local source, natural organic nitrogen sources may readily be available at competitive prices.

Recently, some natural organic nitrogen sources have been inoculated with various microorganisms or were included with readily available organic materials to stimulate natural microbial population. Claims are often made in addition to providing nitrogen; these provide better nutrient retention; pests such as nematodes, soil insects, and diseases are suppressed by the inoculated organisms; thatch decomposition is enhanced by inoculation with bacteria or by stimulation of earthworm activity; and improved soil chemical and physical properties occur. These claims are rarely based on scientific research and results are often highly erratic.

Some issues to consider before using these traditional organic sources include low nitrogen release during cool weather due to reduced microbial activity and low nitrogen content, which can result in large amounts of material having to be applied. Other considerations include greater costs on a per pound of nutrient basis than with soluble sources, and the fact that natural organic nitrogen sources may be difficult to store and to uniformly apply. This is especially true when the turf is already established. Depending on the source, some natural organic sources produce objectionable odor after application and contain undesirable salts, heavy metals, and weed seeds. In general, natural organic sources such as manures and composted crop residues should not be used on golf greens because of potential soil drainage hindrance from the large amounts of material applied. As some of the handling and application problems are resolved, future use of municipal refuse and sewage sludge in turf production will probably increase.

Milorganite

Milorganite, a product from the Milwaukee Sewage Commission, is the most popular commercial organic nitrogen source used on fine turf. It is an activated sewage sludge produced when raw sewage is inoculated with microorganisms, aerated to promote flocculation, filtered, dried, ground, screened, and sterilized. Milorganite contains approximately 6 percent nitrogen, of which 92 percent is water soluble, 4 percent P_2O_5, and an array of micronutrients. Milorganite is characterized by having a low burn potential to turfgrass leaves, and its uniform release of nitrogen over a three- to four-week period has a minimum effect on soil pH and salinity. It also has low leaching and volatilization losses; is a source of iron, copper, and zinc; and, due to its dark color, serves as a soil warmer during cool weather. Lower disease and insect incidence also have been reported when replacing soluble nitrogen sources with Milorganite.

Disadvantages of Milorganite include being relatively costly per pound of nitrogen, having poor winter response since microorganisms are required for nitrogen utilization, and having relatively short residual nitrogen response. Milorganite also contains no potassium; therefore, a potassium source should be used in conjunction with it. *Huactinite* is another sewage-based fertilizer, as are other various locally available products.

Other commercial slow-release natural organic nitrogen fertilizers from animal byproducts include *Nature Safe, Sustane, Ringer,* and *Red Rooster.* These contain various amounts and combinations of composted poultry litter, blood, bone meal, wheat germ, and other additives, and also are often inoculated with various microorganisms and fortified with other nitrogen sources.

Performance Index Number

A new performance index number (PIN) quantitatively and qualitatively rates fertilizers containing insoluble nitrogen. Ideally, this numerical system gives turf managers a more thorough understanding of the rating of the insoluble nitrogen fertilizers and helps predict how long a fertilizer will continue releasing nitrogen. The PIN measures the percentages of (1) particle dispersion, (2) particle integrity, and (3) the nitrogen activity index. Each of the three percentages is on a scale of 100; a perfect PIN rating is 300, while the lowest acceptable PIN value is 235. Particle dispersion is expressed as the percentage of the sample passing the dispersion test. A higher dispersion is desirable for water-insoluble nitrogen to assure the nutrient is delivered to the turf area. The minimum particle distribution is 80 percent. Particle integrity is the measure of how hard the fertilizer granule is. Integrity is important to assure durability through production and shipping to application. The minimum acceptable integrity is 90 percent. The nitrogen activity index is the percentage of water-insoluble nitrogen soluble in hot water with a minimum percentage of 65.

Salt Index

Fertilizers behave just like any salt, such as table salt, by attracting water; thus, they pull moisture from plants they contact. If the fertilizers are applied at excessive rates or when days are hot and dry, plants can suffer fertilizer salt burn (Figure 10–4). The salt index measures the relative tendency of a fertilizer to increase the osmotic pressure of the soil solution compared to the increase by an equal weight of the reference material, sodium nitrate.

Fertilizers vary in their capability to attract plant water, thereby causing burn. This can be minimized by using fertilizers with low salt indexes on days that are hot and/or by applying fertilizer on dry grass leaves and immediately watering it in. If a soil test indicates soil salinity problems, a low salt-index fertilizer should be considered. Another fertilizer burn involves animal urine (Figure 10–5). This often goes undetected until the turf is severely damaged.

Phosphorus

Phosphorus (P), the second-most essential element for plant growth, is involved in the transfer of energy as the organic compound, adenosine triphosphate (ATP), during metabolic processes. It also is an essential component of DNA, RNA, and cellular membranes. Phosphorus content may range between 0.10 to 1.00 percent by weight, with sufficiency values from 0.20 to 0.40 percent in newly mature leaf tissue. Phosphorus is considered deficient when tissue levels are below 0.20 percent and excessive above 1.00 percent. The highest concentration of phosphorus is in new leaves and their growing point, but is readily mobile in plants.

Since phosphorus is fairly mobile in plants, deficiency symptoms initially occur in older tissue. Symptoms of phosphorus deficiencies include slow growth, as well as weak and stunted plants possessing dark-green lower, older leaves. These older leaves eventually show a dull blue-green color with a reddish-purple pigmentation along the leaf blade margins due to sugar accumulation in phosphorus-deficient plants (Plate 10–1). Eventually, leaf tips turn reddish, and may then develop in streaks down the blade.

FIGURE 10–4 Turf burn can result when using excessive fertilizer rates, when fertilizer is applied during hot and dry conditions (top), or when traffic follows application (bottom).

FIGURE 10–5 Turf burn caused by animal urine. Damage often goes undetected until irreversible turf injury has occurred. A strong urine smell is often detectable in such cases.

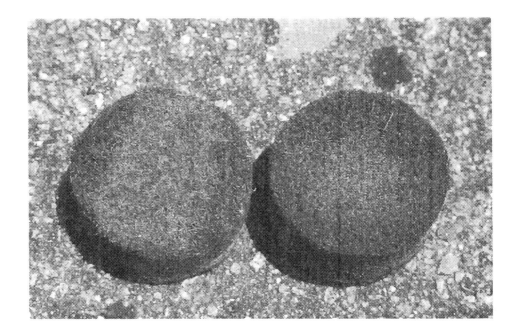

Phosphorus deficiency symptoms normally occur when root growth of turf plants is restricted, and when soil temperatures and oxygen levels decrease. Since roots are a principal site for energy (carbohydrate) storage, they are very dependent on adequate phosphorus levels (Plate 10–2). Early spring and fall are two seasons in which root growth is slowed; hence, phosphorus in the soil is not readily encountered. Similarly, phosphorus deficiencies often occur during turfgrass establishment, resulting from the initial restricted rooting of new seedlings. Research indicates a 1:2:1 or 1:2:2 ratio of N–P–K as best for turfgrass establishment.

Phosphorus absorption by plants is largely due to the very slowly soluble orthophosphate ions, $H_2PO_4^-$ and HPO_4^{-2}, that are present in the soil solution. $H_2PO_4^{-2}$ ions dominate in acid soils. As soil pH increases, HPO_4^{-2} ions dominate until conditions become alkaline, where PO_4^{-3} ions then dominate. $H_2PO_4^-$ and HPO_4^{-2} ions are both found at intermediate pH levels. When calcium carbonate ($CaCO_3^-$) dominates at higher pH, phosphorus availability may be reduced. Heavier phosphorus fertilizer application under high pH conditions may be required to increase its availability.

Phosphorus Forms at Various Soil pH Levels

$$H_2PO_4^- \quad\leftrightarrow\quad H_2O + HPO_4^- \quad\leftrightarrow\quad H_2O + PO_4^{-3}$$
(acid conditions, soil pH <6.0)   (neutral soils, pH 7.0)   (alkaline conditions, soil pH >8.0)

Cool-season turfgrasses (ryegrass) tend to respond positively to phosphorus fertilizer applications even in high-phosphorus-containing soils. Bermudagrass, meanwhile, has been observed to decline in growth rate as a result of excessive phosphorus application. A reduction in tissue nitrogen content appears as a consequence of applying phosphorus to a soil containing high levels of extractable phosphorus. In light of these findings, the majority of yearly fertilizer phosphorus should be applied to the ryegrass when overseeded in bermudagrass. Bentgrass often shows phosphorus deficiency during the summer stress period when its roots are typically shallow and somewhat weak. Besides having disease control properties, fungicides such as fosetyl-AL or mancozeb eventually degrade into byproducts containing phosphorus and other elements such as manganese and zinc. Minute quantities of these elements, readily available from these breakdown products on summer-stressed bentgrass, often improve grass color and growth.

The first fertilizer was manufactured in England around 1830 from treating ground bones with sulfuric acid to increase the solubility (or availability) of the phosphorus. Today, the most common phosphorus fertilizers used in turf include superphosphate, triple (or treble) superphosphate, and monoammonium and diammonium phosphate (MAP and DAP, respectively) (Table 10–9). Superphosphate consists of calcium phosphate and gypsum. It is produced by reacting rock phosphate with sulfuric acid. Triple superphosphate is calcium phosphate formed when rock phosphate is treated with phosphoric acid while ammonium phosphates are produced by reacting ammonia with phosphoric acid.

TABLE 10–9 *Primary phosphorus sources and characteristics used in turf fertilizers.*

Source	Approximate nutrient percentage			Salt index (foliar burn potential)		Acidifying effect	Comment
	Nitrogen (N)	Phosphate (P_2O_5)	Potash (K_2O)	Per nutrient unit[a]	Relative to sodium nitrate (100)		
Phosphorus (P) carriers [formulas]							
Monoammonium phosphate (MAP) [$(NH_4)H_2PO_4$]	11	48	0	2.5 (low)	34	Medium	Soluble phosphorus source that also provides nitrogen and reduces soil pH; preferred to DAP when applied to alkaline soils.
Diammonium phosphate (DAP) [$(NH_4)_2HPO_4$]	18 to 21	46 to 53	0	1.6 (low)	30	Medium	Soluble phosphorus source containing higher nitrogen than MAP while also reducing soil pH. Significant ammonia losses on alkaline soils can occur.
Superphosphate [$Ca(H_2PO_4)_2 + CaSO_4$]	0	20	0	0.4 (low)	8	Neutral	Soluble phosphorus source often used in mixed fertilizers; contains calcium (18 to 21%) and sulfur (12%) as gypsum; has little acidity effect.
Triple (or treble) superphosphate [$Ca(H_2PO_4)_2H_2O$]	0	46	0	0.2 (low)	10	Neutral	Concentrated phosphorus source containing calcium (13%).
Ammonium polyphosphate [$NH_4H_2PO_4 + (NH_4)_3HP_2O_7$)]	10	34	0	2.4 (low)	2	—	A liquid phosphorus and nitrogen solution source; used in fluid fertilizers.
Milorganite	6	4	0	0.6 (low)	3	Low	Activated sewage sludge; nitrogen release rate increases with higher temperatures; contains micronutrients, especially iron.
Colloidal phosphate	0	8	0	low	—	Neutral	Contains 20 percent calcium; low phosphorus availability; best used as a powder on acid soils.

[a]Generally, the higher the salt index/unit of nutrient, the higher the burn potential of the particular fertilizer material.

Other minor use phosphorus sources include bone meal, basic slag, ammonium polyphosphate, and calcium metaphosphate (or apatite). Bone meal contains 15 to 34 percent P_2O_5 and is an animal bone byproduct. Basic slag is a steel manufacturing byproduct containing 10 to 18 percent P_2O_5. It also contains some calcium and should be finely ground before use. Calcium metaphosphate contains 62 to 65 percent phosphate and is effective on acidic soils. Ammonium polyphosphate is a liquid form containing approximately 10-37-0 nitrogen, P_2O_5, and K_2O.

The available phosphorus content in fertilizers is expressed as P_2O_5. To determine the actual phosphorus content from the percent P_2O_5 in a fertilizer, the following conversion is needed:

percent P_2O_5 as expressed on fertilizer bag $\times 0.43$ = percent phosphorus in fertilizer bag

Phosphorus does not move or leach readily due to its low solubility in the soil solution; therefore, phosphorus applications are not needed as regularly as nitrogen applications. A soil test is probably the best indicator of phosphorus levels in a soil. Indiscriminate phosphorus application can form unhealthy, high levels. Iron deficiencies, for example, often result from high phosphorus-containing and/or alkaline soils. Phosphorus is most readily available to plants with the soil pH range of 5.5 to 6.5. At low pH (<5.0), soils containing iron and aluminum form an insoluble complex with phosphorus, resulting in neither nutrient being easily available to the grass. For example, with aluminum and/or iron, the following reaction can occur to form variscite from aluminum or strengite $[Fe(OH)_2H_2PO_4]$ from iron:

Insoluble Phosphorus Formation at Low pH

$$Al^{+3} \quad + \quad H_2PO_4^- \quad + \quad 2H_2O \leftrightarrow 2H^+ \quad + \quad Al(OH)_2H_2PO_4 \quad \text{or} \quad [Fe(OH)_2H_2PO_4]$$

(or Fe^{+3}) (soluble) variscite (insoluble) strengite (insoluble)

Sandy soils, such as that used in many golf greens, lack iron or aluminum and do not form insoluble phosphorus complexes. Under these conditions, phosphorus is more available at a lower pH.

In alkaline soils (pH >7.5), calcium forms insoluble complexes with phosphorus to render it unavailable as dicalcium phosphate $[CaHPO_4]$. Soil pH adjustment may be necessary to prevent the formation of these complexes as applied phosphorus fertilizer is rendered unavailable.

Potassium

Potassium (K) is an essential element not normally associated with a prominent visual response in terms of shoot color, density, or growth. However, it helps plants overcome some of the negative effects of excessive nitrogen fertilization such as decreased stress tolerance to cold, heat, drought, diseases, and wear. Potassium is often called the "health" element since an ample supply increases the plant's tolerance to these stresses (Table 10–2). Potassium is directly involved in maintaining the water status of the plant, the turgor pressure of its cells, and the opening and closing of its stomata. As its concentration increases in plants, cell walls thicken, the tissue water content decreases, and plants become more turgid due to the regulation of stomatal opening. This is due to potassium providing much of the osmotic pressure necessary to pull water into plant roots, and thus it improves the plant's drought tolerance. Thicker cell walls also resist pest pressure better. Potassium is required by more than 60 enzymes for activation.

Cold tolerance is also influenced by the plant's phosphorus-to-potassium relationship. A 1:2 phosphorus-to-potassium ratio in leaf tissue increases the cold temperature tolerance in turfgrasses.

The critical level of potassium in plants is about fourfold that of phosphorus and almost the same as nitrogen. A 3:2 fertilizer ratio of nitrogen to potassium has been shown to be beneficial. Dry matter of leaf tissue consists of 1.0 to 5.0 percent potassium. Sufficient values range from 1.5 to 3.0 percent in recently matured leaf tissue. Potassium deficiency occurs when tissue levels are less than 1.0 percent and excessive when greater than 3.0 percent. However, most plants can absorb more potassium than needed; this is often referred to as **luxury consumption.** An inverse relationship exists between potassium, magnesium, and calcium in plants. As potassium levels increase, magnesium deficiencies are the first to show, while calcium deficiencies occur at higher concentrations. In saline soils, an inverse relationship can occur where calcium, magnesium, or sodium ions compete with potassium for plant uptake.

Deficiencies may occur in soils low in micas (the more-soluble mineral source), soils low in clay (fewer exchange sites), and soils high in sand, which are prone to leaching. Potassium deficiency symptoms include interveinal yellowing of older leaves, and the rolling and burning of the leaf tip (Plate 10–3). Leaf veins finally appear yellow and margins appear scorched (called necrosis). The turf stand will appear thin with spindly growth of individual plants. Potassium is a mobile element within plants; thus, it can be translocated to younger meristematic tissues from older leaves if a shortage occurs, while necrotic spots may form an unique pattern on the leaf margin in certain plants. Although similar in appearance, plant salinity damage differs by affecting newer leaves compared to older leaves with potassium deficiency.

Potassium fertilizer often is referred to as "potash." Early settlers coined the name after producing potassium carbonate needed for making soap by evaporating water filtered through wood ashes. The ash-like residue in the large iron pots was called "pot-ash," and this process was the first U.S. registered patent.

Muriate of potash (potassium chloride) is the most often used potassium-containing fertilizer (Table 10–10) and originates from potassium salt deposits that have been mined and processed. These deposits developed where seawater once occupied the surface. Sodium chloride from this

TABLE 10–10 *Primary potassium sources and characteristics used in turf fertilizers.*

| Source | Approximate nutrient percentage | | | Salt index[a] (foliar burn potential) | | Acidifying effect | Comment |
	Nitrogen (N)	Phosphate (P_2O_5)	Potash (K_2O)	Per nutrient unit[a]	Relative to sodium nitrate (100)		
Potassium (K) carriers [formulas]							
Muriate of potash (potassium chloride) [KCl]	0	0	50 to 60	2.2 (high)	109	Neutral	Most common potassium source; soluble; high burn potential; contains 44 percent chlorine.
Sulfate of potash (potassium sulfate) [K_2SO_4]	0	0	40 to 50	0.9 (low)	46	Neutral	Contains 17 percent sulfur; used instead of potassium chloride where chlorine is not desirable, to reduce foliage burn potential, and to provide sulfur; may not leach as rapidly as potassium chloride.
Potassium-magnesium sulfate (or K-Mag) [$K_2SO_4 \cdot 2MgSO_4$]	0	0	18 to 22	2.0 (high)	43	Neutral	Contains 11 percent magnesium and 23 percent sulfur; also known as langbeinite.
Potassium nitrate [KNO_3]	13	0	37 to 44	1.6 (high)	74	Basic	Also known as saltpeter or nitre; potassium source with supplemental nitrogen; water soluble; low salt concentration, low chloride, fire hazard; has alkalinity effect.

[a]Generally, the higher the salt index/unit of nutrient, the higher burn potential of the particular fertilizer material.

seawater normally is found as a contaminant of the potassium mines. Magnesium salts also are often found concurrently with potassium salts. As seawater evaporated, potassium salts crystallized to become beds of potassium chloride. Potassium sulfate forms when potassium chloride is reacted with sulfuric acid, and potassium nitrate forms when it is reacted with nitric acid. These forms are used to reduce the salt index compared to potassium chloride and are also carriers of sulfur and nitrogen, respectively.

The soluble potassium content in a fertilizer is expressed as K_2O. To determine the quantity of actual potassium supplied in a fertilizer source, the following conversion is used:

percent K_2O as expressed on the fertilizer bag $\times 0.83$ = percent potassium in the fertilizer bag

The available form for plant use is the potassium ion (K^+), absorbed primarily from the soil solution. Other forms exist, but most are unavailable for plant use. Potassium is not readily held in sandy soils (low-CEC soils) and can be lost by leaching. This problem is not always appreciated, especially when growing grass is subjected to heavy rainfall or watering. Newer fertilizer formulations are available that coat the potassium to better regulate its release rate. Soils containing appreciable clay retain more potassium because clay particles serve to hold this element. However, much of the potassium is held so tightly that it becomes relatively unavailable to plants.

Competition exists for plant entrance between potassium with calcium and magnesium. Soils high in either or both of these elements will need additional potassium fertilization in order to satisfy plant needs. In sandy soils, or where turf clippings are not returned, a 2:1 or 1:1 ratio of nitrogen to potassium may be required to maintain adequate potassium supply. Frequent, light potassium treatments with these ratios should be considered with each nitrogen application.

Granular Fertilizers

Granular fertilizers are manufactured when dry materials are mixed with a water or with acids to form a slurry. The slurry is produced in a heated, revolving drum where different-sized particles form as the product dries. To prevent water adsorption from air and to prevent caking, materials like diatomaceous earth or kaolinitic clay are added to produce a granular coating. Oil may also be added to reduce dust. The final product should contain hard granules with uniform size and composition and have good storage and handling qualities.

SECONDARY PLANT NUTRIENTS

Calcium

Calcium (Ca), magnesium (Mg), and **sulfur (S)** are elements required in almost the same quantities as phosphorus. Calcium functions include strengthening cell walls to prevent their collapse; enhancing cell division; encouraging plant growth, protein synthesis, and carbohydrate movement; and balancing cell acidity (Table 10–1). Calcium also improves root formation and growth.

Plants only use the exchangeable calcium ion, Ca^{+2}. Deficiencies occur most often in sandy soils with low cation exchange capacity, extremely acidic (<5.0 pH) soils, or soils saturated with sodium. Long-term use of effluent water high in sodium or aluminum may also induce calcium deficiency.

Deficiency symptoms include young leaves that are distorted (e.g., twisted or deformed) in appearance and turn reddish-brown along their margins before becoming rose-red, finally leading to leaf tips and margins that wither and die. Roots also are short and bunched. Excessive calcium may tie-up other soil nutrients, especially potassium and magnesium, and less so phosphorus, manganese, iron, zinc, and boron.

Calcium is an immobile nutrient within plants. It does not move from older leaves to new ones and must be continuously supplied or young leaves will show deficiency symptoms early. Calcium is usually added in a liming program, by irrigation with high-calcium-containing water, or naturally through high pH soils. Commercial sources of calcium include calcitic and dolomitic limestone, gypsum, superphosphates, calcium nitrate, shells, slags, and water-treatment residue (Table 10–11). When lime is not needed, gypsum or some other calcium source should be considered.

Magnesium

Magnesium is essential for chlorophyll production in plants, as chlorophyll molecules contain approximately 7 percent magnesium (Table 10–1). Magnesium also is essential for many of the energy reactions, such as sugar formation. It acts as a carrier of phosphorus and regulates uptake of other plant nutrients. Deficiencies occur mostly in acidic sandy soils with low CEC or soils of extremely high pH, especially when clippings are continuously removed. Deficiencies can occur in soils with less than 40 pounds per acre of Mehlich-I extractable magnesium. Magnesium generally constitutes about 4 to 20 percent of a soil's CEC, compared with up to 80 percent for calcium and 5 percent for potassium. High calcium and potassium levels tend to reduce magnesium uptake.

Magnesium is a mobile element in the plant and is easily translocated from older (bottommost) to younger plant parts as needed. Symptoms of deficiency include a general loss of green color starting at the bottom (older) leaves. Interveinal chlorosis then occurs; veins remain green, and older leaf margins turn a blotchy cherry-red with a striped appearance of light yellow or white between the parallel veins. Necrosis eventually develops. Interveinal chlorosis can be caused by other deficiencies, but happens more so in neutral-to-alkaline soils. Therefore, a simple soil pH test can help narrow the potential deficiency problem to magnesium. Sources of magnesium include dolomitic limestone, sulfates of potash and magnesium, magnesium sulfate (Epsom salt), oxide, and chelates (Table 10–11). When lime is not needed, magnesium sulfate should be considered. A practical test to determine if magnesium deficiency is occurring on your turf is to apply one pound (454 g) of Epsom salts in three to four gallons of water over 1,000 square feet (12 to 16.3 L/m^2). If the turf greens up within 24 hours or so, magnesium deficiency should be suspected.

Sulfur

Sulfur is essential for the selective amino acids cystine, cysteine, and methionine (Table 10–1). It is used as a building block of proteins and chlorophyll, and also reduces diseases. The acidifying

TABLE 10-11 *Primary calcium and magnesium sources and characteristics used in turf fertilizers.*

Source	Nitrogen (N)	Phosphate (P$_2$O$_5$)	Potash (K$_2$O)	Comment
Calcium (Ca) carriers [formulas]				
Gypsum (calcium sulfate) [CaSO$_4$ · 2H$_2$O] -anhydrite	0	0	0	Contains 24 percent sulfur and 41 percent calcium oxide; has little effect on soil pH; used to displace soil sodium.
-hydrated	0	0	0	Contains 19 percent sulfur and 33 percent calcium oxide; has little effect on soil pH; used to displace soil sodium.
Calcium nitrate [Ca(NO$_3$)$_2$]	16	0	0	Very hygroscopic; contains 19 percent calcium and 1.5 percent magnesium; fast acting with high burn potential; nitrogen release is not temperature dependent; used on sodic soils to displace sodium.
Dolomitic limestone [CaMg(CO$_3$)$_2$]	0	0	0	Used to increase soil pH; contains 22 percent calcium and 11 percent magnesium; very slowly available; low salt hazard.
Superphosphate [Ca(H$_2$PO$_4$)$_2$ + CaSO$_4$]	0	20	0	Soluble phosphorus source often used in mixed fertilizers; contains calcium (18 to 21%) and sulfur (12%) as gypsum.
Triple (or treble) superphosphate [Ca(H$_2$PO$_4$)$_2$H$_2$O]	0	46	0	Concentrated phosphorus source also containing calcium (13%).
Calcitic limestone (calcium carbonate) (CaCO$_3$)	0	0	0	Contains 36 percent calcium; used to raise soil pH; very low salt hazard.
Magnesium (Mg) carriers				
Magnesium sulfate (or Epsom salt) [MgSO$_4$]	0	0	0	Contains 13 to 23 percent sulfur and 10 to 17 percent magnesium; water soluble; neutral salt with little effect on soil pH.
Potassium magnesium sulfate [K$_2$SO$_4$ · 2MgSO$_4$]	0	0	18–22	Contains 23 percent sulfur and 11 percent magnesium; water soluble.
Dolomitic limestone [CaMg(CO$_3$)$_2$]	0	0	0	Increases soil pH; contains 22 percent calcium and 11 percent magnesium; very slowly available; low salt hazard.

effect of sulfur also may increase the availability of essential elements such as iron, manganese, zinc, and phosphorus, as well as help reclaim sodic soil. Sulfur content in leaf tissue ranges from 0.15 to 0.50 percent of the dry weight. Most plants use comparable sulfur quantities as phosphorus and magnesium.

The sulfate anion (SO$_4^{-2}$) is the primary available form found in soil solution. Like nitrate, the sulfate ion can leach from soil. Deficiencies may occur when soil organic matter is low, grass clippings are removed, excessive watering occurs, and nonirrigated (no sulfate from water) and sandy soils predominate. Deficiency symptoms resemble nitrogen deficiency and include an initial light yellow-green color, with yellowing being most pronounced in younger leaves, since sulfur has limited mobility in plants. Older leaves become pale, then turn yellowish-green, in interveinal areas. Leaf tips are scorched along the margins. Roots tend to be longer than normal and stems become woody. Tissue testing is often necessary to distinguish between sulfur and nitrogen deficiencies. Grass grown in sandy soils has been shown to respond to sulfur applications.

Over 90 percent of available sulfur exists in the organic matter, which has an approximately 10:1 nitrogen-to-sulfur ratio. Deficiencies may occur when the nitrogen-to-sulfur ratio is greater than 20:1 or is at high soil pH (>7.0). Sulfur may be precipitated as calcium sulfate ($CaSO_4$ or gypsum), while at lower pH levels (<4.0), the sulfate anion may be adsorbed by aluminum and/or iron oxides. Turf clippings with a high nitrogen-to-sulfur ratio (≥ 20 to 1) decompose slowly and may slow thatch biodegradation. Microorganisms require sulfur to decompose plant residues.

Sulfur deficiencies have become more acute in recent years. This is probably due to less air pollution, a previously important source of sulfur. Sulfur also was supplied as a contaminant in some fertilizer sources, such as superphosphate. However, many new high-analysis fertilizers frequently do not contain appreciable sulfur. Less sulfur is used today in fungicides and insecticides, and its primary soil source, organic matter, may be reduced over time.

Sulfur sources include gypsum (16 to 24% S); elemental sulfur (up to 99% S); ferrous sulfate (19% S, 20% Fe); liquid form ammonium thiosulfate (26% S, 12% N); potassium magnesium sulfate (or K-Mag, 22% S, 22% K, 11% Mg); ammonium sulfate (24% S, 21% N); SCU (10 to 17% S, 32% N); and potassium sulfate (17% S, 50% K) (Table 10–12).

In poorly drained waterlogged soils where soil oxygen is exhausted, SO_4^{-2} and sulfur-containing organic matter can be reduced by sulfate-reducing bacteria to toxic hydrogen sulfide (H_2S). Excessive applications of elemental sulfur to golf greens also may encourage hydrogen sulfide buildup. In addition, insoluble sulfides may form by reacting with soil iron or manganese.

Sulfide Formation

$$Fe^{+2} \quad + \quad S^{-2} \quad \longrightarrow \quad FeS$$

| dissolved ferrous iron | sulfide | | iron sulfide (solid) |

TABLE 10–12 *Primary sulfur sources and characteristics used for turf fertilizer.*

Source	Sulfur (S)	Others	Comment
Sulfur (S) carriers [formulas]			
Gypsum (calcium sulfate) [$CaSO_4 \cdot 2H_2O$]	16 to 24	20 % calcium	Commonly used on sodic soil.
Elemental sulfur [S]	up to 99	—	Oxidizes to sulfuric acid and lowers pH; foliage burn potential; available as a granular or liquid; slow acting; requires microbial oxidation; eye irritant.
Epsom salts (magnesium sulfate) [$MgSO_4$]	13 to 23	10 to 17 % magnesium	Neutral salt with little acidifying effect.
Ferrous sulfate [$FeSO_4 \cdot 7H_2O$]	19	21 % iron	Water soluble; usually applied foliarly.
Ferrous ammonium sulfate [$(NH_4)_2 FeSO_4 \cdot 6H_2O$]	15	14 % iron + 7 % nitrogen	Water soluble; usually applied foliarly.
Ammonium thiosulfate [$(NH_4)_2S_2O_3 + H_2O$]	26	12 % nitrogen	Most widely used sulfur source in clear liquid fertilizers; foliage burn potential.
Potassium magnesium sulfate (or K-mag) [$K_2SO_4 \cdot 2MgSO_4$]	22	22 % potash + 11 % magnesium	Commonly used on alkaline soils.
Ammonium sulfate [$(NH_4)_2SO_4$]	24	21 % nitrogen	Water soluble; high acidifying potential.
Sulfur-coated urea (or SCU) [$CO(NH_2)_2 + S$]	10 to 20	32 % nitrogen	Slowly soluble.
Superphosphate [$Ca(H_2PO_4)_2 + CaSO_4$]	12	20 % P_2O_5 + 20 % calcium	Soluble phosphorus that contains gypsum (calcium sulfate); has little acidifying effect.
Potassium sulfate (or sulfate of potash) [K_2SO_4]	17	50 % potash	Used instead of potassium chloride to reduce foliage burn potential and to supply sulfur.

Turf soils containing toxic levels of hydrogen sulfide or iron sulfate are acidic and commonly form a "black layer" several inches below the soil surface. They typically are characterized by the distinct hydrogen sulfide (e.g., sewer or rotten egg) smell. Low soil oxygen also has reduced states of manganese, copper, and iron and result in gray and blue-colored subsoils. This often occurs in poorly drained, anaerobic soils.

MICRONUTRIENTS

Micronutrients, as previously discussed, are essential elements needed in relatively small (e.g., <50 ppm) amounts. These include boron (B), chlorine (Cl), copper (Cu), iron (Fe), manganese (Mn), molybdenum (Mo), and zinc (Zn). Many soils in the United States supply sufficient levels of micronutrients to the point they do not need to be added. In other cases, enough micronutrients are supplied in fertilizers as impurities. Deficiencies in micronutrients can become a problem, especially in areas with sandy and peat or muck soils; pockets of high pH and phosphorus-containing soil; and poor drainage or periods of extended, heavy rainfall (Chapter 3). For example, as soil pH is increased, iron changes from its available (soluble) ionic form to hydroxy ions, and finally to insoluble or unusable hydroxide, or oxide forms.

Insoluble Iron Hydroxide Formation at High Soil pH Levels

$$Fe^{+3} \xrightarrow[\uparrow pH]{OH^-} Fe(OH)^{+2} \xrightarrow[]{OH^-} Fe(OH)_2{}^+ \xrightarrow[\uparrow pH]{OH^-} Fe(OH)_3$$

Fe^{+3} (soluble in acidic soils) $\xrightarrow[\uparrow pH]{OH^-}$ Fe(OH)$^{+2}$ (soluble hydroxy ions in neutral soils) $\xrightarrow{OH^-}$ Fe(OH)$_2{}^+$ $\xrightarrow[\uparrow pH]{OH^-}$ Fe(OH)$_3$ iron hydroxide (insoluble in alkaline soils)

Soil pH probably influences plants most by affecting the availability of important nutrients. For example, at lower pH values (<5), aluminum, iron, and manganese are highly soluble and may be present in sufficient quantities to actually be toxic to plants. High levels of aluminum can also reduce plant uptake of phosphorus, calcium, magnesium, and iron. At higher pH values (>7.0), nutrients such as iron, manganese, copper, and zinc are less soluble and, therefore, relatively unavailable for plant uptake, although molybdenum (Mo) availability actually *increases* at high pH. The availability of phosphorus and boron also may be hindered by pH values greater than 7.0 (refer to Chapter 4). Marl may become mixed with surface organic soils or peat. These normally acidic organic soils, therefore, become neutral or even alkaline due to the liming action of marl. Many of the peat or muck sod farms in south Florida are on soils with marl intermixing. These soils are almost always low in magnesium as well as potassium, phosphorus, copper, and zinc.

A balance of micronutrients is particularly important because many plant functions require more than one element. Regular soil and tissue testing is the best preventative approach to solving many of the nutrient deficiency problems. Iron and manganese are two of the most common micronutrient deficiencies turf managers experience. However, **if excessive or indiscriminate amounts of micronutrients are applied or soil pH is excessively low, toxicity to the plant can occur.** This is most important with respect to the micronutrients manganese, zinc, copper, and boron in acid soils. An example involves growing turf on old vegetable or fruit production fields that were often sprayed with fungicides containing copper, zinc, and/or sulfur. Because of their relative immobility (with the exception of sulfur) in soils, residues have become toxic to the turfgrasses in some cases.

Micronutrient deficiency symptoms can easily be confused with pest occurrence or other stresses (Plate 10–4). Micronutrient deficiency problems, however, usually are more localized and appear as irregular spots or in circular patterns. General nutrient deficiency symptoms are listed in Table 10–13 while specific ones are outlined in Table 10–14 (Plate 10–5). Table 10–15 offers a starting guideline for spot treating of micronutrients when sprayed on the foliage to the drip point. Sometimes, high-surface-area glasslike beads, called **frits,** are used for boron, copper, zinc, and other micronutrient applications. As the fritted materials weather in soil, they slowly release their micronutrients, avoiding some of the precipitation and sorption problems that might otherwise occur, especially in alkaline soils.

Chelates

Chelates, chelating agents, or **sequestering agents** are cyclic structures of a normally nonsoluble metal atom and an organic component that, when held together, become soluble in water. The chelation process allows nutrients to move through the soil solution to the plants without being tied-up with

TABLE 10–13 *General plant nutrient deficiency symptoms.*

I. Leaf chlorosis evident	Deficient nutrient
1. Entire leaf is chlorotic	
(A) Only older leaves are chlorotic, then necrotic, then drop; growth noticeably slows; symptoms develop uniformly over the whole turfgrass area.	nitrogen
(B) Initially, young leaves turn a light yellow-green color; eventually, all leaves are affected; appears similar to nitrogen deficiency symptoms.	sulfur
2. Interveinal leaf chlorosis	
(A) Only older and recently mature leaves show symptoms; leaf veins remain green; older leaf margins turn cherry-red.	magnesium
(B) Only young leaves show interveinal chlorosis; leaves finally turn white; usually only patches of turf are affected.	iron
1. Tan or gray necrotic spots also develop in chlorotic areas; leaf veins remain dark-green to olive color.	manganese
2. Leaf tips remain green, then turn bluish, wither, and die.	copper
3. Young leaves are dwarfed, dark, and desiccated-looking; shortened internodes; plants appear rosette.	zinc

II. Leaf chlorosis not dominant	
1. Symptoms appear at plant base on older growth	
(A) All leaves appear dark green, then possible yellow; growth stunted; purple coloring in older (bottommost) leaves from increased anthocyanin development; leaf tips turn reddish.	phosphorous
(B) Margins and tips of older leaves chlorotic, then scorched; small, whitish spots may be scattered over older leaves; turf stand composed of thin, spindly individual plants.	potassium
2. Symptoms on new plant growth	
(A) Terminal buds die, resulting in dwarf (rosette) plants.	boron
(B) Margins of young leaves do not form; young leaves twisted or deformed; these do not, or only partially unfold; young leaf margins turn reddish brown; roots are short and bunched; leaf tips and margins eventually wither and die.	calcium

other soil chemicals. However, the activity of the metallic ion decreases in the aqueous solution. For example, in the absence of chelation and the addition of an inorganic ion such as ferric sulfate to calcareous soil, most of the iron becomes unavailable by the following reaction with hydroxide:

$$Fe^{+3} \ (\text{available}) \quad + \quad 3OH^- \quad \longleftrightarrow \quad FeOOH \ (\text{unavailable}) \quad + \quad H_2O$$

However, if the iron is chelated (from the Greek *chele*, meaning claw), it remains available for plant uptake as shown:

$$FeOOH \ (\text{unavailable}) \quad + \quad chelate^{-3} \quad + \quad H_2O \quad \longleftrightarrow \quad Fe \ chelate \ (\text{available}) \quad + \quad 3OH^-$$

Commercially available sequestered metallic ions are iron, copper, zinc, and manganese. Organic compounds that have the ability to chelate or sequester these metallic ions include ethylenediaminetetraacetic acid (EDTA); diethylenetriaminepentaacetic acid (DTPA); cyclohexanediaminetetraacetic acid (CDTA); and ethylenediaminedi (*o*-hydroxyphenylacetic acid) (EDDHA), citrate, and gluconate. These range from 5 to 14 percent iron. Their stability fluctuates with various soil pH levels. For example, EDDHA is best for soil pH from 4 to 9, EDTA at soil pH <6.3, and DTPA at soil pH <7.5.

Nonessential Elements

Sodium, aluminum, arsenic, and silicon are nonessential elements for turfgrass growth and development. These, in general, become toxic when levels are excessive and should not be applied in supplemental fertilizers.

TABLE 10–14 *Micronutrient forms, deficiencies, and sources for turf managers.*

Nutrient	Deficiency occurrence	Deficiency symptoms	Fertilizer sources
Iron (Fe)	Iron levels in soils often are sufficient; however, soil conditions often render them unavailable. Deficiency occurs with excessive soil pH (>7.0), calcium, zinc, manganese, phosphorus, copper, and bicarbonates (HCO_3) levels in irrigation water; poor rooting, poor soil drainage, and cold soils also are associated with deficiency. At low soil pH, phosphorus can combine with iron to form insoluble (unavailable) iron phosphate while at high pH, excessive phosphorus uptake by plants may inactivate absorbed iron. For each increase in pH, there is a 100-fold decrease in soluble Fe^{+2}. A plant tissue ratio of phosphorus-to-iron at 29:1 also provides healthy turf while a phosphorus-to-iron ratio of 40:1 often expresses iron deficiency. An iron-to-manganese ratio of 2:1 in plant tissue also has been suggested. Heavy metals and/or bicarbonates from effluent water or sewage sludge as a soil amendment may also compete with iron for plant uptake. Deficiency symptoms are most severe during warm days/cool nights (e.g., early spring and fall) when root growth is insufficient to support shoot growth.	Chlorosis resembling nitrogen deficiency except iron chlorosis is interveinal (e.g., between leaf veins) and first occurs in the youngest leaves since iron is immobile within plants. Older leaves are affected later. Nitrogen deficiency causes the entire leaf, including veins, to simultaneously yellow. Iron-deficient leaves finally turn white. Iron chlorosis tends to be in random scattered spots, creating a mottled appearance, and appears more severe when closely mowed. Nitrogen deficiency develops uniformly over a large area and appears unaffected by mowing. Management practices to reduce deficiency are meant to lower the soil pH, improve drainage, reduce phosphorus fertilization, and use one of the listed foliar sprays. Excessive iron levels can induce manganese deficiency and leaf blackening. Anaerobic, acidic, poorly drained soils can produce toxicity levels of soluble iron.	**Ferrous sulfate** [$FeSO_4 \cdot 7H_2O$]: (19 to 21% Fe and 19% S); usually foliarly applied; low acidifying effect; water soluble. **Ferrous ammonium sulfate** [$FeSO_4 \cdot (NH_4)_2SO_4$]: (5 to 14% Fe, 16% S, and 7% N); usually foliarly applied; also provides some nitrogen; medium acidifying effect; water soluble. **Chelated iron** [Fe salts of -EDTA, -HEDTA, -EDDHA, or -DTPA]: (5 to 14% Fe); longer greening effect than the other iron sources; low acidifying effect. **Iron frits**: (14% Fe).
Zinc (Zn)	Alkaline soils decrease solubility and availability, as does excessive soil Cu^{+2}, Fe^{+2}, and Mn^{+2} and excessive soil moisture, nitrogen, and phosphates. Zinc solubility increases 100-fold for each decreased pH unit. Above pH 7.7, zinc becomes $Zn(OH)^+$. Lower light intensities reduce root uptake. Sands also are likely to have lower zinc levels than clays. Some mine spoils and municipal wastes may contain high levels of zinc.	Interveinal chlorosis in both younger and some older leaves; mottled-chlorotic leaves, rolled and thin leaf blades; stunted, shortened internode growth; dark, desiccated-looking leaves (starting with the youngest ones); leaves finally turn white in appearance. Excessive zinc may inhibit root and rhizome development and induce iron and magnesium deficiencies.	**Zinc sulfate** [$ZnSO_4 \cdot H_2O$]: (35% Zn and 12% S); water soluble, foliarly applied. **Zinc chelate** [ZnEDTA]: (9 to 14% Zn); foliarly applied. **Zinc oxide** [ZnO]: (78% Zn); water soluble, foliarly applied. **Zinc frits**: (4 to 7% Zn).
Manganese (Mn)	Deficiencies occur in sand, peat, and muck soils (insoluble complexes are formed), alkaline soils high in calcium (for each increase in pH, there is a 100-fold decrease in soluble Mn^{+2}); at low temperatures; and in poor drainage. Excess iron, copper, zinc, potassium, and sodium in low cation exchange capacity soils can reduce manganese adsorption. An iron-to-manganese ratio in leaf tissue should be at least 2:1. Adjusting soil pH to below 7.0 usually reduces manganese deficiencies.	Yellowing (chlorosis) between veins (interveinal) of the youngest leaves, with veins remaining dark-green to olive-green in color since manganese is an immobile element within the plant; small, distinct necrotic leaf spots develop on older leaves; leaf tips may turn grey to white, droop, and wither. On closely mowed turf, mottled or blotchy appearance develops, with little or no response to nitrogen occurring. Toxicity can occur with anaerobic soils with pH <4.8. Excessive manganese levels can induce iron, calcium, or magnesium deficiencies.	**Manganese sulfate** [$MnSO_4 \cdot H_2O$]: (26 to 28% Mn and 13%S); foliarly applied. **Manganese oxide** [MnO]: (33 to 77% Mn). **Mancozeb fungicides**; (16% Mn and 2% Zn). **Manganese chelates** :(5 to 12% Mn). **Tecmangam**: (20% Mn). **Manganese frits**: (3 to 6% Mn).

Element	Description	Sources
Copper (Cu)	Deficiency mostly occurs in sand, peat, muck, and high organic soils due to tight binding properties of these for copper. Excess iron, nitrogen, phosphorus, and zinc, highly leached soils, and high soil pH encourage deficiency. Toxic levels can result from excess sewage sludge applications, use of poultry manures, copper sulfate, and copper-containing pesticides such as Bordeau mixture. Liming to pH 7.0 is often the simplest means of overcoming copper phytotoxicity. Reducing nitrogen fertilization may also help.	Deficiencies are rare. Deficiency symptoms include yellowing and chlorosis of younger leaf margins; leaf tips initially turn bluish, wither, and droop, eventually turn yellow, and die; youngest leaves become light-green, and necrotic; plant dwarfing with inward rolling of leaves that develop a blue-green appearance; symptoms progress from the leaf tips to the base of the plant. Toxicity symptoms of excessive levels include reduced shoot vigor, poorly developed and discolored root systems, and leaf chlorosis resembling iron deficiency. Excessive copper levels suppress uptake of iron, manganese, zinc, and molybdenum.	**Copper sulfate** [$CuSO_4 \cdot 5H_2O$]: (13 to 53% Cu and 13% S); foliarly or soil applied. **Copper oxide** [CuO] (40% Cu); foliarly or soil applied. **Copper chelates** [$CuEDTA$]: (9 to 13% Cu); foliarly applied.
Boron (B)	Organic matter is the principal source of boron; availability increases with decreasing soil pH; deficiencies are most common in high (76.5) pH, leached, or very dry, sandy soils. Calcium also decreases translocation of boron in plants. Liming acidic soils frequently causes a boron deficiency. Excessive levels (>6ppm) may occur with high boron containing irrigation water, arid and semi-arid soils, and some composts.	Thickening, curling, and chlorotic leaves develop on dwarf (rosette) plants; chlorotic streaks develop in the interveinal areas. Leaf tips turn pale green. Plants develop a "bronze" tint. Boron is immobile within the plant; symptoms, therefore, first appear in meristematic tissues and young leaves. Deficiencies are infrequent in turf.	**Borax** [$Na_2B_4O_7 \cdot 10H_2O$]: (11% B and 9% Na). **Boric acid** [H_3BO_3]: 17% B. **Fertilizer borate** [sodium tetraborate, $Na_2B_4O_7 \cdot 5H_2O$, 14 to 21% B; sodium pentaborate, $Na_2B_{10}O_{16} \cdot 5H_2O$, 18% B] **Solubor:** (20% soluble B).
Molybdenum (Mo)	Availability increases with increasing soil pH; deficiencies are most common in acid sands or highly weathered soils; excess copper, iron, manganese, or sulfate may reduce Molybdenum utilization by plants. Deficiencies often occur in ironstone soils of Australia, New Zealand, and Holland.	Resembles mild nitrogen deficiency with pale yellow-green stunted plants; mottled yellowing of interveinal areas then appear in older leaves. Deficiencies are rare. Lime acidifies soils.	**Ammonium molybdate** [$(NH_4)_2MoO_4$]: (54% Mo); liquid. **Sodium molybdate** [$Na_2MoO_4 \cdot H_2O$]: (40% Mo). **Molybdenum trioxide** [MoO_3]: (66% Mo). **Molybdic oxide:** (47% Mo).
Chlorine (Cl)	Less available in alkaline soils, or soils high in NO_3^- and SO_4^{-2}; very mobile in acid-to-neutral soils. Toxic levels reduce water availability to plants; cause premature leaf yellowing, leaf tip, and margin burning; and leaf bronzing and abscission.	Chlorosis of younger leaves and wilting of plants; not mobile within plants and accumulates in older parts. Deficiencies are rare. Chlorine is most commonly applied in large quantities along with the potassium source in fertilizers.	**Ammonium chloride** [NH_4CL]: (66% Cl, 25% N); acid-forming fertilizer. **Calcium chloride** [$CaCl_2$]: (65% Cl). **Magnesium chloride** [$MgCl_2$]: (74% Cl). **Potassium chloride:** [KCl]: (47% Cl, 60% K). **Sodium chloride** [$NaCl$]: (60% Cl, 40% Na).

TABLE 10–15 *Solution used to spot treat for micronutrient deficiencies.*

Deficient micronutrient	Fertilizer source	Rate fluid ounce/gallon/ 1,000 square feet (ml/L)	Rate pound element/ 1,000 square feet (kg element/ha)
Iron	iron sulfate (20% Fe)	2(16)	0.025 (1.2)
Manganese	manganese sulfate (27% Mn)	0.75(6)	0.025 (1.2)
Zinc	zinc sulfate (35% Zn)	0.5(4)	0.010 (0.5)
Copper	copper sulfate (25% Cu)	0.2(1.6)	0.003 (0.15)
Boron	boric acid (17% B)	0.2(1.6)	0.002 (0.05)
Molybdenum	sodium molybdate (47% Mo)	0.04 (0.3)	0.001 (0.05)

LIQUID FERTILIZATION

Foliar liquid fertilization (commonly referred to as foliar feeding) involves the use of a soluble nutrient form for plants. This concept is over 100 years old and provides quicker utilization of nutrients. It also permits correction of deficiencies in less time than soil treatments. However, the response is often temporary. Due to the small amounts required, micronutrient applications have traditionally been the most prominent use of foliar sprays. Difficulties in applying sufficient amounts of macronutrients such as nitrogen, phosphorus, and potassium without leaf burn also has been a problem. Other advantages and disadvantages of foliar liquid fertilization include:

Advantages

1. It has no segregation of particles, as is common with granulars.
2. It provides nutrients directly to plants and is not influenced by soil properties.
3. It contains water-soluble forms of nutrients, which quickly correct plant nutrient deficiencies.
4. Co-application with pesticides is possible.
5. It is generally easier to handle and quicker to apply, with a greater flexibility in timing and rate use.
6. It utilizes a lower cost of energy, labor, and equipment.

Disadvantages

1. The number of bags cannot be counted, requiring the operator and meter to be trusted.
2. Some solutions may salt-out at lower temperatures, especially when used with water high in calcium, magnesium, and bicarbonate.
3. Problems with sufficient application occur without severe leaf burn.
4. Frequent applications at low rates may be necessary because turf response is temporary and low rates prevent leaf burn.
5. Fertilizer distribution depends on water-distribution patterns.
6. Ammonium nitrogen sources may volatilize.

Foliar feeding involves using low fertilizer rates (e.g., 1/8 lb N or Fe per 1,000 sq.ft., 0.6 kg/100 m^2) at low spray volumes (e.g., 1/2 gal per 1,000 sq.ft., 2 L/100 m^2). Low nutrient and spray volumes are used to minimize costs and to supplement the normal fertilization program with nutrients absorbed directly by turfgrass leaves. Urea is generally the most effective nitrogen form used for foliar application. However, to reduce burn, its use should be limited to low light intensities and mild (<85°F, 29°C) temperatures.

The fertilizer is washed off the leaves at higher spray volumes (e.g., 3 to 5 gal per 1,000 sq.ft., 12 to 20 L/m^2), resulting in increased root absorption. This is called **liquid fertilization.** With liquid fertilization, fertilizers and pesticides often are applied together.

Fertilizer application through an irrigation system is termed **fertigation**. Other products, such as certain pesticides, also can be applied through an irrigation system (termed **chemigation**). This ideally combines the two operations to make more efficient use of resources and labor. Frequent light ap-

FIGURE 10–6 This in-line fertigation system consists of a storage tank, filter, back-flow preventer, and injection pump and regulator.

plications (e.g., **spoon feeding**) of fertilizer are metered into irrigation lines and distributed along with irrigation water through sprinkler heads (Figure 10–6). Nitrogen and sulfur are the primary elements applied by this method, while potassium and highly soluble forms of phosphorus, gypsum, iron, and zinc are also used. Fertigation helps maintain a more even color and growth, minimizes color surges that occur after heavy granular applications, and reduces labor costs associated with required frequent applications when using granular forms. Fertigation is especially beneficial on sandy soils where nutrient leaching can occur since heavy amounts of fertilizer applications are avoided.

Design Consideration

Fertigation systems can vary widely in cost and complexity but generally are composed of a large storage tank, a mixing tank, a blending or injection system, and a proper backflow-preventer. The irrigation pump house should be big—at least 24 by 24 feet (7.2 × 7.2 m)—to house the large (e.g., 1,500 gallon, 5,678 L) fertilizer tank and room for service. A containment wall should surround the pump house in case of chemical leaks. A flow meter is used to ensure the ratio of chemical to water stays proportional. If water pressure drops below a predetermined threshold, the injection system can shut off to prevent overfertilization. The injection methods include a venturi system or a metering pump. Systems should have a vacuum break to allow air into the system and to aid in drainage if leaks occur. Backflow values are also needed to prevent backwards tank contamination. In addition, to prevent impurities from contaminating the transfer pump, filters should be installed.

Depending on the specific needs, the system should be kept as simple as possible. Complicated systems can be overwhelming and confusing, increasing the chance of problems. In addition, shop for a well-established product that offers after-sale support and supplies.

Uniform coverage of irrigation systems are critical to provide even turf color and growth. Normally, fertigation systems are separated to specific parts of the course, such as just tees, greens, fairways, and so on, as these sites require varying amounts of fertilizer. A **design uniformity** (or **coefficient of uniformity**) provides a coverage test to determine an irrigation system's efficiency. A design uniformity of 0.80 (or higher) helps provide even distribution. If good head-to-head coverage is not available, green circular patterns ("doughnuts") may develop during drought. Properly designed irrigation systems and skilled operators will minimize these.

Salt buildup on soil surfaces and shallow turf rooting are potential concerns also associated with light, frequent fertigation applications. However, due to the extreme dilutions, little plant damage typically occurs. The use of nitrate solution containing free ammonia or anhydrous ammonia fertilizer materials with water high in calcium, magnesium, and bicarbonates also may result in precipitant (lime) formation. This lime can cause plant scalding and plugging of irrigation equipment and soil pores. Sulfuric acid or long-chain linear polyphosphate water conditioners, such as rose-stone (Calgon), are often added before fertilizer injection to prevent these precipitates from forming.

Fluid Fertilizers

Many problems associated with fertigation are related to the quality of fertilizers being used. Different blended fertilizer materials may not remain mixed in solution. The fertilizer can precipitate, settling to the bottom of the tank to form a messy sludge which then causes incorrect fertilization rates from being applied.

A large part of this problem involves phosphorous fertilizers and their solubility. Phosphorous fertilizers can vary in solubility from 30 percent in some highly ammoniated superphosphates to almost 100 percent in diammonium or monoammonium phosphate, while most potassium and inorganic nitrogen fertilizers are almost 100 percent soluble. Granular phosphorus fertilizers, therefore, should supplement fertigation fertilizer use. Phosphorus can also react with certain fertilizers, such as magnesium sulfate and calcium sulfate, to form insoluble precipitates. Storage tanks then must be cleaned to prevent the irrigation system from clogging. Separate tanks for reactive materials such as phosphorus help eliminate this problem.

Three main categories of fluid fertilizers include:

1. **Clear liquid**—These are true solutions, free of solids, clear enough to see through, and are limited to low analyses since salting-out will occur at low temperatures when fertilizer grades are high.
2. **Suspension fertilizer**—Higher concentration mixtures of liquids and finely divided solids exist when the solids do not settle rapidly and can be redispersed readily by agitation to give a uniform mixture. Certain types of clays are usually added at 1 to 2 percent as suspending agents. Suspension fertilizer's advantage over clear liquid are: (a) higher analysis grades can be produced, (b) costs are lower because fewer pure products can be used, (c) larger quantities of micronutrients can be suspended, and (d) powdered forms of pesticides can normally be suspended and used.
3. **Slurry fertilizers**—Mixtures of liquids and finely divided solids exist that settle rapidly in the absence of agitation and form a firm layer in the bottom of the tank. This layer is difficult to resuspend and may cause line or emitter plugging.

Manufacturing of Liquid Fertilizers

In the United States, >50 percent of all fluid-mixed fertilizers are clear liquid solutions. Mixtures applied in liquid form total about 30 million tons, with the typical analysis being approximately 9 percent nitrogen, 3.9 percent phosphorus, and 7.5 percent potassium.

There are two general methods of manufacturing liquid-mixed fertilizers. The simplest method is known as the batch or suspension process, and simply consists of dissolving the correct proportions of the solid plant-food carriers, such as ammonium phosphates, urea, or potassium chloride, in water to produce the desired grade of final product. The weighed constituents are dissolved in the proper amount of water with a suitable mixing device. The solution may be heated to aid in the dissolving process since many dry fertilizer products absorb heat from water when mixed. The relatively higher cost of raw materials generally limits this to small operations or to companies engaged in manufacturing specialty grades. Solution grade forms of these products are used.

The second, and most widely used, method is based on the neutralization of phosphoric acid with ammonia to produce ammonium polyphosphates. Anhydrous or aqueous ammonia, or ammonia-ammonium nitrate or ammonia-urea type nitrogen solutions, are reacted with phosphoric acid solutions followed by the addition of solid sources of nitrogen and/or potash. Potassium chloride is the usual source of potash. Polyphosphates also can sequester certain micronutrients, thereby allowing these to be added in fluid fertilizer. Aqueous ammonia also is reacted with sulfate and elemental sulfur to form 12-0-0-26S ammonium thiosulfate. It can be used in a wide variety of N-P-K-S formulations and is essentially noncorrosive. It should, however, not come in contact with tin, copper, or brass. The density of most common liquid mixtures will approximate 10 pounds per gallon.

Soluble Sources

The liquid application form in foliar feeding enters plants directly by penetrating leaf cuticles (via micropores) or stomata, and then enters the cells. This method provides quicker utilization of nutrients than through soil treatment. Research also has shown the physical form of the nutrient, dry or fluid, has no measurable effect on its agronomic properties, such as total amount of plant growth. Quickly available nitrogen sources denote rapid or quick availability of nitrogen to the turfgrass plant after fertilizer application. These quickly available nitrogen sources have a high potential for foliar burn from their salt-like characteristics dissolving readily in water to form cations (positive ions) and anions (negative ions). These ions are hydrophilic (water-loving) and, when in direct contact with the leaf surface, they quickly absorb moisture from the plant, resulting in a brown burn appearance. The more free cations and anions in soil solution or on the plant surface, the greater the potential for fertilizer burn. This is a problem when quickly available liquid nitrogen forms, generally in excess of one pound of nitrogen per 1,000 square feet (4.9 kg N/100 m^2), are used. Most recommendations call for foliar fertilization to occur during periods of low temperature and relatively high humidity during early morning or late evening hours. New liquid fertilizer technology will hopefully minimize some of these problems.

Because of its water solubility, urea is the most widely used fertilizer material and is often mixed with ammonium nitrate or potassium nitrate (Table 10–16). Liquid urea is characterized by a quick response in terms of turf color and a medium-to-high burn potential. Low rates, applied more frequently, are required to promote even turf growth and color and to minimize burn potential when using liquid urea. A fine, powder form of urea formaldehyde (*Powder Blue*) also can be used for liquid fertilization. Powder Blue is a 38-0-0 with its nitrogen divided as 27 percent insoluble and 13 percent soluble. Other quickly available liquid nitrogen carriers include ammonium sulfate, ammonium polyphosphate, and ammonium thiosulfate.

TABLE 10–16 *Popular quickly-available liquid nitrogen forms.*

Fertilizer source	Nitrogen	Phosphorus percentage	Potassium	Water insoluble nitrogen (WIN)	Other nutrients	Examples
Solutions						
Methylol urea + urea (formaldehyde + urea)	30	0	0	0	–	RESI-GROW GP-4340; GR-4341 (30-0-2), and GR-4318; FLUF; Form-U-Sol; Homogesol-27; Slo-Release; Flormolene; CoRoN (28-0-0); Nitro-26
Triazones + urea (formaldehyde + ammonia + urea)	28	0	0	0	–	N-Sure; Trisert; Formolene-Plus
Ammonium polyphosphate	10	34	0	0	–	–
Ammonium thiosulfate	12	0	0	0	26% S	–
Ammonium nitrate	20	0	0	0	–	–
Aqueous (or Aqua) ammonia	23	0	0	0	–	–
Urea-ammonium nitrate solution	32	0	0	0	–	–
Calcium ammonium nitrate	17	0	0	0	9% Ca	–
Urea solution	23	0	0	0	–	–
Urea sulfuric acid	10 to 28	0	0	0	9 to 18% S	–
Suspensions						
Methylene ureas	18	0	0	5	–	–
Sprayable powders						
Methylene ureas	40	0	0	12 to 14	–	Triaform; Nutralene; Scotts MU40; METH-EX40; Chip
Ureaform (urea formaldehyde)	38	0	0	25	–	Nitroform; Powder Blue;
Isobutylidene urea (IBDU)	31	0	0	21	–	Slo-Release; IBDU

The remaining soluble nitrogen sources are mixtures of urea and water-soluble short-chain methylene ureas. Nitrogen release from these methylene urea is by rapid microbial degradation. This provides a quick plant response, and has less potential for foliar fertilizer burn. These also are sometimes called controlled-release nitrogen forms.

An aqueous nitrogen solution that contains more than half of its nitrogen as monomethylol urea, with the remaining being free urea and ammonia, is marketed as *Formolene*. Formolene is formulated as a 30-0-2 and contains 3.25 pounds nitrogen per gallon. This is basically a soluble nitrogen source but has a lower salt index than urea. Other quick-release urea and methylene urea nitrogen carriers include *Form-U-Sol* and *Nitro-26*. Form-U-Sol contains 28 percent nitrogen in which 67 percent is urea and 33 percent is methylol urea. Nitro-26 contains 26 percent nitrogen with 30 percent urea and 70 percent methylol urea.

Slow-Release Sources

Several new materials that have better slow-release characteristics are now commercially available. These allow heavier rates to be applied less frequently without undesirable surges in growth or color and minimize turf foliar burn potential. To be classified as a slow-release source, this fact must be identified on the label and comprise at least 15 percent of the total nitrogen.

CoRoN

CoRoN is an aqueous solution of a number (approximately 70 percent) of polymethylene ureas and amine-modified polymethylene ureas. CoRoN consists primarily of a straight chain, amine-modified polymethylene urea containing two to four urea units amounting to about 30 percent of the contained nitrogen. Small amounts of methylene diurea and dimethylene triurea are also present while cyclic urea formaldehyde products, such as triazones, are not. No free ammonia and little methylol urea are included as a part of CoRoN. CoRoN contains a small amount of sodium bicarbonate to protect its near-neutral pH and sufficient water to safely maintain its 28-0-0 formulation in water. Its nitrogen release is dependent upon microbial action, but due to the relatively high urea content, it has been shown to be effective in winter months. It tends not to last as long as a dry slow-release nitrogen source, but its initial green-up is quicker. GP4340 and GP4341 are additional liquid methylol urea solutions.

N-Sure

N-Sure is a liquid nitrogen fertilizer containing triazones combined with urea in a ratio of 0.48:1.0. N-Sure may contain methylene diurea and methylol urea amounting to 6 percent by weight. Triazones are stable heterocyclic nitrogen-carbon ring compounds usually made under low pH conditions from urea, formaldehyde, and ammonia. N-Sure contains 30 percent nitrogen and its nitrogen release rate is microbial dependent. It has been demonstrated to be effective during cool temperatures, but its response does not last as long as a solid slow-release nitrogen source. Trisert and Formolene-Plus are other triazone and urea liquid products.

FLUF

FLUF (flowable liquid urea formaldehyde) is another slow-release nitrogen solution source. It consists of cold water soluble free urea and methylene diurea, cold water insoluble-hot water soluble polymethylene ureas, and small amounts of hot water insoluble polymethylene ureas. Several formulations are available including 10-0-10, 16-2-4, and 18-0-0. Slo-Release is another liquid UF suspension source.

Application

A simple irrigation delivery system consists of fiberglass or plastic storage with a visual volume gauge, a filter, and an adjustable corrosive-resistant pump to inject fertilizer into the main irrigation line. Several types of pumps are available to inject the liquid fertilizer into the irrigation system and include centrifugal pumps, positive displacement pumps, pressure differential methods, and the venturi or siphon system (Table 10–17). If a centrifugal pump is used for irrigation, the injector pump can be eliminated by drawing fertilizer into the suction side of the irrigation pump, so with each irrigation some fertilizer is applied (termed a **venturi** or **siphon system**). If the injection pump supplies fertilizer at a constant rate, it is important the irrigation system be well-

TABLE 10-17 *Comparison of chemical injection methods for fertigation or chemigation (modified from Haman et al., 1998).*

Pump type	Injector	Advantages	Disadvantages
Centrifugal pumps	Centrifugal pump injector	Low cost; can be adjusted while running.	Calibration depends on system pressure.
Positive displacement pumps:			
Reciprocating pumps	Piston pumps	High precision; linear calibration; very high pressure; calibration independent of pressure.	High cost; may need to stop to calibrate; noncontinuous chemical flow.
	Diaphragm pumps	Adjust calibration while injecting; high chemical resistance.	Nonlinear calibration; calibration depends on system pressure; medium to high cost; noncontinuous chemical flow.
	Piston/diaphragm	High precision; linear calibration; high chemical resistance; very high pressure; calibration independent of pressure.	High cost; may need to stop to adjust calibration.
Rotary pumps	Gear pumps Lobe pumps	Injection rate can be adjusted while running.	Fluid cannot be abrasive; injection rate is dependent on system pressure; in lobe pumps, continuity of chemical flow depends on number of lobes.
Miscellaneous	Peristaltic pumps	High chemical resistance; major adjustment can be performed when changing tubing size; injection rate can be adjusted when running.	Short tube life expectancy; injection rate dependent on system pressure; low to medium injection pressure.
Pressure differential methods	Suction line port	Very low cost; injection rate can be adjusted while running.	Permitted only for surface water source and injection of fertilizer; injection rate depends on main pump operation.
Discharge line	Proportional mixers	Low to medium cost; calibrate while operating; injection rates accurately controlled.	Pressure differential required; volume to be injected is limited by the size of the injector; frequent refills required.
	Pressurized mixing tanks	Medium cost; ease of operation; total chemical volume accurately controlled.	Pressure differential required; variable chemical concentration; cannot be calibrated for constant injection rate.
Venturi injectors	Venturi	Low cost; water powered; simple to use; calibrate while operating; no moving parts.	Pressure drop created in the system; calibration depends on chemical level in tank.
Combination methods	Proportional mixers/venturi	Greater precision than proportional mixer alone.	Higher cost than proportional mixer or venturi alone.

balanced, making each zone cover approximately the same amount of land area so the fertilization rate is also constant. The exception would be where it is desirable to fertilize a certain area at a heavier rate. Proportioning systems have been developed that keep a constant ratio between the volume of liquid fertilizer injected and the actual volume of irrigation water applied. Metering systems use electrical and mechanical pumps to deliver exact amounts of chemicals according to precise time intervals and irrespective of water flow rates. Flow rates, however, must be constant to maintain the accuracy of feed. If dry fertilizers are used, mixing or agitation devices also are needed to predissolve them before injection into the lines.

To operate the system, the amount of nitrogen and other nutrients needed per unit of turf area per unit of time (e.g., lbs N per 1,000 sq.ft., or per acre applied per month) must be determined. Then, by knowing the concentration of the fertilizer solution, the rate at which the injection pump must operate can be determined. This rate can be adjusted if necessary to compensate for unusually high or low amounts of rainfall that affect the irrigation need. The visual gauge on the fertilizer tank helps determine how well the fertilization schedule is being maintained, since the time period needed to empty the tank (e.g., a week, a month, etc.) can be determined in advance. Heavy-use areas such as tees and greens often require greater nitrogen rates than fairways. Various methods can be devised for increasing the rate of fertilizer applied by the irrigation systems on these areas. Such complications, however, may cause more excessive work and problems. In most cases, it seems best to use fertigation to supply a uniform rate of nitrogen to the entire golf course with traditional granular means to augment fertilization on the relatively small, heavy-use green and tee areas.

The solubility of liquid fertilizer sources is highly temperature dependent. Variations in temperature may cause solution fertilizers to salt out when storing. Fertigation fertilizers should be formulated with the time of year and temperature indicated when purchased. Using chelated micronutrients helps the solubility of solutions. Surfactants that aid in water utilization and nutrient efficiency also are added directly to the fertilizer mixture. A compatibility test can also be performed in jars before adding components in a fertigation tank to help indicate the potential of precipitation formation with different materials. The appropriate surfactant and temperatures at the time of tank-mixing should be used during the compatibility test to better indicate if problems may occur.

Insoluble precipitate salts of calcium and magnesium (e.g., calcite) may form when ammonium nitrogen (NH_3) is injected into irrigation water high in Ca^{+2}, Mg^{+2}, and bicarbonate (HCO_3^-).

Step 1: $NH_3 + H_2O \rightarrow NH_4OH$

Step 2: $2NH_4OH + Ca(HCO_3)_2$ or $Mg(HCO_3)_2 \rightarrow CaCO_3\downarrow$ or $MgCO_3 \downarrow + (NH_4)_2CO_3 + 2H_2O$

The insoluble calcium and magnesium carbonate salts may clog the irrigation system. Insoluble calcium and magnesium phosphates (e.g., dicalcium phosphate or dimagnesium phosphate) also may form if phosphorus fertilizers are used in high calcium- and magnesium-containing irrigation water. The removal of calcium and magnesium ions from the irrigation water also raises the sodium adsorption ratio (SAR) and the hazard of increased exchangeable sodium percentage (ESP). Acid treatment with sulfuric acid can be used to overcome this.

The pH of the various mixtures of liquid fertilization materials should also be regulated. If the pH is too low, it can be corrosive to equipment. If too high, micronutrients may become insoluble. A near neutral pH of 6.5 to 7.0 is desired for fertigation purposes.

Macronutrient Applications

Nitrogen

Ammonia nitrogen forms applied directly to the soil surface may be subject to volatilization, especially as temperatures rise. Urea and nitrate forms also are prone to leaching if heavy water amounts are applied. Younger plants (<1 month old) often respond better to ammonium sources since it is readily available to them. Young plants often have not developed the enzymes necessary to convert nitrate to ammonium. However, on older plants, a balance of nitrate and ammonium or urea nutrition is usually suggested.

Phosphorus

When applied as fertigation, phosphorus movement into the rootzone profile may be limited due to low phosphorus solubility. Phosphorus also may form clogging precipitates when mixed with water high in calcium and magnesium. To overcome this precipitant (lime) formation, phosphoric acid is used. To keep the pH of the fertigated water low, urea sulfuric acid may be added, although this can damage metal hardware and plant roots, and increase the toxicity of certain micronutrients. It is suggested granular phosphorus sources be used in conjunction with fertigation to ensure adequate soil-available phosphorus levels.

Potassium

Soluble potassium sources such as potassium chloride, potassium nitrate, and potassium sulfate normally can be used in irrigation water with minimum problems.

Micronutrient Application

Foliar application of micronutrients, such as iron, is commonly employed with foliar fertilization. These can be predissolved and metered into irrigation water. All micronutrients are metals except boron and chloride, and the availability of most micronutrients tends to decline, except molybdenum, with increasing soil pH. Chloride is unaffected by soil pH. Micronutrient fertilizers may be characterized generally as being more expensive than macronutrient materials. Application rates of micronutrients, however, usually are low enough so foliar applications are feasible. One potential problem when zinc, iron, manganese, and copper are added to clear liquid fertilizers is precipitation often occurs as a reaction with phosphates. Chelates or sulfate sources of the metal micronutrients can be mixed with liquids without causing precipitation.

Nitrogen also is added to many micronutrient products to stabilize the solution. Micronutrient solutions can retain elements at higher temperatures and become supersaturated. Upon cooling, micronutrients in the solution may precipitate out, forming insoluble compounds. Urea has been shown to help prevent precipitation and it also gives the turf a small color boost.

Regulations

Before using fertigation, a host of regulatory issues need to be addressed. These include the installation of costly backflow preventers and assurance that certain nutrients such as nitrates and phosphates do not escape the intended treated areas and possibly contaminate water supplies. Work with your local regulatory agency and fertigation manufacturer to address these and other issues associated with fertigation.

Note: Available commercial fertilizer sources constantly change in the marketplace as new formulations and delivery systems evolve. The commercial products, manufacturers, and distributors listed are not exclusive but are included for example only and do not constitute a warranty or guarantee.

CHAPTER 11

Developing Turf Fertilizer Programs

INTRODUCTION

Turfgrasses require regular fertilization to promote recovery from traffic, provide a pleasing green color, and replace nutrients lost during clipping removal. Furthermore, many courses are located in areas with extended growing seasons, high annual rainfall, and predominantly sandy soils that increase nutrient use and the need for a well-planned fertilization program.

For these and other reasons, no one single fertilization schedule or program will sufficiently meet the needs of every golf course or even every area on a golf course. In addition, excessive quality expectations and playing standards are often demanded by professional players. Club members, in turn, place much undue pressure on their superintendents to duplicate conditions viewed on television. This often results in lush, unhealthy plant growth that can drive up maintenance costs and potentially waste natural resources.

Furthermore, soils used to construct golf courses vary widely by geographic location and within the few hundred acres of a particular golf course site. Heavy clay soils in the Southeastern United States, for example, tend to hold water and nutrients adequately but have low pH levels. Sandy Coastal Plain soils tend to hold water and nutrients poorly or may have high natural organic matter. Midwestern soils and calcareous sands have naturally high pH values and, as a result, micronutrient management becomes very important. Therefore, a turf manager should be familiar with soils prior to developing a fertilizer program.

Questions to consider when developing a turfgrass fertility program include:

1. What are the aesthetic quality expectations of the area being maintained?
2. What are the playing requirements and recovery needs of this area?
3. What is the current nutritional status of the soil and plant?
4. What fertilizer source will best meet the aforementioned goals?
5. What rate of this fertilizer should be used?
6. What timing and frequency will provide these results?

GENERAL NUTRITIONAL REQUIREMENTS

Timing

Proper fertilization, along with providing healthy disease- and stress-free turf, is important for providing an acceptable playing surface. As a rule, excessive fertilization with nitrogen will not only be agronomically detrimental to overall turfgrass health, but will increase the mowing requirements and can drastically slow ball roll, drawing complaints from players about playing conditions. Exceptions, such as certain high-traffic greens and tees (e.g., par-3) or newly constructed and established areas, require higher nitrogen fertilization to promote turf recovery from ball marks, divots, and concentrated traffic.

In general, light applications of fertilizer in the northern half of the United States should commence in early spring and be stopped or severely curtailed prior to the elevated temperatures of summer. The majority of the annual nitrogen fertilizer (approximately 60 to 75%) should be applied in the fall. This application begins in late summer/early fall as temperatures begin to cool, encouraging renewed growth. A final fertilization application, high in potassium, just after the turf has stopped growing in the late fall and prior to freezes, improves future turf quality.

Fertilizer applications in the southern United States should begin during spring "green-up" after the last killing frost. This generally continues through the summer and early fall, with the last application timed approximately 30 days before the first fall killing frost.

Timing is partially based on the minimum and optimum temperatures necessary for turfgrass growth. Table 11–1 lists growth temperatures for cool- and warm-season turfgrasses. If temperatures are outside the growth range of the grass, fertilizer applications will be inefficiently utilized.

Nitrogen Rates

A general yearly range of nitrogen needs for bermudagrass golf greens is from 8 to 24 pounds of nitrogen per 1,000 square feet (39 to 118 kg N/100 m^2). Bentgrass and bentgrass/*Poa annua* greens annually require three to eight pounds of nitrogen per 1,000 square feet (15 to 39 kg N/100 m^2). Courses with sufficient resources, low-CEC-containing soils, longer growing seasons, excessive traffic, and elevated demands from players would use the higher rate range. Those courses interested in maintaining a less-intensive playing surface, or those with limited labor and financial resources, should use nitrogen rates in the lower range. Exceptions to these ranges may occur depending on various conditions or needs. For example, courses recovering from excessive traffic, pest or low-temperature stresses, or that are establishing new greens, may require higher (approx. 25% more) nitrogen than listed until their grass is sufficiently reestablished.

Frequency

Bermudagrass

The percentages of nitrogen fertilizer applied to warm- and cool-season turfgrasses during the year are listed in Table 11–2. In general, to maintain optimum color and density during periods of active growth, highly maintained bermudagrass golf greens need approximately one-half pound soluble nitrogen per 1,000 square feet (2.5 kg N/100 m^2) every 7 to 14 days. For those courses without these resources and for those with lower quality expectations, adequate bermudagrass can be maintained with one-half pound of nitrogen per 1,000 square feet (2.5 kg N/100 m^2) applied every 14

TABLE 11–1 *Air temperatures affecting turfgrass shoot growth and soil temperatures at 4 inches affecting root growth.*

Turfgrass	Shoot growth		Root growth	
	Minimum	Optimum	Minimum	Optimum
		°F (°C)		
Warm-season grasses	55 (12.7)	80 to 95 (26.7 to 35)	50 to 60 (10 to 15.6)	75 to 85 (24 to 29.4)
Cool-season grasses	40 (4.4)	60 to 75 (15.6 to 24)	33 (0.6)	50 to 65 (10 to 18.3)

TABLE 11-2 *Percentages of nitrogen fertilizer applied to turfgrass during the year.*

Season	Cool-season grasses		Warm-season grasses	
	greens/tees	other	overseeded	non-overseeded
			%	
Fall (Sept., Oct., Nov.)	40 to 75	45 to 75	15	10 to 15
Winter (Dec., Jan., Feb.)	0 to 30*	0 to 45	15	0
Spring (Mar., Apr., May)	10 to 20	10 to 20	25	35
Summer (June, July, Aug.)	10 to 20	0 to 10	45	50 to 55

*Nitrogen use stops during winter in areas where soils routinely freeze.

to 21 days during periods of active growth. On intensively maintained courses, higher rates (e.g., 1 lb N per 1,000 sq.ft. every 7 to 14 days, 5 kg N/100 m^2) may be necessary to encourage quicker turf recovery during times of heavy play. However, these higher rates often lead to other problems. Excessive thatch/mat can quickly accumulate, especially on new ultra-dense cultivars like "Mini Verde," "Champion," or "TifEagle"; thus, ball roll and putting speeds will be slower since more leaf area will be produced, and a decrease in turfgrass rooting often follows.

Bentgrass and Poa annua

The total amount of nitrogen used for bentgrass or bentgrass/*Poa annua* greens generally ranges from three to eight pounds nitrogen per 1,000 square feet annually (15 to 39 kg N/100 m^2). Typically, six to eight pounds (30 to 39 kg/100 m^2) are used annually for bentgrass in areas with longer growing seasons such as the lower transition zone in the hot and humid Southeastern United States. Meanwhile, three to six pounds are typically used per 1,000 square feet (15 to 30 kg N/100 m^2) in shorter-growing-season cool humid or cool arid regions of the United States.

Timing for this three to eight pounds of nitrogen (15 to 39 kg/100 m^2) is based on the temperatures affecting shoot and root growth (Table 11-1). Table 11-2 lists the general rule-of-thumb of the percentage of these total nitrogen amounts applied during the various seasons of the year. The majority of nitrogen (40 to 75%) should be supplied during the autumn months.

A typical bentgrass fertilization schedule for a golf green in the Southeastern United States based on Table 11-2 would include one pound of nitrogen per 1,000 square feet (4.9 kg N/100 m^2) each for the months of September, October, November, December, and January. February (depending on location) would probably receive slightly less (e.g., 3/4 lb N/1,000 ft^2, 3.7 kg N/100 m^2) to reduce succulent growth in the subsequent spring months. By contrast, in the middle to upper transition zone and into the Northern United States, little or no nitrogen would be applied after November 15, as plant roots have a limited capacity to take up fertilizer in cold or frozen soils. March, April, and May might receive one-half pound nitrogen per 1,000 square feet (2.5 kg N/100 m^2) each while the summer months, June, July, and August, would receive a minimum amount of nitrogen (e.g., 1/4 lb N/1,000 ft^2 each, 1.2 kg N/100 m^2) in an attempt to minimize disease incidence and reduce heat and drought stress. A good rule of thumb for high sand content (>80% by volume) greens is to use lower fertilizer rates applied at more frequent intervals such as one-eighth pound nitrogen and potassium per 1,000 square feet (0.6 kg N/100 m^2) every 10 to 14 days during stressful environmental periods. Readily available water-soluble sources like urea delivered using a boom-sprayer work best for this purpose.

Superintendents, in an effort to more closely regulate and maintain consistent growth and color, often alternate between using granular and liquid fertilizer sources. Granular fertilizers are used in fall through mid-spring to encourage turf recovery and rooting. Foliar applied liquid sources are popular during summer stress months as a means of reducing salts and reducing growth surges, while also providing consistent color and desirable playing conditions.

Overseeded Bermudagrass Greens

Once established, overseeded greens should be fertilized every two to three weeks with one-half pound soluble nitrogen (plus potassium) per 1,000 square feet (2.5 kg/100 m^2) during fall and winter months. The objective is to provide enough nitrogen to maintain desirable color but not be excessive so as to weaken the overseeded grasses and promote premature bermudagrass growth. In addition, highly soluble nitrogen use on overseeded grass often leads to excessive turf growth, slower putting speeds, and increased disease (e.g., brown patch and pythium) incidence. Many superintendents have discovered applications of manganese, and possibly iron, can often substitute for a nitrogen application where only an aesthetic color response is desired. Two to three ounces (57 to 85 g) of a chelated iron source (such as ferrous sulfate) or one-half ounce (14 g) manganese sulfate in two to five gallons of water applied per 1,000 square feet (8 to 20 L/100 m^2) provides 10 to 21 days of desirable dark-green color without an undesirable flush of growth. These elements are only foliarly absorbed by plants, resulting in the relatively short color response time due to being removed with regular mowing practices.

Nitrogen Sources

The source of nitrogen used to fertilize golf greens affects the amount safely applied at one time. Usually, a combination of quick-release (water-soluble) and slower-release (water-insoluble) nitrogen sources is recommended to provide uniform grass growth. Ureaformaldehyde (Nitroform), methylene urea, IBDU, sulfur-coated urea (SCU), and polymer-coated materials often are used to provide slow-release, residual nitrogen while a soluble source like urea, ammonium nitrate, or ammonium sulfate is used for quicker turf response. During cold temperatures, water-soluble sources or IBDU provide the fastest turf response as they do not rely on soil microorganisms for nitrogen conversion and release.

Note: IBDU's release rate is dramatically lower in high pH soils like calcareous sands, and the desired response might not be achieved.

Another consideration involving nitrogen sources includes economics. Slow-release and natural organic sources cost considerably more compared to soluble sources. However, slow-release sources need to be applied less often and a labor savings may be achieved. Additionally, many water-soluble sources pose a salinity hazard, and may provide a desirable or undesirable soil acidifying effect. This is particularly true for the ammonium-containing fertilizers like ammonium sulfate and ammonium phosphate. With the exception of certain slow-release (water-insoluble) materials, actual nitrogen should not be applied in excess of one pound per 1,000 square feet (4.9 kg/100 m^2) in any one application. Frequently applying small amounts of nitrogen (e.g., 1/8 to 1/2 lb N per 1,000 sq.ft., 2.5 to 15 kg/100 m^2) is preferred since this produces a higher-quality turf, avoids growth flushes, and minimizes leaching and salt-accumulation potentials. Higher rates (e.g., up to 3 lbs N per 1,000 sq.ft., 15 kg N/100 m^2, every 90 days) of some slow-release nitrogen sources like methylene urea formaldehyde can be applied to fairways and roughs without substantial turf discoloration or tip-burn. In most cases a high-quality turfgrass can be maintained for a 90-day period without flushes of growth or major variations in color when slow-release nitrogen sources are used.

Spoon (also called foliar) feeding during the summer months with liquid fertilizer programs is often used on high-sand-content putting greens and tees to help maintain desirable turf color, minimize growth surges to enhance ball roll, minimize thatch/mat accumulation, discourage *Poa annua,* and provide a continuous supply of elements such as nitrogen or potassium that are often easily leached from sand-based rootzones. Nitrogen rates for foliar feeding programs typically range from 0.1 to 0.25 pounds of nitrogen per 1,000 square feet (0.5 to 1.2 kg/100 m^2) on a 7- to 14-day interval. Phosphorus (as P$_2$O$_5$) is applied at about one-third the rate of nitrogen while potassium rates will be equal to one-half the rate of nitrogen. Other nutrients such as calcium, magnesium, or iron also may be added by foliar feeding to help regulate and maintain desirable turf color. Ideally, these nutrients should be supplied in two to five gallons of water per a 1,000 square foot (8 to 20 L/100 m^2) carrier to ensure application uniformity and minimize the potential for turf burn.

Other Elements

Potassium

Potassium often is referred to as the "health" element and, without a relatively available supply, turfgrasses will be more susceptible to environmental and pest stresses. Root growth also is related to potassium availability. Excessive potassium, however, may increase soil salinity levels, especially if the leaching capability is limited. Potassium also competes for occupancy on the soil cation exchange sites and may displace other essential elements like calcium or magnesium. The following are commonsense guidelines for potassium fertilization (Carrow, 1995b):

1. For native or unamended soils, use soil testing to determine available soil potassium levels and to base potassium fertilization needs. Soil testing results for potassium are generally accurate except for heavily leached, sandy soils.
2. On heavily leached sands:
   a. Apply a 1:1.5 ratio of nitrogen to potash when annual nitrogen rates are one to three pounds of nitrogen per 1,000 square feet (4.9 to 15 kg/100 m^2).
   b. When annual nitrogen rates are three to six pounds per 1,000 square feet (15 to 29 kg/100 m^2), use a 1:1 nitrogen to potash ratio.
   c. When annual nitrogen rates are above six pounds per 1,000 square feet (29 kg/100 m^2), use a 1:0.75 or 1:0.5 nitrogen to potash ratio to avoid the potential of salt buildup.
   d. In summer, apply one-fourth to one-half pound potash per 1,000 square feet (1.2 to 2.5 kg/100 m^2) every two to six weeks.

Phosphorus

Soil phosphorus levels tend not to fluctuate as readily as nitrogen or potassium. Soil-test results should be used to determine the amount needed for a particular turf area. Usually 0 to 4 pounds phosphorus per 1,000 square feet (0 to 20 kg P/100 m^2) are needed yearly. Phosphorus is generally not very water soluble; therefore, if needed, its efficiency is increased if applications follow aerification. This allows the material to be placed more directly in the rootzone where roots can access the nutrient. Over time, phosphorus levels may actually increase near the soil surface, especially where clippings are returned during mowing.

Phosphorus deficiency symptoms appear as a purple discoloration of the youngest leaf blades. However, this can be easily confused with purpling associated with many turfgrasses during cool periods when anthocyanins are exposed. Applying a small area or strip with phosphorus fertilizer is an easy way to determine if insufficient nutrition is the cause of purpling. If the purpling disappears following phosphorus application, then an application across the entire green is probably warranted. Cool-season turfgrasses often have more of a color response to phosphorus fertilization than warm-season grasses. To take advantage of this, turf to be overseeded should have its yearly phosphorus fertilizer applied immediately prior to and during the cool-season overseeded growing period.

Micronutrients

Regular soil and tissue testing is the best preventive approach to solving many of the micronutrient deficiency problems. Iron and manganese are two of the most common micronutrient deficiencies turf managers experience. However, **if excessive or indiscriminate amounts of micronutrients are applied or soil pH is excessively low, toxicity to the plant can occur.** An example involves growing turf on old vegetable or fruit production fields. These are often sprayed with fungicides containing copper, zinc, and/or sulfur. Because of their relative immobility (with the exception of sulfur) in soils, copper and zinc residues have become toxic to the turfgrasses in some cases.

Golf greens, due to their high sand content, typically have low cation exchange capacities (e.g., ≤5.0). Exchange capacity, along with soil pH, are two key components of a soil test report important to understanding micronutrient availability. By default, soils low in pH are saturated with hydrogen ions and are low in calcium, magnesium, potassium, and other cations necessary for healthy plant growth. Thus, low-CEC and low-pH sand soils often experience magnesium deficiency symptoms, especially during initial turfgrass establishment and where the rootzone has low organic matter. Conversely, soils low in CEC but high in soil pH (>7.0) may experience an iron deficiency. Tissue testing and experimenting with small areas of a green by applying the suspected element are the two best means to determine if this is a problem.

Micronutrient deficiency symptoms can easily be confused with pest occurrence or other stresses. These problems, however, usually are more localized and appear as irregular areas or in circular patterns. Chapter 10 provides a starting guideline for spot treating areas exhibiting a micronutrient deficiency.

Tees

Tees, like greens, should be fertilized sufficiently to sustain vigorous recuperative growth, but not to the point where wear tolerance is sacrificed. Often this is associated with succulent leaf growth or increased disease incidences. Tees, in general, are maintained almost as intensively as golf greens. This is especially true for sand-based tees and heavily used par-3 tees receiving excessive traffic and where a significant number of deep divots are removed during regular play. For par-3 tees, especially undersized small tees, the fertilization program should range between three-fourths to equal that used for greens. For most par-4 and par-5 tees, the fertilization program can be reduced to approximately one-half that used for golf greens (Table 11–3). Potassium applications should be approximately one-half of nitrogen applications except where clippings are removed or when sand-based tees are constructed. In such cases, potassium application rates should equal those of nitrogen.

Fairways and Roughs

Fairways generally are maintained with fewer fertilizer inputs than golf greens or tees. This is due to clippings being returned during mowing, resulting in more nutrients being recycled. Fairways also are typically grown on finer (heavier)-textured native soils that retain nutrients better than sand-based rootzones used for greens and tees. In addition, higher mowing heights promote deeper rooting, which improves plant nutrient acquisition. Less irrigation is normally applied to these areas, minimizing nutrient leaching. For bermudagrass, nitrogen and potassium fertilization rates should range between 45 and 260 pounds of nutrient per acre per year (Table 11–3). Zoysiagrass and cool-season grasses such as turf-type tall fescue and perennial ryegrass need between 45 and 135 pounds of nitrogen per acre each year. Yearly bentgrass and Kentucky bluegrass rates may need to be slightly higher (e.g., 60 to 180 lbs N/acre, 67 to 206 kg N/ha). These annual needs are normally split between two and four applications at between 25 and 45 pounds of nitrogen per acre per application (28 to 50 kg N/ha) (Table 11–3). A range is suggested because local weather conditions, insect and disease severity, soil types, turfgrass quality, player expectations, overseeding practices, and so on, influence exact rates and timing. Phosphorus needs should be based on yearly soil test results.

In general, light fertilizer applications should begin in late winter or early spring just prior to the flush of new turf growth. These fertilizer applications are often combined with a preemergence herbicide application for control of annual grassy weeds like crabgrass. In general, one application of a complete fertilizer during this period and another in early fall are needed. These are supplemented throughout the year with nitrogen and potassium, as needed, to maintain desirable color, leaf texture, density, and recuperative ability. These sequential applications are made every five to eight weeks on high-maintenance courses and every 10 to 12 weeks on low-maintenance courses through spring and summer. The last fertilization should be made approximately one month prior to the first anticipated hard frost and should consist of a 1:1 or 1:2 nitrogen-to-potassium ratio to encourage desirable carbohydrate formation. This late-fall fertilization with nitrogen on cool-season grasses is timed after the last mowing (approximately in mid- to late-November), helps improve fall and spring turf color, increases root growth and shoot density, and often decreases weed problems the following summer. This fertilizer application should consist of a readily available water-soluble nitrogen source, like urea, which is quickly absorbed by plant roots and stored in plant tissue. Late-fall fertilization is not normally practiced on warm-season grasses due to increased problems with winter injury and certain diseases such as spring dead spot. Tropical and subtropical areas not prone to these problems continue with fall fertilization to provide the benefits listed earlier for cool-season grasses. Late-summer fertilization of warm-season grasses with potassium (1 lb K/1,000 sq.ft., 49 kg K/ha), however, often helps increase cold tolerance of the grass but has little influence on turf color.

Since roughs are mowed at greater heights than fairways, and clippings are returned, fertilization requirements for roughs are lower (Table 11–3). Roughs are usually fertilized one to three times a year to provide color and recuperation from pest or traffic damage. Forty pounds of a soluble nitrogen source, or eighty pounds of an insoluble source, are usually applied per acre per application (45 to 90 kg N/ha). A complete fertilizer should be used at each treatment. Obviously, as fertilization amounts increase, so do maintenance expenditures in terms of mowing and trimming costs.

TABLE 11-3 Typical nitrogen application rates, frequency, and yearly total amounts for golf course tees, fairways, and roughs.

Grass	Tees			Fairways			Roughs		
	Single rate[1] (lb N/1,000 ft²)	Frequency[2] (weeks)	Yearly total (lb N/1,000 ft²)	Single rate[1] (lb N/acre)	Frequency (weeks)	Yearly total (lb N/acre)	Single rate[1] (lb N/acre)	Frequency (weeks)	Yearly total (lb N/acre)
Bentgrass	0.25 to 0.5	2 to 4	2 to 8	25 to 45	4 to 12	90 to 180	25 to 45	4 to 12	45 to 90
Bermudagrass[3]	0.5 to 1	2 to 4	4 to 12	25 to 45	4 to 16	45 to 180	45	8 to 16	0 to 90
Fine-fescue	0.25 to 0.5	2 to 4	2 to 8	25 to 45	4 to 12	45 to 135	25 to 45	8 to 16	45 to 90
Kentucky bluegrass	0.25 to 0.5	2 to 4	2 to 8	25 to 45	4 to 12	60 to 180	25 to 45	4 to 12	45 to 90
Ryegrass	0.25 to 0.5	2 to 4	2 to 8	25 to 45	4 to 12	45 to 135	25 to 45	4 to 12	45 to 90
Zoysiagrass[3]	0.5 to 1	4 to 8	2 to 8	45	4 to 16	45 to 135	45	8 to 16	0 to 90

[1] Rates listed are typical for single applications. Single application rates, frequency, and yearly total nitrogen rates vary considerably between individual golf facilities, geographical regions, and desired results. Lower rates are acceptable for most golf facilities, especially for those turf areas not irrigated. Slow-release or control-release fertilizer sources should be considered with higher rates. Soluble sources should be used at lower rates and applied more frequently. Multiply lb/1,000 ft² by 4.91 to obtain kg/100 m², multiply lb/acre by 1.12 to obtain kg/ha.

[2] Frequency represents fertilizing only during periods of active growth for each respective grass. The highest application rates should be reserved for optimum growth seasons of each grass. Typically this is late summer through early spring months for cool-season grasses and late spring through late summer/early fall for warm-season grasses. Fertilizer applications should be minimized or possibly eliminated during periods of natural slowed growth or where soils freeze.

[3] Refer to "Overseeding" chapter for fertilization recommendations of overseeded areas.

NUTRIENT ANALYSIS

A variety of analytical tools are available to assist turfgrass managers in developing an effective and efficient nutrient management program for every area of the golf course. These indicate what is available to plants via a soil test and what is actually in plants by a leaf tissue test. The needs for conducting either of these tests varies depending upon management intensity, quality expectations, environmental conditions, turfgrass species, and geographic location.

SOIL TESTING

Soil testing is one of the fundamental practices of turfgrass management. Soil sampling depends on several parameters: (1) type of rootzone, (2) uniformity of soil test results from replicated seasons, (3) turfgrass performance, and (4) turf maturity. Ideally, native soil "push-up" greens are tested once yearly and sand-based greens are tested two or more times annually. When sampling at initial establishment, a depth of six inches (15 cm) should be used. When sampling mature turf, soil should be sampled to a depth of two to four inches (5 to 10 cm) or to the depth the majority of plant roots are located. Soil analysis provides information on relative levels of nutrients, organic matter, pH, soluble salts, and cation exchange capacity. However, significant variations often occur in reported values and nutrient recommendations between testing laboratories. This is primarily due to geographical differences in soil types and different extraction and analysis techniques, as well as philosophical differences in data interpretation. The ranking of the nutrient level, however, should be somewhat similar regardless of the extractant used.

A turf manager should select a particular laboratory and stick with it, as chances of it switching analysis techniques are minimal, and nutrient recommendations will be consistent from year to year. In most cases, soil testing laboratories use university extraction and analysis techniques to base their fertility recommendations. Historically, many nutrient recommendations for turfgrasses have been based on other agronomic, forage, and closely related horticultural crops that often are replanted every year and not maintained as a perennial crop. In many cases, laboratories with only limited experience with turfgrass samples tend to overestimate phosphorus requirements and underestimate potassium needs. Thus, turfgrass managers should ensure the selected laboratory uses information on calibration of soil test results for turf. Table 11–4 lists various extraction techniques used for specific nutrients and soil types. It is best to use a lab located in your general geographic area.

Soil Analysis Report

Two major philosophies for interpreting soil test results currently exist. They are the sufficiency level of available nutrients concept (SLAN) and the basic cation saturation ratio (BCSR) or nutrient maintenance concept. Although both philosophies measure the nutrient status of soil, they differ in how analytical results are interpreted and expressed on reports and can be confusing if the laboratory uses a combination of both concepts to make nutrient recommendations. Consequently, if a golf course manager regularly switches laboratories or is not familiar with reading and interpreting a soil test report, the information can be confusing, and inconsistency in a fertilizer program may result.

For determining soil micronutrient levels, weak acids or chelating agents such as DTPA alone or EDTA combined with Mehlich III are used for iron, copper, manganese, and zinc, Hot water or a water-saturated paste extract is used for boron.

Sufficiency Level of Available Nutrient (SLAN) Concept

The SLAN philosophy is based on the traditional concept that as the soil test index level for a given nutrient increases, the turfgrass plant response to the nutrient will increase up to a given critical level or threshold. This philosophy has traditionally been used for agronomic crops that are replanted annually and maximum crop yield is paramount. The quantities of individual nutrients are typically expressed in terms of "low," "medium," "high," or "very high" (Tables 11–5 and

TABLE 11–4 *Extraction techniques used to determine soil nutrient levels for various locations and soil types.*

Extraction techniques	Comments
Ammonium acetate (NH_4OAc), pH 7.0	Widely used in the Midwest and far western United States for CEC and potassium. At pH 4.8, extracts more calcium and magnesium.
Ammonium acetate + acetic acid	Used to extract sulfate (sulfur).
Ammonium bicarbonate (NH_4HCO_3) or Sodium bicarbonate ($NaHCO_3$)	Used in central western United States on calcareous soils.
Bray P1	Extracts relatively soluble CaP, FeP, and AlP; some organic phosphorus.
Mehlich 1 (dilute double acid method; $HCl + H_2SO_4$)	Used in the clayey soils of the Southeastern United States for relatively soluble CaP, FeP, and AlP; excessive phosphorus in calcareous soils. Used to extract the micronutrients copper, manganese, boron, and zinc and also used to extract sodium to determine CEC and base saturation.
Mehlich II	Extracts relatively soluble CaP, FeP, and AlP; some organic phosphorus; superior on volcanic ash or loess-derived soils.
Mehlich III	Used to extract phosphorus and cations.
Morgan	Used in northeastern and northwestern United States; extracts phosphorus dissolved by carbon dioxide.
Olsen	Extracts CaP fractions and some FeP. Better on calcareous soils than acid extractants.
Water	Extracts sulfur in arid and semiarid regions.
Dilute acid or salt	Extracts sulfur in humid regions.
DTPA-TEA (diethylenetriaminepenataacetic acid-triethanolamine, pH 7.3)	Most widely used extractant for the micronutrients iron, manganese, zinc, and copper.
Glass electrode pH meter on a 1:1 (v/v) basis of soil:deionized water	Soil pH.
Buffer solution, pH 8.0 + glass electrode and pH meter	Buffer pH (exchangeable or potential acidity).

After extraction, nutrient concentrations are often determined by inductively coupled plasma (ICP) emission spectrometry.

TABLE 11–5 *Predicting plant response to nutrient application using soil test index values.*

Soil test index		Probable plant response to nutrient applications				
Range	Rating	Phosphorus	Potassium	Manganese	Zinc	Copper
0 to 10	very low	very high	very high	very high	very high	very high
11 to 25	low	high	high	high	high	high
26 to 50	medium	medium	medium	none	none	none
51 to 100	high	none	low–none	none	none	none
>100	very high	none	none	none	none	none

Source: North Carolina Department of Agriculture, Agronomic Division.

11–6). Based on this method, for example, if a soil test index indicates phosphorus is low, then a phosphorus application will probably improve crop yield. Conversely, if the soil test indicates phosphorus is present at "high" or "very high" levels, then a crop response is not expected and further applications on "very high" testing soils may even lead to other nutrient imbalances. Specific laboratory values for these criteria have been established by decades of field and greenhouse soil test calibration research on various crops over various soil types. The SLAN philosophy works especially well during the turfgrass's initial establishment period. However, as turfgrass areas mature and a relatively stable pool of soil nutrients accumulates, the concept may have limitations.

TABLE 11–6 *Range in extractable Phosphorus, Potassium, Calcium, and Magnesium (lbs element per acre) by soil test ratings.*

Soil test index rating	Phosphorus	Potassium	Calcium	Magnesium
	--------------------------------Pounds element/acre*--------------------------------			
Very low	0 to 10	0 to 24	0 to 200	0 to 10
Low	11 to 30	25 to 70	201 to 400	11 to 32
Medium	31 to 60	71 to 156	401 to 800	33 to 60
High	61 to 120	157 to 235	801 to 2000	>60
Very high	121 to 240	>235	>2000	>60

*Multiply values by 1.12 to obtain kg/ha.
Source: Clemson University Soil Testing Laboratory.

Basic Cation Saturation Ratio (BCSR) Concept

This philosophy is based on the concept of an "ideal" ratio of "basic" cations (primarily calcium, magnesium, and potassium) for the given soil or crop occurring that occupies the majority of cation exchange sites in soil. Some soil testing laboratories and research suggest a balanced "ideal" soil will have 68 percent calcium, 12 percent magnesium, 5 percent potassium, 2 percent sodium, and 3 percent trace cations, with the remainder being hydrogen (10% or less). When these soil nutrient levels are "balanced," "ideal" nutrient ratios for plant growth have been suggested: Ca:Mg of 6.5:1; Ca:K of 13:1; and Mg:K of 2:1. Once the cations are in "balance," these soils are better aggregated, which improves water infiltration and percolation. Furthermore, microbial activity increases due to increased oxygen availability that improves fertilizer use efficiency. Unfortunately, research in this area of soil science is limited and the long-term benefit of fertilizing according to the BCSR philosophy is largely unproven.

Regardless, the primary focus of BCSR is on "fertilizing the soil" rather than "fertilizing the crop" like in the SLAN concept. Annual soil tests are conducted to assess the presence of various nutrients on the cation exchange sites and normally recommend large quantities of calcium, magnesium, and potassium. Adjustments are suggested whenever nutrients become out of "balance." The concept appears to work for many weathered, low-pH soils in the Southeastern United States. However, applying additional calcium and magnesium to the naturally high pH soils of the Midwest, where calcareous sands are used for putting greens, and/or soil tests indicate 90 percent calcium in soil appears unnecessary. However, the concept of annually monitoring the soil nutrient status appears sensible.

Test Results

Regardless of the interpretation method used, most soil analysis reports express nutrient levels by one of two methods: (1) parts per million (ppm), or (2) milliequivalent (meq) per 100 grams of soil. Results for the major elements and micronutrients are most commonly reported in ppm on an elemental basis. An acre of mineral soil, six to seven inches (15 to 18 cm) deep, weighs approximately two million pounds (900,000 kg). To convert ppm to approximate pounds per acre, simply multiply by two.

Soil cations, such as calcium, magnesium, potassium, and hydrogen, are expressed by their relative ability to displace other cations. For example, one meq of potassium is able to displace exactly one meq of magnesium. The unit of measure meq/100 g serves this purpose. Cation exchange capacity (CEC) and the total amounts of individual cations may be expressed using these units.

From these reported nutrient levels, most soil test readings using the SLAN concept are assigned a fertility rating index of very low (VL), low (L), medium (M), high (H), or very high (VH) (Table 11–5). Usually, the division between medium and high is the critical value. Above this point, there is little expected plant response to added fertilizer (e.g., sufficient nutrients are in the soil), while below this value, increasing amounts of fertilizer are needed to produce a desirable plant response. Table 11–6 cross lists the amount of an element extracted from the soil related to its fertility rating index. Tables 11–7 through 11–10 list the recommended yearly amounts of phosphate (P_2O_5) and potash (K_2O) based on the current extractable phosphorus and potassium from the soil. Table 11–11 summarizes recommended ranges for nutrient levels using the Mehlich-I extractant procedure. The reader should note that differences occur between plants, soils, locations, management practices, and laboratory extraction techniques. Multiple sampling years, consistent use of a particular soil testing laboratory, and practical observations are required to establish the "critical" nutrient levels for each individual area on a golf course.

TABLE 11–7 *Recommended fertilizer amounts for bermudagrass golf course fairways based on existing extractable soil phosphorus and potassium levels.* *

	Soil potassium levels			
Soil phosphorus levels	Low	Medium	High	Very high
	---------------Pounds of N - P_2O_5 - K_2O recommended per acre----------------			
Very low	120 - 120 - 120	120 - 120 - 60	120 -120 - 0	120 -120 - 0
Low	120 - 80 - 80	120 - 80 - 60	120 - 80 - 0	120 - 80 - 0
Medium	120 - 40 - 80	120 - 40 - 60	120 - 40 - 0	120 - 40 - 0
High	120 - 40 - 80	120 - 40 - 60	120 - 0 - 0	120 - 0 - 0
Very high	120 - 0 - 80	120 - 0 - 40	120 - 0 - 0	120 - 0 - 0

*Apply one-half of the nitrogen with phosphate and potash in spring and in late summer. Apply additional nitrogen as needed in mid-summer at 60 pounds per acre per application. Multiply values by 1.12 to obtain kg/ha.
Source: Clemson University Soil Testing Laboratory.

TABLE 11–8 *Recommended fertilizer amounts for bermudagrass golf course greens and tees based on existing extractable soil phosphorus and potassium levels.* *

	Soil potassium levels			
Soil phosphorus levels	Low	Medium	High	Very high
	------------- Pounds of N - P_2O_5 - K_2O recommended per 1,000 sq.ft.------------			
Very low	9.0 - 4.5 - 4.5	9.0 - 4.5 - 2.3	9.0 - 4.5 - 1.3	9.0 - 4.5 - 0
Low	9.0 - 4.5 - 4.5	9.0 - 4.5 - 2.3	9.0 - 4.5 - 1.3	9.0 - 4.5 - 0
Medium	9.0 - 2.3 - 4.5	9.0 - 2.3 - 2.3	9.0 - 2.3 - 1.3	9.0 - 2.3 - 0
High	9.0 - 0 - 4.5	9.0 - 0 - 2.3	9.0 - 0 - 1.3	9.0 - 0 - 0
Very high	9.0 - 0 - 4.5	9.0 - 0 - 2.3	9.0 - 0 - 1.3	9.0 - 0 - 0

*Nitrogen applications should be alternated with complete fertilizers and modified to maintain desired growth and color. Multiply values by 1.12 to obtain kg/ha.
Source: Clemson University Soil Testing Laboratory.

TABLE 11–9 *Recommended fertilizer amounts for bentgrass golf course greens and tees based on existing extractable soil phosphorus and potassium levels.* *

	Soil potassium levels			
Soil phosphorus levels	Low	Medium	High	Very high
	---------- Pounds of N - P_2O_5 - K_2O recommended per 1,000 sq.ft. -----------			
Very low	6.9 - 4.5 - 4.5	6.9 - 4.5 - 2.3	6.9 - 4.5 - 1.3	6.9 - 4.5 - 0
Low	6.9 - 4.5 - 4.5	6.9 - 4.5 - 2.3	6.9 - 4.5 - 1.3	6.9 - 4.5 - 0
Medium	6.9 - 2.3 - 4.5	6.9 - 2.3 - 2.3	6.9 - 2.3 - 1.3	6.9 - 2.3 - 0
High	6.9 - 0 - 4.5	6.9 - 0 - 2.3	6.9 - 0 - 1.3	6.9 - 0 - 0
Very high	6.9 - 0 - 4.5	6.9 - 0 - 2.3	6.9 - 0 - 1.3	6.9 - 0 - 0

*Nitrogen applications should be alternated with complete fertilizers and modified to maintain desired growth and color. Multiply values by 1.12 to obtain kg/ha.
Source: Clemson University Soil Testing Laboratory.

TABLE 11–10 *Recommended fertilizer amounts for Kentucky bluegrass, ryegrass, and/or fescue golf course fairways based on existing extractable soil phosphorus and potassium levels.* *

	Soil potassium levels			
Soil phosphorus levels	Low	Medium	High	Very high
	--------------- Pounds of N - P_2O_5 - K_2O recommended per acre ----------------			
Very low	160 - 80 - 80	160 - 80 - 80	160 - 80 - 80	160 - 80 - 0
Low	160 - 80 - 80	160 - 80 - 80	160 - 80 - 80	160 - 80 - 0
Medium	160 - 40 - 80	160 - 40 - 80	160 - 40 - 80	160 - 40 - 0
High	160 - 40 - 80	160 - 40 - 80	160 - 0 - 0	160 - 0 - 0
Very high	160 - 0 - 80	160 - 0 - 80	160 - 0 - 0	160 - 0 - 0

*Multiply values by 1.12 to obtain kg/ha.
Source: Clemson University Soil Testing Laboratory.

Interpreting a Soil Analysis Report

A soil analysis report supplies a wealth of information concerning the nutritional status of a soil and may aid in the early detection of problems limiting turfgrass growth or desirable color. A typical soil analysis supplies information relative to cation exchange capacity, soil acidity, lime requirements, and soil phosphorus, potassium, calcium, and magnesium status. Nitrogen content is rarely determined because of its dynamic status due to environmental conditions and microbial transformations. Additional information can be requested from lab reports such as soil organic matter content, soluble salts, and irrigation water analysis. Table 11–12 lists the results from a typical soil and plant tissue report. Recommendations, in terms of lime and nutrients, are usually listed at the end of the report.

Various Ratios of Elements

Ratios of various elements can be important for certain soil chemical reactions and influence nutrient availability. One of the most important ratios in turf management is the carbon-to-nitrogen ratio of organic amendments like peat moss, composts, or other organic materials used for improving soil structure. The carbon-to-nitrogen ratio will influence organic matter decomposition and is an indicator of nitrogen availability. Generally, a carbon-to-nitrogen ratio between 10 and 12:1 for most organic amendments is desirable. Ratios greater than 20:1 may have an inefficient breakdown of organic matter due to the lack of nitrogen necessary to sustain soil organisms responsible for decomposition. When excessive carbon is present, soil microorganisms will immobilize all available nitrogen for their own metabolic activity. This condition is evident through chlorosis or yellowing, symptoms consistent with a nitrogen deficiency. Certain sawdust sources have a C:N ratio as high as 400:1. Turf managers who use these as soil amendments should add some readily available nitrogen like urea to the mixture.

A trend currently exists in applying composts to golf course fairways and roughs to improve soil structure, especially on heavy clay soils. Many superintendents are producing composts on-site using collected grass clippings and woody debris. For composts, a carbon-to-nitrogen ratio of less than 30:1 is desirable before it is applied to the turf. When in doubt regarding the suitability of a particular compost for turf use, many soil testing laboratories also determine the carbon-to-nitrogen ratio. Coincidentally, a similar condition regarding sulfur availability also could occur if the nitrogen-to-sulfur ratio exceeds 20:1.

Though not well-defined, certain soil nutrient ratios appear beneficial for plant growth. As mentioned previously, Ca:Mg ratios of 6.5:1, Ca:K at 13:1, and Mg:K at 2:1 seem to be beneficial under certain conditions. Plant tissue analysis with a P:Fe ratio greater than 40:1 may have iron deficiency symptoms while a Fe:Mn ratio of 2:1 appears beneficial.

TABLE 11-11 Relative response range of soil elements analyzed by Mehlich I and other indicated extractant techniques* (modified from Carrow, et al., 2001; McCarty, 2001).

Analysis	Acceptable ranges	Comments
Nitrogen/organic matter	≤5%	Due to its readily changing status in soils, nitrogen availability is hard to predict. Often, the percent organic matter serves as a reserve for many essential nutrients, especially nitrogen. Labs, therefore, list an estimated nitrogen release figure based on the percentage of organic matter present to estimate the nitrogen released over the season.
Phosphorus	5 to 30 ppm	Phosphorus absorption is greatest between a soil pH of 5.5 to 6.5. Values for other extractant procedures include:

Extraction technique	Very low	Low	Medium	High
		ppm P		
Bray P1	0 to 4	5 to 15	16 to 30	>31
Mehlich III	0 to 12	13 to 26	27 to 54	>55
Olsen	0 to 6	7 to 12	13 to 28	>29

Analysis	Comments
Potassium	Generally, higher potassium levels are required in high clay or organic matter containing soils. Soils with high levels of magnesium may also require higher potassium applications. Sandy soils require more frequent, light potassium applications compared to heavier ones. A fertilizer ratio of nitrogen to potassium should be 3:2. Due to luxury consumption and leaching loss, levels above medium as reported by soil testing are mostly unnecessary. Values for various extractant procedures include:

Potassium: see comment

Extraction technique	Very low	Low	Medium	High
		ppm K		
1M Ammonium acetate (pH 7.0)				
Sands/most soils	0 to 40	41 to 75	76 to 175	>176
Fine-textured (>35% clay)	0 to 55	56 to 100	101 to 235	>235
Mehlich III				
Sands/most soils	0 to 25	26 to 50	51 to 116	>116
Fine-textured (>35% clay)	0 to 40	41 to 75	76 to 175	>176
Mehlich I				
Sands/most soils	0 to 30	31 to 60	61 to 140	>140
Fine-textured (>35% clay)	0 to 45	46 to 90	91 to 200	>201

(continued)

TABLE 11-11 *Continued* *

Analysis	Acceptable ranges	Comments
Calcium **Magnesium**	5 to 50 ppm (see comment) 5 to 20 ppm (see comment)	With most soils, liming with dolomite to ensure an adequate soil pH for proper plant growth will provide adequate calcium and magnesium. Their deficiencies are more common in sandy, acidic, and/or low organic matter containing soils. Calcareous sands and most soils in the Midwestern states will not require calcium additions. Use gypsum (calcium sulfate) if calcium is needed when soil pH is too high. Consider using magnesium oxide, magnesium sulfate, or sulfate of potash-magnesia if soil tests are low in magnesium and lime is not required. Calcium deficiencies are uncommon; however, magnesium deficiencies often occur in acidic soils low in CEC and subject to frequent leaching. Heavy liming with calcium carbonate (also called calcite) lime or heavy use of potassium also may induce magnesium deficiency. Apply magnesium sulfate (Epsom salts) to test for magnesium deficiency. Guidelines for Mg:K and Ca:K ratios based on saturation percentages on the soil CEC include:
		Ca:K <10:1 calcium deficiency may occur
		>30:1 potassium deficiency may occur
		Mg:K <2:1 magnesium deficiency may occur
		>10:1 potassium deficiency may occur
		Ca:Mg <3:1 calcium deficiency may occur
		>3:1 magnesium deficiency may occur
Soil pH	5.5 to 6.5	Soil pH less than 5.5 becomes highly acidic and can produce toxic elements to the turf. Alkaline soil pH (>7.0) often limits the availability of many minor elements.
Cation exchange capacity (CEC)	5 to 35 meq/100 g	CEC measures a soil's ability to hold the cations calcium, magnesium, potassium, hydrogen, and sodium. Increasing CEC generally occurs with increasing soil organic matter or clay content. Generally, the higher the CEC value, the more productive the soil. A suggested range of the total makeup of a soil's CEC is 65 to 75 percent calcium, 12 to 18 percent magnesium, and 3 to 5 percent potassium.
Percent base saturation	(see comment)	Percent base saturation refers to the proportion of the CEC occupied by the cations calcium, magnesium, potassium, hydrogen, and sodium. With sandy soils, base saturation percentages have little value when determining nutrient levels.
Iron	12 to 25 ppm	Soil pH and relative levels of other elements such as phosphorus are important when interpreting an iron soil test. Generally, iron becomes less available in alkaline or extremely acidic soils, and soils with excessive phosphorus or moisture levels. See copper.
Manganese	2 to 10 ppm	Levels where a plant response to applied manganese may occur include: 3 to 5, 5 to 7, and 7 to 9 ppm for mineral or organic soils with pH 5.5 to 6.0, 6.0 to 6.5, and 6.5 to 7.0, respectively. Deficiencies are more prone on coarse, sandy, acid soils receiving excessive water. See copper.
Zinc	1 to 3 ppm	Levels where a plant response to applied zinc may occur include: 0.5, 0.5 to 1.0, 1 to 3 ppm for soils with pH 5.5 to 6.0, 6.0 to 6.5, and 6.5 to 7.0, respectively. Zinc interactions with phosphorus and soil pH can alter needed application rates. See copper.
Copper	0.1 to 0.5 ppm	Levels where a plant response to applied copper may occur include: 0.1 to 0.3, 0.3 to 0.5, and 0.5 ppm for mineral soils only with pH 5.5 to 6.0, 6.0 to 6.5, and 6.5 to 7.0, respectively. Copper deficiencies can occur on alkaline soils, high organic matter (peat and muck) soils, soils heavily fertilized with nitrogen, phosphorus,

and zinc, and when flatwood soils are first cultivated. Toxic conditions may exist when copper levels exceed 2 to 3, 3 to 5, and 5 ppm in mineral soils with pH of 5.5 to 6.0, 6.0 to 6.5, and 6.5 to 7.0, respectively. Additional levels used by many laboratories for micronutrient availability include:

Extraction technique micronutrient	Low (deficient)	Medium	High (sufficient)
		--------ppm--------	
DTPA			
iron	<2.5	2.6 to 5.0	>5.0
manganese	<1.0	1 to 2	>2
zinc	<0.5	0.6 to 1.0	>1
copper	<0.2	0.2 to 0.4	>0.4
Mehlich III			
iron	<50	50 to 100	>100
manganese	<4.0 (pH 6.0)	4.0 to 6.0	>6.0
	<8.0 (pH 7.0)	8.0 to 12.0	>12.0
zinc	<1.0	1.1 to 2.0	>2.0
copper	<0.3	0.3 to 2.5	>2.5
Boron	1 to 1.5 ppm		
Sulfur	see comment		

Boron deficiencies occur more commonly on sandy, low organic matter soils and alkaline soils. Boron is most soluble (available) under acid soil conditions.

Soil sulfur levels, like nitrogen, are dependent on soil organic matter levels, are erratic to measure, and the results are often meaningless. Soils that are low in organic matter, well-drained, have low CEC values, and are fertilized with excessive nitrogen can develop low sulfur levels. Foliar application of magnesium sulfate (Epsom salt) will indicate if sulfur deficiencies exist by greening up within 48 hours after application.

* Acceptable ranges represent typical values generated by the Mehlich I soil nutrient extractant procedure. Values may vary if other extractant procedures are used that are typically performed for various soil types and geographical regions. Refer to the specific soil testing facility and report to determine which nutrient extractant procedure was used and what the generated values actually represent.

TABLE 11–12 *An example of a soil and tissue analysis laboratory report.*

Grower: _____ Received: _____ Processed: _____ Sample ID: _____

Grass: _____ Phone: _____ Fax: _____ E-mail: _____

Element	Plant tissue	Soil (lb/a)	Deficient	Low	Medium	High
			P=Plant		Test Ratings	S=Soil
Nitrogen (N)	3.13%	—	PPPPPPPPPPPPPPPPPPPPPPPPPPPPPPPPP			
Phosphorus (P)	0.32%	129	PPPPPPPPPPPPPPPPPPPPPPPPPPPPPPPPPPPPPP			
			SSSSSSSSSSSSSSSSSSSSSSSSSSSSSSSSSSSSSSSSSSSS			
Potassium (K)	1.61%	111	PPPPPPPPPPP			
			SSSSSSSSSSSSSSSSSSSSSSSSSSSSSSSSSS			
Calcium (Ca)	0.47%	584	PPPPPPPPPPPPPPPPPPPPPPPPPPPPPPPPPPPPPPPPPP			
			SSSSSSSSSSSSSSSSSSSSSSSSSSSSSSSSSSSSSS			
Magnesium (Mg)	0.35%	196	PPPPPPPPPPPPPPPPPPPPPPPPPPPPPPPPPPPPPPP			
			SSSSSSSSSSSSSSSSSSSSSSSSSSSSSSSSSSSSSSSSSSSSSS			
Sulfur (S)	0.12%	46	PPPPPPPPPPP			
			SSSSSSSSSSSSSSSSSSSSSSSSSSSSSSSSSSSSSSSS			
Boron (B)	5 ppm	0.20	PPPPPPPPPPPPPPPPPPPPPPPPPPPPPPPPPPPP			
			SSSSSSSSSSS			
Copper (Cu)	7 ppm	0.80	PPPPPPPPPPPPPPPPPPPPPPPPPPPPPPPPPPPPP			
			SSSSSSSSSSSSSSSSSSSSSSSSSSSSSSSSSSSSS			
Iron (Fe)	106 ppm	103	PPPPPPPPPPPPPPPPPPPPPPPPPPPPPPPPPPPPPPP			
			SSSSSSSSSSSSSSSSSSSSSSSSSSSSSSSSSSSSSSSSSSSSSSSS			
Manganese (Mn)	38 ppm	10	PPPPPPPPPPPPPPPPPPPPPPPPPPPPPPPPPPPP			
			SSSSSSSSSSS			
Zinc (Zn)	24 ppm	4.00	PPPPPPPPPPPPPPPPPPPPPPPPPPPPPPPPPPPP			
			SSSSSSSSSSSSSSSSSSSSSSSSSSSSSSSSSSSSSSSSSSSSSS			
Sodium (Na)	—	11 ppm	SSS			
Soluble salts	—	0.080 mmho/cm	SSS			
Soil pH (or active acidity)	6.7					
Buffer pH (or lime index)	7.9		%K — 2.5		%H — 66.7	
Organic matter	1.1%		%Ca — 24.0		%Na — 0.8	
Calculated cation exchange capacity	6.0 meq/100 g		%Mg — 6.5			

Lime and fertilizer recommendations:

1. Lime (lbs/1,000 sq.ft.) _____   3. Phosphate (lbs P_2O_5/1,000 sq.ft.) _____   5. Other

2. Nitrogen (lbs N/1,000 sq.ft.) _____   4. Potash (lbs K_2O/1,000 sq.ft.) _____

LEAF TISSUE ANALYSIS

Leaf tissue analysis, in addition to a soil analysis, is another tool turfgrass managers can use to help develop or improve nutrient applications. It is most useful for intensively managed areas like golf greens and/or where the rootzone was constructed using a sand-based system having a relatively low nutrient-holding capacity. Tissue analysis, along with the overall turfgrass appearance and a soil analysis report, can be used as a means of diagnosing problems and determining the effectiveness of fertilization programs, especially for micronutrient deficiency. A tissue test determines if hidden nutrient deficiencies exist and determines how closely nutrients absorbed by the turf correlate with the soil test value.

Primary and secondary nutrients occur in relatively large quantities within plants—their concentrations are usually expressed in grams (g) of the element per kilogram (kg) of plant dry weight or percentages. Micronutrients occur in relatively small quantities—their concentrations are usually expressed in milligrams (mg) of the element per kilogram of plant dry weight, which is also ppm (Table 11–13). Tables 11–14 and 11–15 provide general guidelines for appropriate nutrient concentrations in leaf tissue for the common turfgrasses used on golf courses.

TABLE 11–13 *Adequate or sufficient ranges for nutrients from tissue analysis.*

Element		Amount
Primary nutrients	Nitrogen (N)	27 to 35 g/kg
	Phosphorus (P)	3 to 5.5 g/kg
	Potassium (K)	10 to 25 g/kg
Secondary nutrients	Calcium (Ca)	5 to 12.5 g/kg
	Magnesium (Mg)	2 to 6 g/kg
	Sulfur (S)	2 to 4.5 g/kg
Micronutrients	Iron (Fe)	35 to 100 mg/kg (or ppm)
	Manganese (Mn)	25 to 150 mg/kg
	Zinc (Zn)	20 to 55 mg/kg
	Copper (Cu)	5 to 20 mg/kg
	Boron (B)	10 to 60 mg/kg
	Molybdenum (Mo)	2 to 8 mg/kg
	Chlorine (Cl)	na

TABLE 11-14 Adequate or sufficient ranges for nutrients from tissue analysis (modified from Carrow et al., 2001; Jones et al., 1991; McCarty, 2001).

Element	Bermudagrass Greens/tees			Fairways		
	Low	Desired	High	Low	Desired	High
Primary nutrients			(%)			
Nitrogen (N)	3.50 to 3.99	4.00 to 4.50	>6.00	2.50 to 2.99	3.25 to 4.00	>5.00
Phosphorus (P)	0.15 to 0.24	0.25 to 0.35	>0.60	0.12 to 0.14	0.25 to 0.35	>0.50
Potassium (K)	1.00 to 1.49	1.50 to 2.00	>4.00	0.70 to 0.99	1.45 to 1.75	>4.00
Secondary nutrients						
Calcium (Ca)	0.30 to 0.49	0.50 to 0.60	>1.00	0.30 to 0.45	0.45 to 0.50	>1.00
Magnesium (Mg)	0.10 to 0.30	0.30 to 0.40	>0.40	0.10 to 0.12	0.25 to 0.35	>0.50
Sulfur (S)	0.15 to 0.50	0.50 to 0.60	>0.60	0.12 to 0.14	0.45 to 0.50	>0.50
Micronutrients			(ppm)			
Aluminum (Al)	—	<1,500	—	—	<1,500	>1,500
Boron (B)	4 to 5	15 to 20	>30	4 to 5	10 to 20	>30
Copper (Cu)	3 to 4	10 to 20	>50	3 to 4	10 to 15	>50
Iron (Fe)	40 to 49	300 to 4,000	>400	40 to 49	250 to 450	>450
Manganese (Mn)	16 to 24	80 to 100	>300	16 to 24	80 to 100	>300
Zinc (Zn)	15 to 40	40 to 80	>250	15 to 19	40 to 80	>250

Element	Creeping bentgrass	Desired			Perennial ryegrass		
	Low	Spring	Summer	High	Low	Desired	High
Primary nutrients		(%)					
Nitrogen (N)	<4.5	5.00 to 6.00	4.00 to 5.25	>6.00	4.00 to 4.49	4.50 to 5.00	>5.00
Phosphorus (P)	<0.3	0.35 to 0.40	0.35 to 0.60	>0.60	0.30 to 0.34	0.35 to 0.40	>0.40
Potassium (K)	1.8 to 2.1	2.00 to 3.00	2.25 to 3.00	>3.00	0.70 to 1.99	2.00 to 2.50	>2.50
Secondary nutrients							
Calcium (Ca)	<0.45	0.45 to 0.60	0.45 to 0.60	>0.75	0.20 to 0.24	0.25 to 0.30	>0.30
Magnesium (Mg)	<0.25	0.30 to 0.40	0.30 to 0.40	>0.40	0.13 to 0.15	0.16 to 0.20	>0.20
Sulfur (S)	<0.30	0.50 to 0.60	0.50 to 0.60	>0.70	0.22 to 0.26	0.27 to 0.32	>0.32

Micronutrient tissue nutrient levels (ppm)

Element (Micronutrients)	Kentucky bluegrass Low	Kentucky bluegrass Desired	Kentucky bluegrass High	Tall fescue Low	Tall fescue Desired	Tall fescue High	St. Augustinegrass Desired
Aluminum (Al)	—	<1,500	>1,500	—	—	—	<1,500
Boron (B)	<8	15 to 25	>25	<9.0	9 to 17	>17	15 to 25
Copper (Cu)	<8	10 to 20	>30	4 to 5	6 to 7	>8	10 to 15
Iron (Fe)	<100	300 to 450	>450	<40	40 to 60	>60	300 to 450
Manganese (Mn)	<50	90 to 130	>150	<2.0	2 to 10	>10	90 to 130
Zinc (Zn)	<25	50 to 80	>80	10 to 13	14 to 20	>20	50 to 80

Element	Kentucky bluegrass Low	Kentucky bluegrass Desired	Kentucky bluegrass High	Tall fescue Low	Tall fescue Desired	Tall fescue High	St. Augustinegrass Desired
Primary nutrients							%
Nitrogen (N)	2.01 to 2.59	2.60 to 3.50	>3.50	2.50 to 3.39	3.40 to 3.80	>3.80	1.90 to 3.00
Phosphorus (P)	0.18 to 0.27	0.28 to 0.40	>0.40	0.24 to 0.33	0.34 to 0.45	>0.45	0.20 to 0.50
Potassium (K)	1.50 to 1.99	2.00 to 3.00	>3.00	2.20 to 2.99	3.00 to 4.00	>4.00	2.50 to 4.00
Secondary nutrients							
Calcium (Ca)			no data				0.30 to 0.50
Magnesium (Mg)							0.15 to 0.25
Sulfur (S)							no data
Micronutrients			no data				—mg/kg or ppm—
Iron (Fe)							50 to 300
Manganese (Mn)							40 to 250
Zinc (Zn)							20 to 100
Copper (Cu)							10 to 20
Boron (B)							5 to 10
Molybdenum (Mo)							no data

337

TABLE 11-15 *Average nutrient ranges from leaf analysis for zoysiagrass (Jones et al., 1991).*

Element	Average
	------- % -------
Phosphorus	0.11 to 0.39
Potassium	0.38 to 1.51
Calcium	0.31 to 0.54
Magnesium	0.11 to 0.25

CHAPTER

12

Fertilizer Calculations

INTRODUCTION

The standard method of fertilizer measurement is by "percentage of weight," whether the fertilizer is in liquid or solid form. If it is a liquid, its weight must be determined before the amount of nutrients it contains can be known.

The percentages of most fertilizer nutrients, such as nitrogen, are expressed on an elemental basis. The percentages of phosphorus (P) and potassium (K) are expressed as the compounds phosphoric acid (P_2O_5) and potash (K_2O), respectively. For example, a 5-5-10 fertilizer has a N–P–K ratio of 1-1-2. This 5-5-10 contains 5 percent nitrogen, 5 percent phosphorus, and 10 percent potassium. A 100-pound bag would contain 5 pounds of nitrogen, 5 pounds of P_2O_5, and 10 pounds of K_2O. To convert P_2O_5 to elemental phosphorus and K_2O to potassium, the following conversions are used.

P_2O_5 contains 44 percent phosphorus
K_2O contains 83 percent potassium

Turfgrass fertilizer application rates are typically expressed as pounds (lbs) of nitrogen (N) per 1,000 square feet or per acre and are often calculated on a one pound of nitrogen per 1,000 square feet (4.9 kg N/100 m^2) basis.

CALCULATING NUTRIENT PERCENTAGES

To determine the percentage of a particular nutrient in a fertilizer, the fertilizer formula and nutrient (chemical) atomic weights are needed. For example, to determine the percentage of nitrogen and phosphorus in diammonium phosphate (DAP), one needs to know the fertilizer formula [$(NH_4)_2HPO_4$] and atomic weights of nitrogen (14), hydrogen (1), phosphorus (31), and oxygen (17). The percentages of nitrogen and phosphorus are then calculated by adding up the total atomic weight of DAP and determining what percentage of this total is nitrogen and phosphorus.

$$\text{For nitrogen: } \%N = \frac{2\,N}{(NH_4)_2HPO_4} \times 100 = \frac{2 \times 14}{2[14 + (4 \times 1)] + 1 + 31 + (4 \times 17)} \times 100 = 21\%N$$

$$\text{For phosphorus: } \%P = \frac{P}{(NH_4)_2HPO_4} \times 100 = \frac{31}{2[14 + (4 \times 1)] + 1 + 31 + (4 \times 17)} \times 100 = 23\%P$$

339

GRANULAR FERTILIZERS

To find the amount of material needed to supply a certain amount of nutrient in a given area, divide the rate needed by the percent nutrient in the fertilizer source:

$$\frac{\text{rate of nutrient wanted in a given area}}{\text{percent nutrient in fertilizer}}$$

For example, a superintendent wishes to supply two pounds of nitrogen per 1,000 square feet using ammonium sulfate (20-5-10). How much ammonium sulfate is needed per 1,000 square feet to provide this?

$$\frac{\text{rate of nutrient wanted}}{\text{percent nutrient in fertilizer}} = \frac{2 \text{ lbs}/1,000 \text{ ft}^2}{0.2} = 10 \text{ lbs. of ammonium sulfate needed}/1,000 \text{ ft}^2$$

The amount of P_2O_5 and K_2O in this 10 pounds of 20-5-10 includes:

P_2O_5:   10 lbs fertilizer $\times$ 0.05 = 0.5 pounds P_2O_5
K_2O: 10 lbs fertilizer $\times$ 0.10 = 1.0 pounds K_2O

The amount of actual phosphorus and potassium in this 10 pounds includes:

P: 0.5 lb $P_2O_5 \times$ 0.44 = 0.22 pounds phosphorus
K: 1.0 lb $K_2O \times$ 0.83 = 0.83 pounds potassium

LIQUID FERTILIZERS

To use liquid fertilizer, one must know the weight of the liquid. This weight is then multiplied by the nutrient content to determine the amount of nutrients in a gallon.

Example:

Determine how much nitrogen, P_2O_5, and K_2O in a gallon of 12-4-8 liquid fertilizer weighing 10 gallons per pound. How much of this liquid fertilizer is needed to apply one pound of nitrogen per 1,000 square feet?

Step 1: Determine the actual weight of each nutrient per gallon of fertilizer by multiplying the fertilizer weight by the nutrient percentage.

N: 0.12 (or 12%) N $\times$ 10 lbs = 1.2 pounds of nitrogen per gallon
P_2O_5:   0.04 (or 4%) $P_2O_5 \times$ 10 lbs = 0.4 pounds P_2O_5 per gallon
K_2O: 0.08 (or 8%) $K_2O \times$ 10 lbs = 0.8 pounds K_2O per gallon

Step 2: Determine how much fertilizer should be applied by dividing the desired rate of one pound of nitrogen per 1,000 square feet by the actual amount of nitrogen per gallon of fertilizer.

$$\frac{1 \text{ lb N}/1,000 \text{ ft}^2}{1.2 \text{ lbs N/gal}} = 0.8 \text{ gallon required}/1,000 \text{ ft}^2 \text{ to deliver } 1 \text{ lb N}/1,000 \text{ ft}^2$$

Example:

1. How many pounds of an 18-6-12 granular fertilizer are required to fertilize a 7,500 square foot green at the rate of two pounds of nitrogen per 1,000 square feet?

   Step 1: Determine how many pounds of the 18-6-12 are needed to obtain one pound of nitrogen. Since the 18 is the desired percentage, it is divided into 1.

   $$\frac{1}{0.18} = 5.5$$

   This means that 5.5 pounds of 18-6-12 contains one pound of nitrogen. This may be checked by multiplying the answer, 5.5, by the percent nitrogen, 0.18:

   $$5.5 \times 0.18 = 1 \text{ lb N}$$

Step 2: Since 5.5 pounds of 18-6-12 will provide one pound of nitrogen, then 2×5.5 (11 lbs) will provide the desired two pounds of nitrogen. Next, multiply this value by the area being treated. In this case, there are 7.5 1,000s in 7,500 square feet.

$$11 \text{ lbs} \times 7.5 = 82.5 \text{ lbs}$$

Another way to set this up involves:

$$\frac{11 \text{ lbs}}{1,000 \text{ ft}^2} \times \frac{7,500 \text{ ft}^2}{\text{green}} = \frac{82.5 \text{ lbs}}{\text{green}}$$

Therefore, 82.5 pounds of 18-6-12 will provide two pounds of nitrogen on 7,500 square feet.

2. How many pounds of a 20-2-8 fertilizer are needed to apply one pound of nitrogen per 1,000 square feet on a 2.3 acre fairway?

Step 1: First, determine how many square feet are in 2.3 acres. One acre has 43,560 square feet.

$$43,560 \text{ ft}^2/\text{acre} \times 2.3 \text{ acres} = 100,188 \text{ ft}^2$$

Step 2: Next, determine how many pounds of 20-2-8 will provide one pound of nitrogen per 1,000 square feet.

$$\frac{1}{0.2} = 5 \text{ lbs}$$

Step 3: Finally, determine the total amount of fertilizer needed over the 2.3 acres.

Five pounds are needed per 1,000 square feet $\times$ 100.118 (1,000s) in 2.3 acres = 500 pounds total 20-2-8 needed to provide one pound of nitrogen per 1,000 square feet over 2.3 acres.

3. How much of a 15-6-9 liquid fertilizer is required to apply one pound of nitrogen per 1,000 square feet on a 6,000 square foot green?

Step 1: In order to determine this, the weight of the fertilizer is needed. One gallon of liquid fertilizer weighs about 10 pounds. If one gallon of fertilizer weighs 10 pounds and is 15 percent nitrogen, then one gallon contains 1.5 pounds of nitrogen.

$$0.15 \text{ (15\%) N} \times 10 \text{ lbs} = 1.5 \text{ lbs. N}$$

Step 2: Since one gallon contains 1.5 pounds of nitrogen, then 0.67 gallons contain one pound of nitrogen.

$$\frac{1}{1.5} = 0.67 \text{ gallons}$$

Step 3: The green is 6,000 ($6 \times 1,000$) square feet, so the total amount of liquid fertilizer required is 6×0.67 gallons, or about four gallons.

4. If all other factors are equal, which of the following is a "better buy"?

	Fertilizer A	**Fertilizer B**	**Fertilizer C**
Analysis:	12-4-8	24-8-16	36-12-24
Cost/ton:	$120	$216	$338

In order to compare the costs, first determine the cost of a unit of nitrogen for each fertilizer.

Fertilizer A is a 12 percent (0.12) nitrogen fertilizer. In one ton (2000 lbs), there are 0.12 (12%) or 240 pounds of nitrogen (0.12×2000).

If 240 pounds cost $120, then one pound costs:

$$\frac{\$120}{240 \text{ lbs}} = \$0.50/\text{lb of N}$$

Fertilizer B is a 24 percent (0.24) nitrogen fertilizer. In one ton, there are 0.24 (24%) tons, or 480 pounds of nitrogen.

If 480 pounds cost $216, then one pound costs:

$$\frac{\$216}{480 \text{ lbs}} = \$0.45/\text{lb of N}$$

Fertilizer C is a 36 percent (0.36) nitrogen fertilizer. In one ton, there are 0.36 (36%) tons, or 720 pounds of nitrogen.

If 720 pounds cost $338, then one pound costs:

$$\frac{\$338}{720 \text{ lbs}} = \$0.47/\text{lb of N}$$

Therefore, in this example, <u>fertilizer B</u>, at $0.45/lb of nitrogen, is the better buy.

5. How much of the following fertilizer materials will be required to apply a 3-1-2 ratio of materials at a rate of one pound of nitrogen per 1,000 square feet on a 7,000 square foot green?

Fertilizer materials:

A. 38-0-0 (urea formaldehyde)
B. 0-20-0 (superphosphate)
C. 0-0-50 (potassium sulfate)

A. Since urea formaldehyde is 38 percent (0.38) nitrogen, $1 \div 0.38$ or 2.6 pounds of UF contain one pound of nitrogen.

$$2.6 \text{ lbs (UF)} \times 7 \text{ (from 7,000 ft}^2) = 18.2 \text{ total lbs}$$

B. The ratio of nutrients in this problem is 3-1-2. This means for every three units of nitrogen, we want one unit of P_2O_5, or for every one unit of nitrogen we want one-third unit of P_2O_5. Since the rate of nitrogen application is one pound per 1,000 square feet, then the rate of P_2O_5 application is one-third pound per 1,000 square feet. Superphosphate is 20 percent (or 0.20) P_2O_5.

$$\frac{1}{0.20} = 5 \text{ lbs of 0-20-0 will contain 1 lb of } P_2O_5$$

We need one-third of P_2O_5 per 1,000 square feet, so:

$$1/3 \text{ (or 0.33)} \times 5 = 1.65 \text{ lbs of 0-20-0 provides 1/3 lb } P_2O_5/1,000 \text{ ft}^2.$$

1.65 pound $\times$ 7 (from 7,000 ft^2) = 11.5 total pounds 0-20-0 required to apply one-third pound P_2O_5/1,000 square feet on the 7,000 square foot green.

C. The ratio of nutrients in this problem is 3-1-2. This means for every three units of nitrogen we want two units of K_2O, or for every one unit of nitrogen, we want two-thirds unit of K_2O. Since the rate of nitrogen application is one pound per 1,000 square feet, then the rate of K_2O application is two-thirds pound per 1,000 square feet. Potassium sulfate is 50 percent (or 0.50) K_2O.

$$\frac{1}{0.50} = 2 \text{ lbs of 0-0-50 contains 1 lb of } K_2O$$

We need two-thirds of K_2O per 1,000 square feet, so two-thirds (or 0.67) $\times$ 2 = 1.34 pounds 0-0-50 will provide two-thirds pound K_2O per 1,000 square feet. Since our green is 7,000 square feet, we must multiply by 7:

$$1.34 \text{ lbs} \times 7 \text{ (from 7,000 ft}^2) = 9.4 \text{ total lbs 0-0-50}$$
required to apply 2/3 lb K_2O/1,000 ft^2 on the green.

The answer to this problem is therefore: 18.2 pounds 38-0-0, 11.5 pounds 0-20-0 and 9.4 pounds 0-0-50.

SAMPLE PROBLEMS

1. When establishing a turf on new ground without a soil test, a standard fertilization is eight pounds of P_2O_5 and three pounds of K_2O per 1,000 square feet. How many pounds of a 5-10-10 fertilizer and 20 percent superphosphate would be needed per 1,000 square feet? (answer: 30 lbs 5-10-10; 25 lbs 0-20-0)

2. How many tons of a 16-4-8 fertilizer would be required for 90 acres of fairways at a rate of two pounds of nitrogen per 1,000 square feet? (answer: ~25 tons)

3. How much of the following fertilizer materials would be required to apply a 4-1-3 ratio at a rate of 1.5 pounds of nitrogen per 1,000 square feet on a 6,000 square foot green? (answer: 27 lbs 33-0-0; 11.25 lbs 0-20-0; 14 lbs 0-0-48)

   Materials
   33-0-0 _____ pounds
   0-20-0 _____ pounds
   0-0-48 _____ pounds

4. A nine-hole golf course has bermudagrass greens averaging 5,000 square feet each. You plan to use 10 pounds of nitrogen per 1,000 square feet for the year, with one-half of the nitrogen from 18-5-9 and the other half from urea-form (38% N). How much of each is needed for the year? (answer: 1,250 lbs 18-5-9; 592 lbs 38-0-0)

5. A soil test result indicates 50 pounds lime is needed per 1,000 square feet in the previous problem to raise a sand loam soil pH one unit. Your fairway area includes 43 acres.
   a. How many tons would be needed to raise this? (answer: 47)
   b. How many pounds are needed to raise the soil pH from 5.2 to 6.5? (answer: 121,750 lbs or 61 tons)

6. How many gallons of a liquid fertilizer with 20 percent nitrogen would be needed to apply one-half pound of nitrogen per 1,000 square feet on 13 greens averaging 6,250 square feet each (1 gallon of liquid fertilizer weighs 10.5 lbs)? (answer: 19.3 gal)

7. A superintendent has 15 tons of a 12-4-8 fertilizer on hand. He wants to apply 60 pounds of nitrogen per acre of this fertilizer to his 80 acres of fairways. How much extra will he need to buy, if any? (answer: 5 tons)

8. Calculate the cost per pound of nitrogen for each of the following fertilizer sources.

Fertilizer	Cost/ton	Cost/lb N
Organic source (6% N)	$120	(answer: $1.00)
Ammonium nitrate (33% N)	$150	(answer: $0.23)
Urea (45% N)	$210	(answer: $0.23)
Urea-form (38% N)	$270	(answer: $0.36)

9. A soil test indicates the need for a 1-2-2 ratio fertilizer at a rate of one pound of phosphorus per 1,000 square feet. Your fertilizer dealer has two fertilizers in stock: a 5-10-10 at $4.25/50 pound bag and a 12-24-24 at $7.85/50 pound bag.
   a. Which material is most economical? (answer: 12-24-24)
   b. A total area to be treated is 6,535 square feet per green × 19 greens, but you have only $90 in your budget for fertilizer. Does your budget allow for either product to be used, and if so, which one(s)? (answer: 12-24-24)

10. On a 50-pound bag of 13-4-6 fertilizer, it states this bag will cover 5,000 square feet. What actual rate of nitrogen is being applied per 1,000 square feet in this 5,000 square foot area? (answer: 1.3 lbs N)

11. A soil test recommends 1.75 pounds of phosphorus (P_2O_5) be incorporated per 1,000 square feet of a new seedbed. Only triple superphosphate (0-46-0) is available. How much is needed on a 8,550 square foot site? (answer: 33 lbs)

FERTILIZER INJECTION (OR FERTIGATION) FORMULAS

For stationary irrigation systems, the following formulas are used to determine various calculations needed for fertigation:

A. **hours of injection operation** $= \dfrac{\text{acres irrigated} \times \text{pounds of fertilizer to apply}}{\text{\% ai of fertilizer} \times \text{lb/gallon of fertilizer} \times \text{gph injected}}$

Example:

A golf course sprinkler system covers 22 acres per setting. The injector pump delivers 50 gallons per hour (gph). The superintendent wants to apply 60 pounds of nitrogen per acre using a 30-0-0 fertilizer weighing 10 pounds per gallon. How long should the injection pump be turned on?

$$\text{hours of injection operation} = \dfrac{\text{acre irrigated} \times \text{lbs fertilizer to apply}}{\text{\% ai fertilizer} \times \text{lb/gallon of fertilizer} \times \text{gph injected}}$$

$$= \dfrac{22 \times 60}{0.30 \times 10 \times 50} = 8.8 \text{ hrs or 8 hours 48 minutes}$$

B. **gallon per hour to inject** $= \dfrac{\text{acres irrigated} \times \text{lbs fertilizer to apply}}{\text{\% ai fertilizer} \times \text{lb/gal fertilizer} \times \text{hours of injection}}$

Example:

A superintendent irrigates 12 acres of fairways in six hours. He wishes to apply 60 pounds of nitrogen in that six-hour period. He is using a 32 percent nitrogen source that weighs 10 pounds per gallon. How many gallons per hour should the injector pump deliver?

$$= \dfrac{12 \times 60}{0.32 \times 10 \times 6} = 37.5 \text{ gallons per hour to inject}$$

Other useful chemical injection formulas include:

C. **gallons per hour to inject** $= \dfrac{\text{acres irrigated} \times \text{pints per acre}}{\text{hours of injection} \times 8 \text{ pints/gal}}$

Example:

A superintendent wishes to inject a soil wetting agent into his chemigation system at the application rate of six pints per acre. He plans on diluting this rate into 100 gallons. His irrigation system covers 10 acres in four hours.

Step 1: First, the dilution rate must be determined:
The total amount of wetting agent needed for 10 acres is:

$$\dfrac{6 \text{ pints}}{\text{acre}} \times 10 \text{ acres} = 60 \text{ pints}$$

Step 2: Second, determine the total diluted rate needed for the 10 acres:

$$\dfrac{100 \text{ gallons}}{4 \text{ hours}} = 25 \text{ gallons or 200 pints (25 gallons} \times 8 \text{ pints/gal)}$$

Step 3: Thirdly, determine how many gallons per hour the injection pump delivers to apply 200 pints per acre of diluted chemicals in this four-hour set.

$$\dfrac{10 \text{ acres} \times 200 \text{ pints/acre}}{4 \text{ hours} \times 8 \text{ pints/gal}} = 62.5 \text{ gallons per hour}$$

D. **hours of injection** $= \dfrac{\text{acres irrigated} \times \text{pints per acre}}{\text{gph of injection} \times 8 \text{ pints/gal}}$

Example:

A golf course green irrigation system is designed to cover 2.3 acres. A chemigation injection pump is set to deliver two gallons per hour and the superintendent wishes to apply a fungicide at 10 pints per acre. How long should the injection pump be turned on?

$$\text{hours of injection} = \frac{2.3 \text{ acres} \times 10 \text{ pints/acre}}{2 \text{ gal/hr} \times 8 \text{ pints/gal}} = 1.4 \text{ hr or 1 hour 24 minutes}$$

E. To determine the **amount of nutrient(s) being applied** in an effluent irrigation source or from fertigation, use the following formula:

lbs nutrients applied/acre = ppm of the element in the water ×
acre-inches water applied × 0.226464

Example:

If six acre-inches of effluent water are applied monthly and it contains 150 ppm nitrogen, how many pounds of nitrogen are being applied per acre?

lbs/acre = 150 ppm × 6 acre-inches × 0.226464 = 204 lbs N/a

Parts Per Million (ppm)

In some instances, fertilizers and pesticides are applied in dilutions as parts per million (ppm). In this case, the active ingredient (% ai) of the material must be known. Several methods are then used to determine the amount of material needed in a given amount of water.

A. **fluid oz to use per tank** $= \dfrac{\text{ppm desired} \times \text{gallons/tank} \times 8.34 \times 128}{1,000,000 \times \text{lbs ai/gallon}}$

or

lbs to use per tank $= \dfrac{\text{ppm desired} \times \text{gal/tanks} \times 8.34}{1,000,000 \times \% \text{ ai}}$

or

ppm $= \dfrac{\text{lbs to use/tank} \times 1,000,000 \times \% \text{ ai}}{\text{gal/tank} \times 8.34}$

Example:

A liquid fertilizer is to be applied at 50 ppm. How many fluid ounces of a 20-0-0 material is needed in a two-gallon tank? This fertilizer weighs 10.5 pounds per gallon.

Step 1: First determine the pounds of active ingredient fertilizer per gallon of material.

10.5 lbs/gallon × 20% nitrogen (or 0.20) = 2.1 lbs ai N/gal

Step 2: Next, insert the information into the formula.

$$\text{fluid oz to use per tank} = \frac{50 \text{ ppm} \times 2 \text{ gallons/tank} \times 8.34 \times 128}{1,000,000 \times 2.1 \text{ lbs ai N/gal}} = 0.051 \text{ oz}$$

B. Another method is based on the conversion of one ounce per 100 gallons equals 75 ppm. By using this, one determines the ppm of an element in a fertilizer by multiplying the percent of the element by 75. The answer will be the ppm of the element per ounce of the fertilizer in 100 gallons of water.

fluid oz to use per 100-gallon tank $= \dfrac{\text{ppm desired}}{\% \text{ ai of fertilizer} \times 75}$

Example:

How much of a 20-20-20 fertilizer should be used to obtain a 200 ppm nitrogen solution in a 100-gallon tank?

$$\text{fluid oz to use per 100-gallon tank} = \frac{200}{0.20 \times 75} = 13.3 \text{ oz}$$

C. A weight relationship can also be used to determine ppm by using the following proportion:

$$\textbf{ppm} = \frac{\text{wt. of the material to be used (e.g., lbs)} \times 1{,}000{,}000}{\text{weight of the tank mixture (e.g., lbs)}}$$

or

$$\textbf{wt. of material to be used} = \frac{\text{ppm desired} \times \text{wt. of the tank mixture}}{1{,}000{,}000}$$

Example:

If an insecticide is added at 20.5 ounces to 50 gallons of water, what is the resulting ppm?

$$\text{ppm} = \frac{20.5 \text{ oz} \times 1{,}000{,}000}{6{,}672 \text{ oz (from 50 gal} \times 8.34 \text{ lbs/gal} \times 16 \text{ oz/lb)}} = 3{,}073 \text{ ppm}$$

Remember, this last equation is based solely on weight and does not account for active ingredient. Also, the weight of the material to be used must be in the same units as the weight of the tank mixture.

D. Systems often have flowing water and inject a mixture at the proper rate to maintain a desired concentration level of a chemical. The following determines the injection rate necessary to maintain the desired concentration of a chemical:

$$\textbf{injection rate (gpm)} = \frac{\text{ppm desired} \times \text{water supply flow rate (gpm)} \times 8.3}{[\% \text{ ai of fertilizer} \times \text{specific weight (lb/gal) of the stock iron solution mix} \times 10{,}000 - [\text{ppm desired} \times \text{specific weight (lb/gal) of the stock solution mix}]}$$

Example:

Iron is to be injected to provide 10 ppm of free iron into an irrigation system that has a flow rate of 500 gallons per minute (gpm). The iron stock solution contains 5 percent free iron and has a specific weight of 9.3 pounds per gallon.

$$\text{injection rate} = \frac{10 \text{ ppm} \times 500 \text{ gpm} \times 8.3}{[5 \times 9.3 \times 10{,}000] - [10 \times 9.3]} = 0.09 \text{ gpm}$$

Therefore, the injector should be set to deliver 0.09 gallons per minute of stock solution into the irrigation system to maintain an injected free iron level of 10 ppm.

Calibrating Center Pivot Irrigation Systems

For center pivot irrigation systems, the required fertilizer injection rate is calculated from:

$$\text{injection rate} = \frac{\text{area irrigated (acres)} \times \text{fertilizer rate per acre (lb/acre)} \times 100}{\% \text{ ai of fertilizer} \times \text{fertilizer application time (hr)} \times \text{weight of fertilizer (lb/gal)}}$$

Fertilizer application time (hr) is the time required to make one complete revolution of the irrigation system.

Example:

A grower wants to apply 30 pounds of nitrogen per acre through a 138 center pivot irrigated acre field using a urea-ammonium nitrate (28% N; 10.65 lb/gal). The irrigation time to make one revolution is 48 hours. The rate of injection is calculated as:

$$\text{injection rate} = \frac{\text{area irrigated (acres)} \times \text{fertilizer rate per acre (lb/acre)} \times 100}{\% \text{ ai of fertilizer} \times \text{fertilizer application time (hr)} \times \text{weight of fertilizer (lb/gal)}}$$

$$= \frac{138 \text{ acre} \times 30 \text{ lb/a} \times 100}{28\% \times 48 \text{ hr} \times 10.65 \text{ lb/gal}} = 28.9 \text{ gal per hour}$$

Therefore, 28.9 gallons of urea-ammonium nitrate with 28 percent nitrogen must be injected per hour to apply 30 pounds of nitrogen per acre to the 138 acres. A total of 28.9 gallons per hour times 48 hours = 1,388 gallons must be applied.

Traveling Gun Irrigation Systems

For traveling gun irrigation systems, the injection rate is calculated from:

$$\text{injection rate} = \frac{\text{speed of traveling gun (ft/hr)} \times \text{distance between travel lanes (ft)} \times \text{fertilizer application rate (lb/a)} \times 100}{\% \text{ ai of fertilizer} \times \text{weight of fertilizer (lb/gal)} \times 43,560}$$

Example:

Twenty pounds of nitrogen are to be applied per acre to improve roughs irrigated with a traveling gun system. Travel lane spacings are 200 feet and the gun travels at 7 feet per minute (420 ft/hr). The fertilizer applied is ammonium nitrate (21% N; 10.73 lb/gal). The required injection rate is calculated as:

$$\text{injection rate} = \frac{\text{speed of traveling gun (ft/hr)} \times \text{distance between travel lanes (ft)} \times \text{fertilizer application rate (lb/a)} \times 100}{\% \text{ ai of fertilizer} \times \text{weight of fertilizer (lb/gal)} \times 43,560}$$

$$= \frac{420 \text{ ft/hr} \times 200 \text{ ft} \times 20 \text{ lb/a} \times 100}{21\% \times 10.73 \text{ lb/gal} \times 43,560} = 17.1 \text{ gallons per hour}$$

Therefore, to apply a fertilizer rate of 20 pounds of nitrogen per acre, 17.1 gallons of ammonium nitrate would be injected per hour of traveling gun operation.

PARTS PER MILLION (PPM) PROBLEMS

1. How many ounces of a 12-4-8 should be added to 50 gallons of water to obtain a 300 ppm nitrogen solution? (answer: 16.7 oz)

2. How many pounds of a 25-0-0 should be added to 150 gallons of water to obtain a 450 ppm nitrogen solution? (answer: 2.25 lbs)

3. How many ounces of salt (sodium chloride) should be added to 13 gallons of water to obtain a 1,300 ppm salt solution? (answer: 2.26 oz)

4. If five pounds of potash (0-0-60) are added to 100 gallons of water, how many ppm potassium will result in the solution? (answer: 3,597)

5. If five ounces of NaCl are added to four gallons of water, what is the resulting salt concentration in ppm? (answer: 9,368)

6. If 20 ounces of urea (45-0-0) are added to 30 gallons of water, what is the resulting ppm of nitrogen? (answer: 2,248)

7. If three pounds of triple superphosphate (0-46-0) are added to 125 gallons of water, what is the resulting ppm phosphorus solution? (answer: 1,324)

8. If two acre-inches of an effluent water source containing 150 ppm nitrogen is applied, how many pounds of nitrogen were applied per acre? (answer: 68 lbs N/a)

9. Water from a fertigation system contains 20 ppm phosphorus and 60 inches are applied per year. How many pounds of phosphorus are being applied per 1,000 square feet? (answer: 6.25 lbs)

SECTION

V

BEST GOLF COURSE IRRIGATION PRACTICES

CHAPTER
13

Water Management in Turf

INTRODUCTION

Water is the primary material required for the growth and survival of turfgrasses; yet, at the same time, it is the most limiting. Plants consist of cells that are containers of water, and they maintain turgor (are rigid) when these cells are filled with water. Plants typically contain between 75 to 85 percent water by weight. Cells collapse when they lose water and, if enough cells lose their turgidity, the leaf rolls and turns a blue-green color, while the stem droops. The plant is then considered **wilted** (Plate 13–1). Plants begin to die if the water content drops to 60 to 65 percent within a short period of time. Water acts as a buffer in plants against extreme temperature fluctuations, ensuring these processes occur rather slowly.

Unfortunately, rainfall does not occur frequently enough in most cases to provide adequate water to sustain turfgrasses, especially with the limited root systems associated with most golf course turf areas and soils used with low water-holding capacity. This situation is further intensified by warm weather and the high aesthetic demands by players. Irrigation with acceptable quality water, therefore, is an important part of golf course maintenance. To ensure efficient watering, golf courses require well-designed irrigation systems based on soil infiltration rates, soil water-holding capacity, plant water-use requirements, depth of rootzone, conveyance losses from the surrounding area, and desired level of turfgrass appearance and performance.

WATER USE AND TURF STRESS
How Turfgrasses Obtain Water From the Soil
Evapotranspiration

Plants absorb water from the soil and lose water to the atmosphere. Only about 5 percent of all water consumed by turf is used in photosynthesis, carbohydrate synthesis, and other metabolic reactions. About 95 percent of this water is lost as vapor from the leaves, to the atmosphere, by the process of **transpiration.** Water is also lost by **evaporation** from soil and leaf surfaces. Evaporation is typically much lower than transpirational losses in a mature turf. The combined total of water lost through transpiration and evaporation is termed **evapotranspiration,** abbreviated ET. Evapotranspiration is usually expressed in inches or millimeters per day, week, or

351

month. Since ET is the total water lost from the turf system, it represents the water demand, or the total amount that must be replaced to maintain a healthy turf. Environmental parameters largely controlling ET are light intensity and duration, relative humidity, wind velocity, and temperature. Increasing solar radiation, temperature, and wind increases ET while increasing relative humidity decreases ET. Other parameters affecting ET to a lesser extent include soil-water content, turf-root system development, inherent turf water needs and dehydration avoidance mechanisms, and turf cultural practices.

Transpiration occurs through tiny pores in the leaf, called the **stomata** (Chapter 2). Stomata are usually open, allowing water vapor and oxygen to move out of the leaf and carbon dioxide to move in for photosynthesis. To conserve water, stomata often close during periods of peak water demand (hot, windy afternoons), but will usually reopen after environmental conditions moderate. Under prolonged stress, however, stomata may close for extended periods, which in turn affects other plant functions.

Although it might seem like transpiration is just a waste of water, it is in fact critically important as it cools the leaf. If not for transpirational cooling, a leaf could reach 120°F (49°C) or higher during midsummer, a lethal temperature for most plants. Fortunately, transpiration keeps leaves much cooler, usually below 90°F (32°C), due to the **latent heat of vaporization** for water, or the large amount of energy needed to convert one gram of liquid water to one gram of water vapor via evaporation. For example, for every calorie of solar energy absorbed by the plant, one gram of turfgrass tissue (mainly water) will increase by nearly 2°F. Ten calories of solar energy could warm a gram of turf tissue by about 18°F. However, it takes a lot of energy, 539 calories, to evaporate one gram of water. By transpiring only one gram of water, a turf plant loses enough energy to cool 539 grams of plant tissue by roughly two degrees. Multiply this by the millions of grams of water a turfgrass area loses daily and the incredible cooling capacity of transpiration becomes evident. Humans use a similar process when perspiration evaporates, cooling their bodies.

Transpiration is also directly involved in mineral nutrition, both by causing soluble nutrients to be drawn to the roots along with soil water and by moving nutrients and certain hormones from roots to shoots. When the transpiration stream is lacking, as when plants are grown in a saturated atmosphere (100 percent RH, Ψw ~ 0MPa), nutrient deficiency symptoms, especially for nitrogen and iron, often develop.

Roots absorb water from the soil and transport it to the shoots through the xylem. To do this, several rules about water need reviewing. First, water runs downhill. By analogy, it also flows from a position of high energy to a position of lower energy. This situation is described in terms of **water potential** and expressed as bars and megapascals. In the case of roots absorbing water, hills are not involved, but water still exists in high energy and low energy states. Soil water at field capacity is at a fairly high energy level. By contrast, the water inside a root is relatively low energy. Thus, there is a natural tendency for water to flow from the soil (high energy) into the root (low energy).

The second rule about water is it is sticky. When you suck water through a straw, the water is pulled up against the force of gravity, in a continuous column, due to the vacuum, or negative pressure, created by your mouth. All the water behind the leading edge "sticks" to the water in front of it, and is pulled along. This ability to pull long columns of water up, against gravity, is fundamental for water to move to the top of a plant.

The pathway for water loss from the leaf to the atmosphere includes the air space inside the leaf, the stomatal pore, the thin layer of still air adjacent to the leaf surface (referred to as the **boundary layer**), and finally the bulk atmosphere (Chapter 2). The concentration of water vapor will be essentially saturated inside the leaf air space, somewhat lower in the boundary layer, and usually much lower in the bulk atmosphere. Water will diffuse (run downhill) from inside the leaf (high energy), through the boundary layer (lower energy), and into the bulk atmosphere (lowest energy) due to the lower concentrations in the boundary layer and bulk atmosphere (Table 13–1). The rate of water vapor diffusion is regulated by the resistance encountered at the stomatal pore and the boundary layer. When the stomata are open and the boundary layer is thin, as during windy conditions, water loss will be high. By comparison, water loss will be low when the stomata are closed and the boundary layer thick due to very still air.

With continued transpiration and in the absence of rainfall or irrigation, soil-available water will be nearly depleted, and may approach the permanent wilting point. Water remaining in the soil will be at a much lower energy level than the water at field capacity, and may even be at a lower energy level than the water in the root. Under such conditions, no longer would a "downhill" path for water to flow into the root exist, and the plant would be unable to absorb soil water

TABLE 13-1 *Relative humidity, absolute water vapor concentration, and water potential values at various points along the pathway of water loss from a leaf (Nobel, 1983).*

Site	Percent relative humidity	Water vapor concentration (mol^{-3})	Water potential (MPa)
Leaf inner air space	99	1.3	−3.2
Leaf stomatal pore	95	1.2	−16
Leaf boundary layer	47	0.6	−239
Outside air	50	0.5	−215

quickly, no matter how hard it "pulled." Water would still be transpired; it just would not be replaced from the soil. The result is a water deficiency, and the plant wilts.

Mild-to-moderate wilting during hot, windy summer afternoons is fairly common and often unavoidable, even with adequate soil moisture. Under such conditions, turfgrasses transpire more water than they absorb, resulting in a water deficit and temporary wilting. Fortunately, roots make up the deficit at night, when transpiration is low, and restore tissue moisture to normal. But when soil moisture is low, turfgrasses are unable to fully recover during the night, and wilting becomes more prolonged and ultimately lethal. These environmental conditions could also lead to preconditioning the turf for heat stress. Preconditioned turf has been demonstrated to have higher turf quality, higher leaf water content, higher stomatal conductance, and a higher transpiration rate under heat stress.

Water Potential

As mentioned, when transpiration occurs, a gradient is formed from the leaves down through the plant to the roots and water is literally "pulled" from the soil through the stem and eventually up to the leaves, a process similar to "sucking" liquids through a straw. Generally, this gradient becomes steeper from the soil through the plant's vascular system to the leaf stomata and into the atmosphere (Table 13–1). This gradient (or energy level) is termed **water potential** and is expressed in negative values. The more negative the value, the lower the water potential. The chemical potential of water within this system is lower than that of pure free water due to dissolved solutes and pressure or gradient created by transpiration. This difference in water potential (or degree of "suction") provides the energy for water movement and largely determines the rate of water loss. In soils, water-potential gradients occur when one part of a soil is drier than another.

Technically, the components of water potential (indicated by Ψ_w) include osmotic (or solute) potential (Ψ_O), matric potential (Ψ_M), and pressure (or turgor) potential (Ψ_P), and is written as the following formula:

$$\Psi_w = \Psi_O + \Psi_M + \Psi_P$$

Matric potential (Ψ_M) is how tightly water is held (or adsorbed) by soil or, stated another way, the amount of work required to move water in soil. Water in soil has less free energy to move than water in a pool, and work is required to make it free. Often, matrix potential is the most important component of water potential. When used, matrix potential values are negative. **Osmotic potential** (also called **solute potential,** Ψ_O) is created by the presence of solutes (or salts) in the water solution. The more solutes present, the more their molecules (or ions) are attracted to the water molecules; thus, the more negative the value. The lower the osmotic potential, the greater the amount of tension or suction (or work) required by the plant roots to extract water from the soil. Fertilizer (such as nitrogen or potassium) is a common source of these solute salts. Solute (or osmotic) values also are always negative. **Pressure potential** (also called turgor potential, Ψ_P) is pressure that develops internally in plant cell walls due to the cell contents. This pressure helps maintain plant structure or rigidity and, if it drops drastically, cells collapse and their walls pull apart, a term referred to as **plasmolysis,** or killing the cell. When determining soil water potential, pressure potential forms due to gas pressures in the soil or to overhead water. Pressure values are either zero or positive.

When determining total soil water potential, an additional component is used, **gravitational potential** (Ψ_g). Gravitational potential reflects the ability of water to perform work relative to a reference point in the soil profile. The further water is above or below this reference point, the greater its ability to do work. Gravitational potential values are positive or negative, depending on whether the water is above ($+$) or below ($-$) the reference point.

After heavy rainfall or irrigation, the soil is saturated and the soil's water potential (specifically, matric potential) is near zero. After all the free water drains away, the soil is said to be at **field capacity**. At field capacity, water is readily accessible by plants. As water is removed from the soil by transpiring plants, the soil's water potential begins to drop and a greater suction (or energy) must be applied by the plant to remove it, accomplished by increasing the osmotic pressure of root cells. Eventually a point is reached where the plant cannot lower its water potential below that of the soil's or where insufficient water is available in the soil to prevent plants from wilting. This point is the **wilting point,** while **available water** is the difference between soil water amounts at field capacity and amounts in the soil at the permanent wilting point.

Water potential is generally expressed as bars or megapascals (MPa) where one megapascal equals 10 bars. To obtain pounds per square inch (psi), bars can be multiplied by 14.7 while megapascal (MPa) values are multiplied by 147. For example, a cell with a turgor pressure of 4 bars equals 58 psi, a significant pressure.

Classic soil water potentials have been defined as zero bar when the soil is saturated and up to -15 bar when soils are so dry that plants are considered to be permanently wilted. For *plant* water potential, zero bar represents fully turgid plants and ranges to -20 bars for severely wilted ones. In the *atmosphere,* zero bar represents water-saturated air, or 100 percent **relative humidity,** while $-1,000$ bars is a very low relative humidity (e.g., arid). Due to this gradient, water will move from a site of high-water potential (e.g., zero bar) in soil to one of lower potential (e.g., negative value) in air. However, when soils are so dry their water potential values are less than that of the root, plants cannot extract sufficient water from the soil and they begin to wilt. Table 13–2 indicates the relative humidity of air as a function of water potential.

Example:

A soil solution has a Ψ_w of -0.3 MPa (or -3 bars) and the root cell has a Ψ_w of -0.6 MPa (or -6 bars). Since the Ψ_w of the root is less than that of the soil (-6 versus -3 bars), water can move from the soil into the root. If the Ψ_w in leaves is -0.8 MPa (-8 bars), water will move from the roots through the crown and leaf sheaths into the leaf blades. If the relative humidity of the atmosphere is 50 percent, this is equivalent to about $\Psi_w = -21.6$ MPa (-216 bars). This means the force drawing water from the grass leaves is: $\Psi_w = -0.8$ MPa $- (-21.6$ MPa$) = 20.4$ MPa or 204 bars or 2,999 psi, a truly awesome transpiration force.

TABLE 13–2 *Water potential values in relation to the relative humidity of air. The more negative the water potential value, the greater affinity air has for water vapor in plant leaves.*

Percent relative humidity	Water potential (bars)
100	0
99.9	-0.3
99	-3.2
98	-6.3
95	-16
90	-33
75	-89
50	-216
20	-500
10	-718

As air temperature rises, its water-holding capacity sharply increases. Thus, if a plant abruptly heats up, the relative humidity inside its leaf air space dramatically drops. As a result, water more readily evaporates from the leaf air space into the atmosphere, resulting in an increased water potential gradient (Table 13–1) and more transpiration.

SOIL-WATER RELATIONSHIPS

Soil serves as the water storehouse for plant growth. This water must be readily available to satisfy the demand created by transpiration. Major soil water inputs include precipitation, irrigation, and capillary rise of moisture from below the rootzone. Capillary rise of moisture into the rootzone is important in some areas where high water tables are present. Golf greens built to classic USGA specifications or those built with the PURR-WICK methods also use the principle of "perched" water tables. Depending on capillary action to provide water to plants can result in problems such as a lack of adequate water rising quickly enough to supply turfgrass needs during high evaporative demand periods. In addition, if the water table is left near the surface for extensive periods, decreased rooting may occur. Inadequate drainage in the event of heavy precipitation may also occur.

Water loss from a turf area occurs through evaporation, transpiration, run-off, leaching, and conveyance losses. Turf managers have a degree of control over these water-loss mechanisms; therefore, they should have a good understanding of each mechanism in order to maximize water conservation.

Soil Characteristics

Soils are composed of four components: mineral particles, water, air, and organic matter. Mineral particles and organic matter account for roughly 50 percent of the total soil volume, with the spaces between the particles, the **pores,** accounting for the other 50 percent. The pores are filled with water, air, and organic matter. The balance between these components largely determines the ability of a soil to sustain plant growth.

Texture

Soil **texture** is a measure of the relative particle sizes for a given soil. Soil mineral particles vary in size, ranging from large grains of sand, to intermediate-sized silt particles, to clay particles invisible to the naked eye (Table 13–3).

The average particle size of a soil is directly related to its pore size. Coarse-textured soils (e.g., sands) typically have large pores separating the particles, while fine-textured soils (such as clays) have much smaller pores (Figure 13–1). Large pores, termed **noncapillary** or **macropores,** drain readily after a rain and are then filled with air drawn in from the soil surface. Small pores,

TABLE 13–3   *Particle-size classifications as determined by the United States Department of Agriculture and familiar objects with similar relative sizes.*

Textural name		U.S. standard (sieve number)	Sieve opening (mm)	Number of particles per gram	Typical settling velocity	Objects with similar relative sizes
Gravel	Gravel	4	>4.76	<2	20 cm/sec	—
	Fine gravel	10	2.00 to 4.76	11	3 cm/sec	
Sand	Very coarse sand	18	1.00 to 2.00	90	1 cm/sec	soccer ball
	Coarse sand	35	0.50 to 1.00	720	13 cm/min	tennis ball
	Medium sand	60	0.25 to 0.50	5,700	3 cm/min	golf ball
	Fine sand	140	0.10 to 0.25	46,000	31 cm/hr	play marble
	Very fine sand	270	0.05 to 0.10	722,000	6 cm/hr	match head
Silt		—	0.002 to 0.05	5,776,000	1.3 mm/hr	sesame seeds
Clay		—	<0.002	90,260,853,000	<1.3 mm/hr	table salt

termed capillary or micropores, drain slowly or not at all after a rain, and are where moisture is held. A good soil will have a balance between macro- and micropores, thereby creating a balance between soil moisture and soil aeration.

Golf course superintendents should know, at least approximately, what their soil texture is because it will affect how the turf grows and how it is managed. However, soils are not always uniform, and there may be several soils with very different textures on a golf course (for example, a fairway soil compared to a putting green). Also, there is no single best texture. The good manager can usually overcome less-than-ideal soil conditions through intelligent management.

Structure

The properties of a soil are determined not only by its texture but also by its **structure,** the way individual soil particles are organized. In some cases, soil particles cluster together to form fairly large **aggregates** (a well-structured soil), while in others the particles may be completely dispersed (a poorly structured soil). Sand grain or particles, being relatively large and spherical, cannot "pack" close together; as a result, many macropores usually drain well. Clay and silt particles are very small and platelike (or flat), and can pack closely together. This results in numerous micropores that drain slowly. If micropores predominate, soil water-holding capacity will be high, but drainage and air movement may be inhibited due to lack of adequate macropores. If macropores predominate, excessive drainage and aeration occur at the expense of adequate water-holding capacity. For example, a clay loam soil holds about 20 percent of its weight as available moisture, whereas a coarser-textured soil, such as fine sand, holds only about 7 percent. Although clay soils can hold more water than sandy soils, certain clays also retain this water more tightly; thus, it becomes unavailable to the plant.

Infiltration and **percolation rates** identify a soil's ability to absorb and move water through its profile. Soil texture and structure influence these rates. Fine-textured soils, such as clays, tend to have slower infiltration and percolation rates while coarser-textured sandy soils have increased rates. **Bulk density** is the mass (or weight) of dry soil per unit volume, including solids and pores. Compacted soils have less large pore space; thus, they have higher bulk densities, resulting in slower infiltration and percolation. Noncompacted sandy soils have lower bulk densities and can have an infiltration and percolation rate as high as four feet (1.2 m) per hour, while compacted clay loams have dramatically reduced rates due to higher bulk densities.

Soil organic matter is crucial for good soil structure. Organic matter acts like a glue, cementing the numerous particles together into stable aggregates. These stable aggregates perform somewhat like large grains of sand, having macropores between the aggregates, but also having micropores within the aggregate. Good structure usually means better aeration, better soil moisture, and better fertility.

Unlike texture, which is essentially constant for a given soil, soil structure can and does change. Gypsum, for example, can be added to heavy, poorly structured clays where it binds the separate clay particles together. The addition of organic matter such as peat to a soil can also improve structure. Simply growing turf on a soil can improve structure because the roots penetrate and break up the soil, and they are constantly adding organic matter to the soil. Soil microorganisms, earthworms, and even freezing/thawing cycles improve soil structure. However, soil structure can be destroyed fairly quickly, usually by excessive compaction or poorly timed cultivation. Soil compaction occurs from foot traffic, cart traffic, and equipment, and is most severe when soil is wet. Similarly, roto-tilling or aerifying a soil when it is wet can destroy its structure. The solution is to restrict traffic when soils are excessively wet.

Water-Holding Capacity

Together, soil texture and structure influence the **water-holding capacity** (WHC) of a soil, which in turn affects turfgrass water relations and irrigation. Water-holding capacity is simply the amount of water remaining in a soil following a heavy soaking and after drainage is complete. In general, fine-textured clays can hold approximately twice as much water as loams and four times that of sands (Table 13–4). As a result, fine-textured soils will require less frequent irrigation or rainfall than will coarse-textured soils. Only about half the WHC is actually available to turf; the remainder is held tightly in soil and is unavailable to plants.

Water-holding capacity is related to the soil type and controls the soil depth reached by a given amount of irrigation (Figure 13–2). For example, an inch of irrigation will penetrate a sand to approximately 15 inches (38 cm), a loam to 8 inches (20 cm), and a clay to 5 inches (13 cm). Superintendents can use this information to match irrigation to the depth of the turf root system. It is inefficient to apply an inch (2.5 cm) of water to a sand, wetting it to a depth of 15 inches (38 cm), if the roots are located only in the top three inches (7.6 cm).

Amendments such as peat moss, compost, loamy soil, or manure are sometimes added to sandy soils to increase their WHC by changing the soil texture (Figure 13–3). Heavy clays are

TABLE 13–4   *Water-holding capacity of various soil types (Carrow, 1985).*

Soil texture	Total	Available	Unavailable
	------------------------	inches of water per foot of soil*	------------------------
Sand	0.6 to 1.8	0.4 to 1.0	0.2 to 0.8
Sandy loam	1.8 to 2.7	0.9 to 1.3	0.9 to 1.4
Loam	2.7 to 4.0	1.3 to 2.0	1.4 to 2.0
Silt loam	4.0 to 4.7	2.0 to 2.3	2.0 to 2.4
Clay loam	4.2 to 4.9	1.8 to 2.1	2.4 to 2.7
Clay	4.5 to 4.9	1.8 to 1.9	2.7 to 3.0

*Multiply values by 8.33 to obtain cm/m.

FIGURE 13–2   The expected depth reached from applying one to three inches of water to three soil types (modified from Emmons, 1995).

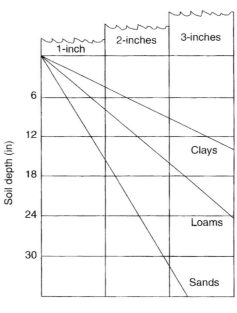

FIGURE 13–3 Soil conditioners influence the amount of water held by soil, which is available to plants. On the right is bentgrass grown on a 85:15 sand-to-peat rootzone mix while the left shows bentgrass grown on 100 percent sand rootzone showing severe moisture stress.

more difficult to improve with amendments. Historically, sand was often added to clays to "lighten" the soil. In fact, this is a good recipe for making adobe brick, not a better soil. Working large quantities of organic matter into heavy clays is a widely used practice to improve structure and increase aeration.

Water Behavior in Soils

An understanding of how water behaves in a soil is important for proper water management. First, as mentioned, water is pulled downward by gravity; in other words, water runs downhill. Second, water is sticky due to hydrogen bonding. It sticks to itself (**cohesion**) and it sticks to other surfaces, such as soil particles (**adhesion** or **adsorption**). As discussed, this is why water is held in a narrow straw against gravity, and why water can be sucked up through the straw. Soil pores are like straws, and water sticks inside soil pores by adhesion. Water sticks tightly inside small pores, but not very tightly inside large pores.

For comparison, consider a sponge and water. When dry, contact with water causes a sponge to wet-up both downward and sideways. Likewise, if the sponge is highly saturated, some water will initially drip out of it, but a certain amount will be held. Capillarity and adsorption forces causing the sponge to hold water work very similarly in soils.

In soil, gravity pulls water downward, but adhesion within the pores tends to counteract gravity. There is a tug-of-war on the water, with gravity working to make the water drain out of the soil pores, and adhesion working to keep the water inside the soil pores. The greater force wins. Since large pores (like sands) hold onto water somewhat loosely, gravity usually wins against large pores, and water drains out of the macropores and down through the soil. However, small pores in a soil are stronger, and hold onto water tighter.

Soil functions as the water reservoir for plants. Whether water is supplied through rainfall or irrigation, it can only be effective when it has entered the soil. Unfortunately, large amounts of water can be lost through surface run-off. How much depends on the type of soil, the topography, the moisture content, the precipitation or irrigation rate, and the presence or absence of healthy turf. One should try to minimize run-off losses by improving soil structure, contouring for gentle slopes, matching irrigation to infiltration, and maintaining a good turf cover. Studies show a healthy stand of turf is a great way to reduce run-off, since the dense shoot system retards surface flow extremely effectively.

Once water has entered soil, it tends to fill most empty pores, both macropores and micropores. Water continues to move downward, under the force of gravity, through the macropores. Eventually the macropores drain completely, and are refilled with air.

Micropores, however, retain their water against the force of gravity. Recall that the force with which water is held in the pores is related to the pore size. Larger pores have just enough force to hold the water against gravity's force, but not enough to resist the stronger force of roots to obtain water. Small pores hold on to their water very tightly, more tightly than the force of gravity, and often more tightly than roots trying to extract water from the soil. This means only some of the micropores give up their water to the plant. Some retain their water even though the plant may be wilting from drought. A soil with good texture and structure will have a mixture of large macropores and smaller micropores. Following drainage, macropores are filled with air, while micropores are filled with water.

Several values exist with regards to soil moisture. The first is when soil is completely **saturated**, with all pores filled, as during or right after a heavy rain. This represents about 50 percent of the total soil volume (good soils are composed of around 50 percent solids, 50 percent pores). After drainage has removed water from the macropores but the micropores remain filled with water, the soil is at **field capacity** (which is equivalent to water-holding capacity), with water occupying approximately 20 to 35 percent of the total volume. But soil does not stay at field capacity very long. Evaporation of water from the soil surface and absorption by plant roots start to deplete water from the larger micropores, and the soil begins to dry out. At some point roots can no longer remove water from the smallest pores, and the plant starts to wilt. A soil is considered to be at the **permanent wilting point** when a severely wilted plant is unable to recover, even after irrigation. This point occurs when soil moisture is around 10 to 15 percent of the total volume and is unavailable to plants. These values are estimates, and actual values depend on the soil texture and structure, as well as the type of plant growing in the soil.

The difference in soil water content between field capacity (-0.33 bar for loam or -0.1 bar for sand) and permanent wilting point (-15 bar or $-1,500$ kPa) is the amount of **available water**. For example, consider a soil with a field capacity of 35 percent and a permanent wilting point of 15 percent. The difference, 20 percent, is the amount of water, expressed as a percent of total volume, which is potentially available to the plant. This can be used to calculate the amount of available water in a given rootzone. However, one cannot normally allow the soil to even dry out close to the permanent wilting point. Doing so and making even the slightest error can result in plant death, and the turf begins to display symptoms of drought stress much earlier, which usually results in immediate action.

Rooting Depth

Other important parameters affecting available water include depth, activity, and spatial distribution of the root system. Very deep root systems will have much more available water than shallow ones. Consider a bermudagrass root system that reaches a depth of 15 inches (38 cm). Multiplying 15 inches (38 cm) by 20 percent available water gives three inches (7.6 cm) of available water, which would probably be enough for 10 to 12 days in the summer. Now consider a bentgrass fairway, with a root system six inches (15 cm) deep in May. Multiplying six inches (15 cm) by 20 percent gives 1.2 inches (3 cm) of available water, enough water for around five days. Finally, let's consider the same bentgrass, but during the heat of August when the root system has declined to only the top two inches (5 cm) of soil. Two inches multiplied by 20 percent gives 0.4 inches (1 cm) of water, about enough for one day. Rooting depth is dynamic, changing during the season and also between species.

Cultural Practices Influencing Water Use

Turfgrass cultural practices influence water-use rates and efficiency. Mowing, fertilization, and irrigation are the primary cultural practices superintendents can use to control water loss and to encourage conservation.

Mowing

Managers should normally mow turf at the higher end of the optimum mowing height range. Taller-mowed turf allows development of more efficient water-using plants. Higher-mowed turf results in a deeper and denser root system that can extract water from a larger volume of soil. Lower mowing heights initially reduce water use because leaf surface area is reduced and the remaining leaves are more compact. Initial water savings are later negated because root depth and density are proportionately reduced by the lower mowing height. Lower-mowed turf tends to require more frequent but shallower water applications than those mowed at higher heights.

Turf managers also should mow frequently and only use sharpened mower equipment. Dull or improperly adjusted mower blades tend to shred turf leaf tips, increasing leaf area, and therefore increase transpiration. Mutilated leaf tips also result in ragged turf appearance. New regimens using plant growth retardants (PGRs) reduce ET by having smaller leaf areas (shorter leaves).

Nutrition

Nitrogen influences turf color, shoot-and-root growth, and water use. As a general rule, nitrogen should be applied at levels to maintain good color, moderate growth, and high recuperative ability. Moderate shoot growth usually equates to maximum root growth, and thus maximum water availability. Excessive nitrogen promotes shoot growth at the expense of root growth and can adversely affect water extraction.

Potassium is often referred to as the "stress" nutrient, since plants suffering from potassium deficiency are more susceptible to drought, cold, and other possible stresses. Fertilizer applications to a potassium-deficient soil may help the turfgrass plant maintain turgor and avoid wilt. However, it is unclear whether added potassium has a similar benefit on soils already containing sufficient amounts of potassium. Excessive nitrogen may override the beneficial effects of potassium.

Foliar iron applications also have been shown to increase turfgrass rooting under certain environmental conditions. Increased rooting adds to the depth of available water and may reduce irrigation needs. Iron and manganese also can provide desirable turf color without excessive growth from excessive nitrogen use. Supplemental iron and manganese should be applied to encourage turf color and root growth without stimulating excessive shoot growth. Liquid calcium applications also improve the drought tolerance of certain turfgrass species.

Soil Compaction

Compaction decreases total pore space in a soil, mainly by eliminating macropores. This reduces soil aeration and may retard root growth and function. Turfgrasses may wilt in compacted, poorly aerated soils even when adequate moisture is present as impaired roots are unable to absorb water (Figure 13–4). Cultivating or coring compacted soils will improve aeration and enhance rooting and turf quality.

Watering Practices

Irrigation practices, in terms of amount and frequency, can significantly increase drought tolerance by conditioning the turf. Irrigation schedules are often based on calendar dates, such as three or seven times per week, without regard to actual turf needs and soil moisture status and availability. Studies have shown "calendar-based" irrigation may provide excessive moisture and lower turf quality. Allowing mild drought stress (soil drying) between watering promotes drought resistance without damage to the turf. Mildly stressed turf slows shoot growth and promotes root growth (Figure 13–5). Also, by preconditioning turf to drier conditions, it often has a higher quality, higher leaf water content, more than 100 percent greater root weights, and higher accumulated solutes (e.g., 8 to 9 percent higher potassium levels).

Determining When to Irrigate

There are a number of methods used to determine how much water a turf requires at any given time, under any given environment. Several are indirect and base their estimates on measuring soil moisture. Others simulate evapotranspiration from the canopy.

Visual Symptoms

A simple method used to determine when to irrigate is when visual symptoms of moisture stress are evident. Moisture-stressed grass appears blue-green or grayish-green in color (Plate 13–2), recuperates slowly (>1 minute) after walking or driving across it ("foot-printing") (Plate 13–3), or

FIGURE 13–4 Excessive soil moisture leads to compaction, insufficient soil oxygen, and buildup of toxic gases and metals. Turf often thins under these conditions, leading to the occurrence of algae, weeds, and certain diseases.

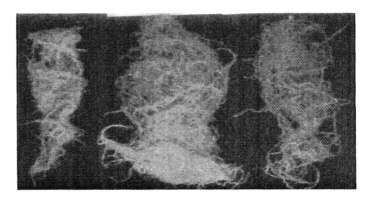

FIGURE 13–5 Turfgrass root growth is influenced by soil moisture. Shown are tall fescue roots following 39 days' exposure to various soil moisture levels. Increased rooting follows exposure to moderate soil moisture stress (middle) compared to either well-watered (left) or extreme moisture stress (right).

wilts continuously. These symptoms occur when plant moisture is insufficient to maintain turgor due to more water being lost than being absorbed. As a result, the plant rolls its leaves to minimize exposed leaf surface (Figure 13–6) and wilts to conserve moisture. Golf course managers should avoid prolonged moisture stress, especially on greens. This method is best used for low-maintenance turf such as golf course roughs.

While visual observation for stress symptoms may be the simplest method, it does have some drawbacks. Waiting for wilting symptoms is a good indicator for when the turf needs water but not necessarily how much water is needed. Superintendents also cannot afford to wait until drought symptoms appear on putting greens since this causes unacceptable turf quality. Certain areas or patches of turf will tend to wilt prior to others due to poor irrigation distribution, localized dry spots, poorly developed root systems, or variation in soil texture. Watering the whole turf area to eliminate these "hot spots" will waste water; thus, extensive hand watering is often needed.

Evaporatory Pans

Another method of irrigation scheduling is the use of evaporatory pans. A U.S. Weather Service Class A Evaporatory Pan is 122 centimeters in diameter, 25 centimeters deep, and is supported 15 centimeters above the ground (Figure 13–7). Evaporatory pans are filled with water and placed in a representative location, where water loss is measured over time. The amount of water evaporating from the pan correlates to that lost by evapotranspiration (ET). This correlation is generally accurate except during windy conditions. Wind tends to exaggerate the amount of water lost by the evaporatory pan compared to actual ET rates.

The water amount lost through evaporation correlates with turfgrass ET, but is not exactly the same; turfgrasses use less water than the amount evaporated from the pan. Warm-season grasses use 55 to 65 percent, and cool-season grasses use 65 to 80 percent, of pan evaporation. Thus, if the evaporative pan shows a one-inch (2.5 cm) water loss, a bermudagrass turf would actually have lost approximately 0.6 inch (1.5 cm) while bentgrass would have lost approximately 0.75 inch (1.9 cm).

Tensiometers

Tensiometers, which are used to measure soil water status, are tubes filled with water and have a porous ceramic cup at the base and a vacuum gauge at the top (Figure 13–8). As soil moisture is depleted, a tension is formed between the water in the soil and water in the tube. This tension is registered by the vacuum gauge and provides a relatively accurate reading on soil moisture availability, registered in centibars. Soil field capacity (water "held" after drainage) generally exists between 5 to 30 centibars, with higher values indicating decreasing soil moisture levels. Tensiometers remain accurate when tensions are below 80 centibars. Commercial tensiometer models are available that can automatically regulate irrigation systems based on a preset tension threshold.

Drawbacks of tensiometers include their readings only being appropriate in the area adjacent to the ceramic tips. This necessitates using multiple units over different soil types, irrigation zones, and terrain. Tensiometers also affect play and routine turfgrass maintenance practices. Tensiometers periodically require maintenance and have to be removed during periods of cold weather to prevent ice formation in the tube. Adequate contact between the ceramic tube and surrounding soil also is essential.

Time-Domain Reflectometry

A relatively new method of measuring soil content is time-domain reflectometry (or TDR) which is based on the unusually high dielectric constant of water. The *dielectric constant* of a material is a measure of the tendency of its molecules to orient themselves in an electrostatic force field. Due to its inherently high **polarity** (having a positive side and a negative side due to the orientation of the hydrogen atoms relative to the oxygen in water molecules), the dielectric constant of water is relatively high. As a soil becomes wetter, its dielectric constant increases.

In traditional TDR techniques, parallel metal rods are inserted into the soil and connected to a signal receiver. These rods serve as conductors while the soil around them serves as a dielectric medium. A voltage signal is released from the ends of the rods and then returns to the TDR re-

FIGURE 13–7 An evaporative pan helps indicate how much water is lost by plants via evapotranspiration (ET), aiding turf managers in planning golf course irrigation needs.

FIGURE 13–8 Tensiometers are water-filled tubes placed in the soil to indicate soil moisture (or tension) levels. Electronic sensors can be used to automatically regulate irrigation systems based on preset tension thresholds.

ceiver. As the soil moisture increases, it requires longer intervals for the signal to travel through the soil and return back to the receiver. Soil moisture content is then determined by this return time. Expense and maintenance around these probes have been the main deterrents of widespread use of TDR in commercial turfgrass.

Most recently, instead of using probes as with traditional TDR, fairly long (e.g., 10 feet, 3 meters) TDR ribbons have been buried horizontally in the rootzone. The turf manager then determines two thresholds: (1) soil field capacity; and, (2) a lower limit, above the permanent wilt point. If the soil moisture exceeds field capacity, then the irrigation system is programmed to turn off. If it approaches the lower value limit, then the irrigation system operates until field capacity is once again reached. This is often referred to as "watering between the lines." It is very accurate in measuring soil moisture, averages across a fairly large volume of soil, and also works well in wet and dry soils. It provides actual soil moisture content measurements and does not rely on weather stations and predictive models to base irrigation needs. TDR also can measure salinity levels, though, this aspect is still being perfected.

Predictive Models or Evapotranspiration Feedback

Predictive models, such as the modified Penman model, based on weather station data and soil types also are available. These are relatively accurate and applicable, especially as long-term predictors of yearly turf water requirements. Models, however, are only as effective as the amount of data collected and the number of assumptions made. Weather data such as rainfall, air and soil temperature, relative humidity, and wind speed are incorporated into certain model formulae, and estimated soil moisture content is made. Accessible weather data, as well as specialized computer equipment and programs, must be available.

Evapotranspiration feedback strategies are also used to schedule irrigation. Weather station or evaporative pan data can be used to calculate water use. This value is referred to as potential ET (ET_p) and is used as a reference point. Actual turf water use usually is not quite as high as ET_p, so a factor called the **crop coefficient** (K_c) is used to convert ET_p to actual turf ET. Crop coefficients are fairly constant for a given species, but vary considerably between species. For example, the K_c of bermudagrass is about 0.7. This means bermudagrass will use about 70 percent as much water as is predicted from using environmental data to calculate ET_p. If environmental data indicates the theoretical reference crop used 2.2 inches (5.6 cm) of water for a given week in the summer, multiply 2.2 by 0.7 to give 1.54 inches (3.9 cm) of water actually used by bermudagrass. Tall fescue has a K_c of approximately 1.0, indicating tall fescue and the theoretical reference crop use water at the same rate, or 2.2 inches (5.6 cm) in the previous situation. These calculated water use rates are the "feedback" used to determine irrigation rates.

Atmometer

Recently, the atmometer (also referred to as the "ET gauge" or Bellani plate) has been used to estimate evaporative demand. This relatively inexpensive device consists of a water reservoir connected to a porous plate covered by green fabric designed to simulate a leaf surface. Water from the reservoir is wicked through the plate to the fabric, where it evaporates. The drop in the reservoir is then easily measured on a daily basis, much like checking a rain gauge. Rates of water loss are directly related to weather conditions, especially temperature, wind, and humidity, and have been found to correlate very well with turfgrass water demand. Atmometers may be an attractive alternative to the more costly weather station-based system while still supplying similar information.

The atmometer should be located in a sunny turfed area representative of the majority of the golf course. Additional units may be necessary for varying microclimates such as shady, windy, or stagnant areas, and irrigation rates should be adjusted accordingly.

Additional Methods

Other methods of estimating soil moisture are available through **gypsum, nylon,** and **fiberglass blocks** that contain electrodes measuring electrical resistance. The porous blocks are buried in soil, and water is allowed to move in or out of them depending on soil moisture tension. These are accurate when measuring low soil moisture content and can be left in place for extended periods. They are, however, sensitive to saline conditions, and like tensiometers, measure soil moisture only at the area immediately surrounding them. They also are not as accurate in predominately sandy soil.

Rough soil moisture estimates can be determined by using a soil probe to feel the depth of moisture. Resistance to penetration of a sharp object such as a screwdriver also can be used. Rain gauges are necessary measurement tools to track natural moisture inputs on a golf course.

No matter which method is used to estimate turfgrass ET, several parameters should be considered. Each location and golf course operation is designed and built differently, and some allowance is needed to accommodate these differences.

To promote the best drought tolerance and conditioning, a mild-to-moderate soil dry-down should be allowed between irrigations. Several irrigation scheduling methods are available. These range from visual symptoms to more precise soil moisture-based irrigations. Watering heavily but infrequently is a commonly accepted turfgrass management practice. However, this can be an ambiguous approach if the exact amount or frequency of water application needed at a given time is not determined.

TURFGRASS EVAPOTRANSPIRATION RATES

Environmental Influence on Evapotranspiration

Environmental parameters that control plant ET include relative humidity, temperature, solar radiation, and wind. Of these, solar radiation is the driving force for evaporative demand by stimulating stomata opening. Cloudiness can decrease ET by blocking incoming radiation.

Atmospheric relative humidity and wind velocity also influence ET rates. As air becomes more saturated at higher humidities, the vapor pressure gradient between leaves and air is reduced, resulting in less ET. Under calm air conditions, the existing vapor pressure tends to form an external layer of still air adjacent to the leaf called the **boundary layer.** The boundary layer, if not disturbed, acts as an insulator by protecting the leaf from sudden vapor pressure changes, and thus reduces ET. The boundary layer thickness is determined by wind speed. With increasing wind, the boundary layer decreases and ET increases. As a result, ET rates tend to increase with higher temperatures, light, and wind, but decrease with higher atmospheric relative humidity and cloud cover. Minimal ET rates occur when dark, cloudy days with high relative humidity, low temperatures, and little wind occur. Conversely, the highest ET rates occur on bright sunny days with low relative humidity, high temperatures, and moderate-to-high winds.

Turfgrass Water-Use Rates

Water-use rates are usually expressed in inches or centimeters (cm) of water lost per day or per week. In general, warm-season grasses use less water due to their greater resistance to water stress than the cool-season grasses (Table 13–5). This ranges between 35 and 50 percent less water required to maintain desirable warm-season grass color compared to cool-season grasses. Bermudagrass ET is between 0.3 and 0.9 centimeters of water per day, while tall fescue water use ranges from 0.4 to 1.3 centimeters per day. Lower values are associated with cooler or more humid regions of the United States, while higher values are typical of warm arid regions. Tall fescue has the highest potential ET rates, but avoids drought stress due to its deep and extensive root system.

In addition to having lower water-use rates than cool-season grasses, warm-season grasses also tend to be more drought tolerant (Table 13–6). This is partly due to differences in rooting depth and warm-season grasses having a type of photosynthesis (C_4) that makes them more water-use efficient. Several of the cool-season grasses, such as Kentucky bluegrass and creeping bentgrass, avoid severe drought stress by going dormant. Although they may look dead, they will recover quickly when water is resupplied.

Established perennial species generally have better drought tolerance due to their deep rooting and rhizomatous growth. Annual species that are shallow-rooted are more susceptible to drought conditions. Also, turfgrasses grown under arid conditions lose more water (approximately 30 percent) than similar turf grown under humid conditions.

In general, a low water-use rate by a turfgrass is based on its ability to maintain a dense shoot coverage, slow vertical leaf growth rate, narrow leaf width, horizontal leaf orientation, and color. As discussed, cultural practices and environmental parameters also have considerable influence on each of these contributing factors. On a similar leaf index area, turfgrasses generally are no different than other plants on their ET rates and may be less than others such as sawgrass (*Cladium jamaicense* Crantz.). Again, it bears repeating that climate conditions control ET and not always the plant species, provided there is a continuous canopy or coverage of the soil surface and water is readily available.

Potential Evapotranspiration Rates

As previously discussed, another method to schedule irrigation is the development of ET feedback systems based on an estimate of the potential ET (indicated as ET_p) developed from climatic

TABLE 13–5 *General mean summer turfgrass evapotranspiration (ET) rates. Low values within a range represent humid conditions; high values are for arid conditions (modified from Beard, 1985; Carrow, 1995a). ET rates during non-summer months generally are much lower.*

Turfgrass	Summer ET rates			
	in./day	mm/day	in./week	cm/week
Bahiagrass	0.25	6.2	1.75	4.4
Bermudagrass	0.12 to 0.30	3.1 to 8.7	0.84 to 2.10	2.1 to 5.3
Buffalograss	0.20 to 0.30	5.3 to 7.3	1.40 to 2.10	3.6 to 5.3
Centipedegrass	0.15 to 0.33	3.8 to 8.5	1.05 to 2.31	2.7 to 5.9
Creeping bentgrass	0.19 to 0.39	5.0 to 9.7	1.33 to 2.73	3.4 to 6.9
Kentucky bluegrass	0.15 to 0.26	3.7 to 6.6	1.05 to 1.82	2.7 to 4.6
Perennial ryegrass	0.15 to 0.44	3.7 to 11.2	1.05 to 3.08	2.7 to 7.8
Seashore paspalum	0.25 to 0.31	6.2 to 8.1	1.75 to 2.17	4.4 to 5.5
St. Augustinegrass	0.13 to 0.37	3.3 to 9.6	0.91 to 2.59	2.3 to 6.6
Tall fescue	0.15 to 0.50	3.7 to 12.6	1.05 to 3.50	2.7 to 8.9
Zoysiagrass	0.14 to 0.30	3.5 to 7.6	0.98 to 2.10	2.5 to 5.3

TABLE 13–6 *Relative drought resistance of turfgrasses (listed alphabetically within each category).*

Relative drought resistance	Turfgrass
Excellent	Bahiagrass
	Blue grama
	Buffalograss
	Common bermudagrass
	Wheatgrass
	Zoysiagrass
Very good	Hybrid bermudagrass
	St. Augustinegrass
Good	Canadian bluegrass
	Centipedegrass
	Fine fescue
	Kentucky bluegrass
	Seashore paspalum
	Tall fescue
Fair	Perennial ryegrass
Poor	Annual bluegrass
	Annual ryegrass
	Carpetgrass
	Colonial bentgrass
	Creeping bentgrass
	Roughstalk bluegrass

data or weather pan evaporation. The ET is then adjusted to actual plant ET use with an appropriate crop coefficient (K_c) that more accurately reflects actual ET for the particular turfgrass under irrigation:

$$ET_p = K_c \times \text{pan evaporation}$$

Currently, the K_c range for warm-season grasses ranges from 0.60 (moderate stress) to 0.90 (non-stressed) and 0.80 to 0.85 for cool-season grasses.

Calculating Turfgrass ET_p Rates

Warm-season grasses: $ET_p = 0.75 \times$ pan evaporation rate
Cool-season grasses: $ET_p = 0.85 \times$ pan evaporation rate

Potential ET rates can be calculated from a variety of equations. In general, by using historical climatological data as a reference and incorporating this in the modified Penman or McCloud equation to determine specific ET rates, potential ET rates have been calculated at various locations throughout the country. From this, normal net irrigation requirements to maintain low-to-medium maintenance grass are estimated.

When using any predictive equation to determine ET rates or net irrigation requirements to maintain grass, a series of assumptions must be made. These assumptions influence actual amounts of net irrigation requirements since each location and golf operation is designed and built differently. Allowances are needed to account for these and to adjust for any differences.

1. The net irrigation requirement is affected by irrigation system efficiency or **distribution uniformity** (designated DU). To determine the actual irrigation quantity needed to provide the intended amount uniformly across the turf, the following equation is used:

$$\text{actual irrigation needed} = \frac{ET_p \times K_c}{DU}$$

   For example, if 1.0 inch of water is needed as determined by multiplying ET_p by K_c with a 75 percent efficient (or DU) system, then 1.33 ($1.0 \div 0.75$) inches of total "applied" water is required to uniformly apply this 1.0 inch (2.5 cm) over the whole turf area.
2. Environmental parameters at the time of application also influence the amount of water delivered to plants. Applications made during hot temperatures, windy conditions, and when relative humidity is low, as well as with fine mist irrigation nozzles, can result in extensive evaporation (up to 30 to 50 percent) of irrigation prior to reaching the turfgrass. Irrigation should not be scheduled during such periods. However, special practices such as establishing new turf areas, and watering-in fertilizer or pesticide applications, often necessitate irrigation during adverse conditions.
3. Net irrigation requirements listed are for taller-mowed grass. Closely maintained grass, such as golf greens and tees, have significantly less rooting depth compared to taller-mowed plants; thus, they require more frequent, shallow irrigations.
4. Rainfall amounts used in these calculations are averages based on historical climatological data. Deviations from these averages usually occur, and net irrigation amounts during exceptionally dry years will have to be increased to compensate for this. Values listed also assume even rainfall distribution over the entire period. If uniform rainfall distribution does not occur, irrigation amounts higher than those listed in Table 13–5 are required.
5. "On-site" computer-assisted ET-predicted models calculate water needs based on local conditions. Generally, a range of ET models are used that estimate between 0.8 and 1.2 of actual ET.

IRRIGATION STRATEGIES FOR TURFGRASS MANAGERS

With potential shortages of irrigation water, it is in the best interest of a golf course to conserve water whenever possible and to design irrigation programs that provide quality turf with minimum water use (Figure 13–9). Irrigating too heavily not only wastes valuable water, but it invites the potential for increased disease incidence, turf thinning, shallow rooting, reduced stress tolerance, and increased soil compaction and turf wear. Inefficient use of electricity and excessive wear and tear on the irrigation pumps and total system also are reasons to maximize water use.

Playing conditions also are influenced by watering practices. Overwatered golf courses tend to play much longer and have slower putting greens. Conversely, drier turf results in quicker putting surfaces and more bounce and roll; in effect, shortening the course. However, if allowed to dry excessively, this increases the risk of losing turf from moisture stress and causes a reduction in aesthetic quality. Many courses also are restricted to the amount of water they can use and may be mandated to irrigate based on ET data, soil moisture levels, or other water need indicators.

Steps in formulating an irrigation strategy include:

1. Calibrate an irrigation system's output and distribution uniformity (or DU).
2. Determine daily ET rates or soil moisture status by one of the methods discussed. A reasonable estimate of daily summer mean ET rates for various grasses are provided in Table 13–5.
3. Accurately track daily rainfall and ET rates so a water budget can be set-up and followed.
4. When irrigation is needed, use the appropriate crop coefficient percent (0.75 to 0.85) of daily ET rate and incorporate distribution uniformity (DU) of the irrigation system as shown earlier and below.
5. Make adjustments for rainfall, varying microclimates, and forecasted weather.

Irrigation System Calibration

The first step in irrigation scheduling is to determine how much water the irrigation system applies, expressed as inches/hour. This information is central to water management. The easiest and most common way to determine application rate is by "canning" the turf area. For small areas, a dozen or so empty tin cans are placed in a grid system across the turf (Figure 13–10). It is important the cans are the same size and fairly tall; soup or vegetable cans work well. The irrigation system is then activated for a timed period, usually 15 to 30 minutes, to let the cans collect a quarter- to a half-inch of water. The average amount of water in each can is then measured with a ruler and adjusted to the amount of water caught per hour. These cans are all emptied into a single can and the water depth is measured with a ruler. The depth is then divided by the total number of cans to get the average depth per can. This value must be divided by the time period to calculate the application rate. For example, assume 12 cans were used to collect irrigation for a 30-minute period. The total depth of all cans was 4.4 inch (11 cm). Dividing 4.4 inch (11 cm) by 12 gives 0.37 inch per can (0.94 cm). Now multiply the average depth, 0.37 inch (0.94 cm) per one-half hour, by 2 to calculate the application rate of 0.74 inch (1.9 cm) per hour.

FIGURE 13–9 An irrigation system should apply sufficient water in an efficient, uniform, and expedient manner.

FIGURE 13–10 Simple irrigation system calibration and uniformity is found by placing cans throughout an irrigation zone, turning the system on for a predetermined time period, and measuring the captured moisture in each can.

The canning method also helps indicate the distribution uniformity (DU) of the irrigation system. Distribution uniformity is determined by calculating the average amount of water caught in 25 percent of the total cans that accumulated the **least** amount of water during the test. This value is then divided by the mean depth of water in all cans. The equation of DU involves:

$$\text{distribution uniformity (DU)} = \frac{\text{average \textbf{least} amount of water depth collected in 25\% of all cans}}{\text{mean depth collected for all cans}}$$

Example:

The can test is performed with 20 cans spaced five feet (1.5 m) apart in a grid system. After a 15-minute run cycle, the average depth in the five **least**-filled cans was measured to be 0.2 inch (0.5 cm). The average depth measure in all cans was 0.33 inch (0.84 cm). The precipitation rate is then adjusted from a 15-minute period to inches per hour by multiplying the 0.33 inch (0.84 cm) by 4 to achieve 1.32 inches (3.6 cm) per hour. The DU value is then determined by the previous formula.

$$\text{DU} = \frac{\text{average \textbf{least} amount of water depth collected in 25\% of all cans}}{\text{mean depth collected for all cans}}$$

$$\text{DU} = \frac{0.2 \text{ inch}}{0.35} = 0.57$$

Typical DU values range from 55 to 75 percent (Figure 13–11). The lower the value, the less uniformity with which an irrigation system applies water; thus, the more water is needed to uniformly meet the plant's need.

Irrigation system calibration, but not DU, can also be determined by knowing the amount (gallons) of water applied per irrigation head, the sprinkler spacing (feet), and by using one of the formulas listed in Table 13–7. Different formulas are needed depending if the sprinkler head design is on square spacing, triangular spacing, or single row design. For example, to determine inches of water applied per hour for an irrigation system designed with triangular spaced heads 50 feet apart that apply 30 gallons of water per head, use the following equation from Table 13–7.

$$\frac{96.3 \times \text{gal per minute applied per head}}{(\text{sprinkler spacing, ft.})^2 \times 0.866} = \text{inches water applied per hour}$$

$$\frac{96.3 \times 30 \text{ gal per minute applied per head}}{(50 \text{ ft})^2 \times 0.866} = 1.33 \text{ inches per hour}$$

Example:

a. If 46 acres (18.6 ha) of turf were to receive one inch (2.5 cm) of water, what is the total amount of water, in gallons, needed? From Table 13–7, one acre-inch of water equals 27,154 gallons; thus, 27,154 gallons × 46 acres = 1,249,084 total gallons of water are needed (47 million liters).

b. If water costs are three cents per cubic foot of water, what is the total cost of this volume? From Table 13–7, one cubic foot equals 7.48 gallons of water; thus,

$$\frac{1\ ft^3}{7.48\ gal} \times 1{,}249{,}084\ gal\ total \times \frac{\$0.03}{ft^3} = \$5{,}010$$

Determining Irrigation Rates and Frequency

In addition to the application rate and uniformity, the turf manager should know how much water the turf is using. This can be determined using reference ET from a weather station/computer system plus a crop coefficient specific for the turf species from data in Table 13–5, or with data from an atmometer or other devices as previously discussed. Historical weather information may also provide reasonable estimates of average water use. Managers also need to know where the roots are in the soil profile and approximately how much available water is held by the soil (Table 13–4 lists approximate values).

The amount of water needed to moisten the soil to a given depth depends on soil type, water infiltration and percolation rates, and surface slope. Figure 13–2 presents the amount of water needed to wet different soils to various depths. Soils severely sloped, compacted, or clayey in nature may have low infiltration rates. As a result, the soil may not be able to absorb the required amount of irrigation at one time. Managers may have to irrigate using multiple cycles until the desired amount is applied. After an irrigation, managers should double-check the depth of moisture penetration using a soil probe or screwdriver so they can fine-tune their timing.

As previously noted, evaporation during hot, windy, and dry periods can reduce irrigation efficiency. Superintendents can avoid this by irrigating early in the morning before the temperature rises and humidity drops. Early morning irrigation also removes dew from the leaves, and helps prevent diseases favored by irrigating in the evening.

Water Budgeting

Budgeting water is analogous to handling money in a checking account (Figure 13–12). There are inputs (deposits), outputs (withdrawals), and a certain amount of water in the soil (standing bal-

TABLE 13–7 *Conversions and calculations for determining turfgrass irrigation needs.*

1 acre-inch (amt. of water needed to cover 1 acre to the depth of 1 inch)	= = =	27,154 gal 43,560 cu. in. 3,630 cu. ft.	1 acre-foot (amt. of water needed to cover 1 acre to the depth of 1 foot)	= =	325,851 gal 43,560 cu. ft.
1 inch/1,000 sq. ft.	= =	620 gal 83 cu. ft.	7 ½ gallons	= =	1 cu ft. 231 cu. in.
1 gallon	= =	0.134 cu. ft. 8.34 lbs	1 cu. ft. (ft³) 1 psi	= =	7.4805 gal 2.31 ft. of head
1 pound of water	=	0.1199 gal	1 foot of head	=	0.433 psi
volume of water	=	7.48 gal/cu. ft.	1 million gallon	=	3.07 acre-feet

for **square** spacing irrigation head design:

$$\frac{96.3 \times \text{gal per minute applied per full circle head}}{(\text{sprinkler spacing, ft})^2} = \text{inches water applied per hour}$$

for **triangular** spacing irrigation head design:

$$\frac{96.3 \times \text{gal per minute applied per full circle head}}{(\text{sprinkler spacing, ft})^2 \times 0.866} = \text{inches water applied per hour}$$

for **single** row spacing irrigation head design:

$$\frac{96.3 \times \text{gal per minute applied per full circle head}}{\text{sprinkler throw diameter (ft)} \times 0.80 \times \text{sprinkler spacing (ft.)}} = \text{inches water applied per hour}$$

Next, to convert inches of water applied per hour to inches per minute, divide by 60.

Finally, calculate the time sprinklers should run to apply ET-adjusted watering rates:

$$\frac{\text{ET rate}}{\text{precipitation rate} \times \text{crop coefficient}} = \text{minutes of run time}$$

ance). The flow of water (money) into and out of the "checking account" (the rootzone) is simply followed over time. If the roots penetrate 12 inches (30 cm), the checking account is the water held in 12 inches (30 cm) of soil. If the roots penetrate only two inches (5 cm), the checking account is considerably smaller. Irrigation is applied to wet the rootzone, no more, no less. Generally, most of the roots on putting greens and tees are in the top six inches (15 cm) of soil, whereas roots on fairways and roughs often penetrate 12 inches (30 cm) or more.

Consider a silt-loam soil at field capacity, which is roughly 2.0 inches (5 cm) of water per foot of soil (see Table 13–4). A 12-inch (30 cm) deep bermudagrass root system growing in this soil will have access to 2.0 inches (5 cm) of available water. Weather station data and a predictive model estimate over a six-day period that 1.8 inch (4.6 cm) of water was used by the theoretical reference crop. Correcting this reference value using a K_c of 0.7 for bermudagrass, the turf actually uses about 1.3 inch of water (1.8 × 0.7 = 1.26 in., 3.2 cm). Subtracting this from the original 2.0 inches (5 cm) of available water gives about 0.7 inch (1.8 cm) of water left in the soil. Should the turf go another day before irrigating? No, it's time to water, since it's never a good idea to deplete most of the available water. Approximately 1.5 inches (3.8 cm) of irrigation should be applied to replace the 1.3 inches (3.3 cm) lost from the system. The soil is returned to field capacity without irrigating excessively and wasting water.

Determining Approximate Intervals (in days) Between Irrigation Cycles

$$\text{irrigation interval (days)} = \frac{\text{soil's field capacity (in. water)} - \text{rooting depth (in.)}}{\text{daily ET rate}}$$

For example, a sand soil with a field capacity of one inch, a rooting depth of one-half inch, and a summer daily ET rate of 0.20 inches per day:

$$\frac{1 \text{ in.} - 0.5 \text{ in.}}{0.2 \text{ in./day}} = 2.5 \text{ days between irrigation cycles, which then brings the soil back to field capacity}$$

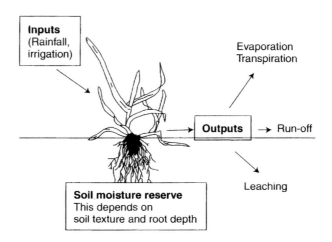

FIGURE 13-12 Water budgeting is like managing a checking account with inputs, reserves, and outputs.

Inputs (Rainfall, irrigation)

Evaporation Transpiration

Outputs → Run-off

Leaching

Soil moisture reserve This depends on soil texture and root depth

If rainfall occurs and it is more than the amount of water depleted during the period (1.3 inch), the rootzone is returned to field capacity and any excess is ignored since it won't be stored in the rootzone. If it rains less than actual ET, the running deficit is calculated over several days, and irrigation is scheduled when ET has depleted the soil moisture to a bit more than 50 percent of the 2.0 inch of available water. A good rain gauge is needed to keep track of precipitation, and it's a good idea to use automatic pump shutdown switches to prevent irrigation after a significant precipitation. Conversion factors in Table 13-7 indicate gallonage required to apply certain amounts.

With information on ET rates and sprinkler calibration available, each sprinkler's run time can be calculated. The daily ET rate is divided by the sprinkler output. For example, if the day's ET rate is 0.3 inch and the sprinkler output is 0.01 inch per minute, the irrigation time needed would be 30 minutes. However, this is adjusted according to the appropriate crop coefficient (0.85 in our case for bentgrass); therefore, 30 minutes is multiplied by 0.85 to give 25 minutes of run-time needed. Distribution uniformity considerations also are incorporated to ensure enough water is being applied uniformly across the turf area.

Time of Day to Irrigate

As discussed earlier, water loss rates decrease with reduced solar radiation, little wind, high relative humidity, and low air temperatures. The superintendent can take advantage of these factors by irrigating when conditions do not favor excessive evaporation. Generally, irrigation should occur in early morning hours before air temperatures rise and relative humidity drops. Irrigating at this time also removes dew from leaf blades and allows sufficient time for infiltration into the soil but not enough to encourage disease development.

A problem with this timing is golfers often begin play early in the morning since it is generally cooler. Therefore, superintendents may have to water at night. However, some evidence suggests irrigating at night may increase the incidence of certain diseases. On most summer days, afternoon irrigation is not suggested unless lowering canopy temperature is important, fertilizer or pesticide application must be irrigated-in, or overseeding and turf establishment are being conducted. Watering efficiency may be reduced somewhat by mid-day irrigation. In addition, mid-day irrigation may result in compaction problems from concentrated play that normally occurs then. Therefore, superintendents should preferably irrigate in early morning, secondly at night, and least desirable, during the day.

Water Conservation

Daily water conservation practices integrate many of the previously mentioned practices and technology (Table 13-8). Using computerized irrigation systems to better pinpoint irrigation needs for various soil types or turfgrass use, utilizing weather stations to determine daily ET rates, installing soil moisture sensors to monitor soil moisture levels, and using automatic

TABLE 13–8 *Improving water efficiency through proper irrigation design, maintenance, and use.*

- Hire an irrigation design specialist.
- Use an irrigation system design that provides uniform application to minimize wet and dry areas and limits run-off or leaching (Figure 13–13).
- Check on local codes for required backflow preventers, valves, heads, and so on (Figure 13–14). Also check on permit requirements.
- Add enough wire in the irrigation system to accommodate future expansions or added heads per zones.
- Use a variable frequency drive pump to gradually reduce water flow after pump shut-off and gradually increase water flow when turned on to reduce strain on the pipe.
- Safeguard against water hammer when systems are pressurized by installing check values where water drains from low heads to prevent damage.
- Periodically check valve boxes for leaks or disconnected wires and open and close valves manually to confirm proper operations.
- Consider using ductile fittings and gasketed joints instead of glue due to their longer life expectancy.
- Consider looping the irrigation system to allow watering from two directions.
- Use multirow irrigation design systems compared to single rows.
- When possible, irrigate in early morning or at night.
- Zone irrigation heads of similar areas together (greens, tees, fairways, and roughs).
- Isolate as many areas of the golf course as possible with individual shut-off valves from the main line.
- Match the application rate to the soil infiltration rate.
- Use low-volume heads when possible.
- Use the biggest irrigation pipe that is affordable—ideally, pipe size should handle water speeds of three feet (0.9 m) per second.
- Mainline pipe should be a minimum of four to six inches (10 to 15 cm) in diameter, preferably larger.
- Successive branches of an irrigation line should be reduced by two inches (5 cm).
- Use multiple irrigation cycles to allow infiltration without surface run-off.
- Have controller flexibility to develop the most efficient irrigation program.
- Eliminate pipe leakage.
- Use a pilot tube and gauge to check pressure at the head to ensure maximum efficiency and to regulate water use.
- Avoid placing heads in a depressed area as seepage or bleeding may occur. Use seals if this is unavoidable.
- Periodically check the height of heads to prevent mower and other equipment damage and to check coverage and water-discharge patterns.
- Use low-maintenance turf, landscape plants, and native grasses whenever possible.
- Use mulch (>3 inches, 7.6 cm deep) around landscaping to reduce evaporation and weeds.
- Use drip irrigation or low emitter heads for landscapes.
- Have efficient drainage designs that allow water harvesting or recapturing in ponds or catch basins.
- Have an on-site weather station or access to regional weather information to calculate ET rates.
- Consider a remote (radio) controller to enable quicker response time to a problem.
- Have color weather radar or other devices to track and predict local showers.
- Use pressure-regulating stems on spray heads to prevent water waste when operated outside the designated window of pressure.
- In windy areas, use low trajectory heads.
- Use an irrigation company with local service support and readily available parts.

pump shutdown switches when significant rainfall occurs are examples of water conservation techniques.

A weather station and soil moisture sensors integrated with an automatic computerized pre-scription irrigation system automatically sets each head's daily run from ET rates and/or soil moisture. Integrated into the ET formulas for calculating plant water needs are other on-site variables such as recent rainfall events, soil types, terrain slope, and geographic location. Partial heads and proper design help place water on intended turf areas and off unintended natural areas, mulched areas, water bodies, and other such areas. Applying an efficient design will (1) limit water loss from run-off, leaching beyond the rootzone, or loss from ET; and (2) provide adequate irrigation within time constraints from night irrigation. Using high-quality premium efficiency pump motors with variable frequency drives are currently state-of-the-art. These motors only expend enough energy to meet the demands of the pumps.

Turf areas should be irrigated when needed and deep enough to wet the entire rootzone. This has shown to be the most efficient and effective mode of irrigation. Sprinkler heads with improved water distribution and reduced wind drift continually evolve. Current sprinklers have scheduling coefficients in the range of 1.3 to 1.5, with some as low as 1.2. Not so long ago, the industry norm was 2.0 to 2.5, indicating the increased efficiency of modern sprinklers.

The use of effluent or reuse water for golf course irrigation and possible wetland recharge will probably increase in the future. Monitoring the quality of this water and building a connection with the wastewater treatment facility are important to determine the desirable and undesirable components of this water. For most instances, effluent water proves to be more than adequate in terms of having acceptable nutrient and heavy metal levels.

Probably the major problem with effluent water is not quality but quantity. Courses find themselves having to accept a certain gallonage per day, whether it is needed or not. Storage of this water is a concern and must be addressed early in the planning process of using effluent water.

Irrigation Systems

When designing or renovating an irrigation system, many parameters affect the potential performance of it. The first step is determining critical site information such as static pressure, meter size, service line size, and elevation changes. These provide the static pressure and gallons per minute (GPA), two critical numbers needed to design a system and to calculate friction loss after the proposed design is drawn. When calculating this, choose the irrigation zone with the highest flow rate, the zone furthest away from the pump, and the zone containing heads at the highest elevation. Once these calculations are made, add the friction losses together and subtract them from the pressure calculated for design capacity. Determine if the adjusted pressure is sufficient to operate the selected sprinklers.

1. Report card for an irrigation system should include the following steps:
   a. Identify a system that will satisfy your needs
   b. Consider historical performance of the existing system
   c. Identify hydraulics, head spacing, nozzle selection, controller capacities, and climate
   d. Evaluate the existing system's conditions as compared to a state-of-the-art design
2. Determine the grade of an irrigation system that will satisfy your needs:
   a. Consider golfer expectations, labor and budget availability, and climate (ET)
3. Historical performance:
   a. Estimate system performance over the past five years
   b. Identify if the system kept the turf healthy, kept the course green most of the time, and kept the course firm and playable
4. Determine the quality of the existing system:
   a. Uniform head-to-head coverage is the result of:
      • Reasonable sprinkler spacing distances specified in the original design
      • Uniformly installed spacing and proper configuration
      • Sprinkler and nozzle performance that produces optimum coverage within the system's design parameters
      • Flexible controls with ability to manage the amount of water applied
      • Reasonable number of sprinklers per control station
      • Proper hydraulic design
      • Properly installed, reliable hardware components
5. Sprinkler spacing distances:
   a. Operating at lower pressures reduces operating costs and minimizes development of fine droplets
   b. Newer irrigation systems are designed with closer spacing and lower pressures

FIGURE 13–13 Circular or "donut" irrigation pattern from a single row system that does not provide sufficient overlap.

FIGURE 13–14 A backflow preventer is required in most areas for irrigation systems connected to a municipal water source.

6. Sprinkler/nozzle performance must be matched or uniformity is impossible:
   a. Use catch can test for evaluation
7. Automatic controls help to quickly and efficiently manage water application.
8. Sprinkler station assignments:
   a. Reducing the total number of sprinklers controlled per satellite station increases flexibility
   b. Ideally, individual head control should be used throughout the course, and dual heads at greens allow separate green and surround controls
9. System hydraulics, flow velocities, and operational windows:
   a. Hydraulic design and pipe sizing are based upon:
      • number of acres to be irrigated
      • peak water replacement requirements
      • number of hours available to complete an irrigation cycle during peak water replacement
   b. Avoid overloading a system's hydraulics, which then generate heat and blow fuses.

Diagnosing and Repairing Irrigation Systems

All irrigation systems are subjected to repairs from natural wear-and-tear or through external mechanical damage such as a mower or truck driving over a head or valve. However, many repairs could be prevented by using higher-quality parts and installation. Irrigation systems are the lifeline of a golf course, and cutting corners during installation or hurrying up installation jobs often leads to system problems or failures.

The goal of any irrigation system repair should be to restore the system to its original, or better, level of operation. Parts susceptible to failure should be replaced before the system is in critical need. A general rule-of-thumb to follow when trying to decide whether or not to replace a part: if the cost of the repair will exceed 50 percent of the cost of the new component, it should be replaced. Items typically not worth repairing, but should be replaced, include:

- Head nozzles
- Riser bubblers
- Pop-up spray heads
- Controllers more than 15 years old
- Rain or freeze sensors
- Pumps so old the name place and specifications cannot be read
- Burned out pump motors
- Any low-cost or non-major brand of irrigation component available by mass retail merchandisers

Diagnosing the problem is the first step in repairing systems. Often, improper or poor irrigation uniformity is due to insufficient pressure, inadequate head spacing, or clogged head or irrigation lines.

Valves

When dealing with inoperative valves, two common problems exist: either they do not close or they will not open. Valves that do not close are usually due to physical obstruction preventing the diaphragm from sealing. Valves may not close due to: (1) insufficient force above the diaphragm caused by a missing plunger, one stuck in the up position, or a plugged diaphragm filter; (2) flow control turned up too high; (3) constant voltage from the controller; (4) leak between the bonnet and valve body; or (5) an open manual bleed.

Pumps

A wise superintendent once said, "If you have a pump, you have a problem." Irrigation pumps often have suction problems, electrical problems, control or relay problems, or sectional valve problems. When repairing pumps, first determine if power is being received by the pump, and if the pump is running at all. Always check the filter system for clogs.

Uniformity

When spotty turf is evident, start checking for reasons of non-uniformity. Broken heads or insufficient coverage may indicate the wrong head is in place. Incorrect or inconsistent head and nozzle types can result from:

- Plant growth interference, requiring pruning/trimming of trees, limbs, or shrubs to allow unimpeded water flow
- Pressure too high, requiring flow control devices and/or pressure regulators
- Low head drainage, requiring new heads with check valves
- Sprinkler heads and/or risers tilted, modified as needed
- Soil compaction, requiring aeration or dethatching of area

Electrical

When checking for electrical problems with irrigation systems, the condition of field wiring, proper and adequate grounding, and checking the transformer and troubleshooting controllers is available. The following steps are used to evaluate the condition of field wiring and solenoid from the controller:

- Disconnect the common wire from the controller
- Set the Volt-ohm meter to the "Ohms" position

- Connect one of the meter leads to the common wire
- Touch the second meter lead to each of the station terminals and record the resistance readings
- Measure the ohms of the solenoid lead wires; if resistance is less than 20 ohms, then the solenoid needs to be replaced

If the solenoid resistance is within the acceptable range, resistance will be less than the resistance for the "least resistive" solenoid. Wire tracing equipment and technology will be needed to locate the shorted field wiring location.

CHAPTER 14

Irrigation Water Quality

INTRODUCTION

Golf courses increasingly face the use of poorer quality irrigation sources. Wells, ponds, streams, rivers, and waste treatment plants are common water sources for irrigation. Problem levels of salinity, sodium, and pH and bicarbonate can occur in any of these sources, especially when located near the coast or in arid regions.

Access to these and other water resources, as well as economic, environmental, and regulatory considerations, may dictate the use of poor quality irrigation water. The continued application of poor quality irrigation water can reduce the quality and growth of turfgrass. However, with proper precautions and altered management practices, poor quality irrigation water may be used safely in most situations.

Most of the knowledge and technology developed concerning the use of poor quality irrigation water is from arid regions. In some instances, the concerns and practices used to overcome poor quality irrigation water in these regions are not the same as those used in other areas. One difference is the occurrence of higher rainfall amounts in contrast to the near absence of rainfall in arid regions, which makes it somewhat easier to effectively utilize poor quality irrigation water in higher rainfall areas. Rainfall is a source of high quality irrigation water and can alleviate the effects of poor quality irrigation water.

Another difference, however, that makes it more difficult to manage poor quality irrigation water is the higher level of bicarbonate often found in higher rainfall areas, in comparison to levels in the arid regions of the United States. Additional management is necessary when bicarbonate levels are high in irrigation water.

With an ever-increasing demand on potable (drinking) supplies, superintendents will probably be using increasing amounts of poorer quality water. Since 250,000 to 1,000,000 gallons per day are needed to irrigate most 18-hole courses, effluent water offers an economical and environmentally sound source for use. The following tests provide information concerning soil and water quality:

- Total salt content as measured by the electrical conductivity (EC_w) or total dissolved salts (TDS) of water
- Sodium level (SAR or ESP)
- Toxic ion levels, especially boron, chloride, and fluoride
- Bicarbonates (RSC)

- Adjusted SAR
- pH

Other factors influencing water quality use are soil water infiltration rates, differential salinity tolerance of the turfgrass species, and nutrient content (e.g., nitrogen, phosphorus, and potassium). Refer to Chapter 2 for a listing of the relative salt tolerance of turfgrass species.

SALINITY

Salts include any negative ion, except hydroxide (OH^-), combined with any positive ion other than hydrogen (H^+). Salts may be soluble, such as those containing chlorides, or relatively insoluble, such as limestone or gypsum. **Soluble salts** are those inorganic chemicals more soluble than gypsum ($CaSO_4$). For example, table salt (NaCl) has a solubility almost 150 times greater (357 g/L) than gypsum (2.4 g/L). Principal soluble salts found in water are chloride and sulfate salts of sodium, calcium, potassium, and magnesium (Table 14–1). Table salt (sodium chloride) is also found in some soils. Insoluble salts occur (e.g., gypsum and lime), but excessive soluble salts are the primary ones that may impede plant growth rather than the insoluble ones.

These salts originated from the weathering of primary rocks and minerals. As pure water from rain or snow moves over rocks and soil, it dissolves soluble salts. Oceans have become the eventual reservoir of soluble salts as water has moved through the hydrological cycle. Along coastal regions, seawater is intruding into fresh water aquifers because withdrawal of water is occurring faster than replenishment. In interior regions of the country, ancient saline marine deposits in geological layers add soluble salts to groundwater as water passes through the layers. This process has occurred throughout the country; as a result, virtually all fresh water supplies have some amount of dissolved salts. The amount of salt in water determines the degree of salinity and, to a large extent, the overall water quality.

TABLE 14–1 *Salts and their ionic components commonly found in soil and irrigation water.*

Salts	Cations	Anions
Soluble salts		
Sodium chloride (NaCl)	Calcium (Ca^{+2})	Chloride (Cl^-)
Calcium chloride (CaCl)	Magnesium (Mg^{+2})	Sulfate (SO_4^{-2})
Epsom salts ($MgSO_4$)	Sodium (Na^+)	Nitrate (NO_3^-)
	Potassium (K^+)	Borate (BO_3^{-3})
	Ammonium (NH_4^+)	
Insoluble salts		
Limestone ($CaCO_3$)		
Gypsum ($CaSO_4$)		
Fertilizer (soluble) salts		
Ammonium nitrate [$(NH_4)_2NO_3$]		
Ammonium sulfate [$(NH_4)_2SO_4$]		
Potassium chloride (KCl)		
Potassium nitrate (KNO_3)		
Potassium sulfate (K_2SO_4)		
Urea [$CO(NH_2)_2$]		

Salts also can move upward from groundwater. Water is drawn to the surface by evaporation and deposited on the soil and plant surface. Formation of a white crust on the soil surface indicates salt accumulation, as does shoot browning (Chapter 2). This generally is a problem in low humidity and low rainfall areas, such as the arid western states, unless extended droughts occur elsewhere.

Measuring and Classifying Irrigation Salinity

Salinity is determined by measuring the ability of water to conduct an electrical current. Salty water is a good conductor of electrical current, whereas pure water is a relatively poor conductor. Salinity is expressed in two different ways, either as **electrical conductivity** (EC_w) or **total dissolved salts** (TDS). There are several units commonly used to express EC_w: deciSiemens per meter (dS/m), millimhos per centimeter (mmhos/cm), or micromhos per centimeter (micromhos/cm). The relationship between these units is:

$$1 \text{ deciSiemens per meter} = 0.1 \text{ Siemens/meter} = 1 \text{ mmhos/cm} = 1{,}000 \text{ micromhos/cm } (\mu\text{mhos/cm})$$
$$= 640 \text{ ppm TDS}$$

Total dissolved salts are expressed in parts per million (ppm) or milligrams per liter (mg/L) and are generally not measured directly, but calculated from an EC_w measurement.

$$1 \text{ milligram/liter (mg/L)} = 1 \text{ part per million (ppm)}$$
$$EC_w \text{ (mmhos/cm or dS/m)} \times 640 = \text{TDS (mg/L or ppm)}$$

The following is used to convert the salt content of water from total dissolved salts (TDS) to EC_w:

$$\text{TDS [ppm (or mg/L)]} \times 0.0016 = EC_w \text{ (mmhos/cm or dS/m)}$$

Example:

1. An irrigation source has an EC_w of 0.53 mmhos/cm. What would the EC_w be in dS/m, μmhos/cm, and TDS ppm?
   a. Since 1 dS/m = 1 mmhos/cm, then 0.53 dS/m = 0.53 mmhos/cm
   b. Since 1 mmhos/cm = 1,000 μmhos/cm, then

$$0.53 \text{ mmhos/cm} \times \frac{1{,}000 \text{ } \mu\text{mhos/cm}}{1 \text{ mmhos/cm}} = 530 \text{ } \mu\text{mhos/cm}$$

   c. To convert mmhos/cm to ppm, multiply by 640:

$$0.53 \text{ mmhos/cm} \times 640 = 339 \text{ ppm TDS}$$

2. The salt content of a water sample is 1,121 mg/L TDS. What is the salt content in dS/m and μmhos/cm?

   a. To convert TDS (mg/L or ppm) to dS/M, divide by 640:

$$1{,}121 \text{ mg/L} \div 640 = 1.75 \text{ dS/m}$$

   b. To convert dS/m (or mmhos/cm) to μmhos/cm, multiply by 1,000:

$$1.75 \text{ dS/m (or mmhos/cm)} \times 1{,}000 = 1{,}750 \text{ } \mu\text{mhos/cm}$$

The ratio of total dissolved salt to EC_w of various salt solutions ranges from 550 to 700 ppm per dS/m. The most common salt in saline water, sodium chloride, has a TDS of 640 ppm at an EC_w of 1 dS/m. Most laboratories use this relationship to calculate TDS from EC_w, but some multiply the amount by 700. Water sample salinities are often compared to those of seawater that has an average EC_w of 43 dS/m or about 32,000 ppm dissolved salts. Individual salts are also reported in milliequivalents per liter (meq/L).

Irrigation water is classified into four categories based on the salinity hazard, which considers the potential for damaging plants and the level of management needed for utilization as an irrigation source (Table 14–2). Water with EC_w readings of less than 0.75 dS/m is suitable for irrigation without problems. Successful use of water with EC_w values above 0.75 dS/m depends upon soil conditions and plant tolerance to salinity. Generally, higher salinity levels can be used

TABLE 14–2 *General guidelines for irrigation water quality concerning total salinity, sodium hazard, and ion toxicity (modified from Huck, 2000; McCarty, 2001; Westcot and Ayers, 1984).*

Item	Units	Minor problems	Increasing problems	Severe problems
General water quality				
pH	1 to 14	6.0 to 7.0	7.0 to 8.0	>8.0
Bicarbonate (HCO_3)	mg/L or ppm	<120	120 to 180	>180
	meq/L	<1.9	1.9 to 2.9	>2.9
Carbonate (CO_3)	mg/L or ppm	<15	15 to 50	>50
	meq/L	<0.5	0.5 to 1.65	>1.65
TSS (total suspended solids)	mg/L or ppm	<5	5 to 10	>10
Water hardness (Ca + Mg)	mg/L or ppm	<200	200 to 400	>400
($CaCO_3$)	mg/L or ppm	<50	50 to 300	>300
EC_w (electrical conductivity)	mmhos/cm or dS/m	<0.75	0.75 to 2.25	>2.25
TDS (total dissolved salts)	mg/L or ppm	<500	500 to 1,400	>1,400
Soil sodium/ion hazard for turfgrass				
Sodium (Na) (SAR) [saturated paste extract]	meq/L	<10	10 to 18	>18
RSC (residual sodium carbonate)	meq/L	<0	1.25 to 2.5	>2.5
EC (electrical conductivity, saturated paste extract)	dS/m	<4	4 to 12	>12
TDS (total dissolved salts)	mg/L or ppm	<2,500	2,500 to 7,500	>7,500
ESP (exchangeable sodium percentage)	%	<13	13 to 15	>15
Calcium (Ca)	mg/L or ppm	<25	25 to 250	>250
Magnesium (Mg)	mg/L or ppm	<20	20 to 40	>40
Foliar ion toxicity for turfgrass				
Calcium (Ca)	mg/L or ppm	<60	60 to 100	>100
Fluoride (F)	mg/L or ppm	<0.25	0.25 to 0.5	>0.5
Iron (Fe)	mg/L or ppm	<0.1	0.1 to 1.0	>1.0
Magnesium (Mg)	mg/L or ppm	<25	25 to 50	>50
Nitrogen (N)	mg/L or ppm	<11	11 to 23	>23
Phosphorus (P)	mg/L or ppm	<0.40	0.40 to 1.0	>1.0
Potassium (K)	mg/L or ppm	<20	20 to 50	>50
Sulfates	mg/L or ppm	<100	100 to 200	>200
Soil ion hazard for sensitive ornamentals				
Boron (B)	meq/L	<0.75	0.75 to 3.0	>3.0
Chloride (Cl^-)	meq/L	<3	3 to 10	>10
	mg/L or ppm	<100	100 to 300	>300
Sodium (Na)	mg/L or ppm	<70	71 to 200	>200
Foliar ion toxicity for sensitive ornamentals				
Ammonium-N (NH_4-N)	mg/L or ppm	<5	5 to 30	>30
Nitrate-N (NO_3-N)	mg/L or ppm	<50	50 to 100	>100
Bicarbonate (HCO_3^-)	meq/L	<1.5	1.5 to 8.5	>8.5
HCO_3 - Unsightly foliar deposits	mg/L or ppm	<90	90 to 500	>500
Residual chlorine (Cl_2)	mg/L or ppm	<1.0	1 to 5	>5
Fluoride (F)	mg/L or ppm	<1.0	1.0	>1.0

on sandy soils where salts can be flushed compared to similar values on poorly draining clay soils that may cause problems. Under typical summer stress, EC_w of turfgrass irrigation should ideally not exceed 1.25 dS/m soluble salts. Salinity levels above 3.0 dS/m are unsuitable for any length as an irrigation source.

Assessing Soil Salinity

Saline soils are classified based on two criteria: (1) the **total soluble salt or salinity content,** and (2) **exchangeable sodium percentage** (or, more recently, **sodium adsorption ratio**). Additional information is also often used, such as carbonate content and potential toxic ions. **Good drainage is essential to leach soluble salts through the soil profile.** The better the drainage, the easier one can keep the soil level of soluble salts within tolerable limits. Sand soils are usually best suited for saline irrigation because of easy drainage, but they must be maintained near field capacity in order to prevent intolerable salt levels.

Soluble salts are measured in soils by the same basic method as used for water samples. A conductivity instrument measures electrical conductivity (EC) in an extract either from a **saturated paste** or from a **soil:water dilution.** Dilution ratios are either a 1:2 dilution (one part dry soil:two parts water) or a 1:5 dilution (one part soil:five parts water). Electrical conductivity readings from these three methods are not comparable, so the method used must be known in order to interpret the EC reading.

The saturated paste extract is the most precise method to determine soil EC, SAR, and boron levels. A soil sample is brought just to the point of saturation, allowing it to equilibrate for several hours, and then is subjected to vacuuming to extract the soil solution through filter paper. Spectrophotometers and other analytical equipment are then used to quantify the soil solution.

Using the saturated paste extract, soils with EC readings <4.0 dS/m are considered to have low salt levels (Table 14–2). Soils with EC readings of 4.0 to 12.0 dS/m have medium levels. When soil readings are above 12.0 dS/m, soils are considered to have high salt levels. Only salt-tolerant turfgrasses survive above 16 dS/m.

Soil testing laboratories frequently use a 1:2 dilution method because it is more rapid than obtaining a saturated paste extract. The EC of a 1:2 extract is on average one-fifth the EC of a saturated paste extract on sand-based greens. To estimate the EC of a saturated paste from a 1:2 extract, multiply the EC of the 1:2 extract by 5.

Substantial amounts of salt can rapidly accumulate in the rootzone during periods of drought when saline irrigation water is the predominant source of water. The application of one inch of moderately saline irrigation water (1.0 dS/m) contributes approximately 3.3 pounds of salt per 1,000 square feet. Since turf water use during peak demand is about 0.15 to 0.30 inches/day, this amount of salt can accumulate in the soil in three to seven days. Compare this amount of salt added via irrigation to routine fertilization which is usually less than two pounds of salt (fertilizer) per application, and is usually avoided when the weather is hot and dry.

Reclaiming saline soils requires leaching soluble salts out of the soil. This requires: (1) good internal soil drainage, (2) replacement of excess sodium in sodic soils, and (3) leaching out of soluble salts.

Sodium Hazard or Reduced Water Infiltration and Soil Aeration (Permeability)

Another major water quality problem with poor quality irrigation sources is deteriorating soil structure due to excessive sodium levels. Since sodium ions (Na^+) are monovalent (have only one positive charge), two sodium ions are needed to displace divalent (two positive charged) ions such as calcium (Ca^{+2}). This concern is greater on fine-textured soils such as clays and silt loams. As mentioned, fewer problems occur in well-drained, sandy soils. High soil sodium causes finer-textured soil clays and organic matter to disperse (or **deflocculate**) to where aggregates break down and smaller mineral and organic particles plug soil pores. The clays and organic matter clog soil pores, reducing water infiltration and soil aeration. The higher the clay and organic matter content of the soil, the greater the effects of sodium. This results in clogging (or dispersing) of soil pores, which reduces soil aeration and water infiltration or permeability. These soils are characterized by pools of standing water after irrigation. Potassium also disperses clays and organic matter, but levels of potassium in soils are usually ignored because they are relatively low in comparison to sodium in sodium-effected soils. Increasing calcium and magnesium concentrations in clay soils cause the soil to flocculate (have good structure), and therefore counteract the negative effects of the sodium.

Assessing Irrigation Water for Sodium Problems

The potential for irrigation water to have poor infiltration properties or sodium hazards is assessed by determining the **sodium adsorption ratio** (SAR) and the electrical conductivity (EC_w) of the water. The sodium adsorption ratio relates the concentration of sodium to the concentration of calcium and magnesium. The higher the sodium in relation to calcium and magnesium, the higher the SAR, the poorer the water infiltration, and the increased problems with soil deflocculation (deterioration). High EC_w or total salt content in the water inhibits the dispersing influence of sodium. SAR is defined as:

$$SAR = \frac{Na^+}{\sqrt{\dfrac{Ca^{+2} + Mg^{+2}}{2}}} \qquad SAR = \frac{NA^+}{\sqrt{Ca^{+2} + Mg^{+2}}}$$

Ion concentrations on the above left equation are expressed in milliequivalents per liter (meq/L) while the equation on the right is expressed in millimoles per liter (mmoles/L). Milliequivalent describes the molecular weight adjusted for the valence number (number of positive charges) of the ion. The SAR determines the number of milligrams per liter (or ppm) of Na^+, Ca^{+2}, and Mg^{+2} in a water sample. To convert parts per million (or mg/L) to meq/L, use the following equation and equivalent weights for Na^+, Ca^{+2}, and Mg^{+2} of 23, 20, and 12.2 mg/meq, respectively (Table 14–3).

$$meq/L = \frac{ppm \text{ (or mg/L)}}{equivalent \text{ weight (in mg/meq)}}$$

Example:

A water sample test reports 1,000 mg/L Na^+, 200 mg/L Ca^{+2}, and 100 mg/L Mg^{+2}. First, calculate the number of milliequivalents per liter for each ion (or refer to Table 14–3):

Na^+ = 1,000 mg/L ÷ 23 mg/meq = 44 meq/L; Ca^{+2} = 200 mg/L ÷ 20 mg/meq = 10 meq/L; Mg^{+2} = 100 mg/L ÷ 12.2 mg/meq = 8.20 meq/L

These values are then placed into the SAR equation as:

$$SAR = \frac{Na^+}{\sqrt{\dfrac{Ca^{+2} + Mg^{+2}}{2}}} = \frac{44}{\sqrt{\dfrac{10 + 8.2}{2}}} = 14.6 \; meq/L$$

Example:

A water analysis indicates a sodium concentration of 85 meq/L, a calcium concentration of 33.3 meq/L, and a magnesium concentration of 7.1 meq/L. What is the SAR value for this water?

$$SAR = \frac{Na^+}{\sqrt{\dfrac{Ca^{+2} + Mg^{+2}}{2}}} = \frac{85}{\sqrt{\dfrac{33.3 + 7.1}{2}}} = 18.9 \; meq/L$$

The effects of high SAR on irrigation water infiltration are dependent on the electrical conductivity of the water. For a given SAR, the lower the EC_w, the poorer the infiltration properties; the higher the EC_w, the better the infiltration. For example, irrigation water with a SAR = 15 has poor infiltration properties if the EC_w = 0.5 dS/m but good infiltration properties with an EC_w = 2.0 dS/m. A good rule-of-thumb is if the SAR is more than 10 times greater than the EC_w, then poor water infiltration is likely to occur.

General guidelines for precautions and management of irrigation water with various SAR values and an EC_w = 1.0 dS/m are provided in Table 14–4. Clay-textured soils can have structural

TABLE 14–3 *Laboratory analysis to determine water quality and factors for converting ion concentration reported in parts per million (ppm) or milligrams per liter (mg/L) to moles per liter (mol/L) or milliequivalents per liter (meq/L).*

ppm (or mg/L) ÷ molecular weight (g) = moles per liter (mol/L)

ppm (or mg/L) ÷ milliequivalent weight (mg/meq) = milliequivalents per liter (meq/L)

milliequivalents per liter (meq/L) = molecular weight ÷ total valence number

Analysis	Reporting symbol	Reporting unit	Molecular weight (g)	Milliequivalent weight (mg/meq)
Electrical conductivity	EC_w	mmhos/cm	—	—
Calcium	Ca^{+2}	meq/L	40	20
Magnesium	Mg^{+2}	meq/L	24.3	12.2
Sodium	Na^{+1}	meq/L	23	23
Carbonate	CO_3^{-2}	meq/L	60	30
Bicarbonate	HCO_3^{-1}	meq/L	61	61
Chloride	Cl^{-1}	meq/L	35.4	35.4
Sulfate	SO_4^{-2}	meq/L	96	48
Boron	B	mg/L	10.8	10.8
Nitrate-nitrogen	NO_3-N	mg/L	14	14
Acidity	pH	pH	—	—
SAR	—	meq/L	—	—
Potassium	K^{+1}	meq/L	39.1	39.1
Lithium	Li^{+1}	mg/L	7	7
Iron	$Fe^{+2 \text{ or } +3}$	mg/L	55.8	27.9 or 18.6
Ammonium-nitrogen	NH_4-N	mg/L	14	14
Phosphate phosphorus	PO_4-P	mg/L	31	varies

Conversion values between mg/L and meq/L for most water constituents		
Constituents	Multiply by the following value to convert mg/L to meq/L	Multiply by the following value to convert meq/L to mg/L
Sodium (Na^{+1})	0.043	23
Magnesium (Mg^{+2})	0.083	12
Calcium (Ca^{+2})	0.05	20
Chloride (Cl^{-1})	0.028	36
Sulfate (SO_4^{-2})	0.021	48
Bicarbonate (HCO_3^{-1})	0.016	61
Carbonate (CO_3^{-2})	0.033	30

permeability problems if a water SAR >9 is used over an extended period that reduces infiltration, percolation, and drainage, often causing low soil oxygen problems. In our earlier example where the water sample had a SAR of 17.5 meq/L, problems could occur if this water source was used long term on finer-textured soils.

Well-drained sand soils, such as many modified golf greens, can tolerate higher SAR values. However, clay or organic matter in the sand is more likely to form a layer to the depth of irrigation water penetration as the sodium disperses these, allowing them to move downward. This layer then restricts the ability to leach the soils.

Some labs report **adjusted SAR** values instead of SAR. The adjusted SAR includes the added effects of the precipitation or dissolution of calcium in soils and is related to carbonate and bicarbonate concentrations. Bicarbonates can interact with soil calcium and magnesium to precipitate out lime ($CaCO_3$) or magnesium carbonate ($MgCO_3$), causing an increase in sodium

TABLE 14–4 *SAR values, categories, and precautions for irrigation sources with $EC_w \geq 1$ dS/m.*

SAR (meq/L)	Category	Precaution
0 to 10	low sodium water	Little danger from structure deterioration to almost all soils. For ornamentals, water SAR values should be <10.
10 to 18	medium sodium water	Problems on fine-textured soils and sodium-sensitive plants, especially under low-leaching conditions. Soils should have good permeability.
18 to 26	high sodium water	Problems on most soils. Good salt-tolerant plants are required along with special management, such as the use of gypsum. Generally, high and very high EC water should not be used for irrigating turfgrasses long term.
>26	very high sodium water	Unsatisfactory except with high salinity (>2.0 dS/m), high calcium levels, and the use of gypsum.

hazard. The adjusted SAR is a good predictor of what the SAR of a soil will be after several years of irrigation without any soil amendments. Adjusted SARs or RSC values are best used when high levels of bicarbonate, HCO_3^- (>2 meq/L or 120 mg/L), and carbonate, CO_3^{-2} (>0.5 meq/L or 15 mg/L) occur, since these values include the influence of HCO_3^-, CO_3^{-2}, Ca^{+2} and Mg^{+2}, or Na^+ activity.

Assessing Soils for Sodium Problems

Salt-affected soil comprises about 10 percent of the total arable lands in the world and occurs in over 100 countries. These affected soils occur most often in arid and semiarid climates but can also be found where the climate and mobility of salts cause saline water and soils, especially along seacoasts or river delta regions where seawater has inundated the soil.

Salt-affected soil can be classified as **saline, sodic,** and **saline-sodic** soils. **Saline soils** are the most common type of salt-affected soil and the easiest to reclaim. Saline soils are plagued by high levels of soluble salts, primarily chloride (Cl^-), sulfate (SO_4^{-2}), and sometimes nitrate (NO_3^-). Salts of low solubility, such as $CaSO_4$ and $CaCO_3$, may also be present. Because exchangeable sodium is not a problem, saline soils are usually flocculated with good water permeability (Table 14–5). Saline problems generally occur when: (1) insufficient rainfall leaches salts through the soil profile, (2) drainage is impaired, or (3) water contains high levels of salts.

Sodic soils, or soil structure deteriorated soils, have high levels of exchangeable sodium, low total soluble salt content, HCO_3 >120 mg/L or CO_3^{-2} >15 mg/L, and these soils tend to disperse, reducing water infiltration. Sodic soils also have a pH between 8.5 and 10 and are often called black alkali soils because the organic matter in the soil tends to disperse. Calcium and magnesium ions in sodic soils tend to form lime, leaving soluble calcium and magnesium levels low, allowing the sodium problems. Sodic soil cannot be improved by leaching the sodium from the soil profile alone. Soil amendments are required to replace the sodium in the soil in conjunction with leaching with acidified water. Saline-sodic soils have both high contents of soluble salts and exchangeable (>15%) sodium.

Two laboratory measurements are used to assess whether soils contain excessive sodium levels and if poor drainage and aeration are likely to occur. These measures are the **exchangeable sodium percentage** (ESP) and the sodium adsorption ratio (SAR). The ESP identifies the degree or portion of the soil cation exchange capacity occupied or saturated by sodium and is calculated as follows:

$$ESP = \frac{\text{exchangeable sodium (meq/L)}}{\text{cation exchange capacity (meq/L)}} \times 100$$

TABLE 14–5 *Classification of soil based on salinity (EC_e = electrical conductivity of a saturated soil paste extract) and sodium (ESP = percent of the soil cation exchange capacity occupied by sodium).*

Classification	EC_e (dS/m)*	ESP	Soil pH	Comments
Normal soil	<4	<15	5.5 to 7.5	—
Saline soil	>4	<15	<8.5	The exchange complex is usually dominated by Ca^+ and Mg^+; thus, the soil pH is usually below 8.5. A white salt crust, referred to as "white alkali," forms on the soil surface as the soil dries. Soil permeability or hydraulic conductivity is not adversely affected by adsorbed sodium. Turfgrass stands often have a spotty growth. Saline soils can be reclaimed by leaching excess salts with low-SAR water.
Sodic soil	<4	>15	>8.5	Sodic soils are nonsaline, but have high levels of exchangeable sodium, and soil pH is generally 8.5 to 10 due to the hydrolysis of sodium carbonate. Referred to as "black alkali" due to black puddles of water, like oil, from dispersed soil organic matter that crusts after drying. Sodic soils do not form a white salt crust on the soil surface but clay particles are dispersed in these soils due to high levels of sodium and low levels of calcium and magnesium. Structureless soils result with low water infiltration, nutritional disorders, compaction risk, and air permeability that few plants can tolerate. Sodic soil is reclaimed by replacing the sodium with another cation, usually calcium in the form of gypsum ($CaSO_4$). The sodium must then be leached from the soil profile.
Saline-sodic soil	≥4	>15	<8.5	These soils have characteristics intermediate between those of saline and sodic soils. Like saline soil, soil pH is usually below 8.5. The soils resemble saline soils if the soluble salts are not leached. With leaching, these soils become sodic, unless calcium and magnesium are applied. Reclaiming a saline-sodic soil is similar to reclaiming a sodic soil where calcium-containing amendments replace the sodium, forming sodium sulfate which is then leached from the soil profile.

*EC_e values are based on saturated extracts.

Example:

A soil test indicates the Na^+ content of a soil is 17.3 meq/L and the CEC of the soil is 6.9 meq/L. Find the exchangeable sodium percentage (ESP) of this soil.

$$ESP = \frac{\text{exchangeable sodium (meq/L)}}{\text{cation exchange capacity (meq/L)}} \times 100 = \frac{17.3 \text{ meq/L}}{6.9 \text{ meq/L}} = 2.5\%$$

Soil SAR is a second, more easily measured property analogous to the irrigation water SAR discussed earlier (see previous equation). Soil SAR is calculated from soil-test extractable levels of sodium, calcium, and magnesium (expressed in meq/100 grams).

ESP indicates the probability a soil will disperse, thereby reducing the permeability of soil to water and air. In the environment, salts and sodium do not act independently. For example, high-soluble salt concentration can negate the soil particle dispersal (thus, impermeability) from the effects of sodium. Table 14–5 lists the combined effects of salinity (EC) and soluble salt contents (ESP). Usually, little or only minor problems occur when ESP values are less than 13 to 15 percent (Table 14–5). An ESP >15 percent or a soil SAR >13 indicates a **sodic** soil where sodium causes soil colloids to disperse and plug the soil's drainage pores, thereby reducing the permeability of the soil to water and air. Sodic soils become saturated with sodium ions compared to calcium and magnesium ions, especially if bicarbonate ions are present. Symptoms of reduced permeability include waterlogging, reduced infiltration rates, crusting, compaction, disease occurrence, weed invasion, and poor aeration. Sodic soils often have considerable clay that is sticky due to the sodium.

Direct Assessment of the Effects of Sodium on Soil Infiltration

A method to provide a rough estimate of the need for adding amendments to sodic soil includes the following:

1. Take a one-quart soil sample from the surface of the impermeable area. Thoroughly dry and pulverize it until the largest particles are about the size of coffee grounds.
2. Add one heaping teaspoon of powdered gypsum to one pint of pulverized soil and mix thoroughly. Leave an equal amount of soil untreated.
3. Prepare two cans three-to-four inches (7.6-to-10 cm) in diameter and four-to-six inches (10-to-15 cm) tall. One open end should be covered with a piece of window screen so water can percolate but soil cannot. Put treated soil in one can and untreated soil in a separate can. Fill each can about three-fourths full with soil and pack each by dropping the can from a height of about one inch (2.5 cm) onto a hard surface about ten times.
4. Fill the can with the irrigation water to be used, being careful not to disturb the soil.
5. Collect the water as it drains. When one-half pint (237 ml) or more is collected from the gypsum-treated sample, compare this volume with the untreated sample.
6. If less than half as much water has passed through the untreated soil as through the gypsum-treated soil in the same length of time, this indicates your soil contains excess exchangeable sodium. If so, the addition of a chemical amendment is likely to improve permeability and help reclaim the soil.

CARBONATES

Bicarbonate (HCO_3^-) and, to a lesser extent, **carbonate** (CO_3^{-2}) are found in high-pH water. The primary source of carbonates and bicarbonates in soils is carbonic acid (H_2CO_3), which forms when carbon dioxide from microbial and root respiration reacts with water.

$$CO_2 \quad + \quad H_2O \quad \longleftrightarrow \quad H_2CO_3$$
$$\text{carbon dioxide} \qquad \text{water} \qquad \qquad \text{carbonic acid}$$

Carbonic acid is a very weak, noncorrosive acid, and is a chief constituent in soda pop. In higher-pH soils, the abundance of hydroxyl (OH^-) ions react with the carbonic acid to initially form bicarbonate (HCO_3^-) and, then, carbonate (CO_3^{-2}) ions.

Step 1:

$$H_2CO_3 \quad + \quad OH^- \quad \longleftrightarrow \quad HCO_3^- \quad + \quad H_2O$$
$$\text{carbonic acid} \qquad \qquad \text{(pH 6 to 9)} \quad \text{bicarbonate}$$

Step 2:

$$HCO_3^- \quad + \quad OH^- \quad \longleftrightarrow \quad CO_3^{-2} \quad + \quad H_2O$$
$$\text{bicarbonate} \qquad \qquad \text{(pH >9)} \quad \text{carbonate}$$

As the concentrations of bicarbonates and carbonates increase, more hydroxyl ions are formed with a corresponding reduction of hydrogen ions (H^+), causing an increase in pH.

When water containing HCO_3^- dries at the soil surface, calcium and magnesium carbonates (lime) are formed. Since calcium and magnesium are no longer dissolved, they do not counteract the effects of sodium, and problems related to high ESP may occur. This results in an increase in the SAR and soil pH and a decrease in water quality and soil infiltration. White lime deposits may also become visible on turf leaves during hot, dry periods as bicarbonates are deposited during evaporation. Fortunately, regular mowing removes much of these deposits.

Two measurements are used for assessing the carbonate level of irrigation water: the direct measurement of carbonate and bicarbonate and the **residual sodium carbonate** equation (RSC).

The residual sodium carbonate (RSC) equation reflects the alkalinity of water by indicating this potential precipitation of calcium and magnesium and whether sodium in irrigation water will cause soil structure problems.

$$\text{Ca}^{+2} \quad + \quad \text{CO}_3^{-2} \quad \rightarrow \quad \text{CaCO}_3$$
calcium   carbonate   calcium carbonate (insoluble)

$$\text{Mg}^{+2} \quad + \quad \text{CO}_3^{-2} \quad \rightarrow \quad \text{MgCO}_3$$
magnesium   carbonate   magnesium carbonate (insoluble)

RSC specifically measures the presence of excess carbonates (CO_3^{-2}) and bicarbonate (HCO_3^-) content over calcium (Ca^{+2}) and magnesium (Mg^{+2}) ions expressed as meq/L:

Residual Sodium Carbonate (RSC) Equation

$$RSC = (CO_3^{-2} + HCO_3^-) - (Ca^{+2} + Mg^{+2})$$

Assessment for poor water infiltration due to high carbonates and low calcium and magnesium as determined by the RSC equation is listed in Table 14-2.

If hazardous RSC water is repeatedly used, the soil becomes alkaline and likely to become sodic (structureless) over time. Values greater than 1.5 meq/L may justify irrigation acid injection. Acid injection changes the carbonates and bicarbonates to carbon dioxide and water but does not affect the calcium or magnesium. Normally, if irrigation RSC values are high but SAR values are low, acid injection is unnecessary since insufficient sodium is present to cause a problem. This also is true in areas of high rainfall where sodium is readily leached out of the soil profile. This sealing can also be broken up by a combination of cultivation (aerifying, spiking, slicing) and use of acidic fertilizers or elemental sulfur.

Example:

A water analysis indicates three mg/L CO_3^{-2}, 128 mg/L HCO_3^-, 21 mg/L Ca^{+2}, and 10 mg/L Mg^{+2}. Determine the residual sodium carbonate (RSC) in meq/L.

Step 1: Convert mg/L to meq/L:

$$\text{meq/L} = \frac{\text{mg/L}}{\text{equivalent weight}}$$

$$CO_3^{-2} = \frac{3}{30} = 0.1 \qquad Ca^{+2} = \frac{21}{20} = 1.05$$

$$HCO_3^- = \frac{128}{61} = 2.1 \qquad Mg^{+2} = \frac{10}{12} = 0.83$$

Step 2: Insert the values into the RSC equation:

$$RSC = (CO_3^{-2} + HCO_3^-) - (Ca^{+2} + Mg^{+2}) = (0.1 + 2.1) - (1.05 + 0.83) = 0.32 \text{ meq/L}$$

Bicarbonate levels alone are sometimes used to assess potential limitations of an irrigation water source (Table 14–2). Water containing two to four meq/L of bicarbonates can be managed by applying ammoniacal fertilizer as part of a regular fertilizer program to help reduce soil pH. Water with greater than four meq/L bicarbonates may need to be acidified with sulfuric or phosphoric acid. Blending poor quality water with better quality water and applying soil amendments such as gypsum or sulfur also are means to help manage bicarbonate problems. The negative effects on soil infiltration of bicarbonate and carbonate are negated by high levels of calcium and magnesium. Bicarbonate and carbonate are good indicators of hazard when irrigation water calcium and magnesium concentrations are low, but the RSC equation should be utilized when water calcium and magnesium are high. High HCO_3^- and CO_3^{-2} water can have good infiltration properties if calcium and magnesium levels are also high.

Nutrient Loads

To determine the amount (lbs/acre) of calcium and magnesium supplied in an acre-inch of irrigation water, multiply each element (in mg/L or ppm) by 2.72. For example, an irrigation source containing 75 mg/L calcium and 30 mg/L magnesium would supply the following:

$Ca^{+2} = 75$ mg/L $\times$ 2.72 = 204 pounds calcium supplied per acre-foot irrigation water

$Mg^{+2} = 30$ mg/L $\times$ 2.72 = 82 pounds magnesium per acre-foot irrigation water

The 2.72 conversion factor is from the following:

$$\frac{1 \text{ lb}}{454{,}000 \text{ mg}} \times \frac{325{,}851 \text{ gal}}{\text{acre-foot}} \times \frac{3.785 \text{ L}}{\text{gal}} \times \frac{X\text{mg}}{\text{L}} = \frac{2.72 \text{ lbs}}{\text{acre-foot}}$$

Typical nutrient ranges found in effluent water sources are listed in Chapter 15.

pH

Continued use of high bicarbonate and carbonate water also leads to a high soil pH. When sodium is the predominant cation in the soil, sodium bicarbonate and sodium carbonate form, causing the pH to be as high as 10 since these ions are water soluble and tend to ionize, which keeps high levels of bicarbonate and carbonate. However, when calcium predominates, usually insoluble calcium carbonate forms which, unlike sodium carbonate, does not ionize to form more carbonate ions; thus, the soil pH generally stabilizes around 8.0. High pH can induce iron, manganese, and to a lesser extent, zinc deficiencies by rendering these micronutrients unavailable to turfgrass roots. Unfortunately, simply adding these micronutrients in fertilizers is sometimes ineffective since these elements quickly become unavailable in high-pH soils. Using chelates and foliar applications help avoid interactions between micronutrients and high-pH soils.

With moderate levels of HCO_3^- and CO_3^{-2}, acidifying amendments can be soil-applied, rather than irrigation-applied, to reduce soil pH. Acidifying nitrogen fertilizers or elemental sulfur are generally employed. The acidifying potentials of various fertilizers and amendments are listed in Table 14–6. Although nitrogen fertilizers containing or generating ammonium (NH_4^+) reduce soil pH, it is important to note nitrate (NO_3^-) fertilizers increase soil pH. Usually, irrigating with water sources containing low bicarbonate concentrations can be managed by using acidifying fertilizers (e.g., ammonium sulfate) or application of granular elemental sulfur.

Irrigation Acid Injection

Acidification of irrigation water is effective in solving some problems but not others. Situations where water acidification may be beneficial include:

1. Water with a high (>1.25) RSC. Lower water pH will neutralize carbonates and bicarbonates in the water, making the water safe to use without the risk of damaging soil structure.
2. Water with a high SAR. One method of coping with high-SAR water is by adding sulfur to the soil. Both acidification and sulfur burners provide this. Adding sulfur, however, does not lower the SAR of the water; it just makes the soil more manageable.
3. Soil ESP >15 percent, which is sodium-affected soil possessing poor infiltration and free calcite (lime) present. Calcite (white crystals of calcium carbonate) form at the soil surface in areas of low rainfall and high rates of evapotranspiration (e.g., arid southwestern United States). Calcite deposits reduce soil water infiltration. The addition of acid helps dissolve calcite crystals. The goal is to lower the pH of the irrigation water to below 7.0 to achieve calcite dissolving.
4. Water with a low RSC and high bicarbonate content. In arid regions (<20 inches, 51 cm, per year rainfall), with fine-textured soil and soil sodium levels that are moderate or high, it is often beneficial to acidify the water to lower soil pH and to maintain it at an acceptable level.

High bicarbonate-containing water may require acidification (via injection into the irrigation system) with sulfuric or phosphoric acids or using sulfur burners (or generators). To reduce handling and corrosion problems, sulfuric acid is often mixed with urea, commonly referred to as N-phuric acid. Water acidification is a two-step process that forms carbon dioxide (CO_2) and water (H_2O) from reacting an acid, such as sulfuric acid (H_2SO_4), with bicarbonate (HCO_3^-) as shown:

Step 1:

$$\begin{array}{ccccccc} H_2SO_4 & + & HCO_3^- & \longleftrightarrow & HSO_4^- & + & H_2CO_3 \\ \text{sulfuric acid} & & \text{bicarbonate} & & \text{bisulfate} & & \text{carbonic acid} \end{array}$$

TABLE 14–6 Nutrient content and acidity or basicity of common fertilizer and soil amendment sources.

Material	Chemical formula	Nutrient content, percent						Acidity or (basicity) generated, lb $CaCO_3$ equiv./100 lb material
		Nitrogen (N)	Phosphoric acid (P_2O_5)	Potash (K_2O)	Calcium (Ca)	Magnesium (Mg)	Sulfur (S)	
Aluminum sulfate	$Al_2(SO_4)_3$	0	0	0	0	0	28	47
Ammonium nitrate	NH_4NO_3	33	0	0	0	0	0	59
Ammonium sulfate	$(NH_4)_2SO_4$	21	0	0	0	0	24	85
Calcium nitrate	$Ca(NO_3)_2$	16	0	0	19	1.5	0	(20)
Calcium sulfate (gypsum)	$CaSO_4$	0	0	0.5	22	0.4	17	0
Diammonium phosphate	$(NH_4)_2HPO_4$	18	46	0	0	0	0	70
Magnesium sulfate	$MgSO_4$	0	0	0	0	10 to 17	13 to 23	0
Monoammonium phosphate	$NH_4H_2PO_4$	27	15	0	0	0	0	65
Potassium chloride	KCl	0	0	60 to 62	0.1	0.1	0	0
Potassium magnesium sulfate	$K_2SO_4/MgSO_4$	0	0	18 to 22	0	11	23	0
Potassium nitrate	KNO_3	13	0	44	0.6	0.4	0.2	(26)
Potassium sulfate	K_2SO_4	0	0	50	0.7	1	18	0
Sodium nitrate	$NaNO_3$	16	0	0.2	0.1	0	0	(29)
Sulfur	S	0	0	0	0	0	90 to 100	312
Sulfur-coated urea	$CO(NH_2)_2 + S$	18 to 39	0	0	0	0	13 to 16	118
Sulfuric acid	H_2SO_4	0	0	0	0	0	20 to 33	62 to 102
Superphosphate (concentrated)	$Ca(H_2PO_4)_2$	0	42 to 50	0.4	14	0.3	1.4	0
Urea	$CO(NH_2)_2$	46	0	0	0	0	0	84

Step 2:

$$H_2CO_3 \longleftrightarrow H_2O + CO_2\uparrow$$
carbonic acid   water   carbon dioxide gas

Other acidifying units (often called sulfur generators) dissolve sulfur chips or flakes (Chapter 3) into stored irrigation water to form sulfite (SO_3). The sulfite then reacts to form sulfurous acid and sulfuric acid, which then has the same effect as acid injection. The generator consists of a sulfur chip storage hopper, oxidizing chamber, blower, and absorption tower. Pure elemental sulfur chips or flakes are combusted in the oxidizing chamber to form sulfur dioxide gas as shown:

$$S + O_2 \longleftrightarrow SO_2\uparrow$$
sulfur   oxygen   sulfur dioxide gas
(from chips)

When sulfur dioxide gas mixes with water, sulfurous acid is formed:

$$SO_2\uparrow + H_2O \longleftrightarrow H_2SO_3^-$$
sulfur dioxide gas   water   sulfurous acid

Sulfurous acid is a mild acid that is only slightly corrosive and easy to handle. In comparison, sulfuric acid (H_2SO_4) is an extremely strong and corrosive acid that is difficult to handle. Sulfurous acid improves water quality by lowering water pH and neutralizing bicarbonates and carbonates. Sulfurous acid reduces pH by dissociating it into hydrogen ions and sulfite:

$$H_2SO_3 \longleftrightarrow 2H^+ + SO_3^{-2}$$
sulfurous acid   hydrogen ions   sulfite
                      (pH$\downarrow$)

The hydrogen ions reduce water pH.

Bicarbonates and carbonates often form lime (calcium or magnesium carbonate), thereby increasing soil pH and tending to reduce soil percolation and drainage. These are neutralized by the sulfurous acid to form sulfite, carbon dioxide, and water.

Bicarbonate Neutralization

$$H_2SO_3 + 2HCO_3^- \rightarrow SO_3^{-2} + 2CO_2\uparrow + 2H_2O$$
sulfurous acid   bicarbonates   sulfite   carbon dioxide   water

Carbonate Neutralization

$$H_2SO_3 + CO_3^- \rightarrow SO_3^{-2} + 2CO_2\uparrow + 2H_2O$$
sulfurous acid   carbonates   sulfite   carbon dioxide   water

The carbon dioxide gas escapes to the air.

Sulfur treatment will reduce water pH, bicarbonates, and carbonates. This treatment, however, will not in itself correct water sodium problems. Sodium-rich water is usually injected with soluble gypsum and/or gypsum is added to the soil surface. Sulfur-treated water, however, helps maintain soluble calcium and magnesium ions and reduce SAR values, thereby countering the detrimental effects of sodium ions in the water.

The amount of acid added to water is most simply measured by pH probes. One probe is placed where water enters the pump station and another is placed downstream from the pump station. The amount of acid needed is based on the pH difference measured at the two probes.

General rates of amendments used are based on neutralizing only 75 percent of the HCO_3^- and CO_3^{-2} in the irrigation water. This precaution is taken because once the HCO_3^- and CO_3^{-2} are neutralized, the pH of the water decreases precipitously with further additions of acid. This process requires specialized equipment and constant monitoring to ensure successful acidification of water without phytotoxic effects occurring to turf. Normally, a desirable soil pH range for turfgrasses is 5.5 to 7.0 and for irrigation water, 6.0 to 8.0. Values within the optimum range for turfgrass growth allow the plant to expend less energy to obtain the necessary nutrients from soil.

Water Hardness

Natural water, passing through rocks and soil, dissolves small quantities of chlorides, sulfates, and bicarbonates of calcium (Ca^{+2}), magnesium (Mg^{+2}), and iron (Fe^{+2}). Water containing such compounds is called **hard water** because of its action on soap. Ordinary soap is a sodium or potassium salt of certain high-molecular-weight acids. When soap is added to hard water, the calcium, magnesium, and ferrous Fe(II) salts of these acids react. This leads to the formation of insoluble metallic soaps that precipitate as a greasy scum on tubs or clothes. Until all of these calcium and magnesium ions from the water are used up, additional soap will be needed to form lather.

$$Ca^{+2} \quad + \quad CH_3(CH_2)_{10}COO^- \quad \rightarrow \quad [CH_3(CH_2)_{10}COO^-]_2Ca^{+2}\downarrow$$

$$\text{hardness ion} \qquad\qquad \text{soap} \qquad\qquad \text{soap scum (insoluble precipitate)}$$

Hard water is undesirable due to the stains it causes in clothes, leather, and paper products during the manufacturing process. In addition, when exposed to heat as in pipes and boilers, the bicarbonates decompose, forming carbonate precipitates. These precipitates build up, preventing good contact between the water and pipes. Additional deposits of slightly soluble salts such as calcium sulfate ($CaSO_4$) occur when the water is evaporated. Therefore, the boiler pipes may overheat and fail under pressure. In turf, precipitates in hard water may clog irrigation heads and valves. In addition, excessive Ca^{+2} ions may displace other desirable cations such as K^+ or Fe^{+2} due to an increase in bicarbonates and water pH.

Softening Hard Water

Hardness of water is classified as (1) *temporary* (or *bicarbonate*) and (2) *permanent* (or *noncarbonate*). Temporary hard water is fresh water containing Ca^{+2} and bicarbonate (HCO_3^-) and can be softened by boiling the water.

$$Ca^{+2} \quad + \quad 2HCO_3^- \quad \overset{heat}{\rightarrow} \quad CaCO_3\downarrow \quad + \quad H_2O \quad + \quad CO_2\uparrow$$

From boiling temporary hard water, calcium, magnesium, or ferrous ions are precipitated as carbonates. Carbon dioxide is lost because it is less soluble in hot water than in cold water. However, in industry, temporary hard water is not softened by boiling due to the cost of fuel required. Chemical methods are used instead, such as the addition of ammonia (NH_3) or slaked lime [$Ca(OH)_2$]:

$$Ca^{+2} + 2HCO_3^- + 2NH_3 \rightarrow CaCO_3\downarrow + 2NH_4^+ + CO_3^{-2}$$
$$Ca^{+2} + 2HCO_3^- + Ca(OH)_2 \rightarrow 2CaCO_3\downarrow + 2H_2O$$

The permanent type of hardness involves other anions, particularly chloride (Cl^-) and sulfates (SO_4^{-2}). This hardness is responsible for the scale that deposits in boilers, hot-water heaters, and teakettles and is not affected by boiling. The calcium carbonate ($CaCO_3$) deposit is a poor conductor of heat and hinders the transfer of heat to water. In addition, it clogs pipes and contributes to corrosion problems. In general, softening of hard water requires the removal from solution of the metallic ions causing the hardness. These ions may be removed as precipitates or by ion-exchange methods using sodium carbonate (SO_4^{-2}).

$$Ca^{+2} + SO_4^{-2} + 2Na^+ + CO_3^{-2} \rightarrow CaCO_3\downarrow + 2Na^+ + SO_4^{-2}$$

When washing clothes, detergents made from sulfonating higher alcohols such as lauryl alcohol ($C_{12}H_{25}OH$) with sodium hydroxide are used. Calcium and magnesium salts of sodium lauryl sulfate are soluble, so these detergents may be used efficiently with hard water without forming precipitates with calcium and magnesium.

In wastewater treatment, the use of both lime and sodium carbonate for treating both kinds (calcium and magnesium carbonates) of hard water simultaneously is called the lime-soda ash treatment. Two reactors, two flocculators, two sedimentation tanks, and a filter operate in series to remove calcium and magnesium carbonates using lime [$Ca(OH)_2$] and soda ash (Na_2CO_3). Alkaline substances such as borax and trisodium phosphate (TSP) are also used in water softening. This method is used for large volumes of water such as for municipalities or factories.

Zeolites, synthetic sodium aluminosilicate minerals, are used in industry by "ion or cation exchange." The process is a cation exchange in which water passes through the softener while calcium and magnesium are exchanged for sodium.

$$Na_2(zeolite) \ + \ Ca^{+2}(aq) \ \rightleftharpoons \ Ca(zeolite)_2 \ + \ 2Na^+(aq)$$

Zeolites are called ion exchangers because the essential process involves the exchange of calcium ions for sodium ions. The zeolite must be reactivated after it becomes saturated by calcium and magnesium by treatment with concentrated sodium chloride (rock salt or brine) solution. This reverses the reaction in the previous equation, thereby regenerating the initial Na(zeolite), which can be reused in a water-softening tank. The use of an ion-exchange softening unit does not require careful and frequent chemical control and is often used in homes, beauty parlors, and hospitals.

Water purity can also be achieved by a combination of techniques such as deionization, removal of dissolved organic materials with activated carbon (or charcoal), and reverse osmosis to remove salts (discussed later). Deionization involves removing ions with an ion-exchange resin. In this process, water containing Na^+, Ca^{+2}, Cl^-, and SO_4^{-2} is added to two columns, with the first column containing cation-exchange plastic resin such as $-SO_3^-$ groups covalently bonded to the surface of the resin. Hydrogen (H^-) ions are ionically bonded to the $-SO_3^-$ groups. In this, the cations, Na^+ and Ca^{+2}, are exchanged for the H^+ ions to form $-SO_3Na$, $-SO_3Ca^{+2}$, and an excess of hydrogen ions. In the second column, an anion-exchange resin with $-N(CH_3)_3OH$ or similar hydroxide-containing compound exchanges the OH^- with the SO_4^{-2} and Cl^-, leaving a number of OH^- in solution. The H^+ from the first column combines with the OH^- in the second column to form water. This formation also buffers the pH of the solution toward 7.0, Thereby reducing bicarbonate (CO_3^{-2}) and allowing certain nutrients to become more available. The cations on the cation-exchange resin can be replaced (or recharged) by hydrogen ions through passing dilute sulfuric acid through the column. The anions on the anion-exchange resin can be replaced (recharged) by hydroxide ions by passing a solution of sodium hydroxide (NaOH) through the column.

Classifying Water Hardness

Industrial water hardness is measured as parts per million (ppm) or meq/L of $CaCO_3$ regardless of what other minerals are present. Water having a hardness of <50 ppm is considered "soft"; 50 to 150 ppm as "medium hard"; and 100 to 300 ppm as "hard" (Table 14–2).

In agriculture, water hardness is also determined as the total lime-neutralizing value based on the following equation:

$$Hardness \ = \ (\%Ca \ \times \ 2.5) \ + \ (\%Mg \ \times \ 4.2)$$

Interpretations for the total lime-neutralizing value are listed in Table 14–2.

It is not always desirable for water to be completely free from minerals that make it hard, because very soft water is likely to be corrosive, especially if the pH value is very low. Highly alkaline water usually will leave a rustation on well screens and pipes. Acid water will be corrosive. Carbonic acid is a major source of low pH. Good water should be nearly neutral in pH.

TOXIC IONS

Irrigation water quality is also influenced by other specific ions such as sodium, boron, and chloride. Most irrigation water sources contain low levels of a variety of elements. Normally these pose minimum problems but can increase under conditions of inadequate leaching with quality water, poor soil permeability, and during periods of high evaporation (Tables 14–2 and 14–7).

Sodium

Sodium (Na) is of prime concern because it is often found in the largest amount. Sodium is an antagonistic ion that displaces calcium in cell membranes, causes leaking of potassium, and can limit the availability of iron and manganese in soils. Sodium toxicity appears as marginal scorch of older leaves. A water sodium content of >3 meq/L (>70 ppm) can damage the foliage of sensitive ornamental plants.

TABLE 14–7 *Potential trace element tolerances for irrigation water (modified from Westcot and Ayers, 1984).*

Element	Continuous use (ppm)	Short-term use on fine-textured soils (ppm)	Comment
Aluminum (Al)	1.0 to 5.0	20	Can cause nonproductivity in acid soils (pH <5.5), but most alkaline soils (pH >7.0) will precipitate the ion and eliminate any toxicity.
Arsenic (As)	0.1	10	Toxicity to plants varies widely, ranging from 12 mg/L for Sudangrass to less than 0.05 mg/L for rice.
Beryllium (Be)	0.1	1.0	Toxicity to plants varies widely, ranging from 5 mg/L for kale to 0.5 mg/L for bush beans.
Boron (B)	0.75	2.0	Accumulates in leaf tips. Sensitive landscape plants can be damaged if >2 mg/L boron is present in irrigation water.
Cadmium (Cd)	0.01	0.05	Toxic to beans, beets, and turnips at concentrations as low as 0.1 mg/L in nutrient solutions.
Chlorine (Cl)	10	—	Accumulates in leaf tips. Landscape plants can be especially sensitive.
Chromium (Cr)	0.1	20	Not generally recognized as an essential growth element.
Cobalt (Co)	0.05	10	Toxic to tomato plants at 0.1 mg/L in nutrient solutions. Tends to be inactivated by neutral and alkaline soils.
Copper (Cu)	0.2	5	Toxic to a number of plants at 0.1 to 1.0 mg/L in nutrient solutions.
Fluoride (F)	1.0	?	Inactivated by neutral and alkaline soils.
Iron (Fe)	5.0	?	Not toxic to plants in aerated soils, but can add to soil acidification and to the loss in availability of phosphorus and molybdenum. Overhead irrigation may discolor plants, sidewalks, equipment, and buildings.
Lead (Pb)	5.0	20	Can inhibit plant cell growth at very high concentrations.
Lithium (Li)	2.5	5.0	Tolerated by most crops up to 5 mg/L; mobile in soil. Acts similarly to boron.
Manganese (Mn)	0.2	20	Toxic to a number of plant roots, but usually only in acidic, poorly drained soils. Keep soil lime to pH 6.0 to 7.0 and provide good drainage.
Molybdenum (Mo)	0.01	0.05	Not toxic to plants at normal concentrations. Can be toxic to livestock if forage has high concentrations.
Nickel (Ni)	0.2	2	Toxic to certain plants at 0.5 mg/L to 1.0 mg/L; reduced toxicity at neutral or alkaline pH.
Selenium (Se)	0.02	0.05	Toxic to plants at concentrations as low as 0.025 mg/L.
Tin (Sn)	?	?	Effectively excluded by plants; specific tolerance is unknown.
Tungsten (W)	?	?	See remarks for tin.
Vanadium (V)	0.1	10	Toxic to many plants at relatively low concentrations.
Zinc (Zn)	2.0	10	Toxic to many plants in widely varying concentrations; reduce toxicity at pH >6.0 and in fine-textured or organic soils.

Boron

Boron (B) in irrigation water is rarely a problem with turfgrasses because boron accumulates in leaf tips that are removed by regular mowing. However, other landscape plants may be more sensitive to boron levels. Boron toxicity symptoms typically show first on older leaf tips and edges either as yellowing, spotting, or drying of leaf tissue. The yellowing or spotting is sometimes followed by drying that progresses from near the tip along the leaf edges and toward the center between the veins (interveinal chlorosis). Landscape plants may be damaged if irrigation water has boron contents above 0.75 meq/L or if leaf boron contents exceed 250 to 300 ppm (dry weight). Turfgrasses generally will grow in soils with boron levels as high as 10 ppm.

Chloride

High concentrations of chloride, sulfate, and bicarbonate ions also can cause specific ornamental plant injury under certain soil conditions. Chloride (Cl^-) is not adsorbed by soils but moves readily with the soil water. It inhibits plant water uptake as a salt; thus, it reduces nutrient uptake. It is absorbed by plant roots and accumulates in the leaves. Chloride toxicity symptoms include leaf burn or drying that typically occurs initially at the leaf tip of older leaves and progresses back along the edges as severity increases. Leaf drop and defoliation also occur with excessive leaf burn. Mowing of turf removes damaged leaf tips. Tables 14–2 and 14–7 offer general ranges of elements and some expected results at various concentrations. A water chloride content of ≥100 mg/L can damage the foliage of sensitive ornamental plants. Chloride concentrations of 350 mg/L or higher in soil can cause damage.

Chlorine

Chlorine (Cl_2) toxicity normally occurs if reclaimed sewage water containing excessive disinfectants is used for irrigation. If stored between treatment and application in a holding pond, much of the free chlorine in water will dissipate since it is very unstable. Foliage damage can occur to ornamentals if residual chlorine levels exceed one mg/L.

Fluoride

Fluoride (F) may also be another ion of concern to ornamental plants. Severe leaf tip burn and scorch can occur on ornamental plants exposed to high fluoride-containing (>1 mg/L) water.

Heavy Metals

Heavy metals such as copper, nickel, zinc, and cadmium may be contained by reclaimed water. The National Academy of Science recommends irrigation water should contain no more than 0.01 mg/L of cadmium, 0.2 mg/L of copper, 0.2 mg/L of nickel, and 2.0 mg/L of zinc.

Managing Toxic Elements

Managing toxic ions is difficult in established landscapes. If a problem develops, replacing plants sensitive to particular elements is probably the easiest and cheapest means of overcoming it. Blending better quality water with that containing the toxic ions and applying additional water to leach the ions are additional means of managing toxic elements.

MANAGING IRRIGATION WATER QUALITY PROBLEMS

Managing salinity, sodicity, and alkalinity problems requires constant attention. Management practices that aid in remedying these problems include:

1. Diluting poor quality water with good quality water
2. Utilizing salt-tolerant grasses
3. Leaching excess salts by applying extra water
4. Modifying soils with various amendments to replace and leach sodium from the soil
5. Amending irrigation water to correct sodium and bicarbonate problems
6. Enhancing soil drainage by using sands and installing subsurface tile drainage
7. Using cytokinin and iron-containing biostimulants as salt-stressed plants often exhibit low cytokinin activity
8. Raising the mowing height to promote more stress-tolerant plants

Irrigation Water Sampling

The first step to managing poor quality irrigation water is to obtain a good water sample and have it analyzed. The accuracy of the laboratory analysis of a water sample is only as good as the sample submitted for analysis. Extreme care should be taken so the sample is free of outside contamination and is representative of the irrigation water being applied to the turfgrass. Take samples directly from the irrigation system after it has operated for 10 to 15 minutes.

Sample Containers

Use only clean plastic containers for holding water samples. Glass containers should be avoided since glass may excrete boron and also breaks easier during shipping. Do not reuse pesticide, surfactant, or fertilizer containers. The container and cap should be rinsed at least three times with the water to be sampled prior to sampling.

Handling and Storage

All samples should be sealed immediately to minimize exposure to air. Equilibration of the water sample with air can alter the pH, carbonate, and bicarbonate level of the water. Label each bottle with permanent markers and high-quality labels indicating the time, date, and location of sampling.

Sampling Technique

If the sample cannot be delivered to the laboratory within 24 hours, it should be kept refrigerated in the dark. Aquatic plants and microorganisms can alter nutrient levels and pH of the water if it is not refrigerated. Seasonal variations also occur; thus, periodic sampling may be needed during the year.

Blending Water Sources for Reducing Salinity

High salinity water that is unacceptable for use can be made suitable as an irrigation source by diluting it with nonsaline water. Enough nonsaline water must be available to create a mixed water of acceptable quality (e.g., not making a less-saline water that is still unacceptable). The quality of a poor water source should improve proportionally to the mixing ratio with better quality water. For example, a water source with an EC_w of five dS/m mixed equally with a source with an EC_w of one dS/m should reduce a salinity blend to approximately three dS/m. A chemical analysis of the blend should be determined to confirm this. The salinity of the mixture can be calculated with this equation:

$$\frac{\text{gallons (water A)} \times EC_w \text{(water A)} + \text{gallons (water B)} \times EC_w \text{(water B)}}{\text{gallons (water A)} + \text{gallons (water B)}}$$

Example:

Two water sources are available for irrigation. One has an EC_w of 3.0 dS/m and the other, 0.6 dS/m. The water will be blended in equal amounts. What would the resulting EC_w of the blended water be?

$$\frac{\text{gallons (water A)} \times EC_w \text{(water A)} + \text{gallons (water B)} \times EC_w \text{(water B)}}{\text{gallons (water A)} + \text{gallons (water B)}}$$

$$\frac{(1 \text{ gal}) \times (3.0 \text{ dS/m}) + (1 \text{ gal}) \times (0.6 \text{ dS/m})}{1 \text{ gal} + 1 \text{ gal}} = \frac{3.6 \text{ dS/m}}{2} = 1.8 \text{ dS/m}$$

Mixing of irrigation sources can occur in irrigation ponds or within the irrigation system itself. When mixing water sources in irrigation ponds, the nonsaline water should be added immediately prior to being used so as to reduce evaporative losses. Evaporation of surface water is not only an inefficient use of water, but it also increases the salinity of the water remaining in the pond.

Planting Salt-Tolerant Grasses

Refer to Chapter 2 for a listing of the relative salt tolerances of various grasses used for turf.

Leaching Soils to Remove Salts

Salt buildup from salt-laden irrigation water occurs when rainfall is low and evaporative demand is high. This normally corresponds to mid-spring through early fall. As water evaporates from the soil surface, salt deposits are left behind. Determining the EC of the soil is the best way to determine the extent of salt accumulation. When the EC exceeds the tolerance level of the turfgrass, the soil should be leached to move the salt below the rootzone. For example, six inches (15 cm) of water is required to leach 80 percent of salt out of the top foot (30 cm) of a sand loam soil and about 1.5 feet (45 cm) to leach 80 percent of the salt out of the top foot (30 cm) of a clay loam.

Frequent flushing of the soil with good quality irrigation water or rainfall is the best method of preventing excessive salt accumulation. Unfortunately, low salinity irrigation sources are not always available and frequently saline irrigation water must be used to manage soil salinity. However, as long as the salinity of the irrigation water is acceptable, it can be used to leach accumulated salts from the turf rootzone. This is especially critical for cool-season grasses in mid-to-late summer that are already weakened from heat and close mowing heights. Leaching in this situation should commence prior to anticipated heat stress. The goal is to maintain a soil salinity level that is not increased through salts added by irrigation and yet can support turfgrass growth. The use of soil amendments, such as gypsum, should be considered in conjunction with leaching irrigation applications in saline-sodic soils. However, if excessive soil sodium and poor water drainage is not a problem, the use of soil amendments should be avoided since they add to soil salinity.

If saline water is used to reduce the salt level of the soil, irrigation must be applied at rates exceeding evapotranspiration to leach excess salts out of the rootzone. To determine the amount of excess water required to leach salt below the rootzone, the following **leaching requirement** equation is often used.

Leaching Requirement Is the Amount of Extra Water Needed to Leach Salts From the Rootzone and Is Defined as

$$\text{leaching requirement} = \frac{EC_{iw}}{EC_{dw}} \times 100\%$$

EC_{iw} equals the electrical conductivity of the irrigation water and EC_{dw} is electrical conductivity of a saturated paste extract that can be tolerated by the turfgrass being grown.

Example:

An irrigation water source has a salinity level of two dS/m. The turfgrass being grown has a tolerance of four dS/m. What would be the recommended amount of water needed to leach salt from the rootzone?

Step 1: Determine the leaching requirement for this sample and turfgrass.

$$\text{leaching requirement} = \frac{EC_{iw}}{EC_{dw}} \times 100\%$$
$$= \frac{2}{4} \times 100\%$$
$$= 50\%$$

Step 2: Fifty percent additional water than normally applied would be needed to leach the salt from the soil. If two inches of water are normally used, 50 percent greater than two would equal three inches. Table 14–8 lists these irrigation guidelines for leaching salts from soil with saline water.

As the irrigation water becomes saltier, the leaching requirement becomes larger, meaning more water must be added for leaching to avoid salt accumulation.

TABLE 14–8 *Irrigation guidelines for leaching salts from soil with saline water.*

Irrigation water EC_{iw} (dS/m)	Maximum plant EC_{dw} tolerance level, measured by saturated soil paste extract (dS/m)		
	4 (low)	8 (medium)	16 (high)
	(inches of water required to replace weekly ET losses and provide adequate leaching in rootzone)		
0.00	1.5	1.5	1.5
1.00	2.0	1.7	1.6
2.00	3.0	2.0	1.7
3.00	6.0	2.4	1.8

Good Soil Percolation and Drainage

As previously mentioned, leaching works well only with soils possessing good drainage. If compacted zones or abrupt changes in soil texture exist, less leaching occurs as water movement through the soil is reduced. Good soil drainage through use of drainage tile is used for carrying away salty water. Tile lines, spaced no more than 20 feet apart, are used on golf greens for this purpose. Aerification also initiates deep root development prior to summer heat and salt stress by reducing soil compaction and disrupting soil layering.

Counteracting Excess Soil Sodium with Soil Amendments

Several soil amendments are used to replace sodium in sodic soils in conjunction with leaching to remove salts from the rootzone. The amendments counteract sodium by providing calcium either directly (contain calcium) or indirectly (provide acid to dissolve calcium carbonate present in the soil). Calcium arising from the soil amendments reacts with soil sodium to displace it from the cation exchange sites on clay and organic matter particles. The released sodium can then be leached out of the soil profile.

Amendments used for the treatment of clay-textured sodic soils include gypsum, sulfur, sulfuric acid, lime sulfur, ferric sulfate, calcium chloride, calcium nitrate, and calcium carbonate. Table 14–9 lists several amendments and their equivalent amounts to pure gypsum.

Because of their expense, calcium chloride and calcium nitrate are not widely used. Sulfuric acid is dangerous to handle and can be corrosive to some types of equipment. Ferric sulfate and lime sulfur also are usually too expensive for practical applications. Ground limestone is effective on acid soils, but its usefulness drops in high pH soils—which describes most sodic soils. Even though gypsum supplies calcium, it is a neutral salt and does not appreciably affect soil pH. Thus, for several reasons, gypsum is the material most often used for reclaiming sodic soils.

Gypsum

Gypsum is low-to-moderately soluble in water and supplies soluble calcium to replace sodium, as shown:

Reaction From Using Gypsum to Reduce Soil Salinity

$$2NaX + CaSO_4 \rightarrow CaX_2 + Na_2SO_4\downarrow$$

soil sodium   gypsum   soil calcium   sodium sulfate

(removed by leaching)

The letter X in the above reaction indicates the exchange site for cations on the soil colloid. Gypsum, by mass action, drives sodium off the soil exchange complex and replaces it with calcium. It leaves sodium sulfate, which is soluble, and readily leaches downward with percolating water. Gypsum applications to soil with pH values <5.5 often have a rapid green-up due to the more favorable conditions to stimulate nitrosomonas and nitrobacter bacteria to convert ammonia to nitrate.

TABLE 14–9 *Relative equivalent amounts of several soil amendments in relation to pure gypsum or elemental sulfur.*

Amendment	Tons of amendment equivalent to	
	1 ton of pure gypsum	1 ton of pure sulfur
Calcium containing		
Gypsum ($CaSO_4 \cdot 2H_2O$)	1.00	5.38
Calcium chloride ($CaCl_2 \cdot H_2O$)	0.86	—
Calcium nitrate [$Ca(NO_3)_2 \cdot H_2O$]	1.06	—
Lime sulfur (CaSx; 9% Ca & 22% S)	0.68	3.65
Acid forming		
Aluminum sulfate [$Al_2(SO_4)_3 \cdot 18H_2O$]	1.29	6.94
Ferric sulfate [$Fe_2(SO_4)_3 \cdot 9H_2O$]	1.09	5.85
Lime sulfur (CaSx; 9% Ca & 22% S)	0.68	3.65
Sulfur (S)	0.19	1.00
Sulfuric acid (H_2SO_4)	0.61	3.20

Guidelines for Application of Gypsum

Gypsum is a byproduct of phosphorus mining. Pure gypsum contains 26 percent calcium and 21 percent sulfur; however, little of this is sold. Most commercial sources contain 50 to 90 percent $CaSO_4$. If gypsum contains impurities or is wet, it will contain less calcium and/or sulfur and larger quantities will be necessary.

The effectiveness of gypsum increases with fineness. Gypsum used on turfgrass should be fine enough so at least 80 percent passes a U.S. Standard No. 8 sieve. Finer, pulverized gypsum (like limestone) reacts quicker with soil but becomes difficult to apply. Larger particles not able to pass a No. 8 sieve are too slow to dissolve, rendering them relatively ineffective. Finer particles will also give a better uniformity than large particles.

Irrigation is needed to dissolve gypsum. Several irrigations usually are required to dissolve gypsum and leach sodium. Generally, if the sodium problem is slight, passage of one foot of water through the soil is sufficient to leach out the salt. Two feet (0.6 m) of water are needed on moderate sodium problem soils while three or more feet are needed on severe sodium soils.

Gypsum is often needed when the following situations occur:

- Water with a SAR >10 causes poor water infiltration and sealing
- Water with EC_w <0.25 dS/m is very pure and lacks sufficient calcium or magnesium
- Sodic or saline-sodic soils (ESP >15%) exist

Application Rates

When applied to reclaim high-sodium soils, the amount of gypsum required depends upon the sodium concentration of the soil, determined by a soil test and by soil texture. Suggested rates are listed in Table 14–10. The objective is to achieve ESP values below 10 percent on fine-textured soils and below 20 percent on coarser-textured soils. These values reflect gypsum use on non-established (or pre-plant) soils. Rates should not exceed five tons per acre (11 metric tons/ha), per application. Rates more than five tons per acre (11 metric tons/ha) should be split with successive applications not made until sufficient time for some leaching has occurred. Additional needs should then be verified by a second soil test.

On established grass, gypsum is added at rates ranging from 5 to 10 pounds per 1,000 square feet (25 to 49 kg/100 m^2) and applied monthly when needed. Light frequent applications are more effective than heavy ones, especially in sandy soils. Gypsum is slow to react and does not normally burn foliage; however, one should still apply it only during mild temperatures (e.g., ≤80°F, 27°C). Due to its low water solubility, some time will be required before gypsum will disappear from the soil surface.

TABLE 14–10 *Pre-plant gypsum amounts required as related to soil texture and sodium percentage.*

Soil texture	Exchangeable sodium percentage				
	15	20	30	40	50
	Gypsum needed (tons/acre)*				
Coarse	2	3	5	7	9
Medium	3	5	8	11	14
Fine	4	6	10	14	18

*Multiply tons (2,000 lbs) per acre by 2.241 to obtain tons (metric) per hectare.

Example:

A soil with CEC of 20 meq/100 g contains 15 percent ESP, and needs to be reduced to 10 percent (a 5 percent total reduction). Determine the amount of gypsum needed per six-inch acre slice:

Step 1: Determine the meq of Na^+ and $CaSO_4$ per 100 g of soil.

$5\% \times 20$ meq CEC/100 g $=$ 1 meq Na^+/100 g and 1 meq $CaSO_4 \cdot 2H_2O$/100 g, thus,

Step 2: Determine equivalent weight of gypsum.

1 meq $CaSO_4 \cdot 2H_2O$/100 g $\times$ 86 mg $CaSO_4 \cdot 2H_2O$/meq $=$ 86 mg $CaSO_4 \cdot 2H_2O$/100 g

86 mg/meq is the molecular weight of $CaSO_4 \cdot 2H_2O$ (172) divided by 2 (the valence number of calcium in relation to sodium) to obtain equivalent weights.

Step 3: Convert equivalent weights (mg/100 g) to pounds needed per six-inch furrow slice.

86 mg $CaSO_4 \cdot 2H_2O$/100 g $\times$ 20 $=$ 1,720 pounds $CaSO_4 \cdot 2H_2O$ needed per six-inch acre furrow slice depth to reduce ESP to 10 percent

Twenty is a conversion factor to convert equivalent weight (mg/100 g) to pounds per six-inch acre furrow slice from the following:

$$\frac{X \text{ mg sample}}{100 \text{ g}} \times \frac{2,000,000 \text{ lb soil}}{6\text{-in. acre furrow slice}} \times \frac{1 \text{ g}}{1,000 \text{ mg}} \times \frac{\text{lb ion}}{454 \text{ g ion}} \times \frac{454 \text{ g soil}}{\text{lb soil}} = \frac{20 \text{ lbs}}{6\text{-in. acre furrow slice}}$$

Another way to determine the amount of gypsum needed involves:

Step 1: Determined the same as above.
Step 2: Recognize one meq of Na^+ needs to be replaced by one meq Ca^{+2} or one meq Na^+ = one meq Ca^{+2}.
Step 3: Determine the percent calcium (Ca^{+2}) contained in gypsum or calcium sulfate ($CaSO_4 \cdot 2H_2O$).

$$\frac{Ca \text{ (g)}}{CaSO_4 \cdot 2H_2O \text{ (g)}} = \frac{40 \text{ g } Ca^{+2}}{172 \text{ g } CaSO_4 \cdot 2H_2O} = 23.2\% \text{ Ca in } CaSO_4 \cdot 2H_2O$$

Therefore, one pound $CaSO_4 \cdot 2H_2O$ contains 0.232 pounds Ca^{+2}.

Step 4: Determine the pounds gypsum required to apply one meq Ca^{+2} per 100 g soil.

$$\frac{1 \text{ meq } Ca^{+2}}{100 \text{ g soil}} \times \frac{1 \text{ eq } Ca^{+2}}{1,000 \text{ meq } Ca^{+2}} \times \frac{20 \text{ g } Ca^{+2}}{1 \text{ eq } Ca^{+2}} \times \frac{1 \text{ lb } Ca^{+2}}{454 \text{ g } Ca^{+2}} \times \frac{1 \text{ lb } CaSO_4 \cdot 2H_2O}{0.232 \text{ lb } Ca^{+2}} \times \frac{454 \text{ g soil}}{1 \text{ lb soil}} \times \frac{2,000,000 \text{ lbs}}{1 \text{ acre soil}}$$

= 1,720 pounds gypsum ($CaSO_4 \cdot 2H_2O$)needed per six-inch acre furrow slice depth to reduce ESP to 10 percent.

Irrigation Injection

Gypsum or magnesium may also be injected into the irrigation system. Gypsum or magnesium injection has been shown to improve water quality; help displace sodium; add to plant-available magnesium and calcium; and decrease pH, which then increases phosphorus availability. Several forms of gypsum are available including natural dihydrate gypsum and the natural anhydrite form.

The dihydrate form dissolves quicker because of attached water molecules. The finest, most soluble grade available should be used.

A gypsum machine with agitators and mixing tanks inject a slurry of suspended (not dissolved) particles into the water. Near 100 percent dissolution of the gypsum should occur within a few minutes. If not, the hard particles could be abrasive to the irrigation emitters.

The suggested injection gypsum rate range is between 2 and 2.5 meq/L. This must be continuously used if sodium levels are excessive in the irrigation water source.

Sulfur and Other Acid-Forming Amendments

Elemental sulfur and other acid-forming amendments and fertilizers (Tables 14–6 and 14–9) may also be used to provide soluble calcium by lowering soil pH and dissolving calcium carbonate precipitated in the soil. If soil pH is only slightly elevated, routine applications of acid-forming nitrogen fertilizers containing or generating ammonium (NH_4^+) may be sufficient to maintain soil pH. Ammonium sulfate is about three times more acidic than other commonly used nitrogen sources and is widely used as a primary nitrogen source where irrigation sources have moderate levels of bicarbonate. However, when irrigation sources have severe bicarbonate problems, elemental sulfur is the most frequently utilized acid-forming amendment. Sulfur is more available and less costly than the other amendments, such as aluminum sulfate. Extreme care should be exercised when using sulfur to lower soil pH. Elemental sulfur has a high potential to burn plant tissue and can lower pH to 3.0 if used unwisely.

Sulfur furnishes calcium indirectly in a two-step process. The chemical reactions are:

Chemical Reactions When Using Elemental Sulfur to Reduce Soil Alkalinity and Sodium in Soils Containing Precipitated Lime ($CaCO_3$)

Step 1: Sulfur must first be oxidized by soil bacteria to sulfuric acid.

$$2S \quad + \quad 3O_2 \quad + \quad 2H_2O \quad \rightarrow \quad 2H_2SO_4$$
$$\text{sulfur} \qquad \text{oxygen} \qquad \text{water} \qquad \text{sulfuric acid}$$

Step 2: Sulfuric acid then reacts with lime in the soil to produce gypsum which is removed by leaching.

$$CaCO_3 \quad + \quad H_2SO_4 \quad \rightarrow \quad CaSO_4 \quad + \quad H_2O \quad + \quad CO_2\uparrow$$
$$\text{lime} \qquad \text{sulfuric acid} \qquad \text{gypsum} \qquad \text{water} \qquad \text{carbon dioxide}$$

Step 3: Gypsum then reacts with sodium ions to produce soluble sodium sulfate.

$$2NaX \quad + \quad CaSO_4 \quad \longleftrightarrow \quad CaX \quad + \quad Na_2SO_4\downarrow$$
$$\text{sodic soil} \qquad \text{gypsum} \qquad \text{calcium soil} \qquad \text{sodium sulfate}$$

The letter X in the above reaction indicates the exchange site for cations on soil clay and organic matter.

In soils lacking free lime, the reactions are:

Step 1: Sulfuric acid is produced by the oxidation of sulfur by soil bacteria.

$$2S \quad + \quad 3O_2 \quad + \quad 2H_2O \quad \rightarrow \quad 2H_2SO_4$$

Step 2: Sulfuric acid produced then reacts directly with sodium ions on the cation exchange sites as follows:

$$2NaX \quad + \quad H_2SO_4 \quad \longleftrightarrow \quad 2HX \quad + \quad Na_2SO_4\downarrow$$

The letter X in the above reaction indicates the exchange site for cations on soil clay and organic matter.

Managing Sulfur Applications

Sulfur-oxidizing bacteria are most active in wet, warm, well-aerated soil. No activity occurs when soil temperatures are below 40° F (4.4°C). Even at 75° F (24°C), the oxidation rate of sulfur is about 15 percent of that at 85°F (29°C). Sulfur application, therefore, should be limited during cooler fall and winter months. Acidity equal to 30 pounds (13.6 kg) of limestone is generated by each 10 pounds (4.5 kg) of sulfur.

The acidifying effects of elemental sulfur are slow to move into the soil when sulfur is surface-applied. Therefore, large decreases in pH may occur in the thatch layer and immediate soil surface with little initial impact on the soil pH of the rootzone. Application rates must be minimal to avoid damage to the crowns of the turfgrass plant. Rates applied to bermudagrass at fairway or rough height may be as high as five pounds per 1,000 square feet (244 kg/100 m^2), whereas applications to greens should not exceed 0.5 pounds per 1,000 square feet (2.4 kg/100 m^2). Total annual applications should not exceed 10 pounds per 1,000 square feet (49 kg/100 m^2) on fairways. Sufficient irrigation water should be applied immediately after each application to wash the sulfur from the turfgrass leaves. Applications are best made when temperatures are warm enough for the bacteria to oxidize the sulfur (70 to 80°F, 21 to 27°C), but not hot enough to accentuate tissue burn. It is wise to have the soil pH checked before reapplication of sulfur to avoid overacidification. Sulfur application coincident with core aerification minimizes the potential for tissue burn and accelerates the acidification of the rootzone.

Commercial sulfur ranges in purity from 50 to 99 percent. The value of sulfur for reclamation depends on its purity and fineness. Like gypsum, the finer the material, the faster it reacts in soil.

Amending Irrigation Water High in Sodium

Mixing high-SAR water with water low in both calcium and EC$_w$ does not reduce the sodium hazard of the mixture, because the SAR is generally not changed appreciably but the EC$_w$ is reduced. Recall high-SAR water with low EC$_w$ has worse infiltration properties than high-SAR water with high EC$_w$.

Adding gypsum to water with high SAR is one method of increasing the suitability of the water. Gypsum decreases the SAR and increases the EC$_w$, which increases the infiltration properties of the water. The impact of gypsum on calcium and EC$_w$ are listed in Table 14–11. The sodium adsorption ratio and EC$_w$ for the water sample should be recalculated using the changes indicated. Adjust the EC$_w$ and SAR of the water with gypsum to produce a water that has sufficient EC$_w$ and SAR to be considered acceptable as assessed by the criteria in Table 14–2.

Gypsum may be added to the irrigation source or injected into the irrigation system as previously discussed.

Amending Irrigation Water High in Carbonate and Bicarbonate

The bicarbonate content of irrigation water can be decreased with sulfur dioxide, sulfuric acid, phosphoric acid, sulfur chips, or other acidifying amendments, if necessary. This is often performed by injecting the amendment into the irrigation system. This process requires specialized equipment and constant monitoring to ensure successful acidification of water without phytotoxic effects occurring to turf or aquatic life.

TABLE 14–11 *Changes in water calcium and electrical conductivity due to gypsum addition.*

Gypsum rate, lb/1,000 gal	Gypsum added in acre-foot of water (lb/acre)	Ca added, meq/L	Increase in EC$_w$ (dS/m)
0.72	234	1.0	0.1
1.44	468	2.0	0.2
2.16	702	3.0	0.3
2.88	936	4.0	0.4
3.60	1,170	5.0	0.5
4.32	1,404	6.0	0.6
5.04	1,638	7.0	0.7

Acidification of the irrigation water converts bicarbonate and carbonate to carbon dioxide and water, but does not affect the sodium, calcium, or magnesium content of the irrigation water. However, this allows calcium and magnesium to remain soluble so they can displace sodium from the soil CEC sites.

Irrigation water high in bicarbonate/carbonate and high in calcium and/or magnesium react to form insoluble lime ($CaCO_3 \cdot MgCO_3$) in the upper centimeter of soil. This insoluble lime, called **calcite,** can eventually coat soil and sand particles, reducing water infiltration. Concentrations of these in irrigation water that can cause reduced water infiltration are shown in Table 14–2.

Ways to disrupt the calcite layer include physically breaking it up by periodic cultivation or dissolving it into more mobile forms such as gypsum ($CaSO_4$) and magnesium sulfate ($MgSO_4$) by using acidifying fertilizers such as ammonium sulfate or by applying elemental sulfur to the turfgrass surface. Acidification of irrigation water is also helpful but is expensive, may not be needed on all areas of the golf course, and may not completely dissolve this layer; thus, it will require supplemental measures.

Desalination

Desalination is the process of taking salt out of saltwater. Several means are available to provide this including: (1) distillation, (2) reverse osmosis, (3) ion exchange, and (4) electrodialysis. Distillation and reverse osmosis remove water from solution while ion exchange and electrodialysis remove salt from the solution. Irregardless of which desalination method is used, costs will depend on how much salt is in the source water and how clean the treated water must be. Fresh water typically has up to 500 ppm of total dissolved solids and usually does not require desalination. Brackish water contains 500 to 35,000 ppm and is the source of water most often used in desalination. Seawater contains more than 35,000 ppm of salt which makes it the most costly source of water to treat.

A byproduct of desalination is **brine,** a concentrated salt solution byproduct from each of these desalination processes that can be discharged into deep saline aquifers or into water with a higher salt content. Brine can also be mixed with treated effluent and sprayed over golf course areas.

Distillation

Distillation is the oldest form of desalination. Simply, distillation is where water is boiled and produces steam. The steam cools and condenses back into water which is then collected and used (Figure 14–1). The salt does not vaporize, forming brine in the original container, so the distilled water is fresh and without salt. Distillation is a high-energy requiring process; thus, it is rarely used to commercially purify golf course water.

FIGURE 14–1 The process of distillation where saltwater is heated and condensed by exposing it to a cold water bath, thereby producing fresh water.

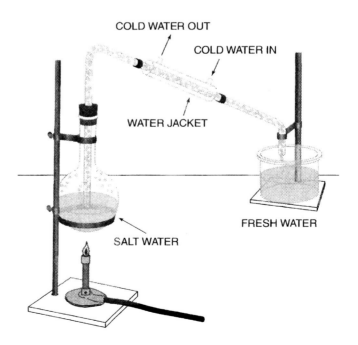

COLD WATER OUT

COLD WATER IN

WATER JACKET

SALT WATER

FRESH WATER

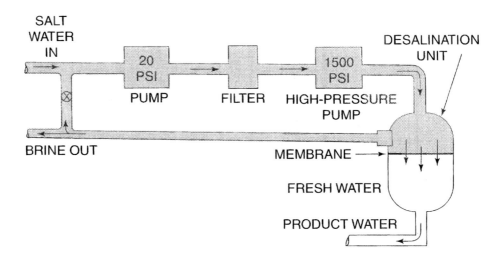

FIGURE 14–2 The process of reverse osmosis where pressure is applied to saltwater and forced through a semipermeable membrane that "screens" or "sieves" out the salts.

Reverse Osmosis

Reverse osmosis is the desalination method gaining the most in use. Osmosis occurs when fresh water and saltwater are on opposite sides of a semipermeable membrane. Saltwater has a higher osmotic pressure and, to balance this pressure, fresh water flows through the membrane and dilutes the saltwater until the pressures of both are equal.

In reverse osmosis, a high pressure pump applies more pressure on the saltwater than the osmotic pressure of seawater. The water in the salt solution side flows through the membrane, leaving salt (brine) behind (Figure 14–2). Reverse osmosis is the desalination process many municipalities and some individual golf courses are starting to use. Although startup costs are still high—often $1,000,000—technological advances have reduced energy, maintenance, and operation costs of this process. Reverse osmosis plants now require lower dosages of anti-scaling chemicals, and use membranes that can operate at lower pressures, thereby reducing energy costs.

Ion Exchange

Ion exchange is a chemical process similar to the water softener processes. Salt is composed of positively charged sodium (Na^+) ions and negatively charged chloride (Cl^-) ions. An ion exchange uses resins to break up the salt by attracting the salt ions. A saline solution flows through a bed of granulated zeolite or an ion-exchange resin. The ions in solution become attached to the material in the bed and displace ions of the same sign. One resin attracts the chloride ions and releases hydroxyl (OH^-) ions. A second resin attracts sodium ions, releasing hydrogen ions. In addition to the clean water that remains, the hydroxyl (OH^-) and hydrogen (H^+) ions combine to form a small amount of water (Figure 14–3). Brine is the byproduct. The resins must be periodically regenerated or "recharged" by washing them with acids or bases.

Electrodialysis

Electrodialysis is similar to reverse osmosis as both use membranes. Electrodialysis is an ion exchange process where salt is removed by separating the ions using an electrical field instead of pressure as with reverse osmosis. In electrodialysis, source water flows into a unit with two membranes where an electric current causes the ions to separate (Figure 14–4). When a direct current is passed through the solution, the ions move through the membranes toward the electrodes of opposite charge, thereby depleting the salt in the center compartment. The positive sodium ions go through one membrane into one compartment, while the negative chloride ions flow through a different membrane into another compartment. The end product remaining in the unit is fresh water.

Example:

The following water quality analysis report was generated for potential water sources for a golf course.

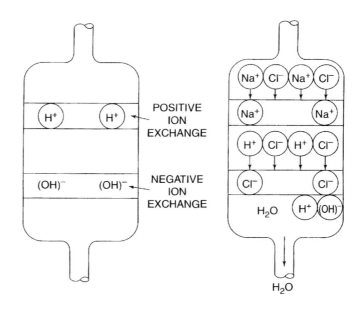

FIGURE 14–3 The process of ion exchange where sodium and chloride ions in saltwater are removed by exchanging them with other ions such as calcium.

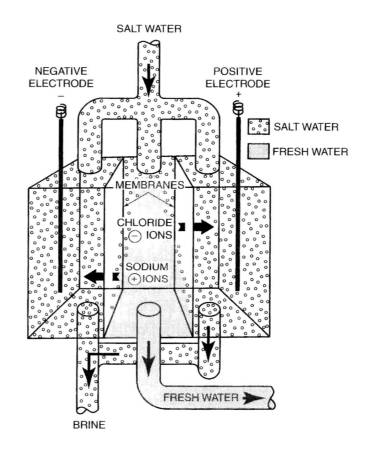

FIGURE 14–4 The process of electrodialysis where water is placed into a container with two opposite facing membranes. Each side of the membranes is then exposed to an electrical charge that attracts either sodium or chloride ions, leaving fresh water in the center of the container and brine inside either membrane.

Sample no.	Sodium (Na)	Calcium (Ca)	Magnesium (Mg)	Phosphorus (P)	Potassium (K)	Chlorine (Cl)	Carbonate (CO₃)	Bicarbonate (HCO₃)	Nitrate (NO₃)	Sulfate (SO₄)	TDS	pH	Conductivity (mmhos/cm)	SAR
							ppm							
1	1,800	131	190	1.55	73	6,800	117	610	6	86	9,100	8.4	8.0	—

1. Find the missing SAR value.

   Step 1: The units must be converted to meq/L: Na (77), Ca (6.6), Mg (15.8), P (1.55), K (73), CO_3 (3.9), HCO_3 (9.8).

   Step 2: Insert the values into the SAR equation:

$$SAR = \frac{Na^+}{\sqrt{\dfrac{Ca^{+2} + Mg^{+2}}{2}}} = \frac{77}{\sqrt{\dfrac{6.6 + 15.8}{2}}} = 23 \ meq/L$$

2. Calculate the RSC value:

$$RSC \ (meq/L) = (CO_3 + HCO_3^-) - (Ca^{+2} + Mg^{+2}) = (3.9 + 9.8) - (6.6 + 15.8) = 8.7 \ meq/L$$

3. The water sample contains 1,800 ppm sodium (Na). If 7.5 acre-inches of water are applied per month, (a) how many pounds of sodium are being applied per year, (b) how much calcium would be needed per year to displace this sodium, (c) how much gypsum ($CaSO_4$) would be needed to provide this calcium amount, and (d) how much calcium carbonate ($CaCO_3^-$) would be needed to provide this calcium amount?

   a.

$$\frac{1,800 \ mg \ Na}{L} \times \frac{1 \ lb}{454,000 \ mg} \times \frac{7.5 \ acre\text{-}in. \ water}{month} \times \frac{12 \ months}{year} \times \frac{27,154 \ gal}{acre\text{-}in.} \times \frac{3.785 \ L}{gal} = 36,670 \ \text{pounds sodium per year}$$

   b.

$$36,670 \ lbs \ Na \times \frac{454 \ g \ Na}{lb \ Na} \times \frac{1 \ eq \ Na}{23 \ g \ Na} \times \frac{1 \ eq \ Ca}{1 \ eq \ Na} \times \frac{20 \ g \ Ca}{1 \ eq \ Ca} \times \frac{1 \ lb \ Ca}{454 \ g \ Ca} = 31,887 \ \text{pounds } Ca^{+2}$$

   c. **Step 1:** The molecular weight of gypsum ($CaSO_4^-$) must be determined: Ca 5 40 g, S = 32 g, O = 16 g

$$CaSO_4 = 40 + 32 + (4 \times 16) = 136 \ grams$$

   Step 2: One of two means of obtaining the desired amount of $CaSO_4$ can be used. The first sets up a ratio:

$$\frac{X \ lbs \ CaSO_4}{31,887 \ lbs \ Ca} = \frac{136 \ lbs \ CaSO_4}{40 \ lbs \ Ca} \qquad X = 108,416 \ \text{pounds or 54 tons}$$

   d. If calcium carbonate ($CaCO_3$) was being used to displace the sodium, how much would be needed?

   Step 1: Determine the molecular weight of $CaCO_3$: Ca = 40 g, C = 12 g, O = 16 g

$$CaCO_3: 40 + 12 + (3 \times 16) = 100 \ grams$$

   Step 2: The following is the second method to determine the rate of $CaCO_3^-$ needed to neutralize the sodium:

$$\frac{31,887 \ lbs \ Ca^{+2}}{acre} \times \frac{100 \ lbs \ CaCO_3}{eq \ Ca^{+2}} \times \frac{1 \ eq \ Ca^{-2}}{40 \ lbs \ Ca^{+2}} = 79,718 \ \text{pounds or 40 tons}$$

4. If your 7.8 acres of tees are irrigated an average of 4.5 acre-inches every month, how much nitrogen is being applied?

   Step 1: The amount of nitrogen in nitrate (NO_3) must be determined: molecular weight nitrogen = 14 grams

$$NO_3 = 14 + (3 \times 16) = 62 \ g \quad \%N = (14 \div 62) \times 100 = 22.6\% \ nitrogen$$

   From the analysis, six ppm NO_3 is in the water; thus, this is multiplied by 22.6 percent to obtain ppm nitrogen.

$$\text{six ppm} \times 22.6\% = 1.4 \ \text{ppm nitrogen is being applied in the six ppm } NO_3$$

   Step 2: Now determine how much nitrogen is being applied each month:

$$1.4 \ \text{ppm nitrogen} \times \frac{4.5 \ acre\text{-}inch}{month} \times 7.8 \ acre = 49 \ \text{pounds nitrogen applied monthly over 7.8 acres}$$

Additional Water Treatment Options

Turfgrass managers are constantly being inundated with certain products that will solve their specific problems. Several commonly touted devices will be discussed. For most of these, little credible evidence exists in reputable scientific literature to support these devices' work, and in most cases, there is no scientific merit, based on current chemical knowledge, to believe they even can work. This certainly does not mean they do not work, but anyone contemplating the purchase of such devices should insist on data from credible sources; have a sound, solid performance guarantee; and preferably have a demonstration on their own course and unique situation.

Depressurizing Water for Scale Control

Supposedly, when water is subjected to rapid reductions in pressure and turbulent flow, dissolved carbon dioxide escapes as a gas, rendering the solution more alkaline, thereby causing dissolved calcium carbonates ("scale") to precipitate out and not be able to form scale deposits. The following reaction is suggested:

$$Ca^{+2} + 2HCO_3^- \rightarrow CO_2\uparrow + H_2O + CaCO_3(s)$$
calcium   bicarbonate   carbon dioxide gas   water   calcium carbonate

However, this reaction requires heat, not pressure, to proceed. Also, it is not clear what happens to the carbon dioxide gas, or what prevents it from redissolving. Others also claim their device employs a "catalytic surface" or core in the housing unit to accelerate formation of the calcium carbonate (calcite) crystals. Neither process has been proven to perform as advertised.

Magnetic (or Electromagnetic) Water Treatment (MWT)

A long history exists of promoting magnets to alleviate the "hardness" of mineral-saturated water, thereby controlling the deposition of scale in various devices. The magnets supposedly cause carbonate salts, that ordinarily form scale deposits, to precipitate as small particles within the water. This is supposed to occur from a change in the morphology of calcium carbonate crystals formed upon evaporation of a solution exposed to a magnetic field. Specifically, the magnetic field deflects the ions of opposite charge to move in opposite directions, thereby producing collisions which then form a microscopic nuclei that causes calcium carbonate to precipitate out before forming scale.

Although polar, water has no paramagnetic properties as the partial charges produced between the oxygen and hydrogen atoms in water and between larger ions in solution are too strong to undergo any significant deflection as they pass by a magnet. Most ionic motion in water is due to random thermal motions; thus, only a very small percentage of this motion would be nonrandom.

Electrical Impulses

Other similar devices claim to negatively charge the ions in water by producing high-frequency electrical impulses through the water. However, ions in water are always equally balanced in electric charge, and cannot be altered by electrochemical processes. Ions cannot be injected into water using simple devices and, even if they could, they would exist for less than a second. Hydrogen bonds in water also cannot be permanently broken to make "wetter water" and to enable fertilizer to break up into smaller groupings and interface with smaller water groupings. Hydrogen bonds are constantly being broken apart, reformed naturally, and cannot be enhanced by such simple devices.

CHAPTER
15

Effluent Wastewater Use on Turf

INTRODUCTION

Use of effluent wastewater for irrigation purposes is a possible alternative water source for many turf growers. Irrigation with effluent water is an old practice used by the Greeks in Athens that has also been used on golf courses in San Francisco as early as 1932. Currently, 13 percent of all golf courses in the United States use effluent water, 34 percent of which are in the Southwest. Turf may be a suitable commodity to use effluent water with since it absorbs large amounts of nitrogen and other nutrients found in reclaimed water. This reduces the chances of groundwater contamination from effluent water use. Since turf is a perennial crop, a continuous supply is needed. Turf is often located near metropolitan areas; therefore, conveyance costs could be reduced. Certain states already have mandated that, if available, golf courses must use reclaimed water for irrigation. With this in mind, all golf facilities should prepare to use reclaimed water or possibly face refused water rights. Since turf is not a food crop, potential health problems arising from reclaimed water are reduced (Table 15–1).

Conditions to address before using reclaimed water for golf course irrigation include:

- Does the reclaimed water have adequate quality and remain consistent over time?
- Is it absent of heavy metals?
- Is it available free or at a reasonable cost?
- Does it possess any detrimental health effects?
- Will it cause any adverse effects on downstream water rights?
- Is it potentially injurious to plant life, fish, and wildlife?

LEVELS OF TREATED WATER

The usability of effluent water on turf depends on the physical, chemical, and microbiological quality of the water. The terms **potable water** and **domestic water** are often used synonymously to describe drinking water while **effluent**-, **reclaimed**-, **gray**-, **recycled**-, or **wastewater** are terms used to describe water that has gone through one cycle of domestic use. Most effluent water from treatment plants is approximately 99.9 percent water and 0.06 percent solids (or sludge) (Table 15–2). Ideally, effluent or wastewater used for turf irrigation should principally come from

TABLE 15–1 *Concerns with effluent wastewater use for irrigation (modified from Asano et al., 1984; Baldwin and Comer, 1986).*

Concern	Measured paramters	Comment
Suspended solids	Suspended solids, including volatile and fixed solids	Suspended solids can lead to the development of sludge deposits and anaerobic conditions when untreated wastewater is discharged in an aquatic environment. Excessive suspended solids can plug irrigation systems and reduce soil water infiltration and percolation rates. Typically, 60 to 70 percent of the suspended solids are removed in primary effluent, up to 90 percent is removed by secondary treatment, and 99 percent + is removed by tertiary treatment.
Biodegradable organics	Biochemical oxygen demand, chemical oxygen demand	Composed mostly of proteins, carbohydrates, and fats. If discharged to the environment, their biological decomposition can lead to the depletion of dissolved oxygen and the development of septic conditions. Advanced treatment has <1 BOD mg/L. Dissolved oxygen levels <5 mg/L are marginal for fish and other aquatic life survival.
Pathogens	Indicator organisms, total and fecal coliform bacteria	Communicable diseases can be transmitted by bacteria, viruses, and parasites. Chlorinated primary and secondary treated wastewater have coliform bacteria limits of 23 or less/100 mL water while advanced or tertiary wastewater has a count of less than 2.2/100 mL water.
Nutrients	Nitrogen (N), phosphorus (P), potassium (K)	Nitrogen, phosphorus, and potassium are essential nutrients for plant growth, and their presence normally enhances the value of the water for irrigation. When discharged to the aquatic environment, nitrogen and phosphorus can lead to the growth of undesirable aquatic life. When discharged in excessive amounts on land, nitrogen can also lead to the pollution of groundwater. Advanced treatment typically has 2 to 10 mg N/L, 0.1 to 1.0 mg P/L, and 0 mg K/L.
Stable (refractory organics)	Specific compounds (e.g., phenols, pesticides, chlorinated hydrocarbons)	These organics tend to resist conventional methods of wastewater treatment. Some organic compounds are toxic in the environment, and their presence may limit the suitability of the wastewater for irrigation.
Hydrogen ion activity	pH	The pH of wastewater affects metal solubility as well as the alkalinity of soils. The normal range in municipal wastewater is 6.5 to 8.5, but industrial waste can significantly alter the pH.
Heavy metals	Specific elements (e.g., Cd, Zn, Ni, Hg)	Some heavy metals accumulate in the environment and are toxic to plants and animals. Their presence may limit the suitability of the wastewater for irrigation.
Dissolved inorganics	Total dissolved solids, electrical conductivity, specific elements (e.g., Na, Ca, Mg, Cl, B)	Excessive salinity may damage some crops. Specific ions such as chloride, sodium, and boron are toxic to some crops. Sodium may decrease soil permeability. Total dissolved solid levels above 1,000 ppm will have limitations as a long-term irrigation source.
Residual chlorine	Free and combined	Excessive chlorine (5 mg/L) may cause leaf tip burn to sensitive plants. However, most chlorine in reclaimed wastewater is in a combined form, which does not cause crop damage.

an urban area without significant industrial input. This should guard against the possibility of excessive heavy metal content from industry. The treatment level of wastewater also should be at least **secondary.**

Primary

Primary treatment begins with the preliminary operations such as screening and sedimentation that remove organic and inorganic solids. After screening and possible grinding of debris, dense

TABLE 15–2 *General characteristics of effluent water.*

Treatment Level	Characteristics
Primary	-Contains ≤50 percent of origin solids
	-Contains no large debris
	-Can have a bad odor
	-Contains <23 coliform bacteria per 100 mL
	-Not to be used for turf irrigation
Secondary	->90 percent solids removed
	-Coliform bacteria count <23/100 mL
	-Has a slight odor
	-Can be used to irrigate turf (no human contact)
Tertiary (or Advanced)	->99 percent solids removed
	-No or low odor
	-Highly purified
	-Coliform bacteria count <2.2/100 mL
	-Can be used to irrigate turf
	-<1 mg/L biological oxygen demand (BOD)
	-Typically contains 2 to 10 mg N/L, 0.1 to 1.0 mg P/L, and 0 mg K/L

materials such as sand and stones are allowed to settle in a grit chamber. This material is normally washed and also is used as landfill.

Undissolved suspended matter is then removed in a second settling tank or a primary clarifier. Settled material forms a mass of raw sludge that is concentrated and used as landfill.

The remaining liquid in the settling tank is called primary effluent and may be chlorinated to destroy bacteria and reduce odor before it is used. Primary sedimentation removes approximately 60 to 70 percent of the suspended solids and 25 to 40 percent of the **biochemical oxygen demand** (BOD).

Secondary

Nonchlorinated primary effluent water may be further treated to break down complex organic matter during secondary treatment. Up to 90 percent of organic matter is removed by secondary treatment by trickling the effluent through large cylindrical vats containing bacterial colonies that digest the complex and simple organic compounds. Water is then chlorinated so the coliform bacterial count is less than 23 per 100 mL of water and is the principal source of water for agricultural irrigation purposes.

Tertiary

Although secondary water is usable for irrigation, many water plants continue treatment to the final stage, known as **advanced** or **tertiary** treatment. Advanced or tertiary wastewater treatment involves using a charcoal bed for chemical coagulation and flocculation, sedimentation, filtration, or adsorption of compounds. It removes nonbiodegradable organic pollutants and most nutrients, such as nitrogen and phosphorus. It has no foul odor and contains a coliform bacterial count of less than 2.2 per mL. This process can provide highly purified water and is similar to potable water treatment. It is the most commonly used effluent source on golf courses. In some instances, **quaternary treatment** is used where UV light, ozone, or additional chlorination are used to further purify the water.

An alternative method to the conventional treatment of wastewater is land treatment. **Overland flow** and **rapid infiltration** are methods utilizing the soil surface and vegetative layer as a natural filter. During these processes, water is applied to land. The renovated water is collected either at the bottom of an overland flow slope (overland flow) or from within the soil by a series of wells. It also is collected by permanent underdrains (rapid infiltration). Rapid infiltration requires less land to renovate wastewater compared to overland flow but requires a permeable soil, a series of wells or underground drainage tiles, and a host of environmental regulations.

CHARACTERISTICS OF EFFLUENT WATER

Effluent water has three major categories of characteristics that are modified during use: (1) biological composition, (2) organic composition, and (3) dissolved inorganic salts. Although biological composition of effluent water is of great concern because of pathogenic bacteria and viruses, chlorinated waters are not released for irrigation without prior approval of the public health officials.

Secondary treated wastewater has been disinfected to a level of 23 total coliform or less per 100 mL, so direct contact with effluent water should be avoided. States generally restrict the use of this water to non-daylight hours and signs are posted indicating, "***Warning: Course Irrigated With Reclaimed Water.***" Treated areas should be allowed to dry before golf course play resumes. To eliminate the possibility of accidental contamination of a domestic water system, an entirely separate delivery system should be constructed.

For irrigation purposes, the organic portion of the effluent water is generally of minimal consequence. The most influential characteristic of effluent water irrigation is the higher salt load that results from its use. The buildup of total soluble salts in the rootzone: (1) inhibits turfgrass water uptake, (2) causes loss of turfgrass color and failure of turf to respond to nutrient applications, and (3) increases the opportunity for direct salt toxicity to root tissues by excessive levels of sodium, chlorine, or boron. Samples should be analyzed before use for:

1. pH
2. Bicarbonate concentration
3. Dissolved solids
4. Salt and sodium hazard (permeability)
5. Heavy metal or toxic ion concentration

Some of these may accumulate in the soil or on leaves at levels injurious to plants. Table 15–3 lists EPA guidelines for water reuse. Water for golf course irrigation, where direct or indirect human contact is likely, must be oxidized, coagulated, filtered, and disinfected so the median member of total coliform organism does not exceed 2.2/mL (Table 15–3). Public health concerns are minimized if appropriate use controls are followed, such as irrigating during off hours and not irrigating when wind-blown spray might reach residential areas. **Note:** These are guidelines for states to consider. Many states (eg. Florida, Arizona, California) have developed their own standards.

Total Suspended Solids

Soluble materials accumulate in water as the result of being used once. **Total suspended solid (TSS)** level requirements have been set between 5 and 10 mg/L for most states. Continuous use of high TSS-containing water may eventually clog surface pores that inhibit water infiltration into the soil profile. Golf greens and tees to be watered with effluent should be constructed with high sand content and have infiltration and percolation rates at the higher rate range. Drip irrigation emitters are prone to clogging when irrigation water has >50 mg/L (ppm) suspended solids. Increased aerification practices also may be necessary if TSS levels are excessive.

Turbidity is also reported by many labs that analyze water quality. Turbidity measures the transmission of light through water. It is most affected by particulant matter suspended in the water. Unfortunately, standard guidelines on acceptable turbidity thresholds are not developed; thus, this measurement currently means little.

Salts and Soil Permeability

Water management and adequate drainage are keys to successful effluent use in turf management. Generally, water going through one cycle of average home use accumulates approximately 300 ppm (or 0.48 dS/m) of **total dissolved salts** (TDS). The ability to leach-out these salts is necessary to prevent accumulation of toxic concentrates. High TSS-containing effluent water also has a tendency to

TABLE 15-3 *U.S. Environmental Protection Agency's Guidelines for Water Reuse* [1] *(Anonymous, 1992).*

Types of reuse	Treatment	Reclaimed water quality[2]	Reclaimed water monitoring	Setback distances[3]	Comments
Landscape irrigation (e.g., golf courses, parks, cemeteries)	Secondary[4] Filtration[5] Disinfection[6]	pH = 6 to 9 ≤10 mg/L BOD[7] ≤2 NTU[8] No detectable fecal coli/100 mL 1 mg/L Cl_2 residual (min.)[11]	pH—weekly BOD—weekly Turbidity—continuous Coliform—daily Cl_2 residual—continuous	50 ft (15 m) to potable water supply wells	* At controlled-access irrigation sites where design and operational measures significantly reduce the potential of public contact with reclaimed water, a lower level of treatment (e.g., secondary treatment and disinfection to achieve ≤14 fecal coli/100 ml) may be appropriate. * Chemical (coagulant and/or polymer) addition prior to filtration may be necessary to meet water quality recommendations. * The reclaimed water should not contain measurable levels of pathogens.[12] * Reclaimed water should be clear, odorless, and contain no substances that are toxic upon ingestion. * A higher chlorine residual and/or a longer contact time may be necessary to ensure that viruses and parasites are inactive or destroyed. * A chlorine residual of 0.5 mg/L or greater in the distribution system is recommended to reduce odors, slime, and bacterial regrowth.
Restricted access area irrigation (e.g., sod farms, silverculture sites)	Secondary[4] Disinfection[5]	pH = 6 to 9 ≤30 mg/L BOD ≤30 mg/L TSS ≤200 fecal coli/100 mL [9,13,14] 1 mg/L Cl_2 residual (min.)[11]	pH—weekly BOD—weekly TSS—daily Coliform—daily Cl_2 residual—continuous	* 300 ft (90 m) to potable water supply wells * 100 ft (30 m) to areas accessible to the public (if spray irrigation)	* If spray irrigation, TSS less than 30 mg/L may be necessary to avoid clogging of sprinkler heads.
Recreational impoundments (incidental contact, such as fishing and boating, and full body contact with reclaimed water allowed)	Secondary[4] Filtration[5] Disinfection[6]	pH = 6 to 9 ≤10 mg/L BOD[7] ≤2 NTU[8] No detectable fecal coli/100 mL [9,10] 1 mg/L Cl_2 residual (min.)	pH—weekly BOD—weekly Turbidity—continuous Coliform—daily Cl_2 residual—continuous	500 ft (150 m) to potable water supply wells (minimum) if bottom not sealed	* Dechlorination may be necessary to protect aquatic species of flora and fauna. * Reclaimed water should be non-irritating to skin and eyes. * Reclaimed water should be clear, odorless, and contain no substances that are toxic upon ingestion. * Nutrient removal may be necessary to avoid algae growth in impoundments.

(continued)

413

TABLE 15–3 *U.S. Environmental Protection Agency's Guidelines for Water Reuse*[1] *(Anonymous, 1992).*

Types of reuse	Treatment	Reclaimed water quality[2]	Reclaimed water monitoring	Setback distances[3]	Comments
Environmental reuse (wetlands, marshes, wildlife habitat, stream augmentation)	Variable Secondary[4] Disinfection[5] (min.)	Variable, but not to exceed: • ≤30 mg/L BOD[7] • ≤30 mg/L TSS • ≤200 fecal coli/100 mL [9,13,14]	BOD—weekly TSS—weekly Coliform—daily Cl$_2$ residual—continuous		* Chemical (coagulant and/or polymer) addition prior to filtration may be necessary to meet water quality recommendations. * The reclaimed water should not contain measurable levels of pathogens. [12] * A higher chlorine residual and/or a longer contact time may be necessary to ensure that viruses and parasites are inactivated or destroyed. * Fish caught in impoundments can be consumed. * Dechlorination may be necessary to protect aquatic species of flora and fauna. * Possible effects on groundwater should be evaluated. * Receiving water quality requirements may necessitate additional treatment. * The temperature of the reclaimed water should not adversely affect ecosystem.

[1]These guidelines are based on water reclamation and reuse practices in the United States, and they are especially directed at states that have not developed their own regulations or guidelines.

[2]Unless otherwise noted, recommended quality limits apply to the reclaimed water at the point of discharge from the treatment facility.

[3]Setback distances are recommended to protect potable water supply source from contamination and to protect humans from unreasonable health risks due to exposure to reclaimed water.

[4]Secondary treatment processes include activated sludge processes, trickling filters, rotating biological contactors, and many stabilization pond systems. Secondary treatment should produce effluent in which both the BOD and TSS do not exceed 30 mg/L.

[5]Filtration means the passing of wastewater through natural undisturbed soils or filter media such as sand and/or anthracite.

[6]Disinfection means the destruction, inactivation, or removal of pathogenic microorganisms by chemical, physical, or biological means. Disinfection may be accomplished by chlorination, ozonation, other chemical disinfectants, UV radiation, membrane processes, or other processes.

[7]As determined from the 5-day BOD test.

[8]The recommended turbidity limit should be met prior to disinfection. The average turbidity should be based on a 24-hour time period. The turbidity should not exceed five NTU at any time. If TSS is used in lieu of turbidity, the average TSS should not exceed five mg/L.

[9]Unless otherwise noted, recommended coliform limits are median values determined from the bacteriological results of the last seven days for which analyses have been completed. Either the membrane filter or fermentation tube technique may be used.

[10]The number of fecal coliform organisms should not exceed 14/100 mL in any sample.

[11]Total chlorine residual after a minimum contact time of 30 minutes.

[12]It is advisable to fully characterize the microbiological quality of the reclaimed water prior to implementation of a reuse program.

[13]The number of fecal coliform organisms should not exceed 800/100 mL in any sample.

[14]Some stabilization pond systems may be able to meet this coliform limit without disinfection.

TABLE 15-4 *Hydraulic loading rates typically used for soils during site design (Kleiss and Hoover, 1986).*

Soil group	Texture	Application rate (in./day)
I	Sandy	1.5 to 2
II	Coarse loamy	1 to 1.5
III	Fine loam	0.75 to 1
IVa	Clay (1:1)	0.33 to 0.75
IVb	Clay (2:1)	unsuitable

clog soil pores and coat the land surface (Table 15–4). Coarse-textured soils, such as sandy loams, with a moderately permeable soil capable of infiltrating approximately two inches per day or more on an intermittent basis is best for the use of wastewater. Soils with a hard pan, clay pan, or underlaying rock may create a perched water table that promotes surface accumulation of salts and heavy metals.

Initial tests should be taken to show the **sodium absorption ratio** (SAR) or **exchangeable sodium percentages** (ESP), which are indexes of the effect of sodium in reducing soil permeability (the rate at which water passes into and through soil) based on the ratio of sodium to calcium and magnesium. A SAR of 10 or less is considered desirable. If greater than 10, gypsum or gypsite could be incorporated into the management program, or alternate application of fresh water with effluent water should be followed to help leach out sodium. A SAR above 10 indicates increasing potential permeability problems. Additional tests include adjusted SAR, which accounts for adjustments in the influence of HCO_3^- and the RSC value using calcium, magnesium, HCO_3, and CO_3 concentrations.

In addition to increasing salt stress, sodium-rich irrigation waters can replace soil-exchangeable calcium and magnesium, with sodium resulting in reduced permeability. Usually this is more of a concern in arid states in which most irrigation water sources have a high sodium content. This may, however, be a concern during dry months if salt has intruded into the normal irrigation water source or into the sewage system. Waterlogging, slow infiltration, crusting or compaction, poor aeration, weed invasion, and disease occurrence are typical symptoms of reduced permeability. A severe infiltration problem may develop if electrical conductivity (EC_w) of irrigation water is less than 0.2 mmhos/cm.

Noticeably, a rapid green-up is common with gypsum applications to soils with pHs less than 5.5 because of more favorable conditions for Nitrosomonas and Nitrobacter stimulation, transforming NH_4 to NO_3. However, high salinity concentrations cannot be easily overcome. Dilution of high salinity wastewater with fresh water is probably the most practical solution. When total salinity is high, iron plus a cytokinin as a foliar treatment is often beneficial since salt-stressed plants exhibit low cytokinin activity.

Other potential problems with effluent irrigation include exposure of golf course maintenance equipment and golf carts to salt when these are driven through depressions holding standing effluent water. Internal switches and the underside bodies of carts are susceptible to rusting from salinity, as are seals and bearings associated with maintenance equipment. Using cart paths and frequently rinsing the equipment with fresh water will minimize these problems.

Nutrient Content

Application of wastewater to crops can be beneficial because of nutrients in the liquid. Virtually all essential plant nutrients are found to some degree in wastewater. Constant monitoring of effluent water should be maintained to determine the amounts of these individual nutrients, and the fertility management of turf should be adjusted to account for these. Potential nitrogen levels range from 10 to 35 mg/L, phosphorus 0 to 5 mg/L, and potassium 5 to 25 mg/L (Table 15–5). The major problem with excessive wastewater nutrient content (especially nitrogen and phosphorus) is these may favor algal blooms in storage ponds. Also, if cool-season grasses are over-fertilized from nitrogen in the water, especially during summer, diseases, excessive growth, weakened plants, and eventual stand deterioration may occur.

TABLE 15–5 *Typical nutrient ranges in effluent water used for irrigation.*

Element	Low	Normal	High	Very high
		Rating (ppm)		
Calcium	<20	20 to 60	60 to 80	>80
Magnesium	<10	10 to 25	25 to 35	>35
Potassium	<5	5 to 20	20 to 30	>30
Phosphorus	<0.1	0.1 to 0.4	0.5 to 0.8	>0.8
Nitrogen	<1	1 to 10	10 to 20	>20
Nitrates	<5	5 to 50	50 to 100	>100
Sulfur	<10	10 to 30	30 to 60	>60
Sulfate	<30	30 to 90	90 to 180	>180

Sulfur

Effluent water also often has an unusually high level of sulfate (SO_4^{-2}). Irrigation water, for example, with 100 ppm SO_4^{-2} provides 2.1 pounds sulfur per 1,000 square feet ($10 \ kg/100 \ m^2$) with each foot of water applied. Sulfur can react with iron and manganese under anaerobic conditions to create FeS and MnS, which then contribute to poor drainage and possible black layer.

Lime can be added to the soil to transform sulfate to insoluble gypsum ($CaSO_4$), which prevents the sulfur from being reduced to FeS and MnS. Calcium carbonate applied at 10 pounds per 1,000 square feet (49 kg/100 m) provides 3.8 pounds calcium (1.7 kg) which can react with 9.1 pounds (4.1 kg) SO_4^{-2}, or 3 pounds, 0.4 kilograms, sulfur to form gypsum.

To determine the amount of nutrients being added using effluent water, the following steps are taken.

1. Find the concentration of the element in question (in ppm or mg/L) from the water quality test report.
2. Multiply this value by 2.72 to determine the pounds of nutrient per acre-foot of applied water. An acre-foot of water is approximately 325,000 gallons.
3. Convert the amount of nutrients applied per acre-foot to 1,000 square feet of turf by dividing the value in step 2 by 43.5.

Example:

1. 10 ppm nitrogen would supply the following:
   Step 1: Find 10 ppm nitrogen from the water quality test report.
   Step 2: Multiply ppm nitrogen by 2.72 to obtain the amount of nitrogen applied per acre-foot of water.

   10 ppm nitrogen × 2.7 = 27 pounds nitrogen per acre-foot ($9.9 \ g/m^3$) of water.

   Step 3: Convert pounds nitrogen applied per acre-foot of water to pounds nitrogen applied per 1,000 square feet of turf per acre-foot of water.

   27 pounds nitrogen per acre-foot ÷ 43.5 = 0.62 pounds of nitrogen applied per 1,000 square feet of turf with every acre-foot ($0.23 \ g/m^3$) of effluent water applied.

2. How many pounds of nitrate nitrogen (NO_3^-) is applied per 1,000 square feet if one acre-foot of 5.2 ppm NO_3^- containing water is used?

   Step 1: ppm NO_3^- × 2.72 = pounds of NO_3^- per acre-foot of water = 5.2 ppm × 2.72 = 14.1 pounds NO_3^- applied per acre-foot of water,
   Step 2: 14.2 pounds NO_3^- per acre-foot of water applied ÷ 43.56 = 0.32 pounds NO_3^- applied per 1,000 square feet with each acre-foot ($0.12 \ g/m^3$) of water applied.

Heavy Metals

Heavy metal concentrations usually are not a problem with urban effluent water sources but are potentially major concerns with certain industrial effluent sources. This is why industrial and mining effluent water sources are not generally recommended for turf irrigation.

There are several trace elements in domestic effluent water that could be present in potentially toxic amounts under certain conditions. Therefore, they should be periodically monitored. These include chlorine, boron, cadmium, copper, nickel, and zinc. Groundwater contamination is the main concern resulting from their presence. Recommendations include a minimum soil depth of five feet (1.5 m) to groundwater supplies and an upper irrigation limit of four inches (10 cm) per week. Groundwater monitoring wells are normally required in areas using effluent water. Suggested maximum levels of trace metals in effluent water are listed in Chapter 14 of this publication.

Chlorine and boron are among the toxic ions to plants found in effluent. Turfgrasses usually are tolerant to these since they tend to accumulate in leaf tips and are removed during mowing. Many trees and shrubs, however, may be sensitive, especially when grown on heavy soils where their amounts of chloride often increase. Certain trees and shrubs are especially sensitive to chloride levels approaching 5 to 10 meq/L (350 ppm) and boron levels of two ppm, and can experience disfiguring leaf burn from long-term exposure to these.

Long-term use of high iron-containing water may cause:

1. Precipitation of phosphorus and molybdenum, causing deficiencies.
2. Staining of sidewalks, buildings, and equipment exposed to the water.
3. Plugging of irrigation components by anaerobic iron sludge deposits.
4. Manganese deficiency or, to a lesser extent, zinc and copper deficiencies.

Storage Ponds

A seasonal problem for turf managers who use wastewater is most contracts require that a specific amount be accepted daily, regardless of weather conditions. In other words, a preset level of wastewater must be accepted per-day whether it is needed or not. Storage capability, therefore, is a major requirement when using effluent water and must be adequate to store enough water for the maximum days of non-irrigation (usually a minimum of three to five).

Storage ponds can be a source of algae, weeds, odors, and health problems if not properly designed and maintained. In fact, effluent water stored in ponds with a 1.1 ppm nitrogen may have excessive algae and aquatic plant growth. If water must be stored, an enclosed tank is preferred as this eliminates sunlight exposure and reduces algae formation. Storage ponds generally are acceptable for wastewater storage as long as the storage amount does not impair the pond's ability to function as a stormwater management system. Generally, storage ponds do not have to be lined, although lining (minimum lake lining thickness of 40 mil) allows easier maintenance and cleaning following draw-downs. Storage ponds should also be at least six feet (1.8 m) deep, with good aeration, and have a 3-to-1 bankside slope to minimize aquatic weed problems. The deeper the pond, the better, since this reduces sunlight penetration, keeps the water cooler (cool water holds 40 percent more oxygen than warm water), and helps manage algae better (Figure 15–1).

Adequate circulation and aeration are needed for odor and algae control; therefore, include electrical service in the course design. Aeration helps attack the cause(s) of poor water quality while other methods, such as dyes and algaecides, only treat the symptoms—algae. Artificial aeration helps provide oxygen when natural wind and wave action cannot provide sufficient levels. One method to encourage circulation is to have the effluent water intake pipe at one end of the pond and the irrigation extraction pipe at the other. Fountains, air injection, waterfalls, and artificial wetlands are other means to provide pond circulation and aeration. Aerators need to be matched for the size of the pond or lake. A one acre pond three feet deep contains about 1 million gallons of water. If the aerator cannot move sufficient amounts of water, then disappointing benefits will be seen from it.

A week's supply of water (assuming 1.5 inches, 3.8 cm, of water applied on 100 acres, 40.5 ha, of turf) would be 4 million gallons (15 million liters) or 535,000 cubic feet (15,133 m^3), translating into a lake 10 feet (3 m) deep measuring approximately 180×300 ft (1,528 m^3) in size. Several smaller ponds may fit a golf course layout better than one large lake.

FIGURE 15-1 Properly
storing effluent water when
not needed can be a problem
for many golf facilities. The
necessary size and strict
environmental regulations
may make such storage ponds
or tanks cost-prohibitive.
Algae and other weeds can be
problematic if nutrients and
water oxygen levels are not
monitored and regulated.

Example:

1. How many gallons of water are in a storage pond with a surface area of 380,000 square feet and an average depth of 12 feet?

   Step 1: Determine the total acres of surface area of the pond.

   $$\frac{380,000 \text{ ft}^2}{\text{pond}} \times \frac{1 \text{ acre}}{43,560 \text{ ft}^2} = 8.724 \text{ total acres}$$

   Step 2: Determine the total acre-feet of the pond.

   $$8.724 \text{ acres} \times 12 \text{ ft.} = 105 \text{ acre-ft.}$$

   Step 3: Convert acre-feet to gallons. From Table 13–7, one acre-ft equals 325,851 gallons; thus,

   $$105 \text{ acre-ft} \times \frac{325,851 \text{ gal}}{\text{acre-ft}} = 34,214,355 \text{ gallons}$$

   Therefore, 34,214,355 gallons of water are in a pond of this size.

2. If 83 acres of turf are irrigated from this storage pond, how many inches of water could be applied (evaporation losses are not considered in this problem)?

   Step 1: Determine the amount of water needed to apply one acre-in. to 83 acres. From Table 13–7, 27,154 gallons of water are in each acre-in.

   $$83 \text{ acres} \times \frac{27,154 \text{ gal}}{\text{acre-in.}} = 2,253,782 \text{ gal}$$

   Step 2: Divide the total capacity of the pond (34,214,355 gal) by the amount of water needed over the 83 acres.

   $$34,214,355 \text{ gal} \times \frac{\text{acre-in.}}{2,253,782 \text{ gal}} = \frac{15.2 \text{ inches of water available for the}}{83 \text{ acres of turf}}$$

Golf Greens

In light of previously discussed advantages and disadvantages of using effluent water for golf course irrigation, it is suggested only tertiary treated wastewater be used on golf greens. Turf mowed excessively low, such as golf greens, is constantly on the management edge in terms of maintaining a healthy, acceptable playing surface. Although primary and secondary wastewater impurities are low, golf greens do not need added stress in terms of salinity and salts. Salinity can be extremely detrimental to golf greens due to their relatively shallow and weak root systems. Continued use of wastewater with low-to-moderate TSS may, in time, reduce water infiltration and percolation to the point of reducing turf quality. For these and other reasons, primary and secondary reclaimed water sources are not recommended for golf greens.

If a turf manager must use one of these wastewater sources for irrigating golf greens, several prerequisites exist for any chance of success. The golf green should have excellent (>6 inches per hour, 15 cm) infiltration and percolation rates to prevent salinity buildup. A superintendent must also be allowed to frequently aerify, spike, and slice the soil surface to minimize crusting and algae development. Regular flushing with a fresh water source also is necessary to remove salts.

Higher-mowed turf, such as fairways and roughs, is better able to tolerate higher salinity and TSS levels. Secondary wastewater, therefore, may be used successfully on such areas, assuming cultural practices such as aerifying and spiking are allowed. Exposure and environmental concerns, however, must be addressed before using this source on these areas.

Irrigation System Design

Corrosion of metallic parts and plugging of nozzle orifices are two potential problems in irrigation components when using wastewater. Chlorides and ammonia are corrosive components of many wastewater sources. Chlorides damage brass irrigation valves and fittings, as well as galvanized pipe and fittings. Ammonia can be corrosive to copper pipe with concentrations as low as 1.5 mg/L nitrogen. Combinations of chlorides and ammonia substantially increase the chances of corrosion.

Nozzle orifice clogging is another potential problem when using wastewater. This usually is not a problem with secondary treated effluent if relatively large irrigation nozzle sizes are used. Normally, the high pressure used to irrigate serves as a self-cleaning mechanism.

Clogging problems may occur from algae growing in the nutrient-rich wastewater while in storage ponds or in the piping system. A filtration system should be provided to minimize algae introduction into pipes, and valves should be designed to handle wastewater.

Sprinkler heads should be placed so a minimum of 75 feet (23 m) exists between the outside radius-throw and potable wells and public areas. Part-circle heads also should be used adjacent to wetlands and estuaries. This may result in unwatered spaces that appear undesirable due to drought and untidiness. Berms, or swales, also may be necessary to limit run-off of wastewater from treated areas to private and environmentally sensitive areas.

Above-ground spigots, hose bibs, quick-couple connections, and so on, are not allowed when using effluent water. These must be in below-ground boxes that are locked and clearly marked.

Cross-Contamination Prevention

The distribution system includes pipelines, pumping stations, and storage facilities. A cross-connection between a potable water system and any nonpotable water source must be avoided. Ways of preventing this include:

- Irrigation lines should be tagged, colored, and designed so unauthorized persons cannot operate them. Most effluent lines and values are colored purple (Plate 15–1).
- Separation of domestic pipelines from reclaimed pipelines are necessary to reduce the possibility of cross-contamination. This usually involves 10-foot (3-m) horizontal and one-foot (0.3-m) vertical separation where these lines cross.
- Prevention of easy connection to effluent water couplers.
- Hose bibs are usually allowed if located in below-ground lockable vaults or if a special tool is necessary to access the effluent water.
- Backflow protection.
- Minimum leaking of pipes and joints.

Other Information and Suggestions

- Bentgrass declines at 1.5 to 2.0 dS/m^{-1} EC$_w$ and bermudagrass declines at 4 to 15 EC$_w$, but may vary depending on soil factors, temperature, irrigation, cultivar, and so on.

- Juvenile plants are more sensitive to salt injury. Increasing overseeding rates 10 to 20 percent may be necessary to produce acceptable quality.
- pH values for most urban effluent water range between 6 to 8.
- Nematode concentrations have not been found to increase with effluent water use.
- Use of salt-tolerant grasses, such as hybrid bermudagrass or seashore paspalum, should be considered before application.
- Effluent water should not be sprayed on domestic water wells, reservoirs, or near drinking fountains or eating areas. Drinking fountains need self-closing covers.
- Irrigation systems should have proper filters to catch any damaging solids.
- Communicate to all persons about the procedure. Establish and maintain good relations with all involved governmental agencies.
- All irrigation should be timed to minimize public contact and to allow ample opportunity for land to dry out before it is reused.
- A backup system is critical for greens and tees, as some treatment plants shut down periodically for maintenance.
- Low-pressure sensors should be installed in the event of pressure drop.
- A 50- to 100-foot (15- to 30-m) vegetative buffer zone is often required between the edge of the spray and the nearest dwelling.
- Chlorine levels of 0.5 mg/L or higher are generally required in effluent water to reduce odors, slime, and bacterial growth.

CALCULATING FERTILIZER AMOUNTS FROM EFFLUENT IRRIGATION

Most effluent irrigation sources contain a certain amount of nutrients. To compensate for these in a yearly fertilization program, the pounds per acre applied from irrigation water needs to be determined. The following formula is one method of determining this; another method was discussed previously in the Nutrient Content section of this chapter.

Pounds

Pounds nutrients applied/acre = ppm of the element in the water × acre-inches water applied × 0.2264 is a conversion factor from:

$$\frac{1 \text{ lb}}{454,000 \text{ mg}} \times \frac{27,154 \text{ gal}}{\text{acre-in.}} \times \frac{3.785 \text{ L}}{\text{gal}} = \frac{0.2264 \text{ lb L}}{\text{mg acre-in.}}$$

Example:

If six acre-inches of effluent water are applied monthly and contain 150 ppm nitrogen, how many pounds of nitrogen are being applied per acre?

lbs/acre = 150 ppm × 6 acre-inches × 0.2264 = 204 pounds nitrogen per acre (288 kg/ha)

PLATE 10–5 Nutrient deficiency symptoms in bentgrass. From the top: phosphorus (left), potassium (right); middle: iron (left), sulfur (right), and magnesium (bottom).

PLATE 13–1 Waiting until just before turf plants wilt before watering helps encourage turf rooting and water conservation. Shown is a green allowed to dry-out excessively which has begun to wilt and is in need of water.

PLATE 13–2 Turfgrass wilting and blue-green color as a response to water stress.

PLATE 13–3 Footprinting of greens indicating initial signs of turf moisture stress.

PLATE 15–1 Most areas require all pipe and other components transporting effluent water to be colored a distinctive purple color.

PLATE 16–1 Alternating light- and dark-appearing grass appears due to continued alternating mowing direction.

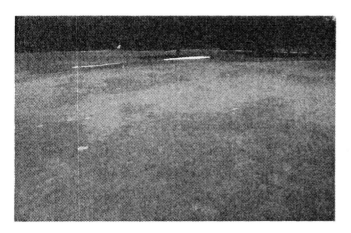

PLATE 16–2 Grain development in a golf green from insufficient vertical mowing, grooming, brushing, and rotating mower direction.

PLATE 16–3 Excessive thatch layering.

PLATE 16–4 Uneven mowing pattern and scalping from excessive thatch layering in a golf green.

PLATE 18–1 Overseeding provides desirable year-round color, some protection to the permanent grass, and suggested landing areas for players.

PLATE 18–2 Annual bluegrass (*Poa annua*) is the most troublesome weed problem in overseeded areas due to its prolific seedhead production, clumping growth habit, and early spring die-back.

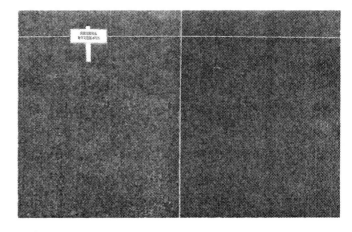

PLATE 18–3 Perennial ryegrass (right) is compared to annual ryegrass (left) used for overseeding.

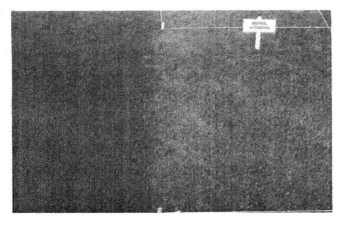

PLATE 18–4 Bentgrass (left) is compared to annual ryegrass (right) used for overseeding.

PLATE 18–4 *Poa trivialis* (or roughstalk bluegrass) has gained in overseeding popularity due to its fine leaf texture, good density, close mowing tolerance, and minimum seedbed preparation needed for establishment. *Poa trivialis* (left) is compared to creeping bentgrass (right) used for overseeding.

PLATE 18–8 Premature transition from the overseeded grass to the still-dormant bermudagrass due to early hot and dry weather. The spring overseeding transition should be a gradual change (or transition) from the overseeded grass to the permanent species. Weather conditions largely dictate transitions, requiring superintendents to closely monitor and address unusual weather patterns. Selecting the proper overseeding grass or blend also can influence spring transition.

PLATE 18–5 Intermediate ryegrass is a hybrid of annual and perennial ryegrass. Intermediate ryegrass germinates quickly but lacks heat tolerance and often has a light-green color. Breeding efforts are being made to improve these characteristics.

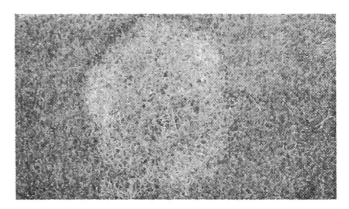

PLATE 18–7 Brown patch disease (*Rhizoctonia solani*) on overseeded ryegrass following warm, wet weather.

PLATE 18–9 Poor spray coverage during spring when chemically removing overseeding.

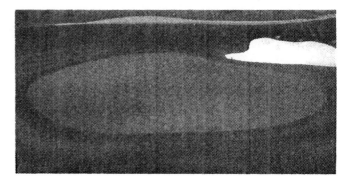

PLATE 19–1 Desirable creeping bentgrass.

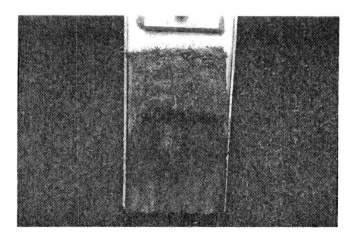

PLATE 19-2 Toxic black layer of sulfides that often forms when soil oxygen becomes depleted and soil moisture is excessive.

PLATE 19-3 Initial symptoms of bentgrass summer decline with initial stand density reduction followed by algae (above). If left unchecked, the bentgrass eventually thins and dies from a combination of reduced soil oxygen, increased root respiration, improper soil moisture, and diseases (below).

PLATE 19-4 Severe algae on a bentgrass golf green that has inadequate surface air movement and soil drainage.

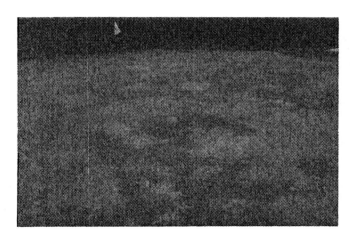

PLATE 19-5 Severe infestation of bermudagrass in a creeping bentgrass golf green.

PLATE 19-6 Segregation or mottling of creeping bentgrass. This naturally occurs and is not from diseases or nutrient imbalances.

PLATE 20–1 Off-type bermudagrasses have plagued many golf courses in recent years. It is believed these occur as chance mutations or as contaminants.

PLATE 22–1 Viruses rarely attack turfgrasses, with centipedegrass and St. Augustinegrass being exceptions. Shown is virus-infected Virginia buttonweed (*Diodia virginiana* L.), a common turfgrass weed. Note the light-green, yellowish color and interveinal chlorosis.

PLATE 22–2 Many grasses on golf greens eventually segregate into distinct patches, which are often confused with diseases. Shown is Tifdwarf bermudagrass with purple patches forming in fall when days are bright and nights cool.

PLATE 22–3 Anthracnose (*Colletotrichum graminicola*) leaf blight on Tifdwarf bermudagrass. Occurrence happens most often during periods of limited growth such as fall for bermudagrass or summer for bentgrass.

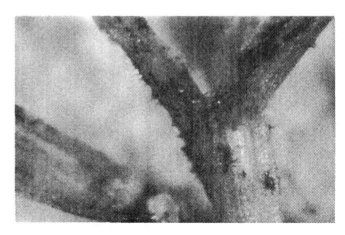

PLATE 22–4 Anthracnose basal rot (*Colletotrichum graminicola*) of creeping bentgrass is shown (left). Anthracnose basal rot is shown (right) with a close-up of black-colored acervuli.

PLATE 22–5 Tifgreen bermudagrass shows symptoms of bermudagrass decline (*Gaeumannomyces graminis* var. *graminis*) (courtesy of Monica Elliott).

PLATE 22–6 Close-up of a typical bermudagrass decline patch (*Gaeumannomyces graminis* var. *graminis*). Note the thinning and lighter green-colored turf. Roots are often weak, black, and rotted (courtesy of Monica Elliott).

PLATE 22–7 Bermudagrass decline (foreground) (*Gaeumannomyces graminis* var. *graminis*) often occurs on excessively closely mowed greens. This typically occurs in mid- to late summer when moisture is excessive, drainage is poor, and photosynthetic activity is limited due to restricted daylight from cloudy or overcast weather. Raising the mowing height reduces or eliminates this disease (background) (courtesy of Monica Elliott).

PLATE 22–8 Brown patch disease (*Rhizoctonia solani*) affecting colonial bentgrass.

PLATE 22–9 Brown patch disease (*Rhizoctonia solani*) affecting bermudagrass.

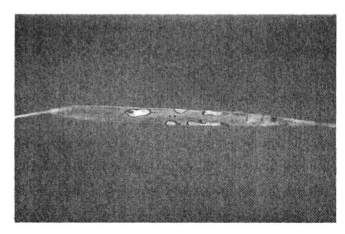

PLATE 22–10 Brown patch (*Rhizoctonia solani*) lesion on tall fescue.

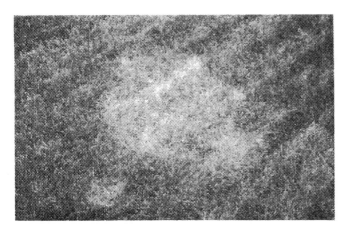

PLATE 22–11 Brown patch disease (*Rhizoctonia solani*) affecting tall fescue.

PLATE 22–12 Brown patch disease (*Rhizoctonia solani*) affecting coarse-textured turfgrass.

PLATE 22–13 Rhizoctonia leaf and sheath spot disease (*Rhizoctonia zeae*) on creeping bentgrass.

PLATE 22–14 Yellow patch (*Rhizoctonia cerealis*) on creeping bentgrass.

PLATE 22–15 Severe dollar spot disease (*Sclerotinia homoeocarpa*) on a golf green.

PLATE 22–16 Dollar spot disease (*Sclerotinia homoeocarpa*) lesion. Note the light-tan center with distinct brown borders.

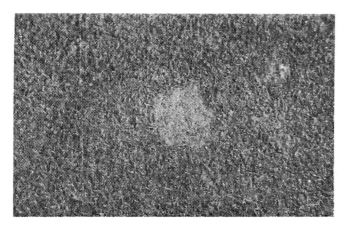

PLATE 22–17 Mycelium associated with dollar spot disease (*Sclerotinia homoeocarpa*).

PLATE 22–18 Control of dollar spot disease (*Sclerotinia homoeocarpa*) with increased nitrogen fertilizer application (left) versus none (right).

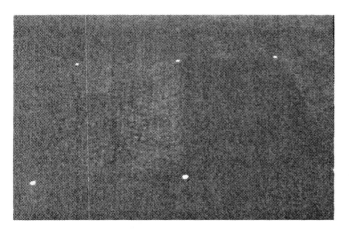

PLATE 22–19 Successful control of dollar spot disease (*Sclerotinia homoeocarpa*) with fungicides (right) compared to an untreated area (left).

PLATE 22–20 Fairy ring with mushrooms present and darker-green rings of turf due to increased nitrogen available from decomposition of organic complexes in the soil.

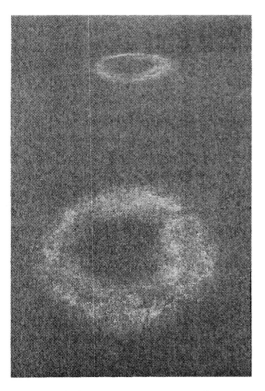

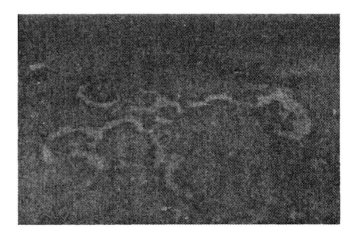

PLATE 22–21 Early Type I edaphic fairy ring on a golf green with a narrow zone of dead grass (necrotic ring).

PLATE 22–22 A layer of hydrophobic (water "hating") mycelium mat that often forms under fairy rings, causing the turf to die from moisture stress.

PLATE 22–23 Type II edaphic fairy ring with a band of dark-green turf.

PLATE 22–24 Type III edaphic fairy ring with only a circle of mushrooms present and no dead grass zone or a stimulated dark-green zone.

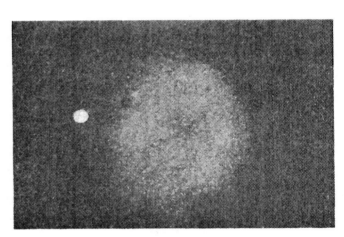

PLATE 22–25 Fusarium patch (or pink snow mold) caused by *Microdochium nivale* on bentgrass.

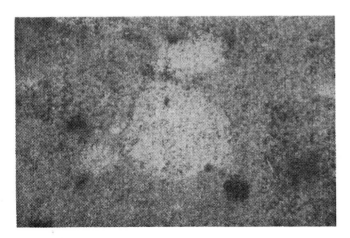

PLATE 22–26 Fusarium patch (or pink snow mold) caused by *Microdochium nivale* on dormant bermudagrass.

PLATE 22–27 Gray leaf spot (or blast) (*Pyricularia grisea*) of ryegrass (courtesy of Peter Dernoeden).

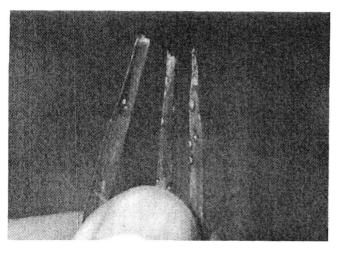

PLATE 22–28 Gray leaf spot (or blast) (*Pyricularia grisea*) lesions on tall fescue.

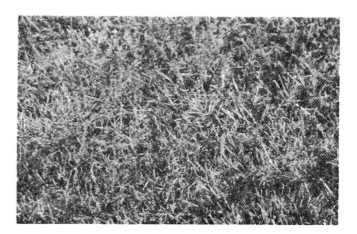

PLATE 22–29 "Melting out" of Kentucky bluegrass caused by *Drechslera poae* (courtesy of Peter Dernoeden).

PLATE 22–30 "Helminthosporium" leaf spot (*Bipolaris* and *Drechslera* spp.) lesions on bermudagrass.

PLATE 22–31 Thinning of creeping bentgrass from "Helminthosporium" leaf spot (*Bipolaris* and *Drechslera* spp.) disease.

PLATE 22–32 Thinning of overseeded bermudagrass from "Helminthosporium" leaf spot (*Bipolaris* and *Drechslera* spp.) disease. Bermudagrass often appears reddish-purple to almost orange when disease is severe.

PLATE 22–33 Necrotic ring spot disease (*Leptosphaeria korrae*) of Kentucky bluegrass (courtesy of Peter Dernoeden).

PLATE 22–34 A powdery mildew (*Erysiphe graminis*) on Kentucky bluegrass leaves that shows grayish/white cobwebby growth (courtesy of Peter Dernoeden).

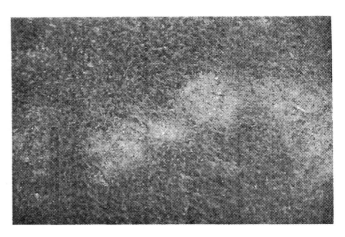

PLATE 22–35 Initial symptoms of Pythium blight where small, distinct reddish-brown patches of grass appear dark and water-soaked.

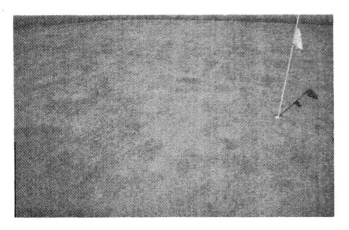

PLATE 22–36 Streaked patches of dark-green, mosaic patterns of bentgrass indicating initial symptoms of Pythium.

PLATE 22–37 Mature Pythium blight patches spreading to form a "streak" pattern from water movement or mowing.

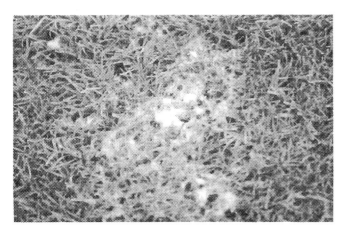

PLATE 22–38 White cottony mycelium associated with Pythium diseases sometimes observed in early morning when moisture is present.

PLATE 22–39 Dead bentgrass from Pythium disease in a poorly drained golf green area.

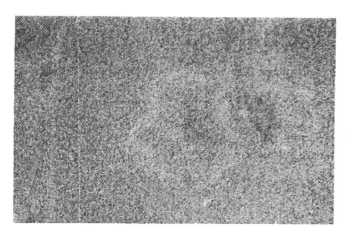

PLATE 22–40 Pythium root rot often causes an initial general yellowing of the turf that later thins. This is often associated with poor growing conditions such as inadequate drainage and excessive moisture.

PLATE 22–41 Early symptoms of Pythium root rot appear in a saturated bermudagrass golf green. Note the light-green to yellow turf.

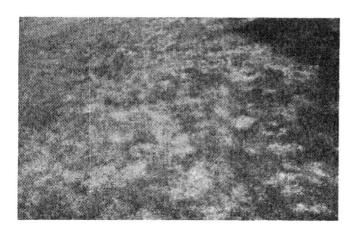

PLATE 22–42 Red thread (*Laetisaria fuciformis*) on fine fescue.

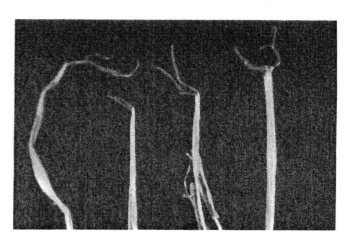

PLATE 22–43 Red thread (*Laetisaria fuciformis*) with red antlerlike "threads" or sclerotia (courtesy of Peter Dernoeden).

PLATE 22–44 Ragged straw-brown appearance from red thread (*Laetisaria fuciformis*) sclerotia (courtesy of Leon Lucas).

PLATE 22–45 Rust disease (*Puccinia* spp.) on slow-growing Kentucky bluegrass.

PLATE 22–46 Rust disease (*Puccinia* spp.) pustules containing orange powdery urediospores on zoysiagrass.

PLATE 22–47 Non-parasitic slime mold often seen during warm, wet weather. Slime mold does not injure or feed on turfgrasses.

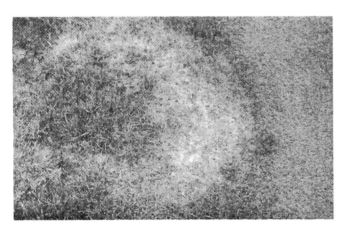

PLATE 22–48 Southern blight (*Sclerotium rolfsii*) on creeping bentgrass.

PLATE 22–49 White mycelial growth and immature white, small seedlike sclerotia associated with Southern blight (*Sclerotium rolfsii*).

PLATE 22–50 Spring dead spot disease (*Gaeumannomyces graminis* var. *graminis*) of bermudagrass.

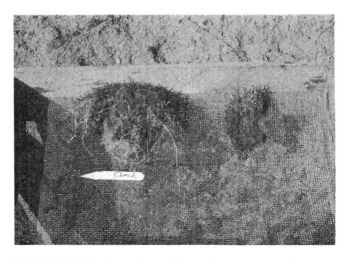

PLATE 22–51 Severely rotted bermudagrass roots and rhizomes (right) from spring dead spot (*Gaeumannomyces graminis* var. *graminis*) compared to non-infected grass (left).

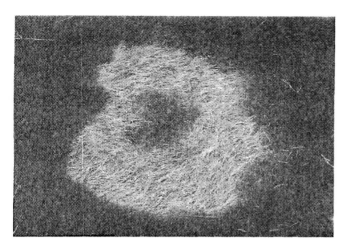

PLATE 22-52 "Frog eye" appearance of spring dead spot disease (*Gaeumannomyces graminis* var. *graminis*) patch that is several years old.

PLATE 22-53 Stripe smut disease (*Ustilago striiformis*) of Kentucky bluegrass (courtesy of Peter Dernoeden).

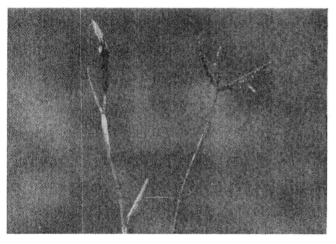

PLATE 22-54 Smut disease (*Ustilago cynodontis*) infecting a bermudagrass seedhead (left) compared to an unaffected seedhead (right).

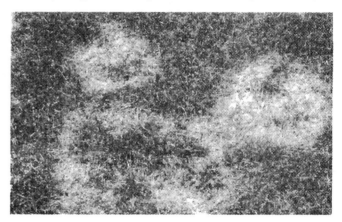

PLATE 22-55 Summer patch disease (formerly called Fusarium leaf spot) caused by *Magnaporthe poae* on Kentucky bluegrass (courtesy of Peter Dernoeden).

PLATE 22-56 Take-all patch disease (or Ophiobolus patch) disease (*Gaeumannomyces graminis* var. *avenae*) of bentgrass (courtesy of Peter Dernoeden).

PLATE 22-57 Weed infestation in a bentgrass take-all patch area (*Gaeumannomyces graminis* var. *avenae*).

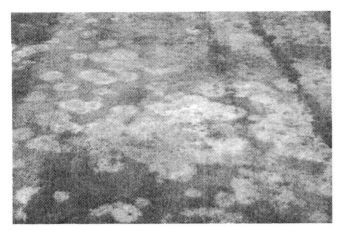

PLATE 22–58 Typhula blight (also called gray snow mold) and Fusarium patch (also called pink snow mold) occurring together on bentgrass (courtesy of Peter Dernoeden).

PLATE 22–59 Dark-colored "scum" or "mat" forming algae on summer decline areas of bentgrass.

PLATE 22–60 "Yard moss" (*Amblystegium trichopodium* and *Brachythecium* spp.) in a bentgrass golf green.

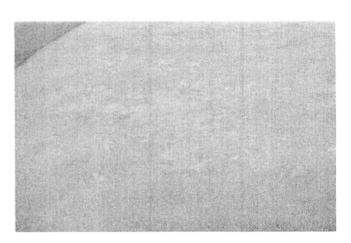

PLATE 22–61 Silver thread moss (*Byrum argetum*) has a silvery appearance and is frequently found on greens.

PLATE 22–62 Severe localized dry spot on a golf green presumably from organic substances produced by soil fungi that coat sand particles, which then prevents water penetration.

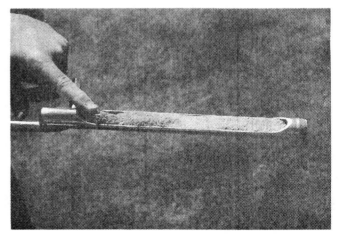

PLATE 22–63 Dry, hydrophobic (water hating) sand is typically found beneath localized dry spots on greens.

PLATE 22–64 Curvularia blight spots (*Curvularia geniculata*), shown on a bentgrass green, occurs most often on newly established greens in midsummer following abundant rainfall.

PLATE 22–65 Close-up of a Curvularia blight spot (*Curvularia geniculata*). Notice the yellowish-colored turf that is rarely killed by the disease but becomes unsightly.

PLATE 22–66 Dead spot (*Ophiosphaerella agrostis*) on bentgrass. Initially, disease symptoms resemble dollar spot or ball marks (courtesy of John E. Kaminski).

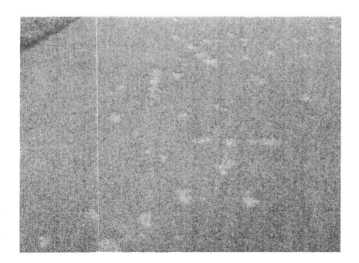

PLATE 22–67 Dead spot (*Ophiosphaerella agrostis*) on bentgrass (courtesy of John E. Kaminski).

PLATE 22–68 Black, flask-shaped fruiting bodies (pseudothecia) embedded in necrotic leaf, sheath, and stolons of bentgrass infected by dead spot (*Ophiosphaerella agrostis*) (courtesy of John E. Kaminski).

SECTION
VI

BEST TURFGRASS MANAGEMENT PRACTICES

CHAPTER
16

Cultural Practices for Golf Courses

INTRODUCTION

Golf courses require daily cultural practices to maintain a quality playing surface and an aesthetically pleasing turf. Frequent maintenance practices such as mowing, watering, fertilizing, and aerifying are necessary for this, and a well-defined and conceived short- and long-term maintenance plan often elevates a course from nearby ones. Courses often begin to decline when necessary practices such as aerifying or topdressing are curtailed or stopped. This chapter outlines contemporary cultural practices and considerations for timings and frequencies courses can use when developing their master maintenance program.

MOWING

Introduction

Mowing is the most basic, yet most important, cultural practice superintendents use to provide a desirable turf. Other cultural practices and many aspects of turf quality are affected by mowing including density, texture, color, root development, and wear tolerance. Failure to mow properly usually weakens the turf with poor density and quality.

Turfgrasses can be mowed relatively close to the ground due to their terminal growing point (crown) being located at or just below the soil surface (Figure 16–1). Regrowth from cell division and elongation takes place from growing points located below the height of the mower blade. In contrast, upright growing dicot plants have their meristematic tissue (growth points) at the top or tip of their stems. Consequently, mowing removes this growing point and many upright dicot weeds are eliminated since they do not have enough recuperative potential to recover.

Turfgrass's growth habit also is affected by mowing. **Tillering** is the development of primary lateral shoots from vegetative axillary buds on the crown. Mowing increases shoot density by promoting the growth of new tillers. As a result, mowing decreases root and rhizome growth because food reserves, following mowing, are utilized for new shoot tissue development at the expense of root and rhizome growth. Improper mowing frequency and radical height reduction magnify this problem. If the correct mowing frequency is followed, then the turf does not go through a stress period from the immediate loss of top growth and can recover quicker. Infrequent mowing results in alternating cycles of elevated crowns followed by scalping, resulting in a further depletion of food reserves.

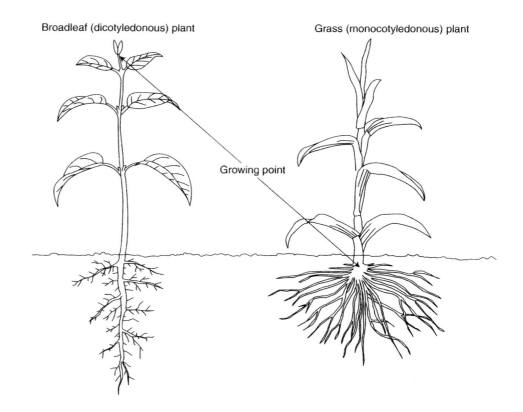

FIGURE 16–1 The prostrate growing point of turfgrasses (right) allows close mowing without permanent damage while many broadleaf plants (left) have their growing points elevated and are damaged from removal by regular mowing (redrawn from Emmons, 1995).

Broadleaf (dicotyledonous) plant

Grass (monocotyledonous) plant

Growing point

Mowing Height

Mowing heights for golf course turf are mainly governed by the grass variety and the intended use. For example, golf greens are mowed at or below 0.25 inch (6.4 mm) to provide the smooth, fast, and consistent playing surface golfers desire. The turf species being mowed also influence height. For example, bentgrass generally withstands a shorter height than bermudagrass. Mowing height also is influenced by cultivar (e.g., TifEagle bermudagrass tolerates shorter mowing than Tifgreen bermudagrass), while the newer ultradwarf (e.g., L-93, A's and G's, etc.) creeping bentgrasses tolerate closer mowing than Penncross bentgrass. Other factors influencing mowing height include mowing frequency, shade versus full sun-grown turf, mowing equipment, time of year, root growth, and moisture or temperature stress. Recommended mowing heights for each grass species and use are listed in Table 16–1.

Mowing height (height of cut, abbreviated HOC) refers to height of top growth immediately after the grass is cut. Determining HOC can be misleading to inexperienced mower operators. Often height is adjusted and checked on a level surface such as a worker bench or roadway and is referred to as **bench setting.** However, mower wheels actually ride on top of grass shoots, causing the cutting units to be raised higher than the bench setting. Conversely, when a mower is operated on soft ground or when a thick, spongy thatch layer is present, the mower cuts lower than the bench setting, often resulting in undesirable scalping.

Variables Influencing Mowing Height

Many factors influence the mowing height of grasses. Shoot tissue is the site of photosynthesis and any removal of this strongly influences the physiological and developmental condition of the turfgrass plant. If grass is mowed too low or too infrequently, excessive shoot tissue is removed and crown damage can occur. This reduces the green plant tissue left, reducing the plant's ability to carry on photosynthesis, and results in scalped, off-colored turf (Figure 16–2).

Root-to-Shoot Ratio

Plants mowed too low also require a substantial amount of time so roots can provide the food needed for shoot tissue production for future photosynthesis. Turfgrasses have a ratio of shoot-to-root tissue that is optimum to support growing grass. If turf is mowed too low at one time, an imbalanced ratio occurs with more roots available than the plant physiologically requires. This

TABLE 16–1   *Recommended mowing heights for turfgrass species and their use.*

Species	Mowing height (in.)*	Mowings per week
Greens		
"Ultradwarf" bermudagrass	1/8** to 3/16	5 to 7
Tifdwarf bermudagrass	5/32 to 3/16	5 to 7
Tifgreen (328) bermudagrass	3/16 to 1/4	5 to 7
Creeping or Colonial bentgrass/Poa	1/10 to 3/16	5 to 7
Tees		
Creeping or Colonial bentgrass	1/4 to 1/2	3 to 5
Hybrid bermudagrass	1/2 to 3/4	2 to 3
Kentucky bluegrass	3/4 to 1	3 to 5
Kikuyugrass, Zoysiagrass	7/16 to 5/8	2 to 5
Perennial ryegrass, Fine fescue	3/8 to 1	3 to 5
Seashore paspalum	5/16 to 1/2	3 to 5
Zoysiagrass	7/16 to 5/8	2 to 5
Fairways		
Common bermudagrass	3/4 to 7/8	2 to 4
Hybrid bermudagrass	7/16 to 5/8	3 to 5
Kentucky bluegrass	1 to 1 1/2	1 to 2
Kikuyugrass	1/2 to 3/4	3 to 5
Perennial ryegrass, Fine fescue	1/2 to 7/8	2 to 4
Seashore paspalum	7/16 to 5/8	2 to 5
Tall fescue	1 1/4 to 2 1/2	1 to 2
Zoysiagrass	1/2 to 3/4	2 to 3

Roughs	Intermediate	Primary	Intermediate	Primary
Common bermudagrass	3/4 to 1 1/4	1 1/2 to 3	2 to 3	1 to 2
Carpetgrass, Centipedegrass	1.0 to 2	2 to 3.0	2 to 3	1 to 2
Hybrid bermudagrass	3/4 to 1 1/4	1 1/2 to 2.0	3 to 4	1 to 3
Kentucky bluegrass	1 1/4 to 2	2.0 to 4	2 to 3	1 to 2
Kikuyugrass	1 to 1 1/2	1 1/2 to 2	2 to 3	1 to 3
Ryegrass	1 to 1 3/4	1 1/2 to 3	2 to 4	1 to 2
Seashore paspalum	3/4 to 1 1/4	1 1/2 to 2	2 to 3	1 to 2
Tall fescue	1 1/4 to 2	2 1/2 to 4	2 to 3	1 to 2
St. Augustinegrass, Bahiagrass***	—	2 to 3	—	1
Wheatgrass	—	2 1/2 to 4	—	1
Zoysiagrass	3/4 to 1 1/2	1 1/2 to 2	2 to 3	1 to 2

*Multiply inches by 25.4 to obtain millimeters (mm) or by 2.54 to obtain centimeters (cm).
**Tifgreen and Tifdwarf bermudagrass mowing heights below 3/16 inch (0.48 cm) are recommended only for short-term durations such as during tournament play. Newer cultivars are more tolerant to long-term lower mowing heights.
***Long-term mowing heights below three inches (7.6 cm) may weaken certain cultivars of St. Augustinegrass and bahiagrass.

FIGURE 16–2 Scalping results in excessive clipping debris, turf discoloration, and reduced rooting.

FIGURE 16–3 A direct relationship exists between mowing height and turf rooting. Higher-mowed grass generally requires less frequent irrigation and nutrient applications (redrawn from Turgeon, 1996).

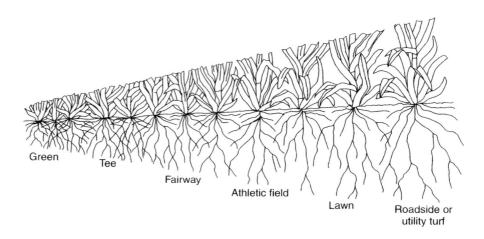

Green   Tee   Fairway   Athletic field   Lawn   Roadside or utility turf

excessive root mass is then sloughed off. Until the plant has time to regenerate new shoot tissue, the plant will become weak and more susceptible to environmental and biotic stresses. Root growth is least affected when no more than 30 to 40 percent of the leaf area is removed at any one time.

Root Growth

There is also a direct relationship between mowing height and rooting depth. As the mowing height is reduced, a corresponding reduction in rooting depth occurs (Figure 16–3). This again ties into the physiological aspect that less rooting is needed to support less top growth when the mowing height is lowered. Less rooting following a lower mowing height is the reason why golf greens need to be watered frequently, many times on a daily basis, and why fertilizer is frequently applied since the shallower roots have a decreased depth of soil from which to obtain moisture and nutrients.

Shade

Other influences on mowing height and frequency include shade, type of mower being used, season of year, and environmental stresses imposed upon the grass. Under shady conditions, grass leaves grow more upright in order to capture as much of the filtered sunlight for photosynthesis as possible. Mowing height, therefore, for grasses grown under these conditions needs to be raised at least 30 percent, and preferably 50 percent. If mowed continuously short, grasses grown under shaded conditions will gradually thin due to their inability to capture sufficient sunlight for photosynthesis.

Mower Type

Mowing height is also influenced by the mower type being used. Rotary and flail mowers cut best at heights above 1.5 inch (3.8 cm). Conversely, reel mowers cut best at heights below 1.5 inch (3.8 cm). Reel mowers predominate those used on low-cut golf course play areas such as greens, tees, and fairways while rotary and flail mowers are mainly used in roughs and out-of-play areas.

Season

Mowing height may also be influenced by the season of year or by environmental stresses imposed upon the turf. In spring through mid-summer, days become longer; therefore, warm-season turfgrasses tend to have a more prostrate (decumbent or spreading) growth habit. During this time they can be mowed closer than during other portions of the year without serious consequences, as surface leaves capture sufficient sunlight to support the plant's photosynthetic needs. Close mowing in early spring also helps control thatch, increase turf density, remove excess residues or dead leaf tissue, and promote earlier green-up. Green-up is hastened because close mowing removes top growth and dead tissue that create shade, thereby cooling the soil surface. Consequently, greater amounts of solar radiation reach the soil surface resulting in it warming up more quickly than if the top growth is allowed to remain tall. Starting in late summer, however, days become shorter and warm-season grasses start growing more upright to allow lower leaves to intercept more sunlight for photosynthesis.

In summer, when days are longer, cool-season grasses tend to have a more upright growth habit and are healthier if the mowing height is raised to compensate for it. Higher mowing height at this time also increases turf rooting; therefore, it reduces watering needs and stresses imposed by increased nematode activity. In fall, mowing height should be raised for warm-season grasses to reduce the chance of low-temperature damage during winter and to provide a cushion for grass crowns in winter when warm-season grasses are dormant. Cool-season grasses, meanwhile, can be mowed closer in fall when temperatures are cool. Their mowing heights, however, should be raised just prior to winter to improve winter color and hasten turf green-up the following spring.

Mowing Frequency

Besides using properly maintained equipment, the most important aspect of mowing management is the frequency of cut—the more often, the better. Also, the shorter a grass is maintained, the more frequently it must be mowed. Mowing frequency often is a compromise between what is best for the turf and what is desired or practical for man. For example, daily mowing would be best for most turf, whether it is a golf green, tee, fairway, or even a sports field. However, this is impractical except for smaller, highly maintained areas such as greens.

The growth rate of the grass should determine the frequency of cut. Growth rate is influenced primarily by the amount and source of nitrogen fertilizer applied and by season or temperature. With warm-season grasses, higher levels of either result in faster top growth, thereby requiring an increased mowing frequency. By raising the mowing height, the frequency of cut is reduced, which helps compensate for faster growing turf. When considering cool-season grasses during summer in warm climates, higher temperatures do not result in faster growth rates. Depending on the species, peak growth occurs around 70°F (21°C) for cool-season grasses. Extreme temperatures above this will slow growth, thereby reducing the need for mowing.

Mowing height and frequency will have a direct impact on the density and texture of a turf. The shorter and more frequently grass is mowed, the more dense (more tillers per unit area) and finer textured it will be, illustrated by the principle known as the **self-thinning law.** The self-thinning law states any ecosystem can only support a fixed biomass. Several factors, such as light quality and quantity, water, and nutrients, combine to produce biomass in turf systems. Under any given environmental conditions, an ecosystem may produce either fewer yet larger tillers, or a large number of smaller tillers. In other words, as the size of the tillers decrease by lower mowing heights, the number of tillers supported will increase, resulting in higher turf density. The opposite is true with higher mowing heights, where tillers will be larger and fewer per unit area, thereby producing a less-dense turf. In addition to density, the thinning law also applies to texture. The shorter and more frequently grass is mowed, the finer the texture will be.

One-Third Rule

The traditional rule is to mow often enough so as not to remove more than one-third of top growth at any one time (Figure 16–4) since this decreases the recuperative ability of plants due to extensive loss of the leaf area needed for photosynthesis. This reduction in photosynthesis (food production) can result in weakening or death of a large portion of the root system since carbohydrates in roots are then used to restore new shoot tissue. Consequently, root growth may stop for a period following severe defoliation since the regeneration of new leaves (shoots) takes priority over sustaining roots for food reserves. However, when only one-third or less of shoot growth is removed during one mowing, enough carbohydrates are available to simultaneously sustain shoot-and-root growth without significantly reducing either. Table 16–2 lists typical mowing heights and the resulting mowing frequency needed during active growing periods to maintain turf within the one-third rule-of-thumb. A golf course rough maintained at three inches (7.6 cm) needs to be mowed infrequently (once every 10 to 14 days) compared to a golf green mowed at 0.25-inch (6.4 mm), which requires daily mowing to prevent more than one-third of the height (0.08 inches, 2.0 mm) from being removed at any one period. Again, frequency is dependent on the grass growth rate.

Scalping

Scalping occurs when the turf has grown above the one-third maintenance height and is then mowed. Excessive growth most often is from excessive nitrogen use, environmental conditions that favor rapid growth, and/or weather conditions that prevent normal mowing (Fig. 16–2). If turf becomes excessively tall, it should not immediately be mowed down to the intended height. The resulting severe scalping may stop root growth for extensive periods. Also, since scalping removes the majority of plant leaf tissue, sunlight more readily reaches the soil surface and weeds typically become more problematic.

FIGURE 16–4 Mowing should ideally be performed when the turf height is one-third higher than the desired height.

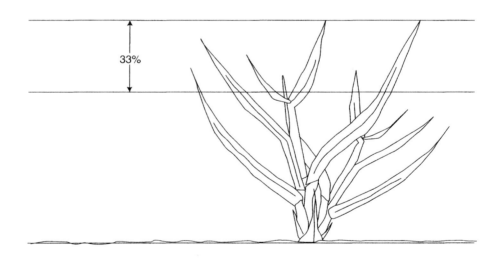

TABLE 16–2 *Typical mowing frequencies during periods of active growth needed for a given height to remove one-third of the leaf surface.*

Desired height (inches)*	Height reached above the desired cutting height before mowing	Approximate frequency (days)
≤1/4	3/8	daily
1/2	3/4	2 to 3
1	1 1/2	4 to 5
2	3	7 to 10
3	4 1/2	10 to 14

*Multiply inches by 2.54 to obtain centimeters.

Mowing Equipment

Mowing equipment has continued to increase in sophistication since mowing began with a scythe. The first reel mower was developed in 1830 by Edwin Budding, a textile engineer who adapted the rotary shears used to cut carpet nap. Early mowers relied on hand, steam, or animal power to operate. In the early 1900s, gasoline-powered units became available, followed by diesel-powered units. Today there is a vast array of mower types, levels of sophistication, and costs available. When choosing a particular model, several considerations should initially be examined.

1. **The terrain to be cut.** A smooth and level terrain is best for reel mowers. A rough, hilly, swampy, or wooded terrain may be more suited for a rotary or flail mower.
2. **The size of the area.** With the ever-increasing costs of labor, it is more practical to buy the largest mower available to perform the job in the shortest amount of time. There are, of course, limits to this. For example, a weight limit or size limit restricts the type of mower usable in high-maintenance areas such as golf greens or those areas requiring trimming types of mowers.
3. **Simplicity of design, durability, and maneuverability.** Usually the simpler the mower design, the easier it is to operate, adjust, and maintain. However, mowers need to be versatile enough to perform the job, such as hydraulically operating individual cutting units near stationary or unaccessible objects. Likewise, mowers should be well-braced and ruggedly built. Maintenance should be easily and routinely performed in order to minimize the power and time required to operate the equipment. Machines with easily accessible lubrication points, belt adjustments, bearings, chains, and shafts will likely be better maintained by employees compared to designs that are not or that require extensive effort to reach.
4. **Turf type and/or use.** Several types of mowers are available and used by golf course superintendents. These include **reel, rotary,** and **flail mowers.** Fine-textured turf species such as bentgrass, bermudagrass, or zoysiagrass should be mowed with a reel mower. This mower provides the finest, closest cut and is mandatory for high-maintenance areas such as golf greens, tees, and fairways. Turf species with wider leaf textures such as St. Augustinegrass or centipedegrass, or upright growing species such as bahiagrass, Kentucky bluegrass, or tall fescue, are usually mowed with a rotary mower. Most home lawns, and low-maintenance areas such as roadsides or golf course roughs, are maintained with a rotary mower. Flail mowers are also often used in low-maintenance areas that do not demand the highest quality cut.
5. **Engine types.** Diesel engines provide better fuel efficiency than gasoline engines, run cooler during hot weather, require no regular tune-ups, and generally have greater life expectancy. Diesel fuel, however, may be more expensive, and diesel engines generally weigh more, are more expensive to purchase, and require special maintenance personnel or equipment for repair.

Recently, due to noise levels associated with fuel-driven engines, battery-powered mowers have become available. Most units have sufficient power to mow at least 20 typically sized golf greens on one charge. Maintenance requirements with these also are minimal.

Equipment care is almost as important as initially choosing the right machine. Routine maintenance such as lubrication, oil changes, blade sharpening, tune-ups, belt adjustments, changing bearings, and proper cleaning are important in extending the useful life of equipment as well as lowering operating costs. Adequate, accurate records need to be maintained and observed to help pinpoint the costs of operation and to justify purchases of new equipment. In addition, proper storage facilities should be available to minimize the exposure of equipment to weather, to prevent accidents, and to maintain security. When a job is finished, the unit should be properly cleaned, rinsed, maintained, and stored in a clean, dry, and secure area.

Reel Mowers

Reel mowers consist of blades attached to a cylinder known as a reel. As this cylinder rotates, grass leaves are pushed against a sharp, stationary bed knife and clipped. A properly adjusted mower cuts grass as cleanly as a sharp pair of scissors and exhibits better mowing quality than

FIGURE 16–5 Reel
mowers, when properly
adjusted and used, provide
the finest, closest cut of
available mowers.

other types of mowers (Figure 16–5). Reel mowers also require less power, consume less fuel and, therefore, are more efficient to operate than rotary or flail mowers. Reel mowers use up to 50 percent less fuel per acre of cut than rotary mowers when used at the same mowing speed.

The quality cut for reel mowers is determined by mowing height, number of blades on the reel, rotational speed of the reel, and forward speed of the mower. Increasing the number of blades and sections of a mower typically improves uniformity and quality of cut, especially if the mower reels can flex or float over uneven terrain. At mowing heights of 0.5 to 1.5 inch (1.3 to 3.8 cm), a reel mower typically has five to seven blades. In order to use the same mower at a lower height of cut, the reel would have to be powered to revolve at a higher rate of speed than at a higher cutting height. A wavy or rippled appearance of the turf would develop. Nine or more blades per reel or a hydraulically powered reel are required at mowing heights below 0.5 inch (1.3 cm) to provide a smooth cut. Golf green mowers typically have 11 to 13 blades on a relatively small diameter reel in order to provide the desired smooth surface needed for putting.

The wavy or rippled appearance associated with an improper mower setting or height is from exceeding the designed "clip" of the blade. The **clip** is defined as the horizontal forward distance covered between the time each reel blade engages the bed knife, which depends on the number of blades and rotational speed of the reel, as well as the forward speed of the mower. As mentioned, the greater the number of blades on a reel, the shorter the distance the mower travels before the reel again engages the bed knife and the smoother the resulting cut. A faster rotating reel will produce a shorter clip length than a slower reel with the same number of blades. Usually the most uniform cut occurs when the clip equals the mowing height. Ground-driven reel mowers have a constant clip and can only provide a smooth cut at or above a certain height or will result in ripples when mowed below that height. This rippling also occurs when the forward speed of the mower is excessive. Conversely, if the clip is appreciably shorter than the mowing height, air movement generated by the reel prevents proper contact of grass leaves to the reel blades and results in a ragged, nonuniform cut regardless of ground speed. Hydraulic-driven reels provide a variable clip and usually extend the mowing height range that a reel mower can provide.

Operating a reel mower satisfactorily requires the following:

- The bed knife being parallel with the reel.
- The reel just barely missing making contact with the bed knife as it turns.
- The bed knife and cutting edges of the reel being sharp and straight.

A properly adjusted and sharpened reel should cleanly and easily cut a piece of paper. Adjusting the distance between reel blades and the bed knife, as well as sharpening blades by the standard process of backlapping, are used to provide this desired cut. Backlapping involves applying an emery powder/liquid soap slurry to the reel as it is rotating backward to help maintain a sharp cut between grindings. All reel blades should be aligned equally with the bed knife along its entire length. A reel properly adjusted to the bed knife will cleanly cut a piece of newsprint paper along the entire length of the reel without binding.

During the mowing operation, tight turns should be avoided or, at least, performed slowly. When turning, the mower strikes turf and has a tendency to dip and dig into it. Fast, tight turns often cause scalping or severe grass defoliation from this dipping.

Except during adjustment or sharpening, reel mowers should only be operated when in contact with grass. The dew on, and moisture within, grass acts as a lubricant for the metal-to-metal contact between reel blades and the bed knife. If the reel is operated during transport or over nonvegetative surfaces such as roadways or sidewalks, the heat expansion of metal may result in severe wear or warping of reels and bed knives.

Reel mowers do have some disadvantages. Most notably, they are unable to mow grass maintained above approximately 1.5 inch (3.8 cm) and cut coarse-textured turf. Similarly, tall seedheads, weeds, and tough seed stalks are not cut efficiently with reel mowers. Reel mowers, especially hydraulically driven ones, are more expensive than other mowers and usually require a higher level of skill to operate and maintain. Sophistication and maintenance increase, as do the number of blades, mowing units, and options such as reversible blades for ease of backlapping or removal of grass clumps. Hydraulic leaks that normally kill the grass also are a concern (Figure 16–6).

Rotary Mowers

Two impact-type cutting mowers are rotary and flail. Rotary mowers have blades horizontally mounted to a vertical shaft that cuts grass by impact at a high rate of speed. The key to success with rotary mowers is to maintain a sharp, balanced blade. Rotary mowers cut grass similar to a machete; as long as the blade is sharp and balanced, the quality of cut is acceptable. A dull mower blade shreds leaf blades instead of cutting them and leaf tips become jagged and frayed (Figure 16–8). When leaf tissue is mutilated from the use of an unsharpened rotary blade, wounds heal slowly and greater water losses occur through evaporation since the leaf area exposed to the environment is increased. Mutilated tissue that heals slower also provides invasion points for diseases for longer periods of time. If rotary blades are nicked from hitting hard objects, they should be ground or filed to restore the original sharp cutting edges.

Rotary mowers have the advantage of being relatively inexpensive and more versatile than reel mowers. They can be used to cut very tall grass, coarse-textured grass, tough seedhead stalks, and weeds where reel mowers cannot. Rotary mowers are also more maneuverable, making it easier to trim around trees and buildings than with reel mowers. Rotary mowers generally have lower initial costs and simpler maintenance requirements. For example, replacement blades for rotary mowers are generally much cheaper compared to a reel mower blade.

FIGURE 16–6 Hydraulic leak from maintenance equipment is a persistent problem that usually is lethal to the turf.

Backlapping is a means to hone and sharpen reel mowers. This involves rotating the reels backwards or in reverse against the bed knife while a fluid-dispersed grinding compound is applied. The steps involved in this process include:

Clean the reel and bed knife. Rinse or blow off the reel and bed knife to remove any debris.

Inspect the reel and bed knife. Release the bed knife from the reel and feel along the knife to make sure the surface is even and not damaged. Grind (lathe) or replace as needed to ensure the surface is even and true. Spin the reel to see if it turns evenly and smoothly. Grab and move the reel in multiple directions to see if any give is present. If so, bearings may be worn or the main shaft bent or distorted. Repair or replace as needed.

Grease reel bearings and rollers. Use a high-quality, high-impact water-resistant grease lubricant. If the new grease squeezes out water, more frequent greasing may be needed.

Adjust the reel. Adjust the reel so it almost touches the bed knife. Place a piece of newspaper between the reel and bed knife and adjust the reel so a slight tug occurs as the paper is pulled out (Figure 16-7). Work the paper up and down the length of the bed knife so this tugging is uniform (parallel) across all reels along the bed knife.

Backlap the reel. Spin the reel backwards. It should not touch the bed knife. Apply 120-grit compound across the bed knife using a long-handled paintbrush so a grinding noise occurs. Continue applying the grit on the brush until it is used up. If the bed knife and reel are sharp, the job is completed. If not, adjust one end of the reel just enough to hear the grinding noise again and then repeat the same increment on the other end. Reapply grinding compound and continue this process until the blades are sharp. Zero metal-to-metal contact should result. If the bed knife does not become sharp after about 15 minutes, it probably needs to be sharpened (grounded) on a lathe machine. A higher grit compound such as 180 can also be used to try to sharpen the bed knife.

Clean the mowing unit. Wash the reel and bed knife thoroughly to remove all grinding compound. Leave the backlapping machine running during this process to enhance cleaning. Once washing is completed, the reel should turn freely with no metal-to-metal contact. Adjust the height of cut and test the mower on a nursery or practice green for quality of cut.

FIGURE 16–7 Using a newspaper to check the sharpness of a reel blade following backlapping.

Disadvantages of rotary mowers include their inability to provide a quality cut at heights lower than about 1 to 1.5 inch (2.5 to 3.8 cm). Rotary mowers are dangerous, since hands or feet can accidentally be placed under the mowing deck while the blade is operating. The high speed in which blades rotate also can be dangerous if objects such as rocks or tree limbs are encountered. Rotary mowers are not usually designed to follow the surface contour as precisely as a reel mower. Therefore, at close mowing heights, the rotary mower is more likely to scalp turf as it travels across

small mounds or ridges that often compose the turf surface. Individual floating mower decks help minimize scalping with larger machines.

Flail Mowers

Flail mowers are another impact-type cutting unit involving a number of small L- or Y-shaped blades (knives) loosely attached to a horizontal shaft. As the shaft rotates, the knives are held out by centrifugal force. Cut debris from flail mowers is recut until it is small enough to escape the close clearance between the knives and mower housing.

Advantages of flail mowers include their ability to cut tall grass into finely ground mulch and the ability of each blade to recoil without damage to the mower or creating a dangerous projectile if it strikes a hard object such as a rock. This is especially important when operating near bystanders. Flail mowers also avoid windrowing associated with rotary units and generally can handle wet grass better since their discharge area runs the entire width of the machine.

Disadvantages include the flail mower's inability to provide a close, quality turf surface as does a reel mower and the difficulty in sharpening the small, numerous knives. Most units are bulky and heavy, often necessitating a designated tractor for smoother operation and handling. Flail mowers are most often used on low-maintenance utility turf mowed infrequently without a high aesthetic requirement such as golf course roughs or out-of-play areas.

Mowing Pattern

Mowing patterns imposed by operators can influence aesthetic as well as functional characteristics of a turf surface. Aesthetic qualities are influenced due to differing light reflections in response to mowing direction. This produces alternating light- and dark-green strips in response to alternating mowing directions and are generally more pronounced when walk-behind reel mowers are used compared to triplex-riding mowers. Double-cutting at right angles produces a checkerboard appearance of light- and dark-green strips as if two different grasses or nitrogen fertility levels were being imposed (Plate 16–1).

Identical long-term mowing directions should not be used even though this may produce the alternating color differences. Mowing turf repeatedly in the same direction results in grass leaning or growing in the direction in which it is cut. This horizontal orientation of grass foliage in one direction is called **grain** (Plate 16–2). Grain results in an uneven cut, a streaked appearance, and a poor quality putting surface on golf greens. The ball tends to follow the grain and, when different grain is encountered, the ball reacts by bouncing, having its path slightly altered, or changing its rolling speed.

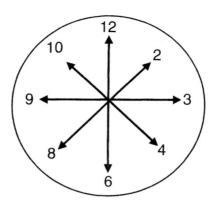

FIGURE 16–9 To prevent grain development, mowing patterns should be rotated. Rotating the direction hourly from the face of a clock helps facilitate this shift.

Grain is easily prevented by varying the pattern of successive mowings (Figure 16–9). This encourages upright growth of the shoots that minimizes the amount of leaf surface the rolling golf ball encounters, thereby increasing the putting speed and accuracy of the green. Golf green mowing patterns or directions should be changed daily and cleanup laps reversed or skipped on a routine basis. Often a rotating clock pattern is followed for mowing directions and is changed daily. Similarly, fairways should be mowed side to side, and diagonally as well as longitudinally, to minimize wear, compaction, and grain development.

Mowing continually in the same direction has the additional detriment of repeatedly scalping the same high spots as well as increasing compaction and rutting by mower wheels. Turning the mower at the same location and in the same direction also encourages severe damage from wear and soil compaction.

Grass Clippings

Clippings are often composed of 3 to 5 percent nitrogen on a dry-weight basis and also contain significant amounts of phosphorus and potassium. Clippings, therefore, serve as an important source of nutrients. If clippings are removed, additional fertilization is required to compensate for those nutrients. Removing clippings also poses a disposal problem to many superintendents since most municipal landfills no longer accept them, or if they do, an additional fee is assessed. Emptying the catcher or raking the clippings also requires additional time and labor. Under normal conditions, clippings should be allowed to fall back to the turf. Only when clippings are so heavy they smother the grass or interfere with the playing surface, such as golf greens, should they be removed.

By following the one-third rule on mowing frequency, heavy amounts of clippings are not deposited at one time. Soil organisms that naturally break down cellulose in grass clippings then have sufficient time to decompose them before accumulation problems develop. However, if excessive amounts are produced from mowing, such as following heavy nitrogen fertilization or from excessive scalping, natural decomposition may not be sufficient. A mat problem may develop under these conditions.

Clippings collected from golf greens should be disposed of properly to prevent undesirable odors near the playing area and to prevent fire hazards when clipping piles accumulate. Compost piles can be developed by alternating layers of clippings with a mixture of soil and nitrogen fertilizer. When composted, clippings can then be used as a ground mulch in flower beds or inaccessible mowing areas. If not composted, clippings should be dispersed so these piles are not allowed to form.

AERIFICATION

Introduction

Turf on heavy use areas such as golf course greens, sports fields, and other high-traffic areas often deteriorate due to compacted soil, thatch development, and excessive use. Unlike annual row crops that are periodically tilled to correct these problems, turf managers cannot provide such physical disturbances without destroying the playing surface. Soil-related problems are usually confined to the upper three inches (7.6 cm) of the turf profile. Once formed, they may not be completely corrective, especially where improper site preparation occurred prior to establishment.

However, over the years, a number of mechanical devices that provide soil cultivation with minimum turf surface disturbance have been developed. Cultivation is accomplished by core aerification, vertical mowing, spiking, slicing, and topdressing.

Aerification or **"coring"** is the removal of small soil cores or plugs of soil with grass from the turf surface, leaving a hole in the sod (Figure 16–10). Holes are normally 0.25 to 0.75 inch (6.4 to 19 mm) in diameter, with their depth and distance apart depending upon the type of machine used, forward speed, degree of soil compaction, and level of soil moisture present. Traditional aerifying machines penetrate the upper two to four inches (5 to 10 cm) of soil surface with cores spaced anywhere from two to six inches (5 to 15 cm) to the center. Recent innovations in aerification equipment provide options for creating holes to depths of greater than 10 inches (25 cm) and diameters ranging from one-eighth- to one inch (3.2 to 25 mm). Turf generally responds best when cores are close together and deep. This pattern removes more soil, exposes more surface area for water and nutrient intake, and alleviates compaction better than wider or shallower tine spacing and depth. In addition to the depth and diameter of the holes, options are now available on how to create the hole and core spacing. Advantages and disadvantages associated with coring include the following:

Benefits of Coring

1. Relieves soil compaction.
2. Allows deeper, faster penetration of water, air, topdressing sand, fertilizer, lime, and pesticides into the rootzone.
3. Allows for penetration of oxygen into the soil for plant roots.
4. Allows for atmospheric release of toxic gases (e.g., carbon dioxide, methane, carbon monoxide) from the rootzone, minimizing the occurrence of **"black layer."**
5. Improves surface drainage to help dry out saturated soils and prevent formation of puddles.
6. Improves penetration of water into dry or hydrophobic soils (e.g., relieves localized dry spots).
7. Penetrates through soil layers that develop from topdressing with dissimilar materials. These form stratified layers where water will not drain out of the finer layer until it is fully saturated. A one-eighth inch (3.2 mm) layer of fine soil is sufficient to prevent drainage in an otherwise perfect soil profile.
8. Aids in soil replacement when combined with topdressing.
9. Encourages thatch control by stimulating those environmental conditions that promote healthy soil microorganism activity that naturally decomposes the components attributing to thatch development.
10. Increases rooting by constructing a rootzone more conducive for active root growth.
11. Improves turf resiliency and soil cushioning.
12. Improves seedbed preparation for renovation, overseeding, and interseeding.

Disadvantages of Coring

1. Temporary disruption or damage to the playing surfaces.
2. Increased surface desiccation as roots and soil surfaces are exposed.
3. Temporarily provides a better habitat in which cutworms, mole crickets, and other insects can reside.

Generally, the benefits of aerification far outweigh any detrimental effects. Turf managers must decide which option is best to solve the existing problem.

Soil Compaction

The primary goal of core aerification is to relieve soil compaction. Compacted soil occurs when mineral particles have been pressed close together from excessive or concentrated traffic, especially when soil is wet. Soil compaction reduces oxygen (porosity) levels in the soil. A soil should ideally be composed of between 25 to 40 percent air on a volume basis, although compacted soils have as little as 5 percent. Root function decreases under compaction due to the lack of oxygen needed for respiration and due to buildup of toxic gases such as carbon dioxide, methane, or sulfides. Roots may also be unable to physically penetrate soil during growth when it is tightly compacted. New roots are often abundant along the sides of the aerifying holes indicating the need for increased soil oxygen and reduced compaction.

Soil aerification also helps reduce thatch by providing a better microenvironment for soil organisms that naturally decompose this matter. The aerification process also brings up a small amount of soil to the surface, thereby acting similar to a thin topdressing. Thatch accumulates quicker on compacted soils than on well-aerated soil.

Compacted soil surfaces also reduce water infiltration and percolation rates. Dry soils in compacted areas are difficult to rewet and conditions such as localized dry spots often develop, especially on high sand content areas. However, compacted, saturated soils may not drain excessive water and often turn into mud with continued use. Such soils often remain wet for extended periods of time and become covered with an undesirable layer of algae or moss. The success of highly maintained turf areas is dependent on the superintendent having control over the soil moisture content of the soil, both through adequate drainage and irrigation.

The best methods for preventing compaction are to build the greens and tees with a predominately (>80 percent) medium-to-coarse sandy soil with minimum (<5 percent) content of silt and clay, and also surface grade for proper surface drainage. Compaction is much more likely on fine-textured clayey soils than on a coarser, sandy soil.

Reducing or redirecting the concentration of traffic is the next method of relieving soil compaction. For example, the correct placement of cart paths and sidewalks is imperative. Cart paths should normally be a minimum of eight feet (2.4 m) wide to allow adequate passageway for two-way traffic as well as larger maintenance vehicles such as trucks. Barriers such as curbs or railroad cross-ties should be used adjacent to high-traffic areas such as tees and greens to prevent carts from leaving the path.

Traffic should also be minimized or prevented when soil is wet. Water in soil acts as a lubricant and traffic during these periods further aggravates soil compaction, reducing turfgrass growth and vigor. Traffic should be regulated after heavy rains, as well as after any mowing with large, heavy units. Wide turf tires should be used on all equipment to help distribute the weight of such vehicles over a larger area than allowed by regular tires.

Core aerification will usually soften hard, compacted turf surfaces. This is especially true when the spacing between holes does not exceed two inches (5 cm). Aerifier tines should penetrate a minimum of three inches (7.6 cm) in depth. This depth should be varied between aerifications to minimize any compacted layering effect from forming. Coring is most effective when soils are moist to facilitate penetration of tines, but should never be performed when soils are saturated, as rutting and additional compaction may occur.

Dry Spots

Localized dry spots due to soil water repellency are areas usually one to several feet in diameter (>0.3 m) that become very hydrophobic (Figure 16–11). This situation is most pronounced during hot, dry weather and occurs mainly in sand-based greens or in high organic matter accumu-

FIGURE 16–11   Localized
dry spots are soil water
repellency areas managed by
aggressive aerification, heavy
hand watering, and use of
wetting agents.

lations in thatch. Coating of the sand or thatch occurs from microbial deposits of various hydrophobic acids during organic matter decomposition. Aerifying with small-diameter tines (≤1/2
inch, 1.3 cm) on close spacing (≤2 inches, 5 cm) allows better water infiltration. Routine use of a
granular wetting agent applied to the dry spots in combination with aerification is also helpful.
The best results occur from preventive rather than curative treatments. The recent advent of
"quad-tines" is suited for alleviating dry spots with minimum disruption to the putting green surface. Localized dry spots may also be routinely aerified with a pitchfork or similar device and
heavily hand watered to force moisture into the soil.

Types of Cultivation Methods

Many types of core aerifiers or cultivators are available. Equipment is classified as core cultivation
or aerification, solid tine cultivation, slicing or spiking, water injection, and deep subsurface cultivation. Most aerifiers fall into one of two categories: vertical- or circular-motion (or disc-type)
units. Minimal surface disruption accompanies vertical-motion core cultivators, and they are the
preferred choice on closely mowed turf surfaces such as golf greens (Figure 16–12). Vertical units
have the drawback of being relatively slow due to the synchronization of vertical and forward operations. However, improvement in speed and operator ease have been achieved in recent years.

Circular-motion or disc-type cultivators have tines or spoons mounted on a drum or metal
discs (Figure 16–13). Hollow tines or spoons are forced into soil as the drum or discs turn in a circular motion. Hollow drum units are available that remove extracted cores from the soil surface
while other units do not remove cores, or deposit cores back directly onto the soil surface.
Circular-motion cultivators are preferred for aerifying large areas since the rotating units can cover
more ground in a given time period than vertical-motion cultivators. However, circular-motion
cultivators disrupt the turf surface more and do not penetrate as deeply as vertical-motion cultivators. Weights are often placed on top of circular-motion cultivators to increase penetration depth.

Core Removal

Aerifiers with hollow tines cut and bring a core of soil to the surface, leaving a hole or cavity in
the turf. Superintendents often ask whether or not to remove cores produced from aerifying
(Figure 16–14). For turf areas other than golf or bowling greens, it is most practical to leave the
holes open. Cores also do not have to be removed if thatch control, temporary compaction reduction, or air and chemical entry are desired and the underlying soil is acceptable. If the rootzone mixture (soil) present is acceptable, then the cores should be broken up by lightly
verticutting or dragging the area with a mat, brush, or piece of carpet. The remaining debris may
then be blown off or picked up with a follow-up mowing. Before soil cores are matted, they should

FIGURE 16–12 The keys to maintaining turf density and growth on compacted soil are aggressive aerification, traffic control, and prudent irrigation practices. Most highly trafficked turf areas such as greens, tees, or sports fields require a minimum of three to four yearly aerifications. A vertical-motion soil cultivator that minimizes surface disruption is shown.

FIGURE 16–13 A circular-motion soil cultivator is used for aerifying large areas such as fairways.

be allowed to dry sufficiently so they can easily crumble between the fingers. If cores are too dry when matted, they are hard and not easily broken up. If they are too wet, they tend to smear and be aesthetically undesirable.

Hollow versus Solid Tines

Solid tines are sometimes used for aerifying instead of hollow-cone tines. Creating holes by forcing solid tines into the turf is called **"shatter-coring."** Solid tines do not remove soil cores; rather, they divot the soil surface, and may compact soil along the sides and bottom of the holes more severely than hollow tines. Uplifting and jarring soil using solid tines is often claimed to improve soil aeration. However, unless the soil's bulk density is reduced by removing the soil cores, areas receiving solid-tine aerification will only enjoy temporary benefits.

Solid tines, however, do not disrupt the playing surface as much as hollow-tine cultivation. This is an advantage during extreme weather conditions when the grass has ceased or reduced its growth rate. Using solid tines in overseeded turf temporarily reduces compaction and softens the

FIGURE 16–14 Removing cores following aerification can be performed mechanically or by windrowing them (shown) and using a shovel.

green with minimum disruption of the putting surface. Labor savings provide another advantage of solid tines.

Disadvantages of solid-tine cultivation include only providing short-term relief of compacted soil and an increased potential to develop a hard pan. Varying the depth of cultivation, allowing the soil to dry before aerifying, and the use of small-diameter (1/4 to 3/8 inch, 6.4 to 9.5 mm) solid tines are methods to help prevent hard pan development.

Grass should only be aerified when it is actively growing and not subjected to heat, cold, and water stress. Topdressing and irrigation immediately following aerification may reduce desiccation potential, but may not be totally effective during periods of hot temperatures.

If the desire is to reduce soil compaction, soil cores should be removed. If soil cores are not removed but rather solid tines are used to produce a hole, soil bulk density is unaffected or, possibly, even increased. This hastens soil compaction. On short-mowed turf areas, recent advances in mechanization allow quick and easy windrowing of soil cores and their subsequent mechanical removal. Following coring, light topdressing may be needed to help smooth the playing surface.

Frequency and Timing of Cultivation

The frequency of core cultivation should be based on the intensity of traffic to which the turf is exposed. Other factors include soil makeup, hardness of the soil surface, drainage capability, and degree of compaction. Areas receiving intense, daily traffic such as golf greens, approaches, landing areas, aprons, and tees annually require a *minimum* of three to four core aerifications. Additional aerifications may be needed on exceptionally small greens where traffic is more concentrated, areas consisting of heavy soils high in silt and/or clay that do not drain well, areas with localized dry spots, or soils exposed to saline or effluent water use. Such areas may need aerification with smaller diameter tines (3/8 inch, 9.5 mm, or less) every four to six weeks during active growing months. Failure to maintain an aggressive aerification program in such situations will result in a gradual reduction in turf quality from poorly drained soils, thin grass stands, mat accumulation, and continued problems with algae and moss.

Less intense traffic areas should be aerified on an as-needed basis. Most warm-season grass fairways should be aerified twice yearly, with the first timed in mid-spring once the grass is actively growing and chances of a late freeze have passed. The second aerification should be in late summer. If the area is to be overseeded with ryegrass, then the second aerification should be timed approximately four to six weeks prior to seeding. Aerification is not recommended within six to eight weeks before the first expected frost to allow enough time for grass recuperation before cold weather ceases growth. The aerification of cool-season grass fairways is usually performed twice yearly, usually in fall and early spring, when temperatures are conducive for optimum growth.

TABLE 16–3 *Aerficiation tine size diameter and hole spacing effects on the turf surface area displacement.*

Tine diameter (in.)	Tine hole spacing (in.)	No. of holes per square feet	Surface area impacted per tine (sq. in.)	Surface area displacement (%)	No. of aerifications needed to impact 20 percent of surface area
1/4 (0.25)	1 × 1	144	0.049	4.9	4
	1.25 × 1.25	92		3.1	6.5
	1 × 2	72		2.5	8
	2 × 2	36		1.2	16.7
	2.5 × 2.5	23		0.8	25
3/8 (0.375)	1 × 1	144	0.110	11	1.8
	1.25 × 1.25	92		7.1	2.8
	1 × 2	72		5.5	3.6
	2 × 2	36		2.76	7
1/2 (0.5)	1 × 1	144	0.196	19.6	1
	1 × 2	72		9.8	2
	2 × 2	36		4.9	4
	2.5 × 2.5	23		3.1	6.5
5/8 (0.625)	1 × 1	144	0.307	30.7	0.7
	1 × 2	72		15.3	1.3
	2 × 2	36		7.7	2.6
	2.5 × 2.5	23		4.9	4
	5 × 5	5.8		1.2	0.8
3/4 (0.75)	2.5 × 2.5	23	0.44	7.1	2.8
	5 × 5	5.8		1.8	11
1 (1.0)	5 × 5	5.8	0.79	3.16	6.5

Another means to determine how much to aerify each year is based on the amount of turf surface impacted by aerification. A 15 to 20 percent surface area being impacting on an annual basis is a reasonable routine goal for many well-established golf courses. A percentage basis is sometimes easier for non-agronomists to understand instead of trying to comprehend tine diameters and spacing. Neglected courses may need a more aggressive aerification program. As outlined in Table 16–3, using various tine sizes and hole spacings will determine the surface area of turf impacted. For example, a fourfold increase in surface area impacted occurs when using a 0.5-inch (1.3-cm) tine instead of 0.25-inch (0.6-cm) tines. An approximately 50 percent increase in surface area impacted occurs when using 5/8-inch (1.6-cm) tines instead of a 0.5-inch (1.3-cm) tine. Another example involves changing tine spacing; for example, changing tine spacing from two × two inch (5 × 5 cm) to one × two inch (2.5 to 5 cm) (with 3/8-inch diameter tines, 1 cm) increases the surface area impacted by 100 percent.

Recent Aerification Developments

Deep Tine

Several recent developments in technology provide turf managers with a wider choice of aerification strategies. One involves deep-tine cultivators that are able to extract 0.75- to one-inch (1.9- to 2.5-cm) diameter cores to a depth of 8 to 12 inches, or 20 to 30 centimeters (Figure 16–15). Deep-tine units enable the superintendent to relieve the soil compaction layer (e.g., hardpan) that develops when traditionally used aerifiers constantly penetrate to three inches (7.6 cm). Soil profiles consisting of many undesirable layers that develop from using different materials for top-dressing are also penetrated. This enhances water penetration, soil aeration, and rooting. The soil

FIGURE 16–15 Deep-tine aerifier that extracts soil cores 8 to 12 inches (20 to 30 cm) deep.

FIGURE 16–16 Small-diameter tines, often called "needle" or "pencil" tines (top), are used to provide small, less surface-disrupting holes (bottom). This machine temporarily relieves soil compaction when the turf is under environmental stress with minimum turf damage.

profile of an undesirable green can also be improved by topdressing following deep aerification with a desirable rootzone mix.

Needle Tine

Small-diameter solid, "needle"- or "pencil"-tine aerifiers, ranging in size from 3/16 to 5/8 inch (0.48 to 1.6 cm) and up to 12 inches (30-cm) deep, can make an enormous number of tiny aeration channels in the soil profile (Figure 16–16). These disrupt hardpans or layers that have formed, and provide passageways for soil water and air exchange, thereby aiding drainage and irrigation efficiency. The small-diameter tines are much less disruptive to the playing surface, allowing play immediately following their use. Since these machines place little stress on the turf, they are especially useful on bentgrass greens during summer stress and on bermudagrass greens in late winter.

Deep Drill

Another development is the deep-drill aerifier. Drill bits of varying lengths and diameter are drilled in the turf, leaving a small casting of soil on the surface around each hole. This soil is usually then matted back into the turf while certain units can inject soil or sand into the holes. The biggest advantage of the deep-drill aerifier is the ability to provide a deep hole with the least disruption of the playing surface. Also, "drill-n-fill" units are now available that refill the drilled hole with a desired soil amendment such as sand (Figure 16–17). These units, however, are relatively slow and are generally more expensive to operate since a high degree of mechanization and numerous drill bits are needed to operate the machine. Additionally, since cores are not physically extracted, the soil brought to the surface is difficult to remove. For this reason, deep-drill aerifiers are not recommended when removal of soil is desired.

Drawbacks of deep aerification include more surface damage than with more shallow depths. The initial expense also prevents many clubs from purchasing a unit since it is more of a renovation tool than a regularly scheduled maintenance practice. However, these units are generally available for rent or contract use, or several clubs may choose to share the cost by jointly purchasing a unit. Care must be used when aerifying golf greens built to USGA specifications outlined so as not to penetrate the two- to four-inch (5- to 10-cm) coarse-sand layer located 12 to 14 inches (30 to 36 cm) deep. This would destroy the theory behind these greens maintaining a "perched" water table.

High Pressure Water Injection

A recent aerification technique consists of using high pressure water injection (Figure 16–18). Fine streams of high-velocity water (up to 5,000 psi, 34,450 kPa) are injected with minimum surface disruption occurring. Play, therefore, is not disrupted from high water pressure aerification holes as when traditional machines are used. High pressure units also help wet hydrophobic soils such as localized dry spots and can also inject wetting agents. Disadvantages include the initial high cost, the need for a water source at all aerification sites with certain units, and reduced effectiveness on heavy soils where the high pressure water stream cannot adequately pen-

FIGURE 16–17 A deep-drill aerifier penetrates 8 to 12 inches (20 to 30 cm) deep, such as this "drill-n-fill" machine that can incorporate a desired soil amendment (e.g., sand) into the drilled hole.

etrate. Thatch control is also minimal, and sand cannot be incorporated back into the profile since the holes produced are generally not large enough. The hole spacing and penetration depth is, however, adjustable through multiple pulses by leaving the units in the raised position, changing the nozzle spacing, or by varying speed. Frequency of water injection on greens depends on the level of stress to be alleviated with a typical treatment on a three- to four-week basis. Water-injection cultivation should be viewed as a supplement to traditional core aerification and not as a replacement.

Spiking and Slicing

Two other cultural practices available to help relieve surface compaction, promote better water penetration and aeration, stimulate new shoot-and-root development, sever stolons and rhizomes, and help incorporate topdressing are **spiking** and **slicing.** These generally are pull-type, non-powered units consisting of a series of blades mounted on a horizontal shaft. A slicer has thin, V-shaped knives bolted at intervals to the perimeter of metal wheels that cut into the soil (Figure 16–19). Turf is sliced with narrow slits about one-fourth inch (6.4 mm) wide and two to four inches (5 to 10 cm) deep. Slicing can be performed much faster than coring and does not interfere with the turf surface since soil cores are not removed; thus, no cleanup is necessary after the operation. Slicing is also performed on fairways and other large, high-traffic areas during midsummer stress periods when coring may be too injurious or disruptive. Slicing is an excellent tool to prevent surface crusting and algae development and can be used during periods of heavy rainfall when other aerification techniques cannot. Weekly use is recommended, especially during stressful growing conditions. Slicing, however, is less effective than coring and is most effective when used in conjunction with coring. As with coring, slicing is best accomplished on moist soils to facilitate penetration.

A spiker has solid tines mounted on a horizontal shaft. It provides an effect similar to a slicer, but the penetration is limited to approximately one inch (2.5 cm). The distance between perforations along the turf's surface is also shorter. Because of these reasons, and since spiking causes less surface disruption than coring, spiking is primarily practiced on greens and tees. Both a slicer and spiker help (1) break up soil surface crusting, (2) break up algae layers, and (3) improve water penetration and aeration. Solid tines are associated with a spiker, and holes are punched by forcing soil downward and laterally. This causes some compaction at the bottom and along the sides of the holes. Since only minor disruptions of soil surfaces occur, spiking and slicing can be performed more often (e.g., every 7 to 14 days) than with core aerification (e.g., every 4 to 8 weeks).

FIGURE 16–19 A slicer with V-shaped blades mounted on a rotating shaft (top) and the pattern from using a slicer on golf greens (bottom).

VERTICAL MOWING

A vertical mower is a powered unit with a series of knives vertically mounted on a horizontal shaft. The shaft rotates at high speeds and the blades slice into the turf and rip out thatch and other debris (Figure 16–20). Depending on the task, the shaft can be raised or lowered to cut shallowly or more deeply into the turf. Vertical blade thickness varies between 1/32 and 1/4 inch (0.8 to 6.4 mm), according to use. Golf greens require thinner blades to prevent excessive surface damage while fairways require heavier, thicker blades to obtain desired results.

Depth

Different objectives can be met with vertical mowing depending on the depth of penetration and blade spacing. Grain is reduced when knives are set shallow enough to just nick the surface of the turf. Shallow vertical mowing also is used to break up cores following aerification, thereby providing a topdressing effect. Deeper penetration of knives stimulates new growth of creeping species when stolons and rhizomes are severed and also removes accumulated thatch. Seedbed preparation prior to overseeding also is accomplished by deep vertical mowing.

When dethatching is the objective, thatch depth will determine the depth of blades. The bottom of the thatch layer should be reached by vertical mowing, and the soil surface beneath the thatch layer should preferably be sliced. However, there is a limit to the depth blades should be set or excessive removal of turf roots, rhizomes, stolons, and leaf surface may occur. For example, blades should be set at a depth to just cut stolons and no deeper if new growth stimulation is the objective. Vertical blade spacing for thatch removal should be between one and two inches (2.5 to 5 cm). This range provides maximum thatch removal with minimal turf damage.

Deep vertical mower penetration requires the use of a heavy-duty machine that can penetrate two to three inches (5 to 7.6 cm). Deep vertical mowing grooves the turf surface, so topdressing is often required to smooth the surface and cover exposed stolons (Figure 16–21). Shallow-rooted

FIGURE 16–20 A vertical mower is used to remove excess thatch in turf.

FIGURE 16–21 Distinct grooves follow heavy verticutting and topdressing.

or immature turf can be severely damaged or torn out by deep vertical mowing. Preliminary testing at the site to be verticut should be done by hand pulling to measure if favorable rooting of the grass exists. Irrigation and topdressing should follow such deep vertical mowing to prevent quick desiccation of exposed roots, rhizomes, and stolons, as well as to help smooth the turf surface and encourage turf recovery.

Frequency

The rate of thatch accumulation dictates the frequency of vertical mowing. Vertical mowing should begin once the thatch layer on golf greens exceeds 0.25 to 0.5 inch, 6.4 to 13 millimeters. This layer can be periodically checked when cups are changed or at any time by using a knife to slice a plug from the green. Areas prone to thatching accumulation may require heavy vertical mowing several times per year. For bermudagrass, the first is during mid- to late-spring when the grass is actively growing. This removes thatch and encourages turf spread by slicing stolons and by warming the soil surface quicker than if the thatch is allowed to remain. The second vertical mowing should be timed two to four weeks before the anticipated fall overseeding. This discourages late-season bermudagrass growth that can compete with the overseeded grasses, and exposes the soil surface so grass seed can reach the soil better and have optimum germination. However, fall vertical mowing will result in a degree of surface damage that may not heal until the overseeding has time to become established. Bentgrass greens are vertically mowed in fall and again in spring when temperatures are mild and the grass is actively growing. However, newer cultivars tend to form a tighter stand surface than older ones; thus, vertical mowing may be required more often with these.

Soil and thatch should be dry when deep vertical mowing is performed or turfgrass injury will be more extensive since moist conditions encourage excessive plant material to be removed. Following verticutting, debris should be disposed and the area immediately irrigated. Approximately five to seven days following heavy vertical mowing, nitrogen should be applied to encourage rapid recovery. With bermudagrass, the last heavy vertical mowing of the season should be timed at least four weeks before the first anticipated frost. With cool-season grasses, the last verticutting should occur at least one month prior to the onset of unfavorable growing conditions, be it the hot weather of summer or cold winter temperatures.

If the thatch layer has become excessive (>2 inches, 5 cm), it may become uncontrollable through vertical mowing (Plate 16–3). In such extreme conditions, the grass and thatch layer need to be removed with a sod cutter. Soil must be added to level the area and then reestablished. This problem can be best avoided by verticutting and topdressing frequently enough (e.g., every four weeks during the growing season) to keep the thatch under control. Additionally, judicious use of fertilizer nitrogen and pesticides will sometimes slow rapid and extreme thatch accumulations.

Interchangeable vertical mower units are now available for many of today's triplex greensmowers. This equipment allows for frequent vertical mowing and simultaneous debris collection. The vertical blades on greensmowers should be set to only nick the surface of the turf so the surface is not impaired. By conducting frequent, light vertical mowing, the severe vertical mowing needed for renovation may be avoided (Table 16–4). Large turf areas such as fairways are vertical mowed by using units that operate off a tractor's power take off (PTO). Such units have heavily reinforced construction and large, thick (approximately 1/4-inch, 6.4-mm) blades that are able to penetrate the soil surface.

Grooming and Conditioning

The grooming mower (also called turf conditioner) is a recent advancement in vertical mowing. Grooming keeps greens smooth and quick by reducing grain and removing excessive top growth. In front of the reel-cutting unit is an attached miniature vertical mower (often referred to as **vertical grooming**) with typical blade spacing of ≤1/4 inch (6.4 mm) that rotates through slots in the front roller (Figure 16–22). In front of the vertical groomer, a roller is mounted to increase turf penetration in dense turfgrasses and to improve the height of cut. A solid or full roller minimally penetrates, and performs best on stiffer turfgrasses that quickly rebound after the roller goes over them. A swaged roller has thickened outer edges where the center of the roller does not touch the grass. It, therefore, penetrates the grass surface very little. Grooved rollers provide maximum turf penetration due to the many grooves or slits in them.

TABLE 16–4 *Turf surface area impacted by vertical mowing blade widths.*

Vertical mower blade width (in.)	Spacing (in.)	Surface area impacted (%)	No. of vertical mowings needed to impact 25 percent of surface area
5/64	0.5	15.6	1.6
	1	7.8	3.2
9/64	0.5	28	0.9
	1	14.1	1.8

FIGURE 16-22 A
grooming unit with a grooved
roller and vertical mower
mounted ahead of a reel
mower unit can slightly raise
the leaf tissue for better
mowing characteristics.

Each time turf is mowed with this unit, the turf is lightly vertically mowed (or groomed or conditioned). This unit improves the playing surface by standing up leaf blades before mowing, thereby removing much of the surface grain. New shoot development is also stimulated by slicing stolons and removing thatch near the surface. Weekly grooming, along with timely topdressing and aerification, helps eliminate the need for traditionally performed turf renovation by severe vertical mowing.

Other groomers use a rotary brush that operates in the opposite direction of the mower blade. The brush stands the grass up prior to mowing, reducing grain and providing a smooth surface. Combs are also mounted behind the front roller to lift up (or comb) the grass to reduce grain and improve cutting.

TOPDRESSING

Topdressing adds a thin layer of soil to the turf surface, which is then incorporated into the turf by dragging or brushing it in (Figure 16–23). The benefits of a proper topdressing program include:

1. Increasing thatch decomposition
2. Truing and smoothing the playing surface
3. Reducing graininess
4. Enhancing turf recovery from injury
5. Encouraging a denser and finer-textured turf
6. Enhancing overseeding
7. Modifying existing soil

On newly vegetatively established turf, topdressing partially covers and stabilizes the newly planted material, smooths gaps from sodding, and minimizes turfgrass desiccation. Topdressing is performed on established turf to smooth the playing surface, control thatch and grain, promote recovery from injury, and possibly change the physical characteristics of the underlying soil. Unfortunately, in recent years, many superintendents have reduced the number of coring and topdressing procedures due to member complaints of disrupting play. These procedures, however, are sound, fundamental agronomic practices necessary to maintain an optimal putting surface; if eliminated, putting green quality will diminish over time. An effective topdressing program requires: (1) selecting an appropriate topdressing material, (2) using the appropriate frequency and rate, and (3) adjusting the schedule to best suit a particular site or situation.

FIGURE 16–23
Topdressing is the process of
evenly applying a thin layer
of sand on the surface of the
turf. It is incorporated from
the turf surface into the
canopy by dragging a brush,
piece of carpet, or chain-link
fence across it.

Topdressing Materials

Deciding on the material to use for topdressing is one of the superintendent's most important long-term agronomic decisions. Using undesirable materials can be disastrous and ruin the integrity of many initially well-built facilities. This usually occurs when a topdressing material is finer in particle size than that from which the green is constructed. Therefore, locating a topdressing source that meets your needs is the first step.

When the underlying soil of the playing surface is unsatisfactory, a decision will be needed on whether to rebuild the facility or try to slowly change its composition through aggressive coring and topdressing (Figure 16–24). If the soil problem is considered severe, then the superintendent's green committee will probably be disappointed with the coring and topdressing approach and should consider reconstruction. If a topdressing program is chosen to try to eventually improve the soil makeup, then the next question is what material to use. Many native soil playing surfaces are predominately made up of fine-textured soils high in clay and/or silt. The thought is to introduce a coarser soil texture, most notably sand, to improve water percolation and aeration. A general rule-of-thumb is to never topdress with a sand that drains slower or is finer in texture than the existing rootzone mix. Current trends involve frequently topdressing with 80 percent or more of pure fine-to-coarse (0.15 to 0.5 mm) sand. Preferably, a minimum of 60 percent should be in the medium sand range (1/4 to 1/2 mm), with no more than 20 percent below 0.25 millimeters. This size sand is usually coarse enough to provide the desirable effects of changing the soil constituents and yet fine enough to be easily worked into the turf surface, but not so fine as to seal the surface and impede air and water movement. Also, sand particles larger than 1.0 millimeters in diameter are not likely to work themselves down into the turfgrass canopy; thus, they are picked up by mowers, causing equipment wear. A competent soil testing laboratory should be consulted to test the sands in question before attempting to slowly change the rootzone of the green.

Some problems from topdressing with pure sand can result. Sandy soils tend to produce harder (firm) playing surfaces that do not hold approaching shots well. Sandy soils also require an increase in nutrient and water application since they drain so well, and localized dry spots may develop if the sand becomes hydrophobic. Proper coring and vertical mowing will help minimize some of these problems associated with high sand content soils.

If the golf green soil profile is satisfactory, then the topdressing material used should match the initial construction sand. When new greens are constructed, stockpiling enough rootzone mix to cover two to five years of routine topdressing is highly recommended to prevent the introduction of dissimilar soil into the green. The only difference in the stockpiled material and regular soil mix used in construction may be the absence of organic matter in this topdressing material. Enough organic matter is usually produced by normal growth for future needs.

If the underlying soil is acceptable, it is common for this material to be reincorporated in aerification cores, which is achieved by topdressing the greens with sand immediately before coring.

FIGURE 16–24 A deep core aerifying hole filled with topdressing sand. Deep aerifying penetrates through soil layering, allows deeper drainage, reduces soil compaction, and allows the underlying soil mix to be slowly modified by topdressing with desirable sand.

The cores come to rest on the sand topdressing, which promotes drying. Following partial drying, the cores are shattered by a vertical mower. This process blends the topdressing sand and soil from the cores, which is then brushed or matted into the turf and aerifying holes (Figure 16–25). The organic matter remaining on the surface is blown-off or removed by mowing. This procedure minimizes soil layering.

One of the most commonly observed problems with improper topdressing is the formation of various alternating layers of soil (stratification) that arise from using different topdressing materials over time (Figure 16–26). Differences in textural characteristics between sands and organic matter layers result in poor root growth caused by physical barriers, lack of oxygen, entrapment of toxic gases, micro-perched water tables, and dry zones. Only a one-eighth-inch (3.2 mm) layer of different soil textures may disrupt normal soil water and gas movement. Once these layers are allowed to form, aggressive vertical mowing and coring are required to correct the problem, short of reconstruction. Aerification holes should extend at least one inch (2.5 cm) below the depth of the deepest layer. The use of one of the new deep-tine or deep-drill aerifiers often is required to reach these greater depths. Shallow spiking or coring above the layering is of very little benefit.

FIGURE 16–25 Turf
surface following proper
aerification, topdressing, and
incorporation of the
topdressing material.

FIGURE 16–26
Undesirable layering from
topdressing occurs over time
with different textured
materials. Only one-eighth
inch (3.2 mm) of varying
textured layer can disrupt
normal soil moisture
movement.

Dry topdressing material penetrates core aerification holes better than damp or wet topdressing material. Topdressing should then be matted in by dragging a steel mat, brush, or piece
of carpet over the areas in several directions to evenly distribute the material. This area should
then be watered immediately to reduce soil drying and to provide further settling of newly topdressed soil. With the introduction of deep core aerifiers, changing the underlying soil characteristics may be expanded. Deep coring once per year, followed by heavy topdressing with a
desirable sand, should be practiced to improve poor draining greens. Between these corings, conventional aerification and topdressing should still be performed. Over several years, progress can
be made in improving the soil characteristics of the playing area by this technique, assuming drain
lines are installed beneath the surface.

Only weed- and nematode-free (e.g., fumigated) materials should be used for topdressing. If the material's origin is not known or if it has been piled and exposed for a period of time, fumigation with methyl bromide is highly recommended before use. Nematodes and weeds are becoming very difficult to control with an ever-shrinking number of pesticides, and re-inoculation by using contaminated topdressing soil further complicates this process. Washed sands may not need sterilization before use but should be closely inspected to determine this need. Excess topdressing material should be properly stored to keep it dry and uncontaminated. Covered soil bins or polyethylene covers provide good storage conditions until their use.

Topdressing Frequency and Amounts

Rates

The frequency and rate of topdressing depend on the objective. Following coring and heavy verticutting, moderate to heavy topdressing is used to help smooth the surface, fill coring holes, and cover exposed roots resulting from these two processes. Irregular playing surfaces or soil profile renovation will require frequent and relatively heavy topdressing. Rates ranging from one-eighth to one-fourth inch (10 to 21 cubic feet of soil per 1,000 sq.ft., 0.3 to 0.64 m^3/100 m^2) are suggested (Table 16–5), except if the turf has a limited capacity to absorb the material, as grass smothering would result and development of excessive layers is likely to occur (Figure 16–27).

A suggested yearly total amount ranges from 30 to 45 cubic feet of sand per 1,000 square feet (0.9 to 1.3 m^3/100 m^2). This, along with aerifying, grooming, and vertical mowing, helps prevent organic matter content from exceeding 3 percent (by weight). The topdressing is generally applied as light (e.g., 1/2 to 1 ft^3/1,000 sq.ft.), frequent (e.g., every 1 to 3 weeks) events to minimize sand layer development and to prevent smothering.

Specific soil volumes needed for a given desired depth can be determined by the following. It is normally easier to convert the desired depth in inches to feet. For example, to topdress a 6,000 square foot green with one-eighth inch depth topdressing, the following calculations are needed:

1. One-eighth-inch topdressing depth is converted to feet by dividing by 12 since there are 12 inches per foot.

   1/8 inch ÷ 12 inches per foot = 0.011 foot depth of topdressing desired

TABLE 16–5 *Approximate soil volumes needed to topdress golf greens to various depths.*

Relative rate	Depth		Soil volume		
	inches	mm	ft^3/1,000 sq.ft.	yd^3/5,000 sq.ft.	m^3/100 m^2
Light	1/167 (0.006)	0.15	1/2	0.09	0.015
	1/83 (0.012)	0.30	1	0.19	0.030
Medium	1/42 (0.024)	0.61	2	0.37	0.061
	1/28 (0.036)	0.91	3	0.56	0.091
	1/20 (0.048)	1.22	4	0.74	0.122
Heavy	1/10 (0.10)	2.54	8	1.5	0.244
	1/8 (0.12)	3.05	10	1.9	0.30
	1/6 (0.17)	4.23	14.2	2.3	0.38
Extremely heavy	1/4 (0.25)	6.35	21	3.9	0.64
	1/2 (0.50)	12.7	42	7.7	1.28

inch × 25.4 = millimeters (mm)
inch per 1,000 square feet × 83.3 = cubic feet per 1,000 square feet
cubic feet per 1,000 square feet × 27 = cubic yards per 1,000 square feet
cubic feet per 1,000 square feet × 0.185 = cubic yards per 5,000 square feet
cubic feet per 1,000 square feet × 0.030463 = cubic meters per 100 square meters
cubic yards per 1,000 square feet × 0.822 = cubic meters per 100 square meters

FIGURE 16–27 An undesirable distinct sand layer occurs from topdressing too heavily during one event.

2. Next, find the total volume, in cubic feet (cu. ft.), of the area to be topdressed.

green size (6,000 sq.ft.) × topdressing depth (0.011 ft.) = 66 cubic feet

3. Finally, convert the 66 cubic feet to cubic yards (cu.yd.) by dividing with 27 cubic feet per cubic yard.

66 ft^3 ÷ 27 yd^3 = 2.4 yd^3 of soil volume is needed to topdress the 6,000 square feet green to a depth of one-eighth inch

Aerified Green

The topdressing needs of an aerified green are greater than those for greens not aerified due to the filling of aeration holes. It generally is easier to first determine total volume of cored holes for one square foot and then convert this to the total surface area of the green being topdressed.

Step 1: Determine the total volume of all core holes for one square foot. A 0.5-inch (1.3-cm) diameter core is extracted to a depth of three inches (7.6 cm) on two-inch (5-cm) centers, producing:

$$\frac{144\ \text{inches}}{\text{sq.ft.}} \times \frac{\text{cores}}{2 \times 2\ \text{inches}} = \frac{36\ \text{cores}}{\text{sq.ft.}}$$

The volume of a core is [3.14 × (radius)^2] × height = [3.14 × (0.25 in.)^2] × 3 inches = 0.59 in.^{3} per core.

Step 2: Determine the volume of cores per square foot:

$$\frac{0.59\ \text{in.}^3}{\text{core}} \times \frac{36\ \text{cores}}{\text{sq.ft.}} = \frac{21.2\ \text{in.}^3}{\text{sq.ft.}}$$

Step 3: Determine the total amount of topdress material by multiplying the amount per square foot by the area of the green. If a green is 6,000 square feet in area, then:

$$\frac{21.2 \text{ in.}^3}{\text{ft}^2} \times \frac{6,000 \text{ ft}^2}{\text{green}} = \frac{127,200 \text{ in.}^3 \text{ topdressing}}{\text{green}}$$

Since 1,728 cubic inches are in each cubic foot, this can be converted by:

$$\frac{127,200 \text{ in}^3}{\text{green}} \times \frac{\text{ft}^3}{1,728 \text{ in}^3} = \frac{73.6 \text{ ft}^3 \text{ topdressing}}{\text{green}}$$

Since 27 cubic feet are in each cubic yard, this can be converted by:

$$\frac{73.6 \text{ ft}^3 \text{ topdressing}}{\text{green}} \times \frac{\text{yd}^3}{27 \text{ ft}^3} = 2.73 \text{ yd}^3 \text{ topdressing material}$$

Therefore, 2.73 cubic yards of topdressing material is needed per 6,000 square feet of green to fill 0.5-inch diameter holes three inches deep on two-inch spacing.

Frequency

If the objective of topdressing is to change the characteristics of the underlying soil, then a heavier topdressing program following numerous core removal operations is required. But, even following a rigorous coring and topdressing program, adequate modification of underlying soil may require several years to accomplish.

If thatch control is the main objective of topdressing, the amount and frequency are governed by the rate of thatch accumulation (Plate 16–4). Thatch layering between 0.25 and 0.5 inch (0.64 and 1.3 cm) on golf greens is desirable. This relatively thin thatch layer cushions (holds) the approaching golf shot better and also provides a certain amount of protection of grass crowns from traffic. However, once this thickness is exceeded, frequent topdressing along with possible coring and verticutting are necessary. A suggested amount of topdressing when thatch is not excessive (1/4 to 1/2 inch) is approximately one cubic foot per 1,000 square feet (0.03 m^3/100 m^2). If this relatively light rate does not adequately enhance the decomposition of the thatch layer, then the frequency of application and topdressing rate should be increased.

If the objective of topdressing is just to provide routine smoothing of the playing surface, then light, frequent topdressings are suggested. Matting or brushing the green following topdressing results in the material being dragged into low spots. Surface irregularities of the green are reduced and the area is somewhat leveled. Topdressing with 0.25 to 0.5 cubic yard per 5,000 square feet of green surface every two to four weeks provides a smoother, truer playing surface. Light topdressing is also performed approximately 10 to 14 days prior to major club tournaments to increase the speed of greens and provide a smoother putting surface. Frequent, light topdressing should also be applied on new bermudagrass greens to cover stolons and to smooth the surface. This should be performed every two to four weeks until complete coverage or the desired smoothness is achieved.

New Cultivar Considerations

The new dense, aggressively growing golf green creeping bentgrass and hybrid bermudagrass cultivars that tolerate very close mowing are changing some traditional topdressing practices. These new grasses are noted for very dense stands and tolerance to close mowing heights, so heavy, infrequent topdressings are very difficult to incorporate into the turf's surface, causing considerable mower damage. Coarse topdressing material (> 3/4 mm) also should be minimized on these new cultivars as these sands do not settle to the soil surface well. Superintendents, therefore, have adjusted their topdressing programs in these situations away from heavy, infrequent applications to lighter, more frequent ones. For example, weekly or every other week topdressing at 1 to 1.5 cubic feet per 1,000 square feet (0.03 to 0.045 m^3/100 m^2) is commonly used when these grasses are actively growing. During periods of non-active growth, topdressing at longer intervals (e.g., three to five weeks) is practiced to minimize abrasion to the grass by the sand. Too much material should not be applied at one time as undesirable layering may occur.

Adjusting the Program

Courses may change the topdressing sand to try to improve a less-than-desirable sand used during construction, or use a less-expensive sand to topdress after using expensive sand for construction. If the initial construction sand was coarse, then the topdressing sand should not have excessive (e.g., <20 percent) fine (< 1/4 mm) particles. Fine sand can cause layering or stratification where this created perched water table disrupts proper drainage.

Topdressing coarse sands over finer permanent soil mixes is not always successful and consists of a long-term investment. An aggressive aerification program is suggested in conjunction with this type of program to minimize layering and to help intermix the two sands together.

Thatch/Organic Matter Content Control

Most practices covered in this chapter are geared toward reducing soil compaction and minimizing thatch/mat or organic matter levels. Greens predominantly built with sand are designed to provide adequate internal drainage and to minimize soil compaction. However, organic matter can accumulate excessively over time and the benefits of sand greens gradually diminish. Cultural practices such as vertical mowing, grooming, aerifying, and topdressing are necessary to keep the organic matter buildup in check.

Aerification

A 15 to 20 percent annual surface area impaction by aerification is a suggested range for sand-built greens. This is achieved by a wide array of tine spacing and diameters. This amount of aerification is needed to maintain sufficient soil/air oxygen and water exchange, as well as reduce soil compaction. This 15 to 20 percent surface area annually impacts value increases as the amount of sand used in construction is reduced.

Organic Matter

Plants have a very dynamic life cycle. They constantly produce new leaves, stems, and roots, sloughing off the old ones. The plant's old shoots, stems, and roots begin to accumulate as organic mat, eventually leading to mat and thatch development (Figure 16–28). A suggested range of organic matter by weight in a golf green in stressful environments is less than 3 percent. In less-stressful environments, a 4 to 5 percent organic matter by weight may be allowed before problems occur like reduced soil oxygen, improper water infiltration and drainage, wet wilt, diseases, shallow rooting, thatch/mat, scalping, and black layer development. These often contribute to summer bentgrass decline, causing bentgrass/Poa greens to thin or totally die.

FIGURE 16–28   A
desirable turf rootzone profile
(left) appears with no
excessive thatch/mat or soil
layering. Undesirable
thatch/mat development
(right) increases the difficulty
of maintaining desirable turf.

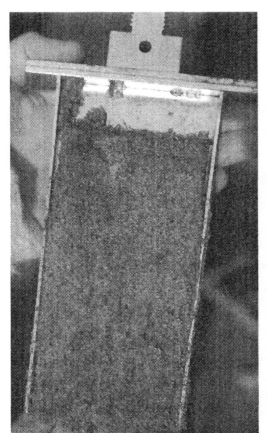

CHAPTER 17

Management Practices Affecting Putting Speed

INTRODUCTION

Today's golf course superintendent is in the middle of a hotly debated issue concerning golf green putting speed. On one hand, club members see professional golfers playing every weekend on the best-maintained golf courses in the world, where not a blade of grass is missing or out-of-place. Even drainage ditches and creek banks are completely covered with lush, dark-green turf. The greens putt like glass and the pros actually complain they are too fast. Everything seems to be perfect and the members have trouble understanding why their home course cannot be maintained in a similar condition.

On the other hand, the superintendent wisely knows what is required in terms of money, time, labor, and resources to obtain "tournament" playing conditions. These courses can spend up to five years preparing for one tournament and spare no expense in achieving the best possible playing surface. Members do not realize the greens have been pampered for months leading up to the tournament, often not allowing membership play during this time. The finest equipment and supplies have been purchased or leased and used on the greens. The greens are built with the latest technology which allows perfect soil water content control.

As with most things in life, a reasonable compromise must be struck to keep the majority of golf course members happy yet not be overly cost prohibitive. Before using putting speed as the sole criteria for judging the quality of a green, other components influencing putting speed need to be discussed (Figure 17–1). A high-quality green should be uniform in terms of density and coverage, deeply rooted, and free of disruptions from insects, diseases, or weeds. The individual leaves and tillers of the green should be oriented vertically to eliminate grain. The green does not necessarily need to be dark-green in color and lush in growth. **A diminishing-quality putting surface can be expected if putting speed is emphasized long term over other components of a good golf green.**

Golf course officials should first decide on the desired speed for both normal play and for tournament play. This decision should be based on the desires of the course members, as well as the amount of normal play received by the course, the superintendent's knowledge and experience, the course's budget and equipment, and other resources the club can make available to

FIGURE 17–1 Putting quality is influenced by many parameters including grass species, turf density, mowing height, and cultural practices such as topdressing, grooming, watering, and rolling. A "Stimpmeter," a device from which ball roll distance is easily measured, is shown. Normally, two readings are taken at 180 degrees of each other and averaged.

maintain the greens. Before unrealistic speeds are outlined by the club, reasonable expectations of the resources available to the superintendent should be discussed.

GROOMING PRACTICES

Grooming putting surfaces to maximize green speed and quality involves the following.

1. Grass selection
2. Mowing practices
3. Fertilization
4. Aerification
5. Topdressing
6. Brushing/combing/grooming
7. Plant growth regulators
8. Water management
9. Rolling

Grass Selection

The grasses used for the putting surface ultimately influence ball roll distance. Management practices such as the mowing height tolerated by these grasses also greatly influence ball roll distance. For example, bentgrass traditionally has been able to tolerate lower mowing heights than bermudagrass; thus, it has greater ball roll distance. *Poa trivialis* and bentgrass used for overseeding also tolerate lower mowing heights than other overseeding grasses such as perennial ryegrass. However, management practices can be altered on older turf varieties to provide adequate ball roll distance for most situations.

Tifgreen bermudagrass provided the first real improved bermudagrass cultivar that allowed lower mowing heights, followed by the release of Tifdwarf bermudagrass. Recently, improved selections from these grasses promise to further increase ball roll distance due to lower mowing height tolerances.

Similar trends have also occurred with bentgrass. Older colonial and creeping bentgrass varieties would not always tolerate lower mowing heights; however, recently introduced ones will. Nonetheless, selecting and managing grasses solely on mowing height and ball roll distance can negatively impact the health of the grass. Other management strategies and practices should also be integrated into developing putting green quality and distance.

Mowing

Height

Many times mowing height is the main criteria manipulated in an attempt to alter putting speed. On average, as the mowing height is reduced by one-eighth inch (3.2 mm), stimpmeter readings increase by 8 to 12 inches (20 to 30 cm).

Although mowing height is an important component influencing speed, it is not the only one. If the course attempts to maintain speed solely on mowing height, long-term decline of the putting surface can be expected.

Putting surfaces of older bermudagrass cultivars can maintain everyday acceptable putting quality with routine mowing at a height of 3/16 inch (4.8 mm). Heights maintained above this are healthier for the turf but provide slower putting speeds by today's standards. Constant mowing below 3/16 inch (4.8 mm) weakens bermudagrass and results in some of the previously discussed problems. New cultivars offer the promise that bermudagrass can be mowed lower (1/8 to 3/16 inch, 3.2 to 4.8 mm) without detrimental long-term effects.

Creeping bentgrass is routinely mowed between 1/8 and 3/16 inch (3.2 to 4.8 mm), making it popular among pro players. However, bentgrass mowing height should be raised during periods of summer stress.

Timing and Frequency

Three to five days prior to a major tournament, mowing height can be reduced from 3/16 inch to 5/32 or ⅛ inch (4 to 3.2 mm). Research shows that reducing the mowing height from 3/16 inch (4.8 mm) to 5/32 inch (4 mm) increases putting length (distance) approximately eight inches (20 cm). This reduction should occur in steps of 1/32 inch (0.8 mm) increments to prevent scalping. Among bermudagrasses, the "dwarf" types are better adapted to lower mowing heights than Tifgreen.

Research also indicates that double cutting two days in advance of a major tournament, and continuing this practice during the tournament, will increase the putting speed by approximately six inches (15 cm). If double cutting is incorporated, the clean-up mowing lap on the perimeter of the green should be made only once since this extra lap imposes additional turning stress on the grass and increases soil compaction.

A regular mowing schedule is also an important mechanism in developing and maintaining a high-quality putting green. Putting green speed will be optimized with daily mowing rather than mowing three times per week. Except on the day the green is left unmowed, research indicates a decrease in mowing frequency from seven to six days a week will have a very minor long-term effect on putting speed and may encourage a healthier turf. Changing the direction of cut each time also helps reduce undesirable surface grain and excessive wear patterns. Many courses use the clock system and post it near the mowing equipment. As an example, Monday has a 6 to 12 orientation; Tuesday, 9 to 3; Wednesday, 7 to 1; and so on.

Vertical Mowing

Light, frequent vertical mowing is one of the most beneficial grooming practices to maintain desirable mowing qualities. Weekly, light vertical mowing during the grass's optimum growing season should be performed for superior putting quality. Vertical mower blades used on triplex mowers should be set just above the soil surface. This shallow setting encourages an upright, vertical growth habit and is not intended to remove thatch from the soil surface. If the grooves from vertical mowing remain visible longer than four days, the vertical mowing heads are probably set too deep.

One relatively new improvement in mower design is placing grooved rollers in front of the reels (Chapter 16). These grooved rollers do not lay the grass over before the reel has a chance to dip the ends as do traditional solid rollers. Grooved rollers also help reduce thatch accumulation since they do not float over the thatch surface, but rather sink into it and allow better thatch removal. The use of grooved rollers varies between golf courses. For some, grooved rollers are used daily, almost on a year-round basis, while for most courses, they are used once or twice weekly. In either case, grooved rollers should be used daily starting several weeks before a major tournament.

Nitrogen Fertilization

Nitrogen is important for maintaining healthy, aesthetically pleasing greens. One of the results of nitrogen application is increased turf shoot growth and wider leaf blade width. This growth increases the leaf surface that the ball contacts, and increases the resistance it must overcome, thereby decreasing putting speed. Enough nitrogen must be available to maintain a desirable cover of grass and enable it to recover from environmental stresses or physical damage. However, excess nitrogen application results in many adverse conditions including a significant reduction in putting speed. Research indicates for each pound of actual nitrogen applied per 1,000 square feet during the season, there is an approximately four-inch (10-cm) decrease in putting green speed.

Under normal conditions, nitrogen applications should cease at least two weeks prior to the start of a major tournament. Greens, thus, are slightly "hungry" going into the tournament, and therefore grow less without significant color loss. If unacceptable coloring of the putting surface does occur, liquid iron application approximately five days prior to the tournament will boost the desirable dark-green color of the grass without stimulating excessive growth. Two ounces of iron sulfate in several gallons of water should be applied per 1,000 square feet. To minimize burn potential, care must be taken not to apply this when temperatures are hot.

Aerification and Topdressing

Aerification and topdressing are two common and important practices necessary to maintain a satisfactory putting surface. Each practice, as expected, has a dramatic effect on putting green speed. Aerification not followed by topdressing has been shown to decrease putting speed an average of five inches (13 cm) for up to 28 days. Aerification followed by topdressing initially decreases putting speed, but after eight days, an increase of 6 to 15 inches (15 to 38 cm) can be expected for the next 21 days for light and heavy topdressings, respectively. Up to eight days are required for topdressing material to be uniformly worked into the turf canopy and for excessive topdressing material to be picked up or evenly distributed by mowing.

One of the most important benefits aerification provides to the golfer is that it softens the playing surface, allowing the green to hold approaching shots. Timing is important prior to a major tournament. Smaller tines (<3/8 inch, 9.5 mm) should be used for the aerification and should be timed at least 30 days prior to the tournament. This allows time for the grass to recover and fill in aerifying holes. Topdressing should also accompany this aerification.

Topdressing provides many attributes for the golf green. One of its greatest effects is to provide a layer of soil to smooth the small irregularities from traffic, machinery, and pest damage and to firm the putting surface. Light, frequent topdressing should be applied in addition to the heavier ones made after aerification. Ideally, during the growing season, topdressing should be made about every one to three weeks at the rate of approximately one-eighth cubic yard per 1,000 square feet ($0.1 \text{ m}^3/100 \text{ m}^2$). These light applications, especially when using dry topdressing material, do not need to be dragged-in, but instead can be broomed-in or even watered-in with the irrigation system.

As mentioned earlier, it takes approximately eight days after topdressing for these benefits to be fully recognized in terms of increased putting speed. Therefore, topdressing of two to four cubic yards should be applied per 5,000 square feet ($8.3 \text{ to } 16.5 \text{ m}^3/100 \text{ m}^2$) of green between 8 and 14 days prior to the tournament to optimize putting speed. This topdressing should be incorporated by matting the soil immediately after application, which is accomplished by dragging a brush, piece of carpet, or steel drag mat over the surface in several directions.

Brushing and Combing

Brushing one to three times per week during the growing season with steel bristled putting green brushes encourages vertical growth that produces a cleaner mowing pattern and reduces grain from lateral growth. Combing is practiced in much the same manner and frequency as brushing. These practices, however, should not be performed on bentgrass during summer stress due to plant injury.

Plant Growth Regulators

Plant growth regulators (PGRs) can potentially increase ball roll distance due to their ability to decrease leaf surface area. Plant growth regulators also provide smoother putting surfaces and help moderate growth so afternoon putting characteristics more closely reflect those following mowing. Flurprimidol (Cutless), Paclobutrazol (Turf Enhancer), and trinexapac-ethyl (Primo) are commercial PGRs used to help increase ball roll distance and smooth the playing surface. Timing and rates are very important and vary widely between different products, seasons, and grasses. Much of this information is local in nature and turf managers interested in using PGRs should contact their state turf specialist. Refer to Chapter 25 on Turfgrass Plant Growth Regulators for more information on these and other products.

Currently, trinexapac-ethyl is widely used at one ounce of the 1EC formulation per acre during periods of active growth. Courses apply this rate weekly, two ounces per acre every two weeks, or three ounces per acre every three weeks. Superintendents not familiar with PGR use on greens are advised to "test" them on their nursery or practice green before treating regular ones.

Water Management

A key to any intensively managed turf such as a putting green or athletic field is having total control over soil water content. Excess water is often applied to greens in an attempt to soften the soil to better hold the approach shot, but like excess nitrogen, wet soils slow ball roll, reducing the putting speed. Turf managers should attempt to maintain a "soft" green by aggressive aerification accompanied by judicious watering and not topdressing exclusively with pure sand. Superintendents should water heavily to wet the entire rootzone rather than water lightly on a daily basis. Letting the soil dry between waterings will help maintain desirable putting speed.

Rolling

An older practice that has been rediscovered is rolling greens prior to a tournament to provide a smoother, faster playing surface. Greens in the past that were not typically maintained at today's low mowing heights and were not frequently topdressed usually benefited from such practices. Rollers typically were unpowered, large, heavy, and bulky machines that often damaged the putting surface when pulled or pushed across the surface. Severe compaction also resulted, especially in clay-based greens, that encouraged weeds such as goosegrass and *Poa annua*.

In the 1970s, as mowing heights began to drop, the need for rolling greens began to wane and the practice was largely abandoned. However, in the 1990s, with increased environmental and physiological pressures to manage greens with less inputs, superintendents are beginning to raise mowing heights to allow healthier turf growth. To compensate for slower putting speeds, interest in rolling greens has resurfaced.

Two primary types of rollers are used today. One is a set of three that replaces the mowing units on a triplex mower (Figure 17–2). These are operated in a similar fashion as mowing where the rollers are hydraulically raised and lowered and are easily transported between sites. This requires the constant replacement of the mower units with the rollers or else the designation of a triplex unit for exclusive rolling purposes.

FIGURE 17–2 A roller can replace the mowing unit on a triplex mower.

The other is from Australia where the roller is a stand alone unit that has a driver facing perpendicular to the direction the machine moves (Figure 17–3). This odd-looking machine must be loaded and unloaded from a trailer at each green and requires a small tractor for transport between greens. Other push-type rollers are available or often are constructed. These perform fine, although time and labor costs must be considered when choosing between mechanical and manual rollers.

Benefits

Limited research on bentgrass provides some guidelines on the expected increase in ball speed after rolling. Rolling once the morning before a tournament increases the speed of a green approximately 10 percent. However, to increase the speed by 20 percent, greens need to be rolled a total of four times. Rolling two or three times tends to increase the speed between 10 and 20 percent. Most courses, if choosing to use rollers, should roll greens once daily. Lightweight rolling does not negatively affect the turf stand or soil if performed three or fewer times per week. However, rolling four or more times weekly increases soil compaction and eventually (after three to four weeks) reduces turf quality. The effects of rolling tend to last about 24 hours. It is interesting to note the roller weight does not influence green speed and most (even low handicap) golfers cannot detect differences in green speed of six inches (15 cm) or less.

Limitations

Any time pressure is applied to a soil surface, a chance of compaction occurs. Therefore, to minimize the potential of compaction developing from rollers, use the lightest roller(s) available. As previously mentioned, roller weight apparently does not influence ball speed but may influence the degree of compaction. Rollers also should be used only on greens consisting primarily (≥ 80 percent) of sand and less than 10 percent silt or clay.

To further prevent compaction problems and to reduce labor costs, roller use is encouraged only during major tournament play and not as a routine daily practice. Rolling should also never be attempted when the soil is saturated, since moisture will act as a lubricant and allow compaction. Extra aerification to relieve any soil compaction may be required.

Rollers are an additional tool for superintendents to consider for improving ball speed. Long-term effects of constant rolling are not well-documented; thus, caution should be utilized before use. Renting or borrowing a unit for a period of time is recommended before purchase to ensure desired benefits occur.

SUGGESTED SEQUENCE OF EVENTS

The following sequence of agronomic events is suggested to provide acceptable putting surfaces in terms of uniformity, density, and speed (modified from Throssell, 1985). If all of these are incorporated into a total management practice package, putting characteristics should be acceptable for the majority of participants. Table 17–1 lists guidelines for ball speeds based on the stimpmeter.

Three Months Prior to the Tournament

Begin a PGR program to help regulate growth throughout the day. It requires several applications of PGRs to "condition" the grass so as not to have any phytotoxicity. These are usually spaced one to four weeks apart depending on use rate.

Six Weeks Prior to the Tournament

Fertilize with a 3-1-2 ratio fertilizer at the rate of one pound actual nitrogen per 1,000 square feet (4.9 kg N/100 m^2). This fertilization will strengthen the grass for the upcoming aerification and aid recuperation.

One Month Prior to the Tournament

Core aerify with relatively small (e.g.,< 3/8 inch, 9.5 mm) tines when the green has adequate moisture to minimize damage to the putting surface. Aerification is needed when greens are considered hard and do not hold approaching shots well, if the greens are not properly draining, or if localized dry spots are developing. If these problems are not present, then core aerification can be skipped. However, one month may be needed for the grass to recover and fill-in holes left from coring. Individual cores should be removed following aerification. The exception to this is when a desirable soil mixture is currently present. The cores in this case should be incorporated back into the profile by lightly verticutting or dragging with a brush or piece of carpet or steel drag mat.

Following aerification, the greens should be topdressed with a medium rate of desirable, clean soil. One to three cubic feet of material per 1,000 square feet (0.03 to 0.09 m^3/100 m^2) should provide a medium topdressing rate. This should be immediately incorporated by dragging. Care must be taken during this process to prevent excessive desiccation or turf damage. Irrigate heavily following aerification to help prevent exposed roots from drying.

One week following aerification, greens should receive the equivalent of one pound actual nitrogen per 1,000 square feet (4.9 kg N/100 m^2) as a quick-release nitrogen source (e.g., ammonium sulfate or ammonium nitrate). Rapid-release nitrogen will aid in recovery of aerifying holes and be timed in advance of the tournament so excessive growth will have subsided.

Two Weeks Prior to the Tournament

All nitrogen fertilization should be completed by this time. If not, the grass will be growing too aggressively by tournament time, and consequently, the putting speed will be disappointingly reduced.

TABLE 17–1 *Putting green speeds as determined by the stimpmeter (USGA).*

| Putting characteristic | Ball roll distance* | | | | | | | |
| | Normal conditions | | | | Tournament conditions | | | |
	Feet	Meters	Inches	Centimeters	Feet	Meters	Inches	Centimeters
Slow	<7.5	<2.3	<90	<229	<8.5	<2.59	<102	<259
Medium	7.5 to 9.0	2.3 to 2.7	90 to 108	229 to 274	8.5 to 10	2.6 to 3.1	102 to 120	259 to 365
Fast	>9.0	>2.7	>108	>274	>10	>3.1	>120	>305

*Based on an average of ball roll distance up and down a green's slope.

The greens should also be lightly vertical mowed in two directions at this time. Vertical mowing blades should just barely touch the plant crowns. This will remove some of the surface debris left over from aerifying and will reduce grain. Greens should be groomed daily at this time by using grooved rollers, brushing, and/or combing.

Between 10 and 14 days prior to the tournament, the greens should receive a light application of topdressing. One to two cubic yards per 5,000 square feet (0.03 to 0.06 m^3/100 m^2) should be ample to provide the final touches in smoothing the putting surface. The topdressing material should be immediately incorporated by dragging it in several directions.

Five Days Prior to the Tournament

If the greens start to lose some color due to lack of nitrogen fertilization, application of liquid iron sources should be considered. Two ounces of iron sulfate or a chelated iron source in several gallons of water should be applied per 1,000 square feet (6.4 L/ha). To prevent burn, this should not be applied during the heat of the day.

The mowing height can be reduced at this time from 3/16 inch (4.8 mm) to 5/32 or 1/8 inch (4 or 3 mm). This height, combined with the other management practices already outlined, should provide satisfactory putting conditions for the tournament.

Three Days Prior to the Tournament

Begin double cutting the greens at the intended tournament height three days prior to the tournament, so the maximum benefits from this practice are experienced. The clean-up mowing lap should be performed only once daily to prevent excessive tearing of the grass or soil compaction.

Water management during the weeks leading up to the tournament is critical. Excessive soil moisture should not be used as a method to soften the greens. Water should be applied to wet the rootzone and soil should be allowed to dry before reapplying it. Firm greens are often desired to challenge golfers for precise approach shots. However, with the added stresses of a lower mowing height and double cutting, constant inspection for wilting should occur and afternoon syringing should be considered.

Tournament Day (Optional)

If green speed is totally unacceptable, then the use of a roller(s) is available. The greens should be allowed to drain (not wet) before this is attempted and should follow routine mowing. One pass is recommended per day.

Once the tournament is completed, the mowing height should be raised. Greens should then be fertilized and adequately watered to aid in recovery from the concentrated tournament play.

CHAPTER
18

Overseeding

INTRODUCTION

Bermudagrass growth stops when temperatures drop below 60°F (15.5°C), and discoloration (browning) can be expected if temperatures drop below 50°F (10°C) for an extended period. Warm-season grasses such as bermudagrass and zoysiagrass, therefore, are often overseeded with cool-season grasses during the fall and winter to provide a green playing surface with desirable color and better traffic tolerance (Plate 18–1). In addition, golf course fairways sometimes are overseeded to clearly mark suggested landing areas for golfers. Overseeding is an important economic aspect of golf because many resort courses enjoy their heaviest play from tourists during the fall, winter, and spring months, which helps attract golfers. Overseeding also improves winter and spring play conditions.

OVERSEEDING MYTHS

Although there are reasons or benefits associated with overseeding, some myths and drawbacks exist about it as well. One myth is that overseeding improves course drainage. During winter, evapotranspiration (ET) rates are low and rainfall is usually adequate. Therefore, overseeding does not normally significantly help "dry-out" soil. Others contend overseeding significantly protects the bermudagrass from winter kill, and overseeding will not have any negative impact on spring bermudagrass transition. Overseeding grasses compete very aggressively with the bermudagrass until air temperature consistently reaches the high 80°Fs (27°Cs). This competition typically delays total green-up and fill-in of the bermudagrass and, if the overseeding quickly dies, the bermudagrass stand generally is thin.

If an area is overseeded for only one year, it will normally take at least two additional years for all of the overseeding seed to totally germinate. Therefore, courses will have reoccurring sporadic overseeding for up to three years after the last overseeding year. Escaped clumps (often referred to as "renegade" ryegrass) of overseeding from the intended seeded areas also are very unsightly, difficult to mow, difficult to eradicate, and often live into mid-summer.

Overseeding is also believed to reduce weed population due to the competition. This is rarely the case and, in fact, overseeding usually slowly increases weed pressure. This is especially true for annual bluegrass that typically becomes a serious weed problem when courses continuously overseed for a number of years. This seed is then easily tracked onto green and tee surfaces, thereby increasing its occurrence in these areas. The overseeding process of light, frequent watering and fertilizer application plus soil surface compaction also provide ideal growing conditions for annual bluegrass.

A good uniform irrigation system is also required for desirable overseeding. If not available, sporadic overseeding stands usually result. Overseeding is also a disruptive process where golf courses typically have to close to prepare the seedbed, plant the seed, and then provide continuous watering to establish the stand. Finally, overseeding can be expensive. Depending on seeding rates, fertilizer rates, mowing intervals, extra labor demands, and so on, yearly overseeding costs typically range from $500 to over $2,000 per acre. This includes seed costs; extra watering needs; specialized equipment needs such as drop spreaders, vertical mower reels, and fairway vacuums; mowing expenses for fuel, labor, and equipment wear-and-tear; extra fertilizer and herbicide costs; possible use of plant growth regulators (PGRs); and possible downtime for the course to actually seed.

Optimum overseeding performance is a sequential procedure requiring proper seedbed preparation and timing. Proper winter management and spring turf species transition also ensure optimum playing conditions during tournament play periods. Luck, mostly in terms of favorable weather, is as important as sound agronomic procedures.

TIMING

To maintain consistent turf quality, a gradual transition from the permanent grass to overseeded grass species in the fall and back to the permanent grass in the spring are necessary. Seeding too early can result in excessive bermudagrass or zoysiagrass competition and the increased likelihood of turf failure due to diseases such as *Pythium* blight. Seeding too late in fall may result in unacceptable, weak, delayed or reduced seed germination because of low temperatures.

There are several available means for determining when to overseed. A general indicator of optimum overseeding time is when late summer/early fall night temperatures consistently are around the 50°F (10°C) range. Other timing indicators include overseeding when soil temperatures at a four-inch (10-cm) depth are in the mid-70°Fs (14°Cs), or the average mid-day air temperatures remain in the low 70°Fs. Cool-season grass seed germination is favored by temperatures between 50 and 70°F. Overseeding also should be timed at least 20 to 30 days before the first expected killing frost. This timing minimizes bermudagrass competition, and optimizes seed germination and establishment of the overseeded grasses. It also will reduce seedling diseases. Figure 18–1 indicates typical overseeding timings for various regions of the United States.

Other factors, such as tournament play and golf course usage, may dictate that seeding dates be altered. For example, light frosts can occur in subtropical areas such as southern Florida and California, but deep freezes are rare. Bermudagrass normally does not completely go dormant in these areas. Soil temperatures in these subtropical areas remain in the 80°F (27°C) area through November; thus, temperature-based indicators are not always applicable. Overseeding timing then becomes a management decision based primarily on the timing of play intensity, customer demands, availability of seed, and desired level of aesthetics. In general, overseeding is conducted prior to increased winter use in these areas, which typically occurs from late October through early December.

FIGURE 18–1 Typical overseeding timing for most bermudagrass regions in the mainland United States.

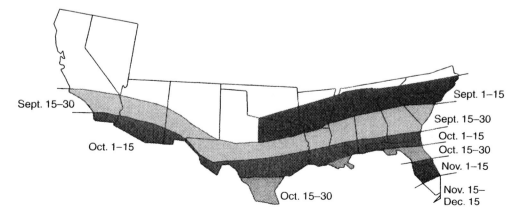

Sept. 15–30

Oct. 1–15

Oct. 15–30

Sept. 1–15

Sept. 15–30

Oct. 1–15

Oct. 15–30

Nov. 1–15

Nov. 15– Dec. 15

SEEDBED PREPARATION

Seedbed preparation actually is a year-long process and does not just occur two weeks prior to overseeding. Planning should take place several months before the actual overseeding operation to ensure a seed source and a seed type. Purchasing of seed and its timely delivery also will allow flexibility for overseeding scheduling if done in advance. A healthy bermudagrass base also is needed to withstand harsh cultural practices and the turf competition associated with overseeding. This can only be accomplished by careful management of bermudagrass throughout the year.

Greens and Tees

Proper seedbed preparation ensures seedling roots will be in contact with the soil, which reduces susceptibility to drought and temperature stress. Thatch greater than one-half inch (1.3 cm) associated with a bermudagrass or zoysiagrass base prevents this good seed-to-soil contact and therefore should be reduced before overseeding. Proper seedbed preparation to minimize thatch and allow optimal germination and growth includes the following procedures.

Three to Six Weeks Prior to Overseeding

1. Nitrogen fertilization should be reduced or completely stopped three to four weeks prior to overseeding to minimize competitive bermudagrass growth. Excessive growth at the time of overseeding will provide competition for the germinating seed and also may predispose the grass to winter injury.
2. Cultivate the soil by coring four to six weeks prior to overseeding to alleviate soil compaction and to open the turf (Figure 18–2). Allow the cores to dry and pulverize them by verticutting, power raking, or dragging. Coring is performed in advance of the actual overseeding date to allow coring holes to heal over, thereby preventing a speckled growth pattern of winter grass. The overseeded grasses typically grow faster with a darker-green color in and around core holes than between them.
3. Following coring, verticut in several directions to reduce thatch and to open the soil surface to allow better soil-to-seed contact (Figure 18–3). Verticut debris should be removed by raking, blowing, or mowing with a catcher basket attachment. The depth of verticutting depends primarily on the depth of thatch. Thicker thatch layering requires deeper verticutting. Other parameters, such as algae formation, however, may dictate how severe this verticutting is. If algae is a problem, light, frequent grooming may substitute for verticutting greens.
4. Topdress with approximately one-half cubic yard per 1,000 square feet (0.015 m³/100 m²) following the removal of the verticut debris in order to provide a smooth seedbed and to

FIGURE 18–2 Coring or aerifying is usually needed prior to overseeding to reduce soil compaction and help control thatch.

FIGURE 18–3
Verticutting turf prior to overseeding removes thatch/mat to enhance seed-to-soil contact following overseeding.

FIGURE 18–4
Topdressing following overseeding improves seed-to-soil contact and prevents seed movement following irrigation or rain.

minimize the effects of the remaining thatch (Figure 18–4). Most consistent results occur when the seedbed is topdressed before and immediately after overseeding to provide desirable soil contact. Use a desirable topdressing mix (e.g., contains <10 percent of particles smaller than 0.1 mm and none above 1 mm in diameter).

5. Apply phosphorus (P_2O_5) and potassium (K_2O) at a suggested rate of 10 pounds of 0-9-27 (or equivalent) per 1,000 square feet, or at the rate suggested by a soil fertility test. The soil should be tested approximately four weeks prior to overseeding. Phosphorus and potassium will enhance overseeding rooting without promoting excessive bermudagrass or zoysiagrass top growth.

Ten to Fourteen Days Prior to Overseeding

1. Approximately 10 to 14 days prior to overseeding, reduce the mowing height and verticut lightly in two directions (just touching the soil surface) to open the turf and allow the seed to fall into the turf canopy. This practice provides good seed-to-soil contact, prevents wind

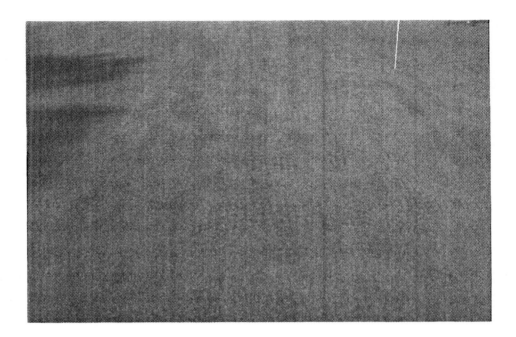

FIGURE 18–5 Aerifying too close to overseeding may result in a speckling of grass stand.

and water from carrying seed away, and provides sufficient time for verticut slits to recuperate before overseeding.

2. Next, use a power sweeper, a mower with basket attachments, or a blower to remove remaining debris, and then thoroughly irrigate. On sloped areas, if possible, discontinue mowing two or three days prior to overseeding, or raise the mowing height 1/4 or 5/16 inch (6.4 to 7.9 mm) one week prior to overseeding to provide an upright framework of grass to prevent seed from washing. Spiking or slicing in several directions just prior to seeding also enhances seed-to-soil contact. Care, however, might be taken to evenly distribute seed without concentrating it in spiked holes to prevent a speckled appearance (Figure 18–5).

Overseeding with small-seeded species such as fine fescue or *Poa trivialis* often does not require as extensive a seedbed preparation as larger-seeded grasses like ryegrass. However, some seedbed preparation is needed for all species, with the two steps listed above being the minimum requirements for all overseeding. A greater thatch layer and using larger-seeded species require more seedbed preparation.

Fairways

Fairways require an aesthetically pleasing appearance but are not prepared as intensely for overseeding as are greens and tees. However, preparation is needed to provide for uniform germination and overseeded grass establishment. Brushing with an industrial street brush throughout summer stands leaves up and provides a true cut (Figure 18–6). Continuous brushing does not leave grooves like verticutting can. Mow the base grass very close (e.g., 0.375 to 0.5 inch, 9.5 to 13 mm) just prior (two to three days) to overseeding and pick up clippings and debris. Brush again, if necessary. This also will open up the turf and will allow the seed to reach the soil surface—provided thatch is not a problem. If thatch is a problem, coring should be performed several weeks in advance of overseeding. Cores can be broken up by dragging a piece of chain-link fence or a flexible metal mat over the surface after it has dried. Soil from this coring also provides a good germination media for the overseeded grass. Excessive fairway thatch layering, however, may require verticutting in conjunction to close mowing and coring prior to overseeding. Perform verticutting in several directions to minimize lines of overseeding from verticutting grooves (Figure 18–7).

Plant Growth Retardants

To prevent excessive base grass growth, PGRs can be used. Trinexapac-ethyl (Primo 1L) at 8 to 12 ounce product per acre (0.6 to 0.9 L/ha) every three to four weeks throughout helps regulate this growth. The last application should be two to seven days prior to overseeding and the rate

FIGURE 18–6 A front-mounted tractor power brush is often used to stand up the permanent grass and to remove thatch for better seed-to-soil contact when overseeding.

FIGURE 18–7 A thin, sporatic overseeding stand results from insufficient irrigation coverage.

should be increased if competitive grass growth is anticipated. The herbicide triclopyr (Turflon Ester 4L) can also be used for pre-overseeding at one to two pints per acre (1.2 to 2.3 L/ha) to reduce bermudagrass competition.

Annual Bluegrass Weed Control

Annual bluegrass (*Poa annua* L.) is an undesirable bunch-type winter annual weed because of its clumping growth habit, its early spring die-back, and its prolific seedhead production (Plate 18–2). Control of annual bluegrass with traditional herbicides is difficult due to the potential injury of germinating overseeded grasses.

Golf greens

There are several herbicide options for preemergence control of annual bluegrass in overseeded bermudagrass golf greens. Currently, fenarimol, pronamide, dithiopyr, and rimsulfuron are used prior to overseeding for *Poa annua* control. One, fenarimol, is actually a fungicide that also has preemergence herbicidal activity on *Poa annua*. Refer to Chapter 25 for detailed information on these and other products for preemergence and postemergence Poa control.

Charcoal has been used in conjunction with pronamide when pronamide was applied less than 60 days prior to overseeding to negate its effect on the germination of overseeded grasses. Activated charcoal should be applied at two to five pounds per 1,000 square feet. At least 14 days should be allowed between herbicide and charcoal applications, while overseeding should occur no sooner than seven days following charcoal application. There is an inherent chance the charcoal application may not totally work due to the difficulty of application. Charcoal also might negate the herbicidal effect of the pronamide on annual bluegrass germination. Available activated charcoal sources include "Clean Carbon" from Aquatrols, "Gro-Safe" from American Norit Company, and "52 Pickup" from Parkway Research Corporation.

Fairways

In addition to those products listed for annual bluegrass control in overseeded golf greens, several others can be used in overseeded fairways. Ethofumesate (Progress 1.5EC) is used for preemergence and/or postemergence control of annual bluegrass in **dormant** bermudagrass tees, fairways, and roughs overseeded only with perennial ryegrass. In addition, bensulide, prodiamine, oxadiazon, benefin, and possibly others can be used for selective *Poa annua* control in overseeded grasses. Refer to Chapter 25 for detailed information.

OVERSEEDING GRASS SELECTION

The primary grasses used for overseeding are perennial ryegrass, annual ryegrass, intermediate ryegrass, roughstalk bluegrass or *Poa trivialis,* creeping bentgrass, and fine (chewings, creeping red, or hard) fescue. Improved cultivars of perennial ryegrass seeded alone, or in mixtures with bentgrass, roughstalk bluegrass or fine fescue, are the grasses and mixtures most widely used on golf greens and tees. For golf courses wishing for the greatest chance of success on overseeding greens, perennial ryegrass should be the major component of the blend or mix chosen. Fairways are seeded predominately with a perennial ryegrass cultivar. Each grass has advantages and disadvantages. Table 18–1 illustrates and describes each of these.

Perennial Ryegrass

Perennial ryegrass has traditionally been the preferred grass used for most overseeding purposes. It is noted for its fast germination (typically five to seven days), finer leaf texture, darker-green color, seedling vigor, and for having better disease and traffic resistance than annual ryegrass (Plate 18–3). Perennial ryegrass also provides a highly desirable striped appearance when mowed in alternating directions. Many improved turf-type varieties recently have been released that provide fine putting surfaces if seeded at high rates. However, many new varieties have improved heat tolerance; thus, they may be more competitive during spring transition than the traditionally used annual (Italian) ryegrass. Poor (slow) putting surfaces also occur in fall until mowing heights are reduced three to five weeks following germination. If seeded alone, a blend of at least two (preferably three or four) improved turf-type cultivars should be used to help ensure good performance over a wide range of conditions. Chapter 1 lists some of the more than 200 cultivars available. Mixtures of perennial ryegrass with creeping bentgrass, fine fescue, and *Poa trivialis* are often used on golf greens.

Annual (Italian) Ryegrass

Annual ryegrass (*Lolium multiflorum*) has lost some of its importance as an overseeding grass in recent years since it produces a coarser, more open turf than many newer turf-type perennial ryegrasses (Plates 18–3 and 18–4) and is extremely susceptible to pythium diseases. Annual ryegrass also has poor heat and cold tolerance and often experiences early spring death that may result in poor seasonal transition. Like annual bluegrass, annual ryegrass quickly dies when a few warm days occur in early spring. This quick death may result in thin spots where the bermudagrass has not had time to fully green-up and cover any weak areas. However, annual ryegrass germinates

TABLE 18–1 *Characteristics of selected grasses used for winter overseeding.*

Grass species	Green color	Texture	Density	Establishment rate	Winter performance	Spring performance
Perennial ryegrass (turf-type)	Dark	Medium–fine (2 to 4 mm)	Good	Fast (3 to 4 weeks)	Good–excellent	Good–excellent
Annual ryegrass	Light	Coarse (3 to 5 mm)	Poor	Very fast (2 to 3 weeks)	Fair–good	Poor
Intermediate ryegrass	Intermediate	Coarse–medium (3 to 4 mm)	Fair	Fast (2 to 4 weeks)	Fair	Fair
Fine fescue	Light–dark	Very fine (1 to 2 mm)	Excellent	Slow (4 to 6 weeks)	Fair	Good
Roughstalk bluegrass (*Poa trivialis*)	Light–intermediate	Fine (1 to 4 mm)	Excellent	Slow (4 to 6 weeks)	Fair	Excellent
Creeping bentgrass	Intermediate	Very fine (1 to 2 mm)	Excellent	Very slow (6 to 8 weeks)	Fair	Fair

quickly and is acceptable on fairways and other general use areas where color and appearance are not of greatest concern, or when budget constraints are important. Few improved turf-type cultivars of annual ryegrass are currently available. Turf-type annual ryegrasses include Axcella, Barverdi, Hilltop, King, Panterra, and TransEze, while forage-type cultivars include Astor, Gulf, Magnolia, and Wimmera.

Intermediate (Transitional) Ryegrass

Intermediate ryegrass (*Lolium hybridum*) is a hybrid of annual and perennial ryegrass. Like annual ryegrass, intermediate ryegrasses germinate quickly but lack heat tolerance. Intermediate ryegrass makes a sharper transition than the turf-type perennial ryegrasses. Intermediate ryegrasses also have a medium texture, a lighter-green color, and reduced shoot growth (Plate 18–5). Due to its heat intolerance, intermediate ryegrasses disappear quickly as bermudagrass begins to grow in the spring. They do not retard bermudagrass as much as more heat-tolerant turf-type perennial ryegrasses. Higher-budgeted fairways are the main use areas of intermediate ryegrass. Several varieties of intermediate ryegrasses are available, including A-97, Agree, Froghair I-II, Harbour, Midway, Oregreen, Savvy, Transist, and Transtar.

Fine Fescue

Fine fescue is a general term used for several fine-leafed *Festuca* spp. that have delicate and wiry leaves that are usually less than 0.5 millimeters wide and have a clumping, bristle-like appearance. **Red fescue** (*F. rubra* L.) and **spreading fescue** (*F. pratensis* Huds.) have slow-spreading rhizomes while **chewings fescue** (*F. rubra* ssp. *communtata* Gaud.), **sheep fescue** (*F. ovina* L.), and **hard fescue** (*F. longifolia* auct. non Thuill.) have a bunch-type growth habit. As a group, the fine fescues are noted for good shade tolerance, low-mowing height tolerance, winter hardiness, and adaptability to infertile and dry soil conditions. They do not tolerate heat or wet, poorly drained soils well, but are particularly adapted to dry, shady conditions as well as to low-maintenance situations. Fine fescues rarely are used alone for overseeding but are usually mixed with other cool-season grasses such as perennial ryegrass and bentgrass. Fine (red, chewings, or hard) fescues, particularly chewings fescue, provide a fine texture and a stiff, upright growth habit that increases fall putting speeds. Density is good to excellent, but the establishment rate is moderate. Fine fescues, as a group, provide good spring transition. They should not, however, be used if the herbicide ethofumesate (Progress) is to be applied for annual bluegrass control. Fine fescue normally is used as a mixture with perennial ryegrass to improve desirable characteristics of a putting surface. Chapter 1 lists some of the currently available fine fescue cultivars.

Spring transition	Wear tolerance	Shade tolerance	Putting quality	Competitiveness with *Poa annua*	Leaf fraying	Disease resistance
Slow	Fair–excellent	Fair–good	Fair–excellent	Very	Moderate–minimum	Fair–good
Medium	Poor–fair	Fair	Poor	Very	Heavy	Poor
Medium	Fair–good	Fair	Poor–fair	Very	Moderate	Fair
Fast	Fair	Very good	Good	Not very	Minimum	Fair
Fast	Poor	Good	Excellent	Not very	Minimum	Poor–fair
Slow	Fair	Fair	Excellent	Not very	Minimum	Fair

Bentgrass

Due to its fine texture and low growth habit, bentgrass often is used to provide a permanent or temporary overseeded putting surface (Plate 18–4). Bentgrass (especially Seaside and Mariner) also has good salt tolerance. However, bentgrass is slow to establish and is susceptible to many diseases. In addition, it is usually slow to transition in spring when compared to most other grasses used for overseeding. In warmer regions, the lack of extended cold temperatures may allow the bermudagrass to stay competitive throughout the winter. This may result in small, immature bentgrass seedlings that poorly tolerate traffic and are more susceptible to diseases and overwatering. Bentgrass can be seeded alone, but due to its slow establishment rate (e.g., four to eight weeks), it usually is used in combination with fine fescue, ryegrass, and roughstalk bluegrass. If a bentgrass is used for overseeding, Redtop (*Agrostis alba*) is more vigorous, less expensive, and less competitive in the spring. Numerous bentgrass varieties have been introduced in the last decade (Chapter 1).

Poa Trivialis (Roughstalk Bluegrass)

Poa trivialis (often called roughstalk bluegrass, rough bluegrass, or "Poa triv") is native to wet, shaded environments of northern Europe. It has a fine texture, good density, and is more cold tolerant than ryegrass. This is due, in part, to its high seed count, at approximately 8-to-1, compared to perennial ryegrass. This gives it a greater density in the number of seed per square foot than ryegrass. It is easier to establish in the fall compared to ryegrass since radical increases in mowing heights are not necessary and golfers like it due to the minimum seedbed preparation needed for establishment. Roughstalk bluegrass also tolerates poorly drained soils and has good shade tolerance. These characteristics make it desirable as a component of an overseeding mixture (typically 15 to 30 percent) along with perennial ryegrass or bentgrass (Plate 18–6). However, *Poa trivialis* is susceptible to diseases, especially dollar spot. It has poor wear tolerance and a natural yellow-green color. Hot spots, or dry areas, may develop and require daily hand syringing. *Poa trivialis* also tends to die-out earlier in the spring than most other overseeding grasses due to its low heat tolerance. This low heat tolerance normally is desirable since the spring transition is quicker and smoother. However, extended warm weather into the fall and early warm weather in the spring may prematurely weaken it. *Poa trivialis* also is susceptible to damage when Prograss herbicide is used for annual bluegrass control. Numerous varieties of *Poa trivialis* are currently being developed and released. Improved cultivars include Bariviera, Barusa, Colt, Cypress, Darkhorse, Dasus, Fuzzy, Laser, Laser II, Marine, Pilgrim, Polder, Polis, ProAm, Pulsar, Sabre, Sabre II, Shangrila, Snowbird, Sun-Up, Star Dust, Winterlinks, Winterplay, and Winterstar.

Supina Bluegrass

Supina bluegrass (*Poa supina*) is a naturally apple-green grass native to the European Alps. It can tolerate extreme shade (80 to 90 percent) and heavy traffic, but may be undesirable due to its light-green color, although darker-green ecotypes are being developed. It has high seed cost, a shallow root system, and is a common grass type used on golf courses in Europe and in the cooler regions of the United States. It displays good disease resistance but is susceptible to *Microdochium* patch (Pink snow mold). Commercial varieties include Supra and Supranova.

Blends and Mixtures

Blends (two or more cultivars of the same grass species) of perennial ryegrass, or mixtures (two or more cultivars of different grass species) of bentgrass and *Poa trivialis* (roughstalk bluegrass), or mixtures of perennial ryegrass and fine fescue are commonly utilized as a measure of protection against disease and environmental stresses. They are also used to enhance fine texture and smoothness. Mixtures typically consist of 70 to 90 percent perennial ryegrass, 20 to 30 percent fine fescue, and 20 to 30 percent *Poa trivialis*. If spring transition is a problem, reducing or eliminating the ryegrass component may be considered. An 80 percent fine fescue and a 20 percent roughstalk bluegrass (by seed weight) mixture will provide a quicker, smoother spring transition. Roughstalk bluegrass also is typically mixed with perennial ryegrass and bentgrass to enhance its performance and to provide a more desirable spring transition. A typical seed-weight formula is 85 percent perennial ryegrass plus 15 percent bluegrass, or 60 percent bentgrass plus 40 percent bluegrass. Since no one grass provides all optimum characteristics necessary for overseeding, turf managers often choose different mixtures or blends to suit their needs.

The grass species selected to be used for overseeding will depend on a number of considerations including the following.

1. **Budget**—The budget will often limit the availability of options. For those with limited financial resources, annual ryegrass is usually the cheapest. However, turf quality is sacrificed. Annual ryegrass seeded alone is suggested only for those who wish to provide a green ground cover during winter on fairways or roughs and are not concerned about traffic intensity. More expensive perennial ryegrasses or bentgrass, *Poa trivialis,* and/or fine fescue should be chosen for a high-quality surface.

2. **Intended Quality**—A quality blend of grasses should be considered for those areas receiving heavy traffic. For example, on many golf greens where uniformity, putting quality, and species transition are of prime importance, combinations of bentgrass, fine fescue, perennial ryegrass, or roughstalk bluegrass will enhance the turf's fine texture and smoothness. In fairways, where color and appearance are less important than on golf greens, perennial ryegrass is most often used; however, annual ryegrass may be acceptable. It produces a coarser-bladed, more-open, and less-uniform turf than turf-type perennial ryegrasses. The inferior quality of annual ryegrass usually goes unnoticed by most club members if it is used on large areas such as fairways. Due to its darker color, however, some clubs prefer perennial ryegrass and use lighter seeding rates to save money.

3. **Planting Date**—At times, the expected planting date may affect grass selection. If major tournaments should occur during optimum overseeding periods, then the grasses chosen should reflect earlier or later planting dates. If seeding occurs late in the fall, ryegrasses may be the only option since they germinate and establish themselves quickly. Roughstalk bluegrass and bentgrass may not have sufficient time to become established if they are seeded in late fall. Early overseeding of fine fescues should not be planned because they generally are more heat sensitive than the other grasses. In spring, if tournaments are scheduled during transition, the superintendent must carefully select the overseeding grass species. For example, if a tournament occurs in the earlier portion of spring transition, then a greater amount of annual ryegrass, intermediate ryegrass, and *Poa trivialis* can be used. If the tournament is later, or during the transition period, then more heat-resistant varieties of perennial ryegrass or bentgrass should be considered.

4. **Traffic or Play Intensity**—Resort or municipal courses that depend on heavy play during fall, winter, and spring months should carefully select their overseeding grass(es). Perennial ryegrass offers the quickest establishment and best tolerance to intense or heavy traffic. Bentgrass, fine fescue, and *Poa trivialis* generally make a better putting surface but

at the cost of sacrificing establishment rate and traffic tolerance. Blends containing perennial ryegrass plus bentgrass and/or *Poa trivialis* or fine fescue are often used to try and take advantage of each grass. Other resort clubs use bentgrass or *Poa trivialis* exclusively but buy enough additional seed to periodically "dust" weak or excessively damaged areas. Shady or excessively wet greens also perform better if a percentage of their overseeding blend contains *Poa trivialis* and/or fine fescue.

Seed Quality

Only certified (blue tag) seed should be used when selecting species and cultivars for overseeding. Maximum percent purity and acceptable germination should be specified at the time of purchase. Seed also should be certified free of hard-to-control weeds such as annual bluegrass.

Fungicide-treated seed should be requested to reduce potential seedling loss due to *Pythium* and *Rhizoctonia* diseases. Metalaxyl (Apron) or etridiazole (Koban) are fungicides commonly used for this purpose. Bentgrass used for overseeding is normally not treated with a fungicide. Extra seed (approximately 10 percent) also should be purchased for repairing small areas that may be lost from pests, weather, or traffic. All seed should be protected from rodents and stored in a cool, dry place to retain seed viability.

Seeding Rate

The grasses being used and the desired turf density will dictate seeding rate. Small seeded grasses, such as bentgrass and roughstalk bluegrass, can be seeded at lower rates when compared to large seeded grasses such as annual and perennial ryegrass. They will provide a comparable number of plants per given area. Areas receiving heavy traffic require a higher seeding rate than those areas where winter color is the main objective. Table 18–2 lists suggested overseeding rates. If either of these high or low seeding ranges are exceeded, thin, open, and disease-susceptible turf can be expected.

OVERSEEDING

Golf Greens and Tees

Before overseeding, the steps listed in "Seedbed Preparation" should be implemented to provide a desirable seedbed. Following this, a uniform application of seed is needed to provide a smooth and uniform playing surface (Figure 18–8). Seed should be applied when the surface is dry. Drying can be hastened by dragging a hose across the turf surface. Wind speed should be less than five miles per hour to minimize seed movement onto adjacent areas.

Spreaders should be carefully calibrated to deliver the appropriate amount of seed. Another method is to pre-weigh seed for a known area, such as a putting green, and carefully meter it out over the area. This usually requires numerous passes over the area to ensure uniform seed coverage, and at least two directions should be used when broadcasting the seed (Figure 18–9). Apply half of the seed in one direction and the other half while moving at right angles to the first pass.

Boundaries of the overseeded areas should be defined by using a drop spreader. The remaining seed is applied with a drop, or centrifugal, spreader within the outer fringe of the seeded area. Avoid seed spread to non-target areas such as collars, fringes, and other nearby turf areas (Figure 18–10). Unwanted seed will reduce aesthetic value and create the need for additional maintenance. Clumps of ryegrass are most noticeable the spring following application and tend to remain visible into early summer. Control of these clumps, once they are established, is difficult and slow. When trying to reduce the amount of unwanted ryegrass drift, carpets and mats should be placed in the designated areas used to fill and empty spreaders. Mats also can be placed around the perimeter of the seeding area to minimize escaped seed. Workers' shoes and dragging equipment should be cleaned before and after entering the perimeter area surrounding the green. If ryegrass drift is suspected outside the intended overseeded area, a preemergence herbicide should be applied after overseeding. A short boom or backpack sprayer should be used to treat areas not accessible by tractor-drawn or self-powered sprayers.

TABLE 18–2 *Suggested overseeding rates for various grasses and mixtures (by seed weight) used on golf courses.*

Grass	Greens	Tees	Collar/aprons	Fairways
	---------- lbs. per 1,000 sq.ft. ----------			-lbs/acre-
Perennial ryegrass	25 to 40	15 to 20	10 to 20	250 to 450
Italian (Annual) ryegrass	35 to 50	15 to 25	15 to 25	250 to 400
Chewings (Fine) fescue	25 to 30	10 to 20	5 to 20	—
Bentgrass	2 to 5	2 to 3	2	—
Poa trivialis	6 to 12	5 to 7	4 to 7	—
Typical mixture for enhanced performance and better spring transition: 75 percent Perennial ryegrass + 25 percent Chewings fescue	30 to 40	10 to 20	10 to 20	150 to 250
Typical mixture for enhanced performance and better spring transition: 75 percent Perennial ryegrass + 25 percent *P. trivialis*	30 to 40	10 to 20	10 to 20	150 to 250
Typical mixture for better performance in shady or wet areas: 60 percent bentgrass + 40 percent *P. trivialis*	5 to 7	3 to 4	2 to 4	—
Typical mixture: 60 percent P. ryegrass + 25 percent Chewings fescue + 15 percent *P. trivialis* (widely adaptable to poorly drained or shady areas)	25 to 30	10 to 15	10 to 15	150 to 250
Typical mixture for enhanced fall establishment and better spring transition: 80 percent Chewings fescue + 20 percent *P. trivialis*	20 to 25	8 to 10	8 to 10	150 to 200

FIGURE 18–8 Poor overseeding patterns result from insufficient distribution coverage of seed.

If non-fungicide-treated bentgrass seed is used, a fungicide is needed for disease control. For best seed coverage, fungicides should be applied before the green is topdressed. Fresh seed also should be used, as good seedling vigor is necessary for plants to quickly develop past the susceptible seedling stage. Proper seeding rates should also be adhered to since higher rates should not be used; this could produce weak, succulent plants.

Once the seed has been applied, light topdressing of greens and tees at one-third to one-half cubic yard per 1,000 square feet (0.27 to 0.41 m³/100 m²) encourages desirable seed-to-soil contact and turf establishment. Seed and topdressing material is then incorporated by dragging a carpet across the seeded area. A steel mat may need to be placed on the carpet to provide sufficient weight. Topdressing should be dry before dragging to minimize seed pickup on shoes and equipment. A cover on the ground also should be used when entering and leaving overseeded areas to prevent unwanted seed movement.

FIGURE 18–9 Seeding should be in several directions to ensure uniform application. A drop spreader should be used to apply seed to the perimeter and collars of golf greens.

FIGURE 18–10 Seed trails resulting from a leaking hopper (top) and unwanted ryegrass clumps appearing adjacent to a green during overseeding (bottom). A drop seeder should be used along the perimeter of greens to prevent unwanted seed movement.

Fairways

Following seedbed preparation, large areas such as fairways typically use a centrifugal spreader to disperse seed. As with golf greens, seed should be spread in at least two directions. Use a drop spreader for defining the perimeter of these areas. Fairways are seeded at 250 to 450 pounds per acre (280 to 504 kg/ha) with perennial ryegrass, or 250 to 400 pounds per acre (280 to 450 kg/ha)

with annual ryegrass (Table 18–2). Only fungicide-treated seed should be planted. Buying extra seed to repair worn, skipped, or poorly established areas is suggested.

Fairway seed should be matted into the soil surface following overseeding. Topdressing usually is not used on these large areas after seeding except for intensive traffic areas such as approaches. Matting of large areas can be achieved by dragging a rug or old carpet section over the seeded area. Another method to encourage good seed-soil contact is by operating a stiff-wire power sweeper in several directions over seeded areas (Figure 18–11). After dragging-in the seed, topdress lightly (e.g., one-third to one-half cubic yards per 1,000 square feet) over heavy play or traffic areas with a soil mix similar to the underlying soil.

Another means of seeding fairways is through a slit applicator. This machine cuts a thin slice through the thatch layer, drops the seed, and presses the seed into the soil. Slit seeding helps overcome heavy thatch layering and generally provides good germination since the seed is in direct contact with the soil and is less susceptible to drought. Slit seeding, however, requires a slit seeder, is slower to plant, is easy to have skips and gaps in the seeding pattern, and results in pronounced rows of seed until the ryegrass is mature enough to till.

The use of plant growth retardants (PGRs) as overseeding aids has increased in recent years. The PGR is applied just prior to overseeding to retard the bermudagrass growth; thus, it reduces the competition between it and the newly overseeded grasses. Only foliar-absorbed PGR materials should be used since root-absorbed PGRs can retard the germination and growth of the overseeded grasses. Trinexapac-ethyl (Primo 1EC) applied at 8 to 16 ounces per acre (0.6 to 1.2 L/ha) two to five days prior to overseeding has worked well if the bermudagrass is still actively growing with little or no effect on overseeded ryegrass. If the area to be overseeded is cultivated by verticutting prior to seeding, the advantages of using PGRs are greatly diminished. The herbicide triclopyr (Turflon Ester 4L) can also be used at one to two pints per acre (1.2 to 2.3 L/ha) two to seven days prior to overseeeding to retard bermudagrass growth.

To produce a sharp contrast line between the overseeded fairway and non-overseeded rough, the outside perimeter of overseeded fairways may be treated with a preemergence herbicide prior to overseeding. This will help minimize "renegade ryegrass," *Poa annua,* and other winter weeds that give the overseeded area a ragged appearance.

Pre-Germinated Seed

If bare areas result from excessive play or diseases, reseeding with ryegrass through early spring is possible. It is always a good idea to order an extra 10 percent of seed in the event of thinning. Ryegrass seed (5 to 10 pounds per 1,000 sq.ft.) may be pre-germinated by soaking it in water for 24 to 48 hours and mixing it with topdressing prior to dispersal. The soil in these areas should first be loosened by spiking or aerifying. Ryegrass seed also may be "cleated-in" by simply broadcasting seed before play and letting the players' spikes push the seed into the soil.

Overseeding Cool-Season Areas

Areas established with cool-season grasses also require periodic overseeding to repair or thicken worn and damaged areas. The procedures of overseeding cool-season areas are similar to the warm-season areas, except for timing. Cool-season areas can be overseeded at different times of the year, but generally are seeded in late summer (best time) or early spring (second best time). Dormant seeding is sometimes used successfully in northern areas when the seed is applied during late fall or winter when temperatures prevent germination. In spring, when thawing soils are often saturated and very difficult to get heavy machinery into, the earlier seeding allows germination and establishment. Winter weather for dormant seeding should cooperate where temperatures stay consistently cold during winter to prevent premature germination and subsequent kill by a late cold snap. The areas should also remain under snow cover to maintain steady soil moisture with little rain to move seed. When using dormant seeding, seed mortality is high, requiring seeding rates up to 50 percent higher than normal.

In order to obtain good seed-to-soil contact, slit-seeding or slicing is often used when overseeding into existing cool-season areas. The sliced grooves should be at least one-fourth-inch deep to provide this desired contact rather than merely scratching the surface. Several passes help ensure good coverage and less noticeable slits.

Generally, the turfgrass species chosen should closely match what is currently present unless a change in grass is desired or extensive turf damage has occurred. A Kentucky bluegrass fairway, for example, is generally overseeded with 100 percent bluegrass at a rate of two to three pounds per 1,000 square feet. If extensive damage or exposed areas exist (25 to 50 percent bare soil), a mixture of two pounds bluegrass plus five pounds perennial ryegrass per 1,000 square feet may be necessary for rapid cover. Pure perennial ryegrass areas are generally overseeded with ryegrass only.

POST-PLANTING MAINTENANCE

Irrigation

Following seeding, irrigate lightly to carefully moisten the soil surface without puddling or washing the seed into surrounding areas. Three to four light irrigations per day may be needed until all seedlings establish. Once germination begins, the seed cannot be allowed to dry out or the stand will thin. If seed washes into concentrated drifts following intense rains or heavy irrigation, a stiff-bristled broom should be used to redistribute it. Once grass is established, gradually reduce watering frequency to decrease disease potential.

After seedling emergence (five to seven days for ryegrass, 10 to 14 for bentgrass and for roughstalk bluegrass), apply a preventative fungicide to help protect against Pythium root rot and Rhizoctonia brown patch, which can destroy overseeding stands (Plate 18–7). Factors that encourage these diseases include:

1. Unseasonably warm weather
2. Using excessive seeding rates that produce young, succulent plants
3. Prolonged periods of high, free moisture on leaf and stem surfaces, such as extended foggy conditions
4. Bermudagrass aggressiveness

Proper timing and application rate of seeding, minimum use of nitrogen, efficient irrigation scheduling, and the use of pretreated fungicide seed are methods to reduce disease potential. Many areas often experience warm, foggy mornings in the fall. Turf managers especially should be on the lookout for diseases during these conditions since they are ideal for rapid fungal reproduction and spread. To prevent development of resistant strains of *Pythium*, always follow the label and alternate between chemical groups.

Mowing

With ryegrass overseeding, mow greens at a one-half-inch (1.3-cm) height when the new stand reaches two-thirds to three-fourths inches (1.7 to 1.9 cm). Gradually lower the cutting height to 1/4 to 5/16 inch (6.1 to 8 mm) over a two to three week period at 1/32-inch (0.8-mm) increments and skip the "clean-up" mowing lap the first few mowings to minimize traffic and wear on the tender seedlings. Continue this gradual reduction in height for four to six weeks until a 3/16-inch (4.8-mm) height is reached. Use a sharp mower that will not pull up seedlings. Once well-established, mowing heights gradually can be reduced to the desired height and the heavier triplex mowers then can be used. On tees and fairways, initiate mowing when the grass reaches 0.75 to 1 inch (1.9 to 2.5 cm). This normally occurs 14 to 21 days after seeding and will allow time for seedlings to root. Wait until the morning dew is gone before mowing to prevent pulling of the seedlings from the ground. Tees and fairways usually are permanently mowed at one-half to three-fourths inch (1.3 to 1.9 cm).

Fertilization

Do not fertilize with nitrogen during overseeding since this may encourage excessive bermudagrass competition. Adequate levels of phosphorus and potassium, however, should be maintained for good plant growth. Begin to fertilize shortly after significant shoot emergence (two to three weeks after seeding for perennial ryegrass) and continue until cold weather halts bermudagrass growth. Normally, one-fourth to one-half pound nitrogen per 1,000 square feet every two to three weeks with a soluble nitrogen source (e.g., ammonium nitrate/sulfate), or one pound per 1,000 square feet per month with a slow-release nitrogen source (e.g., IBDU, milorganite, SCU), is adequate to promote desired growth without overstimulating growth and encouraging disease. Traffic during grass establishment should be minimized whenever possible. Cups in greens and tee markers should be moved daily.

WINTER MANAGEMENT

Maintaining an acceptable turf appearance during winter involves proper watering and fertilization practices, proper traffic control, and proper disease management. In addition, damaged areas that do not provide an acceptable stand after the initial seeding may require additional seed applications. It is always a good idea to order an extra 10 percent of seed in the event of thinning.

Irrigate regularly during the dry winter months to prevent plant desiccation. In addition, light, mid-day irrigations may be necessary if the overseeded grass begins to wilt. Do not overwater since this may promote algae and disease occurrence.

Traffic control in winter reduces injury to the bermudagrass crowns and stolons. Ways to control this injury include frequently alternating or changing mowing patterns, regularly skipping "clean-up" laps, and changing pin placement daily to distribute traffic.

Nitrogen fertilizer influences the appearance of the overseeded grass and spring recovery of the bermudagrass. Excessive nitrogen should be avoided to prevent unhealthy grass competition and to prevent succulent overseeding growth. Nitrogen applications every two to three weeks with one-half pound nitrogen per 1,000 square feet usually is sufficient. More frequent applications may be needed if the recovery time from traffic or weather damage is slow.

Applications of phosphorus, potassium, manganese, and iron should be considered during winter. All of these provide desirable color without stimulating excessive shoot growth. In addition, potassium helps in carbohydrate formation. These, along with iron, also prevent grass desiccation. Soil phosphorus and potassium levels and rates can be determined by soil testing. Iron is generally applied every three to four weeks as ferrous sulfate at two ounces per 1,000 square feet. Iron sulfate or a chelated iron source usually can be tank-mixed with most fungicides. Manganese can be applied as manganese sulfate at one-half to one ounce in three to five gallons of water per 1,000 square feet.

Once the overseeded grass becomes established, the chances of severe disease is reduced. Dollar spot usually develops when nitrogen levels are low or when *Poa trivialis* or bentgrass is used as an overseeded grass. Its occurrence usually is suppressed with sufficient nitrogen levels. Brown patch and Pythium blight generally are the exception and not the rule for today's overseeded grasses. Greens, however, that drain poorly, or during continuous wet periods, can trigger outbreaks of these diseases. Excessive amounts of soluble nitrogen can also trigger disease. Turf managers should constantly check the weather forecast and be ready to use a fungicide if extended warm, moist (foggy) conditions are forecasted.

In addition to these diseases, the overseeded grass and the non-dormant bermudagrass base grass can develop "Helminthosporium" leaf spot during the fall, winter, and spring months when temperatures slow grass growth. Leaf spot is similar to dollar spot where maintaining adequate nitrogen levels usually keeps the grass growing aggressively enough to outgrow the disease symptoms. Fungicides, however, may be required during extended periods of cool weather that prevent adequate bermudagrass shoot growth.

SPRING TRANSITION

The main objective in spring is the gradual and smooth transition from overseeded grasses back to bermudagrass turf. Dormant bermudagrass shows signs of "green-up" when soil temperatures reach the 60°F range. Some overseeded grasses, especially the new and aggressive heat-tolerant perennial ryegrasses, can successfully compete with bermudagrass through the spring. This results in a poor transition. Golf greens seeded with mixtures containing bentgrass often experience the same problem. However, mixtures high in *Poa trivialis* or fine fescue are difficult to maintain once temperatures reach the 80°F range. During these times, these grasses become very sensitive to management practices designed to encourage bermudagrass recovery (Plate 18–8). As early spring approaches, a cultural program is initiated using lower mowing heights, brushes, topdressings, and other reel implements such as grooved rollers. The following procedures have proven beneficial in encouraging bermudagrass at the expense of overseeded grasses with minimal disruption to the turf.

1. **Use the appropriate seed or mixture**—Reducing the amount of perennial ryegrass or bentgrass in an overseeding mixture tends to aid in spring transition. Intermediate ryegrass, fine fescues, and roughstalk bluegrass are less heat tolerant and therefore tend to transition earlier than perennial ryegrass or bentgrass. A 75 to 85 percent perennial ryegrass plus 15 to 25 percent roughstalk bluegrass, or 60 percent bentgrass to 40 percent bluegrass mixture transitions better in spring, yet provides a desirable putting surface. For those greens with good drainage and less traffic, an 80 percent fine fescue plus a 20 percent roughstalk bluegrass provides a quicker, smoother spring transition.

2. **Time transition according to temperatures**—Temperatures (both day *and* night) are the most important criteria influencing overseeding. Unfortunately, turf managers have little direct control over this. However, management practices can be timed around traditional temperature patterns and short-term weather forecasts. Probably the most important temperature range to remember is bermudagrass will not aggressively grow until night temperatures consistently reach the mid 60°Fs (Chapter 2). Bermudagrass shoots will "green-up" much sooner when daytime temperatures reach the mid 50°Fs (10°Cs), and slowly initiate growth when night temperatures reach 58°F. Members become excited with the first warm spell of the season and this puts added pressure on the superintendent to hasten transition. However, bermudagrass will not aggressively grow (especially laterally) until mid-to-high 60°Fs are reached. Therefore, do not begin your transition steps until just before these temperatures are anticipated. If performed prematurely, bare areas may become exposed and will not recover until temperatures are high enough to favor bermudagrass growth (Plate 18–7). Also, if a late cool snap occurs and night temperatures drop into the 50s or low 60s, it will require three to seven days of high 60°F temperatures for the bermudagrass to resume active growth.

3. **Reduced mowing height**—Begin reducing the mowing height several weeks before the expected spring transition period. Begin in mid-to-late February by reducing the cut height 1/32 inch (0.8 mm) every two weeks until a height of 5/32 or 1/8 inch (4 to 3 mm) is reached in late March. Maintain a short mowing height until at least 50 percent of the overseeded grass has been removed (e.g., early May). The mowing height might be raised back to 3/16 inch (4.8 mm) as the bermudagrass begins to recover, but should not be raised while the overseeded grass still dominates. A lower mowing height reduces the overseeding shading of developing bermudagrass, warms the soil, and inhibits the growth of the overseeded grasses. The use of grooved rollers and brushes also improves the putting surface and helps maintain the overseeded grass in an upright growth habit.

4. **Cultivation**—Spike approximately three weeks before bermudagrass normally begins to green-up and every week following to enhance soil warming and turf recovery. Spiking also reduces surface compaction and algae growth. Aerify several weeks before the expected spring green-up to promote bermudagrass growth by warming the soil and reduce

the competition from the overseeded grass. Small (1/4-inch) tines should be used and good soil moisture should be present. The superintendent and club pro should coordinate spring tournaments around aerification times to minimize play disruption.

5. **Fertility**—Maintain low fertilizer application rates in late winter through early spring to reduce overseeded grass growth. Liquid iron will aid in maintaining desirable green color without an excessive flush of growth. When bermudagrass growth is apparent, restore fertilizer applications. Approximately two weeks after the initiation of spiking, fertilize with one pound of soluble nitrogen per 1,000 square feet to help stimulate new bermudagrass growth. Fertilize weekly at this rate until an adequate bermudagrass cover is achieved.

6. **Verticutting**—While overseeded grasses are still actively growing, initiate light and frequent (e.g., weekly) verticuttings to help maintain the overseeded grasses in a upright growth habit that allows increased sunlight and warmth to penetrate through to the soil and thus encourage an earlier and more rapid regrowth of the bermudagrass. Begin verticutting when daytime temperatures are consistently above 70°F. Another method of judging when to initiate verticutting is when the non-overseeded adjacent fairways green-up. *This verticutting should be no lower than 1/16 inch below the bed knife.* It should cut above the soil surface and remove only surface leaves and not remove or damage bermudagrass stolons. Light verticutting, in addition to aiding the bermudagrass, also will improve the putting quality of greens. Light topdressings on a two to three week basis at approximately one-eighth yard per 1,000 square feet also aids in maintaining a desirable putting surface. **Note:** Although traditional light, frequent verticutting and core aerification may promote the gradual transition to bermudagrass, visual turf quality may be reduced until the bermudagrass has had sufficient time to recover. This is especially true if medium-to-heavy verticutting is implemented. Typically, patches of thin turf form and remain unsightly until the bermudagrass greens-up and fills in.

7. **Maintain adequate soil moisture**—Reducing or withholding water in an attempt to encourage the overseeded grass to die from moisture stress is not recommended. Spring is when bermudagrass suffers from the natural decline of older roots and initiation of new ones. Withholding water during this root transformation may cause greater damage to the extremely shallow-rooted bermudagrass more than the deeper-rooted winter overseeded species. Water deeply and infrequently to encourage deep bermudagrass rooting at the expense of the overseeded grass.

8. **Use of herbicides or plant growth retardants**—Selective herbicides have proven useful for slow removal of overseeded grasses in spring. This allows the superintendent better control on transition timing. Herbicide use also provides an earlier indication on how well the bermudagrass wintered and allows more time should resprigging or sodding be required. Removal of overseeded grass with herbicides also will remove the competitiveness and therefore will allow quicker bermudagrass recovery. Control of other weeds, such as *Poa annua,* also is possible with some of the herbicides.

Several products are available to assist in spring transition. Application rates and timings are extremely important. Products that require four to six weeks to control the overseeding include pronamide (Kerb 50WP) and metsulfuron (Manor or Blade 60DF). Kerb is applied from a one-half to one pound product per acre while metsulfuron is used at 0.5 to 1 ounce product per acre. Results are desirably slow. Four to six weeks, depending on temperatures and rates, are typically required to gradually reduce the overseeded grass. Warmer temperatures and the higher rates usually hasten this conversion. However, a weak stand of grass may result if greens are treated too soon in spring and if the weather remains cool (Plate 18–9). Thin turf will remain until temperatures are warm enough for bermudagrass to recover. These products are typically applied in late April to mid-May, depending on the location.

Quicker-reacting products include rimsulfuron (TranXit) and foramsulfuron (Revolver). These typically control the overseeding in two to three weeks. These, therefore, are not typically applied until later in spring (e.g., May) so sufficient bermudagrass growth has resumed to provide the desired smooth transition. Visual injury to ryegrass with this treatment normally lasts from one to three weeks. Pendimethalin applied at five pounds of product (Pre-M 60DG) in early March also aids in transition but may not be consistent between years. Oryzalin or oryzalin plus benefin (e.g., XL) severely injures ryegrass while oxadiazon, metribuzin (e.g., Sencor), or MSMA does not affect transition.

Experience suggests turf managers wishing to use herbicides to enhance transition proceed with caution. Do not begin treatments until one to two weeks after bermudagrass resumes active growth. Lighter rates than listed may be wise if "weaker" overseeded grasses such as *Poa trivialis* or fine fescue are present. Sprayer calibration and application uniformity are extremely critical; once the overseeded grass begins to die from the herbicide, there is no turning back.

Plant growth retardants have also been used to help make a smoother spring transition. Mefluidide (Embark 2S) and trinexapac-ethyl (Primo 1EC) have been used in early spring to help discourage the overseeding without retarding the bermudagrass green-up. Rates appear important since heavy applications may retard the bermudagrass as well as the overseeding. Primo 1EC at three to four ounces of product per acre and Embark 2S at one quart per acre are the starting points for this application. Additional research is needed with these to further pinpoint rates in relation to the transition timing.

CHAPTER

19

Managing Bentgrass/Poa annua Golf Greens in Stressful Environments

INTRODUCTION

Bentgrass use on putting greens is expanding outside of its natural region of adaptation into more hot and humid areas. This expansion frequently occurs in vacation or resort travel destinations where the facilities are primarily operated as daily fee courses. Much of the clientele visiting these golf courses are from areas that exclusively use bentgrass or bentgrass/*Poa annua* greens. These players expect similar putting surfaces in heat-stress environments as those found in cooler regions. Contributing to the bentgrass use trend are advancements in innovative summer stress management practices and the availability of improved cultivars that possess better heat and drought tolerance. These improved cultivars produce an extremely fine-textured, dense turf when closely mowed because of their extremely high shoot density. *Poa annua* greens are becoming more widespread primarily due to the lack of reliable selective control in bentgrass greens. Superintendents, therefore, have adjusted their management programs to maintain them.

Despite these benefits, considerable time, expertise, effort, and money are required to successfully maintain these grasses where grown outside their natural range of adaptation (Plate 19–1). During summer, bentgrass/Poa golf greens require intense management. Turf thinning often results from heat stress, disease, intense traffic, ball marks, and insect damage. A major goal of bentgrass/Poa managers during this time is maintaining a turf that resists invasion by pests such as *Poa annua,* goosegrass, bermudagrass, moss, or algae. The following information outlines management practices needed to successfully manage bentgrass/Poa grown in chronically stressful environments.

GEOGRAPHICAL ADAPTATION

Understanding the adaptation and physiology of these grasses is essential to successfully maintain a persistent turf. Temperature and moisture are the principal climatic factors determining distribution. Although soil moisture availability can be controlled with irrigation, other moisture sources, particularly relative humidity (RH), are not easily controlled and can influence species distribution and survival. Turfgrasses, like all living things, respond to environmental parameters and have specific critical tolerance limits. When these limits of a species are exceeded, its survival will decrease. The strategy when growing a turfgrass outside its natural zone of adaptation is to manipulate management and microenvironmental conditions to better simulate its natural environment.

Temperature

Creeping bentgrass (*Agrostis palustris* L.) originated in Eurasia while colonial bentgrass (*Agrostis tenuis* Sibthorp) originated in Germany where temperatures generally range from 60 to 75°F (15 to 24°C) (Ward, 1969). The area of bentgrass adaptation in the United States is depicted in Chapter 1. Bentgrass is particularly suited to the maritime climates of New England and the Pacific Northwest. Cool-season (C_3) grasses seldom grow naturally above the 80°F July isotherm (the geographic delineation of areas with the same mean temperature). Warm-season (C_4) grasses, however, seldom grow naturally below the 40°F January isotherm.

Southern areas in the United States often have annual temperatures 20 to 40°F (4.4 to 6.7°C) higher than the optimum for bentgrass. Also, the average annual rainfall can be 20 to 30 inches (50 to 76 cm) higher than the optimum amount for bentgrass. With these extreme conditions, maintaining a persistent bentgrass turf can be a struggle, and turf managers must alter the microclimate surrounding greens to avoid prolonged periods of environmental stress and better simulate its naturally adapted environment. The primary reason bentgrass or bentgrass/Poa greens decline during summer months is indirect heat stress that predisposes plants to poor stress tolerance and a number of secondary fungal pathogens. Interestingly, roots of cool-season grasses are the plant organs most sensitive to heat stress (Figure 19–1). Bentgrass roots are deepest and most healthy during spring, but rapidly decline when soil temperatures exceed 79°F (26°C) (Figure 19–2). This sensitivity is exacerbated when soils are compacted and/or wet, thereby reducing oxygen levels.

Humidity

Humidity is the amount of water vapor in the air relative to the maximum amount the air could hold at a specific temperature. High relative humidity (RH), among other parameters, helps buffer or prevent wide day–night (diurnal) fluctuations in air temperature. For example, when RH is low, air temperatures quickly increase after sunrise and drop after sunset, which are conditions common to desert (arid) climates. High RH acts like a blanket providing minimum drop in day–night temperatures, resulting in higher night temperatures, which are conditions common in summer months. Prolonged higher night temperatures increase bentgrass/Poa respiratory activity, depleting carbohydrates and slowly weakening plants over time. Low RH areas such as deserts have greater fluctuations in daily temperature changes. Although daytime temperatures in these locations regularly exceed 100°F (38°C), with cooler nights, plants have an opportunity to recover. Cooler regions generally can grow bentgrass with less difficulty than hot, humid areas (Figure 19–3).

High humidity also increases the amount and time that free moisture like dew or guttation persists on turf leaves and delays normal drying times. Extended free moisture on physiologically weak turf greatly enhances summer disease activity.

High RH also reduces the rate of evapotranspiration (ET), a natural evaporation process by which plants cool themselves. Syringing, the process of applying a very thin film of water to the turfgrass canopy, is a management procedure used by superintendents in an attempt to cool the turf surface. This process becomes less effective during periods of high humidity because the humidity-laden atmosphere does not provide a favorable gradient for water to evaporate from the leaf surface. Furthermore, when ET is slowed, nutrient availability is also slowed, because less water is moving from the soil solution to plant roots via the transpiration gradient. The lack of available nutrients may also negatively affect turf vigor during stress periods.

Microenvironment or Climate

Tremendous variations can be found within a climatic zone. The localized climatic region is often referred to as the **microclimate** or **microenvironment.** For example, in the northern hemi-

FIGURE 19–1 Creeping bentgrass root mortality (top) and turf quality (bottom) following two night temperatures when day temperatures were maintained at 75°F (24°C) (*HortScience*, 2003, 38(2):299–301).

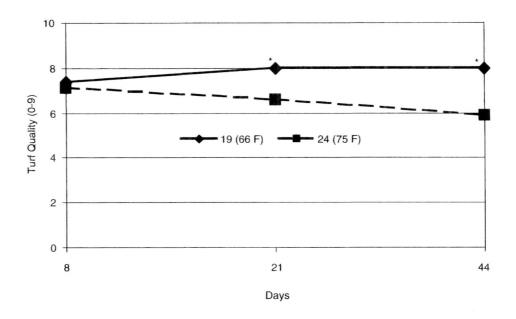

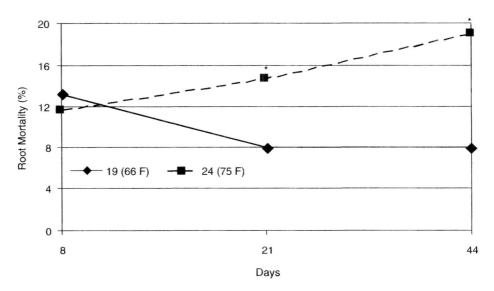

FIGURE 19–2 Typical annual rooting characteristics of creeping bentgrass in heat-stress environments (*Crop Science*, 2001, 41:1901–1905).

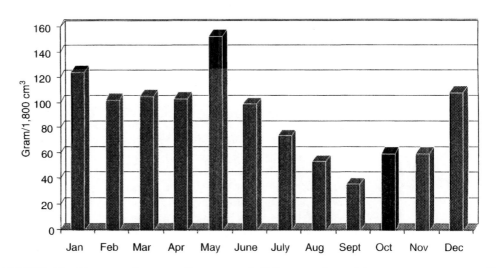

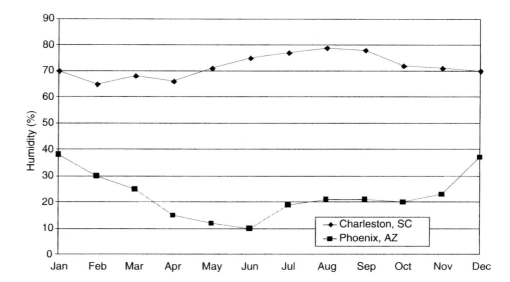

FIGURE 19–3 Comparing monthly relative humidities of an arid location (Phoenix, AZ) to a humid location (Charleston, SC). Generally, as the relative humidity increases, so does plant respiration and disease occurrence.

sphere, south- or southwestern-facing slopes are warmer than north- or northeastern-facing ones. Trees located to the south or southwest side of a green cast longer shadows, especially in fall and winter; influence light quality and quantity; and affect daytime temperatures, as well as wind movement. Tall shrubs, understory trees, and underbrush surrounding greens may limit or prevent air movement, resulting in stagnant, hot-humid air pockets. Other obstructions around greens, such as buildings, or architecturally placed mounds also restrict air movement. Elevated mounds tend to dry out quicker than lower or more level areas. Low areas on putting greens, which are typically located near the front or at the base of tiered slopes, typically hold excessive soil moisture. Furthermore, these areas often receive enormous foot traffic as players walk on and off these areas; frequently, the hole is located in this accessible location.

Other examples of microenvironments include greens adjacent to the coastal regions that experience perennial winds that quickly dry out turf areas and expose the turf to salt spray. Bodies of water such as swamps, ponds, or lakes also tend to influence the microenvironment by raising the relative humidity of adjacent turf areas. Adjacent rivers or large lakes can help moderate the temperature of the microenvironment. When possible, and prior to siting and building a putting green, the architect and superintendent should recognize and carefully consider future management strategies to deal with each of these unique situations. As the saying goes, "An ounce of prevention is worth a pound of cure!"

BENTGRASS/POA PHYSIOLOGY

Some plants flourish in warmer areas, whereas others "prefer" cooler climates. It was not until the middle 1960s that scientists began to unravel this physiological difference. In the late 1960s, scientists discovered C_4 metabolism was associated with warm-season grasses, such as bermudagrass, while cool-season plants, such as bentgrass and Poa, have C_3 metabolism. Refer to Chapter 2 for additional information on C_3 and C_4 plants. Table 19–1 lists some agronomic and physiological requirements and differences between creeping bentgrass/Poa, C_3 plants, and bermudagrass, a C_4 plant.

Photorespiration

Bentgrass and Poa are C_3 plants and absorb carbon dioxide (CO_2) through their stomates, which then competes with oxygen (O_2) for a two-carbon molecule called ribulose bisphosphate, Rubisco, or RUBP. As temperatures increase, bentgrass/Poa leaf stomates close to conserve water, reducing carbon dioxide absorption from the atmosphere. As a result, more dissolved oxygen produced from photosynthesis is found within the plant and it competes with carbon dioxide for RUBP. This process is known as **photorespiration** (Chapter 2) and, under prolonged occurrence, it gradually weakens the turf since plants require carbon dioxide to produce carbohydrates (food). C_4 plants such as bermudagrass, however, inherently have higher carbon dioxide concentrations

TABLE 19–1 *Comparison of creeping bentgrass and bermudagrass physiological and agronomic requirements for golf greens.*

Parameter	Creeping bentgrass	Bermudagrass
Carbon metabolism type	C_3 (cool-season)	C_4 (warm-season)
Sunlight requirements for maximum photosynthesis	25 to 50 percent full sunlight	100 percent full sunlight
Photorespiration presence	Present	Absent
Temperature Ps/Rs compensation point* (Figure 19–4)	86°F (30°C)	na
Optimum soil temperatures for shoot growth	59 to 75°F (15 to 24°C)	80 to 95°F (26.7 to 35°C)
Optimum soil temperatures for root growth	50 to 65°F (10 to 18°C)	75 to 95°F (24 to 35°C)
50 percent root loss soil temperatures (Figure 19–5)	75 to 77°F (24 to 25°C)	—
Growth limiting soil temperatures	80 to 95°F (26.7 to 35°C)	100 to 110°F (38 to 43°C)
Lethal soil temperature	100 to 110°F (38 to 43°C)	120°F (49°C)
Temperature that causes shoot dormancy	<30°F (−1.1°C)	≈50°F (10°C)
Overseeding requirement	Generally not unless summer stress has dramatically reduced stand density	Necessary in most areas for winter color
Carbohydrate "food" storage type	Soluble sugars (fructosans)	Insoluble starch
Preferred soil texture	Sand to sandy loam	Sand to loam
Minimum soil oxygen needs (ODR)	1.5 to 2.0×10^{-7} g/cm²/min	na
Soil carbon dioxide tolerance	<2.5 percent	na
Mean summer ET rates	0.19 to 0.39 in./day (4.8 to 9.9 mm)	0.15 to 0.28 in./day (3.8 to 7.1 mm)
Irrigation requirements	Conventional deep irrigation + supplemental spot hand watering/ syringing	Conventional deep infrequent irrigation
Air circulation requirement	Required	Not required
Fertilizer application	Granular and liquid	Granular and liquid
Pesticide tolerance	Poor (especially under moisture and heat stress)	Very good
Disease susceptibility/Fungicide requirement	Mod-high/high	Low/low
Salinity tolerance	Low (600 to 1,000 ppm)	High (1,000 to 2,000 ppm)

*Ps = photosynthesis; Rs = respiration.

FIGURE 19–4 Creeping bentgrass photosynthesis to the respiration point where temperatures above 86°F, 30°C have more carbohydrates consumed by plant respiration than are produced by photosynthesis (*Crop Science*, 2000, 40:1115–1120).

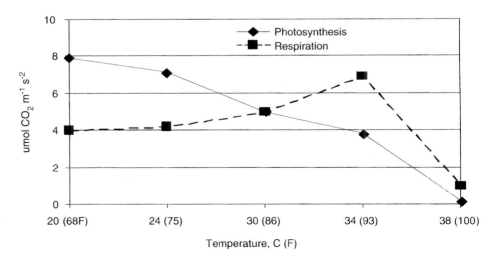

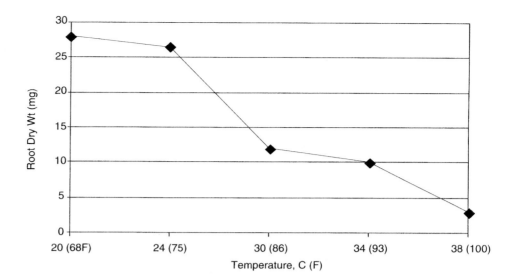

FIGURE 19–5 Reduction in creeping bentgrass root weights as temperatures increase (B. Huang, unpublished data).

since their stomates do not normally close at higher temperatures; thus, they do not photorespire. C_4 plants, therefore, freely absorb the carbon dioxide needed to produce plant foods and other materials during summer growing conditions and continue growing.

Sunlight requirements

In photosynthesis, energies in the form of light photons are used to break apart water molecules. Water molecules release positively charged hydrogen ions, which are used to make energy in the form of ATP. Higher light intensities require higher carbon dioxide levels within the plant for optimum photosynthetic efficiency. Due to higher concentrations of carbon dioxide within C_4 plants, these plants have a nonsaturating light requirement. In other words, bermudagrass requires full sunlight levels for optimum growth. Bermudagrass grown in shade weakens and thins, especially when maintained at putting green height, since the leaf surface available to intercept sunlight is reduced.

C_3 plants such as bentgrass/Poa, however, are more shade tolerant than most C_4 grasses. However, shady environments are often combined with reduced air movement and increased humidity that limits leaf drying potential. These factors increase disease incidence, reduce traffic tolerance, and increase management needs, thereby offsetting the inherent shade tolerance of bentgrass/Poa. The best growing and easiest-to-maintain bentgrass/Poa greens requiring fewest inputs tend to be those located in open, full-sun sites with no surrounding trees, buildings, or mounds to impede air movement.

Poa annua

Maintaining desirable *Poa* or mixed Poa/bentgrass greens requires an in-depth appreciation for the art and science needed to produce a consistent, persistent turf. Compared to bentgrass, Poa is physiologically strongest during the fall, winter, and spring months while bentgrass is strongest during summer. Thus, the key to success is employing management practices to keep Poa alive and dense during the stressful summer months. Otherwise, voids that affect ball roll will develop.

The Poa Life Cycle

Ecologically, Poa is a winter annual, with peak germination in late summer/early fall, vegetative growth during winter, profuse seed production in spring, and, if not managed properly, eventual death in summer due to heat, disease, and moisture stress. Throughout the years, different ecotypes have evolved: the true winter annual, biennial, and perennial. For greens, which are regularly irrigated, fertilized, and treated for pests, the perennial (or creeping) ecotype is most frequently encountered. This ecotype is also preferred as it produces the least amount of undesirable seed stalks, and typically produces short stolons, allowing it to creep and fill in weak or thin areas. Annual Poa biotypes have an enormous ability to produce seed that do not all germinate in one particular year and can remain viable for more than six years. Of those that do germinate in one year, approximately 70 to 90 percent will germinate in fall and the other 10 to 30 percent in spring. This extended germination period helps ensure survival, but also ensures an almost certain level of failure when trying to completely eradicate it. Also, since the majority of root carbohydrate reserves are used to produce seed, Poa plants have little if any root density remaining after spring seed production. Turf managers then face the upcoming summer stress with plants that have minimum root systems and little tolerance for intense traffic, pest or pest control, ball marks, or invasive mechanical cultural practices like core cultivation.

CULTURAL PRACTICES FOR BENTGRASS/POA GREENS

Green Construction

In a model round of golf, 75 percent of strokes involve or are conducted on the putting green. This rigorous use can stress even the best-built and maintained greens. To maintain a desirable putting surface, greens receive maintenance practices like mowing, rolling, irrigation, pesticide applications, fertilization, overseeding, and soil cultivation. Most cultural practices used for bentgrass/Poa greens are conducted at much different times than for bermudagrass because of the seasonal differences in optimum growth and recovery. Regardless of the turf species being grown, in stressful environments the most successful putting greens are those constructed using a sand-dominant system.

Precise soil moisture control is a critical prerequisite for growing and maintaining bentgrass/Poa. Without this precise control, bentgrass/Poa can and will suffer from excessive or inadequate soil moisture that may lead to other conditions such as diseases or soil compaction. Precise moisture control is best achieved with golf greens built as outlined in the green construction section (Chapter 8). The intent is to resist compaction, provide proper internal drainage, and prevent excessive prolonged soil wetness that may weaken bentgrass/Poa root systems, primarily due to root decline from anaerobic soil conditions such as "black layer" or attack from soil-borne diseases such as *Pythium* root rot or *Rhizoctonia* brown patch.

Rootzone materials used for bentgrass/Poa golf greens should consist of at least 80 percent properly sized sand particles, an organic amendment like peat moss, and/or possibly a small percentage of native loamy sand or sandy loam soil. This small amount of appropriate loamy sand or sandy loam native soil will greatly improve cation exchange capacity and water-holding capacity, as well as reduce irrigation and fertilization requirements. Before selecting any rootzone materials for greens, consult a qualified rootzone testing laboratory. This will ensure the correct percentages of rootzone materials are blended for optimum physical properties. Putting green construction specifications adopted by the United States Golf Association are most widely used. These specifications provide adequate drainage, yet retain suitable moisture and nutrient levels to sustain bentgrass/Poa growth and development. Unamended pure sand greens, although successfully maintained in some climates, generally tend to be very porous, have inadequate nutrient retention, and tend to dry out quickly. Regardless of the construction profile chosen, research and experience indicates improperly constructed greens that drain poorly will eventually prove unsatisfactory in terms of maintaining viable bentgrass/Poa, especially as one moves into stressful environments. This will be most obvious during the summer months when the root systems of bentgrass or bentgrass/Poa will quickly decline due to indirect heat stress, a lack of soil oxygen diffusion, and increased activity of root fungal pathogens favored by warm, wet soil conditions.

Mowing

Rooting depths directly correlate with mowing height. As the mowing height is lowered, root systems become shorter (Figure 19–6). The lowest mowing height for bentgrass/Poa should be from fall through early spring. By mid-spring (May) through early fall (October), the highest-tolerable mowing height should be used to provide deeper and stronger rooting. Greens are maintained at heights generally between 1/8 and 5/32 inch (3.2 and 4 mm) and are mowed daily during nonstressed periods. As summer temperatures and stresses increase, raising the mowing height is one of the most effective but least used management techniques. Heights may be raised up to 3/16 inch (4.8 mm), at which time mowing frequency is often reduced to five times weekly. Lightweight walk-behind mowers are preferred during heat-stress periods, and also year-round, if possible, since "clean-up laps" with heavy triplex mowers compact and damage the turf. Double

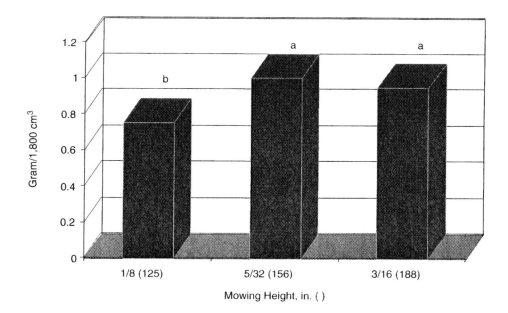

FIGURE 19–6 Correlation indicating that, as the mowing height of creeping bentgrass is lowered, a corresponding decrease in root biomass occurs (F. Yelverton, 1999. TURFAX:74).

FIGURE 19–7 "Triplex ring" of compacted, physically abraded bentgrass from using a triplex mower during summer stress. Soils mowed while saturated, and native or "push-up" style constructed greens with a relatively small surface size, are most prone to this damage.

cutting should also be avoided during periods of heat stress, and perimeter clean-up passes should be skipped periodically if excessive wear or soil compaction is evident on the perimeter of greens (Figure 19–7). Clippings are always collected on greens as they interfere with ball roll, reduce sunlight penetration, and may act as a source of inoculum for several diseases. Mowing direction should be changed or rotated daily to promote upright shoot growth and reduce grain.

Irrigation/Water Management

Proper surface and internal soil drainage plus irrigation are key parameters in growing bentgrass/Poa in stressful areas. Inadequate drainage, directly or indirectly, is responsible for the death of more grass than any other factor (Figure 19–8). Good water management can increase root development, which begins in spring as new growth is initiated. Mowing heights of less than one-fourth inch (6.4 mm) will greatly decrease leaf area and root depth; this should be considered when determining an irrigation program (Figure 19–9). Maximizing the time between irrigations without producing significant moisture stress encourages a deep root system. Daily irrigation encourages shallow rooting, algae, traffic stress, ball marks, moss, and many diseases. The recommended philosophy is to use heavy and infrequent applications, allowing grass/soil to dry-down between

FIGURE 19–8 Adequate drainage is necessary to maintain desirable putting greens, especially bentgrass/Poa.

FIGURE 19–9 Maximizing the time between irrigation events and maintaining the highest possible mowing heights are two strategies for developing efficient water-use programs. Shown is a bad mower pattern which reduces water use efficiency by the turf.

irrigations. Most superintendents prefer to keep their greens slightly on the dry side to minimize disease occurrence, encourage deeper rooting, and limit ball marks. Drier greens also absorb summer thunderstorms and other rainfall events quicker and easier than saturated greens. Furthermore, they retain less heat, and cool off at night more efficiently than saturated greens. It generally is easier to apply water when needed rather than trying to remove excessive amounts. However, if greens remain too dry for too long, problems with localized dry spots and inadequate soil moisture to support daily ET may occur. As a general rule, superintendents try to "stretch" the time between heavy, overhead irrigation cycles. Two to five days between the heavier, overhead irrigation cycles are typically utilized to encourage deeper rooting and to allow the flushing of salts out of the surface. These deep, infrequent irrigation cycles are supplemented by hand watering or syringing on localized areas displaying drought stress.

Theoretically, during summer in the absence of rainfall, the normal overhead irrigation applied to meet water-use rates (evapotranspiration) is approximately 0.2 inches (5 mm) daily (reduced to 0.1 inch (2.5 mm) during cooler times of the year). In reality, varying the irrigation schedule and amounts based on prevailing environmental conditions minimizes the aforementioned problems and prevents wilting.

For maximum moisture regulation, irrigation heads around putting greens should be individually controlled. This allows adjustment for seasonal changes in prevailing winds or unusual situations such as formation of persistent localized dry spots. Separate (or dual head) irrigation systems are also suggested for greens that are independent from the surrounding collar or slope region, as these areas often have a different turfgrass species, soil profile, and mowing height than on greens. Where this system is not used, the frequent, light irrigations needed for maintaining bentgrass/Poa during summer often keeps surrounding turf excessively wet and prone to disease, weed invasion, and compaction. A separate irrigation system ensures more efficient watering and less likelihood of weak turf or pest invasion.

Superintendents require adequate personnel to hourly monitor moisture conditions on greens (or even more frequently) during extreme prolonged stress periods. Monitoring greens consists of hand watering or lightly syringing "hot spots" at the first signs of wilt. In general, one to three extra people per 18 holes will be needed to properly monitor and prevent wilt and lethal heat accumulation.

Hand Watering

Most greens have certain chronic "hot spots" that characteristically wilt quickest. These typically occur on small ridges, mounds, or slopes of greens. They also occur where pockets of pure sand or excessively deep rootzone mix (>12 inches, 30 cm) were placed during construction. Additionally, a "wicking" phenomenon at the interface between the sand rootzone and surrounding native soil occurs when a plastic green liner is not used and may cause localized dry spots. Hand watering with a hose is often supplemented to normal sprinkler irrigation on these "hot spots" throughout the summer heat-stress period (Figure 19–10). Constant inspection, probing for moisture status, and supplemental hand watering are necessary from early morning until dark during peak summer stress. Greens must be inspected at least hourly and any "hot" spots immediately watered. To improve water penetration, hot spots are typically cored with a pitchfork or soil core probe to facilitate water infiltration through the thatch and propel water into the soil. Commercial water injection forks attached to irrigation hoses are available to help water penetrate thatch/mat to combat localized dry spots. Hand watering is preferred to syringing because hand watering only treats stressed areas of the green, thereby reducing the chance for overwatering the entire green.

Syringing

Syringing is the process of periodically applying a very thin film of water, generally through the irrigation system, to gently wet the leaf blades and relieve heat stress via evaporative cooling. As

FIGURE 19–10 Hand watering localized dry spots is necessary when bentgrass is grown in heat stress environments. This style of watering wets areas demonstrating drought stress but does not over water those areas that appear healthy.

this applied syringed water evaporates, it extracts heat from the turf surface, thereby cooling it. Evaporation of water is a considerable cooling process. When water evaporates, it absorbs heat (e.g., 580 calories at 86°F, 30°C, for one gram water) from the leaf and its environment. This is termed **latent heat of vaporization.** A similar cooling effect occurs in greenhouses when air is drawn through a wet fibrous pad that dissipates heat as water evaporates. This principle works better when air moisture is at a lower relative humidity. A typical syringing program involves two to six daily cycles when temperatures exceed 85 to 90°F (29 to 32°C). Syringing cycles generally are spaced 45 minutes to 1.5 hours apart and apply about 0.005 to 0.01 inches (0.13 to 0.29 mm) of water each. Unfortunately, many older irrigation systems and components cannot properly apply these very small quantities of water very efficiently. Thus, this management practice is losing favor to hand watering, since syringing has the potential of applying water where it is not needed. Excessive water from syringing also can provide ideal conditions for diseases, algae, or black layer development. Areas with high humidity do not evaporate water quickly; thus, the cooling effects of syringing and evaporation are only slowly realized. Other possible side effects of constant, light syringing are the development of a shallow root system and excess salt accumulation. It is important to remember syringing is a supplementary cultural practice and employed to manage severe summer stress. It is not a replacement for the regular deep infrequent irrigation cycles.

Localized Dry Spots

Another problem associated with bentgrass/Poa grown on sand-based greens is the occurrence of hydrophobic localized dry spots (referred to as **LDS,** or **isolated dry spots**). In these areas, the rootzone becomes hydrophobic, water is repelled from organic-coated sand particles, and bentgrass/Poa roots are unable to absorb water. In **hydrophobic** (meaning water "hating") sands, shoots wilt and the color of shoots quickly change to a purplish- or bluish-gray. If allowed to go untreated, LDS will kill turf. Detecting dry spots early is the key to turf survival. Oftentimes, a reduction in morning dew formation serves as an early indicator of LDS. A direct way of determining LDS severity is by pulling a soil core and placing water droplets every one-half inch (1.3 cm) or so along the length of the core. If these droplets do not penetrate the core and remain in droplet formation, this clearly indicates the soil is hydrophobic (Figure 19–11). If the soil is dry, then the localized dry areas should be deeply spiked with a solid-tine aerator, soil probe, or pitchfork (Figure 19–12). The area should then be deeply hand watered, and treated with a wetting agent to improve water penetration and retention. Overhead sprinklers should not be used in these situations because water is wasted on unneeded areas and also may encourage disease occurrence. LDS often reoccurs annually in the same areas. Once LDS areas develop, it becomes difficult to wet these areas again without extensive aerification or the use of wetting agents, and many times the turf is

FIGURE 19–11 Using the water drop test to determine the hydrophobicity of a soil. If a drop of water remains intact for more than one minute, as shown on the left side of the core profile, the soil is considered hydrophobic (water "hating"). If the bead disperses, as shown on the right side of the core profile, the soil is considered hydrophilic (water "loving"). Hydrophobic soils typically do not accept water readily and often develop into localized dry spots.

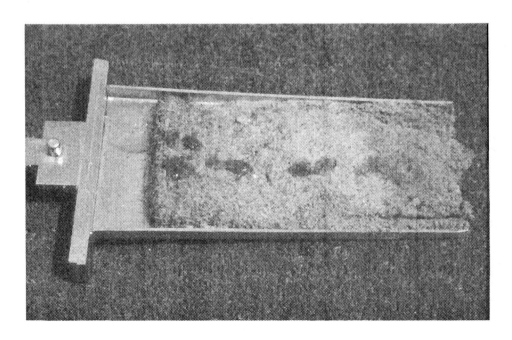

FIGURE 19–12 To wet the soil, a localized dry spot in a creeping bentgrass green is disturbed by aerification, forking, slicing, and so forth, treated with a wetting agent, and heavily hand watered.

FIGURE 19–13 Wetting agents reduce dew formation by lowering the surface tension between water and soil (right). This allows better water penetration for turfgrass use and minimizes the time water (dew) remains on the plant surface, potentially reducing disease occurrence.

lost. Therefore, identifying and mapping these chronically affected areas will help future management and schedule preventive treatment with wetting agents. Many recently introduced wetting agents have much improved control of LDS over previous chemistries (Figure 19–13).

Salinity

Another potential problem with growing bentgrass/Poa and regular shallow irrigation cycles is a gradual buildup of excess salinity. The light and frequent irrigation cycles often used to maintain these grasses, combined with the high summer evapotranspiration rates and applications of salt-based fertilizers, are conducive for salt accumulation. This is magnified when highly soluble fertilizer sources are used at relatively light but frequent rates and there is a lack of frequent, heavy rainfall to periodically leach the salt below the rootzone. Occurrence is more common on newly constructed greens receiving light, frequent nitrogen and potassium applications as well as light, frequent overhead irrigations to encourage rapid turf coverage. Specifically, during summer months, turf becomes more susceptible to salinity damage than normal. Under hot, dry, summer conditions, soil salinity levels as low as 600 ppm in the upper one-half to one inch (1.3 to 2.5 cm) of soil can begin to stress bentgrass/Poa. During cooler growing conditions, critical salinity levels often increase to approximately 1,000 to 1,200 ppm.

Summer salinity symptoms are often difficult to diagnose and are frequently confused with moisture stress. The turf initially appears light blue-gray as if moisture stress is occurring, and areas that drain poorly or receive light irrigation often are affected first. The turf does not respond favorably to fertilization and eventually shoot density declines, resembling moisture stress or localized dry spots. Often the symptoms of high-soluble salt damage are large areas or streaks on a green that turn yellow, begin to decline, and even die a few days to several weeks after fertilization. The streaks are usually from where fertilizer applications overlapped. When salinity stress is suspected, soil and water testing are used to help diagnose this problem. Cores from the affected area should be sampled from the top one-half to one inch (1.3 to 2.5 cm) where salts are most likely to accumulate.

To combat potential salinity buildup, superintendents have modified their watering practices from light, frequent applications in summer to heavier, infrequent ones, supplemented by heavy hand watering and coring to ensure water moves through the entire rootzone. Greens also must have relatively good internal drainage so salts can be leached below the turfgrass roots during rainfall or heavy hand watering events. Using low salt-containing water sources also helps. Coastal courses or those using effluent water sources should closely monitor their salt levels, especially during summer.

Using low salt-containing and slow-release fertilizer sources also becomes critical during stressful periods. In recent years, fertigation and foliar feeding by liquid fertilizer sources have become popular to help better maintain favorable bentgrass/Poa color and growth during summer. These fertilizer sources also minimize salinity problems. Buffering water pH to a range of 6.0 to 6.5 and periodically applying light gypsum on salt-affected soils also help reduce the salinity-associated problems.

Fertilization

Devising and implementing a sound fertility program is one of the most important agronomic considerations when growing bentgrass/Poa. Fertilization, along with aerification/topdressing practices, are two of the most debated agronomic topics among superintendents. Superintendents should formulate individual strategies for each green according to their financial resources, traffic intensity, geographic location, microclimates, player/quality expectations, specialized rootzone construction method, and the age of the rootzone/turfgrass.

Regularly fertilizing bentgrass/Poa provides an aesthetically desirable and playable surface and greatly influences the recuperative potential and stress tolerance of the grass. However, overstimulation with nitrogen fertilizer can lead to short roots and lush, green top growth that is more susceptible to diseases and drought stress. Adequate potassium, meanwhile, is necessary for plant stress tolerance.

As mentioned, trying to maintain adequate soil nutrients in sand-based greens is a challenge without "spoon" feeding nutrients or having wide swings in color and growth patterns. Frequent syringing of bentgrass/Poa to reduce wilting and heat stress, as well as daily mowing with clippings removed, also deplete soil nutrient levels. In order to provide a more uniform, desirable green color through summer and possibly reduce salt accumulation from granular sources, liquid fertilization or fertigation can be considered.

Another negative side effect of growing turf on high sand content greens is their relatively low CEC and nutrient retention. As a result, soil magnesium, iron, and/or calcium levels may become limiting for desirable growth and color.

Where iron deficiencies occur, chelated iron sources generally are best to prevent turf burn. Light, frequent iron applications are often made during summer to provide desirable color without undesirable succulent turf growth. Iron can often be incorporated in a regular fungicide spray program. The lack of other nutrients such as phosphorus, manganese, and zinc appear to contribute to the decline of bentgrass/Poa in summer months. Phosphorus deficiencies are not normally associated with most plant growth. However, with high sand content golf greens, phosphorus deficiencies can occur. Regular soil and tissue testing are the only ways to quantify this and should be performed often on bentgrass/Poa. Various liming and fertilizer materials contain one or more of these elements. In general, the ideal soil pH for maintaining bentgrass/Poa is 5.5 to 6.5. By comparison, the ideal soil pH for maximum nutrient availability is approximately 6.5 to 7.5. On silica sand-based greens amended with peat moss, lime may be required to raise the soil pH to a desirable level. On calcareous sands, however, it is difficult, and almost impossible, to reduce the soil pH below 7.0, and additional lime should not be used.

Soil and Tissue Testing

As previously mentioned, sand is often used for golf greens because it resists compaction and drains well. One negative, however, is its low nutrient-holding (cation exchange) capacity, requiring frequent soil and tissue analysis to monitor nutrient needs. Nutrient ranges for soils and plant tissue are listed in the fertilization section (Chapter 11).

Rates

The total amount of nitrogen used for bentgrass greens generally ranges from three to eight pounds nitrogen per 1,000 square feet (15 to 39 kg N/100 m^2) annually for established putting greens, while slightly more may be required for newly planted turf. Due to its leaching potential and high needs by plants, potassium rates should equal nitrogen rates or even be slightly higher. Phosphorus rates, in lieu of a soil test, should be approximately one-half the rate of nitrogen. An all-purpose fertilizer such as a 2-1-2 N–P–K ratio would be appropriate. Again, in general, no more than one pound of actual nitrogen per 1,000 square feet (4.9 kg N/100 m^2) should be applied at one time. Smaller quantities of liquid fertilizers are typically applied during the summer every two to four weeks at approximately 0.2 pounds nitrogen per 1,000 square feet (1 kg N/100 m^2) or every 7 to 14 days at 0.08 to 0.1 pounds nitrogen and potassium per 1,000 square feet (0.4 to 0.5 kg N and K/100 m^2).

Timing

Timing for this three to eight pounds of nitrogen (15 to 39 kg N/100 m^2) is based on the temperatures affecting shoot-and-root growth (Table 19–1). Table 19–2 lists a general rule-of-thumb for the percentages of this total nitrogen amount applied during the various seasons of the year.

With the commercial availability of improved bentgrass cultivars, superintendents are slightly altering their fall:winter:spring:summer seasonal percentages from a 40:30:20:10 to 40:30:10:20. This alteration provides less spring fertilization, which typically produces a flush of undesirable top growth, in favor of more summer fertilization to promote grass recovery from summer decline, traffic damage, ball marks, and so forth, on these newer cultivars.

A typical fertilization schedule based on Table 19–2 would include three-fourths to one pound nitrogen per 1,000 square feet (3.7 to 4.9 kg N/100 m2) for each month of September, October, November, December, and January. February (depending on location) would probably receive slightly less (e.g., 3/4 lb N/1,000 ft2, 3.7 kg N/100 m2) to reduce succulent growth in the subsequent spring months. March, April, and May might receive one-fourth to one-half pound nitrogen per 1,000 square feet (1.2 to 2.5 kg N/100 m2) each, while the summer months, June, July, and August, would receive minimal, but some, nitrogen (e.g., 1/4 lb N/1,000 ft2 each, 1.2 kg N/100 m2) in an attempt to reduce heat, drought, and disease susceptibility. Again, with the release of newer bentgrass/Poa cultivars, the spring and summer fertilizer rates just listed are often flipped to reduce spring flush growth and to promote summer recovery. For the upper transition zone and in areas where the soil freezes in the winter, most of the annual nitrogen requirements

TABLE 19–2 *Percentages of nitrogen fertilizer applied to bentgrass/Poa golf greens during the year.*

Season	Annual nitrogen application to bentgrass/poa golf greens
	--------------- % ---------------
Fall (Sept., Oct., Nov.)	40 to 75
Winter (Dec., Jan., Feb.)*	0 to 30
Spring (Mar., Apr., May)	10 to 20
Summer (June, July, Aug.)	10 to 20

*Nitrogen should not be applied to greens where soils regularly freeze during these months.

should be applied during the late-summer and autumn months, with little application during winter. This too will avoid the spring flush of growth and minimize disease problems.

A good rule-of-thumb for high sand content greens is to use lower fertilization rates (e.g., 1/8 lb nitrogen and potassium per 1,000 ft^2, 0.6 kg N/100 m^2) applied at more frequent intervals (e.g., every 10 to 14 days) during stressful environmental periods. These rates, as well as using soluble fertilizer sources like urea, are preferred because the turf has a shallow root system and the plant is unable to tolerate large salt additions. Phosphorus rates are best determined by soil and tissue testing. Often, one to two pounds (4.91 to 9.8 kg/100 m^2) of phosphorus and four to eight pounds (20 to 40 kg/100 m^2) of potassium are applied annually per 1,000 square feet. Again, rely on frequent soil and tissue tests to determine the nutrient needs of plants. Phosphorus applications are best made after aerification, which enables the very slowly soluble phosphorus to be placed directly into the rootzone where the plant roots can more readily absorb it.

Fertilizer Sources

Traditionally, golf courses have predominantly relied on granular fertilizer sources for the majority of their fertilization. However, improved technology and the availability of liquid fertilizers have changed this trend to where more liquid sources are being used, especially during stress periods. Liquid sources allow superintendents to more precisely control the rate being applied and application uniformity. This control becomes very important during the summer stress period as the bentgrass/Poa needs some fertilizer to encourage recovery and growth from this stress, yet does not need quick flushes of growth that may be severely detrimental during this time. Fertilizer helps the grass recover from traffic, heat, disease, or ball mark damage. Once bentgrass/Poa stops growing and becomes semi-dormant in summer due to the lack of fertilization, it becomes very difficult to "kickstart" growth again with fertilizer until the summer stress period subsides.

Typically, granular fertilizers are used during the fall, winter, and early spring months, especially for potassium and phosphorus needs. Liquid materials may be used during this time to enhance color. During the summer stress periods, many managers switch predominantly to liquid sources and "spoon feed" the greens as needed (e.g., when soil and tissue tests indicate nutrient needs, when color is needed, or when growth dramatically slows). Granular fertilizers are then used in fall after summer stress periods have ceased to promote recovery.

Micronutrients

Iron (Fe), sulfur (S), manganese (Mn), and magnesium (Mg) nutrient deficiencies may appear, especially when soil pH and/or phosphorus levels are high. Tissue testing will indicate these nutrient levels in plants. Light, frequent applications (e.g., 1 to 2 oz. product/1,000 sq.ft., 3 to 6 L/ha, every 3 to 4 weeks) of one or more of these nutrients often produce desirable color response without undesirable succulent shoot growth. Research also suggests the lack of the micronutrients manganese and zinc, as well as the macronutrient phosphorus, can contribute significantly to typical summer decline symptoms. Tissue testing is the most accurate means of monitoring these and other elements in plants. Excessive use, however, can cause phytotoxicity and/or imbalances with other necessary nutrients. Chapter 11 lists relative nutrient ranges for bentgrass/Poa.

Soil Cultivation

Aerification

Creeping bentgrass has poor tolerance to compacted soils and generally has a shallow (<3 inch, 7.6 cm) root system in summer (Figure 19–14). *Poa annua*, meanwhile, appears much better adapted to compacted soil conditions, and has the competitive advantage over bentgrass when these conditions occur. Poor or inadequate aerification and improper sand topdressing practices decrease bentgrass summer survival. Soil cultivation improves water infiltration and percolation, enhances soil oxygen diffusion, minimizes excess thatch and mat layering, and alleviates soil compaction, resulting in a healthier turf.

Soil cultivation should ideally be performed prior to a stress period when the turf is actively growing. This cannot be overemphasized since once stress begins, the chances of successful aerification are reduced. The most popular method of soil cultivation on golf greens is hollow-tine aerification. These tines generally penetrate three inches (7.5 cm) deep, are 3/8 to 1/2 inch (9.5 to

13 mm) in diameter, and most often are spaced on two-inch (5-cm) centers. Cores are removed if the existing rootzone media is unacceptable and sand topdressing mix is brushed (or ground-up) into the holes. If the existing rootzone media is appropriate, cores are mechanically pulverized, thatch is removed, and rootzone materials are brushed back into the holes. Aerification frequency most often depends on the amount of traffic an area receives, generally three to four times yearly. Bentgrass/Poa greens are most often aerified from September through May when temperatures are between 50 and 80°F (10 to 27°C). Expect to aerify with relatively large (1/2- to 3/4- inch, 1.3-to 1.9-cm) tines at least three times annually (e.g., fall, early spring such as March, and late spring such as May). In addition, on older or native "push-up" greens, deep-tine aerification (e.g., 8 to 10 inches, 20 to 25 cm deep) is also annually recommended. This helps improve internal drainage and breaks up any compacted "plow-layers" that may have formed as a result of repetitive cultivation to the same depth year after year.

Core aerification during summer months with small (e.g., 1/4 inch, 6.4 mm) hollow or solid tines is now possible. These small tines (often called "needle" or "pencil" tines) allow the benefits of aerification without extensive disruption to the playing surface (Figure 19–15) and the holes heal quickly. Using one-fourth-inch (6.4 mm) diameter tines on declining bentgrass/Poa greens during summer appears to be an effective treatment. This size tine is large enough to encourage significant air/water exchange with minimal disturbance to the putting surface. This may be more effective than slicing, which is the cutting of bentgrass/Poa stolons during a time when the grass is weak. During the stressful summer months, especially where high humidity accompanies heat, practices causing leaf abrasion should be avoided, including heavy sand topdressing, aggressive vertical mowing, or dragging-in aerification cores. If hollow-tine aerification is practiced during this time of year, the cores should be quickly removed from the surface.

The least-disruptive form of core cultivation is high pressure water injection. These systems use small, highly pressurized jets of water that penetrate more than 18 inches (46 cm). Regular use of hydro-aerifiers reduces soil compaction, improves soil oxygen, and reduces localized dry spot occurrence. Weekly aerification with these units during stressful summer months and every 21 days in fall, winter, and spring is often beneficial. Lastly, it is important to follow any aerification event with a light rolling of the surface. This prevents mower scalping, which often occurs due to the uneven turf surface from the aerification event.

Slicing and Spiking

Soil aerification should be supplemented with spiking, slicing, vertical mowing, grooming, and topdressing. Spiking, slicing, and using a high pressure water injection system may be preferred in warmer months. Spiking machines have vertical projections that punch small openings on the

FIGURE 19–15
Aerification holes from using
one-fourth-inch (6.4-mm)
"needle" or "pencil" tines
during summer to provide
drainage and soil/air
exchange with minimum
disruption to the playing
surface.

green's surface. Spiking relieves surface compaction but does not penetrate deep into the soil. Slicing involves thin, V-shaped blades that slice (or cut) into the top inch (2.5 cm) or so of turf. These thin slices help disrupt algae formation, divide stolons to encourage turf regrowth, and provide water and air entrance ports into thatch and soil. Slicing or spiking is normally performed weekly in summer and more frequently on problem areas.

Verticutting and Grooming

Moderate-to-heavy verticutting is performed at least once in spring (March until early May) and repeated in fall (October). Verticutting helps thin the turf, removes unwanted thatch and mat, and allows better soil oxygen diffusion and water penetration. Proper aerification coupled with sand topdressing and light verticutting also are needed to minimize development of the thatch/mat layer. The high water holding capacities of the thatch/mat layer often prevent or minimize internal water and air movement into the rootzone, effectively sealing off the sand and roots below. It is not uncommon to have a wet thatch/mat layer while the sand below the thatch layer is dry. The thick, organic thatch/mat layer is much like a dishwashing sponge that holds significant quantities of water. This water can often be squeezed out of the thatch or mat layer for several days after irrigation or rainfall even though the sand mixture below is relatively dry. This environment is very favorable for fungi and algae development and discourages deep turf rooting. An excessively wet thatch/mat layer also retains significant quantities of heat during summer months, further stressing crowns and roots growing in this layer.

Verticutting is generally followed by topdressing, rolling, light fertilization, and moderate watering. Light vertical mowing, enough to just "tickle" the leaf blades to promote an upright growth habit, also may be performed every two to three weeks in fall and early spring, followed each time by a light topdressing with the same soil mixture used in green construction. Light vertical mowing and grooming are performed often (e.g., weekly) during periods of favorable bentgrass/Poa growth during most of the winter and early spring to help reduce thatch and graininess.

Frequent grooming with groomers, brushes, grooved rollers, or light verticutting are also excellent means of minimizing thatch/mat layer development while also enhancing green speed. Turf groomers are used in fall, winter, and spring to reduce grain and to improve the quality of cut. Refer to Chapter 7 for further information on these procedures.

Light, frequent vertical mowing is being rediscovered with the newer, denser, rapidly growing bentgrass/Poa varieties. However, disagreement exists on the benefits of verticutting these newer cultivars. Some feel with their upright growth habit, verticutting or the use of grooved (or Wiley) rollers is not necessary. Others feel these bentgrass/Poas grow so aggressively and become so thatchy, they must be frequently groomed or lightly vertical mowed. In either case, bentgrass/Poa should be regularly (e.g., weekly) sliced and aerified via high pressure water injection to ensure adequate water and oxygen in the rootzone.

A recent development in thatch/mat management is a specialized heavy duty verticutter, called the "Graden." This machine has 15 blades spaced approximately one inch (2.5 cm) apart that can be adjusted to penetrate up to two inches (5 cm) deep. This aggressive verticutting machine can remove significant thatch and mat with regular use. Current trends are to use the machine in early spring and fall on bentgrass/Poa. Aggressive use will remove significant debris and soil and will require extensive labor for proper clean-up. Aggressive use also produces extensive slits or grooves (rows) that remain visible for extended periods of time (weeks, sometimes months) (Chapter 16). Topdressing regularly (30 to 40 times yearly) and rolling will help smooth these slits until the turf has time to recover. Some users are modifying the blade spacing so that, instead of one-inch (2.5-cm) centers, blades are spaced on two-inch (5-cm) centers. Additionally, two blades are being placed side-by-side on the two-inch (5-cm) spacing. This achieves less surface disruption while removing the same quantity of organic material. Furthermore, with the wider grooves, sand topdressing works into the rootzone easier.

Topdressing—Grooming—Rolling

Sand topdressing is the most effective means of preventing or reducing thatch/mat buildup. Thatch control can be accomplished by light, frequent (weekly or biweekly) topdressing, which also reduces algae development and helps provide a smoother putting surface. A key to success is using a sand topdressing material that matches the particle-size distribution of the underlying rootzone. Additionally, all sand topdressing should be free of, or have very little, silt or clay. With repeated use, the presence of these particles clog the desirable macropores of a sand-based rootzone.

Rolling of greens is a recently reintroduced cultural practice. With the demands for faster putting green speeds, this practice provides better ball roll without excessively low mowing during the summer-stress period. Solid rollers are suggested in summer to reduce turf damage. Depending on the weight of the machine, rolling may be performed one to two times weekly to help increase ball roll—up to 8 to 12 inches (20 to 30 cm) as measured by a stimpmeter. The major limiting factor to roller use is abrasion and mechanical injury occurring in the collars and chronically wet areas such as the low points of the green where water tends to settle. These areas should be avoided, especially during periods of high heat and humidity.

Black Layer

A distinctive black layer may develop in the rootzone when excessive moisture and/or soil compaction causes anaerobic (oxygen-lacking) soil conditions (Plate 19–2). Hydrogen and iron sulfide and methane gas concentrations rise and can reach toxic concentrations for bentgrass/Poa roots. If conditions persist, a layer of metal sulfides form in the saturated zone, often in the top four inches (10 cm) of the soil surface. This anaerobic zone takes on a characteristic dark (or black) color due to the reduced metals present, as well as a characteristic rotten egg or sewer-type smell. Since the problem is mainly due to anaerobic conditions, the primary solution to this problem is to improve soil oxygen diffusion. This involves prudent aerification, pH regulation, and water management practices to reduce the toxic effects of anaerobic conditions. Where the underlying soil or rootzone does not have adequate internal drainage, this problem will also need to be addressed.

Air Movement and Drainage

In the absence of proper soil moisture and air movement, bentgrass turf can reach surface temperatures in excess of 125°F (52°C). At these temperatures, turf will quickly wilt and, if not addressed, substantial turf loss will occur. Superintendents, in an effort to reduce these lethal conditions, have implemented various surface and subsurface air movement techniques to complement other management practices used to maintain bentgrass/Poa.

Proper air circulation helps reduce the direct heat load on bentgrass/Poa surfaces. Air circulation also helps plants transpire during summer heat-stress periods, which cools them. Newly

FIGURE 19–16 Surface fans should be considered on bentgrass greens grown in heat-stress environments to displace temperatures and encourage evapotranspiration. Research indicates a 3.5 to 4.5 mph (5.6 to 7.2 km/hr) wind speed at the plant surface is necessary for these benefits to occur.

constructed bentgrass/Poa greens should not be located in pocketed sites surrounded by anything that may prevent adequate wind or air movement. Additionally, established courses should remove these obstacles to encourage better air circulation and/or install fans around pocketed greens to improve surface air movement.

Surface Movement

A cultural practice unique to bentgrass/Poa greens is using surface area fans in warmer months to disperse the heat load and increase transpiration, which encourages evaporative cooling (Figure 19–16). Fans also dry the grass surface, and greens with fans on them typically show fewer signs of stress. For example, a healthy bentgrass turf has a surface temperature of over 100°F (38°C), with hot spots being over 120°F (49°C) when air temperatures are 90°F (32°C). If a 3.5 mph (5.6 km/hr) breeze is present, the turf surface temperature drops to approximately 90°F (32°C). If misters are combined with the surface fans, the turf surface temperature drops to approximately 80°F (27°C). With fans, however, care must be taken not to allow soil to excessively dry; with misters, increased disease incidence, especially dollar spot, may occur.

Fans work best when installed and used in late-spring before heat and moisture stress start. Ideally, a fan should provide a 3.5 to 4.5 mph (5.6 to 7.2 km/hr) wind speed at the turf canopy, not three inches (7.6 cm) or three feet (0.9 m) above it. Fans placed considerable distances away from and/or elevated above the turf surface seldom provide the necessary air movement at the turf canopy surface to reduce heat stress. Current trends involve placing smaller oscillating fans near or on the collars of greens or placing larger fans just off the collars.

Subsurface Movement

One of the latest management tools in bentgrass/Poa management is providing subsurface air movement through drainage tiles (Figure 19–17). Blowers connected to the drainage tile force air through this system into the rootzone mixture. This system should be considered on courses grown in especially hot areas as the air movement displaces potentially toxic gasses like carbon dioxide, methane, and hydrogen sulfide and provides deep soil oxygenation. A 3 to 4°F (~2°C) drop in soil temperature occurs if air is pushed through the system (Figure 19–18). This drop depends on air movement speed, pipe length, and pipe depth in the soil, which influence the temperatures in the pipe. It is not clear if this change in temperature is sufficient to overcome indirect summer heat-related stress. The blowers can also be reversed to provide suction used to extract these gasses and remove excess surface and soil moisture.

This system works best on sand-based rootzones with a properly installed network of underground drainage pipe. For many older greens, the installation and use of this system may be cost

FIGURE 19–17
Subsurface air movement
helps dry greens, cool them,
and displace toxic gases such
as carbon dioxide and
methane.

FIGURE 19–18
Reductions in soil
temperature occur by either
injecting or evacuating air on
a bentgrass golf green
compared to ambient air and
soil temperatures. Injecting
air tends to lower soil
temperatures more than
evacuating them
(*HortScience*, 2003, 38).

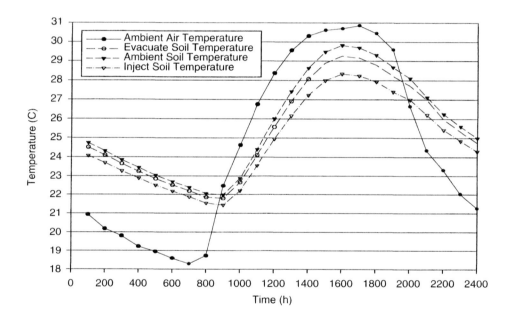

prohibitive. In addition, the possibility of quickly drying out soil must be considered and monitored when this system is used.

Poa annua Greens

Promoting Root Growth

Poa annua roots are woefully shallow during summer months; thus, maximum root growth should be encouraged in fall when maximum rooting naturally occurs. Bentgrass, meanwhile, typically produces its peak root production in spring since it does not seed profusely like Poa alone.

Granular fertilizer products work best to grow roots and should be used predominately during fall, winter, and early spring. Sprayable products produce desirable color and shoot growth, but may negatively affect root growth when used long term. Two to three pounds of nitrogen per 1,000 square feet (9.8 to 15 kg N/100 m^2) should be applied during fall months to promote rooting. The majority of this should be a water-soluble nitrogen source to quickly release and encourage plants to maximize rooting. Save the foliar fertilization for summer when a small boost in color and shoot growth is needed to help the Poa plants recover from ball marks, traffic, and other stresses. Annual fall applications of gypsum (calcium sulfate) following aerfication at 15 pounds of product per 1,000 square feet (73 kg N/100 m^2) also helps relieve any salt (fertilizer) stress and flocculates the soil.

Aerify

Again, to maximize root growth, aggressive aerification practices are necessary to reduce bulk density and improve soil porosity. Poa greens should be aggressively aerified in fall and early spring months. Mini- or needle-tine aerification should occur in late spring and this, combined with topdressing, helps to smooth the putting surface during the Poa seeding season and helps water infiltration and percolation during summer months. If aggressively deep-tine aerifying Poa greens, Poa turf can sustain excessive ripping and tearing, especially to its root system, thereby requiring an extended healing time. The optimum time to deep-tine aerify is the fall or spring months. However, with Poa greens, plants may have little roots to withstand deep-tine aerification in early fall. If performed in spring, it may require extensive time for turf recovery as soil temperatures are typically still low.

Topdressing with sand following aerification helps to smooth the greens and increase desirable soil pore space. In addition to heavier applications following aerification, light applications at three-week intervals throughout the playing season also work well.

During summer months, superintendents should use a hydroject aerifier whenever possible. These machines provide pores or channels for root growth and improve water infiltration and soil percolation with little disruption to the playing surface. Weekly hydrojecting should be performed during the summer months; a machine equipped with the biggest nozzles available works best.

Water Management

With shallow-rooted Poa greens, water management becomes critical. Excessively wet greens encourage disease, soil compaction, and other problems while overly dry greens will stress the shallow-rooted, drought-sensitive Poa. Extensive hand watering will be required to maintain uniform soil moisture and should predominate a summer watering program.

Winter Blankets

In the northern regions of the United States, winter blankets are often used to lengthen the favorable soil temperatures necessary to promote rooting. This should be performed during times when traditional daytime temperatures will not rise above 40°F (4.4°C). If covers remain in place during warmer temperatures, excessive shoot growth and disease or scalding conditions may develop. Always apply a preventive fungicide for brown patch and snow mold prior to blanket installation.

PGRs and Herbicide Use

Desirable Poa should be allowed to grow unregulated during summer stress months. Plant growth regulators (PGRs) should only be used during periods of active growth (fall and spring months). Summer and winter applications may overregulate or prevent desirable growth. Herbicide use should also be carefully timed. Preemergence herbicides should be used only on well-established Poa plants. If used during fall or spring months, these materials may retard active root growth. Postemergence herbicides and hand weeding may be necessary if preemergence herbicides fail to provide an appropriate level of control.

Traffic Damage

Most Poa courses have a nonmetal spike golf shoe policy, especially during summer months. To further reduce traffic stress, Poa greens must be walk-mowed during summer, using solid rather than grooved roller or grooming devices. Additionally, the perimeter clean-up lap should only be performed every other day. The cup-changer should also carefully level the moved plugs during course set-up to prevent the "scalped plug syndrome" which may result in turf loss.

Diseases

Several diseases can be chronic problems on bentgrass/Poa greens. Most diseases occur in summer, although some also occur in other seasons. A fertilization program consisting of constant but low levels of nitrogen in summer and the use of slow-release liquids help reduce the majority of disease problems.

Root and crown rot are the diseases most often affecting bentgrass in stressful summer conditions and result from various species of *Pythium, Rhizoctonia,* and most recently, *Colletotrichum* (commonly referred to as **Anthracnose**). Root and crown injury from these diseases stress bentgrass even more, beginning a cycle of stress-disease-stress. These diseases form a complex and, when combined with other stresses such as heavy traffic, low mowing heights, poor drainage, and poor fertility, bentgrass can succumb to the summer bentgrass decline syndrome. Dollar spot is also a constant disease, especially during periods of warm weather and cool nights that produce heavy morning dews and during times when bentgrass is not aggressively growing. Some cultivars (e.g., Crenshaw) are more susceptible than others, so check with your local turfgrass specialist regarding disease resistance.

Summer Decline

Summer bentgrass/Poa decline is the term used to describe a physiological/disease complex (Plate 19–3). Symptoms begin as a gradual discoloration, loss in vigor, and decline in shoot density. Eventually large areas with slowed or stopped growth can be affected. In conjunction with shoot decline, root systems become extremely short (<2 inches, 5 cm, in many cases) and may eventually rot. Summer decline usually begins in low-lying areas with poor or restricted air circulation and areas with compacted soils and/or poor surface and subsurface drainage (Plate 19–4). Algae and/or moss often quickly invade decline areas. Various summer patch diseases may be confused with decline symptoms. However, patch diseases usually occur in isolated locations and have fairly distinguishable borders. Anthracnose, which primarily affects Poa, initially resembles the early development stages of localized dry spot. Leaves (or borders) in infected areas turn a brownish-bronze color and the plants eventually collapse in irregular-shaped patches. These patches, like Pythium blight, often are streaked from mowing equipment or water movement into long, thin, brown stripes. The black fruiting bodies of the fungus (called **setae**) are often observed in crowns of infected plants during hot weather.

Cultural Control

Preventive measures are the easiest with summer turfgrass decline, as with all fungal-disease related problems. Promoting optimal root growth before summer starts is the first step for preventive control. This includes avoiding or reducing excessive heat and moisture stress, providing proper soil aeration and air circulation, preventing excess thatch/mat development, raising the mowing height, and routinely skipping mowing (Figure 19–19).

Fungicides

Bentgrass/Poa management during summer often requires preventive disease control measures since curative ones often are too late or work too slowly. Typically this involves beginning a fungicide program in late spring when bentgrass/Poa-lethal temperatures approach those listed in Table 19–1. Normally, in early and late summer, dollar spot disease is the most prevalent disease. During hotter and drier summer months, disease strategies shift from dollar spot to brown patch, Pythium, and Anthracnose. During this time, products providing brown patch control are tank-mixed with those providing Pythium root rot control since these diseases often occur simultaneously. Usually a 10- to 14-day spray interval is needed for this preventive measure. Superintendents should rotate between chemical classes to minimize the chance of disease resistance. Extra care should be taken when using the sterol inhibitor (e.g., triadmefon-Bayleton; myclobutanil-Eagle; fenarimol-Rubigan; Lynx; and others) fungicides on bentgrass/Poa. Summer applications of these materials can reduce bentgrass/Poa growth and result in thin turf and an increase in algae (Figure 19–20).

FIGURE 19–19 The speckling effect of healthy bentgrass in aerification holes is observed in a heat-stressed green. Aerification holes enhance growing environments by providing balanced soil moisture to soil oxygen/gas levels.

FIGURE 19–20 A bentgrass injury from applying demethylation inhibitor (DMI) (also called ergosterol biosynthesis inhibitors, or SBIs) fungicides during heat stress.

Interestingly, a combination of the two fungicides, mancozeb plus fosetyl-Al, often improves summer bentgrass density, color, and disease suppression, but these results do not necessarily always occur. A pigment in the mancozeb (Fore) is at least partially responsible for this. This blue inert pigment, copper phthalocyanine, is an insoluble organic pigment (#15) added to make the naturally yellow-colored mancozeb have a green hue.

Chipco Signature is a combination of fosetyl-Al plus a similar pigment, chlorinated phthalocyanine, which is soluble. These two phthalocyanine pigments are very similar in size and composition as the molecules heme and chlorophyll. Therefore, they are believed to somehow improve the efficiency or enhance the plant's photosynthesis capability. Signature appears most beneficial as a growth promoter when the plant is growing under stress. For example, superior bentgrass is typically observed when used for summer-stress applications. In addition to their fungicidal properties, these materials also may contribute to soil nutrients since they break down to phosphorus, manganese, and zinc. As mentioned earlier, tissue testing should be performed to determine the status of these and other nutrients.

One should remember, however, that successful bentgrass/Poa growth, especially through fungicide use, is still based on combining good science with the art of turfgrass management.

Success with these and many other products on one golf course, in one year, or on one green on a golf course does not mean similar successes will universally occur. Too many unknown or poorly understood biological parameters influence this. Fungicide strategies constantly change; therefore, the reader should consult the Extension Turf Specialist in his or her state for the latest available and recommended material(s).

Bentgrass/Poa is susceptible to other diseases in addition to summer decline. The reader should refer to Chapter 22 for further information.

Nematodes

Nematodes are microscopic, nonsegmented roundworms that are generally transparent and colorless. They are essentially invisible to the unaided eye, appear transparent when viewed under magnification, and damage plants as they feed by puncturing the cells of the root system with their stylet (a hollow, oral spear), injecting digestive juices into cells, and drawing liquid contents from cells as a food source.

Since nematodes damage turfgrass root growth and development, symptoms of injury often go unnoticed until soil water becomes limiting. These symptoms are often confused with environmental stress symptoms; thus, they may be difficult to diagnose. Nematode populations are also distributed very erratically in soil (great variation in numbers within a few feet is common), so aboveground symptoms also appear in areas of irregular size and shape. Nematode damage rarely is uniform or ends abruptly; a problem that has distinct, sharp boundaries between good and poor turf is probably not caused by nematodes.

Nematodes most often associated with bentgrass include: Sting (*Belonolaimus longicaudatus*), Lance (*Hoplolaimus* species), and Root-Knot (*Meloidogyne* species). Activity is generally greatest on bentgrass/Poa in mid-to-late spring, and again in early fall. These times follow active growth of turfgrass roots that subsequently supports higher soil nematode levels. The result of nematode feeding becomes most apparent when conditions become unfavorable (e.g., hot and dry) for the turfgrass. It may be prudent to sample your turf monthly during the growing season to determine the fluctuation of nematode populations. This will allow treatment before typical population peaks.

Analysis of soil and plant tissue is the only sure way to determine if, and what kinds of, nematodes are present and the level of risk they may pose to turf. Most states have an assay laboratory associated with the land-grant university. Other laboratories also provide nematode assay service; consult them about the services they offer, as well as gather instructions for preparing and submitting samples to them.

Control of nematodes begins before the green is planted. Only nematode-free soil should ever be introduced into or onto a golf green. All practical means of preventing the introduction of nematodes into a golf green should be followed, including using nematode-free (or fumigated) soil mix, topdressing material, and planting material. Once nematodes become established, chemical control is erratic, often unavailable, and expensive. Nematode damage to roots also adds additional stress to bentgrass/Poa survival, especially during summer months. Soils should be fumigated prior to planting and, if sprigs or sod is used to plant a green, these should be soil free. Refer to Chapter 24 for more information on this subject.

Weed Control

Herbicide Use

Using preemergence herbicides on bentgrass/Poa in stressful areas is a difficult choice. On one hand, if not used, annual grasses such as goosegrass and annual bluegrass may eventually outcompete the turf. On the other hand, most preemergence herbicides act by preventing cell division when the growing point of the plant comes into contact with the chemical. Selective tolerance does not exist between weeds and desirable turfgrass roots trying to grow through this layer. Since most creeping bentgrass/Poa varieties have extremely shallow rooting depths during summer, herbicides applied on the soil surface may further inhibit this rooting. Read the label and consult with your state turfgrass specialist before putting any herbicide on bentgrass/Poa, especially during or just prior to summer heat stress. Postemergence herbicides are used only as a last resort, since turf tolerance to these during summer stress is poor. Refer to Chapter 25 for additional herbicide use strategies on greens.

Bermudagrass Encroachment

One of the hardest weeds to control in bentgrass is bermudagrass encroachment (Plate 19–5). Bermudagrass from surrounding collars often invades weakly competitive bentgrass greens during summer. During construction, collars should be established on rootzone media identical to the putting greens. They should then be planted to bentgrass and/or perennial ryegrass to provide a buffer against invasive bermudagrass. Golf courses in southern climates often sod zoysiagrass on the outside perimeter of the collar to provide an additional buffer against bermudagrass encroachment. Clubs also often heavily overseed bermudagrass collars with ryegrass to help suppress the bermudagrass throughout most of the year.

Bermudagrass removal involves edging, mechanical hand picking, or physically removing the undesirable grass and resodding. Proper timing of certain herbicides such as siduron (Tupersan) or ethofumesate (Progress) and plant growth retardants like flurprimido/(cutless) help suppress bermudagrass encroachment. Monthly applications of siduron beginning in spring with the resumed growth of bermudagrass work best. Summer applications do not appear to have much effect, but treatments should resume in late summer until the expected heavy frost that causes the bermudagrass to go dormant. An embedded steel track system that surrounds the green is also available where a metal blade is run around the green periodically to sever encroaching bermudagrass stolons and rhizomes. Although effective, costs, installation disruptions, and diligence/dedication in use should be considered before use.

OTHER CONSIDERATIONS

Segregation and Patch Development

Penncross bentgrass, the most widely planted cultivar, is a polysynthetic from three parental clones that produces nine possible crosses. Only the first generation of this seed is certified. Penncross greens will eventually (within five years) segregate into distinct mottled patches, which can sometimes give the false appearance of disease or grass contamination, and may add to surface grain. Lightly verticutting and reseeding each fall with one pound per 1,000 square feet (5 kg/100 m^2) will help mask this mottled appearance and help thicken weak areas thinned by summer stress. While Penncross has frequently been observed to segregate, it is likely the newer bentgrass cultivars may also segregate after several years of use (Plate 19–6).

Reseeding

As mentioned, greens often experience loss of shoot density following the summer-stress period and require seeding to regain density. Some superintendents are also interseeding newer improved cultivars into older ones in an attempt to increase the genetic pool and improve stress resistance. Seeding requires soil preparation to provide a suitable seedbed. Various intensities of aerification, verticutting, and topdressing are required for success, and it may take several years to successfully convert greens to the newer desired cultivar. Recent research on this topic indicates that only limited success (10 to 15 percent) in converting older cultivars to newer cultivars can be achieved while the green is still being used. The combination of close, frequent mowing and existing plant competition make it difficult for seedlings to establish and survive. The best chance of success would be to seed in late summer when the existing bentgrass/Poa is at its weakest. Competition from existing hardy Poa seedlings that are germinating at this time of year will also be a challenge.

Nonmetal Spiked Golf Shoes

To reduce extensive damage to the putting surface caused by the metal spikes of most traditionally used golf shoes, many courses now recommend (or require) only nonmetal spiked shoes or soft spikes be worn during part or all of the year. Needless to say, this has caused considerable debate between management and players. Agronomically, spikeless shoes worn during the summer-stress period reduce or eliminate cleat marks across greens, resulting in a much smoother, healthier turf. Potential drawbacks, however, include reduced traction during aggressive swings and while walking on grassy slopes or wet wooden walkways. However, with time, most players who wear these spike alternatives become accustomed to them, adjust their games accordingly, and enjoy their added comfort and reduced damage to the putting surface.

Turf Nursery

An on-site turf nursery is highly recommended and nearly a requirement when growing bentgrass/Poa in stressful areas. This allows repair of injured or dead turf on greens with the same grasses, and provides a test area for any new products or grasses being considered. The size of the nursery should be equal to or larger than the largest green on the property, or at least 10,000 square feet (929 m²) in size. The rootzone media used for this nursery should be identical to what is used on the regular greens. Furthermore, this area should receive identical management practices as regular greens.

Adequate Financial Resources

Needless to say, one of the most important prerequisites when growing bentgrass/Poa outside its naturally adapted region is adequate financial resources. Many of the cultural practices necessary to maintain bentgrass/Poa greens require significantly more labor, irrigation, fertilizer, mowing, and chemical inputs than other greens. The major cost, however, will be associated with labor. When monitoring summer stress on greens at a bentgrass/Poa golf course, one to three additional employees will be needed from May through early October. These employees will be primarily monitoring moisture conditions, hand watering, and scouting for localized dry spots and disease symptoms. Additionally, they probably will be assisting in walk-mowing greens each morning.

Weekly preventive fungicide applications should also be budgeted during the summer from late May through early September. Where air movement is an issue, fans are used on the greens from May through October. These have installation and power costs. Also, at least one additional employee is needed during the summer to repair damage from ball marks and to hand-pick weeds. The additional cost on an annual basis to maintain bentgrass/Poa greens is easily $75,000+ more than for bermudagrass putting greens, and this total does not include subsurface blower fans connected to the tile line of problem greens. These systems are expensive and also require installation, electricity, and routine maintenance, plus employees to use them. The facility management needs to consider if the cost of maintaining bentgrass/Poa outside its region of adaptation is financially sound in terms of additional rounds played and revenue generated. If it is, then a substantial financial commitment to the appropriate management practices needs to be made. If a sufficient financial commitment is not made, then in most years a degree of turf failure and loss in revenue due to poor putting quality can be expected.

Sympathetic Management and Members

Not only does a golf course need adequate financial resources but it also needs management and/or members who are sympathetic to the dynamic seasonal life cycle and cultural requirements of bentgrass/Poa. As mentioned earlier, bentgrass/Poa will survive better during summer months outside its natural region of adaptation if the mowing height is raised. Uninformed members should not dictate lower mowing heights to increase ball roll and ultimately increase green speed at the expense of turf health. This may be difficult when a vocal group of low-handicap members or regular patrons demand fast greens. If this occurs, turf will decline. Also, chronic "hot" spots on greens have to be hand watered quickly before the grass dies, regardless of play, which can be difficult when the golf course is full of players. However, this is a necessary management practice. Additionally, golfers hate nothing more than aerification, which can produce a temporarily bumpy putting surface. However, during summer months or in periods of excess rainfall, aerification may be necessary to maintain drainage and ensure proper oxygen diffusion so turf roots survive. Fans also are annoying to many golfers, as some models are noisy and sometimes hard to play around.

Political communication skills are needed by the superintendent to educate the membership or golfers on bentgrass/Poa growth requirements. The superintendent must keep the channels of communication open. Green committee members should be personally informed of vital cultural management practices and any situations that affect play. Providing members with a relevant article or research summary in a monthly newsletter has proven extremely beneficial and reduces confusion and misunderstandings by uninformed members. The scheduling of key tournaments should involve input from the superintendent along with the golf professional so critical management practices like core aeration can be properly scheduled and the best playing conditions possible are provided.

Experience, research, and trial by fire have proven the aforementioned principles are required when growing bentgrass/Poa outside its naturally adapted area (Table 19–3). Members and management should be fully informed and aware of the benefits and potential detriments of attempting this daunting task. Management and members should also be sympathetic to the superintendent's struggle to provide acceptable greens during summer stress, especially if the tools and/or budgets listed in this chapter are lacking. Many successful superintendents have maintained high-quality bentgrass/Poa greens in very unfavorable environments. In the end, however, Mother Nature still has the final word in how easy or difficult any given year will be.

TABLE 19–3 *Summary of cultural practices for bentgrass/*Poa annua *golf greens.*

Practice	Description
Fertilization	
Optimum timing for nitrogen fertilization	(Feb. through March) + May + (Sept. through Nov.)
Damaging response to excessive nitrogen fertilizer	June through August (during summer stress)
Yearly nitrogen requirements (lbs N/1,000 sq.ft.)	3 to 8 pounds nitrogen per 1,000 square feet (15 to 39 kg/100 m^2)
Monthly nitrogen requirement (lbs N/1,000 sq.ft.)	0.5 to 0.7 pounds nitrogen per 1,000 square feet (2.5 to 3.4 kg/100 m^2) per growing month
Fertilizer application	Slow-release (primarily) granular + liquids for color
Liquid versus granular fertilizer use	0.1 to 0.3 pounds nitrogen per 1,000 square feet (0.5 to 1.5 kg N/100 m^2) every 10 to 14 days for liquid carrier during summer or 0.3 to 0.7 pounds nitrogen per 1,000 square feet (1.5 to 3.4 kg N/100 m^2) every three to four weeks in fall and spring for a slow-release granular carrier
Acceptable pH range	6.0 to 6.5
Acceptable phosphorus levels	Low to medium (excess levels encourage micronutrient deficiencies and *Poa annua*)
Optimum potassium levels	Medium (improves drought and heat tolerance)
Cultural requirements	
Overseeding	Generally not unless summer stress has thinned the stand
Irrigation requirements	Moisten full rootzone depth, rewetting just prior to wilting; supplement with heavy hand watering of hot (dry) spots
Air circulation requirement	Required where natural air movement is restricted in heat-stressed environments
Cultivation timing optimum	September through November + March through May
Mowing height	0.100 to 0.156 (1/10 to 5/32) in. (2.5 to 4 mm)
Mowing frequency	Daily, reduced to five times weekly during stress
Mowing pattern	Changed (rotated) daily
Mower type	Walk-behind during stress periods, triplex during periods of active growth
Clippings	Removed
Thatch/mat control	Frequent topdressing, lightly vertical mowing and grooming, regular aerification
Compaction control	Use a predominate sand-base rootzone during construction, routine aerification, limit play (traffic) during wet conditions
Topdressing	Light (0.2 yd^3/1,000 ft^2, 0.17 m^3/100 m^2) but frequently (weekly) during active growth, water-in; monthly at 0.3 to 0.5 cubic yards per 1,000 square feet (0.25 to 0.4 m^3/100 m^2) during slowed growth
Aerification (coring)	Performed two to six times annually with at least one deep tine yearly; stop within 30 days of cold or hot weather
Regular (deeper) verticutting	Once or twice yearly, once in late winter/early spring and another during active fall growth
Grooming	Performed weekly with ultradwarf cultivars except during periods of extreme stress
Slicing	Performed weekly in two directions to reduce surface compaction and algae and to facilitate soil air exchange and infiltration

CHAPTER
20

Managing Bermudagrass Golf Greens

INTRODUCTION

Bermudagrass has traditionally been the grass of choice for most golf courses in tropical and subtropical areas, as well as many other areas of the temperate growing zones. Bermudagrass provides a smooth putting surface and resists many pests that other grasses like bentgrass or *Poa annua* are often susceptible to. New dwarf bermudagrass cultivars offer similar short mowing height options that traditionally have been provided by bentgrass or Poa. In addition, bermudagrass is not as sensitive to heat, salinity, and moisture stress as bentgrass and is generally more tolerant to management practices such as aerification, topdressing, and vertical mowing. Soil pH for bermudagrass is between 5.5 and 7.0, although it often tolerates a wider range than this.

Bermudagrass begins going dormant when air temperatures approach 50°F (10°C). This dormancy requires most clubs to overseed with a cool-season grass in late summer/early fall to provide winter color. Overseeding, however, can be a disruptive process that often requires clubs to close for several days to prepare the bermudagrass seedbed, perform the seeding, and provide postseeding management such as extensive watering. The overseeding also goes through another transition period in the spring, as the overseeded grass begins to weaken with the onset of heat stress and the bermudagrass gradually greens-up and fills-in. The spring transition can be difficult when temperatures do not follow normal patterns, often causing premature thinning of the overseeded grass before the bermudagrass has had the necessary temperatures to encourage its recovery.

Bermudagrass also has been susceptible to periodic "winter kill" where freezes below 10 to 15°F (−12 to −15°C) can kill or thin the stand. This typically is more of a problem on fairways and roughs. Depending on the location, winter kill is most severe in the northern and western areas of the transition zone, especially in shade-prone situations.

In recent years, mutants or off-types of grasses in previously pure bermudagrass stands have occurred (Plate 20–1), presumably from the chance occurrence of mutation in the parent material or possibly contamination through mechanical means or encroachment from collars. As mowing heights have been lowered below the adapted heights for Tifgreen and Tifdwarf bermudagrass, mutations or biotypes have emerged that could survive these conditions. Tifway II, Tifgreen II, and TifEagle are induced mutations of the original grasses created by exposing parent material to artificially high levels of radiation. Tifdwarf, FloraDwarf, and Pee Dee 102 bermudagrasses are believed to be natural mutants from Tifgreen bermudagrass. Champion, Mini Verde, Reesegrass, MS Supreme, Classic dwarf, and others are selections from previously planted Tifdwarf greens.

One often unrecognized characteristic of bermudagrass is its inherent poor shade tolerance. Many courses have trees that are small when the course is constructed. Over time, as the trees enlarge, they cast larger and longer shadows that can interfere with normal bermudagrass growth and development. This is especially true in late fall and winter when the sun is lowest on the horizon and the overseeded grass is also contributing to shade. Courses, therefore, should provide a minimum of eight hours of full sunlight on each green throughout the year. Morning sun should also be emphasized as this encourages early growth each day, helps dry the dew to minimize disease problems, and thaws frost so play can resume earlier. Morning sun is also important in summer as clouds typically buildup by mid-day, severely limiting the quality and quantity of light reaching the green by early afternoon.

CULTURAL PRACTICES FOR BERMUDAGRASS GREENS

Green Construction

Precise soil moisture control is not as critical for growing and maintaining bermudagrass as it is for bentgrass/Poa. However, the chances of growing successful bermudagrass increases with the quality of green construction. Many bermudagrass greens were initially constructed as "push-ups" from native soil or built with the fill resulting from pond construction or creek excavation, which often contain high levels of silt and clay. These greens have often proven unsatisfactory in today's market where the pressure to open soon after rainfall events is greater, and due to increased play, soil compaction has also increased.

Minimum construction specifications for bermudagrass greens include those described in Chapter 8. Typically, finding the right sand is the key ingredient in successful green construction. A sand free of silt and clay that does not excessively compact is highly desirable. Sands should be extensively laboratory tested during the planning stage to ensure quality. Green construction as outlined in Chapter 8 is currently considered the highest standard possible, but it is often difficult to locate each component, difficult to install, and is expensive. This type of profile has proven more beneficial for bentgrass, which requires more precise moisture management than bermudagrass.

Mowing

Bermudagrass greens are maintained at heights between one-eighth and one-fourth inch (3.2 and 6.4 mm) and are mowed daily. Older bermudagrass cultivars such as Tifgreen are mowed routinely between 3/16 (0.188) and 1/4 inch (0.25); these are only mowed shorter (e.g., 5/32 or 0.156 inch, 4 mm) for short-term periods such as weekend tournaments. Tifdwarf is routinely mowed at approximately 3/16 inch (4.8 mm) while newer dwarf cultivars such as TifEagle, Champion, Mini Verde, FloraDwarf, and others tolerate routine mowing heights between 1/8 and 3/16 inch (3.2 and 4.8 mm). Mowing height alone, however, should not be the only means of providing a smooth, quick putting surface. As outlined in Chapter 17, numerous techniques are available besides mowing height in providing the desired putting surface and should be integrated into a total green management plan. Walk-behind mowers are often used, especially with mowing heights below 3/16 inch (4.8 mm), as it becomes difficult to set triplex mowers at these low heights without scalping and excessive compaction. Clippings are normally removed and the mower pattern changed or rotated daily to reduce grain.

Irrigation/Water Management

Good water management is a key component of any golf course management plan. Maximizing the time between irrigations without producing significant moisture stress encourages a deeper root system. Fortunately, bermudagrass is not as sensitive to precise water management as bentgrass/ Poa, since bermudagrass does not require routine hand watering and extra labor to check for "hot spots" hourly during summer months. As stated, the recommended philosophy is to utilize heavy and infrequent applications, thereby allowing the grass/soil to dry-down between irrigations. Most superintendents prefer to keep their greens slightly on the dry side to minimize disease occurrence, encourage deeper rooting, and avoid algae. Drier greens also absorb summer thunderstorms and other rainfall events better than saturated greens. It generally is easier to apply water when needed rather than trying to remove it when excessive.

Steps in formulating an irrigation strategy include:

1. Calibrate an irrigation system's output and distribution uniformity (or DU).
2. Determine daily ET rates or soil moisture status.
3. Accurately track daily rainfall and ET rates so a water budget can be set up and followed.
4. When irrigation is needed, use the appropriate crop coefficient percent (0.75 to 0.85) of daily ET rate and adjust for distribution uniformity (DU) of the irrigation system.
5. Make adjustments for rainfall, varying microclimates, and forecasted weather.

Determining Irrigation Rates and Frequency

In addition to the application rate and uniformity, the turf manager should know how much water the turf is using. This can be determined using reference ET from a weather station/computer system plus a crop coefficient specific for the turf species or with data from an atmometer or other devices. Historical weather information may also provide reasonable estimates of average water use. Managers also need to know where the roots are in the soil profile and approximately how much available water is held by the soil.

The amount of water needed to moisten the soil to a given depth depends on soil type, water infiltration and percolation rates, and surface slope. Soils that are severely sloped, compacted, or clayey in nature may have low infiltration rates. These soils, therefore, may not be able to absorb the required amount of irrigation at one time. Managers may have to irrigate using multiple cycles until the desired amount is applied. After an irrigation, managers should double-check the depth of moisture penetration using a soil probe so they can fine-tune their timing.

Evaporation during hot, windy, and dry periods can reduce irrigation efficiency. Superintendents can avoid this by irrigating early in the morning before the temperature rises and humidity drops. Early morning irrigation also removes dew from the leaves, and helps prevent diseases favored by irrigating in the evening.

Water Quality

Another potential problem with all greens is a gradual buildup of salinity from the use of high pH or bicarbonate-containing irrigation water, effluent sources, or brackish water. This is magnified when highly soluble fertilizer sources are used at relatively light but frequent rates and a lack of frequent, heavy rainfall occurs to periodically leach the salt below the rootzone.

To combat potential salinity buildup, superintendents have modified their watering practices from light, frequent applications in summer to heavier, infrequent ones. Greens also must drain relatively well so salts can be leached below the rootzone by heavy rainfall or by heavy hand watering. Using low salt-containing water sources also helps. Coastal courses or those using effluent water sources should closely monitor their salt levels, especially during summer.

In recent years, fertigation and foliar feeding (or spoon feeding) by liquid fertilizer sources have become popular to help better regulate grass color and growth during summer. Fertigation allows many frequent fertilizer applications at low rates. Fertigation may be used as a primary source of fertility or to supplement a dry fertilizer program. Fertigation also allows a turf manager to spoon feed the turf without weighing fertilizers and driving over the area multiple times during the year. Leaching of nutrients is minimized because of the low application rate. A potential problem is having to irrigate in order to fertilize the greens, whether or not irrigation is needed. Spoon feeding then becomes an alternative.

There are many materials that can be added to the fertilizer holding tank without negative results. Micronutrients are often added through fertigation systems. Due to solubility problems, micronutrients are often chelated to help them stay in solution. Surfactants, which may aid in water utilization and therefore nutrient efficiency, are often added directly to the fertilizer mixture. Before adding anything to the tank, test the compatibility of materials using the jar test. To do this, take some fertilizer solution from the holding tank and put it into a jar, and then add the material in question at a recommended rate to the fertilizer solution. Observe for any change in composition for at least a day. If no change occurs, it is most likely safe to add the material to the fertilizer holding tank at a similar concentration.

Fertigation and foliar feeding also reduce the salinity load on the grass. Buffering the water pH from 6.0 to 6.5 and using periodic light application of gypsum also helps reduce the salinity stress. High bicarbonate water is also commonly treated by artificially acidifying it, often by sulfur injection. This technology is rapidly evolving and dramatic effects can be realized.

Also influencing water quality use are soil water infiltration rates, differential salinity tolerance of the turfgrass species, and nutrient content (e.g., nitrogen, phosphorus, and potassium). Refer to Chapter 5 for additional information on water quality.

Fertilizing

To promote recovery from traffic and clipping removal, and to fulfill clientele color expectations, bermudagrass requires ample nutrients. Furthermore, many courses are located in areas with extended growing seasons, high annual rainfall, and predominately sandy soils that increase the precision of using the right amounts and ratios of nutrients.

Questions to ask when developing a turfgrass fertility program include:

1. What fertilizer analysis and source is best?
2. What application method(s) is (are) best for my course?
3. What rate of this fertilizer should be used?
4. What timing and frequency will provide optimum results?

Timing

Fertilization programs should provide adequate levels of essential nutrients to sustain growth, as well as acceptable turf quality and color. Improper timing and/or rates of fertilizer influence turfgrass stress tolerance and recuperative ability. In addition, disease occurrence and severity often are closely linked to the amounts and the timing of fertilization programs. For example, dollar spot (*Moellerodiscus* and *Lanzia* spp.) and Helminthosporium leaf spot (*Drechslera* and *Bipolaris* spp.) diseases often are correlated with periods of inactive or slowed turf growth. A fertilizer application containing soluble nitrogen often promotes the turfgrass to outgrow these disease symptoms, eliminating the need for fungicide applications. In contrast, excessive fertilization of overseeded ryegrass, roughstalk bluegrass (*Poa trivialis*), and bentgrass often promotes the occurrence of brown patch (*Rhizoctonia* spp.) and Pythium (*Pythium* spp.) diseases.

Proper fertilization, along with providing healthy disease- and stress-free turf, provides an acceptable playing surface. As a rule, excessive fertilization with nitrogen will not only be agronomically detrimental to the turfgrass, but will drastically slow ball roll and draw complaints from players. Exceptions, such as certain high traffic greens and tees (e.g., par-3) or newly constructed greens, require higher nitrogen fertilization to promote turf recovery or grow-in.

Timing is partially based on the minimum and optimum temperatures necessary for turfgrass growth. Table 20–1 lists growth temperatures for cool- and warm-season turfgrasses. If temperatures are outside the growth range of the grass, fertilizer applications will be inefficiently utilized.

Nitrogen Rates

A general yearly range of nitrogen needs for bermudagrass golf greens is from 8 to 18 pounds nitrogen per 1,000 square feet (0.5 to 1.5 lbs N/1,000 sq.ft. per growing month, 24 to 74 kg N/100 m²). Courses with sufficient resources, excessive traffic, sandy soils, older bermudagrass cultivars, and elevated demands from players would use the higher rate range. Those courses interested in main-

TABLE 20–1 *Air temperatures affecting turfgrass shoot growth and soil temperatures at four inches (10 cm) affecting root growth (McCarty, 2001).*

Turfgrass	Shoot growth		Root growth	
	Minimum	Optimum	Minimum	Optimum
		°F*		
Warm-season grasses	55	80 to 95	50 to 60	75 to 85
Cool-season grasses	40	60 to 75	33	50 to 65

*°C = °F-32 (5/9).

taining a less-intensive playing surface, or those that have ultradwarf cultivars or limited labor and financial resources, should use nitrogen rates in the lower range. Exceptions to these values may occur. For example, courses recovering from excessive traffic, pest or low-temperature stresses, or that are establishing new greens may require higher (approx. 25 percent more) nitrogen rates than those listed until their grass is sufficiently reestablished.

Frequency

The percentages of nitrogen fertilizer applied to warm-season turfgrasses during the year are listed in Table 20–2. In general, to maintain optimum color and density during periods of active growth, highly maintained bermudagrass golf greens need approximately one-half pound soluble nitrogen per 1,000 square feet (2.4 kg N/100 m^2) every 7 to 14 days. For those courses without these resources and for those that have lower expectations, adequate bermudagrass can be maintained with one-half pound nitrogen per 1,000 square feet (2.4 kg N/100 m^2) applied every 14 to 21 days during periods of active growth. On intensively maintained courses, higher rates (e.g., 1 lb N per 1,000 sq.ft. [4.9 kg N/100 m^2] every 7 to 14 days) may be necessary to encourage quicker turf recovery during times of heavy play. However, these higher rates can lead to other problems. Excessive thatch can quickly accumulate, putting speeds will be slower since more leaf area will be produced, and a decrease in turfgrass rooting often occurs.

As discussed later, fertilizer rates for ultradwarf cultivars are reduced to approximately one-half pound nitrogen per 1,000 square feet (24 kg N/100 m^2) for granular fertilizer per growing month with slow-release sources. This is usually supplemented with 0.1 to 0.25 pound nitrogen per 1,000 square feet (0.5 to 1.2 kg N/100 m^2) of a liquid source every 7 to 14 days. This program helps maintain consistent color and growth rates, reduces scalping, and minimizes thatch/mat accumulation. Due to their density, mini-prilled or greens-grade granular fertilizer should be used on greens to better allow penetration through the turf canopy while not being removed by mowing.

Overseeded Bermudagrass Greens

Once established, overseeded greens should be fertilized every two to three weeks with one-half pound soluble nitrogen (plus potassium) per 1,000 square feet (2.4 kg N/100 m^2) during the fall and winter months. The objective is to provide enough nitrogen to maintain desirable color but not be so excessive as to weaken the overseeded grasses and promote premature growth of bermudagrass. In addition, highly soluble nitrogen use on overseeded grass often leads to excessive turf growth, slower putting speeds, and disease (e.g., brown patch and Pythium) occurrence. Many superintendents have discovered an application of manganese, and possibly iron, can often substitute for a nitrogen application. Two to three ounces (56 to 84 g) of an iron source (such as ferrous sulfate) or one-half ounce (14 g) of manganese sulfate in two to five gallons of water applied per 1,000 square feet (8 to 20 L/100 m^3) provides 10 to 21 days of desirable dark-green color without an undesirable flush of growth. These elements are only foliarly absorbed by plants; hence, the relatively short color response time.

Nitrogen Sources

The source of nitrogen used to fertilize golf greens affects the amount applied at one time. Usually, a combination of soluble and insoluble nitrogen sources is recommended to provide uniform grass growth. Ureaformaldehyde (Nitroform), IBDU, SCU, and polymer-coated materials often are used to provide slow-release, residual nitrogen while a soluble source is used for

TABLE 20–2 *Percentages of nitrogen fertilizer applied to bermudagrass during the year.*

Season	Overseeded	Nonoverseeded
Fall (Sept., Oct., Nov.)	15	10 to 15
Winter (Dec., Jan., Feb.)	15	0
Spring (Mar., Apr., May)	25	35
Summer (June, July, Aug.)	45	50 to 55

quicker turf response. During cold temperatures, IBDU or soluble sources provide the fastest turf response because of their reduced dependence on microorganisms for nitrogen conversion and release.

Spoon (also called **foliar**) **feeding** with liquid fertilizer programs is often used on high sand content areas to help regulate turf growth and color, as well as provide a continuous supply of elements such as nitrogen or potassium that are often easily leached. Nitrogen rates in a foliar feeding program typically range from 0.1 to 0.25 pounds nitrogen per 1,000 square feet (0.5 to 1.2 kg N/100 m^2) on a 7- to 14-day interval. Phosphorus (as phosphoric acid or P_2O_5) is applied at about one-third the rate of nitrogen while potassium rates will be equal to one-half the rate of nitrogen. Other elements, such as magnesium or iron, also may be added by foliar feeding to help regulate and maintain desirable turf color.

Other Elements

Potassium

Potassium often is called the "health" element. Without a relatively available supply of potassium, turfgrasses will be more susceptible to environmental and pest stresses. Root growth also is related to potassium availability. Research and experience indicate N:K ratios on greens should be 1:0.5 to 1:0.75. Excessive potassium may increase the soil salinity levels, especially if the leaching capability is limited, and also compete with the soil exchange sites at the expense of other essential elements such as calcium, magnesium, and iron.

Phosphorus

Soil phosphorus levels tend not to fluctuate as readily as nitrogen or potassium. Soil test results should be used to determine the amount needed for a particular course. Usually zero to four pounds phosphorus per 1,000 square feet (0 to 20 kg P/100 m^2) are needed per year. Phosphorus is generally not very water soluble; therefore, if needed, its efficiency is increased if applications follow aerification. This allows the material to be placed more directly into the rootzone. Phosphorus levels can become limiting during a grow-in situation; an N:P ratio of 1:2 has proven best for bermudagrass sprig grow-in and is normally applied at one pound nitrogen per 1,000 square feet (4.9 kg N/100 m^2) every 7 to 14 days until complete coverage is achieved.

A plant symptom of phosphorus deficiency is the purple discoloration of leaf blades. However, this can be easily confused with purpling that often occurs during cool periods when anthocyanins (bluish pigments) are exposed. Applying a small area or strip with phosphorus fertilizer is an easy way to determine the cause of purpling. If the purpling disappears after phosphorus fertilization, then an application across the entire green is probably warranted. Cool-season turfgrasses often have more of a color response to phosphorus fertilization than warm-season grasses. To take advantage of this, turf to be overseeded should have its yearly phosphorus fertilizer applied during the cool-season months.

Micronutrients

Regular soil and tissue testing is the best preventative approach to solving many of the nutrient deficiency problems. Iron and manganese are two of the most common micronutrient deficiencies turf managers experience. However, **if excessive or indiscriminate amounts of micronutrients are applied or soil pH is excessively low (<5.0), plant toxicity can occur.** An example involves growing turf on old vegetable or fruit production fields. These were often sprayed with fungicides containing copper, zinc, and/or sulfur. Because of their relative immobility (with the exception of sulfur) in soils, residues have become toxic to turfgrasses in some cases.

Golf greens, due to their high sand content, typically have low cation exchange capacities (e.g., ≤5.0 meq/100 g or cmol/kg). Along with soil pH, this key component of a soil test report is important to understand the availability of micronutrients. By default, soils low in pH are saturated with hydrogen ions and are low in calcium, magnesium, potassium, phosphorus, and other cations necessary for plant growth. Thus, low-CEC and low-pH sand soils often experience magnesium deficiency, especially during grow-in of low organic matter containing greens. Conversely, soils low in CEC but high in soil pH (>7.0) may experience iron deficiency. Tissue testing and experimenting with small areas of a green by applying the suspected element are the two best means to determine if this is a problem.

Micronutrient deficiency symptoms can easily be confused with pest occurrence or other stresses. These problems, however, are usually more localized and appear as either irregular spots or in circular patterns. Refer to Chapter 11 for information on applying micronutrients and chelates on greens.

Nonessential Elements

Sodium, aluminum, and arsenic are nonessential elements for turfgrass growth and development. These, in general, become toxic when levels are excessive and should not be applied in supplemental fertilizers.

SOIL ANALYSIS

Soil testing is one of the basic practices of turfgrass management. Soil analysis provides information on relative levels of nutrients, organic matter, pH, soluble salts, and cation exchange capacity. However, variations occur between testing laboratories due to different extraction and analysis techniques. The ranking of the nutrient level, however, should be similar regardless of the extractant. Turf managers should pick a particular laboratory and stick with it, as the chances of the lab switching analysis techniques are thereby minimized. In most cases, these laboratories use university extraction and analysis techniques as well as fertility recommendations. Managers should be careful the chosen laboratory uses information on the calibration of soil test results for the plant material being grown. Recommendations based on plant responses other than turfgrass may provide inaccurate results since turfgrass needs differ from most crops. For example, laboratories not specializing in turfgrass tend to overestimate phosphorus recommendations and underestimate potassium requirements. Also, laboratories use various extraction techniques, depending on their geographical location (soil type). Refer to Chapter 4 for various extraction techniques used for specific nutrients and soil types.

Soil Analysis Report

Cation Exchange Capacity

Soil cation exchange capacity (CEC) measures a soil's capacity to hold the positively charged cations of calcium (Ca^{+2}), magnesium (Mg^{+2}), potassium (K^+), copper (Cu^{+2}), manganese (Mn^{+2}), zinc (Zn^{+2}), and iron (Fe^{+2}), and their relative ability to displace other cations. For example, one meq of potassium is able to displace exactly one meq of magnesium. The unit of measure meq/100 g (or cmol/kg) serves this purpose; cation exchange capacity (CEC) and the total amounts of individual cations may be expressed using these units. Higher values usually represent better soils in terms of fertility because, at high values, the soil attracts and holds more nutrients. Soil constituents that attract cations, such as organic matter and clay, have higher CEC values than sandy soil, which are the least fertile.

Base Saturation (or Cation Saturation)

The degree to which the total CEC sites are saturated with the cations of calcium, magnesium, and potassium, as opposed to the acid cations of hydrogen and aluminum, is referred to as the **base saturation** of a soil. In general, the pH and fertility of a soil increase as the percentage base saturation increases. Higher base saturation generally increases the ease with which cations are absorbed by plants. The greatest availability of most nutrients to plants is in the soil pH range of 6 to 7. In highly acidic soils (pH<5.5), exchangeable aluminum may be present and, along with magnesium and/or hydrogen ions, can suppress plant uptake of calcium or potassium. However, toxic aluminum becomes less prevalent, and therefore less detrimental to the plant, as the base saturation increases.

Nutrient Listing

Most soil analysis reports list nutrient levels by one of two methods: parts per million (ppm) or milliequivalent (meq) per 100 grams of soil. Results for the major elements and micronutrients are most commonly reported in ppm on an elemental basis. For example, an acre of mineral soil, six to seven inches deep, weighs approximately 2 million pounds. Therefore, to convert ppm to approximate pounds per acre, multiply by two.

From these reported nutrient levels, most soil test readings are given a fertility rating index of very low (VL), low (L), medium (M), high (H), or very high (VH). Usually, the division between medium and high is the critical value. Above this point there is no expected plant response to added fertilizer, while below this point increasing amounts of fertilizer are needed with decreasing levels. Chapter 11 summarizes the recommended ranges for nutrient levels using the Mehlich-I extractant procedure. The reader should note differences occur between plants, soils, locations, management practices, and laboratory extraction techniques. Time and experience are required to establish a baseline from which superintendents can gauge specific nutrient level fluctuations according to the specific extraction technique used by a particular laboratory.

Various Ratios of Elements

Ratios of various elements can be important for specific chemical reactions. For example, the carbon-to-nitrogen ratio of amendments influences the decomposition and utilization of organic matter, and generally ranges between 10 and 12 to 1 for soil organic matter. Ratios greater than 20 to 1 may result in an inefficient breakdown of organic matter due to the lack of nitrogen necessary to sustain soil organisms. Certain sawdust sources have as high a C:N ratio as 400:1. Turf managers who use these as soil amendments should add some nitrogen to the mixture, since sawdust can raise the carbon-to-nitrogen ratio above 20:1. Similar results also could occur if the nitrogen-to-sulfur ratio exceeds 20:1.

LEAF ANALYSIS

Tissue or leaf analysis can help determine those inputs needed in maintaining the turf. Leaf analysis, along with turfgrass appearance and soil analysis, can be used as a means of diagnosing the problems and the effectiveness of fertilization programs, especially for micronutrient deficiency. Soil analysis for some nutrients does not always adequately indicate their availability to plants. Therefore, potential nutrient deficiencies can be detected with leaf analysis before visual symptoms appear. Leaf analysis also provides information on nutrient levels available to turf plants compared to soil test levels and possibly determines what may interfere with nutrient uptake to create a deficiency in the plant.

Primary and secondary nutrients occur in relatively large quantities within plants—their concentrations are usually expressed in grams (g) of the element per kilogram (kg) of plant dry weight. Micronutrients occur in relatively small quantities—their concentrations are usually expressed in milligrams (mg) of the element per kilogram of plant dry weight (Chapter 11).

Golf courses in the past have relied predominately on granular fertilizer sources for the majority of their fertilization. However, improved technology and the availability of liquid fertilizers have changed this trend. More liquid sources are being used, especially during stress periods. Liquid sources allow more control of application rates and application uniformity without the need of watering-in like granulars, which becomes important during rainy seasons or on poorly drained greens.

Typically, granular fertilizers are used most months for bermudagrass greens, especially for potassium and phosphorus needs. Liquid materials are used to boost or maintain uniform color. Many courses "spoon feed" the greens as needed (e.g., when soil and tissue tests indicate nutrient needs, when color is needed, or when growth dramatically slows). Liquid fertilizers are typically applied at approximately 0.2 pounds nitrogen per 1,000 square feet (1 kg N/100 m^2) every two to four weeks during this time.

AERIFICATION STRATEGIES AND TECHNIQUES

Many golf facilities are not constructed with desirable soil. Turf built with "native" soil and exposed to heavy traffic and improper management practices often deteriorate due to compacted soil, thatch or mat development, and excessive use. Unlike annual row crops that are periodically tilled to correct these problems, turf managers do not have the opportunities to provide such physical disturbances without destroying the playing surface. Soil-related problems are usually confined to the upper three inches (7.6 cm) of the turf and, once formed, may not be completely corrective, especially where improper site preparation occurred prior to establishing the turf. However, over the years, a number of mechanical devices that provide soil cultivation with minimum turf surface disturbance have been developed. Cultivation is accomplished by core aerification, vertical mowing, spiking, slicing, and topdressing.

Frequency and Timing of Core Cultivation

Frequency of core cultivation should be based on the intensity of traffic the turf is exposed to, soil makeup, hardness of the soil surface, drainage capability, and degree of compaction. Areas receiving intense, daily traffic such as golf greens, approaches, landing areas, aprons, and tees require a *minimum* of three to four annual core aerifications. Typical timings are in spring, summer, late summer, and late winter, which should be followed with medium-to-heavy topdressing with desirable sand. If followed for four to five consecutive years, this method will help relieve the undesirable condition of many native soil greens.

Additional aerifications may be needed on exceptionally small greens where traffic is more concentrated, areas consisting of heavy soils high in silt and/or clay that do not drain well, greens established with one of the newer dwarf bermudagrasses, or soils exposed to saline or effluent water use. Such areas may need aerification with smaller diameter tines (3/8 inch or less, 1 cm) every four to six weeks during active growing months in addition to at least twice yearly with larger (≥ 1/2 inch, 1.3 cm) diameter tines. Heavier (e.g., "native") soil greens should be aerified at least four times yearly with a deep-tine or deep-drill aerifier. Some clubs opt to double aerify to obtain the benefits of two aerifications without having to wait twice as long for the holes to heal, even though double the amount of sand and time are needed to perform this. Failure to maintain an aggressive aerification program in such situations will result in a gradual reduction in turf quality from poorly drained soils, thin grass stands, mat accumulation, and continued problems with algae and moss.

Another means to determine how much to aerify is based on the amount of turf surface impacted by aerification. A 15 to 20 percent surface area being impacted on an annual basis is a reasonable routine goal for many well-established golf courses. A percentage basis is sometimes easier for non-agronomists to understand instead of trying to comprehend tine diameters and spacing. Courses that have been neglected may need a more aggressive aerification program. As outlined in Chapter 16, using various tine sizes and hole spacings will determine the surface area of turf impacted. For example, a fourfold increase in surface area impacted occurs when using a one-half-inch (1.3 cm) tine instead of a one-fourth-inch (0.6 cm) tine. An approximately 50 percent increase in surface area impacted occurs when using five-eighths-inch (1.6-cm) tines instead of a one-half-inch (1.3-cm) tine. Another example involves changing tine spacing. Changing tine spacing from two × two inches (5 × 5 cm) to one × two inches (2.5 to 5 cm) (with 3/8-inch diameter tines, 1 cm) increases the surface area impacted by 100 percent.

Spiking and Slicing

Two other cultural practices available to help relieve surface compaction, break up algae layers, and promote better water penetration and aeration are **spiking** and **slicing.** These are generally pull-type, non-powered units consisting of a series of blades mounted on a horizontal shaft. A slicer has thin, V-shaped knives bolted at intervals to the perimeter of metal wheels that cut into the soil. Turf is sliced with narrow slits about one-eighth- to one-fourth-inch (0.3 to 0.6 cm) wide and two to four (5 to 10 cm) inches deep.

A spiker has solid tines mounted on a horizontal shaft. It provides an effect similar to a slicer, but the penetration is limited to approximately one inch (2.5 cm) and the distance between perforations along the turf's surface is shorter. Because of these reasons, and since spiking causes less surface disruption than coring, spiking is primarily practiced on greens and tees. Slicing and spiking are performed to: (1) break up soil surface crusting, (2) break up algae layers, and (3) improve water penetration and aeration by relieving shallow soil compaction. Solid tines are associated with a spiker and holes are punched by forcing soil downward and laterally, resulting in some compaction at the bottom and along the sides of the holes. Since only minor disruptions of soil surfaces occur, spiking and slicing can be performed more often (e.g., every 7 to 14 days) than core aerification (e.g., every 4 to 8 weeks).

Vertical Mowing

A vertical mower is a powered unit with a series of knives vertically mounted on a horizontal shaft. The shaft rotates at high speeds while the blades slice into the turf and rip out thatch and other debris. Depending on the task, the shaft can be raised or lowered to cut shallowly or more deeply into the turf. Vertical blade thickness varies between 1/32 and 1/4 inch (0.08 to 0.6 cm) according to use. Vertical blade spacing varies from one-half to one inch (1.3 to 2.5 cm) depending on the desired results. Golf greens require thinner blades to prevent excessive surface damage while fairways require the heavier, thicker blades. The surface area impacted by various vertical mowing blade widths are listed in Chapter 16. For example, as simple math demonstrates, using 5/64-inch (0.2-cm) wide blades almost doubles the surface area impacted compared to using a 9/64-inch (0.4-cm) blade.

Depth

Different objectives can be met with vertical mowing depending on the depth of penetration. Grain is reduced when knives are set shallow enough to just nick the turf's surface. Shallow vertical mowing also is used to break up cores following aerification, providing a topdressing effect. Deeper penetration of knives stimulates new growth and removes accumulated thatch when stolons and rhizomes are severed. Seedbed preparation prior to overseeding is also accomplished by deep vertical mowing.

When dethatching is the objective, thatch depth will determine the depth of the blades. The bottom of the thatch layer should be reached by vertical mowing, and preferably the soil surface beneath the thatch layer should be sliced. However, there is a limit to the depth blades should be set or excessive removal of turf roots, rhizomes, stolons, and leaf surface may occur. For example, blades should be set at a depth to just cut stolons and no deeper if new growth stimulation is the objective. Vertical blade spacing for thatch removal should be between one and two inches (2.5 to 5 cm). This range provides maximum thatch removal with minimal turf damage.

Deep vertical mower penetration requires the use of a heavy-duty machine that can penetrate 1.5 to 3 inches (3.8 to 7.6 cm). Deep vertical mowing grooves the turf surface, so subsequent topdressing is often required to smooth the surface and cover exposed stolons. Shallow-rooted or immature turf can be severely damaged or torn out by deep vertical mowing. Preliminary testing at the site to be verticut should be done by hand pulling to measure if favorable rooting of the grass exists. Irrigation and topdressing should follow such deep vertical mowing to prevent quick desiccation of exposed roots, rhizomes, and stolons. It will also help smooth the turf surface and encourage turf recovery.

Frequency

The rate of thatch accumulation dictates the frequency of vertical mowing, which should begin once the thatch or mat layer on golf greens exceeds one-fourth to one-half inch (0.6 to 1.3 cm). Areas prone to thatch accumulation may require heavy vertical mowing several times per year. For bermudagrass, the first is during mid-to-late spring when bermudagrass is actively growing. This removes thatch and encourages turf spread by slicing stolons and by warming the soil surface quicker than if the thatch is allowed to remain. The second vertical mowing should be timed one to seven days before the anticipated fall overseeding. This discourages late-season bermudagrass growth that can compete with the overseeded grasses, and exposes the soil surface so grass seed can reach the soil better and have optimum germination. However, fall vertical mowing will result in a degree of surface damage that may not mask until the overseeding has time to become established.

Soil and thatch should be dry when deep vertical mowing is performed or turfgrass injury will be more extensive, since moist conditions encourage excessive plant material to be removed. Following verticutting, debris should be removed and the area should be immediately irrigated. Approximately five to seven days following heavy vertical mowing, one pound of nitrogen per 1,000 square feet (4.9 kg N/100 m²) should be applied to encourage rapid recovery. Quick-release nitrogen sources are preferred.

Interchangeable vertical mower units are now available for many of today's triplex greensmowers. This equipment allows for frequent vertical mowing and simultaneous debris collection.

The vertical blades on greensmowers should be set to only nick the turf surface so it is not impaired. By conducting frequent, light vertical mowing, the severe vertical mowing needed for renovation may be avoided.

Grooming and Conditioning

The grooming mower (also called turf conditioner) is a recent advancement in vertical mowing. Grooming keeps greens smooth and fast by reducing grain and removing excessive top growth. In front of the reel-cutting unit of greensmowers is an attached miniature vertical mower (often referred to as **vertical grooming**) with blade spacing typically $\leq$ one-fourth inch (0.6 cm) that rotates through slots in the front roller. A solid roller was traditionally used in place of grooved rollers. Each time turf is mowed with this unit, the turf is lightly vertically mowed (groomed or conditioned). This unit improves the playing surface by standing up leaf blades before mowing, thereby removing much of the surface grain. New shoot development is also stimulated by slicing stolons and removing thatch near the surface. Weekly grooming, along with timely topdressing and aerification, helps eliminate the need for traditionally performed turf renovation by severe vertical mowing. The height of the groomer is usually adjustable and is independent of the mowing unit, allowing the superintendent to adjust the groomer height higher or lower than the mower, depending on how aggressive one wants to be.

Other groomers use a rotary brush that rotates in the opposite direction of the mower blade. The brush stands up the grass prior to mowing, thereby reducing grain and providing a smooth surface.

TOPDRESSING

Topdressing adds a thin layer of soil to the turf surface, which is then incorporated into the turf by dragging or brushing. Frequency and rate of topdressing depend on the objective. Following coring and heavy verticutting, moderate-to-heavy topdressing is used to help smooth the surface, fill coring holes, and cover exposed roots resulting from these two processes. Irregular playing surfaces or gradual soil profile modification will require frequent and relatively heavy topdressing. Rates ranging from one-eighth to one-fourth inch (0.4 to 0.8 cubic yards of soil per 1,000 sq.ft., 0.33 to 0.66 m^3/100 m^2) are suggested, except if the turf has a limited capacity to absorb the material, since grass smothering would result.

If the objective of topdressing is to change the characteristic of the underlying soil, then a heavy topdressing program following numerous core removal operations is required. However, even following a rigorous coring and topdressing program, adequate modification of underlying soil may take several years to accomplish. Deep-tine aerification and core removal should be performed as much as possible prior to topdressing.

If thatch control is the main objective of topdressing, the amount and frequency are governed by the rate of thatch accumulation. A suggested amount of a medium rate of topdressing when thatch is not excessively (1/4 to 1/2 inch, 0.6 to 1.2 cm) thick is approximately one cubic yard per 5,000 square feet (0.17 m^3/100 m^2). If this relatively light rate does not adequately enhance the decomposition of the thatch layer, then the frequency of application and topdressing rate should be increased.

If the objective of topdressing is just to provide routine smoothing of the playing surface, then light, frequent topdressings are suggested. Matting or brushing the green following topdressing results in the material being dragged into low spots. Surface irregularities of the green are reduced and the area is somewhat leveled. Topdressing with one-half to one cubic yard per 5,000 square feet (0.09 to 0.17 m^3/100 m^2) of green surface every two to four weeks provides a smoother, truer playing surface. Light topdressing is also performed approximately 10 to 14 days prior to major club tournaments to increase the speed of greens and provide a smoother putting surface. Applying frequent, light topdressing on newly planted bermudagrass greens to cover stolons and to smooth the surface should be performed every two to four weeks until complete cover or the desired smoothness is achieved. Putting speed on a freshly topdressed green will initially be much slower but will increase in several days following irrigation, incorporation, and several mowings.

When attempting to reduce thatch and mat layering of the newer ultradwarf bermudagrass cultivars, a "frequent dusting" is often employed. With this light (1 to 3 ft^3/1,000 ft^2, 0.03 to 0.09 m^3/100 m^2) rate, topdressing is usually applied weekly, followed by light brushing or irrigation to incorporate the sand. Using dry, bagged sand is becoming popular as a topdressing source.

Plant growth regulators or retardants (PGRs) are tools that provide superintendents with opportunities for smoother putting surfaces. PGRs used on golf greens promote lateral and root growth instead of top or horizontal growth. This encourages thicker, more laterally growing bermudagrass, often simulating grass mowed at much lower heights. Regular PGR use provides the desired smoother putting surface for courses unable to replant one of the newer ultradwarf bermudagrasses. PGRs also help regulate or delay top growth when a regular mowing schedule is disrupted or when putting characteristics in the afternoon need to closely reflect those following morning mowing. PGR use prior to overseeding slows bermudagrass growth competition, allowing a smoother transition to the overseeded grass, although these benefits are less dramatic.

During periods of active growth, PGRs are used every three to four weeks to achieve these desirable traits. Current PGR examples include paclobutrazol (Turf Enhancer), trinexapac-ethyl (Primo), flurprimidol (Cutless), and mefluidide (Embark). Not all of these are used on greens or tees. Each have their own precaution statements before using them. Currently, the most popular for smoothing greens is trinexapac-ethyl 1EC. Light rates (~4 oz/acre, 0.3 L/ha) are applied every three to four weeks during periods of active growth and/or just prior to anticipated rainy weather. Other PGRs are used to help regular *Poa annua* growth and development. Refer to Chapter 25 for additional information on these topics.

OVERSEEDING/PAINTING

Overseeding is performed in late summer through early fall to provide green color to the bermudagrass which turns brown when temperatures drop below 50°F (10°C) for an extended period. In addition, golf course fairways also are overseeded to clearly mark suggested landing areas for golfers. Overseeding is an important economic aspect of golf because many resort courses enjoy their heaviest play from tourists during the fall, winter, and spring months, which helps attract golfers. Overseeding also improves winter and spring play conditions.

Overseeding, however, requires various degrees of seedbed preparation in the form of aerifying, verticutting, and topdressing. Extensive watering is needed until the overseeded grass becomes established. Spring transition from the overseeded grass back to the bermudagrass also can be unpredictable, erratic, and can undesirably extend into summer. Chapter 18 of this publication covers overseeding practices.

Painting of bermudagrass greens for winter color instead of overseeding is gaining in popularity due to the disruption of overseeding in fall and problems with spring transition. Seed, fertilizers, pesticides, and labor costs are greatly reduced or eliminated by painting. Equipment wear-and-tear also is reduced. Painted greens tend to putt much smoother and farther (quicker) since overseeding grasses do not disrupt or slow ball roll. To minimize these complaints, raise the mowing height the last several regular mowing events to provide more leaf area which restricts ball roll. Higher mowing heights in fall also benefit the bermudagrass by encouraging desirable carbohydrate production and storage prior to the dormancy period. Ball roll can also be slowed by heavily hand watering just prior to a major tournament. Improvements in paints, their longevity, and application equipment/techniques also make painting more attractive than in previous situations.

Painting greens is still somewhat more of an art than science. Considerable practice on the nursery green, driving range, or out-of-play areas should be made prior to actually painting greens. Paints tend to last four to six weeks, resulting in the need for reapplication. A good turf base is also needed for the paint to adhere to. Worn, thin, or bare areas will be less successful from painting.

MANAGING ULTRADWARF CULTIVARS
Cultivation Practice Summary for Ultradwarf Bermudagrasses

The newer dwarf growing bermudagrass cultivars such as TifEagle, FloraDwarf, Champion, Mini Verde, and others are noted for their tight, horizontal growth habits. In fact, unless these are mowed below 3/16 inch (0.48 cm), their effectiveness and desired qualities for a putting surface are diminished and clubs should use Tifdwarf instead.

The recent introduction of the "ultradwarf" bermudagrass cultivars for golf greens is revolutionizing management philosophies and practices. All of these cultivars are noted for their high shoot densities, finer leaf textures, and tolerance to extremely low (e.g., 1/8 inch, 0.3 cm, or lower) mowing heights. These characteristics have allowed ultradwarf bermudagrass to rival bentgrass in terms of putting speed and smoothness with much lower inputs in terms of heat, water management, and disease control. However, the ultradwarf bermudagrass, like many of the newer bentgrass cultivars, characteristically develop an extensive thatch (or mat) layer in a relatively short period of time. Unlike Tifdwarf or Tifgreen bermudagrass, which normally takes several years to develop this layering, newer cultivars such as Champion, TifEagle, FloraDwarf, and Mini Verde begin showing layering problems shortly after grow-in. This mat layer holds approach shots, provides better traffic tolerance, and allows quick recovery from divots and ball marks. It should not, however, be allowed to accumulate excessively (e.g., >1/2 inch thick, 1.2 cm) or the green becomes puffy, scalps easily, is difficult to efficiently water, and provides a poor seedbed for overseeding. This mat layer, therefore, must be aggressively controlled through core cultivation, vertical mowing, grooming, and topdressing techniques.

During periods of active growth, this mat layer should be lightly vertical mowed or groomed on a weekly basis. Additional events may be needed if weekly frequency does not control the mat layer. Core cultivation or aeration will be needed with small tines every six to eight weeks with the cores removed. Light, frequent topdressing should also be incorporated. Light topdressing every one or two weeks will help control this mat layer, along with the coring and vertical mowing.

The ultradwarf bermudagrasses require intensive maintenance; thus, they cost more to maintain and are not suited for all courses. However, for those courses desiring premium putting greens, these grasses should be considered. The following are a summary of management practices that are beneficial in managing these newer grasses (Table 20–3).

Fertilization

For Tifdwarf or Tifgreen bermudagrass, the rule-of-thumb for nitrogen fertilization has been one to two pounds of nitrogen per 1,000 square feet (4.9 to 9.8 kg N/100 m^2) per growing month. These rates are considered essential in maintaining lateral growth to help recover from traffic, ball marks, and spring transition. They are also necessary to maintain a desirable green color. Most of this fertilizer is in granular form from various nitrogen sources.

Due in part to their extremely tight (high) density, the need to water-in granular products, and the desire not to encourage thatch/mat development, fertilization practices for the ultradwarf bermudagrass have changed. For example, granular fertilizers, even greens-grade or mini-prill, often do not adequately penetrate the high shoot density of the ultradwarf grasses; thus, they are easily removed by the mowing process. Granular products also need to be incorporated by being watered-in even during wet weather and/or on poorly draining greens. Bermudagrass courses, therefore, have adopted a practice from many Southern U.S. bentgrass growers where spoon feeding with liquid fertilizers has become more widely used. Spraying with low rates (e.g., 0.1 to 0.25 lbs N/1,000 sq.ft., 0.5 to 1.2 kg N/100 m^2) of nitrogen or readily available nutrients on a frequent basis (e.g., 7 to 14 days) during the growing season is common. This enables superintendents to better control growth levels, thereby minimizing thatch/mat layering, and also provide desirable green color without the need to water-in.

A fertilizer program combining granular and spoon (or liquid) feeding is suggested. A mini-prilled fertilizer containing a slow-release nitrogen source should be applied monthly at approximately 0.5 pounds nitrogen per 1,000 square feet (2.4 kg N/100 m^2) during the growing season. This is supplemented with spoon feeding at 0.1 to 0.25 pounds nitrogen per 1,000 square feet (0.5 to 1.2 kg N/100 m^2) every 7 to 14 days to provide a total of approximately one pound of nitrogen per 1,000 square feet (4.9 kg N/100 m^2) per growing month. This, as well as any fertilization program, should be backed with regular tissue and soil testing to monitor and track nutrient levels to ensure adequate levels are being absorbed.

Topdressing

Like fertilization programs, topdressing programs have changed with the introduction of the ultradwarf bermudagrasses. Topdressing has long been recognized as the main cultural practice that smooths the putting surface, allows better rootzone management, and prevents (or reduces)

TABLE 20–3 *Summary of cultural practices for bermudagrass golf greens.*

Practice	Description
Fertilization	
Optimum timing for nitrogen fertilization	April through September
Damaging response to excessive nitrogen fertilizer	November through March
Yearly nitrogen requirements (lbs N/1,000 sq.ft.)	8 to 18 (391 to 879 kg/ha)
Monthly nitrogen requirements (lbs N/1,000 sq.ft.)	0.5 to 1.5 pounds nitrogen per 1,000 square feet
Acceptable pH range	5.5 to 7.0
Acceptable phosphorus levels	Low to high
Optimum potassium levels	Medium to high (improves low temperature tolerance); usually applied at one-half to equal amounts of nitrogen
Cultural requirements	
Minimum sunlight hours required	8
Overseeding/painting	Necessary in temperate and most subtropical areas for winter color
Irrigation requirements	Moisten full rootzone depth, rewetting just prior to wilting
Air circulation requirements	Not normally required
Aerification/cultivation	Minimum of two to four times yearly; shallow and deep aerifying are used
Cultivation timing optimum	May through September
Fertilizer application	Slow-release (primarily) granular + liquids for color
Mowing height	0.100 to 0.25 (1/10 to 1/4) in. (2.54 to 6.35 mm)
Mowing frequency	Daily
Mowing pattern	Changed (rotated) daily
Clippings	Removed
Thatch/mat control	Frequent topdressing, lightly vertical mowing and grooming, regular aerification
Compaction control	Use a predominate sand-base rootzone during construction; routine aerification; limit play (traffic) during wet conditions
Topdressing	Light (0.2 cu.yd./1,000 sq.ft., 0.17 m³/100 m²) but frequently (weekly) during active growth; monthly at 0.3 to 0.5 cu.yd./1,000 sq.ft. (0.25 to 0.4 m³/100 m²) during slowed growth
Aerification (coring)	Performed two to six times annually with at least one deep tine yearly; stop within 30 days of overseeding
Regular (deeper) verticutting	Once or twice yearly, once in spring and another just prior to overseeding
Grooming	Performed weekly with ultradwarf cultivars
Slicing	Performed weekly in two directions to reduce surface compaction and algae and to facilitate soil air exchange and infiltration

thatch/mat buildup. A rule-of-thumb is to match topdressing rates and frequencies with the growth rate and density of the turf. With the higher shoot densities of the ultradwarf bermudagrass cultivars, traditional heavy and infrequent topdressing has evolved to lighter, more frequent events. This has been accented with newer topdressing techniques and equipment as well as the ability to purchase dried sand in bags. These light topdressings (a.k.a., "dusting") are quicker to perform, are less intrusive to players and playing surfaces, and are easily incorporated by light brushing or irrigation. Walk-behind fertilizer applicators are often used to quickly apply these "dustings" of topdressing.

With the ultradwarf bermudagrass cultivars, expect to topdress frequently but lightly on a 7- to 14-day schedule during the growing season, with one to two cubic feet of sand per 1,000 square feet (0.03 to 0.06 m³/100 m²) or 0.012 to 0.024 inches (0.03 to 0.06 cm) in depth, respectively. Performing light verticutting or grooming prior to topdressing opens the turf canopy and helps allow incorporation of the topdressing sand. Superintendents should experiment with their conditions on this rate and frequency and be aware of the extra wear-and-tear this may place on mowing units.

Grooming and Verticutting

Due to the relatively quick buildup of thatch/mat layering, frequent grooming and/or verticutting are necessary with the ultradwarf bermudagrasses. Frequency and timing will vary depending primarily on the fertilization and topdressing program used by a particular course. Weekly grooming or light verticutting is suggested during growing months, supplemented with one or two relatively heavy vertical mowings, often following aerification in mid-to-late spring and again in mid-to-late summer just prior to overseeding.

Like the newer trend of light but frequent topdressing, light and frequent grooming or verticutting often go unnoticed by players, yet it helps prevent or maintain thatch/mat layering. These techniques have proven extremely beneficial, yet they are less disruptive than previous practices.

Aerification

The introduction of the ultradwarf bermudagrass cultivars has not decreased the need for or frequency of core aerification. In addition to soil compaction relief, core aerification penetrates the thatch/mat layering, creating a more favorable environment for soil organisms to naturally decompose. Three to four core aerifications are still the norm for most bermudagrass greens. At least two of these are typically performed with one-half-inch (1.2-cm) diameter tines, especially when performed in conjunction with topdressing. Greens heavier in composition (e.g., more silt and clay content) and courses with heavy yearly play would consider the more frequent aerification schedule with one or two of these using the deep-tine or deep-drill units. When used in conjunction with heavy topdressing, green soil composition can slowly be improved, as can deep soil aeration and compaction relief. Topdressing cores brought to the soil surface can be hand or mechanically removed or reincorporated by lightly verticutting or dragging-in.

Additional Considerations

PGR Use

Plant growth regulators (PGRs) are often used on bermudagrass to promote lateral growth (e.g., surface tightening) over vertical growth. PGRs also help to produce a consistent putting surface during periods of growth surges, provide more consistent putting throughout the day, promote a darker blue-green color, and provide greens with "off-types" of bermudagrass patches with an illusion of having only one type of grass present. The most popular PGR product currently used for these purposes is trinexapac-ethyl (trade name: Primo 1EC). Using this product on a three- to four-week interval at light rates (e.g., 3 to 4 oz product per acre [0.22 to 0.29 L/ha] of the 1EC formulation) has proven beneficial during the growing months. PGRs, however, do not necessarily increase putting speeds (or distances), but rather help maintain those current playing conditions.

Double Cutting and/or Rolling

A popular practice "rediscovered" in the 1990s was double cutting and/or rolling greens to help provide smoother playing surfaces without having to mow at extremely low heights that often proved detrimental to Tifgreen and Tifdwarf greens. Double cutting, due to costs, is still used but mostly prior to and during tournament play. Rolling is also provided then, but more courses provide this two to four times weekly, especially when bermudagrass mowing heights are raised during periods of cloudy/rainy weather and/or when days become shorter (late summer). Courses, obviously, must weigh the benefits of double cutting and/or rolling greens compared to increased equipment needs, costs, and wear-and-tear, as well as the possibility of increased soil compaction or turf wear, especially on clean-up passes.

On ultradwarf bermudagrass, double cutting is used only during tournament play (for most courses due to costs) while rolling may be used more routinely. However, due to their normal close mowing heights, these practices are less beneficial for the ultradwarf cultivars than for higher-mowed Tifgreen or Tifdwarf. However, as mentioned, during periods of overcast weather and/or shorter days, the mowing height of the ultradwarf bermudagrass needs raising. These practices, along with PGR use, help to maintain more desirable putting characteristics without overly damaging the grass.

Overseeding

Due to their high shoot densities, several traditional overseeding practices are altered to accommodate the ultradwarf bermudagrasses. First is grass (or seed) selection. The smaller-seeded *Poa trivialis* and/or bentgrass are the current grasses used to overseed ultradwarf bermudagrass greens. These smaller-seeded varieties require less aggressive seedbed preparation compared to using larger-seeded grasses such as ryegrass. Even with these smaller-seeded varieties, aggressive seedbed preparation will be needed prior to overseeding greens where an excessive (e.g., >1/2 inch, 1.2 cm) thatch/mat layer has developed. This should begin three or four weeks prior to seeding by aggressively coring, followed by weekly vertical mowing. Topdressing both before and after overseeding is ideal; at a minimum, however, topdressing following overseeding is suggested to increase soil contact with the seed.

In areas where no or only light and infrequent frost occurs, overseeding the ultradwarf bermudagrasses may not be necessary. Due to their close proximity to the normally warmer soil surface, short periods of cool or cold weather may not cause browning of these grasses. However, if heavy frosts are normally experienced, overseeding is generally required. In areas that only occasionally experience cold weather, temporary, removable covers are available that can be placed on the greens to protect them from frost. These, however, should be removed daily if temperatures are forecasted to be above 50°F (10°C). Spraying greens with charcoal also helps to prevent discoloration due to temporarily cool temperatures. Charcoal should be applied at a rate of two to five pounds of product per 1,000 square feet (9.8 to 24 kg/100 m^2) and preferably when the sun is shining so heat can be absorbed and retained during cool periods.

SECTION

VII

BEST PEST MANAGEMENT AND CONTROL PRACTICES

CHAPTER

21

Integrated Pest Management

INTRODUCTION

One of the most appealing aspects of golf is the beauty of the course. To maintain "acceptable" playing conditions, the superintendent must minimize pest problems such as weeds, insects, nematodes, and diseases. One method to meet these objectives is the incorporation of a common-sense approach or way of thinking to protect the turf, which is accomplished by gathering information, analyzing the information, and making a knowledgeable decision. **Integrated pest management (IPM)** combines proper plant selection, correct cultural practices, monitoring of pests and environmental conditions, use of biological control, and the judicious use of pesticides. Like the pieces of a puzzle, all are critical to complete the entire picture of turfgrass management. The principles and practices of IPM also are typically included in **best management practices (BMP), turfgrass management practices (TMP), best turfgrass management practices (BTMP),** and **sustainable agriculture.**

Unfortunately, the player pressure placed on golf course superintendents to maintain "tournament" conditions year-round have often forced superintendents to abandon some sound agronomic practices. Players commonly request less than one-eighth inch (3.2 mm) mowing heights along with "soft" greens that putt with unreasonable quickness and have no scars or disruptions in consistency. Often, this requires grasses to be grown outside their natural range of adaptability. As a result, superintendents have been forced to increase their fertilizer, water, and pesticide usage to maintain the grass at the players' satisfaction level.

Public concerns about chemical use has been increasing while restrictions on the availability of traditionally used resources has also become an issue. Superintendents must consider incorporating and informing the public about programs like IPM that reduce these inputs for maintaining golf courses. However, until golfers themselves modify their expectations for playing conditions, they will continue to pressure superintendents, resulting in practices that are not necessarily best for the grass or the environment.

IPM HISTORY

Modern IPM concepts and practices began to develop in the late 1950s with alfalfa and apple production, and vastly expanded in the 1960s with cotton production. These concepts evolved from

531

the mid-1940s when superintendents felt "silver-bullet" or ultimate specific weapons such as pesticides were needed to control all pest problems. Most traditional pest and plant ecological studies were then deemphasized and abandoned, along with nonchemical control alternative research efforts. This led to a new generation of producers and scientists who had little experience with nonchemical approaches to pest or plant management.

In recent years, turf managers, feeling dependant on pesticides, suffered from a lack of research and training in the pest management area. For example, in the early 1980s, two very effective and relatively inexpensive pesticides, EDB (ethylene dibromide) and chlordane, were banned from the turf market. EDB was a highly effective soil-injected nematicide. Since EDB was so effective and inexpensive, research on turf tolerance to higher nematode populations was essentially abandoned. Chlordane, an insecticide, was especially useful for mole cricket and grub control. With chlordane, managers did not worry about managing the turf to withstand higher pest populations or treating during the most susceptible point in the insect's life cycle. However, after losing these chemicals, nematodes, mole crickets, and grubs became very serious turf pests. Researchers are now trying to find alternative methods of pest management.

Plant breeding provides another method of manipulating grass for better pest resistance. In the past, turf breeders basically tried to satisfy the golfer by developing grasses that had finer texture, greater density, and the ability to survive at lower mowing heights. Today, turf breeders will have to redirect their efforts by including pest resistance in turf species lines. More time and research will be necessary to solve problems that have basically been ignored for the last 40 years.

As noted, IPM practices have not been widely used in the turfgrass profession. One reason for this is the lack of adequate federal, state, or industry money available for turf researchers wishing to explore IPM approaches. Traditional "crops" such as cotton, soybeans, and corn have enjoyed the majority of available grants for this type of research and subsequently have made the greatest strides in IPM. Hopefully, turf researchers will soon receive similar considerations from these granting agencies.

Only a few reports are available dealing with turf IPM programs. One experimental IPM program in selected urban Florida areas has resulted in an approximately 90 percent reduction in pesticide application without sacrificing visual quality. No differences were noted between lawns sprayed only when pests reached aesthetic thresholds and lawns sprayed preventively. Results from a similar IPM scouting program in Maryland suggested 40 to 80 percent of the pest problems could be eliminated by simply substituting resistant ornamental varieties or eliminating pest-susceptible plants in residential lawns. The most significant lawn problems in Maryland were low soil pH, low soil fertility, and weed invasion.

A country club in Massachusetts has used IPM practices to control Japanese beetle grubs, using sex tabs and floral lures instead of the traditional pesticide treatment approach to attract insects into traps. For example, during August, the club placed 47 traps in the rough and collected 160 gallons of beetles. The number of grubs were reduced from 50 to 75 per square foot to only one or two. Pioneering IPM strategies for insect management also are being practiced on other golf courses, such as Pine Ridge in Baltimore, and those along the Georgia coast.

A golf club in Idaho traditionally had disease problems during the summer on its bentgrass greens. The superintendent, with some major reservations from club officials, decided that continued and frequent fungicide use only provided temporary masking of disease symptoms and began searching for the underlying disease causes. Poor drainage and soil layering were discovered on the most troublesome greens. Excessive nitrogen and water-use rates were applied in recent years and a distinct buildup of black layer occurred.

The club initially began implementing IPM practices by informing and soliciting support from the club members. After obtaining approval, greens were aggressively and frequently aerified deep enough to allow better and healthier root penetration. Natural organic fertilizers and a biostimulant were used to supplement and eventually replace a portion of the synthetic materials. Synthetic fungicide use was partially replaced by natural sea plant extract disease suppressants and a "compost soup" consisting of digested sewage sludge and wood wastes.

Other projects in New York have been able to reduce pesticide applications by about one-third. Diligent scouting and emergency pesticide applications were needed, but avoided the "calender" spray schedules typical of many greens today. The IPM greens also usually had higher quality than regularly maintained greens. The IPM greens, however, had occasional pest outbreaks that caused poor conditions before control measures were implemented. Additional experience; evolving technology such as GPS/GIS, optical sensing, and more precise spray technology; and improved pest-resistant grasses will improve IPM results and acceptance.

South Carolina conducted a pilot project incorporating traditional IPM strategies into managing golf turf. Turfgrass Information and Pest Scouting (TIPS) was administered on seven golf courses. Scouting was performed and recommendations made to the superintendents about agronomic practices and judicious use of pesticides. Among this project's accomplishments was a 30 percent reduction in fungicides used by monitoring weather parameters and not applying chemicals until favorable conditions existed for disease development. Nitrogen use was also reduced 35 percent without sacrificing golf course quality by using judicious amounts timed to produce maximum benefits in relation to the plant's growth cycle and environment.

STRATEGIES OF INTEGRATED PEST MANAGEMENT

Developing IPM strategies requires superintendents to have reliable information about the following:

1. Obtain information concerning the total ecological situation involved with the particular turfgrass and pest. Identify the pest and know its biology and life cycles, as well as management practices that disrupt or influence these to reduce pest numbers. Understanding the strengths and weaknesses of the pest increases the chances of success. This allows one to know:
    a. When to expect the pest problem or when, in its life cycle, it is most susceptible for control.
    b. Where to expect their occurrence. Mapping and record keeping can help spot the "when" and "where" of infestation patterns.
2. Use a monitoring system to carefully follow pest trends, which determines if a pesticide will be necessary, and if so, when and where it would be most effectively applied.
3. Maintain careful records to measure IPM effectiveness.
4. Inform the public these IPM practices are being implemented to demonstrate golf course managers are just as environmentally aware and sensitive as players are.

IPM control strategies can be subdivided into **chemical** and **nonchemical** strategies. Both are equally important in implementing a successful program.

Nonchemical Strategies

The following contribute to the integration of nonchemical strategies for pest management: host-plant resistance, pest-free propagation (or sanitation), site preparation, cultural practices, and biological control.

Host-Plant Resistance

One of the oldest means of pest control is through careful selection and breeding of pest-resistant or pest-tolerant plants. People have traditionally selected those plants that grew best or had the highest yields, and then used them in subsequent years. Many turfgrass varieties are the result of this type of selection process, where a patch of turf grew better, was denser, or had better color than the surrounding grass. Further genetic work with selections often has revealed certain genes for pest resistance and/or better turfgrass characteristics. This genetic resistance can be incorporated into a cultivated plant to provide more effective pest control. For example, "Floratam" St. Augustinegrass was the first commercially available variety resistant to chinch bugs (*Blissus* spp.). However, some plants are less resistant to certain pests and their use must be weighed against other desirable characteristics. For example, Ormond bermudagrass is highly susceptible to stunt mites (*Aceria* spp.) while Tifway bermudagrass is not. L-93 creeping bentgrass has good resistance to dollar spot while Crenshaw bentgrass does not.

Resistance usually involves one or a combination of the following:

1. Chemicals produced by the host repel the pest or prevent it from completing its life cycle.
2. The host is more vigorous or tolerant than other varieties and thus withstands higher pest populations and/or more pest damage.
3. The host has physical characteristics making it less vulnerable to attack.

As noted, turf breeding efforts have traditionally been more concerned with improving the playability of grasses than with breeding for pest resistance. With the threat of losing many of today's effective pesticides, breeding for pest resistance will become a higher priority. Hopefully, as today's breeding and genetic engineering technologies evolve, better means of transferring genes will provide turf plants with desirable playing qualities and inherent pest resistance.

Pest-Free Propagation

One of the easiest, yet often overlooked, means of preventing pest establishment in turf is by using pest-free planting materials. Each state established a seed certification program, one of the first regulatory measures designed to provide pest-free propagation. Each bag of seed, in order to meet certification, must provide information on purity and germination percentages. In addition, a weed seed listing must be provided. No noxious weed seeds are allowed in the seed bags.

Turf managers should take this process one step further and ensure all planting materials introduced contain few, if any, pests. For example, with the limited nematode control options currently available, a sod and sprig purchaser should make every effort to assure their purchase does not bring a serious nematode problem with it. A nematode assay of the material before delivery can help by showing the kinds of nematodes present, and if any of them are at excessive levels. It is not realistic to expect turf planting material to be entirely free of nematodes, but it is reasonable to seek material that contains few serious types and none in high numbers. By visually examining root systems at the time of purchase, the buyer can determine if root pests have been severe in the production field, thereby preventing a high risk of damage once the material is planted. Likewise, the turf also should be inspected for other pests such as weeds and fire ants. The old saying "an ounce of prevention is worth a pound of cure" has never been more true than when deciding on which planting material to use.

This same philosophy also should apply to planting in soil free of noxious pests. Soil fumigation to control many soil-borne pests such as nematodes and weeds should be considered in almost all cases before turf establishment. Likewise, soil added to an existing turf site via topdressing should be pest-free. Do not accept pest-contaminated soil because of price.

Exclusion is another nonchemical IPM strategy related to pest-free propagation. It involves keeping pests out of the region or country. However, exclusion usually involves legally enforced stoppage of plant pests at ports of entry, which is accomplished by the inspection, interception, destruction, and quarantine of the plants. Some of today's worst turf pests have been accidentally or intentionally introduced. For example, many turf weeds initially were introduced into the United States as experimental pasture materials, for soil stabilization, or as ornamental plantings. Hopefully, with the more stringent quarantine laws of today, additional foreign pests will remain excluded.

Site Preparation

Properly preparing the planting site is an important, yet often unrecognized, IPM step that involves planning and constructing highly utilized areas, such as putting greens or tees, with precise water management capabilities. Precise water management is the major key to successful turf maintenance under intense playing conditions. Disease and soil compaction are among the problems occurring if soil saturation is allowed during intense play. Adequate surface and subsurface drainage must be provided so play can quickly resume after a heavy rain without soil compaction. However, golf greens must be able to retain adequate levels of moisture and nutrients to avoid continuous reapplication of them.

Other considerations for site preparation and construction include: (1) provision of proper sunlight and ventilation around golf greens, (2) adequate sizing of greens for even distribution of traffic, (3) proper drainage in fairways, and (4) provision of adequate quantity and quality of irrigation. All too often, these preconstruction criteria are neglected, causing even the most intense IPM programs to fail, leaving members dissatisfied with the services rendered.

Cultural Practices

Probably the best defense against pest invasion is providing a dense, healthy, competitive turf. This is achieved by providing cultural practices that favor turf growth over pest proliferation, which disrupts the normal relationship between the pest and its host plant, making the pest less

FIGURE 21–1 An example of pest occurrence when growing conditions favor it. Annual bluegrass (*Poa annua*) is shown around a leaking irrigation head, resulting in continued excess soil moisture that favors the weed.

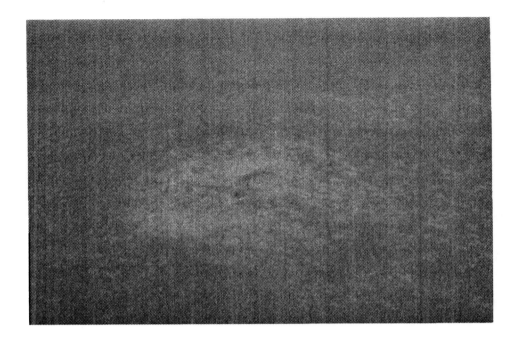

likely to grow, survive, or reproduce. These practices include proper irrigation, fertilization, mowing, aerification, and topdressing (Figure 21–1). Prolonged use of incorrect cultural practices weakens the turf, promotes pest invasion and its spread, and often encourages excessive thatch development. Thatch not only harbors many insects and disease pathogens, but it also limits pesticide effectiveness while reducing the efficiency of a watering program.

Biological Control

Biological pest control uses natural enemies, such as pathogens, predators, and parasites, to reduce pest populations to aesthetically acceptable levels. Criteria for a successful biological control agent include: (1) the absence of nontarget effects on desirable plants or other organisms, (2) its ability to reproduce quickly to prevent the pest from attaining damage thresholds, (3) its persistence in the environment, even at nondamaging pest levels, and (4) its adaptability to the environment of the host. The biological control agent also should be free of its own predators, parasites, and pathogens.

Pests in their native habitats are regulated through Mother Nature's system of checks and balances. Predators and parasites help keep pest populations at a relatively constant level. Problems occur when pests are introduced into those areas lacking these natural regulatory means. As a result, foreign pests often become epidemic since the ecosystem is defenseless. For example, mole crickets in their native South American habitat are not considered a major problem. Other insects, nematodes, and fungi that attack mole crickets in South America tend to minimize their effects. However, when mole crickets are accidentally introduced in the United States without the presence of these beneficial organisms, they soon reach epidemic levels. If it were not for these natural biological control agents, the world would be overrun by only a few organisms. Scientists currently are exploring the numerous naturally occurring organisms in the pests' native habitats that can be successfully transferred to other areas. Various successes have occurred using biological control agents such as parasites, predators, or diseases to control pest organisms.

A few examples of biological control measures currently are being used in commercial turf production. *Bacillus popilliae*, a bacterium commonly known to cause the milky spore disease, has been used to control Japanese beetle grubs. More effective strains are currently being developed. The white amur carp, a fish native to southeast Asia, has recently been introduced for submerged aquatic weed control in golf course ponds. Extracts from various wood decaying fungi are being reformulated as commercial fungicides. Other potential agents for biological control of turf pests include endophytic fungi for insect control, bacteria such as *Xanthomonas* species for annual bluegrass control, various rust (*Puccinia* spp.) fungi for nutsedge control, and several parasitic bacteria, nematodes, and fungi for the control of mole crickets and damaging nematodes in turf.

Biological control systems are complex; they are not totally effective, nor always predictable. The concept of biological control has been so widely publicized that the general public views it as a viable and readily available alternative for all pesticides. Although this is not yet the case, it is an area currently receiving much attention and hopefully will provide additional control strategies in the future.

One underlying requirement of the use of biological control agents is the public's willingness to accept a certain level of pest damage. This level of pest pressure is necessary for the biological control agent to have a continual food source after the pest level has become acceptable. Thus, total pest elimination is not feasible when integrating biological control measures. There also is a time lag between the use of a biological agent and actual control. Club members must be educated to this fact and be willing to accept minor levels of pest pressure and time delay for long-term success.

Chemical Pest Control

Not all pest problems can be solved by host-plant resistance, manipulating cultural practices in the plant environment, or by the use of biological control agents. In these cases, pesticides become the second line of defense. In the IPM scheme, pesticide use is not eliminated. However, indiscriminate spraying is eliminated and only practical pesticide use is employed so there is minimal damage to the natural biological control agents of the pest, as well as minimum damage to the environment. This requires extensive knowledge of the ecology and interrelation of the pest, the pesticide, the host plant, and the beneficial natural biological control agent. Several considerations for strategic pesticide use involve making management decisions concerning the following:

1. Locate and identify the pest using reliable monitoring techniques and establish an aesthetic threshold. Pest identification is a fundamental requirement when developing an IPM program. The task of identifying pests can be both frustrating and time-consuming. Pest diagnosis often can be assisted by training and by having well-illustrated pest literature on site.

   Even with a good reference library, certain pest problems require laboratory analysis for the identification of threshold estimations. State plant problem diagnostic services are accessible through the local County Extension Office, e-mails, or by direct submission. Diagnostic services can often bring clarity to difficult turfgrass problems where overlapping diseases exist, nematode/disease interactions occur, or fertility/pest interactions develop.

   Trained personnel, often referred to as **scouts,** examine or scout the golf course on a routine basis monitoring pest levels. Monitoring ranges from visual inspection, sampling, and analyzing soil and plant tissue to the use of sophisticated "high-tech" detection techniques. Decisions based on what pests and symptoms are visible can immediately be made. When specialized tests must be run at public or private diagnostic laboratories (e.g., nematode assays, detection and accurate identification of certain viruses, species identification of some fungi), scout(s) must know how each type of sample should be taken and handled to provide the most useful and reliable information. They also must know how to specifically interpret the results of each test conducted.

   Once pests have been identified and their infestation levels recorded, a control action must be initiated at a predetermined pest threshold level. These threshold levels are known as economic, damage, or action thresholds in other IPM programs. For turf managers, economic and related threshold-level terms mean little since crop yield is not the ultimate goal, but rather an aesthetic level of turf quality. An aesthetic threshold deals with the amount of visual damage a particular turf area can withstand before action is required. Highly maintained areas such as golf greens have a lower aesthetic threshold level than less-maintained areas such as roughs, which can withstand a higher degree of pest damage before action is required. These thresholds also vary with the expectations for a particular golf course, the availability of financial resources, and available alternative control measures.

2. Attack a pest during the most susceptible point in its life cycle, which usually is during the early stages of development. For example, the most effective time for mole cricket control is during its first instars, which normally occur during the month of June. However, prior scouting and mapping of mole cricket infested areas have proven most beneficial when

pinpointing sites of future pesticide use. The same philosophy of attacking the most susceptible point in its life cycle also is true for most weeds. Young, actively growing weeds are usually the easiest to control. Once weeds begin to mature, they become more difficult and expensive to control.

3. If a pesticide is necessary, use the one that is most effective but the least toxic to nontarget organisms and the environment. Read the label and use the recommended rate, and spot treat, if possible, instead of applying "blanket" or "wall-to-wall" treatments. Obviously this relies on effective scouting techniques and proper recording or mapping of pest outbreaks.

STARTING AN IPM PROGRAM

Developing an IPM program involves certain steps. However, each golfing facility differs and will require an IPM program tailored to its interest, level of expectation, and available budget. Pest problems are going to occur on any golf course; even the best management program cannot guarantee problems will not occur. The very nature of managing a golf course predisposes it to stress since the turf is maintained at its very edge of survival. For example, golf greens are generally mowed below one-eighth inch (3.2 mm), which is much lower than the natural adaptation of these grasses. This results in a precarious balance between the needs for grass maintenance and those for grass survival. The following steps have proven successful in developing an IPM program or mindset and should provide a good starting point for golf course superintendents.

1. Define the role and responsibility of all persons who are involved in the pest management program. This includes establishing communication between club officials, players, and crew members, who must be aware of the new approach the superintendent is trying and that it is an ongoing experiment. They need to expect some successes and some setbacks. Assurance and understanding will be needed by all participants during the initial stages of development to prevent misunderstanding and provide ample time for desirable results to occur.

   Scouts who are conscientious and trained to recognize turf pest problems provide the base of a successful monitoring program. The superintendent will probably want to begin as the primary scout until a feel for IPM strategies is attained. Once this occurs, scouting may be delegated to an assistant. However, all employees should play an important role in recognizing pests and/or damage produced. Take time to explain the pests and their symptoms to those who perform daily tasks, such as mowing or irrigation, since these people have a close, daily view of the grass. The spray technician also should be familiar with pest identification and, most important, its life cycle. Emphasize how each pest usually has a point in its life cycle when it is most vulnerable.

2. Determine management objectives for specific areas of the course and correct all practices that favor pest development or place undue stress on the turf. Obviously, highly maintained areas such as greens and tees receive a priority for pest control. Lower-maintained grass, such as the driving range or roughs, are a lower priority. A thorough inspection should be conducted of each site on the course before implementing the IPM program. This will provide the groundwork from which all management decisions can be based and also will provide a record justifying the correction of problems made during course construction or from subsequent management. A field history form similar to Table 21–1 should be used to record data, including the current turf species, its area, mowing schedule, soil analysis, soil drainage, fertilizer programs, irrigation scheduling, and shade and traffic patterns. Be prepared to improve existing problems that weaken the turf, or the potential success of the IPM program will be greatly reduced. Solicit funds for these improvements, as they will save money in the long run. Again, this requires open communication between club officials and the superintendent.

   A weather monitoring system should also be installed, which will provide detailed, localized data on important variables such as rainfall patterns, soil temperature and moisture, wind movement, humidity, and sunlight indices. These climatic conditions usually play the most important role in specific turf growth patterns. Being able to track or pinpoint them enables the superintendent to modify cultural practices to supplement or offset its effects.

TABLE 21-1 *Field history report form used for golf courses.*

Turf IPM Field History Report Form

Club _____ Superintendent _____ Phone Number _____ Date _____

Hole Number _____ Scout _____ Phone Number _____

Site	Turf species	Area	Mowing schedule	Soil analysis pH	P	K	Soil drainage	Fertilization amount (N/1,000 sq. ft.) Spring	Summer	Fall	Winter	Frequency	Irrigation scheduling
Green													
Tee													
Fairway													
Rough													
Driving range													
Nursery green													
Practice green													

Comments on specific topics such as shade, overseeding blend, nitrogen carrier, topdressing mix, weather, irrigation salinity levels, and so forth:

_____

_____

_____

_____

3. Set aesthetic or action thresholds and begin monitoring and recording pest levels. An aesthetic or action threshold is the point when pest populations or environmental conditions indicate some action must be taken to prevent intolerable damage. These thresholds will vary according to the location of the course, the specific pest being scouted, the level of use of the turf area, the expectations of club members, and budget constraints.

The pest in question will partially determine its aesthetic threshold. For example, the number of mole crickets tolerated on an area basis is less than the number of sod webworms. Related to this threshold level is the site in which the pest is found. Golf greens have a much lower aesthetic threshold for mole crickets than a rough or out-of-play area. Unfortunately, exact threshold numbers have not been developed for every pest encountered in turf. However, Table 21–2 provides a starting point for several common turf insects.

A professional scout or consultant, who may be employed by several nearby courses, also may be used. Since these scouts visit several courses, pest trends are more easily recognized and information useful from one course can more easily be used to assist others. A scout should hold a degree in agronomy, horticulture, entomology, or plant pathology with an emphasis in pest management.

Tools required for scouting vary with pest problems, scout training, and golf course budget. A good set of eyes and an inquisitive mind are essential, supported by a standard 10X hand or pocket lens, soil probe, soil profile probe, spade, cup cutter, pocket knife, tweezers, scalpel, collection vials and paper bags, digital camera, access to e-mail and the World Wide Web, and field identification guides. Soap and water also are necessary for insect monitoring.

More expensive but precise instruments may be used in a room designated as a diagnostic laboratory, including stereo- and compound-microscopes, soil sieves, pH meter, conductivity meter, and elementary soil analysis kits. These need to be supplemented by ongoing scout training at short courses, formal classes, appropriate diagnostic guides, and opportunities to visit similar set-ups to exchange ideas.

Monitoring intensively maintained golf courses includes scouting greens, tees, fairways, roughs, ornamental plantings, and trees. Greens and tees generally require the greatest amount of attention and are monitored daily or every other day. Remaining areas are monitored less frequently, usually weekly. Monitoring frequency may require adjustment depending on climatic conditions and reports of nearby pest problems.

TABLE 21–2   *Aesthetic or action levels for several common turf insects.*

Insect	Aesthetic or action threshold levels*	Inspection method
Annual bluegrass weevil	30 to 50/sq.ft.	Visual and water float
Armyworms	1 to 4/sq.ft.	Visual and soap flush
Bermudagrass mites	4 to 8 tufts/sq.ft.	Visual
Billbugs	10/sq.ft.	Visual
Black turfgrass ataenius grubs	30 to 50/sq.ft.	Visual
Bluegrass billbugs	6 to 10/sq.ft.	Visual
Chinch bugs (St. Augustinegrass)	20 to 25/sq.ft.	Water float
Cutworms	3 to 8/sq.ft.	Visual and soap flush
European crane fly	25/sq.ft.	Visual and soil
May/Green June beetle grubs	3 to 4/sq.ft.	Visual and soil
Masked chafer beetles	8 to 10/sq.ft.	Visual
Mole crickets	1 to 2/sq.ft.	Visual and soap flush
Sod webworms	6 to 16/sq.ft.	Visual and soap flush

*Smaller numbers represent threshold levels for highly maintained areas such as golf greens and tees. Larger numbers are for lower-maintained areas such as fairways, roughs, athletic fields, and lawns.

Greens and tees are scouted by simply walking around the area to observe insect and disease activity as well as other pest and noninfectious symptoms. Fairways and roughs are usually scouted from a golf cart or utility vehicle. This allows the scout closer examination if symptoms are observed.

The superintendent should provide the scout guidance for traditional pest problem areas or hot spots. This allows the scout to concentrate his or her efforts in these areas when conditions favor those pests. In order to minimize play disruptions and to better recognize specific pest damage such as disease symptoms and nocturnal insect feeding, early morning scouting is suggested.

Determining ways of monitoring pests vary widely and range from simple visual inspection to the use of soil bioassays and immunoassays. For example, the following are used for routine insect detection:

a. **Visual inspection or evaluation of the turf area.** This determines surface-active insects feeding on aboveground plant portions.

b. **Manual inspection of the soil in suspected or damaged areas.** This involves examining the thatch layer and top two to three inches (5 to 7.6 cm) of soil. Usually three sides of a piece of turf are severed with a shovel and the grass is laid back, exposing the thatch and soil. Grub and billbug larvae are the principal insects found by this method.

c. **Soap flush.** This is accomplished by mixing 1.5 fluid ounces (44 ml) of liquid dishwashing soap or one tablespoon (15 ml) of 1 percent pyrethrin in three-to-five gallons (11-to-19 L) of water and applying this mixture to a two × two square foot $(0.6 \times 0.6 \text{ m}^2)$ area of turf. If present, affected insects will soon emerge and usually die due to the soap interfering with respiration. The area should be observed for at least two minutes to see if any insects emerge. Mole crickets, webworms, armyworms, and chinch bugs are detected by this means.

d. **Water flotation.** A metal cylinder, such as an open-ended coffee can six inches (15 cm) or so in diameter, is forced through the turf one to two inches (2.5 to 5 cm) deep and filled with water. The can should be inspected for at least two minutes for any insects floating to the surface. Chinch bugs are detected by this method.

e. **Pitfall traps, pheromone traps, and floral lures.** Pitfall traps consist of one-inch (2.5-cm) diameter PVC pipe with a portion sliced along its side and placed face-up flush with the soil surface. A jar trap one-third full of 70 percent ethanol is placed at one end. As insects move across the soil surface, they will fall in the PVC pipe and then crawl into and be trapped by the jar with ethanol. Pheromone traps and floral lures are two examples of attracting the insect into traps by using either sex hormones or lights. As the chemistry of natural hormones and insect attractants become better understood, these and similar monitoring devices will become more widely available.

Recording pest levels should be done on a form similar to the one in Table 21–3. This will allow the scout and superintendent to monitor pest trends and determine if these levels reach or exceed aesthetic thresholds. Maps developed for each golf hole should accompany these forms. Maps can easily be drawn via the computer using one of the popular "draw" or "paint"-type programs (Figure 21–2). Maps enable the scout to pinpoint pest problem areas, thereby allowing spot versus traditional blanket pesticide treatment. Over time, these maps can indicate where pest problems annually occur and possibly allow superintendents to correct management or environmental variables influencing them. For example, mole cricket egg laying activity (tunneling) during April and May should be mapped and these areas treated in June, as mole crickets tend to deposit eggs in the same areas each year. Chemical control is not effective with early spring applications due to most mole crickets being adults that are not susceptible to most insecticides. Certain insecticides also work best on young insects, as they are selectively ineffective against adults. Scouting and mapping, therefore, are essential for optimizing such materials. Maps also provide area information for the superintendent and allow new crew members a visual aid in treating problem areas. Aerial photographs and digital cameras are valuable in identifying, tracking, and mapping problem areas.

4. Use pesticides correctly and only when threshold limits are reached. One of the goals of IPM is intelligent and prudent pesticide use. Once these thresholds are reached, the pesticide used should be the safest one available; spot treatments should be practiced, if

TABLE 21-3 *Field infestation report form used for golf courses.*

Turf IPM Field Infestation Report Form

Club _____ Superintendent _____ Phone Number _____ Date _____

Hole Number _____ Scout _____ Phone Number _____

Site (turf species)	Mowing height	Soil moisture	Weeds		Diseases		Insects		Nematodes	
			Species	No. or percent	Species	No. or percent	Species	No.	Species	No.
Green:										
Tee:										
Fairway:										
Rough:										

Notes:

Weeds
1. Goosegrass
2. Crabgrass
3. Thin paspalum/Dallisgrass
4. Broadleaves
5. Quackgrass
6. Nutsedge (Yellow, Globe, Purple, Annual, Kyllinga)
7. Nutsedge (Purple)
8. *Poa annua*
9. Broadleaves
10. Other

Diseases
1. Dollar spot
2. Leaf spot
3. *Pythium* blight
4. *Pythium* root rot
5. Fairy ring
6. Brown patch (*R. solani*)
7. Rhizoctonia leaf and sheath blight (*R. zeae*)
8. Bermudagrass decline
9. Algae/Moss
10. Other

Insects
1. Mole crickets
2. Sod webworms
3. Armyworms
4. Cutworms
5. White grubs
6. Fire ants
7. Mites
8. Grass scales
9. Billbugs
10. Other

Nematodes
1. Sting
2. Lance
3. Stubby-root
4. Root-knot
5. Cyst
6. Ring
7. Spiral
8. Sheath
9. Other

FIGURE 21–2
Computerized drawn map of
a golf hole enabling a scout
to identify and mark pest
problem areas.

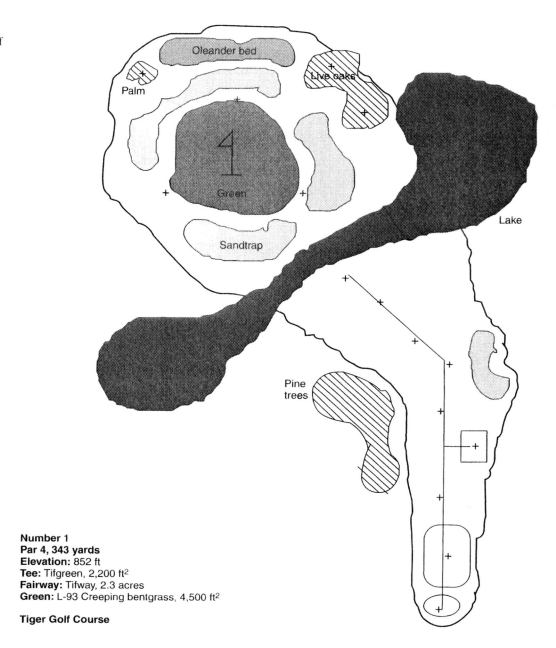

Number 1
Par 4, 343 yards
Elevation: 852 ft
Tee: Tifgreen, 2,200 ft^2
Fairway: Tifway, 2.3 acres
Green: L-93 Creeping bentgrass, 4,500 ft^2

Tiger Golf Course

possible; and all safety precautions should be followed. Pests should also be treated during
the most vulnerable stage of their life cycle. In addition:

- Use natural biological controls when possible.
- Spray only when necessary and strictly control the location of pesticide application.
- Select pesticides that are least toxic, less mobile, and have a short half-life.
- Identify areas that may be particularly susceptible to ground/surface water
  contamination.

5. Evaluate the results of the habitat modification and pesticide treatments by periodically
   monitoring the site environment and pest populations. Keep written records of site pest
   management objectives, monitoring methods, and data collected. Also record the actions
   taken and the results obtained by the pest management methods. This will provide
   additional information for club members who do not understand the program but would
   understand results. This will also demonstrate that golf course superintendents are striving
   to reduce the chemical inputs in maintaining the course and obtain an ecological balance
   between man and nature.

SUMMARY

Pest management strategies for turf production are in their infancy but are nonetheless being developed and used. Strategies necessary for a successful IPM program have been outlined and should provide a starting point for golf course superintendents. No one recipe, however, will work uniformly across all golf courses. Individual programs will most likely evolve for each particular course depending on their demands, needs, acceptance of pest damage, and budgets to work with. Golf course members should realize that it will take time to implement and measure the success of IPM methods. Open communication between all crew members, club officials, players, and the superintendent are necessary for programs to be understood and to succeed. Read and study information on pests associated with golf courses in your state, their life cycles, the ecology surrounding their occurrence, and the pest management strategies to successfully suppress their numbers below threshold levels. More importantly, follow those management guidelines that encourage competitive turf growth and discourage pest establishment.

IPM represents a case of redirecting resources invested in turf maintenance, in which professional knowledge and judgment is partially substituted for chemicals. It may or may not be cheaper in up-front costs, but does provide an excellent means of reducing unwelcome environmental and personnel risks without sacrificing turf health. IPM reduces pesticide use or "softens" the kinds of pesticides needed, as well as our potential liability for unforeseeable clean-ups or other corrective actions for specific pesticide use or handling sites. IPM thus improves the image of the golf industry as good stewards of modern urban society.

CHAPTER
22

Turfgrass Diseases

INTRODUCTION

Plant diseases are among the most feared, yet least understood, phenomena turf managers face. Although some types of diseases are present at almost any given time on most golf courses, they may or may not develop into epidemic proportions that cause unacceptable damage. Many interacting factors determine the severity of disease development over time.

This chapter will discuss turf diseases in the context of their importance, diagnosis, prediction, risk of damage, and recuperative ability.

WHAT IS A DISEASE?

One definition of a disease is any disturbance preventing the normal development of a plant that reduces its economic or aesthetic value. Diseases interfere with the normal function of some part of the plant, resulting in lower yields or reduced quality. Technically, a **disease** is defined as a detrimental condition developing from a continuous interaction between a causal agent and a host plant.

A diseased condition can also develop from deficiencies or excesses of certain parameters. This is directly analogous to the concept of disease in animals or humans, in which the absence or excesses of factors can induce a diseased condition in the host.

Diseases are caused by either living agents (**biotic agents**) or nonliving agents (**abiotic agents**). Abiotic agents can be environmental parameters, such as air pollutants, soil or water pollutants, lightning, inadequate moisture, light, air movement or nutrition, mechanical injury, and so forth. An important point to note is that abiotic causal agents induce disease that is *noninfectious,* meaning the disease does not spread from affected plants to nonaffected ones.

Biotic causal agents are living organisms capable of causing disease, including both microorganisms and parasitic plants. In contrast to abiotic agents, biotic causal agents cause disease that is *infectious,* whereby infected plants produce inoculum that is spread in various ways to nonaffected, susceptible plants. Biotic agents of disease include fungi, bacteria, phytoplasmas, nematodes, viruses and viroids, parasitic plants, and protozoa.

Infectious diseases in turfgrasses, as in other plants, originate from an interaction between a susceptible plant, a disease-producing organism (usually a fungus), and an environment favorable for the disease-causing organism to attack. Often the environment is unfavorable for ideal growth

FIGURE 22–1 Disease occurrence requires the simultaneous overlapping of a susceptible plant, a disease-causing pathogen, and a favorable environment.

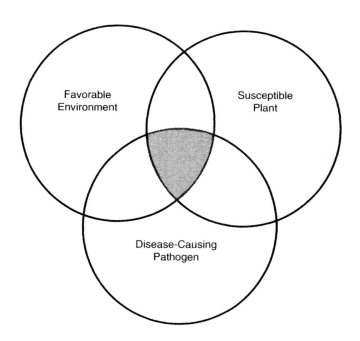

and development of the host plant. Diseases do not occur until all three parameters overlap (Figure 22–1). Information on all three factors should be gathered to obtain information for diagnosis of the problem. Turf managers should try to alter any or all of these three factors to combat the disease. Thus, disease produces an abnormality that injures the plant or reduces its value.

Turfgrass plants affected with disease give visible evidence that something is wrong. **Signs** involve directly seeing a pathogen or its parts and products on a plant. The plant's visible reactions to a disease is referred to as its **symptoms.** Some symptoms of turfgrass disease may be leaf lesions, turfgrass thinning or discoloration, the development of small areas of dead plants within the turfgrass community, and many other symptoms characteristic of specific diseases that will be discussed later. Sometimes parts of the causal agent itself are directly visible with the unaided eye or with the assistance of a hand magnifying lens. In this case, disease **signs** involve directly seeing a pathogen or its parts and products on a plant.

In most turfgrass situations, the environment is the key factor for disease development since the turfgrass host and turfgrass pathogens are virtually always present, especially in older turfgrass stands. While turfgrasses may be affected by diseases all year long, individual turf diseases are generally prominent for only a few months each year, usually due to weather patterns and subsequent environmental effects. However, any stress (environmental or man-made) placed on turf will weaken it, making it more susceptible to disease development and less able to recover from disease once ideal conditions for disease cease (for example, a change in weather or chemical treatment). If the stress occurs during a time of year when the grass in question is likely to vigorously grow, then recovery from disease is faster and frequently complete. However, if the stress occurs in combination with unfavorable environmental conditions for turf recuperation, then diseases can be devastating. Frequently, these unfavorable conditions for the host also favor rapid reproduction of the pathogen.

This chapter deals with infectious turfgrass diseases, caused mostly by fungi. Turfgrass injury (a one-time occurrence) such as a lightning strike, or disorders such as nutritional deficiencies, herbicide injury, cold stress, heat stress, chemical spills, air pollution, and so forth, will not be discussed except as they affect infectious diseases.

BIOTIC ORGANISMS CAUSING TURFGRASS DISEASES
Fungi

Fungi are small, threadlike organisms composed of tiny filaments (hyphae) that cannot manufacture their own food. Although many fungi resemble plants without chlorophyll, they are not plants

TABLE 22–1 *Parasitic habits of turfgrass fungi.*

Saprophytes—Fungi that feed on dead organic matter such as thatch.

Parasites—Fungi that feed directly on plants to obtain some or all of their food.

Parasitic habit	Turf pathogen	Primary infection sites
Facultative parasites—Parasitic fungi that can survive as saprophytes until conditions are favorable for infecting living plants, after which they become parasitic.	• *Colletotrichum, Curvularia, Xanthomonas* • *Pythium, Typhula*	• Mostly shoots • Mostly roots
Facultative saprophytes—Fungi that function primarily as parasites, but can temporarily subsist as saprophytes on dead organic matter.	• *Gaeumannonyces, Leptosphaeria, Magnaporthe,* • *Pyricularia, Rhizoctonia, Sclerotinia, Microdochium (Fusarium)* • *Drechslera, Bipolaris*	• Roots • Shoots • Shoots and roots
Obligate parasites—Fungi that live only in association with a living host, feeding on them.	• *Erysiphe, Puccinia, Urocystis, Ustilago,* Panicum mosaic virus (SADV) • Parasitic nematodes	• Shoots • Roots
Obligate saprophytes—Fungi that only live with dead organic residues, such as thatch and mat, and do not infect living plants.	• *Fuligo, Mucilago, Physarum* • *Agaricus, Lepiota, Lycoperdon, Tricholoma*	• Shoots • Roots

and are classified in their own Kingdom. Fungi are either parasitic or saprophytic (Table 22–1). **Parasites** obtain their nutrition from another living organism, and saprophytes obtain their nutrition from nonliving organic materials. Some fungi are **facultative parasites,** meaning they are normally saprophytic, but can sometimes infect living plants. An example is *Sclerotium rolfsii,* which causes southern blight. Most fungi that are pathogens of turfgrass are **facultative saprophytes,** which are normally parasitic, but can survive in the absence of the host on dead organic matter (usually crop debris). Examples include *Rhizoctonia solani,* which causes brown patch, and *Sclerotinia homoeocarpa,* which causes dollar spot. Fungi occurring in turf systems as saprophytes may nevertheless be mistaken as parasites, such as the harmless slime mold fungi. Fairy ring fungi, although saprophytic, do cause detrimental chronic disorders in turf. Some fungi, such as rust fungi and downy mildew fungi, are **obligate parasites;** these organisms must parasitize living plants in order to grow and reproduce. They utilize a specialized hypha within the infected plant cells called a **haustorium** that is used to extract nutrients from the living host. **Obligate saprophytes** live only in association with dead organic residues, such as thatch; thus, they do not infect living plants. Examples include the true slime molds, *Mucilago* and *Physarum.*

Most fungi produce **spores** (seedlike bodies) that are spread by wind, water, mechanical means such as mowers, or by infected plant materials such as grass clippings. Under moist conditions, spores germinate and grow by producing threadlike filaments, or **hyphae.** Collectively, a mass of hyphae is known as a **mycelium** (or **mycelia** for plural). Mycelia may function by absorbing nutrients from plant cells and also can become dormant, thereby providing some fungi a means to survive periods of inactive growth. Some fungi produce hardened, aggregated mycelial structures called **sclerotia,** which may aid in resisting unfavorable environmental conditions.

When a fungal pathogen is not actively attacking the plant, it has not disappeared from the turfgrass area but is simply surviving in a dormant state or as a saprophyte living off organic materials in the thatch and soil layers in the environment. Fungicides generally do not eliminate turfgrass pathogens, but simply suppress the pathogen's activity on the plant while the environment is conducive for disease. Generally, they should be thought of as plant pharmaceuticals acting as plant protectants and/or chemotherapeutic agents.

Fungi produce spores either through sexual reproduction, by asexual means, or as a combination of both. The portion of a fungi's life cycle involving sexual reproduction is termed the **perfect stage.** The **imperfect stage** is the life cycle phase involving asexual reproduction. In some fungi, spores produced asexually in vast numbers may quickly colonize susceptible plants and produce epidemics.

Bacteria

Bacteria are microscopic single-celled organisms with rigid cell walls but no organized nucleus. They are **prokaryotes.** Fungi are **eukaryotes,** meaning they have organized nuclei within their cells. Bacteria reproduce by fission (or simple cell division), and can rapidly reproduce. Bacteria lack chlorophyll, although bacterial pathogens can be obligate or facultative parasites, and other bacteria can be beneficial as saprophytes as well. They overwinter, like fungi, in and on thatch, plants, seed, soil, and sometimes in insects. Bacterial pathogens enter plants only through wounds (which may be made by living organisms, such as insects) or natural openings, such as lenticels, hydathodes, or stomata. Although some bacteria are able to swim, splashing water, wind-blown water, insects, infected tools, or plant cuttings are the normal means of dispersal. Once inside the host, bacteria cause damage by producing toxins or they plug vascular tissue. This blocking retards water movement and infected plants wilt. Practically all plant-infecting bacteria are rod-shaped.

More than 80 bacteria species have been reported to cause plant diseases. Fortunately for turf managers, only a few damage finely maintained turf. The only major known economically important bacterial turf disease is **bacterial wilt** caused by specific forms of the pathogen, *Burkholderia (Xanthomonas) campestris*. These forms attack a number of grass species but are found most often on annual bluegrass and the vegetatively propagated creeping bentgrass cultivars Toronto C-15, Nimisilla, and Cohansey. The switch in the 1980s to sand topdressing programs has been associated with several outbreaks of bacterial wilt in vegetatively propagated bentgrasses. The sand was thought to cause excessive wounds, allowing infection, or possibly the number of beneficial organisms in pure sand topdressing were too low to compete with the pathogen. Recently, bacterial wilt in annual bluegrass has been increasing in occurrence, but bacterial wilt in bentgrass has not been reported since the 1980s' outbreaks. Bacterial wilt symptoms initially appear as tiny red- to copper-colored spots resembling dollar spot except for the unusual color. As the disease progresses, the spots become larger and portions of the green wilt as the bacteria clog the xylem tissue of the plants. When cut and observed microscopically ($\geq$100X), infected leaves ooze out streaming bacteria cells.

The disease is enhanced by extensive rainfall, followed by warm weather that induces wilting. Control of the disease in bentgrass involved switching from vegetatively planted turfgrass to seeded varieties with a wider genetic base for resistance. Avoiding plant injury through sand topdressing where the disease is present also helps. The antibiotic oxytetracycline (Mycoshield) may provide temporary (four- to six-week) control of this bacteria. However, repeat treatments are necessary, which soon become cost prohibitive. In addition, the antibiotic can be phytotoxic in warm weather.

Nematodes

Nematodes are small eel-like worms that lack eyes. Those capable of causing disease in plants are mostly microscopic, with the largest approaching only 1/16 inch (1.6 mm) in length. Nematodes cause disease by infecting plant roots; however, some species infect leaves, stems, buds, and even replace embryos in the seeds of some plants. They possess a specialized feeding apparatus, a needlelike stylet, in their heads, which is utilized to tear and stab plant cells and extract their contents for nematode nutrition. Some, like root-knot and cyst nematodes, set up specialized feeding sites within plant roots, inducing giant cells and cell proliferation in root tissues, leading to gall formation in the case of root-knot nematodes. Nematodes as turfgrass pathogens are discussed in Chapter 24.

Phytoplasmas

Phytoplasmas (previously known as mycoplasma-like organisms) are also prokaryotes, but do not have rigid cell walls. They are also believed to be obligate parasites, and are vectored by insects (many are leafhopper-transmitted). Some diseases, called yellow diseases, once thought to be caused by viruses have since been shown to be caused by phytoplasmas. Although diseases of turf in other parts of the world have reportedly been caused by phytoplasmas, such as yellow dwarf of bentgrass in Japan, none have been reported in the United States.

Viruses

Viruses are much smaller than bacteria, and can only be viewed with the aid of electron microscopes. Viruses are extremely small obligate parasites composed of nucleic acid (DNA or RNA) and a protective protein coat. Viruses are really complex molecules, but are infectious in nature. Viruses infect plants through wounds or by introduction into cells by means of a vector (insect, fungus, nematode), depending on the virus. For example, barley yellow dwarf virus is vectored by aphids, tomato spotted wilt virus is vectored by thrips, and wheat soilborne mosaic is vectored by a soilborne fungus. Once inside the cell, a virus forces the plant's genetic material to make more viral particles. Being produced inside the plant, viruses cause systemic infections. They seldom kill their host plants, but do severely affect their quality and health.

The diseases **St. Augustinegrass decline (SAD)** and **centipede mosaic** are the only economically important virus-induced diseases in turfgrasses. These are caused by various strains of **panicum mosaic virus** which is easily mechanically transmitted, most often by mowers and possibly by insects. St. Augustinegrass decline occurs most often in Texas and the southeastern United States. Symptoms first appear as a mild chlorotic mottling, blotching, and a speckling or stippling of the leaf blades for the first several years. Initially, symptoms resemble iron or zinc deficiency, mite damage, or yellow tuft (downy mildew) disease (Plate 22–1). Virus symptoms on infected leaf blades have a mosaic pattern with yellow streaking. Leaf nutrient deficiency symptoms, however, include continuous yellow stripes parallel to the veins. Symptoms intensify over time and infected plants may eventually die, leaving voids for weeds to fill. St. Augustinegrass grown under low nitrogen or drought conditions appear most susceptible. Chemical controls are not available. Planting a resistant variety such as "Floratam," "Raleigh," "Floralawn," or "Seville" St. Augustinegrass is the only known means of controlling this disease, but cultivar selection is important because of differences in low-temperature tolerance as well as chinch bug susceptibility. Maintenance of good turf vigor and density by using proper fertilization, mowing, and fertility practices helps mask the symptoms.

Parasitic Higher Plants

Parasitic plants, like mistletoe and dodder, and protozoa are also known to cause infectious diseases in some plants, but none are known to cause turfgrass diseases.

THE DISEASE CYCLE

The nature of infectious disease is dynamic, meaning it is always changing. The dynamics involve the growth and reproduction of the host and the pathogen, as affected by environmental conditions. The host and the pathogen have definite life cycles, detailing their growth and reproduction. The disease cycle illustrates the phases of the interaction between the host and the pathogen as disease is developing and changing. A **disease cycle** might include the following phases: **pathogen survival** (overwintering, or oversummering); **pathogen dispersal** (by wind, water, on plant material, or by vectors); **inoculation** (the pathogen coming in contact with the host); **infection** (penetration of host tissues); **colonization of host tissues; reproduction** (within tissues and by propagules such as spores); and finally, **pathogen dispersal** once again.

The infection process begins when a fungus spore or mycelium comes into contact with a host plant. With germination, the fungus spore produces a germ tube that enters the plant through a wound or by penetrating the cuticle and epidermis of a leaf, sometimes through stomates, but also directly through the leaf surface. Depending on the pathogen, root and crown tissues may be attacked as well. Certain fungi, such as *Pythium,* directly disrupt cells by producing enzymes that cause plant cell walls to dissolve. The cell contents then leak into the surrounding tissue where the fungal hyphae can absorb nutrients.

Almost all fungi require moisture on leaves and a favorable temperature to start disease development. Because of this, turfgrass diseases are most common during rainy or foggy weather or when excessive moisture remains on leaves or in the soil for extended periods (Figure 22–2). Since most fungi do not infect turfgrass in the absence of moisture, proper irrigation and soil drainage are important keys to disease management.

FIGURE 22–2
Continuous surface moisture
provides ideal conditions for
the development of many
turfgrass diseases. Shown
is the dispersal of dew by
"whipping" the turf
with a pole.

Once inside the host plant, the pathogen begins to obtain nutrition directly from living cells or from products of cellular decomposition, followed by an incubation period where the pathogen produces spores, sclerotia, or other survival structures that can serve to infect other plants. Symptoms eventually develop and, with continuous infection cycles and favorable environmental conditions for the pathogen, an epidemic results, causing widespread loss of turf. Under unfavorable conditions, some pathogenic organisms can survive in a "resting stage" as **sclerotia**. These persist in the turf until the return of environmental conditions that favor their germination and subsequent infection of susceptible turfgrasses.

EPIDEMIOLOGY OF PLANT DISEASES

Plant diseases are destructive when epidemics develop. An epidemic develops when there is an increase in the amount of disease caused by a pathogen in a plant population over time. Genetics of plants can affect the genetics of pathogens attacking them, and vice versa. Disease epidemics are described by disease progress curves, which depict increases in amounts and severity of disease over time.

Since pathogens have evolved to efficiently survive, or produce abundant inoculum (reproduction), and turfgrass host plants are abundant, environmental conditions favoring pathogens and disfavoring hosts are the primary driving factors in the development of epidemics. The primary environmental factors affecting disease development (and plant growth) are:

1. **Temperature**—Different plants and pathogens thrive at different temperatures. There are warm-weather and cool-weather diseases.
2. **Moisture**—Moisture occurs in the form of rain, dew, and irrigation, as well as fog and relative humidity. In many cases, disease is highly correlated with the amount of rainfall. Fungal and bacterial diseases are more common in the eastern United States than in the arid west.
3. **Light**—Quality, intensity, and duration affect the growth of hosts and pathogens. Some pathogens are killed by UV radiation, while others have evolved to survive this radiation (melanin-like pigments). Morning shade, in particular, can enhance dew existence and maintain cooler temperatures, possibly favoring diseases.
4. **Wind**—Wind spreads pathogens and insect vectors; in combination with rain, wind disperses viable propagules of pathogens.
5. **Soil pH and nutrient status**—Some pathogens can efficiently survive low soil pH levels, and others cannot. For instance, *Phytophthora* and *Pythium* fungi are somewhat sensitive to low soil pH levels, although in turf this has not led to a practical control measure. Nutrition

affects the rate of growth of plant tissue and the ability of plants to defend themselves against disease. Primary nutrients and micronutrients affect host susceptibility to disease as well as their ability to recover or defend themselves.

DISEASE CONTROL STRATEGIES

Correct Diagnosis

The first step in turfgrass disease management is identification of the problem. For accurate diagnosis, a number of steps are taken, the first being careful observation of **symptoms.** Leaf spots in various sizes, colors, and shapes are among the most common symptoms visible. Seeing the fungi directly is usually difficult due to their microscopic size. However, certain observable parts of the pathogen (called **signs**) may be visible with a hand lens. Common signs include spores such as yellow masses associated with various rusts, and mycelium, which may be visible in early morning with dollar spot or Pythium blight. Patterns of symptomatic turf are key observations for diagnosis in the field. Are discrete patches formed? What is the size and aggregation of patches? Do leaves have identifiable lesions? Do these lesions and thinning stands occur throughout the turf or only in patches? Are symptomatic plants associated with unique environmental or microclimatic factors of importance?

As mentioned, most pathogens (fungi) causing turfgrass diseases are microscopic; therefore, individual spores cannot be seen by the naked eye. However, with some diseases, spores collect to sufficient levels that they become visible as threads, powders, or masses. When the causal fungus is visible, its appearance often becomes the most important clue for diagnosis.

True **pathogenicity** (ability to cause disease) can be proved only by reliable scientific methods, usually requiring a laboratory and greenhouse or growth chamber. Three disease factors (grass, pathogen, and environment) provide the sources of diagnostic information. Thus, the next step in identification is an examination of the environment during the onset of disease occurrence. For example, what were the temperature, light intensity, and moisture conditions prior to and during disease development? The nature of the disease site also is important. Air and water drainage, soil conditions, sun and shade, slope, and nearness of other plantings or buildings all may be important in the development of turfgrass diseases. Prior chemical applications to the site, including pesticides and fertilizers, may be important to make a correct diagnosis. Heavy thatch accumulation and poor mowing practices stressing the turf may trigger or amplify certain disease problems.

Finally, the submission of affected turf samples to a reputable laboratory or pathologist can assist in receiving a correct diagnosis and advice on corrective measures to take.

Since it is usually not practical to eliminate the turfgrass host, disease control recommendations are aimed at: (1) using disease-resistant grasses, (2) suppressing the pathogen, and (3) altering the environment so it is less favorable for disease development. Thus, an integrated management program including cultural and chemical methods is the key to preventing and controlling turfgrass diseases. This method uses all available tools to manage diseases below an economic or aesthetic threshold level.

Cultural Control

Cultural practices should promote an environment not conducive for pathogen infection and disease development as well as promote healthy, vigorous plant growth to better fight off an attack. This may be achieved by planting disease-resistant cultivars, if they are available; following sound principles of site preparation during turfgrass establishment; and managing an established turf through proper mowing, fertilization, irrigation, and cultivation practices. For all fine turf areas, cultural control should encompass landscape design to promote drying conditions, sunlight penetration, good drainage, and so forth. Since living organisms are involved (turfgrass plants as well as the pathogens affecting them), a goal should be selecting appropriate plants for the particular site. If this is performed, disease potential should be minimized (but will never be eliminated). If a disease should affect the turfgrass, other cultural practices should be implemented first or, at the very least, implemented at the same time fungicides are applied. If a particular putting green, tee, or fairway has a history of developing a particular disease at a particular time of year, then one should implement cultural practices to prevent this yearly reoccurrence. If changing a practice will prevent problems later, then it may be reasonable to change the practice. The cultural practices that follow are all designed to alter the turfgrass environment to prevent diseases or at least lessen their severity.

Disease-Resistant Grasses

When establishing a new turf area or when renovating disease-damaged turf, it is important to select grasses known to be resistant to pests commonly occurring in the area (Table 22–2). Resistant cultivars can produce chemical toxins to the fungus, have morphological or chemical characteristics that prevent fungi entrance, or lack a nutrient the fungus needs. For example, certain Kentucky bluegrass varieties are resistant to melting out, stripe smut diseases, and spring leaf spot, diseases that devastate many bluegrass varieties. Crenshaw bentgrass, meanwhile, is highly susceptible to dollar spot disease. Blends of various varieties or even turf species often provide a wider spectrum of pest resistance than planting a monoculture of one specific variety. If one cultivar loses its disease resistance, the entire turf stand is not ruined since other resistant cultivars are present. For example, blending Crenshaw and L-93 bentgrasses reduces dollar spot disease occurrence compared to Crenshaw-only stands. It is generally not a good idea to replant the same grass previously killed by the same disease, if another option exists.

In several cases, grasses naturally turn a different color or form patches that are often confused with disease symptoms. For example, Penncross and some other cultivars of creeping bentgrass often begin to segregate over time to distinct patches in terms of color, density, and disease resistance. This segregation is often confused with disease symptoms, causing major concern by players and management. Bermudagrass also often turns a purple color in fall when days are bright and nights are cool (Plate 22–2) and can also form distinct patches of grass with a different texture, color, and density, causing similar concern as with bentgrass when a disease is active. These are nondisease-related situations where fungicides provide little, if any, relief.

Proper Turfgrass Establishment

Disease problems can often be avoided by implementing proper site preparation prior to planting. Buried debris, soil layering, and failure to incorporate amendments or construct drainage facili-

TABLE 22–2 *Relative disease proneness of turfgrass species.*

Susceptibility ranking	Turfgrass species
Very high	Annual bluegrass
	"Colonial" bentgrass
	Creeping bentgrass
	Velvet bentgrass
	Roughstalk bluegrass
High	Kentucky bluegrass
	Perennial ryegrass
	Fine fescues
	Tall fescue
Moderate	Bermudagrass
	St. Augustinegrass
	Zoysiagrass
Low	Bahiagrass
	Carpetgrass
	Centipedegrass
	Buffalograss
	Kikuyugrass

ties where necessary can provide unfavorable turfgrass growing conditions. The turf may then become weakened from stresses associated with site construction, causing the turf to become more susceptible to disease.

Soil to be planted should be of uniform texture and well-structured in order to provide sufficient moisture, aeration, and nutrients for optimum turfgrass growth. A minimum of six inches (15 cm) of good topsoil is recommended. The site should also be well-drained. Surface drainage should be implemented to remove excess water following heavy rainfall or irrigation. Internal drainage should be provided by using soil mixes or amendments that allow adequate infiltration and percolation rates. Drain tiles installed below the surface can aid in reducing excessive surface moisture that can weaken turf roots over time.

Golf greens need special provisions for ensuring adequate drainage. Specially amended topsoil composed primarily of sand with some organic amendment and perhaps a small percentage of soil should be used along with subsurface drainage tiles. This is critical when trying to grow grasses outside their naturally adapted areas, such as growing bentgrass in the hot, humid areas.

Mowing

Mowing is the most common turf maintenance operation and, when improperly done, probably the most damaging. Every time a mower removes leaf tissue, a wound is created through which a pathogen may enter the plant. Mowing also spreads certain fungal spores and mycelium. In addition, turfgrasses cut below their optimum height will become stressed and more susceptible to diseases, especially root rots. This practice reduces the recuperative potential of the grass and should not be practiced during times of the year when recuperative potential is low. Mower blades should be sharp and properly adjusted; otherwise, the aesthetic appearance and vigor of the turfgrass may be reduced along with the wounds it creates. Also, on bentgrass/Poa, switch from grooved to solid rollers in summer to reduce wounding and additional mower stress.

The proper mowing height for the particular turfgrass should also be followed. Mowing too close weakens the turfgrass to where its competitiveness against diseases may be reduced. Mowing closely depletes root carbohydrate reserves, which weakens its recovery potential following stress or damage. Raise the height on putting greens prone to disease during specific times of the year and on greens with active disease areas. Over the past few years, the height of cut on greens has been reduced substantially, with one-eighth inch (3.2 mm) or lower as the standard. This low height of cut reduces the leaf tissue necessary for photosynthesis, the process by which the plant produces energy for growth. In addition, diseases eventually reduce the leaf canopy and photosynthesis is reduced even further. Raising the height of cut increases the green plant tissue needed for photosynthesis, resulting in more energy for turfgrass growth and development and, subsequently, prevention or recovery from the disease. Of course, raising a height of cut after the golf green has succumbed to various pathogens and stresses is too little, too late. Excessively close mowing favors many diseases, and just as importantly disfavors turf recovery, even if pathogens are controlled with fungicides. This is true for root diseases such as Pythium root rot, bermudagrass decline, and summer patch, as well as other diseases such as Helminthosporium leaf spot, anthracnose, brown patch, dollar spot, rusts, and damage from plant parasitic nematodes.

Clipping removal helps speed the drying of the turf surface and may help reduce certain diseases such as dollar spot, brown patch, and Pythium blight. This is most beneficial for high-maintenance turf such as golf greens and tees. Clipping removal generally does not significantly influence disease development for lawns, as long as proper mowing practices are followed for the particular site and turf species being utilized. Also avoid mowing when excessive free moisture is present on the surface of a green.

Irrigation Practices

Moisture is critical for many fungal spores to germinate and develop. While irrigation is essential to prevent drought damage, the amount of water and the timing of its application can prevent or contribute to disease development. Dew (more importantly, the length of the dew period), a critical factor for disease development, is dependent on temperature and humidity. Extending the length of the dew (free water) period by irrigating in the evening before dew forms or in the morning after the dew evaporates extends the dew period. Therefore, irrigate when dew is already present, usually in the pre-dawn hours. This will also dilute or remove the guttation fluid accumulating at the cut leaf tip, which may provide a food source for some pathogens. For many golf courses, eight hours or more may be needed to irrigate the entire course. Since the putting greens are most susceptible to diseases, irrigate them during the pre-dawn hours, so they will dry quicker. As more and more courses implement new computer-driven irrigation systems, this is often easier to accomplish.

If localized dry spots have developed, supplemental hand watering will be required on these areas in addition to the normal irrigation cycle. Spiking these areas before watering is also useful, as is the addition of materials that increase water absorption. As a general guideline, deep, infrequent irrigation discourages most diseases and encourages plant rooting. Shallow, frequent (e.g., daily) irrigation encourages many pathogens and reduces plant rooting, thereby reducing its vigor to resist diseases. Soil acts as a reservoir for water; thus, managers do not have to frequently irrigate. Rooting depths should be routinely monitored, and irrigation cycles appropriately adjusted to supply adequate moisture to the entire rootzone, encouraging plants to "search" for water held in reserve. When initial signs of impending stress are noted (ideally, just before this stage), adequate irrigation should again be supplied to wet the rootzone.

Nutritional Status

Many diseases are also influenced by the nutritional status of the grass, especially concerning nitrogen. Achieving a perfect balance to maintain green, healthy, and growing plants is the goal because both excessively high and low nitrogen fertility contributes to turfgrass diseases and recovery (Table 22–3). Excessive nitrogen applications, for example, encourage *Rhizoctonia*, *Pythium*, snow molds, powdery mildew, and stripe smut. Low nitrogen levels, meanwhile, encourage dollar spot, rust diseases, and red thread. When a foliar disease is active, select a fertilizer blend with a high percentage of the slow-release component and a lower percentage of the rapid-release component. Adequate nutrition should be available to plants for continued growth, but the goal is to minimize luxuriant growth that induces greater susceptibility to pathogens. With bentgrass/Poa, for example, summer fertility typically involves weekly to biweekly applications of soluble fertilizers at 0.1 to 0.2 actual nitrogen per 1,000 square feet (49 to 98 g N/100 m^2) per application. Micronutrients, such as iron, also are added.

Potassium is an important component in disease prevention as it reduces plant stress. Again, a nonstressed plant is not as susceptible to diseases. This has probably best been documented with "*Helminthosporium*" leaf spot diseases. An N:K ratio of at least 1:1 is best, although a ratio of 1:2 may be necessary in certain circumstances. It is important to remember potassium is not held tightly in sandy soils. While many superintendents are using slow-release nitrogen components, quick-release, highly soluble potassium sources are often used. If fertilizer is not frequently applied, a nitrogen/potassium imbalance may occur, creating a stress situation for the turf. Soil and leaf tissue testing should be performed periodically to indicate plant availability of nutrients.

Today, most new or reconstructed putting greens are usually composed of at least 80 percent sand, with the remaining component composed of an organic material such as peat moss. These high sand content greens are not composed of constituents such as clays that help to hold potentially leachable nutrients, such as potassium, in the rootzone. These rootzone mixes initially have a very low cation exchange capacity (CEC). Two to three years will be required before a rootzone

TABLE 22–3 *Turfgrass disease occurrence as influenced by nitrogen levels.*

Diseases normally encouraged by excessive nitrogen fertility	Diseases normally decreased by adequate nitrogen fertility
Gray leaf spot	Anthracnose
Gray snow mold (*Typhula* blight)	Dollar spot
Pink snow mold (*Fusarium* or *Microdochium* patch)	"Helminthosporium" leaf spot
Pythium diseases	Melting out
Rhizoctonia diseases	Necrotic ring spot/summer patch
Spring dead spot	Red thread
Stripe smut	Rust

with desirable CEC characteristics develops. Thus, during the first few years, plant nutrition should be carefully monitored.

Cultivation/Thatch Control

Thatch is the tightly bound layer of living and dead stems and roots that develops between the zone of green vegetation and soil surface. It is a natural and desirable component of a turfgrass ecosystem. However, an excessive thatch accumulation indicates an imbalance has occurred, with plant tissue being produced more quickly than being decomposed. Parameters impeding microbial decomposition are excessively wet or dry conditions, very high or low thatch pH, inadequate nitrogen levels, and repeated use of chemical pesticides (particularly fungicides).

Most fungi causing turfgrass diseases do not simply disappear when disease activity subsides. Some pathogens remain dormant when environmental conditions are not conducive for their growth. Other fungi are saprophytes; thus, they survive by decomposing organic matter such as the dead tissue in the thatch layer. In fact, these fungi are important components in the thatch decomposition process. In both cases, the fungi are not causing any harm to the turf. However, by allowing an accumulation of excessive thatch, the population of fungi potentially causing a disease if the proper environmental conditions develop increases. Therefore, the goal in thatch management is to reduce disease potential but not entirely eliminate the fungi. Excessive thatch accumulations also encourage turf crowns, rhizomes, and stolons to be exposed to stressful environmental (incipient drought, low temperatures, high temperatures, etc.), as well as biological, stress factors.

Excessive soil compaction should also be avoided as this may reduce the oxygen level, leaving roots weak and more susceptible to disease attack. Soil compaction also impedes subsurface water movement and can encourage pests such as algae, goosegrass, and annual bluegrass. Sound agronomic practices such as coring, topdressing, slicing, spiking, and deep vertical mowing help to reduce thatch and alleviate soil compaction. One, however, must be careful not to aggressively mechanically damage bentgrass/Poa turf and some cultivars of ultradwarf bermudagrasses during summer stress from brushing, grooming, aerating, verticutting, dethatching, and so forth. Mechanically damaged turf has more wounds from which disease spores can enter.

Other Cultural Control Practices

Other practices help in reducing turfgrass stress as well as turfgrass diseases. For example, cool-season grasses grown in hot, humid areas should have adequate air circulation across the turf surface to prevent heat accumulation. Dense shrubs or trees surrounding these areas should be thinned to allow maximum air circulation. Shade from these sources also weaken most grasses and can induce diseases such as powdery mildew and "*Helminthosporium*" leaf spot or melting out. Roots from these surrounding plants also can compete with turfgrass for water and nutrients. Soil pH should also be monitored and maintained between 5.5 and 6.5. High soil pH encourages certain diseases such as take-all patch, spring dead spot, bermudagrass decline, and pink snow mold. Appropriate use of acidifying fertilizers such as ammonium nitrate/sulfate help reduce these and other diseases.

CHEMICAL CONTROL PRACTICES

A primary misconception many turf managers have concerning fungicides is that these materials kill fungi. Fungicides do not eliminate pathogens from the turfgrass area, and should never be utilized with this strategy in mind. When a fungal pathogen is not actively attacking the plant, it has not disappeared from the turfgrass area but is simply surviving in the environment in a dormant state or as a saprophyte living off dead organic matter in the thatch and soil layers. Most fungicides act as **fungistatic** compounds, meaning they primarily suppress fungal growth to prevent plant infection during environmental conditions conducive for disease development (Figure 22–3). Fungicides are applied either prior to anticipated disease outbreaks (**preventive**) or following the appearance of disease symptoms (**curative** or **eradicants**). Thus, fungicides should be considered as prophylactic plant pharmaceuticals. Those with some eradicant activity still work as plant protectants, but may also behave as chemical therapeutic plant pharmaceuticals.

Preventive fungicides are needed when chronically damaging diseases occur. This is especially true on golf greens that have seasonal problems with certain diseases such as Pythium blight, summer decline, brown patch, and snow molds. Preventive use of fungicides often allows

substantially lower rates than those required for curative treatment. Knowledge of the site, the grass being cultured, and the probability of certain diseases occurring during particular environmental conditions is crucial information for proper deployment of chemical and cultural control strategies. Newly overseeded areas also are prime candidates for preventive fungicide use until the overseeded grass becomes fully established. It is perfectly acceptable to use fungicides on a preventive basis as long as one understands what diseases/pathogens one is protecting the grass from at any given time of the year.

To be effective, a curative fungicide use strategy should be used at the onset of disease symptoms. Obviously, correct disease diagnosis is crucial for this strategy. Once significant turf damage has occurred, it is generally useless to curatively apply fungicides. Many fungicides, such as mancozeb, ethazole, and others, act as contacts (nonplant penetrants). They are more economical to use and less likely to have pathogens develop disease resistance; however, they generally only provide short duration (7 to 14 day) control under high disease pressure.

Only use fungicides when absolutely necessary as overuse has the potential to increase or shift the disease spectrum on turfgrasses, lead to development of fungicide-resistant strains of pathogens, and increase thatch development.

Fungicides

Fungicides can be classified in various ways, and managers should become familiar with all of the different classifications for knowledge on their mode of action, as well as strategies for minimizing undesirable effects and maximizing disease management effectiveness. Fungicides may be classified based on how they behave on or within turfgrass plants. Basically, there are two categories of their topical modes of action: they penetrate the plant or they do not.

1. Contact fungicides—mostly curative
2. Systemic (penetrant) fungicides—curative and preventive
   a. Local systemics (or penetrants)
      1. Xylem mobile
      2. Xylem limited
   b. Mobile systemic (or penetrants)
      1. Acropetal—upward movement from roots
      2. Basipetal—downward movement from shoots

Contact Fungicides

Contact (also called nonpenetrant, surface, protectant, or nonsystemic) fungicides form a protective coating on turfgrass foliage and control susceptible fungi as they initiate growth. These are generally applied to the leaf and stem surfaces of turfgrasses. These fungicides remain on the plant surface and do not penetrate into the plant; thus, they do not control a pathogen already inside the plant. However, they do help prevent disease spread to healthy plants by inhibiting the growth of fungal hyphae or spores before they enter the grass host. They usually do not kill fungi after plant invasion. They remain active only as long as the fungicide remains on the plant in sufficient concentration to inhibit fungi. Leaves that emerge after the fungicide has been applied will not be protected. In addition, fungicide on the plant surface will be gradually lost due to mowing, irrigation, rainfall, sunlight exposure, and decomposition. Consequently, they are only effective for short durations, usually 7 to 14 days. This short duration is especially magnified on daily mowed greens and during frequent rainfall. To obtain optimum protection, it is important that contact fungicides evenly coat the entire leaf surface and are allowed to dry completely before irrigating or mowing. Ideally, the turf area should be mowed and irrigated prior to a fungicide application to allow a maximum time interval between fungicide application and the next turfgrass maintenance operation.

Contact fungicides are normally used to control foliar diseases and not root/crown diseases. The exceptions would be chloroneb (Terraneb) and ethazol (Koban, Terrazole) when used to control Pythium root rot. Contact fungicides have a broad spectrum of disease control activity and have been used extensively in the turf industry for a number of years. Since contact fungicides have a non-site specific mode of action, development of disease resistance has not been a problem. Today, they are often mixed with systemic fungicides to obtain a fungicide mixture with broad spectrum control, to provide slightly longer residual effect, to delay the development of resistance to the systemic fungicide, or to enhance the activity of the systemic fungicide.

Systemic (or Penetrant) Fungicides

Systemic fungicides are absorbed and translocated within plants, destroying or suppressing subsequent fungal growth and development. Some fungicides are able to penetrate the plant in various ways. **Local penetrants** (also called **local-systemic fungicides**) move into plant tissues at the site of fungicide application, but do not move in the xylem or phloem. The majority of fungicide applied remains in the area of initial plant entry on or near the plant surface. This group of fungicides includes iprodione (Chipco 26019, 26GT), chloroneb (Teremec SP), and vinclozolin (Vorlan, Touche, Curalan).

Propamocarb (Banol) is an example of a local-systemic fungicide. It does penetrate the plant surface and has limited mobility within the plant **(xylem-limited).** However, it is degraded by the plant itself and thus may not last as long in the plant as other xylem-mobile fungicides. The strobilurin fungicides trifloxystrobin (Compass) and pyraclostrobin (Insignia) are localized penetrant fungicides that are not xylem-mobile. However, they exhibit various affinities for waxes and other lipids in leaf tissues and have been shown to move through leaves and within the vapor phase (as gases) as well. These characteristics give strobilurins excellent rainfast properties and provide redistribution of active fungicide residues to prolong disease control.

The localized penetrant fungicides are primarily protective in activity, whereas the xylem-mobile fungicides have both curative and protective activities. Local-systemic materials also are normally absorbed by the plant; therefore, they are not as subject to degradation by sunlight or removal by irrigation and rainfall. However, due to limited movement within plants, they are removed by mowing.

Systemic fungicides penetrate plant surfaces and then are translocated (moved) within the plant, either in the xylem or phloem tissue. Xylem tissues are water-conducting tubes; thus, compounds in the xylem move primarily in an upward direction with the water stream. Phloem tissues are tubes that move photosynthates (plant products) from their site of production (source) to other plant organs (sinks) in upward and downward directions. With turfgrasses, this usually means fully expanded green leaves are sources and roots are sinks so most photosynthates move downward in the phloem. Except for fosetyl-Al (Aliette), which is translocated in xylem and phloem (primarily phloem) tissue, most fungicides that are mobile in the plant are xylem-limited; thus, they move upward within the plant from the point of entry and not to the root (termed **acropetal penetrants**). Examples include the sterol biosynthesis inhibitors and azoxystrobin (Heritage).

In general, mobile penetrant fungicides have curative and protective properties with extended residual activity. Because these fungicides are absorbed by the plants, they "work" inside the plant to (1) stop the growth of pathogenic fungi that have already entered the plant and initiated a disease (curative action), and (2) prevent fungi entering the plant from initiating a disease (preventive action). Their residual activity is also due to being absorbed by the plant. Once a systemic fungicide is inside the plant, it will not be removed by rain or irrigation, and newly emerged leaves may contain sufficient concentrations of the fungicide to protect them from fungal infection. Therefore, systemic fungicides do not need to be applied as often as contact fungicides and usually provide control for 15- to 30-day intervals.

When attempting to control root and crown diseases, plant mobile fungicides should be watered into the rootzone for maximum effectiveness. As indicted, the majority of mobile penetrant fungicides are xylem-limited. If the fungicides are only applied to the leaf tissue, the compounds may never reach their root target in the amount needed for control. Due to their specific sites of action, disease resistance with continued use of systemic fungicides has occurred. Turf managers, therefore, should rotate between classes of fungicides and/or tank-mix with various contact fungicides to reduce disease-resistance potential.

Fungicide Resistance

Fungicide resistance by turf pathogens is an increasing problem, especially with systemic fungicides since the physiological processes these materials inhibit are genetically controlled by only one or a few genes. Being so specific in their mode of action, fungi may exist in nature at low frequencies that circumvent this, reducing the efficacy of the fungicide. Resistant fungi are then able to multiply as the susceptible fungi in the population are reduced by the fungicide. With repeat applications, resistant fungi multiply until the population is mostly fungicide-resistant and disease control is severely reduced or completely lost. Usually, strains of fungi resistant to a fungicide will be resistant to all fungicides in the same chemical class (called "**cross-resistance**"). Examples of diseases where resistance has been documented include anthracnose, dollar spot, powdery mildew, necrotic ring spot, and summer patch to members of the fungicide family benzimidazoles (thiophanate-methyl); Pythium blight to metalaxyl (or Subdue); dollar spot and pink snow mold to iprodione (26GT); and gray leaf spot and anthracnose resistance to the strobilurin fungicides (Table 22–4).

Multi-site fungicides, meanwhile, interfere with several physiological functions of the fungal cell. They are less likely to promote resistance because, even if resistance develops to one site, control can be achieved through another site of action. Examples of fungicides with multi-sites of actions, thus, are less likely to develop resistance include fosetyl-aluminum, propamocarb, chlorothalonil, and mancozeb.

Normally, rotating between fungicides with different modes of action reduces the risk or may delay the development of fungicide resistance. Rotation involves using two or more fungicides in sequence, each alone. This tends to work best in a preventive spray program.

In addition, mixing products in different chemical classes and with different modes of action is another strategy for delaying the development of fungicide resistance. A tank-mix of a contact fungicide with a systemic or penetrant fungicide is initially used. For the next spray, a contact fungicide is then used with another penetrant using a different mode of action. This is continued

TABLE 22–4 *Examples of resistance of turfgrass pathogens to fungicides.*

Disease	Pathogen	Fungicide
Dollar spot	*Sclerotinia homoeocarpa*	Benzimidazoles, dicarboximides, DMIs, triazines
Fusarium patch	*Microdochium nivale*	Benomyl
Powdery mildew	*Erysiphe graminis*	Benomyl
Pythium blight	*Pythium aphanidermatum*	Metalaxyl
Gray leaf spot	*Pyricularia grisea*	Azoxystrobin
Anthracnose	*Colletotrichum graminicola*	Azoxystrobin

throughout the spray season where a systemic or penetrant fungicide (acropetal or local) is combined with a contact fungicide and then rotated. If a curative application is needed, spray intervals should be shortened, curative rates should be used instead of preventive, and a tank-mix of a contact plus a penetrant fungicide should be used.

Much research and promotion have been associated with a relatively new class of fungicides, the strobilurins, which are fungal antibiotics discovered in 1977. The original form was strobilurin A produced by the pine cone fungus, *Strobilurus tenacellus*, and belongs to the mushroom-producing fungi. The initial form of strobilurin A is light sensitivity. Today's synthetic analogs were developed to decrease light sensitivity. Their mode of action is to block electron transport through the mitochondrial system; thus, treated fungi cannot produce energy.

The first strobilurin fungicide labeled on turf was azoxystrobin (Heritage) in 1997. It is a synthetic strobilurin fungicide which is acropetal systemic. It has upward mobility from the roots and is especially strong with soil-borne diseases. Trifloxystrobin (Compass) was the next strobilurin fungicide registered in 1998. It embeds itself in the waxy cuticle of plants, and is not xylem-mobile. However, it can move in waxes through leaves and in the vapor phase within and around treated leaf tissue. It provides broad spectrum control of many diseases and is very rainfast. The most recent strobilurin fungicide is pyraclostrobin (Insignia), manufactured by BASF, which is also a local systemic, and has excellent rainfast properties. Dimoxystrobin is the next anticipated strobilurin for turf disease control. One noted disease most strobilurin fungicides do not consistently control is dollar spot. Since the history of resistance development in dollar spot fungal populations is high, the use of strobilurin fungicides for dollar spot suppression needs to be carefully monitored and all strategies for delay of fungicide resistance need to be employed.

Mixing Fungicides

Fungicides are often mixed to increase the spectrum of disease control. The most likely mixture contains a contact and a systemic fungicide. The contact fungicide provides a protective coating while the systemic fungicide protects root and crown pathogens and extends control of foliar pathogens. As previously mentioned, these mixtures are a common technique to delay or reduce the risk of resistant forms of pathogens from increasing.

Commercially available mixtures of fungicides are on the market. Their components can be mixed separately by the applicator if each product is legally labeled for the turfgrass site, and they are a compatible tank-mix. The applicator, however, should be aware if one of the materials needs to be watered-in while the other one does not.

Fungicide/PGR Interactions

Certain sterol demethylation inhibitor (DMI) fungicides and morpholine-derived plant growth regulators (PGRs) should not be applied together as severe turf phytotoxicity may result. These two groups act by different mechanisms to block the sterol biosynthetic pathways. When used together, the combined DMI fungicides (Banner, Bayleton, Eagle, Rubigan) and PGRs flurprimidol (Cutless) and paclobutrazol (Trimmit) can be highly phytotoxic to annual bluegrass. Applying these fungicides should be delayed three to four weeks after the last treatment of either flurprimidol or paclobutrazol. These phytotoxic interactions are not as severe on other cool-season grasses but can cause stunting and discoloration of bermudagrass greens and thinning of bentgrass in hot weather.

Spray Volumes

Application spray volumes for disease control are generally higher than for other pests such as weeds. Delivery rates for most fungicides are in the 45 to 135 gallons per acre range (1 to 3 gallons per 1,000 sq.ft.), specifically one to two gallons per 1,000 square feet (4 to 8 L/100 m^2) for contact fungicides and two to three gallons per 1,000 square feet (8 to 12 L/100 m^2) for combination products. For fairways, 100 gallons per acre (935 L/ha) is standard. This high volume should be applied by regulating (slowing) sprayer speed and changing nozzle types instead of using higher spray pressures.

A broadcast boom fitted with flat fan nozzles and delivering 30 to 60 psi has provided very good results. Flooding nozzles have not been as effective.

Chemical Groups

Fungicides are also divided into groups based on their chemical properties (Table 22–5). To prevent fungicide resistance from developing in a pathogen population, it is important to know which fungicides belong to the same chemical group or have the same biochemical mode of action. Biochemical mode of action refers to the way the fungicide inhibits fungi, whether at sites controlled genetically by one or a few genes or through multiple genetic control mechanisms. Fungicides should be periodically alternated or rotated, or used in mixtures with fungicides belonging to different chemical groups to prevent fungicide resistance. For example, alternating between myclobutanil (Eagle) and cyproconazole (Sentinel) is not alternating between chemical groups as both fungicides belong to the same chemical group, the sterol biosynthesis inhibitors (triazole group). The occurrence of resistance has been problematic with plant-penetrant fungicides since their modes of action in controlling fungi are more genetically specific and the probability of resistant strains becoming selected is higher. In Table 22–5, fungicides are listed based on their chemical group.

The recent marketing of fungicide mixtures also makes it very important to know the chemical names or common names of fungicides, as the trade name of the fungicides used in the mixture are not listed on the label. For example, the fungicides TwoSome and Broadway are mixtures of chlorothalonil (Daconil 2787) and fenarimol (Rubigan). Another example is Pace, a mixture of metalaxyl (Subdue) and mancozeb (Fore or Dithane). Duosan is a mixture of mancozeb (Fore or Dithane) and thiophanate methyl (Fungo). Ask your sales representative for complete information concerning the components in the fungicide mixture you buy. Table 22–6 lists some common fungicide mixtures and their corresponding trade names while Table 22–7 is a cross-listing of fungicides for major turfgrass diseases.

If you do not achieve disease control with a fungicide, make sure the disease was properly diagnosed and the fungicide properly applied before assuming a fungicide-resistant strain has developed. The number of documented cases of fungicide resistance is limited, especially for warm-season turfgrasses. Turf managers can keep it this way by exercising intelligent, prudent use of fungicides.

A special consideration should be given to applications of fosetyl-aluminum (Aliette). Due to the acidic and reactive nature of this chemical, care should be exercised in mixing Aliette with certain other chemicals. Do not mix Aliette with either soluble fertilizers or flowable chlorothalonil or mancozeb formulations. In addition, do not add acidifying products to alkaline spray water when using Aliette. In a neutral spray water (pH=7.0), Aliette will acidify the spray water to a pH of about 4.5.

Read Labels

You would not think of giving a family member any medication without reading the instructions first. Turfgrass fungicides deserve the same amount of respect. After all, they are plant pharmaceuticals. In addition to rates and intervals for application, labels provide information concerning the use or non-use of surfactants with the material, compatibility between other pesticides or fertilizers, amount of water to use in the application process, posting or reentry restrictions, and so forth. Keep up-to-date with the labels. Take the time to read them completely at least once each year. Remember, labels are the law.

DIAGNOSTIC FEATURES AND MANAGEMENT OF SPECIFIC TURFGRASS DISEASES

This section will discuss the primary diseases that occur on turfgrasses. The exact time when a disease will occur is dependent on the environment. Some of these diseases are rare or their duration is so limited that they are relatively unimportant. Chemical control treatments are listed as the common name only. Refer to Tables 22–5 and 22–6 for a partial list of corresponding trade names. Refer to the cultural control section for more details on specific cultural practices and Table 22–7 for a cross-reference of control products for specific turf diseases.

Anthracnose Leaf Blight

The causal agent of anthracnose leaf blight is *Colletotrichum graminicola* (Ces.) Wils.

TABLE 22-5 *Turfgrass fungicides classified by chemical activity group.*

Chemical group (activity)	Mode of action	Common name	Trade name(s)*	Diseases controlled
Contact (Nonsystemic or nonplant penetrants)				
Aromatic hydrocarbons (also called **substituted aromatics** or **substituted benzenes**) (protective)	Interferes with DNA synthesis, as well as enzyme, membrane, or chitin production needed for growth and reproduction.	Chloroneb	-Terraneb SP, Teremec SP, Fungicide V, Chloroneb	*Pythium* spp. (ethazol, mancozeb, & maneb); brown patch (chloroneb, PCNB, thiram, mancozeb, & maneb); dollar spot (PCNB, mancozeb, & maneb); snow mold; "Helminthosporium" diseases (PCNB, mancozeb, & maneb); rust (mancozeb & maneb); melting out (PCNB, mancozeb); preventive blue-green algae (mancozeb). Little turf phytotoxicity or undesirable growth regulatory effects.
		Ethazol (Etridiazole)	-Koban, Terrazole	
		PCNB (Quintozene)	-Terraclor, PCNB, Penstar, Engage, Revere, Turfcide, F + F II, Defend, Par Flo 4F	
Dithiocarbamates or **carbamates** (protective)	Interferes with fungi cell respiration, enzyme activity, and cell membrane fluidity.	Mancozeb	-Fore, Dithane-45 Special, Manzate 200F, Protect T/O, Formec 80, Mancozeb, Tersan LSR, Pentathlon DF	
		Maneb	-Manex, Dithane-22 Special, Maneb	
		Thiram	-Sporete 75, Thiramad, Thiram, Lawn Disease Control, Defiant	
Benzonitriles (also called **nitriles**) (protective)	Interferes with DNA synthesis and nuclear division.	Chlorothalonil	-Daconil Ultrex/Weatherstik, Thal-o-nil, Echo 720, Manicure, Turf Fungicide, Flo-130, Lawn Fungicide, Bravado, Chlorostar, Concorde	Dollar spot; copper spot; "Helminthosporium" diseases; brown patch; preventive anthracnose; gray leaf spot; snow mold; red thread; stem rust; preventive blue-green algae. Little turf phytotoxicity or undesirable growth regulatory effects. Often combined with propiconazole for dollar spot control.
Phthalimides (protective)	Inhibits fungal respiration.	Captan	-Captan, Captec	"Helminthosporium" diseases; brown patch; *Pythium* blight.
Pyrollnitrin (protective). Anti-fungal compound derived from the bacterium *Pseudomonas pyrocinia*.	Interferes with fungal membrane transport.	Fludioxonil	-Medallion	Brown patch; "Helminthosporium" leaf spot diseases, dead spot.
Triazines (protective)	Inhibits fungal spore metabolism and cell processes.	Anilazine	-Dyrene	Dollar spot; copper spot; rust; "Helminthosporium" diseases; brown patch; Typhula blight. Often combined with propiconazole for dollar spot control.
Local-systemic (or local-penetrant)				
Dicarboximides (protective)	Inhibits DNA synthesis in cell division of spores, disrupts membranes, and blocks certain respiratory enzymes.	Iprodione	-Chipco 26019, Chipco 26GT, Rovral, Scotts Fungicide X, Iprodione Pro	Dollar spot; "Helminthosporium" diseases; brown patch; copper spot; snow mold; melting out; red thread; curvularia blight. Also combined with propiconazole for dollar spot control.
		Vinclozolin	-Vorlan, Curalan, Touche	

TABLE 22-5 *Turfgrass fungicides classified by chemical activity group.* *(continued)*

Chemical group (activity)	Mode of action	Common name	Trade name(s)*	Diseases controlled
Contact (Nonsystemic or nonplant penetrants)				
Benzamide (also called **benzanilide, anilides,** or **carboxamide**) (curative and protective)	Inhibits the respiratory enzyme succinate dehydrogenase which is needed in mitochondrial transport chain, specifically the Complex II of the mitochondria.	Flutolanil	-ProStar	Brown patch; red thread; southern blight; and basidiomycete (*Lycoperdon* spp.) fungi which cause fairy rings. Little control of non-basidiomycete fungi such as dollar spot and anthracnose.
		Boscalid	-Emerald 70WG	Dollar spot.
Carbamates (curative and protective)	Inhibits membrane function and sporulation through altering fatty acid composition.	Propamocarb hydrochloride	-Banol	Pythium blight and damping-off; less clear on Pythium root rot control. Also combined with mancozeb and fosetyl-Al for Pythium blight control.
Mobile plant penetrants (systemics)				
DeMethylation inhibitors or **DMIs** including triazole, pyrimidine groups (curative and protective). Also often referred to as **ergosterol biosynthesis inhibitors** (or **SBIs**).	Inhibits ergosterol synthesis, which are components of fungi cell membranes.	Cyproconazole	-Sentinel	Curative against dollar spot; anthracnose; rust (cyproconazole, propiconazole, & triadimefon); snow mold; "Helminthosporium" diseases (propiconazole); copper spot (cyproconazole, triadimefon); powdery mildew; red thread; southern blight (cyproconazole, triadimefon); and gray leaf spot (cyproconazole, propiconazole). Protective against brown patch, especially if tank-mixed; Summer patch; zoysia large patch; stripe smut. Undesirable turf growth regulatory effects may occur if used during stress (e.g., summer) periods.
		Fenarimol	-Rubigan, Patchwork	
		Myclobutanil	-Eagle, Systhane WSP, Golden Eagle	
		Propiconazole	-Banner MAXX, Alamo, Spectator, Propiconazole PRO	
		Tebuconazole	-Lynx	
		Triadimefon	-Bayleton, Fungicide VII, Accost 1G, Granular Turf Fungicide, Strike 25WP, Fungisol	
Benzimidazoles (curative and protective)	Inhibits DNA synthesis, mitosis, and development of the fungal skeleton. Upon wetting, these materials transform to methyl-2-benzimidazole carbamate (MBC).	Thiophanate-methyl	-Fungo 50, Cleary's 3336, Spot Kleen, Systemic Fungicide, Systec 1998, Cavalier, T-Storm, T-Methyl Pro	Dollar spot; brown patch; anthracnose; copper spot; snow molds; stripe smut; fusarium patch, bermudagrass decline.

Mobile plant penetrants (systemics) (continued)

Category	Mode of action	Active ingredient	Trade names	Diseases/uses
Acetanilides (also called **phenylamides**) (curative and protective)	Blocks RNA synthesis of mycelia and spore production. Does not inhibit spore germination or zoospore release.	Metalaxyl	-Apron (seed treatment only), Subdue 2E, Pythium Control	Pythium blight and damping-off; not always effective against Pythium root rot. Yellow tuft; downy mildew. Often combined with mancozeb for Pythium blight control.
		Mefanoxam	-Subdue Maxx (Mefenoxam)	
		Oxadixyl	-Anchor (seed treatment only)	
Organophosphates (curative and protective)	Increases plant resistance and blocks mycelial development and spore germination.	Fosetyl-Aluminum (Al)	-Aliette, Aliette Signature, Prodigy, Prodigy Signature	Pythium spp.: better as a preventative rather than a curative. Yellow tuft. Often combined with metalaxyl, propamocarb, mancozeb, or chlorothalonil.
Strobilurin (curative and protective). Anti-fungal compounds derived from various wood-decaying fungi such as Strobilurus and Oudemansin spp.	Inhibits spore germination and mycelial growth by blocking electron transport in the cytochrome bc complex, disrupting mitochondrial respiration, and ATP production.	Azoystrobin	-Heritage	Brown patch: Pythium blight; summer patch: snow mold; anthracnose; red thread: "Helminthosporium" leaf spot; grey leaf spot; rust; take-all patch. Suppression of fairy ring caused by Lycoperdon spp. Minimum activity on dollar spot (Pyraclostrobin). Little turf phytotoxicity or undesirable growth regulatory effects.
		Pyraclostrobin	-Insignia	
		Trifloxystrobin	-Compass	
		Dimoxystrobin	-TBA	
Antibiotics. Antifungal compounds derived from Streptomycin (protective and curative)	Inhibits chitin, a substance in fungal (and insect) cell walls. It also inhibits spore germination and mycelium growth.	Polyoxin D zinc salt	-Endorse 25 WP & 10 DF	Best for brown patch and gray leaf spot. Suppresses gray snow mold, Rhizoctonia damping-off, large patch, pink snow mold, leaf spot/melting out, snow mold, red thread, and yellow patch. Recently labeled for anthracnose.
Biofungicides	Either: (1) antibiotic biosynthesis; (2) resource competition; or (3) hyperparasitism.	Bacillus licheniformis SB3086	-GR 710-140	–
		Bacillus subtilis GB03	-Companion	–
		Bacillus spp.	-Green Releaf, Bio-B Plus	–
		Burkholderia cepacia	-Blue Circle	Pythium blight.
		Gliocladium catenulatum J1446	-Primastop	–
		Pseudomonas aureofaciens Tx-1	-TX-1, Spot-Less/BioJect	Anthracnose, leaf spot, take-all patch, pink snow mold, brown patch, dollar spot.
		Trichoderma harzianum 1295-22	-BioTrek 22 (Turf Shield) TurfMate	Dollar spot, brown patch. Pythium root rot.
		Streptomyces cacaoi var. asoensis	-Stop-It	Brown patch.
		Streptomyces lydicus WYEC 108	-Actinovate	–

*This is a partial list of trade names. Other fungicides are available alone and as mixtures under various trade names.

563

TABLE 22–6 *Trade names of common fungicide mixtures.*

Mixture	Trade names
Fenarimol + chlorothalonil	Twosome Flowable Fungicide
Fludioxonil + propiconazole	Foundation
Mancozeb + copper hydroxide	Junction
Mancozeb + myclobutanil	Manhandle
Metalaxyl + mancozeb	Pace
PMA + thiram	Proturf Broad Spectrum Fungicide
Propamocarb + chlorothalonil	Banol C
Thiophanate methyl + chloroneb	Fungicide IV
Thiophanate methyl + chlorothalonil	ConSyst, Spectro 90WDG
Thiophanate methyl + iprodione	Fluid Fungicide
Thiophanate methyl + maneb (mancozeb)	Duosan WP, WSB
Thiophanate methyl + thiram	Bromosan
Triadimefon methyl + flutolanil	SysStar
Triadimefon + metalaxyl	Fluid Fungicide II
Triadimefon + thiram	Fluid Fungicide III

Occurrence

Several manifestations of anthracnose diseases exist in turfgrasses. Anthracnose diseases occur on many cool-season grasses as anthracnose leaf blight and occasionally as anthracnose basal rot. Bermudagrass and centipedegrass also may develop anthracnose leaf blight. On bermudagrass, the disease occurs in the fall as the growth of the grass slows (Plate 22–3). On centipedegrass, leaf blight may occur under conditions of unusually wet and humid weather in the late spring, summertime, or fall. Anthracnose leaf blight occurs by itself and in combination with *Bipolaris sorokiniana* (or leaf spot) to severely thin annual bluegrass, fine-leaf fescue, perennial ryegrass, creeping bentgrass, and certain cultivars of Kentucky bluegrass. Anthracnose infection is associated with plant stress. It is favored during environmental periods of limited grass growth such as warm (80 to 90°F, 27 to 32°C) summer weather when the soil is dry, leaves are wet, and high atmospheric humidity occurs with cool-season grasses. Anthracnose leaf blight often selectively infects annual bluegrass in bentgrass/annual bluegrass stands in late spring. Although common, anthracnose leaf blight is usually of minor significance except on greens dependent on annual bluegrass as a component of the putting surface.

Symptoms/Signs

This pathogen attacks grass shoots, stems, and roots. Initial symptoms are small (size of a dime) yellowing of the annual bluegrass turf which turns bronze in color if warm weather persists. Commonly, this occurs after flowering of annual bluegrass during heat stress. Lower leaves of plants initially show symptoms as elongated reddish-brown lesions that may enlarge and eventually encompass the entire leaf blade. The disease occurs as irregular-shaped patches. A water-soaked black rot of crown tissue may be evident if sheath tissue is removed (anthracnose basal rot). One-celled, crescent-shaped conidia are produced. The black fruiting bodies of the fungus (**acervuli**) can be seen growing in rows on infected leaves during hot weather. These acervuli have black spines called **setae** protruding from leaf tissue. Affected turf areas may thin and have a yellow-to-orange or reddish-brown cast to the overall area. The fungus overwinters as a saprophyte in dead plant tissue in the thatch and on stems beneath the leaf sheath of live plants.

Cultural Controls

Adequate nitrogen fertility will help reduce the severity of anthracnose leaf blight in some areas during cool periods. Fungicides will be needed in addition to light nitrogen applications during

TABLE 22-7 *Cross-reference table of fungicides for major turfgrass diseases.*

Fungicide	Algae	Anthracnose	Brown patch	Curvularia blight	Dollar spot	Fairy ring	Gray leaf spot	Gray snow mold	Leaf spot	Necrotic ring spot	Pink snow mold/Fusarium patch
Aliette											
Banner Maxx		✓	✓		✓		✓	✓	✓	✓	✓
Banol											✓
Bayleton		✓	✓		✓			✓			✓
Chipco 26019		✓	✓		✓			✓	✓	✓	✓
Cleary 3336		✓	✓	✓	✓				✓	✓	✓
Compass			✓		✓		✓		✓		✓
Curalan			✓		✓			✓	✓		✓
Daconil	✓	✓					✓	✓			✓
Eagle		✓	✓		✓				✓	✓	
Emerald					✓						
Endorse		✓	✓		✓				✓		✓
Fore	✓		✓						✓		
Heritage		✓	✓		✓	✓	✓	✓		✓	✓
Insignia		✓	✓				✓	✓		✓	✓
Koban/Terrazole											
Medallion			✓		✓				✓		✓
PCNB			✓		✓				✓		✓
Prostar			✓			✓		✓			
Rubigan		✓	✓					✓		✓	✓
Sporete 75					✓			✓			✓
Subdue Maxx					✓						
Terraneb			✓								

TABLE 22-7 *Cross-reference table of fungicides for major turfgrass diseases. (continued)*

Fungicide	Turf diseases										
	Pink patch	Pythium blight	Pythium root rot	Rapid blight	Red thread	Rhizoctonia leaf & sheath spot	Rust	Southern blight	Spring dead spot	Stripe smut	Summer patch
Aliette		✓	✓								
Banner Maxx	✓				✓		✓			✓	✓
Banol		✓	✓								
Bayleton					✓		✓	✓	✓	✓	✓
Chipco 26019					✓						
Cleary 3336					✓					✓	✓
Compass	✓			✓	✓		✓				
Curalan	✓				✓						
Daconil					✓	✓	✓				
Eagle					✓		✓		✓	✓	
Emerald											
Endorse											
Fore				✓	✓		✓				
Heritage		✓	✓	✓	✓			✓	✓		✓
Insignia		✓		✓	✓						
Koban/Terrazole		✓		✓							
Medallion			✓								
PCNB											
Prostar	✓				✓						
Rubigan					✓			✓	✓	✓	✓
Sentinel					✓		✓	✓		✓	✓
Spotrete		✓									
Subdue Maxx			✓					✓			
Terraneb		✓									

TABLE 22-7 *Cross-reference table of fungicides for major turfgrass diseases. (continued)*

Fungicide	Take-all patch	Yellow patch (Cool weather brown patch)	Yellow tuft (downy mildew)
Aliette			✓
Banner Maxx	✓	✓	
Banol			
Bayleton	✓		
Chipco 26019			
Cleary 3336			
Compass			
Curalan			
Daconil		✓	
Eagle			
Emerald			
Endorse			
Fore			
Heritage	✓	✓	
Insignia			
Koban/Terrazole			
Medallion		✓	
PCNB			
Prostar		✓	
Rubigan	✓		
Sentinel			
Spotrete			
Subdue Maxx			✓
Terraneb			

summer to prevent turf stand loss. Utilize cultural practices that minimize stress to cool-season grasses such as reducing soil compaction, heavy traffic, and low nitrogen fertility. Most damage occurs on annual bluegrass under heat stress. Begin a solid-tine aerification or slicing program in late May or early June, just prior to traditional heat-stress periods. Failure to aerify at this time may enhance anthracnose in July and August. Raise the mowing height and water to prevent wilt.

Chemical Controls

Propiconazole, chlorothalonil, iprodione, triadimefon, thiophanate-methyl, azoxystrobin, trifloxystrobin, myclobutanil, and pyraclostrobin help reduce but not eradicate the disease. Apply systemics preventively on 21-day intervals. For best curative control, tank-mix a systemic fungicide with a contact and reapply in 14 to 21 days.

Anthracnose Basal Rot

The causal agent of anthracnose basal rot is *Colletotrichum graminicola* (Ces.) Wils.

Occurrence

Increasingly, anthracnose basal rot is occurring in stands of creeping bentgrass and/or annual bluegrass (Plate 22–4). This disease is frequently misidentified as Pythium root rot. Generally, bentgrass affected with anthracnose basal rot appears in the summer, although cases have been noted in the spring under conditions normally associated with good bentgrass growth. Usually, some stress factor is associated with the development of anthracnose basal rot. It is associated with putting greens under high management, which implies various combinations of low cutting heights, rolling, topdressing with sand-based materials, and low fertility. In some cases, anthracnose basal rot has developed in bentgrass after it has been affected with localized dry spots. Wounding associated with sand topdressing may predispose the turf to infections.

Symptoms/Signs

Initial symptoms are small (size of a dime) dark-blue to purple annual bluegrass or bentgrass turf that turns red or bronze to copper in color if warm weather persists. Close examination of affected plants, however, differentiates symptoms from anthracnose leaf blight. Crowns are affected, and leaf lesions are usually absent. Crowns are rotted, exhibiting a watery, water-soaked appearance if the plants are only initially infected. As the disease worsens, the darkening (rotting) progresses up the stem. Shoots are easily pulled free from infected crowns. Usually dark, black masses of setae and abundant sporulation in acervuli are noted. Black masses of sclerotia-like bodies, resembling charcoal, are often embedded in rotted crown tissues.

Cultural Controls

Avoid extremely low cutting heights, extremely low fertility, and limit topdressing with sand during periods of low turf recuperative potential. Utilize cultural practices that minimize stress to cool-season grasses such as reducing soil compaction, heavy traffic, and low nitrogen fertility. Raise the mowing height, and water to prevent wilt or development of localized dry spots. Some surfactants for prevention of localized dry spots may be beneficial.

Chemical Controls

Propiconazole, chlorothalonil, triadimefon, thiophanate-methyl, azoxystrobin, and pyraclostrobin may prevent more severe disease development. However, with anthracnose basal rot, affected plants generally die and recovery depends on surrounding, unaffected plants. Apply systemics preventively. For best curative control, tank-mix a systemic fungicide with a contact and reapply in 14 to 21 days. Be judicious with the use of the strobilurin fungicides and utilize good practices designed to delay development of fungicide-resistant strains of anthracnose fungi. Resistance to azoxystrobin and trifloxystrobin have been reported, as well as to thiophanate methyl fungicides.

Bermudagrass Decline

The causal agent of bermudagrass decline is *Gaeumannomyces graminis* (Sacc.) Arx & D. Olivier var. *graminis.*

Occurrence

Primarily observed during summer and early fall months when temperatures are above 75 to 80°F, 24 to 27°C (including night) with high humidity, cloudy skies, and frequent rainfall. This disease is mostly limited to putting greens due to the stress imposed by very low cutting heights (Plate 22–5). Tees may also be affected if mowed excessively low. As a general rule, the outer margins of a golf green exhibit the disease symptoms first, presumably due to added pressure from turning mowers, but can spread slowly across an entire green. It occurs on all types of putting greens—old, new, poorly drained, and well-drained. At this time all plant material is assumed to be infected since the causal fungus is ubiquitously found with all bermudagrass plants.

Symptoms/Signs

This is a root rot disease; therefore, the plant is easily stressed for water and nutrients. By the time aboveground symptoms appear, pathogens have been active on roots for at least a few weeks and possibly months. Initial symptoms are irregular, yellow (chlorotic) patches ranging in diameter from a few inches to a few feet. Lower leaves will exhibit the aboveground symptoms first by becoming yellow and then brown (dead). Roots with initial symptoms will usually be thin and off-white in color with isolated black lesions. Eventually, roots will turn black and rot. Stolons and rhizomes may also have black lesions. Black strands of fungi (runner hyphae) will be present on the outside of roots, as well as hyphopodia (specialized hyphae visible microscopically on root surfaces). Entire plants may die, resulting in an irregular thinning of grass, and if not controlled, bare patches may develop (Plate 22–6). This disease should not be confused with Pythium root rot, which causes a general decline across the entire green or limited portions of the green. Pythium root rot does not usually result in plant death.

Cultural Controls

Bermudagrass decline is very difficult to control once it is established. Therefore, preventive measures that alleviate stress are the best methods for completely controlling the disease or at least decreasing the potential damage.

1. Raise the mowing height, especially during stressful growth periods during summer and early fall months. **This is the most important preventive measure** (Plate 22–7).
2. Aerify greens frequently to avoid compaction problems. Remove the cores.
3. Topdress after aerification with a topsoil mix containing at least 70 percent sand. More frequent topdressing may be necessary on putting greens where the disease has been previously observed. Topdressing also covers dying lower leaves, leaving the "appearance" of a healthy, green playing surface.
4. Balance nitrogen applications with equal amounts of potassium. On new sand greens, monitor other nutrients as well—especially phosphorus and micronutrients. Fertilize to encourage rapid growth. Remember, deeper roots are damaged; thus, shallower ones have to "work" for nutrients in the top few inches of soil. Nitrogen should be applied with potassium in a 1:1 or 1:2 ratio. Apply micronutrients, especially iron and manganese, if they are in low supply or unavailable to the plant due to a high soil pH. A readily available source of phosphorus may be useful. Foliar feeding of nutrients may be useful if the root system is severely damaged.
5. Do not raise soil pH by adding dolomitic lime to greens. If it is necessary to add magnesium, use magnesium sulfate (Epsom salts) or, if calcium is needed, then consider calcium sulfate (gypsum). These pathogens prefer neutral to alkaline soil pH, so the addition of lime may increase their activity as the pH increases.

Chemical Controls

The fungicides fenarimol, propiconazole, thiophanate methyl, and triadimefon have controlled similar patch diseases (spring dead spot, summer patch, take-all patch) as indicated on their labels. However, best control is achieved when fungicides are used preventively, prior to symptom development. Do not use these excessively as they may have negative growth-regulating effects on bermudagrass. Treat in spring prior to infestations when daytime temperatures are <80°F (27°C). Cultural control methods, especially raising the cutting height, should also be implemented at the same time. Control seems to be best when fungicides are lightly watered into the rootzone (but not below it) immediately after application. These fungicides penetrate the plant, but are xylem-mobile (see fungicide section). The use of a contact fungicide such as mancozeb or chlorothalonil on the leaf tissue may also be useful to prevent secondary leaf infections from occurring and to prevent algae formation in thin areas of the green (see algae section). Propiconazole and other DMI fungicides should not be used during the warm summer months. If *Rhizoctonia zeae* is also present, do not use thiophanate methyl products, since it is not sensitive to this chemistry. Azoxystrobin also has shown some suppression when preventively used.

Brown Patch (Rhizoctonia Blight)

The causal agent of brown patch is *Rhizoctonia solani* Kuhn.

Occurrence

Brown patch is the most widespread turfgrass disease. It affects all turfgrass species and is observed most often on creeping bentgrass, tall fescue, perennial ryegrass, and annual bluegrass during warm (above 85°F, 29°C) weather when night temperatures are above 68°F (20°C) and foliage remains wet for extended (>10 hours) periods (Plate 22–8). In cool-season grasses, infection is triggered by a rapid rise in air temperature combined with either rainfall or extended periods of high humidity, resulting in the leaf canopy being continuously wet for 48 hours or more. *Rhizoctonia* species are found in all soils and survive unfavorable environments as dormant, thick-walled mycelia or as compact masses of thick-walled cells (**bulbils**) resembling sclerotia in plant debris. There is some evidence inferred that asymptomatic plants, may become blighted when weather favors symptom expression and serves as primary inoculum for initiating new disease cycles.

On warm-season grasses, including bermudagrass, zoysiagrass, St. Augustinegrass, and centipedegrass, the strain of *R. solani* (AG-2-2 LP) is most active as a pathogen in the spring or fall months when the temperatures are relatively cool and the turf surface stays continuously wet for several days due to heavy fog or extended rainfall (Plate 22–9). This disease in zoysia may be referred to as "large patch," and is caused by a particular strain (AG-2-2) of *R. solani* that is different from strains typically associated with brown patch in cool-season grasses (typically AG-1 or AG 2-2 IIIB). Strains from other warm-season grasses are similar to those collected from large patch in zoysia.

Symptoms/Signs

Symptoms of brown patch differ in cool-season grasses, depending on the height of cut. On putting greens, the disease begins as small circular light-green to dark-purplish patches that eventually turn yellow and then brown or straw-colored. Patches may expand to several feet in diameter, and may or may not have green, relatively healthy appearing turf in the center of the patches. On lower heights of cut, a dark gray, purplish or dark-brown "smoke ring" may be visible, particularly under conditions of high relative humidity or when dew is on the green. This ring is composed of mycelium and freshly wilted, infected grass. These symptoms may change as the day progresses so, by late morning, the patch appears more uniformly light-brown, yellow-orange, or straw-colored. On higher heights of cut, typical of roughs, leaf lesions are more apparent (Plate 22–10) and a smoke ring symptom may not be visible, although mycelium may still be visible upon careful examination of affected leaves low in the turfgrass canopy. The turf may also appear "sunken." The later symptoms are typical in tall fescue (Plate 22–11). Brown patch is distinguished from summer patch in annual bluegrass by the characteristic leaf lesions on individual blades associated with brown patch. Lesions are irregularly shaped grayish-colored leaf spots with a dark-brown margin. *Pythium* spp. often occur simultaneously with *Rhizoctonia*.

Symptoms in warm-season grasses differ significantly from those observed in cool-season grasses. In warm-season grasses, discrete leaf lesions are not usually formed; rather, a soft, dark rot will occur on the lower portion of the leaf sheath. Whole leaf fascicles pull up easily due to this basal leaf sheath rot. Eventually, entire shoots will easily pull off the stolons. When disease is active, margins of patches exhibit yellowed shoots, whose basal leaf sheaths are recently infected and rotted. So, a yellow- to light-brown band of more recently affected shoots surround the more-brown patch of affected turf. Roots are not normally affected by this pathogen or those causing disease in cool-season turfgrasses. Roots may decline, however, as foliage is destroyed. Patches up to 20 feet (6 m) in diameter may develop on hybrid bermudagrass, zoysiagrass, St. Augustinegrass, or centipedegrass during cool, wet weather and shoot green-up in the spring (Plate 22–12). As temperatures warm, turf vigor increases and eventually grows over diseased areas, but cultivars or species with lower turf recuperative potential (like Meyer zoysia, or centipede) may still exhibit symptoms into the summertime, and weeds typically invade these weak areas of turf. These large patches are perennial in nature, and may reappear in the same location in following years, but expanded in size.

Cultural Controls

For cool-season grasses, avoid excess nitrogen, especially readily available forms such as soluble liquids or quick-release nitrogen sources just prior to hot, humid weather. For bentgrass greens, use very low rates and adopt a "spoon feeding" approach to avoid stimulating succulent foliage, but still maintain the ability of bentgrass turf to recover from disease. Complete elimination of nitrogen fertility, even in the summertime for bentgrass greens, is not advised as new root-and-shoot growth is needed for plants to recover from disease and (hopefully) transient highly stressful high temperatures. Maintain adequate levels of phosphorus and potassium. Avoid excessive irrigation, and irrigate greens when dew is already present so leaves do not stay continuously wet. Dragging a hose across the turfgrass or whipping greens with a bamboo or fiberglass pole will also remove morning moisture. Increase air circulation by removing adjacent underbrush and consider tree removal to improve morning sunlight penetration to the green. Remove clippings on infected areas or when conditions favor disease development. Use sharp mower blades to reduce turf stress and excessive wounding. Regularly core aerify to increase soil drainage, improve soil oxygen status, and reduce thatch buildup. Increasing mowing height also encourages turf recovery.

For brown patch management in warm-season grasses, avoid early fall applications of excess nitrogen. Improve drainage, as it has been observed brown patch chronically appears in poorly drained areas. On golf course roughs where centipedegrass has been utilized, brown patch may become severe as superintendents water to establish fall overseedings of ryegrass in bermudagrass fairways. This may be an argument against using centipedegrass for this purpose. Managing thatch accumulations will help to improve recuperative potential as well.

Chemical Controls

Preventive control (such as fall application for warm-season grasses) in chronic disease areas helps prevent spring disease symptoms. Flutolanil, iprodione, propiconazole, cyproconazole, PCNB, triadimefon, azoxystrobin, pyraclostrobin, and chlorothalonil may be used for preventive control. For creeping bentgrass in summertime, preventive applications are necessary to allow conservation of healthy foliage for maintenance of root systems and hence the turf stand. During other times of the year, when favorable weather for epidemics is likely to be of short duration (spring, winter, and fall), curative approaches are successful. Apply on a 10- to 14-day schedule during hot, humid weather when night temperatures exceed 68°F (20°C). Waiting for symptoms to develop before chemical control, however, may result in dead or thinned areas of turf unable to recover until favorable turf-growing conditions resume in fall. In summer, algae development becomes problematic under these conditions.

Rhizoctonia Leaf and Sheath Spot

The causal agents of Rhizoctonia leaf and sheath spot are *Rhizoctonia zeae* Voorhees and *R. oryzae* Ryker & Gooch.

Occurrence

Rhizoctonia leaf and sheath spot occurs primarily during the warm late spring, summer, and early fall months, especially when nighttime temperatures exceed 77°F (25°C) and humidity is high. However, it has also been observed in winter months after a sustained, high-temperature period (>80°F, 27°C) with high humidity. Another environmental factor associated with secondary infection is a dry rootzone as found with localized dry spots. The *Rhizoctonia* species infect by mycelial growth arising from infested plant debris or from sclerotia or thick-walled cells that survive in thatch or soil. These fungi rarely form spores, and therefore spread primarily by mycelial growth or movement through mechanical means.

Symptoms/Signs

Lesions may be present on leaves and leaf sheaths. Normally, the disease appears as a total blight of leaf tissue, resulting in a reddish-yellow coloration of leaves. On creeping bentgrass greens, symptoms can include yellow rings similar to those of yellow patch disease, but also can resemble brown patch symptoms, including the formation of smoke ring symptoms in high humidity. Individual infected leaves have gray or tan irregular lesions with tan or brown borders. Warm-season grasses rarely exhibit lesions on upper leaf blades as do cool-season grasses. Roots are not normally affected by these pathogens. Two types of overall "patch" symptoms have been observed. One is large areas of chlorotic (yellow) turf which never turn brown. The symptoms most often observed are necrotic (brown) rings of all sizes (6 inches to 6 feet diameter, 0.2 to 1.8 m)—ranging from full circles to semicircles to quarter-circles (Plate 22–13). Rings often appear sunken, are never dark-green as with true fairy rings, and they do not normally expand in size, only in number. The centers may "thin-out," but this may be due to the presence of *Pythium* or *Gaeumannomyces* spp. on the roots. If rings are from a secondary infection induced by localized dry spots caused by fungi (usually *Lycoperdon* spp.), "puffball" mushrooms will usually be formed throughout the dry area, inside and outside the ring. These rings will not appear sunken, and the entire area will appear drought stressed. See section on localized dry spot. On bentgrass greens, symptoms may resemble those of yellow patch except yellow rings or arcs are present in summertime. Symptoms on young, recently established bentgrass may resemble typical brown patch, complete with smoke ring symptoms in early morning hours.

Cultural Controls

Control information is quite limited. If localized dry spots are associated with rings, alleviate dryness first by spiking and hand watering them with a wetting agent. As with all turfgrass diseases, maintain an adequate and balanced fertility regime, such as slow-release nitrogen sources. Foliar nitrogen feeding should be discontinued when the disease is active. An abundance of readily available nitrogen amplifies both the frequency and severity of this disease. Limit traffic movement (people and equipment) on affected areas since the pathogens seem to spread quite easily. Irrigate only when dew is already present on the turf and irrigate the entire rootzone. Do not allow the turf to become drought stressed, especially putting greens. In other words, avoid having a dry root system when the leaf canopy is wet due to high humidity.

Chemical Controls

Consistent disease control has not been observed with the fungicides currently registered for *R. solani* (brown patch/Rhizoctonia blight). Again, if the rings are a secondary infection associated with localized dry spots, the dry soil condition must be alleviated before any fungicides are used. Do not use fungicides containing benomyl or thiophanate methyl as *R. zeae* and *R. oryzae* are not sensitive to this group of fungicides. Mancozeb, PCNB, chlorothalonil, iprodione, vinclozolin, and flutolanil, among others, provide some suppression.

Yellow Patch

The causal agent of yellow patch is *Rhizoctonia cerealis* Van der Hoeven.

Occurrence

Yellow patch, also referred to as cool-season brown patch, is primarily a problem on cool-season grasses, especially bentgrass and annual bluegrass. It also occurs on Kentucky bluegrass, zoysiagrass, ryegrass, rough bluegrass overseedings, tall fescue, and bermudagrass. It is favored by cold (50 to 68°F, 10 to 20°C), wet conditions from fall to early spring.

Symptoms/Signs

On bentgrass greens, irregular, narrow, yellow rings ranging from several inches to several feet in diameter appear in late fall through winter when cool, humid (or wet) conditions occur (Plate 22–14). Ring symptoms persist under these conditions while bentgrass has slow growth. Often patches appear sunken due to rapid decomposition of the thatch layer. Individual tillers appear yellow in color, with crowns and lower portions of leaves sometimes red in color. Leaf lesions are rare compared to brown patch (*R. solani*) on cool-season grasses. Once ring symptoms appear, fungicides become relatively ineffective. Preventive applications are needed before rings appear to control symptoms.

Cultural Controls

Avoid excess nitrogen, especially readily available forms of nitrogen such as soluble liquids or quick-release nitrogen sources. Do not force grasses to grow in winter with excessive nitrogen. Irrigate greens when dew is already present so leaves do not stay continuously wet. Increase air circulation. Remove clippings and avoid thatch buildup. The disease survives periods of unfavorable growth as minute, dark-brown to black bulbils and as mycelium in the thatch and plant debris.

Chemical Controls

Curative control has been difficult with this disease, and symptoms generally subside once good growing conditions resume with warmer weather. Propiconazole, flutolanil, azoxystrobin, and pyraclostrobin provide preventive control.

Copper Spot

The causal agent of copper spot is *Gloeocercospora sorghi* Bain & Edgerton ex Deighton.

Occurrence

Copper spot (also called Zonate leaf spot) can be a serious disease during periods of moderately warm, wet weather. While not as widespread as most other turfgrass diseases, it can be destructive to creeping and velvet bentgrasses, and less frequently on bermudagrass and zoysiagrass. Disease development initiates when temperatures reach 69°F (21°C) and is favored by temperatures above 80°F (27°C).

Symptoms/Signs

Leaves initially have small reddish lesions. The spots are salmon-pink to copper-red in appearance and range in size from one to three inches (2.5 to 7.6 cm). Lesions may spread rapidly to blight entire leaves. The disease can be easily confused with the early stages of Pythium blight if patches are copper-colored. Overall symptoms resemble dollar spot disease except for the distinct copper or pink-colored patches associated with copper spot. During wet weather, leaves may be covered with pustules of gelatinous, pink spore masses that turn bright orange when dry. Also, very tiny black sclerotia may be formed in necrotic portions of leaf lesions. When active, sclerotia germinate from sporodochia. Conidia (spores) are produced in the sporodochia and germinate to produce hyphae that quickly penetrate leaves in warm, moist weather. Conidia are spread by splashing, shoes, and turf equipment. The fungus survives in host debris as sclerotia and thick-walled mycelium in thatch.

Cultural Controls

Turf normally slowly recovers following cool, dry weather. To prevent spread, allow greens to dry before mowing. Dragging or poling greens hastens this drying. Avoid quickly available nitrogen sources when disease is active. Liming may help reduce disease severity if soil pH is low.

Chemical Controls

Chlorothalonil, iprodione, thiophanate, and triadimefon provide good control. Apply once or twice on a 14- to 21-day interval.

Dollar Spot

The causal agent of dollar spot is *Sclerotinia homoeocarpa* F. T. Bennett.

Occurrence

This disease is favored by low soil nitrogen levels, close mowing, micronutrient deficiency, dry soil, heavy dews, and excessive thatch accumulation—characteristics of most modern golf greens. It occurs during periods of warm, humid weather when heavy dews occur. All turfgrasses are susceptible, with creeping bentgrass, ryegrass, Kentucky bluegrass, annual bluegrass, and roughstalk bluegrass (*Poa trivialis*) being most susceptible for cool-season grasses and bermudagrass and zoysiagrass most susceptible for warm-season grasses. Activity begins at 60°F (16°C) and is optimum between 70 and 80°F (21 and 27°C), especially when free moisture is present. Although a very persistent disease, dollar spot does not normally cause quick, total kill of a turf area.

Symptoms/Signs

Small (2 inches, 5 cm, diameter), bleached patches of dead grass on low-cut turf such as golf greens will develop first (Plate 22–15). Irregular, light-tan lesions with distinct brown borders will be present on individual leaf tissue at the outside edge of the patch (Plate 22–16). Leaves may be girdled and collapse at the lesion even though leaf tips remain green. In contrast, lesions caused by *Pythium* fungi generally are water-soaked in appearance, feel greasy to the touch, and do not have distinct borders around the bleached diseased leaf tissue. In taller turfgrass, four- to six-inch (10- to 15-cm) patches of mottled, straw-colored turf often occur. Lesions on taller-mowed grass often die-back from the tip and have straw-colored or bleached lesions shaped like an hourglass. White, cottony mycelium may be observed in early morning hours when dew is present and can easily be confused with early stages of Pythium blight or the web of spiders (Plate 22–17). Spider webs, however, are flat, have a web pattern, and do not cause leaf lesions while mycelium from dollar spot or Pythium blight is three-dimensional.

Dollar spot fungi do not form spores; rather, disease is spread from mycelial growth and movement of infected plant parts, infested equipment, or traffic. Dollar spot fungi survive as dormant mycelium in plant parts and as thin flakes of fungal tissue on foliage or in soil. Disease often develops earlier in spring where it was not adequately controlled the previous fall. Spots in sod-forming grasses, such as bermudagrass and bentgrass, usually disappear once disease is controlled; however, spots in bunch-type grasses, such as ryegrass, often remain due to their inability to fill-in damaged areas. Severity usually peaks in late spring and again in late summer on cool-season grasses when night temperatures are cool enough to allow heavy early morning dew formation and high humidity in the turf canopy. Leaf wetness periods of 12 or more hours are conducive for severe dollar spot outbreaks on putting greens cultured to cool-season grasses. On warm-season grasses, dollar spot occurs all season long.

Cultural Controls

Plant resistant cultivars, blends, and mixtures of various grasses whenever possible. Bentgrass cultivars Crenshaw and SR1020 are highly susceptible while Penncross, L-93, A-1, A-2, and G-1 are more resistant. Avoid extreme nitrogen deficiency. If the disease develops, apply a quick-release source of nitrogen such as ammonium sulfate; symptoms will subside, although control is not sustained as long as with some fungicides (Plate 22–18). Do not use this approach with creeping bentgrass in the Southeast as quick-release fertilizers may cause excessive, succulent growth, promoting heat- and moisture-stress problems. Organic fertilizers may help delay dollar spot in early season, but do not reduce its severity when disease pressure is high. Maintain adequate phosphorus, potassium, and lime. Irrigate during early morning hours to limit periods of high humidity and remove leaf moisture (dragging a hose over the area or using a whipping pole to remove moisture may enhance spread). Avoid thatch buildup by aerifying, topdressing, and verticutting.

Prevent disease spread by removing clippings from infected areas, washing equipment before entering a noninfected area, and by encouraging golfers to clean their shoes between rounds. Raising the mowing height also reduces disease severity on golf greens.

Chemical Controls

Most fungicides labeled for control do a good job (Plate 22–19). These include boscalid, chlorothalonil, fenarimol, iprodione, mancozeb, maneb, propiconazole, thiophanate, triadimefon, thiram, and vinclozolin. Synergistic combinations of fungicides for dollar spot control include propiconazole plus either triadimefon, iprodione, chlorothalonil, vinclozolin, or anilazine. Contact fungicides provide 10- to 14-day preventive control while systemics provide 14- to 28-day control. Use higher rates only for curative control situations. Resistance has been problematic for the benzimidazole class of fungicides (including thiophanate methyl) and the sterol biosynthesis inhibitors (fenarimol, propiconazole, triadimefon, cyproconazole, myclobutanil). Resistance to these fungicides appears to be long lasting, once induced. Resistance has also developed in response to overuse of dicarboxamides, iprodione, or vinclozolin, but the pathogen populations become sensitive to these fungicides if they are not used for several years before being used once again. Rotating and tank-mixing fungicides are necessary for managing disease resistance. For resistant-prone fungicides, do not apply products from the same chemical class (or family) two or more consecutive times. Tank-mixing a low resistant-prone contact fungicide with a systemic (or penetrant) as previously discussed also reduces the chances of resistance. Strains of the fungus *Trichoderma* and several formulations of antagonistic bacteria appear promising as biocontrol agents when disease pressure is low.

Preventive control treatments should start in spring when nightly low temperatures are between 50 and 70°F (10 and 21°C). Repeat applications on 14- to 21-day intervals, depending on the products and rates selected. In addition, flat fan nozzles work best due to their even coverage. Spray application volume should also be at least two gallons of water per 1,000 square feet (8 liters per hectare).

Fairy Ring

The causal agents of fairy ring include *Chlorophyllum, Marasmius, Lepiota, Agaricus, Amanita, Lycoperdon, Calvatia,* and over 50 other basidiomycetes (mushroom-, toadstool-, or puffball-producing fungi). The name fairy ring is from English folklore where the rings were believed to be where fairies had danced. There are records of fairy rings in Europe over 100 years old and up to several hundred feet in diameter.

Occurrence

Fairy rings are most common in soils with high organic matter, often where old tree stumps, lumber, and other organic debris were buried during construction, or they may occur in soils of very poor fertility. Newly constructed putting greens, in which the rootzone mix consists of sand and an organic amendment (such as peat), may develop severe infestations after only a few years or even months. The fungi live by decomposing organic litter such as thatch and plant debris. Fairy rings caused by *Lycoperdon* (a common puffball) may develop on 100 percent sand-based greens as well. Fairy rings are most frequently observed during summer months, presumably due to warm, wet weather, which favor fungal growth. In some instances, toxic materials associated with certain species of fairy ring may cause/promote localized dry spot (LDS). However, fairy ring can occur under any soil condition supporting turfgrass growth.

Usually growth stimulation of the turfgrass occurs in the form of darker-green rings or arcs (Plate 22–20). Grass stimulation associated with fairy rings is due to the increased availability of nutrients, especially nitrogen, from decomposition of organic complexes in soil by the fungi or from decomposition of the fungi themselves as the rings expand outward. Grass inside a fairy ring is usually in a state of decline and frequently infested with weeds or algae. This decline is thought to be from depletion of nutrients; lack of soil moisture due to an impervious mat of fungal tissue at or near the soil surface; a toxic agent, such as cyanide-containing compounds produced by the fungus; or a combination of two or more of these. Fairy rings caused by *Marasmius oreades* rarely cross each other as the fungi produce compounds that inhibit the growth of other fairy ring fungi.

Symptoms/Signs

Fairy rings have been classified in several ways, depending on the symptoms and conditions induced. One classification describes them as belonging to two basic types: **edaphic** or **lectophilic.** Edaphic fairy rings are those induced by soil-inhabiting fungi. Edaphic fairy rings occur as rings or arcs of green stimulated turf which may or may not be accompanied by adjacent areas of dead or declining grass. A mat of white to cream-colored fungal mycelium may be present at or just below the soil line. This mat becomes very evident when a plug of grass is incubated in a sealed bag for two or three days. Soil beneath rings may become very dry and difficult to wet during summer and autumn. Edaphic fairy rings are more common in lawns and pastures. Three types of symptom expression are described for edaphic fairy rings.

> *Type I rings*—These have a zone of dead grass just inside a zone of dark-green grass (Plate 22–21). These are more prevalent on new greens than on established ones. The dead grass may form from mushroom mycelia accumulating below the soil surface and cause soil to become hydrophobic (water "hating") (Plate 22–22). Type I rings generally cause the most damage due to this soil drying which prevents water from reaching plant roots.
>
> *Type II rings*—These have only a circular band of dark-green turf, with or without mushrooms present in the band (Plate 22–23). On frequently mowed areas (greens and tees), mature mushrooms may never be observed but the "button" stage may be present at ground level. Turf is normally not killed.
>
> *Type III rings*—These do not exhibit a dead zone or a stimulated dark-green zone, but simply have a ring of mushrooms present (Plate 22–24). Mushrooms or puffballs often develop after rains or heavy irrigation during mild weather. Rings normally expand each year. The size and completeness (circular, semicircular, quarter-circles) of the bands vary considerably (e.g., 1 to 100 feet).

Lectophilic fairy rings (sometimes called "superficial" fairy rings) are those inhabiting thatch and upper soil surfaces. Lectophilic fairy rings tend to be less problematic although, on putting greens, they can be unsightly and may still induce hydrophobic conditions that require treatment.

Cultural Controls

Edaphic fairy rings are very difficult to control. If necessary for aesthetic purposes, mask the dark-green ring symptoms with nitrogen fertilizers (especially for Type II rings). However, do not over-fertilize cool-season grasses in summer as this may stimulate other, more severe problems. Remove mushrooms as some (e.g., *Chlorophyllum* spp.) are poisonous. Fumigation may be used where sod in affected areas is removed, and the top six inches (15 cm) of soil are then mixed with a fumigant such as metam sodium or dazomet. Once the fumigant has dissipated, the area is re-sodded. Affected areas may also be excavated by digging up all infested soil in the ring area and two feet (0.6 m) beyond. Soil in the affected area is then removed to a 12-inch (30-cm) depth. Uncontaminated soil is then replaced and the area reseeded or sodded.

Although it is possible to excavate and fumigate fairy ring sites, it is quite likely rings will return if the food source is still present underground. In some situations on putting greens, these rings are also associated with localized dry spots in which the fungi have produced humic and fulvic acids that coat sand particles. In those situations, it may be useful to spike the area and use wetting agents to increase water absorption. Also, aerify and remove soil cores to allow better nutrient and water penetration. Infected areas should be heavily hand watered, being careful not to overwater adjacent, unaffected areas that could result in other diseases and problems. Do not bury and plant over organic debris such as tree stumps, large roots, and lumber left over during the construction and establishment phases of turf areas.

Chemical Controls

Removing afflicted sod, followed by soil fumigation, tilling, and replanting, helps reduce fairy ring occurrence. Some success in temporarily suppressing fairy rings caused by *Lycoperdon* puffballs has occurred from using flutolanil, azoxystrobin, and pyraclostrobin. Best results occur when fungicides are applied following aerification and irrigation to move them into the zone of fungus infestation. Also, the use of a wetting agent program to combat hydrophobic soil conditions is helpful. However, wetting agents will not control fairy ring fungi. By inhibiting the fungi with fungicides and providing better water infiltration and soil movement with wetting agents, symptoms can sometimes be suppressed for months. High pressure water injection of the fungicides and wetting agent combined is also helpful.

Fusarium Patch (or Pink Snow Mold or Microdochium Patch)

The causal agent of Fusarium patch is *Microdochium nivale* (Fr.) Samuels and Hallett (formerly, *Fusarium nivale* Ces. ex Berl. & Voglino).

Occurrence

Fusarium (or *Microdochium*) patch is probably the most important disease in the Pacific Northwest, although it is also important in northern areas of the United States, Canada, and Europe. It is referred to as Fusarium patch in the absence of snow cover and pink snow mold with snow cover. It occurs during periods of cool (32 to 60°F, 0 to 16°C), wet spring and fall weather with or without snow cover. Alternating thawing and snow cover, repeated frosts, cold fogs, and light rain are particularly favorable for leaf-to-leaf spread of the fungus. Creeping bentgrass, annual bluegrass, Kentucky bluegrass, ryegrass, and fine leaf fescue are all susceptible, with annual bluegrass and bentgrass being most susceptible and Kentucky bluegrass, tall fescue, and red fescue least susceptible. Although sometimes susceptible, reports of Fusarium patch on warm-season grasses have been rare.

Symptoms/Signs

When Fusarium patch occurs without snow cover, the spots are one to eight inches (2.5 to 20 cm) in diameter and reddish-brown in color (Plate 22–25). At this stage, the disease can be easily confused with Pythium blight or copper spot. When the disease occurs under snow, spots are usually from two to three inches (5 to 7.6 cm) up to two feet (0.6 m) in diameter, and range in color from tan to whitish-gray or reddish-brown. Immediately after the snow melts, spots will initially appear water-soaked and may have pinkish, salmon-colored mycelium present in the margins (hence, the common name), later turning to light tan in color. In the center of patches, grass collapses and is frequently matted and water-soaked. If severe, spots may coalesce to form large areas of diseased turf. Grass on the outer edge of patches generally appears water-soaked, with profuse gray- or pink-colored mycelium of the fungus present. The disease may spread by mycelial growth or movement of spores that are produced in enormous amounts on diseased tissue in fruiting bodies called **sporodochia**. The white- or salmon-pink-colored sporodochia are very small and, with the aid of a hand lens, appear as flecks on dead plant tissue. These cannot be readily seen after the plant tissue dries. Spores are easily transported by water, machinery, animals, and foot traffic, and tracking patterns on greens are not uncommon. Conidia usually occur in orange-colored spore masses. It probably survives the summer months as resistant hyphae (mycelia) and spores in turfgrass debris. On dormant bermudagrass, under periods of high moisture, a grayish-colored patch can form (Plate 22–26). Permanent bermudagrass damage has not been seen.

Cultural Controls

Avoid late summer and early fall fertility that may lead to lush growth during cool, wet weather or under snow cover. Avoid excess spring nitrogen when Fusarium patch is a problem. Acidifying fertilizers such as ammonium nitrate/sulfate may aid in reducing soil pH and disease occurrence. Soil pH should be maintained below 7.0. Increase soil potassium in late fall to increase turf cold hardiness and to suppress the disease. Poor drainage and long leaf blades that mat down produce high humidity that favors disease development. Reduce shade and improve soil aeration and drainage. Remove tree leaves as the disease often develops under these, remaining on the turf for long periods during cold, wet weather. Use snow fences or plant landscape plants adjacent to golf greens to prevent excess snow accumulation. Avoid compaction during winter by preventing skiers and snowmobiles from being on greens and tees. If covers are used on greens for insulation, treat with a fungicide prior to installation of the covers.

Chemical Controls

Chlorothalonil, mancozeb, triadimefon, thiophanate-methyl, fenarimol, vinclozolin, pentachloronitrobenzene (PCNB), iprodione, and propiconazole provide good control and should be applied before the first seasonal snow storm. Contact fungicide, such as mancozeb or chlorothalonil, combined with benzimidazole systemic fungicides such as thiophanate, generally provide the best control. Apply a late September to early October tank-mix of a systemic fungicide and a strobilurin fungicide. This helps control Fusarium patch, dollar spot, anthracnose, and brown patch. Sequential treatments should be used in disease-prone areas during mid-winter thaws. In warmer climates, such as the Piedmont, Coastal Plains, and coastal regions of the southeastern United States, a curative approach is generally successful due to the probability of more favorable weather for turf recovery in winter.

Gray Leaf Spot (or Blast)

The causal agent of gray leaf spot is *Pyricularia grisea* (Cke.) Sacc. (= *Magnaporthe grisea* (Hebert) = *Pyricularia oryzae*).

Occurrence

Gray leaf spot (also called "blast") is a disease most often seen in St. Augustinegrass, tall fescue, and perennial ryegrass (Plate 22–27). Certain strains of the fungus also infect bermudagrass, crabgrass, foxtails, rice, and barnyardgrass. It occurs mostly in late summer during prolonged hot (80 to 90°F, 27 to 32°C), rainy, humid conditions, and is generally more severe in newly established turf areas, shady locations, turf being heavily fertilized with nitrogen, and locations with poor air movement. Morning dew and high overcast conditions also are often associated with its occurrence, and higher-mowed areas of perennial ryegrass, such as roughs and south-facing areas, seem most affected, presumably due to their increased canopy humidity. Turf growth slowed by herbicides also becomes susceptible. The fungus forms spores (conidia) that are spread easily by wind and moisture or by maintenance equipment. The disease overwinters as dormant mycelium in dead leaves. Conidia produced from these leaves serves as the primary inoculum early in the growing season. Conidia are dispersed by maintenance equipment, golf carts, wind, and water. Replacing perennial ryegrass with another turf species such as bentgrass or Kentucky bluegrass can be considered. However, thatch build up and other diseases associated these choices should carefully be weighed before use.

Symptoms/Signs

Infections may occur on all aboveground plant parts and begin as small brown to tan water-soaked leaf spots with a distinct brown to purple border or band surrounding the infected tissue (Plate 22–28). Lesions may become very numerous on leaves and individual spots may expand to consume leaves completely and to girdle stolons. Infected perennial ryegrass leaf blades often are twisted or flagging and die-back from the tips. Prolonged favorable weather for disease may leave turf with a scorched and ragged appearance that thins to resemble melting out or severe drought stress. However, unlike drought stress, a water-soaking and yellowing appearance of the leaf tips is first observed along with distinctive leaf spots. The circular spots may take on a grayish or grayish-brown appearance with purple to dark-brown borders and a yellowish halo. The lesions may resemble those caused by the *Dreschlera* species. Advanced symptoms on perennial ryegrass commonly resemble Rhizoctonia leaf and sheath spot or Pythium blight where blighted leaves turn yellow, then brown, with characteristic twisted leaf tips. However, there are no foliar mycelium or smoke rings associated with these patches. Under conducive environmental conditions, complete ryegrass stand loss can occur within 48 hours. This rapid decline causes confusion with pythium diseases or may be misdiagnosed as a symptom of drought. Grass blades may appear in early morning hours as felted or fuzzy, due to the massive production of spores on the lesions. It overwinters as spores and dormant mycelium in infected plants and in thatch. Disease is often along low-lying or poorly drained areas where prolonged leaf wetness occurs. Spring use of ethofumesate herbicide to control annual bluegrass also has been associated with disease outbreaks.

Cultural Controls

Avoiding nitrogen fertility in summer leads to lush growth. Improve air movement and light penetration in areas prone to chronic infections. Irrigate in early morning hours to promote maximum drying conditions during the day. Plant Kentucky bluegrass as a mix.

Chemical Controls

Azoxystrobin, chlorothalonil, propiconazole, trifloxystrobin, pyraclostrobin, and thiophanate methyl are used to control this disease. Resistance has been documented to strobilurin fungicides such as azoxystrobin, pyraclostrobin, and trifloxystrobin. An effective alternative is thiophanate methyl and combinations of thiophanate methyl and chlorothalonil or propiconazole and chlorothalonil. Apply as needed on a 10- to 14-day interval. Due to its potential explosive nature, early diagnosis is critical. If allowed to reach epidemic proportions, nearly all control strategies may fail. One strategy is to tank-mix products with different modes of action during high disease pressure. Another strategy to reduce resistance potential is to rotate between different mode-of-action fungicides such as a strobilurin, then thiophanate methyl, then a DMI fungicide plus chlorothalonil.

"Helminthosporium" Diseases—Leaf Spot and Melting Out

The causal agent of "Helminthosporium" diseases is primarily *Bipolaris* and *Drechslera* spp. (previously known as species of *Helminthosporium*).

Occurrence

Leaf spot fungi previously belonged to the genus *Helminthosporium*, and they are still often referred to as "Helminthosporium" diseases. These fungi induce a variety of symptoms in many warm- and cool-season turfgrasses and attack all plant parts of turfgrasses. Thus, leaf spots, crown rots, and root, crown, rhizome, and stolon rots may occur, depending on the specific disease. Table 22–8 lists several common Helminthosporium diseases.

In general, leaf tissue as well as crowns, rhizomes, and roots may be affected. These diseases become severe under moderate temperatures in spring, fall, and summer under wet, humid conditions. Conidia (spores) of these fungi are abundantly produced in lesions and are dispersed by wind, water, and through dispersal of infested tissue removed by mowing. Crown and root rotting becomes more apparent in late spring and summer when stressful conditions eliminate severely infected plants, causing a "melting out" symptom common with *Drechslera poae* in Kentucky bluegrass (Plate 22–29). These fungi survive as dormant mycelia in thatch and leaf litter, on colonized plants, and as conidia.

Symptoms/Signs

Drechslera species cause leaf spots during cool, humid conditions, especially following cloudy weather, with crown and root rot phases occurring during warm, dry weather or during wet periods following dry periods. *Drechslera* species occur mostly on cool-season grasses. Symptoms vary on different cool-season turfgrasses. Leaf lesions are generally distinct and begin when temperatures are between 70 and 85°F (21 and 27°C), and are tiny water-soaked areas that become dark-brown to purplish-black. Lesions are usually surrounded by a yellow area of varying width that fades to the normal green of the leaf tissue. Older lesions may have a white or bleached area

TABLE 22–8 *Common names, causal pathogens, and primary turfgrass hosts of various "Helminthosporium" diseases.*

Disease	Pathogen	Primary turfgrass hosts
Melting out	*Drechslera poae* (Baudys) Shoemaker	Kentucky bluegrass, rough bluegrass, ryegrass, buffalograss
Helminthosporium leafspot	*Bipolaris sorokiniana* (Sacc.) Shoemaker	Kentucky bluegrass, bentgrasses, annual bluegrass, tall fescue, ryegrasses, bermudagrass, buffalograss
Red leafspot	*Drechslera erythrospila* Paul and Parberry	Bentgrasses
Helminthosporium blight (Net blotch)	*Drechslera dictyoides* (Drechs.) Shoemaker	Fescues, ryegrasses, Kentucky bluegrass
Zonate eyespot	*Drechslera gigantea* (Heald and Wolf) Ito	Bermudagrasses, but also bentgrasses and Kentucky bluegrass
Stem and crown necrosis	*Bipolaris specifera* Nicot	Bermudagrasses, zoysiagrasses
Leaf blotch	*Bipolaris cynodontis* Marignoni	Bermudagrasses

in their centers. Severely affected plants may become almost entirely yellow in appearance. Leaf spots, crown rotting, and root rotting occurs. On leaves, small water-soaked lesions occur initially, are brown in color, or are a purplish color (Plate 22–30). Lesions on leaf sheaths similarly occur, but may encircle leaf sheaths and girdle leaf fascicles. When temperatures are above 85°F (27°C), lesions mature, the centers may turn tan or white in color and yellow, and chlorotic tissue may surround the actual lesions. Microscopically, abundant, dark, multicellular spores borne on simple modified hyphae are associated with the lesion's necrotic tissue. Gradual browning and thinning occurs over a period of weeks to months. As diseases progress, large irregular areas turn yellow, then brown, and then thin out. Lesions on stolons, stems, crowns, rhizomes, and roots are dark-purple to black. Crown/root rots will also occur at this time and infected plants lack vigor, often wilting even when adequate soil moisture is present.

On closely mowed bentgrass, leaves from red leafspot turn reddish-brown or dark gray in irregularly shaped areas, causing a smoky blue appearance resembling drought stress. Lower (older) leaves tend to initially show symptoms, presumably to their slowed growth (Plate 22–31).

On bermudagrass, leaf spot is most pronounced in fall and early spring months when the grass is green but not actively growing due to cool temperatures. Leaf spot rarely causes permanent damage to bermudagrass but can cause streaking, browning, light-brown blotches, and stand thinning under severe infestations (Plate 22–32). Turf normally fully recovers when good grass growing temperatures return.

Cultural Controls

Use resistant cultivars, blends, and mixtures of cool-season grasses whenever possible to alter the genetics of the host and prevent devastating epidemics. Balance nitrogen levels with potassium. Avoid drought stress and reduce leaf-surface moisture by deeply but infrequently watering. Avoid late afternoon and evening waterings and encourage good soil drainage. Encourage air movement and light penetration by removing shade sources and unneeded adjacent vegetation. Avoid thatch accumulation greater than one-half inch (1.3 cm). Raise mowing height between 1.5 and 2 inches (3.8 and 5 cm) for bluegrass to improve the survival of affected plants, but note this practice may be dependent on the particular cultivars being used. Overuse of certain fungicides (benomyl) and phenoxy herbicides (MCPP, 2,4-D, and dicamba) for broadleaf weed control may enhance disease development on cool-season grasses or if used when bermudagrass is not actively growing. Avoid using these pesticides or treat preventatively for "Helminthosporium" disease control prior to their use.

Chemical Controls

Chlorothalonil, iprodione, mancozeb, and vinclozolin provide control. Chronic problems with these diseases may be site specific, and preventive or curative control approaches should be used accordingly. Some disease enhancement has been noted with some of the sterol biosynthesis inhibitor fungicides. Preventive control is best. Begin applications in early spring after new growth is apparent and repeat at 7- to 21-day intervals until warm weather occurs. Curative control of the warm weather group such as leaf blight and melting out are often ineffective when symptoms are obvious since the fungus is well-established and inaccessible in infected plant crowns, roots, rhizomes, and stolons.

Necrotic Ring Spot

The causal agent of necrotic ring spot is *Ophiosphaerella* (=*Leptosphaeria*) *korrae* J. C. Walker & A. M. Smith.

Occurrence

A major disease of Kentucky bluegrass and annual bluegrass, along with summer patch, necrotic ring spot has a similar pattern of occurrence to Fusarium blight and yellow patch (Plate 22–33). Undoubtedly, all of these distinct diseases have been confused due to the similarity of occurrence and symptoms in Kentucky bluegrass. Necrotic ring spot has been recorded on lawns and sports turf of Kentucky bluegrass, annual bluegrass, and red fescue. To date, necrotic ring spot occurs mostly in the northeastern, north central, and Pacific northwestern United States.

Symptoms/Signs

This is a root and crown rot, caused by *Ophiosphaerella korrae*, one of the "ectotrophic" root-infecting fungi that destroys the plant's ability to absorb water, causing it to wilt and die more rapidly than healthy grass. This fungus colonizes roots and crown tissues, growing slowly and initially infecting cortical tissues, and eventually entire roots. Initial symptoms are wilting patches of turf that range in size from a few inches up to a foot or more in diameter. Sunken, crater-like patches of this disease appear in spring or late summer in cool, wet weather. Patches may develop a "frog eye" appearance in which diseased turf occurs in circles or arcs, with surviving plants or weeds in the center. Individual plants exhibit brown to black, rotted roots and crowns, with varying degrees of chlorosis, necrosis, and tip die-back of shoots. Necrotic ring spot patches tend to be large (>1 foot, 0.3 m, in diameter), often with the frog eye symptoms, and mostly occur in spring and early fall. Summer patch tends to be smaller (<1 foot, 0.3 m) in diameter and occurs most often during summer-stress periods.

Distinctive leaf lesions are not associated with this disease, but leaves often die from the tip back. Plants at the edge of patches often have a bronze or copper color, while affected greens often have a spotted effect as infected annual bluegrass plants die-out and adjacent bentgrass is unaffected. A dark-brown to black discoloration of lower shoots, stems, and roots is often associated with advanced stages of the disease and affected plants easily pull from soil.

These fungi survive as saprophytic mycelium and sclerotia in soil and as conidia. Disease spreads by transporting affected roots, stems, crowns, and soil by maintenance equipment.

Cultural Controls

As with most root diseases, control requires an integrated strategy involving cultural, genetic, and fungicidal use. Utilize watering practices to minimize drought stress and encourage deeper rooting. When disease has severely damaged the root system, it requires light and frequent (e.g., 0.1 inch/day, 25 mm) irrigation, most often during afternoon stress. Cutting heights can be raised to increase carbohydrate production and improve the chances of turf recovery. Utilize fertility practices to maintain a moderate soil pH of about 5.5 and utilize slow-release nitrogen sources. Using slow-release nitrogen forms consistently improves disease symptoms in research trials. Differences also occur in susceptibility among Kentucky bluegrass cultivars, with Midnight, Wabash, Eclipse, Adelphi, Park, I-13, Mystic, Somerset, and some others reported to have good to moderate resistance or tolerance. Plant a 75 to 85 percent blend of these and other resistant cultivars with 15 to 25 percent (by weight) of turf-type perennial ryegrass. Avoid herbicide use during hot weather.

Chemical Controls

Preventive applications of fenarimol, propiconazole, triadimefon, thiophanate-methyl, myclobutanil, and cyproconazole have shown efficacy. To be effective, these must be applied before symptoms develop and repeat at 21- to 30-day intervals during the summer. A single mid-spring (e.g., April/May) application of one of the DMI fungicides has shown good control through late summer/early autumn. Adequate nitrogen and soil moisture are necessary or these fungicides are less effective.

Powdery Mildew

The causal agent of powdery mildew is *Erysiphe graminis* DC.

Occurrence

Powdery mildew is a disease occurring under low light intensities; therefore, it is mostly a problem on turf grown in shaded areas such as under trees or on the north sides of buildings. It can also occur in open areas, especially in fall and spring with consecutive cool, cloudy, humid days. Unlike most foliar blights or leaf-spot diseases, powdery mildew does not require wet foliage and usually does not cause severe damage. Cooler temperatures (55 to 70°F, 13 to 21°C) favor its development. Kentucky bluegrass is especially susceptible. *Erysiphe graminis* is an obligate parasite, obtaining nutrients from its host and only completing its life cycle in association with a living host.

Symptoms/Signs

Turf appears to have a dull-white appearance and may be severely thinned. In severe cases the turf may take on a chlorotic (yellow) appearance or appear to have been dusted with ground limestone or flour. The fungus appears as a white to grayish-white, cobwebby growth to powdery patches on upper surface of the leaves (Plate 22–34). The powdery appearance is from the production of numerous conidia (spores) in chains. Conidia are easily spread by wind, water, and turf-maintenance equipment. In older leaves, black **cleistothecia** (spore-bearing bodies) may be seen embedded in the leaves.

The fungus overwinters in living, infected plants as ascospores in cleistothecia. Spores are produced in spring, become airborne, and only live for a few days, but can infect susceptible leaves over wide environmental conditions. Peak activity is generally when days are warm and nights are cool. Late summer and early fall are when the white covering of mycelium and spores occur.

Cultural Controls

Use resistant cultivars and resolve the shade issues, where possible. Increase air circulation and drying by removing underbrush, lower tree limbs, and if possible, selective trees. Plant shade-tolerant grasses such as creeping red fescue or other ground cover, increase the mowing height, and use a balanced N–P–K fertility program to reduce disease injury.

Chemical Controls

When the turf stand has chlorotic plants and stand thinning, fungicides such as propiconazole and triadimefon may be justified. A single application usually is sufficient.

Pythium Blight (Cottony Blight, Greasy Spot, Damping-Off, Seedling Blight)

The causal agents of Pythium blight are *Pythium aphanidermatum* (Edson) Fitzpatrick and other *Pythium* species such as *P. myriotylum* Drechs., *P. graminicola* Subrum., *P. arrhenomanes* Drechs., and *P. ultimum* Trow.

Occurrence

All turfgrasses are susceptible, with the cool-season grasses—creeping bentgrass, annual bluegrass, Kentucky bluegrass, and perennial ryegrass—being the most susceptible. Although this disease is rarely observed on bermudagrass, it is a disease of cool-season turfgrasses used for overseeding bermudagrass surfaces. With all cool-season grasses, disease can be especially severe on newly established stands. It is most likely to occur when day and night temperatures exceed 85 and 68°F (29 and 20°C), respectively, and when the relative humidity is high. Pythium blight can be a highly destructive disease.

Pythium species are water molds; thus, they require sufficient surface moisture for development. All soils contain *Pythium* species unless the soil has recently been fumigated. *Pythium* species causing Pythium blight are facultative parasites, meaning they are saprophytes in thatch or soil and quickly become pathogenic when favorable conditions develop. The fungi produce thick-walled sexual spores that survive for long periods in the soil. The germination and "grow-in" period of newly established bentgrass greens or overseeded cool-season grasses are ideal for disease development since fall temperatures can still be quite warm and the turf is being irrigated more frequently than normal. Extended periods of warm, foggy mornings also favor this disease, potentially destroying large areas in a short period of time. On creeping bentgrass, conditions may be favorable for relatively long periods of time during summer, depending on location. Greens situated in low, protected areas with poor sunlight penetration and air movement are most at risk. Bentgrass is more susceptible when saline soil conditions (and presumably high-soluble salts from fertilizers) exist.

Symptoms/Signs

Small, distinct reddish-brown patches of grass, usually about one to six inches (2.5 to 15 cm) in diameter, first appear dark and water-soaked (slimy), but later shrivel and turn straw-colored as humidity and/or temperature decrease (Plate 22–35). In some cases, after heavy rains and prolonged high relative humidity, the first sign of disease is a white, cottony mycelial growth. Turf grown in shaded, low lying areas adjacent to water where air circulation is poor and humidity highest is likely to become diseased first (Plate 22–36). Water-soaked, blackened leaves often feel greasy or slimy. If conditions become less humid during the day, bleached lesions can be observed on partially damaged leaves, but these lesions have no distinct border, which easily distinguishes them from dollar spot. Pythium blight can initially be confused with both copper spot and Fusarium patch on creeping bentgrass in the fall. Patches may spread quickly in a "streak" pattern, usually following water drainage movement (Plate 22–37). White cottony mycelium may be observed in early morning when dew is present, but this disease sign is not always apparent (Plate 22–38). Pythium fungi is spread by direct mycelial growth as well as through a spore or spore-containing sack called **sporangia** and small swimming spores released from sporangia called **zoospores.** These fungi also produce thick-walled resting spores called **oospores** that may survive in soil and thatch for extended periods. Disease may spread rapidly when sporangia, zoospores, oospores, or infected plant parts are moved by water along drainage patterns, or by mowers or traffic (Plate 22–39). Often, two or more *Pythium* species may simultaneously occur, requiring growing the fungus on special laboratory media and microscopically examining the sporangia and oospores for specific identification. Being water molds, *Pythium* spores can survive in ponds used for irrigation, which makes control difficult as the turf is reinoculated with each watering.

Cultural Controls

Improve drainage, air circulation, and light penetration by removing shrubs, trees, and limbs and possibly add fans in pockets of poor air movement. Reduce soil and leaf moisture, as moisture control is a key to *Pythium* management; therefore, early morning removal of dew and guttation water by poling or dragging a hose and utilization of early morning irrigation is beneficial. Plant fungicide-treated seed at the recommended amount, avoiding very high seeding rates. Avoid excessive use of nitrogen prior to warm weather. Minimize equipment or foot traffic across wet infected turf. Wash equipment before entering unaffected areas and encourage golfers to clean their shoes between rounds. Delay overseeding in late summer/early fall until the weather turns cool and dry. Alleviate soil compaction as this reduces turfgrass rooting, which then requires turf managers to irrigate lightly and frequently. Maintain a slightly acidic soil pH, using properly balanced fertilization and avoiding calcium deficiency.

Chemical Controls

Mancozeb, chloroneb, and ethazol provide quick short-term (e.g., 5 to 10 days) contact control. Apply during hot (>80°F, 27°C), humid (≥85 percent) weather when night temperatures exceed 65°F (18°C). Be careful using chloroneb and ethazole, as these are potentially phytotoxic to the turf. Metalaxyl, fosetyl-Al, propamocarb, pyraclostrobin, and azoxystrobin provide longer residual (14- to 21-day) control if preventively applied. Whenever possible, plant seed treated with metalaxyl, mefanoxam, or ethazole. Otherwise, apply one of these fungicides immediately after planting, and reapply approximately 7 to 14 days later (after the seed has germinated). Alternate between compounds to avoid development of fungicide-resistant strains of *Pythium*. A two-way combination of mancozeb and metalaxyl (or mefanoxam), mancozeb and propamocarb, propamocarb and metaxyl (or mefanoxam), and propamocarb and fosetyl-Al has been shown to be synergistic. Mancozeb plus chloroneb tank-mixes, however, are antagonistic and should not be used together. For bentgrass in very hot weather, the mancozeb and fosetyl-Al combination is effective for summer decline (*Rhizoctonia* and *Pythium*-induced disease). A combination of azoxystrobin and chlorothalonil, or chlorothalonil and fosetyl-Al, has performed similarly to mancozeb and fosetyl-Al. Consult turf pathologists for specific rates and timing.

Due to the potential for rapid development of this disease and loss of large areas, turf managers growing cool-season grasses should consider a preventive fungicide program when hot, humid (e.g., foggy) weather is forecasted. Alternating between contact and preventive fungicides should also help reduce the risk of resistance problems. Use curative rates only when absolutely necessary to prevent resistance buildup.

A *Pythium* disease-predicting model (called the Nutter-Shane model) has been developed that requires a maximum daily temperature greater than 82°F (28°C) and a minimum temperature of 68°F (20°C) combined with at least 9 to 14 hours of 90 percent or higher relative humidity before a preventive fungicide is needed. Commercial weather stations (e.g., Environcaster) can be programmed to indicate when disease likelihood occurs based on this Nutter-Shane model.

Pythium Root Rot

The causal agents of Pythium root rot are *Pythium* spp. including *P. aristosporum* Vanterpool, *P. aphanidermatum* (Edson) Fitzpatrick, *P. arrhenomanes* Drechs., *P. graminicola* Subrum., *P. irregulare*, *P. myriotylum* Drechs., and *P. vanterpooli* Kouyeas & Kouyeas.

Occurrence

These *Pythium* species are capable of infecting roots and crowns of cool-season grasses such as bentgrass and annual bluegrass year-round, causing stunting and yellowing. Different levels of aggressiveness are associated with different species of *Pythium*. Pythium root rot is still poorly understood for the different turfgrasses. Symptoms may appear at any time of the year, but they will usually be associated with wet conditions—either from too much precipitation or too much irrigation. Poor drainage and soil compaction conditions will compound this problem and encourage algae development in areas where disease has weakened or killed the grass. Root damage from nematodes or *Gaeumannomyces* spp. also may contribute to this disease.

Symptoms/Signs

Symptoms are typically nonspecific declines in turf quality (Plate 22–40). However, circular patches in rings, arcs, or solid patches of a few inches up to about eight inches (20 cm) may occur in the spring in creeping bentgrass in the southeast. Small or large turf areas will become a general yellow or brown color and gradually begin to thin (Plate 22–41). However, the areas do not normally thin to bare soil. Roots appear thin with few root hairs and have a general discoloration, but are not black and rotted as they are with other root rotting diseases such as necrotic ring spot or bermudagrass decline. Foliar mycelium is absent, often causing confusion with melting out disease or, possibly, anthracnose. Turf does not respond to fertilizer applications, especially nitrogen. This disease cannot be diagnosed from field symptoms alone. Microscopic examination of affected roots and crowns is required to determine if *Pythium* spp. are associated with the symptoms.

Cultural Controls

Improve drainage, aerate, and reduce irrigation as *Pythium* spp. require very wet situations for disease development. Aerify in spring to improve surface drying and to promote rooting. When symptoms are present, irrigate only as needed to prevent permanent wilt. To prevent the disease, avoid frequent shallow irrigations that constantly keep the turf wet. Reduce nematode populations, if justified by a nematode assay. Increase mowing height to one-fourth inch (6.4 mm) or higher to reduce stress and promote root growth. Mow affected greens with walking mowers, skipping clean-up laps and possibly mowing on an alternate-day basis. Wash mowers when used between infected and uninfected turf areas to minimize the spread of disease spores. Aerify and topdress to stimulate new root growth. Check for soluble salt levels in the upper soil and thatch, especially in the first year of turf establishment when excessive fertilizer is used for grow-in.

Chemical Controls

Chemical control includes chloroneb, ethazol, metalaxyl, fosetyl-Al, propamocarb, and azoxystrobin. To increase effectiveness, these fungicides, except for fosetyl-Al, should be either lightly watered into the rootzone or applied in 5 to 10 gallons of water per 1,000 square feet (20 to 40 L/100 m^2). At least two applications will probably be required. Treat preventively beginning in mid- to late June and continue at three-week intervals. Several of these compounds do not have Pythium root rot listed on their labels for turfgrass. This is due to inconsistent disease control. Alternate between compounds to avoid development of fungicide-resistant strains of Pythium. Note that, except for azoxystrobin, these fungicides are specific for *Pythium* spp. only.

Red Thread

The causal agent of red thread is *Laetisaria fuciformis* (McAlphine) Burdsall (formerly, *Corticium fuciformis*).

Occurrence

Red thread can be a destructive disease on slow-growing turf. Perennial ryegrasses and fine leaf fescues are notably susceptible, especially in nitrogen-deficient turf. The disease is primarily a problem during winter or early spring months in cooler (60 to 70°F, 16 to 21°C), humid environments. The disease is fairly common in humid winter months in the upper elevation or northern United States regions.

Symptoms/Signs

Red thread appears as irregular-shaped patches about four to six inches (10 to 15 cm) in diameter that are bleached-tan to reddish in color (resembling dollar spot). From a distance the disease often appears similar to dollar spot and the turf often develops a ragged straw-brown appearance as if it had been mowed with a dull mower blade or may be suffering from drought stress (Plate 22–42). Decline of leaves is rapid in affected areas. Bright coral-pink to red antlerlike "threads" or sclerotia of the fungi are easily seen with the naked eye protruding from dying leaf tips that may have a split, torn appearance (Plate 22–43). Threads are gelatinous in the early morning dew, but later dry and become thin and brittle. Threads occur most often during the cool, drizzly days of spring but can also occur throughout summer in higher elevations. The fungi overseasons on leaves and thatch as pink or red, gelatinous crusts of fungal threads or sclerotia (Plate 22–44). Red thread, like dollar spot, may increase with the current trend of using lower nitrogen rates.

Cultural Controls

Increase nitrogen fertility in the spring and fall when possible. This increases plant vigor which allows the plant to outgrow disease damage. Collect and destroy clippings to minimize spread of sclerotia. Potassium should also be applied with nitrogen. Water deeply but infrequently to prevent prolonged leaf wetness. Avoid watering in late afternoon and evening. Improve air circulation and reduce humidity by pruning trees and removing underbrush. Collect and dispose of clippings from infected areas and wash equipment before entering unaffected areas. Encourage golfers to clean their shoes between rounds.

Chemical Controls

Azoxystrobin, chlorothalonil, iprodione, flutolanil, triadimefon, pyraclostrobin, and vinclozolin provide good control, and only one or two applications on 14- to 21-day intervals should be necessary. Fall and winter treatments help prevent spring disease development.

Rust

The causal agents of rust are *Puccinia* spp. (such as *Puccinia graminis, P. striiformis, P. coronata, P. zoysiae*) or *Uromyces dactylidis.*

Occurrence

Stem rust (*Puccinia graminis* f. sp. *poae*) has been a problem on slow-growing Kentucky bluegrass, especially in seed production fields. Crown rust (*P. coronata*) is an important problem on the new perennial ryegrasses, including their seed production fields. Rusts can also be a serious problem on zoysiagrass and fescue. The disease is most severe during cool weather in late summer and fall when conditions are less than adequate for good turfgrass growth. Nitrogen-deficient grasses grown in shade are especially affected.

Infected turfgrass foliage in areas with mild climates serves as the overwintering site for rust fungi spores or mycelium. Spore dispersal by wind can spread from warm regions in the country to cooler ones. Rust fungi are obligate parasites; thus, they must grow and reproduce only in living tissue.

Symptoms/Signs

Overall symptoms of severe rust infection are a thinned, clumpy turf. Heavily infected turf areas will appear yellow and produce a cloud of orange dust (**urediospores**) when the foliage is disturbed (Plate 22–45). The orange powdery material easily rubs off on hands, machinery, shoes, and clothing. Turf will appear thin and weak, and is more susceptible to drought and winter injury. Oval to elongated pustules, yellow to orange or reddish-brown in color, are raised on the surface of leaves (Plate 22–46). These spores are dry, powdery, and spread easily by wind, machinery, shoes, and infected plants. Survival during periods of unfavorable growth is by dormant mycelium and urediospores in or on infected plants and equipment.

Cultural Controls

Management practices that provide steady grass growth during prolonged warm to hot periods when rust problems are most common should be followed. Maintain adequate nitrogen levels (1/4 to 1/2 lb N/1,000 sq.ft., 1.2 to 2.4 kg/100 m^2) for sufficient growth to ensure weekly mowing will help reduce the severity of rust. If rust occurs in late fall, do not fertilize as the disease usually disappears during winter. Many cultivars of Kentucky bluegrass, perennial ryegrass, and tall fescue have moderate-to-good rust resistance. Planting blends of cultivars with different genetic backgrounds have limited disease occurrence. Remove clippings and remove shade sources, as low light intensity favors the disease. Wash equipment before entering an uninfected area. Water deeply but infrequently to encourage deep rooting and avoid drought stress.

Chemical Controls

Zoysiagrass, due to its inherent slow-growing nature, and seed production fields of perennial ryegrass and tall fescue may require fungicide treatment. Triadimefon and propiconazole control rusts when applied in spring or fall when the first signs of rust are visible. Repeat applications every 7 to 14 days are necessary while rust is present. Contact fungicides require applications on a 7- to 10-day interval and are not especially effective.

Slime Mold

The causal agents of slime mold are *Mucilago, Physarum,* and *Fuligo* spp.

Occurrence

All grasses may be affected because slime molds are not parasites of turfgrass plants, but occur most often during warm, wet weather or after periods of heavy summer rainfall. These fungi move about as slow-moving protoplasmic amoebae and feed as saprophytes on bacteria, fungi, and decayed organic matter in soil. They do not feed on turfgrasses. Slime molds survive as spores.

Symptoms/Signs

White, gray, powdery fruiting bodies cover leaves in patches 6 to 12 inches (15 to 30 cm) in diameter during warm, wet weather. The protoplasmic forms of the fungi migrate to plant tips and produce the spore stage, which allows enhanced dispersal of the dark, powdery black spores by wind (Plate 22–47). During the day, ruptured fruiting bodies may cover grass leaves with the black, soot-like spores. Affected areas may appear a dull-gray color due to high populations of these spores.

Cultural Controls

Remove the grayish fruiting bodies by brushing, mowing, or washing the turf. Slime molds are not considered harmful and usually disappear during dry weather.

Chemical Controls

None are needed.

Southern Blight

The causal agent of Southern blight is *Sclerotium rolfsii* Sacc.

Occurrence

Kentucky bluegrass, annual bluegrass, and ryegrass are most susceptible, followed by bentgrass, fescue, and bermudagrass, especially in the southern states. The disease appears in midsummer, usually following a period of excessive rainfall. Dry conditions, followed by a rainy or humid period, enhance disease occurrence, and stimulate "eruptive" germination of sclerotia. The fungus survives as sclerotia during fall, winter, and spring on dead grass plants and thatch. Air temperatures in the range of 85 to 95°F (29 to 35°C) favor disease development in combination with rainfall/high relative humidity.

Symptoms/Signs

Symptoms first appear during hot weather as circular, crescent-shaped patches, with yellow to dead areas one to nine feet (0.3 to 2.7 m) in diameter. Patches are yellow or reddish-brown in color on golf greens (Plate 22–48). Abundant white mycelial growth and small spherical, light to brown-colored sclerotia, resembling mustard seed, are often found at the base of infected plants (Plate 22–49). Turf usually dies in rings, leaving a tuft of green grass in the center ("frog eye"). Weeds such as clover are also killed in these spots. Small, round, tan to brown seedlike bodies (**sclerotia**) are usually present at the outer edge of this ring. This disease usually occurs in turf that is heavily thatched. Sclerotia germinate during hot, humid weather and the fungus grows on organic matter before spreading to live plants.

Cultural Controls

Fertilize and irrigate turf properly. Verticut to remove thatch when it exceeds one-half inch (1.3 cm) and use ammonium sulfate as a fertilizer source. Minimize the physical spread of sclerotia which can act as "seeds." The fungus survives as sclerotia during fall, winter, and spring on dead grass plants and thatch. Dry conditions followed by a rainy or humid period enhance disease occurrence.

Chemical Controls

Flutolanil or triadimefon may be beneficial on greens and tees. Replanting larger, lower-maintained areas with less susceptible grass may be more economical than fungicide use.

Spring Dead Spot

The causal agents of spring dead spot are *Gaeumannomyces graminis* (Sacc.) Arx & Olivier var. *graminis; Ophiosphaerella* (=*Leptosphaeria*) *korrae; Ophiosphaerella* (=*Leptosphaeria*) *narmari*; and/or *Ophiosphaerella herpotricha*.

Occurrence

Spring dead spot is the most serious disease of bermudagrass in the United States, where it undergoes complete dormancy in winter (Plate 22–50). The highest-maintained turf is generally most susceptible. Hybrid bermudagrasses that tend to produce excessive thatch are most prone to disease attack while cold hardy cultivars such as "Midiron," "Midfield," "Patriot," "Riviera," "Vamont," and "Yukon" are more resistant. Late-summer nitrogen applications, abundant fall moisture, and low winter temperatures also predispose bermudagrass for spring dead spot development. Spots generally begin to appear after the turf is at least three to five years old. Infected areas recover slowly and weeds frequently invade these areas during summer. Presumably, fungi causing spring dead spot infect in late summer and fall, and weaken the turf without visible symptoms. Parameters affecting winter hardiness and spring green-up also influence spring dead spot symptom development and turf recovery. All of the four reported causal agents are slow-growing root ectotrophic fungi, similar to organisms causing take-all patch, necrotic ringspot, and summer patch in bluegrass and bentgrass. In fact, *Ophiosphaerella korrae* is known to cause both necrotic ringspot and spring dead spot. The dark-brown, black mycelium from ectotrophic-growing fungi directly penetrate roots, stolons, and rhizomes, filling vascular tissue with a brown substrate and dark, spindle-shaped sclerotia.

Symptoms/Signs

Dead, straw-colored spots two to three feet (0.3 to 0.6 m) in diameter appear in spring as affected bermudagrass begins to "green-up" and is often confused with winter kill. Spring dead spot patches are sunken, generally well-defined, and circular, in contrast to more diffuse dead areas caused by direct low-temperature injury. Roots and stolons of affected bermudagrass are severely rotted (Plate 22–51). Patches may enlarge over three to four years, develop into rings, and then disappear. Affected spots may also remain greener in late fall going into winter. Patches in overseeded affected bermudagrass may resemble brown patch in spring. Patches are usually perennial in nature, often recurring in the same location over several years. After a year or two from their first occurrence, patches develop into doughnut or frog eye patterns with relatively nonsymptomatic bermudagrass in the centers (Plate 22–52). After several years, spring dead spot may entirely disappear from a site.

Rhizomes and stolons from adjacent bermudagrass slowly fill-in dead spots. This slow process allows summer annual weeds such as crabgrass to easily become established. Use of certain preemergence herbicides for summer annual grassy weed control may affect recovery from spring dead spot. Herbicides that inhibit cell division (the dinitroanaline group, as well as dithiopyr) may inhibit new stolons from colonizing patches and slow recovery. Oxadiazon, however, does not inhibit rooting and might be a better choice of a preemergence herbicide in SDS areas if one is needed. Managers may also opt to use postemergence techniques for weed control in areas prone to severe spring dead spot.

Cultural Controls

Spring dead spot is a disease of intensively managed mature bermudagrass. Use acidifying fertilizers such as ammonium nitrate/sulfate to help speed recovery and reduce disease severity. However, avoid excessive nitrogen fertilization and do not apply nitrogen in the fall. Raise the mowing height and ensure adequate potassium levels in the fall. Reduce thatch by aerifying and pulverizing soil cores.

Chemical Controls

Some success (30 to 75 percent patch reduction) has been obtained following late-summer and early fall application of fenarimol, propiconazole, or myclobutanil, but should be used only after suggested cultural practices have been followed. These should be applied as drenches. Several years of consecutive use may be required for complete control as the patches are typically reduced in size following each yearly fungicide use.

Stripe Smut

The causal agents of stripe smut are *Ustilago striiformis* (Westend.) Niessl and *Urocystis* spp. such as *U. agropyri* (Preuss) Schrot (often called flag smut).

Occurrence

Stripe smut is an important disease of creeping bentgrass and Kentucky bluegrass, especially Kentucky bluegrass cultivars resistant to melting out (Plate 22–53). It also attacks older stands of tall fescue but not to the same extent as brown patch. It is a perennial systemic disease; once a plant is infected, it remains so for life. Daughter plants from stolons or rhizomes of infected mother plants will also be infected. Infected plants often are invaded by other organisms such as "Helminthosporium" diseases. Infected turf appears clumpy and patchy when viewed from a distance. Infected plants usually die during the heat- and drought-stress period of summer and are replaced by weeds. An additional smut, *Ustilago cynodontis* (Pass.) Henn., may infect common bermudagrass, replacing the flower heads with dark smut spores (Plate 22–54).

Symptoms/Signs

Symptoms most commonly occur in spring and fall while experiencing cool (<70°F, 21°C), wet weather. Infected turf has a clumpy appearance due to the death of surrounding grass plants. Many "clumps" appear pale green in spring, but develop yellow streaks when disease is active, giving the appearance of nitrogen deficiency. Quackgrass and tall fescue often invade severely infected stripe smut turf areas in Kentucky bluegrass turf. Individual plants are stunted and upright in their growth habit. Disease first appears as dull-gray streaks in leaves. The epidermis above streaks is eventually ruptured, exposing black masses of stripe smut teliospores. These spores may be transported on seeds and turf-maintenance equipment. Leaves eventually split, shred, twist, and curl, exposing the black smut teliospores. Although plants are infected, they may appear amazingly healthy if properly maintained as weather warms during the summer. Turf stand loss mostly occurs during the hot, dry summer from heat and drought stress. By fall, typical symptoms may reoccur and, by winter, these develop a gray-brown desiccated appearance from the shredding of leaves by maturing fruiting bodies during fall. The fungus overwinters as dormant mycelium in plants and as teliospores in soil and plant debris.

Cultural Controls

Use resistant cultivars in blends that have been propagated in smut-free environments and avoid heavy (over 1/2 lb N/1,000 sq.ft., 2.5 kg N/100 m^2, per month) nitrogen applications in late spring through summer. Prevent moisture stress on infected turf, use a balanced N–P–K fall fertilizer program, and raise the mowing height of infected turf.

Chemical Controls

Some systemic fungicides, including triadimefon, fenarimol, and propiconazole, are effective in slowing infection rates and in promoting healing of diseased turf stands when applied in spring (May) or fall (mid- to late October).

Summer Patch

The causal agent of summer patch is *Magnaporthe poae* Landschoot and Jackson.

Occurrence

Summer patch is primarily a disease of bluegrass caused by a slow-growing ectotrophic root-infecting fungus. Being a soil-borne fungus, early disease diagnosis can be difficult and often goes undetected until plants begin to die. It is easily confused with necrotic ring spot, as their hosts and symptoms are very similar. It is a major disease of annual bluegrass, but also affects Kentucky bluegrass and fine fescues. Parameters increasing stress to these grasses also influence the development of summer patch. Summer patch primarily occurs in the northeastern and midwestern United States, and also in California and the Pacific Northwest. Outbreaks occur from mid-June through September during high temperature stress, especially when nighttime temperatures remain above 70°F (21°C) and during heavy rainfall. Sunny areas and those adjacent to heat-stress areas such as sidewalks are most susceptible. Usually, mature turf is infected more than young immature stands.

Symptoms/Signs

Patches of affected turf are circular, semicircular, or serpentine in shape from a few scattered plants ranging in size from a few inches up to about a foot (0.3 m) in diameter (Plate 22–55). Patches are generally smaller than those caused by necrotic ring spot. Initially, plants are wilted, gray-green in color, and may develop heat-stress banding (white bands across individual leaf blades). These affected plants wilt, die, and become matted, tan, or brown, leaving patterns of patches, rings, and arcs of symptomatic turf. Tufts of green grass may remain in the center, leaving a "frog eye" pattern. Roots and crowns are rotted and are brown to black in color, similar to necrotic ring spot. Southerly exposed slopes or turf near concrete areas tend to exhibit moisture stress.

Cultural Controls

Utilize cultural practices to improve root systems, such as core aerification, proper watering (adequate moisture, avoiding even transient drought stress), and thatch management to eliminate plant stress. Core aerify prior to infection periods but not during an active disease outbreak. Avoid heavy spring and summer nitrogen fertilization. Raising cutting heights prior to and during anticipated periods of heat stress can be beneficial. Consider conversion of *Poa annua*-dependent greens to bentgrass, which is highly resistant.

Chemical Controls

Preventive fungicide applications have been effective, including several sterol biosynthesis inhibitor fungicides, azoxystrobin, and pyraclostrobin. Thiophanate methyl has been curatively effective. Apply fungicides with adequate water to move the active ingredients to the rootzone, which should have moderate moisture in the soil when the fungicides are applied. Apply in spring when soil temperatures at a depth of two inches (5 cm) reach 62°F (16.7°C), before symptoms develop, and repeat on a 21- to 30-day interval during summer.

Take-All Patch (or Ophiobolus Patch)

The causal agent of take-all patch is *Gaeumannomyces graminis* (Sacc.) Arx & Olivier var. *avenae* (E. M. Turner) Dennis.

Occurrence

Take-all patch most often affects bentgrass, and to a lesser extent annual bluegrass, ryegrass, and fescue. The disease occurs most frequently in cooler (40 to 70°F, 4.4 to 21°C) climates and in soils of high pH and excessive moisture. It appears from late spring (April to June) through summer months (September through November) and survives as a saprophyte in grass debris and living plants. It may also occur in late fall and winter. Take-all patch is a problem in the northeastern, north central, and northwestern states of the United States, Europe, Japan, and Australia. It has also been a problem in the mid-Atlantic states and the mountains of North Carolina. Its occurrence elsewhere has not been officially confirmed or reported, although the disease is suspected to occur at times under special conditions, such as new golf courses or recently constructed courses with moderate soil pH levels (pH>6.0), recently limed sandy soils with low organic matter and low fertility, and conditions of high moisture during infection periods. Plants grown in soils with low levels of plant-available manganese are especially susceptible to infection. Nitrate fertilizers also encourage the disease by raising soil pH.

It is most common on newly constructed or recently renovated greens using sand-based soil that has been fumigated. As soil organisms recover from the fumigation process, disease severity declines, presumably due to the antagonistic effects of these soil organisms. During this time, turf rarely is killed but takes on a yellow, thin appearance.

Symptoms/Signs

Roots, crowns, and stems are affected with no distinctive leaf spots or sheath lesions. Dead, yellow or reddish-brown, sunken circular patches ranging from several inches initially up to three or four feet (0.9 to 1.2 m) in diameter develop in late spring and may increase in size slowly over the summer months (Plate 22–56). These may persist several years and increase in size each year. The fungus is active around the margins of patches and causes dark-brown to black rotted tissue of affected roots and crowns. Dying bentgrass at advancing margins has a purplish tinge, and freshly infected plants may become "bronze" in color. Black strands of mycelium are visible under the base of leaf sheaths or on the surface of roots, rhizomes, and stolons. Large black **perithecia** (fruiting bodies) may be visible with a hand lens on dead tissue. These contain septate, elongated ascospores. Weeds such as annual bluegrass, fescue, crabgrass, and various broadleaf weeds commonly invade the centers of patches (Plate 22–57). The fungus overseasons as mycelium in plant debris, thatch, and on perennial plant parts.

Cultural Controls

Fertilize with acidifying fertilizers such as ammonium nitrate/sulfate or use other acidifying compounds such as elemental sulfur at three to five pounds per 1,000 square feet (15 to 25 kg/100 m^2). Split the total yearly amount of acidifying compound into several applications so as to maintain a soil pH of around 5.5. Minor elements such as manganese, magnesium, and zinc should also be tested and applied if deficient. Either spring or fall applications of two pounds of manganese per acre (5 kg/100 m^2) in heavy soils and six to eight pounds per acre (30 to 40 kg/100 m^2) in sandy soils have proven beneficial. Annual applications are usually needed. Granular products containing these work better than foliar feeding. Control thatch accumulation by aerifying, topdressing, and verticutting. In situations with chronic infections, replant affected areas with less-susceptible grasses, blends, or mixtures of non-host grasses.

Chemical Controls

Preventive control of patches has been effective with propiconazole, fenarimol, thiophanate-methyl or triadimefon when applied in late fall or early winter. If take-all patch was prevalent the previous year, mid-March to mid-May applications may be beneficial. Reports of azoxystrobin and trifloxystrobin effectiveness for this disease are also encouraging.

Typhula Blight (Gray or Speckled Snow Mold)

The causal agents of Typhula blight are *Typhula incarnata* Lasch ex Fr.; and *T. ishikariensis* Imai. These are **psychrophilic** (cold-loving) microorganisms. Other related diseases are Coprinus snow mold (*Coprinus psychromobidus*); snow scald (*Myriosclerotinia borealis* (syn. *Sclerotinia borealis*); and snow rot or snow blight (various *Pythium* spp.).

Occurrence

Typhula blight, or gray snow mold, is a very destructive disease of turfgrass under snow cover. Optimum temperatures for development range from 32 to 45°F (0 to 7°C). Disease severity increases with duration of snow cover and often occurs under slushy conditions during thaws. Perennial ryegrass and creeping bentgrass are especially susceptible and can lead to severe destruction of this turf with a subsequent invasion of annual bluegrass. Typhula blight is rare in the southern United States, occurring only in mountainous regions where persistent snow cover occurs.

Symptoms/Signs

Snow mold severity is generally governed by fall and winter environmental conditions, depth and duration of snow cover, and level of disease inoculum. The fungi begin as saprophytes feeding on dead organic matter and invade turf when under snow. It survives summer as dark- to rust-colored sclerotia less than one-eighth inch (3 mm) in diameter. Sclerotia germinate in late fall when cool, moist weather occurs but before the soil is frozen. The fungi then proliferate under snow and spread in host tissue under dark, humid conditions. Foliar symptoms include light brown or red sclerotia embedded in leaves and crowns of infected plants. Later they dry and shrink to pin-head size and turn dark brown, giving a speckled appearance. Infected turf stands have straw-colored, roundish areas ranging in size from a few inches to two feet (0.6 m) in diameter (Plate 22–58). Spots may coalesce to cover large areas. When spots are first observed in the margins of melting snow, they may contain fluffy white to bluish-gray fungal mycelium or silvery crust that disappears as the turf dries. This gray-colored mycelium is where the disease gets its common name. Leaves in affected areas are matted together. Gray snow mold is more damaging under prolonged, deep snow coverage. Although the fungus can kill the turf when it infects crowns and roots, it's more frequent that only shoots are killed and new leaves appear in spring. Disease spots can be noticeable until late spring. The fungi survives as sclerotia during the summer.

Symptoms of gray snow mold caused by *T. ishikariensis* resemble diseases caused by *T. incarnata* except it is found when a snow cover remains for four months or more and it produces numerous small dark-colored sclerotia following snow melt. The sclerotia are so numerous the turf appears as if it had been sprinkled with pepper. It is found more often in the western portion of North America.

Cultural Controls

Avoid nitrogen fertility in fall which leads to lush, succulent growth going into winter. If dormant nitrogen feeding is applied to promote early spring green-up and quicker recovery from snow mold damage, fungicides should also be applied. Erect snow fences or barriers to protect areas damaged yearly by snow drifts. Promote drying by providing good soil drainage, pruning limbs, trees, or shrubs to increase air circulation, and remove fallen leaves and clippings. The fine fescues are typically more resistant than bluegrass and bentgrass.

Chemical Controls

Preventive control is provided by chloroneb, flutolanil, iprodione, PCNB, fenarimol, propiconazole, and triadimefon but provide little control in spring after sclerotia form. The combination of chlorothalonil and iprodione or a three-way combination of a systemic fungicide, a strobilurin fungicide, and either PCNB or chlorothalonil applied in mid- to late October and repeated three to four weeks later appear to satisfactorily control both *Typhula* species as well as pink snow mold or Fusarium patch, which may occur at the same time and site. Apply before the first heavy snow or before cold, rainy weather, and repeat as needed during mid-winter and early spring during snow melts.

Algae

The causal agents of algal infestations are the cyanobacteria *Nostoc* and *Oscillatoria,* but also include the green and brown algae genera *Chlamydomonas, Hantzschia* spp., and others. This is a disease-associated problem. Aquatic algal species found in streams and ponds are not the same ones occurring on golf greens. Algae contain complex cells with nuclei, mitochondria, chloroplasts, an endoplasmic reticulum, and other organelles. Algae are considered primitive plants since they contain chlorophyll. However, they lack roots, stems, and leaves; thus, they must be in aquatic or near aquatic environments to thrive.

In addition to true green algae, primitive bacteria called **cyanobacteria,** also called the blue-green algae, infest turf stands with dark, slimy colonies. Cyanobacteria (*Oscillatoria, Phormidium, Lynbya, Nostoc,* and *Anacystis* spp.) contain none of the complex eukaryotic cells as algae and are more closely related to other bacteria such as *E. coli* and *Xanthomonas. Oscillatoria* is a small, primitive, photosynthetic microbe that produces dark crusts and slime layers on putting green soils and foliage. It produces energy by photosynthesis at low light intensities; thus, it invades closely mowed, shaded greens. Cyanobacteria can grow rapidly in water or wet soils with sufficient light, nutrients, and temperature and can move by sliding on their own produced mucilaginous (slimy) materials. Cyanobacteria are filamentous, producing **trichomes,** which are long chains of cells making up the black slime coating often seen on greens. They typically move to plants from thatch at night or on shade greens and retract back to cooler thatch during hot temperatures. They also produce toxins that enter plants through mowing injury. Cyanobacteria are known to be the most ancient organism with photosynthetic capability and have the ability to synthesize and secrete large quantities of polysaccharides from cells. The polysaccharides provide a protective coating allowing the cyanobacteria to withstand moisture and heat stresses. Some cyanobacteria can survive deserts, hot springs, arctic conditions, and other environmental extremes. In addition, an antibiotic produced by *Oscillatoria* attacks photosystem II in plant cells. Due to lack of oxygen and drainage under cyanobacteria crusts, the plant may yellow and thin. Certain green algae and cyanobacteria directly cause plant damage and should be considered pathogens to turfgrasses.

Occurrence

Algae are most noticeable on close-cut, poorly drained, and shaded areas on tees and putting greens. Soil layering, poor surface drainage, compaction, poor disease control, and other stresses can predispose greens and other highly managed sites to algae infestations.

Symptoms/Signs

Symptoms begin slowly, often at the edges of greens. Turf areas in partially shaded, damp locations become weak and begin to thin, usually starting in early summer. Algae begin to predominate in these areas. These algae are commonly green or brown in color and can be sheetlike, leaflike, or cushionlike in appearance. Initially, these spots may be difficult to see, but as they enlarge, the turf begins to yellow and thin due to a lack of oxygen and drainage under the crust. Algae will develop on turf areas where grass is less dense than normal and surface soil moisture is high resulting in a dark-color "scum" or "mat" forming on the soil surface (Plate 22–59). Frequently, on bentgrass greens affected by brown patch, algae invade the thinned areas. If left untreated, these areas will continue to "thin-out" and expand in size until a large mat of algae forms, preventing turfgrass growth and penetration of irrigation water. Black algal scum development often occurs in summer following periods of rainy, overcast, warm days. Although erroneously thought to cause algae on golf courses, algae species found in irrigation ponds, lakes, and streams are different species and do not appear to contribute to this problem.

Cultural Controls

Due to their rapid development, preventive management is the best approach. Prevention begins by correcting those conditions that predispose the turf to algal growth. This involves reducing surface moisture by improving air circulation and light exposure by removing adjacent underbrush and selectively removing trees. Improve drainage and reduce irrigation frequency and amount. Reduce freely available nitrogen and phosphorus at the site. Avoid organic-based products if excessive phosphorus is present in them. Reduce irrigation and improve the growth of the turfgrass where algae is present so the turf can form a dense area. If the area occupied by algae is large, spiking, verticutting, and topdressing will help break-up and dry the mat. Applying ground limestone or hydrated lime will help desiccate algae. Diluted bleach, copper sulfate, and chloride also may help reduce algae growth. However, these should not be used during hot temperatures, as they may cause varying levels of turf discoloration. Be judicious in the use of copper-containing fungicides to avoid a buildup of copper and potential copper toxicity in soils. This would be more of a risk in sandy putting green mixes with low organic matter. Increase the mowing height, as low mowing aggravates the problem.

Chemical Controls

Some fungicides such as mancozeb, maneb, and chlorothalonil help to prevent development of algae and prevent its spread when a mat has already formed. They need periodic applications (e.g., every 7 to 14 days) and should be used **prior** to algae formation and continually as long as conditions remain favorable for occurrence. Members of the quartenary ammonium chemical group also provide varying controls of certain algae. Unfortunately, other fungicides, such as azoxystrobin, myclobutanil, thiophanate-methyl, and propiconazole have little effect on cyanobacteria, and certain fungicides (e.g., sterol inhibitors) used in summer may encourage algae by thinning the turf. Control diseases, such as brown patch, to prevent thinning of the turf canopy. In areas with high disease pressure and low turf recuperative potential, such as the transition zone region of the United States, preventive disease control approaches are necessary in the summertime.

Moss

The causal agents of moss include *Selagimella, Byrum, Amblystegium, Brachythecium, Ceratodon, Hypnum, Polytrichum* spp., plus others. *Amblystegium trichopodium* and *Brachythecium* spp. are usually found in higher-cut turf and are often referred to as "yard moss" (Plate 22–60). *Bryum argetum,* referred to as silver thread moss, has a silvery appearance and is found more frequently on greens (Plate 22–61). Unlike most mosses, silver thread moss grows well in both wet, shady environments and hot, dry sites in full sun.

Moss are threadlike, branched, primitive (400 million years old) plant forms encompassing many species. They spread by spores disseminated by wind and water movement. Most moss species are **bryophytes,** meaning they do not form true roots, but form rhizoids which are filamentous structures and do not provide anchoring. Consequently, they can survive on rocks, concrete, and masonry walls. Bryophytes also are nonvascular plants requiring constant contact with water to prevent drying. Others are able to absorb water through their rhizoids. Mosses are able to photosynthesize and fix nitrogen. Moss are nonparasitic to the turf and spread by plant fragments (mainly) and less so as spores. They can also survive long periods of desiccation.

Occurrence

Moss is most noticeable on close-cut areas such as tees and putting greens that poorly drain (thus remaining continuously wet) and are heavily shaded. However, moss can rapidly fill a void if thin turf develops, sun or shade. Moss can survive weather extremes in a dormant state or by living symbiotically with blue-green algae. Algae, therefore, can be a precursor to moss encroachment and should be discouraged to prevent moss colonization. Silver thread moss occurs first in weak turf areas such as ridges and mounds where grass is thin from scalping and/or drought. It is favored by acidic, infertile soils with thatch. It typically forms in summer following periods of rain or overcast, warm days. It is encouraged by (1) extremely low mowing heights, (2) minimal nitrogen fertilization, (3) increased use of sand growth medium, (4) intense topdressing with finer-textured sands that slow drainage, and (5) loss of mercury-based fungicides. Moss appears sensitive to metal-contaminated soils, with the heavy metals, especially mercury, being most toxic. These metals participate in the destruction of chlorophyll molecules in moss, which is why many copper-based products are currently being used.

Symptoms/Signs

Turf areas in partially shaded, damp locations become weak and begin to thin. Moss begins to predominate in these areas. Moss forms a tangled, thick, green mat occurring in patches over the soil surface. Moss will develop on turf areas where grass is less dense than normal and surface soil moisture is high. Acidic, infertile soils with excessive thatch also favor moss development. If left untreated, these areas will continue to "thin-out" and expand in size until a large mat forms preventing growth of the grass and penetration of irrigation water. Moss mats typically develop in summer following periods of rainy, overcast, warm days.

Cultural Controls

Control involves a long-term, persistent program combining cultural and chemical control methods in realizing healthy turf is the only means to prevent and cure moss. Control begins by correcting those conditions that predispose turf to moss growth. This involves reducing surface moisture by improving air circulation and light exposure by removing adjacent underbrush and selectively removing trees. Improve surface and subsurface drainage and reduce irrigation frequency and amount. Reduce freely available nitrogen at the site. Reduce irrigation and improve turfgrass growth where moss is present so the turf can form a dense area. If the area occupied by moss is large, spiking, verticutting, and topdressing will help to break up and dry the mat. Moss turning orange-brown or golden brown in color indicates positive desiccation is occurring. However, mosses are adapted to survive periods of desiccation, so simple drying of the moss will not cause it to die.

Several trends in fertility and moss development have been noted. For example, calcium-rich soil may encourage certain moss species while moss tends to be discouraged in potassium-adequate soils. Control is often erratic and often unsuccessful, especially if agronomic practices are not corrected that favor moss. Increase the mowing height as low mowing aggravates the problem. Spike or rake the dehydrated moss layer to remove any remaining impervious layer. Products controlling moss that can be phytotoxic to turf include hydrogen peroxide, copper sulfate, copper soaps, and zinc sulfate. Baking soda applied lightly at six ounces per gallon of water (40 g/L) also helps desiccate moss. Turf yellowing can be expected following this and most other treatments.

Chemical Controls

Chemical control is erratic and often unsuccessful, especially if agronomic practices are not corrected that favor moss growth and development. Ammonium sulfate at 1/10 to 1/8 pounds nitrogen per 1,000 square feet (0.5 to 6.1 g N/100 m^2) applied weekly is thought to help desiccate moss and encourage competitive turf growth. Applying ground limestone (75 to 100 lbs/1,000 sq.ft., 368 to 491 kg/100 m^2) or hydrated lime (2 to 3 lbs/1,000 sq.ft. in 3 gallons of water, 9.8 to 15 kg/100 m^2 in 1,220 liters) will help desiccate the moss and raise the soil pH level that favors competitive turf growth. Diluted bleach and dishwashing detergent at four ounces per gallon of water (31 ml/L) applied as a drench; chloride; ferrous sulfate at four to seven ounces per 1,000 square feet; granular iron sulfate at up to three pounds per 1,000 square feet (15 kg/100 m^2); or ferrous ammonium sulfate at 10 ounces per 1,000 square feet (31 kg/100 m^2) also may help reduce moss growth. Five to seven treatments applied at two-week intervals are often necessary. However, these should not be used on greens during hot temperatures, as they may cause varying levels of turf discoloration. Applications should be performed on sunny days when temperatures are between 55 and 80°F (13 and 27°C). Iron-containing products should be used if a copper-containing product is also used.

Chlorothalonil at 16 pounds ai/acre (18 kg ai/ha) applied for three consecutive weeks also has suppressed moss. This works best when air temperatures at the time of application are >80°F (27°C), preferably >85°F (29°C). In cooler weather, copper hydroxide alone (e.g., Kocide 2000) or copper hydroxide combined with mancozeb (e.g., Junction) at 0.1 to 0.15 pounds copper per 1,000 square feet (0.1 to 0.17 kg Cu/ha) can be used every two weeks for a total of five to seven applications. Due to the potential of copper buildup, limit applications to a total of one pound copper per 1,000 square feet (1.1 kg Cu/ha) yearly. Iron chlorosis may occur with copper use; therefore, apply iron at 0.05 pounds iron per 1,000 square feet (0.06 kg Fe/ha). Products containing potassium salts of fatty acids (e.g., DeMoss, HO2) applied weekly at two to three ounces per 1,000 square feet (6.4 to 9.5 L/ha), or No-Mas (22 percent fatty acid) at 0.8 gallons per 1,000 square feet (3.2 L/100 m^2) may be used to control moss in turfgrasses. These should be applied in high rates of water, ≥ 6 gallons of water per 1,000 square feet (24 L/100 m^2). Two applications, two weeks apart, are typically needed. They control moss through a contact mode of action but should be carefully used. All label information should be closely followed. Again, if iron chlorosis (turf yellowing) occurs, alternate the fatty acid applications with 0.05 pounds iron per 1,000 square feet (0.06 kg Fe/ha). Tank-mixing iron with fatty acids often has iron precipitation, clogging spray nozzles. High soil or spray water pH may reduce control. The herbicide oxadiazon provides some preemergence control of some moss species.

Localized Dry Spots

At least one causal agent of localized dry spots are Basidiomycete fungi, probably *Lycoperdon* spp. There may be other reasons for development of localized dry spots not due to fungi such as coating of sand particles by humic substances, initial poor mixing of the greens mix, buried rocks and other debris, and tree roots near the soil surface.

Occurrence

Localized dry spots are most noticeable on close-cut areas such as tees and putting greens, usually during warmer months where this water-repellent soil develops in the top two inches (5 cm) of the soil profile. Localized dry spots caused by fungi have been primarily observed on greens less than three to four years old, especially those aggressively topdressed with sand.

Symptoms/Signs

Dry spots are several inches to several feet across and often irregularly or serpentine shaped (Plate 22–62). An affected area will appear drought stressed, despite daily irrigations or rainfall. "Puffball" mushrooms may be present throughout the dry area, but these signs are not always apparent. The fungus has colonized (covered) the sand particles in the rootzone mix. Due to this fungal covering, the sand is now hydrophobic and repels water, despite heavy rainfall or watering (Plate 22–63). Soil hydrophobicity primarily occurs in the upper two inches (5 cm) of the soil profile. It is thought as fungi mycelium decomposes, organic substances are released that coat and bind the coarse sand particles so tightly together they prevent water penetration. This organic matter decomposition is a natural process and cannot be stopped. Necrotic rings may develop due to a secondary infection by *Rhizoctonia zeae*. Mushrooms are not directly associated with these rings as mushrooms will be found inside and outside the ring. They are fruiting structures of the Basidiomycete fungi colonizing sand particles and not the *R. zeae*. Also, it has been recently observed anthracnose basal rot of creeping bentgrass may be initiated by development of stress from localized dry spots.

To determine the water repellency tendencies of a soil, the water drop test can be used. A soil core one inch (2.5 cm) in diameter and at least six inches (15 cm) in depth is extracted. Drops of water are place on soil at increments of one-half to one inch (1.3 to 2.5 cm), starting at the soil surface. If droplets remain intact on the surface for more than five seconds, the soil is hydrophobic. The longer droplets remain, the more water-repellent the soil.

Cultural Controls

Since hydrophobic soils tend to be in the upper two inches (5 cm) of soil, management practices to encourage rooting beyond the two-inch (5-cm) depth should be implemented. Hydrophobic sand must be broken up and wetted, which can be accomplished by spiking the dry patch every five to seven days or core aerifying. For a small area, a pitchfork or similar tool will accomplish this task. Irrigate dry patches by hand several times a day, in addition to any normal irrigation or rainfall. The addition of a wetting agent to the water is also useful and should be watered-in. Some programs of prevention by utilizing several applications of certain wetting agents have been successful. Ideally, it is best to treat the entire green with the specified wetting agent and then, if needed, go back and spot treat areas continuing to show localized dry spot. The water-repelling action of the fungal colonized sand must be eliminated before the grass will recover from the drought stress and the secondary infection by *R. zeae*. Wetting agents can last up to five months but are affected by organic matter content, cultural practices, and the degree of hydrophobicity. When excessive thatch, mat, or compacted soil is present in conjunction with LDS, core cultivate prior to wetting agent application. Treat the entire green to help ensure more uniform soil moisture throughout the area. Soil treated with wetting agents will not hold more water than its normal field capacity after treatment. However, the soil surface of sands may drain and dry out quicker following wetting agent use. If excessive organic matter (thatch or mat) is present, moisture may be retained longer when treated with a wetting agent. Using high pressure water injection cultivation in combination with a wetting agent also helps to alleviate symptoms.

Chemical Controls

No chemical controls are currently registered as localized dry spot is from organic coating of sand particles and not directly from fungi; thus, fungicides rarely work. If chronic infestations of fairy ring fungi such as *Lycoperdon* spp. are present, then control with flutolanil, azoxystrobin, or pyraclostrobin may be beneficial.

Other Locally Important Turf Diseases

Yellow Tuft or Downy Mildew

The causal agent of yellow tuft is *Sclerophthora macrospora* (Sacc.) Thirum., Shaw & Naras. All turfgrasses can be affected, but bentgrass greens and Kentucky bluegrass are most susceptible. Yellow tuft appears on golf greens as small yellow spots one-fourth to two inches (0.6 to 5 cm) in diameter. These spots have plants with prolific (e.g., 20 or more) tillers, giving them a tufted appearance. Infected plants have short root systems, are easily pulled up, and die during stress periods. Yellow tuft symptoms most often develop during cool, moist periods of spring and fall. Plants appear to recover in summer. The pathogen is an obligate parasite and a member of the oomycete fungal group. The fungus survives as dormant oospores and mycelium in plant tissue, thatch, and leaf litter. Low areas that often puddle are most often infected since the fungus disperses as swimming zoospores. Control begins with good surface drainage. Fosetyl-Al or metalaxyl provide chemical control when applied preventatively in one or two applications in spring or fall when nighttime temperatures are in the 50°Fs (10°Cs). Liquid iron applications may help mask disease symptoms. Once tuft formation occurs, fungicides provide little cosmetic turf recovery.

Curvularia Blight

The causal agents of Curvularia blight are *Curvularia geniculata* (Tracy and Earle) Boedijn; *C. lunata* (Wakk.) Boedijn, and others. Bentgrasses and bluegrasses are most susceptible, especially during hot (≥85°F, 29°C) temperatures. Symptoms are similar to diseases caused by *Bipolaris* spp. and include tip die-back of infected plants, yellowish-colored turf, and stands that thin in an irregular pattern (Plates 22–64 & 22–65). Brownish leaf lesions similar to leaf spot diseases may be present, particularly on older, senescent leaves. Plants damaged from heat, drought, and/or herbicide stress are most susceptible. Curvularia blight is most common on newly established bentgrass greens, and generally becomes apparent in midsummer after abundant rainfall during the high heat periods of mid- to late summer. Turf exposed to full sun, growing on south-facing slopes or adjacent to paved surfaces, are often most affected. The disease rarely kills the grass, but symptoms of yellow patches of a few inches in diameter are unsightly. *Curvularia* spp. survive periods of unfavorable growth as saprophytic mycelium on plant debris and tissue. It has been observed a good preventive fungicide program for brown patch and Pythium blight will help to prevent stress associated with Curvularia blight. Alleviating stress through soil aeration, good irrigation practices, increasing mowing height, and proper fertility helps plants resist infection. Fungicides that control leaf spot diseases also may be beneficial in controlling Curvularia.

Dead Spot

(The following provided by John E. Kaminski, University of Maryland)

The causal agent of dead spot is *Ophiosphaerella agrostis* Dernoeden, M.P.S. Camara, N.R. O'Neill, van Berkum et M.E. Palm. Dead spot is a relatively new disease of creeping bentgrass that is incited by a previously undescribed species of *Ophiosphaerella*. First identified in Maryland, the disease has been found on creeping bentgrass as far north as Michigan, west as far as Missouri, and along the eastern seaboard of the United States. The pathogen also affects hybrid bermudagrass greens in the southeastern United States. The disease is most commonly found within two years of seeding new greens or on older greens that have been fumigated with methyl bromide. Dead spot generally declines within one to three years following initial symptoms and the disease has not been found on sites less than six years old. The disease only has been found on sand-based greens, collars, and tees and has not been found on bentgrass grown on native soil. Dead spot generally appears in areas receiving full sun and good air circulation, and infection centers first appear on ridges, mounds, or south-facing slopes of greens. On bentgrass, dead spot is most severe in July and August, but the pathogen may be active between May and December. Disease symptoms on bermudagrass generally appear in March.

Disease development in the mid-Atlantic and southeastern states appears to be most common from July to August, but may remain active as late as December. Environmental conditions appearing to enhance disease development include hot, dry weather. Symptoms begin as small, reddish-brown spots one-half to one inch (1.3 to 2.5 cm) in diameter and often are confused with dollar spot, copper spot, black cutworm damage, or golf ball injury (Plate 22–66). Spots enlarge at a slow rate, with dead tissue in the center of the spots turning tan and leaves in the active, outer edge appearing bronze or red (Plate 22–67). Spots generally do not coalesce and usually enlarge to no more than four inches (10 cm) in diameter. Unlike other turfgrass pathogens within the genus, black, flask-shaped fruiting bodies (**pseudothecia**) often are found embedded in necrotic leaf, sheath, and stolons of plants infected by *O. agrostis* (Plate 22–68). Mycelium is not observed in the field. Dark-brown to black hyphal masses and runner hyphae, however, are commonly found on the nodes of bentgrass stolons. Turf in the center of infected spots is killed and recovery from the disease is very slow.

All major bentgrass species used on golf course putting greens are susceptible to the disease as no resistant cultivars are known. Limited information on cultural controls is available; however, applications of an acidifying fertilizer (e.g., ammonium sulfate) may reduce disease incidence and severity. If the disease becomes established, light fertilization, coupled with chemical control, aids in the healing of dead spots.

Chemical control involves the use of chlorothalonil, fludioxonil, mancozeb, propiconazole, and thiophanate-methyl. Dead spot is most successfully managed when treated prior to the onset of disease symptoms and is difficult to control once infection centers appear. When the disease is active, fungicides should be reapplied on a 7- to 10-day schedule. Although fungicide efficacy varies within each chemical class, most Q_0I and sterol-inhibiting fungicides have not provided adequate disease control to date.

Rapid Blight

The causal agent of rapid blight is believed to be a species of marine slime mold in the genus *Labyrinthula*. Rapid blight has occurred on perennial ryegrass and rough bluegrass when used to overseed bermudagrass in certain western and southern U.S. states during fall, winter, and spring. It has also been a problem in annual bluegrass putting greens in parts of California. *Labyrinthula* spp. are known to occur in saline environments in terrestrial sites, and outbreaks of rapid blight have been problematic in golf courses with saline irrigation water and/or with soils with high-soluble salts. Damage to dormant and actively growing bermudagrass has not been observed.

Initial symptoms include small yellow spots that enlarge quickly to one foot (0.3 m) in diameter (Plate 22–69). Spots appear roughly circular with chlorotic turf in the center of patches, surrounded with a darker water-soaked appearance in the grass bordering the affected patches (Plate 22–70). No association with mycelium of true fungi has been observed. Due to the remarkable speed the disease spreads, the name "rapid blight" has been proposed.

Seedlings of overseeded bermudagrass turf appear to be the most susceptible. The disease has appeared in annual bluegrass and overseeded rough bluegrass, and perennial ryegrass greens closely following the first mowing. Most severe cases include the wetter and lower areas on greens. The pathogen appears to be tracked by mowers across turf areas. The disease has been reported at sites with high irrigation water salinity, sodium, or bicarbonate levels, with sodium absorption ratios (SAR) ranging from 20 to 40 meq/L. Soil tests indicate high sodium-based saturation levels in the 10 to 35 percent range may also be a critical factor in the incidence of the disease. Courses that manage their water quality have fewer disease problems. In addition, it may be prudent to wash mowers after mowing affected greens. Minimize turf shoot abrasion or damage situations like mowing wet greens and using excessive sand topdressing rates that appear to increase the severity and spread of the disease.

Traditional Pythium blight fungicides have so far been unsuccessful in controlling the disease. The strobilurin fungicides trifloxystrobin and pyraclostrobin appear promising. Applications of mancozeb alone or in combination with trifloxystrobin have also been shown experimentally to aid in prevention of the disease. Curative applications of mancozeb alone, trifloxystrobin, or pyraclostrobin may stop development in early stages.

CHAPTER
23

Turfgrass Insects

INTRODUCTION

Several insects and related arthropods are common pests on turf installations and can cause considerable damage if left unchecked. Pests feeding on leaves and stems include sod webworms, armyworms, grass loopers, cutworms, chinch bugs, bermudagrass mites, and scale. Those feeding on roots include mole crickets, white grubs, billbugs, and ground pearls. Nuisance pests such as fire ants also are found.

An insect management program involves:

1. Correctly identifying the insect and its damage pattern.
2. Understanding the insect's life cycle, biology, and aesthetic thresholds.
3. When justified, selecting and properly applying the appropriate control method at the most strategic time.

Early insect detection is vital to any pest management program. Therefore, turf should be inspected as often as practical. All employees should be trained to spot potential problems while performing their assigned duties. When pests are noticed, the employee should promptly notify the person responsible for pest management. If insecticides are used as part of a control program, be sure the formulation is labeled for the particular turfgrass area. Numerous restrictions are placed on several insecticides (e.g., soil type, number of applications, minimum distance from bodies of water, irrigation requirements, reentry, etc.), so read the label carefully before use.

INSECT BIOLOGY

More than 1 million species of insects exist; however, only several dozen are serious pests of turfgrasses. Insect bodies consist of three segments (head, thorax, and abdomen), an exoskeleton, three pairs of jointed legs, a pair of antennae, and usually one or two pairs of wings. Turf-damaging insects either have **chewing** or **piercing and sucking** mouthparts. Chewing mouthparts are jawlike arrangements that insects use to tear, chew, and grind plant tissue. Piercing and sucking mouthparts are needlelike beaks that insects insert into plant tissue to suck juices from them.

Insects grow only by shedding their **exoskeleton** (body wall or outer covering), thereby exposing a new, larger one through a process known as **molting. Instars** are growth stages between molts. This change in form and the increase in size is through a process called **metamorphosis.** Two types of metamorphosis occur: (1) **complete,** and (2) **incomplete.** Insects with complete metamorphosis have very distinct stages in their life cycle. The stages are egg, larvae, pupae, and finally, adult. The larvae, also called caterpillars (larva of a moth or butterfly), maggots (larva of a fly), or grubs (larva of a beetle), are generally the most destructive stage and have a very different appearance than in the adult stage, which has wings and reproductive organs. This transformation from larva to adult is referred to as **pupation.** Examples of turf insects with complete metamorphosis include:

- Annual bluegrass (Hyperodes) weevil (grubs)
- Ants
- Armyworm (caterpillars)
- Beetles (grubs)
- Billbugs (grubs)
- Crane fly (maggots)
- Cutworms (caterpillars)
- Sod webworm (caterpillars)

Insects that go through incomplete metamorphosis change little in appearance from immatures to adults. The only major difference is an increase in size and possible development of wings. Stages of incomplete metamorphosis are egg, several immature stages called **nymphs,** and finally, adult. The nymphs generally feed on the same food as adults. Examples of turf insects with incomplete metamorphosis include:

- Chinch bugs
- Ground pearls
- Leafhoppers
- Mole crickets
- Spittlebugs

Close relatives of insects include spiders, fleas, ticks, sowbugs, pillbugs, centipedes, and millipedes. These differ from insects by their number of legs and body segments.

DETECTION AND IDENTIFICATION

The first step in formulating any pest management strategy is identifying the damage your turf is experiencing, especially before pest populations reach chronic levels. Insect pests attack grass plants either above or below ground, usually by either feeding directly on roots (below ground) or by sucking sap or chewing grass leaves (above ground). A few, such as Southern mole crickets and fire ants, do not normally feed directly on the plants, but in their search for food or nest building, disrupt the turfgrass surface. This is compounded by mammals, such as moles, skunks, armadillos, and raccoons, digging through the turf as they search for these turfgrass insects as a food source.

Surface (or aboveground)-feeding insects

These insects feed on the leaves and stems of turfgrass plants. Many of these hide in the thatch during the day, and then surface and feed on leaves and stems at night. Other surface-feeding insects remain on the leaf surface and feed. These larvae (caterpillars) have **chewing mouthparts** and eat entire leaves and stems. These are the larvae of various moths. Adult beetles also have chewing mouthparts.

Indications of surface-feeding insects include:

1. Birds feeding on the turf surface.
2. Moths (mostly tan in color) flying zigzag patterns over the turf area, especially in late evenings.
3. Rapid turf color loss similar to fertilizer burn or drought stress even though irrigation is provided.
4. Notched leaves or residue of chewed grass (frass) at or near the soil surface.

Other surface-feeding insects have **piercing and sucking mouthparts** that tend to discolor the grass, resembling drought stress. These insects include aphids, chinch bugs, spittlebugs, and mealybugs.

Subsurface (root or belowground)-feeding insects

These insects inhabit the thatch and rootzones, and can be very damaging due to their root and crown feeding. Due to its subterranean location, this group of insects is the most difficult to control. Pesticides must move through the leaf canopy, through the thatch layer, and into the soil. Thatch control, adequate incorporation through irrigation, and subsurface placement in the soil are means to increase the efficacy of control products. White grubs, billbug larvae, mole crickets, and ground pearls are the most damaging subsurface-feeding insects.

Indications of subsurface-feeding insects include:

1. Visible mounds of soil that are soft and cause excessive scalping injury.
2. Poor turf rooting where the grass can be rolled up like carpet.
3. Damage from insect-feeding mammals such as moles, raccoons, and armadillos.
4. Turf thinning.
5. Yellow, chlorotic turf appearance.

Detection techniques

Inspecting the turfgrass involves several common sampling techniques to identify the most common turfgrass insects. Early detection is important to head-off undesirable and unacceptable aesthetic damage.

1. **Visual Inspection**—Walking around the perimeter of the turfgrass area in question is the first step in detecting insect presence/damage. Pull up some grass stems and see if a particular feeding pattern is noticed. Kneel on your hands and knees and, with a 10X hand lens, see if tiny insects are detectable at the base of the turfgrass plant or on the soil surface. Physical disruption, such as tunneling from mole crickets, is relatively easy to detect when the insects are large nymphs or adults. However, remember the objective is to detect pest populations before major damage occurs. Surface-active insects feeding on aboveground plant portions are easiest to determine by visual inspection.

2. **Soil/Thatch Inspection**—Manual inspection of the top two to three inches of soil or turfgrass thatch involves severing three sides of a piece of turf with a shovel and peeling back the grass to expose the thatch and soil. White grubs and billbug larvae are the principal insects found by this method. Several samples in an area should be taken to obtain a representative average.

3. **Soap Flush**—Soap flushing helps indicate insects hiding in the thatch or those moving too rapidly to be seen or caught. Mix one to two fluid ounces (30 to 59 ml) of lemon-scented liquid dishwashing soap or one tablespoon (15 ml) of 1 percent pyrethrin in two to three gallons (7.6 to 11 L) of water and apply this to a two × two square foot (0.6 × 0.6 m) area of turf (Figure 23–1). The solution interferes with insect respiration and, if present, they will soon emerge in an attempt to breath. The area should be observed for at least two minutes to see if any insects emerge. Mole crickets, webworms, armyworms, chinch bugs, cutworms, and beetles are detected by this method. Use of more than two fluid ounces (59 ml) of detergent may cause damage to the grass during hot weather.

4. **Water Flotation**—Small insects, such as chinch bugs, can easily hide in the turf thatch and shoot layers. Water flotation involves inserting a metal cylinder, such as an open-ended three-pound (1.4-kg) coffee can, through the turf one to two inches (2.5 to 5 cm) deep and filling with water. Do not add detergent to the water. Stirring the turf may help dislodge insects. Those present should float to the top of the water level within two minutes.

5. **Pitfall Traps, Pheromone Traps, and Floral Lures (Light Traps)**—Pitfall traps consist of one-inch (2.5-cm) diameter PVC pipe with a portion removed from its side and placed face-up flush with the soil surface. A trap jar, one-third full of 70 percent ethanol, is placed at one end of this pipe. As insects move across the soil surface, they fall in the open-sided PVC pipe, crawl down the pipe, and fall in the jar of ethanol.

   Pheromone traps and light traps are examples of attracting insects into traps by using either sex hormones or lights. Pheromone traps are available for cutworms, armyworms, and

FIGURE 23–1 A soap flush can detect the presence of certain insects.

sod webworms. The traps are good indicators of adult moth activity, but are not good predictors of potential damage. Light traps attract a wide variety of both pest and non-pest insect species. If large numbers of insects are captured, species identification can be difficult.

Scouts

A professional scout, who may be employed by several nearby courses, may be used to identify and quantify pest populations. Since these scouts visit several courses, pest trends are more easily recognized and useful information from one course can be used to assist others. A scout should typically hold a degree in agronomy, horticulture, entomology, or plant pathology with an emphasis in pest management.

Tools required for scouting vary with pest problems, scout training, and golf course budget. A good set of eyes and an inquisitive mind are essential. These are supported by a standard 10X hand or pocket lens, soil probe, soil profile probe, spade, cup cutter, pocket knife, tweezers, scalpel, collection vials, paper bags, and field identification guides. Soap and water also are necessary for insect monitoring.

More expensive, but precise, instruments may be used in a room designated as a diagnostic laboratory. Included are stereo- and compound-microscopes, soil sieves, pH meter, conductivity meter, and elementary soil analysis kits. These need to be supplemented by ongoing scout training at short courses, formal classes, appropriate diagnostic guides, and opportunities to visit similar facilities to exchange ideas.

INSECT CONTROL STRATEGIES

Set Threshold Levels

Once the insect and its damage have been positively identified and its life cycle understood, pest management involves setting threshold levels, recording pest levels, and possibly applying an appropriate control method. An aesthetic or action threshold is the point when pest populations or environmental conditions indicate some action must be taken to prevent intolerable damage. These thresholds will vary according to the location of the course, the specific pest being scouted, the turf area's level of use, club members' expectations, and budget constraints.

The pest in question will partially determine its aesthetic threshold. For example, the number of mole crickets tolerated on an area basis is less than the number of sod webworms. Related to this threshold level is the site in which the pest is found. Golf greens have a much lower aesthetic threshold than a rough or out-of-play area. Unfortunately, exact threshold numbers have not

TABLE 23–1 *Aesthetic or action levels for several common turf insects.*

Insect	Aesthetic or action threshold levels (per square foot)*	Inspection method
Annual bluegrass weevil	30 to 50	Visual and water float
Armyworms	1 to 4	Visual and soap flush
Bermudagrass mites	4 to 8 tufts	Visual
Billbugs	10	Visual
Black turfgrass ataenius grubs	30 to 50	Visual
Bluegrass billbugs	6 to 10	Visual
Chinch bugs (St. Augustinegrass)	20 to 25	Water float
Cutworms	3 to 8	Visual and soap flush
European crane fly	25	Visual and soil
May/Green June beetle grubs	3 to 4	Visual and soil
Masked chafer beetles	8 to 10	Visual
Mole crickets	1 to 2	Visual and soap flush
Sod webworms	6 to 16	Visual and soap flush

*Smaller numbers represent threshold levels for highly maintained areas such as golf greens and tees. Larger numbers are for less intensively maintained areas such as fairways, roughs, athletic fields, and lawns. Multiply values by 11 to obtain numbers per square meter.

been developed for every pest encountered in turf. However, Table 23–1 provides a starting point for several common turf insects. Also, damage by birds and mammals feeding on pest insects may cause more acute damage than the insect.

Monitoring intensively maintained golf courses includes scouting greens, tees, fairways, roughs, ornamental plantings, and trees. Greens and tees generally require the greatest amount of attention and are monitored daily or every other day. Remaining areas are monitored less frequently, usually weekly. Monitoring frequency may require adjustment depending on climatic conditions and reports of nearby pest problems.

Greens and tees are scouted by simply walking around the area to observe insect and disease activity as well as other pest and non-infectious symptoms. Fairways and roughs are usually scouted from a golf cart or utility vehicle. This allows closer examination if symptoms are observed.

The superintendent should provide guidance to the scout for traditional pest problem areas or hot spots. This allows the scout to concentrate his or her efforts in these areas when conditions favor those pests. In order to minimize play disruptions and to better recognize specific pest damage such as disease symptoms and nocturnal insect feeding, early morning scouting is suggested.

Pest levels should be recorded on a form similar to the one in Chapter 21. This will allow the scout and superintendent to monitor pest trends and determine if these levels reach or exceed aesthetic thresholds. Maps developed for each golf hole should accompany these forms. These maps can easily be drawn via a computer using one of the popular "draw-" or "paint-" type programs or by scanning them in from score cards. Maps enable the scout to pinpoint pest problem areas, allowing spot versus traditional blanket pesticide treatment. Over time, these maps can indicate where pest problems annually occur and possibly allow superintendents to correct management or environmental variables influencing them. For example, mole cricket tunneling activity during April and May should be mapped and these areas treated in June, as mole crickets tend to deposit eggs in the same areas each year. Early spring applications of insecticides are not effective due to the majority of mole crickets being adults, which are less susceptible to most insecticides. Maps also provide area information for the superintendent and allow new crew members a visual aid in treating problem areas.

Biological Control Strategies

Much research and talk has been on "organic," "non-synthetic," "bio," or "biorational" pesticide control of pests. These bio pesticides have little, if any, adverse effect on beneficial organisms or to the environment. The best approach in pest control is to integrate all possible control and management strategies into a plan since no single method of control is 100 percent reliable. These include host-plant resistance, pest-free propagation (or sanitation), proper site preparation, cultural practices, and biological control. These are discussed in detail in Chapter 21.

Biorational pesticides are derived from a variety of sources, including endophytes, bacteria, nematodes, fungi, other insects, and insect-derived pheromones and growth regulators. Biorational pesticides tend to be short lived; thus, they may require multiple applications, one often life-stage-specific and insect-specific, requiring proper timing of application and positive insect identification.

Endophytes

A relatively new nonchemical control method of certain insects involves naturally occurring fungi called **endophytes.** Endophytes (living within the plant, between cell walls) are fungi and other organisms that form symbiotic relationships with certain grasses but do not cause disease. Unlike most fungi, endophytes are not externally visible on plants. The endophyte fungus (*Acremonium coenophialum*) was initially discovered in forage production, as cattle and horses feeding on endophyte-containing tall fescue produced a syndrome referred to as "fescue toxicity." However, this fungus has been found to also produce ergot alkaloids (such as peramine, lolitrem B, ergovaline, paxilline, and others) that are toxic or incompatible to certain insects, and have since been transferred to certain turfgrasses. Other fungal endophytes include *Neotyphodium lolli* in perennial ryegrass and *Neotyphodium coenophialum* in tall fescue, while two endophytes, *Neotyphodium typhinum* and *Epichloe typhina,* occur in the fine fescues. In addition to providing resistance to various insects, secondary effects of certain endophytes include providing dollar spot control and increasing plant tolerance to drought and other stresses.

Infected plants appear the same as endophyte-free plants, and laboratory examination is the only way to detect its presence. Plants are not harmed by the fungus. In fact, the endophyte and the grass derive mutual positive benefits from their association. In addition to infested grass being more tolerant to insects, they also have more tolerance to nematodes and drought.

It appears the endophyte is spread only through infected seed. Therefore, cool-season grasses (fine fescue, perennial ryegrass, and tall fescue) currently have the most endophyte incorporated in them since most warm-season grasses are vegetatively established. Endophytes remain viable in storage as seed for only one or two years. Endophytes offer plant breeders and entomologists one of the most significant means for nonchemical control in years. However, market oversaturation, the fungi's fragility, and government regulations to define quantifiable levels have limited the commercial success of endophytes. Hopefully, further research will determine how to transfer this fungi to additional turfgrasses, stabilize their shelf life, increase their efficacy, and possibly offer tolerance to other pests such as nematodes.

Bacteria

Several species of the soil bacterium, *Bacillus,* provide various levels of soil and forest insect control. The first, *Bacillus thuringiensis* (or Bt), was discovered in 1901 in Japan. Since then, over 30 subspecies and varieties of Bt have been identified (Table 23–2). These bacterium produce protein crystals that must be consumed by the insects. Other products produced by the bacteria also must be consumed to control certain insects. Once inside the insect's gut, the crystals dissolve if the proper acidity exists and binds to specific sites in the gut lining. Susceptible insect guts then become paralyzed and the insect stops feeding.

Unlike many biological control agents, these bacteria generally are short-lived in the environment; they are readily degraded by direct sunlight, are slow to kill insects, do not reproduce in the insect host, are less effective on larger larvae, and are not spread from treated to nontreated sites. This has limited their acceptability in the commercial arena.

Bacillus thuringiensis varieties currently available include Bt *kurstake* and *aizawai* (best for caterpillars), Bt *israelensis* (for mosquitoes and European crane fly larvae), Bt *tenebrionis* and *san diego* (for potato beetle larvae), and most recently, Bt *buibui* (for Japanese beetle, Oriental beetle, masked chafer, and green June beetle grubs). The newer strains have less of these negative attributes and appear to be more efficacious.

Another Bacillus species (*Bacillus popilliae*) was the first microbial agent registered as an insecticide in the United States and has been used to control Japanese beetle grubs. It is often referred

TABLE 23–2 *Insecticides (chemical, common, and trade names) for control of turfgrass insect pests.* *

Chemical family	Common name	Trade name examples
Amidinohydrazone	Hydramethylon	Amdro Pro, Siege
Bioinsecticides	*Bacillus thuringiensis* var. or subsp.	
Bacteria and their various strains (gut disrupters)	*-aizawai*	XenTari
	-israelensis	VectoBac, Mosquito Attack, Bactimos, Skeetal, Teknar, and others
	-kurstaki	Biobit, Crymax, Deliver, Dipel DF, Javelin, Lepinox, Mattch, MVP II, and others
	-kurstaki, strain EG7826	Lepinox
	-sphaericus	VectoLex
	Bacillus popilliae and *B. lentimorbus*	Milky Spore Disease and others
Bacterial-derived products: Spinosad (believed nervous system disrupter)	*Spinosyn sp.* (strain A & D) or *Saccharopolyspora spinosa*	Conserve SC, Justice Fire Ant Bait
Fungi (cuticle disrupter)	*Beauveria bassiana* (strain JW-1)	Naturalis-T&O, etc.
Beneficial nematodes	*Steinernema scapterisci* and other species	Nematac-S
	Heterorhabditis bacteriopora and other species	Bioquest
	H. bacteriophora	Cruiser
Carbamate	Carbaryl	Sevin, Carbaryl, and others
	Fenoxycarb	Award, Logic
Chlorinated hydrocarbon	Dicofol	Kelthane
	1,3-Dichloropropene	Curfew
Chloronicotinyl (Neonicotinoid)	Imidacloprid	Merit 3G, Marathon
	Thiamethoxam	Meridian
Insect growth regulators & feeding deterrents (Botanical)	Azadirachtin (Neem)	Azatin, Azatrol, BioNeem, Proneem, Turplex BioInsecticide
	Halofenozide (Diacylhydrazine) (molt accelerating compound)	Mach 2
	Methoprene	Extinguish
	Pyriproxyfen	Distant Fire Ant Bait
Organophosphate	Acephate	Orthene Turf, Tree & Ornamental Spray, Pinpoint, Velocity
	Chlorpyrifos	Dursban, Mole Cricket Bait
	Diazinon	Diazinon
	Malathion	Malathion
	Trichlorfon	Dylox, Proxol, Grub Control, Trichlorfon
Phenyl pyrazoles	Fipronil	Chipco Choice, TopChoice, FireStar
Pyrethroid (synthetic)	Bifenthrin	Talstar
	Cyfluthrin	Tempo, Decathlon
	Cypermethrin	Cynoff, Demon TC
	Deltamethrin	DeltaGard GC, Suspend
	Fluvalinate	Mavrick Aquaflow
	Lambda-cyhalothrin	Scimitar, Battle
	Permethrin	Astro, Permethrin, Perm-X, Pounce, Prelude, Torpedo
	Pyrethin	Exciter, Pyganic

*In the United States, the Food Quality Protection Act (FQPA) will affect the registration of many traditional pesticides, most notably the organophosphate insecticides. The future of these are uncertain, with many manufacturers voluntarily discontinuing these labels rather than face the financial burden of re-registration.

to as the milky disease since the bacteria causes the insect's body fluids to turn a milky white color prior to grub death. The use of this bacterium has been limited due to the extended period of time needed for populations to build to infectious levels and become lethal (three to five years). Milky disease also is relatively expensive and can be extremely variable in its control. It is harmless to earthworms, wildlife, humans, and beneficial insects.

Recently, another bacteria, *Serratia entomophila,* has shown promise for the control of grass grubs in New Zealand. A new class of insecticides, Spinosad, called naturalytes contain fermented-derived products from the bacterium *Saccharopolyspora spinosa.* It is a gut poison; thus, it must be eaten by the insect. It is used at low rates and has relatively short residual activity. Research continues on the commercial development of these and other beneficial bacterium and their products.

Beneficial nematodes

Research initiated at the University of Florida has led to the identification of several beneficial (or entomogenous) nematodes in the families Steinernematidae and Heterorhabditidae which attack a specific host, yet will not attack plants or vertebrates. These nematodes lack a stylet, or the piercing mouthpart, characteristic of plant-parasitic nematodes; therefore, they do not feed on plants. In addition, these nematodes are relatively easy to mass-produce, they can search out their target hosts, and can be applied with most standard pesticide application equipment assuming the tank is ultra clean, coarse nozzles are used with no filter, and at least 140 gallons per acre (1,200 L/ha) are used. The nematodes rapidly kill their host by entering the host's mouth or spiracles and move through the gut into the blood where a colony of bacteria is released. The bacteria then multiply and produce toxins that kill the infected insect. The nematode continues to feed inside the infected host and eventually reproduces, producing thousands of new nematodes that emerge and search for new hosts.

Since beneficial nematodes are considered parasites, and not microbial insecticides, they are exempt from registration by the USEPA. This greatly speeds the registration process since these predators are exempt from long-term toxicological and environmental studies, which greatly increase the time and costs of bringing a new pesticide to the market.

Several beneficial nematodes are available, with additional ones currently being screened as potential control agents. *Steinernema scapterisci* was the first isolated and commercialized nematode, followed by *S. riobravis.* These are used for mole cricket control. Additional beneficial nematodes include *S. glaseri* (white grubs), *S. carpocapsae* (for billbugs and caterpillars such as cutworms, webworms, and armyworms), and *Heterorhabditis bacterophora* and *H. zealandica* X1 (for white grubs).

Application rates in the field range from 1 to 6 billion nematodes per acre. These can be applied using most application equipment if screens smaller than 50 mesh are not used. Subsurface injection has been used but efficacy has not been consistently improved over surface application. Environmental conditions at the time of application are very important in the success of these nematodes. Most are extremely sensitive to ultraviolet light and will survive only briefly when exposed to direct sunlight. These nematodes also are very sensitive to moisture levels as they quickly desiccate. Only early morning or late afternoon applications should be made and irrigated-in immediately to provide high relative humidity, as well as a film of moisture on the leaf and soil surface for the nematodes to survive and move. Nematodes not immediately applied after purchase also must be properly stored to extend their life expectancy. Avoid spray tank temperatures above 77°F (25°C) and soil temperatures above 86°F (30°C) or below 59°F (15°C).

Other biological control agents

Fungal pathogens

Various species of fungal pathogens also have been discovered and screened as potential biological control agents. *Beauveria bassiana* and *Metarhizium anisopliae* are two promising fungal control agents for soil-dwelling and soft-bodied greenhouse insects. Host infection is initiated when the spores of the fungus adhere to the insect body. These spores germinate under the correct environmental conditions and grow into the insect, eventually penetrating its circulatory system. The fungi then rapidly reproduce and produce toxins that kill the insect. Additional fungal spores are then produced that can spread through the environment, infecting other insects. Continued moisture is required for the pathogen to survive and work. Chinch bugs, cutworms, white grubs, and mole crickets show susceptibility to current fungal control agents.

Parasitic insects

Research continues in discovering insects that are parasitic to destructive turf insects. The red-eyed Brazilian fly, *Ormia depleta*, is currently being screened as a biological control agent against mole crickets. The red-eyed fly, a tachinid, locates the mole cricket by its singing and deposits live maggots on or near the site. These maggots attack the mole crickets and eventually consume their tissues. The maggots eventually pupate into adult flies and continue the infection process. Additional parasitic insect research continues; however, none are currently commercially available.

Insect growth regulators (IGRs)

Insect growth regulators are a relatively new class of artificial compounds currently being developed that mimic the action of the natural hormone, ecdysone. IGRs interfere with either the normal insect molting process, causing insect mortality, or by altering juvenile hormones, preventing insects from maturing. These also can inhibit the production of chitin, a polymer composite of the insect's exterior. The process is rate dependent and insect specific. Suboptimal application rates cause sublethal effects such as rapid maturation of insects to adult stages, and deformities of larvae. As mentioned, certain IGRs are more effective on specific insects; therefore, the turf manager must identify the insect present for maximum effectiveness.

IGRs generally require ingestion for optimum activity; therefore, the insect must be actively feeding when the IGR is applied. Young larval stages are most susceptible to IGRs that attack chitin synthesis. Armyworms, cutworms, sod webworms, and possibly white grubs are most susceptible to current IGRs.

Chemical Control

One of the goals of IPM is intelligent and prudent pesticide use. Once these thresholds are reached, the pesticide used should be the safest one available; spot treatments should be practiced, if possible; and all safety precautions should be followed. Pests should also be treated during the most vulnerable stage of their life cycle, such as mid- to late June for mole crickets. Refer to Figures 23–2 and 23–3 for typical life cycles and control timings for the major turf insect pests.

Evaluate the results of the habitat modification and pesticide treatments by periodically monitoring the site environment and pest populations. Keep written records of site pest management objectives, monitoring methods and data collected. Also record the actions taken and the results obtained by the pest management methods. This will provide additional information for club members who do not understand the program but would understand results. This also will aid in

FIGURE 23–2 Typical damage periods, control timings, and generations per year currently found for insects in the northern sections of the United States.

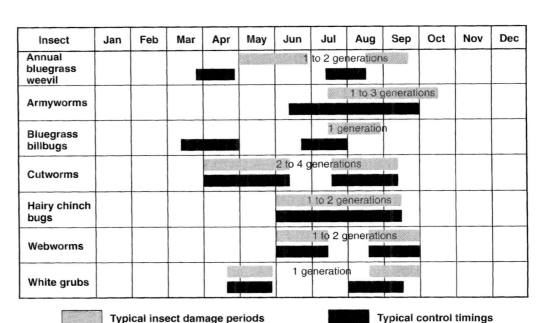

FIGURE 23-3 Typical damage periods, control timings, and generations per year currently found for insects in the southern sections of the United States.

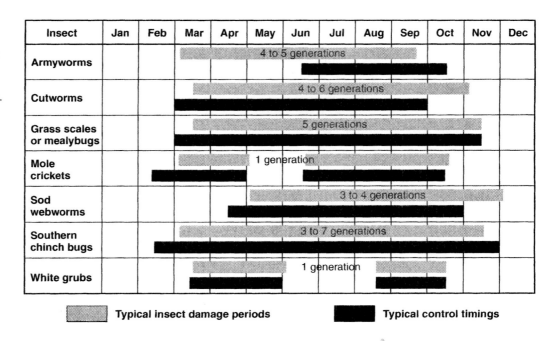

Insect	Jan	Feb	Mar	Apr	May	Jun	Jul	Aug	Sep	Oct	Nov	Dec
Armyworms						4 to 5 generations						
Cutworms						4 to 6 generations						
Grass scales or mealybugs						5 generations						
Mole crickets						1 generation						
Sod webworms						3 to 4 generations						
Southern chinch bugs						3 to 7 generations						
White grubs						1 generation						

▨ Typical insect damage periods   ▮ Typical control timings

demonstrating that golf course superintendents are striving to reduce the chemical inputs in maintaining the course and obtain an ecological balance between man and nature.

Chemical control is not the total answer but is a contributing method in insect pest management. Table 23–2 lists current insecticides and their families used on turfgrasses, while Tables 23–3 & 23–4 cross-list control options for various turfgrass insects and nuisance insects. Influence of control is regulated by a number of inherent chemical properties and by environmental parameters interacting with these.

Thatch

This partially decomposed thatch layer of turfgrass leaves and stems is located just below the shoot tissue and right above the soil layer. Excessive thatch (>1/2 inch, 1.3 cm) provides an ideal habitat (e.g., warmth and humidity) within which most insects can reside. Due to its high organic matter content, the thatch layer also tends to "tie-up" or bind many applied pesticides. This lowers the effectiveness of these pesticides, especially when dealing with soil-inhabiting insects. Thatch control should be a routine practice for most golf courses, especially on greens and tees. Some insecticides are rendered unavailable by being tied up by thatch; thus, they are inserted through this layer by a high pressure injector or a slit granular applicator.

Irrigation

In order to move most surface-applied pesticides to the soil where subsurface insects reside, irrigation must be provided shortly after application. This washes the insecticide below the thatch before it can dry or be trapped and rendered ineffective in the thatch layer. Some insecticides also are highly sensitive to direct sunlight and break down quickly when exposed. Irrigation immediately after application of these (many organophosphates and carbamates) washes them below the leaf surface, away from direct sunlight. Surface-feeding insects generally do not need to have treatments irrigated-in. Read the label to determine if a specific product should be irrigated after application.

Ultraviolet Light (UV) Degradation

Exposure to sunlight by several materials often breaks chemical bonds that may make the compound inactive. Pyrethroids, insect growth regulators (IGRs), bio (microbial) pesticides, and botanical insecticides are often susceptible to UV degradation. Applying susceptible products late in the evening and/or watering them off the leaf surface are two means turf managers can use to reduce UV degradation.

TABLE 23–3 *Cross-reference table of insecticides for major turfgrass pests.*

Insecticide	Armyworm	Bermudagrass mites	Billbugs	Clover mites	Cutworms	Fire ants	Leafhoppers	Mole crickets	Sod webworm	Southern chinch bug	Spittlebug	White grubs
Advanced Lawn 24 Hour Grub Control					✓			✓	✓			✓
Advanced Lawn Season-Long Grub Control								✓				✓
Amdro Pro						✓						
Astro	✓		✓			✓	✓	✓	✓	✓	✓	
Award Fire Ant Bait						✓						
Bacillus thuringiensis (Dipel, Javelin, XenTari)	✓	✓			✓				✓			
Battle GC	✓	✓		✓	✓	✓		✓	✓	✓	✓	
Chipco Choice, TopChoice						✓		✓	✓			
Chipco FireStar						✓						
Conserve SC	✓				✓	✓			✓			
DeltaGard	✓		✓	✓	✓	✓	✓	✓	✓	✓	✓	
Demand	✓	✓	✓	✓	✓	✓	✓	✓	✓	✓	✓	✓
Diazinon AG600, 50W, 5G			✓	✓	✓	✓	✓			✓		
Distance Fire Ant Bait						✓						
Dursban PRO	✓	✓	✓	✓	✓	✓	✓		✓	✓		
Dursban Coated Granules	✓		✓		✓	✓			✓	✓		
Dursban Granular Bait, 1%	✓				✓	✓			✓	✓		✓
Dylox								✓				
Justice Fire Ant Bait						✓						
Kelthane		✓		✓								
Logic					✓	✓						
Mach 2	✓		✓		✓				✓			✓

TABLE 23–3 *Cross-reference table of insecticides for major turfgrass pests. (continued)*

Insecticide	Armyworm	Bermudagrass mites	Billbugs	Clover mites	Cutworms	Fire ants	Leafhoppers	Mole crickets	Sod webworm	Southern chinch bug	Spittlebug	White grubs
Merit 75WP, 0.5G			✓		✓		✓	✓		✓	✓	✓
Nematac S								✓				
Orthene TT&O	✓				✓	✓	✓	✓	✓	✓	✓	
Pinpoint 15G	✓				✓	✓		✓	✓	✓	✓	
Scimitar GC or CS	✓		✓	✓	✓	✓	✓	✓	✓	✓	✓	
Sevin 10G	✓		✓		✓	✓	✓		✓	✓	✓	✓
Sevin 80WSP	✓		✓		✓	✓	✓		✓	✓	✓	✓
Sevin SL	✓		✓		✓	✓	✓		✓	✓	✓	✓
Talstar Flowable & Granular formulations	✓		✓	✓	✓	✓	✓	✓	✓	✓	✓	
Tempo 2, 20WP, and 20WP GC	✓		✓	✓	✓	✓	✓	✓	✓	✓	✓	
Varsity Fire Ant Bait						✓						
White Grub & Sod Webworm Insecticide					✓			✓	✓			✓

TABLE 23–4 *Cross-reference table of insecticides for nuisance insects.*

Insecticide	Ants	Chiggers (red bugs), ticks	Imported fire ants	Fleas	Centipedes, millipedes, pillbugs, sowbugs	Snails, slugs	Wasps, bees
Advanced Lawn Fire Ant Killer			✓				
Andro Pro	✓		✓				✓
Astro	✓		✓	✓	✓		
Award Fire Ant Bait			✓				
Battle GC	✓	✓	✓	✓			
Chipco Choice, TopChoice	✓	✓	✓	✓	✓		
Delta Gard	✓	✓	✓	✓	✓		✓
Diazinon AG600, 50W, 5G			✓				
Distance Fire Ant Bait			✓				
Dursban PRO	✓	✓	✓	✓	✓		✓
Justice Fire Ant Bait			✓				
Logic			✓	✓			
Metaldehyde 7.5G						✓	
Orthene TT&O	✓		✓				
Pinpoint 15G	✓		✓			✓	
Scimitar GC, Demand CS	✓	✓	✓	✓	✓	✓	
Sevin SL, 80WSP, XLR Plus	✓	✓	✓	✓	✓	✓	✓
Talstar	✓	✓	✓	✓	✓	✓	✓
Tempo 2, 20WP, and 20WP GC	✓	✓	✓	✓	✓	✓	✓
Varsity Fire Ant Bait			✓				

Weather

Weather conditions, especially temperature, often influence the frequency of insect generations and severity of insect infestations and damage. A rapid temperature drop to subfreezing temperatures often kills significant numbers of overwintering insects. Drought conditions often delay development or reduce pest reproduction. Generally, as temperatures increase, insects reproduce and develop faster.

pH of Spray Tank and Soil

Most insecticides require a neutral (pH=7) or slightly acidic pH in the tank mixture. When the pH in a tank mixture exceeds 7.0, the product begins to disassociate through hydrolysis into inactive or ineffective byproducts. However, not all insecticides are sensitive to pH. After the tank-mix is made and agitated, the pH of the resulting solution should be taken. If a high pH is detected, a commercial buffering agent or acidifier should be added. Use the mixed pesticide solution immediately, never store overnight and spray the following day. Read the label to determine if a particular pest control compound is sensitive to pH.

Insect Resistance

Species that are adapted to their environment are able to survive and thrive. If certain animals were not able to adapt to unfavorable environments or pesticides, their future would be in jeopardy. Continued exposure to a single material has allowed certain insects to develop resistance to it. Turf managers, therefore, should rotate between classes of insecticides, never use more insecticide than the label calls for, and if possible, treat only when necessary and only the damaged area. Avoid "wall-to-wall" spray application whenever possible.

Enhanced Microbial Degradation

Microbes (usually bacteria and simple fungi) present in the soil often can use a portion of pesticides as a food source. During this process, complex compounds are broken down into those used for food. Certain continuously used pesticides can become victims to enhanced microbial degradation. Populations of aerobic microbes buildup to levels that quickly break down pesticides within hours after being applied. Reduce the chance of enhanced microbial degradation by (1) rotating between classes of pesticides, (2) using one class of pesticides only once per year, and (3) applying only the recommended amounts of materials as excessive rates may favor microbial buildup.

Longevity of Control

Modern synthetic insecticides belonging to the chemical classes organophosphates, carbamates, and pyrethroids are generally very effective against the target pest if application timing and methods are followed as recommended. One drawback to these materials, however, is their relatively short control. Three to 14 days, depending on the material, insect, and environmental conditions (as discussed earlier), is the general range of control for most of these materials. Improper application and subsequent watering practices reduce the control longevity of these materials as do excessive thatch layering, sunlight (UV) exposure, and improper spray tank pH levels.

Control also is rarely 100 percent effective, even if ideal application parameters and environmental conditions exist. However, populations should be lowered to below aesthetic levels. Slow repopulation from survivors and subsequent hatching of eggs and migration of adults from nearby untreated areas may require retreatment. Newer insecticides, such as imidacloprid and fipronil, show good soil longevity, yet they are extremely environmentally safe.

Insecticide Classes

Insecticides, like most pesticides, are grouped into similar chemical classes or modes of action. The following are the main groups of insecticides used in turfgrass: organochlorines, organophosphates, carbamates, pyrethroids, phenyl pyrazoles, chloronicotinyls, and biological insecticides.

Organochlorines (chlorinated hydrocarbons)

Organochlorines are also referred to as **chlorinated organics, chlorinated insecticides,** and **chlorinated synthetics.** These insecticides contain carbon (hence the name *organo-*), chlorine, and hydrogen. These insecticides are neurotoxins that act on the insect's nervous system by disrupting sodium ion movement within and through nerve membranes. This disruption results in slowed nerve cell repolarization and increased sensitivity of neurons to stimuli which causes persistent tremors and seizures. As a class, organochlorines have long life residues.

Organophosphates (OPs)

Organophosphate is usually used as a generic term to include all insecticides containing phosphorus. They are all derived from phosphoric acid, tend to be more toxic than organochlorine insecticides, and are relatively unstable in the environment, meaning they are nonpersistent.

Organophosphates work by inhibiting the cholinesterase enzyme activity that is necessary for transmission of nerve impulses across synapses. Many of the current insecticides used in turf are organophosphates and include acephate, chlorpyrifos, diazinon, malathion, and trichlorfon. However, in the United States, the Food Quality Protection Act (FQPA) has and will continue to reduce the members of organophosphates registered for turf.

Carbamates

Carbamates are insecticide derivatives of carbamic acid. Their mode of action is similar to the organophosphates as they also inhibit cholinesterase enzyme activity during nerve impulse transmission. Important turf members include bendiocarb, carbaryl, and fenoxycarb.

Synthetic Pyrethroids

Synthetic pyrethroids are synthetic pyrethrin-like materials that are more stable in sunlight than natural insecticide pyrethrum and are generally effective against most insects at very low rates. They disrupt impulse transmission via the sodium channel along nerve axons in ganglia of the central nervous system. Fast knockdown of insects is the result of rapid muscular paralysis caused by these materials. Important turf members include bifenthrin, cyfluthrin, cypermethrin, permethrin, and lambda-cyhalothrin.

Phenyl pyrazoles

Phenyl pyrazoles are a relatively new class of synthetic insecticides discovered in 1981 and are noted for excellent insecticidal properties, low mammalian toxicity, and favorable environmental characteristics. Phenyl pyrazoles interfere with the insect's chloride ions through the gamma-aminobutyric acid (GABA)-regulated chloride channel, thereby disrupting central nerve activity. These insecticides display selective tighter bonding in the insect GABA chloride channel than in mammals. Fipronil is the first member of the phenyl pyrazoles used in turf.

Chloronicotinyls or Neonicotinoids

These postsynaptic inhibitors attack the nervous system by binding with the insect's nicotinic acetylcholine receptor agonist site in membranes. Imidacloprid, one of the first commercial products from this insecticide class, is active both by insect contact and ingestion. Imidacloprid translocates within plants, providing good control of stem-tunneling larvae of billbugs and annual bluegrass weevil as well as grubs. It is not as effective on leaf-feeding caterpillars such as sod webworms, armyworms, and cutworms. The newest chloronicotinyl (also listed as a neonicotinoid) is thiamethoxam, which is primarily a grub control product but also controls a wide spectrum of sucking and chewing insects. Both products are root absorbed and translocated to the foliage.

Biologicals or Biorationals

Biorations control insects through the use of hormones, pheromones, and naturally occurring insect and plant growth regulators. **Pheromones** and **attractants** are highly specific chemicals that are released in very small quantities, vaporize, and are detected by insects of the same species for communication purposes. Sex pheromones are used in pheromone traps to attract the opposite sex. These are mostly used to monitor specific insect populations and to provide male "confusion" so they are prevented from finding mates.

Insect growth regulators (IGRs) are man-made chemicals that alter the growth and development of insects. They have effects on reproduction, behavior, and diapause. These include the molting and juvenile hormones and the chitin inhibitors. These target sites are not found in mammals; thus, IGRs generally have very low toxicity to non-insect groups. Azadirachtin (Neem) from *Azadirachta indica* is one of the first IGRs registered for use in turf, with halofenozide recently introduced as a molt-accelerating compound (MACs). MACs work by mimicking the action of the hormone ecdysone, which regulates molting. Insect exposure to MACs causes lethal premature molting. Insect feeding stops immediately, with death occurring in one to three weeks. Being molt-accelerating compounds, these products are most effective on immature insects. Armyworms, cutworms, and sod webworms are most susceptible to azadirachtin while these insects plus white grubs are susceptible to halofenozide. Affected caterpillars do not surface; they die in their burrows. Being systemic in plants, these insecticides do not require watering-in.

Bioinsecticides

Bioinsecticides use one organism to control another. They pose few environmental or mammalian problems and are very specific hosts. Complete control, however, is rarely achieved with these materials and their effects are usually slow to occur. This class of insecticides is currently receiving an enormous increase in attention with new products quickly reaching the market due to the lower costs needed to obtain registration. Three main bioinsecticides currently in turf include bacteria, fungi, and beneficial nematodes. These are discussed in more detail under the biological control strategies section.

A recent class of naturalyte insecticides is **Spinosad.** Spinosad contains two (A and D) fermented-derived compounds from the bacterium *Saccharopolyspora spinosa* that act as stomach poisons; thus, they must be eaten. They are used at low rates, have fairly short residual activity, and contain low toxicity to humans and mammals. Armyworms, cutworms, and sod webworms appear most susceptible. As synthetic pesticides decline, the use of Spinosad products as well as other bioinsecticides will probably increase.

Food Quality Protection Act (FQPA)

In 1996, the United States Congress passed the FQPA, which considered the potential exposure of infants and children to pesticides. Since it is believed children do not metabolize pesticides as efficiently as adults, traditional toxicology tests were believed not to provide an adequate margin of safety for them. The Environmental Protection Agency (EPA) modified toxicological studies to include "aggregate" and "cumulative" exposure.

All avenues of exposure now must be considered during the insecticide registration process, including minuscule amounts in water, meat and produce, drift, applications in schools or restaurants, and on lawns and gardens. Also, the EPA started reviewing all members of insecticides within the same family or class together. Studying "cumulative" exposure considered the tolerances of similar compounds on the same crop, and the total (cumulative) exposure must be considered when determining allowable residues for each compound. This led to the "risk cup" concept, which considered the total use of a class of products and set lower limits for this amount.

As a result of FQPA, companies were told by the EPA what production limits would be allowed for each class of insecticides; thus, companies started to decide which products and which markets were profitable enough to meet the lower production forecasts. Since people are sensitive to cholinesterase inhibitors, the organophosphates and carbamates were among the first group to be reviewed. Many home and ground labels were withdrawn or greatly revised to minimize exposures or to bring ingredients within the limits of this "risk cup."

Many widely used, broad spectrum products have disappeared or soon will, from the turf and ornamental markets. Dursban (chlorpyrifos), Turcam (bendiocarb), Oftanol (isofenphos), Crusade/Mainstay (fonofos), Mocap (ethoprop), and Triumph (isazophos) are some early casualties of FQPA. Fortunately, new products are being introduced to help replace some of the uses of cancelled ones. Newer products, however, only control specific pests, are more expensive, and are not as broad in their control as previous products. They, however, are deemed much more favorable in their toxicological properties but require more knowledge on insect life cycles and movement patterns for optimum effectiveness.

SURFACE- OR LEAF-FEEDING INSECTS

Sod Webworms

Species

Sod webworms (order Lepidoptera, family Acrolophidae, Pyralidae) compose a large number of grass-feeding larvae (caterpillars) and adult moths. Most sod webworms are native to North America and found throughout the country, especially the eastern half. Over 15 species of webworms attack turfgrasses, including:

- Tropical sod webworms, *Herpetogramma phaeopteralis* Guerne, the one most often found in southern States.

  Those most commonly found on cool-season grasses include:

- Bluegrass sod webworm, *Parapediasis teterrella* (Zincken), which is especially prevalent in Kentucky and Tennessee. These larvae damage bentgrass greens in a manner similar to grub feeding.
- Striped sod webworm, *Fissicrambus mutabilis* (Clemens), which is especially prevalent in Pennsylvania, Illinois, and Tennessee.
- Large sod webworm, *Pediasia trisecta* (Walker), which is especially prevalent in Ohio and Iowa.
- Burrowing sod webworm (*Acrolophus sp.*), which is sometimes a problem in the Midwest and southeast.
- The Silverstriped webworm, *Crambus praefectellus* (Zincken), which is found along the Pacific coast and areas west of the Rocky Mountains.

Insect Description

Larvae of the tropical sod webworm have a dark yellowish-brown head and greenish, hairy body with numerous black spots scattered over it (Figure 23–4). Larvae are 1/25-inch (1-mm) long when first hatched and grow to three-fourths inch (1.9-cm) long. Most sod webworm larvae curl

FIGURE 23–4 Sod webworm and adult (left) larva (right).

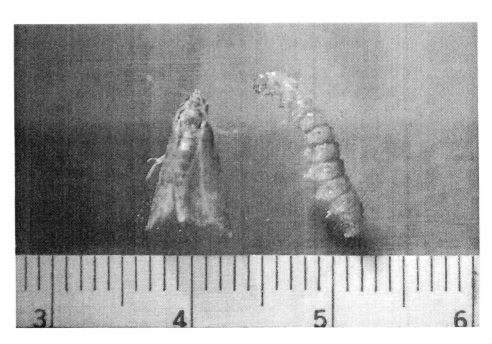

into a ball when disturbed. Adult moths are small, dingy brown to almost white-colored with a wing span of three-fourths-inch (1.9-cm) and delicate fringes along the wing borders. Resting adult sod webworm moths have a very long, distinct, snoutlike labial palpi extending in front of their heads, giving a tubelike appearance. However, unlike other webworms, adult tropical sod webworms do not fold their wings against their bodies but hold them out in a triangular pattern like most other moths. Adults often hide in grass or shrubbery and are attracted to lights at night. When disturbed, adult moths fly short distances in a zigzag pattern. Sod webworm adults are identified by varying wing color patterns and male genitalia while larvae are extremely difficult to separate.

Biology and Distribution

Most sod webworms overwinter as larvae tightly coiled in silk-lined tunnels or cases. In spring, the larvae pupate within these and the adults emerge, mate, and lay eggs. During the day, moths rest in shrubbery adjacent to turf areas. At dusk they fly in a zigzag pattern over the turf, depositing clusters of 6 to 15 eggs on grass leaves. Eggs hatch in approximately seven days when temperatures are at least 78°F (26°C) and larvae progress through seven instars, requiring 25 days. When temperatures are lower (72°F, 23°C), eight larval instars occur requiring 45 to 50 days to complete their development. They pupate on the soil surface and emerge as adult moths in seven days. Life cycle from egg to adult requires five to six weeks at 78°F (26°C) and 12 weeks at 72°F (23°C).

During most years, there are two generations in north and central Florida and up to four generations yearly in south Florida. The tropical sod webworm does not overwinter further north than central Florida during most years. In south Florida, economic damage to grass usually begins in May or June. Further north, it is usually August before larval populations develop in sufficient numbers to cause damage.

Damage Symptoms/Signs

Adult sod webworms do not feed, but larvae damage grass by chewing blades or severing blades above the thatch and pulling this into their silk-lined tunnels. When first hatched, they only rasp the surface or skeletonize the blades. Damaged areas appear grayish and usually are only two to three feet in diameter. Often, damage is first noticed adjacent to shrubbery and flower beds since moths rest in the foliage and lay more eggs in nearby turf. Moths are attracted to dark-green, healthy turf; therefore, golf greens provide a choice site for them. When larvae become larger, they notch the blades and the grass becomes ragged in appearance. Injury initially appears as small, closely cropped grass patches as grass blades are clipped just above the crowns. Damaged areas then become larger and fuse. Continued feeding gives the turf a close-cropped yellowish, and then brown, appearance from the exposed underneath thatch. Webworms normally do not kill turf crowns, but rather feed on their leaves and stems. Turfgrasses, therefore, normally can recover from insect feeding if the webworm is controlled and proper fertilization and watering practices are used. Bermudagrass and bluegrass are most often attacked.

Sod webworms (except Tropical sod webworm) live in small tunnels of silk and grass in the thatch or soil and overwinter as larvae in these silk-lined tunnels. When feeding, birds often pull out the paperlike white sacs, leaving them laying on the grass. Sod webworms are mostly night feeders and retreat to these tunnels during the day after feeding on individual grass blades. During the day, they rest in a curled position on the soil surface.

Inspection and Control

Approximately 5 to 12 larvae per square foot are required to cause economic damage. Irregular brown spots resembling dollar spot disease are early signs of damage (Figure 23–5). The presence of larvae can be confirmed by parting the grass and observing the soil surface in suspect areas for frass or pellets (Figure 23–6) or for curled-up resting larvae. They also can be flushed to the grass surface by using a soap mixture or pyrethrin solution. Flocks of birds frequently returning to a turf area, especially in early morning, or the presence of large numbers of moths flying over the turf area at dusk usually are an indication sod webworms or other caterpillars are present. Numerous moths flying at dusk or collecting on doors, windows, and around lights often

FIGURE 23–5 Sod webworm feeding on golf greens often resembles dollar spot disease except with a tunnel in the center.

FIGURE 23–6 Cast or frass mounds are associated with sod webworm feeding.

indicate egg-laying periods. The birds often produce pencil-sized holes in the turf as they dig in the silken tunnels for the webworms. The turf area should be monitored for webworms once a week during the season they are most active in an area. Damage is most evident in late summer when populations have increased and grass growth is slowed.

Long residual control of the tropical sod webworm is difficult. There are many overlapping generations and the moths are continually flying into the turf area and depositing eggs. Insecticide sprayed on the grass may be removed within a few days by mowing, leaving the new grass without defense. Also, insecticides exposed to the weather, especially the sun, break down more rapidly than when irrigated into the soil.

Control of early instar larvae is possible with various microbial insecticides derived from *Bacillus thuringiensis* var *kurstaki* (often indicated as **Bt**). This microbial insecticide is a stomach poison; therefore, the insect must ingest it to be effective. Preirrigating the turf and allowing the grass to grow several days after Bt application increases its effectiveness. Control is best on young larvae. Several insect pathogenic nematodes also are being screened as possible control measures, as are some fungal endophytes.

FIGURE 23–7 Young fall armyworm larva have dorsal stripes.

Fall Armyworm

Species

Spodoptera frugiperda (Smith) is the fall armyworm while *S. ornithogalli* is the "yellowstriped" armyworm, and the "beet" armyworm is *S. exigua*. The "common" or "true" armyworm is *Pseudaletia unipuncta* (Haworth) (order Lepidoptera, family Noctuidae), also listed previously as *Leucania extranea* and *Cirphis unipuncta*. These were described by American colonists as a pest which devoured crops like an "army of worms."

Insect Description

Fall armyworm larvae are the injurious stage and are 1.5 inches (3.8 cm) long when mature. They are greenish when small and dark-brown when fully grown (Figure 23–7). They have a light dorsal stripe with darker bands on each side running the length of the body. Larvae also have a distinct inverted yellow "Y" shape on their heads. Adult moths are brownish with light and dark markings and a distinct white blotch near the tip of each front wing (Figure 23–8). They have a wing span of about 1.5 inches (3.8 cm). Common armyworms do not have the light-colored Y-shaped mark but rather a brownish head with H-shaped darker brown lines.

Biology and Distribution

The life cycle of the fall armyworm varies considerably according to the region and is very similar to the sod webworm; however, armyworms pupate in the soil. Armyworms continuously reside in Central and tropical South America and the West Indies. They also survive mild winters in the Gulf Coast region of the United States. They spread each spring from these areas into the eastern United States and into southern New Mexico, Arizona, and California, reaching the northern states in fall; hence, their name. In the Gulf Coast region, during mild winters, larval and pupal stages overwinter and emerge as new adults in early spring. Typically, only one generation occurs per year in northern areas and they die each fall with freezing temperatures. The common armyworm is more cold tolerant and can survive as larvae or pupae further north.

Several generations occur yearly in the southeastern United States. The first generation causes turf damage in May to mid-June. A second generation may occur from June to July, and a third from August until the first frost. The second or third generation typically causes the most damage. Eggs are laid on the grass blades or almost any object near the turf area. They are laid in

FIGURE 23–8 Adult fall armyworm moth with its wings folded in a resting position.

FIGURE 23–9 Fall armyworm damage to a golf green.

clusters and are covered with grayish, fuzzy scales from the body of the female moth. A generation takes five to six weeks.

Damage Symptoms/Signs

Despite its name, the fall armyworm is capable of causing damage to turfgrass in early summer, especially following cool, wet springs, which may reduce populations of natural parasites. However, most damage occurs during late summer and early fall after populations have increased during the season. Larval feeding is similar to webworm feeding except it usually does not occur in patches, but in more uniform and larger areas. Larvae feed day or night, but are most active early in the morning or late in the evening. Younger larvae feed on leaf margins, giving them a ragged look (Figure 23–9). Larger larvae eat all aboveground leaves and stems, resembling a "mowing." Bentgrass, bermudagrass, fescue, bluegrass, ryegrass, and grain crops (especially sweet corn) are most often attacked.

Inspection and Control

Soap flushing can bring the larvae to the soil surface. Feeding birds and the presence of green fecal pellets also indicate an armyworm presence. Adult moths are often attracted to lights at night during flight periods. Threshold levels vary on lower maintenance turf, but control may be justified if one armyworm is found per square foot on a green. Current strains of *Bacillus thuringiensis* are for inconsistent control. However, endophyte-containing grasses such as ryegrasses or fescues are quite resistant to armyworms. Stoloniferous grasses, such as bermudagrass, generally recover from armyworm feeding since the pests do not destroy plant crowns. Nonstoloniferous grasses, such as fescue, may not fully recover.

The spinosyn toxins and the parasite *Steinernema* nematodes provide biorational control. As new Bt strains are produced, these also may provide acceptable biorational control. Most synthetic pesticides such as the pyrethroids also provide effective control. In addition to treating obviously damaged areas, treat one or two boomwidths outside the infested area to control the probable additional caterpillars feeding beyond.

Cutworms

Species

Several members of the order Lepidoptera, family Noctuidae, are considered cutworms:

- Black cutworm, *Agrostis ipsilon* (Hufnagel), is the most common cutworm.
- Variegated cutworm, *Peridroma saucia* (Hubner).
- Granulate cutworm, *Feltia subterranea* (Fabricius), is found most often in southern regions.
- Bronzed cutworm, *Nephelodes minians* (Guenee), often infests bluegrass turf.

Insect Description

Adults are moths with forewings that are dark brown and mottled or streaked in color. The hindwings are lightly colored and unmarked. The moths are generally stout-bodied and have a wingspan of about 1.5 inches (3.8 cm). When resting, cutworm moths hold their wings back in a triangular position. Cutworm larvae are fat, smooth, dull gray or brown to nearly black-colored caterpillars and measure about 1.75 inches (4.4 cm) when fully grown (Figure 23–10). All have a dorso (side) median stripe that may be broken or continuous. If disturbed, the larvae usually curl into a C-shaped position.

FIGURE 23–10 A black cutworm larvae feeds on a golf green.

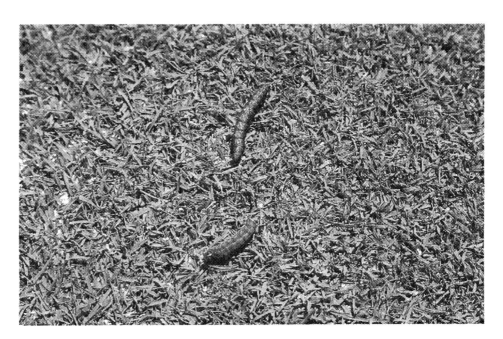

Biology and Distribution

Cutworms are found throughout the United States. Each cutworm varies slightly from the others in details of habits and appearance but their life histories are generally similar. Adults and larvae are nocturnal and hide during the day, but may become active on cloudy days. They overwinter in the soil either as pupae or mature larvae. In the spring, the hibernating larvae pupate. Adults begin to appear in mid-March. Female moths deposit eggs singly or in clusters, and each female can lay as many as 500 eggs. Under optimum conditions, the eggs hatch in three to five days, and larvae develop in three to four weeks, passing through six instars. Pupae mature in two weeks during the summer but may require up to nine weeks in the fall. As many as four generations occur each year.

Damage Symptoms/Signs

Cutworms are caterpillars that feed on the stems and leaves of young plants and often cut them off near the soil line; hence, their common name. Cutworms, unlike sod webworms, do not construct tunnels. Many prefer wilted plant material and may climb ornamental plants and feed on unopened buds. Bentgrass is a major target of cutworms and they often reside in and eat extensively around aerifier holes (Figure 23–11). Damage to greens from insect-feeding birds can also be substantial. Damage appears as one- to two-inch (2.5- to 5-cm) dead spots resembling ball marks on closely cut turf with a pencil-size hole in the middle.

Inspection and Control

Since cutworms are mostly nocturnal, late afternoon is best for their detection. Examine the turf for damage. Initial feeding symptoms often are mistaken for ball mark damage. Later symptoms often appear similar to dollar spot disease except a hole where the worm resides can be found in the center of the damaged area. The soap or pyrethrum flush test will also aid in detection. Threshold levels for golf greens are approximately one cutworm per square foot ($11/m^2$), while 5 to 10 larvae per square foot (54 to $108/m^2$) are tolerable on fairways and lawns. Control is best when applied in late afternoon to early evening. Endophyte-enhanced fescues and ryegrasses are available to reduce problems. Bt also is effective on young (first to third instars) larvae if enough material is ingested.

   Many liquid insecticides are available that provide good control. These should be applied late in the evening and **not** irrigated-in, as the insecticide should be left on the leaf surface for the insect to feed on. Granular insecticides may not be as effective.

FIGURE 23–11 Cutworm larvae cause feeding damage to bentgrass golf greens. Cutworms often hibernate during the day in aerifying holes and feed around the perimeter of the hole at night.

Bermudagrass Mites

Species

The bermudagrass mite, *Eriophyes cynodoniensis* Sayed (order Acarina, family Eriophyidae), appears in all bermudagrass-growing states. It is also commonly referred to as the "bermudagrass stunt mite." Bermudagrass mites are not true insects but are more closely related to spiders.

Insect Description

The mites are extremely small, only about 1/130-inch (0.2-mm) long, yellowish-white, and somewhat wormlike in shape with only two pairs of short legs. A microscope with at least 30X magnification is needed to detect them.

Biology and Distribution

Bermudagrass mites are probably native to Australia but have spread to New Zealand, Africa, and America. They are found in all U.S. bermudagrass-growing regions. They multiply very rapidly, requiring only about seven days to complete their life cycle. This short life cycle allows for rapid buildup during late spring and summer. Eggs are deposited under the leaf sheath, and after hatching, mites molt two times before reaching adulthood. All stages are found under the leaf sheaths. Mites appear well-adapted to hot temperatures and become relatively inactive during cold temperatures. They spread through infected plants, clippings, machinery, mobile insects, and even by the wind.

Damage Symptoms/Signs

Since the bermudagrass mite is so small, it remains hidden beneath the leaf sheath. Therefore, it can be identified more easily by symptoms of grass damage. The mite sucks plant juices with their needlelike mouth parts that cause a characteristic type of damage. Grass blades turn light-green and abnormally curl. Typical vigorous spring growth is noticeably absent. Internodes shorten, tissues swell, and the grass becomes tufted so small clumps, often bushy in appearance, are noticed. This is often called "witches brooming" (Figure 23–12). This characteristic growth is believed to be caused by a toxin injected into the developing grass node. The grass loses its vigor, thins out, and may die. Injury is more pronounced during dry weather and especially when grass is stressed

FIGURE 23–12 Turf symptoms (often referred to as "witches brooming") resulting from bermudagrass mite feeding.

due to poor maintenance. Since damage is often associated with drought stress, providing adequate moisture and nutrients help the grass outgrow mite damage.

Inspection and Control

Infestations usually develop in taller-mowed grass, such as rough areas, around sand traps, and along canals and fence rows. To aid in reducing populations, mow as close as practical and collect and destroy grass clippings from infested areas. In general, as the mowing height is decreased, mite numbers are decreased. A wetting agent in the spray mixture will improve pesticide results. Spread appears most common by moving infested turf. The threshold for control is suggested when four to eight witches broomed tufts are seen per square foot (43 to 86 per square meter).

Use resistant varieties such as Tifgreen (328), Tifdwarf, FloraTeX, and Midiron bermudagrasses. Coarser varieties, such as Common and Ormond, appear more susceptible. Maintain good soil moisture as dry conditions tend to favor mite damage. Commercial insecticides are available but may require frequent application since mites have such a short life cycle.

Grass Scales or Mealybugs

Species

Over 37 species of mealybugs have been associated with grasses. Two major grass scales occur: (1) the rhodesgrass mealybug, also called rhodesgrass scale, *Antonia graminis* (Maskell); and (2) the bermudagrass scale, *Odonaspis ruthae* Kotinsky (order Homoptera, family Pseudococcidae and Diaspididae). These are not common pests but do occasionally occur from South Carolina to California, most often on bermudagrass and St. Augustinegrass, especially growing in shade. Rhodesgrass scale derives its name from feeding on its favorite host, rhodesgrass, a coarse-textured pasturegrass. The buffalograss mealybug, *Tridiscus sporoboli* (Cockerell) and *Trionymus* sp., is often found on buffalograss but appears to cause little economic damage. Ground pearls also are scale insects and are discussed separately.

Insect Description

The rhodesgrass mealybug body is round and dark brown but is covered with a white cottony secretion that appears like tufts of cotton on the grass (Figure 23–13). Male mealybugs resemble tiny gnats with a single pair of wings and three pairs of red eyes. Adult males are not considered harmful to turfgrasses. The bermudagrass scale is oval shaped, white, wingless, and approximately 1/15 inch (1.7 mm) in diameter. They prefer the taller grass in rough areas, especially in

FIGURE 23–13
Rhodesgrass mealybug (scale) feeding on bermudagrass stems.

heavily thatched and shaded areas. They also are found around sand traps, along fence rows, and in other similar areas. When the scales hatch into the crawler stage, they migrate beneath the leaf sheath, usually at the nodes. Only the youngest, immature stages are mobile. Adults settle on the leaf or stem, insert their needlelike mouthparts, become immobile, and eventually start excreting a white, cottony, waxy covering.

Biology and Distribution

The life cycles of both insects range from 60 to 70 days, and there are up to five generations per year in the southern United States. Continuous generations occur from Orlando, Florida, south.

Damage Symptoms/Signs

As mentioned, bermudagrass and St. Augustinegrass are their favorite hosts. They infest the crown, nodes, or under leaf sheaths (not the leaves) and withdraw plant sap with their piercing/sucking mouthparts. Infested grass slowly loses vitality, discolors, and later appears to be suffering from drought. Stunting and thinning of the grass stand occurs under high infestation levels. Under heavy infestations, plants are often covered with tiny masses of white, waxy secretions. Injury is most severe during extended hot, dry (stressful) periods. The rhodesgrass mealybug produces considerable honeydew, and other insects such as ants or bees may be present on heavily infested turfgrass.

Inspection and Control

Plant leaves should be pulled away from the stem and sheaths examined for tiny, white cottony masses. Ants feeding on the honeydew also can indicate mealybugs. Since these insects produce more damage during dry weather, keep the turf well-irrigated and fertilized. Cultural control includes collecting grass clippings, which will contain some scales, and destroying these. Several insecticides provide control but are rarely needed. If needed, thorough spray coverage is necessary and a surfactant should be added.

Annual Bluegrass (or Hyperodes) Weevils

Species

Listronotus maculicollis (Dietz) (order Coleoptera, family Curculionidae); formerly *Hyperodes* sp. near *anthracinus* (Dietz), is the annual bluegrass weevil.

Insect Description

Larvae are C-shaped, legless, and from 1/32- to 3/16-inch (0.8- to 5-mm) long. Larvae are creamy-white in color with light brown to tan heads. Adults are small (1/8 inch, 3 mm, long), about half the size of Kentucky bluegrass billbug, black to dark-gray weevils with a relatively broad and short snout. Adults initially appear reddish in color when they first emerge from the pupal stage but turn black as their exoskeleton hardens.

Biology and Distribution

Annual bluegrass weevils are most often encountered in the northeastern United States including New York, southwestern Connecticut, northern New Jersey, Pennsylvania, and all of the New England states. Adults are in the overwintering stage and often hibernate in the leaf litter under trees of golf course roughs, and become active in early spring, often corresponding with early plant flowering. Eggs are deposited in early May in chewed-out stems. Larvae hatch in four to five days and chew into the stems feeding on plant crowns, killing the plants. Sawdust-like frass is evident from this feeding and is apparent by late spring. Five instar stages occur, each lasting five to seven days, and resembling each other except becoming larger in size. Mature larvae pupate near the soil surface in mid-June. Young adults emerge in late June, lay eggs in mid-July, and the second generation small larvae emerge in late July. Most of these larvae pupate in late August. Since life cycles overlap, all stages of development can be found from late June through early

September. Currently, only annual bluegrass is the host of annual bluegrass weevils. It appears only in short-mowed (≤1/2 inch, 1.3 cm) annual bluegrass such as greens, tees, and fairways. Feeding damage resembles anthracnose symptoms, causing easy misdiagnosis.

Damage Symptoms/Signs

Damage is generally most severe in early June and again in mid-summer (late July) when other turf stresses, such as water, fertility, and mowing, weaken the turf. Damage is from larvae feeding and begins as small yellow patches that appear wilted and increase into larger areas. Turf does not normally respond to watering. This is from larva severing stems from the plant. The edges of fairways, near woods, or collars are often initial sites of damage. Severe damage resembles a water-soaked appearance from the hollowed grass stems.

Inspection and Control

Suspected infested areas should have a physical inspection in spring (April to early May). A cup cutter (or similar device) should be used to collect cores. Break up the cores and place the loosened soil and plant parts in a pan filled with lukewarm water. This forces adults to crawl to the surface. A soapy flush can also be used in the field to indicate an adult presence. If present, after about five minutes, weevils (except eggs) will float to the surface. Insecticides should be applied in spring just prior to adults beginning to lay eggs and can usually be timed when flowering shrubs and trees such as forsythia, wisteria, and dogwood bloom, typically from mid-April through early May. Where the second generation occurs, a follow-up insecticide application may be needed in early July. Treatments should be lightly watered-in. Threshold levels range from 30 per square feet ($323/m^2$) for golf greens and up to 50 per square foot ($540/m^2$) for well-maintained fairways. Lower-maintained (non-irrigated) turf may have lower (e.g., 20 to 40 weevils per square foot, 215 to $430/m^2$) threshold levels. Healthy turf is the first step against damage.

SUBSURFACE- OR ROOT-FEEDING INSECTS

Mole Crickets

Species

Mole crickets (order Orthoptera, family Gryllotalpidae) are subterranean insects and are considered the most serious turfgrass pest in sandy, coastal plain areas from North Carolina to Texas. Isolated outbreaks have also occurred in southern California and Arizona, causing severe damage to bermudagrass, bahiagrass, and centipedegrass. Several species exist, including:

- The Southern mole cricket, *Scapteriscus borelli* Giglio-Tos.
- The Tawny mole cricket, *Scapteriscus vicinus* Scudder (previously called the Changa or Puerto Rican mole cricket), is the most damaging.
- The Short-winged mole cricket, *Scapteriscus abbreviatus* Scudder, is found in isolated areas.
- The Northern mole cricket, *Gryllotalpa hexadactyla* Perty, is the only species native to the United States and is least damaging.

Insect Description

Mole crickets are 1 to 1.5 inches (2.5 to 3.8 cm) long when mature and possess spadelike front legs that are well-adapted for tunneling through soil. Nymphs resemble adults but are smaller and wingless. Two species of mole crickets are widespread in the southern United States, the Southern mole cricket and the Tawny mole cricket (Figure 23–14). The color patterns of the two species usually are distinct; the tawny mole cricket is a lighter creamy brown, while the Southern mole cricket is grayish to dark-brown and usually has four distinct light spots on its prothorax. The two species also can be distinguished by their dactyls (digging claws). The Southern mole cricket has a "U"-shaped space between its dactyls while the Tawny has a "V"-shaped space. A third species, the short-winged mole cricket, is abundant locally, especially along the southeast and southwest

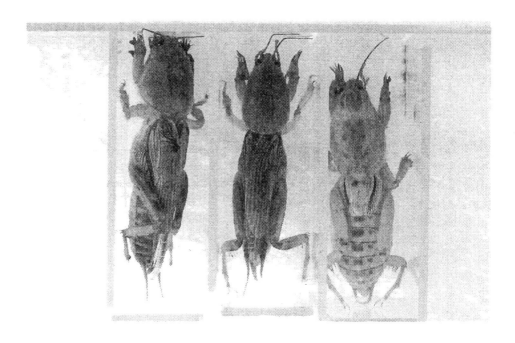

coasts in Florida. It is similar in appearance to the Tawny mole cricket, but has short wings and cannot fly; thus, it has limited distribution. The Southern, Tawny, and Short-winged species were introduced into the southeastern United States around 1900 as stowaways in sand used as the ballast material of South American ships. They are found throughout the Coastal Plain region of the southeast and northern Argentina, Uruguay, and Brazil. A fourth species, the Northern mole cricket, is native to the United States, but is not considered to be a major pest. It primarily inhabits moist soil adjacent to water.

Biology and Distribution

Mole crickets have a gradual metamorphosis life cycle where adults appear similar as nymphs except for their underdeveloped wings. In most locations, the Tawny and Southern mole crickets have one generation per year. The process of this life cycle begins in spring, when adults fly, mate, and lay eggs. Two major flights occur each year. In the spring, starting in February in Florida and peaking in March, Tawny mole cricket adults are attracted to lights, with major flights during the full moon. Southern mole cricket flights begin in March in Florida and peak in early May. Flight periods of each cricket species are delayed about a month in more northern areas such as North Carolina. Flights also may be delayed during cool, wet, windy weather conditions. The spring flight is the larger of the two flights. The second flight (the dispersal flight) is made in fall between August and December. This dispersal flight enables new generation adults to reach previously uninfested areas, locations previously protected from crickets, and areas already populated by these insects. The flights may be up to six miles per night.

Mole crickets mate and disperse via flying in the spring. Adult males attract females by using a harp-shaped area located on the wing between the two forelegs. This "harp" resonates to produce a mating call. Males construct trumpet-shaped chambers at the soil surface during the mating period to increase the intensity of the mating calls. This also helps ensure females are attracted to areas with good soil moisture to lay eggs. Hollow tops of these chambers are often visible in early spring.

Inspection by flushing should be performed throughout this period and females constantly inspected for egg development. Most of the eggs are laid within the first 12 inches (0.3 m) of soil, but cool and/or dry weather may cause these chambers to be constructed at a greater depth. Females often lay eggs near where they mate as this usually is moist soil, increasing the chances of egg and nymph survival. Females usually lay about four clutches of eggs per year, and average 35 eggs per clutch. Adult males die after mating while adult females die after depositing their eggs.

In most southern areas, oviposition (egg laying) begins in late March with a peak in May. Eggs hatch in 20 to 25 days, and their emergence is complete by mid-June. Extended drought conditions may delay oviposition and egg hatch. The small nymphs are easiest to control, yet cause little visible damage; thus, they are often ignored. Nymphs feed and mature throughout the summer, molting five to eight times, although their wing buds do not appear until the last two instars. As the nymphs mature, it becomes more difficult to manage and control them. Adults begin to appear in the fall. Tawny mole crickets overwinter mostly as adults, while Southern mole crickets overwinter primarily as large nymphs. In most of the Southeast, the Southern and Tawny mole crickets have only one distinct generation per year.

Tawny mole crickets tend to tunnel deeper into the soil than the Southern mole cricket which tends to dig and feed near the soil surface. This is important as the Tawny mole cricket may escape the lethal effects of some surface-applied insecticides. The Tawny mole cricket also tends to dig two V-shaped tunnels, presumably to provide an alternative route of escaping enemies.

The life cycle of the Tawny mole cricket is similar in south Florida, although oviposition and egg hatch occur a few weeks earlier. The southern species has two generations per year in south Florida. Its egg laying occurs in early spring and again in summer, through September. Generations of short-winged mole crickets are not discrete. Egg laying occurs year-round and peaks in late spring or summer and then again, to a lesser degree, in winter.

Damage Symptoms/Signs

Mole crickets damage turf in several ways. Tawny and Short-winged mole crickets are herbivorous and consume all parts of the grass plant. The Southern mole cricket is a predator and a scavenger, feeding on earthworms and insects, and is believed not to prefer plant material as food. All three species tunnel through the surface layer of the soil, causing considerable mechanical damage to the grass roots (Figure 23–15). The tunneling also loosens the soil so the grass is often uprooted, resulting in desiccation that can disrupt and break preemergence herbicide barriers, enabling weeds to germinate (Figure 23–16). As one walks across infested turf, the ground often feels spongy because of burrowing and displacement of soil near the surface (Figure 23–17).

Most mole cricket tunneling occurs at night, with the highest activity occurring a few hours after dusk and again just before dawn. As mentioned, they make deep V- or Y-shaped tunnels to provide an alternative route to escape from predators. They are especially active after rain showers or after irrigation in warm weather. Most activity within the top two inches (5 cm) of soil occurs when night temperatures are above 60°F (15.6°C). Both nymphs and adults tunnel in the top inch of soil and come to the surface to feed when soil is moist and may tunnel up to 20 feet (6 m) per night in moist soils. Their feeding and tunneling are greatly reduced during cold weather or when soil is dry.

Inspection and Control

Four critical steps are necessary for mole cricket control.

1. Map the infestation areas in spring, since adults usually lay eggs in the same area(s) where spring damage is seen. Mapping heavily infested areas in fall also indicates where damage is likely to occur in spring.
2. Monitor egg hatch using a soapy water flush.
3. After the majority of egg hatch has occurred and before nymphs grow past one-fourth-inch (6.4-mm) long, apply the appropriate control product. This is typically from mid- to late

FIGURE 23–15 Turf damage occurs from mole cricket tunneling.

FIGURE 23–16 Mole cricket tunneling in a golf course sand trap or bunker.

FIGURE 23–17 Extensive golf course turf damage adjacent to a bunker from mole cricket tunneling.

June. Irrigate prior to application and lightly afterwards (according to label instructions) for best results.

4. Continue to monitor the treated area with the soap flush and be prepared to spot treat areas with unacceptable control.

In order to control mole crickets, a clear understanding of their life cycle and behavioral patterns is essential. A poor appreciation of what mole crickets are doing at any particular point in time is a recipe for failure (Figure 23–18). Without this appreciation, successful control is unrealistic. Maps of each golf hole are useful in scouting and should be made in October or November indicating heavily infested areas. Additional mapping should be made in late winter through spring when overwintering mole crickets become active. Tawny mole crickets typically infest the same sites yearly. Mapping can pinpoint these preferred sites, enabling spot treatment of the heaviest infested areas. Spring mapping during periods of adult activity provides knowledge on where the majority of nymphs reside and where to apply your insecticide during early summer. If these areas are not mapped, by the time one sees activity in mid- to late summer, insecticides become less effective.

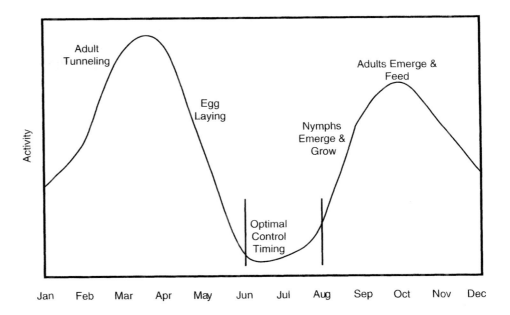

FIGURE 23–18 In typical mole cricket activity periods, the optimum timing for control is when the nymphs are young and actively growing.

To determine which species is prevalent in your particular area and the relative population level, use the following soap flush. Mix three tablespoons (44 ml) of lemon-scented liquid dishwashing detergent in two gallons (7.6 L) of water. Apply the soap mixture over a two × two foot (0.6 × 0.6 m) area of infested turf using a two-gallon (7.6-L) sprinkling can. Mole crickets present will surface in a few minutes. Flushing late in the afternoon or early in the morning, especially in moist soil, is best. This technique also may be used to verify the presence and developmental stage of nymphs. As crickets mature, the soap flush becomes less effective.

The majority of turf damage occurs in late summer and fall when the nymphs are reaching maturity. Tunneling damage also occurs in late winter and spring from overwintering adult crickets. Damage subsides in May after eggs are deposited and most adults have died. It usually is mid-July before nymphs reach sufficient size to again cause noticeable turf damage. Timing of the pesticide application is one of the most important aspects of successful mole cricket management. Mid- to late June usually is the optimum time to obtain maximum control with an insecticide application.

In south Florida, peak hatch for the Tawny mole cricket is early May; therefore, an insecticide should be applied during late May. The Southern species peak hatch occurs in June and July. Proper timing for an insecticide to control this species would be mid- to late July. If approximately equal populations of the two species are present, apply a pesticide in late June.

As mentioned, mid- to late June is generally the best time to control mole crickets with insecticides, especially preventive (long-residual) ones. This is when nymphs are large enough to feed on or near the soil surface when insecticides are applied. Materials with the longest soil residual (three to six weeks) should be used to control the nymphs at or even before this time and include fipronil (Choice) and imidacloprid (Merit). It is crucial when using these materials to apply them right at or soon after egg hatch (Table 23–5). Turf should be moist before insecticide treatments are made. Apply the pesticide as late in the day as possible, with dusk being the optimum time. Follow label directions explicitly regarding safety, dosage, application, and irrigation information. Later-hatching nymphs should also be treated with another long-residual material in mid-July. Commercial baits also are effective for this mid-July application as crickets are then big enough to ingest enough bait to make it effective. Moist soil and dry turf foliage at the time of application provide the best control with baits. Irrigation after bait application should not occur for several days as this may degrade the material.

By August, nymphs have grown considerably and become more difficult to control. Baits generally are still effective at this time, as are most curative insecticides including the pyrethroids and acephate (Orthene). Most commercial insecticides also are effective at this time. These should be applied when soils are moist to encourage cricket activity nearer the surface. Most insecticides (baits and Orthene are exceptions) need about one-half inch (1.3 cm) irrigation following application to move the material into the soil and to encourage surface activity by the crickets. The residual activity of these products is relatively short; thus, it should be applied after the bulk of

TABLE 23–5 *Comparison of insecticides for mole cricket control in turf.*

Material	Formulation	Residual	Comment
Chipco Choice[*]	0.1%G	Very long	Slit applications only; caution use label.
Chipco TopChoice[*]	0.0143%G	Long	Broadcast application; water-in; four months control.
Merit	75WP, 0.5G	Intermediate	Several formulations for various sites.
Advanced Lawn Season Long Grub Control	0.2G	Intermediate	Best for nymphs; apply at egg hatch.
Battle/Scimitar/Demand	0.88 EC	Intermediate	Best for nymphs; apply at egg hatch.
Advanced Lawn 24 Hour Grub Control	6.2G	Intermediate	Low odor; controls nymphs and adults.
Orthene, Pinpoint, Velocity	75, 15G	Short	Standard for nymphs in summer.
Baits			
Sevin	5%	Short	Good for mid- and late-season nymphs.

[*]Not effective on white grubs.

mole crickets have hatched. Late afternoon or evening application provide the best control with all products.

By fall, numerous adults are present. At this time, they cause extensive damage and are difficult to control. Feeding continues throughout the fall until cold temperatures drive the crickets further down in the soil. Spot treatment generally is the best method of controlling adults. Timing for control is at dusk as feeding is optimum at this time.

In spring, feeding by adults declines as they prepare tunnels to lay eggs. Cutting open several fertilized females in spring helps better pinpoint when they will begin to lay eggs. Young eggs are white to almost clear in color, and turn tannish-brown just before being laid. When approximately 50 percent of the developing eggs inside the females become hard and BB-like, eggs will be laid in about one week and should begin to hatch in approximately one month. No registered insecticide provides outstanding control of adults in a single application at this time. Spot treating the most damaged areas is the most economical means of control at this time. Parasitic nematodes also work best on adult crickets; thus, they may be considered at this time. Table 23–5 lists control options for mole crickets.

The parasitic nematodes, *Steinernema scapterisci* and *S. riobravis,* and the red-eyed Brazilian fly, *Ormia depleta,* are being utilized as biological control agents against mole crickets. These natural enemies were imported from South America and are specific mole cricket parasites, while harmless to non-target organisms. The nematodes enter the crickets through the mouth or spiracles. They penetrate the gut and enter the hemocoel where bacteria is released in the hemolymph. The mole cricket then dies from bacterial poisoning. The nematodes pass through several generations inside the dead mole cricket. About 100,000 nematodes emerge from a single insect. The red-eyed fly, a tachinid, locates mole crickets by their singing and deposits live maggots on or near their host.

As with most biological control agents, the beneficial nematodes and the red-eyed fly are slower to control the mole cricket host and control will never be 100 percent. However, as the populations of these beneficial organisms increase, control effectiveness also increases. The parasitic nematodes are most effective on adult crickets that are prevalent during early spring (e.g., February in Florida, March in North Carolina) and early fall (October to November before frost). Providing good soil moisture also is necessary for survival of these parasitic nematodes. Tawny mole crickets avoid contact with endopathogenic fungi (*Beauveria busiana* and *Metarhizium anidopliae*), suggesting these could potentially be used in mole cricket management.

White Grubs

Species

White grubs (order Coleoptera, family Scarabaeidae), the larvae of scarab beetles, are among the most serious insect pests in the northern United States (Figure 23–19). In the southern United States they typically are more of a problem in localized areas. Although over 1,500 different scarab beetles occur in North America, the most common in turf include (Figure 23–20):

FIGURE 23–19 Various white grub larvae and adults feed on turf roots.

FIGURE 23–20 This illustration displays various white grub adults.

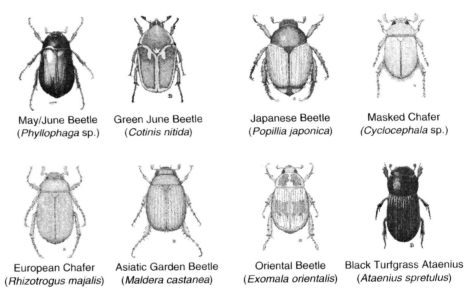

May/June Beetle
(*Phyllophaga* sp.)

Green June Beetle
(*Cotinis nitida*)

Japanese Beetle
(*Popillia japonica*)

Masked Chafer
(*Cyclocephala* sp.)

European Chafer
(*Rhizotrogus majalis*)

Asiatic Garden Beetle
(*Maldera castanea*)

Oriental Beetle
(*Exomala orientalis*)

Black Turfgrass Ataenius
(*Ataenius spretulus*)

- Japanese beetle, *Popillia japonica* Newman, is the most commonly found grub.
- May beetles, *Phyllophaga* sp.
- Black turfgrass ataenius, *Ataenius spretulus* Haldeman.
- Green June beetle, *Cotinis nitida* (Linnaeus).
- Masked chafers, *Cyclocephala borealis* and *C. lurida.*
- European chafer, *Rhizotrogus majalis* (Razoumowsky).
- Asiatic garden beetle (*Maladera castanea*).

Native species to the United States include masked chafers, black ataenius, and various May or June beetles. Introduced species include Japanese beetle, European chafer, Asiatic garden beetle, and Oriental beetles.

Insect Description

The grub larvae are similar in appearance. They have white to cream-colored robust bodies with brown heads, have three pair of small legs, and have a dark area at the rear of their 10-segmented abdomen. Depending on the species, they range from three-eighths to two inches (1 to 5 cm) long when mature and rest in a C-shaped position, especially when disturbed.

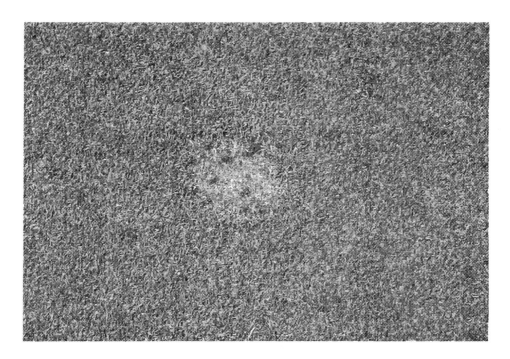

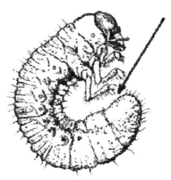

Black ataenius grubs are quite small, one-fourth inch (0.6 cm), compared to May and June beetles. They are sometimes mistaken for young grubs of Japanese beetles, masked chafers, or other larger species. BTA grubs can be distinguished by a pair of padlike bumps at the tip of the abdomen, just in front of the anal slit. These are fairly easy to discern with a 10X hand lens. The main blood vessel, which runs longitudinally down the back, typically appears almost black in contrast to the gray-white body. The black ataenius grubs tend to be a more serious problem in northern states, especially on bluegrass and bentgrass roots (Figure 23–21). Specific identification of larvae is difficult and is based on the form, shape, and arrangement of course hair, bristles, or spines (the raster) on the end abdominal segments (Figures 23–22 and 23–23) (Table 23–6).

Biology and Distribution

Scarabs have a complete life cycle involving eggs, larvae, pupae, and adults. Depending on the species, less than one year up to four years are required to complete their life cycle. The most common life cycle lasts one year. Adult beetles start flying in June or July, feeding on foliage of many ornamental plants. They mate and, for most white grub species such as *Cyclocephala,* females burrow through the thatch into the soil where their eggs are deposited. Their eggs are usually laid during May into mid-July one to two inches (2.5 to 5 cm) below the soil surface. During July through August, eggs hatch, and the young first instar larvae, which are about one-eighth-inch (3-mm) long, begin feeding on turfgrass roots. The grubs continue feeding on the grass roots, molt twice, and grow larger to about one-inch (2.5-cm) long until winter before working their way deeper into the soil just below the frost line to overwinter. The following spring they return to the rootzone and continue to feed on grass roots until April to June. They then pupate a few inches below the soil

FIGURE 23–23

Illustration of the anal region of white grubs showing the spine patterns.

May/June Beetle
(*Phyllophaga* sp.)

Green June Beetle
(*Cotinis nitida*)

Japanese Beetle
(*Popillia japonica*)

Masked Chafer
(*Cyclocephala* sp.)

European Chafer
(*Rhizotrogus majalis*)

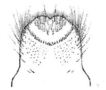
Asiatic Garden Beetle
(*Maldera castanea*)

Oriental Beetle
(*Exomala orientalis*)

Black Turfgrass Ataenius
(*Ataenius spretulus*)

TABLE 23–6 *Identification of white grubs based on the shape and patterns of their anal slit and spines.*

Insect	Anal slit shape	Spine pattern
Japanese beetle	Transverse	Distinct V-shaped pattern of spines pointing toward the insect's head.
European chafer	Branched	Two rows, roughly parallel to each other, resembling a partly open zipper.
Oriental beetle	Transverse	Two rows, roughly parallel to each other.
Masked chafer	Transverse	Random pattern of spines scattered in the anal region.
Green June beetle	Transverse	Two short rows or spines, parallel to each other. Few additional spines are present. The three pairs of legs are greatly reduced (very small).
Asiatic garden beetle	Branched	Tightly packed semicircle of spines just in front of the anal slit; also have a cream-colored tumorlike expansion on the sides of the mandibles on the head.
Black turfgrass ataenius	Branched	Has a pair of padlike bumps at the tips of the abdomen, just in front of the anal slit. No distinct pattern of spines is present, but 40 to 45 irregularly placed setae are; also has a distinguishable black-colored blood vessel running down the back.

surface. Adult beetles emerge during late May through early July to mate and then lay eggs to start the cycle again. Turf damage from grubs with annual life cycles usually is most evident in late summer (late August and September), with less damage apparent during the spring feeding season.

Cyclocephala spp. have a one-year life cycle. *Popillia* have a one-year life cycle in most of the United States but require two years in the more northern latitudes. Their larvae are peculiar as they crawl on their backs like green June beetles. *Phyllophaga* have a three-year life cycle. Species with more than one-year life cycles spend the extra year or two in the grub stage, feeding throughout the growing season and moving deeper into the soil each winter.

Ataenius have different life cycles than other white grubs and involve two generations per year in most areas. The adults overwinter in protective areas such as ground covers or tall fescue clumps, emerge in late March through April, and lay eggs during May through mid-June. Larvae emerge from late May through mid-July, feed, and grow through two molts. In late June and July, mature larvae cease feeding and burrow deep into the soil to pupate. Adults emerge in late July and August. These first-generation adults begin laying eggs in July and produce a second generation. The second generation beetles emerge, feed on grass roots during July and August, mate, and fly to overwintering wooded sites at the perimeter of the turf facility in September and October. Turf damage from *Ataenius* is most obvious in July, especially if the weather is hot, and again in August. Only one generation occurs in upstate New York and New England with grubs present from June to August.

Damage Symptoms/Signs

Grubs feed on all species of grass, although green June beetle grubs tend to feed mainly on decaying organic matter. They feed on the roots at, or just below, the soil-thatch interface and cause large patches of turf to die. Damage is most pronounced from mature grubs in late summer and early fall (August through October) and less so during spring (April and May). During heavy infestations, the soil surface may become very loose and spongy to walk on. In severe cases, roots are pruned so extensively that the turf mat can be rolled back like a carpet exposing the C-shaped white grubs (Figure 23–24). Damage is ill-timed, being just prior to summer stress for cool-season grasses and just prior to dormancy for warm-season grasses. Symptoms of grub infestation include a gradual decline forming a yellow mosaic pattern, or consistently wilting grass in an area even though adequate water is available (Figure 23–25). Continued feeding causes larger patches of turf to thin and die, allowing weeds to invade. Additional damage may occur from predatory animals such as armadillos, birds, hogs, skunks, raccoons, moles, or opossums (Figure 23–26). Unlike the other white grubs, green June beetle grubs do not feed primarily on plant roots but uproot the grass and push-up small mounds of soil. Adult scarab beetles do not feed on turfgrasses; however, some adult scarab beetles (e.g., Japanese beetle) aggressively feed on ornamental plants and trees during June and July.

Inspection and Control

Good turf management such as adequate moisture and fertilization help the turf withstand moderate grub infestations. Adult beetles are often found in swimming pools, in areas under lights, or slowly crawling across turf areas. To check for grubs, use a spade to cut three sides of a one-foot square (0.3 m^2) piece of sod. The cuts should be two inches (5 cm) deep at the edge of one of the off-color areas. Force the spade under the sod and lay it back. See if the grass roots are chewed off and sift through the soil looking for the larvae. Check several places in the turf area. As a rule of thumb, if an average of three to seven grubs are found per square foot, an insecticide should be applied. However, irrigated areas and lower-maintenance areas can withstand 25 to 50 grubs per square foot (270 to $540/\text{m}^2$), depending on the species and size.

FIGURE 23–24 White grubs feeding on turf roots.

FIGURE 23–25 Turf damage symptoms appearing from white grub feeding. Damage often resembles drought stress even when adequate soil moisture is present.

FIGURE 23–26 Digging damage to turf occurs from predatory animals such as armadillos, birds, hogs, skunks, raccoons, moles, or opossums searching for white grubs.

The Japanese beetle is one of the easier species to manage while oriental beetles and European chafers are more problematic. Biological control has been provided by strains of the bacterium, *Bacillus popilliae* and *B. thuringiensis* (Bt), and parasitic nematodes, *Heterorhadbitis bacteriophora* and *Steinernema* sp. The milky disease from this bacteria is most active on Japanese beetle grubs. Grubs ingest this while feeding and the bacteria causes the body fluids to turn a milky white color (hence, the name) prior to grub death. Bts produce crystalline proteins that destroy the insect's gut lining. Bacteria population buildup and control require an extended time period, typically three to five years. The parasitic nematodes show promise but must be applied yearly within moist soil. A dark-colored, hairy wasp, *Scolia dubia*, is often seen hovering over turf in late August or September. Female wasps sting a grub to paralyze it and deposit an egg; upon hatching, the wasp larva consumes the grub. These wasps are virtually harmless to humans unless picked up or stepped on with bare feet.

Commercial insecticides are partially (75 to 90 percent) effective. This is due, in part, to the insect's subterranean habit of the larvae that reduces the effectiveness of most surface-applied insecticides. Timing is critical, and application should be just after egg laying for targeted species when using systemic insecticides. A contact insecticide such as trichlorfon or carbaryl also may be needed in spring if damage is excessive by overwintering second-instar grubs. Once grubs reach the third-instar stage in late spring, insecticides become less effective than when grubs are small and actively feeding. Larger grubs in fall are much more difficult to control and tend to go deeper in the soil when temperatures cool. These grubs emerge in spring and are also very difficult to control.

Two windows of opportunity exist for maximum grub control: pre-grub damage and post-grub damage. Pre-grub damage occurs during the time from pre-egg lay to second-instar grubs, typically early June through mid-July. Longer residual products such as imidacloprid (Merit), thiamethoxam (Meridian), and halofenozide (Mach II) typically provide the best control then. Control is slow with these materials, typically occurring 10 to 20 days after application. Although effective on small grubs, these materials are less efficacious on larger, more mature grubs.

Post-grub damage occurs when grubs are larger—late second to third instar, typically from late August through spring (March and April) of the following year. Damage from vertebrate pests also often occurs then. Trichlorfon (Dylox) and carbaryl (Sevin) provide quick knockdown as a rescue treatment during this time. Control is fairly quick, within one to two days after application. These, however, have a very short residual (<1 week) and require multiple applications for extended control. One common problem of using post-grub damage products is the presence of piles of dead, smelly grubs littering the soil surface that require a morning-after clean-up.

Control will be more effective if the soil is kept moist for several days before treatment to encourage grubs to come closer to the soil surface, and thereby more susceptible to insecticides. Apply as late in the afternoon as practical and irrigate immediately with one-fourth to one-half-inch (0.6 to 1.3-cm) of water for maximum effectiveness. Thatch control also is extremely important as excessive thatch tends to bind or tie-up most insecticides. Enhanced soil degradation of certain insecticides used for grub control also is currently suspected.

Ataenius control is best timed in spring (late May), when adults are laying eggs, using a longer residual product. If control methods are delayed until damage is evident, control becomes less effective since the grubs have finished feeding and are less affected by the insecticide. Insecticides should be lightly watered-in to move them into the thatch layer where the insects are located. Alternative control timing is when larvae begin to hatch from late May on. These applications should be thoroughly watered-in to move the materials through the thatch to the soil layer.

Billbugs

Species

In cool-season grasses: the bluegrass billbug, *Sphenophorus parvulus* Gyllenhal; the lesser billbug, *S. minimus;* and the Denver or Rocky Mountain billbug, *S. cicatristriatus* are most important. In warm-season grasses: the hunting billbug, *Sphenophorus venatus vestitus* Chittenden; and the Phoenix billbug, *S. phoeniciensis* on bermudagrass are most important. Billbugs are in the insect order Coleoptera, family Curculionidae.

Insect Description

Billbugs are weevils or beetles with distinguishable snouts (or bills). Adult beetles are about three-eighths-inch (1-cm) long, typically weevil-like in appearance with a short, fairly broad recurved snout (Figure 23–27), and are relatively broad in their shoulder regions. They have chewing mouthparts at the tip of their distinctive snouts. They are gray to black but often are covered with soil, giving the beetle a dirty appearance. Grubs are 3/8-inch (1-cm) long when mature, the body is white with a tan head, and they are legless.

Billbugs are not persistent problems in turfgrass. Damage from this pest usually is sporadic. Several years may elapse before infestations reoccur. Zoysia and bermudagrass grown in the warm-season and transition areas are the hunting billbug's favorite hosts; however, bahiagrass, St. Augustinegrass, and centipedegrass also are attacked. The bluegrass billbug is a pest of bluegrass and other cool-season grasses in the north from Washington State across to the East Coast. Billbugs are native to North America.

FIGURE 23–27   Hunting billbug adult and larva have a distinctive snout.

Biology and Distribution

Both larvae and adults injure turfgrasses. Adults feed by inserting their mouthparts into the center of the grass stem. However, adult billbug feeding is not considered very damaging. In cool-season grasses, adult female billbugs bore cavities in grass stems near the crown in spring (May and June) and deposit eggs in these cavities. Eggs are generally white, bean-shaped, and about 1/16-inch (1.6-mm) long. Legless, grub-like larvae hatch in three to ten days and feed inside the grass stem and crown area to the degree stems can easily be pulled out by hand by late June. Eventually the larvae destroy the crown and drop out the stem once they become too large to fit within the plant. In late June into early July, the mature (3/8-inch, 9.5-mm long) larvae dig one to two inches (2.5 to 5 cm) into the soil and form a pupal cell. In the cell or chamber, pupae gradually mature into adults over a two-week period. Adults begin to emerge in late July, and often are observed climbing walls and windows. They overwinter as adults, often in the junction of turf and sidewalks as well as hedgerows. During early spring (April and May) when daytime temperatures consistently reach 65 to 68°F, adults emerge from winter hibernation and are often visible crawling over paved surfaces on their way to feed and to deposit eggs on turf. Normally, only one generation occurs per year. Peak feeding activity for adults is during July.

In warm-season grasses, females chew holes into stems (stolons) of bermudagrass and zoysiagrass and insert their eggs. After hatching, larvae feed on the stems, drop into the soil, and feed externally on grass parts. Adults first appear in late summer (September to October). However, larvae may still be present through the fall.

Larvae commonly remain active through the winter, feeding on dormant stolons and crowns. Damage often is not evident until spring when the bermudagrass or zoysiagrass starts to green-up. Damage is often mistaken for small spring dead spot disease or "delayed spring green-up syndrome."

Larvae mature from February into early May, pupate, and lay eggs as adults throughout the summer. Since turf growth is rapid in summer, feeding damage often goes unnoticed then.

Damage Symptoms/Signs

Most damage is in June and July. Damage resembles fertilizer burn or disease; however, the grass easily breaks off at the crown ("tug test"). Grab several affected stems and tug up. Damaged stems easily break off just below the thatch level and tan sawdust-like frass is evident at the base. Lack of mobility of the legless larvae result in small irregular areas of dead grass, resembling dollar spot disease. When the stem is consumed, the larvae migrate downward and feed on roots. Damage to the turf from mature larvae resembles white grub damage with sloped, sunny areas often showing damage first. Larvae are found in the soil one to three inches deep, among roots and runners. The larval stage lasts three to five weeks. Pupation occurs in the soil. The average length of their life cycle is about 30 days. One generation occurs yearly. Turf injury is much more pronounced during extended dry weather than when ample rainfall or irrigation is available and damage often resembles drought or heat stress. Billbugs overwinter in any stage in the south, but overwinter mostly as adults in the north. Adults tend to be a problem in spring while grubs cause damage in summer, especially when the turf suffers from moisture stress.

Inspection and Control

To determine if billbugs are causing problems, inspect the rootzone as with white grubs. Pitfall traps are used to monitor spring adult activity. Watching driveways, steep-walled sandtraps, and sidewalks for adult migration also aids in determining a pest presence. Damage usually occurs as spotty, brown patches, first along driveways and sidewalks. Control involves cultural (proper irrigation and fertilization), plant resistance (endophyte-enhanced ryegrass or fescue), and preventive and curative insecticides.

As a rule-of-thumb, if an average of 10 billbug larvae are found per square foot ($107/m^2$), an insecticide should be applied. Damage from moderate infestations may be masked with light fertilization and adequate water. Beneficial fungus, *Beauveria* sp., and nematodes, *Steinernema* sp., show promise for biological control. Endophyte-containing ryegrasses and fescues often are resistant or tolerant to attack. Once billbug damage is noticeable, pesticide control often is unsatisfactory. Successful control, therefore, focuses on anticipating the problem. Control with insecticides have been most beneficial when timed in spring from April to mid-May when adults emerge from winter and are searching for oviposition sites. If more than five adults are observed during a five-minute period, a pesticide application may be warranted. Treat newly mowed turf and lightly water-in to move the insecticide into the thatch where the grubs reside. Preventive control includes chlorpyrifos (Dursban), most pyrethroids (e.g., DeltaGard, Scimitar, Tempo, Talstar, etc.), imidacloprid (Merit), and halofenozide (Mach 2). If using imidacloprid, consider delaying treatment until late May or early June to also help reduce mole cricket and white grub eggs. Curative control is difficult to achieve. This is best attempted in mid- to late June into July as a soil drench. Carbaryl (Sevin) and, to a lesser extent, trichlorfon (Dylox) have had the best results as a curative treatment.

ADDITIONAL TURFGRASS INSECTS

Other insects can occasionally become important pests of various turfgrasses. However, their occurrence and damage is usually very regionalized and normally minor. Exceptional weather conditions (e.g., extremely dry) generally are associated with these.

Grasshoppers

Numerous species (most often *Melanoplus* spp.) of grasshoppers (order Orthoptera, family Acrididae) are found throughout the world. They are turfgrass pests mostly during periods of exceptional drought in locations of low annual rainfall such as the Great Plains. They feed by chewing the foliage of a wide range of plants. Well-maintained turfgrass rarely has problems unless the grasshoppers are present in high numbers on adjacent crops. Generally, one or two generations occur yearly and they overwinter as eggs in the soil.

European Crane Fly

Tipula paludosa Meigen (order Diptera, family Tipulidae) is a pest most commonly found in the Pacific Northwest. Larvae initially are white, wormlike maggots and have four instars. Later, they become small, gray-brown, wormlike creatures with a tough skin and are commonly referred to as "leather jackets." The third instar is the overwintering stage; the third and fourth instars do the most turf damage in spring. Adults have very long legs and resemble large mosquitoes with their large bodies, approximately one-inch (2.5-cm) long. The larvae feed on turfgrass roots and crowns, causing browning when threshold numbers approach 20 to 25 per square feet (215 to

FIGURE 23–28 Adult two-line spittlebug, which is an occasional pest of turfgrasses.

269/m^2). Feeding by larvae progresses slowly in winter, with most damage to turf occurring in spring. Leather jackets rest during the day in the soil and feed mostly at night. Adults may congregate near houses, often exciting homeowners into thinking immediate control is necessary. However, they do not bite or sting and cause no damage to houses. Control may be necessary for sod operations to prevent accidental shipment of larvae to uninfested areas, as well as for golf greens that are expensive to replace if extensive damage occurs.

Two-line Spittlebug

Spittlebugs, *Prosapia bicincta* (Say) (order Homoptera, family Cercopidae) (Figure 23–28) are an occasional pest of turfgrasses, especially centipedegrass and, to a lesser degree, St. Augustinegrass, bermudagrass, and ornamentals, especially Burford holly. Other grasses attacked by spittlebugs include bahiagrass, pangolagrass, and ryegrasses. They occur from Maine to Florida and westward to Iowa, Kansas, and Oklahoma. The nymphs are initially reddish, but turn white and live within a white frothy mass or "spittle" (Figure 23–29). Nymphs and adults feed by sucking juices from the grass through their needlelike mouthparts. Infested grass will have spittle masses present, and tips of the grass will turn yellow, followed by browning and curling. Generally two generations occur yearly (peaking in late spring and late summer) and they overwinter as eggs in hollow stems or among plant debris.

Chinch Bugs

Chinch bugs include the southern chinch bug, *Blissus insularis* Barber, and the hairy chinch bug, *Blissus leucopterus hirtus* Montandon (order Hemiptera, family Lygaeidae). The most serious insect pest of St. Augustinegrass is the southern chinch bug (Figure 23–30). It may also attack bermudagrass. The hairy chinch bug is a pest of bluegrass, ryegrass, zoysiagrass, bentgrass, and fescue in the north and upper midwestern United States.

Chinch bugs damage turf by piercing plant tissue and sucking sap with their needlelike mouthparts. They may also introduce toxic saliva into the plant during this feeding process that may block xylem and phloem tissue. Nymphs do the most damage. Affected areas appear as yellow spots or patches 3 to 10 feet in diameter and often are noticed first along concrete or asphalt paved edges or in water-stressed areas where the grass is growing in full sun (Figure 23–31). By blocking xylem and phloem tissue, leaves wither as in drought and food from photosynthesis does not translocate to the roots. Plants eventually die.

FIGURE 23–29 Nymphs of two-line spittlebugs are reddish-white in color and live within a white frothy mass or "spittle."

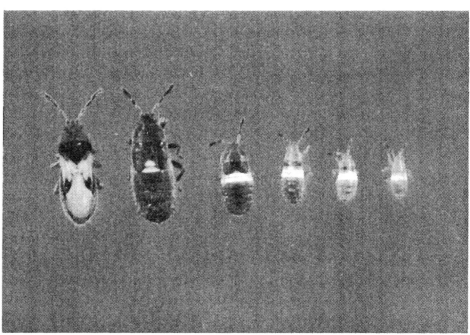

FIGURE 23–30 The life stages of chinch bugs.

Adults are about one-fifth inch (0.5-cm) long, and black, with white patches on their wings. Nymphs range from 1/20-inch (1.3-mm) long to nearly adult size. There are five nymphal instars. The small nymphs are bright red with a white band across the back, but become black and white in color as they mature. Chinch bugs overwinter as inactive adults and become active in spring, where they feed and mate. One or two generations occur in the north while up to seven occur in south Florida. Eggs are laid in sheaths or pushed into soft soil and protected places. In summer, eggs hatch in 10 days to two weeks, and the young develop to adults in three weeks. Adults become active when daytime temperatures reach 70°F (21°C).

Detection of chinch bugs begins by parting grass on the edge of infested areas and observing the soil surface. All stages can be seen moving through the loose duff on the soil surface. In extremely heavy infestations, some can be seen crawling over grass blades, sidewalks, and outside walls of houses. Their presence can also be confirmed by using the flotation method.

Control begins by preventing drought stress since damage symptoms are less when grass is well-watered. Reduce summer fertilization with quick-release nitrogen sources as the resulting

FIGURE 23–31 Chinch bug feeding creates damage on St. Augustinegrass. Damage is most severe during hot, dry weather conditions especially adjacent to pavement areas.

lush grass growth is more susceptible to damage. Spot spraying before extensive damage occurs is best. Threshold levels of 15 to 20 per square foot (160 to 215/m^2) may warrant control. Most insecticides for chinch bugs should not be watered-in.

Ground Pearls

Margarodes meridionalis Morrill (order Homoptera, family Margarodidae) are tiny scales that live in the soil and suck juices from grass roots. Warm-season grasses, especially centipedegrass and less often, bermudagrass, grown from North Carolina across to Southern California are preferred hosts. Ground pearls are spherical and range in size from a grain of sand to about one-eighth-inch (3-mm) diameter. They are yellowish-purple in color and look very much like pearls. Eggs are laid in the soil from March to June. The first nymphal instar, called the crawler, locates a grass root, attaches itself, and begins to cover itself with a yellowish to light-pearl-colored hard wax coating. The nymphs continue developing inside this shell and overwinter in this stage. The life cycle from egg to adult requires one, possibly two, years. Severely infested grass turns yellow, then brown, resembling drought stress occurring in irregular patches. Chemical control is currently unavailable for ground pearls since they are covered by a hard, waxy, practically impenetrable shell. In addition, ground pearls live at depths up to 10 inches (25 cm). Infested grass should be grown to follow best management practices such as raising the mowing height, providing good soil moisture, and providing adequate soil potassium to encourage rooting.

Imported Fire Ants

Fire ants are small reddish-brown to nearly black ants in the genus *Solenopsis*. They range in size from about 1/8 to 3/8 inch (3 to 9.5 mm) (Figure 23–32). Fire ant nests are easily recognized by their characteristic dome shape, size, and apparent lack of an entrance hole (Figure 23–33). Although they do not directly feed on turfgrasses, their mounds often desiccate turf areas, disrupt the turfgrass surface, cause mowing problems, and are a nuisance to golfers and maintenance personnel. In sandy soil, mounds may not maintain their shape.

Disturbance of a mound creates a characteristic aggressive "boiling" effect of ants coming out of the mound in a defensive action, attacking and stinging all intruders. Each nest may contain anywhere from a few hundred ants to 350,000 ants. It is not uncommon for infestations with 300 or more mounds per acre to occur.

Nests are usually located in open areas such as lawns, pastures, and golf courses. They frequently will take advantage of protective structures such as rocks, pavement, stumps, rotten logs, and so forth. Fire ants also reduce the yield of some 40 different crops, cause damage to electrical units (a favorite nesting location), and also damage mowing machinery.

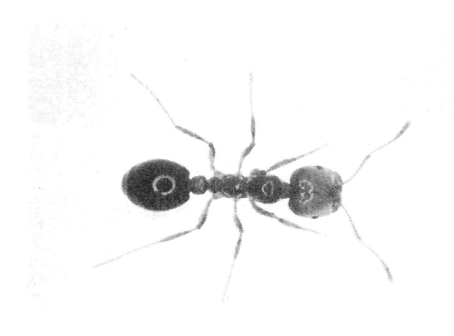

FIGURE 23–32 The imported fire ant ranges in size from one-eighth to three-eighths inch.

FIGURE 23–33 An imported fire ant colony mound is recognized by its apparent lack of entrance hole.

Wildlife is also greatly impacted by the fire ants' presence. Bob White Quail populations have been reduced by competition for their primary food source, namely small insects. Other species have fallen prey to the fire ants' omnivorous appetite.

History

Two major species of fire ants occur in the United States, *Solenopsis invicta,* the red imported fire ant, and *Solenopsis ricteri,* the black imported fire ant, as well as several native species of fire ants.

The two imported species were accidentally imported through the port of Mobile, Alabama. This occurred around 1918. Their spread has continued at a rate of about five miles per year.

It is currently estimated imported fire ants infest more than 300 million acres throughout the states of Alabama, Arkansas, California, Florida, Georgia, Louisiana, Mississippi, North Carolina, Oklahoma, South Carolina, Tennessee, Texas, and Puerto Rico. Spot infestations have occurred in Arizona, Delaware, Maryland, Nevada, and Virginia as well.

To limit the spread of imported fire ants, a federal quarantine restricts the movement of soil, potted plants, plants with soil attached, grass sod, hay, and used soil-moving equipment to uninfested areas of the United States. These items must be certified to be free from infestation.

Biology

An understanding of the biology is critical in understanding the management of the fire ant. The following are some of the highlights of the fire ants' life history as it relates to matters of control.

Establishing a colony

When a colony reaches a critical size and resources are suitably abundant, the queen ant will begin to lay eggs that will develop into sexually reproductive winged ants called alates. These alates will have a mating flight when the temperature is between 70 and 95°F (21 and 35°C) with high humidity, and usually occurs within 24 hours of a rain. Throughout much of the southeastern United States, these conditions can occur anytime throughout the year, and indeed mating flights have been recorded during 12 months of the year. The bulk of the mating flights take place in the spring and the fall. It is important to note reinfestation of a treated area can occur throughout the year.

Mating flights take place in the air. The males die immediately after the mating takes place, having served their only function within the colony. All of the other ants are female.

The female usually lands within a mile or two of her mother colony, but with a tail wind some have been recorded to fly as much as 10 to 12 miles (16 to 19 km). This is important because it demonstrates a treated area can be reinfested from fairly long distances.

After landing, the newly mated queen breaks her wings off and begins the search for a suitable nest site. This is a very dangerous time for the queen, as she is vulnerable to desiccation and numerous predators. Fewer than 1 percent ever survive to establish a viable colony. This demonstrates the tremendous reproductive potential of the fire ant.

After finding a suitable site, the queen forms a waterproof chamber sealed with soil and saliva where she will lay her eggs. This chamber may be as deep as six to eight inches (15 to 20 cm) below the surface of the soil, making it difficult to reach with pesticides. The queen will lay between 45 and 150 eggs. She will rear the larvae to adulthood, living off of the energy provided by digesting her wing muscles. Once the young mature into adults they begin to take on the work of the colony and take care of the queen. The queen, relieved of other maternal duties, begins producing eggs as her only duty. She may lay as many as 1,500 eggs per day or 350,000 eggs per year. Since she may live as long as seven years, it is imperative for any control measures to eliminate the queen.

The caste system

Fire ants, like all ants, are social insects. This means they have overlapping generations that care for the young and a caste system with specific jobs for each caste to perform. In general the youngest ants serve as nursery workers and take care of the larvae and pupae (called brood). The middle-aged workers serve as reserves, providing help wherever needed. The oldest workers serve as foragers, venturing from the colony in search of food. Even the larvae have a job to do. Fire ants cannot eat solid food, so one stage of the larvae has a big "lip" called a bucal pouch. Solid food is placed on this "lip" and the larvae secretes digestive enzymes that liquefy the solid food. Nurse ants then stroke the larvae with their antennae and the larvae regurgitates an oily liquid. Other ants then repeat this process with the nurse ants and so on. This process of passing food from one individual to another within the colony is called **tropholaxis.** Tropholaxis serves as an efficient filtering system for food. Foods that prove toxic or unsuitable are discarded, as are any sick ants. The queen is among the last ant to get any food—so she can survive. Baits with toxicants used for control must act slowly enough so all of the ants including the queen receive a lethal dose before any effects of the toxicant are revealed.

In the absence of larvae to digest food, adults can survive on liquid oils and sugars provided in the environment. Therefore, you can treat a mound and kill the queen, and a colony can still persist for up to six months.

The mound

In general there is as much mound below ground as there is above ground. However, the ants constantly change the mound—raising the mound to capture radiant heat when it is cold, and lowering the mound to reduce the effect of the sun's rays when it is too hot. The ants move up and down within the soil profile searching for the ideal temperature of 70 and 95°F (21 to 35°C). Some colonies have been found as deep as 12 to 14 feet (3.6 to 4.3 m).

The fire ants can also regulate moisture and humidity levels similarly as they do for heat. This is why fresh mounds are often seen after a rain even though the colony was always there. Each colony also contains deep tunnels to groundwater regardless of how deep that is.

Each colony has forage tunnels radiating out like the spokes of a wagon wheel in all directions. The tunnels have periodic openings that are used by the foragers. They will search for food around the opening, then return. If they don't find food, they continue down the tunnel and try at another opening. If they find food, they release a chemical called a pheromone that recruits other workers to help. Forage tunnels may reach as far as 100 yards (91 m) away from the colony.

The sting

Though most people refer to fire ant "bites," in reality this is a sting. The stinger is like a hypodermic needle delivering the venom below the skin that then burns "like fire." The stingers are used for both defense and subduing prey. The venom also contains 1 to 2 percent protein, which causes the allergic reaction many people experience.

When getting ready to sting, the fire ant will grab the victim with its mandibles, or jaws, and place the stinger precisely between the mandible and into the victim. At the same time, the ant releases an alarm pheromone, which is simply a chemical that tells the other ants to sting as well. Thus, the perception that the entire colony gets on you and they all sting at the same time is true.

Management Strategies for the Fire Ant

There are more than 150 products labeled for fire ant control. Most are effective when used properly, but none are permanently effective. As a result, retreatment will be necessary. It is very easy to control individual mounds of fire ants, as there is no known pesticide resistance. Population levels, however, are difficult to reduce. The fire ant's ability to move vertically and horizontally within the soil profile, lack of ecological competition, high reproductive potential, ability to traverse relatively great distances, and biological behaviors make population reduction a difficult proposition.

Most management strategies fall into one of four categories.

1. Bait applications
2. Individual mound treatments (IMT)
3. Combination of bait and IMT
4. General broadcast treatments

Baits

Most fire ant baits are formulated using defatted corn grit as the bait matrix and soybean oil as the carrier. The solid yellow stuff is defatted corn grit and the active ingredient is added to soybean oil, which is then added to the defatted corn grit. The soybean oil is what attracts the ants and is an important part of the bait. Over time, soybean oil can go rancid and become unattractive to the ants. Therefore, it is imperative fresh bait be used.

Baits, when used properly, have a number of advantages that make them an appealing choice for fire ant management.

1. They have a low level of toxicity to nontarget organisms.
2. They are easy to find in most retail stores.
3. They can be quickly applied.
4. You can kill mounds you cannot see or reach.
5. They work well for sensitive areas such as ponds or wells.
6. They are relatively inexpensive when properly used.
7. They kill the queen and the rest of the colony.

8. They kill colonies outside of the treatment area.
9. Active ingredients do not persist in the environment.

Disadvantages include:

1. If used as an individual mound treatment, they can be expensive.
2. They are often very slow acting.
3. A knowledge of fire ant biology is necessary for optimum control.
4. Control levels rarely exceed a 95 percent reduction.
5. Rebound of the population is usually about three months.
6. Active ingredients break down quickly in sunlight and water.

The active ingredients used in baits can be grouped into two general categories. The first group includes the compounds that use a toxin as the active ingredient. The second group uses insect growth regulators (**IGR**) as active ingredients (Table 23–7).

In general, research demonstrates most baits provide a similar level of control—between 85 percent and 95 percent reduction in the fire ant population. Differences become evident when you start to look at how quickly a population reduction occurs and how long this lasts.

The insect growth regulators take longer to see an effect, but they also tend to give control for an extended period of time when compared to those products using toxins as the active ingredient.

Several things should be remembered to ensure success with any fire ant bait used. First, because the products break down quickly, they need to be applied when the fire ants are foraging. Remember fire ants forage when the surface soil temperature is between 70 and 95°F (21 and 35°C). The easiest way to tell if fire ants are foraging is to place a small amount of test bait in the treatment area and wait about 30 minutes. If fire ants are foraging they will find the bait in that amount of time and bait can be applied. If fire ants are not foraging, do not apply the bait.

Secondly, the most effective method of bait application is to broadcast it. However, one of the greatest difficulties with broadcast treatment of fire ant bait formulations is the low rate. Most call for 1 to 1.5 pounds per acre (1.1 to 1.7 kg/ha). This is a small amount for a large area and overapplication is common. For best results:

- **Use fresh baits**—As previously stated, the baits can spoil and become unattractive to the fire ants. Buy only what you need for a single application.
- **Apply baits on a dry surface and when rain is not expected for at least 12 hours.**
- **Apply baits when ants are actively foraging**—These products break down quickly in sunlight and water. If the ants are actively foraging, they will pick up the bait before the bait's effectiveness is reduced. If the fire ants are active, their ability to outcompete other ants will reduce the effect of the bait on nontarget ant species.

TABLE 23–7 *Insecticides used for broadcast treatment for fire ant control.*

Active ingredient	Trade name/s	Type	Advantages/Disadvantages
Hydramethylnon	Amdro, Maxforce	Toxin	Amdro is easily available at most lawn and garden centers and is relatively cheap.
Fenoxycarb	Logic, Award	IGR	Most commonly available IGR.
Methoprene	Extinguish	IGR	The only product labeled for use in gardens and pastures.
Spinosad	Justice, Eliminator Fire Ant Killer with Conserve, Penn Kill Fire Ant Killer	Toxin	Derived from a bio-active fungi. Many people consider these products as organic due to their origin.
Pyriproxyfen	Distance	IGR	Difficult to find, but works well.
Abamectin	Ascend, Clinch, Varsity	—	—
Fipronil	Choice, Chipco FireStar, TopChoice	Toxin	Make broadcast applications when ants are actively foraging (looking for food); this is typically in the morning or evening. Do not apply immediately before or after irrigation or rain. Fire ants will begin to die in about 14 days; however, allow four to six weeks to achieve control. Superintendents may make a total of four applications per year if necessary.

- **Do not mix baits with other materials such as fertilizer**—Ants have a very good sense of smell and will not pick up bait tainted with undesirable odors. Make sure the spreader you are using is clean, or better yet, used only for spreading fire ant bait.
- **Calibrate and measure properly.**

Individual Mound Treatments (IMT)

Products labeled for individual mound treatments are, as a whole, very effective in eliminating 98 percent or more of the mounds treated (Table 23–8). The not-so-obvious disadvantage is they kill only the mounds that are treated. Many newly established colonies, or colonies in intensively managed areas, are difficult to see and are therefore missed with this form of treatment.

Advantages to IMT include:

- High percentage of mounds treated are eliminated.
- Most act very quickly and eliminate mounds within a few hours.
- Most are inexpensive.
- Most are readily available.
- They kill the queen and the rest of the colony.
- They are very fast acting.

TABLE 23–8 *Insecticides for individual mound treatments of fire ants.*

Active ingredient	Trade name(s)	Type	Advantages/Disadvantages
Acephate	Orthene Fire Ant Killer, Orthene TTO	Dust/soluble powder	-Easy to use, no drenching of mound required. -Smells very bad!
Clorpyifos	Dursban	Granular	-Labeled uses being removed from market. -Requires drenching of mounds to be effective.
	Diazinon	Granular	-Labeled uses being removed from market. -Requires drenching of mounds to be effective.
Acephate	Pinpoint 15 G, Velocity	Granular	-May injure grass in treated area. -Velocity comes in shaker can. -Pinpoint has 12-hour reentry interval. -Neither product requires water-in after application.
Carbaryl	Sevin 70 WP	Wettable powder	-Requires premixing of wettable powder before treating mound. -Very inexpensive.
		Aerosol	-Very fast and effective. -Very expensive. -Works best for those individual mounds that need to be eliminated quickly. -Difficult to find in retail stores. -Restricted largely to commercial uses.
Fipronil	Choice, Chipco FireStar, TopChoice	Granular	Shake the granules uniformly around the mound, but do not disturb the mound. Broadcast the granules in a circle about four or five feet in diameter around the mound. Apply when ants are actively foraging (looking for food); this is typically in the morning or evening. Do not apply immediately before or after irrigation or rain. Fire ants will begin to die in about 14 days; however, allow four to six weeks to achieve control. Superintendents may make a total of four applications per year, if necessary.
Baits			Can be used as individual mound treatments, but are more effective as broadcast treatments.

Disadvantages to IMT include:

- Greater concentration of toxins.
- Not recommended for sensitive areas such as wells, ponds, playgrounds, and pet runs. See reentry intervals listed on labels for these sites.
- It is easy to miss some mounds that are difficult to see.
- Some products require premixing, or drenching.

The Two Step

The two step method is a combination of the two methods previously discussed, and is the most commonly recommended method by researchers and extension personnel. All of the methods discussed for both baits and IMTs apply to this method of fire ant management.

Broadcast fire ant baits while fire ants are foraging, wait 10 to 14 days, and then use individual mound treatments on mounds that continue to be a problem.

The two step is recommended twice a year, usually in the April to May time frame and again in the September to October time frame.

Other Ants

Other ants do not pose a threat to humans but disrupt play by their extensive mound construction on putting surfaces that often invade golf courses (Figure 23–34). In addition to the mounds, predatory birds may cause further damage by probing the nest openings. The most common ant species that causes these mounds is *Lasius neoniger*. These social insects consist of numerous sterile female workers and usually only one reproductive queen. The workers feed and tend to the queen ant and her eggs and larvae. Mounds are passageways for the workers and interconnected chambers compose the underground living quarters, usually 10 to 15 inches (15 to 38 cm) below the soil surface. The worker ants often feed on small insects and insect eggs and on the sugary honeydew produced by root aphids.

Control is often achieved with commercial ant baits. Small amounts of the bait are sprinkled around the mounds where the worker ants carry the bait into the nest for the queen and her brood to feed on. After the queen is eliminated, the colony cannot reproduce and dies out. Irrigation should be withheld for at least eight hours after application to allow time for the worker ants to carry the bait to the queen. About two days are needed to eliminate the colony. Baits are usually spot treated, most often by shaker cans. Early spring is best for applications, since nests are small and the buildup of mounds that occurs in late spring and summer is avoided.

FIGURE 23–34 Ant hill mounds disrupt play on a golf green.

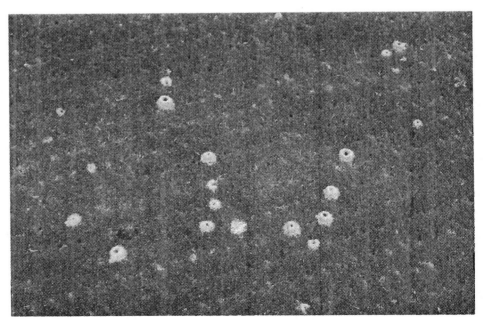

Earthworm(s)

Earthworm activity on a golf course is generally considered beneficial as this indicates ecologically healthy turfgrass growing conditions. Their feeding and burrowing habits initiate thatch decomposition, stimulate microorganism activity, increase the availability of certain soil nutrients, increase soil aeration, and generally improve overall soil quality. However, from these benefits, earthworm casting on golf course fairways is an extremely challenging turfgrass management issue. Casting occurs when earthworms ingest soil and leaf tissue to extract nutrients and then emerge from their burrows to deposit fecal matter (casts) as mounds of soil on the turfgrass surface (Figure 23–35). These castings interfere with maintenance practices, play, and overall turf aesthetics. No products are specific to control earthworm casting, and the effects of cancelled long-residual pesticides such as chlorinated hydrocarbons or mercury-based materials have worn off.

A major earthworm species in the United States is the common night crawler (*Lumbricus terrestris*). *Apporectodea calignosa* and *A. longa* are additional earthworms often found on golf courses. Peak casting is during the cool, wet weather in spring and late fall through winter. Night crawlers can live up to six to nine years; thus, they reoccur in the same place. Earthworms dig burrows in the soil and migrate upward with fluctuations in moisture content, soil temperature, and availability of food such as clippings and soil organic matter. It has been shown, however, that neither clipping removal nor aerification reduces earthworm casting.

Other control attempts have involved changing soil pH (high or low) that does not influence night crawler activity. Other earthworm species, however, may respond differently to changes in soil pH. Control is currently focusing on the abrasiveness and desiccation ability of sand particles through aggressive topdressing. Due to the need of multiple applications, a long-term commitment of up to five years of topdressing are needed for success. Successful yearly total topdressing rates have been between 0.75 and 1.5 inches (1.9 and 3.8 cm). Due to the expense and labor required to perform this heavy rate of topdressing, it is suggested infestation areas be mapped and a priority be placed on most infested sites. Member education about the benefits of earthworm and long-term commitment for casting control also are needed.

FIGURE 23–35 Mounds (castings) of soil caused from earthworm activity.

CHAPTER 24

Turfgrass Nematodes

INTRODUCTION

Plant parasitic nematodes, alone as well as in combination with other drought-related stresses, nutritional status, and fungal diseases, can cause serious damage to turfgrass stands. In subtropical and warm regions, parasitic nematodes are among the most important turfgrass pests. Symptoms of nematode damage to turfgrasses can be easily confused with the effects of nutritional deficiencies, water or heat stress, or other diseases. A good knowledge of nematode sampling, biology, and turfgrass management strategies for different environmental conditions is a prerequisite for successful management of turfgrass nematodes without heavy reliance on nematicides.

Nematode Description

Nematodes (sometimes called eelworms) are probably the most abundant multicellular animals known. Fortunately, the overwhelming majority are nonparasitic (free-living). They are tiny nonsegmented roundworms measuring 0.1 to 3 millimeters (1/250 to 1/8 inch). With the unaided eye, adults are barely visible. When viewed under magnification, they appear almost transparent but with definite body outlines. Most nematodes are slender (eel-like) throughout their life stages, but a few become swollen as they mature. Although flowers, stems, leaves, and roots of some plants are attacked by certain plant parasitic nematodes, all of the important nematode pests in turfgrasses are root parasites. Figure 24–1 shows a schematic diagram of a nematode.

Most nematode parasites of turfgrasses remain entirely outside of roots with only their stylet (hollow protrusible spear) thrust inside the root (these are termed **ectoparasites**). A few are **endoparasites,** where they spend part of their life cycle completely inside the roots. Some endoparasitic nematodes move freely within and out of the root for all developmental stages (termed **migratory endoparasites**) while other species remain in a permanent feeding position within the root tissue for most of their life cycle (termed **sedentary endoparasites**). Sting, ring, and stubby-root nematodes are examples of ectoparasites; lance and lesion nematodes are migratory endoparasites, while root-knot nematodes are sedentary endoparasites (Table 24–1).

Plant nematodes are aquatic animals living in the soil water film or in plant fluids. They are very well-adapted plant parasites. Females produce a few dozen to over 500 eggs each. When a host plant is unavailable, eggs of some species survive for years but hatch quickly when stimulated by exudates from plants. Their activity, growth, and reproduction increase as soil

FIGURE 24–1 A drawing showing a typical nematode.

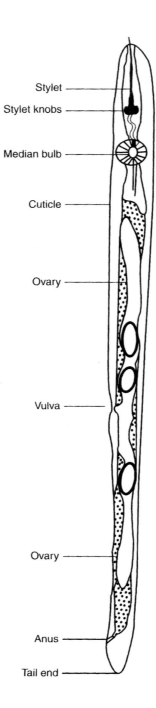

Stylet

Stylet knobs

Median bulb

Cuticle

Ovary

Vulva

Ovary

Anus

Tail end

temperature rises from about 50°F to about 90°F (10 to 32°C). Generation time is between three and six weeks for many nematodes.

How Nematodes Cause Damage

Plant nematodes are obligate parasites, which means they must find and feed on a living plant host at some stage of their life cycle. Most species attack a wide range of plant material, and can survive on weeds or on overseeded grasses. Many also may survive short periods in frozen soils. Plant-parasitic nematodes damage plants directly by their feeding activities, which involve puncturing cells (mostly in the root system) with their stylet, injecting digestive juices into the cells, and then sucking the liquid contents out. A **stylet** is a hollow, needlelike organ in the head, adapted for feeding activities. Although nematodes rarely kill their host, these feeding activities cause localized cell death, induce host reactions that change the integrity of root tissue, and provide entry points for secondary invasion by fungi, all of which result in abnormal root function. Uptake of nutrients and water by the roots is adversely affected, even-

TABLE 24–1 *Nematodes affecting turfgrasses and damage threshold levels typically used to justify nematicide application.*

Common name (Scientific name)	Most susceptible grasses	Threshold[*] (No./100 cc soil)
Endoparasitic		
Root-knot	St. Augustinegrass	80
Meloidogyne spp.	Bentgrass	80 to 100
	Bermudagrass	80
	Zoysiagrass	80
Lesion	All	150
Pratylenchus spp.		
Cyst	St. Augustinegrass	na
Heterodera spp.		
Ectoparasitic		
Sting	St. Augustinegrass	10 to 20
Belonolaimus longicaudatus	Bermudagrass	10 to 20
	Zoysiagrass	10 to 20
Lance	St. Augustinegrass	50
Hoplolaimus spp.	Bentgrass	40 to 60
	Bermudagrass	80
Ring	Centipedegrass	150 to 300
Criconemella spp.		
Stubby-root	All	100
Paratrichodorus spp.		
Sheath	All	80 to 200
Hemicycliophora spp.		
Spiral	All	200 to 600
Helicotylenchus spp.		
Awl	Turfgrass (especially bermudagrass) in wet locations	80
Dolichodorus heterocephalus		
Dagger	Rarely a turf pest	150 to 300
Xiphinema spp.		
Stunt	Rarely a turf pest	100 to 400
Tylenchorhynchus spp.		

[*]Threshold level ranges commonly used in research by universities. na = data not available.

tually weakening the plants and causing turf stand thinning. Since nematodes mostly damage turfgrass roots (and not aboveground plant parts), symptoms of injury often go unnoticed until soil water is limiting. These symptoms are often confused with environmental stress symptoms or nutritional problems and may be difficult to diagnose. The extended growing season, warm climate, and sandy soils of tropical and subtropical areas favor development of very high nematode populations and also create conditions in which grasses are most susceptible to nematode damage. Moreover, many activities and management practices on golf courses promote the development of high numbers of nematodes and increase turfgrass susceptibility to nematodes.

TURFGRASS NEMATODES

Several different kinds of nematodes can affect turf, with the most damaging described in the following pages. Table 24–1 also lists the numbers of each kind of nematode expected to cause similar levels of damage.

Sting Nematode (commonly *Belonolaimus longicaudatus,* also *B. gracilis,* and other species)

Sting nematodes are the largest of the turf parasites in the southeastern United States, with adults reaching lengths of nearly one-eighth inch (3.2 mm). They occur naturally in dune sands and the sandy soils of sandhill regions. Sand-based rootzones in constructed putting greens are ideal habitats for sting nematodes as well as other species. The following combination of characteristics describe the genus *Belonolaimus:* possession of a very long stylet with knobs at the base, a median bulb (valvulated "pump"), vermiform (eel-like) adult, two ovaries, and a round tail end. Sting nematodes use their very long stylets to siphon plant sap from turfgrass roots. These nematodes are ectoparasitic; thus, they remain outside of roots while feeding, with only their long stylets penetrated deep into the vascular tissue. Although lesions are evident throughout the root system, the most active feeding occurs at root tips. In sufficient numbers (usually ≥20/100 cubic centimeters [cc] soil), sting nematodes retard overall root development, making plants more sensitive to moisture stress. Turfgrass top growth is stunted, appears yellow, and thins out. Sting nematodes are generally found only in very sandy (>80 percent sand) soils. They feed on all grasses grown for turfgrasses, but damage is most severe on bermudagrass (Plates 24–1 and 24–2 and Figure 24–2), St. Augustinegrass, zoysiagrass, bentgrass, and ryegrasses. Many other grasses are hosts to sting nematodes including oats, centipedegrass, barley, and common ryegrass. Centipedegrass in sandy soils can be severely damaged by sting nematodes. Weedy plants such as prostrate spurge, Florida pusley, knotweed, or bahiagrass may invade sting- and also ring-nematode-infested areas (Plate 24–3).

Ring Nematodes (*Criconemella, Mesocriconemella* spp.)

These nematodes are characterized by a body with prominent rings, one ovary, vermiform adults, blunt tail, and a knobbed stylet. Ring nematodes feed ectoparasitically (from the outside of the roots) (Figure 24–3). Brown lesions appear along the roots and tips, and roots become stunted. When high numbers of ring nematodes are present, severe root rotting may occur. Ring nematodes are widely distributed on many turfgrasses (namely Kentucky bluegrass, annual bluegrass,

FIGURE 24–2 Turf root damage (right) caused by sting nematodes compared to healthy turf roots (left).

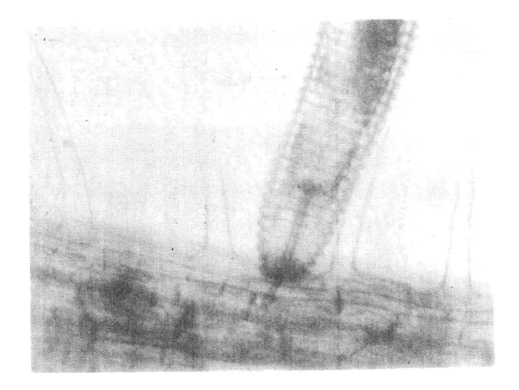

FIGURE 24–3 Ring nematode feeding ectoparasitically on turfgrass roots.

St. Augustinegrass, zoysiagrass, bermudagrass, and creeping bentgrass), but is considered to be a major pest on centipedegrass, especially in sandy soils.

Lance Nematodes (*Hoplolaimus* spp.)

The stylet knobs of lance nematodes resemble a tulip, their tail length is <1.5 times the anal body diameter, they have a medium bulb, two ovaries are present, and mature females are vermiform (bulb-shaped). These nematodes feed mostly ectoparasitically but can enter and move through the root cortex, making them very difficult to control even with chemical nematicides. For this reason, lance nematodes frequently occur in high numbers more in older turfgrass areas, such as older putting greens where other nematodes were controlled over the years with various nematicides. In zones of heavy feeding, roots exhibit slight tissue swelling followed by necrosis and sloughing off of cortical tissues. Lance nematodes have a wide host range and attack all commonly grown turfgrasses (St. Augustinegrass, bahiagrass, creeping bentgrasses, bermudagrass, annual and Kentucky bluegrasses, annual ryegrass, and zoysiagrasses). It is the most important nematode pest of St. Augustinegrass.

Root-Knot Nematodes (*Meloidogyne* spp.)

These nematodes enter and feed inside roots (endoparasites). The female enlarges into a pear-shaped mature form that remains embedded within the root (Figure 24–4). It possesses a knobbed stylet and median bulb. Second-stage larvae enter root cells with the aid of their stylet and migrate through the root cortex toward the vascular tissue, where they become stationary. Saliva secretion during feeding by the nematodes induce enlargement and accelerated division of root cells at certain points inside roots. Mature female nematodes enlarge, appear pearly white, and produce eggs in a gelatinous sac matrix that usually protrudes on the outside of the root surface. Symptoms on both fibrous and lateral roots appear as distinctively small, spherical, or elongated swellings having the same color as the adjacent root surface. Root swellings may be difficult to see without a hand lens. Root-knot nematodes are assumed to be injurious only when numerous, but their importance as a pest of turfgrasses has not been well-assessed. Root-knot nematodes have a very wide host range. Root-knot nematodes can colonize all common turfgrasses, but they are most commonly found on zoysiagrass, St. Augustinegrass, bermudagrass, and bentgrasses (Plate 24–4). Similar to lance nematodes, it has been observed that root-knot nematodes occur in

FIGURE 24–4 Root-knot nematode feeding endoparasitically in turfgrass roots.

large numbers in older greens. Their numbers may increase relative to ectoparasites, which may be differentially susceptible to certain nematicides.

Stubby-Root Nematodes (*Paratrichodorus* and *Trichodorus* spp.)

These ectoparasites are characterized by the possession of a distinctive short, curved, knobbed spear and the absence of a median bulb. They mostly feed at growing root tips, which stop elongating, may become slightly swollen and discolored (or both), and often become very short and "stubby." Lesions are large, brownish, irregular in shape, and often extend deep into the root tissue. Aboveground symptoms appear as a pronounced chlorosis with reduced growth rates. Most warm-season grasses are hosts of stubby-root nematodes. Kentucky bluegrass, tall and red fescues, St. Augustinegrass, bermudagrass, centipedegrass, and zoysiagrasses are common hosts. Numbers can fluctuate in assays of bentgrass putting greens, and their importance as pathogens of bentgrass is not well understood.

Spiral Nematodes (*Helicotylenchus* spp.)

Spiral nematodes are ectoparasites and are among the most frequently found nematodes on all common turfgrasses. They possess a median bulb, knobbed stylet, two ovaries, ventrally located tail tip, and take on a characteristic spiral shape when heat-killed. Spiral nematodes are rarely serious pests of turfgrasses when they are the dominant species encountered. However, they cannot be dismissed entirely as pathogens when they occur in high numbers or at lower populations in combination with other plant parasitic species. In high numbers, roots are poorly developed and discolored brown with premature sloughing of cortical tissues. Aboveground, the turfgrass stand becomes sparse and difficult to maintain because of reduced plant vigor. Leaf blades become more narrow and appear pale to chlorotic. Symptoms are not evident during vigorous root-and-shoot growth in the moist months of spring and early summer even in the presence of very high numbers of spiral nematodes. The nematode populations peak in the advent of both higher temperatures and decreased availability of soil moisture in the top few inches of soil (which also coincides with plant decline). Nematode numbers decline during dormancy periods, but increase again in the cooler weeks of early fall when plant growth resumes. Both warm- and cool-season grasses are good hosts for spiral nematodes.

Awl Nematodes (commonly *Dolichodorus heterocephalus*)

Awl nematodes are ectoparasites possessing a median bulb, long knobbed stylet, two ovaries, and female tail ending in a short terminal "awl-like" point. Awl nematodes are very damaging to turfgrasses in wet locations such as the low land areas near lakes, ponds, and canals. Turfgrass hosts include bentgrasses, centipedegrass, tall fescue, St. Augustinegrass, and especially bermudagrass.

Lesion Nematodes (*Pratylenchus* spp.)

Lesion nematodes are occasional turfgrass pests. They are endoparasites possessing a median bulb, a single ovary, and a short but very robust knobbed stylet (stylet length ÷ body diameter at stylet base is <1.5). Root lesions are initially minute and brown. They progressively enlarge and promote secondary fungal invasion, and may eventually girdle the root. With high populations of lesion nematodes, the root system may appear severely pruned. Both larvae and adults can penetrate and move through and between root cells. There is a preference for feeding in the more mature cortical areas behind the root tips. Two common species, *P. brachyurus* and *P. penetrans*, favor soil temperatures of 80 to 90°F (27 to 32°C) and 70°F (21°C), respectively, and can complete their life cycles (egg to egg) in six to nine weeks under optimal conditions. Both warm- and cool-season grasses can be colonized by root lesion nematodes.

Stunt Nematodes (*Tylenchorhynchus* spp.)

Stunt nematodes possess two ovaries, a median bulb, a round tail end, but a short stylet with round (not tulip-shaped) knobs. The tail is somewhat cylindrical; the tail end is round. They are an occasional turfgrass pest, but may reach very high populations on bentgrass and *Poa annua* in cooler regions in sand-based rootzones. Brown lesions may be evident on the roots, but definite lesions are not usually present (as a rule). Roots appear shriveled and severely shortened. *Tylenchorhynchus dubius* on bentgrasses feeds primarily on root hairs and areas immediately behind root tips with only the stylet penetrating the epidermal cell. Other species browse more and may group into clusters on epidermal cells that cause a mechanical breakdown of epidermal, cortical, and vascular tissue. Stunt nematodes can survive in the presence of adequate soil moisture for several months without a host. Both warm- and cool-season grasses are suitable hosts.

Dagger Nematodes (*Xiphinema* spp.)

Dagger nematodes are long, slender, and shaped like a "dagger." The stylet is very long with basal flanges (not knobs). The guiding ring for the stylet is nearer to the base than it is to the apex of the stylet. A median bulb is absent. Dagger nematodes feed ectoparasitically and induce reddish-brown to black, slightly sunken root lesions. In very high numbers, extensive feeding reduces root growth. Warm-season grasses (especially zoysiagrasses) and perennial ryegrass are suitable hosts. Other hosts are bentgrasses and Kentucky bluegrass.

Other Nematodes

Other nematodes may damage turf, especially when numerous other pests, pathogens, or environmental conditions stress the turfgrass. Occasional turf pests include spiral, stunt, and dagger nematodes (already previously mentioned); sheath (*Hemicycliophora* spp.) and sheathoid (*Hemicriconemoides* spp.) nematodes; and cyst nematodes (*Heterodera* spp.). All, except the cyst, feed ectoparasitically. *Hemicycliophora* is identified by the presence of a loose sheath around the body of the nematode. *Hemicriconemoides* do not have a loose sheath, but do have fairly pronounced annulations in the cuticle and a tail end that is more pointed than *Mesocriconemella* (ring nematode). The bodies of female cyst nematodes enlarge into lemon shapes that eventually become completely filled with eggs. Egg-filled cysts can be observed still attached to affected roots; St. Augustinegrass is especially susceptible to cyst nematodes.

DIAGNOSIS OF NEMATODE PROBLEMS

Although diagnosing nematode problems is often difficult, there are several clues that are used during the investigative process. These include the type of symptoms, pattern and timing of damage, previous history, nematode species present, and the results of nematode counts.

Root symptoms

Root symptoms include lesions; galls; stubby, swollen root tips; lateral root proliferation; and/or stunted shallow root systems with few feeder roots (Figure 24–5). Common symptoms associated

with certain nematodes were previously described. The penetration and movement of endoparasitic nematodes within roots leave openings that allow root invasion by secondary microorganisms in the soil such as fungi. The result is accelerated rotting (blackening) of roots and proneness of plants to wilting. The physiological and biochemical responses of the turfgrass to the invasion by the nematodes and microorganisms weaken the host further and may even break overall host resistance. Heavily affected root systems have much less soil clinging to them when a plug is pulled from the turf compared to unaffected turfgrass stands. The root symptoms, however, are not unique to nematodes and should always be considered in conjunction with other observations when diagnosing nematode problems.

Aboveground symptoms

Aboveground symptoms include wilting, thinning, or gradual decline; or the yellowing of leaves without lesions or deformities (Plate 24–5). Again, these symptoms are not unique to nematodes and can be caused by heat or drought stresses, nutrient deficiency, fungal diseases, insect feeding, soil compaction, prolonged saturation of soil with water, or chemical contamination. The turfgrass is weakened by the nematode damage and is unable to outcompete invading weeds (such as sedges, knotweed, pusley, and spurges). Nematode-affected areas may appear more weedy than other turf areas.

Pattern of damage

Nematodes do not cause uniform damage to an expanse of turfgrass (as occurs, for example, in rust diseases). Rust fungi produce millions of dry spores that are easily dispersed over long distances in open air by the wind. Nematodes, however, produce a mere 50 to 500 eggs (per female). These eggs are in the soil environment and are not immediately and easily dispersed from the source by an active agent (such as the wind). Nematodes do not migrate more than one meter in one growing season and must depend on movement in surface water run-off, irrigation water, and soil clinging to equipment, sod, or plugs for long-range movement. Nematodes, therefore, show an irregular (somewhat patchy) horizontal and vertical distribution in the soil. Symptoms above ground also follow this irregular distribution, but nematode-affected areas usually do not show distinct sharp boundaries. However, these symptoms resemble early stages of many fungal turfgrass diseases and could be misdiagnosed as nematode-related.

Timing of damage

Plant parasitic nematodes are obligate parasites and feed most when the turfgrass roots are actively growing. They are therefore most numerous during mild weather, in late spring (May to June) and early fall (October to November) on warm-season grasses, and mid- to late spring and again in fall on cool-season grasses. The turf usually shows no aboveground symptoms of nematode damage until unfavorable environmental conditions prevail (for example, during hot, dry periods when soils are dry).

Soil sampling

Nematode counts are the surest way to determine whether a problem in the turf is indeed caused by parasitic nematodes. It is good practice to take soil and root samples monthly so changes in the populations of plant parasitic nematodes in the turfgrass stand can be monitored and kept below acceptable damage threshold levels. Given the irregular distribution of nematodes in the soil, it is imperative that adequate soil/root sampling be conducted in order to confirm the nematode problem to some degree of certainty. Golf course superintendents could be wasting precious time and thousands of dollars on fungicide applications if a problem is not correctly diagnosed as nematode-related. The same waste of resources would occur if the problem is misdiagnosed as nematodal and nematicides are being applied when the real cause is another stress.

To sample nematodes, a one-cup (100-cc) sample of soil is taken from suspected areas. Soil cores should be at least one-half inch (1.3 cm) in diameter to four-inches (10-cm) deep, placed into a clean plastic bag, and sealed. Typically, 10 cores are required to achieve sufficient soil volume for an adequate sample. If several areas show symptoms of nematode damage, separate the samples from each area and store these out of direct sunlight and at room temperature. If they cannot be shipped to a lab within two days, place them in a refrigerator, but do not freeze them. Another common mistake is to place samples in a vehicle where they quickly heat to lethal temperatures.

Both private and university laboratories provide good nematode assay services and should be consulted about the services they offer, as well as instructions for taking and submitting samples. It is usually best to stick to one lab since assay methods and results differ between laboratories. The decision to use a nematicide should be based on the quality of turfgrass required and budget allowances. It should not always be predicated on some fixed threshold level of nematodes set by a laboratory. The level of damage tolerated by one golf course may be completely unacceptable on another. The most important management principle to go by is the fact that the health and vigor of turfgrasses directly affect their relative susceptibility to a given level of parasitic nematodes. In fact, the majority of nematode-induced damage is culturally managed, without nematicides. Nematicides only become necessary if populations reach unmanageable levels and/or if particularly virulent species, such as *Belonolaimus* spp. (sting), are present.

NEMATODE MANAGEMENT

Although no turfgrass cultivars are currently available that are resistant to all nematode species, significant differences exist among turfgrass varieties in terms of the numbers and species of nematodes feeding on them and their proneness to damage caused by feeding activities. Visual symptoms and even adequate soil/root sampling may sometimes not be enough to confirm a nematode problem. A positive growth response to an effective nematicide may sometimes be required for confirmation.

Turfgrasses tolerate some feeding by most nematodes; therefore, the most practical strategy for nematode control is often the promotion of vigorous root growth (using recommended cultural practices and timely nematicide applications).

1. **Cultural practices**—Certain cultural practices help minimize stresses that make the turfgrass more susceptible to nematodes. To facilitate deeper penetration of the soil by roots, irrigate deeply (but less frequently) instead of using shallow, daily watering. To achieve proper infiltration and adequate oxygen levels in soil, coring with narrow, hollow

tines or spiking should be performed (in late spring and early summer). Cultivation should be performed at times of the year when the best turf recovery occurs (e.g., in late spring for warm-season turfgrasses and in mid-spring or early fall for cool-season turfgrasses).

Excessive fertilization with water-soluble nitrogen must be avoided since nematode numbers increase rapidly on succulent roots and, during periods of environmental stress (for example, in summer), the roots are placed under an additional strain. Organic forms of nitrogen have been shown to be associated with lower nematode numbers than inorganic forms. However, judicious use of a balanced fertilizer is always advocated.

Plant diseases, nutrient deficiencies, and soil compaction should be managed or minimized in order to decrease the impact of nematode diseases on turfgrass stands. Avoid mowing low to prevent additional stress to the nematode-infested turfgrass stand that is forced to survive with reduced shoot biomass.

Certain soil amendments to turf grown in sandy soils are known to improve soil composition and reduce the impact of plant parasitic nematodes. Preplant incorporation of colloidal phosphate and/or composted municipal sludge, or long-term use of the latter as a top-dressing, have been shown to reduce nematode damage to turfgrass stands.

2. **Use of tolerant grasses**—Whenever possible, avoid planting species or cultivars that are the most susceptible to the nematode species deemed problematic in a given locality. Table 24–1 lists parasitic nematodes and the most susceptible grasses. By establishing turf initially with a tolerant variety, the impact of certain nematodes and the cost of nematode management will be reduced overall. Information on the relative tolerance of the hundreds of varieties of different turfgrasses is scarce. The bermudagrass variety "Tifdwarf," however, appears to be more tolerant of stunt and ring nematodes than "Tufcote," "Tiffine," "Continental," or "U-3." "Tifway" is fairly tolerant of the sting nematode while "Tifdwarf," "Tufcote," "Tifgreen I," "Tifgreen II," and "Midiron" are susceptible. Polyploid St. Augustinegrass varieties are typically tolerant of sting nematodes compared to diploid varieties.

3. **Chemical control**—Because crop rotation, varietal resistance, biological control, and several other disease-management strategies are not always practical or effective for turfgrass nematode control, the use of chemical nematicides is currently the most reliable approach to reducing parasitic nematode levels in turfgrass stands (Figure 24–6). Chemical nematicides can be applied as preplant fumigants and as post-plant nonfumigant contact chemicals. Fumigants are toxic to plants and are labeled for use only before establishment of the turfgrass stand. In established turfgrass stands, contact nematicides are available as granular or spray formulations and are always watered-in immediately after application. They also have some insecticidal activity. All nematicides are extremely toxic to humans

FIGURE 24–6 Control of turfgrass nematodes is accomplished with nematicides.

and animals and should be handled with all precautions indicated on the product label. No single product is effective against all nematodes on a given turfgrass species.

Soil Fumigation Before Planting

Soil fumigants are chemicals applied as gases or liquids that readily vaporize. They are toxic to the turfgrass but may be used to treat soil prior to seeding or planting to reduce plant parasitic nematodes, weeds, fungal pathogens, and other soil-borne microorganisms. Turfgrasses established in fumigated soil show more uniform and vigorous growth. The fumigants used in turf are the gas methyl bromide, and the liquids 1,3-Dichloropropene (Telone II), 1,3-Dichloropropene-chloropicrin (Telone C-17), and metam-sodium (labeled as Vapam, Sectagon, or Busan 1020). All three fumigants are "restricted use" pesticides requiring special equipment and application only by licensed professionals, especially when large areas are to be treated.

1. Methyl bromide is a very effective broad-spectrum biocide which has "served" the turf industry well. It is standard practice to fumigate new greens, tees, and areas being replanted with methyl bromide. For treatment of small areas, methyl bromide is available in small cans (e.g., Brom-O-Gas). This is achieved not by injection but by allowing the gas to diffuse into the pores of the soil. Cans contain 1 or 1.5 pounds (545 or 681 g) of methyl bromide, enough to give excellent control of pests and weeds at a rate of one pound per 50 square feet (9.8 kg per 100 square meters). Custom applicators often have their own name brand of methyl bromide, such as Terr-O-Gas. The commercial production of methyl bromide is scheduled to stop January 1, 2005, since it has been found to be ozone-depleting and a potentially serious environmental pollutant. Methyl bromide will therefore not be available for nematode control after the phase-out period.

2. Telone C-17 is not without problems. It contains tear gas and is now under special review. Residues have been detected in the air near schools and residential areas.

3. Metam-sodium is a useful option, although not as effective as methyl bromide. It can be applied as a drench in water or by injection. After application, metam releases gases, especially methyl isothiocyanate, which provide control. Metam products do not, however, penetrate tough tubers, stolons, and rhizomes, as well as methyl bromide, and are more sensitive to soil temperature and moisture levels. Also, the fumes from metam-sodium escape slowly from the soil, especially when the soil is cool, wet, or high in organic matter or clay content; thus, it should be used several weeks prior to an anticipated planting. Busan, Sectagon, and Vapam are examples of commercial formulations of metam-sodium.

When using fumigants, best results are usually obtained when the old sod is first stripped from the area to be treated, followed by thorough tilling of the soil at least two weeks prior to the application of the fumigant to allow adequate decomposition of old roots. Tilling loosens the soil and permits more rapid and uniform diffusion of the fumigant. At the time of application, the soil should be moist (not water-saturated). Too much fumigant escapes in dry soil and too little diffuses when pores are filled with water. The temperature of the soil should be about 50 to 80°F (10 to 27°C) (at a depth of 4 inches, 10 cm). Too much fumigant evaporates from hot soil, whereas diffusion is too slow in cold soil. For maximum effectiveness, the treated area should be sealed immediately with plastic tarp for several days. It is extremely important the fumigated area is not recontaminated by accidental introduction of nematodes in soil clinging to tools, equipment, footwear, run-off water, or infested soil. Pests introduced into partially sterilized soil usually reproduce rapidly because of the lack of competition from microorganisms.

Nematicides for Established Commercial Turf

Only a few chemical nematicides are currently available for use on established turfgrass stands. They are the nonfumigant organophosphates fenamiphos (Nemacur 10G or 3EC) and the fumigant 1,3-Dichloropropene (Curfew). They can only be used on commercial turf (including golf courses and sod farms) where the risks of exposure can be minimized. The active ingredient in the granules or emulsifiable concentrate must be carried into the soil by an adequate amount of irrigation or rain water (enough to reach the rootzones and give effective control of nematodes but without product loss through leaching).

Nematicide applications should be made in autumn or spring (before nematode populations peak) during periods when soil temperatures are above 60°F (15.6°C) according to the product label. For granular formulations, gravity or "drop-type" granule spreaders are preferred (or required) over centrifugal types for more accurate application and for ensuring the safety of animals, humans, and non-target plants. Other applicator types are still being tested. For example, the suitability of a shallow injection of narrow bands of granules into the turf, which is popular for application of granular insecticides for mole cricket control, is being tested for nematode control. Experiments comparing the effectiveness of broadcast application of granules versus subsurface injection of granules have shown similar effectiveness. Subsurface injection in fairways is practical and should reduce the potential for off-site material movement.

Prior to application, physical soil treatments that aid soil penetration by water (such as core cultivation, vertical mowing, and mechanical thatch removal) should be done. Applications should be followed by adequate overhead irrigation in order to wash the active ingredient into the soil and avoid chemical exposure of people, pets, and wildlife.

Fenamiphos (Nemacur)

Fenamiphos is a systemic penetrant nematicide (absorbed by the roots and distributed throughout the grass) that gives some control of nematodes feeding within the roots. It is therefore effective against a fairly broad range of ecto- and endoparasitic nematodes. Fenamiphos affects nematodes by blocking enzymes in their nervous system, thereby interfering with motor function and causing irregular movements such as twitching, tremors, and eventual paralysis. During the prelethal phase or exposure to sublethal nematicide levels, feeding by the nematode stops. Recent research suggests population suppression of sting nematodes in the field by fenamiphos (at 11.25 kg ai/ha) is probably due to temporary incapacitation or irreversible sublethal effects caused by contact action and/or the systemic action of the nematicide. Fenamiphos has an intermediate water solubility (400 to 700 ppm) and medium adsorption potential. High soil and/or water pH can rapidly inactivate fenamiphos; thus, it should be applied immediately after mixing or a buffering solution should be added to the tank-mix to modify the pH.

The following guidelines apply only for fenamiphos use on Florida golf courses. These measures are designed to reduce the risk of exposure to birds and aquatic organisms. No more than 10 acres per golf course per day may be treated with Nemacur (3 EC or 10G). There must be a three-day interval before an additional 10 acres (4 hectares) can be treated. Do not apply Nemacur closer than 10 feet (3 m) from bodies of water and surface fairway drains. Nemacur should not be applied to golf course turf between noon and sunset from June 1 to September 30 to avoid pesticide movement by sudden downpours. It must not be used to control mole crickets. On sod farms, total product application must not exceed 200 pounds per acre per year (224 kg per hectare).

The safest guidelines for using Nemacur are always on the product label. The product must be distributed evenly over the area to be treated and it must be washed immediately into the soil with at least 0.5 inches (1.3 cm) of water (usually up to the point when one inch [2.5 cm] of the topsoil has become wet). Total irrigation should not result in puddling and run-off. Do not apply Nemacur where water run-off is likely to occur. The 3 EC formulation is not recommended for use on greens and tees in North Carolina. The purchase and use of **all** formulations of Nemacur are restricted to certified applicators for uses authorized by their certification, or to persons under their direct supervision.

Fenamiphos is also used for the control of mole crickets in turf, although this is not advised in the state of Florida. The efficacy of fenamiphos against turfgrass nematodes is indicated in Table 24–2. The manufacturer's label must be followed in all cases involving the use of these pesticides.

1,3-Dichloropropene (Curfew)

Recently, the use of a soil fumigant, 1,3-Dichloropropene (trade name Curfew), has been approved for use as a selective nematicide in bermudagrass turf. Depending on use rate, 1,3-Dichloropropene has nematicidal, fungicidal, insecticidal, and herbicidal properties. This material is injected five to six inches deep (13 to 15 cm) through chisels spaced 12 inches (30 cm) apart with a coulter, knife, and roller assembly. The coulter slices the turf open at least five-inches (13-cm) deep, with a six-inch (15-cm) knife, and an attached tube that injects the material at a rate of five gallons of product per acre (9.4 liters per hectare), followed by rolling to seal the slit (Figure 24–7). With adequate fertility and irrigation, slits typically heal within two to three weeks.

TABLE 24–2 *Relative effectiveness of nonfumigant nematicides used in turfgrass nematode control.*

Nematode	Phenamiphos (Nemacur)	1,3-Dichloropropene (Curfew)
Sting	Good	Good
Awl	Good	na
Spiral	Good	Good
Ring	Good	Good
Stubby-root	Good	Good
Sheath, Sheathoid	Good	Good
Lance	Good	Good
Root-knot	Moderate	Good

FIGURE 24–7 Slits or grooves remain after the mechanical injection of a nematicide.

A half-inch (1.3-cm) irrigation should follow injection to help "cap" the treatment. The fumigant then diffuses throughout soil pores, killing nematodes on contact with 98 percent dissipation within 24 hours after treatment.

The reentry period of turf following injection is 24 hours unless full personal protective equipment (including suit, gloves, boots, and respirator) are worn. Injections cannot occur within 100 feet (30 meters) of an occupied structure such as a residence or place of business. Obviously, being a soil injection, buried obstacles such as irrigation heads and drains must be flagged and avoided. Work is progressing with an injection unit suitable for greens that minimizes disruption of the playing surface.

Following treatment, turfgrass roots typically respond dramatically with greater root depths and mass. However, since the soil is not sterilized by 1,3-Dichloropropene, nematode populations usually rebound over time; however, with improved rooting, higher nematode populations may be tolerated.

Maximizing the Effectiveness of Nematicides

Neither fumigant or nonfumigant nematicides completely eradicate plant parasitic nematodes. Some nematodes in deeper layers of soil and root tissue may escape exposure to lethal concentrations of the nematicide. Others are only temporarily paralyzed or disoriented by sublethal levels of the nematicide and will resume feeding when the chemical dissipates through diffusion, dilution, degradation, or leaching. Avoid the introduction of nematodes from other sources (for example, contaminated soil or sod). It is important to monitor the population levels of nematodes to know when nematicide treatments are needed.

Just before the nematicide application, cultivate the soil by coring, spiking, and perhaps vertical mowing to improve water infiltration. Aggressive cultivation may not be practical if damage by sting nematodes is severe. The soil should be moist (not water-saturated) and at temperatures of 60°F (16°C) or greater (at 4 inches, 10 cm, deep). Irrigate adequately immediately after application of the nematicide. Do not excessively irrigate.

Nematicides mainly affect nematodes; they do not stimulate plant growth directly. Nematicide-treated turfgrass therefore needs time to grow new roots in order to support new foliage and recover from nematode-induced stresses. Factors limiting root growth must be taken care of immediately after nematicide applications in order to achieve complete recovery of turf affected by nematode parasites. Ensure good drainage, adequate irrigation and aerification, balanced soil fertility, control of other pests and diseases, and reduced pedestrian traffic, if possible. Aboveground plant responses after a nematicide application are usually slow or delayed.

Timing of applications is important. In the southeastern United States, a very good response of bermudagrass to Nemacur application in sting- and ring-infested soil is obtained by a mid-April application, normally several weeks after spring green-up. Presumably, nematode populations are suppressed and allow new stolon and root development at the time of year when growth is maximized. Fall applications of nematicides to suppress damaging nematodes in bermudagrass turf may also be made, but overseeding establishment of cool-season grasses can be adversely affected if seeding and nematicide application coincide or the interval is short. If a nematicide application is necessary in the fall, it should be done two to three weeks prior to the overseeding date. Postemergence applications of fenamiphos may damage *Poa trivialis.*

Related to the timing of applications, the use of certain preemergence herbicides for crabgrass or goosegrass control, which act as inhibitors of cell division, may inhibit bermudagrass response to nematode suppression by nematicides. Although nematodes are suppressed by the nematicide application, turf may not respond because residual herbicides inhibit new stolons. Managers may opt to skip the preemergence herbicide application and use postemergence strategies instead, or use a material (e.g., oxadiazon, or Ronstar) that does not inhibit "tacking" of new stolons into treated areas. This becomes a problem when damage to bermudagrass is substantial and managers rely on new stolon development for recovery (e.g., rhizomes are absent or weakened).

Avoid overuse of any nematicide because soil microorganisms that can degrade the nematicide will buildup to high population levels, decrease the efficacy and longevity of the chemical in subsequent applications, and consequently shorten the period of nematode control. Prolonged frequent use of a given pesticide also allows the buildup of one or more parasitic nematode species against which the chemical is less effective.

BIOLOGICAL CONTROL

There are several products on the market for management of plant parasitic nematodes using various natural products. For instance, mixtures of chitin from shells and urea have been shown to suppress root-knot nematodes when the material is incorporated into soil. Microbes increase to enzymatically break down chitin (chitinases) which may, concomitantly, degrade nematode eggs in soil. ClandoSan is one commercial formulation of this. Another product utilizes preparations of sesame, which has been shown to be toxic to nematodes under some circumstances. Nematrol, Neotrol, and others are commercial formulations. Also, various bacteria have been shown to suppress nematodes, and various commercial preparations of bacteria or bacterial products have come on the market. Incorporation of effective quantities of these materials into existing turf is problematic, as is the relatively high amounts of nitrogen as urea used to break down chitin.

Biological nematode control is also receiving much attention. Two insect-parasitic nematodes (*Steinernema riobravis* and *S. carpocapsae,* trade name Vector MC and others) have been used for mole cricket control. Their effectiveness, however, for certain plant-parasitic nematodes have been somewhat erratic.

Although many of these materials may suppress nematodes for short time intervals, none have given results in the field to date that compare with the efficacy of chemical nematicides. However, the need for safe and effective control of nematodes for turfgrasses has never been greater.

CHAPTER 25

Turfgrass Weeds

INTRODUCTION

A weed can be defined as a plant growing where it is not wanted or growing out of place. For example, tall fescue is considered a weed when grown in a pure stand of bermudagrass, but may be highly desirable when grown in a monoculture such as a golf course rough. In addition to being unsightly, weeds compete with turfgrasses for light, soil nutrients, soil moisture, and physical space. Weeds also are hosts for pests such as plant pathogens, nematodes, and insects. Certain weeds are irritants to humans when allergic reactions to pollen or chemicals occur.

One of the most undesirable characteristics of weeds in turf situations is the disruption of visual turf uniformity (Plate 25–1), which happens with the presence of different (1) leaf width or shape, (2) growth habit, or (3) colors. Many broadleaf weeds such as dandelion, plantains, and pennywort have a wider leaf than the dominant turf species. They also have a different leaf shape. The growth habit of tall fescue, orchardgrass, ryegrass, smutgrass, goosegrass, dallisgrass, vaseygrass, and thin paspalum results in clumps or patches that also disrupt turf uniformity. In addition, large clumps are difficult to effectively mow and increase maintenance problems. The lighter-green color and presence of seedheads typically associated with certain weeds such as annual bluegrass in a golf green often distracts from the playing surface.

Weeds often are the result of a weakened turf, not the cause of it. Understanding this helps to explain the major reason for weed encroachment into a turf area (e.g., thin turf density and bare spots). Reasons for weak or bare turf areas are numerous, including (1) improper turf species selection not adapted to environmental conditions; (2) damage from turfgrass pests such as diseases, insects, nematodes, and animals; (3) environmental stresses such as excessive shade, drought, heat, and cold; (4) improper turf management practices such as misuse of fertilizer and chemicals, improper mowing height, or improper mowing frequency and improper soil aeration; and (5) physical damage and compaction from concentrated or constant traffic. Unless the parameters contributing to the decline of a turf area are corrected, continued problems with weed infestations should be expected.

DEVELOPING A WEED MANAGEMENT PROGRAM

Weed management is an integrated process where good cultural practices are employed to encourage desirable turfgrass ground cover as well as the intelligent selection and use of herbicides. A successful weed management approach involves the following:

1. Proper weed identification
2. Prevention of weed introduction
3. Proper turfgrass management or cultural practices to encourage competitive turf growth
4. If necessary, the proper selection and use of a herbicide

Weed Identification

The first step to successful weed management is proper identification. Turf managers should be able to identify each weed to genus, and preferably to species, in order to select the appropriate control technique. Weed identification also is the first step in understanding why weeds occur and how to control them. For instance, most sedges prefer moist, wet areas while sandspurs prefer drier sites.

Identification begins with classifying the weed type. **Broadleaves,** or dicotyledonous plants, have two seed cotyledons (young leaves) at emergence and have netlike veins in their true leaves (Table 25–1). Broadleaves, which often have colorful flowers, include clover, dandelion, knotweed, lespedeza, plantains, henbit, pusley, beggarweed, spurges, and matchweed (Plate 25–2). **Grasses,** or monocotyledonous plants, only have one seed cotyledon present when seedlings emerge from the soil. Grasses also have hollow, rounded stems with nodes (joints) and parallel veins in their true leaves. Leaf sheaths are open. Most grass species have ligules, a projection at the inside junction of the leaf blade and collar. Ligules may be membrane-like, have a membrane with hairs on top, or be totally absent. Examples include crabgrass, goosegrass, dallisgrass, nimblewill, quackgrass, thin (bull) paspalum, and annual bluegrass.

Separating Grass-Like Plants

Although most nonbroadleaf weeds in turfgrasses are usually grasses, not all are grasses and they are often easily confused. **Sedges** and **rushes** generally favor a moist habitat and have a closed leaf sheath. Their leaf arrangements are three-ranked, ligules are mostly absent, and they either have stems that are triangular-shaped and solid (**sedges**), or round and solid (**rushes**). The distinguishing characteristics that help distinguish between grasses from grasslike plants—sedges and rushes—are listed in Table 25–2.

TABLE 25–1 *Distinguishing characteristics of monocots compared to dicots.*

Characteristic	Monocot	Dicot
Seedling cotyledons	One	Two
Leaf veination	Parallel	Netted
Leaf attachment	Directly on stems	On short stalks called petioles
Ligules	Present, rarely absent (grasses, sedges, rushes)	Absent
Vascular bundles	Scattered	Distinct (arranged in a ring of bundles surrounding a central pith)
Vascular tissue growth	Only primary	Primary & secondary; thus, they can become woody
Meristems	Basal	Terminal
Root system	Fibrous without cambium layer	Taproot with a cambium layer
Flowers	Not showy (grasses, sedges, rushes)	Usually showy
Flower parts	Group of 3s	Usually groups of 4s or 5s

TABLE 25–2 *Distinguishing characteristics between grasses, sedges, and rushes.*

Characteristic	Grasses	Sedges	Rushes
Stem	Usually hollow, round, or flattened	Usually 3-sided, pithy, rarely hollow	Round and filled with sponge-like pith
Nodes	Very noticeable	Indistinct	Indistinct
Leaf arrangement	2-ranked	3-ranked	3-ranked
Leaf sheath	Usually split	Usually closed	Usually open
Leaf blade	Flat, often folded, hairy, or smooth	Flat, usually smooth	Round or flat, usually smooth, often with visible partitions
Leaf margin	Smooth, rough hairy, or sharp	Usually rough	Usually smooth
Collar	Often a distinct band	Indistinct	Indistinct
Auricles	Present or absent	Absent	Present or absent
Ligule	Present, rarely absent	Absent or only weakly developed	Absent or only weakly developed

In the past, proper weed identification was difficult to achieve due to the lack of a suitable guide. Most guides pictured weeds in unmowed conditions or did not list all the important turf weeds. *Color Atlas of Turfgrass Weeds* covers most major world turfgrass weeds and provides color photographs of over 215 major weeds with detailed descriptions, life cycles, worldwide distribution information, and current control strategies. Most photographs were taken in mowed turf situations. This guide is available through the Golf Course Superintendent's Association (GCSAA).

Weed Life Cycles

Weeds complete their life cycles in either one growing season (**annuals**), two growing seasons (**biennials**), or three or more growing seasons (**perennials**). Annuals completing their life cycles from spring to fall are generally referred to as **summer annuals,** and those completing their life cycles from fall to spring are **winter annuals.** Summer annual grasses, as a class, are generally the most troublesome in turf.

Weed Prevention

Prevention involves avoiding the introduction of weeds into an area. There are national, state, and local prevention efforts against the introduction and spread of weeds. A local preventive program is one of the best methods of avoiding future weed problems. Many of these methods are commonsense approaches that ensure sanitary conditions and minimize weed introduction. Some of these methods include use of weed-free turf seeds, stolons, sprigs, plugs, or sod. Washing or blowing equipment between mowings, maintaining weed-free fence lines and ditch banks, and the use of clean mulch and topdressing material are additional examples of preventative methods (Figure 25–1).

Cultural

Cultural practices promoting a vigorous, dense turf are perhaps the most important and least recognized means of preventing weed encroachment and establishment. Soil fertility, aeration, and moisture levels should be maintained at an optimum level to promote turf cover. Since light is required for optimum germination of weeds such as crabgrass and goosegrass, cultural practices increasing turf density will prevent light from reaching the soil surface. Preventing light from reaching the soil surface also delays spring germination of weed seeds requiring warmth because the soil surface is better insulated; thus, it remains cooler. Maintaining the highest cutting height possible and adequate fertility levels will help encourage a high shoot density and will also minimize light penetration to the soil surface.

FIGURE 25–1 Good sanitary practices such as washing maintenance equipment between use; planting only weed-free seed, sprigs, and sod; and maintaining weed-free fence lines and ditch banks help reduce the spread and occurrence of weeds.

High infestation levels of certain weeds also might indicate specific soil conditions that favor their presence. Table 25–3 lists some of these soil conditions and associated weeds. Continual weed problems can be expected until these growth conditions are corrected.

Herbicide Classification and Nomenclature

Herbicides may be classified according to chemistry, method of application, timing of application, persistence, selectivity, and/or mode of action.

1. **Selective**—A selective herbicide controls or suppresses certain plant species without seriously affecting the growth of another plant species. Selectivity may be due to differential absorption, translocation, and morphological and/or physiological differences between turfgrasses and weeds. The majority of herbicides used in turfgrasses are selective. For example, 2,4-D (several trade names) is used for selective control of many broadleaf weeds, such as dandelion, without significant injury to turfgrasses.
2. **Nonselective**—Nonselective herbicides control plants regardless of species. These are primarily used to control all plants, as in the renovation or establishment of a new turf area, "spot treatments," or for edging. Glyphosate (Roundup Pro, others), glufosinate (Finale), and diquat (Reward) are examples of nonselective herbicides. Herbicides such as atrazine (Aatrex) or MSMA (Bueno 6, others) can be nonselective at rates in excess of those used for selective control.
3. **Systemic**—Systemic herbicides are extensively translocated (moved) in the plant's vascular system. The vascular system translocates the nutrients, water, and organic materials necessary for normal growth and development. In contrast to the quick kill observed with contact herbicides, systemic herbicides require several days or even a few weeks to fully translocate throughout the plant's vascular system, and therefore require a longer period of time before kill. Systemic herbicides are also classified as selective or nonselective. Glyphosate is a nonselective, systemic herbicide while 2,4-D, dicamba (Vanquish), imazaquin (Image), and sethoxydim (Vantage) are examples of selective, systemic herbicides.
4. **Contact**—Contact herbicides only affect the portion of green plant tissue in contact with the herbicide spray. These herbicides are not, or only are to a limited extent, translocated in the vascular system of plants. Therefore, underground plant parts such as rhizomes or tubers are not killed. Usually repeat applications are needed with contact herbicides to kill regrowth from these underground plant parts. Adequate spray volumes and thorough coverage of the weed foliage are necessary for effective control. These herbicides kill plants quickly, often within a few hours of application. Contact herbicides may be

TABLE 25–3 *Weeds as indicators of specific poor soil conditions.*

Soil condition	Indicator weed(s)
Acid soils	Bentgrasses (*Agrostis* spp.) Red sorrel (*Rumex acetosella*)
Compacted soils	Annual bluegrass (*Poa annua*) Bermudagrass (*Cynodon dactylon*) Common chickweed (*Stellaria media*) Goosegrass (*Eleusine indica*) Knotweed (*Polygonum aviculare*) Mouseear chickweed (*Cerastium vulgatum*) Prostrate spurge (*Chamaesyce humistrata*) Rushes (*Juncus* spp.)
Infertile/sandy soils	Bahiagrass (*Paspalum notatum*) Black medic (*Medicago lupulina*) Bromesedge (*Andropogon* spp.) Carpetweed (*Mollugo verticillata*) Legumes (clover, lespedeza, medic) Poorjoe (*Diodia teres*) Quackgrass (*Agropyron repens*) Red sorrel (*Rumex acetosella*) Sandbur (*Cenchrus pauciflorus*) White clover (*Trifolium repens*) Yarrow (*Achillea millefolium*) Yellow woodsorrel (*Oxalis stricta*)
High fertility soils	Annual bluegrass (*Poa annua*) Bentgrasses (*Agrostis* spp.) Bermudagrass (*Cynodon dactylon*) Crabgrasses (*Digitaria* spp.) Henbit (*Lamium amplexicaule*) Purslane (*Portulacca oleracea*) Ryegrass (*Lolium* spp.) Yellow woodsorrel (*Oxalis stricta*)
High or infrequent mowing	Chicory (*Cichorium intybus*) Clover (*Trifolium* spp.) Thistle (*Cirsium, Carduus* spp.)
Low mowing	Algae Annual bluegrass (*Poa annua*) Chickweeds Pearlwort (*Sagina procumbens*)
Shaded soils	Annual bluegrass (*Poa annua*) Common chickweed (*Stellaria media*) Ground ivy (*Glechoma hederacea*) Mouseear chickweed (*Cerastium vulgatum*) Nimblewill (*Muhlenbergia shreberi*) Roughstalk bluegrass (*Poa trivialis*) Violets (*Viola* spp.)
Wet soils	Algae Alligatorweed (*Alternanthera philoxeroides*) Annual bluegrass (*Poa annua*) Barnyardgrass (*Echinochloa crusgalli*) Bentgrasses (*Agrostis* spp.) Common chickweed (*Stellaria media*) Ground ivy (*Glechoma hederacea*) Kyllingas (*Cyperus* spp.) Moss Mouseear chickweed (*Cerastium vulgatum*) Nutsedges (*Cyperus* spp.) Pennywort (*Hydrocotyle* spp.) Rushes (*Juncus* spp.) Speedwells (*Veronica* spp.) Violets (*Viola* spp.)

classified as selective or nonselective. Bromoxynil (Buctril) and bentazon (Basagran T&O) are classified as selective, contact herbicides. Diquat (Reward) and glufosinate (Finale) are nonselective, contact herbicides.

Herbicides from the same class of chemistry are grouped into families in much the same way plants are grouped into genus and species. In general, members of a herbicide family are similarly absorbed and translocated and have a similar mode of action (Table 25–4).

Timing of Herbicide Application

Herbicides are classified by the time the chemical is applied in respect to turfgrass and/or weed seed germination. Although the majority of herbicides may be classified into one category, atrazine (AAtrex), simazine (Princep), dithiopyr (Dimension), and pronamide (Kerb) are notable exceptions. They are used as both preemergence and postemergence herbicides.

Preplant herbicides

Preplant herbicides are applied before turfgrass is established, usually to provide nonselective, complete control of all present weeds. Soil fumigants, such as metam-sodium (Vapam), methyl bromide (Terr-O-Gas, Dowfume, Brom-O-Gas, others), and dazomet (Basamid), and nonselective herbicides such as glyphosate (Roundup Pro, others) may be used as nonselective preplant herbicides.

Preemergence herbicides

Preemergence herbicides are applied to the turfgrass prior to weed seed germination and form a barrier at, or just below, the soil surface. Most preemergence herbicides prevent cell division during weed-seed germination as the emerging seedling comes into contact with the herbicide (Figure 25–2). Weeds already emerged (visible) at the time of application are not controlled consistently by preemergence herbicides because their primary growing points escape treatment. Preemergence herbicides also do not control dormant weed seeds.

Postemergence herbicides

Postemergence herbicides are applied directly to emerged weeds. In contrast to preemergence herbicides, this group of herbicides provides little, if any, soil residual control of weeds. A complete chemical weed control program can be accomplished with postemergence herbicides, provided multiple applications are used throughout the year. However, due to the necessity of repeat applications and temporary turfgrass injury, most turfgrass managers use postemergence herbicides in conjunction with a preemergence herbicide. Postemergence herbicides are useful for controlling perennial grasses and broadleaf weeds not controlled by preemergence herbicides. Certain postemergence herbicides also may be used on newly established turfgrasses.

Soil Fumigation for Nonselective Preplant Weed Control

Soil fumigants are volatile liquids or gases that control a wide range of soil-borne pests. Soil fumigants are also *highly toxic* to plants and other biological organisms, and are also expensive. Their use is limited to small, high value crop acres such as tobacco, certain vegetables, fruits, bedding plants, and turf. The expense usually results from the impermeable cover necessary to trap the fumigant vapors in the soil. Fumigants control not only most weed species, but also many nematodes, fungi, and insects. Weed species possessing a hard, water-impermeable seed coat such as sicklepod, white clover, common mallow, redstem filaree, and morning glory are not effectively controlled with soil fumigants. Important considerations before choosing a particular soil fumigant include expense, soil moisture level, soil temperature, and time available before planting.

Several compounds are, or have been, used as fumigants. The two most used materials in turf are **methyl bromide** and **metham** or **metam-sodium. Dazomet** also is available as a granular soil fumigant.

TABLE 25-4 *Classification of herbicides based on mode of action.*

Mode of action	
A. Specific site(s) of action	
Herbicide families	**Herbicide common names**

Growth regulators

A. Synthetic auxins	
Phenoxy acetic acids	- 2,4-D, MCPA
Phenoxy propionic acids	- Diclorprop (2,4-DP), mecoprop (MCPP)
Phenoxy butyric acids	- 2,4-DB, MCPB
Benzoic acids	- Dicamba
Carboxylic acids	- Clopyralid, fluroxypyr, picloram, triclopyr
Picolinic acid and related compounds	- Picloram, triclopyr, clopyralid, quinclorac
Quinaline carboxylic acid	- Quinclorac (broadleaves)

Photosynthesis inhibitors

A. Inhibitors of photosystem II—Site A	
s-Triazines	
Chloro	- Atrazine, simazine
Methoxy	- Prometon
Triazinones	- Hexazinone, metribuzin
Uracils	- Bromacil, terbacil
B. Inhibitors of photosystem II—Site B	
Benzothiadiazoles	- Bentazon
Nitriles	- Bromoxynil
Phenyl-pyridazine	- Pyridate
C. Inhibitors of photosystem II—Same site different binding behavior	
Amides	- Propanil
Ureas	- Diuron, fluometuron, linuron, siduron, tebuthiuron

Pigment inhibitors

A. Bleaching—Inhibitors of carotenoid biosynthesis (unknown target)	
Triazole	- Amitrole
B. Bleaching—Inhibitors of carotenoid biosynthesis at the phytene desaturase step (PDS)	
Pyridazinone	- Norflurazon
Others	- Fluridone
C. Bleaching inhibitor of DOXP synthase	
Isoxazolidionone	- Clomazone

Growth inhibitors

A. Microtubule assembly inhibitors	
Dinitroanilines	- Benefin, ethalfluralin, oryzalin, pendimethalin, prodiamine, trifluralin
Pyridines	- Dithiopyr, thiazopyr
Unknown	- DCPA

(continued)

TABLE 25–4 *Classification of herbicides based on mode of action. (continued)*

Herbicide families	Herbicide common names
Growth inhibitors	
B. Inhibitors of emerging seedling shoots	
Carbamothioates or thiocarbamates	- Butylate, EPTC, cycloate, molinate, pebulate, prosulfocarb, thiobencarb, triallate, vernolate
C. Inhibitors of emerging seedling roots	- Bensulide
D. Inhibitors of very long chain fatty acids (seedling roots and shoots)	
Acetamides or amides	- Napropamide
Chloroacetamide	- Acetochlor, alachlor, butachlor, dimethenamid, metolachlor, propachlor
Inhibitors of amino acid synthesis	
A. Inhibitors of acetolactate synthase (ALS), also called acetohydroxyacid synthase (AHAS)	
Sulfonylureas	- Bensulfuron, chlorimuron, chlorsulfuron, ethametsulfuron, flazasulfuron, foramsulfuron, halosulfuron, metsulfuron, nicosulfuron, primisulfuron, prosulfuron, rimsulfuron, sulfometuron, sulfosulfuron, thifensulfuron, triasulfuron, tribenuron, trifloxysulfuron sodium, triflusulfuron, others
Imidazolinones	- Imazamethabenz, imazamox, imazapic, imazapyr, imazaquin, imazethapyr
Pyrimidinyl oxybenzoates	- Pyrithiobac, bispyribac-sodium
B. Inhibitors of EPSP synthase	- Glyphosate
C. Inhibitors of glutamine synthetase	- Glufosinate
Lipid biosynthesis inhibitors	
A. Inhibitors of acetyl CoA carboxylase	
Cyclohexenediones	- Clethodim, sethoxydim
Aryloxyphenoxy-propionates	- Diclofop, fenoxaprop, fluazifop, quizalofop
Inhibitors of cell wall biosynthesis	
A. Site A—Nitriles	- Dichlobenil
B. Site B—Benzamide	- Isoxaben
Rapidly disrupt cell membranes	
A. Direct effect on membranes	- Dilute sulfuric acid, monocarbamide dihydrogen sulfate, herbicidal oils
B. Induce lipid peroxidation	
Photosynthesis I electron diverters	
Bipyridyliums	- Diquat, paraquat
Inhibitors of protoporphyrinogen oxidase (Protox)	
Diphenylethers	- Acifluorfen, fomesafen, lactofen, oxyfluorfen
Oxadiazole	- Oxadiazon, flumiclorac
Aryl triazinones	- Carfentrazone-ethyl, sulfentrazone
Inhibits dihydropteroate (DHP) synthase	
Carbamates	- Asulam
Unknown/miscellaneous	- Difenzoquat, endothall, TCA quinclorac (monocots)
Benzofurans	- Ethofumesate
Organic arsenicals	- DSMA, MSMA, CMA

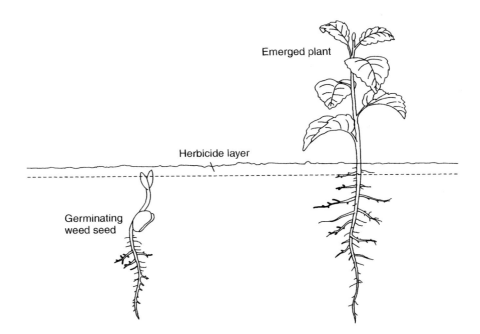

Methyl bromide

Methyl bromide is a colorless, nearly odorless liquid or gas. At 38°F (3.3°C), the liquid turns into a gas and, at 68°F (20°C), is 3.2 times heavier than air. These properties require a cover to be used with methyl bromide or the material will escape. Methyl bromide is extremely toxic (acute vapor toxicity is 200 ppm), is a serious inhalation hazard, and is commonly combined with a warning agent such as chloropicrin (teargas) to warn the user of escapage.

When using a fumigant, the soil should be in the suitable planting condition, including seed bed preparation by proper tilling through plowing soil 8 to 10 inches (20 to 25 cm) in depth, then releasing the chemical under a gas-proof (plastic) cover with the edges sealed and leaving it for 24 to 48 hours. Control will be only as deep as the soil is adequately tilled. Soil should be moist for adequate soil fumigant penetration and dispersion. Saturated or extremely dry soils limit penetration and dispersion, and subsequently affect weed-seed absorption. Soil temperatures at four inches (10 cm) should be a minimum of 60°F (16°C). Fumigation is not effective if soil temperatures are below 50°F (10°C). The cover should then be removed and the soil aerated for 24 to 72 hours before planting. **Methyl bromide is a toxic material used by professional applicators only. Some methyl bromide formulations are restricted use pesticides.** Hiring a contractor who specializes in fumigation is recommended for those unfamiliar with the process. Due to potential ozone depletion concerns, methyl bromide is being phased out of use in the United States. January 2005 is the scheduled time for cancellation of methyl bromide.

Metham or metam-sodium

Metham (sodium methyl-dithiocarbamate) is a member of the thiocarbamate herbicide family. Metham is water-soluble, and upon contact with moist soils, it breaks down to form the highly toxic and volatile chemical **methyl isothiocyanate.** Like methyl bromide, metham should be applied to moist soils with temperatures of at least 60°F (16°C). It is most effective when its vapors are confined with a cover; however, a water and soil-seal method may be used in the absence of a cover. With the water and soil-seal method, the soil is cultivated, sealed with water at 15 gallons per 100 square feet (61 L per 10 m^2), and kept moist for a week before treatment. Approximately seven days after treatment, the area should be cultivated to help release any residual gases. One-to-two weeks later (two-to-three weeks after initial application), the treated area may be planted. The longer waiting period before planting, and the lowered effectiveness in the absence of using a cover, are drawbacks to metham and should be considered before use.

Dazomet

Dazomet recently has been reintroduced as a soil fumigant. Unlike methyl bromide and metham, dazomet is a granular product and is not a restricted use product. Being a granular formulation, dazomet must be evenly applied and incorporated for maximum effectiveness. Its breakdown characteristics, application preparation, and effectiveness are closely associated to metham, as are its advantages and disadvantages.

SELECTIVE WEED CONTROL

Maintaining today's modern, multimillion dollar turf complexes at the desired level of aesthetics requires knowledge of specific weeds, their biology, and available control measures. The following sections discuss current selective weed control options turf managers have at their disposal. Weed control should be a carefully planned and coordinated program instead of being a hit-or-miss operation. Understanding how and why weeds are present on a site is more important than what control options are available once the weed is present.

PROPER HERBICIDE SELECTION AND APPLICATION

When choosing a herbicide, the effectiveness at certain weed growth stages, tolerance or susceptibility of treated turf species, time required for its control, economics, and safety characteristics are important considerations when trying to choose among herbicides. The most effective herbicide is only as good as its application. Many variables influence successful herbicide application, including (1) proper equipment; (2) environmental factors at the time of application; (3) accurate and constant monitoring of calibration; and (4) adequate agitation. Most herbicide failures involve using the wrong chemical at the wrong date, or they are applied at an improper time or manner. It is not by failure of the herbicide itself.

PREEMERGENCE HERBICIDES

Preemergence herbicides are the foundation of a chemical weed control program in turfgrasses and are used primarily to control annual grasses and certain annual broadleaf weeds. Preemergence weed control was first suggested in 1927. Some of the first chemicals evaluated for preemergence weed control include calcium cyanide, arsenate, and naphthylacetic acid. In 1959, the first true preemergence herbicide that provided consistent control became available for turf managers. DCPA (dimethyl tetrachloroterephthalate) (Dacthal) provided more consistent control with less damage to the turf than was previously available. With the subsequent release of dinitroaniline herbicides, the widespread acceptance of preemergence weed control in turfgrass was established.

When considering any herbicide, one of the first questions is the tolerance of the desirable turfgrass species to the chemical in question. Table 25–5 lists the most widely used turfgrass species on golf courses and their tolerance to currently available preemergence herbicides. Herbicides such as bensulide (Betasan), dithiopyr (Dimension), and members of the dinitroaniline herbicide family (e.g., benefin [Balan], oryzalin [Surflan], pendimethalin [Pre-M], prodiamine [Barricade], trifluralin [Treflan]) should be used only on well-established turfgrasses.

Effectiveness of Preemergence Herbicides

The effectiveness of preemergence herbicides varies because of many factors, including application timing in relation to weed seed germination, soil type, environmental conditions (e.g., rainfall and temperature), target weed species and biotype, and cultural factors (e.g., aerification) that follow application. Preemergence herbicides generally are most effective for annual grass control, although some annual small seeded broadleaf weeds also are suppressed. Table 25–6 lists the expected control of common annual grass and several broadleaf weeds for various preemergence herbicides.

TABLE 25–5 Turfgrass tolerance to preemergence herbicides (refer to herbicide label for specific species listing).

Herbicides	Bahiagrass	Bentgrass[1]	Bermudagrass[1]	Buffalograss	Centipedegrass	St. Augustinegrass	Zoysiagrass
Atrazine (Aatrex)	NR[2]	NR	I (D)	I (D)	S	S	I-S
Benefin (Balan)	S	NR	S	NR	S	S	S
Benefin + oryzalin (XL)	S	NR	S	I (D)	S	S	S
Benefin + trifluralin (Team)	S	NR	S	NR	S	S	S
Bensulide (Betasan, PreSan)	S	S	S	NR	S	S	S
Bensulide + oxadiazon	NR	S	S	NR	NR	NR	S
Dithiopyr (Dimension)	S	S	S	S	S	I	S
Ethofumesate (Prograss)[3]	NR	S	S (D)	NR	NR	I	NR
Fenarimol (Rubigan)	NR	NR	S	NR	NR	NR	S
Isoxaben (Gallery)	S	NR	S	S	S	S	S
Metolachlor (Pennant)	S	NR	I	NR	S	S	S
Napropamide (Devrinol)	S	NR	S	NR	S	S	NR
Oryzalin (Surflan)	S	NR	S	S	S	S	S
Oxadiazon (Ronstar)	NR	NR	S	S	NR	S	S
Pendimethalin (Pre-M)	S	NR	S	S	S	S	S
Prodiamine (Barricade)	S	NR	S	S	S	S	S
Pronamide (Kerb)	S	NR	S	S	S	S	S
Rimsulfuron (TranXit)	NR	NR	S	NR	NR	NR	NR
Siduron (Tupersan)	NR	I	NR	NR	NR	NR	S
Simazine (Princep)	NR	NR	I (D)	NR	S	S	S

(continued)

TABLE 25-5 *Turfgrass tolerance to preemergence herbicides (refer to herbicide label for specific species listing). (continued)*

Herbicides	Overseeded ryegrass	Perennial ryegrass	Seashore paspalum	Tall fescue	Red fescue	Kentucky bluegrass	Kikuyugrass
Atrazine (Aatrex)	NR	NR	NR	NR	NR	NR	NR
Benefin (Balan)	NR	S	NR	S	S	S	NR
Benefin + oryzalin (XL)	NR	S	NR	S	NR	NR	NR
Benefin + trifluralin (Team)	NR	S	NR	S	S	S	NR
Bensulide (Betasan, PreSan)	I-S	S	NR	S	S	S	NR
Bensulide + oxadiazon	NR	S	NR	S	S	S	NR
Dithiopyr (Dimension)	I	S	S	S	I	S	S
Ethofumesate (Prograss)[3]	S (D)	S	NR	I	I	I	NR
Fenarimol (Rubigan)	S	NR	NR	S	S	S	NR
Isoxaben (Gallery)	I-S	S	NR	S	S	S	NR
Metolachlor (Pennant)	NR	NR	NR	S	S	S	NR
Napropamide (Devrinol)	NR	NR	NR	S	NR	NR	NR
Oryzalin (Surflan)	NR	NR	NR	S	NR	NR	NR
Oxadiazon (Ronstar)	I	S	S	S	S	S	NR
Pendimethalin (Pre-M)	NR	S	NR	S	S	S	NR
Prodiamine (Barricade)	I	S	S	S	S	S	NR
Pronamide (Kerb)	NR	NR	NR	NR	NR	NR	NR
Rimsulfuron (TranXit)	NR	NR	NR	NR	NR	NR	NR
Siduron (Tupersan)	NR	S	NR	S	S	S	NR
Simazine (Princep)	NR	NR	NR	NR	NR	NR	NR

[1]Check herbicide label to determine if product can be used on golf course putting greens.

[2]**S**=Safe at labeled rates on mature, healthy turf; **I**=Intermediate safety; may cause slight damage to mature, healthy turf! Use only one-half the normal rate when temperatures are hot (>85°F) or if the turf is under water stress; **NR**=Not registered for use on and/or damages this turf species.

[3]Ethofumesate is labeled only for dormant (**D**) bermudagrass overseeded with perennial ryegrass.

These are relative rankings and depend on factors such as environmental conditions, turfgrass vigor or health, application timing, and so forth, and are intended only as a guide.

TABLE 25–6 *Preemergence herbicide efficacy ratings (refer to herbicide label for specific species and use listing).*

Herbicide	Crabgrass	Goosegrass	Annual bluegrass	Common chickweed	Henbit	Lawn burweed	Speedwell spp.	Spurges	Woodsorrel	FL pusley	Phyllanthus sp.	Purslane
Atrazine (Aatrex)	F[1]	P	E	E	E	G	E	G	F	G	–	G
Benefin (Balan)	G-E	F	G-E	G	G	P	P	P	–	–	–	–
Benefin + oryzalin (XL)	E	G	G	G	G	–	–	F	F-G	G	–	G
Benefin + trifluralin (Team)	F-G	F	G	G	G	–	–	F	F	–	–	–
Bensulide (Betasan, PreSan)	G-E	P-F	F	P	P	P	P	–	–	–	–	F
Bensulide + oxadiazon	E	G-E	G-E	G	–	–	–	G	–	–	–	–
Dithiopyr (Dimension)	E	G-E	G-E	G	G	–	G	G	G	–	–	F
Fenarimol (Rubigan)	P	P	G-E	P	P	P	P	P	P	P	–	–
Isoxaben (Gallery)	P-F	P	P-F	E	G	E	G-E	G	G	F-G	–	G
Metolachlor (Pennant)	F-G	P-F	G	F	–	–	–	F	P	G	P	F
Napropamide (Devrinol)	G-E	G	G	E	P	E	E	P	G	P	–	G
Oryzalin (Surflan)	E	G	G-E	G	G	F	P	F-G	G	G	–	G
Oxadiazon + prodiamine	E	G-E	G-E	G	G	G	G	G	G	G	F-G	G
Oxadiazon (Ronstar)	G-E	E	G-E	P	P	P	G	G	G	G	F-G	G
Pendimethalin (Pre-M)	E	G-E	G-E	E	G	G	G-E	G	G	G	F-G	G
Prodiamine (Barricade)	E	G-E	G-E	G	G	F-G	F-G	G	G	G	F-G	G
Pronamide (Kerb)	P-F	P	G-E	E	F-G	P	E	P	P	–	–	G
Rimsulfuron (TranXit)	P	P	G	P	P	P	P	P	P	P	P	P
Simazine (Princep T&O)	P-F	P	E	E	E	G-E	E	F-G	F	G	–	G

[1]E=Excellent, >89 percent control; **G**=Good, 80 to 89 percent control; **F**=Fair, 70 to 79 percent control; **P**=Poor, <70 percent control; – = Data not available.

These are relative ratings and depend on many factors such as environmental conditions, turfgrass vigor or health, application timing, and so forth, and are intended only as a guide.

Timing of Preemergence Herbicides

An important consideration in using preemergence herbicides is application timing. Most preemergence herbicides act as mitotic inhibitors, meaning they prevent cell division. Since the germinating shoot-and-root tips are the two major sites of cell division, preemergence herbicides must contact these plant structures in the soil. Application should therefore be timed just prior to weed-seed germination since most preemergence herbicides are ineffective on emerged (visible) weeds. If applied too soon, natural herbicide degradation processes may reduce the herbicide concentration in the soil to a level resulting in ineffective or reduced control. If applied too late (e.g., weed seedlings are visible), the weeds have grown above the thin layer of preemergence herbicide located at the soil surface, resulting in the effectiveness of the materials being drastically reduced (Figure 25–2).

Crabgrass germinates from February through May when soil temperatures at a four-inch (10-cm) depth reach 53 to 58°F (12 to 14°C). Alternating dry and wet conditions at the soil surface, as well as sunlight, greatly encourages crabgrass germination. Crabgrass germination often coincides with flowering of early spring plants such as redbuds, pears, and cherry trees.

Goosegrass germinates when soil temperatures at the four-inch (10-cm) level reach 60 to 65°F (16 to 18°C). Goosegrass also requires sunlight for optimum seed germination and is very competitive in compacted soils. Normally, because of higher temperature requirements for germination, goosegrass germinates two to four weeks later in spring than crabgrass. This often coincides with flowering of later plants such as dogwoods and azaleas. If herbicides are applied at the time for crabgrass control, the material will begin to break down in the soil and goosegrass control will be reduced. Therefore, when developing a goosegrass weed control program, delaying preemergence spring herbicide application three to four weeks after the targeted date for crabgrass control is more efficient.

Annual bluegrass (*Poa annua*) begins to germinate in late summer through early fall when daytime temperatures consistently drop into the mid-70°Fs (21°Cs). Typically, a second major flush of annual bluegrass germination occurs in early winter (December 20 to January 20) when days are bright, air temperatures are in the 60°Fs (16°Cs), and night temperatures are cold (<35°F, 2°C). Thin turf areas, slightly shady areas, and excessively wet areas generally have the earliest Poa germination.

Sequential or Repeat Applications

Repeat applications of preemergence herbicides are generally necessary for full season control for crabgrass, goosegrass, and annual bluegrass. Most herbicides begin to degrade soon after application when exposed to the environment. Usually, the level of degradation occurring from 6 to 16 weeks after application reduces the herbicide concentration to the point where poor control of later germinating weed seeds, such as goosegrass, occurs. Repeat applications, therefore, are necessary between 60 to 75 days after the initial application for season-long preemergence weed control.

Note: On those areas to be established with turf, most preemergence herbicides should not be used two to four months prior to planting. Severe root damage and reduced turfgrass seed germination may result.

Core Aerification and Preemergence Herbicides

Core aeration has not traditionally been recommended or practiced following a preemergence herbicide application. This procedure was believed to disrupt the herbicide barrier in the soil, thereby allowing weed germination. Research, however, indicates core aerification immediately prior to, or one, two, three, or four months after application of many preemergence herbicides does not stimulate large crabgrass emergence. Aeration at one or two months after application also has little effect on large crabgrass cover. Core aeration at one, two, or three months after an application of preemergence herbicide does not decrease goosegrass control on putting greens. However, greater amounts of crabgrass occur on greens aerified with the cores returned than non-aerified greens, or aerified greens with the cores removed.

Fertilizer-Based Preemergence Herbicide

A growing trend in the turfgrass industry is the use of granular preemergence herbicides. The low cost of granular applicators and public perception of spraying has contributed to this trend. Additionally, many turfgrass managers are using dry fertilizer-based preemergence herbicides. Fertilizer-herbicide mixtures enable a weed-n-feed treatment in the same application or trip over the turfgrass. "Weed-n-feed" treatments may be convenient; however, certain factors must be considered prior to application. Depending upon the turfgrass, the time of year a herbicide should be applied may not coincide with the time of year a fertilizer is needed. For example, unless a slow-release nitrogen fertilizer is used, bermudagrass should not receive spring fertilization until the grass has greened-up approximately 40 percent, the chances of frost have passed, or the grass has recovered from winter dormancy. At the full green-up stage of bermudagrass, it is usually too late to apply most preemergence herbicides since many summer annual weeds have already emerged.

When using herbicides formulated on a fertilizer carrier, it is also important to determine if the manufacturers' recommended rate of the product supplies sufficient amounts of fertilizer needed by the turfgrass and herbicide required for weed control. Supplemental applications of fertilizer or herbicide may be required if the product does not supply enough of each to meet these needs.

Corn Gluten as Preemergent Weed Control

The concept of using corn gluten meal as a natural herbicide originated at Iowa State University in the 1980s. Accidentally discovered while using corn meal as a growing medium for *Pythium,* raw corn meal was applied in adjacent plots several weeks before seed bed planting. Secondary observations were made when germination of grass seed was inhibited by the raw corn meal. It was later found an organic substance in the corn meal was destroyed when it was cultured with the fungal organism *Pythium*. Corn gluten is a byproduct of the wet milling process of corn grain. Corn gluten contains 60 percent protein and 10 percent nitrogen (N) by weight, which may make an excellent fertilizer for plants with an established root system. The inhibitory substance of corn gluten prevents the formation of roots on germinating seedlings of a variety of grass and broadleaf plants. Five individual dipeptides (combinations of two amino acids) inhibit root formation of germinating seedlings. These dipeptides are glutaminyl-glutamine, glycinyl-alanine, alaninyl-glutamine, alaninyl-asparagine, and alaninyl-alanine. The application rate is 20 pounds of product (2 pounds of N, 0.9 kg) per 1,000 square feet (100 kg per 100 m^2) in spring two to four weeks before the anticipated germination of summer annuals.

Preemergence Herbicides for Golf Greens

Few preemergence herbicides are recommended for use by the manufacturer on golf greens due to the liability associated with these valuable areas. However, several are available for either bermudagrass or bentgrass greens (Table 24–7). Several can be used on either grass; however, the user should check the latest herbicide label to ensure these are still available for green use.

POSTEMERGENCE HERBICIDES

Postemergence herbicides are generally effective only on those weeds that have germinated and are visible. Most postemergence herbicides are relatively ineffective as preemergence herbicides. The timing of application should be when weeds are young (two- to four-leaf stage) (Figure 25–3) and actively growing. At this stage, herbicide uptake and translocation is favored, and turfgrasses are better able to fill in voids left by the dying weeds. The tolerances of different turfgrass species to postemergence herbicides are listed in Tables 25–8 and 25–9.

Broadleaf Weed Control

Broadleaf weeds in turf have traditionally been controlled with members of the phenoxy herbicide family (e.g., 2,4-D, dichlorprop, MCPA, and mecoprop) and benzoic acid herbicide family (e.g., dicamba). All are selective, systemic foliar-applied herbicides. Only a very few broadleaf weeds, especially perennials, are controlled with just one of these materials. Usually, two- or three-way combinations of these herbicides and possible repeat applications are necessary for satisfactory weed control. Special formulations of three-way type mixtures of 2,4-D, dichlorprop (2,4-DP), MCPP, MCPA, and dicamba are available. Various MCPP formulations also are

TABLE 25–7 *Preemergence herbicides for putting greens (refer to herbicide label for specific turf species and use listing).*

Trade names	Ingredients	Bentgrass	Bermudagrass	Bermudagrass to be overseeded (refer to label for specific timing)
Weedgrass Preventer	Bensulide	✔	✔	✔
Goosegrass/Crabgrass Control	Bensulide + oxadiazon	✔	✔	—
Southern Weedgrass Control	Pendimethalin	—	✔	—
Devrinol	Napronamide	—	✔	—
Betasan	Bensulide	✔	✔	✔
Kerb	Pronamide	—	✔	✔
Revolver	Foramsulfuron	—	✔	✔
Rubigan	Fenarimol	—	✔	✔
TranXit	Rimsulfuron	—	✔	✔
Tupersan	Siduron	✔	—	—

FIGURE 25–3 Young
weeds (one- to five-leaf
stage) are easiest and
cheapest to control. Waiting
until weeds are more mature
requires multiple applications
for control, driving up costs,
and increasing the potential
of turf injury. Shown is a
young goosegrass plant.

available. Sequential applications should be spaced 10 to 14 days apart and only healthy-growing, nonstress turf should be treated.

Until recently, these various herbicide combinations were the main chemicals for broadleaf weed control. Clopyralid (Lontrel), triclopyr (Turflon), and various combinations with other herbicides have been introduced as alternatives to phenoxy herbicides for broadleaf weed control. Carfentrazone also has been added to several of these combination products to decrease the time during which control symptoms appear.

Triclopyr belongs to the Picolinic Acid herbicide family. Compounds in this family are noted for their high degree of activity. These herbicides are up to 10 times more potent than 2,4-D on certain broadleaf weed species. They are rapidly absorbed by the roots and foliage of broadleaf plants, and are readily translocated throughout the plants via both xylem and phloem tissues. Problems with this herbicide family include its soil mobility and the extreme ornamental sensitivity. Clopyralid also is one of the newer members of this herbicide family. It is currently marketed in a mixture with triclopyr (Confront) for use on labeled cool- and warm-season turfgrasses. Clopyralid is especially effective on leguminous plants (nitrogen producing) such as black medic, clover, kudzu, lespedeza, and vetch.

Chlorsulfuron (Corsair) and metsulfuron (Manor, Blade) are sulfonylurea herbicides labeled for selective broadleaf and tall fescue control in certain cool- and warm-season turfgrasses. Rates range from 0.25 to 5 **ounces** of product per acre, depending on the weed species present and herbicides used. Table 25–10 lists the effectiveness of commonly used postemergence herbicides for broadleaf weed control.

Grass Weed Control

Traditionally, for tolerant turfgrass species, postemergence grass weed control was through single and repeat applications of the organic arsenicals (e.g., MSMA, DSMA, CMA). Two to four applications, spaced seven days apart, generally are required for complete control. The rate and number of applications necessary for weed control usually increases as weeds mature. On cool-season turfgrasses, and zoysiagrass, organic arsenicals can be very phytotoxic, especially when used during high temperatures (>90°F, 32°C). Control also is reduced if rainfall occurs within 24 hours of treatment. Recently, new herbicide releases have provided alternatives to the arsenicals for postemergence grass weed control (Table 25–11). Decreased phytotoxicity as well as reduced number of applications are often associated with these herbicides. The following sections discuss herbicides available for various turfgrass species.

TABLE 25–8 Established turfgrass tolerance to postemergence broadleaf herbicides (refer to herbicide label for specific species listing).

Herbicides	Bentgrass greens	Bentgrass fairways	Ryegrass	Tall fescue	Fine fescue	Kentucky bluegrass	Buffalo-grass	Seashore paspalum
Broadleaf weed control								
Atrazine (Aatrex)	NR	NR	NR	NR	NR	NR	I (D)	NR
Bentazon (Basagran T&O)	NR-I	I	S	S	S	S	S	S-NR
Bromoxynil (Buctril)	NR	NR	S	S	S	S	NR	NR
Carfentrazone + 2,4-D + MCPP + dicamba (Speed Zone North)	NR	S	S	S	S	S	NR	NR
Carfentrazone + MCPA + MCPP + dicamba (Power Zone)	NR	NR	S	S	S	S	NR	NR
Carfentrazone + 2,4-D + MCPP + dicamba (Speed Zone Southern)	NR	S	S	S	S	S	S	S
Chlorsulfuron (Corsair, TFC)	NR	I	NR	NR	I-S	S	NR	NR
Clopyralid (Lontrel)	NR	I	S	S	S	S	S	S
2,4-D	I^1	NR	S	S	S	S	I	S
MCPP (mecoprop)	S	I	S	S	S	S	I	S
Dicamba (Vanquish)	I	I	S	S	S	S	I-NR	S
2,4-D + dicamba	I	I	S	S	S	S	NR	S
2,4-D + dichlorprop (2,4-DP)	I	I	S	S	S	S	S	S
2,4-D + MCPP	I	I	S	S	S	S	NR	NR
2,4-D + triclopyr (Turflon)	NR-I	NR	S	S	I	S	NR	NR
2,4-D + MCPP + dicamba	I	I	S	S	S	S	I	NR
2,4-D + MCPP + 2,4-DP	I	I	S	S	S	S	NR	NR
MCPA + MCPP + 2,4-DP	I	I	S	S	S	S	NR	NR
MCPA + triclopyr + clopyralid	S	S	S	S	S	S	S	S
Halosulfuron (Manage)	NR	I	NR	NR	NR	NR	NR	NR
Imazaquin (Image)	NR	NR	NR	NR	NR	NR	S-NR	S-NR
Metsulfuron (Manor, Blade)	NR	NR	NR	NR	I	I	S	S
Quinclorac (Drive)	NR	S	S	S	NR	S	S	S
Simazine (Princep T&O)	NR	NR	NR	NR	NR	NR	S	S
Triclopyr (Turflon)	NR	NR	S	S	S	S	NR	NR
Triclopyr + clopyralid (Confront)	NR	I	S	S	I	S	S	NR

(continued)

TABLE 25–8 *Established turfgrass tolerance to postemergence broadleaf herbicides (refer to herbicide label for specific species listing). (continued)*

Herbicides	Bahia-grass	Bermuda-grass	Carpet-grass	Centipede-grass	St. Augustine-grass	Zoysia-grass	Kikuyu-grass	Overseeded ryegrass/blends
Atrazine (Aatrex)	NR[1]	S-I (D)	I[2]	S	S	I	NR	NR
Bentazon (Basagran T&O)	S	S	S	S	S	S	NR	S-I
Bromoxynil (Buctril)	S	S	S	S	S	S	NR	S
Carfentrazone + 2,4-D + MCPP + dicamba (Speed Zone North)	NR	S	NR	NR	NR	S	NR	S
Carfentrazone + MCPA + MCPP + dicamba (Power Zone)	NR	S	NR	NR	NR	S	NR	S
Carfentrazone + 2,4-D + MCPP + dicamba (Speed Zone Southern)	S	S	NR	S	S	S	NR	S
Chlorsulfuron (Corsair, TFC)	I	S	I	I	I	I	NR	NR
Clopyralid (Lontrel)	S	S	S	S	S	S	NR	S
2,4-D	S	S	I	S-I	I	S	S	S-I
MCPP (mecoprop)	S	S	I	I	I	S	NR	I
Dicamba (Vanquish)	S	S	I	I	I	S	NR	I
2,4-D + dicamba	S	S	I	I	I	S	NR	S-I
2,4-D + dichlorprop (2,4-DP)	S	S	I	I	I	S	S	S
2,4-D + MCPP	S	S	I	I	I	S	NR	S
2,4-D + triclopyr (Turflon)	NR	NR	NR	NR	NR	NR	NR	S
2,4-D + MCPP + dicamba	S	S	I	I	I	S	NR	S
2,4-D + MCPP + 2,4-DP	S	S	I	I	I	S	NR	S
MCPA + MCPP + 2,4-DP	S	S	I	I	I	I	NR	S
MCPA + triclopyr + clopyralid	S	S	I	S	NR	S	NR	S
Halosulfuron (Manage)	S	S	S	S	S	S	S	S
Imazaquin (Image)	NR	S-I	I	S	S	S	NR	NR
Metsulfuron (Manor, Blade)	NR	S	I	I-S	S-I	S	NR	NR
Quinclorac (Drive)	NR	S	NR	NR	NR	S	NR	S
Simazine (Princep T&O)	NR	S-I (D)	I	S-I	S-I	I	NR	NR
Triclopyr (Turflon)	NR	NR	NR	NR	NR	NR	NR	S
Triclopyr + clopyralid (Confront)	I	I	NR	S	NR	S	NR	S

[1]**S**=Safe at labeled rates; **I**=Intermediate safety, use at reduced rates; **NR**=Not registered for use on and/or damages this turfgrass; **D**=Dormant turf only.

[2]Carpetgrass tolerance to herbicides listed has not fully been explored.

These are relative rankings and depend on factors such as environmental conditions, turfgrass vigor or health, application timing, and so forth, and are intended only as a guide.

TABLE 25–9 *Established turfgrass tolerance to postemergence grass herbicides (refer to herbicide label for specific species listing).*

Herbicides	Bentgrass greens	Bentgrass fairways	Ryegrass	Tall fescue	Fine fescue	Kentucky bluegrass	Buffalograss	Seashore paspalum	Kikuyugrass
Grass weed control									
Asulam (Asulox)	NR[1]	NR	NR	NR	NR	NR	I-NR	NR	NR
Bispyribac-sodium (Velocity)[4]	NR-I	NR	S	NR	NR	NR	NR	NR	NR
Clethodim (Envoy)	NR	NR	NR	NR	NR	NR	NR	NR	NR
Diclofop (Illoxan)	NR	NR	NR	NR	NR	NR	S-NR	NR	NR
DSMA, MSMA, CMA	NR-I	I	S-I	I	I	I	I	NR	NR
Ethofumesate (Prograss)[4]	NR-I	I	S	S	I	S	NR	S-NR	NR
Fenoxaprop (Acclaim Extra)	NR-I	I	S	S	S	S	NR	NR	NR
Fluazifop (Fusilade II)	NR	NR	NR	S-I	NR	NR	NR	NR	NR
Foramsulfuron (Revolver)	NR	NR	NR	NR	NR	NR	NR	NR	NR
Metribuzin (Sencor Turf)	NR	NR	NR	NR	NR	NR	NR	NR	NR
Pronamide (Kerb)	NR	NR	S	S	NR	NR	NR	S-NR	NR
Quinclorac (Drive)	NR	I	S	S	I	S	S	S-NR	S
Rimsulfuron (TranXit)	NR	NR	NR	NR	NR	NR	NR	NR	NR
Sethoxydim (Vantage)	NR	NR	NR	NR	S	NR	NR	NR	NR

Herbicides	Bahiagrass	Bermudagrass	Carpetgrass[3]	Centipedegrass	St. Augustinegrass	Zoysiagrass	Overseeded ryegrass/blends
Asulam (Asulox)	NR	S-I[2]	NR	NR	S-I	I-NR	NR
Bispyribac-sodium (Velocity)[4]	NR	S[4]	NR	NR	NR	NR	S[4]
Clethodim (Envoy)	NR	NR	NR	S	NR	NR	NR
Diclofop (Illoxan)	NR	S	NR	NR	NR	NR	NR
DSMA, MSMA, CMA	NR	S-I	NR	NR	NR	S-I	NR
Ethofumesate (Prograss)[4]	NR	D	NR	NR	NR	NR	I
Fenoxaprop (Acclaim Extra)	I-NR	I-NR	NR	NR	NR	I	I
Fluazifop (Fusilade II)	NR	NR	NR	NR	NR	I	NR
Foramsulfuron (Revolver)	NR	S	NR	NR	I	S	NR
Metribuzin (Sencor Turf)	NR	S-I	NR	NR	NR	NR	NR
Pronamide (Kerb)	S	S	NR	S	S	S	S
Quinclorac (Drive)	NR	S-I	NR	NR	NR	S	S
Rimsulfuron (TranXit)	NR	S	NR	NR	NR	NR	NR
Sethoxydim (Vantage)	NR	NR	NR	S	S	NR	NR

[1]S= Safe at labeled rates; **I**=Intermediate safety, use at reduced rates; **NR**=Not registered for use on and/or damages this turfgrass; **D**=Dormant turf only.
[2]Asulam is labeled for "Tifway" (419) bermudagrass and St. Augustinegrass.
[3]Carpetgrass tolerance to herbicides listed has not been fully explored.
[4]Used on dormant bermudagrass overseeded with perennial ryegrass.
These are relative rankings and depend on factors such as environmental conditions, turfgrass vigor or health, application timing, and so forth, and are intended only as a guide.

TABLE 25–10 Expected control of broadleaf weeds with turf herbicides (consult specific herbicide label for weed species listing).

Weed	Life cycle	Atrazine/simazine	2,4-D	MCPP	Dicamba	2,4-D + MCPP	2,4-D + 2,4-DP	2,4-D + MCPP + dicamba	Bentazon	Bromoxynil	Chlorsulfuron	Clopyralid	Imazaquin	Metsulfuron	Triclopyr	2,4-D + triclopyr	Triclopyr + clopyralid	MCPA + triclopyr + clopyralid	Carfentrazone, + 2,4-D + MCPP + MCPA &/or dicamba	Quinclorac
Aster	P[1]	—	G	—	—	F	G	F	P	P	—	G	—	G	—	F	G	G	G	—
Bedstraw, smooth	P	—	P	P-F	G	F	F	F	—	—	G	—	—	P	F-G	G	G	G	G	—
Beggarticks	A	G	G	F	F	F	G	G	G	—	—	—	—	—	—	G	G	G	G	—
Betony, Florida	P	F-G[2]	F	F	F	F	F	F-G	G	—	—	—	—	—	—	G	G	G	G	—
Bittercress, hairy	WA	—	E	G	E	E	E	E	P	—	—	—	—	E	G	—	—	—	G	—
Bindweed, field	P	—	G	E	G	E-F	G	E	—	P	—	—	—	G	G	G	G	G	G	E
Burclover	A	—	F-P	F	E	E-F	E-F	E	P-F	P	F	G	—	—	F	—	G	G	G	—
Buttercups	WA, B&P	F	G	F	F-G	E	E	E	P	P	G	G	—	E	G	G	E	G	E	—
Buttonweed, Virginia	P	—	F	P-F	F	F	E	E-F	P	P	F	F	—	G	F	F-P	G	E	E	—
Carpetweed	SA	E	G	F	E	E	E	E	P	—	—	—	—	P	G	F	—	E	E	—
Carrot, wild	A, B	E	G	F	E	G	E	E	P	P	G	—	—	E	—	G	—	E	E	—
Catsear	P	—	E-F	F	E	E	E	E	—	—	—	—	—	—	—	—	—	G	—	—
Chamberbitter	SA, P	E	—	E-F	—	E-F	E-F	—	—	—	—	—	—	—	P-F	—	—	—	—	—
Chickweed, common	WA	E	G	G	G	E	E	E	F-G	P	G	—	—	E	G	E	E	E	G	E
Chickweed, mouseear	WA, P	F	G	G	G	E	E	E	—	P	G	—	—	E	—	—	E	E	G	E
Chicory	P	—	G	G	G	G	E	E-F	—	P	F	P	G	E	—	E-F	E	E	G	E
Cinquefoil, common	P	—	E-F	E-F	E-F	E-F	E-F	E-F	—	—	—	—	—	E	—	G	—	E	E	—
Clover, crimson	SA	—	G	G	G	G	G	E	—	—	G	G	—	—	—	—	E	E	E	F
Clover, hop	WA	E	G	F	G	F	F	E	—	—	G	G	—	F	—	—	E	E	E	—
Clover, white	P	E	F-G	G	G	G-E	G-E	E	—	—	G	G	—	E	F-G	E	G-E	E	E	—
Cudweed	WA	G-E	G-E	—	E	G	G	G	—	P	—	—	—	E	—	E-F	—	G	—	—
Daisy, English	P	—	P	F	G	F	F	F	P	P	F	F	—	—	—	G-E	G	E	G	F
Daisy, oxeye	P, B	—	F	F	F	F	F	E-F	—	—	—	—	—	—	G	—	—	—	—	—
Dandelion	P	E-F	G	G	G	E	E	E	P	P	G	F	F	E	G	G-E	G	E	E	G
Dayflower, spreading	SA	G-E	F	F-G	G	F-G	F-G	F-G	G	P	—	—	F	G	—	F-E	G	G	G	G
Deadnettle, purple	WA	G-E	G	F	G	F	—	F-G	—	P	—	—	F	P	G	F-G	F	G	G	E
Dichondra	P	E-F	E	F	E-F	E	E	G	—	—	—	—	—	—	—	—	—	—	G	—
Dock, broadleaf & curly	P	F	G	F-G	F	G	G	E-F	P	P	F	G	P-F	G-E	G	E	E	E	G	—
Dogfennel	P	—	G	—	G	—	—	E	—	—	—	—	—	G	—	E	G	E	—	—
Doveweed	SA	G-E	F	F	F	F-G	F-G	F-G	—	—	—	—	—	P-F	—	F-G	—	F-G	—	—
Evening primrose, cutleaf	WA	E	—	—	G	—	F	—	P	F	—	—	G	—	—	—	—	—	—	—
Falsedandelion, Carolina	WA, B	E	G	G	G	G	G	G	P	P	—	—	G	—	G	G	G	G	—	—
Filaree, redstem	WA	P	P-F	G	G	—	—	—	P	P	F	—	—	G-E	P	—	—	—	G	—
Garlic, wild	P	P	P	P	—	—	G	—	—	—	F	—	—	—	—	—	—	—	G	—
Geranium, Carolina	WA	E	E	E-F	E	E-F	E-F	E-F	P	P	F	—	G	G-E	—	—	—	G	G	—
Groundsel	WA	—	G	G	—	E	G	E-F	G	G	G	G	G	P-F	—	—	—	G	G	P
Hawkweed	P	—	G	P	G	E-F	E-F	E-F	—	—	—	—	—	E	—	—	G	G	G	—

682

Weed	Life cycle¹																		
Healall	P	—	G	P	P	—	E	E	P	P	P	—	—	—	G	—	E	E	—
Henbit	WA	E	F	G	G	F	E-F	F	P	F	G	G	—	—	E-F	G	G	G	F-G
Horseweed	WA, SA	E	—	F	E	—	G-E	—	—	—	E	E	G	G	E	—	E	—	—
Ivy, ground	P	—	G	G	G	—	E-F	F-E	—	—	G	G	G	F	G	—	F	G	—
Knawel	WA	—	F	F	F	F	F-G	E-F	—	—	F	F	—	—	F	—	G	G	—
Knotweed, prostrate	SA	—	G	G	G	G	F-G	G	—	G	G	G	G	G	G	G	G	G	—
Kochia	SA	—	G	G	F	G	F	F	G	F	—	—	—	—	G	—	G	G	—
Lambsquarters	SA	G	G	G	F	F	G	E	G	G	G	G	F	G	F	G	H	E	—
Lespedeza	SA	E	F-P	E	E-F	E	E	G	—	—	—	—	—	E	E	E	E	E	—
Mallow	P	—	F	F	G	G	E-F	E-F	—	F	F	—	—	—	E	G	G	G	E
Medic, black	A	—	P	P	G	G	E	E	—	—	—	—	—	—	E	G	E	E	—
Moneywort	P	—	G	F	F	G	G	G	—	—	—	G	—	G	G	G	G	G	—
Mugwort	P	—	F	F-P	—	G	F	F	F	G	G	—	P-F	—	—	—	—	—	—
Mustard, wild	WA	E	G	F	G	G-E	E	E	G	F	F	G	G	—	F	E	F	G	—
Nettle, stinging	P	F-G	G	—	F	F	F	F	—	—	—	G	—	—	G-E	G	E	—	—
Onion, wild	P	P	G	P	F	G	E	E	P	F	P	—	—	—	G-E	—	E	G	—
Parsley-piert	WA	E	G	E-F	E-F	E-F	E-F	E-F	G	E-F	P	—	—	E	—	E	E	—	—
Pearlwort	WA	—	E-F	E-F	—	E-F	E-F	E-F	—	—	—	F	E-F	F	E-F	—	—	—	—
Pennywort (dollarweed)	P	G	G	E-F	E-F	E-F	E-F	P-F	P	P	—	G	F	F	G	—	E	E	E
Pepperweed, Virginia	WA	E	G	E-F	G	E	E	E	G	G	—	—	F-G	G-E	E	—	E	G	—
Pigweed	SA	E	G	G	E	G	G	G	P	G	P	G	G	F-G	G	—	F	G	—
Pineapple-weed	WA, SA	—	F	—	P	F	F-G	F-G	P	P	—	G	G-F	G	F-G	—	E	E	—
Plantains	P	F-P	G	F-P	P	E	E	E	G	F-P	G	G	G	G	E	—	E	G	—
Purslane, common	SA	G	G	G	G	E-F	E-F	G	F	G	—	G	G	G	G	—	G	G	—
Pusley, Florida	SA	G	G	G	F	G	G	G	F	G	G	G	G	G	F	—	F	F	G
Ragweed, common	SA	G	G	G	F	F	G	G	—	G	G	G	G	G	G	—	G	G	G
Rocket, yellow	WA, B	E-F	F-G	F	E-F	G	G	G	P	F-G	G	P	G	G	E-F	—	E-F	E-F	G
Shepherd's-purse	WA	—	G	E-F	E-F	E-F	E-F	E-F	P	G	G	—	F	G	F	—	F	F	G
Sida	A	—	F	—	—	—	—	F-G	—	F-G	F-G	—	—	—	—	—	—	—	—
Smartweed	SA	G	F	G	G	G	G	G	G	G	E	G	F-G	G	F-G	—	G	G	G
Sorrel, red	P	—	P	—	F	F	F	G	E	F-G	G	F-G	G	G	G	—	G	G	E
Speedwell, common	WA	G	G	G	E-F	G	G	G	G	F-G	P	F-G	G-E	F-G	G	—	P-F	F-G	—
Speedwell, corn	P	F-P	P	P	F	G	G	G	P	F-G	G	F-G	F	G	F-G	—	E	F-G	F-G
Speedwell, germander	WA	E	F-P	P	E-F	G	G	G	P	P	P	F-G	G	F-G	G	—	F	F	—
Speedwell, purslane	P	F	P	—	F-P	G	G	G	—	—	—	F-G	G	F-G	G	—	F	F-G	—
Speedwell, thymeleaf	P	F	P-F	F	F	G	G	G	F	G	G	F-G	G	F-G	G	—	G	G	G
Spurge, prostrate	SA	G	F	G	G	E	G	G	G	G	G	E-F	F	E-F	E-F	—	G	G	G
Spurge, spotted	SA	E	G	G	G	E	G	G	G	G	P	E-F	F	E-F	E-F	—	G	G	G
Spurry, corn	SA	F-P	—	G	F-G	G	F-G	F	P	F	P	F	F	F	F	—	G	F	—
Spurweed (lawn burweed)	WA	F-G	F	E-F	E	G	F-G	G	F-G	F-G	F-G	G-E	F-G	E	E	—	G-E	—	E
Strawberry, Indian mock	P	—	P	F	E-F	F	E-F	F-G	F-G	F-G	—	G	G	G	—	—	P-F	—	—
Thistles	B, P	E	G	G	E-F	G	E	E	G	G	E	P	G	—	G	—	G	—	—
Vetch, common	WA, SA	G	G	G	F	G	G	G	G	G	G	G	G	E	G	—	E	G	G
Violet, Johnny-jumpup	WA	F-P	F-P	E-F	F	F	F-P	P	P	F	P	F	P	—	—	—	F	—	—
Violet, wild	P	F-P	F-P	E-F	P-F	P	F-P	P	F	P-F	P	F-G	P	F	F	—	F	F	—
Woodsorrel, creeping	P	P	P	G	G	G	P-F	P-F	P-F	P-F	G	F-G	P	F-G	F-G	—	F-G	F-G	G
Woodsorrel, yellow	P	F	P	P	G	E-F	F-P	P-F	P	P	P-F	E-F	—	E-F	E-F	—	E-F	E-F	—
Yarrow	P	—	F	F	E	G	E-F	E-F	G	P	G	—	G	F-P	G	—	G	G	—

¹A = Annual; B = Biennial; P = Perennial; SA = Summer annual; WA = Winter annual. ²E = Excellent (>89 percent) control; F = Fair to good (70 to 89 percent), good control sometimes with high rates; however, a repeat treatment one to three weeks later of each at the standard or reduced rate is usually more effective, especially on perennial weeds; P = Poor (<70 percent) control in most cases. Not all weeds have been tested for susceptibility to each herbicide listed.

TABLE 25–11 Guide to grass weed control with postemergence turfgrass herbicides (refer to herbicide label for specific species listing).

Herbicide[1]	Crabgrass	Goosegrass	Annual bluegrass	Sandspur	Dallisgrass	Thin (bull) paspalum	Ryegrass	Smutgrass	Bahiagrass	Carpetgrass	Tall fescue	Bermudagrass	Quackgrass
Asulam (Asulox)	G	F	P	F	P	P-F	–	F	P	G	P	P	–
Atrazine (Aatrex)	P-F[2]	P	G-E	F	P	P	G-E	F-G	F	P	F	P-F	F
Bispyribac-sodium (Velocity)	–	–	G	–	–	–	P	–	–	–	–	P	–
Chlorsulfuron (Corsair, TFC)	P	P	P	P	P	P	G	F	P	P	G	P	–
Clethodim (Envoy)	E	G-E	G	G	–	–	G-E	–	–	–	P	G	G
Diclofop (Illoxan)	P	G-E	P	P	P	P	G	P	P	P	P	P	–
DSMA, MSMA	G	F	P	G	F	F-G	P	P	F	G	P	P	–
Ethofumesate (Prograss)	P	P	F-G*	P	P	P	P	P	P	–	P	P-G	–
Fenoxaprop (Acclaim Extra)	G-E	G-E	P	G	P	P	P	P	G	–	P	F-G	–
Fluazifop (Fusilade II)	G-E	G	F	G	P	P	G-E	P	G	–	P	G	G
Foramsulfuron (Revolver)	P	G-E	E	–	F	–	E	–	–	–	G-E	P	–
Metribuzin (Sencor)	F-G	G-E	G	–	F	P	F	P	P	–	F	P	–
Metsulfuron (Manor)	P	P	P	P	P	P	G	P	G	P	F	P	–
Pronamide (Kerb)	P	P	G-E	P	P	P	G-E	P	P	–	G	P	F-G
Rimsulfuron (TranXit)	P	P	F-E	P	P	P	G-E	P	P	P	P	P	P
Sethoxydim (Vantage)	G-E	G	P	G	P-F	P	P	P	G	P	P	F-G	F-G
Simazine (Princep T&O)	P-F	P	G-E	P-F	P	P	G-E	F	F	P	F	P-F	F
Quinclorac (Drive)	E	P	P	–	F	P	P	P	P	P	P	P	–

[1] Repeat applications usually 5 to 14 days apart are needed for most herbicides and weeds. This is especially true as weeds mature, producing flowers and seedheads.

[2] **E** = Excellent (>90 percent) control with one application;

G = Good (80 to 90 percent) control with one application;

F = Fair to good (70 to 89 percent), good control sometimes with high rates; however, a repeat treatment one to three weeks later of each at the standard or reduced rate is usually more effective; **P** = Poor (<70 percent) control in most cases.

– = Control unknown as all weeds have not been tested for susceptibility to each herbicide listed.

*Ethofumesate provides good to excellent control of most true annual biotypes of annual bluegrass, but only poor to fair control of perennial biotypes.

Warm-Season Turfgrasses

Bermudagrass and zoysiagrass

Postemergence control of crabgrass species and goosegrass has traditionally been with **organic arsenicals (e.g., MSMA/DSMA).** As previously mentioned, repeat applications with a short time interval between applications (five to seven days) are required—especially for goosegrass, dallisgrass, thin paspalum, or bahiagrass control. Increasing phytotoxicity usually results in bermudagrass and zoysiagrass with repeat applications.

In order to increase herbicidal activity on goosegrass, various other herbicides are combined with the organic arsenicals. High rates of **metribuzin (Sencor Turf),** an asymmetrical triazine, gives excellent control of goosegrass, but bermudagrass has marginal tolerance. Lower rates of metribuzin combined with arsenical herbicides provide good to excellent goosegrass control. However, this combination should only be used on well-established bermudagrass which is actively growing and also is maintained at mowing heights greater than one-half inch (1.3 cm).

Foramsulfuron (Revolver), a sulfonylurea herbicide, has recently been labeled for postemergence control of goosegrass in bermudagrass and zoysiagrass. Minimum turfgrass injury occurs but foramsulfuron is not effective for crabgrass control and requires two to four weeks for goosegrass control.

Diclofop-methyl (Illoxan), a member of the aryl-oxy-phenoxy herbicide family, controls goosegrass with good turf tolerance. Little damage to bermudagrass, including putting greens, occurs and repeat applications are not usually necessary. This herbicide is most active on younger, lower-mowed goosegrass. Weed control is relatively slow, often requiring two to three weeks to take effect. The weed control spectrum also appears to be limited, with goosegrass being the most susceptible grass species. Treated areas should not be overseeded with perennial ryegrass for at least six weeks after herbicide application. Diclofop also should not be mixed with any other postemergence herbicides, especially 2,4-D or MSMA as reduced goosegrass control and increased turfgrass phytotoxicity may result. An exception involves controlling mature, clump-forming plants. Tank-mixing diclofop with metribuzin at one-fourth to one-half pound ai/acre (0.28 to 0.56 kg/ha) will help control these mature plants. Expect turf phytotoxicity for 7 to 21 days following this combination treatment.

Fenoxaprop-ethyl (Acclaim Extra), another member of the aryl-oxy-phenoxy herbicide family, controls annual grass weeds, crabgrass species in particular. Zoysiagrass and, at much lower rates, bentgrass fairways have acceptable tolerance to fenoxaprop. Zoysiagrass also has good tolerance to **fluazifop (Fusilade II T&O).** This material has excellent activity on annual grasses such as crabgrass and goosegrass and suppresses perennial weeds such as bermudagrass. Control with either fenoxaprop or fluazifop should begin in spring after the bermudagrass has greened-up and be repeated in two to three weeks until satisfactory control is achieved. Short-term turf phytotoxicity can be expected after treatment.

Quinclorac (Drive), a quinolinecarboxylic acid herbicide family member, provides postemergence crabgrass, signalgrass, barnyardgrass, and foxtail control in bermudagrass and zoysiagrass. Drive also controls some broadleaf weeds such as pennywort, speedwells, dandelion, and black medic. With repeat applications about three weeks apart, Drive suppresses torpedograss and kikuyugrass but has little activity on goosegrass. Avoid drift onto ornamentals.

Bahiagrass

Bahiagrass is somewhat sensitive to most postemergence herbicides. This sensitivity limits the choices of materials available for use on it. Although labeled for use on bahiagrass, most postemergence broadleaf (e.g., 2,4-D, dicamba, and/or mecoprop) herbicides will result in yellowing, especially if applied at high air temperatures or if the turf is growing under stressful conditions. Normally, the phytotoxicity is not lethal, and recovery can be expected within one to two weeks.

Selective postemergence grass weed control in golf course bahiagrass is not currently available. Spot treatment with a nonselective herbicide, such as glyphosate, is the only chemical method of control.

Cool-Season Turfgrasses

Postemergence grass weed control in cool-season turfgrasses has previously been limited to various members of the **organic arsenicals.** Specific formulations (e.g., CMA) and rates are necessary for use on most cool-season turfgrasses or unacceptable levels of injury may result. Proper timing at a young weed-growth stage, during mild environmental conditions, and actively growing turfgrasses are specific considerations before using any of these herbicides.

Fluazifop (Fusilade II T&O) may be used on tall fescue at low rates to control annual grassy weeds and suppress bermudagrass. Applications should be in spring and prior to the summer-stress period when weeds are small. Good soil moisture should be present when applications are made.

Sethoxydim (Vantage 1L) at 2.4 pints per acre (2.8 L/ha) controls many annual grasses in fine fescue. Spring applications are best due to cooler temperatures and younger weeds that are easier to control.

Chlorosulfuron (Corsair, TFC 75DF) controls tall fescue selectively in Kentucky bluegrass and fine fescues. Low rates (1 to 5 oz/a, 11 to 58 g/ha) and spot treatments help minimize turf phytotoxicity. Chlorosulfuron also selectively removes ryegrass from bentgrass.

Fenxoaprop (Acclaim Extra 1EC) at 15 to 45 ounces per acre (1.1 to 3.3 L/ha) may be used on Kentucky bluegrass, fine fescues, tall fescue, annual bluegrass, bentgrass fairways, and perennial ryegrass to control most annual grass weeds and to suppress bermudagrass encroachment. Spring applications are best and the turf should not be under moisture or heat stress when treated.

Quinclorac (Drive) provides postemergence crabgrass, signalgrass, barnyardgrass, and foxtail control in bluegrass, ryegrass, and tall fescue. Creeping bentgrass and fine fescue have intermediate tolerance. Drive also controls some broadleaf weeds such as pennywort, speedwells, dandelion, and black medic. Avoid drift onto ornamentals.

SPECIAL WEED MANAGEMENT SITUATIONS

Poa annua Control

Annual bluegrass (*Poa annua* L.) is the most troublesome winter annual grass weed on golf courses. Its low growth habit and unique ability to thrive in moist conditions and compacted areas make it difficult to control with management practices alone. Annual bluegrass has a lighter-green color than most grass species used to overseed golf greens, and produces numerous seedheads that disrupt the playing surface. Also, due to low heat tolerance, annual bluegrass quickly dies in warm weather, leaving areas bare until the bermudagrass has time to fill-in.

Chemical control of annual bluegrass is difficult to achieve due to: (1) the inability of most preemergence herbicides to prevent annual bluegrass germination selectively while allowing the desirable overseeded grass to become established, and (2) most postemergence herbicides effective on annual bluegrass also damage the desirable overseeded grass species.

In recent years, annual bluegrass has quickly reached epidemic proportions for many golf courses. The reasons for this are numerous: (1) a variety of biotypes are present; (2) the switch of many golf courses to the similar *Poa trivialis* for overseeding greens reduces herbicide options; (3) increased overseeding of fairways generally increases *Poa annua* populations; and (4) the occurrence of herbicide-resistant plants has increased the incidence of Poa and continues to mount frustration for members and superintendents alike.

A *Poa annua* Primer

Biology

The annual Poa biotype (*Poa annua* ssp. *annua* L.) has a nonstoloniferous bunch-type growth habit and generally a light-green color. It is a true annual and begins to germinate when daytime temperatures consistently drop into the mid-70°Fs and nighttime temperatures are in the mid-50°Fs for several consecutive days in late summer and early fall (Table 25–12). Maximum seed germination occurs when full sunlight is present; thus, thin, weak turf stands often have the earliest Poa germination. Areas remaining cooler, including shaded areas and continuous wet areas, also have earlier Poa seed germination. Another flush of germination typically occurs in early winter, generally from mid-December through mid-January when daytime temperatures are warm and nighttime temperatures are cold. This alternating warm/cold temperature scarifies additional seed; thus, it causes another flush of germination. Many herbicides applied in late summer for the initial fall flush of germination will not satisfactorily control this second germination; thus, repeat applications may be necessary.

TABLE 25–12 *Growth responses of annual bluegrass to varying temperatures.*

Growth response	Temperature
Germination	
- Optimum	mid-70°Fs (21°C), daytime
	mid-50°Fs (10°C), nighttime
- Range	35 to 102°F (1.7 to 39°C)
Maximum growth	60 to 70°F (15.5 to 21°C)
Maximum root growth	65 to 70°F (18 to 21°C) (soil temperatures)
Seedhead development	≈75°F (26.7°C)
Maximum heat tolerance	85 to 95°F (29 to 35°C)
Minimum growth	50°F (10°C) (soil temperatures)
Lethal cold temperature	≈5°F (−15°C)

After germination, Poa grows and then tills (mostly unnoticeable) throughout the fall and early winter months. Once late winter arrives, Poa begins to shift its growth from vegetative toward reproductive by forming numerous seedheads that can literally turn a turf stand snow-white (Plate 25–3). Since *Poa* has both male and female flowers on each plant, they are capable of either self-pollinating or cross-fertilizing nearby plants. Each small plant can produce several hundred viable seeds. From the time Poa seed germinates in the soil, 44 to 149 days are required before seedheads form. However, the timing of seedhead formation is influenced by many factors; weather, geography, and the biotypes of Poa present at your location are most important. The annual biotype reduces its growth in late spring and dies when daytime temperatures reach the lower 90°Fs for several consecutive days. Seed can remain viable in the soil for more than six years, thereby ensuring a continual supply.

Several cultural factors favor Poa growth and occurrence. The first step, therefore, in a total Poa management program would be to shift the following to those favoring turfgrass growth.

1. **Continuous wet and compacted soils**—Poa thrives under wet and/or compacted soil conditions. Due to its shallow root system, Poa can tolerate lower soil oxygen levels while turfgrass stands will begin to thin. Use appropriate soil mixtures to reduce soil compaction. Soils should be frequently aerified, and greens should be mowed with walking mowers. Greens also should be spiked frequently to reduce surface compaction and to sever bermudagrass stolons to encourage a thicker turf stand. Also, do not overwater.
2. **Excessive nitrogen rates**—A high available nitrogen supply will profusely encourage Poa occurrence, growth, and tillering.
3. **Excessive soil phosphorus levels**—Poa has been shown to be favored by excessive phosphorus levels and will outcompete turfgrasses under these conditions. Supply sufficient phosphorus as indicated by soil tests for the turf but do not use excessive rates.
4. **Leaving clippings**—Due to its tolerance to low mowing height and abundant seed production, leaving clippings only helps spread Poa seed, thereby slowly increasing its occurrence.
5. **Overseeding**—Overseeding bermudagrass provides winter and early spring turf color for golfers. However, overseeding greatly encourages Poa invasion since prepping bermudagrass via aerifying and verticutting helps thin the turf stand. This opens the turf to more sunlight, which encourages Poa to germinate. The increased watering need for overseeding establishment also encourages Poa. Overseeding also weakens the bermudagrass in spring, extending the time needed for recovery, allowing Poa to encroach slowly. In addition, overseeding restricts the number of herbicide options available, as controlling one cool-season turfgrass in another is very difficult, especially if the overseeded grass is *Poa trivialis,* a relative of *Poa annua.*

A buffer zone of overseeding around the approach helps intercept Poa seed from golfers and equipment. Courses with epidemic Poa levels may opt to skip overseeding fairways until the population is brought under control. Others may overseed fairways but skip approaches as more control options are available for non-overseeded areas.

Herbicide-Resistant *Poa annua*

Besides those listed management practices that encourage *Poa annua* stands, the recent occurrence of herbicide-resistant Poa biotypes has further reduced the number of effective control options. Resistant biotypes to simazine and atrazine (Princep and Aatrex), the dinitroaniline herbicides, and ethofumesate (Progress) have been noted.

Resistance problems generally begin to show up when a class of compounds is continuously used over an approximately 7- to 10-year period. These herbicides selectively control those susceptible biotypes, thereby gradually allowing the resistant biotypes to spread and increase over time. Just as turf managers should rotate between fungicide groups to prevent disease resistance, herbicides with different modes of action should also be rotated to prevent Poa resistance.

Control Options

The following sections discuss various Poa control options on golf courses. These include using selective and nonselective herbicides and plant growth retardants.

Overseeded Bermudagrass

Preemergence control

Preemergence annual bluegrass control is currently achieved with several herbicides. Each has its own precautions before use, and if these are not followed, unsatisfactory results may occur.

Pronamide (Kerb 50WP)

Pronamide must be applied before annual bluegrass germination and planting of overseeding grass. Thirty to 45 days is the minimum recommended period between application and overseeding. It also is recommended that applications not be made where drainage flows onto areas planted with cool-season grasses, or onto bermudagrass golf greens. A one to two pound per acre application rate of actual product is used.

Superintendents who have to apply pronamide closer than 30 days before overseeding can offset the problems of reduced ryegrass seed germination by applying a thin layer of charcoal (Plate 25–4). The charcoal will bind the pronamide and prevent it from damaging the overseeded ryegrass. However, the mess and dark color associated with charcoal applications and the risk of it not working must be considered before use. Activated charcoal should be applied at two to four pounds per 1,000 square feet (10 to 20 kg per 100 m^2), and reseeding should occur no sooner than seven days following charcoal use.

Fenarimol (Rubigan 1AS)

Fenarimol is a systemic fungicide used to control several turfgrass diseases, which gradually reduces annual bluegrass populations without adverse effects to overseeded grasses or to bermudagrass. Application should occur before overseeding and germination of annual bluegrass. A treatment scheme has been suggested consisting of two (6 oz/1,000 ft^2 each, 19 L/ha) or three (4 oz/1,000 ft^2 each, 13 L/ha) sequential treatments, with the final application being two weeks before overseeding with perennial ryegrass. A follow-up application of two ounces per 1,000 square feet (6 L/ha) in early January may be necessary for heavy Poa populations. For the 50 WSP Rubigan formulation, two 1.5-ounce (3.7 kg/ha) or three 1.0-ounce applications (3.1 kg/ha) should be made per 1,000 square feet and spaced as discussed for the 1 AS formulation. The total should not exceed three ounces per 1,000 square feet (9 kg/ha). Unlike pronamide, fenarimol does not appear to affect either overseeded perennial ryegrass or bermudagrass, but the necessity of properly timed repeat application can be a drawback for those with limited budgets and labor. Also, if *Poa trivialis* or creeping bentgrass is used for overseeding, the last fenarimol application should be at least 30 days before overseeding or a delay in seed germination can occur. *Poa* control should not be expected to exceed 95 percent.

Bensulide (Betasan, Pre-San)

Bensulide also provides varying preemergence annual bluegrass control and an acceptable stand of ryegrasses is obtainable when seeding is delayed four months after herbicide application. This could, however, be influenced by environment and management practices. The ryegrass tolerance range is narrow. Current label directions indicate 100 pounds per acre (112 kg/ha) of the 12.5G formulation or 2.5 gallons (23 L/ha) of the 4L formulation should be applied (12 1/2 lbs ai/A). This four-month waiting period allows enough bensulide to be in the soil to control the Poa but also be low enough to not interfere with germination of the overseeded grass. If the treated area needs to be seeded sooner than four months after application, powdered, activated charcoal can be used to deactivate the bensulide as previously discussed. The turf should be irrigated immediately after application to wash the charcoal into the soil. Reseeding should occur no sooner then seven days after applying the charcoal.

Benefin (Balan 2.5G)

Benefin also may be used at 115 to 120 pounds per acre (129 to 134 kg/ha) in areas to be overseeded with ryegrass for preemergence annual bluegrass control. A minimum waiting period of 45 days must be observed between the 115 pounds per acre benefin application and ryegrass overseeding, while 12 to 16 weeks are necessary for the 120 pounds per acre rate. This use of benefin is recommended only on larger areas such as golf course fairways and athletic fields, but not on golf greens. Neither benefin nor bensulide remain for long periods when applied to wet soils. Poa control with these materials under wet conditions generally is unsatisfactory.

Dithiopyr (Dimension)

Dithiopyr provides good control of annual bluegrass when applied six to eight weeks prior to overseeding bermudagrass with perennial ryegrass. Dithiopyr is available in various formulations, and best control often accompanies the use of a granular formulation. The maximum labeled rate for this type of application is 0.5 pounds ai/acre (0.56 kg ai/ha). Due to its soil persistence characteristics, the six to eight week waiting period is necessary to prevent dithiopyr from affecting perennial ryegrass establishment. Dithiopyr is no longer labeled for use on putting greens.

Prodiamine (Barricade)

Prodiamine has a long soil half-life but can be applied before overseeding bermudagrass with perennial ryegrass for annual bluegrass control. Similar to dithiopyr, prodiamine is available in various formulations. Use rates range from 0.38 to 0.66 pounds ai/acre applied six to eight weeks in advance of overseeding. Research conducted at several universities shows prodiamine applied at 0.5 pounds ai/acre (0.56 kg ai/ha) eight weeks in advance of overseeding provides consistently high levels of annual bluegrass control with only slight effects on perennial ryegrass establishment. With this herbicide, a minimum of 250 pounds per acre (280 kg/ha) of perennial ryegrass should be used. Prodiamine is not labeled for use on bermudagrass putting greens.

Rimsulfuron (TranXit)

Rimsulfuron controls annual bluegrass in bermudagrass scheduled to be overseeded with perennial ryegrass. This herbicide has an extremely short half-life in the soil and can be applied 10 to 14 days in advance of overseeding. When used in this manner, very young annual bluegrass plants that have germinated in the early fall months are effectively controlled. This herbicide also has short-term preemergence control of annual bluegrass. Rimsulfuron should not be applied any closer than 10 days before overseeding perennial ryegrass, or stand establishment will be affected. The best Poa control strategy with rimsulfuron or formasulfuron is to delay overseeding as late as possible to allow maximum Poa germination, and then apply 10 days prior to overseeding. Rimsulfuron belongs to the sulfonylurea herbicide family and is used at rates ranging from 0.031 to 0.062 pounds ai/acre (1 to 2 oz product per acre, 0.035 to 0.069 kg ai per hectare).

Foramsulfuron (Revolver)

Foramsulfuron is used on bermudagrass and zoysiagrass, and similar to rimsulfuron, it may be applied 14 days in advance of overseeding bermudagrass with perennial ryegrass or *Poa trivialis* for the control of annual bluegrass. Like rimsulfuron, foramsulfuron also has an extremely short half-life in the soil. It also is a member of the sulfonylurea herbicide family and is used at rates ranging from 0.006 to 0.025 pounds ai/acre (0.007 to 0.028 kg ai/ha).

Postemergence control

Ethofumesate (Progress 1.5EC) provides preemergence and early postemergence annual blue-grass control in bermudagrass. However, to prevent undesirable turfgrass injury, the application rate, timing, and frequency are important. If applied in fall before bermudagrass dormancy, an immediate cessation of bermudagrass growth occurs. A delay in spring transition from ryegrass to bermudagrass also occurs with early fall application. Spring green-up of bermudagrass can be severely retarded with February applications. Therefore, ethofumesate should only be used where sufficient cold weather occurs for complete bermudagrass dormancy, and then applied during late fall (e.g., late November) through early winter (e.g., no later than January 15). Ethofumesate is not labeled for golf greens, zoysiagrass, or fine fescues. The application rate is two quarts per acre, 4.7 liters per hectare (or 1 lb ai/a, 1.12 kg ai/ha) applied 30 to 45 days after overseeding, with a repeat application 21 to 28 days later.

Plant growth retardants

Certain plant growth retardants (PGRs) also help suppress the seedheads of *Poa annua* in over-seeded bermudagrass fairways. Timing is critical with these, and the club must be willing to accept some degree of short-term turfgrass discoloration (or phytotoxicity).

Mefluidide (Embark 2S, Embark Lite 0.2S)

Apply mefluidide at 0.05 to 0.125 pound ai/acre (Embark 2S at 0.5 pt/a, 0.085 L/ha; Embark Lite at 2 to 5 pt/a, 2.3 to 5.9 L/ha) to suppress annual bluegrass seedhead development. Mefluidide must be applied before seedheads emerge. Application timing varies between geographical locations, but generally occurs during January though early March (actual timing of the application depends upon the location and climatic conditions). Mefluidide is primarily foliage absorbed. Do not apply mefluidide to turf within four growing months after seeding, and do not reseed within three days after application. Treated turf may appear less dense and temporarily discolored. Adding one to two quarts of a nonionic surfactant per 100 gallons of spray solution may enhance suppression; however, discoloration may also be increased. Iron applications may lessen discoloration. Mefluidide formulations are not recommended for use on golf course putting greens. Read and follow label recommendations before use.

Paclobutrazol (Trimmit 2SC)

Apply paclobutrazol at 6.4 to 48 fl oz/a, 0.5 to 3.5 L/ha (0.1 to 0.75 lb ai/acre) in late winter to early spring after the growth of desired grasses has resumed and one to two mowings has occurred. Do not apply after March 15 to avoid delaying green-up of bermudagrass. Paclobutrazol is root absorbed, and one-fourth inch (0.64 cm) of rainfall or irrigation water should be applied within 24 hours of application. Repeat applications may be made three to four weeks apart. It is not recommended for use with bermudagrass golf greens such as "Tifdwarf," "Champion," or "TifEagle." Do not use if *Poa annua* populations exceed 70 percent.

Non-overseeded Bermudagrass

Preemergence Control

Poa control in non-overseeded bermudagrass turf is generally much easier and cheaper to achieve as more effective herbicide options are available. Control is available with most commonly used preemergence herbicides such as benefin (Balan), dithiopyr (Dimension), oryzalin (Surflan), oxadiazon (Ronstar), pendimethalin (Pre-M, Pendulum), prodiamine (Barricade), and various combinations such as Team (benefin + trifluralin) and XL (benefin + oryzalin). Approximately 80 to 90 percent control is the best level of control expected from a single preemergence herbicide application. For season-long control, some preemergence products will need a repeat application approximately 60 days following the first.

Postemergence Control

Postemergence control of Poa in non-overseeded bermudagrass is numerous. However, timing and selective placement are very important to prevent damage to the overseeded stand or permanent bermudagrass.

Selective control

Pronamide (Kerb 50WP) can be applied either as preemergence or early postemergence for excellent Poa control. Application rates are between one and two pounds of product per acre (1.1 to 2.2 kg/ha) and should be timed for mid-fall (e.g., November), with a possible repeat in mid-winter (e.g., late January/early February). If applications are made later in spring, control will drop and the time required for control significantly increases. Kerb also will help control perennial (or renegade) ryegrass before it tillers and clumps. Kerb, however, should *not* be used upslope of desirable overseeding or bentgrass as it can and will move with water and run across these areas, causing death of the overseeding.

Rimsulfuron (TranXit 25DG), trifloxysulfuron (Monument 75 WG), and foramsulfuron (Revolver 0.19L) are members of the sulfonylurea herbicide family that provide good to excellent postemergence control of Poa in non-overseeded bermudagrass or zoysiagrass. Application rates are low, 0.5 to 5 ounces per acre, depending on the product and age of the Poa. Control is slow, at two to six weeks. Like Kerb, neither TranXit, Monument, or Revolver should be used upslope of desirable overseeding or bentgrass, as these can and will move with water and run across these areas, causing death of the overseeding.

Simazine and atrazine (e.g., Princep T&O, Aatrex), like Kerb, provide good selective control of Poa at one to two pounds ai/acre (1 to 2 qts/a of 4L) if appropriately timed. Timing of these is very similar to Kerb, with mid-fall and early winter follow-up applications best. Simazine and atrazine also provide good to excellent control of many winter annual broadleaf weeds such as spurweed, chickweed, and henbit. These materials, however, should not be used during or just before normal spring green-up of bermudagrass as they can significantly delay this. As with pronamide, do not use simazine or atrazine upslope of desirable cool-season grasses.

Nonselective control

Nonselective control of Poa and other winter weeds is available with several herbicides if these are appropriately timed. Glyphosate (Roundup Pro), glufosinate (Finale), diquat (Reward), and pelargonic acid (Scythe) provide varying levels of Poa control. These must be timed when the bermudagrass is fully dormant, with no green leaves or stolons present. This situation generally occurs in mid-January after several consecutive hard frosts. If applied at other times, delayed green-up of the bermudagrass can be expected with possible permanent damage. Subtropical areas such as Florida, southern California, south Texas, and other Gulf Coast areas do not typically experience sufficient cold weather to have completely dormant bermudagrass. Nonselective Poa control, therefore, is not recommended for these areas.

These herbicides should be applied on relatively warm days (>50°F, 10°C) or extended periods will be required for control. Diquat, glufosinate, and pelargonic acid provide relatively quick burn of winter weeds while glyphosate provides better long-term control, but with much slower results. With glyphosate, an application rate in excess of one pint per acre (1.2 L/ha) of the 4L formulation could delay spring green-up. Glyphosate also provides better control when applied with low application volumes such as 10 to 20 gallons per acre (94 to 187 L/ha). High volumes, in excess of 40 gpa (374 L/ha), should be avoided. Do not apply to dormant zoysiagrass or centipedegrass as significant turf injury may occur.

Bentgrass golf greens

Bentgrass is sensitive to most postemergence grass herbicides. Additionally, most of these products are ineffective against annual bluegrass. As a result, preemergence herbicides are the most common means of controlling this weed on bentgrass golf greens. Erratic control of annual bluegrass, however, has been reported. The presence of perennial biotypes of the species may contribute to this erratic control. Low-growing, creeping perennial types become dominant over the annual biotype under frequent close mowing. Moist soil conditions and high soil nutrient levels, which are conditions normally maintained with creeping bentgrass golf greens, also contribute to creeping perennial biotype dominance. As the annual biotype is controlled by herbicides, the perennial biotype begins to dominate the green.

Limited research on preemergence control of the perennial biotype suggests poor short-term control. Repeat applications over multiple years (minimum of four years) are necessary for significant reduction of the perennial biotypes in bentgrass golf greens. Multiple-year treatments during February and March are considered superior for control and turf safety rather than August or September treatments. Currently available preemergence herbicides labeled for bentgrass golf greens include bensulide (Betasan, Weed Grass Preventer) and bensulide plus oxadiazon (Goosegrass/Crabgrass Control) (Table 25–7).

Selective postemergence control of annual bluegrass in bentgrass golf greens is currently unavailable, but is actively being investigated.

PGRs

With the realization that annual bluegrass elimination in golf greens is not always achievable with current herbicide technology, research recently has focused on suppressing its growth and seedhead production (Plate 25–5). The turf growth regulators (TGRs) paclobutrazol (Trimmit) and flurprimidol (Cutless) currently are available for annual bluegrass suppression in bentgrass golf greens. Other materials (e.g., mefluidide, maleic hydrazide) also are available, but only for higher-mowed turf. Combining these PGRs with other products such as the sterol inhibitor (DMI) fungicides may also help suppress Poa in bentgrass. In a typical program, paclobutrazol or flurprimidol is applied to actively growing bentgrass two to three times in fall and two to three times in early spring when the turf is actively growing (50 to 70°F, 10 to 21°C). Thirty-day intervals should occur between applications. DMI fungicides applied two weeks following each PGR treatment increases Poa control. Repeating applications during these time periods over several years is necessary to gradually eliminate the perennial biotype. Treatments should not be made during periods of heat, moisture, or cold stress to the bentgrass. Treated turf also may appear more "grainy" with a wider leaf texture while treated Poa plants often have noticeable discoloration in terms of a lighter-green to yellow color.

Differential species' susceptibility to the herbicide is attributed to a greater uptake of the TGR by the shallower-rooted annual bluegrass when compared to the deeper-rooted bentgrass. Paclobutrazol and flurprimidol are considered Type II growth regulators since they inhibit gibberellin biosynthesis and suppress internode elongation. These materials are root-absorbed (xylem-mobile) and work by reducing the competitive ability of the annual bluegrass for three to eight weeks after application. This allows the creeping bentgrass to outcompete the weed. These materials should only be applied during periods of active bentgrass root growth. Flurprimidol at rates greater than 0.5 pounds per acre (0.56 kg/ha) can reduce germination of annual bluegrass seed as well as bentgrass; thus, it should only be applied to established greens. Prevention of annual bluegrass seedhead formation may be inconsistent with these materials but they do prevent seedhead stalk elongation, which may result in improved turf uniformity and appearance.

Eleven-Step Plan to Control Poa annua in Golf Greens

1. Fumigate all soil mix before planting.
2. Begin with and retain good drainage to prevent soil compaction and excessive soil moisture that favor the Poa.
3. Use certified seed, sprigs, or sod free of Poa when planting.
4. Obtain and maintain good turf density to reduce Poa invasion.
5. Aerify consistently to relieve soil compaction.
6. Use fumigated sand/soil when topdressing.
7. Use preemergence herbicides in spring and fall.
8. Use PGRs in spring and fall to reduce Poa competition and seedhead development.
9. Hand pick or wick nonselective herbicide (e.g., glyphosate) on small (e.g., 1-inch diameter) Poa plants.
10. Plug larger spots with Poa-free turf.
11. Control *Poa annua* in green surrounds and in other areas of the golf course to minimize seed transfer to greens by players, water movement, and maintenance equipment.

Poa annua Control in Fairways

For creeping bentgrass, Kentucky bluegrass, and tall fescue fairways and roughs, preemergence *Poa annua* control is provided by those preemergence herbicides previously discussed. Early postemergence control is provided by ethofumesate (Progress 1.5EC). Young (one- to five-leaf stage) Poa should be treated in fall with a sequential application three weeks following the initial application. Turf should be at least eight weeks old before treatment with ethofumesate. Control of perennial biotypes with ethofumesate is erratic. Turf growing in shaded, wet, and/or low areas may have increased damage from ethofumesate.

Other Problem Weeds on Golf Courses

Annual blue-eyed grass (*Sisyrinchium rosulatum*)

Annual blue-eyed grass, a member of the Iris family, is a winter annual that appears similar to goosegrass except it is a cool-season annual. It has flat, light-green leaves, all clustered at the base, and zigzag-shaped stems. Its flowers are pale purple to white with a rose-purple eye ring. It reproduces by seed, and other *Sisyrinchium* species also commonly occur.

Control Strategies

Products containing atrazine or simazine are applied twice 30 days apart. Prompt (a premix of atrazine and Basagran) and rimsulfuron (TranXit) also work well. Sencor also provides excellent control in tolerant turfgrasses. Products containing two- or three-way broadleaf herbicide mixtures applied at least twice seven days apart also work.

Bahiagrass (*Paspalum notatum*)

Bahiagrass is a perennial, often from roadside and pasture plantings of seed.

Control Strategies

Postemergence control in bermuda and zoysiagrasses occurs with repeat MSMA/DSMA applications at one to two pounds ai/acre every five to seven days starting in spring. Normally, at least three applications are needed. In zoysiagrass, fluazifop (Fusilade T&O) or fenoxaprop-ethyl (Acclaim Extra) also are used as repeat applications. In centipedegrass, repeat sethoxydim (Vantage 1L) applications every 14 to 21 days at two pints per acre. Also, use metsulfuron at one ounce per acre in industrial areas, roadsides, and unimproved areas, and Manor or Blade 60DF at one ounce per acre in fine turf.

Bermudagrass (*Cynodon dactylon*)

Common bermudagrass is a perennial with enormous reproductive potential from seed, stolons, and rhizomes. It aggressively creeps into flower beds, sidewalks, and into other fine-textured turf species.

Control Strategies

For preplant control, fumigate with methyl bromide (Dowfume, Brom-O-Gas, Profume, Terr-O-Gas), dazomet (Basamid), or metam-sodium (Vapam). If not fumigated, use three repeat glyphosate (Roundup Pro plus others) treatments at two to three quarts per acre each time when bermudagrass regrowth appears. For postemergence control in zoysiagrass or tall fescue, repeat fenoxaprop-ethyl (Acclaim Extra 0.57 EC) at 1.5 pints per acre or fluazifop (Fusilade T&O 2EC) at five to six ounces per acre on 30-day intervals. Use only on fescue >four weeks old. Start treatments in spring, as they need good soil moisture, and discontinue during summer stress. In centipedegrass, use sethoxydim (Vantage 1L) at two pints per acre, and repeat in three weeks. In St. Augustinegrass, use ethofumesate (Progress 1.5EC) at two gallons per acre + two quarts per acre of atrazine 4L. Begin treatments in mid-March, and repeat in 30 days.

Bermudagrass Encroachment into Bentgrass Golf Greens

An increasing problem for many golf course superintendents is the encroachment of collar region bermudagrass into bentgrass greens.

Control Strategies

Small areas are plugged-out with bentgrass. However, bermudagrass roots and rhizomes must be removed with plugging to prevent reinfestation. Siduron (Tupersan) and ethofumesate (Progress) suppress bermudagrass; however, varying levels of bentgrass injury normally occur. Control is generally best in spring or fall when the bentgrass is actively growing and the bermudagrass is not. Temporary (up to three months) bermudagrass suppression has been achieved with combinations of siduron with flurprimidol (Cutless), as well as ethofumesate plus flurprimidol. This suppression has been superior to the standard practice of using siduron alone. April treatments are less injurious to bentgrass and provide a level of bermudagrass suppression similar to a September, followed by an April, application. Tupersan 50WP is used at 18 to 24 ounces of product per 1,000 square feet in spring or fall. Repeat as needed and water-in. With Progress 1.5EC + Cutless 50W, apply the first application in March/April at three ounces + 0.6 ounces per 1,000 square feet. Repeat in six weeks at 1.7 + 0.14 ounces per 1,000 square feet. Repeat again in 30 days. Temporary turf discoloration will follow Progress plus Cutless treatments.

Dallisgrass (*Paspalum dilatatum*)

Dallisgrass, a perennial, is also a problem in forage/hay production.

Control Strategies

For postemergence control in bermudagrass, repeat MSMA/DSMA applications at two pounds ai/acre every five to seven days starting in spring. Three to four applications are usually required. It is important to stay on schedule. Adding Sencor 75DF at 0.19 to 0.25 pounds per acre to MSMA or DSMA increases control but also increases turf injury. Water the turf if it is drought-stressed. In other grasses, spot treat or rope wick with glyphosate (4S) using two fluid ounces per gallon of water. Begin in spring, and repeat in two to three weeks, avoiding desirable plants. The repeat MSMA application program can also be used on certain zoysiagrass cultivars such as Meyer and El Toro.

Goosegrass (*Eleusine indica*)

Goosegrass, a summer annual grass, thrives in wet, compacted soils.

Control Strategies

For preemergence control, split applications of PRE herbicides such as Barricade, Dimension, Pendimethalin, Ronstar, or Surflan 60 days apart. The first application is in early spring when soil temperatures at four inches reach 63°F (17°C) for 24 consecutive hours. POST control with Illoxan 3EC at 1 to 1.4 quarts per acre, or Sencor 75DF (0.19 lbs/a) + MSMA (1 lb ai/a). Foramsulfuron (Revolver) can also be used for postemergence control. Avoid drought- and heat-stressed turf.

Kyllinga spp.

a. Perennials:
   K. brevifolia; "Perennial" or "Green" kyllinga
   K. gracillima = *K. brevifolioides;* no common name
   K. nemoralis; "White" kyllinga
b. Annuals:
   K. pumila; no common name
   K. squamulata; "Cock's-comb" kyllinga
   K. odorata = *C. sesquiflorus;* "Annual" kyllinga (**note:** *K. odorata* acts as an annual in the United States but is a short-lived perennial in the tropics).

These appear similar to nutsedges except kyllinga species do not form underground nutlets. Perennial kyllinga species form weed patches from rhizomes. Currently, *K. nemoralis* (or "White" kyllinga) is thought to be restricted in the United States to Hawaii. However, it probably can survive in portions of the mainland including southern California and south Florida.

Control Strategies

Annual kyllinga species can be controlled with Basagran, Image, Manage, or repeat applications of MSMA or DSMA. Perennial species require repeat applications of Image, Image + MSMA, Manage, or Monument.

Ground Ivy (*Glechoma hederacea*)

Ground Ivy is a patch-forming perennial, also known as creeping charlie. It is a member of the mint family with square stems and a minty odor when crushed. It has paired leaves, 0.5 to 1.5 inches (1.3 to 3.8 cm) in diameter, which are opposite, somewhat kidney-shaped, with toothed margins along stems. Petioles (leaf stalks) are long, bluish flowers appearing in mid- to late spring, and are very shade tolerant.

Control Strategies

Reduce shade source and grow shade-tolerant turfgrasses. Herbicides include three-way combinations of 2,4-D + MCPP + dicamba. Other herbicides include those containing 2,4-DP or triclopyr; dicamba alone also works well. Mid- to late fall applications are best followed by spring.

Lawn burweed or Spurweed (*Soliva pterosperma*)

Lawn burweed is a low-growing, freely branched winter annual broadleaf weed that has opposite leaves that are twice divided into narrow segments or lobes. Its flowers are small and inconspicuous, and its fruits have sharp spines that reproduce by seed.

Control Strategies

Preemergence or postemergence applications of simazine or atrazine in mid-fall provide excellent control. Manor or Blade, Prompts, Monument, and Sencor also work well in tolerant turfgrasses. Repeat applications of two- or three-way broadleaf herbicide mixtures also provide control. The key to control is applicating in fall when weeds are small.

Knotweed, Prostrate (*Polygonum aviculare* L.)

Knotweed is a prostrate, mat-forming, blue-green-colored summer annual broadleaf weed. Its leaves are alternate, smooth, oblong to linear, short-petioled, and joined to the stem by a sheathing membrane. It has inconspicuous white flowers that form in the leaf axils. It flowers from late spring until frost. Its fruit is dull brown and three-sided, and remains viable for years. Knotweed is common on infertile and compacted soils of cultivated fields as well as disturbed areas, and is one of the first summer annuals to germinate in the spring. It propagates by seed.

Control Strategies

Repeat applications of dicamba or two- or three-way mixtures of 2,4-D, dicamba, MCPP, or MCPA. Other suggested options include atrazine/simazine, metribuzin, and triclopyr alone or combined with clopyralid or 2,4-D. Oxadiazon may provide good PRE control if applied at or before the time for crabgrass control.

Nimblewill (*Muhlenbergia schreberi*)

Nimblewill is a delicate, mat-forming blue-green perennial, often rooting at nodes. Leaves are very narrow, short, hairless, pointed, grayish-green, and alternate. It has rolled vernation, a hairy leaf collar, and a short membranous ligule. Nimblewill thrives in moist, shady sites and turns brown in winter.

Control Strategies

No selective preemergence or postemergence control is currently available. Spot treat with glyphosate (Roundup Pro, others) or glufosinate (Finale) and replant.

FIGURE 25–4 For some weed situations, no selective chemical means of control currently exists. Shown is a patch of creeping bentgrass in a Kentucky bluegrass fairway.

Poa trivialis in Bentgrass or Bentgrass in Other Cool-Season Grasses

These are often seed contaminants that may be encouraged with prolonged PGR use (Figure 25–4).

Control Strategies

Currently, these cannot be selectively controlled in other cool-season grasses. *Poa trivialis* is suppressed in perennial ryegrass with fenoxaprop (Acclaim Extra) every two to three weeks from April to September or ethofumesate (Progress) in October and November. Lower rates must be used in bentgrass; thus, poorer control often results. Spot treat with glyphosate (Roundup Pro, others) in late summer just prior to overseeding.

Sandbur (Sandspur) (*Cenchrus* sp.)

Sandbur is a summer annual.

Control Strategies

Preemergence control in early spring occurs with split applications 60 days apart of PRE herbicides such as Barricade, Dimension, Pendimethalin, Ronstar, or Surflan. Postemergence control occurs in bermuda/zoysia with MSMA (1 lb ai/a), and is repeated in 10 days. In centipedegrass, use Vantage 1L at two pints per acre. Repeat in 21 days. In fescue/zoysia, repeat Acclaim Extra (0.57 EC) at 1.5 pints per acre or Fusilade T&O (2EC) at five to six ounces per acre on 30-day intervals. Use only on fescue >four weeks old. Start treatment in spring, as it needs good soil moisture, and then discontinue during summer stress.

Smutgrass (*Sporobolus indicus*)

Smutgrass, a clumping perennial grass, has very thin, flat blades. Its seedhead stalk is often infected with black fungus (or smut), and reproduces by seed.

Control Strategies

Selective control has been very elusive. Summer atrazine or simazine applications provide approximately 50 percent control. However, expect temporary turfgrass damage with this. Corsair has smutgrass listed on its label, but control is often very erratic with this product. Nonselective control includes spot spraying or rope wicking glyphosate (Roundup Pro, others). If rope wicking, treat in two directions.

Spurges (*Chamaesyce* sp.)

Spurges are summer annuals that include spotted, prostrate, garden, and roundleaf spurges. These often act as indicator plants for high-nematode-containing soils.

Control Strategies

Manor or Blade 60DF at 0.25 ounces per acre provides the best control in tolerant warm-season grasses. Two- and three-way mixes of 2,4-D, dicamba, and MCPP work in cool-season grasses. Repeat applications of the mixes may be necessary as plants mature.

Tall Fescue Clumps (*Festuca arundinacea*)

Tall fescue clumps are perennial grasses.

Control Strategies

For postemergence control in Kentucky bluegrass, fine fescue, zoysiagrass, or bermudagrass, use Corsair 75DF at four to five ounces per acre or as a spot treatment at 2.5 grams/2 gallons water. In dormant bermudagrass, spot treat with glyphosate (Roundup Pro 4L, others) at two ounces per gallon of water, and avoid desirable green plants. Repeat in 60 days. Foramsulfuron (Revolver) may also be used for tall fescue control in bermudagrass and zoysiagrass.

Thin or Bull Paspalum (*Paspalum setaceum*)

Thin (bull) paspalum, a clump-forming perennial grass, has flat blades that are hairy to almost smooth, with a fringe of stiff hairs along the leaf margins. Common in sandy soils, it reproduces by seed and clump fragments.

Control Strategies

Repeat applications of MSMA or DSMA are required every seven days until complete control is achieved.

Torpedograss (*Panicum repens*)

Torpedograss—normally an aquatic weed with robust, sharply pointed, creeping rhizomes—reproduces primarily by rhizomes.

Control Strategies

Nonselective control occurs with at least three applications of glyphosate (Roundup Pro, others) each spaced three weeks apart. Other nonselective control involves fumigating with methyl bromide and replanting. Selective control (or suppression) is available with quinclorac (Drive) and trifloxysulfuron (Monument). These should be applied two or three times, spaced three to four weeks apart. Expect some minor temporary turfgrass discoloration.

Kikuyugrass (*Pennisetum clandestinum*)

Kikuyugrass, a tough perennial grass, has vigorous, thick, aggressively growing rhizomes and stolons.

Control Strategies

Avoid movement of contaminated soil, and fumigate before using or planting. Selective post-emergence control occurs with repeat applications of quinclorac (Drive), triclopyr (Turflon Ester), or triclopyr plus MSMA.

Virginia Buttonweed (*Diodia virginiana*)

Virginia buttonweed reproduces from fleshy roots, cut plant pieces, and seed. Physically dig if only a few plants are present. Remove all plant parts and soil. Refill with fresh soil and weed-free sod.

Control Strategies

Postemergence suppression is with two-way or three-way herbicides with 2,4-D, dicamba, carfentrazone, clopyralid, + MCPP. 2,4-D is most effective; therefore, use combination products with a high concentration of it. Confront (triclopyr + clopyralid) also works well. Repeat applications every three to four weeks when regrowth occurs.

Wild Garlic and Onion (*Allium* sp.)

Wild garlic and onion are cool-season perennials. Wild onion has offset bulblets, a fibrous coat on the central bulb, and flat, solid leaves that arise near the base of a solid flowering stem.

Control Strategies

Postemergence control occurs with Image 1.5L at two pints per acre in December. Repeat with one pint per acre in early March. Add 0.25 percent nonionic surfactant (1 qt/100 gal water). Manor and Blade 60DF at one-half to one ounce per acre at these timings also work well. Also, use 2,4-D LV ester alone or in two- or three-way combination products. Treat in November, March, and again the following November. In dormant turf, use glyphosate (Roundup Pro 4L, others) at one pint per acre, and repeat in three to four weeks.

Nutsedge Control

The predominant sedge weed species in turfgrasses are yellow and purple nutsedge. Other problem members of the *Cyperus* and *Kyllinga* genus include annual or water sedge, perennial and annual kyllinga, globe sedge, Texas sedge, flathead sedge, and cylindrical sedge. Path or slender rush, a member of the rush (*Juncus*) family, also can occur in some turf situations.

Sedges generally thrive in soils that remain wet for extended periods of time due to poor drainage or excessive irrigation. The first step in sedge weed control is, therefore, to correct the cause of continuously wet soils. Do not overirrigate an area; if necessary, provide surface and subsurface drainage.

Yellow and purple nutsedge are low-growing perennials resembling grasses. Sedges, in general, are yellow-green to dark-green, with triangular stems bearing three-ranked leaves—unlike the two-ranked leaves of the grass family. Yellow and purple nutsedge have fibrous root systems with deep-rooted tubers or nutlets for reproduction. Seedhead color is often used to distinguish between these two major nutsedges. Yellow nutsedge has a yellowish- to straw-colored inflorescence, while purple nutsedge has a reddish to purple inflorescence. Leaf tip shape is another distinguishing method. Leaf tips of purple nutsedge are generally thicker and more rounded than yellow nutsedge leaf tips that are very narrow, ultimately forming a needle-like end. Yellow and purple nutsedge have a great capacity to reproduce and spread due in part to their massive underground tuber and rhizome systems. They are not believed to produce viable seed.

Historically, chemical control of most sedges was with repeat applications of 2,4-D or the organic arsenicals (MSMA, DSMA). Although effective, these treatments are slow to kill the weeds and repeat applications are generally necessary, resulting in extensive damage in certain turf species (Table 25–13).

Selective yellow nutsedge control is available with bentazon (Basagran T&O) with minimum turf damage. Control of most other sedges, except purple nutsedge, also will result from bentazon treatments. Bentazon is a contact material and will control only those portions of the weeds contacted by the spray. Complete coverage of the weeds is necessary for the greatest bentazon activity. Even with good herbicide coverage, regrowth will normally occur from the roots and tubers and repeat applications will be necessary.

TABLE 25-13 Relative sedge control and turf tolerance to various herbicides (refer to herbicide label for specific species listing).

Herbicide(s)*	Sedge control					Turf tolerance (excluding greens)							
	Annual sedge	Purple nutsedge	Yellow nutsedge	Annual kyllinga species	Perennial kyllinga species	Bermudagrass	Bentgrass	Bluegrass, fescue, ryegrass	Centipedegrass	St. Augustinegrass	Bahiagrass	Zoysiagrass	Kikuyugrass
Preemergence control													
Metolachlor (Pennant)	G	P	G	F-G	P	S	NR	NR	NR	NR	NR	S	NR
Oxadiazon (Ronstar 2G)	G	P	P	F	P	S	NR	S	NR	NR	NR	S	NR
Postemergence control													
Bentazon (Basagran T&O)	G	P	G	F-G	F-G	S	S-I	S	S	S	S	S	NR
Imazaquin (Image)	G	G	F	G	G	I-S	NR	NR	I	I	NR	S	NR
Halosulfuron (Manage)	G	G-E	G-E	G	F-G	S	S	S	S	S	S	S	S
MSMA/DSMA/CMA	G	P-F	F	G	G	S-I	I	NR	NR	NR	NR	S-I	NR
Image + MSMA/DSMA	G	G	G	G	G	S-I	NR	NR	NR	NR	NR	S-I	NR
Trifloxysulfuron (Monument)	G	G	G	G	G	G	NR	NR	NR	NR	NR	G	NR

*Repeat applications are necessary for complete control from all herbicides. This interval is from five days for MSMA/DSMA up to three to eight weeks for Manage or Image.

G = Good; **F** = Fair; **NR** = Not registered for use on and/or damages this turf species.

S = Safe at labeled rates on mature, healthy turf.

I = Intermediate safety; use lower rates during stress periods.

These are relative rankings and depend on many factors such as environmental conditions, turfgrass vigor or health, application timing, and so forth, and are intended only as a guide.

699

Purple and yellow nutsedge, as well as several other sedges, can be suppressed with imazaquin (Image). Selective broadleaf weeds, such as pennywort, are also controlled with imazaquin. As with bentazon, repeat applications—possibly over several years—will be required to control all the underground reproductive parts with imazaquin. The addition of MSMA increases the activity of either bentazon or imazaquin and broadens the range of controlled weeds. However, this tank-mix should be used only on actively growing bermudagrass or zoysiagrass and imazaquin.

Halosulfuron (Manage) also has good control on most sedges and very good warm- and cool-season turf tolerance. Halosulfuron is somewhat slow, requiring two to three weeks for control and, as with sedge control materials, repeat applications three to four weeks after the initial application are necessary, especially when trying to control perennial sedges.

Recently, trifloxysulfuron (Monument) has become available for control of all major sedges and kyllinga species in bermudagrass and zoysiagrass. Two applications four weeks apart will be necessary for satisfactory control of perennial species. Cool-season grasses and other warm-season grasses should not be treated with trifloxysulfuron.

Precautionary Statements

When using any postemergence herbicide, certain precautions should be followed to minimize any problems. Treat the weeds when they are young (e.g., two- to four-leaf stage). Larger weeds require repeat applications, which will result in an increased chance of phytotoxicity and increased labor costs with added wear-and-tear on equipment. Treat when the weeds, and preferably the turf, is actively growing and good soil moisture is present. Treating when the weed is actively growing results in better herbicide uptake and translocation, resulting in better efficacy. If weeds are treated after they begin to flower or produce seedheads, herbicide activity will be reduced and repeat applications will be necessary. If seedheads or flowers are present, mow the weeds as low as possible, wait several days until new regrowth is evident, and then make the herbicide application. Allowing weeds to produce seedheads may add to the soil's weed-seed reserve; therefore, mowing or herbicide treatments should be in advance of seedhead development.

An adjuvant (surfactant, wetting agent, or crop oil concentrate) is generally needed by most postemergence herbicides. The label should be consulted, however, as many postemergence herbicides already contain them. If other pesticides are to be tank-mixed with herbicides, always conduct a compatibility test unless the specific tank-mix is recommended on the herbicide label. Indiscriminate tank-mixing can lead to chemical compatibility problems (e.g., flakes, gels, precipitates) in the spray tank and may result in excessive turfgrass injury. As application volumes and pre- or post-treatment irrigation recommendations dramatically vary between herbicides, fungicides, and insecticides, it usually is not advisable to tank-mix the various types of pesticides. Compatibility tests should also be conducted when mixing herbicides with liquid fertilizers. The herbicide label will usually contain information on how to conduct a compatibility test.

Disclaimer

All mentioned chemicals are for reference only and may not be available for turf use. They may be restricted by some state, province, or federal agencies; thus, be sure to check the current status of the pesticide being considered for use. Always read and follow the manufacturer's label as registered under the Federal Insecticide, Fungicide, and Rodenticide Act. Mention of a proprietary product does not constitute a guarantee or warranty of the product by the authors or the publishers and does not imply approval to the exclusion of other products that also may be suitable. Table 25–14 cross-lists current common herbicide names with trade names and their manufacturers and/or distributors.

TABLE 25–14 *Common and trade names of turf herbicides.* *

Common name	Trade name(s)
Ammoniated soap of fatty acids	Quick-fire
Asulam	Asulox 3.34L, Asulam 3.3
Atrazine	Aatrex, Atrazine Plus, Purge II, Aatrex 90, Atrazine 4L, Bonus S, St. Augustine Weedgrass Control + others
Benefin	Balan 2.5G. 1.5EC, Crabgrass Preventer + others
Benefin + oryzalin	XL 2G
Benefin + trifluralin	Team 2G, Crabgrass Preventer 0.92%, Team Pro
Bensulide	Betasan, Pre-San 12.5 & 7G, Bensumec 4L, Lescosan, Weedgrass Preventer, Betamec, Squelch + others
Bentazon	Basagran T/O 4L, Lescogran 4L
Bentazon + atrazine	Prompt 5L
Bispyribac-sodium	Velocity 80WP
Bromoxynil	Buctril 2L, Brominal 4L, Bromox 2E, Moxy 2E
Cacodylic acid	Montar, Weed Ender
Carfentrazone + 2,4-D + MCPP + dicamba	Speed Zone Southern, Power Zone, Speed Zone
Chlorsulfuron	Corsair 75DF, Telar 75DG
Clethodim	Envoy 0.94EC
Clopyralid	Lontrel T&O 3L, Transline 3L
CMA (CAMA)	Calar, Ortho Crabgrass Killer – Formula II, Selectrol
Corn gluten	Dynaweed, WeedzSTOP 100G
Dazomet	Basamid
Dichlobenil	Casoron 4G, Dyclomec 4G, Norosac 4G
2,4-D	2,4-D Amine & Ester; Weedone LV4; Dacamine; Weedar 64; AM-40; 2,4-D LV4; Dymec; Lesco A-4D + others
2,4-D + clopyralid + dicamba	Millennium Ultra 3.75 lbs/gal
2,4-D + clopyralid + triclopyr	Momentum
2,4-D + dicamba	81 Selective Weedkiller; Four Power Plus; Triple D Lawn Weed Killer; Banvel 2,4-D
2,4-D + dichlorprop (2,4-DP)	2D + 2DP Amine, Turf D + DP, Fluid Broadleaf Weed Control, Weedone DPC Ester & Amine + others
2,4-D + dichlorprop (2,4-DP) + dicamba	Super Trimec, Brushmaster
2,4-D + mecoprop (MCPP)	2D Amine + 2MCPP; 2 Plus 2; MCPP-2,4-D; Phenomec; Ortho Weed-B-Gon Lawn Weed Killer + others
2,4-D + MCPP + 2,4-DP	Broadleaf Granular Herbicide, Dissolve, Triamine, Tri-Ester, Jet-Spray 3-Way Weed Control, Turf Weeder + others
2,4-D + MCPP + dicamba + MCPA and/or 2,4-DP	Trimec Southern, Three-Way Selective, Eliminate DG, 33-Plus, Dissolve, Triamine 3.9 lb/gal, TriEster, Triplet, Trex-San, Weed-B-Gon, 2 Plus 2, Bentgrass Selective Weed Killer, Trimec Bentgrass Formula, Strike 3, Broadleaf Trimec, MECAmine-D, Trimec 992, Weed-B-Gon for Southern Lawns, Formula II + others
Dicamba	Vanquish 4L, K-O-G Weed Control, Bentgrass Selective, Banvel 4S + others
Dicamba + MCPA + MCPP	Encore DSC, Tri-Power Dry, Tri-Power Selective, Trimec Encore
Diclofop	Illoxan 3EC
Diquat	Reward LS, Watrol, Vegetrol, Aquatate

(continued)

701

TABLE 25–14 *Common and trade names of turf herbicides. (continued)*

Common name	Trade name(s)
Dithiopyr	-Dimension 1L, Dimension Ultra 40WSP
DSMA	-Ansar, DSMA Liquid, Methar 30, Namate, DSMA 4
DSMA + 2,4-D	-Weed Beater Plus
Ethephon	-Proxy 2L, Ethephon 2
Ethofumesate	-Prograss 1.5L
Fenarimol	-Rubigan 1AS, Patchwork 0.78G
Fenoxaprop	-Acclaim Extra 0.57EC
Flazasulfuron	-Katana
Fluazifop	-Fusilade II T&O, Ornamec
Flurprimidol	-Cutless 50WP
Foramsulfuron	-Revolver 0.19L
Gibberellic acid	-RyzUp, ProGibb
Glufosinate	-Finale 1L
Glyphosate	-Roundup Pro 4L, Roundup ProDry, Gly-Flo, Glypro, AquaNeat, Razor, Rodeo 5.4L, Ortho Kleenup, Weed Wrangler, Prosecutor, Touchdown Pro, Trailblazer, Glyphomate 41 (3.8L) + others
Glyphosate + 2,4-D	-Campaign 3.1L
Halosulfuron	-Manage 75WP, Sempra 75WP
Hexazinone	-Velpar 2L
Imazapic	-Plateau 70DG
Imazapyr	-Arsenal 2S
Imazaquin	-Image 1.5L, 70DF
Isoxaben	-Gallery 75DF
Isoxaben + trifluralin	-Preen 1.9G, Snapshot TG
Maleic hydrazide	-Royal Slo-Gro
Methyl chlorflurenol	-Maintain CF
MCPA	-Weedar MCPA 4 lb/gal, MCPA-4 Amine + others
MCPA + clopyralid + dichlorprop	-Chaser Ultra
MCPA + clopyralid + triclopyr	-Battleship
MCPA + MCPP + 2,4-DP	-Triamine II, Tri-Ester II
MCPA + dicamba + triclopyr	-Eliminate, Three-Way Ester II
MCPP	-Mecomec 4, Chickweed & Clover Control, Lescopex, MCPP-4 Amine, MCPP-4K + others
MSMA	-Daconate 6, Dal-E-Rad, Crab-E-Rad, MSMA 6.6L, Drexar 530, Buano 6L, 120 Herbicide, Daconate Super, 912 Herbicide, MSMA Turf, Summer Crabicide, Target MSMA + others
MSMA + 2,4-D + MCPP + dicamba	-Trimec Plus (Quadmec)
Mefluidide	-Embark
Methyl Bromide	-Brom-O-Gas, Terr-O-Gas, MB 98, MBC

Active Ingredient	Trade Name(s)
Metolachlor	Pennant, Pennant Magnum 7.8 lb/gal
Metribuzin	Sencor 75DF
Metsulfuron	Manor 60DF, Blade 60DF, Escort 60DF
Napropamide	Devrinol 50DF, 2G, 10G, Ornamental Herbicide 5G
Napropamide + oxadiazon	PrePair 6G
Norflurazon	Predict
Oryzalin	Surflan AS 4 lb/gal
Oxadiazon	Ronstar 2G, 50WP
Oxadiazon + benefin	Regalstar 1.5G
Oxadiazon + bensulide	Goosegrass/Crabgrass Control
Oxadiazon + dithiopyr	SuperStar
Oxadiazon + prodiamine	Regalstar II 1.2G
Oxyfluorfen	Goal 2XL
Oxyfluorfen + oryzalin	Rout
Oxyfluorfen + oxadiazon	OO-Herbicide 3G
Oxyfluorfen + pendimethalin	OH2
Paclobutrazol	Turf Enhancer 50WP, 2SC, Trimmit 2SC, TGR
Pelargonic acid	Scythe
Pendimethalin	Pre-M & Pendulum (60DG, WP, 3.3EC, 2G), Pendulum AquaCap (3.8 CS), Hurdle, Turf Weedgrass Control, Halts, Corral 2.68G
Prodiamine	Barricade 65WDG, Endurance 65 WDG, Factor 65 WDG, RegalKade 0.5G
Pronamide	Kerb 50WP
Quinclorac	Drive 75DF
Rimsulfuron	TranXit GTA 25DG
Sethoxydim	Vantage 1.0 lb/gal
Siduron	Tupersan 50WP, 4.6%
Simazine	Princep 4 lb/gal, T&O, 80WP, Simazine, Wynstar, + others
Sulfometuron-methyl	Oust 75DG
Sulfosulfuron	Battalion 75WG, Outrider 75DF
Triclopyr	Turflon Ester 4L, Garlon 3A (triclopyr amine), Garlon 4A (triclopyr ester), Pathfinder 1L (RTU)
Triclopyr + 2,4-D	Turflon II Amine, Chaser 3L, Chaser 2 Amine
Triclopyr + clopyralid	Confront 3L
Triclopyr + MCPP + dicamba	Cool Power 3.6 lb/gal, Horsepower 4.56 lb/gal, 3-Way Ester II
Trifluralin	Treflan 5G, Trifluralin 4EC, Trilin 4EC, 5EC
Trinexapac-ethyl	Primo 1EC, Triple Play

*Refer to the herbicide label for specific site and use registration.

CHAPTER
26

Turfgrass Plant Growth Regulators

INTRODUCTION

Plant growth regulators (PGRs) or inhibitors are increasingly being used on golf courses to suppress seedheads and vegetative growth of desirable turfgrasses, enhance turfgrass quality, and manage annual bluegrass (*Poa annua*) growth and development. Depending upon the turfgrass and situation, PGRs may reduce mowing costs, prevent scalping, increase turf density, and decrease the need to mow steep slopes (Figure 26–1). Traditionally, PGRs were used in the United States to suppress bahiagrass (*Paspalum notatum*), Kentucky bluegrass (*Poa pratensis*), and tall fescue (*Festuca arundinacea*) seedhead production in low-maintenance areas such as highway roadsides, airports, and golf course roughs. However, products have been registered for use in most high-maintenance turfgrasses.

PGRs are recommended for use only on certain turfgrass species (Table 26–1). Additionally, the use of a PGR is often determined by the type of turfgrass area and level of maintenance. For example, imazapic (Plateau) is recommended for use on low-maintenance sites such as roadsides and airports. However, flurprimidol (Cutless), paclobutrazol (Trimmit), and trinexapac-ethyl (Primo) may be used on putting green turfgrasses. The PGR label should always be consulted for information concerning turfgrass species and application sites.

Prior to the development of PGRs for fine turfgrasses, several undesirable characteristics were associated with the PGRs used on low-maintenance, or rough, turfgrass sites, including: (1) phytotoxicity (burn) of treated leaves for four to six weeks following applications, (2) reduced recuperative potential when the PGR-treated turfgrass was physically damaged, and (3) increased weed pressure due to reduced competition from treated turfgrasses. However, because most PGRs were historically used in low-maintenance areas, these undesirable characteristics did not pose a problem to most managers.

Fine-turfgrass PGRs suppress vertical top growth, but usually do not affect the lateral or horizontal spread of stolons. The most noticeable effect is usually a reduction in the amount of clippings, and a reduction in mowing frequency. On tee boxes and fairway landing areas, turf recovery from golf club divots and other injuries occurs while vertical top growth remains suppressed. Depending upon the product, fine-turfgrass PGRs also enable superintendents to reduce mowing frequency on fairways, suppress annual bluegrass in creeping bentgrass greens, improve ball lie or playability, and suppress the growth of bermudagrass during overseeding with a cool-season turfgrass.

FIGURE 26–1 Plant
growth retardants are used to
suppress turfgrass growth.

PGR CLASSIFICATION

Similar to herbicides, PGRs are placed into groups based on mode of action, or the way they inhibit turfgrass growth. Classification schemes can vary; however, three distinct groups of PGRs exist (Table 26–2).

Cell Division Inhibitors (also called Type I PGRs)

Cell division inhibitors are primarily foliage absorbed and inhibit cell division and differentiation in meristematic regions. They inhibit both vegetative growth and seedhead development. Growth inhibition is rapid, occurring within 4 to 10 days, and lasting three to four weeks, depending on the application rate. Mefluidide (Embark, Embark 0.2S) and maleic hydrazide (Royal Slo-Gro, others) are examples of cell division inhibitors. These products are primarily used on low- and medium-maintenance turfgrass areas, as phytotoxicity (yellowing) can be a problem. On golf courses, cell division inhibitors may be useful to reduce mowing on steep slopes, ditches, and other difficult-to-mow areas.

Herbicides

Various herbicides are used at low rates to suppress the growth or seedhead development of turfgrasses. Depending upon the chemical, herbicides inhibit turfgrass growth and development through interruption of amino acid synthesis (glyphosate, sulfometuron, chlorsulfuron, metsulfuron, imazapic, imazethapyr + imazapyr) or fatty acid biosynthesis (sethoxydim). Turfgrass tolerance can be marginal and is highly rate dependent. Herbicides are primarily used only on low-maintenance turfgrasses to reduce mowing and control weeds.

Gibberellin Biosynthesis Inhibitors (also called Type II PGRs)

Gibberellin is a plant-produced hormone needed for cell elongation, as well as normal growth and development. Numerous gibberellins are needed for normal plant growth and development. When gibberellin production is inhibited, plant cells do not elongate, internodes become shortened, and overall plant growth is reduced. Two types of gibberellin biosynthesis inhibitors are available for use on golf courses. Trinexapac-ethyl (Primo), a Class A gibberellin biosynthesis inhibitor, is foliar absorbed and inhibits the synthesis of gibberellin late in its biosynthetic pathway. Paclobutrazol (Trimmit) and flurprimidol (Cutless) are root-absorbed Class B gibberellin biosynthesis inhibitors and inhibit gibberellin biosynthesis in the early

TABLE 26–1 *Labeled plant growth regulators for various turfgrass species.*

Common name	Trade names	Root or foliar absorbed	Suppression characteristics Foliage	Suppression characteristics Seedhead	Maintenance level of turfgrass site[1]	Labeled turfgrass species
Maleic hydrazide	Royal Slo-Gro, others	Foliar	Yes	Yes	Low	Bahiagrass, bermudagrass, fescues, Kentucky bluegrass, ryegrass
Mefluidide	Embark, Embark 0.25	Foliar	Yes	Yes	Low, medium low, medium, high	Bermudagrass, centipedegrass, fescues, Kentucky bluegrass, ryegrass, St. Augustinegrass
Sethoxydim	Poast, Vantage	Foliar	Yes	Yes	Low, medium, high	Centipedegrass, fine fescues (roadside tall fescue)
Glyphosate	Roundup Pro	Foliar	Yes	Yes	Low	Bahiagrass, bermudagrass
Imazapic	Plateau	Both	Yes	Yes	Low	Bahiagrass, bermudagrass
Imazethapyr + Imazapyr	Event	Both	Yes	Yes	Low	Bahiagrass
Sulfometuron	Oust	Both	Yes	Yes	Low	Bahiagrass, bermudagrass
Metsulfuron	Escort	Both	Yes	Yes	Low	Bermudagrass, fescues, Kentucky bluegrass
Chlorsulfuron	Telar	Both	Yes	Yes	Low	Bahiagrass, bermudagrass, fescues, Kentucky bluegrass
Flurprimidol	Cutless	Root	Yes	No	Low, medium, high	Bentgrass, bermudagrass, Kentucky bluegrass, ryegrass, St. Augustinegrass, zoysiagrass
Paclobutrazol	Trimmit	Root	Yes	No/partial	Low, medium, high	Bentgrass, bermudagrass, Kentucky bluegrass, ryegrass, St. Augustinegrass, zoysiagrass
Trinexapac-ethyl	Primo	Root	Yes	Parital	Low, medium, high	Bahiagrass, bentgrass, bermudagrass, centipedegrass, fescues, Kentucky bluegrass, ryegrass, St. Augustinegrass, zoysiagrass

[1]Low-maintenance turfgrass sites: roadsides, airports, storage sites, hard-to-mow areas, and so forth.
Medium-maintenance turfgrass sites: industrial grounds, parks, cemeteries, golf course roughs, home lawns.
High-maintenance turfgrass sites: putting greens, tees, fairways, athletic fields, high-quality home lawns, and commercial properties.

TABLE 26–2 *Characteristics of various plant growth regulators used in turfgrass management.*

PGR common names	PGR trade name	Absorption site	Mode of action	Comments
Maleic hydrazide	Retard, Royal Slo-Gro, Liquid Growth Retardant	Foliar	Inhibit cell division (mitosis)	Effective seedhead suppressors. Growth inhibition is rapid, within 4 to 10 days, and lasts three to four weeks.
Mefluidide	Embark, Embark 0.2S			
Sethoxydim	Poast, Vantage	Foliar	Inhibit fatty acid biosynthesis	Usually low in cost, but turfgrass tolerance is low and rate dependent.
Glyphosate	Roundup Pro, others	Foliar	Inhibit amino acid biosynthesis	Use is restricted to low-maintenance turfgrasses.
Imazapic	Plateau	Foliar and root		
Imazethapyr + Imazapyr	Event	Foliar and root		
Sulfometuron	Oust	Foliar and root		
Metsulfuron	Escort	Foliar and root		
Chlorsulfuron	Telar	Foliar and root		
Flurprimidol	Cutless	Root	Interferes with gibberellin biosynthesis	Initial growth response is slower compared to cell division inhibitors, but duration of activity is usually longer, three to seven weeks. Rainfall, irrigation, or high application volumes are required for activating root-absorbed PGRs.
Paclobutrazol	Trimmit	Root		
Trinexapac-ethyl	Primo	Foliar		
Chemicals for growth and color promotion				
Gibberellic acid	Gibgrow, ProGib, RyzUp 4 percent active solution	Foliar	Promotes gibberellin biosynthesis	Apply 10 grams ai/acre (10 fl oz/a or 0.23 fl oz/1,000 sq.ft.) weekly or 25 grams ai/acre biweekly in 25 to 100 gpa to promote growth and prevent discoloration (e.g., purpling) during periods of cold stress and light frosts on bermudagrasses such as Tifdwarf or Tifgreen. Do not apply when night temperatures exceed 65°F.

stages of this pathway. This early blockage prevents the synthesis of numerous gibberellins. Inhibition during the early stages of gibberellin biosynthesis can lead to increased injury when environmentally stressed turfgrasses are treated with Class B gibberellin biosynthesis inhibitors. Additionally, turfgrasses may exhibit various morphological responses such as the widening of creeping bentgrass leaf blades. Studies have shown that inhibiting gibberellin biosynthesis late in the pathway, as with trinexapac-ethyl, is less physiologically disruptive and injurious to turfgrasses, although as with all PGRs, plant phytotoxicity can still occur at higher rates.

Ethophon (Proxy) is a PGR recently introduced into the turfgrass market that is hydrolyzed into ethylene by treated plants. Ethylene is a growth hormone noted as a fruit ripener and retardant in floriculture crops. In turfgrass, ethophon at 3.4 pounds active ingredient per acre (3.8 kg active ingredient per hectare) provides good Kentucky bluegrass, perennial ryegrass, and hard fescue growth suppression for approximately four weeks. Treated turf often has enhanced green leaf color, and tiller formation and root length are stimulated. Rhizome development, however, may be somewhat inhibited. Tall fescue growth appears less influenced by ethophon. Combinations of ethophon with other PGRs, such as trinexapac-ethyl, are currently being investigated.

Limited work in bermudagrass suggests reduced growth at rates above six pounds active ingredient per acre. On centipedegrass, 4.5 pounds active ingredient per acre of ethophon suppresses growth for four to six weeks, enhances turf quality in terms of a more uniform turf canopy with fewer seedheads, and provides a desirable blue-green turf color.

Site of Absorption

Plant growth regulators are absorbed, or enter the turfgrass plant, by roots, foliage (or shoots), or with some products, both roots and foliage (Table 26–2). Root-absorbed PGRs, such as paclobutrazol and flurprimidol, require irrigation or rainfall after application to move the material into the turfgrass rootzone. In contrast, trinexapac-ethyl is rapidly absorbed by turfgrass foliage, and irrigation after application is not necessary. Compared to cell division inhibitors, there is less likelihood of leaf burn due to improper spray pattern overlaps with the gibberellin biosynthesis inhibitor PGRs. Most foliar-absorbed materials (e.g., mefluidide, maleic hydrazide, and herbicides) require uniform, even coverage to prevent phytotoxicity and must be absorbed by turfgrass leaves before irrigation or rainfall occurs.

Growth Suppression

Cell division inhibitor PGRs quickly (five to seven days) suppress vegetative growth, but usually provide a shorter period of growth suppression than gibberellin biosynthesis inhibitors (three to six weeks). However, unlike gibberellin biosynthesis inhibitors, cell division inhibitors are highly effective in suppressing seedhead development. The growth suppression activity of gibberellin biosynthesis inhibitors is often not immediately evident. Compared to cell division inhibitors, paclobutrazol and flurprimidol are slower (10 to 14 days) in suppressing turfgrass growth, but their duration of activity is usually longer, lasting from four to eight weeks, depending on the application rate. Trinexapac-ethyl has been shown to reduce common and hybrid bermudagrass clipping weights 50 percent at seven days after application. Depending upon the application rates and schedules, trinexapac-ethyl also provides long-term (four to eight weeks) growth suppression. Another key difference is while gibberellin biosynthesis inhibitors decrease seedhead stalk height, they have little effect on the actual formation of seedheads.

Application Timing

Timing of application with PGRs is critical to achieve desired results. When used for seedhead suppression, the PGR must be applied before seedhead formation and emergence. Applications made after seedhead emergence will not be effective. For bahiagrass, mow the area as seedheads initially emerge (usually from May to mid-June) to provide a uniform, even appearance to the site. For tall fescue or bluegrass, mow the area in early spring (late March to late April). The PGR treatment should be applied about 7 to 10 days following mowing or just prior to new seedhead appearance. Additional applications six to eight weeks later may be required if new seedheads begin to emerge.

If PGRs are being used on creeping bentgrass golf greens, applications should be made during periods of active root growth. In most areas of the United States, this would be during the mid-fall and spring months. Applications should not be made during stressful mid-summer and mid-winter months. On warm-season turfgrasses, such as bermudagrass, the appropriate PGR should be applied to actively growing turfgrasses after full spring green-up and several mowings. Applications can be repeated during the summer months if additional growth regulation is needed.

Weed Control Considerations

An integrated weed management program must accompany any PGR use as PGRs usually do not suppress weed growth, particularly that of broadleaf weeds. In addition, after the PGR has been applied, annual and perennial weeds can become a problem, as PGR-treated turfgrass often does not compete well with weeds. On high-maintenance turfgrasses, it usually is advisable to continue preemergence herbicide use to control annual grass weeds. For postemergence control, normally 2,4-D, dicamba, or various two- and three-way herbicide mixtures are used to control broadleaf weeds. Other postemergence herbicides such as MSMA, used for annual grass weed control, or nutsedge control herbicides may also be needed in some situations. Postemergence herbicides often cause temporary phytotoxicity to turfgrasses. Postemergence herbicides can be tank-mixed with PGRs; however, turfgrass injury is often greater than when either type of product is used alone. Therefore, on high-maintenance turfgrasses, where color and appearance may be of utmost importance, it is advisable not to tank-mix postemergence herbicides with PGRs. Additionally, if a postemergence herbicide has injured the turfgrass, PGR application should be delayed until the turfgrass has fully recovered. The PGR label and personal experience provide the best guide to determine the suitability of tank-mixing PGRs and postemergence herbicides.

CURRENTLY AVAILABLE PLANT GROWTH RETARDANTS

Low-Maintenance Turfgrasses

Sulfometuron-methyl (Oust 75DG)

Used on bahiagrass at 0.5 ounces per acre (0.02 lb ai/acre), sulfometuron-methyl is foliar, root absorbed, and should be applied to bahiagrass in spring or early summer 7 to 10 days after the first mowing. Do not use a surfactant, apply to wetlands, or use where run-off water may drain onto cultivated lands or forests. Do not apply to turf less than one year old. Treated areas may appear less dense and be temporarily discolored. Only one application per year should be made, as repeat applications within the same year can reduce bahiagrass density. Read and follow all label recommendations before use. This PGR is often tank-mixed with glyphosate, Telar, Campaign, and/or Velpar. **DO NOT EXCEED THE RECOMMENDED RATE.** Sulfometuron-methyl is not recommended for use on high-maintenance turfgrasses.

Chlorsulfuron (Telar 75DG)

Used in tall fescue, bahiagrass, Kentucky bluegrass, and bermudagrass at rates ranging from 0.25 to 1.0 ounce per acre (0.012 to 0.05 lb ai/acre), chlorsulfuron is foliar, root absorbed, and should be applied to well-established tall fescue prior to seedhead formation. Do not apply to turfgrasses less than one year old. A nonionic surfactant should be added to the spray mixture. A tank-mix of Telar at 0.25 ounce per acre plus Embark at 0.5 pint per acre can be used to suppress growth and seedhead emergence in tall fescue. Apply this tank-mix after spring green-up but before tall fescue seedhead emergence. Chlorsulfuron may also be tank-mixed with glyphosate and sulfometuron-methyl. Chlorsulfuron should not be used on turfgrasses that are stressed due to drought, insects, disease, cold temperatures, or poor fertility since injury may result. Chlorsulfuron is not recommended for use on high-maintenance turfgrasses.

Metsulfuron (Escort 60DF)

Used in tall fescue, Kentucky bluegrass, and bermudagrass at rates ranging from 0.25 to 2.0 ounce per acre (0.009 to 0.075 lb ai/acre), metsulfuron is foliar and root absorbed. Low rates (0.25 to

0.5 oz/a) may be used for growth and seedhead suppression in well-established tall fescue. Applications to tall fescue should be made in the spring after two to three inches of new growth appear but before seedhead emergence. In bermudagrass, metsulfuron is primarily used to control weeds at rates ranging from 0.25 to 2.0 ounce per acre. A tank-mix of Escort at 0.25 to 0.33 ounce per acre plus Embark at 0.125 to 0.25 pint per acre can be used to suppress growth and seedhead emergence in tall fescue. Do not apply metsulfuron to turfgrasses less than one year old. A non-ionic surfactant should be added to the spray mixture. Metsulfuron should not be used on turfgrasses that are stressed due to drought, insects, disease, cold temperatures, or poor fertility, since injury may result. Metsulfuron is not recommended for use on high-maintenance turfgrasses or bahiagrass.

Sethoxydim (Vantage 1.0L; Poast 1.5L)

Apply sethoxydim at 0.1875 pounds active ingredient per acre (Vantage—1.5 pts/a; Poast—1.0 pt/a) to established, low-maintenance tall fescue for seedhead suppression. Sethoxydim is foliar absorbed. Applications should be made in the early spring before tall fescue seedhead emergence. A crop oil concentrate at 2.0 pints per acre or Dash HC spray adjuvant at 1.0 pint per acre must be added to Poast. It is not necessary to add a spray adjuvant to Vantage. Unlike other herbicides used for growth suppression on low-maintenance grasses, sethoxydim has no herbicidal activity on broadleaf weeds. Appropriate broadleaf weed control practices are usually necessary following the use of sethoxydim. Vantage may also be used in high-maintenance centipedegrass and fine fescues (creeping red, chewings, sheep, and hard) for annual grass and bahiagrass control.

Maleic hydrazide (Retard 2.25L; Royal Slo-Gro 1.5L; Liquid Growth Retardant 0.6L)

Apply the respective product at 3.0 pounds active ingredient per acre. Maleic hydrazide is foliar absorbed. Apply it to bahiagrass in the spring or 7 to 14 days after the first mowing. Do not use a surfactant, apply to turf less than three years old, or reseed within three days after application. Treated areas may appear less dense and be temporarily discolored. Do not use on St. Augustinegrass, and do not apply to bahiagrass under drought conditions. Read and follow all label recommendations before use. A 12-hour rainfree period is required for optimum activity. It is also used on fescue, bluegrass, and ryegrass. Maleic hydrazide is not recommended for use on high-maintenance turfgrasses.

Glyphosate (Roundup Pro 4L, others)

Only apply glyphosate to bahiagrass at 4.0 to 8.0 fluid ounces per acre (0.18 to 0.22 lb ai/acre). Glyphosate is also sold in combination with 2,4-D as Campaign 2.5L. The addition of 2,4-D to glyphosate increases broadleaf weed control. Glyphosate is foliar absorbed. **Note: Glyphosate is classified as a nonselective herbicide. Only low rates of glyphosate should be used in bahiagrass, or severe injury will occur.** Make the initial application at a rate of 6.0 to 8.0 fluid ounces per acre after full green-up of bahiagrass (timing will vary according to location). Treated areas may appear less dense and be temporarily discolored. Repeat applications of Roundup Pro at 4.0 to 6.0 fluid ounces per acre six weeks later can be used to extend the period of growth and seedhead regulation. Read and follow the label recommendations prior to use. Glyphosate is not recommended for use on high-maintenance turfgrasses.

Imazapic (Plateau 2ASU)

Apply imazapic to bahiagrass and bermudagrass at 2.0 to 4.0 fluid ounces per acre (0.031 to 0.062 lb ai/acre). Imazapic is foliar and root absorbed. Apply it to bahiagrass in the spring two to three weeks before seedhead formation or 7 to 10 days after mowing. Imazapic also provides some broadleaf weed and annual grass control. Do not apply it to wetlands. Treated areas may appear less dense and be temporarily discolored. Do not use on St. Augustinegrass, tall fescue, or drought-stressed bahiagrass. Add a surfactant or methylated seed oil according to label recommendations. Read and follow the label directions before use. Imazapic is not recommended for use on high-maintenance turfgrasses.

Imazethapyr + Imazapyr (Event 1.46L)

Apply imazethapyr plus imazapyr to low-maintenance tall fescue at 8.0 to 10.0 fluid ounces per acre (0.09 to 0.11 lb ai/acre) after turf has completed its spring transition, is actively growing, and has at least two inches of vertical growth. Add a surfactant at 0.25 percent v/v. Do not use on stands less than one year old or on highly managed turf. Do not reseed within three months after application. Read and follow the label directions before use.

Mefluidide (Embark 2S)

Apply mefluidide at 1.5 to 2.0 pints per acre (0.38 to 0.5 lb ai/acre) approximately two weeks before seedhead appearance. It is foliar absorbed. Do not use mefluidide on turf less than four months old and do not reseed within three days after application. Treated turf may appear less dense and be temporarily discolored. An eight-hour rainfree period is needed after application. The addition of 0.25 to 0.5 percent v/v nonionic surfactant may increase seedhead control but also may increase turf discoloration. For low-maintenance bermudagrass, use a 1.0 pound active ingredient per acre application rate.

Low- to Medium-Maintenance Turf
Mefluidide (Embark 2S, Embark 0.2S)

Mefluidide is recommended for use on turfgrasses under low to medium levels of maintenance. Apply it at 0.125 to 1.0 pound active ingredient per acre (Embark 2S at 0.5 to 4 pts/a: Embark 0.2S at 5 to 20 pts/a). Mefluidide is primarily foliar absorbed. Apply it to common bermudagrass (4 pts/a Embark 2S, 20 pts/a Embark 0.2S), tall fescue and Kentucky bluegrass (1.5 pt/a Embark 2S, 5 pts/a Embark 0.2S), and St. Augustinegrass (1.0 pt/a Embark, 5 pts/a Embark 0.2S), and in spring after green-up until approximately two weeks before the seedhead appearance. Optimum results may not be obtained if rainfall or irrigation occurs within eight hours following application. Do not apply it to turf within four growing months after seeding, and do not reseed within three days after application. Treated turf may appear less dense and temporarily discolored. Adding one to two quarts of a nonionic surfactant per 100 gallons of spray solution may enhance suppression; however, turfgrass injury (discoloration) may also be increased. Use 0.5 pint per acre of Embark or two to five pints per acre of Embark 0.2S in the early January through February time frame to suppress *Poa annua* seedheads in fairways (Figure 26–2). Iron applications 10 days or less before mefluidide application may lessen discoloration. Read and follow the label recommendations before use.

FIGURE 26–2 Control of *Poa annua* seedheads (right) with timely applications of plant growth retardants can be compared to an untreated plot (left).

Flurprimidol (Cutless 50WP)

Apply flurprimidol at 0.75 to 3.0 pounds per acre (0.375 to 1.5 lbs ai/acre). Flurprimidol is root absorbed. Apply it to bermudagrass or zoysiagrass golf course fairways, as well as hard-to-mow and trimmed areas, and provide four to eight weeks of suppression. Flurprimidol must be uniformly applied and irrigated-in with 0.5 inch of water within 24 hours of application. Flurprimidol does not completely control seedheads, but only seedhead stalk elongation. Temporary turf discoloration may follow this treatment. St. Augustinegrass, bahiagrass, and common bermudagrass require the higher rate. Repeat applications every four weeks on Tifway bermudagrass with 1.0 pound per acre will minimize turf injury.

Trinexapac-ethyl (Primo 1EC, Primo MAXX, Primo 25WSB)

Apply trinexapac-ethyl at rates ranging from 0.1 to 0.75 pound active ingredient per acre (Primo MAXX and 1EC—3 to 22 fl oz/a; Primo 25WSB—5.4 to 44 oz/a) depending upon the turfgrass species, mowing height, and length of suppression desired. Trinexapac-ethyl is foliar absorbed. Low rates are for hybrid bermudagrass, centipedegrass, zoysiagrass, and St. Augustinegrass (Figure 26–3); medium rates are for common bermudagrass and tall fescue, while the high rate is for bahiagrass. Primo MAXX and 1EC at 3.0 to 6.0 fluid ounces per acre and Primo 25WSB at 1.35 to 2.7 ounces per acre may also be used on creeping bentgrass and hybrid bermudagrass putting greens. A one hour rainfree period is needed after application. Mowing one to seven days after application improves the appearance. Repeat applications may be applied as needed or approximately three to six weeks apart to maintain growth suppression, but do not exceed 19 pints per acre of Primo MAXX and 1EC or 174 ounces per acre of Primo 25WSB per year. Trinexapac-ethyl will suppress seedheads on hybrid bermudagrass, but only partial seedhead suppression is observed on other turfgrass species. Temporary turf discoloration may follow treatment. It is not necessary to add a surfactant to trinexapac-ethyl. Primo formulations may also be used to enhance the establishment of cool-season turfgrasses in bermudagrass (overseeding). Apply Primo before verticutting, spiking, scalping, and so forth, as well as one to five days before overseeding.

Paclobutrazol (Trimmit 2SC)

Apply paclobutrazol at 2.0 to 3.0 pints per acre (0.5 to 0.75 lb ai/acre) to actively growing hybrid bermudagrass and St. Augustinegrass. Paclobutrazol is also available on several dry fertilizer formulation carriers. Paclobutrazol is root absorbed. This product may also be used on overseeded golf greens and fairways during winter for turf enhancement, for annual bluegrass suppression,

FIGURE 26–3 Control of turf internodal extension through various rates of a gibberellin biosynthesis plant growth inhibitor *(courtesy of Jan Weinbrecht).*

and to suppress the growth of perennial biotypes of annual bluegrass in creeping bentgrass greens. Paclobutrazol should be applied in early January for seedhead suppression of annual bluegrass. Do not apply to saturated soils and treat only dry foliage. Read and follow recommendations before use.

Annual Bluegrass Suppression in Highly Maintained Bentgrass or Overseeded Bermudagrass
Mefluidide (Embark 2S, Embark 0.2S)

Apply mefluidide at 0.05 to 0.125 pound active ingredient per acre (Embark 2S at 0.5 pt/a; Embark 0.2S at 2 to 5 pt/a) to suppress annual bluegrass seedhead development. Mefluidide must be applied before seedheads emerge. Application timing varies between geographical locations, but generally occurs during the January through early March time frame (actual timing of application depends upon location and climatic conditions). Mefluidide is primarily foliage absorbed. Do not apply to turf within four growing months after seeding, and do not reseed within three days after application. Treated turf may appear less dense and temporarily discolored. Adding one to two quarts of a nonionic surfactant per 100 gallons of spray solution may enhance suppression; however, discoloration may also be increased. Iron applications may lessen discoloration. Mefluidide formulations are not recommended for use on golf course putting greens. Read and follow label recommendations before use.

Paclobutrazol (Trimmit 2SC)

Apply paclobutrazol at 6.4 to 48 fluid ounces per acre (0.1 to 0.75 lb ai/a) in late winter to early spring after growth of desired grasses has resumed and one to two mowings has occurred. Do not apply after March 15 to avoid delaying green-up of bermudagrass. Paclobutrazol is root absorbed, and 0.25-inch of rainfall or irrigation water should be applied within 24 hours of application. Fall and spring applications of paclobutrazol may also be used over a period of years to suppress the growth of perennial biotypes of annual bluegrass in creeping bentgrass greens. Repeat applications may be made three to four weeks apart. Do not use if *Poa annua* populations exceed 70 percent.

Flurprimidol (Cutless 50WP)

Apply flurprimidol at 0.25 to 0.5 pound per acre (0.12 to 0.25 lb ai/a) to actively growing creeping bentgrass in the spring after the third or fourth mowing or in the fall months. Repeat, if necessary, at three- to six-week intervals, but do not exceed two pounds of product per acre per growing season. Delay overseeding until two weeks after application, and make the final fall application eight weeks before the onset of winter dormancy. Flurprimidol is not as effective as paclobutrazol in suppressing the growth of perennial biotypes of annual bluegrass.

Plant Growth Promoters

An available plant growth promoter is RyzUp from Abbott Laboratories. RyzUp is gibberellic acid that encourages cell division and elongation. When used, RyzUp helps initiate or maintain growth and prevent color changes (e.g., purpling) during periods of cold stress and light frosts on bermudagrass such as Tifdwarf and Tifgreen. Oftentimes, fall golf tournaments may experience an early light frost before the overseeding has become established. RyzUp helps the turf recover from this discoloration.

SECTION

VIII

BEST PESTICIDE AND NUTRIENT MANAGEMENT AND HANDLING PRACTICES

CHAPTER
27

Effective, Safe, and Legal Use of Pesticides

INTRODUCTION

Pesticides are tools used to help develop desirable plants and are among the main reasons the population enjoys a high quality and quantity of food. Correct pesticide use is critical to the protection of the environment and is best ensured by following the label directions as required by law. In addition, individual states have specific laws and regulations concerning pesticide storage and disposal. The following material is related to pesticides and their safe and judicious use. The Department of Agriculture, County Extension Office, Department of Environmental Protection, or equivalent agency in a specific state should be consulted for their exact safe use requirements.

PESTICIDE NOMENCLATURE

A **pesticide** is defined as any substance or mixture of substances intended for preventing, destroying, repelling, or mitigating any pest, and any substance or mixture of substances intended for use as a plant regulator, defoliant, or desiccant. Three types of names are normally associated with a pesticide. The **chemical name** describes the chemistry of the compound, which is usually technical and lengthy. The **common name** is a generic term assigned to the chemical that is often a simpler version of the chemical name. Chemical and common names must be approved by an appropriate authority. The **trade name** is used by the chemical company for marketing purposes to promote a specific product's sale. It often is the most recognizable pesticide name. A pesticide with one common name can have a number of trade names. For example, Fungo, Cleary 3336, and SysTec 1998 are **trade names** for the fungicide thiophanate methyl. Thiophanate methyl is the **common name,** while the **chemical name** is dimethyl 4,4'-o-phenylenebis[3-thioallophanate]. Due to the number of trade names and their constant change, most scientific journals and university publications refer to pesticides by their common name.

PESTICIDE REGISTRATION

Registering a new pesticide is a time-consuming, complicated, and expensive venture. Only one successful pesticide reaches the market out of every 140,000 compounds tested. Discovering, developing, and registering a new pesticide costs over $185 million, with an additional $40 million to $100 million required to build a production plant. Nine to 10 years of testing normally are required before a compound reaches the market. Since a patent protects a compound for 17 years, less than 10 years of exclusive marketing can be expected to protect the investment of development and continued research.

Much of the money needed for pesticide development is used to generate required data from extensive and rigorous testing. Testing for crop safety, pest control efficacy, environmental hazards, and a wide array of toxicological issues is performed. These increasing costs and regulations have significantly reduced the number of companies developing new pesticides.

Data is submitted to the Environmental Protection Agency (EPA) for review and possible registration. The EPA has the responsibility of ensuring the pesticide poses no undue environmental and health hazards when used as instructed. It is not the responsibility of the EPA to document efficacy. A label providing sufficient use instructions and warnings on the safe and proper handling must accompany each product.

The U.S. congressional law regulating the registration, manufacture, transportation, and use of pesticides is the Federal Insecticide, Fungicide and Rodenticide Act (FIFRA). A legally registered pesticide will have an EPA registration number on its label. The EPA registers pesticides; it does not "approve" them.

The law provides:

1. All pesticides must be used only as directed on the label.
2. All pesticides must be classified as "general" or "restricted-use" pesticides.
3. Persons who buy or use "restricted-use" pesticides must be certified as competent pesticide applicators, or must be supervised directly by a certified applicator.
4. Persons who do not obey the law will be subject to civil and/or criminal penalties including fines and jail terms.

General-Use Pesticides

General-use pesticides are those that will not cause unreasonable adverse effects to the environment and may be purchased and applied by the general public when used according to label directions (Table 27–1). However, in some states, anyone applying any pesticide for monetary compensation or to public property (including golf courses) must have a license or be directly supervised by someone with a license. **Restricted-use pesticides** are pesticides that pose some risk to the environment or human health even when used according to the label. These pesticides must be applied by certified applicators, or persons under their direct supervision, who have shown the ability to use these materials safely and properly. Persons handling restricted-use pesticides also must wear approved protective clothing. The pesticide label will indicate whether a pesticide is classified as a restricted-use product. A third category, **mixed-use,** covers pesticides that are classified as "general" for certain purposes and "restricted" for others.

A state may be allowed to register additional uses for a federally registered (EPA) pesticide under certain circumstances. This is called a **Special Local Needs (SLN) registration** or **24(C) registration.** These registrations often involve adding application sites, pests, or alternate techniques to those already listed on the federally registered pesticide label. The EPA registration number will have the initials "SLN" and the two-letter abbreviation for the state that issues the special registration. The applicator must have a copy of an SLN label *in his or her possession* in order to apply the pesticide for the purpose listed on it.

A **Section 18** is another special temporary registration allowed under *emergency* situations where an unregistered pesticide may be used. Such conditions must be deemed where no alternate control method is available and significant economic or health problems would exist if the pest is left uncontrolled. Nonfood or nonfiber commodities such as turf and ornamentals rarely are granted Section 18 exemptions.

An **Experimental Use Permit** (EUP) is often granted by the EPA for products during the final stages of development to allow companies to expand their database under actual field condi-

TABLE 27–1 *Table of pesticide toxicity categories.*

	Categories			
	I	**II**	**III**	**IV**
Pesticide Classification	Restricted-use	Some restricted-use, some general-use	Mostly general-use	General-use
Oral LD$_{50}$ (mg/kg)	0 to 50	50 to 500	500 to 5,000	>5,000
Inhalation LC$_{50}$ (mg/L)	0 to 0.2	0.2 to 2	2 to 20	>20
Dermal LD$_{50}$ (mg/kg)	0 to 200	200 to 2,000	2,000 to 20,000	>20,000
Eye effects	Corneal opacity not reversible within seven days	Corneal opacity reversible within seven days: irritation	No corneal opacity; irritation reversible within seven days	No irritation
Skin effects	Corrosive	Severe irritation at 72 hours	Moderate irritation at 72 hours	Mild or slight irritation at 72 hours
Signal words/symbols	DANGER/POISON with skull and crossbones symbol	WARNING	CAUTION	CAUTION
Description	Very highly toxic	Highly toxic	Moderately toxic	Low toxicity
Oral dosage lethal to human adults	Few drops to one teaspoon	One teaspoon to two tablespoons	One ounce to one pint	> One pint

tions and commercial applications before full registration. Only a limited amount of the product can be used or sold in specific geographical locations under an EUP.

Certified pesticide applicators for golf courses in most states are regulated by the state's pesticide regulatory agency—Department of Agriculture, Department of Pesticide Regulation, or a similar department. Two tests must be completed before a person can obtain a restricted-use pesticide applicator license. The first test queries a person's knowledge of general areas of safe pesticide use and handling (core test), while the second covers specific information concerning pesticide use for turfgrass and ornamental pest control (category test).

Other tests may be required if restricted-use pesticides are applied to other areas on a golf course, such as lakes. These tests are administered at local county cooperative extension offices in some states, or by the state pesticide regulatory agency. Study guides for the tests can be obtained from these agencies. Once the license has been obtained, it must be renewed by retaking the tests, or by accumulating continuing education units (CEUs) or continuing certification hours (CCHs) over a prescribed period of years. Programs that provide CEUs/CCHs are offered by a number of agencies throughout the year.

Restricted-Use Pesticides

As previously indicated, restricted-use pesticides must be applied by a licensed, certified pesticide applicator, or by persons under the direct supervision of a licensed, certified pesticide applicator. If an unlicensed worker is applying the pesticide, the licensed supervisor may be required by law to tell unlicensed workers the following:

1. Safety procedures to be followed as given on the label.
2. Safety clothing and equipment to be used.
3. Common symptoms of pesticide poisoning.
4. Dangers of eating, drinking, smoking, or toileting while handling pesticides.
5. Where to obtain emergency medical treatment.

The licensed certified pesticide applicator must maintain records of the use of restricted-use pesticides. This information also should be maintained for general-use pesticides. The records must be kept for two (2) years and include:

1. Date and time of treatment.
2. Location of property.

3. Owner or person authorizing application.
4. Name of applicator.
5. Crop or target area and acreage covered.
6. Pests to be controlled.
7. Pesticide used, including trade name, common name, EPA registration number, application rate, and type of equipment used.

Simplifying record keeping makes it less of an added burden. For example, superintendents can use a computer to print out customized forms with blanks to be filled in for each pesticide application. Another simplification of record keeping is the use of a rubber stamp that can be made at local office supply stores. Stamp the book pages and fill in the blanks accordingly. An example of the minimum amount of information recorded for each pesticide application is shown on the Pesticide Application Record form on the following page. **Use your own records—they are valuable management tools.**

PESTICIDE FORMULATIONS AND CARRIERS

Pesticides are not sold to end-users as pure chemicals, but are formulated or combined with appropriate solvents, diluents, or adjuvants to form a material called a **formulation.** The primary function of formulating a pesticide is to permit uniform application. However, formulations also extend the stability and storage life of pesticides, enhance pesticide activity, allow pesticides to be packaged in convenient containers, and allow for safer use. They also may vary in their effectiveness on weeds and the tolerance of turf and ornamentals to the herbicide. Some formulations are more costly than others, and the ease of application and compatibility with your application equipment can vary according to the formulation. Pesticides are available in a variety of formulations, and often the same pesticide is sold as several different formulations (Table 27–2). A **Material Safety Data Sheet (MSDS)** for each formulation of a pesticide should be obtained and cataloged.

Pesticides are applied to the target site with the use of a carrier. A carrier is a gas, liquid, or solid substance used to propel, dilute, or suspend a pesticide during its application. Water is the most commonly used liquid carrier, although fluid fertilizers also may be used. Granules and pellets consisting of clay, corn cobs, ground nut hulls, sand, or dry fertilizer serve as carriers for dry pesticide formulations.

Sprayable Formulations

Sprayable formulations are applied with liquid carriers, usually water. The amount of liquid carrier required to uniformly cover the turfgrass will be indicated on the label. Use the label recommendation for each pesticide you apply, because amounts above the label rate are illegal and those below the label rate may be ineffective.

Aerosols (A)

Aerosols contain one or more active ingredients and a solvent. Most aerosols contain a very low percentage of active ingredient. There are two types of aerosol formulations: the ready-to-use type and those made for use in smoke or fog generators. Insecticides are the pesticides most often used as aerosols.

Water-Soluble Liquids (S or SL)

A water-soluble pesticide formulation typically consists of the pesticide, water as solvent for the pesticide, selected surfactants to improve wetting and penetration, and possibly an antifreeze. These form true solutions (completely dissolved) when mixed with water; they are nonabrasive and do not plug screens or nozzles. The resulting solution can be clear or colored and is stable, requiring no agitation once initially mixed.

Pesticide Application Record

Company Name _____   Commercial Applicator _____

Application Date & Time _____   Site Location _____

Pesticide License Category _____   Number _____

Pesticide Name(s) _____   Manufacturer _____

EPA Registration No. _____   Restricted-Entry Interval (REI) _____

Active Material & Formulation _____

Lot No. _____   % Concentration _____

Safety Equipment Needed _____

Application Information

Type of Area Treated _____   Target Site _____

Target Pest(s) _____   Total Treated Area _____

Application Rate (e.g., per acre or per 1,000 sq.ft.) _____   Application Timing _____

Amount of Pesticide Product Mixed _____ Per _____ Gallons of Water

Additives (Surfactant/Wetting Agent/Crop Oil, etc.) _____ Rate _____

Weather Conditions

Air Temperature (°F) _____   % Relative Humidity _____   Dew Presence (Y/N) _____

Initial Wind Velocity (MPH) _____   Wind Direction _____

First Hour _____   Second Hour _____   Third Hour _____

Soil Temperature at four inches (°F) _____   Soil Moisture _____   % Cloud Cover _____

Application Equipment

Method of Application _____ Speed (mph) _____ Motor Speed (rpm) _____ Nozzle Type _____ Number _____

Nozzle Height _____ Spacing _____ Boom Width _____ Gallon Per Acre (gpa) _____ Spray Pressure (psi) _____

Nontarget Plant, Animal, or Human Exposure: Yes _____ No _____ (If yes, list corrective or emergency action taken)

Other Comments:

Signature _____   Date _____

TABLE 27-2 *Comparisons of pesticide formulations (read individual labels for product specific information).*

Formulation (abbreviation)	Mixing/loading hazards	Plant phytotoxicity	Effect on application equipment	Agitation required	Visible residues	Compatible with other formulations
Dry flowables/water-dispersible granules (DF or WDG)	Minimum	Safe	Abrasive	Yes	Yes	Good
Emulsifiable concentrates (EC)	Spills & splashes	Maybe	May affect rubber pump parts	Yes	No	Fair
Flowables (F)	Spills & splashes	Maybe	May affect rubber pump parts; also abrasive	Yes	Yes	Fair
Dusts (D)	Severe inhalation hazards	Safe	—	Yes	Yes	—
Granules (G) & pellets (P or Ps)	Minimum	Safe	—	No	No	—
Microencapsulated (M)	Spills & splashes	Safe	None	Yes	—	Fair
Solutions (S)	Spills & splashes	Safe	Nonabrasive	No	No	Fair
Soluble powders (SP)	Dust inhalation	Safe	Nonabrasive	No	Some	Fair
Wettable powders (WP)	Dust inhalation	Safe	Abrasive	Yes	Yes	Highly

Water-Soluble Powders (SP or WSP)

Water-soluble powders are finely divided dry solids that look like wettable powders; however, they completely dissolve in water to form true solutions requiring no agitation once initially mixed. Wettable powders, however, do not form true solutions and must be constantly agitated. Water-soluble powders possess all the advantages of wettable powders with none of the disadvantages except inhalation hazard during mixing.

Emulsifiable Concentrates (E or EC)

Emulsifiable concentrates are oily (or nonpolar) liquids that form emulsions (droplets of oil surrounded by water) in water (polar) instead of forming true solutions. The *emulsifying agent* acts as a binder-coupler between the oil-water surface, reducing interfacial tension and allowing the tiny droplets of oil to remain in suspension. This allows water-insoluble pesticides to be uniformly dispersed in water, even though each maintains its original identity. After EC compounds are added to water, the resulting emulsions are milky/colored and require mild agitation to keep the pesticide uniformly suspended in the spray tank. Each EC gallon usually contains 25 to 75 percent (two to eight pounds) of active ingredient. Emulsions present little problems in mixing, pumping, or spraying. They are not abrasive, do not plug screens or nozzles, and leave little visible residue.

Wettable Powders (W or WP)

Wettable powders are finely ground solids that look like dusts, and consist of a dry diluent (usually a hydrophilic clay such as bentonite or attapulgite) plus the pesticide and perhaps adjuvants. Usually, pesticides make up 50 to 80 percent (by weight) of a wettable powder formulation. The various adjuvants in the formulation prevent lumpiness or flocculation of the finely ground materials and improve mixing in the spray tank. Wettable powders do not dissolve in water; rather, they form unstable suspensions in water, giving it a cloudy appearance, and require vigorous agitation to prevent settling of the suspended particles. Inhalation hazards also exist when pouring and mixing the powder. Wettable powder formulations also cause rapid nozzle wear, often clog nozzles and screens, and may leave visible residues.

Flowables or Aqueous Suspensions (F or AS)

Also designated as **liquids (L)** or **water-dispersible liquids (WDL),** these highly viscous (not easily poured) liquids contain finely ground solids suspended in a liquid system. The particles are smaller than those of the wettable powders. These formulations form a suspension in water and require agitation to remain distributed. These also settle out when in storage; therefore, they require vigorous shaking before use but have less mixing and dust exposure problems typical of wettable powders. They may leave a visible residue. Nozzle wear is intermediate between WP and EC, but more similar to WP.

Dispersible Granules or Dry Flowable Granules (DG or DF or WDG)

These finely ground solids are formulated as water-dispersible granules and form a suspension in water. These are similar to wettable powder formulations, except they are granule-sized particles. Once in solution, the granules break apart into a fine powder. Agitation is required to prevent settling of the suspended particles, and nozzle wear is similar to flowables. Granules are made up of finely ground solids combined with suspending and dispersing agents. Their chief advantage over wettable powders and flowables is the ease of measurement and handling and are less susceptible to inhalation and wind blowing. **Note:** These formulations are always applied with a liquid (water or fluid fertilizer) carrier.

Water-Soluble Bags/Packs

Some pesticides are being sold with a premeasured amount of the pesticide formulation (usually a wettable powder or dry flowable) packaged inside a water-soluble bag. This bag will dissolve when placed in a tank of water, thereby releasing the pesticide. This eliminates the need to directly handle the pesticide, thereby reducing worker exposure to the pesticide. These bags are not to be broken before being placed in the tank. Exact sprayer calibration is necessary since parts or pieces of a bag cannot be used.

Microencapsulated (M)

These particles of pesticides (liquid or dry) are surrounded by a plastic coating. The formulated product is mixed with water and applied as a spray. Once applied, the capsule slowly releases the pesticide. Advantages of microencapsulated pesticides include increased safety to the applicator, ease of mixing and handling, and controlled release, thereby extending the period of pest control. Constant agitation is necessary to maintain the solution.

Dry Formulations

Dry pesticide formulations are not applied with liquid carriers but are applied as purchased. Normally the pesticide is formulated in relatively low concentrations on the dry carrier to aid in uniform distribution.

Granules (G)

Small granular particles ($<10\ \mu M^3$) are applied in the dry state. These consist of the pesticide plus a dry carrier such as clay, vermiculite, walnut shells, sand, or corn cobs. The active material either coats the outside of the granules or is absorbed into them. Pesticide concentrations typically range from 2 to 10 percent. Advantages of granules include: (1) ready to use—water is not needed for application; (2) they are generally quicker to apply than liquid applications; (3) they can be combined with fertilizer to combine two steps, thereby, reducing costs; and (4) public perception is usually more favorable using granules compared to liquid applications. Granular formulations require slightly more rainfall for activation than sprayable formulations and tend to be more expensive. Uniform application can also be a problem and application equipment is harder to calibrate. When combined with fertilizer, proper timing of pest control and appropriate plant fertilization timing needs should coincide.

Pellets (P)

Pellets are similar to granules except the particles are usually larger. Pellets are frequently used for spot applications, and are applied either "by hand" from shaker cans or with hand spreaders. These usually contain low active ingredient concentrations of approximately 5 to 20 percent. See the previous comments regarding granules.

Dusts (D)

Dusts are popular homeowner formulations of insecticides and fungicides requiring simple equipment and are effective in hard-to-reach areas. Most formulations are ready-to-use and contain between 0.5 to 10 percent active ingredient plus a fine, dry, inert carrier such as talc, chalk, clay, or ash. Due to drift hazards, few herbicides are currently formulated as dusts.

Adjuvants

An **adjuvant** is a spray additive enhancing the performance, safety, or handling characteristics of a pesticide. "Adjuvant" is a broad term and includes **surfactants, crop oils, crop oil concentrates, anti-foaming agents, drift control agents, pH modifiers,** and **compatibility agents.** These help modify the surface properties of liquids by enhancing and facilitating emulsifying, dispersing, wetting, spreading, sticking, and penetrating of liquids into plants and soil. Surfactants, crop oils, and crop oil concentrates are added according to label directions since indiscriminate use may cause severe turfgrass injury or decreased pesticide performance. Some pesticides, such as postemergence herbicides, and a few fungicides have surfactants included in their formulation; therefore, additional surfactant is unnecessary. Always read the pesticide label before adding any adjuvants. Look for recommendations as to the type of adjuvant to add. Use only the recommended rates as too much of some adjuvants can cause an unsprayable tank-mix. Surfactants are most often used in liquid (soluble, emulsifiable) and dry (wettable powders, others) formulations applied in aqueous sprays.

Surfactants

Substances without affinity for each other (such as water and leaf wax) tend to repel. To "bind" the two surfaces, surfactants with a lipophilic (oil-loving) portion and a hydrophilic (water-loving) portion on the same molecule are used. The term **surfactant** is an acronym for **surface-active agents** to indicate the changes they produce at surfaces. At low concentrations, surfactants reduce surface tension between spray droplets and the waxy leaf surface, allowing the spray droplets to spread out and contact a greater portion of the leaf. This aids in penetration and helps prevent droplets from rolling off the leaf. At higher concentrations, surfactants help dissolve the wax in the leaf cuticles, allowing easier penetration of the leaf by the pesticide. However, this also accounts for undesirable phytotoxicity to the turfgrass if excessive rates are used.

Three major types of surfactants include **emulsifiers, wetting agents,** and **stickers. Emulsifiers** stabilize the dispersal of oil-soluble pesticides in water so the pesticide will not settle out. These allow petroleum-based formulations such as emulsifiable concentrates to mix with water. These usually are added by the chemical company during the pesticide formulation process. **Invert emulsifiers** allow water-based pesticides to mix with petroleum-based carriers. **Stickers (or adhesives)** cause the spray droplet to adhere to the leaf surface and reduces spray run-off during application and wash-off by rain or irrigation. Stickers often are combined with wetting agents (spreader-stickers) to increase adhesion and spray droplet coverage.

Wetting agents help the spray droplet to spread over the leaf surface by reducing the interfacial tension between the leaf surface and spray droplets. Wetting agents also allow wettable powders to mix with water. The three types of wetting agents (**anionic, cationic,** and **nonionic**) are classified based on how they ionize or separate into charged particles in water. Nonionic surfactants do not ionize; thus, they remain uncharged. They are the most commonly used type of surfactant and are compatible with most pesticides. They are unaffected by water containing high levels of calcium, magnesium, or ferric ions. They also can be used in strong acid solutions. **Anionic** surfactants ionize with water to form a negative charge while **cationic** surfactants ionize with water to form a positive charge. These are only occasionally used. A pesticide mixed with an anionic surfactant will stick to the leaf tissue but will not be absorbed by the plant. These should be used with pesticides that remain on the plant surface (contact pesticides).

A pesticide mixed with a nonionic surfactant will help a pesticide penetrate plant cuticles. These are best used with systemic pesticides that need to be absorbed by the plant to be effective. Cationic surfactants are extremely phytotoxic. Do not use them unless it is specifically stated on a pesticide label.

Crop Oils

Crop oils and **crop oil concentrates** are non-phytotoxic light oils containing varying percentages of surfactants and primarily emulsifiers. These are phytobland petroleum or vegetable oils increasing pesticide absorption through leaf cuticles (or waxy layer). Crop oils contain 1 to 10 percent surfactant and commonly are used at concentrations of one gallon per acre. Crop oil concentrates contain 17 to 20 percent surfactant and are generally used at concentrations of one quart per acre. Crop oil concentrates have replaced crop oils since reduced amounts of the adjuvant are required.

Miscellaneous Adjuvants

The use of **anti-foaming agents** (or defoamers) minimize air entrapment during agitation and may be necessary if excessive foaming occurs in the spray tank. **Drift control agents** (or thickeners) reduce spray droplet drift by reducing the percentage of very fine spray particles in the spray mist. **Compatibility agents** are added to fluid fertilizer and pesticide mixtures to prevent these individual components from separating or clumping. Follow label directions closely for mixing compatibility agents. However, before adding any such mixture to a spray tank, *test* the mixture in a small jar to ensure there will be no clumping or separation (see procedure below).

Penetrants allow pesticides to enter the outer surface of plants while **spreaders** allow a uniform coating layer over the treated surface.

Some pesticides will be inactivated if the pH is too high or too low. **Modifiers** are compounds, either buffers or acidifiers, available to adjust the pH of the water to be used as the pesticide carrier. Buffers change the pH to a desired level, and then keep it relatively constant. Acidifiers neutralize alkaline solutions (lower the pH) but will not maintain the pH at this level as well as buffers do. Lower solution pH with an acidifier after the pesticide is added to the tank. Ask your sales representative to provide you with the manufacturer's recommendation for the pH of the carrier.

Pesticide Compatibility

Two or more pesticides, or one that can be mixed with fertilizer, are compatible if no adverse effects occur as a result of the mixture. Possible effects of mixing incompatible chemicals include:

- Effectiveness of one or both compounds may be reduced.
- A precipitate may form in the tank, clogging screens and nozzles of application equipment.
- Plant phytotoxicity, stunting, or reduced seed germination and production may occur.
- Excessive residues.
- Excessive run-off.

Compatibility Test

A compatibility test (the jar test) should be made well before mixing chemicals for application:

1. Place one teaspoon of each chemical in a quart jar containing about a pint of water.
2. Close the lid tightly; shake vigorously; and observe the mixture for settling out, layering, formation of gels, flakes, or other precipitates, or a change in temperature of the mixture (e.g., rapid heating).
3. If any of these effects are seen, the chemicals are not compatible and should not be used together. If nothing happens, let the jar stand for about 30 minutes and reobserve.

Mixing Compatible Chemicals

Mixing some pesticides requires premixing in a smaller, separate container or tank.

1. Always add a wettable powder first. Make a slurry with it in a separate container by adding a small amount of water until it forms a gravy-like consistency. Slowly add this slurry to the tank with the spray tank agitator running.

2. Dry flowable or water-dispersible granules are added second. Flowables should be premixed (one part flowable to one part water) and poured slowly into the tank.
3. Liquid flowables should be added third. Liquids should also be premixed (one part liquid chemical to two parts water or liquid fertilizer) before blending in the tank. Many labels provide the proper mixing sequence.
4. Emulsifiable concentrates and water-soluble liquids should be combined last.

Proper Order for Tank-Mixing Various Pesticide Formulations

WP→DF→F→EC→S

pH Problems

The measure of pH (how alkaline [basic] or acidic a solution is) can greatly influence how pesticide and other products perform. Most waters are slightly basic because of the presence of dissolved carbonate and bicarbonate salts. The water pH greatly affects the breakdown (or hydrolysis) of pesticides. In general, high pH water conditions (basic) cause a shorter half-life (or more rapid breakdown) of the pesticide. Insecticides are especially affected by spray-tank water pH. For example, acephate (Orthene) has a half-life of 65 days at a pH of 3 (acidic), and a half-life of 16 days at pH 9 (basic). Carbaryl (Sevin) has a half-life of 100 to 150 days at pH 6, but only 24 hours at pH 9.

The pH of spray-tank water should be adjusted with buffers or acidifiers to within a certain range for adequate usage (Table 27–3).

To test and adjust the pH of water to be used for mixing pesticides, do the following:

1. Test the water by using a clean container to obtain a one-pint sample of water to be used. Check the pH using a pH meter, test kit, or test paper and determine if the pH needs to be adjusted.
2. Adjust the pH by using a standard eyedropper to add three drops of buffer or acidifier to the measured pint of water. Stir well with a clean glass rod or clean, nonporous utensil. Check pH as previously noted and, if further adjustments are needed, repeat the previous steps until proper pH is obtained, recording the number of times three drops of buffer or acidifier were added.
3. Correct the pH in the spray tank by filling the tank with water. Add two ounces of buffer or acidifier for each time three drops were used in the previous jar test, in every 100 gallons of water in the spray tank. Recheck the pH of water in the tank and adjust, if necessary. Add pesticides to the spray tank.

HANDLING PESTICIDES SAFELY

Pesticide "handling" includes virtually all transport, storage, mixing, loading, applying, and disposal activities.

Pesticide Storage

Proper storage of pesticides not only helps protect against accidental spills and leaks, but can also influence the shelf life and efficacy of relied-upon products. Factors such as air temperature, humidity, sunlight, and ventilation should be carefully considered. The following are some storage suggestions; however, the best source of specific product storage and spill control information is the product MSDS.

TABLE 27–3 *Spray-tank pH levels and precautionary statements.*

pH range	Comments
3.5 to 6.0	Satisfactory for spraying and short-term storage of most spray mixtures in the spray tank.
6.1 to 7.0	Adequate for immediate spraying of most pesticides. Do not allow mixture to sit over one to two hours to prevent loss of effectiveness.
≥7.1	Should add buffer or acidifier and do not allow to sit in direct sunlight.

The Storage Facility and Site (Figure 27–1)

- Keep the amount of storage space to a minimum to discourage storing unneeded pesticides, but large enough to handle what might reasonably be stored. This should include not only newly purchased chemicals, but also opened containers; empty, clean containers; and waste pesticides held for proper disposal.
- Locate the storage site in a safe location: a place not flooded by rivers, ditches, run-off, or tides.
- To prevent moisture accumulation, elevate the storage facility above the immediate ground level by at least 12 inches (0.3 m). Free moisture will rust metal containers; disintegrate paper or cardboard packaging; make labels unreadable; cause labels to detach; cause dry formulation to clump, cake, break down, or dissolve; and possibly cause pesticides to spread or move from the storage area.
- Use a portable storage building for best storage. These can be repositioned easily in case of flooding or change in the area use patterns.
- Use tie-downs on portable storage buildings to prevent tipping, rolling, or movement due to water or wind.
- Select a site with as little run-off as possible to prevent contamination of surface waters in case of a leak or spill.
- Locate the storage facility at least 100 feet (30 m) from surface waters and wells, animal feeding stations or shelters, and food or feed storage and dwellings.
- Determine the direction of prevailing winds and consider what is downwind from your storage site. This may be important in the event of spills or fires.
- Locate your storage site so it is easily accessible by vehicles for pesticide delivery and pick-up, as well as emergency vehicles.
- Determine and comply with any applicable local zoning and building codes.
- Consider using barriers, such as posts, to prevent damage to the storage unit by vehicles delivering pesticides or picking them up for applications.

Physical Construction of the Storage Unit

- Use a separate storage unit made of nonflammable materials to reduce fire hazard.
- The best storage is a detached structure positioned far enough away from other structures that could threaten the storage if they should burn.
- Use sealed floors—metal; sealed concrete; epoxy-coated metal, wood, or concrete; no-wax sheet flooring; or other easily cleaned, non-absorbent material. Dirt or unsealed wood flooring should not be used.

- Use non-absorbing materials throughout. The best shelving is metal with a lip. Consider leak-proof plastic trays on shelves.
- Have a built-in sump, or drain to a sump. Locate any external sump beside the building instead of under it for easy access if you need to remove spilled materials. Protect sumps from filling with water from rain or run-off.
- Have a continuous internal lip or curb two to four inches (5 to 10 cm) high to prevent spills from overflowing and going outside the building.
- If possible, provide electrical power to the storage unit. This allows interior lighting, as well as an exhaust fan and heater. It also allows exterior security lighting and alarms. Explosion-proof wiring and switches are best. The light/fan switch should be on the outside of the storage unit and weatherproof.
- Have good lighting; explosion-proof lighting is best. Good lighting lets you:
  - read labeling
  - note leaks and damaged containers
  - clean-up spills
  - record inventory changes

Storage Environment (Figure 27–2)

- Keep the storage unit dry. Keep doors and windows to the outside closed and locked, unless windows are needed for ventilation.
- Keep the unit well-ventilated by passive ventilation, mechanical ventilation, or both.
  - Locate a louvered vent or exhaust fan high at one end (back) of the unit and an air makeup louvered vent low at the other end (e.g., in the lower part of the door). This allows vapors to flow away from anyone entering or inside the storage unit.
  - One recommendation for mechanical ventilation is an exhaust fan capable of exchanging air in the unit at least once every six minutes; increase to every three minutes when pesticide handlers are in the unit. For best operation, wire the fan to the light switch so the fan is always on or increases speed whenever pesticide handlers are in the unit. If possible, also wire the fan to a thermostat set between 75 and 85°F (24 and 29°C).
- Keep pesticides from freezing and extremely high temperatures. Most pesticides should be stored at above 40 and below 90°F (4.4 and 32°C).
  - Freezing can cause containers to burst or develop intermittent leaks. Freezing may cause formulations to separate. Many pesticide labels say "Store in a cool, dry place." Some must be stored at temperatures below 90°F (32°C).
  - High temperatures can cause plastic to melt or become brittle, or glass to burst. Pressure caused by high temperatures may cause intermittent leaks, swelling, or a spill when the

FIGURE 27–2 Proper pesticide storage facilities are available as portable units.

product is opened. High temperatures can break down some chemicals or cause some chemicals to volatilize. Heat can also cause explosion or fire.

- Insulate the unit to prevent freezing or overheating.
- Install a heater, ideally an explosion-proof one.

- Keep containers out of direct sunlight. Don't put containers, especially glass or aerosol containers, in windows, even temporarily.

Low-Temperature Considerations

1. When temperatures drop too low, solvents may precipitate out of the solution and crystallize on the inside surfaces of plastic containers. If these crystals are allowed to remain inside the container when the product is poured, there will be an altered ratio of active ingredient per amount of solvent. The result is an incorrect application rate. Some products can be shaken to get the active ingredient back into the solution.
2. Because plastic jugs may become brittle under very cold temperatures, they should be stored on shelves low enough to minimize the effect of dropping. In general, try to avoid storing liquid products above other products in the unlikely event a container leaks. Shelves should be constructed of metal, not wood.

High-Temperature Considerations

1. Excessive heat can cause some products to decompose and lose efficacy. This same decomposition process may also result in the creation of gasses within the container. Under extreme conditions, these gasses may create sufficient pressure that some product is sprayed out of the jug upon opening or at least is mixed into the air during mixing. Always work in well-ventilated areas.
2. High heat coupled with high humidity may weaken cardboard containers in which pesticides are packaged.

Storage Security

- Store pesticides in a separate location, preferably in a separate locked storage building just for them.
- Always lock pesticide storage cabinets, closets, rooms, and buildings.
- Besides locking a storage building, it is a good idea to fence it in and lock the gate.
- Limit access to pesticide storage—allow access to only essential persons. Take necessary steps to keep out any unauthorized persons—children, workers who do not use pesticides, visitors, and so forth.
- Consider installing security lighting and possibly an alarm system.
- If pesticide storage is located within a larger structure, have storage access through a separate, outside door.
- Post signs on the door, building, or fence indicating pesticide storage that tell people to stay out: "Danger—Pesticides—Unauthorized Persons KEEP OUT." Consider writing this information in a second, additional language, such as Spanish.
- Signs should have at least two emergency phone numbers. One person should not be the sole contact in an accident, as that person could be the victim of an accidental exposure. At least one phone number should be for emergency response (fire, rescue, etc.). Poison Control Center phone numbers are a good additional choice.
- Indicate the location of the nearest accessible telephone.
- Post NO SMOKING signs and do not allow smoking in or near your storage area or facility.

Safe Storage Practices

Good storage practices are in part good pesticide handling behaviors. While a good storage unit remains essential, these practices are the real key to safe pesticide storage.

- Read the label and comply with all product storage requirements.
- Store pesticides in their original containers. While this is familiar advice, storing pesticides in other than the original container is one of, if not *the,* most frequent pesticide storage violations.

- Be sure all opened (used) containers are kept securely closed or sealed. If a container is not emptied with a given use, mark the opening date on the container before storing.
- Be sure all pesticide labels and containers are intact. Obtain necessary replacement labels from your dealer or chemical sales representative. A product name penciled on masking tape is not a label. A substitute label, if needed, should have at least the product name, the active ingredient name, the EPA registration number for the product, the manufacturer's name, and any emergency phone numbers listed on the original label.
- Be sure to:
  - Store pesticides separately from food and feeds.
  - Follow any specific storage separation requirements on the label. An example is the required separate storage for phenoxy herbicides (e.g., 2,4-D). Vapors can cross-contaminate other stored chemicals.
  - Keep any food, drinks, veterinary supplies or medications, first aid supplies, and clothing or protective equipment, especially respiratory protection, out of the storage area. These can easily be contaminated by dusts, vapors, or spills.
  - Use a sharp knife or scissors to open paper containers and not tear them unevenly.
  - When pouring from a container, keep it at or below eye level and avoid splashing or spilling on your face or protective clothing.
  - Never use your mouth to siphon a pesticide from a container.
- As much as you can (especially if the label so states):
  - Store all pesticides separately from other chemicals, such as fertilizers.
  - Store pesticides separately from gasoline and other fuels.
  - Separate insecticides, fungicides, and so forth, from herbicides.
  - Store volatile and flammable materials separately.
  - Store liquid formulations below dry formulations.
  - Store any glass containers on the lowest level.
  - Store containers off the floor.
  - Store empty, clean containers separately from full and in-use containers.
- Keep measuring devices (spoons, cups, scales) in the pesticide storage area and label them to prevent their accidental use for other purposes.
- Keep spill control supplies in the storage unit; for example, clean-up materials such as cat litter, vermiculite, spill pillows, and so on; broom, dust pan; activated charcoal, lime, or bleach for decontamination; plastic bags; gloves, eye protection; and plastic sealable container(s).
- Collect spilled pesticides for possible reuse. Remember, clean-up materials become hazardous waste.
- Update your pesticide inventory. You will need an up-to-date inventory for determining future purchases, and in case of spills, fire, weather-related damage, or theft. Keep copies at the storage site, filed at the office, and with your local emergency response agency.
- File copies of your storage location map, storage unit floor plan, and current or seasonal inventory in a secure place away from the storage unit, along with your fire department or other first responders, and with your Local Emergency Planning Committee (LEPC), if required.
- Have a plan. Develop a contingency plan for your establishment with your fire department/rescue unit, especially considering your pesticide storage. In case of a fire in a chemical storage facility, the preferred course of action is to let it burn.

Remember, firefighters are trained to put out fires. Work with these agencies before you need them.

- Fire control—have an ABC fire extinguisher and fire/rescue telephone numbers outside the storage building.
- Keep MSDS sheets in an accessible location.

Other Considerations
- Store products away from heat sources such as gas or electric heaters.
- Segregate products according to hazard class (flammables in one corner, nonflammables in another corner, and poisons in another).
- Chemical storage areas should be a safe distance from water sources, and should be kept locked when not in use.

- Regularly inspect containers for leaks.
- Dry bags should be raised on pallets to prevent them from getting wet. Liquids should be stored below dry materials, not above them.
- Segregate pesticide types to prevent cross-contamination and to minimize the potential for misapplication.
- Keep a spill kit handy, and make sure employees know how to use it.
- Maintain emergency showers and eye wash stations within close proximity of storage and mixing areas.
- Fire extinguishers should be located near every exit of your storage building and should have a 2-A rating (at minimum, 10-pound ABC).
- Post emergency telephone numbers where they can be readily found, if needed. This list should include company managers as well as local fire and rescue units.
- Maintain an up-to-date inventory record of all stored products, and keep it in a separate location. In case of a fire or spill, the fire department or other emergency personnel will want to know exactly what products are involved.
- When adding water to a spray mixture, keep the water hose end above the level of the mixture and not in it. This prevents contamination of the hose and avoids the possibility of back-siphoning. Do not leave equipment unattended when it is being filled.

Additional Safe Storage Practices

- Conduct regularly scheduled safety and maintenance inspections of the storage unit or facility.
- Have a nearby source of clean water for decontaminating skin, eyes, and so forth.
  - Eye wash stations are desirable and may be required by pesticide labeling or chemical safety regulations depending on how your storage unit is sited. Mount eye wash stations outside a smaller storage unit to prevent contamination.
  - In a larger facility you may want or need emergency deluge-type showers in addition to eye wash fountains.
- Locate a telephone in or near the storage area for reporting emergencies.
- Know what your insurance policy covers. Check limitations on coverage. You may need riders for complete coverage. Keep your policy in a safe place.
- If you consider modifying your present storage unit and practices or purchasing new storage, you will undoubtedly consider the costs of these measures. When you balance costs and benefits you should consider:
  - the dollar value of your stored pesticides (are they insured?)
  - the ease and cost of spill clean-up in substandard storage
  - your liability in the event of a spill or fire where there is an environmental impact
  - your liability if any person or animal is injured or killed
  - the potential cost of EPA/state fines for improperly storing your pesticides, or OSHA fines for improper chemical storage or related violations
  - your cost and time-frame for changes needed to correct violations
- The final advice must be the original advice: Follow label instructions—the label is the law.

How Safe is your Pesticide Storage?

- Do you store your pesticides in a detached structure?
- Does your storage building have a sound roof?
- Does your storage building have sound, liquid-proof flooring?
- Are the pesticides you store in their original containers?
- Do the pesticides you store have intact, readable labels?
- Do you store your pesticides separately from gasoline and other fuels?

Reusing Stored Pesticides

Stored pesticides should be examined before they are used to indicate if they have deteriorated (Table 27–4). Containers should be checked for leaks, cracks, tears, erosion, seal failures, or the development of gases. Some formulations, such as those containing emulsifiers, may stratify at low temperatures and should be stirred or shaken and allowed to sit for 30 minutes. These should then be rechecked to see if the formulation stays in solution. If not, then it should be properly disposed and not used.

TABLE 27–4 *General signs of deterioration in pesticide formulations.*

Formulation	General signs of deterioration
Dusts and granulars	Excessive lumping.
Emulsifiable	Milky coloration does not occur with the addition of concentrate to water; sludge or separation of components is evident.
Oil sprays	Milky coloration does not occur by addition of water.
Solutions	Crystallization, precipitation.
Wettable powders	Lumping occurs and powder will not suspend in water.

Resuspending crystals that have separated out is done by heating the mixture to 100 to 140°F (38 to 60°C) using electrically heated warming blankets, hot water baths, or steam, but never by using an open flame. This should be performed by experienced pesticide handlers and not by the general public. If the pesticide appears normal but there are doubts about its effectiveness, test a small amount according to label instructions. Product-specific information on reuse may be found on the product MSDS and the label. If a pesticide exhibits any of the signs of deterioration listed in Table 27–4 and cannot be restored to usable condition, it should be properly disposed of.

Pesticide Containment Area

A pesticide containment area is designed to keep storage, mixing, and loading isolated from other operations. It usually consists of a concrete pad on which a storage building is built and where a drainage system can collect spills and washwater into a holding tank. An example is shown in Figure 27–3. The key concept is that spills and equipment washwater can be easily contained, temporarily stored, and then added back to the spray tank as mix water to be sprayed according to the label.

The concrete pads must be sufficiently reinforced and thick enough to accommodate the gross weight of any item or combination of items to be washed without any structural damage. The area also should exclude run-off in the case of excessive rainfall. State and local laws often govern the proper design and construction of pesticide storage and containment areas and should be consulted when construction is planned on such a facility. Pesticide containment and the wash pad site should be concrete. This prevents the accumulation of rainwater and overflow.

No one design fits all situations, and it is better to set up your own containment area so it is used effectively in your operations. Some considerations include:

- The storage building should be on the pad so spills within the building can be washed into the drain for collection and later application. As a precaution, keep absorbents such as cat litter or dry soil in the building for spill clean-up.
- The pad should be sloped to a drain that can be routed directly to a storage tank, usually through a sump pump. Spills and equipment rinses can be washed into the storage tank, and this mix can be used as makeup water in the next tank mix. Appropriate filters will be needed so the spray nozzles do not become clogged; likewise, keeping mud and debris off the pad is important.
- A roof over the pad eliminates the need to handle rain falling on it. If no roof is possible, the pad drain should have a valve to allow rain to drain freely; this valve can be closed during spray operations. Any materials spilled on the pad should be washed into the storage tank before the valve is opened.

A puncture-type pressure rinse nozzle should be available to rinse empty containers into the spray tank. Bags should be shaken clean and disposed of in an approved landfill.

Worker Protection Standard

The **Worker Protection Standard (WPS)** applies to agricultural workers performing tasks related to the cultivation and harvesting of agricultural plants on farms, nurseries, greenhouses, and in forests. The law also applies to employees who handle (mix, load, apply, repair application equipment, etc.) pesticides in these work environments. The WPS mandates specific restricted entry in-

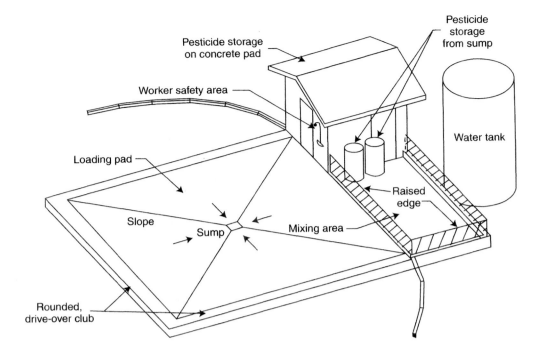

FIGURE 27–3 This sketch of a pesticide mix/load site contains a concrete loading pad with sump and curb, pesticide storage tanks from this sump, and a water tank for emergencies.

Labels in figure:
Pesticide storage from sump
Pesticide storage on concrete pad
Worker safety area
Water tank
Loading pad
Raised edge
Slope
Sump
Mixing area
Rounded, drive-over club

tervals, personal protective equipment, emergency assistance, employee pesticide safety education, and worker access to displayed information. Pesticides requiring compliance with the WPS can be identified by WPS reference in the *Agricultural Use* section of a product's *Directions for Use*.

The WPS specifically excludes many turf uses of pesticides (e.g., golf courses and recreational areas) but not others (e.g., turf [sod] farms). In either case, follow all precautions possible to protect employees from exposure and keep up with the latest changes in laws and regulations.

Personal Protection

To determine the specific protective clothing and equipment required for a particular product, you must refer to the instructions on the product label (Figure 27–4). These instructions carry the weight of law. The toxicity level of the chemical determines the correct body protection. The pesticide label should list a toxicity class, or so-called signal word, with Class I ("Danger") being the most toxic, followed by Class II ("Warning") for moderately toxic, and Class III and IV ("Caution") for the least-toxic chemicals. The material safety data sheet (MSDS) provides additional information in helping to determine personal protection. The following are some general guidelines regarding **Personal Protection Equipment (PPE)** and safe handling practices.

1. At a minimum, wear a long-sleeved shirt and full-length pants (or coveralls), unlined waterproof gloves at least 14 mil thick, and rubber or chemical-resistant boots. Never use leather, paper, or fabric gloves, since these may absorb and retain pesticides. Protective eyewear such as goggles and some type of hat, preferably a hard hat, also should be worn. Wear additional protection such as a chemical-resistant apron and respirator whenever the label so states, or if you want additional protection. When applying "Danger" or "Warning" class (Class I or II) products, wear coveralls that are completely liquid-proof such as polyethylene-coated or poly-vinyl chloride PPE.
2. Keep in mind the most common form of pesticide exposure is through direct contact with the skin. During mixing and loading, hands and forearms are especially vulnerable.
3. Wash the outside of gloves and boots with detergent and water before removing them. Then wash them inside and out with detergent and water. Allow them to dry in a well-ventilated location.
4. Clothing worn during pesticide application should be washed daily in hot, soapy water. Use heavy-duty liquid detergents, and do not mix other non-exposed clothes in same wash load. Run a cycle with hot water and detergent (but no clothes) afterward to minimize the potential for contaminating the next batch of clothes. If clothes become heavily saturated with pesticide, they should be placed in plastic garbage bags and disposed of properly.

FIGURE 27–4 Personal protection equipment generally involves covering all exposed skin surfaces and protecting the eyes, ears, and lungs of the applicator.

5. Two main types of respirators are used when handling pesticides: mechanical filter respirators, which are only effective in filtering dusts; and chemical cartridge or canister respirators, which protect only against gasses and vapors. Combination respirators that perform the functions of both types are also available. Respirators must be certified by the National Institute for Occupational Safety and Health (NIOSH). The pesticide label will have the NIOSH approval number for the respirator to be worn. A written policy should be developed and employees trained on the proper fitting and use of various respirators.

6. Earplugs or other acceptable aural protection devices should be available and used with any power equipment. Annual hearing tests are often required to detect if a gradual hearing loss is occurring.

7. Someone on the staff should be trained in CPR.

Mixing and Loading

Opening pesticide containers, connecting application equipment, or transferring pesticides to another container for application all entail the possibility of exposure. Having an appropriate pesticide mixing center provides a place where the operator can perform all mixing and loading duties without spills escaping into the environment. The following are encouraged standards to consider when designing or building such a facility.

1. Loading and mixing of pesticides should be performed over an impermeable source such as a concrete pad treated with a sealant and sloped to a liquid-tight sump where all spilled liquids can be recycled. Absorbents such as cat litter, clay, soil, or sand should be available for small spills, while hydrated lime and bleach can be used to neutralize and clean surfaces where spills occur.

2. To minimize water (including rainfall) waste from the chemical mixing pad, a roof with a minimum 30 degree overhang on all sides is advised.

3. Spills and rinsates from the pad should be saved and used as make-up water for the next time the same material is used. To minimize a build-up of sediments in the pump, tires and equipment should be cleaned (e.g., air-blown) prior to entering onto the pad.

4. Empty pesticide containers should be cleaned by pressure-rinsing or triple-rinsing and the rinse water dumped into the sprayer as part of the make-up water before beginning spraying. Non-rigid bags should be shaken clean and stored out of the rain until they can be disposed of in an approved landfill or recycled.

5. The loading/handling area should be away from other people and animals.

Disposal of Pesticide Wastes

Proper pesticide waste disposal is an important part of responsible pesticide use by the applicator. Improper disposal can lead to contamination of soil and ground and surface water, causing serious liability problems for the pesticide user. Federal and state laws, including the Federal Insecticide Fungicide and Rodenticide Act (FIFRA), regulate the disposal of pesticide waste.

Pesticide wastes include: (1) empty containers, (2) excess mixture, (3) rinse water from containers and application equipment, and (4) material generated from the clean-up of spills and leaks. These types of pesticide wastes are classified as either hazardous waste or solid waste. Pesticides classified as hazardous wastes are regulated by the Federal Resource Conservation and Recovery Act (RCRA). This waste must be disposed of properly, usually by a licensed hazardous waste contractor. Properly rinsed empty containers are solid waste.

Pesticides not classified as hazardous wastes may be disposed of as regular solid waste or trash. This is regulated under state law and must be disposed of in a careful manner according to label instructions. Ask your local pesticide regulatory agency about the specific laws and regulations affecting your area.

Emergency Planning and Community Right-to-Know

In 1986, in a response to the 1984 toxic gas disaster in Bhopal, India, Title III of the Superfund Amendment and Reauthorization Act (SARA) mandated a federal program subtitled the Emergency Planning and Community Right-to-Know Act (EPCRA). The intent of EPCRA is to assure information regarding hazardous chemicals is made available to emergency response agencies and the general public. The responsibilities of these efforts are assigned to the USEPA and individual states. Four separate categories are covered by this legislation.

1. Emergency planning involving extremely hazardous substances.
2. Reporting spills and leaks of extremely hazardous substances.
3. Reporting hazardous substances in the workplace.
4. Reporting toxic chemical releases.

Contact your local emergency planning committee or law enforcement agencies for more information on local and state requirements involving compliance.

Equipment Clean-up

After each day's or pesticide's use, application equipment should be flushed with water inside and out to prevent chemical accumulation. The cleaning area should be chosen with care to prevent cleaning water from contaminating water supplies and streams, or injuring plants. The cleaning water should be stored and reused to dilute the next batch of spray solution containing the same chemical(s). When changing chemicals or finishing spraying for an extended time, clean the sprayer thoroughly inside and out by following these steps:

1. Completely hose down the inside of the tank, filling it about 10 percent full of water, and then flush it out through the nozzles by operating the sprayer for at least 30 seconds. Repeat this step twice more.
2. Remove nozzle tips and screens and check for wear. Clean them in kerosene or detergent solution using a soft brush. Do not use a knife, wire, or other hard material to clean nozzle tips because the finely machined tip surfaces can be easily damaged, causing spray pattern distortion and an increased application rate.
3. Fill the tank half full of water and add about a pound of detergent for every 50 gallons of water.
4. Operate the pump to circulate the detergent solution through the sprayer for about 30 minutes, then flush it out through the bottom.
5. If 2,4-D or an organophosphate insecticide has been used, follow the steps below, in addition to the final flush using water:
   a. Replace the screens and nozzle tips.
   b. Fill the tank half full of water and add one pint of household ammonia for every 25 gallons of water.

c. Operate the pump to circulate the ammonia solution through to the sprayer for about five minutes, and discharge a small amount through the boom and nozzles.

d. Keep the remaining solution in the sprayer overnight.

e. In the next day, agitate the system and flush out all ammonia solution through the nozzles by operating the sprayer.

f. Finally, fill the tank about half full of clean water while hosing down both the inside and outside, then flush out through the boom. When finished with the sprayer for an extended period, remove and store the nozzle tips, strainers, and screens in light oil. Store the sprayer in a clean, dry shed. If the pump cannot be completely drained, store it where it will not freeze, or run antifreeze through the pump.

PESTICIDE LABELS AND LABELING

Material Safety Data Sheets

Each pesticide product has a Material Safety Data Sheet (MSDS) written by the manufacturer. These sheets provide information on:

1. Chemical product/company identification
2. Composition/information on ingredients
3. Hazardous identification
4. First aid measures
5. Firefighting measures
6. Accidental release measures
7. Handling and storage
8. Exposure controls/personal protection
9. Physical and chemical properties
10. Stability and reactivity
11. Toxicological information
12. Ecological information
13. Disposal considerations
14. Transportation information
15. Regulatory information
16. Other information

MSDS sheets for each pesticide formulation must be kept readily available for workers to read prior to handling the pesticide and to refer to in emergency situations.

Technical Information Bulletins

It has become quite common for some golf courses to submit pesticide use plans to water management districts or other state agencies. In most cases, the information required may either be found on the label or on the MSDS for the pesticide. However, some information may only be found in technical bulletins. These also are written by the company manufacturing the product, but normally are *not* provided to the pesticide user. If a specific piece of information cannot be located on the label or MSDS, contact the company representative (salesperson, sales manager, R&D representative, etc.) and request a technical bulletin.

Labeling Is the Law

It is extremely important to remember the pesticide label is the *law*. Pesticides may not be used in a manner not permitted by the labeling. Pesticide uses inconsistent with the label include:

1. Applying pesticides to plants, animals, or sites not specified in the directions for use. If the label does not state it is for use on turfgrass, then it is not legal to use on turfgrass.
2. Using higher dosages, higher concentrations, or more frequent applications than specified on the label.
3. Not following the directions for use, safety, diluting, storage, and disposal. This also includes any restrictions on course reentry, not only for employees but for golfers as well.

The law does allow you to:

1. Apply pesticides at dosages, concentrations, and frequencies less than those listed on the label if you obtain expert opinion or have data to justify the lower rate.
2. Apply a pesticide against any target pest not listed on the label *if* the application is to a crop/plant, animal, or site listed on the label. In other words, if a new weed suddenly appears, it is legal to use a herbicide for control as long as turfgrass is listed on the label and you know the material will control the weed.
3. Mix a pesticide with a fertilizer if the mixture is not prohibited by the label.
4. Mix two or more pesticides together if all the dosages are at or below the labeled rate(s), and the mixture is not prohibited by any of the labels.

Read the *entire* label of any pesticide before you buy, mix, apply, store, or dispose of it. If you have questions on how to use a pesticide, it is quite likely other applicators have the same questions. Be a good consumer and tell the manufacturer your concerns. They may not realize there are problems or questions with the label directions. The label must contain the items listed below.

1. Trade name
2. Ingredient statement
   a. Active ingredient (chemical name; common name may be present)
   b. Inert ingredient(s)
3. Type of pesticide (herbicide, insecticide, nematicide, fungicide, etc.)
4. Net contents
5. Name and address of manufacturer—establishment number
6. EPA registration number—indicates the label is approved by the EPA
7. Signal words and symbols
   a. Danger: highly toxic; some products may also carry the word "Poison" printed in red plus the skull and crossbones symbol (category I)
   b. Warning: moderately toxic (category II)
   c. Caution: slightly toxic (categories III and IV)
8. Precautionary statements
   a. Route of entry (to the body) statements
   b. Specific action statements (to prevent poisoning accidents)
   c. Protective clothing and equipment statements
   d. Other statements may be listed in regards to precautions to take while handling the product
9. Statement of practical treatment in case of poisoning
10. Environment hazards
    a. Special toxicity statements (e.g., toxic to bees, fish, etc.)
    b. General environmental statements
11. Physical or chemical hazards
12. Classification statement: General- or restricted-use pesticide
13. Reentry statement
14. Storage and disposal
15. Directions for use

Note: The toxicity category is *not* found on the label or the MSDS.

PREPARING AGROCHEMICAL STORAGE FACILITIES FOR A MAJOR DISASTER

Hurricanes, floods, tornadoes, and other severe storms can seriously damage agricultural chemical storage facilities and the chemicals they contain. Storm-damaged facilities may adversely affect the environment and people. The following are steps to consider if a storm approaches and damages an agrochemical storage facility.

Inventory

Do an inventory of what pesticides and other chemicals you have on hand. Such an inventory will be useful for insurance purposes, or in the event of necessary pesticide or chemical clean-ups.

Include product and active ingredient names and container sizes. Receipts for the purchase of these materials are useful for this, or in some cases may suffice themselves. Put the inventory in a safe location. In the case of large scale storms it may be useful to make a copy of your inventory and mail or fax it to a friend or business associate who lives outside of the potentially affected area.

Insurance

Know where your insurance policy is and know exactly what kind of coverage you have. Does it cover your chemical inventory or the damage it could cause? Find out now because if you need to know later, your insurance agent will be very busy.

Chemical Use

At this point, consider not using or making applications of agricultural chemicals, or at least holding off, until the potential of the impending severe weather event is resolved. Delay purchase or delivery of additional chemicals to your operation until after the impending storm risk is past. If deliveries are scheduled for the coming week it may be best to cancel them.

Chemical Storage and Security

Secure all chemicals including fertilizers, pesticides, solvents, fuels, and so forth. Close and secure container lids, moving containers and application equipment to the most secure location. Raise chemicals from the floor or cover materials potentially damaged by water. Do what you can to protect product labels and labeling. Doors, windows, and other points of access to storage locations should be secured and locked. Consider boarding up the pesticide and other chemical storage areas. Don't leave chemicals in vehicles or application equipment. Be sure all of the stored items are compatible. Don't, for instance, put pesticides and fuels in the same building with animals, or animal feeds.

Now is the time to read the storage and spill containment sections of your MSDS. Gather and secure pesticide and other chemical MSDS sheets and provide local emergency first responders with a copy of these, along with a copy of your chemical inventory. Also secure your personal protective equipment. This may be needed as part of the clean-up operations after the storm.

Secure buildings as much as possible. Are the roofs tied into the building? Can you tie-down small storage buildings and storage tanks? Also, if you leave your location during a severe weather event, be sure the pesticide storage building is well signed.

Have all emergency phone numbers needed on hand and consult your chemical dealer and insurance agent for additional suggestions, but do it soon.

Storm-Damaged Agrochemical Storage Facilities
Area Security

Following a severe storm, keep unauthorized people away from the chemical storage facility and adjacent areas. Post the area to indicate which potentially hazardous chemicals are present; erect fencing or rope cordons, and inform persons entering the property of the presence of an agricultural chemical storage facility. The idea is to keep people and animals out of the surrounding area.

Personal Safety

Make personal safety a priority. When dealing with a storm-damaged facility, wear the necessary personal protective equipment (PPE) to protect a person handling the most dangerous material present. This usually means respirator, eye protection, unlined nitrile gloves, rubber boots, long-sleeved shirt, work trousers, and a chemical-resistant apron. Before using *any* personal protective equipment, check to see that it is in serviceable condition. Be alert for *signs* or *symptoms* of pesticide poisoning: nausea, headache, difficult breathing, pinpoint pupils, or convulsions. If these appear and pesticide poisoning is suspected, seek medical attention immediately.

Site Inspection

As soon as possible, inspect the site for storm damage. Focus on (1) the presence of damaged containers, (2) if and where the storm has moved pesticide containers off-site, (3) structural damage to the storage facility, and (4) ways to avoid further weather damage.

Spill Management

Finding broken packages or ruptured containers indicates the need for spill management efforts. To manage spills, use a stepwise procedure and focus on:

1. *Controlling* actively spilled materials by standing containers upright, plugging holes, and so forth.
2. *Containing* spilled chemicals by installing absorbent barriers.
3. *Collecting* spilled product and absorbents and placing these in sturdy containers.
4. *Storing* all containers of spilled agrochemicals in an area where disturbance is likely to be minimal.

Spill Prevention

Consolidate agrochemicals having intact packaging. Sort these according to package type (glass, paper, plastic, metal), substance type (insecticides, herbicides, etc.), and reactivity group (flammables, corrosives, etc.); then, put them in areas protected from weather, flooding, and building collapse.

Consider alternatives such as pallets placed on blocks and covered with tarpaulins or plastic sheeting. The idea is that consolidating intact containers and providing sheltered storage will help prevent container deterioration and subsequent spills.

Product Identity and Labels

Knowing the contents of an agrochemical container is extremely important. Make every effort to preserve and protect container labeling. Containers lacking labeling will likely end up being considered unknowns—and disposal of unknowns is often very costly. Exposure to severe storms, heavy rain, or flood waters will often cause labels to loosen. Refasten all loose labeling. Use non-water-soluble glue or sturdy transparent packaging tape to refasten loose labels. *Never* refasten labels with rubber bands (they quickly rot and easily break) or nontransparent tapes such as duct or masking tape (they can obscure important product caution statements or label directions for product usage).

As a supplement to marred or badly damaged labels, fasten a baggage tag to the container handle. On the tag write the product name, formulation, concentration of active ingredient(s), and date of product purchase. If there is any question about the contents of a container, set it aside for disposal.

Salvage

If the labeling is legible and secure, then agrochemicals in intact waterproof containers, and formulated as liquids, emulsifiable concentrates, flowables, or oil solutions, are often salvageable. Check each container for hidden damage. In particular, determine whether or not the pour spout seal has been broken.

Upon finding a broken seal, examine the contents for evidence of contamination—especially water-induced damage. In general, liquid formulations with a milky appearance have been corrupted by water encroachment. In most cases, these should be set aside for disposal.

Oil solutions, such as livestock sprays, can often be salvaged. Water is easily detected in oil solutions. Since oil floats on water, carefully pour off the oil and leave the water behind. Handle the water as a container rinsate (e.g., use it as make-up water); thereafter, return the oil solution to its original container. Triple rinse the temporary container and handle the rinsate as dilute pesticide (e.g., include in a batch of spray mix).

The salvageability of dry formulations (baits, dusts, wettable powders, granules, dry flowables, etc.) is more difficult to assess. In general, products held in paper packaging are more vulnerable to severe-storm-induced damage. However, paper is not the sole problem. Plastic and foil-lined bags are also difficult to assess for pinholes and unsound seams. As a rule, avoid opening large quantities of dry formulation packaging and examining contents in detail. Again, when in doubt, set the container aside for later disposal.

Temporary Storage

Temporary storage is another key concern for agrochemical facilities damaged by severe storms. In addition to the aspects of storage discussed earlier (see spill prevention), other points merit mention.

1. Designate three separate storage areas, one for salvaged materials, a second for materials intended for disposal, and a third one for materials in the process of being re-collected and evaluated.
2. Make sure each storage area is secure and not readily accessible to persons or animals.
3. Provide each area with protection from further weather- and debris-induced damage; keep each of the three stockpiles away from supplies of water, foods, fuels, machinery, and personal protective equipment.

Handling and Transport

All post-storm movement of agrochemicals and their containers (including re-collection of off-site containers) requires care and greater-than-normal safeguards. Labeling must be preserved (even for those ultimately requiring disposal). Storm-damaged packaging is more spill prone. Also, for certain agrochemicals, moisture increases the reactivity and fire hazard. Handling and transport efforts must take these considerations into account *before* movement of the product is attempted. Consult MSDS sheets. Finally, before moving agrochemicals whose packaging is suspected to be weakened and likely to spill, have temporary containment vessels (such as garbage cans lined with plastic bags) on hand.

Disposal

Disposal of natural-disaster-induced agrochemical waste should proceed only after proper authorities have been contacted. In certain cases, part of the disposal costs might be paid by disaster-relief funds. Persons having severe-storm-damaged agrochemicals should contact their Department of Environmental Protection for information on their disposal.

ACTIVATED CHARCOAL TO DEACTIVATE PESTICIDES
Introduction

Activated charcoal (also called activated carbon) is often used to adsorb or deactivate organic chemicals such as pesticides. Activated charcoal has been used for many years to remove organic contaminants from wastewaters and in water purification systems. Since most pesticides are organic chemicals, activated charcoal can effectively be used to deactivate or "tie-up" these products in soil. Once the pesticide has been adsorbed onto activated charcoal, it is biologically inactive and cannot cause injury to the turfgrass. Therefore, this product can be beneficial to turfgrass managers in the case of an accidental pesticide spill or where a herbicide needs to be inactivated for seeding or sprigging of turfgrasses. Due to its dark color, and its consequent ability to absorb heat, activated charcoal is also used to artificially warm the soil to minimize the effects of light frosts or to allow earlier seeding of an area (Chapter 25).

Charcoal is a porous, soft, black substance made by heating, in a restricted amount of air, substances containing carbon such as material from hardwood trees and coconut shells. Powdered activated charcoal is made up of very small carbon particles with a high affinity for organic chemicals such as pesticides. Activated charcoal has a large surface area and can absorb 100 to 200 times its own weight.

The amount of activated charcoal to apply to a pesticide-contaminated area varies with the chemical characteristics of the particular pesticide. Rates generally range from about 100 to 400 pounds of activated charcoal per acre (2.3 to 9.2 pounds per thousand square feet) for each pound of active ingredient of a pesticide applied per acre. A general rule is to apply about 200 pounds of activated charcoal per acre (4.6 pounds per thousand square feet) for each pound of pesticide active ingredient per acre (Table 27–5).

Example:

Suppose Balan 2.5G was inadvertently applied at two pounds of active ingredient per acre to an area designated to be seeded with a turfgrass. To completely inactivate this herbicide, an application of activated charcoal at 400 pounds per acre (or 9.2 pounds per 1,000 square feet) would be needed. See Table 27–6 for additional conversions of rates per acre to pounds per 1,000 square feet.

Application Methods

Activated charcoal can be applied by various methods. It can be applied in the dry form with a drop spreader. However, activated charcoal particles are easily moved by wind, so it may be difficult to distribute the charcoal evenly when applied in the dry form. The easiest method is to suspend the charcoal in water and apply it by hand with a watering can (for small areas) or a power sprayer. Because activated charcoal does not mix easily with water, a 0.5 percent solution of a nonionic surfactant (equivalent to 1 quart per 50 gallons) will enhance its suspension in water. Note charcoal particles are very abrasive and can damage spray equipment (particularly rotary type pumps). Therefore, if a sprayer is used to apply activated charcoal, care should be taken to thoroughly clean the equipment when finished.

TABLE 27–5 *Rates of activated charcoal used for spills and deactivating turf pesticides.*

Application	Recommendation	Comments
Spills	For reducing the effects from spills of organic pesticides, some petroleum products, and hydraulic fluids.	Use 100 to 400 pounds of activated charcoal to every pound of active material spilled per acre (2.3 to 9.2 lbs/1,000 ft²). If the active material has not been diluted with water at the time of spill, apply the charcoal directly as a dry powder. If the active material has been diluted with water, apply the activated charcoal in a slurry with a sprinkle can or common sprayer equipment. The charcoal must be incorporated into the contaminated soil, preferably to a depth of six inches. With severe spills, some of the contaminated soils may need removal prior to activated charcoal application.
"Deactivating" turf herbicides and soil warming	Turf areas treated with preemergence herbicides can be reseeded earlier than normal by treating with activated charcoal.	Whenever it is desirable to terminate a preemergence herbicide, apply charcoal slurry at a rate of two to four pounds per 1,000 square feet. Water the slurry into the soil. Make sure the grass is washed free of heavy charcoal deposits. Where possible, it is desirable to thoroughly rake the charcoal into the soil. The area can be seeded 24 hours after treatment.

TABLE 27–6 *Conversion from pounds of activated charcoal per acre to pounds of activated charcoal per 1,000 square feet.*

Rate of activated charcoal (pounds per acre)	Activated charcoal needed (pounds per 1,000 square feet)
100	2.3
200	4.6
400	9.2
800	18.4
1,600	36.7
3,200	73.5

When deactivating a pesticide in a seedbed, the activated charcoal should be incorporated with a rotary tiller or other appropriate equipment so the charcoal is placed in the upper few inches of soil. The objective is to get the activated charcoal in the same proximity as the pesticide. Uniform application of activated charcoal followed by thorough mixing is the key to inactivating a pesticide-contaminated area. If the pesticide is on the turf, in the thatch layer, or on the uppermost surface of the soil (for instance, if the pesticide has not been watered-in), the pesticide can be inactivated by simply applying the charcoal to the area and thoroughly watering once charcoal application is complete. Again, the objective is to place the charcoal in the same proximity as the pesticide. If activated carbon is applied and either incorporated or watered correctly, inactivation of the pesticide will be successfully accomplished. For application convenience, it is recommended activated charcoal be applied as a water slurry. To minimize dusting, always add activated charcoal to water slowly, keeping the bag as close to the water surface as possible. The following steps are suggested when mixing and applying charcoal.

Spray Application

1. Make sure spray equipment, tubing, and nozzles are completely clean. Screens should be removed if practical.
2. The final spray mixture should contain one to two pounds of charcoal per gallon of water.
3. Add sufficient water to begin moderate agitation. Simultaneously add the balance of required water and charcoal. Continue agitation until a uniform mixture is obtained.
4. Maintain moderate agitation while spraying.

It is important to understand situations where activated charcoal will not work. If a herbicide has been applied for several weeks and rainfall has occurred and/or irrigation water has been applied, the herbicide is most likely past the thatch layer and, depending on water solubility and soil adsorption of the herbicide, is probably in the upper inch or so of the soil. In this case, activated charcoal would have to be physically incorporated with a rotary tiller or other implement to get the charcoal in contact with the herbicide. The reason is activated charcoal will not leach through soil. If activated charcoal is applied to the soil surface and watered, the charcoal will remain on top of the soil and will not inactivate the herbicide below the soil surface. Activated charcoal is considered ineffective for inorganic pesticides such as arsenates, lead compounds, sodium chlorate, sulfur, borax, and so forth, and water-soluble organic pesticides such as, but not limited to, MSMA and DSMA.

Activated carbon is available from most suppliers of turfgrass products. It is a good idea to keep several bags on hand so it can be applied immediately instead of having to wait for delivery. Several different brands and formulations are on the market (Table 27–7). There appears to be little, if any, difference in the effectiveness of the different brands. However, some may be easier to apply than others, depending on the particular situation where it is to be used.

TABLE 27–7 *Suppliers of activated charcoal.*

Powdered activated charcoal is available as "Gro-Safe" from:	"Clean Carbon" activated charcoal is available from:
American Norit Co., Inc.	Aquatrols
1050 Crown Pointe Parkway	5 North Olney Ave.
Atlanta, GA 30338	Cherry Hill, NJ 08003
1-800-641-9245	1-800-257-7797
Flowable activated charcoal is available as "52 Pickup" from:	
Parkway Research Corp.	
13802 Chrisman Road	
Houston, TX 77039	
1-800-442-9821	

CHAPTER
28

Best Golf Course Environmental Protection Strategies

INTRODUCTION

Golf courses offer many recreational, economical, and environmental benefits. Turfgrasses are oxygen producers that help cool their surrounding environments, absorb sound and glare, prevent erosion, and are effective filters of natural and synthetic contaminants. They also provide areas for recreational activities, help increase property values, provide green space and wildlife habitats in urban areas, and provide an enormous economic impact in terms of jobs, tax base, and many side impacts such as being the site of vacation destinations and retirement communities. However, like any living plant, turfgrasses require certain inputs in terms of fertilizer, water, and in special situations, pesticides to maintain their vigor and health. Golf courses often intersect with environmentally sensitive areas, and management strategies should be formulated that protect these areas.

Best management practices are developed to protect water resources and other environmental concerns. This protection involves removing, filtering, detaining, or rerouting potential contaminants before they enter water sources or other environmentally sensitive areas. An environmental monitoring program providing feedback to the golf course as to conditions and movement of materials also is beneficial. A well-developed management plan includes site description and evaluation, golf course cultural practices including using best management practices and integrated pest management, and safety regulations on storage, handling, disposal, and record keeping of pesticides related to worker protection, employee right-to-know, and OSHA requirements. The following sections discuss pesticides and nutrients in the environment and strategies for developing environmentally sound golf course design, construction, and maintenance practices.

PESTICIDES AND NUTRIENTS IN THE ENVIRONMENT

Fate of Pesticides and Nutrients

Environmentally introduced pesticides and nutrients experience numerous fates and routes of decomposition following application. Most pesticides and nutrients pose little, if any, threat when used according to the label. This is due to the numerous means by which they are absorbed and broken down by natural entities in the environment.

Turfgrasses are unique systems due to the extremely high density of plants with communities containing up to 2,500 plants per square foot. Turfgrasses also produce a thatch layer high in organic matter that acts as a filter and binds many pesticides before they can reach the soil. It has been estimated a 150-acre golf course has the capacity to absorb 12 million gallons of water during a three-inch downpour. This water infiltrates and is absorbed by the turf/thatch/soil profile before it moves horizontally as run-off. Thatch also harbors high populations of microorganisms that use pesticides and nutrients as energy sources as they breakdown these compounds into simple molecules. Turfgrasses also possess dense, fibrous root systems that are capable of adsorbing pesticides. Other avenues of pesticide and nutrient dissipation include (Figure 28–1):

- Volatilization and evaporation
- Photodegradation by ultraviolet light from the sun
- Microbial decay
- Hydrolysis
- Conversion to other compounds
- Plant uptake

Chemical and microbial degradation of pesticides and nutrients occurs through the processes of hydrolysis, oxidation, and reduction to transform the parent compounds into the production of carbon dioxide, water, and some inorganic products such as nitrogen, sulfur, and phosphorus. Soil microbes can use pesticides as a food source; this rate of degradation is influenced by pesticide present, temperature, soil water content, pH, oxygen levels, organic matter, and prior pesticide use. Nutrient fate or cycle in the environment is discussed in Section IV of this book.

Pesticide persistence is often expressed as **half-life** (often indicated as DT_{50}), which is the time required for 50 percent of the original pesticide to break down into other products. Half-life values change according to the location and site being treated; thus, they are guidelines instead of absolute values. Once a pesticide leaves the nozzle or spreader, there are four major places it can go: (1) air, (2) plants, (3) soil, and (4) water.

Atmosphere

When using traditional applicators, the air is the first place a pesticide goes before it hits a target. Losses of pesticides to the air can occur. Here are some factors in these losses.

Volatilization

Volatilization and **evaporation** of pesticides involve the process where the chemicals are transformed from a solid or liquid phase into a gas. This tendency to volatilize is expressed in units of

FIGURE 28–1 Several avenues exist for applied chemical to turf. The major dispersal means include plant uptake, soil sorption followed by microbial degradation and chemical degradation, volatilization, photodecomposition, and run-off and leaching.

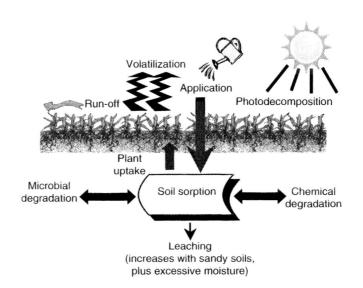

vapor pressure. **Vapor pressure** (or **volatility**) is the measure of the intramolecular bonding forces of a compound and is usually expressed as mm Hg (mercury) at 25°C (Table 28–1). Compounds possessing weak intramolecular forces readily volatilize and can easily change from a solid or liquid form to a gaseous form at room temperature.

Volatilization increases with the inherent vapor pressure of a chemical, with increasing temperature, with increasing air movement, and in the absence of incorporation. Losses to volatilization typically range from 5 to 20 percent but can be higher when a volatile compound is surface applied on a hot, windy day. Some of the factors in volatilization are:

1. **Soil placement**—Pesticides incorporated by being irrigated-in or injected have a much lower rate of volatilization compared to those that are surface applied.
2. **Soil organic matter and clay content**—Higher soil organic matter or clay contents will increase the adsorption of a pesticide, which in turn reduces the amount available for volatilization.
3. **Soil moisture**—Higher moisture contents can work to slow adsorption to soil particles, which will keep more pesticides available for volatilization.
4. **Temperature**—Increasing temperatures can increase volatilization, but the relationship is not direct because changes in moisture usually accompany temperature changes. Meaning, it usually is not raining when it is very hot.
5. **Temperature inversion**—If present, the unsettled, lightweight, and nearly invisible spray droplets will hover along the ground, much like a fog, instead of rising and mixing.
6. **Wind**—Increasing wind speed will increase volatile losses, although a rough surface such as turf can greatly reduce these effects.

As discussed, volatility is highly dependent on temperature, moisture, soil texture, and the properties of a specific herbicide, and is extremely important in determining how a particular herbicide can be used. For example, compounds with high volatility are applied and incorporated by watering-in to prevent loss through volatilization to the air. Solids and liquids increase vaporization as the temperature increases. Pesticides formulated as esters also have a greater potential for volatility than do amine formulations.

Drift

Most pesticide applications are liquid sprays applied several feet or more above the soil or turf. Several types of potential drift occur:

1. **Drift**—The removal of an intended particle from the intended target, making it less effective and depositing it where it is not needed and often not wanted. Type of nozzle, pressure, height of boom, spray volume, and environmental conditions all affect the amount of spray drift that occurs.
2. **Vapor drift**—Movement associated with the volatilization of pesticide molecules and their movement off-target, making it independent of the application. The only effective means of reducing drift by increasing spray volume is to increase the nozzle size rather than increasing pressure in the smaller nozzle size.
3. **Particle drift**—Off-target movement of spray particles formed during application that may move off-target at the time of the application or at a longer time following the application.

TABLE 28–1   *Vapor pressure as a degree of volatility.*

Volatility	Vapor pressure range at 20 to 30°C (mm Hg)
Very high volatility	$>10^{-3}$
High volatility	10^{-4} to 10^{-3}
Moderate volatility	10^{-5} to 10^{-4}
Low volatility	10^{-6} to 10^{-5}
Very low volatility	10^{-7} to 10^{-6}
Extremely low volatility	$<10^{-7}$

4. **Atomization**—Breaking up of the spray solution as it passes through the nozzle orifice under pressure. Atomizing a known amount of spray solution into smaller droplets will increase the coverage; however, evaporation, drift potential, canopy penetration, and deposition characteristics must be taken into account.

This creates an opportunity for wind to carry a portion of the spray away from the target. Under worse-case conditions (high winds, small droplets), portions of the spray can be carried downwind. Several parameters that potentially influence this include.

1. **Wind**—The amount of drift is directly related to wind speed. Spraying in windy conditions (greater than 10 miles per hour wind speed) may cause the spray to drift away from the target. Highly turbulent winds, which occur during inversions or on hot afternoons, are more likely to cause drift. Other environmental parameters influencing drift include temperature, humidity, and temperature inversion.
2. **Droplet size**—Nozzles that produce a significant number of small droplets (e.g., <100 microns) can significantly increase drift. There is always a trade-off between the improved coverage of small droplets and the risk of drift. Larger droplets (e.g., >200 microns) are least likely to drift but may reduce coverage. The only effective means of reducing drift by increasing spray volume is to increase the nozzle size rather than increasing pressure in the smaller nozzle size.
3. **Drift-control additives**—Tank additives have been shown to reduce drift primarily by reducing the amount of smaller droplets produced. Not all adjuvants work well for these purposes and only those intended for this purpose should be used.
4. **Boom height**—The farther the boom is from the intended target, the greater the chance of drift. Nozzle manufacturers' charts will provide information for proper boom settings for different nozzle types. Wide-angle nozzles can be placed closer to the ground than nozzles that produce narrow spray angles.

Check the pattern uniformity of an applicator by spraying water across flat, black asphalt. The spray swath dries evenly when the spray pattern is uniform. If the swath dries in streaks, the pattern is uneven and the nozzles need checking.

Environmental Impacts of Pesticides in the Atmosphere

The most immediate impact of pesticide losses to the atmosphere is the reduction of pest control. If one pound of product is recommended to control a pest and half of it is lost to the atmosphere, the pest is probably not going to be controlled. The second possible impact is on adjacent property, where the pesticide could cause significant damage in the form of injured crops, residues on crops with no label for the pesticide, or negative wildlife impacts such as on fish or bees.

Plants

The most important target of most pesticide applications is the turf itself. A number of fates await a pesticide once it lands on the turf:

Photolysis

The sun provides a wide spectrum of radiation beyond the narrow band called light. The higher-energy ultraviolet radiation is sufficiently strong to cause some pesticides to break apart. This is the case for residues that are exposed on the plant (or soil) surface.

Absorption

Absorption of a pesticide by a plant can either occur through the leaf or the roots. Getting through the leaf is difficult due to leaf hairs and a waxy cuticle blocking entry. One way to improve coverage and penetration is by using an adjuvant or spray additive that allows the droplets to spread on the leaf surface without beading up.

Effects of Plants on Pesticides in the Environment

Uptake and metabolism of pesticides by plants are important in a turf environment due to the high percentage of ground covered. Much of the applied pesticides still end up in the thatch and soil, however. The impacts of plants are still quite important. A turf cover significantly reduces drift through interception and increased surface "roughness" which slows wind. The canopy can reduce surface temperatures 10 to 20°F degrees, which slows volatilization. Turf also creates a more porous soil, allowing more water to infiltrate and slow run-off.

Soil

The majority of applied pesticides end up in the thatch and soil. Even when the pesticide reaches a leaf, it is likely most of it will wash off and soak into the thatch and soil. Applied pesticides are largely processed and disposed of in the thatch and soil. A very serious environmental contamination problem would exist if this did not occur. However, a spill on the ground is a different situation. Concentrated chemicals that occur in a spill usually overwhelm normal soil processes and leach into deeper layers, possibly to groundwater. Mixing and loading on a hard surface where spills can be easily cleaned up or rinsates can be recycled avoids this type of problem. In the absence of a spill, pesticide fate in the soil/thatch region of the turfgrass is dictated by adsorption, chemical and biological degradation, and leaching.

Adsorption

Soil sorption is the affinity a chemical has to adhere to soils. The term **sorption** includes the processes of adsorption and absorption. **Adsorption** is the binding of a chemical onto the surface of a soil particle while **absorption** is the binding of a chemical into a soil particle. Adsorption is generally the more important means of binding a chemical to the soil surface. This is greatly influenced by the chemical and physical characteristics of the chemical (e.g., anionic, cationic, or nonionic), the soil characteristics or composition, and the nature of the soil solution. The major soil characteristics affecting pesticides are soil texture, permeability, and organic matter content. Coarse, sandy soil textures tend to have low cation exchange capacities (CECs) and high permeability rates; thus, they hold applied materials poorly. Increases in organic matter and certain clays tend to increase a soil's ability to hold applied materials. This is one reason organic matter should be considered in golf course construction. Clay soils are least likely to allow leaching, but are most likely to have run-off. Most insecticides readily adsorb to soil and thatch, which is why they are rarely detected in groundwater. The majority of fungicides and herbicides are also tightly bound by soil, but some do have the potential to leach to groundwater.

The constant used to measure the tendency of a chemical to sorb to the soil organic matter is called the **partition coefficient**. This is most often abbreviated as K_{oc} but is sometimes reported as K_d. The relationship between K_{oc} and K_d is:

$$K_{oc} = K_d \div \% \text{ soil organic carbon content} \times 100$$

For an organic compound, the larger the K_{oc} value, the more strongly it will be sorbed to soils; therefore, it is less likely to leach or volatilize. A partition coefficient less than 300 to 500 is considered low and the chemical has a greater tendency to leach in low organic matter-containing soil (Table 28–2).

Pesticides binding tightly to soil may be preferred from an environmental perspective since this reduces the movement of the pesticide. This can be a problem, however, because a pesticide may not be active if it is highly bound to soil. A good example is the herbicide glyphosate (Roundup Pro), which is inactivated in soil through tight binding to clays.

Degradation

Pesticides are often quickly degraded once they reach the thatch and soil layers. The sun can break them down through photolysis the same way as on plant surfaces. Acids commonly found in the soil can sever parts of the pesticide in a process called **hydrolysis.** The most important factor, however, are the organisms living in soil that use them as food sources. Bacteria are the main degraders in soil and thatch. Most turf pesticides will be degraded in thatch and soil in a matter of days or

TABLE 28–2 *Pesticide characteristics influencing the potential for groundwater and surface water contamination (EPA, 1988, as reported by Balogh and Walker, 1992).*

Chemical characteristic	Range for potential contamination
Water solubility	>30 ppm
K_d	<5, usually <1
K_{oc} (ml/g)	<300 to 500
Henry's law constant	$<10^{-2}$ atm per $^{-3}$ mol
Hydrolysis half-life	>175 days
Photolysis half-life	>7 days
Field dissipation half-life	>21 days

weeks. This is good if one wants to minimize the possibility of the pesticide reaching ground or surface water. Of course, this also means the effectiveness of the pesticide is reduced. Pesticide chemists developing new products are always confronted with this dilemma: a chemical that persists may be effective longer but may have an increased risk of contaminating water. The EPA will not allow a new chemical on the market if it poses an undue risk of contaminating water.

Leaching

A pesticide that is not bound to the soil and is not degraded can move through the soil with the infiltrating water. This process depends on the chemical properties of the pesticide and the soil. Even a small fraction of the applied pesticide leaching through the soil can be detected in groundwater. As chemicals move downward in the soil, both the amount of adsorption and the rate of degradation rapidly decline. There is little organic matter or bacterial activity once the pesticide is past the rootzone. Fortunately, the adsorption and degradation processes handle all or nearly all of the pesticide before it can reach the lower layers.

Solubility is the extent a chemical will dissolve in water (Table 28–3). Generally the higher a liquid's solubility, the greater the chance it may move from the site of application. Although solubility is normally a good indicator of the likelihood a chemical may be mobile, its sorption to soil also must be considered.

Pesticides in Water

Much of the bad press pesticides have received is from detections in groundwater and surface water used for drinking water supplies. Surveys of ground and surface water have found pesticides in some areas of the country. The extent of the contamination is becoming reasonably well-defined, but the source or sources of contamination are often quite elusive. The sources and problems associated with groundwater and surface water contamination are quite different and will be dealt with separately in the following.

Surface Water

Most pesticide contamination of streams, lakes, and estuaries occurs as run-off from agricultural and urban areas. Run-off carries with it a mix of suspended soil particles and any pesticides that were either attached to the particles or dissolved in surface moisture just before run-off began. The amount of pesticide loss to run-off is affected by the following factors:

1. **Rain intensity**—Heavy downpours result in minimal infiltration and maximum run-off.
2. **Surface conditions**—Recently tilled soil and soil with a good ground cover have the most resistance to run-off since water infiltrates relatively easily and the surface is "rough" enough to break up water flow. Maximum run-off is expected during the month after planting, since the soil is exposed and the turf has not grown large enough to intercept rain and reduce its impact energy.
3. **Magnitude and length of slope**—The steeper and longer the slope, the greater the chance of run-off picking up energy and soil.

TABLE 28–3   *Solubility rankings of a compound based on water solubilities.*

Relative solubility	Water solubility (ppm)
Very high solubility	>10,000 (1%)
High solubility	1,000 to 10,000
Moderate solubility	100 to 1,000
Low solubility	10 to 100
Very low solubility	1 to 10
Extremely low solubility	0.1 to 1

4. **Method of application**—Pesticides tilled or injected into the soil are less likely to be lost in run-off, although the disturbance of the soil itself may increase soil (and attached pesticide) losses. Flier pesticides can suffer large losses in run-off if a heavy downpour occurs soon after application.

5. **Timing**—As previously mentioned, if a run-off event occurs soon after the pesticide is applied, substantial losses can occur.

Losses of pesticides to run-off generally are found at 1 to 5 percent of applied rates, depending on the various factors. Losses are usually the greatest in the one to two weeks after application and are highly dependent on storm events.

The effects of providing untreated grassed borders can be quite substantial, with reductions of pesticide movement into adjoining streams of 80 to 90 percent (Baird et al., 1997). The combination of infiltration, reduced overland flow rates, and adsorption in these zones can be quite effective in keeping pollutants from the fields from getting into the waterways. The role of forested buffers is likely quite similar.

It is important to emphasize that buffers function only when the waters they receive are spread across the strip. Run-off that moves through a buffer in a ditch or channel has little opportunity to degrade or adsorb before it intercepts surface water.

Once organic chemicals like pesticides enter surface water, their rate of degradation slows considerably compared to soil degradation rates. A portion of the pesticide will partition onto the sediment and remain there until a flood event moves the sediment back into the moving water. This is thought to be the explanation for why low levels of pesticides can be detected long after the application season.

Groundwater

Groundwater is water located beneath the earth's surface. Groundwater is often erroneously perceived as occurring in vast underground lakes, rivers, or streams. In reality, groundwater usually occurs in aquifers composed of pore spaces and cracks in rock and soil. An **aquifer** may be defined as a formation containing sufficient saturated permeable material to yield significant quantities of water to wells and springs. Aquifers, such as unconsolidated sands and gravels, can store and transmit water. They are quite extensive and may be confined above or below by a confining bed made by a relatively impermeable material such as clay or sandy clay.

Unconsolidated aquifers are sand and gravel deposits that can be relatively shallow, often only 10 to 20 feet below the surface. The pores within these deposits are filled with water if they are below the water table. These aquifers are mostly located in coastal plain areas within 200 miles of the coast. Recharge of these aquifers is usually local but there may be several layered on top of each other, with lower aquifers recharging some distance away. Wells drilled into the first or top layer, or superficial aquifer, are the most susceptible to contamination.

Groundwater moves very slowly through irregular spaces within otherwise solid rock or seeps between particles of sand, clay, and gravel. An exception is in limestone areas, where groundwater may, in fact, flow through large underground channels or caverns.

Groundwater is recharged (replaced) mostly from rain or snow that enters the soil. Water moving downward in the soil is either absorbed by plants, is held in the upper layers of soil, or moves down through the rootzone until it reaches a zone saturated with water. This saturated zone is the uppermost layer of groundwater. The **water table** is the "dividing line" between the groundwater and the unsaturated rock or soil above it. Spring and fall generally are the times when the water table is closest to the soil surface.

The following are major factors determining whether a pesticide moving through the soil will reach the groundwater.

1. **Soil type**—Sandy soils leach more than loamy or heavier soils.
2. **Pesticide characteristics**—How tightly the pesticide binds to soil and thatch; how long it lasts in the soil.
3. **Weather**—Cool, wet conditions can push the pesticide deep in the soil before it can degrade or bind.
4. **Depth to groundwater**—The deeper the groundwater, the more time a pesticide has to break down.

Most rural residents get their water from wells placed in groundwater tables. The water that is found in those aquifers may come from the nearby area or many miles away, depending on the type of aquifer. The water may have been in the aquifer for several years or many decades.

Sources of Contamination

Point-Source

Environmental contamination originates either as **point-source** or **non-point-source** pollution. Point-source pollution comes from a specific, identifiable point. A pesticide spill into a well, sink-hole, or storm sewer exemplifies identifiable point-source pollution. Sewage treatment plants and concentrated animal production facilities also are potential point-sources. Other point-source pollution comes from improper disposal of pesticide containers and water from rinsates, leaks and spills at the site of pesticide storage facilities, and spills occurring while mixing and loading pesticides into application equipment. Groundwater can be contaminated directly in many ways. Some of the most serious include back-siphoning, surface water movement into wells, or drainage into limestone channels. These contamination problems can nearly always be prevented. Once they occur, however, the point of entry becomes a point-source for contamination. A plume of contamination moves slowly away from the source and can spread to contaminate many wells down gradient.

Well contamination is often the result of *poor well construction*. Problems such as a poor or absent casing, lack of grouting, location in a low spot where water accumulates, or capping below the soil surface are all invitations for contaminated surface water to enter the well. High nitrates and bacterial contamination are often associated with these problems. An example of protecting sensitive areas from point-source pollution involves locating mix/load and equipment cleaning sites at least 100 feet from surface wells or surface water sources. Constructing a permanent site for mixing/loading of pesticides or equipment washing with a collection pad or tray to catch and contain leaks, spills, or wastewater also is beneficial, as is proper disposal of unused pesticides, pesticide containers, and container rinse water. The best way to handle pesticides spilled on soil is to quickly excavate the soil and spread it on a field used for a crop labeled for this pesticide. The soil application will simply follow the labeled rate based on the pesticide concentration in the soil. This method of handling a spill allows the normal soil processes to handle the pesticide residues.

Non-Point

Non-point-source pollution generally involves contamination from a normal application over a wide surface area(s), which can occur if nutrients or pesticides leach through the soil and reach groundwater, or if they wash off in run-off and enter lakes or streams. Leaching through the soil profile and movement with run-off water are believed to be two major sources of non-point pollution. However, if used according to the pesticide label, it is believed non-point-source pollution is actually very minor and contributes little to the overall pollution problem. Problems normally develop only when an intense rainfall occurs almost immediately after application, before the pesticide has been absorbed by the plant or soil.

Currently, the main non-point water quality problem in many states is sediment in streams, lakes, reservoirs, and estuaries. Sediment sources include agricultural fields, construction sites, and stream bank erosion. Established grass areas are not significant sources of sediment but can contribute during establishment or renovation. Mulching, erosion control fences, hay bales, and sod strip lines on bare soil help reduce sediment movement. Stabilizing stream banks by creating gently sloping banks and then establishing vegetative covers are keys to reducing sediments from these sources.

Surface water nutrients also generate problems from non-point sources. Nitrogen and phosphorus, the two most important nutrients affecting water quality, often lead to algal blooms that reduce oxygen levels in water and prevent sunlight from reaching aquatic plants.

Parameters influencing the potential of non-point-source pollution most often involve weather after application, chemical characteristics of pesticides or nutrients, depth of groundwater from the soil surface, and soil type. Pesticides should not be applied if standing water is on the treated surface, as this greatly increases the likelihood of downward movement. Applications prior to heavy rain or excessive irrigation also tend to move pesticides prematurely from the site of application.

In addition, chemical properties of pesticides influence the likelihood of groundwater contamination. These properties include solubility, adsorption and absorption capability, and persistence. Chemicals with high solubility, low adsorption capability, and extended persistence have more potential of becoming non-point-source polluters (Table 28–4).

Research indicates a solid ground coverage by turf is probably the best "filter" in preventing both lateral and horizontal movement of applied pesticides, fertilizers, and soil sediments. Untreated turf buffer zones around sensitive areas such as ponds, lakes, or streams also provide the best assurance of preventing unwanted lateral pesticide movement (Figure 28–2). Turf plants also directly absorb pesticides and, when actively growing, can reduce the likelihood of water-soluble pesticides leaching.

Safe Handling, Application, and Protection of the Environment

Concerns about wildlife and the environment are important in decisions about which pesticides will be registered and what they may be used for. Two issues receiving particular attention are: (1) groundwater protection, and (2) protection of endangered species.

Groundwater Protection

Federal and state efforts to protect groundwater and endangered species are resulting in new instructions and limitations for pesticide handlers. Pesticides incorrectly or accidentally released

TABLE 28–4 *Parameters that minimize the risk for groundwater and surface water contamination from pesticide use.*

Pesticide or site characteristic	Parameters that minimize off-site movement
Pesticide properties	Low solubility
	High soil adsorption (K_{oc})
	Short half-life or little persistence
	High volatility
Soil properties	Finer-textured soil
	Higher organic matter content
Site characteristics	Deep water table
	Flat versus sloping land
	Adequate distance from surface water, sink holes, or abandoned wells
	Soil completely covered with turf, mulch, or ground cover
Management planning	Adequate planning and consideration for impending weather events
	Proper application and timing
	Proper incorporation through irrigation following application

FIGURE 28–2 Research indicates growing a healthy, thick turf is one of the best methods of preventing unwanted lateral movement of applied materials such as pesticides or nutrients. This is enhanced by having 10 to 20 feet (3 to 6 m) of untreated buffer zones adjacent to the sensitive areas.

into the environment—either during application or during other handling activities, such as mixing, loading, equipment cleaning, storage, transportation, or disposal—pose a threat to groundwater and endangered species.

Whether special actions are required to protect groundwater and endangered species depends mainly on the use site location. Groundwater contamination is of greatest concern in release sites where groundwater is close to the surface or where the soil type or the geology allows contaminants to easily reach groundwater. Protection of endangered species usually is required only in locations where they currently live or are being reintroduced. Read the pesticide labeling carefully to determine whether specific pesticide use is subject to any special groundwater or endangered species limitation.

The U.S. Environmental Protection Agency (EPA) may establish specific limitations or instructions for pesticide users in locations where groundwater or endangered species are most at risk. These limitations and instructions are often too long to be included in pesticide labeling. The labeling may indicate whether one must consult another source for the details about the instructions and limitations that apply in a situation. The legal responsibility for following instructions that are distributed separately is the same as it is for instructions that appear in full on the pesticide labeling.

Endangered Species Protection

An endangered species is a plant or animal that is in danger of becoming extinct. A Federal law, the Endangered Species Act (ESA), requires the EPA to ensure endangered species are protected (Figure 28–3). The EPA's goal is to remove or reduce the threat pesticide use poses to endangered species. Limitations of pesticide use apply most in the currently occupied habitat or range of each endangered species at risk.

The U.S. Fish and Wildlife Service is responsible for identifying the current habitat or range of each endangered species. The National Marine Fisheries Service has the same responsibility for marine species. For aquatic species, the restricted habitat often will include an additional zone around the body of water to keep any drift, run-off, or leachate in the watershed from reaching the water. Under the Endangered Species Act, it is a Federal offense to use any pesticide in a manner resulting in the death of a member of an endangered species. If the pesticide user is in doubt whether or not endangered species may be affected, he or she should contact the regional U.S. Fish and Wildlife Service Office or state pesticide regulatory agency.

The ESA policy will prohibit the use of some pesticides in specific locations. The labels of those pesticides state the use of the pesticide is prohibited in specific counties or specific areas within counties. In order to use the pesticide, the user must obtain an "EPA PESTICIDE USE

FIGURE 28–3 The Endangered Species Act protects those plants and animals that are at risk of becoming extinct. Oftentimes, golf courses are havens for such endangered species, providing the necessary habitat and food sources to live.

BULLETIN FOR PROTECTION OF ENDANGERED SPECIES." These bulletins will describe all pertinent restrictions in each affected county. Bulletins may be available from a variety of sources including pesticide dealers and county Extension and Soil Conservation offices.

STRATEGIES FOR ENVIRONMENTALLY SOUND GOLF COURSE DESIGN

Predesign Questions

Golf courses should be designed to integrate with the natural geography of the site. This means the golf course should complement the natural resources of the site and, in turn, the natural resources should help make the course unique. Although no two golf courses and the associated natural resources will be identical, certain questions concerning environmental issues should be addressed during the planning, review, and construction process (modified from Love, 1992). These questions include the following:

1. Does a golf course provide important open or green space by making use of a site that is currently undeveloped?
2. Will the proposed golf course maintain or expand wetlands and other sensitive environmental areas that may exist on the site?
3. Are there significant historical or archaeological areas on the site that will be preserved by the golf course?
4. What positive impact will the golf course have on the ecological systems of the site, such as plant life and wildlife habitat?
5. How will the golf course enhance the existing character of a site through alteration of the topography and vegetative cover?
6. How will potential earth disturbance and erosion be minimized during the construction of the golf course?
7. How will prudent irrigation design and efficient water use impact existing water supplies, especially in areas experiencing conditions that limit water resources?
8. How will the design and maintenance practices of the golf course be implemented to prevent water pollution from surface run-off or infiltration into the ground?

By addressing these issues during the planning stage, the developer can avoid deleterious environmental impacts as well as costly delays in the development process. The end result is a more successful design, development, and construction project that produces an enjoyable recreational facility that is aesthetically pleasing and environmentally compatible.

Team Approach

The most successful approach to ensure a successful project completion is to form a team of experts. This team should include a golf course architect, engineer, landscape architect, water resources specialist, environmental specialist, and other consultants as dictated by the peculiarities of the golf course and the watershed in which it is sited. This team then works with the developer, community representatives, environmental groups, and regulatory agencies to determine the project goals.

During site selection and golf course design, the team must become intimately familiar with the environmental aspects of the site. Proposed site selection guidelines (Anonymous, 1993a; 1996a) include the following:

1. Have professionals assess the physical and economic viability of a golf course on a particular site. Identifying environmentally sensitive areas and other natural resources helps balance environmental concerns, playability, and aesthetics in the course design.
2. If possible, select sites outside of agricultural land use zones. Should agricultural land be the only option, follow local and state agricultural guidelines when selecting development sites.
3. Identify and respect existing ecosystems such as unique wetland qualities and other sensitive natural areas. Avoid the disturbance of these areas and incorporate these features into the design. This will help protect natural resources, improve course maintenance efficiency, and will likely minimize permit and site development costs.
4. Consider present or potential aggregate resources when determining location.
5. Ensure the project conforms with all state and local land use plans and zoning bylaws.
6. Ensure adequate water supply is available for all potable and irrigation needs of the golf facility and neighboring properties.
7. Be available to meet with the public and answer their concerns regarding the development site.

Developing the Design

The sum total of all reconnaissance and analysis should be a series of maps illustrating existing roads and property boundaries, water sources for both irrigation and consumption, topography, sensitive wildlife habitat, potentially high erosion areas (steep slopes), wetlands and required buffer areas, drainage patterns including flood plains, vegetative cover, historical or archaeological sites, right-of-ways or easements, utilities including power and sewer, scenic views and vistas, adjacent land uses, and other information critical to planning and designing the golf course. It is critical, at this point, to be intimately familiar with all rules and regulations governing the construction and management of the golf course. This will help establish realistic goals and produce the most efficient planning and design. In particular, this approach will avoid costly revisions and delays during the review, permit, and construction process.

Additional suggested design considerations (Anonymous, 1993a; 1996a) include the following:

1. Select plant species that are best suited to the local climate and require the minimum of inputs. Use of native or naturalized vegetation should be retained when appropriate in nonplay areas.
2. Design the irrigation to efficiently use water only where and when needed.
3. Investigate the feasibility of alternative or supplemental sources of irrigation water (e.g., on-site storage reservoirs for storm water run-off collection or effluent). On-site retention of stormwater run-off should be considered on soils with low infiltration rates. Effluent water should be considered if it meets local health and environmental standards and it does not negatively affect sensitive surface water areas.
4. Maintain a vegetative buffer zone adjacent to all water courses to assist in filtering any nutrients or pesticides from storm run-off, to reduce intrusion from effluent water use, and to moderate water temperatures.
5. Retain as much natural cover as possible and enhance vegetation through supplementary planting of trees, shrubs, and grasses, especially along fairways to provide wildlife habitat and along water courses supporting a fish habitat.

6. Incorporate as many natural features and areas in the design as possible to minimize disturbance of the existing ecology. Seek to create and/or preserve habitat areas that enhance the area's ecosystem.
7. Consider future maintenance requirements of all golf course design features. Low-maintenance features that require less-intensive management are preferred. Integrated plant management, including integrated pest management, plant nutrition, and overall plant health, should be emphasized to most efficiently use and protect available resources.

A well-balanced landscape design for the golf course results in a mix of shrubs, trees, grassy areas, and water features that sustain and encourage wildlife and plant diversity. This design should balance the correction of poor drainage and erosion with the need to maintain wetland habitats.

Wetland habitats are particularly critical not only for wildlife but also for water treatment, processing, and storage. Whenever possible, golf courses should be designed so irrigation and stormwater run-off move from the edges into the middle of the course. Drainage ditches should be bisected by small swales or even natural or constructed wetlands. These geographic features slow down water and allow for assimilation of both nutrients and pesticides by vegetation. These geographic features can be picturesque playing hazards that make the course more challenging.

In many locations, water quantity and quality may be the limiting factors in golf course development. A wise water-use plan might include the recapture and reuse of irrigation water as well as the use of secondary treated effluent water from a municipality or surrounding housing development for irrigation. Wetlands are extremely important for both their water-holding capacity and their water purification capacity. These features will increase water recapture by the golf course as well as help to alleviate fears by homeowners over the use of wastewater treatment effluent on the course.

STRATEGIES FOR ENVIRONMENTALLY SOUND GOLF COURSE CONSTRUCTION

Construction Documents

Once the planning and design processes have been completed, the construction phase of development is initiated. The environmental issues concerning construction will have been addressed during the design of the golf course. The construction documents will vary depending upon the architect and local regulations, but typically include (Anonymous, 1996a):

1. Using only qualified contractors experienced in the unique needs of golf course construction.
2. Staking plans to locate the key points of the golf course (tees, landing areas, and greens) in the field for review and construction. This should emphasize protecting water sources, reducing wildlife and plant disruption, minimizing topsoil loss, and avoiding environmentally sensitive areas.
3. Erosion control and stormwater management plans show the location of features and methods of controlling stormwater and erosion on disturbed areas of the site during construction. Construct sediment traps and basins and establish plant materials to provide soil stabilization.
4. Clearing plans to indicate the limits of clearing necessary for golf course construction. Specimen trees to be saved or areas of vegetation to be preserved will be shown on this plan or designated in the field.
5. Grading and drainage plans to show the overall plan for construction of the golf course and the earth work necessary to create features and produce the proper drainage. Break long or steep slopes with diversions to keep run-off velocities low and divert storm water run-off.
6. Green plans to provide details for the construction of each green complex.
7. Construction details and sections to show how the features (trees, bunkers, mounding, ponds, etc.) are to be constructed in conjunction with the grading and drainage plan.
8. Irrigation plans and details to provide the information for the type of irrigation system and pump station to be installed for the golf course.
9. Grassing plans to indicate the areas where specific turfgrasses and, in some cases, ornamental grasses are to be planted on the golf course.

10. Landscape plans to serve as a guideline of where plant material is to be installed to enhance the golf course design. As a part of this plan, conservation areas can be established throughout the golf course.
11. Specifications and bid documents outline the methods and details of construction for the course completion.

Construction Process

The golf course superintendent should be hired early in the design and construction process. The superintendent will inspect the construction process daily and serve as the on-site representative for the owner and the architect. During the construction process, site visits are made by the golf course architect, accompanied at times by other members of the consultant team, to inspect the work and see that the intended level of design and quality in the course is being accomplished. These visits ensure that the close interaction between the architect, design team, and the construction team will ultimately produce the distinctive features and character of the golf course. These visits also provide the opportunity to monitor the controls and management techniques in place for environmental protection.

The construction process starts with the stakeout of the golf course by a surveyor or engineer. This process is reviewed by the architect and minor field adjustments are made to improve the golf course by responding to existing terrain, by integrating natural features, by providing further protection for sensitive areas, and by the preservation of specific natural features such as trees, rock outcroppings, and sand dunes in the design.

Soil erosion control features are then installed and checked to ensure proper placement and installation prior to the clearing and grading of the site. It is critical these controls remain in place throughout the construction and stabilization of the disturbed areas (e.g., turf establishment). Stormwater management controls are also installed very early in the construction phase to control drainage of the site and avoid impacts to sensitive areas. This is the time when natural geographic features such as ponds, grass swales, and wetlands are incorporated into the water management plan.

The next step is grading the golf course. It is important to remember the objectives during grading the course should be to avoid excessive disturbance, produce the necessary drainage contours, and provide the features required by the golf course design. An irrigation system is installed after grading has been completed. The system must be complete and operational to support the planting of the golf course. Care should be taken to design the irrigation system so the spray is directed inward onto the course with little drift off of the course. This is particularly important if fertigation or chemigation is planned.

After grading and installing the irrigation system, the course should be prepared and planted with the specific types of turfgrass or ornamental grass required by the golf course design. Native species should be used to re-establish roughs and areas designed to make the course more visually pleasing. The overall landscape design should include specific areas designed to promote wildlife habitat.

Additional construction considerations suggested by the Royal Canadian Golf Association (Anonymous, 1993a) include the following:

1. Protect or re-establish native groundcover and understory species during and after construction.
2. Schedule construction to protect soils by minimizing the time ground is left without cover. Protect soils during construction through the use of mulching materials, hydro-seeding, or sod.
3. Monitor groundwater quality before and after construction.
4. Avoid construction near water courses, especially during fish spawning season. However, if construction is necessary, ensure adequate mitigative measures are in place to protect water quality, fisheries, and stream-side habitats. Contact the local regulatory agencies for guidance.

STRATEGIES FOR ENVIRONMENTALLY SOUND GOLF COURSE MANAGEMENT

Public concerns for the environment have led to the idea of best management practices (BMPs) for golf courses. The BMP concept consists of five basic goals: (1) decrease off-site transport of pesticides and nutrients, (2) control the application of these chemicals, (3) decrease total chemical loads, (4) use both biological and mechanical soil and water conservation plans (SWCPs), and (5) educate both managers and the public about the relationship between environmental issues and golf course management (Balogh and Walker, 1992). The following sections detail management strategies golf courses should consider.

Water

Water is a very important component in golf course management. The following sections will discuss the various uses of water on a golf course (e.g., irrigation, hazards, and aesthetics). Attention will be given to sources of water used in irrigation and subsequent management of possible runoff, as well as the management of both existing and man-made bodies of water found on the property (Figure 28–4).

Irrigation

Maintenance of optimal soil moisture levels is necessary for turfgrass growth and formation. Approximately 70 percent of water used for irrigation is from surface water sources (e.g., lakes, ponds, streams). Purchase of potable waters or secondary treated effluent make up less than 10 percent of irrigation waters used.

Lakes, ponds, and streams on the golf course may serve as an adequate source of irrigation water. However, in coastal areas the salinity of these water bodies may be detrimental to turfgrass, thereby eliminating them as possible sources. Dilution of these brackish waters with potable or other freshwaters can reduce the need for purchasing water for irrigation purposes.

Purchasing potable water is another option. This may be done as a sole source or simply as a means of augmenting another supply source. In either case, this source of water can be very expensive.

The push for water conservation has resulted in the management technique of using secondary treated effluent for irrigation. This practice can be beneficial to all involved. Nutrient levels in the effluent will supplement the application of fertilizers, thereby reducing the amount of fertilizers purchased and applied. In coastal areas in particular, the sand content of the soil also serves to filter out bacteria and other contaminants found in the effluent. This then decreases the possible chances of groundwater pollution. However, the use of effluent for irrigation is strictly regulated. Refer to Chapter 15 for additional information on effluent water use.

Lakes/Ponds/Streams

Flood control of existing water bodies and those constructed on the course is a very important issue to be addressed. All drainage structures should be maintained so as to ensure the proper control of excess water. In part, these aspects of management are built into the golf course at the design and construction phase. However, as a golf course ages, erosion should be curbed and drains often

FIGURE 28–4 Wetlands provide the necessary habitat for many plants and animals to live. Wetlands also help regulate and resupply water levels. Protecting wetlands during the design, construction, and maintenance of golf courses has become a primary environmental objective.

need some attention. A small sedimentation pond upstream may be necessary to reduce erosion, especially if significant development or logging occurs upstream of the main golf course lakes or ponds. In most situations, lakes and ponds on the course will be used to collect run-off and will be able to hold nearly all input. It is the run-off into creeks and streams that is of most concern. The planting of aquatic macrophytes in these areas may help slow flow and filter contaminants.

Water quality should be monitored in all bodies of water subject to the effects of golf course management. The most common problem superintendents face in managing water quality is fluctuations in dissolved oxygen (Figure 28–5). A decline in dissolved oxygen can initially be minimized by controlling algal blooms, which are the major contributor to oxygen consumption in early morning hours, and then by directly treating the problem. The addition of an aerator in ponds and lakes receiving nutrient-rich run-off will help quench the extreme dissolved oxygen shifts. Assimilation of excess nutrients by wetlands is a management technique used to improve water quality, which is discussed later. An unfertilized buffer zone surrounding lakes and ponds should be considered, especially on steep-sloped edges or edges with soils such as clays that do not readily allow water infiltration.

Common groups of algae include blue-green, green, diatoms, dinoflagellates, and euglena. Algae form the base of an aquatic food chain; thus, they are important to the overall system's health. However, algal blooms require management at various times of the year. This is an area of management that can be addressed at the design/construction phase of a golf course. The use of existing or constructed wetlands and riparian zones can reduce the total loading of nutrients into aquatic systems, subsequently decreasing the growth rate of algae.

Aquatic macrophytes such as duckweed, widgeon grass, and cattail can play a large role in the assimilation of chemical input to aquatic systems as well as serve to control erosion. Nuisance macrophyte growth can be controlled by various means. Mechanical means may be employed to physically remove the plants, or biological controls (e.g., grass carp) may be used. A limited number of herbicides can also be used to control aquatic plants.

Ponds food chain

The food chain in a pond directly influences the amount of oxygen produced in the pond.

Bass

Bream ↗

Zooplankton ↗

Phytoplankton ↗
(base of pond food chain) ↗

FIGURE 28–5 Water features add beauty to a facility and, if carefully planned, may enhance the quality of water by providing aeration.

Phytoplanktonic algae form the base of the food chain in a pond system. These are microscopic plants living suspending in the water. Through photosynthesis, phytoplanktonic algae provide the oxygen needed for fish and other aquatic organisms. **Zooplankton** are tiny insectlike animals floating in the water and feeding on phytoplankton. Bream then feed on zooplankton and aquatic insects. The top of the food chain in most ponds contains bass. Bass feed on bream and help control their populations. In fact, ponds lacking a satisfactory bass population will be overcrowded with small bream. However, overstocking or using the wrong kind of fish could cause long-term fish kill. Consult a fisheries scientist before stocking any fish to determine how much and which kind(s) of fish are needed for a particular site.

Ponds can be divided into various regions or areas, including the **littoral region** and **open water regions.** The shore area or interface zone between the land of the drainage basin and open water is the **littoral region** (Figure 28–6). This region is generally a ring of plants around the shore area with plant communities according to water depth and wave action. It extends from the shoreline to the point where aquatic plants no longer grow. Typical plants growing in this region are cattails or rushes, water lily or lotus, and submersed plants such as pondweeds (Figure 28–7). The littoral region is also the area in which over 90 percent of all algal species are found attached to macrophytes. These contribute significantly to the pond's productivity and provide habitats for microflora, as well as larger invertebrates and vertebrates.

Beyond the littoral region is the **open water region,** an area where an upper layer of warm, well-lit, and relatively high oxygen levels and a lower layer of cooler, poorly lit, and lower oxygen levels occur. Plants and animals in the open water region include planktonic algae, zooplankton, invertebrates, and fish.

The water in ponds gets colder the deeper one goes. As temperatures rise in summer, the surface of the ponds warm and become lighter (less dense); thus, they float on a cooler water layer. **Thermal stratification** begins, allowing the water to "layer," with warm water being separated from the cooler water. Upper levels of ponds may become much warmer (termed **epilimnion**) than the cold-water bottom (termed **hypolimnion**). In small ponds (e.g., <15 acres) the warm layer extends down to about six feet (2 m) where a **thermocline,** the dividing line between the two layers, occurs. Most of the oxygen-producing phytoplankton live in the warmer upper layer; thus, most of the oxygen for fish to breathe also resides here. Little oxygen occurs below this warm layer; thus, it does not support aquatic life very well and is not a good source of irrigation water for turf.

Thermal stratification must be interrupted or **eutrophication** will occur, where excess dissolved nutrients occur with insufficient dissolved oxygen. "Turnover" of a pond often occurs when the surface is cooled from rain or cold temperatures. The temperature of the top layer then equals the bottom layer and the two water layers will mix. As the two layers mix, the oxygen will diffuse from the top of the pond to the bottom, leaving insufficient oxygen to support fish life. Turnover of ponds may also occur as aquatic plants receive insufficient sunlight for normal photosynthesis during cloudy weather, and dissolved oxygen becomes deficient in the system. With depleted oxygen, a cold rain may mix the warm and cold layers, breaking down the thermocline

FIGURE 28–6 Cross-section providing a typical pond showing the littoral and open water regions and the upper and lower water layers.

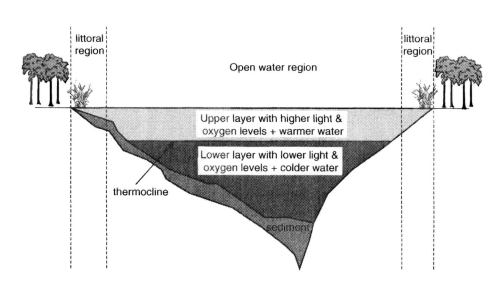

FIGURE 28–7 Aquatic death often occurs when an algae bloom or natural pond turnover from temperature stratification or weather changes occur. Pesticides or nutrients are often erroneously blamed for such kills. Constant monitoring of the water's chemical status, minimizing weeds and algae, and providing oxygen through artificial aeration are means of predicting and minimizing the conditions that cause fish problems.

and depleting the pond of what little dissolved oxygen remains in the upper levels. Less-desirable odoriferous anaerobic bacteria then take over. Without oxygen, microorganisms, invertebrates, and fish die. Oxygen levels also tend to decline over time as ponds lose some of their holding capacity when sludge or sediment buildup occurs. Undecomposed debris accumulates on the bottom as sludge and gradually decreases the depth of the pond.

Ponds often naturally turn over in fall when temperatures begin to cool. The major difference between a fall turnover and a summer turnover is the cooler water temperatures. Cold water will hold more oxygen than warm water, so when a pond turns over in the fall there is more oxygen available in the epilimnion layer, and fish do not die.

Cultural eutrophication such as sewage disposal, land drainage, and fertilization may result in excess nutrient enrichment in ponds. High nitrates and phosphates cause algal blooms, aquatic weeds follow, and water turbidity, pH, alkalinity, and dissolved oxygen are adversely affected in eutrophic ponds. Balancing a pond's ecosystem must provide fewer destructive primary producers such as periphytic algae and manageable aquatic vegetation. Biodiversity of plants and animals is best for golf course ponds, resulting in as many levels of the food chain as possible.

Monitoring ponds should consist of measuring turbidity, total ammonia-nitrogen, phosphorous, temperature, pH, and dissolved oxygen. Pond nutrients are most prolific during the summer, leading to foul odors. Aerobic bacteria digest algae and other nutrients seven times faster than anaerobic bacteria. When aerobic bacteria run out of oxygen, the less-desirable anaerobic bacteria take over.

Aeration

Adequate circulation and aeration are needed for odor and algae control; therefore, include electrical service in the course design. Aeration helps attack the cause(s) of poor water quality while other methods such as dyes and algaecides treat the symptoms—algae. Artificial aeration helps provide oxygen when natural wind and wave action cannot provide sufficient levels. Aerators introduce oxygen into a larger volume of water while fountains create an attractive display or spray pattern (Figure 28–8). Aerators use propellers to move a large volume of water and introduce a larger volume of oxygen. In fountains, a centrifugal pump usually creates an attractive display while volume is sacrificed to obtain the necessary pressure to achieve these heights and shapes.

Aerators need to be matched for the size of the pond or lake. A one-acre pond three feet deep contains about 1 million gallons of water. For aerations, 800 to 1,400 gallons per minute (gpm) should be propelled into the atmosphere for a water surface area 0.5 to 1.5 acres (0.2 to 0.6 ha) in size. For smaller, 0.1 to 0.5 acre (0.04 to 0.2 ha) areas, 350 to 500 gpm is acceptable. If the lake is bigger, multiple smaller units generally distribute oxygen more evenly than one unit of larger horsepower. If the aerator cannot move sufficient amounts of water, then disappointing benefits will be seen from it.

1. Fish swimming at the surface are gulping for air, especially in late night or early morning.
2. Water is rapidly turning dark brown to black in color.
3. A rotten or putrid odor is detected.
4. Sudden algal death.

These conditions are most likely after extended hot, cloudy weather is interrupted by a summer rain storm.

FIGURE 28–8 Aerators are attractive and effective means of introducing oxygen into an aquatic feature. Many types and models exist, with most requiring direct electrical service.

Types of Aerators

Many types of aerators are available, including:

1. **Floating fountains (also called display fountains)**—These electrically charged floating devices with a motor or pump/motor send jets or fountains of water into the atmosphere which dissolve oxygen and, through wave action following surface impact, support aerobic bacteria. Although spectacular, fountains normally do not move the volume of water as true aerators.
2. **Aerating fountains**—This combination of an aerator and a fountain generally creates a spray pattern shaped as the flair of a trumpet or tuba.
3. **Floating surface aerators**—This device, similar to the floating fountains, does not create a fountain-type spray pattern when this is not desired. It agitates the surface in the form of a bubbling or boiling effect.
4. **Aspirating aerator**—This device does not create a fountain pattern but blows oxygenated bubbles directionally into the water body, deep below the surface. The pond's bottom needs to be equipment-friendly, so as not to upset and mix the silt and any sludge throughout the pond. Aspirating aerators can be either floating or fixed base mounted.
5. **Pond bottom aerator**—This completely submerged unit uses a propeller water transport system where bottom water is circulated to the surface. This cooler, denser water absorbs oxygen as it spreads across the pond and returns through the stratified layers.
6. **Diffused air or compressed air systems**—These systems involve a shore-mounted compressor that pumps oxygen through tubing into the pond. It requires quality weighted tubing and self-cleaning diffusers but offers superior aeration, circulation, and de-stratification.

Surface spray aerators can pump water from lower parts of the pond to break through the thermocline and into the air, where it can pick up oxygen. Short, wide, full volume water pumped at lower speeds maximize recycling of water and injection of oxygen into water. Running fountain surface sprayers and subsurface aerators are maximized at night for oxygen benefits. A balanced pond will typically contain two to three ppm of oxygen. Oxygen levels are typically lowest just before dawn. Increasing the oxygen content in lakes can help reduce nutrient levels, limit thermal stratification, and decrease algae growth.

Beneficial algae

Periphytic algae is the general category of predominantly beneficial green algae found growing on or attached to submerged structures in fresh water. These can outcompete problematic blue-green and filamentous algae but require a submerged surface area to live. The usage of barley straw to control algae and clarify ponds was developed in England in the 1990s; however, mixed results were found since its effects on planktonic algae were less than on filamentous algae. The straw is believed to inhibit algae growth through a chemical exuded from the decomposing barley straw; by a metabolic product produced by fungi that decomposes the barley straw, preventing algae growth; or by the barley tying up excessive nitrates (NO_3^-). As a starting use rate, barley straw bales are applied at 225 pounds per acre (252 kg/ha) in shallow (4 to 5 feet, 1.2 to 1.5 m, deep) ponds or one two × four foot (0.6 × 1.2 m) bale per 5,000 square meters of water, which is repeated twice yearly. Other structures used to encourage beneficial algae are rocks, rooted plants, Christmas trees, and other organic materials. Commercial mats are also available that provide enormous surface area for these beneficial algae.

However, ponds must be continually monitored, measuring turbidity, ammonia (NH_4), phosphorous, temperature, pH, and dissolved oxygen. Small ponds are more prone to stagnation when water temperatures rise as aquatic plants die and consume dissolved oxygen. Strong odors and aquatic death result. However, small ponds allow regular turnover of water; the fresher the water, the less problems occur.

Use of a filter system also is suggested to reduce algae that may enter the sprinkler system and clog nozzles. Even distribution by the irrigation system also helps prevent buildup of any harmful substances.

Pond enhancements

Algae are well-adapted to high nutrient concentrations, particularly phosphorus, warm water, and sunshine. Their ability to reproduce exponentially can result in an algal bloom distinguished by a "pea-soup" appearance.

Prevention of algal blooms often requires controlling nutrients in the pond. If not prevented, restoring ponds after an algal bloom can be costly and time-consuming. Ways to enhance pond health, attract wildlife, and prevent algal blooms include:

- Create islands and shallow water areas by adding rocks and logs. These help protect and provide nesting sites for various small creatures and create basking sites for turtles.
- Provide shelter for fish by sinking trees.
- Provide food and safe access to wildlife by planting a vegetative bugger around the edge of ponds. These plants also help filter run-off to improve water quality.
- Plant emergent vegetation to provide food and cover for various buds, mammals, amphibians, and insects.
- Plant submergent vegetation to provide cover for various aquatic life and to help maintain healthy oxygen levels.
- Have a no-treatment buffer zone around the pond to act as a filter of surface-applied material.

Herbicides

Herbicides often are the fastest way to control weeds, but may not provide long-term control. Decaying weeds from herbicide control also often create oxygen depletion as the bacteria that decompose the weeds are oxygen consumers, leaving insufficient levels for fish. If using aquatic herbicides, treat in early spring when water temperatures are cooler, thereby holding more oxygen. If ponds need to be treated in summer, treat one-fourth of the pond at a time. If the whole pond is treated in summer, dissolved oxygen levels are reduced by the decomposing bacteria, causing fish kills.

Wetlands and Riparian Zones

Geographic features such as wetlands and riparian zones are valuable natural resources. Wetlands are currently one of the most valuable natural resources in the United States. They serve many purposes in nature, ranging from habitat for wildlife to a means of water quality improvement. Golf course developers, managers, and scientists are recognizing that wetlands and other geographic features may be essential to environmentally sound golf course management.

Natural Wetlands

Natural and constructed wetlands and riparian zones may be incorporated into golf course design. These features, when fully integrated into the water management strategy, act as natural filters to remove nutrients, pesticides, and suspended particulates (e.g., soil, microorganisms) from run-off water. Many courses in coastal areas are fortunate to have an abundance of natural wetlands and riparian zones. These geographic features provide a critical wildlife habitat. In turn, the wildlife and the wetlands significantly contribute to the aesthetics of the course itself.

The key is to create a hydrologic design that begins with irrigation and rainfall; follows run-off from tees, fairways, and greens; and treats this run-off with vegetative filter strips, wetlands, and riparian zones. Collection of this treated run-off into ponds and lakes may provide a much-needed source of clean irrigation water for reuse on the course.

Constructed Wetlands

Some principles of ecological engineering suggested by Mitsch and Gooselink (1993) that can be applied to the construction and restoration of wetlands for non-point-source chemical run-off include the following:

1. Design the system for minimum maintenance. The system of plants, animals, microbes, substrate, and water flows should be developed.
2. Design a system that utilizes natural energies, such as the potential energy of streams, as natural subsidies to the system.
3. Design the system with the landscape, not against it. Floods and droughts should be expected. Outbreak of plant diseases and invasion of alien species are often symptomatic of other stresses and may indicate faulty design rather than ecosystem failure.
4. Design the system with multiple objectives, but identify at least one major objective and several secondary objectives.
5. Design the system as an ecotone. This means including a buffer strip around the site, but it also means the wetland site itself is often a buffer system between upland and aquatic systems. Stabilize and maintain stream banks and limit fertilizer and pesticide use near wetlands.
6. Give the system time. Wetlands do not become functional overnight and several years may lapse before nutrient retention or wildlife enhancement is optimal. Strategies that try to short-circuit ecological succession or overmanage are doomed to failure.
7. Design the system for function, not for form. If initial plantings and animal introductions fail but the overall function of the wetland, based on initial objectives, is intact, then the wetland has not failed.
8. Do not overengineer wetland design with rectangular basins, rigid structures and channels, and regular morphology. Ecological engineering recognizes natural systems should be mimicked to accommodate biological systems.

Wetlands can be located almost anywhere on a golf course. This utility facilitates the integration of a challenging hole design with water and chemical management. Wetlands can be incorporated into streams by adding control structures. Blocking the entire stream is a reasonable alternative only in low-order streams. This approach is usually not cost effective and is particularly vulnerable during high flow and flooding. An alternative would be to provide another channel for high flow periods. This would preserve the integrity of the wetland during intense storm events and flooding.

Riparian wetlands are those adjacent to flooding streams. These wetlands periodically receive flood waters and, in natural systems, may be seen as bottomland hardwood forests. Forested riparian zones adjacent to small creeks and drainage ditches are extremely useful for water and chemical management. For example, run-off from a playing surface may be directed via drain pipe or shallow depressions to a riparian ditch. This ditch, with a gentle to steep slope depending on the terrain, then empties into a wetland immediately upstream from a lake or larger-order stream. In considering the complete golf course hydrologic plan, the use of several small wetlands instead of a few larger wetlands should be considered. There are several advantages to locating several small wetlands in the upper reaches of the golf course (but not in the streams themselves) rather than fewer larger wetlands in the lower reaches. A particularly useful design might be the construction of multiple small wetlands in the landscape to intercept small streams and drainage tiles prior to reaching the stream. The stream itself is not diverted; the wetlands receive water, nutrients, and golf course chemicals from small tributaries, swales, and overland flow. In addition, drain tiles can be located so that they provide significant amounts of water to the wetlands. These tile drains are often the sources of highest chemical concentrations such as fertilizers.

As previously discussed, multiple smaller wetlands are usually better than one or two larger wetlands. The size and shape of the wetland should be dictated by other phonographic features such as slope. Short, wide wetlands might be appropriate for intercepting diffuse overland flow in areas with gentle slopes; long, narrow wetlands might be more appropriate for ditches, swales, and streams in areas with steeper slopes. In extreme cases of the latter, terraced wetlands placed into the watershed in a stair-step style are most appropriate.

Turf

A more encompassing concept than integrated pest management (IPM) is turfgrass management systems (TMS), which combine cultural management factors for sustained productivity, course profitability, and the integrity of ecosystems on and in the vicinity of the golf course (Balogh and Walker, 1992). These authors list six critical components of TMS: (1) selection of turfgrass species and cultivars; (2) soil management practices; (3) clipping and cultivation practices; (4) nutrient management; (5) irrigation and drainage management; and (6) chemical, biological, and cultural pest management. The goal of a TMS approach is to balance costs, benefits, and human and environmental health while sustaining an acceptable playing surface.

Fertilizers

Some basic principles of nutrient management that are consistent with TMS programs have been suggested (Balogh and Walker, 1992). The first and most important principle is to use minimal rates of nitrogen and phosphorus to maintain appropriate nutrient levels and avoid losses to run-off or leaching. Soil and tissue tests frequently determine specific levels and possible needs. Improving uptake efficacy will also minimize nutrient losses. For example, core aerify compacted soil before fertilizing to allow better penetration by the particles; water-in soluble fertilizer sources after application; use slow-release sources when feasible, especially in sandy soils; use minimum rates on severely sloping or highly erodible soils; use iron as a supplement to nitrogen for improved turf color; recycle grass clippings; and avoid fertilizer application in bodies of water by using a drop spreader near these. Also, applications of fertilizers should coincide with the growth requirements of the specific turfgrass species. Traffic patterns and intensity should be monitored and taken into account in calculating the potential for run-off. Selecting different application techniques can also reduce losses, as can variations in the formulations used. In addition, it is necessary to have properly calibrated equipment. Some measure of quality control and quality assurance needs to be conducted in order to assess the efficacy of the nutrient management plan.

Pesticides

Foremost in the superintendent's mind when planning pesticide management is probably the safety of the workers and golfers. Considerable details on pesticides, their characteristics, formulations, and use are covered in Chapter 27.

Control of Other Pests

Other pests such as raccoons, armadillos, groundhogs, wild hogs, deer, geese, and other birds should be controlled according to local regulations. Trapping or harvesting these pests, humanely, may be effective. Care should be taken when handling wild animals as they are vectors for various diseases, such as rabies.

Audubon International Cooperative Sanctuary Program

Audubon International began its Audubon Cooperative Sanctuary Program (ACSP) in 1991 to "educate people about environmental stewardship and motivate them to take action in their daily lives which will enhance and protect wildlife and their habitats and conserve natural resources." The ACSP has devised four programs tailored for homeowners, businesses, schools, and golf courses.

A golf course can become certified in the ACSP in six areas:

- Environmental planning
- Wildlife and habitat management
- Chemical use reduction and safety
- Water conservation
- Water quality management
- Outreach and education

If a course successfully becomes certified in all six categories, it receives a Certified Audubon Cooperative Sanctuary. Once a course is certified, it must be recertified after two years. This involves completing a case study, site assessment, and environmental planning. For further information on this sanctuary program, contact the Audubon International at:

Audubon International
46 Rarick Road
Selkirk, NY 12158
Phone: (518) 767-9051
Fax: (518) 767-9076
www.audubonintl.org

BEST ENVIRONMENTAL GOLF COURSE MANAGEMENT SUMMARY

Nutrient and pesticide movement or soil sediment erosion could negatively affect environmental quality if allowed to enter lakes or streams in an uncontrolled manner or in significant amounts. Best management practices are plans to reduce this possibility by (1) growing a solid turf stand that reduces the off-site transport of sediment, nutrients, and pesticides; (2) controlling the rate, method, and type of chemicals being applied; and (3) reducing the total chemical load by using TMS (including economic thresholds, alternate pest control), and fertility testing. Following the labeling directions exactly is the best way to prevent contaminating groundwater. In addition, the following should be remembered:

1. **Avoid disturbing sensitive wildlife areas and wetlands during the initial design and construction of a golf course**—When designing and maintaining a golf course, wetlands and other sensitive natural areas should be incorporated into the design and not disturbed (Figure 28–9).
2. **Select plant species that are locally adapted and require minimum inputs**—Growing plants outside their naturally adapted range usually means increased inputs in terms of pesticides, water, nutrient, and other energy needed to maintain the plant. Growing bentgrass outside its naturally adapted range is an example of having to greatly manipulate its surrounding microenvironment to simulate its natural adaptation environment. Native plants often are able to survive with fewer maintenance inputs such as nutrients, water, and pesticides, but are not always very attractive.
3. **During construction, all necessary steps of preventing soil erosion and managing stormwater run-off on disturbed areas should be implemented**—This step involves minimizing soil movement during construction by installing silt fencing, adding hay protection, sodding highly erodible areas, and so forth. As outlined in Chapters 3 and 4, this also includes providing a master plan with drainage for green construction, grading, clearing, and specific features such as trees, bunkers, mounding, ponds, and so forth.
4. **Maintain the turf to encourage a deep, actively growing root system**—Deep, active root systems are better able to recover applied nutrients and thereby prevent leaching. Deep

root systems also allow efficient use of applied water as they can extract moisture from a greater area and require less irrigation. Cultural practices such as using the highest acceptable mowing height and proper frequency, minimizing soil compaction and layering, minimizing thatch layering, and eliminating root feeding insects, diseases, and nematodes are means of promoting a healthy turf root system.

5. **When possible, select pesticides based on the following:**
   - Lowest toxicity to humans, mammals, fish, birds, and bees.
   - Rapidity of degradation and lowest leaching potential. More persistent pesticides have a greater chance of off-site movement via leaching or lateral movement.
   - Highest soil adsorption, as higher soil adsorbing pesticides are less likely to leach.
   - Lowest volatility. Pesticides with lower vapor pressures are less likely to volatilize and move off-site. This results in lower efficiency of pesticide use and could possibly pose problems to adjacent sensitive plants. Ester formulations of phenoxy herbicides, for example, may vaporize and drift when sprayed during warm temperatures, when winds are excessive, and when high soil moisture is present.

6. **Using the appropriate pesticide and nutrient rates (not excessive, especially for nitrogen and phosphorus)**—An obvious management practice that is sometimes lost primarily due to pressure from club members or players is to maintain ideal year-round green grass. Higher nutrient rates usually mean lush, fast-growing turf which is harder to mow and becomes more susceptible to certain pests. Unusual circumstances, however, such as growing-in a newly established area or having to quickly recover from winter kill, sometimes dictate using temporarily slightly higher-than-normal nutrient rates.

7. **Use the least amount of soluble nutrient sources commensurated with acceptable turfgrass quality**—Applying lighter but more frequent amounts of soluble nutrient sources has been shown to produce high-quality turf without groundwater leaching problems. Using slow-release nutrient sources in combination with soluble sources also helps minimize any negative impact. Water-in soluble sources after application to reduce movement following a heavy rainfall event.

8. **Use the best application method to minimize any special risks**—For example, soil injection of some pesticides may not be wise when groundwater is close to the surface. However, in other cases slit injection may reduce exposure to wildlife. Liquid fertilizer application and fertigation are means of applying low amounts of nutrients on a frequent basis. These allow steady turf color and growth and minimize single application nutrient loads. Spot treat with pesticides whenever possible or practical.

9. **Prevent back-siphoning of the pesticide into your water source by keeping the end of the fill hose above the spray tank's water level**—The most pronounced means of

FIGURE 28–9 Wetlands and other aquatic features add distinction and beauty to well-planned and well-maintained golf facilities.

contaminating groundwater with pesticides is during the mixing and loading process, especially when near a water source or well. Check valves should be installed to prevent back-siphoning, although these can fail. An air space is the best protection.

10. **Locate mix-load sites and equipment rinsing sites at least 100 feet from surface water or from wells or sinkholes that have direct links to groundwater**—Dikes, sump pits, and containment pads may be necessary when these sites are closer than 100 feet. Also work on a flat, impermeable surface when mixing or loading pesticides and mix pesticides where a spill can be contained. Consider installing a closed system.

11. **Dispose all pesticide waste in accordance with local, state, and Federal laws to prevent contaminating groundwater through improper disposal of unused pesticides, pesticide containers, and container rinse water**—Do not dispose of excess pesticide rinsates by dumping them on the ground, especially in a concentrated manner. Also, do not place them in a septic tank or sewer system unless allowed by law. The best means of disposing of excess rinsates is by applying them on a legal site or through an approved degradation pit. Triple-rinse used containers and read and follow all label directions before use.

12. **Use ponds, basins, vegetation strips, riparian zones (e.g., bottomland hardwood, flood plain forests), and channels containing vegetation to filter or assimilate nutrients from drainage water**—The pond for irrigation reserve often serves to protect native surface waters. Created wetlands, which are less than 18 inches in depth, also are used to reduce run-off quantity and nutrient and pesticide discharge. Wetland flora create an environment in which bacteria facilitate the precipitation and degradation of pollutants. Algae, bacteria, sphagnum moss (*Sphagnum* sp.), cattails (*Typha* sp.), bulrushes (*Scirpus* sp.), and rushes (*Juncus* sp.) have been shown to remove nutrients, sulfate, and pesticides. Certainly, indigenous wetland plants could also be used. Many of these and other wetland plants are available either locally or through companies. Fish and invertebrates should not be overlooked. While invertebrates will most likely colonize the wetland, small fish should be stocked. Fish serve as excellent mosquito control. Generally, nearby soil is used for the wetland substrate. A suggested ratio of wetland size to drainage area is one acre for a 200-acre drainage area. Water flow velocity for wetlands is between 0.1 and 1.0 feet per second. Average hydraulic retention should be about five days. Reuse drainage water as an irrigation source when possible.

13. **Drainage from greens and tees should be spread in grassed or natural areas**—This allows the nutrients and pesticides to be absorbed before the water reaches a stream or pond. When this is not possible, subsurface drainage can be filtered through a sand-charcoal system to remove pollutants, or this drainage can be captured, stored in ponds, or stored in storage reserves for stormwater run-off collection, and reused as an irrigation source.

14. **Use a natural or constructed waterway or outlet maintained with vegetative cover to prevent soil erosion and to filter nutrients**—Dry ponds and golf course roughs serve in this capacity. Whenever possible, courses should be designed so irrigation and stormwater run-off move from the edges into the middle of the course. Drainage ditches should be bisected by small swales or natural or constructed wetlands. These geographic features slow down the water and allow for assimilation of nutrients and pesticides by the vegetation.

15. **Maintain an untreated (no spray) vegetative buffer zone of 10 to 50 feet adjacent to all water sources to help filter nutrients or pesticides from run-off**—Research has repetitively shown a vegetative buffer strip adjacent to water sources acts as a filter in preventing surface run-off of sediments, nutrients, and pesticides. Steeper-sloping land adjacent to water sources or slopes with slowly permeable soils such as clays should consider using the wider buffer strip range.

16. **Manage a decline in dissolved oxygen levels in water by controlling algae and nutrient run-off, as well as providing adequate aeration**—When problems such as fish kills occur, pesticides are often erroneously blamed. Low dissolved oxygen (DO) levels from algal blooms or natural pond turnover from temperature stratification or weather changes are most often the reason for the problem. Large fish are more sensitive to DO fluctuations that typically occur in early morning hours. Limited fish stocking might be considered. A water quality monitoring program may be considered to track water pH, dissolved oxygen levels, and possibly nutrient and certain pesticide levels. If a fish kill occurs, the following

steps and observations should immediately be taken to help pinpoint the cause (Meyer and Barclay, 1990):

- Date and time of day
- Location
- Estimated time kill began
- Water quality characteristics including:
  - Dissolved oxygen
  - pH
  - Water temperature
  - Water color
  - Water odor
  - Salinity
- Condition of fish seen (e.g., moribund, dead, or decaying)
- Condition of other organisms in the area
- Weather conditions of the day and previous day and night
- Physical appearance of fish (e.g., gills flared, mouth agape, spinal curvature, excessive mucus, lesions)
- Any other unusual characteristics, behaviors, or discolored vegetation
- If effluent water is used, heavy metal concentration and other toxic materials tested
- For possible organophosphate and carbamate exposure, fish samples can be tested for blood and brain cholinesterase, an enzyme responsible for normal nervous system function

17. **Test soil and tissues to optimize fertilization with the growth and use by turfgrasses to prevent excess use and possible run-off**—Use slow-release (e.g., coated) fertilizers when possible to minimize nitrogen losses through leaching. This book lists those optimum soil and tissue nutrient ranges for turfgrasses. These ranges should be checked frequently to ensure adequate but not excessive rates are available. Fertilizer use should also coincide with the growth needs of the turfgrass species.

18. **Prevent run-off by using irrigation water management so application rates do not exceed the infiltration capacity of the soil**—Watering according to evapotranspiration rates and soil moisture sensing devices, and using efficiently designed, installed, maintained, and frequently calibrated irrigation systems, not only saves precious water, but also minimizes surface and subsurface movement of any applied materials. Water to a depth just below the root system and water in early morning. Sloped areas should be irrigated in short, frequent intervals to minimize run-off. Excessive irrigation rates not only waste water, but potential nutrient and pesticide leaching may occur. Using effluent water sources also helps conserve and recycle this precious commodity.

19. **Avoid pesticide or nutrient applications just prior to anticipated rainfall events**—Rainfall, especially as thunderstorms, can release large amounts of water in a relatively short period. Soils cannot always absorb this water quantity in a short time period; thus, surface run-off occurs. Nutrient and pesticide movement in this run-off may occur, reducing the effectiveness of the products, but also potentially causing environmental problems. Applying nutrients or pesticides during the period of day (morning) that has the least chance of heavy rainfall, and irrigating them in immediately (if the label recommends this), are the best means of preventing run-off. Also, do not treat standing water puddles, as pesticides or nutrients may move with this water as it drains.

20. **Do not apply pesticides or nutrients to an area in excess of what can be quickly and efficiently watered-in**—Many turf installations can irrigate only so many acres at one time. Therefore, if more area is treated with a product than the irrigation system can immediately water-in, the chances of rainfall events or exposure problems increase, reducing the effectiveness of the product and potentially causing problems. For example, if the irrigation system can only cover 10 acres at once, then only these 10 acres should be treated and irrigated-in before the next 10 acres are treated.

21. **Return grass clippings when practical**—Grass clippings are a source of most major nutrients and, by returning them after mowing, this aids in recycling. Certain areas, such as golf greens, do not return clippings, as they would interfere with the surface. These clippings can be recycled by mulching or composting them and applying them to landscape beds.

22. **Follow IPM practices as previously outlined in addition to the proper storage, mixing, application, and disposal of pesticides, their containers, and rinsates**—IPM practices help optimize the use of pesticides without discriminate applications. An IPM program includes hiring a knowledgeable and appropriately trained superintendent, devising a written IPM plan, defining pest thresholds for specific turf sites, implementing appropriate cultural practices, monitoring (scouting) pest levels and activity, and maintaining accurate records.

23. **Frequently check and calibrate all pesticide and fertilizer applicators**—A maximum of 10 percent deviation should be allowed before recalibrating or changing worn nozzles or other parts.

24. **Install a well-balanced landscape with a mix of shrubs, trees, grass areas, and water features that sustain and encourage wildlife and a diversity of plants**—Wildlife needs a variety of plants to feed on and to provide habitats. This can be supplemented by providing feeders and nesting sites such as birdhouses. As part of this landscape, conservation areas to be established throughout the golf course should be considered.

25. **Keep detailed, accurate records on nutrient and pesticide applications**—Record keeping using a form similar to that on page 721 in Chapter 27 becomes necessary for agronomic reasons and in case any environmental problems occur. Without accurate records, a golf course invites finger-pointing, as well as possible accusations and liability associated with its operation. Contact Audubon International for greater details on creating and maintaining natural conservative areas and wildlife habitats. Becoming a fully certified Audubon Cooperative Sanctuary should be a long-term goal of most golf facilities. The certification process has six categories to complete to become a Certified Cooperative Sanctuary. These include:
    • Environmental planning
    • Member and public involvement
    • Integrated pest management
    • Wildlife and habitat management
    • Water conservation
    • Water quality management

26. **Provide periodic pesticide handling, and use training and updating sessions for all employees**—Technology, trends, and laws dealing with pesticide and nutrient purchasing, storage, mixing, application, and disposal constantly change. All employees who handle or are exposed to these materials should routinely attend updates on these trends. Numerous turfgrass and pesticide seminars, workshops, and training sessions are available where continuing educational credits or units are provided for certification. Contact your local Cooperative County Agent or golf course superintendent's association for the latest information on training events in your area.

CHAPTER
29

Sprayer and Spreader Calibration

INTRODUCTION

Proper sprayer/spreader calibration is extremely important to assure successful application of pesticides, fertilizers, lime, and seed. Applying excessive product wastes materials and money, may injure the turf, and can potentially cause unnecessary environmental contamination. Applying inadequate pesticide may result in poor control of the pest, resulting in undesirable turf and lost revenue. Constant observation of applicator operating conditions and frequent calibration of the equipment are necessary to avoid these problems (Figure 29–1). The Appendix lists helpful pesticide calibration formulas and metric conversion factors.

FIGURE 29–1 A properly calibrated and operating spray unit looks professional. It also potentially saves money and prevents problems such as spray drift.

SPRAYER CALIBRATION

The amount of chemical solution applied depends upon: (1) the sprayer's forward speed, (2) the pressure at the nozzle, (3) the size of the nozzles, and (4) the spacing of the nozzles on the boom. A change in any one of these will change the application rate.

Sprayer Speed

To measure travel speed, drive at the speed used for spraying. In addition, drive on a turfgrass area rather than a concrete or asphalt road, so the travel "test" conditions reflect "actual" conditions. The following formula may be used to determine miles per hour when the time necessary to travel a certain distance is known. Table 29–1 is a chart that converts the time to drive 300 feet to the speed in miles per hour (mph).

$$\text{speed } (mph) = \frac{\text{distance traveled (ft)} \times 60}{\text{time (sec) to travel distance} \times 88}$$

Example:

A superintendent fills his sprayer and marks off a 100-foot strip. He rides the course several times and determines an average of 20 seconds is needed to cover this area. What is the sprayer's speed, in mph?

Simply insert the distance and time values into the following formula.

$$\text{speed } (mph) = \frac{\text{distance (ft)} \times 60}{\text{time (sec)} \times 88} = \frac{100 \times 60}{20 \times 88} = 3.5 \text{ mph}$$

Pressure

The type of pesticide and nozzle being used often determines the pressure needed for spraying. The pesticide label usually recommends the sprayer pressure. Low pressures of 30 to 50 psi (pounds per square inch) may be sufficient for most turfgrass pesticides. Spray nozzles are designed to be operated within a certain pressure range (Table 29–2). Higher-than-recommended pressure increases delivery rate, reduces droplet size, and distorts the spray pattern. Lower pressures reduce delivery rate and prevent a full spray width pattern. Always follow the nozzle manufacturer's pressure recommendations as explained in their product catalog. Determine pressure at the nozzles or boom and not at the control valve.

TABLE 29–1 *Time (seconds) required to cover a specific distance to obtain a desired speed (mph).*

Desired mph	Feet per minute	Time required (seconds) to travel a distance of		
		100 ft.	200 ft.	300 ft.
2.0	176	34	68	102
2.5	220	27	54	81
3.0	264	23	45	68
3.5	308	20	39	58
4.0	352	17	33	51
4.5	395	15	30	45
5.0	440	14	27	41
6.0	528	—	23	34
7.0	616	—	19	29
8.0	704	—	17	26
9.0	792	—	15	23

Nozzles	Pressure (psi)
Flat fan	15 to 40
Even flat fan	15 to 40
Whirl chamber	5 to 25
Flooding nozzle	5 to 20

Nozzles

Nozzle spray patterns vary according to the intended pest target or application equipment. The main spray patterns include hollow cone, solid or full cone, regular flat fan, and even flat fan (Figure 29–2). Flat fans are most often used in turfgrass situations due to crop uniformity. Hollow cones, however, are sometimes used to apply fungicides or insecticides.

Commonly used nozzles have spray angles ranging from 65 to 120°. Wide angle types can be mounted lower to the ground or spaced further apart on the boom. Narrow angle types produce a more penetrating pattern, and tend to better force droplets through trash or foliage.

Most normal spraying operations in turf are easily and efficiently performed using regular flat fan nozzles. Manufacturers typically code their nozzles with a numbering system to indicate the spray angle and output for the particular nozzle. Spraying Systems, for example, code their regular flat fans with four numbers. The first two indicate the spray angle and the second two indicate the output. For example, 8002 tips have 80° angles and apply 0.2 gallons per minute at 40 psi. Delavan, another nozzle company, indicates the same nozzle as Delavan 80° LF2, meaning an 80° spray angle that applies 0.2 gpm at 40 psi. The LF indicates a regular flat fan. Manufacturer specifications should be consulted on nozzle types available and their required nozzle spacings, operating pressures, and application heights.

Select the spray nozzle most applicable for the pesticide being used. If you only have one sprayer and do not want to change nozzles for each type of pesticide applied, flat fan nozzles will be your best overall choice. These also are the best choice for broadcast spraying.

Nozzles are made of aluminum, brass, ceramic, plastic, stainless steel, or tungsten carbide. Brass tips are the most often used due to their lower costs, but tend to wear faster. Stainless-steel and tungsten carbide tips last up to 3.5 times longer than brass and are more resistant to abrasive powders, but are more expensive. No one nozzle material provides least costs with corrosion resistance. Check valves also are available that help eliminate "dribble" once the sprayer is turned off.

Nozzle manufacturers help applicators choose the right tip for each job by providing detailed performance charts. The pesticide applicator matches the specific needs of the job to the information on the chart to determine the tips and strainers to use. The charts include factors to be considered in order to choose appropriate nozzles—pressure, equipment speed, and spray volume. Charts showing spray volume in terms of both gallons per acre (gpa) and gallons per minute (gpm) allow the nozzle choice without further calculations. Some manufacturers, however, list only gallons per minute. Desired gallons per acre must be converted to gallons per minute as shown below.

$$\frac{\text{gallons per minute}}{(\text{per nozzle})} = \frac{\text{gallons per acre} \times \text{mph} \times \text{w}}{5,940}$$

where w = nozzle spacing (inches) on the boom sprayer.

Example:

If the pesticide label recommends a spray volume of 10 gallons of water per acre (gpa), the sprayer travels at four miles per hour (mph) and the spray boom has a 20-inch spacing between nozzles, find the output per nozzle.

$$gpm = \frac{\text{gpa} \times \text{mph} \times \text{w}}{5,940} = \frac{10 \text{ gpa} \times 4 \text{ mph} \times 20 \text{ inch}}{5,940} = \frac{0.13 \text{ gpm}}{(\text{per nozzle})}$$

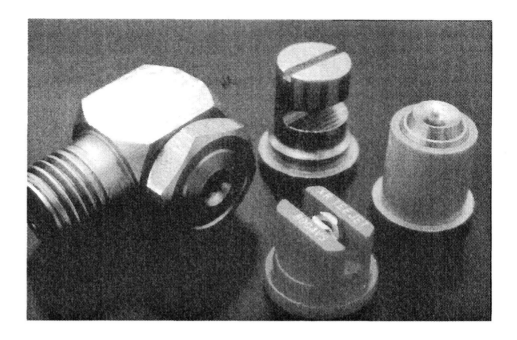

FIGURE 29–2 A wide array of sprayer nozzles are available. Flat fans are most often used in turfgrass situations due to crop uniformity. Hollow cones, however, are sometimes used to apply fungicides or insecticides.

Nozzle spacing usually is predetermined based on the type or make of the boom purchased. Nozzles usually are spaced 20, 30, or 40 inches apart along the boom. To obtain a uniform spray pattern with proper overlap, nozzles must be mounted at the proper height (e.g., boom height) above the target. Boom height varies depending on the nozzle spacing on the boom. For example, a 20-inch nozzle spacing allows nozzles to be mounted closer to the spray target than a 30-inch nozzle spacing does.

Each nozzle on a sprayer should apply nearly equal amounts of pesticide. For any one nozzle, the discharge should not vary by more than 10 percent below or above the average. Under normal operating pressure, collect the discharge from each nozzle for 30 seconds (Figure 29–3). Determine the average output and compare the output for each nozzle with the average. To evaluate the nozzles of a sprayer, the following test should be conducted.

First, measure and average the amount of water applied with the sprayer running for 30 seconds. For example, for individual nozzle readings, the fluid ounces collected in 30 seconds are shown.

Nozzle No. 1: 14 oz.
Nozzle No. 2: 18 oz.
Nozzle No. 3: 17 oz.
Nozzle No. 4: 15 oz.
Nozzle No. 5: 16 oz.
TOTAL   80 oz.

Average = 16 oz. per nozzle (80 oz. ÷ 5)

Next, a 10 percent allowance for the nozzles should be determined.

10% of 16 oz. is 1.6 oz. (16 oz. × 0.10)

16.0 oz. + 1.6 oz (10% greater) = 17.6 oz.

16.0 oz. − 1.6 oz. (10% less) = 14.4 oz.

The range of 14.4 to 17.6 ounce allows for a ±10 percent variation for these five nozzles. Therefore, Nozzles No. 1 and 2 fall outside the ±10 percent variation and should be replaced.

To convert the output per nozzle from ounces to gallons per minute (gpm), the following equation is used:

$$gpm = \frac{(\text{ounces per nozzle in 30 seconds*}) \times 2}{128}$$

*Use the average discharge per nozzle as previously calculated.

FIGURE 29–3 Calibrating a sprayer includes measuring the output from each nozzle on the boom to ensure uniformity. Generally, if the output for any one nozzle varies by more than 10 percent below or above the average of the other boom nozzles, it should be replaced.

Example:

A broad spectrum fungicide is needed on your bentgrass greens for brown patch control. You decide to use Fung-No-Mo as the fungicide and remembered flat fan nozzles spaced 20 inches apart on the boom were the best choice for this application. The label suggests this material be applied in a volume of 20 to 30 gpa, with water as the carrier, and at a pressure of 30 to 40 psi. Decide on the best nozzle type for this application.

First, determine the output required per nozzle at each recommended spray pressure.

For 20 gpa	For 30 gpa
$gpm = \dfrac{\text{gallons per acre} \times \text{mph} \times \text{w}}{5{,}940}$ $= \dfrac{20 \times 5 \times 20}{5{,}940}$ $= 0.34$	$gpm = \dfrac{\text{gallons per acre} \times \text{mph} \times \text{w}}{5{,}940}$ $= \dfrac{30 \times 5 \times 20}{5{,}940}$ $= 0.51$

Next, refer to the nozzle catalog to select a size of flat fan nozzle that delivers between 0.34 and 0.51 gpm at pressures of 30 to 40 psi.

Sprayer Pressure and Speed Changes

If only minor changes are needed in the output of a sprayer, adjusting pressure is one means of achieving this. However, major changes in output should be adjusted by other means as all types of nozzles have a certain pressure range within which they should be operated. The following formula is used to determine the effects of pressure on output.

Flow Rate (as influenced by pressure)

$$\frac{gpm_1}{gpm_2} = \frac{\sqrt{psi_1}}{\sqrt{psi_2}} \quad \text{or} \quad gpa_2 = gpa_1 \times \sqrt{\frac{psi_2}{psi_1}} \quad \text{or} \quad psi_2 = psi_1 \times \left(\frac{gpa_2}{gpa_1}\right)^2$$

To double output, pressure must be increased fourfold. To cut output in half, pressure must be decreased fourfold.

For any change in travel speed (mph), calculate the resulting gpa_2 by:

$$gpa_2 = \frac{gpa_1 \times mph_1}{mph_2} \quad \text{or} \quad \frac{gpa_1}{gpa_2} = \frac{mph_2}{mph_1} \quad \text{or} \quad mph_2 = \frac{gpa_1 \times mph_1}{gpa_2}$$

By doubling travel speed, sprayer output per acre is cut in half. By reducing travel speed to one-half of the original speed, sprayer output per acre is doubled.

Example:

A superintendent finds it takes 7 minutes, 15 seconds to empty a 40-gallon tank operated at 25 psi. However, he wishes to extend this time to 7 minutes, 45 seconds. How is this done?

First, find the gpm for each time period:

$$gpm_1 = 40 \text{ gal}/7.25 \text{ min} = 5.52$$

$$gpm_2 = 40 \text{ gal}/7.75 \text{ min} = 5.16$$

Now, insert this data into the following:

$$psi_2 = psi_1 \times \left(\frac{gpa_2}{gpa_1}\right)^2 = psi_2 = 25 \times \left(\frac{5.16}{5.52}\right)^2 = 21.89 \text{ psi}$$

Now the superintendent wants to adjust the sprayer speed. If it applies 20 gpa at four mph, what will be the output if speed is increased to eight mph?

Again, set up the formula to determine this:

$$\frac{gpa_1}{gpa_2} = \frac{mph_2}{mph_1}$$

$gpa_1 = 20$

$mph_1 = 4$

$mph_2 = 8$ $\qquad \frac{20}{gpa_2} = \frac{8}{4} \qquad gpa_2 = 10$

$gpa_2 = X$

Determining Sprayer Output

Once the sprayer speed (mph) and nozzle discharge (gpm) are determined as previously described, sprayer output in gallons per acre (gpa) is calculated.

Calculate gallons per acre (gpa) using the following formula. If the resulting output appears to be too high or too low, remember that altering speed or adjusting pressure will alter output. However, do not deviate beyond the manufacturer's recommendations. The other alternative is to reevaluate your nozzle selection to determine if you selected the proper one based on expected nozzle output and pressure.

$$gpa = \frac{gpm \text{ per nozzle} \times 5,940}{mph \times \text{ nozzle spacing (inches)}}$$

To determine gallons per 1,000 square feet, divide the gpa value by 43.56.

Example:

A superintendent wishes to apply one pound of active ingredient per acre of 2,4-D amine at 30 gpa and at 25 psi. The formulation of 2,4-D purchased has four pounds of active ingredient per gallon. You have 338,000 square feet to treat. Nozzle spacing on the boom is 19 inches and the spray tank holds 35 gallons.

1. You check the sprayer speed on a fairway and find it takes 34 seconds to travel 200 feet. What is your speed in *mph*?

$$\text{speed } (mph) = \frac{\text{distance traveled (ft)} \times 60}{\text{time (sec) to travel distance} \times 88} = \frac{200 \text{ ft} \times 60}{34 \text{ sec} \times 88} = 4 \text{ mph}$$

2. You catch the following output of the nozzles when operated at 25 psi. Should any need replacing?

Nozzle #	Ounces/30 sec
1	29
2	29
3	30
4	31
5	31
6	30
7	31
8	29

The average output of these nozzles is 30 ounces per 30 seconds. If a 10 percent error term is allowed, then any nozzles with an output ±3 ounces per 30 seconds higher or lower than 30 ounces per 30 seconds would need replacing. Since this range would then be 27 to 33 ounces per 30 seconds and all current nozzles fall within this, none need replacing.

3. What is your sprayer output (*gpa*)?

You first need to determine the average gallons per minute for each nozzle. From the previous step you know the average output is 30 ounces per 30 seconds. This equals 60 ounces per minute. Since 128 ounces are in each gallon, the following is calculated.

$$30 \text{ oz/30 sec} \times 2 = 60 \text{ oz/min}$$

$$60 \text{ oz/min} \times \text{gal/128 oz} = 0.47 \text{ gal/min}$$

$$gpa = \frac{gpm \text{ per nozzle} \times 5{,}940}{mph \times \text{nozzle spacing (inches)}} = \frac{0.47 \text{ gpm} \times 5{,}940}{4 \text{ mph} \times 19 \text{ in.}} = 36.7 \text{ or } 37$$

4. How much herbicide would you need to buy to treat the 338,000 square feet?

First, determine the number of acres in 338,000 square feet.

$$338{,}000 \text{ sq.ft.} \times \frac{1 \text{ acre}}{43{,}560 \text{ sq.ft.}} = 7.8 \text{ acres}$$

Next, determine the amount of formulated herbicide needed per acre.

$$\frac{1 \text{ lb ai}}{\text{acre}} \times \frac{1 \text{ gal}}{4 \text{ lb ai}} = 0.25 \text{ gal (or 1 qt)/acre}$$

Finally, combine these two previous steps to find the total amount of herbicide needed for the total area.

$$0.25 \text{ gal/acre} \times 7.8 \text{ acres total} = 2 \text{ gal total (approximately)}$$

5. How many ounces of this herbicide are needed to make a total spray volume of 35 gallons?

First, find the amount of gallons per tank needed for the appropriate herbicide application rate.

$$\frac{35 \text{ gal}}{\text{tank}} \times \frac{\text{acre}}{34 \text{ gal}} \times \frac{0.25 \text{ gal}}{\text{acre}} = \frac{0.26 \text{ gal}}{\text{tank}}$$

Next, convert this value to ounces (oz):

$$\frac{0.26 \text{ gal}}{\text{tank}} \times \frac{128 \text{ oz}}{\text{gal}} = 33 \text{ ounces per tank}$$

To convert to pints (pts):

$$\frac{0.26 \text{ gal}}{\text{tank}} \times \frac{8 \text{ pts}}{\text{gal}} = 2.08 \text{ pints per tank}$$

To convert to quarts (qts):

$$\frac{0.26 \text{ gal}}{\text{tank}} \times \frac{4 \text{ qts}}{\text{gal}} = 1.04 \text{ quarts per tank}$$

To convert to milliliters (ml):

$$\frac{0.26 \text{ gal}}{\text{tank}} \times \frac{3,785 \text{ ml}}{\text{gal}} = 984 \text{ ml per tank}$$

6. Lastly, you need to know how many acres can be applied with a full tank of mixture. Use the following formula to determine this.

$$\text{acres per tank} = \frac{\text{tank volume (gal)}}{\text{gpa}} = \frac{35 \text{ gal/tank}}{34 \text{ gal/acre}} = 1.03 \text{ acres per tank}$$

Another way to determine how much pesticide to add per tank is to set up a ratio:

$$\frac{\text{pesticide rate}}{\text{gpa}} = \frac{X \text{ amount pesticide}}{\text{tank size (gal)}}$$

In the previous example:

$$\frac{1 \text{ qt pesticide per acre}}{34 \text{ gpa}} = \frac{X \text{ qt pesticide}}{35 \text{ gal tank}}$$

$$\frac{(1 \text{ qt})(35 \text{ gal})}{34 \text{ gpa}} = X \text{ qt pesticide per tank}$$

$$1.03 \text{ qt pesticide per 35 gal tank} = X$$

Adding Adjuvants

Many pesticides require that various adjuvants (crop oils, surfactants, etc.) be added to the spray solution. Most of these are added on a volume basis. To determine this, you would go through the same type of calculations that determined how much pesticide needed to be added per tank.

Example:

We are broadcasting an insecticide and the label suggests a crop oil concentrate be added at 1 percent volume of crop oil per volume of spray tank. Our sprayer is calibrated to apply 20 gpa and the tank holds 100 gallons. For a full tank, how much crop oil concentrate is needed?

$$\frac{100 \text{ gal}}{\text{tank}} \times 1\% \text{ (or 0.01)} = 1 \text{ gal of crop oil per 100 gal tank}$$

To add 0.25 percent nonionic surfactant per tank, the following is calculated.

$$\frac{100 \text{ gal}}{\text{tank}} \times 0.25\% \text{ (or 0.0025)} = 0.25 \text{ gal (or 1 qt) of nonionic surfactant per 100 gal tank}$$

Dilutions

Many turf products, including pesticides, are formulated as concentrated liquids for ease of handling and to save costs. Typically, these concentrated liquids must be diluted before being applied. Hose-on applicators often are calibrated where the concentrate is diluted by siphoning in a ratio to the volume of water (also called the diluent) that passes through the hose. Use the following formula for dilution problems.

$$\text{amount of concentrate needed} = \frac{\% \text{ ai of desired final concentration} \times \text{tank size}}{\% \text{ ai of initial product concentration}}$$

Example:

Five gallons of a 15 percent chlorox solution is desired to sterilize hand tools. How much chlorox is needed?

(**Note:** Chlorox is bought as a 100 percent concentrate.)

$$\text{amount of concentrate needed} = \frac{0.15 \times 5 \text{ gallons}}{100\%} = 0.75 \text{ gal or } 96 \text{ oz}$$

Add 96 ounces of chlorox to the tank and bring the final solution volume to five gallons.

Example:

Two gallons of 15 percent herbicide solution is desired to spot treat weeds. How much herbicide (4 lb ai/gal formulation) is needed? (Assume this herbicide is bought as a 50 percent concentrate.)

$$\text{amount of concentrate needed} = \frac{0.15 \times 2 \text{ gallons}}{0.5} = 0.6 \text{ gal or } 4.8 \text{ pints}$$

Add 4.8 pints to the tank and bring the final solution volume to two gallons.

Example:

A hose-on sprayer applied 2.5 gallons of spray while siphoning two quarts out of a container.

1. If a fungicide is to be applied at a rate of three ounces per gallon of water, how should the stock solution be mixed?

$$\text{amount of concentrate needed} = \frac{\text{amount of desired final concentration} \times \text{tank size}}{\text{amount of initial product concentration}}$$

$$= \frac{3 \text{ oz/gal} \times 2.5 \text{ gal}}{0.5 \text{ gal (or 2 qts)}} = 15 \text{ oz/gal}$$

Therefore, add 15 ounces of the fungicide and add water to bring the final solution volume to one gallon.

2. What is the ppm of this final solution?

One gallon of water weighs 133 ounces. Therefore, insert the following:

$$\text{ppm} = \frac{\text{wt. of material to be used} \times 1{,}000{,}000}{\text{wt. of the tank mixture}} = \frac{15 \text{ oz} \times 1{,}000{,}000}{133 \text{ oz}}$$

$$\text{ppm} = 112{,}782 \text{ ppm}$$

Converting Between Active Ingredients and Formulated Product

Pesticide recommendations are often given in pounds of active ingredient (ai) per acre (lb ai/a) because several different trade names and formulations may accompany a particular chemical. For example, mancozeb is the common name of a fungicide; however, trade names include Fore, Dithane, Formec, and Protect. Each product may have a different formulation (or strength); thus, pounds of active ingredient per acre provide the basic rate regardless of formulation. Therefore, turf managers should be able to make the necessary calculations from pounds or gallons or pints of product to pounds of active ingredient and vice versa. The following formula determines liquid conversion:

$$\text{liquid conversion:} \frac{\text{lb ai recommended/acre}}{\text{lb ai/gal}} = \text{gal of material needed/acre}$$

Wettable powders (WP), soluble powders (SP), dry flowables (DF), and water-dispersible granules (WDG) are formulated in percent active ingredient (%ai) and require the following for conversion:

$$\text{powder conversion:} \frac{\text{lb ai recommended/acre}}{\% \text{ ai of material}} = \text{lb material needed/acre}$$

Example:

To control a certain insect, the superintendent tells you to apply 0.5 pounds of active ingredient per acre (often abbreviated lb ai/a) of Trumpet 4E liquid insecticide over 54 acres. How much Trumpet 4 should you buy?

To determine the total pounds of active ingredient needed to treat 54 acres,

$$54 \text{ acres to treat} \times 0.5 \text{ lb ai/a} = 27 \text{ lb ai needed}$$

To find the total amount of the 4E formulation of Trumpet insecticide needed,

$$27 \text{ lb ai needed} \div 4 \text{ lb ai/gal} = 6.75 \text{ gallons of Trumpet 4 needed to treat 54 acres at 0.5 lb ai/a}$$

If you find the 4E formulation of Trumpet is no longer available, but instead a 75DF formulation is, then the following is calculated (the 75DF formulation contains 75 percent active ingredient).

$$27 \text{ lb ai needed} \div 0.75 \text{ active} = 36 \text{ lb of Trumpet 75DF needed to treat 54 acres at the 0.5 lb ai/a rate}$$

Acid Equivalents of Salts and Esters

Some pesticides, particularly herbicides, are formulated as either salts, esters, or both. Recommendations are often based on pounds of the acid equivalent of the active ingredient per acre to provide standardization, since salt and ester forms vary in weight. The acid equivalent of a salt or ester is the portion of the molecule that is the parent acid form of the molecule.

Generally, the salt or ester portion of a pesticide is inactive; thus, the acid portion of this salt or ester molecule is the active portion. When determining the acid equivalent rate of a salt or ester form of a pesticide, it is necessary to adjust the rate to account for the heavier weight of the salt or ester. This is usually reported in terms of pounds of acid equivalent per gallon.

SPRAYER PUMPS

Pumps used on spray equipment create the required amount of pressure to force spray solution through the nozzles. Pumps also provide agitation if the sprayer has a hydraulic agitation system. The three major types of low-pressure pumps include (Table 29–3) **roller, centrifugal** (or **turbine**), and **diaphragm**. **Piston** pumps are also used in some special situations when high pressure is needed (Figure 29–4).

Pumps are also classified as **positive** or **nonpositive** displacement. With positive displacement, the pump output is independent of pressure. A constant volume of liquid is displaced with each pump stroke or revolution. Positive type pump sprayers require a pressure relief valve, or some sort of pressure control device to recirculate liquid not being used for spraying back to the nurse tank. These pumps also are self-priming; therefore, they do not need to be mounted below

TABLE 29–3 *Characteristics of various sprayer pump types.*

Pump type	Pressure range (psi)	Flow rate (gpm)	Type displacement	Comments
Roller	5 to 300	1 to 35	Positive	Low costs, ease of service, self-priming, operates at PTO speeds, medium volume, short life if WPs used.
Centrifugal (or Turbine)	5 to 100	20 to 120	Nonpositive	Medium costs, handles all materials, high volume, long life, low pressure, not self-priming, requires high PTO speed.
Piston	400 to 1,000	5 to 60	Positive	High costs, handles all materials, wear resistant, self-priming, high pressure, needs surge tank, long life.
Diaphragm	75 to 100	15 to 60	Positive	High costs, long life, resistant to most chemicals, self-priming, needs surge tank.

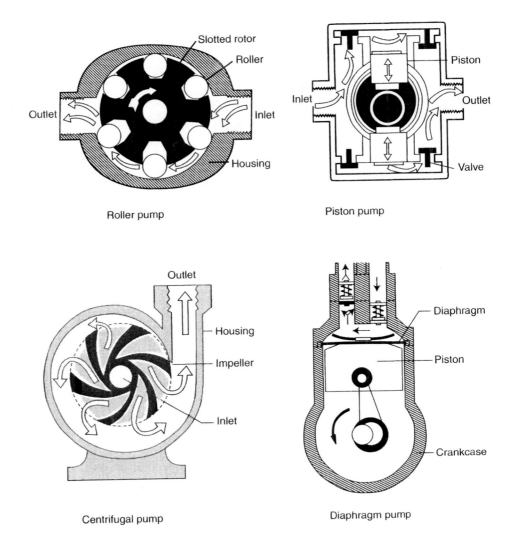

FIGURE 29–4   A side
view of various sprayer pump
types used most often in turf
applications.

Slotted rotor

Roller

Outlet

Inlet

Housing

Roller pump

Piston

Inlet

Outlet

Valve

Piston pump

Outlet

Housing

Impeller

Inlet

Centrifugal pump

Diaphragm

Piston

Crankcase

Diaphragm pump

the tank level in order to be primed or start pumping. Positive displacement pumps include the
piston pump, diaphragm pump, and the roller pump operating at low pressures.

Nonpositive displacement pumps (primarily centrifugal) have output that is dependent upon
pressure; thus, output decreases if pressure increases. They do not require bypass relief valves and
are not self-priming. Nonpositive pumps generally have longer life spans than positive displacement pumps, which require close housing of rotary parts and easily wear, especially from abrasive
suspensions. The power to drive both types of pumps include tractor power take-off (PTO), ground
wheel traction drive, or separate fuel-driven engines or electric motors. Nonpositive displacement
pumps include the centrifugal pump and the roller pump when operated at higher pressures.

Roller Pumps

Roller pumps have elliptically shaped inner walls of the pump housing with a slotted rotor containing rollers in the slots. Spray solution accumulates in these slots since more space is located
between the rotor and pump housing on the intake side. As the rotor turns toward the outlet side,
less space occurs between the rotor and housing, creating pressure. As the roller pushes back into
the slot, the spray solution is forced out. They are often preferred for their low-pressure operation
(40 to 280 psi) and deliver 5 to 40 gallons per acre.

Roller pumps are considered positive displacement, but do experience some decline in output as pressure is increased. They require a pressure relief or control device to divert unsprayed
solution back to the tank. They have the advantages of being low in initial costs and in maintenance. They are compact in size in relation to their capacity and operate at tractor PTO speeds.
They prime easily, and have relatively long life expectancies when properly operated. Their chief

disadvantage is being sensitive to abrasive pesticide formulations (e.g., WP, DF, F, sand, and grit). Using rubber rollers helps extend the pump's lifespan if abrasive materials are used often. Roller pumps are widely used for turfgrass spray operations.

Centrifugal Pumps

Centrifugal pumps create pressure by spinning a fly wheel within the pump housing; this centrifugal force creates pressure. The spray material feeds into the center of a high-speed impeller, and is thrown outward, creating pressure in the outlet line. Centrifugal pumps are considered nonpositive displacement since their output decreases as pressure increases; thus, they are not self-priming. Their chief advantages include being able to handle suspensions well, being resistant to wear, and having relatively long operating lives. They also have a high capacity (70 to 130 gpm at 30 to 40 psi), simple maintenance, and no need for pressure relief valves. They are considered high-volume, low-pressure pumps.

Disadvantages include the limited low pressure, usually 50 psi or less. They tend to be hard to prime, requiring positive inlet pressure, or are placed below the tank, using a small vent at the top of the pump to allow trapped air to escape to prevent vapor lock. Normal tractor speed also may be too slow, requiring a step-up gear box or pulley arrangement. **Turbine pumps** are similar to centrifugal pumps but can operate as a direct drive from the PTO due to their low operating speeds; thus, they do not require step-up mechanisms.

Diaphragm Pumps

Diaphragm pumps work on a piston action where a flexible diaphragm moves up and down in a sealed chamber, creating suction and pressure. As the diaphragm moves up, suction is created and the spray material is drawn into the chamber. As the diaphragm moves down, pressure is created and the spray material is forced out of the chamber through a discharge valve. They are self-priming positive displacement pumps and require less horsepower than comparable pumps with similar flow and pressure ratings. Medium- to high-pressure models (75 to 100 psi and higher) are available, creating flow rates ranging from 15 to 50 gpm. Abrasive materials can successfully be used with diaphragm pumps, although the diaphragm should be resistant to other caustic materials.

Piston Pumps

Piston pumps work on the basic principle of pistons in a motor where the intake stroke draws the liquid in through one valve, and the output stroke forces the liquid out through another valve. Piston pumps are low-volume, high-pressure capacity pumps. They are true positive displacement, meaning the output is independent of pressure. They tend to handle suspensions well, are resistant to wear, and have relatively long life spans. They also prime easily and handle high pressures (up to 600 psi or more). Disadvantages include a higher purchase price, the need for a surge tank, and they are generally too large to mount directly on most tractor PTOs.

CALIBRATING GRANULAR SPREADERS

Dry pesticide or fertilizer application is only effective if uniform coverage is ensured. These can be applied with either a drop (gravity) spreader or a rotary (centrifugal) spreader.

A drop spreader has the advantage of applying a fairly exact pattern since this is limited to the distance between the wheels. This method also allows a "tight" pattern (line) to be cut but requires each pass to exactly meet with the previous one or skips will be noticeable. Wide (>6 feet) drop spreaders can become cumbersome in the landscape by limiting access around trees and shrubs and getting through gates. The agitator in the bottom of the drop spreader's hopper also may break the coating of some slow-release fertilizers.

The cyclone (also known as rotary or centrifugal) spreader generally has a wider pattern of distribution compared to a drop spreader and thus can cover a larger area in a short time. The application pattern of the cyclone spreader also gradually diminishes away from the machine, reducing the probability of an application skip. The uneven, wide pattern of the cyclone spreader is initially harder to calibrate, and heavier particles tend to sling farther away from the machine. However, proper calibration and experience minimize these incidents.

A recent improvement in spreader technology is the use of air to apply the material to the turf. This technique produces a fairly wide pattern (like the cyclone spreader) that is somewhat exact (like the drop spreader) without damaging the granules or slinging heavier particles farther. Wind and rain effects also are reduced using the technology but initial equipment expense and application expertise are higher.

Spreader calibration involves measurement of the granular output as the spreader is operated over a known area. One way to ensure uniform application of material is to divide the material into two equal portions. Use a spreader calibration that will deliver one-half the correct amount of material. Make an application over the entire area, turn the spreader direction ninety degrees (90°) from the initial application, and make a second application; this eliminates skips in the coverage. Accordingly, calibration of the spreader should be based on one-half the desired application rates. A flat surface, a method of collecting the material, and a scale for weighing the material is needed for calibration. The following sequence of steps will aid in calibrating a fertilizer spreader.

Calibrating a Drop-Type (Gravity) Spreader

Follow these steps, in order, to calibrate your drop-type (gravity) spreader.

1. Check the spreader to make certain all the parts are functioning properly.
2. Mark off an area, multiplying it by the width of the spreader to give 100 square feet of area. For example, the length required for a 1 1/2-, 2-, and 3-foot spreader is 66 2/3, 50, and 33 1/3 feet, respectively.
3. Fill the spreader with the material you wish to apply (fertilizer, seed, pesticide, lime, other). Fill the hopper only to the level you will have when the material will actually be applied.
4. Make several trial runs over the area and practice opening the spreader as you cross the starting line and closing it at the finish line. Opening the spreader before it is in motion will result in nonuniform distribution. Walk at a pace that will be used when actually applying the material. Open and close the spreader gradually, not in a fast, jerky motion.
5. The weight of the material applied by the spreader must be determined. It can be swept up from a hard surface or caught on a large piece of paper or plastic. The easiest method is to attach a catch pan (cardboard works nicely) under the spreader openings; the material in the catch pan during the test run can determine how much was applied (Figure 29–5).
6. Begin calibration at the lowest setting and proceed at progressively higher settings (larger openings). The more trials at a given setting, the better will be the average rate of application. Three trials at a given setting are usually enough to obtain a reliable application rate. Weigh the material and record the information on each trial run for future use.
7. One of the calibrated settings will approximate the correct rate of material. Careful calibration is suggested for the complete spreader range. Settings are not necessarily linear; therefore, half of a particular application rate may not necessarily be obtained by using a setting number of half the original.

EXAMPLE:
You want to calibrate a spreader to apply one pound of nitrogen per 1,000 square feet using a 10-10-10 fertilizer. This calculates to 10 pounds of fertilizer per 1,000 square feet since the material is 10 percent nitrogen (10% × 10 pounds = 1 pound nitrogen). Since the area for calibration trials is in only 100 square feet, apply one-tenth of 10 pounds, or one pound of fertilizer, per 100 square feet. The spreader setting should be 11 for this example if you obtain the following results shown from your calibration trials with your spreader. If the desired application rate was 0.5 pound of nitrogen (5 pounds of material per 1,000 square feet or 0.5 pound per 100 square feet), a setting of 7 should be used.

Setting	Output (oz)
1	2
3	3
5	6
7	8
9	10
11	16

8. The same calibration procedure is used for any material you want to apply. Since the quantity applied depends upon the physical properties of the material, the same settings cannot be used for different materials, even if the ratios are the same. Once the spreader is calibrated and set for the proper rate, any size area can be accurately treated.

EXAMPLE:

The application rate for a granular insecticide is three pounds of product per 1,000 square feet. Your applicator is four feet wide and you decide to catch the output when pushed for 200 feet. How much should be caught to calibrate the spreader to give three pounds per 1,000 square feet?

First, determine the amount of total material needed to be caught in the area used for calibration.

4 ft wide spreader × 200 ft long = 800 sq.ft. of total area being treated

Next, set up a ratio involving the rate needed on a 1,000 square foot basis to the actual area being treated.

$$\frac{3 \text{ lb}}{2,000 \text{ sq.ft.}} = \frac{X \text{ lb}}{800 \text{ sq.ft.}}$$

$$\frac{(3)(800)}{2,000} = 1.2 \text{ lb}/800 \text{ sq.ft.}$$

Now you need to use a catch basin to collect the output as you travel the 200 feet. The output is then weighed and the spreader setting adjusted to give more or less output as needed. Repeat this step until the unit is set to apply 1.2 pounds in 200 feet traveled.

Calibrating a Rotary (Centrifugal) or Pendulum Spreader

It is important the "effective" width of application be determined first. Follow these steps, in order, to calibrate your rotary (centrifugal) spreader.

1. Check the spreader to make certain all parts are operating properly.
2. Fill the hopper about half full with the material you plan to apply and run it with the spreader setting about half open (medium setting). Make the application on bare ground or a hard surface where the width of surface covered by the material can be measured.

3. Rotary spreaders do not apply a constant amount of material across the entire width of application. More material is applied toward the center and less at the edges. For this reason, the width of application is accurate for a constant application rate only at about two-thirds (60 to 70 percent) of the actual width measured.

EXAMPLE:
If the application width is 12 feet, only about eight feet (or four feet across both sides of the spreader), within the band of application, is receiving approximately the same application rate. The other two feet on each edge, respectively, receive much less material than the center area. Once this "effective" width is determined, calibration is fairly simple.

4. Mark off a test distance that, when multiplied by the effective width, will give you a 1,000 square feet area. For this example, assume the "effective" width is 10 feet. The test strip will then be 100 feet long since width times length is 10×100 or 1,000 square feet.

Note: This calculation is based on "effective" width of application and not the total width.

5. Determine the amount of material to be applied.

EXAMPLE:
To apply one pound of nitrogen per 1,000 square feet using a 16-4-8 fertilizer, 6.25 pounds of material should be applied per 1,000 square feet.

6. Fill the hopper with a known weight of fertilizer and adjust the spreader to the lowest setting that will allow the material to flow. Push the spreader down the center of the test area, opening the hopper at the starting line and closing it at the finish. Weigh the material left in the spreader and subtract the amount from the starting weight to determine the amount used per 1,000 square feet. The beginning weight minus the ending weight tells how much material was applied per 1,000 square feet.

7. Repeat the preceding step at successively greater settings (openings) and record the material applied at each setting.

8. Select the spreader setting that most closely applies the desired rate of material, set the spreader accordingly, and use it on any size area. To obtain uniform spread of material, remember to set the spreader at half the desired rate of application and make two passes at 90° to each other. Strive for proper spread overlap during application.

If the "effective" width is 10 feet, after each pass, move the spreader over 10 feet from the center of the tire tracks. This will give a fairly constant rate of application over the entire area.

A simpler way to use a centrifugal spreader is to determine the amount of material to apply on a given area and then set the spreader at a low setting and apply this amount in several directions.

EXAMPLE:
A rate of granular fungicide is 2.5 pounds of product per 1,000 square feet. The nursery green to be treated is 40 feet by 150 feet. How much fungicide should go on the area?
First, find the total amount of area to be treated.

$$40 \text{ ft} \times 150 \text{ ft} = 6,000 \text{ sq.ft. to treat}$$

Next, set up a ratio to convert the amount needed on a 1,000 square foot basis to the actual 6,000 square foot green area.

$$\frac{2.5 \text{ lb}}{1,000 \text{ sq.ft.}} = \frac{X \text{ lb}}{6,000 \text{ sq.ft}}$$

$$\frac{(2.5)(6,000)}{1,000} = X$$

$$X = 15 \text{ pounds}$$

Finally, place the 15 pounds of fungicide into the spreader hopper and set the opening in the bottom of the applicator to give a low rate of material flow. Push the spreader over the area to be treated until all of the fungicide has been applied. To improve the uniformity of application with this type of spreader, you should always go over the area in at least two directions.

TURF SPRAYER/SPREADER CALIBRATION PROBLEMS

1. A new insecticide is introduced (Cricket-Kill) that is a 4E. Ponderosa CC wants to use this at a rate of 0.83 pounds active ingredient per acre. The superintendent calibrated his sprayer and found the speed was 240 feet in 53 seconds and measured a nozzle spacing of 20 inches with five nozzles per boom and caught 18 ounces per nozzle in this time.
   a. How many milliliters of product are required to treat 7.8 acres? (*answer:* 6,126 ml or 1.6 gal total)
   b. How many gallons of water are required to treat 7.8 acres? (*answer:* 119 gal)
   c. What is the dilution rate of product:water resulting in this application? (*answer:* 1.6 gal product:119 gal water or 1:75)
   d. Calculate the nozzle flow rate (gpm/noz). (*answer:* 0.16 gpm/noz)
2. LawnGreen's new spray gun, Hose-All, puts out 0.5 gallons in one minute. If the desired output is 25 gpa,
   a. How much material should be applied in 21 feet × 21 feet and how long will it take? (*answer:* 0.26 gal and 30.3 sec)
   b. A new spreader-sticker, Wet-All, has a recommended concentration of 0.33 percent by volume. How much should be added to a 378,500 milliliters tank? (*answer:* 0.33 gal or 1,249 ml)
3. Ronstar 2G is applied at a rate of three pounds per 1,000 square feet. Your clubhouse lawn is 55 × 38 feet. How much material is needed and how much active material is being applied on a per-acre basis? (*answer:* 6.27 lbs and 2.61 lb ai/a)
4. Clemson University Golf Club has a sprayer that holds 40 gallons with eight nozzles spaced 19 inches apart. Dr. Boyd tells you to apply one pound of active ingredient per acre of 2,4-D amine between 20 and 30 gpa and at 25 psi. Dacamine 4L is used. Eight greens average 4,520 square feet each, so you assume all 18 measure this (plus a practice green and a nursery green). It takes 34 seconds for the sprayer to travel 200 feet.
   a. What is your speed (mph)? (*answer:* 4)
   b. What type of nozzle would you select and what is the recommended spray height for these? (*answer:* stainless steel or brass LP 11003; height = 15 to 18 inches)
   c. What size of nozzle would you select? (*answer:* Manufacturer dependent, 8004 or 8005 are possibilities)
   d. At 25 psi you find the following outputs:

Nozzle #	Oz/30 sec	Nozzle #	Oz/30 sec
1	29	5	25
2	29	6	34
3	30	7	28
4	31	8	33

   Which, if any, nozzles need replacing? (*answer:* 5, 6, 8)
   e. What is the sprayer output (gpa)? (*answer:* ~37)
   f. How much herbicide is needed to treat the greens? (*answer:* 0.52 gal or ≈2 qts or ≈66.6 oz)
   g. How many ounces of herbicide would be added to enough water to make a total spray volume of 35 gallons? (*answer:* ~31 oz)
   h. If 0.25 percent v/v surfactant is required, how many milliliters will be needed per tank? (*answer:* 331 ml for 35 gal tank or 379 ml for 40 gal tank)
   i. How many tanks would be needed to cover 10.4 acres? (*answer:* 11.24 tanks)
   j. Will Holroyd, Superintendent, finds it takes 5 minutes, 35 seconds to empty the 40 gallon tank at 23 psi. However, he wants this extended to six minutes. How is this done? (*answer:* change psi to 21.89)
   k. If you have sprayed 10 out of 12 acres of turf and run out of material, how much spray solution is needed to finish up? (*answer:* 73 gal + 2 qts of 2,4-D)

l. Draw the spray pattern from two 11004 nozzles on a 19-inch spacing. Label all appropriate angles and distances. (*answer:* 19-inch spacing with 110° angle spray pattern with 20 percent overlap and a height of 14 inches)

m. A repeat application is needed and Jim has a half-full tank (remember, a full tank equals 40 gal) left over from the first spray. However, he must switch to a 3.3L formulation of 2,4-D. How much of the new formulation must Jim add to fill this tank at the proper rate of active material? (*answer:* 21.3 oz product/20 gal tank)

5. A roadside applicator wishes to calibrate a right-of-way sprayer to apply 10 gpa. The single nozzle sprays 30 feet wide and the truck averages 5 mph. What flow rate (gpm) is required? (*answer:* 3.03)

6. The assistant superintendent is getting ready to overseed his greens with *Poa trivialis*. The application rate is eight pounds of seed per 1,000 square feet of green. Nineteen greens are to be overseeded, with each green averaging 6,532 square feet. How much seed is needed for the entire project? (*answer:* 992 lbs)

7. A liquid fungicide has a 10 percent concentrate of the active ingredient. The superintendent wants to apply a rate of three ounces of product per 1,000 square feet.
   a. How much product will be needed for a 6,500 square foot green? (*answer:* 19.5 oz)
   b. How much pesticide is needed to treat this green at a rate of three ounces active ingredient per 1,000 square feet? (*answer:* 195 oz)

8. An insecticide costs $75 per gallon and the recommended application rate is 1.5 ounces per 1,000 square feet. How much does it cost to treat nine greens that average 6,250 square feet each? (*answer:* $396)

9. Two granular fungicides are available. Fungicide A costs $28/bag and covers 16,000 square feet. Fungicide B costs $12/bag and covers 6,525 square feet. Which fungicide is more economical and why? (*answer:* Fungicide A at $1.75/1,000 ft² compared to $1.83/1,000 ft² for Fungicide B)

CHAPTER
30

Budgets and Personnel Management

INTRODUCTION

Just as the layout and expectations vary from one golf course to another, so do costs, personnel requirements, and budgets. Careful planning and communication are essential to the financial success of the operation, whatever the decision-makers agree to spend on the facility, as the owner and manager use the budget process to plan, project and control the course's financial resources. Successful superintendents learn to develop and implement budgets and personnel issues and how to communicate these needs to their owners or managers.

Budgets are organized systematically in stages. This includes long-term improvements of the course, daily expectations of course conditions and personnel and budgets needs to obtain these, and cost projections to meet the desired goals. Comparison with similar facilities provide a starting point for this as do accounting firms or banks experienced in dealing with golf courses.

BUDGETS

Budgets for golf courses come in all shapes and sizes depending on the quality of the initial course design and construction; the size and location of the course; the proximity of available resources such as water, topdressing materials, irrigation supplies, and fertilizers; the equipment age and preventive maintenance; membership makeup; player demand; play; financial resources; and desired playing conditions for the individual course. There is no standard cost per round, or cost per acre, for managing a golf course. Rather, golf course owners, managers, and members determine the conditions they desire and the money they are willing to spend on any given course.

Budget Purpose

The purposes of a budget are for planning, projecting, and controlling. Planning involves determining the labor needs and resources for maintaining the course at the desired level of quality and within its financial resources. Projecting the budget over a period of time allows the golf course manager and owner to determine how much money will be needed in the short term to cover bills, and how much money should be held in reserve for future expenditures. The budget can also be a tool for controlling expenditures, based on income or previous projections, by measuring the plan and the projection in comparison to the actual financial activity. In summary, the budget is a process of communicating current and future financial needs, and tracking the actual financial activity of the course.

Income

Income sources for a golf course are multifaceted. Revenue sources vary depending upon the type of golf course and services provided. Private facilities charge membership dues and fees. Semi-private, public, or "for a fee" courses charge a fee for each round played. Other revenue categories are typically associated with the game or are generated by additional amenities such as food and beverage services and can generate substantial revenues. These are generally separated into two groups: (1) fees, and (2) golf-related services (Table 30–1).

Expenses

Costs for operating a golf course facility include capital improvements, capital expenses, fixed costs, and variable (or maintenance) costs.

Capital Improvements

Capital improvements are those expenditures (assets) that improve the value of the property. This includes permanent constructions such as a pump house, shelters, bridges, cart paths, parking lot, tree planting, tennis courts, permanent drainage, swimming pools, new green construction, and

TABLE 30–1 *Means and approximate percentages of each from which a typical golf facility generates income.*

	% of total income
Fees	
Membership dues	15 to 20
Golf cart fees	15
Golf green/guest fees	15
Membership fees	5
Revenues	
Food sales	10 to 15
Merchandise sales	5 to 8
Caddie services	~5
Beverage sales	~4
Tournament operations	~2
Golf range	~2
Golf instruction	~1
Club rental	<1
Club repair	<1
Handicapping service	<1
Golf bag storage	<1
Locker fees	<1
Other (e.g., cart storage, catering, facility rental, raffles, etc.)	~5

so forth. These items normally are prime objectives of long-range improvements and are often funded from the sale of property and initiation fees, as well as windfall profits.

Long-range planning is a must for any forward-thinking organization, and for golf courses it typically involves a minimum planning period of two to three years and a maximum of five years. Failure to plan for large-ticket capital improvement items on an annual basis may lead to an excessive, one-time expense to replace equipment or buildings. Without long-range goals, operations become outdated, efficiency is lost, and employee turnover is often higher.

Capital Expenses

Capital expenses or investments are nonhuman durable inputs of production, composed mostly of equipment, tools, and office furniture for a typical 18-hole facility. Capital expenses are often the prime objective of short-range improvements. Equipment becomes worn, outdated, or even dangerous. Player demands and increasing labor costs dictate the need to purchase labor-saving devices that provide equal or better playing conditions than previously achieved. Planning for new or additional capital expenses typically is a continuous three- to five-year process. Equipment leasing and contract maintenance are two relatively recent means through which courses are maximizing their capital dollars. Capital items are allocated to the capital budget and are usually subject to tax depreciation deductions.

Fixed Costs

Fixed costs include those required to maintain capital ownership and employ resources regardless of play, including land rent, insurance, taxes, depreciation, interest charges, and others.

Variable or Maintenance Costs

Variable or maintenance costs are resources allocated for golf course maintenance. Revenues from golf course fees generally fund the expenses in the golf course operating budget. Golf course maintenance budgets can be classified into three categories: low, moderate or medium, and high. Currently, annual maintenance budgets (variable costs) range from $300,000 to $500,000; $500,000 to $700,000; and above $700,000 for low, medium, and high maintenance budgets, respectively. These figures generally include only maintenance expenses as outlined in Table 30–2 and do not include capital improvements, capital expenses, or fixed costs. Courses in the United States currently average approximately $600,000 for their maintenance budgets. Expenses are recorded to the operating budget and are fully tax deductible against revenue.

Table 30–2 does not, of course, cover all typical expenses golf courses incur. Other maintenance considerations involve golf equipment such as pins, flags, cups, tee markers, benches, towels, and rope; repair to fences, shelters, and bridges; repair and upkeep of the maintenance building, tennis courts, and swimming pool; and miscellaneous items such as employee uniforms and laundry, office supplies, and vehicle licenses.

Floods, freezes, droughts, accidental spills or misapplied products, tornadoes, hurricanes, fire, vandalism, and other unusual expenses do not frequently occur, but most courses usually experience one or more of these at some point. Proper insurance coverage, continued employee training, and preventive measures should be planned for these and other unplanned expenses. Figures 30–1 through 30–3 offer examples of forecasting budgets and actual budgets for a typical 18-hole facility.

Figures 30–4 through 30–7 offer tables on tracking employee salaries, equipment inventories, equipment purchases, and various supplies purchased. Much of the mundane record keeping for a modern golf course maintenance unit can be managed by a number of available database, spreadsheet, and/or specialized computer programs targeted for golf course maintenance and record keeping.

Tournament Costs

Local courses often desire playing conditions similar to those professional golfers experience at major tournaments. Superintendents and their course conditions are often unfairly compared to the latest televised professional tournament with little regard to the time, labor, equipment, and

TABLE 30–2 *Typical expenses and their approximate percentages of the total maintenance budget for a moderately budgeted 18-hole golf course.*

Expense	Approximate percent of total maintenance budget
Salaries and wages (including benefits such as retirement, group health insurance, unemployment insurance, etc.)	45 to 65
Fertilizer	5 to 10
Chemicals	5 to 10
Irrigation repair and drainage	2 to 10 (location dependent)
Irrigation water	varies (~0 to 10)
Parts, service, tools	1
Utilities (electrical, heat, AC, phone)	3 to 5
Gas, oil, and lubricants	2
Landscaping (annuals, perennials, mulch, etc.)	1 to 3
Topdressing sand and gravel	1 to 2
Seed, sod, sprigs	5
Tree service (where needed)	3
Travel and association dues/professional development	1 to 3
Equipment parts and repairs	5 to 10
Cart path repairs	1 to 3
Contract maintenance	1 to 5
Office supplies	<1
Auto/vehicle allowance	1 to 2
Soil, water, and disease analysis (testing)	<1
First aid	<1
Temporary labor	1 to 5
Uniforms	1 to 2
Equipment lease	1 to 5
Equipment rental	<1
Cleaning supplies	<1
Golf maintenance supplies (e.g., cups, flags, ropes, stakes, coolers, paint, signs, etc.)	<1
Aquatic weed control and plant material	<1
Special projects	1 to 5
Consultants	1 to 2
Contingency	1 to 5

financial resources required to achieve those conditions. The goal of golf courses hosting professional events is to have the course prepped to test participants' skills and have each player encounter similar conditions as their competitors each day of the tournament.

Additional labor is a primary cost consideration for hosting a major tournament. For example, a recent U.S. Open Tournament required an additional $100,000 the two years preceding the event for enhanced course preparation not including capital investments for irrigation additions, greens construction, tee additions, tee leveling, or bunker renovation. Five times the normal labor pool was required during the tournament to provide acceptable playing conditions. Club officials determined that maintaining the golf course under continuous tournament conditions would require an additional $1 million each year. This is in addition to the normal labor allocation budget of $750,000 for "routine" playing conditions. Maintaining tournament conditions for long peri-

Monthly Expenses—Estimated

	J	F	M	A	M	J	J	A	S	O	N	D	Total
Salaries and wages													
Chemicals													
Irrigation/drainage repair													
Irrigation water													
Parts, service, tools													
Utilities													
Gas and oil													
Landscaping													
Sand and gravel													
Seed, sod, sprigs													
Tree service													
Professional development													
Equipment parts/repairs													
Cart path repairs													
Contract maintenance													
Office supplies													
Auto/vehicle allowance													
Soil, water, and disease tests													
First aid													
Temporary labor													
Uniforms													
Equipment lease													
Equipment rental													
Cleaning supplies													
Golf supplies													
Aquatic weed control													
Special projects													
Consultants													
Other													
Contingency													

Grand Total $_____

FIGURE 30–1   This form is an example of a monthly forecasted golf course maintenance/operating expenses form.

ods also often sacrifices grass quality since the lower mowing heights and increased stresses in terms of lean nitrogen and less water often combine to eventually damage the grass.

Long-Term Planning/Golf Course Standards

It is highly recommended that superintendents develop, along with the club professional/manager, greens committee, and board of directors/owner, long-term plans for the enhancement and care of the facility; including desired playing conditions (or expectations), facility upgrades, equipment replacement, capital improvements, and labor changes. The complex nature and expectations of modern golf course maintenance and play conditions are becoming increasingly evident. Fine-conditioned courses do not happen by accident but rather are the planned result of many contributing factors. Each segment of the course and its facilities should be included. This involves long-term goals and means of achieving these for each hole in terms of greens, tees, bunkers, fairways, cart paths, landscaping, roughs, out-of-play areas, and surrounds. Equipment, labor, and facilities goals also should be included.

Plans for play expectations, capital investments, and expenses need to be discussed, approved, and documented by all affected parties. The board of directors and greens committees

Monthly Expenses—Actual

	J	F	M	A	M	J	J	A	S	O	N	D	Total
Salaries and wages													
Chemicals													
Irrigation/drainage repair													
Irrigation water													
Parts, service, tools													
Utilities													
Gas and oil													
Landscaping													
Sand and gravel													
Seed, sod, sprigs													
Tree service													
Professional development													
Equipment parts/repairs													
Cart path repairs													
Contract maintenance													
Office supplies													
Auto/vehicle allowance													
Soil, water, disease tests													
Dues and subscriptions													
First aid													
Temporary labor													
Uniforms													
Equipment lease													
Equipment rental													
Cleaning supplies													
Golf supplies													
Aquatic weed control													
Special projects													
Consultants													
Other													
Contingency													

Grand Total $ _____

FIGURE 30–2   This form is an example of an actual monthly golf course maintenance/operating expenses form.

continually change, often with little regard to previous committee or board wishes. Problems and unnecessary expenses are avoided if a long-range plan is documented and on file, to be passed on from retiring board members to newly elected ones. This planning would allow continuity and consistency into the total organizational operation and can result in long-term savings by not "doing and undoing."

MAINTENANCE EQUIPMENT NEEDS

Maintaining today's golf courses requires adequate equipment, supplies, facilities, and personnel. As labor, salaries, and other costs such as workers' compensation rise, the manufacturing industry will continue to produce quicker, more efficient machinery that requires less labor to operate and maintain. However, golf equipment also tends to become more specialized, requiring larger operating budgets to buy and use. Table 30–3 has been complied by the U.S. Golf Association as a sug-

APPROVED, PROJECTED, AND PROPOSED OPERATING BUDGETS

	20_-_ Approved budget	20_-_ Projected budget	20_-_ Proposed budget	$ Increase from projected to proposed budgets	% Increase from projected to proposed budgets
Salaries and wages					
Chemicals					
Irrigation/drainage repair					
Irrigation water					
Parts, service, tools					
Utilities					
Gas, oil, lubricants					
Landscaping					
Sand and gravel					
Seed, sod, sprigs					
Tree service					
Professional development					
Equipment parts/repairs					
Cart path repairs					
Contract maintenance					
Office supplies					
Auto/vehicle allowance					
Soil, water, and disease tests					
Dues and subscriptions					
First aid					
Temporary labor					
Uniforms					
Equipment lease					
Equipment rental					
Cleaning supplies					
Golf supplies					
Aquatic weed control					
Special projects					
Consultants					
Other					
Contingency					
Totals					

FIGURE 30–3 This form is an example of a yearly approved, projected, and proposed golf course maintenance/operating expenses form.

gested list for maintaining the majority of 18-hole courses. Courses with more demanding players or unusual environmental requirements may need additional or other specialized equipment.

Miscellaneous Equipment

Additional miscellaneous equipment that is needed on golf courses includes axes, brooms, buckets, crowbars, cup cutters, dew whips, funnels, gas cans, hoses, ladders, picks, pruners, pumps, rakes, scales, shovels, soil probes, traps for vertebrate pests, tree saws, and a wheelbarrow. Other equipment may also be needed.

General Repair Tools

General repair tools include all power equipment (trucks, tractors, mowers, etc.), plumbing, drains, electrical equipment, sewers, roadways, fences, cement and concrete, water systems, painting and woodworking repairs, and so forth.

SALARIES AND WAGES

Year: _____

Monthly Expenses

	J	F	M	A	M	J	J	A	S	O	N	D	Total
Superintendent													
First assistant													
Second assistant													
Irrigation tech.													
Spray tech.													
Equipment manager													
Equipment operator 1													
Equipment operator 2													
Equipment operator 3													
Equipment operator 4													
Landscaper/horticulturist													
Office assistant													
Summer intern 1													
Summer intern 2													
Monthly totals													

Grand Total $_____

FIGURE 30–4   This form is an example of a monthly salaries and wages form for a golf course maintenance/operating budget.

EQUIPMENT INVENTORY

Year: _____

Item	Serial number	Total cost	Depreciation, years	Yearly depreciation, $
•	•	•	•	•
•	•	•	•	•
•	•	•	•	•
•	•	•	•	•
•	•	•	•	•

FIGURE 30–5   This form is an example of an equipment inventory form for a golf course maintenance operation.

NEW EQUIPMENT PURCHASES

Year: _____

Date	Amount	Item	Make	Serial number	Supplier	Cost	Expected life, years
•	•	•	•	•	•	•	•
•	•	•	•	•	•	•	•
•	•	•	•	•	•	•	•
•	•	•	•	•	•	•	•
•	•	•	•	•	•	•	•

Total Costs $_____

FIGURE 30–6   This form is an example of a new equipment purchases form for a golf course maintenance operation.

Date	Amount	Item	Supplier	Cost
•	•	•	•	•
•	•	•	•	•
•	•	•	•	•
•	•	•	•	•
•	•	•	•	•
•	•	•	•	•
			Total Costs	$ _____

FIGURE 30–7   This form is an example of a supplies and materials purchased form for a golf course maintenance operation.

Shop Equipment

Shop equipment includes a backlapping machine, air compressor, steam cleaner, bench grinder, bed knife grinder, reel grinder, pipe threader, paint sprayer, welding equipment, drill press, vises, work benches, and an equipment lift or hoist.

Irrigation Equipment

Irrigation equipment includes a pumping station, field satellite controllers, centralized computer control system and irrigation heads, hoses, trenching shovels, wire locators (metal detectors), pipe and wire pullers, pipe, fittings, and specialized repair tools.

Maintenance Facility

A maintenance facility should provide the following:

- Office for the superintendent, assistant superintendent, spray technician, irrigation technician, and secretary. This includes equipment such as desks, file cabinets, phones, computers, and so forth.
- Toilet facilities, showers, and locker room.
- Break room/meeting room with audio-video equipment for training purposes.
- Adequate heating, cooling, and ventilation.
- Paint spraying room.
- Reel grinding room.
- Pesticide storage facility.
- Wash rack area.
- Fertilizer and seed storage area.
- Storage for oil, gasoline, and diesel fuel.
- Adequate storage for all equipment, parts, supplies, and tools.
- Adequate maintenance work area.
- Soil bins for topdressing material, bunker sand, and soil amendments. These should be kept in a dry area, free of contamination, and preferably covered.

Justifying an Asset

Justifying a needed asset, along with justifying needed personnel, are two of the biggest budgetary challenges facing superintendents. Governing boards at golf courses are typically composed of bankers, accountants, lawyers, small-business owners, engineers, and doctors—professionals accustomed to justifying their own needs within their organizations. To those familiar with the

TABLE 30–3 *Typical equipment needs for an 18-hole golf course.*

Equipment	Quantity needed
Greens and tees	
Putting green mowers, walk-behind, **or**	6 to 8, **or**
Triplex mowers (2 for greens, 2 for tees, 1 for collars)	3
Triplex vertical mowing reel set	1
Brushes or groomers for mowing equipment	2
Three-gang tee, fringe, and collar mowers	1 to 2
Power aerifiers	2
Topdressing machines	1 to 2
Core harvesting machines	1
Power dethatcher	1
Power spiker (or slicer) or spiker attachment	1
Power sprayer for pesticide and fertilizer application	1
Rotary fertilizer spreader/seeder	2
Dragmats, brushes, or brooms to incorporate topdressing material	2
Blowers	1 to 5
Roller, tournament speed	1
Hydroject water inject aerifier	1
Fairways and roughs	
Lightweight, five-gang fairway mowers, **or**	2 to 3, **or**
Seven-gang hydraulic-powered mowers	2
Fairway aerifier	1
Fairway dethatcher/vertical mower	1
Power sprayer (200- to 300-gallon capacity)	1
Large volume fertilizer spreader	1
Five-gang rough mower, **or**	1, **or**
Multi-deck rotary rough mowers	2
Triplex trim mowers	2 to 3
Tractor-mounted blower	1
Fairway sweeper/blower	1
General equipment	
Transportation vehicles for the staff	4 to 5
General construction PTO tractors	2 to 3
Dump trailers	1 to 2
Pickup truck	1
Dump truck (five-ton minimum)	1
Front-end loader and backhoe (this can be rented as needed)	1
Forklift or front-end loader	1
Trencher (this can be rented as needed)	1
Slicer/seeder	1
Snow plow, where necessary	1
Power sod cutter	1
Rotary trim mowers	4 to 5
Power edgers	4 to 5
Backpack blowers	4 to 5
String trimmers	4 to 5

golf maintenance business, justifying a piece of turf equipment or extra personnel seems obvious. However, when trying to balance a club's total budget, while keeping expenses in check, superintendents need to have a plan of justification before success in acquiring an asset can be expected. The following outline is often successfully used when an asset that board members are familiar with and typically expect is needed.

1. **Description of the asset.** The description lists the name of the asset and model number, with all accessories, plus the name and address of the seller. It is helpful to attach a color picture of the asset from a manufacturer's brochure to help the committee visualize the asset.

2. **Justification of the asset.** The justification explains what the asset does and why the club needs the asset (for example, to replace a worn, broken, or outdated piece of equipment). Describe any safety issues or deficiencies the current asset has or is lacking. Attach a performance specification sheet from the manufacturer to explain features, accessories, and expected performance of the proposed asset.

3. **Selection of the new asset.** Explain the various assets available on the market, the results of any in-house testing or equipment demonstrations, and why a certain model or manufacturer was chosen.

4. **Availability and delivery of the asset and part replacement.** Explain the time frame the new asset can be made available and if replacement parts are easily accessible.

5. **List alternative(s) if this proposal is rejected.** Explain how expensive it would be to repair the existing machine or how much additional labor would be needed if the asset proposal is rejected.

6. **Asset maintenance plan.** Explain how routine maintenance of the new asset would be handled. Explain preventive maintenance procedures, schedule, and parts inventory needs.

7. **Use life of the asset.** List a reasonable life expectancy of the new asset, assuming proper maintenance is followed. Sales or technical brochures may be helpful in this task.

8. **Fate of the asset being replaced.** Explain what is planned for the asset being replaced. Can any useful parts be salvaged? Can it be traded in? Can it be sold? and so forth.

EXAMPLE

A golf course superintendent determines a new sand trap rake is needed but feels the new club manager will have difficulty agreeing with the request. The following capital equipment purchase request is prepared to justify this purchase.

1. **Description of the asset.** Sand Trap Master model #12345 with a 16hp v-twin gas engine, three-wheel drive, mid-mount cultivator, manual control front blade, rear rakes, and spike attachment, to be purchased from Great Turf Equipment of Anywhere, United States (attach a picture).

2. **Justification of the asset.** This machine is a basic component of our equipment inventory, used to maintain our sand bunkers on the golf course. The front blade is needed for pushing sand up into washouts after heavy rains and to distribute newly placed sand. It works approximately 25 percent quicker than comparable machines. Additionally, this machine will be used to do small grading projects, spike greens, and drag-in topdressing (attach performance sheet).

   This machine is needed to replace out our current 10-year-old Worn Out Sand Trap Mutilator. This machine has provided 10 years of commendable service; however, it is currently in poor shape. At present, the machine is not running due to a blown engine. In addition, the frame is broken, the brakes are nonresponsive (dangerous), and the hydraulic system needs replacing. Due to liability and mechanical issues, we have parked the machine, feeling it is not worth repairing. Since the machine is inoperable, we are having difficulties accomplishing routine bunker maintenance to the level outlined in our long-term play performance goals.

3. **Selection of the new asset.** Recently, new bunker rakes have been introduced into the marketplace that are more time-effective and provide a better quality product than our current model. Several models have been demonstrated on our course with our personnel. In addition, several manufacturers left demo models on the course for several weeks for further evaluation.

All machines did a commendable job but we felt Sand Trap Master model #12345 would best fit our needs. The reasons include:

a. This machine was most cost effective with the added accessories.

b. If the operator prefers a piece of equipment, he/she will take better care of it and appreciate the job being performed.

c. Lower maintenance due to a superior steering system and simpler hydraulic system.

d. Superior transport speed, reducing the total man-hours needed to perform the total job.

e. The mounting of the front blade is such that a wider turn can be made in the traps without digging into steep bunker faces.

4. **Availability and delivery of the asset and part replacement.** Upon the receipt of our order, Great Turf Equipment of Anywhere, United States, can deliver the machine within 10 to 14 days. Repair parts are usually available overnight while service is available within one week from Great Turf Equipment.

5. **List alternative(s) if this proposal is rejected.** If the proposal is rejected, our options are limited. We would have to spend several thousand dollars repairing a machine that is worn out and beyond its usual life expectancy. The money to do so is not in our operations budget, nor do we have the time to undertake a rebuilding job of this magnitude at this point of the season.

6. **Asset maintenance plan.** Maintenance will be handled by the staff mechanic. A preventative maintenance schedule will be established and computer tracked. An inventory of frequently used parts, of which there are very few, will be established. Many parts are currently inventoried, as this machine shares similar parts with other equipment.

7. **Use life of the asset.** With proper maintenance, this machine will have an active and useful life of 8 to 10 years.

8. **Fate of the asset being replaced.** Due to safety issues, we feel the current machine should not be sold. The unit will be stripped of any useful parts and junked. A notification will be forwarded to accounting to remove it from the books.

PERSONNEL REQUIREMENTS

Staffing a golf course maintenance crew is a never-ending challenge. Labor costs are skyrocketing, forcing some clubs to cut back on personnel numbers and/or benefits. However, golf courses require an extensive staff that is dependable and continuously trained to handle complicated machinery and certain chemicals. It is much cheaper in the long run to pay qualified people good salaries to minimize turnover and to ensure highly skilled labor.

Labor costs are generally the largest line item in the operating budget and include salaries, wages, taxes, and benefits. In order to effectively plan and project labor costs, the owner and superintendent must agree upon the number of employees needed to maintain the golf course, how many will be full- and part-time employees, the wage and salary scale, what benefits are offered, and so forth.

A simple spreadsheet will help plan and project wages and salaries. The number of weeks and hours per week, including overtime hours, are needed to add additional costs from unemployment insurance, employer's liability, Medicare and worker's compensation insurance, and any owner-sponsored benefit plans offered.

Trying to list the personnel requirements for an 18-hole facility is difficult as each course has varying needs, financial resources, and player demands. A detailed manpower analysis by a professional group is suggested as a specific method to determine staff size. Table 30–4 is a suggested working list of personnel for a typical facility.

Labor Justification

As mentioned, justifying additional labor and equipment are two of the biggest challenges superintendents face. For this to be successful, detailed records on the time required to perform certain tasks on a particular sized area will be needed. Having a written expected standard level is another helpful piece of information when justifying these additions. When labor needs do not match the expected standard of a course, then the superintendent has the information needed to justify hiring additional help. The following formula can be used to determine the amount of la-

Position description	Number
Superintendent	1
Assistant superintendent or foreman	1
Secretary (full- or part-time)	1
Equipment manager (mechanic)	1
Irrigation technician	1
Spray technician	1
Section people/greenskeepers/syringers	3
Equipment operators	4
Utility people	2
Landscaper/horticulturist	1
Total	**16**

bor required to perform certain tasks; if the number of personnel available does not meet this value, then several options are available: reduce the expected standards of the course, reduce the area being maintained at this level, increase the labor pool, or, if available, purchase equipment that reduces labor needs.

$$\text{time (hrs) per unit area} = \frac{\text{total hours per year to perform a given job}}{\text{no. of times per year a job is performed} \times \text{area (sq.ft. or acres)}}$$

Figure 30–8 provides a table to track various tasks necessary to maintain a golf course. These figures are necessary for any budgetary or personnel increase justification.

Example:

Through detailed records, the following labor hours have been determined as necessary each year. Each employee works on average 45 hours per week and the main season is 40 weeks long.

Number	Task	Hours required (yearly)
1	Greens and collars	5,245
2	Tees and nursery	2,834
3	Fairways	3,100
4	Approaches	752
5	Roughs	5,543
6	Clubhouse grounds	1,589
7	Sand traps	2,238
8	Topdressing	303
9	Nursery	165
10	Miscellaneous	6,101
	Total	**27,870**

To determine the "ideal" number of employees to perform these tasks:

$$\text{time (hrs) per unit area} = \frac{\text{total hours per year to perform a given job}}{\text{no. of times per year a job is performed} \times \text{area (sq.ft. or acres)}}$$

$$= \frac{27,870}{40 \text{ weeks} \times 45 \text{ hours/week}} = 15.5 \text{ employees}$$

If the total area is known, then the time (minutes or hours) needed to perform the particular operation can be determined. For example, if it requires two minutes to walk-mow each 1,000

Date	Hole	Activity	Area size	Time required	Totals
Greens					
Tees					
Fairways					
Roughs					
Other: _____					
Other: _____					

FIGURE 30–8   This form is an example of a work record form for a golf course maintenance operation.

square feet of greens and this is performed 225 times yearly, then it requires 7.5 hours (or 450 minutes) to perform this task. Multiply this number by the amount of greens area to determine the total hours necessary to mow greens each year. If you have 19 greens (counting the practice green) averaging 5,000 square feet each, then a total of 95,000 square feet (or 2.2 acres) need mowing. Based on 7.5 hours needed yearly to mow 1,000 square feet, it requires 713 hours yearly to mow all greens a total of 225 times.

Obviously, conditions and playing area at every golf course can vary significantly and this formula cannot account for all duties performed or varying conditions throughout a season or year. However, the formula can be a guide to compare operating practices and possibly justify additional personnel and/or faster, more efficient equipment.

Job Descriptions

In today's labor market and legal atmosphere, companies are requiring formal job descriptions for their employees. Job descriptions typically provide an overall statement of what is expected of the position followed by a detailed breakdown and percentages of each expected task. Figure 30–9 provides an example of a job description plus the necessary qualifications for an assistant golf course superintendent, plus a yearly evaluation.

Example:

Assistant Golf Course Superintendent

JOB PURPOSE

Under direct supervision of the golf course superintendent, the assistant GCS directs and participates in the maintenance of the golf course greens, tees, fairways, roughs, and cart paths; supervises the maintenance and repair of motorized and other mechanical equipment; coordinates pesticide and fertilizer application; oversees operational irrigation systems; and does related work as required. The assistant GCS may serve in the golf course superintendent's capacity during his or her absence.

Job Tasks—Assistant Golf Course Superintendent:	Percentage of time
Assists the golf course superintendent in planning and supervising the maintenance of greens, tees, and fairways; schedules work and supervises the employees and use of the equipment.	60
Instructs equipment operators on the proper use and care of mowing and other equipment; supervises pesticide applications and/or operates and calibrates pesticide application equipment; supervises and participates in the operation and maintenance of pumps, and in the maintenance of irrigation and drainage systems.	20
Assists in personnel management and evaluation, employee safety, and personnel discipline, and may also modify the daily work schedule on professional interpretation.	15
Miscellaneous duties as required.	10

MINIMUM TRAINING AND EXPERIENCE REQUIREMENTS

AAS in horticulture, agronomy, or closely related field and a minimum of two years' experience in professional turfgrass/golf course management and construction. Must possess, maintain, and be willing to use a state pesticide license in turfgrass and ornamentals. Must be able to pick up 50 pounds.

PREFERRED QUALIFICATIONS

BS degree and three years' experience as previously described. Formal training in Spanish, irrigation technology, and personnel management is preferred.

WHAT KNOWLEDGE, SKILLS AND ABILITIES ARE NEEDED BY AN EMPLOYEE UPON ENTRY TO THIS JOB?

The job requires knowledge of the goals and objectives of turfgrass maintenance programs and safety practices relevant to turf maintenance; including knowledge and/or experience with managing bentgrass greens in heat stress and overseeding bermudagrass with ryegrass, *Poa trivialis,* fine fescue, and so forth, for winter color. Ability to plan, coordinate, and conduct daily work schedules for the maintenance crew and plan capital improvement projects using

FIGURE 30–9 This form is an example of an assistant golf course superintendent's job description plus a yearly evaluation.

EMPLOYEE PERFORMANCE MANAGEMENT SYSTEM

Name:_____   Social Security No._____

Department: **MAINTENANCE/GROUNDS**_____

Position Classification: **ASSISTANT GOLF COURSE SUPERINTENDENT**_____

Date Assigned to Current Position: _____

Performance Review From:_____ To:_____

EVALUATION STAGE ACKNOWLEDGMENT

Rating Officer:_____   Date:_____

Reviewed by:_____   Date:_____

Reviewing Officer Comments:_____

_____

Employee:_____   Date:_____

(My signature indicates I was given the opportunity to discuss the official performance review with my supervisor, not that I necessarily agree.)

Employee Comments: _____

_____

(continued)

FIGURE 30–9
(continued)

JOB FUNCTIONS: ASSISTANT GOLF COURSE SUPERINTENDENT	Performance level
Job Duty: Assists in planning and supervising the maintenance of greens, tees, and fairways; schedules work and supervises the employees and use of the equipment. **Success Criteria:** Ensure daily and weekly work assignments are made and properly implemented.	
Job Duty: Instructs equipment operators on the proper use and care of mowing and other equipment; supervises pesticide applications and/or operates and calibrates pesticide application equipment; supervises and participates in the operation and maintenance of pumps, and monitors the maintenance of irrigation and drainage systems. **Success Criteria:** Handling equipment repairs and coordinating spray and fertilizer applications. This includes the legal and safe storage, use, and disposal of pesticides, fertilizers, and other chemicals and hazardous materials.	
Job Duty: Assists in personnel management and evaluation, employee safety, and personnel discipline, and may also modify the daily work schedule on professional interpretation. **Success Criteria:** Provide input to the golf course superintendent on personnel management and annual evaluations. Handles minor personnel discipline issues, coordinates weekly and daily work schedules, and ensures proper interpretations by workers on the desired outcome(s).	
Job Duty: Miscellaneous duties as required. **Success Criteria:** Perform the job duty as described.	

ACTUAL PERFORMANCE

Employee _____ .

SUMMARY AND IMPROVEMENT PLAN
Identify the employee's major accomplishments, areas needing improvement, and steps to improve present and future performance.

Employee: _____

Employee: _____

Employee: _____

Employee: _____

APPRAISAL RESULTS:

_____ Substantially Exceeds _____ Exceeds _____ Meets _____ Improvement Needed _____ Below

modern construction methods and techniques. Must also coordinate and oversee the functional legal operation of pesticide mixing/loading sites, rinsate handling, and proper storage and inventory of pesticides, fertilizers, and other hazardous materials. Confers and makes suggestions with the golf course superintendent on daily and long-term planning strategies, evaluating personnel, and handling minor personnel disputes/discipline.

DESCRIBE THE GUIDELINES AND SUPERVISION AN EMPLOYEE RECEIVES IN ORDER TO DO THIS JOB, INCLUDING THE EMPLOYEE'S INDEPENDENCE AND DISCRETION.

After conferring with the golf course superintendent, the assistant GCS must work independently and make informed decisions independent of the supervisor with minimal supervision.

Other brief examples of job descriptions for positions on the golf course maintenance staff include the following.

Example:

Equipment Manager

JOB PURPOSE

Under direct supervision of the golf course superintendent and/or assistant GCS, the equipment manager supervises a comprehensive preventive maintenance program on the golf course equipment. This includes the repair of failing or failed equipment, maintaining records of parts and labor required to perform this duty, and placing orders for necessary parts and supplies. The equipment manager communicates any needs or problems relating to equipment maintenance or repair. Safety is a top priority, and the equipment manager is responsible for maintaining a clean, organized service area and maintenance building.

Job Tasks—Equipment Manager:	Percentage of time
Inspects, diagnoses, and repairs mechanical defects/failures of maintenance equipment including diesel-, electric-, and gasoline-powered automobiles, trucks, mowers, rollers, and other mechanical equipment used on the golf course. This includes hydraulics and routine mower blade sharpening.	60
Instructs equipment operators on the proper use and care of mowing and other equipment; preventive maintenance procedures; and proper cleaning, storing, and use of equipment.	15
Keeps a complete set of records for equipment and inventory purchases and needs, equipment condition, and costs of repairs. Also purchases repair parts and replacement supplies.	10
Maintains a clean, organized shop maintenance facility.	5
Miscellaneous duties as required.	10

MINIMUM TRAINING AND EXPERIENCE REQUIREMENTS

The position requires a working knowledge of light and heavy maintenance equipment, internal combustion engines, mowing equipment, and automotive pieces. This includes the ability to diagnose mechanical problems and determine appropriate maintenance needs. Requires skill in the use of various equipment repair tools with the ability to purchase appropriate tools and supplies within budget to provide the necessary working order of equipment. Requires a working knowledge of the safety precautions of the profession to maintain an OSHA-approved workplace. Must possess a valid driver's license and possibly a commercial driver's license (CDL). Must be able to move at least 75 pounds.

PREFERRED QUALIFICATIONS

Formal mechanical training and three years' experience as previously described. Understands the needs of modern golf maintenance shops and playing conditions and how these affect the golf course.

Example:

Irrigation Technician/Specialist

JOB PURPOSE

Under direct supervision of the golf course superintendent and/or assistant GCS, the irrigation technician/specialist is responsible for the programming, operation, and maintenance of the golf course irrigation system(s). This includes repair of failing or failed irrigation equipment, maintaining records of parts and labor required to perform this duty, and placing orders for necessary parts and supplies. The irrigation specialist communicates any needs or problems relating to irrigation equipment maintenance or repair. If water permitting/licensing becomes required, the irrigation technician shall help develop water usage and other materials/information necessary to conform or apply for this.

Job Tasks—Irrigation Technician/Specialist:	Percentage of time
Coordinates necessary watering for the entire golf course. This includes supplemental hand watering/syringing; water quality issues/adjustments; and monitoring ponds, lakes, and streams for water quality and wildlife habitats.	50
Inspects, diagnoses, coordinates, and repairs defects/failures of irrigation equipment including controllers, pumps, motors, valves, heads, leaks, and other related irrigation situations on the golf course.	20
Keeps a complete set of records for irrigation equipment and inventory purchases and needs, equipment condition, and costs of repairs. Also purchases repair parts and replacement supplies.	10
Coordinates and supervises labor for special projects such as repairing greens with seeds or plugs of new grass when needed.	10
Miscellaneous duties as required.	10

MINIMUM TRAINING AND EXPERIENCE REQUIREMENTS
The position requires working knowledge of basic electricity and irrigation hydraulics including automatic valves and controllers, as well as various types of pumps and pumping systems. Requires knowledge of basic tests and data interpretation necessary to monitor water quality and ways to adjust or modify water to suitable levels. Requires understanding of soil and turfgrass science and the rules of golf; ability to operate light motorized equipment; and ability to follow oral and written instructions.

PREFERRED QUALIFICATIONS
AAS or BS in turfgrass science, irrigation technology, or a closely related field. Training in water quality is desirable. Requires a valid driver's license.

Example:

Chemical Technician/IPM Specialist

JOB PURPOSE
Under direct supervision of the golf course superintendent and/or assistant GCS, the chemical (spray) technician/IPM specialist is responsible for following all integrated pest management (IPM) strategies involving scouting, detection, and threshold determination. This person also oversees the application of all chemicals and fertilizers on golf course properties, including proper sprayer/spreader calibration, right-to-know laws, and appropriate applicator apparel. The chemical technician is responsible for reading, understanding, and keeping current with pesticide and fertilizer storage, as well as application and disposal rules and regulations. This includes maintaining up-to-date pesticide labels and material safety data sheets (MSDS). Records indicating pesticide usage on the golf course will also be provided to the golf course superintendent.

Job Tasks—Chemical Technician/IPM Specialist:	Percentage of time
Coordinates necessary pesticide and fertilizer application for the entire golf course. This includes proper sprayer calibration and application, applicator safety apparel, scouting for pests, and proper disposal of rinsates.	60
Keeps a complete set of records for pesticide and fertilizer inventory, purchases, application equipment, and repairs. Periodic training of the golf course crew on pesticide and fertilizer safety and handling issues will also be performed.	20
Maintains chemical and fertilizer storage and mixing areas in compliance with county, state, and Federal regulations and is responsible for the safety and direction of chemical handlers and/or helpers.	10
Miscellaneous duties as required.	10

MINIMUM TRAINING AND EXPERIENCE REQUIREMENTS

This position requires complete knowledge of chemical and fertilizer application equipment including hand-operated spreaders, spray equipment, and pressurized sprayers. Requires current state certification or licensing as a restricted-use pesticide applicator, American Red Cross first-aid training, and ability to follow oral and written instructions.

PREFERRED QUALIFICATIONS

AAS or BS in turfgrass science, pest management, entomology, plant pathology, or closely related field. Requires a valid driver's license and the ability to move 50 pounds. Prefer to be able to communicate in Spanish.

Example:

Equipment Operator

JOB PURPOSE

Under direct supervision of the golf course superintendent and/or assistant GCS, the equipment operator works using large equipment, including tractors, loaders, trenchers, backhoes, trucks, and other maintenance equipment. This person also assists the equipment manager on routine preventive maintenance of such equipment.

Job Tasks—Equipment Operator:	Percentage of time
Mows tees, fairways, and roughs with gang units. Operates walk-behind and motorized greens mowers.	50
Operates other large equipment such as turf vac, skid-loader, fairway and rough aerifier, and boom sprayer in fairways and rough.	20
Checks and properly maintains equipment cooling system, fuel, and oil levels; cleans equipment daily; and immediately reports equipment problems or failures to the equipment manager.	10
Under the direction of the equipment manager, provides basic preventive maintenance on equipment and returns it to the designated location at the maintenance facility.	10
Miscellaneous duties as required.	10

MINIMUM TRAINING AND EXPERIENCE REQUIREMENTS

This position requires knowledge of safe, efficient mechanical operation of tractors and other motorized equipment, mechanical aptitude, and ability to follow oral and written directions.

PREFERRED QUALIFICATIONS

One year's experience with similar equipment at a comparable golf course facility. Requires a valid driver's license and must randomly submit to a drug test.

Example:

Office Assistant

JOB PURPOSE

Under direct supervision of the golf course superintendent, the office assistant provides administrative, clerical, and office management support for the golf course maintenance operation.

Job Tasks—Office Assistant:	Percentage of time
Answers and directs all incoming phone calls and e-mails, screens the golf course superintendent's calls, greets and directs all visitors, distributes all incoming mail, and oversees outgoing mail, shipping operations, and services.	50
Maintains the golf course superintendent's calendar of meetings, and so forth. Dispatches employees' daily tasks, posting assignments, tracking appointments, workflow, and recording hourly employees' work time.	20
Maintains records and files for the golf course maintenance operation, including current and accurate job position descriptions; job applicant database and file of applications received; inventory of building keys and credit card accounts; golf course maintenance staff payroll information including regular and overtime hours, sick time, vacation time, and so forth; and scheduling annual performance evaluations and other appointments.	20
Miscellaneous duties as required.	10

MINIMUM TRAINING AND EXPERIENCE REQUIREMENTS

This position requires knowledge of telephone experience and ability to organize an office, calls, appointments, job applications, and applicants. Some bookkeeping experience would be helpful.

PREFERRED QUALIFICATIONS

High school diploma or equivalent and two years' postsecondary work in office administration, office machines, and record keeping. Requires typing skills of 50 words per minute and knowledge of word processing, spreadsheet, and database management software. Requires excellent organizational skills and sensitivity with confidential information.

Example:

Landscaper/Horticulturist

JOB PURPOSE

Under direct supervision of the golf course superintendent, the landscaper/horticulturist manages the greenhouse and nursery to produce and install ornamental landscaping for the golf course and clubhouse properties. Routine maintenance of such plantings in terms of pruning, weeding, mulching, fertilizing, irrigation, and others also are included.

Job Tasks—Landscaper/Horticulturist:	Percentage of time
Manages the greenhouse and ornamental nursery facilities; selects, propagates, and grows plant materials (except trees and larger shrubs) for pleasing ornamental use on and around the golf course, clubhouse, and other buildings. Applies mulch and coordinates hand weed control as needed.	60
Designs flower beds. Cultivates shrubs, and flowers. Trims and prunes hedges and shrubbery. Advises the golf course superintendent of the need for tree trimming services.	10
Designs, installs, and maintains low-pressure irrigation systems for landscaping.	10
Applies fertilizer, pesticides, and other chemicals to ornamental plantings, keeping the appropriate records and following all local, state, and Federal laws in providing this.	10
Miscellaneous duties as required.	10

MINIMUM TRAINING AND EXPERIENCE REQUIREMENTS
This position requires knowledge of locally adapted plants for various uses on the golf course property. Two years of such experience with similar climatically adapted plants would be helpful. Experience in golf course maintenance and the game of golf is helpful.

PREFERRED QUALIFICATIONS
AAS or BS in horticulture or closely related field. Requires knowledge of the characteristics, growth habits, and proper cultivation of locally adapted flowering bulbs and annual, biennial, and perennial plant materials, including herbaceous and woody plants. Requires knowledge of various fertilizers, soil amendments, and pest control options for landscape plantings. Requires current state licensing as a pesticide applicator for indoor and outdoor landscape plantings.

EMPLOYMENT CONTRACTS

To protect both the golf course and the superintendent, a memorandum of agreement or contract on the duties, extent of authority, specific responsibilities, immediate supervisor, salary, and list of privileges or benefits should be drawn up and agreed upon. This formal written contract is valid and enforceable while oral ones probably are not. This is important as many members of the board of directors and/or greens committee constantly change, thus, the contract helps protect the superintendent with the different personalities and agendas of each board. Figure 30–10 provides a simple contract on what may be included. Time and consultation are needed in the contract negotiating and writing process so both parties understand what is expected.

FIGURE 30–10 This form is an example of a contract between a golf course and its superintendent.

LETTER OF UNDERSTANDING AND AGREEMENT BETWEEN

_____

Representing ABC Golf Course/Country Club (the Employer) and

_____

The Superintendent (the Employee)

is hereby employed as golf course superintendent of the ABC Golf Course for a period between
_____, 20_____ and _____, 20_____. Annual restitution will be at the rate of $ _____ subject to annual review and renewal. The mutual objective between the superintendent and club is to bring about and maintain a quality golf course at a reasonable cost.

Golf Course Superintendent's Responsibilities:
1. The superintendent will be responsible only to the chair of the greens committee, the club manager, or _____.
2. The superintendent shall be solely responsible for the hiring, firing, and supervising of all grounds and greens maintenance personnel; the salaries of such persons shall be approved by the greens committee, club manager, or _____.
3. All purchases/leases for maintenance of the golf course grounds/greens shall be the responsibility of the superintendent after previous approval by the greens committee, the club manager, or _____.
4. The superintendent shall follow all local, state, and national laws and policies concerning all pesticide/fertilizer/fuel and similar hazardous materials, purchases, storage, and use; maintain the maintenance facility according to insurance and/or local codes, such as OSHA or similar; and follow club policy on hiring, firing, promotions, and employee reprimand.
5. The golf course shall be maintained in accordance to the performance standards agreed upon by the greens committee and superintendent with reasonable allowances for necessary routine maintenance, construction, renovation, and/or acts of God.

Privileges:
1. The superintendent shall enjoy all privileges offered by the course and clubhouse, including guests, in good taste, in accordance with the rules of the club.
2. Lunch shall be available to the superintendent at his/her discretion. Supper will be available when duties require the superintendent to be at the club during evening hours.
3. Vacation, with pay, will be _____ days annually, with timing approved by the chair of the greens committee, club manager, or _____.
4. The club shall provide a vehicle (usually a truck), fuel, insurance, and routine maintenance for the superintendent to use during and after work, not to exceed _____ annual miles for personnel use.
5. As the superintendent is a key representative of the golf club, he/she is expected to maintain acceptable dress/attire in accordance with club policy. An annual clothing allowance not to exceed $ _____ will be provided.
6. Reasonable expenses for educational meetings/training/materials will be provided by the employer, not to exceed $ _____ annually.

Terms:
These terms may be renewed or extended annually by the agreement of both parties. If either the employer or superintendent does not desire to renew or extend this agreement, written notice will be provided to the other party at least 90 days prior to the expiration of this agreement by certified mail. The employer may terminate this agreement for cause, effective the date the employer so notifies the superintendent in writing. The standard minimum two weeks' courtesy notice shall be invoked by either party prior to employment termination.

_____   Date _____
ABC Golf Club President

_____   Date _____
Superintendent

APPENDIX A

STOKES' EQUATION FOR CALCULATING THE VELOCITY OF A FALLING PARTICLE AND DARCY'S EQUATION FOR CALCULATING HYDRAULIC CONDUCTIVITY

STOKES' EQUATION

Stokes' equation is used to calculate the velocity of a falling particle through a suspension (also referred to as the Pipet Method). According to Stokes' equation, the velocity of a spherical particle settling under the influence of gravity in a fluid of a given density and viscosity is proportional to the square of the particle's radius. This governs the method of sedimentation analysis. A particle falling in a fluid will encounter a frictional resistance proportional to the product of its radius and velocity, as well as the viscosity of the fluid. In other words, the larger the diameter of the particle, the faster it falls in a liquid. Relating this relationship to soils, it means sand will fall in a liquid faster than silt, which will fall faster than clay.

$$V = \frac{g(d^1 - d)D^2}{18\,\eta}$$

where: V = velocity of the falling particle (cm/sec)
d^1 = density of the particle (g/cm^3), (2.65 g/cm^3 for most mineral soils)
d = density of the medium (g/cm^3), (0.997 g/cm^3 for water at 25°C)
g = acceleration due to gravity (980 cm/sec^2)
D = diameter of the particle (cm)
η = absolute viscosity of the medium (dyne sec/cm^2)

Subtracting fluid density from particle density accounts for the buoyancy that reduces the effective weight of particles in suspension.

In the equation, g, d^1, and d are constants. If the temperature is constant, the viscosity of water is also constant (0.01 at 20°C, for example).

One assumption of Stokes' equation is the soil particles are smooth spheres, which can be incorrect. By substituting these values into one equation, typical fall rates for various-sized particles can be calculated as centimeters per second from:

$$V \text{ (cm/sec)} = KD^2$$

where K equals the constant, taking into account density, viscosity, gravity, and temperatures. At 20°C, K is approximately 8,711. At 25°C, K is approximately 10,000.

Example:

Determine the time required for all particles (all sand) larger than 0.05 millimeters (0.005 cm) to fall 10 centimeters in a suspension at 25°C.

$$V = KD^2$$
$$= (10,000)(0.005)^2$$
$$= 0.25 \text{ cm/sec}$$

With this velocity, the time required for particles to fall 10 centimeters can be determined using the relationship between velocity, time, and distance:

$$\text{velocity} = \frac{\text{distance}}{\text{time}} = \frac{\text{cm}}{\text{sec}}$$

$$\text{time} = \frac{\text{distance}}{\text{velocity}} = \frac{\text{cm}}{\text{cm/sec}} = \text{sec}$$

Therefore:

$$\text{time} = \frac{\text{distance}}{\text{velocity}} = \frac{10 \text{ cm}}{0.25 \text{ cm/sec}} = 40 \text{ sec}$$

From this, at the end of 40 seconds, the suspension above 10 centimeters depth in a container is free of all particles 0.05 millimeters in diameter or larger. In other words, it is free of all sand. This same process can be repeated for other textural components such as silt. If the amount of soil originally suspended is known, the proportions of sand, silt, and clay can be determined by measuring the amount of material remaining in suspension after a specific time has elapsed.

From Stokes' equation, the settling rate in water of a particle with the diameter of 0.05 millimeters (lower limit of sand) at 25°C, is 0.25 centimeters per second, and with a diameter of 0.002 millimeters (upper limit of clay) the rate is only 0.004 centimeters per second. Sand, therefore, has been calculated to settle in a 7.25-inch (18.4 cm) high cylinder beaker in approximately 74 seconds. If a thoroughly distributed sample is placed in a 1,000-milliliter cylinder beaker 7.25 inches in height, it should retain the silt and clay fractions in suspension longer than 74 seconds (approximately two hours for silt and "days" for clay), enabling the soil scientist to separate these from the larger-diameter sand particles. The time required for settling can also be calculated from the following:

$$\text{time (sec)} = \frac{18\eta}{g(d^1 - d)D^2}$$

where: h = vertical height (cm).

DARCY'S EQUATION

Darcy's equation is used for calculating hydraulic conductivity under saturated soil conditions.

$$K = Q/AT \times dL/dH$$

where: K = hydraulic conductivity (cm/sec)
       Q = quantity of water (cm^3) passing through the soil core
       A = cross-sectional area (cm^2) of the soil core
       T = time (sec) required for the water to pass through the core
     dL = length (cm) of the soil core
    dH = head (cm) of the water imposed on the core

Darcy's equation describes that water flow through soil is directly proportional to soil permeability (K), height of the water column above the soil surface (dH), area of the soil column (A) and time (T), and is inversely proportional to the height of the soil column (dL) (Figure A–1).

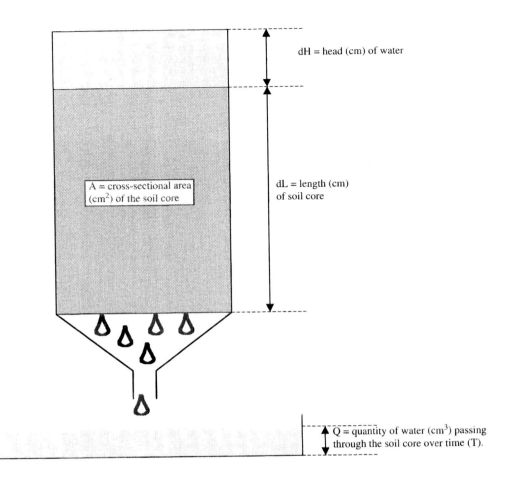

FIGURE A–1 Water flow through soil (Q) is directly proportional to soil permeability (K), height of water column above the soil surface (dH), area of soil column (A) and time (T), and inversely proportional to height of soil column (dL) as determined by Darcy's Law.

dH = head (cm) of water

dL = length (cm) of soil core

A = cross-sectional area (cm²) of the soil core

Q = quantity of water (cm³) passing through the soil core over time (T).

APPENDIX B

CALCULATING SOIL POROSITY

CALCULATING SOIL POROSITY

In calculating total pore space or porosity, two weight measurements of soils, **particle density** and **bulk density,** must be known. By knowing these two variables, the total solid space makeup of a soil can be determined. From here, total solid space is subtracted from 100 to indicate **total pore space.**

% pore space = 100 − [(bulk density of a soil/particle density of the soil) × 100]

For example, if a sandy soil has a bulk density of 1.50 g/cm^3 and a particle density of 2.65 g/cm^3, then the pore (air and water) space will be 43.4 percent (100 − [1.5 g/cm^3 ÷ 2.65 g/cm^3] × 100). A silt loam with 1.30 g/cm^3 bulk density and 2.65 g/cm^3 particle density possesses 50.9 percent pore space.

The next step is determining what percentage of pore space is actually filled with water and what portion is filled with air. To determine this amount, two additional variables must be calculated. The first is the **water content of soil** by weight; in other words, the weight of water in a soil in relation to the total weight of the soil. A sample of soil is weighed, then completely dried and reweighed. The numbers are then inserted into the following equation:

water content of a soil, by weight = (wet weight − dry weight) / dry weight

Next, the water content of a soil, by volume (often called the **volume metric water content** of a soil), is determined. This value is simply found by multiplying the water content weight by the bulk density of the soil.

water content of a soil, by volume = (water content, by weight) × bulk density

The total porosity (the portion that is filled with air and the portion filled with water) can now be calculated. Total porosity, as explained earlier, can be determined by several methods. This value was previously found using the equation:

total soil porosity = 1 − (bulk density/particle density)

The portion of the total soil porosity filled by air (**aeration porosity**) is then simply determined by the following:

air filled (aeration) porosity = total soil porosity − the volume metric water content of the soil

Water-filled porosity is then determined by simply subtracting air-filled porosity from the total soil porosity.

The classical laboratory method of determining soil porosity involves measuring the water retention capacity of a saturated sample held at a tension of 40 centimeters at 15 atmospheres. Water removed by this tension is considered to be that which occupies noncapillary pore space, and retained water is considered to occupy capillary pore space for a golf green. The calculations are as follows:

$$\text{percent total porosity} = \frac{\text{saturated weight of soil (g)} - \text{oven dry weight (g)}}{\text{volume of soil (cm}^3)} \times 100$$

$$\text{percent noncapillary porosity} = \frac{\text{saturated wt. of soil (g)} - \text{wt. with 40 cm tension (g)}}{\text{volume of soil (cm}^3)} \times 100$$

$$\text{percent capillary porosity} = \frac{\text{weight with 40 cm tension} - \text{oven dry weight (g)}}{\text{volume of soil (cm}^3)} \times 100$$

Field capacity is traditionally determined by subjecting soil cores to a pressure of one-third atmosphere on a pressure plate apparatus. The water released at this tension is considered to be **gravitational water** (water pulled from a soil by the force of gravity). The **permanent wilting point** is determined by exposing the cores to 15 atmospheres (15 bars) tension of a pressure membrane extraction apparatus. Although one-third atmosphere and 15 atmospheres are accepted standards for most soils, many sands, by their nature, hold considerably less water, and little available water remains at pressures greater than one-third atmosphere.

By determining the rooting depth of the turf, and knowing the evapotranspiration rate, the amount of water available to the turf may be calculated. A water-retention capacity between 12 and 25 percent by weight is desirable, with an ideal capacity of 18 percent. This translates to the equivalent depth of water being 0.18 inch held per inch of soil. The equivalent depth of water is calculated as follows:

equivalent depth of water = volume metric water content × the soil depth of the sample

Appendix C

Determining Surface Area

DETERMINING SURFACE AREA

When determining surface areas (Figure A–2), the following calculations and formulas are helpful.

Helpful Calculations and Formulas

Rectangle, square or parallelogram:	Area	$= \text{length (L)} \times \text{width (W)}$
Trapezoid:	Area	$= [a + (b \times h)] \div 2$
Circle:	Area	$= \text{radius (r)}^2 \times 3.1416 \text{ (or } \pi)$
		$= \text{diameter (d)}^2 \times 0.7854$
		$= (\text{radius} \times \text{diameter}) \times 0.7854$
	Radius	$= d \div 2$
	Diameter	$= r \times 2$
	Circumference	$= \pi \times d$
Sphere:	Volume	$= r^3 \times 4.1888$ $= d^3 \times 0.5236$
Triangle:	Area	$= (W \times H) \div 2$
Cylinder:	Volume	$= r^2 \times 3.1416 \times L$

Finding Tank Capacity (gallons)

Cylindrical tanks:	(Inches)	$= L \times d^2 \times 0.0034$
	(Feet)	$= L \times d^2 \times 5.875$
Rectangle tanks:	(Inches)	$= L \times W \times \text{height} \times 0.004329$
	(Feet)	$= L \times W \times \text{height} \times 7.48$
Elliptical tanks:	(Inches)	$= L \times \text{short diameter (sd)} \times \text{long diameter (ld)} \times 0.0034$
	(Feet)	$= L \times \text{sd} \times \text{ld} \times 5.875$

Example:

From Figure A–3, determine the area (sq.ft.) of the tee, dogleg fairway, and green.

Step 1: Segment the total area into common geometric figures including parallelograms, triangles, rectangles, trapezoids, circles, and ovals.

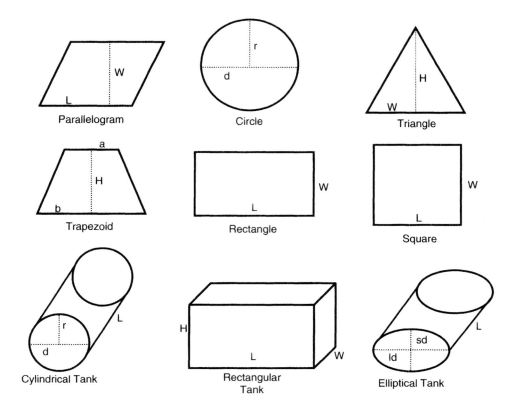

Parallelogram

Circle

Triangle

Trapezoid

Rectangle

Square

Cylindrical Tank

Rectangular
Tank

Elliptical Tank

Step 2: Determine the area of each geometric figure:

Tee

area of a square = length × width = 30 ft × 30 ft = 900 sq.ft.

Fairway

area of a parallelogram = length × width = 85 ft × 200 ft = 17,000 sq.ft.
area of a triangle = (width × height) ÷ 2 = 20 ft × 200 ft ÷ 2 = 2,000 sq.ft.
area of a rectangle = length × width = 110 ft × 200 ft = 22,000 sq.ft.
area of a triangle = (width × height) ÷ 2 = 75 ft × 200 ft ÷ 2 = 7,500 sq.ft.
area of a trapezoid = [a + (b × height)] ÷ 2 = [40 ft + (100 ft × 200 ft)] ÷ 2 = 10,020 sq.ft.
area of a rectangle = length × width = 130 ft × 200 ft = 26,000 sq.ft.
area of a triangle = (width × height) ÷ 2 = (30 ft × 200 ft) ÷ 2 = 3,000 sq.ft.
total area of the fairway = 17,000 + 2,000 + 22,000 + 7,500 + 10,020 + 26,000 + 3,000 =
    87,520 sq.ft.

= 87,520 sq.ft. ÷ 43,560 sq.ft. per acre = 2 total acres

Green

area of a circle = diameter (d)^2 × 0.7854 = (80 ft)^2 × 0.7854 = 5,027 sq.ft.
area of an oval = (radius × diameter) × 0.7854 = (25 ft × 40 ft) × 0.7854 = 785 sq.ft.
total area of the green = 5,027 + 785 = 5,812 sq.ft.

OFFSET METHOD
Another way to measure irregularly shaped areas is the offset method. Large areas are broken
down into a series of smaller trapezoids equally spaced along a centerline (Figure A–4). The precision is increased by decreasing the spacing between lines.
    Each 90° offset line is added together, and this sum is multiplied by the spacing(s) of each line.

FIGURE A–3

Determining the surface area of a dogleg golf hole (top) including tee, fairway and green by segmenting each area into smaller units (bottom).

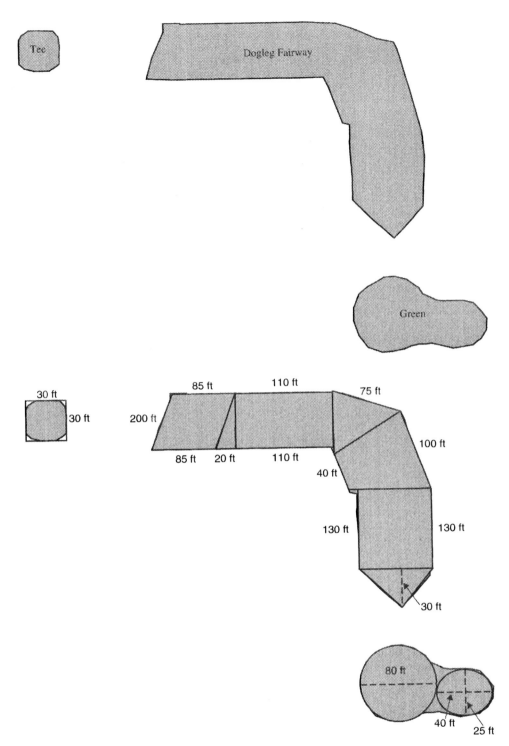

Example:

Determine the area of the following sand trap (Figure A–5).

Step 1: Establish a center line and divide it into equally spaced offset lines. The center line in this example is 80 feet long and is divided into seven offset lines spaced 10 feet apart (Figure A–6).

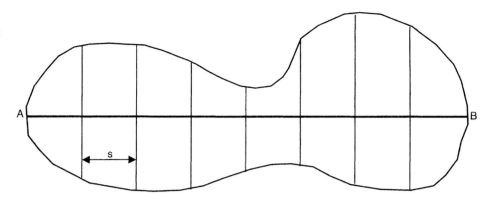

FIGURE A–4 Using the offset method for determining the size of irregularly shaped areas. Large areas are segmented into a series of smaller trapezoids equally spaced along a centerline. Each 90° offset line is added together and this sum is multiplied by the spacing of each line.

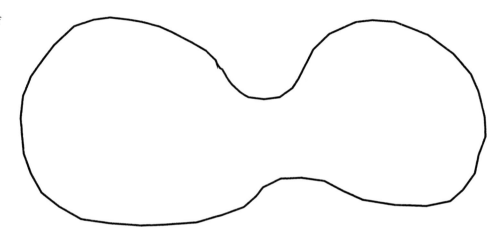

FIGURE A–5 Example of an irregularly shaped sand trap prior to determining its size.

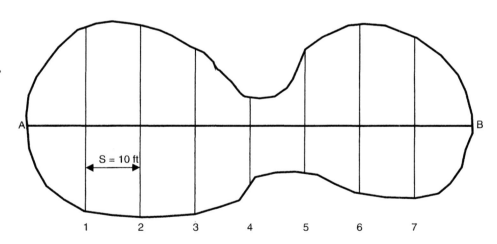

FIGURE A–6 A center line is established in the sand trap and it is divided into seven equally spaced (10 feet, 3m) offset lines. These are added up and multiplied by the spacing of each line to obtain total area.

Step 2: Add up the lengths of the seven offset lines:

$$
\begin{array}{ll}
1 = 12\ \text{ft} & 5 = 7\ \text{ft} \\
2 = 11\ \text{ft} & 6 = 10\ \text{ft} \\
3 = 10\ \text{ft} & 7 = \underline{9\ \text{ft}} \\
4 = 5\ \text{ft} & 64\ \text{ft}
\end{array}
$$

Step 3: Multiply the total lengths of the offset lines by the spacing(s) of each line to obtain total area in square feet:

$$\text{area} = 64\ \text{ft} \times 10\ \text{ft} = 640\ \text{sq.ft.}$$

AVERAGE RADIUS METHOD

A variation of the offset method to determine an irregularly shaped circular area is the **average radius method.** The average radius method is most often used for irregularly shaped greens.

Step 1: From the center of the irregularly shaped circular area, such as a green, divide it into equally spaced 10 or 20° pie-shaped increments (Figure A–7). For greater precision, use the 10° increments.

Step 2: Measure the length of each radial from the center to the edge of the green. This totals 36 measurements for 10° increments and 18 for 20° increments.

Step 3: Total these measurements and divide by the number of measurements to achieve an average radius length.

Step 4: Calculate the area of the green using the formula:

$$area = 3.14 \times (average\ radius)^2$$

Example:

From the previous illustration, determine the area of the green.

Step 1: Divide the green into equally spaced degree increments. For this example, 20° increments are used.

Step 2: Measure the length of each radial from the center of the green to the edge. Add these and divide by the total number of measurements (18 in this example).

0° = 53 ft	120° = 46 ft	240° = 37 ft
20° = 50 ft	140° = 48 ft	260° = 34 ft
40° = 47 ft	160° = 50 ft	280° = 36 ft
60° = 36 ft	180° = 52 ft	300° = 47 ft
80° = 34 ft	200° = 48 ft	320° = 50 ft
100° = 37 ft	220° = 46 ft	340° = 49 ft
		800 ft ÷ 18 = 44.4 ft

FIGURE A–7 Using the average radius method to determine an irregularly shaped circular area. From the center of the circular area, it is divided into equally spaced 10 or 20° pie-shaped increments. The length of each radial from the center to the edge of the circular area is measured and these are totaled and divided by the number of measurements to achieve an average radius length. The area is then calculated by using the formula: area = 3.14 × (average radius)².

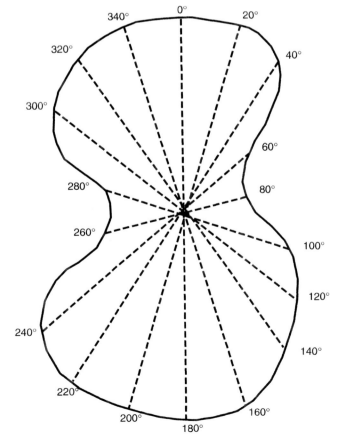

Step 3: Calculate the surface area using the formula:

$$\text{area} = 3.14 \times (\text{average radius})^2$$
$$= 3.14 \times (44.4)^2$$
$$= 6{,}190 \text{ sq.ft.}$$

MODIFIED OFFSET METHOD

When measuring large areas, such as ponds, a modification of the offset method can be used.

Step 1: The pond is first bracketed by a large rectangle so all of the pond is included (Figure A–8).
Step 2: Offset lines are marked at even spacings along the long edge of the rectangle and their lengths are recorded.
Step 3: Add the two lines for each spacing and subtract this amount from the total width of the rectangle.
Step 4: Total these values and multiply this total by the spacing between the offset lines.

Example:

Determine the area of the previously illustrated pond.

Step 1: Draw and measure a rectangle around the area. The length is 360 feet long and the width is 320 feet. Divide the length into equally spaced offset lines.
Step 2: Measure and total the lengths of each equally spaced offset line.

A1 = 40 ft	B1 = 50 ft	C1 = 60 ft	D1 = 20 ft	E1 = 16 ft	F1 = 24 ft	G1 = 24 ft
A2 = 20 ft	B2 = 24 ft	C2 = 18 ft	D2 = 20 ft	E2 = 22 ft	F2 = 26 ft	G2 = 22 ft
60 ft	74 ft	78 ft	40 ft	38 ft	50 ft	46 ft

FIGURE A–8 Using the modified offset method to determine the size of large areas, such as ponds. The pond is first bracketed by a large rectangle so all of the pond is included. Offset lines are marked at even spacings along the long edge of the rectangle and their lengths recorded. The two lines for each spacing are then added and subtracted from the total width of the rectangle. These values are totaled and multiplied by the spacing between the offset lines.

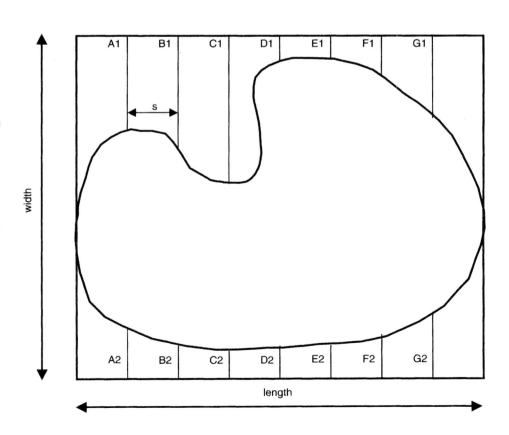

Step 3: Subtract each offset line total from the width of the rectangle and then total these values.

A: $160 - 60 = 100$ ft
B: $160 - 74 = 86$ ft
C: $160 - 78 = 82$ ft
D: $160 - 40 = 120$ ft
E: $160 - 38 = 122$ ft
F: $160 - 50 = 110$ ft
G: $160 - 46 = \underline{114 \text{ ft}}$
734 ft

Step 4: Multiply the total by the spacing distance:

$$\text{area} = \text{total} \times \text{spacing distance}$$
$$= 734 \text{ ft} \times 80 \text{ ft}$$
$$= 58{,}720 \text{ ft}^2$$

To convert square feet to acres, divide the square feet by 43,560:

$$58{,}720 \text{ ft}^2 \times \frac{\text{acre}}{43{,}560 \text{ ft}^2} = 1.35 \text{ acres}$$

If the average depth of the pond is known, the volume of water in the pond can be determined by multiplying the surface area by the average depth and converting to gallons, with the knowledge that 7.48 gallons can be held per cubic foot. For example, if the above pond has an average depth of 50 feet, then:

$$\text{volume} = \text{surface area} \times \text{average depth} \times \frac{7.48 \text{ gal}}{\text{ft}^3}$$
$$= 58{,}720 \text{ ft}^2 \times 50 \text{ ft} \times \frac{7.48 \text{ gal}}{\text{ft}^3}$$
$$= 21{,}961{,}280 \text{ gal}$$

APPENDIX D

CALIBRATION FORMULAS AND METRIC CONVERSION TABLES

PESTICIDE CALIBRATION FORMULAS AND INFORMATION

acres covered/hour:

$$= \text{mph} \times \text{swath (ft)} \times 0.1212$$

$$\text{or} \quad \frac{\text{mph} \times \text{swath (ft)}}{8.25}$$

gallons per acre (gpa):

$$= \frac{\text{gpm} \times 495}{\text{mph} \times \text{swath (ft)}}$$

$$\text{or} \quad \frac{\text{gpm per nozzle} \times 495}{\text{mph} \times \text{nozzle spacing (ft)}}$$

$$= \frac{\text{gpm per nozzle} \times 5{,}940}{\text{mph} \times \text{nozzle spacing (inches)}}$$

$$\text{or} \quad \frac{\text{fl.oz. collected per nozzle} \times 4{,}084}{\text{ft traveled} \times \text{nozzle spacing (inches)}}$$

$$= \frac{\text{fl.oz. collected per nozzle in 100 ft} \times 40.8375}{\text{nozzle spacing (inches)}}$$

$$\text{or} \quad \frac{\text{gallons per 1,000 sq. ft.}}{0.023}$$

$$= \frac{\text{gallons collected per nozzle} \times \text{no. of nozzles} \times 43{,}560}{\text{ft traveled} \times \text{swath (ft)}}$$

gallons per 1,000 sq. ft.

$$= 0.023 \times \text{gpa}$$

ounces per 1,000 sq. ft.

$$= 2.94 \times \text{gpa}$$

gallons per minute (gpm):

$$= \frac{\text{gpa} \times \text{mph} \times \text{swath (ft)}}{495}$$

$$\text{or} \quad \frac{\text{fl.oz. per minute}}{128}$$

$$= \frac{\text{gpa} \times \text{mph} \times \text{nozzle spacing (inches)} \times \text{no. nozzles}}{5{,}940}$$

gpm/nozzle:

$$= \frac{\text{gpa} \times \text{mph} \times \text{nozzle spacing (inches)}}{5{,}940}$$

$$\text{or} \quad \frac{\text{gpa} \times \text{mph} \times \text{nozzle spacing (ft)}}{495}$$

$$= \frac{\text{test jar fl.oz.} \times 0.46875}{\text{seconds to fill test jar}}$$

$$\text{or} \quad \frac{7.5}{\text{seconds to fill 1 pint (16 fl.oz.)}}$$

$$= \frac{15}{\text{seconds to fill 1 quart (32 fl.oz.)}}$$

minutes/acre

$$= \frac{495}{\text{mph} \times \text{swath (ft)}}$$

minutes/load

$$= \frac{\text{gallons/load} \times 495}{\text{mph} \times \text{gpa} \times \text{swath (ft)}}$$

acres covered per tank:

$$= \frac{\text{gallons per tank}}{\text{gpa}}$$

material needed per tank

$$= \frac{\text{rate/a} \times \text{gallons/tank}}{\text{gpa}}$$

travel speed (miles per hour, mph)

$$= \frac{\text{distance traveled (ft)} \times 0.68}{\text{time (seconds) to travel distance}}$$

flow rate (as influenced by pressure):

$$\frac{gpm_1}{gpm_2} = \frac{\sqrt{psi_1}}{\sqrt{psi_2}}$$

$$\text{or} \quad gpa_2 = gpa_1 \times \sqrt{\frac{psi_2}{psi_1}}$$

$$\text{or} \quad psi_2 = psi_1 \times \left(\frac{gpa_2}{gpa_1}\right)^2$$

For any change in travel speed (mph), calculate the resulting gpa_2 by:

$$gpa_2 = \frac{gpa_1 \times mph_1}{mph_2}$$

or $\dfrac{gpa_1}{gpa_2} = \dfrac{mph_2}{mph_1}$ or $mph_2 = \dfrac{gpa_1 \times mph_1}{gpa_2}$

Fluid Application

lbs/acre nutrient applied
= 0.226464 × element concentration (ppm) × acre inches of solution applied

ppm
= $\dfrac{1{,}000{,}000 \times \text{lbs ai used}}{\text{gal/tank} \times 8.34}$ or $\dfrac{\text{wt. of material to be used (lbs)} \times 1{,}000{,}000}{\text{wt. of tank mixture (lbs)}}$

= $\dfrac{1{,}000{,}000 \times \text{fl.oz. used} \times \text{lb ai/gal}}{\text{gal/tank} \times 8.34 \times 128}$ or $\dfrac{1{,}000{,}000 \times \text{oz commercial material used} \times \%\text{ ai (decimal)}}{\text{gal/tank} \times 8.34 \times 16}$

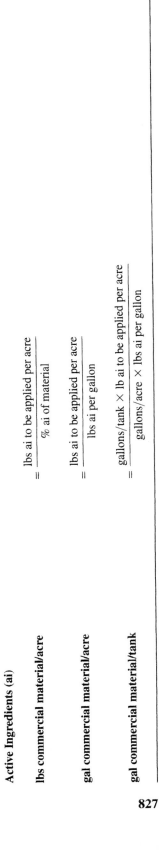

lbs nutrients applied/acre
= ppm of the element in the water × acre-inches water applied × 0.226464

lb ai to use per tank
= $\dfrac{\text{ppm desired} \times \text{gal/tank} \times 8.34}{1{,}000{,}000}$ or $\dfrac{\text{ppm desired} \times \text{gal/tank} \times 8.34}{1{,}000{,}000 \times \%\text{ ai}}$

lb commercial material to use per tank
= $\dfrac{\text{ppm desired} \times \text{gal/tank} \times 8.34}{1{,}000{,}000 \times \%\text{ ai (decimal)}}$ or $\dfrac{\%\text{ desired} \times \text{gal/tank} \times 8.34}{\%\text{ ai (decimal)}}$

fl.oz. to use per tank
= $\dfrac{\text{ppm desired} \times \text{gal/tank} \times 8.34 \times 128}{1{,}000{,}000 \times \text{ai per gal}}$

gal commercial material to use per tank
= $\dfrac{\text{ai (decimal)} \times 8.34 \times \text{gal/tank}}{\text{ai per gal} \times 100}$

% ai in a spray mix
= $\dfrac{\text{lbs commercial material used} \times \%\text{ ai (decimal)}}{\text{gal/tank} \times 8.34}$

gal commercial material for total treated acres
= $\dfrac{\text{ppm desired} \times \text{gpa} \times \text{acres} \times 8.34}{1{,}000{,}000 \times \text{lb ai/gal}}$

Active Ingredients (ai)

lbs commercial material/acre
= $\dfrac{\text{lbs ai to be applied per acre}}{\%\text{ ai of material}}$

gal commercial material/acre
= $\dfrac{\text{lbs ai to be applied per acre}}{\text{lbs ai per gallon}}$

gal commercial material/tank
= $\dfrac{\text{gallons/tank} \times \text{lb ai to be applied per acre}}{\text{gallons/acre} \times \text{lbs ai per gallon}}$

Time (seconds) required to cover a specific distance to obtain a desired speed (mph).

Desired mph	Feet per minute	Time required (seconds) to travel a distance of		
		100 ft	200 ft	300 ft
2.0	176	34	68	102
2.5	220	27	54	81
3.0	264	23	45	68
3.5	308	20	39	58
4.0	352	17	43	51
4.5	395	15	30	45
5.0	440	14	27	41
6.0	528	—	23	34
7.0	616	—	19	29
8.0	704	—	17	26
9.0	792	—	15	23

Metric Prefix Definitions (basic metric unit = 1)

tera	= 10^{12}		deci	= 10^{-1}
giga	= 10^{9}		centi	= 10^{-2}
mega	= 10^{6}		milli	= 10^{-3}
kilo	= 10^{3}		micro	= 10^{-6}
hecto	= 10^{2}		nano	= 10^{-9}
deca	= 10^{1}		pico	= 10^{-12}

Approximate Rates of Application Equivalents

Weights

1 oz/ft^2	= 2,722.5 lbs/a	
1 oz/yd^2	= 302.5 lbs/a	
1 oz/100 ft^2	= 27.2 lbs/a	
1 oz/1,000 ft^2	= 43.46 oz/a	= 2.72 lbs/a
1 lb/a	= 1 oz/2,733 ft^2	= 8.5 g/1,000 ft^2
100 lb/a	= 2.5 lb/1,000 ft^2	
1 yd^3 sand	= 1.3 to 1.5 tons	
1 bushel	= 1 1/4 ft^3	= 0.046 yd^3

Liquid

1 oz/1,000 ft^2	= 43.56 oz/a	= 1.4 qt/a
1 pt/1,000 ft^2	= 5.4 gal/a	
100 gal/a	= 2.3 gal/1,000 ft^2	= 1 qt/100 ft^2

METRIC SYSTEM CONVERSION FACTORS

Area Equivalents

1 acre = 43,560 ft^2 = 4,840 yd^2 = 0.4047 hectares = 160 rods^2 = 4,047 m^2 = 0.0016 square mile
1 acre-inch = 102.8 m^3 = 27,154 gal = 3,630 ft^3
1 hectare (ha) = 10,000 m^2 = 100 are = 2.471 acres = 107,639 ft^2
1 cubic foot (ft^3) = 1,728 in.^{3} = 0.037 yd^3 = 0.02832 m^3 = 28,320 cm^3
1 cubic yard (yd^3) = 27 ft^3 = 0.765 m^3
1 square foot (ft^2) = 144 in.^{2} = 929.03 cm^2 = 0.09290 m^2
1 square yard (yd^2) = 9 ft^2 = 0.836 m^2

Liquid Equivalents

1 ft^3 of water = 7.5 gal = 62.4 lbs = 28.3 liters
1 acre-inch of water = 27,154 gal = 3,630 ft^3
1 liter (l) = 2.113 pts = 1,000 ml = 1.057 qts = 33.8 fl.oz. = 0.26 gal

1 U.S. gallon = 4 qt = 8 pt = 16 cups = 128 fl.oz. = 8.337 lbs of water = 3.785 L = 3,785 ml
    = 231 in.^{3} = 256 tbsp. = 0.1337 ft^3
1 quart = 0.9463 liters = 2 pt = 32 fl.oz. = 4 cups = 64 tablespoons (tbsp.) = 57.75 in.^{3} =
    0.25 gal = 946.4 ml
1 pint = 16 fl.oz. = 2 cups = 473.2 ml = 32 level tablespoons = 0.125 gal = 0.5 qt
1 cup = 8 fl.oz. = 1/2 pt = 16 tablespoons = 236.6 ml
1 tablespoon = 14.8 ml = 3 teaspoons (tsp.) = 0.5 fl.oz.
1 milliliter (ml) = 1 cm^3 = 0.34 fl.oz. = 0.002 pts
1 U.S. fluid ounce = 29.57 ml = 2 tablespoons = 6 tsp = 0.03125 qt
1 teaspoon = 4.93 ml = 0.1667 fl.oz. = 80 drops

Temperature Equivalents

degrees Centigrade = (°F − 32) × 5/9
degrees Fahrenheit = (°C × 9/5) + 32

Pressure Equivalents

1 lb per square inch (psi) = 6.9 kilopascal (kPa)
1 psi = 2.31 feet head of water
1 atm = 760 mm Hg = 1.013 × 10^5 Pa = 1.013 bar
    = 14.70 psi
1 mm Hg = 133.32 Pa = 0.133 kPa = 133,333 mPa

Length Equivalents

centimeter (cm) = 0.3937 inch = 0.01 m = 0.03281 ft
meter (m) = 3.28 feet = 39.4 inches = 100 cm = 1.094 yds = 1,000 mm
kilometer = 0.621 statute mile = 1,000 meters = 100,000 cm = 3,281 ft = 39,370 in.
inch = 2.54 cm = 25.4 mm = 0.0254 m = 0.08333 ft
foot = 0.3048 meters = 30.48 cm = 12 inches
yard = 0.9144 meters = 3 feet = 36 inches = 91.44 cm
statute mile = 1,760 yards = 5,280 feet = 1.61 kilometers = 1,609 meters

Mixture Ratios

1 mg/g = 1,000 ppm
1 fl.oz./gal = 7,490 ppm
1 fl.oz./100 gal = 75 ppm
1 qt/100 gal = 2 tablespoons/1.0 gal
1 pt/100 gal = 1 teaspoons/1gal

Flow

1 gpm = 0.134 ft^3/minute
1 ft^3/min (cfm) = 449 gal/hr (gph) = 7.481 gal/min

Weight Equivalents

1 ton (U.S.) = 2,000 lb = 0.907 metric tons = 907.2 kg
1 metric ton = 10^6 g = 1,000 kg = 2,205 lb
1 lb = 16 oz = 453.6 grams (g) = 0.4536 kg
1 oz (weight) = 28.35 g = 0.0625 lb
1 gram = 1,000 mg = 0.0353 oz = 0.001 kg = 0.002205 lb
milligrams (mg) = 0.001 grams
1 kilogram (kg) = 1,000 grams = 35.3 oz = 2.205 lbs
microgram (μg) = 10^{-6} grams = 0.001 mg
1 nanogram (ng) = 10^{-9} grams = 0.001 micrograms (μg)
picogram = 10^{-12} grams
1 ppm = 0.0001% = 0.013 fl.oz. in 100 gal = 1 mg/kg = 1 mg/l = 1 μg/g = 0.379 g in 100 gal
    water = 8.34 × 10^{-6} lb/gal = 1μl/l
10 ppm = 0.001% = 10 mg/l   100 ppm = 0.01% = 100 mg/l
1,000 ppm = 1mg/g = 0.1% = 1,000 mg/l
1 ppb = 1 μg/kg or 1 μg/L or 1 ng/g   1 ppt = 1 picogram/g
1% = 10,000 ppm = 10 g/l = 1g/100 ml = 10 g/kg = 1.33 oz by weight/gal water = 8.34
    lbs/100 gal water

Approximate Weight of Dry Soil

Type	g/cm³	lbs/ft³	lbs/acre (6 inches deep)
Sand	1.6	100 (or 2,700 lbs/yd³)	2,143,000
Loam	1.3 to 1.55	80 to 95	1,714,000
Clay or silt	1.0 to 1.30	65 to 80	1,286,000
Muck	0.65	40	860,000
Peat	0.325	20	430,000

Sand weights (tons)	=	yd³	×	1.3
Gravel weights (tons)	=	ft³	×	110
0.5 to 1 inch diameter gravel			=	2,700 lbs/ton
0.25 to 0.375 inch diameter gravel			=	3,000 lbs/ton

Energy

1 calorie (cal) = 4.184 Joule (J)
Joule (J) = $1 \text{ kg m}^2 \text{ s}^{-2}$
1 kcal = 4.184 kJ

Metric Conversion Factors

To convert	Multiply by	To obtain
acres	0.4047	hectare (ha)
acres	43,560	sq.feet
acres	0.00405	sq.kilometer
acres	4,047	sq.meter
acres	4,840	sq.yards
acre-feet	325,851	sq.feet
acre-feet	43,560	cu.feet
acre-feet	1,233.5	m³
acre-inch	102.8	m³
bar	14.5	lb/in.²
bar	1,019.7	g/cm³
bar	29.53	inches Hg @ 0°C
bar	75	cm Hg @ 0°C
bar	0.001	J/kg
bar	100	kPa
bushels (dry)	0.03524	m²
bushels	1.245	ft³
calorie (cal)	4.184	Joules (J)
centimeters (cm)	0.03281	feet
centimeters	0.3937	inches
centimeters	0.1094	yards
centimeters	0.01	meters
centimeters	10	millimeters (mm)
cm/sec	1.9685	ft/min
cm/sec	0.0223694	mph
cm²	0.001076	ft²

To convert	Multiply by	To obtain
cm^2	0.1550	in.^{2}
cm^3	0.0610237	inch^3
cm^3	0.0338	fl.oz.
cup	8	fl.oz.
cup	236.6	cm^3
feet (ft)	30.48	centimeters
feet	0.3048	meters
feet	305	mm
ft^2	929	cm^2
ft^2	0.0929	m^2
ft^2	9.294×10^{-6}	hectares (ha)
ft^3 (cubic feet)	0.0283	cu.meter
ft^3	7.4805	gallons
ft^3	1,728	cubic inches
ft^3	0.037	cubic yards
ft^3	28.32	L
ft^3/1,000 ft^2	0.030463	m^3/100 m^2
feet per minute	0.01136	mph
feet head of water	0.433	psi
foot candle	10.764	lux
gallons (gal)	3.785	liters
gal	3,785	milliliters
gal	128	ounces (liquid)
gal	0.13368	ft^3
gal/acre	9.354	liters/hectare
gal/acre	2.938	oz/1,000 ft^2 (liquid)
gal/1,000 ft^2	4.0746	L/100 m^2
gal/minute	2.228×10^{-3}	cubic feet/second
gal/min	0.06309	L/sec
gal/min	0.227125	m^3/hr
grams (g)	0.002205	pounds
gram	0.035274	oz
g/cm^3	0.036127	lb/in.^{3}
g/cm^3	62.428	lb/ft^3
g/ha	0.000893	lbs/a
g/ha	0.087162	oz/a
g/kg	0.10	percent (%)
grams per liter	1,000	ppm
grams per liter	10	percent
grams/sq.meter	0.00020481	lb/sq.feet
hectares (ha)	2.471	acres
ha	107,639	ft^2
inches	2.540	centimeters
inches	0.0254	meters
inches	25.40	millimeters

To convert	Multiply by	To obtain
in./ft	8.3	CM/M
in.^{2}	6.4516	cm^2
in.^{3}	16.3871	cm^3
in.^{3}	0.55411	fl.oz.
in.^{3}	0.01732	qt
kilograms (kg)	2.2046	pounds
kg/hectare	0.892	pounds/acre
kg/ha	0.02048	lb/1,000 ft^2
kg/100 m^2	2.037	lbs/1,000 ft^2
kg/L	8.3454	lb/gal
kilometers (km)	100,000	centimeters
kilometers	3,281	feet
kilometers	1,000	meters
kilometers	0.6214	miles
kilometers	1,094	yards
km/h	0.62137	mph
km/h	54.6807	ft/min
kilopascals (kPa)	0.145	pounds/sq.in. (psi)
liters (L)	0.2642	gallons
L	33.814	ounces
L	2.113	pints
L	1.057	quarts
L	0.035315	ft^3
L/100 m^2	0.2454	gal/1,000 ft^2
L/100 m^2	1.9634	pt/1,000 ft^2
liters/hectare	0.107	gallons/acre
L/ha	0.314	oz/1,000 ft^2
L/ha	0.855	pt/a
L/min	15.85	gal/hr
meters (m)	3.281	feet
meters	39.37	inches
meters	1.094	yards
meters	100	centimeters
meters	0.001	kilometers
meters	1,000	millimeters
meters/sec	2.2369	mph
m^2	10.764	ft^2
m^2	1,550	in.^{2}
m^2	1.196	yd^2
m^3	35.3147	ft^3
m^3	1.30795	yd^3
miles (nautical)	1.1508	miles (statute)
miles (statute)	160,900	centimeters
miles	5,280	feet
miles	1.609	kilometers

To convert	Multiply by	To obtain
miles	1,760	yards
miles/hour (mph)	1.467	feet/second
miles/hour	88	feet/minute
miles/hour	1.61	kilometers/hour
miles/hour	0.447	meter/second
milliliters (mL)	0.0338	ounces (fluid)
milliliters	0.0002642	gallons
ml/m^2	3.14	fl. oz/1,000 ft^2
ml/10,000 L	0.0128	fl. oz./1,000 gal
millimeters (mm)	0.03937	inches
1 mm Hg @ 0°C	0.13332	kPa
1 mm Hg	133333.3	mPa
ounces (fluid)	0.02957	liters
ounces (fluid)	29.573	milliliters
ounces (fluid)	0.03125	qt
ounces (fluid)/acre	0.0731	L/ha
ounces (fluid)/1,000 ft^2	3.18	L/ha
ounces (weight)	28.35	grams
ounces (weight)	0.0625	lb
ounces (weight)/acre	0.07	kg/ha
oz (weight)/acre	11.473	g/ha
oz (weight)/1,000 ft^2	3.05	kg/ha
oz (wt.)/ft^2	305.15	g/m^2
percent (%)	10	g/kg
pint (liquid)	0.473	liter
pt/a	1.1692	L/ha
pt/a	0.3673	oz/1,000 ft^2
pt/1,000 ft^2	0.50932	L/100 m^2
parts per million (ppm)	2.719	lb ai/acre foot of water
ppm	0.001	grams/L
ppm	8.34	lb/million gal
ppm	1	mg/kg
ppm	0.013	ounces/100 gal of water
ppm	0.3295	gal/acre-foot of water
ppm	8.2897	lbs/million gal of water
pounds (lbs)	0.4536	kilograms
pounds	453.6	grams
pounds/acre	1.12	kg/hectare
pounds/a	1.0413	g/100 ft^2
pounds/a	0.02296	lb/1,000 ft^2
pounds/acre-foot	0.3682	g/m^3
pounds/acre-foot	0.0003682	kg/m^3
pounds/sq.ft.	4,883	grams/sq.meter
pounds/1,000 ft^2	48.83	kg/ha
pounds/1,000 ft^2	43.5597	lb/a

To convert	Multiply by	To obtain
pounds/1,000 ft^2	491	g/100 m^2
pounds/1,000 ft^2	4.91	kg/100 m^2
pounds/yd^3	0.0005937	g/cm^3
pounds/yd^3	594	g/m^3
pounds/gallon	0.12	kg/liter
psi (lbs/sq.in.)	6.89	kilopascals (kPa)
psi	0.06895	bar
psi	0.068046	atm
psi	2.31	feet head of water
quarts	0.9463	liters
qt/a	2.3385	L/ha
qt/a	0.7346	oz/1,000 ft^2
ton (2,000 lbs)	907	kg
ton (2,000 lbs)	0.907	ton (metric)
ton (2,000 lbs)/acre	2.241	ton (metric)/ha
ton (metric)	2,205	lb
ton (metric)	1,000	kg
ton (metric)	1.102	ton (2,000 lb)
yards	91.44	centimeters
yards	0.9144	meters
yards	914.4	millimeters
yd^3	27	ft^3
yd^3	0.7645	m^3
yd^3	765	L
yd^3/1,000 ft^2	0.825	m^3/100 m^2
P_2O_5	0.437	P
K_2O	0.830	K
CaO	0.715	Ca
MgO	0.602	Mg

Decimal and Millimeter Length Equivalents

Fraction (inch)	Decimals (inch)	Millimeters
1	1.00	25.4
15/16	0.9375	23.812
7/8	0.875	22.225
13/16	0.8125	20.638
3/4	0.75	19.05
11/16	0.6875	17.462
5/8	0.625	15.875
9/16	0.5625	14.288
1/2	0.5	12.70
7/16	0.4375	11.112
3/8	0.3750	9.525
11/32	0.34375	8.731

Fraction (inch)	Decimals (inch)	Millimeters
5/16	0.3125	7.938
9/32	0.28125	7.144
1/4	0.25	6.350
15/64	0.234375	5.953
7/32	0.21875	5.556
13/64	0.203125	5.159
1/5	0.200	5.08
3/16	0.1875	4.762
23/128	0.1797	4.564
11/64	0.171875	4.366
1/6	0.167	4.242
21/128	0.1641	4.168
5/32	0.15625	3.969
19/128	0.1484	3.769
1/7	0.143	3.633
9/64	0.140625	3.572
1/8	0.1250	3.175
7/64	0.109375	2.778
1/10	0.100	2.540
3/32	0.09375	2.381
5/64	0.078125	1.984
1/16	0.0625	1.588
3/64	0.046875	1.191
1/32	0.03125	0.794
1/64	0.015625	0.397

Slopes

10 percent	=	6°	=	10:1		33 percent	=	18°	=	3:1
18 percent	=	10°	=	6:1		50 percent	=	26°	=	2:1
25 percent	=	14°	=	4:1		100 percent	=	45°	=	1:1

REFERENCES AND ADDITIONAL READING

A

Adams, W. A., and R. F. Gibbs. 1994. *Natural turf for sport and amenity: Science and practice.* Cambridge, Great Britain: CAB International, University Press.

Anonymous. 1972. *Water quality criteria. Agricultural use of water.* Washington, D.C.: National Academy of Science—National Academy of Engineering, sec. V, 323–353.

Anonymous. 1982a. *Lime and fertilizer recommendations based on soil-test results.* Clemson University Extension Service Circular 476.

Anonymous. 1982b. *USGA refining the green section specification for putting green construction.* Far Hills, N.J.: Golf House.

Anonymous. 1992. *Guidelines for water reuse.* EPA/625/R-92/004. Cincinnati, OH: U.S. EPA, Center for Environmental Research Information.

Anonymous. 1993a. *Environmental guidelines for Canadian golf clubs.* Oakville, Ontario: Royal Canadian Golf Association, 10.

Anonymous. 1993b. *Protect yourself from pesticides.* Washington, D.C.: U.S. Environmental Protection Agency.

Anonymous. 1993c. USGA recommendations for a method of putting green construction. *USGA Green Section Record* 31(2):1–3.

Anonymous. 1995. *Best management practices for golf course maintenance departments.* Tallahassee: Florida Department of Environmental Protection.

Anonymous. 1996a. *Environmental principles for golf courses in the United States.* Salt Lake City, Utah: The Center for Resource Management, 1–15.

Anonymous. 1996b. *Turf and landscape digest.* 5th ed. Grounds Maintenance. Overland Park, Kans.: Intertec Publishing.

Asano, T., R. G. Smith, and G. Tschobanoglous. 1984. Municipal wastewater: Treatment and reclaimed water characteristics. In *Irrigation with reclaimed municipal wastewater—A guidance manual,* Report no. 84-1, ed. G. S. Pettygrove and T. Asano, 2:1–2:26. Sacramento: California State Water Resources Control Board.

Augustin, B. J., and G. H. Snyder. 1984. Moisture sensor-controlled irrigation for maintaining bermudagrass turf. *Agronomy J.* 76:848–850.

Ayers, R. S., and D. W. Westcot. 1976. *Water quality for agriculture.* Irrigation and Drainage Paper 29. Rome, Italy: Food and Agriculture Organization of the United Nations.

B

Backman, P. A., E. D. Miltner, G. K. Stahnke, and T. W. Cook. 2002. Worming your way out of a turf situation. *USGA Green Section Record* 40(4):7–8.

Baird, J. H., N. T. Basta, R. I. Huhnke, M. E. Payton, G. V. Johnson, D. E. Storm, and M. D. Smolen. 1997. Influence of buffer length and mowing height on surface runoff of pesticides and nutrients from bermudagrass turf. *Agronomy Abstracts* 89:130.

Baker, S. W., and D. J. Binns. 2001. The influence of grain size and shape on particle migration from the rootzone layer to the drainage layer of golf greens. *9th International Turfgrass Society Research Journal* 9:458–462.

Baldwin, L. B., and D. A. Comer. 1986. *Utilizing treated sewage for irrigation of urban landscapes.* Florida Cooperative Extension Service, Circular 714.

Balogh, J. C., and W. J. Walker, eds. 1992. *Golf course management and construction: Environmental issues.* Chelsea, Mich.: Lewis Publishers.

Beard, J. B. 1974. *Turfgrass: Science and culture.* Upper Saddle River, N.J.: Prentice-Hall, Inc.

Beard, J. B. 1985. An assessment of water use by turfgrasses. In *Turfgrass water conversation. Proc. Symposium ASPA, San Antonio, TX. 15–16 Feb. 1983* ed. V. B. Youngner and S. T. Cockerham, 47–60. Oakland, Calif.: Cooperative Extension University of California.

Beard, J. B. 2002. *Turf management for golf courses.* 2nd ed. Chelsea, Mich.: Ann Arbor Press.

Beard, J. B., and R. L. Green. 1994. The role of turfgrass in environmental protection and their benefits to humans. *Journal of Environmental Quality* 23:452–460.

Bloodworth, M. E., K. W. Brown, J. B. Beard, and S. I. Sifers. 1993. Rootzone modification. *Grounds Maintenance* 28(1):13–20.

Bohn, H. L., B. L. McNeal, and G. A. O'Conner. 2001. *Soil chemistry.* 3rd ed. New York: John Wiley and Sons.

Brady, N. C., and R. R. Weil. 1999. *The nature and properties of soils.* 12th ed. Upper Saddle River, N.J.: Prentice-Hall, Inc.

Brandenburg, R. L. 2003. Cricket control. *Grounds Maintenance* 38(2):22–24, 33–35.

Brauen, S. E., G. K. Stahnke, W. J. Johnston, and C. Cogger. 1994. *Quantification and fate of nitrogen from amended and trafficked sand putting green/tee profiles. Pesticide and nutrient fate 1991–1993 summary.* Overland Park, Kans.: United States Golf Association.

Bremner, J. M., and A. M. Blackmer. 1982. Composition of soil atmosphere. In *Methods of soil analysis,* part 2, ed. A. L. Page, 873–901. Agronomy Monographs 9. Madison, Wis.: ASA, CSSA, SSSA. American Society of Agronomy, Crop Science Society of America, Soil Science Society of America.

Brilman, L. A. 2003. PVP: What does it mean? *Golf Course Management* 71(3):116–119.

Brown, K. W., and J. C. Thomas. 1986. Bunker sand selection. *Golf Course Management* 54:64–70.

Bruneau, A. H., J. E. Watkins, and R. L. Brandenburg. 1992. Integrated pest management. In *Turfgrass,* ed. D. V. Waddington, R. N. Carrow, and R. C. Shearman, 653–688. Agronomy Monograph 32. Madison, Wis.: ASA, CSSA, SSSA.

Buchanan, B. B., W. Gruissem, and R. L. Jones. 2000. *Biochemistry and molecular biology of plants.* Rockville, Md.: American Society of Plant Physiologists.

Butler, J. D., P. E. Rieke, and D. D. Minner. 1985. Influence of water quality on turfgrass. In *Turfgrass water conversation. Proc. Symposium ASPA, San Antonio, TX. 15–16 Feb. 1983.* ed. V. B. Youngner and S. T. Cockerham, 71–84. Oakland, Calif.: Cooperative Extension University of California.

C

Callahan, L. M., R. S. Freeland, R. D. Von Bernuth, D. P. Shepard, J. M. Parham, and J. M. Garrison. 1997. Geotextiles as substitutes for choker layer sand in USGA greens. I. Water infiltration rates and water retention. *International Turfgrass Society Research Journal* 8:65–74.

Carrow, R. N. 1985. Soil/water relationships in turfgrass. In *Turfgrass water conversation. Proc. Symposium ASPA, San Antonio, TX. 15–16 Feb. 1983.* ed. V. B. Youngner and S. T. Cockerham, 85–102. Oakland, Calif.: Cooperative Extension University of California.

Carrow, R. N. 1995a. Drought resistance aspects of turfgrasses in the Southeast: Evapotranspiration and crop coefficients. *Crop Sci.* 35:1685–1690.

Carrow, R. N. 1995b. Soil testing for fertilizer recommendations. *Golf Course Management.* 63:61–68.

Carrow, R. N., and A. Martin Petrovic. 1992. Effects of traffic on turfgrasses. In *Turfgrass,* ed. D. V. Waddington, R. N. Carrow, and R. C. Shearman, 285–330. Agronomy Monograph 32. Madison, Wis.: ASA, CSSA, SSSA.

Carrow, R. N., D. V. Waddington, and P. E. Rieke. 2001. *Turfgrass soil fertility and chemical properties.* Chelsea, Mich.: Ann Arbor Press.

Christians, N. 1999. Why inject acid into irrigation water? *Golf Course Management* 67(6):52–56.

Colbaugh, P. 2002. Algae—Crusty foes for golf greens. *Grounds Maintenance* 37(1):6–8.

Cooper, R. J. 1996. Soils teem with tiny organisms. *Golf Course Management* 64:63–67.

Couch, H. B. 1995. *Diseases of turfgrasses.* 3rd edition. Malabar, Fla.: Krieger Publishing Company, 421.

D

Davis, W. B., J. L. Paul, and D. Bowman. 1990. *The sand putting green—Construction and management.* University of California Division of Agriculture and Natural Resources Publication 21448.

Dernoeden, P. H. 1995. Turfgrass diseases and their management. In *Managing Turfgrass Pests,* ed. T. L. Watschke, P. H. Dernoeden, and D. J. Shetlar, 87–170. Boca Raton, Fla.: Lewis Publishers.

Duble, R. L. 1996. *Turfgrasses: Their management and use in the southern zone.* College Station: Texas A&M University Press.

E

Emmons, R. D. 1995. *Turfgrass science and management.* Albany, N.Y.: Delmar Publishers, Inc.

Engelstad, O.P., ed. 1985. *Fertilizer technology and use.* Madison, Wis.: Soil Science Society of America.

Ennis, J., and K. Bilawa. 2000. Golf course ponds are complete ecosystems. *Golf Course Mangement* 68(5):61–64.

Eskelson, D. 1992. Implementing IPM strategies. *Golf Course Management* 60:68–75.

F

Farnham, D. S., R. F. Hasek, and J. L. Paul. 1985. *Water quality: Its effects on ornamental plants.* University of California Cooperative Extension Publication 2995, 15.

Fidanza, M. 2002. Figuring out fairy rings. *Grounds Maintenance* 37(3):49–54.

Foy, J. H. 1988. Bentgrass or bermudagrass—What is right for Florida? *Golf Course Management* 26(1):1–5.

Frank, L. 2002. Executing irrigation inspections. *Sportsturf* 18(4):14–15.

Frank, M. J. 2000. Pointers for perfect *Poa. Golf Course Management* 68(10):106–112.

Fry, J., D. Settle, and N. Tisserat. 2002. Managing brown patch in tall fescue. *Grounds Maintenance* 37(4):27–32.

G

Gee, G. W., and J. W. Bauder. 1986. Particle-size analysis. In *Method of soil analysis,* part 1, ed. A. Klute, 383–411. Madison, Wis.: ASA and SSSA.

Gelernter, W., and L. Stowell. 2001. Learning to love kikuyugrass. *Golf Course Management* 69:55–59.

Gross, C. M., J. S. Angle, R. L. Hill, and M. S. Welterlen. 1991. Runoff and sediment losses from tall fescue under simulated rainfall. *Journal of Environmental Quality* 20:604–607.

Gross, P. J. 2003. Looking kindly at kikuyugrass. *USGA Green Section Record* 41(4):2–8.

Guertal, E. 2000. Nitrogen: Finding the form that fits. *Grounds Maintenance* 35(9): 15–18.

H

Haman, D. Z., A. G. Smajstrla, and F. S. Zazueta. 1998. Chemical injection methods for irrigation. *Irrigation Business and Technology* 6(2):28–29.

Handreck, K. A., and N. D. Black. 1986. *Growing media for ornamental plants and turf.* Kensington NSW, Australia: New South Wales University Press, 124–142.

Hanks, R. J., and G. L. Ashcroft. 1980. *Applied soil physics.* New York: Springer-Verlag, 159.

Harivandi, M. A. 1999. Interpreting turfgrass irrigation water test results. *California Turfgrass Culture* 49:1–4.

Harivandi, M. A., J. D. Butler, and L. Wu. 1992. Salinity and turf culture. In *Turfgrass,* ed. D. V. Waddington, R. N. Carrow, and R. C. Shearman, 208–230. Agronomy Monograph Series 32. Madison, Wis.: ASA, CSSA, and SSSA.

Harper, J. C., II. 1982. *Athletic fields: Specification outline, construction, and maintenance.* Penn. State University Agricultural Extension Service U. Ed. No. 82–827.

Huang, B., and Hongwen, G. 2000. Growth and metabolism of creeping bentgrass cultivars in response to increasing temperatures. *Crop Sci.* 40:1115–1120.

Huck, M. 2000. Does your irrigation system make the grade? *USGA Green Section Record* 39(5):1–5.

Hummel, N. W., Jr. 1998. Which root-zone recipe makes the best green? *Golf Course Management* 66(12):49–51.

Hummel, N. W., Jr. 2000. What goes best with sand: Peat, soil, or compost? *Golf Course Management* 68(4):57–60.

Hurdzan, M. J. 1996. *Golf course architecture.* Chelsea, Mich.: Sleeping Bear Press.

Hurley, R. H. 1990. Best turfgrasses for southern winter overseeding. *Grounds Maintenance* 26(1).

J

Johnson, P. G., and T. P. Riordan. 1999. Buffalograss: Home on the range. *Golf Course Management* 67(6):66–70.

Jones, J. B., Jr., B. Wolf, and H. A. Mills. 1991. *Plant analysis handbook.* Athens, Ga.: Micro-Macro Publishing, Inc.

K

Karnock, K. 2000. Promises, promises: Can biostimulants deliver? *Golf Course Management* 68(8):67–71.

Karnock, K., and K. Tucker. 2002. Water repellent soils part 1: Where are we now? *Golf Course Management* 70(6):59–62.

Kavanagh, T., and R. M. Jelley. 1981. Soil atmospheric studies in relation to compaction. In *Proceedings of the 4th International Turfgrass Research Conference,* ed. R. W. Sheard, 181–188. Ontario, Canada: University of Guelph.

Kleiss, H. J., and M. T. Hoover. 1986. Soil and site criteria for on-site systems. In *Utilization, treatment, and disposal of waste on land,* 111–128. Madison, Wis.: Soil Science Society of America.

Kneebone, W. R., D. M. Kopec, and C. F. Mancino. 1992. Water requirements and irrigation. In *Turfgrass,* ed. D. V. Waddington, R. N. Carrow, and R. C. Shearman, 441–472. Agronomy Monograph Series 32. Madison, Wis.: ASA, CSSA, and SSSA.

Kopec, D. M. 1996. Managing turf with effluent water. *Golf Course Irrigation* 4(3):14–16.

Krenisky, E. C., M. J. Carroll, R. L. Hill, and J. M. Krouse. 1998. Runoff and sediment losses from natural and man-made erosion control materials. *J. Soil Water Cons.* 52:96–102.

L

Lea, P. J., and R. C. Leegood. 1999. *Plant biochemistry and molecular biology.* Chichester, UK: John Wiley and Sons, Inc.

Love, W. R. 1992. *An environmental approach to golf course development.* Chicago, Ill.: American Society of Golf Course Architects.

Lubin, T. 1995. Controlling soil pH with irrigation water. *Golf Course Management* 63:56–60.

Lucas, L. T., C. T. Blake, and K. R. Barker. 1974. Nematodes associated with bentgrass and bermudagrass golf greens in North Carolina. *Plant Disease Reporter* 58(9):822–824.

Lucas, L. T., K. R. Barker, and C. T. Blake. 1978. Seasonal changes in nematode densities on bentgrass golf greens in North Carolina. *Plant Disease Reporter* 62(4):373–376.

M

Martin, B., L. Stowell, and W. Gelernter. 2002. Rough bluegrass, annual bluegrass, and perennial ryegrass hit by new disease. *Golf Course Management* 70(4):61–65.

McCarty, L. B., ed. 2001. *Best golf course management practices.* Upper Saddle River, N.J.: Prentice-Hall, Inc.

McCarty, L. B., and G. L. Miller. 2002. *Managing bermuda-grass turf.* Chelsea, Mich.: Ann Arbor Press.

McCarty, L. B., T. Whitwell, and J. K. Norsworthy. 2003. *Turf and ornamental herbicide families and their characteristics.* Clemson, S.C.: Clemson University Cooperative Extension Service, EC 697.

McCloud, D. E. 1955. Water requirements of field crops in Florida as influenced by climate. *Proc. Soil Sci. Soc. Fla.* 15:165–172.

McGuirk, S., and A. Harivandi. 1998. Irrigation systems can offer alternative uses. *Ground Maintenance* 33:28–32, 86.

McIntyre, K., and B. Jakobsen. 2000. *Practical drainage for golf, sportsturf and horticulture.* Chelsea, Mich.: Ann Arbor Press.

McNeely, W. H., and W. C. Morgan. 1968a. Review of soil amendments. Classification and development. *Turf-Grass Times* 3:23.

McNeely, W. H., and W. C. Morgan. 1968b. Soil amendments. *Turf-Grass Times.* 3:3, 4.

Meyer, F. P., and L. A. Barclay. 1990. *Field manual for the investigation of fish kills.* Fish and Wildlife Service, Resource Publication 177. Washington, D.C.: Department of the Interior.

Miller, R. W., and D. T. Gardiner. 1998. *Soils in our environment.* 8th ed. Upper Saddle River, N.J.: Prentice-Hall, Inc.

Mitsch, W. J., and J. G. Gosselink. 1993. *Wetlands.* New York: Van Nostrand Reinhold.

Musser, H. B., and A. T. Perkins. 1969. Guide to planting. In *Turfgrass Science,* ed. A. A. Hanson and F. V. Juska, 474–490. Agronomy Monograph 14. Madison, Wis.: ASA.

Musser, H. B., and A. T. Perkins. 1969. Guide to seedbed preparation. In *Turfgrass Science,* ed. A. A. Hanson and F. V. Juska, 462–473. Agronomy Monograph 14. Madison, Wis.: ASA.

N

Nelson, M. 1998. The microbial world. *USGA Green Section Record,* 36(4):1–5.

Nobel, P. 1983. *Biophysical plant physiology and ecology.* San Francisco, Calif.: W. H. Freeman.

P

Pettyman, G. W., and E. L. McCoy. 2002. Effect of profile layering, rootzone texture, and slope on putting-green drainage rates. *Agronomy Journal* 94:358–364.

Potter, D. A. 1998. Using the new soil insecticides. *Golf Course Management* 66(1): 49–55.

Pound, C. E. 1973. *Wastewater treatment and reuse by land application* (vol.1). EPA-660/2-73-006a. Washington, D.C.

S

Salisbury, F. B., and C. W. Ross. 1992. *Plant physiology.* 4th ed. Belmont, Calif.: Wadsworth Publishing Company.

Shearman, R. C. 1985. Turfgrass culture and water use. In *Turfgrass water conservation. Proc. Symposium ASPA, San Antonio, TX. 15–16 Feb. 1983,* ed. V. B. Youngner and S. T. Cockerham, 61–70. Oakland, Calif.: Cooperative Extension University of California.

Shetlar, D. J. 1995. Turfgrass insect and mite management. In *Managing Turfgrass Pests,* ed. T. L. Watschke, P. H. Dernoeden, and D. J. Shetlar, 171–343. Boca Raton, Fla.: Lewis Publishers.

Snow, J. T. 1993. USGA explains its new greens specifications. *Ground Maintenance* 28(1):20–22.

Snyder, G. H. 1979. Fertigation for managing turf nitrogen nutrition. *Proc. GCSAA 50th Inter. Turf. Conf. and Show,* 163–167. GCSAA, Lawrence, Kans.

Snyder, G. H., and B. J. Augustin. 1986. Managing micronutrient application on Florida turfgrass. In *Advances in turfgrass fertility,* ed. B. J. Joyner, 149–179. Columbus, Ohio: ChemLawn Corp.

Sullivan, D. L. 1970. Wastewater for golf course irrigation. *Water and Sewage Work* 117(5), 153–159.

T

Taiz, L., and E. Zeiger. 1998. *Plant physiology* 2nd ed. Sunderland, Mass.: Sinauer Associates, Inc.

Taylor, D. H., G. R. Blake, and D. B. White. 1987. *Athletic field construction and maintenance.* Minnesota Extension Service AG-BU-3125, 16.

Thom, W. O., and A. J. Powell, Jr. Sampling soils with turfgrass. In *Soil sampling procedures for the southern region of the United States,* ed. W. O. Thom, and W. Sabbe, 31–34. Southern Cooperative Series, Bulletin No. 377.

Throssell, C. S. 1985. Management practices affecting bentgrass putting green speed. *Oklahoma Turf:* 3(1 & 2).

Tisdale, S. L., W. L. Nelson, and J. D. Beaton. 1985. *Soil fertility and fertilizers.* New York: Macmillan Publishing Company.

Tucker, B. 1984. The use of gypsum on turf. *Oklahoma Turf* 2(1):1–3.

Turgeon, A. J. 1996. *Turfgrass management.* 4th. ed. Upper Saddle River, N.J.: Prentice-Hall, Inc.

Turner, T. R., and N. W. Hummel, Jr. 1992. Nutritional requirements and fertilization. In *Turfgrass,* ed. D. V. Waddington, R. N. Carrow, and R. C. Shearman, 382–439. Agronomy Monograph Series 32. Madison, Wis.: ASA, CSSA, and SSSA.

V

Vargas, J. M., Jr. 1994. *Management of turfgrass diseases.* Boca Raton, Fla.: Lewis Publishers.

Vincelli, P., and E. Dixon. 2002. Update: Fungicide failure against gray leaf spot. *Golf Course Management* 70(1):53–55.

Vittum, P. J., M. G. Villani, and H. Tashiro. 1999. *Turfgrass insects of the United States and Canada.* 2nd ed. Ithaca, New York: Cornell University.

W

Waddington, D. V. 1992. Soils, soil mixtures, and soil amendments. In *Turfgrass,* ed. D. V. Waddington, R. N. Carrow, and R. C. Shearman, 331–383. Agronomy Monograph 32. Madison, Wis.: ASA, CSSA, SSSA.

Ward, C. Y. 1969. Climate and adaptation. In *Turfgrass Science,* ed. A.A. Hanson and F.V. Juska, 27–29. Agronomy Monograph 14. Madison, Wis.: American Society of Agronomy.

Watson, J. R. 1985. Water resources in the United States. In *Turfgrass water conversation. Proc. Symposium ASPA, San Antonio, TX. 15–16 Feb. 1983,* ed. V. B. Youngner and S. T. Cockerham, 19–36. Oakland, Calif.: Cooperative Extension University of California.

Westcot, D. W., and R. S. Ayers. 1984. Irrigation water quality criteria. In *Irrigation with reclaimed municipal wastewater—A guidance manual,* ed. G. S. Pettygrove and T. Asano, 3:1–3:37. Report No. 84-1 wr. Calif. State Water Resources Control Board, Sacramento, Calif.

Wildmon, J. 1991. Converting golf courses to effluent irrigation. *Florida Turf Digest* 8(5):17–18.

Williamson, R. C. 1999. Biorational pesticides: What are they anyway? *Golf Course Management* 67:61–64.

Y

Youngner, V. B. 1985. Physiology of water use and water stress. In *Turfgrass water conversation. Proc. Symposium ASPA, San Antonio, TX. 15–16 Feb. 1983,* ed. V. B. Youngner and S. T. Cockerham, 37–43. Oakland, Calif.: Cooperative Extension University of California.

GLOSSARY

A

abaxial Something located away from the axis side; for example, the underside of a leaf.

abiotic Nonliving environmental elements such as rainfall, temperature, wind, lightning, and minerals.

abscisic acid A plant hormone that, among other things, promotes bud dormancy, maintains seed dormancy, and causes stomatal closing.

absorption In plants, the passing of a compound from one system into another, such as water movement from soil into roots; in soils, the binding of a chemical into a soil particle.

acclimation Physical and physiological processes in plants that prepare them for temperature extremes, such as winter.

acid equivalent (ae) Amount of parent acid from the active ingredient content found in a pesticide formulation.

acid injection In agriculture, adding acidic materials such as sulfur or phosphoric acid to irrigation water with excessive pH, bicarbonate, and carbonate contents. This lowers the pH and converts bicarbonate and carbonate into carbon dioxide and water.

acid rain Rainwater with a pH below 5.6.

actinomycetes Microorganisms that are intermediate between bacteria and fungi.

activated sludge Aerated sludge subjected to bacterial processes, which is used as a fertilizer or soil amendment.

active acidity Acidity of a soil solution from free hydrogen ions measured as pH; also called potential acidity and buffer capacity.

active ingredient (ai) The actual amount of active concentration in a formulation; for example, Aatrex 4L contains four pounds of active ingredient per gallon of product, and Ronstar 2G has 2 percent active ingredient per pound of product.

acute Sharply pointed.

acute toxicity The ability of a substance to cause injury or death shortly following exposure, usually due to a relatively large dose.

adaptation A unique structure, physiology, or process that aids an organism to fit into its environment.

adaxial Something located toward the axis side; for example, the upperside of a leaf.

adenosine triphosphate (ATP) A nucleotide consisting of adenine, ribose sugar, and three phosphate groups that, upon metabolism, provide usable chemical energy. On hydrolysis, energy is released when ATP loses one phosphate group to become adenosine diphosphate (ADP).

adhesion Molecular attraction and contact between the surfaces of two unlike substances or objects.

adjuvant A substance in a formulation that enhances its effectiveness.

adsorption Bonding or adhering of ions or compounds to the surface of soil particles or plant parts.

adventitious bud A bud produced in an unusual or unexpected place; for example, near a point of stem injury or on a leaf or a root.

adventitious root A root originating in an unusual or unexpected place, such as from stem or leaf tissue instead of from another root.

aerification In turf, a method of turf cultivation where hollow or solid tines or spoons are inserted into and removed from the turf to control soil compaction and increase water and fertilizer penetration; *hollow-tine* aerification involves hollow tines that remove soil plugs, *solid-tine* aerification does not remove plugs when holes are made, *deep-drill* aerification involves removing soil via long drill bits, and *hydro-*, *hydraulic-*, or *water-injection* aerification uses fine streams of high-pressure water to penetrate the soil surface.

aerobic Something requiring oxygen or having oxygen present in the environment.

aggregate To collect together in tufts, groups, or bunches, such as soil clods.

agronomy The science of crops and soils.

aleurone layer Layer of high-protein cells in seeds surrounding the storage cells of endosperm. It secretes enzymes for digesting food reserves in the endosperm during seed germination.

alga (plural: algae) A single- to multiple-celled plant found in damp habitats containing chlorophyll and having no true roots, stems, or leaves.

algal bloom Population explosion of algae that is often followed by green- or red-colored water and low oxygen levels. It is commonly stimulated by phosphorus and/or nitrogen enrichment.

alkaline soil   Soil with a pH >7.0, usually found in areas of relatively low rainfall.

alkalinity   The capacity of water to neutralize acids; a property imparted by carbonates, bicarbonates, hydroxides, and others.

allelopathy   Plant chemical product that inhibits the growth of adjacent plants.

alternate   In botany, an arrangement of a single leaf, bud, or branch attached singly at different points on the stem, there by appearing to alternate.

amendment   Any material, such as sand, sawdust, gypsum, diatomaceous earth, peat, or calcined clay, that is added to soil to alter its chemical and/or physical characteristics.

amino acids   Nitrogen-containing organic acids that are building blocks to form proteins. Amino acids contain one or more amino ($-NH_2$) groups, a carboxyl group ($-COOH$), and possibly sulfur.

ammonification   Conversion of amino acids and other nitrogen-containing organic compounds into ammonia (NH_3) and ammonium ions (NH_4^+).

amylase   An enzyme that converts starch into smaller units; often refers to seed germination.

anaerobic   Something not requiring oxygen, or the absence of oxygen in the environment.

anion   Negatively charged ion that is attracted to a positively charged anode.

anion exchange capacity (AEC)   Sum of exchangeable anions a soil can adsorb, expressed as centimoles of charge per kilogram of soil ($cmol_c/kg$). AEC only occurs to any appreciable extent when soil pH is <5.

annual   A plant starting from seed and completing its life cycle, including death, within one year; *summer annuals* germinate in spring, grow through summer, and die in fall; *winter annuals* germinate in fall, live through the winter, and die the following spring or summer.

anther   Sac-like portion of the male part of a flower (stamen) that bears pollen.

anthesis   Opening of the flower bud when pollination occurs.

anthocyanin   A water-soluble blue or red pigment that aids in light harvesting during photosynthesis.

anthracnose   A crown and/or leaf disease caused by fungi producing asexual spores in an acervulus.

antibiosis   In biology, an association between two organisms where one is adversely affected.

antibody   A chemical substance in a host that opposes the action of parasites, their products, or other foreign materials.

antigen   A substance introduced into animal tissue that stimulates the production of an antibody.

antioxidants   Compounds that react with toxic oxygen and free radicals to produce nontoxic water and molecular oxygen.

apex   The tip of a stem, root, or leaf.

apical   At or near the apex or tip.

apical dominance   Ability of a terminal plant bud to inhibit the sprouting and growth of adjacent lateral buds.

apomixis   Seed development without sexual fusion of the egg and sperm cells.

apoplast   Nonliving, interconnecting cells of xylem tissue that primarily move substances upward in plants.

approach   In golf, the fairway area nearest a golf green that is often mowed closer to improve turf playability.

apron   In golf, the area between the fairway and collar of the putting green that is usually mowed shorter than the fairway but higher than the collar and green; often called the approach.

aquatic   Something growing in water.

aquifer   A reservoir for underground water, which is often a water source for wells and springs.

artificial turf   A synthetic turf surface.

ascending   Something sloping or growing upward or outward.

aseptate   Something lacking cross walls; usually refers to fungus mycelium.

asymmetrical   Lopsided; having two sides different in shape or area.

atom   The smallest unit of a chemical element that retains its characteristic properties.

atomic number   The number of protons in the nucleus of an atom.

atomic weight   The weight of an atom of an element relative to the weight of an atom of carbon ^{12}C, which has been assigned the value 12.

ATP   *See* adenosine triphosphate.

auricle   Small, ear-shaped lobes or appendages at the junction of the leaf sheath and blade in grasses, or at the leaf base of broadleaf plants.

autoecious   Requiring only one host on which to complete a life cycle; often refers to some rust fungi.

auxin   A plant growth regulating hormone that promotes cell elongation.

available water   Portion of soil water that can be readily absorbed by plant roots; often considered to be the water held in soil against a pressure of -33 kPa to approximately $-1,500$ kPa (or -15 bars).

awn   A slender or stiff bristle, usually extending from a grass floret, specifically on the glumes or lemma.

axil   The angle between the leaf and stem.

axillary bud   A bud located in the leaf axil or internal fold.

axis   The main stem of an inflorescence; a panicle is an example.

B

bacillus (plural bacilli)   Rod-shaped bacterium.

backlapping   Backward turning of mower reel blades against a bed knife with a corresponding addition of fluid-dispersed grinding compound to hone the blades.

bacteria (plural: bacterium)   Microscopic, single-celled, nongreen organisms with rigid cell walls that reproduce by cell division. Bacteria are prokaryotes.

ball mark   A depression or tear in the turf surface from the impact of a ball.

ball roll distance   The distance a golf ball moves following a putting stroke, often measured with a stimpmeter.

bar   In science, a unit of pressure used to express water potential (1 atmosphere = 1.013 bars).

basal rosette   A cluster of leaves radiating at the base of a plant at ground level.

base saturation   The relative amount of the basic cations, Ca^{+2}, Mg^{+2}, Na^+, and K^+, in a soil compared to acidic cations, H^+ and Al^{+3}. Mathematically, base saturation is a sum of the basic cations divided by the total cations present:

$$\text{base saturation} = \frac{Ca^{+2} + Mg^{+2} + Na^+ + K^+}{CEC}$$

basiomycetes   Fungi that produce sexual spores (basidiospores) on a club-shaped structure called a basidium.

beak   A hard point or projection, seen frequently on seeds and fruits.

bearded   Something having long hairs.

bed knife   Stationary lower blade on a reel mower where cutting occurs when the rotating reel blade contacts it.

bench setting   The height mower blades are set on a hard, flat surface.

best management practices (BMPs)   In turf, management or cultural practices that minimize inputs and undesirable effects yet maximize outputs and aesthetic value.

biennial   A plant that completes its life cycle and dies in two years. In the first year, seeds germinate and form vegetative growth; in the second year, flowering, seed set, and death occur.

biodegradation   Breakdown (digestion) by biological organisms.

biological control   Using any biological agent to control a pest.

biological oxygen demand (BOD)   Quantity of dissolved oxygen in water used in the oxidation of organic matter. High BOD usually means anaerobic water.

biostimulant   Organic material applied in small quantities that enhances plant growth and development.

biotype   A population within a species possessing a distinct genetic variation.

bipinnate   Two rows of lateral branches along an axis that are again divided into two rows; feather-like.

bisexual   Flowers with male (stamens) and female (pistil) elements.

blade   In biology, the expanded, usually flat, portion of a leaf.

blend   In turf, a combination of two or more cultivars of a single turfgrass species.

blight   Plant disease symptom characterized by general and rapid killing of leaves, flowers, and stems, resembling heat injury.

blotch   Plant disease symptom characterized by large, irregularly shaped spots or blots on leaves, shoots, and stems.

boat-shaped   Leaf tips that are shaped like the front (or bow) of a boat such as *Poa* species.

brackish   Water description with a high content of soluble salts; salty.

bract   A modified, usually reduced leaf associated with a flower or flower cluster.

branch   A lateral stem.

brine   Salt residue remaining following water desalination.

bristle   A short, coarse, stiff hairlike part.

brushing   In turf, the use of brushes in front of mower blades that upright the leaf for a cleaner cut.

bryophytes   Members of the phyla of nonvascular plants; the mosses, hornworts, and liverworts.

bud   An usually tightly bunched, undeveloped shoot or flower usually located at the tip of a stem or branch (called *apical bud*) or in the axil or internal fold of a leaf sheath (called *axillary bud*).

buffer   Substance that resists any change in pH.

buffer capacity   Ability of soils to resist chemical change caused by the high cation exchange capacity and, in some cases, free calcium carbonate.

buffer pH   Substance used to determine buffering capacity of a soil for lime requirements.

bulb   An underground short, thickened shoot where food is stored, such as in wild onion.

bulk blending   Mixing individual granular fertilizer materials to form a mixed material.

bulk flow   Overall movement of a liquid such as water induced by gravity, pressure, or an interplay of both.

bunchgrass   Intravaginal tilling at the crown without stolon or rhizome formation.

bunker   In turf, a hazard, usually a depression filled with sand or grass, that penalizes an errant golf shot; also called a sand trap.

bur   A structure with spines or prickles that is frequently hooked or barbed.

C

C_3 plants   Plants using only the Calvin (or C_3) cycle or pathway in the fixation of CO_2; the first stable product is the 3-carbon compound, 3-phosphoglycerate (3-PGA); hence, the designation C_3.

C_4 cycle (Hatch-Slack) or pathway   Reactions where carbon dioxide is fixed to phosphoenolpyruvate (or PEP) to yield a 4-carbon compound, oxaloacetate (or OAA); hence, the designation C_4.

C_4 plants   Plants where the first product of CO_2 fixation is a 4-carbon compound, oxaloacetate (or OAA), where both the Calvin (or C_3) cycle and the C_4 pathway are used.

calcareous soil   A soil containing 10 to 1,000 grams per kilogram of $CaCO_3$ (calcium carbonate, lime) equivalent.

calcined clay   A granular soil modification amendment consisting of highly fired (*calcining*) clay minerals, such as montmorillonite and attapulgite, that are absorbent and stable.

calcined diatomaceous earth   Fired single-celled ocean organisms called *diatoms* that are absorbent and stable; often used as a granular soil modification amendment.

calcite   A crystalline form of calcium carbonate ($CaCO_3$) often formed when high bicarbonate-containing water is used for irrigation; also called *calcitic limestone*.

calcium carbonate equivalent (CCE)   A relative measurement of the purity of a liming material compared to 100 for calcium carbonate ($CaCO_3$).

Calvin cycle Series of reactions during photosynthesis where carbon dioxide is reduced to 3-phosphoglyceraldehyde (or 3PGA) and the carbon dioxide acceptor, ribulose 1,5-bisphosphate (RuBP), is regenerated.

capillary fringe Zone immediately above the water table that is nearly saturated.

capillary water Water remaining in soil pores following gravity drainage.

carbohydrates Plant food sources including sugars and starches containing carbon with hydrogen and oxygen in a 2:1 ratio, as in water (H_2O).

carbon:nitrogen (C:N) ratio Ratio of organic carbon weight to total nitrogen weight in soil or organic material.

carotenoid Yellow or red plant pigment.

carpel A unit of the pistil in a flower; a simple pistil is formed from a single carpel while two or more carpels compose a compound pistil.

caryopsis The grass fruit, normally dry at maturity, consisting of a single seed within the ovary.

cation Positively charged ion that is attracted to a negatively charged cathode.

cation exchange capacity (CEC) Sum of exchangeable cations a soil can adsorb and retain against leaching; expressed as centimoles per kilogram of soil.

cellulose An unbranched sugar that is the chief substance composing cell walls or woody parts of plants.

centrifugal spreader Machine that spreads granules as they drop onto a spinning disc or blade beneath the hopper.

certified seed Seed from registered or foundation plants produced under an officially designated system of maintaining genetic identity and purity. It is typically identified by a blue tag.

chelates (chelating or sequestering agenis) A chemical formulation that binds a metal atom (such as iron) with an organic component to improve its soil availability and uptake by plants.

chilling injury Plant damage from nonfreezing, low temperatures, usually 35 to 60°F (1.7 to 16°C).

chlorophyll Green photosynthetic pigment found in the chloroplasts of all photosynthetic plants that enables them to capture solar energy to make food.

chloroplast Sac-like structure in plant cells containing chlorophyll; the site of photosynthesis.

chlorosis Yellowing of normally green plant tissue due to chlorophyll loss.

chromosome The structure that carries the genes during cell division.

chronic toxicity Ability of a substance to cause injury or death after long-term exposure, usually to small doses.

ciliate Fringed with hairs on the margin; hairy.

clasping A type of leaf attachment where the leaf base partly or completely encircles the stem.

clay Soil particles 0.002 millimeter diameter; also indicates a soil mixture containing more than 40 percent clay.

clipping height Distance above the soil line at which grasses are clipped or mowed.

clippings Leaf and stem portions of plants severed by mowing.

clump-forming or tufted Something that grows in a compact cluster.

coefficient of uniformity (design uniformity) In irrigation, the efficiency of a sprinkler system based on precipitation rates at various points.

cohesion (surface tension) Mutual attraction of molecules of the same substance.

cold hardiness The ability of plants to survive extreme cold and dry weather.

cold water insoluble nitrogen (CWIN) Insoluble nitrogen fertilizer that forms in cold (77°F or 25°C) water.

cold water soluble nitrogen (CWSN) Soluble nitrogen fertilizer that forms in cold (77°F or 25°C) water.

coleoptile Protective sheath covering the shoot tip and leaves of emerging grass seedlings.

coleorhiza Transitory protective sheath covering the root apex (tip) of emerging seedlings.

collar In botany, the outer side of a grass leaf at the junction of the blade and sheath; in golf, the area surrounding the green or fringe (if present), normally maintained between the green and fairway.

colloidal phosphate Soil amendment used to increase cation exchange capacity and water-holding capacity of sandy soils, which is a byproduct from phosphate washing.

colorant A paintlike dye or pigment used to create a green color when the turf is discolored or dormant.

combing Mowing technique utilizing a series of metal teeth or flexible tines (comb) in front of a mower to lift shoots for a more desirable cut.

common name In pesticides, a name applied to a pesticide's active ingredient, usually agreed upon by the American National Standards Institute and the International Organization for Standardization. For example, oryzalin is the common name of the herbicide with the trade name Surflan. In plants, layman or regional names are associated with a particular plant; for example, annual bluegrass is a common name of the plant with the scientific name *Poa annua*.

compaction An unfavorable increase in soil bulk density (g/cm^3) and corresponding decrease in soil porosity from mechanical pressures to the soil.

composite A member of the *Compositae* or *Asteraceae* family that has a dense inflorescence, usually composed of florets, a receptacle, and bracts.

compost Residues from organic matter and soil piles allowed to undergo biological decomposition.

compound leaf A type of leaf composed of two or more distinct, similar parts often called leaflets.

compressed Laterally flattened.

contours Outline of a figure, body, or mass; contour lines connect the points on a land surface with the same elevation.

cool-season grass Grass with optimum growth in the temperature range of 60 to 75°F (15.5 to 24°C).

core aerification *See* aerification.

core cultivation *See* aerification.

coring *See* aerification.

corm A stout, short, vertical, bulblike underground food storage stem.

corolla The flower petals that surround the stamens and pistil.

cotyledon A seed leaf of the embryo, most often the storage sites of reserve food used by germinating seedlings.

crop oil concentrate Nonphytotoxic light oil containing surfactants used to enhance the effectiveness of liquid solutions applied to plant foliage.

crown A meristematic growing point at or just below the ground where stems and roots join and new shoots emerge.

culm Flowering stem of a grass plant not including the leaves.

cultipacking Seeding technique utilizing a seeder with a larger, ridged, front roller to prepare a shallow seedbed, with an offset, smaller, rear roller to firm the soil around the planted seed.

cultivar Form, type, or variety of a cultivated plant.

cultivation In turf, the disturbance of soil and/or thatch layer without destroying the turf (e.g., aerifying, slicing, spiking, slitting, etc.).

cup cutter Hollow cylinder used to cut a 4.25-inch (10.8-cm) diameter hole at least four inches deep (10.8 cm) for the cup (or pin) in a green or to replace damaged turf.

curative Fungicides applied following the appearance of disease symptoms; also called eradicants.

cuticle Waxy outer layer of a leaf or stem.

cutin A waxy substance found on the surface of certain seeds or leaves to conserve water.

cutting height Height above the plane of travel and the parallel plane of cut on a mower.

cytochrome Heme proteins serving as electron carriers in photosynthesis and respiration.

cytokinins Group of plant growth regulating hormones that regulate cell division.

D

damping-off A seedling disease that causes them to rot at the soil surface and fall over.

Darcy's Law A law describing saturated water flow through a porous media.

day-neutral plants Plants with no daylength requirements for floral initiation.

decumbent Lying on the ground, but rising at the tip.

deflocculation (dispersion) To cause particles to separate into individual components and disperse by chemical and/or physical means.

defoliant Chemical that causes a plant to lose its leaves.

denitrification The biological conversion of nitrate or nitrite to gaseous nitrogen as either N_2 or N_2O.

deoxyribonucleic acid (DNA) Carrier of genetic information in cells.

desalination Process of separating a saline solution into pure fresh water and brine.

desiccation Plant moisture loss from hot, dry weather, fertilizers, or chemicals.

dethatching Removal of excessive turf thatch and/or mat using stiff rakes or a series of vertically mounted knives or tines.

diatomaceous earth Geologic deposit of siliceous skeleton material of diatoms (algae); used as an inorganic soil amendment.

diatoms Algae with siliceous cell walls that persist as a skeleton following death.

dicotyledon, dicot Broadleaf plants with two seed embryos (leaves) or cotyledons when they emerge from the soil; these also have netted leaf veins, showy flowers, flower parts in 4s or 5s, and often a cambium for secondary growth.

diffuse Loose and widely spreading.

digitate Branches arising from a common point, resembling the fingers of a human hand.

dioecious Separate male (stamens) and female (pistil) plants; unisexual.

diploid Containing a double ($2n$) number of chromosomes.

disease A disturbance that interferes with normal plant structure, function, or economic value.

disease triangle A concept where disease development requires concurrent presence of a susceptible host, a virulent pathogen, and conducive environmental conditions.

dissected Something divided into numerous narrow segments or lobes.

dissolved oxygen Atmospheric oxygen held in solution within water.

divot Removal of a small turf piece from twisting cleated foot traffic or a golf swing, often exposing soil.

dogleg hole A right or left bend in a golf hole.

dolomite Magnesium carbonate ($MgCO_3$) containing limestone.

dormancy Arrested plant growth during periods of unfavorable environmental conditions.

dormant seeding Planting in fall or winter when it is too cold for germination until the following spring.

dormant sodding Sodding in fall or winter when it is too cold for active growth.

double green Large putting surface servicing two different golf holes with two separate flagsticks and holes.

drain line Underground pipe that collects and removes excessive soil moisture.

E

ecology Study of plant life in relation to its environment.

ecosystem Interacting system of living organisms and their physical environment.

ecotype A strain or selection within a given species adapted to a particular environment.

edaphic Pertaining to soil.

effective calcium carbonate (ECC) The quality of limestone determined by multiplying its fineness by its purity (or calcium carbonate equivalent).

effluent Partially or completely treated wastewater from a treatment plant, reservoir, or basin.

electrical conductivity (EC) A measure of salinity using electrical conductance expressed as millimhos per centimeter (mmho/cm) or decisiemens per meter (dS/m). EC_e is the electrical conductivity of soil from a saturated paste while EC_w is the electrical conductivity of water.

electrodialysis Water desalination method where ions pass through a semipermeable membrane toward an electrical field, leaving purer water behind.

electron A negatively charged subatomic particle that orbits the atom's positively charged nucleus, determining the atom's chemical properties.

electron transport system ("Z" scheme) Movement of electrons down a series of electron-carrier molecules with the subsequent release of energy.

element A substance composed of only one kind of atom. These combine to compose all materials.

elliptic A narrow shape with relatively rounded ends that is widest at the middle.

elongate To make narrow and long.

embryo Seed portion that develops into a juvenile plant.

emergence Visible protrusion of the shoots of a newly germinated seed.

emulsifier A substance that promotes the suspension of one liquid in another.

emulsifying agent Colloidal substance that forms a film around immiscible particles to obtain a suspension.

emulsion System of oil dispersed in water or system of water dispersed in oil; not a true solution.

endocarp Inner layer of the pericarp (fruit wall).

endodermis Layer of cells forming a sheath around the vascular region in roots and some stems.

endosperm Seed portion containing food reserves.

entire In plants, a type of leaf margin without teeth, lobes, or divisions; smoothed-edge.

enzyme A complex organic agent that enhances cellular reaction rates without being altered in the process.

epicotyl Young stem of a seedling or embryo just above the cotyledon(s).

epidermis Outer cellular layer of plants that helps prevent drying and mechanical injury.

Epsom salt Common name for magnesium sulfate ($MgSO_4$).

equivalent Amount of material that reacts with or provides one gram formula weight of hydrogen.

equivalent weight (moles of ion charge) The amounts of substances that are equivalent to each other in chemical reactions, determined in an acid as the weight of substance furnishing one mole of hydrogen ions, while in a base the weight furnishing one mole of hydroxide (OH^-) ions. Also measured as the change in oxidation (valence) atoms undergo in a chemical reaction.

$$\text{equivalent weight} = \frac{\text{molecular weight}}{\text{number of H or OH per molecule}}$$
$$\text{or } \frac{\text{molecular weight}}{\text{valence}}$$

eradicant A product that destroys a pathogen at its source.

erosion Wearing of land by running water, wind, or other geological agents.

ethylene A hydrocarbon hormone gas (C_2H_4) whose effect on plants is most prominent in fruit ripening.

eukaryote An organism with a membrane-bound nucleus and organelles whose DNA is associated with proteins.

eutrophication Water condition with excess dissolved nutrients and insufficient dissolved oxygen.

evaporation Process of water evaporation as vapor from land, water, and vegetation surfaces.

evapotranspiration (ET) Combined loss of water from an area by evaporation from the soil surface and transpiration from plants; expressed as in./wk and mm/day.

exchangeable sodium percentage (ESP) A measure of excessive sodium hazard in the soil as the ratio (as percent) of exchangeable sodium to the remaining exchangeable cations (Mg, Ca, and K).

exergonic Energy-yielding chemical reaction.

exodermis Outer layer of cells of root cortex.

extravaginal Growth from stem penetration through the basal leaf sheath as seen in rhizomes and stolons.

F

F_1 First generation offspring from a cross; F_2 and F_3 are the second and third generations resulting from such a cross.

facultative parasite A mostly saprophytic organism that may become parasitic when environmental conditions are favorable.

facultative saprophyte A mostly parasitic organism that may become saprophytic when environmental conditions are favorable.

fairway The primary playing area on a golf course between the tees and putting green.

family In the plant and animal kingdom, a taxonomic group between order and genus in rank. A family contains one or more genera and each family belongs to an order.

fat A molecule composed of glycerol and three fatty acid molecules, with its proportion of oxygen to carbon being less in fats than in carbohydrates. Liquid fats are called oils.

fatty acid Organic compound of carbon, hydrogen, and oxygen that combines with glycerol to form a fat.

ferredoxin (Fd) Electron-transferring proteins of high iron content, often involved in electron transport during photosynthesis and respiration.

fertigation Fertilizing through irrigation systems.

fertilizer Any material, except lime, supplying essential elements.

fertilizer analysis Percentage of composition of a fertilizer as total nitrogen (N), phosphoric acid (P_2O_5) and potash (K_2O).

fertilizer burn Plant injury from dehydration due to contact with materials containing salts.

fertilizer grade Guaranteed minimum analysis of the major nutrients of a fertilizer.

fibrous roots   Slender, branched roots of similar size arising from a similar point.

field capacity   The percentage of water a soil retains against the action of gravity; typically the water remaining in a soil two or three days after the soil is saturated and free drainage has occurred; often estimated at -33 kPa water potential.

filament   Anther-bearing stalk of a flower's stamen (male part); thread.

filiform   Threadlike, long, and very slender.

fission   Asexual reproduction involving the division of a single-celled individual into two new single-celled individuals of equal size.

flaccid   Without rigidity; limp or weak.

flail mower   Mower with a series of retractable, free hanging T-shaped blades that extend when a shaft rotates at high speeds. It cuts and re-cuts until clippings are sufficiently pulverized to escape the mower housing; also called a *hammerknife* mower.

flocculation   To aggregate or clump together.

floret   A small flower or one of individual closely clustered small flowers (having both pistil and stamens) enclosed by bracts (lemma and palea).

folded   In botany, lengthwise folding arrangement of the youngest leaf in a plant's shoot.

foliar burn   *See* fertilizer burn.

foliar feeding   Light liquid fertilizer application to plant foliage.

footprinting   Extended turf indentation from surface traffic due to the lack of leaf turgidity (moisture).

forking   Turf cultivation technique of using a spading fork to punch holes in the turf and soil.

formulation   The form in which a product is available to the consumer, including both the active and inert ingredients; examples include concentrates, emulsifiables, flowables, granulars, and powders.

foundation seed   Progeny (seed) from breeder stock; used as planting stock for registered and certified seed.

French drain   *See* slit drain.

frequency of clip   Distance of travel between successive cuts of mower blades.

fringe   Optional area, two to four feet wide (0.6 to 1.2 m), between the golf green surface and collar, which is maintained between the green and collar but is not considered part of the putting surface.

fruit   A matured ovary with its enclosed seeds; a ripened pistil.

fulvic acid   Soluble organic substances remaining after a soil alkali extract has been acidified.

fumigation   The process of applying a fumigant that disinfests an area from various pests.

fungicide   A compound toxic to fungi.

fungistatic   A compound preventing fungus growth without killing it.

fungus (plural: fungi)   An undifferentiated threadlike organism without chlorophyll and conductive tissue. Fungi are eukaryotes.

G

gene   A unit of heredity.

general-use pesticide   Pesticide not causing unreasonable adverse effects on the environment that is safe for application by the general public without requiring special training.

genotype   The hereditary makeup of a plant (or variety) that determines its inheritance.

genus (plural: genera)   A taxonomic group of related species ranked between family and species.

gibberellic acids   Growth promoting substances that regulate many growth responses, such as increased plant stem elongation, that are used in seed priming to speed germination.

glabrous   Smooth, without hairs or bristles.

glandular hair   A small hair terminated in a small pinhead-like gland, frequently secreting resin, wax, or other substances.

glaucous   Covered with a waxy coating resulting in a whitish to blue-green color.

glucose   A common six-carbon sugar ($C_6H_{12}O_6$).

glume   One of the pair of bracts at the base of a grass spikelet that does not enclose flowers.

glycolysis   Anaerobic enzymatic breakdown of complex organic molecules with the release of energy.

grain   In turf, the mostly undesirable horizontal laying of grass blades in one direction, usually caused by repeated mowing in the same direction, which tends to deflect a rolling ball from a true course.

gram-negative bacteria   A negative reaction to the Gram's stain, wherein the purple dye washes out and the cells stain red.

gram-positive bacteria   A positive reaction to the Gram's stain, wherein the cells retain the purple dye.

gravitational water   Water movement through soil due to gravity.

green   Putting surface of a golf course.

grooving   Turf cultivation method utilizing vertical, rotating blades that cut shallow slits through the turf and into the soil.

groundwater   Subsurface water in the zone of saturation that moves freely, and often horizontally.

growth regulator   Synthetic compound that controls plant growth responses.

grub   In biology, an insect larva; typically associated with the Coleoptera and Hymenoptera insect families.

guard cells   Pairs of specialized epidermal cells surrounding a pore or stomata that open and close in response to changes in turgor pressure.

guttation   Exudation of liquid from leaf tips caused by root pressure.

H

habit   In botany, growth form of the plant.

habitat   Natural environment where an organism grows.

half-life   Time required for half of a substance to be inactivated.

halophyte   Plant that grows in salty soil.

haploid   Having only one set of chromosomes (*n*) compared to two in diploids (*2n*).

hard water   Water containing calcium, magnesium, or ferrous ions, which forms a precipitate with soap or crusting.

haustorium (plural haustoria)   A projection of fungal hypha that penetrates and absorbs content from the host tissue.

hazard   A penalty area on a golf course that does not allow normal play, such as a bunker or water hazard.

head   A dense cluster of stalkless flowers, as in dandelion.

heat of vaporization   Quantity of heat (540 calories for water at 100°C) needed to vaporize one gram of a substance.

heavy metals   Metals with densities of 5.0 mg/m or greater and include cadmium, cobalt, chromium, copper, iron, mercury, manganese, molybdenum, lead, and zinc.

herbaceous   Nonwoody plant that may die-back to the ground in winter.

herbicide   Weed (plant)-controlling compound.

heredity   Transfer of characteristics from parents to offspring through gametes.

hole   Final target on a golf green 4.25 inch (10.8 cm) in diameter, and at least four inches (100 mm) deep.

hormone   A chemical substance produced in one part of a plant and used in minute quantities to induce a growth response in another part of the plant; often refers particularly to auxins.

host   An organism invaded by a plant parasite, which obtains its nutrients, and reproduces upon it.

hot water insoluble nitrogen (HWIN)   Insoluble nitrogen fertilizer form in hot (212°F or 100°C) water.

humate (humin)   Portion of soil organic matter that is insoluble in dilute alkali.

humic acid   Portion of humus that is water insoluble and is extracted from soil with dilute alkali and precipitated upon acidification.

humidity   *See* relative humidity.

humus   Relatively stable, dark-colored colloidal soil organic matter containing no recognizable plant parts.

hybrid   Cross between two species.

hydrated lime   Calcium hydroxide from reacting burnt lime (CaO) with water.

hydraulic conductivity   Rate of water flow in soil as imposed by a hydraulic head.

hydrolysis   Splitting of one molecule by adding water.

hydrophillic   Water-loving; attracted to water.

hydrophobic   Water-hating; not attracted to water.

hydroscopic water   Unavailable soil water tightly held by bonding (absorption) to soil particles.

hydroseeding   Planting of turf seed through a hose mixed with water and possibly fertilizer and mulch.

hydroxyl group   An OH⁻ group formed by the dissociation of a water molecule.

hypha (plural: hyphae)   Filaments of fungal cells.

hypocotyl   Stem part below the cotyledons of a seedling.

I

IAA   *See* indole-3-acetic acid.

immersed   Growing under water; submerged.

immobilization   Conversion of an element from the inorganic to organic form in microbial or plant tissues; often used to describe the conversion of nitrate or ammonium into organic forms by soil microorganisms.

imperfect flower   Flowers lacking either male or female parts; unisexual flowers.

imperfect fungi   A fungus that does not produce sexual spores.

imperfect stage   An asexual sporulating stage of a fungus.

indole-3-acetic acid (IAA)   Naturally occurring auxin, a kind of plant hormone.

inert ingredients   Portion of a formulation that is not active (or inert) but aids in dispersal, shipping, and longevity such as water, wetting agents, emulsifiers, buffers, and spreading agents.

infect   To invade or penetrate.

infiltration   Downward entry and movement of water into and through soil.

infiltration rate   Quantity (in. or cm) of water entering soil per unit time (hr.).

infiltrometer   Device used for measuring the rate of water's entry into a soil.

inflorescence   The flowering portion of a plant.

injury   Plant damage from a biotic, physical, or chemical agent.

insecticide   Insect-killing compound.

instar   Stages between insect molts or shedding of the exoskeleton.

integrated pest management (IPM)   Combining methods to control pests, such as resistant plant varieties, chemical and natural or biological pesticides, pest exclusion, and plant health management techniques.

intercalary meristem   Meristematic area at the base of each internode that accounts for stem elongation in grasses.

intermediate rough   An optional narrow (4 to 10 ft, 1.2 to 3 m) strip of turf parallel to the sides of the fairway maintained in height between the fairway and primary rough.

internode   Section of stem between two successive nodes or joints.

interseeding   Seeding into an established stand of grass.

interspecific hybrid   A cross between two different species; [e.g., Tifway (419) bermudagrass is an interspecific hybrid from a cross between a tetraploid *Cynodon dactylon* and diploid *C. transvaalensis*].

intraspecific hybrid   A cross between two plants of the same genus and species; (e.g., Princess-77 bermudagrass is an intraspecific hybrid from crossing two *Cynodon dactylon* bermudagrasses).

intravaginal growth   Shoot growth in plants that does not penetrate through the enclosing sheath.

ions   Electrically charged atoms resulting from the loss of electrons (cations) or gain of electrons (anions).

isomer   Compounds with identical atomic composition but that differ in structural arrangement; for example, glucose and fructose.

isomorphous substitution   Replacement of similar sized atoms in a soil crystal lattice.

J

joint   In turf, node of a grass stem.

K

keel   A prominent ridge, often comprised of tissue on both sides of a glume's midrib or leaf blade, for example, that has grown together.

kinetin   A purine that acts as a cytokinin in plants.

kingdom   One of seven chief taxonomic categories; for example, *Fungi* or *Plantae*.

Kranz anatomy   In C_4 plants, a wreathlike arrangement of mesophyll cells around large bundle-sheath cells, forming two concentric layers around the vascular bundle that aids in concentrating carbon dioxide needed for photosynthesis and subsequent carbohydrate formation.

L

lamella   Layer of photosynthetic, chlorophyll-containing plant membranes.

lamina   The extended flattened portion of a leaf or petal.

lanceolate   A shape longer than wide, broadest below the middle; lance-shaped.

lapping, mower   *See* backlapping.

larva   An immature stage of young insects called a caterpillar, slug, maggot, or grub.

lateral bud   A bud originating in the leaf axil, on the side of the stem.

lateral shoot   A shoot originating from vegetative buds in the axil of leaves or from the nodes of stems, rhizomes, or stolons.

layering   In soil, alternating stratification of different soil texture, that affects water movement and soil aeration.

LD$_{50}$ A measure of toxicity where the dose of product causes mortality in 50 percent of the treated test animals. Generally, the lower or smaller the LC$_{50}$ value, the more acutely toxic the product.

LDS   *See* localized dry spot.

leaching   Downward movement of soluble materials in a soil.

leaf axil   The upper angle formed between the axis of a stem and another structure, such as a leaf.

leaf bud   An emerging grass blade.

leaflet   One of the divisions of a compound leaf.

legume   Member of the pea or bean family having a dry fruit that splits open along two longitudinal sutures; pods.

lemma   Lowermost of the two bracts enclosing a grass flower; the other bract is a palea.

lesion   A wound or delimited diseased area.

lignin   Strengthening or deposition material in plant cells, along with cellulose, that tends to make them hard.

Chemically, lignin has both phenolic and alcoholic characteristics that are very resistant to decomposition by soil organisms and constitutes much of the soil's residual humus.

ligule   Projection at the inside junction of the grass leaf blade and collar, which may be membranelike or a row of hairs.

lime   Calcium oxide (CaO) and/or a variety of acid-neutralizing materials containing calcium or calcium and magnesium.

limestone   Sedimentary rock composed of more than half calcium carbonate ($CaCO_3$).

linear   A long and narrow shape with parallel margins.

liquid fertilization   Applying nutrients as dissolved fertilizer in solution.

littoral region   Shoreline area of a body of water usually composed of a ring of plants.

loam   Soil composed of 7 to 27 percent clay, 28 to 50 percent silt, and less than 52 percent sand.

lobe   A segment of a simple leaf cut rather deeply into curved or angular segments.

localized dry spot (LDS)   Soil that resists rewetting associated with thatch and/or organic acid coating of sand particles, buried debris, fairy ring fungi, or insufficient irrigation.

long-day plants   Plants that initiate flowering under long-day (short-night) regimes.

M

macronutrient   Nutrients needed in the largest amounts (usually 50 mg/kg) for plant growth (e.g., carbon, nitrogen, oxygen, potassium, magnesium, calcium, sulfur, and hydrogen).

marl   Fresh water lake deposit consisting of soft calcium carbonate mixed with clay or other impurities.

matric (or capillary) potential   How tightly water is held (or adsorbed) in soil; carries a negative (minus) sign.

matting   Process of dragging or brushing the turf surface to incorporate topdressing or disperse cores lifted from aerifying.

mat   A tan- to brown-colored tightly intermingled layer of thatch intermixed with soil.

membranous   Thin, transparent, and flexible; membranelike.

meristem   A cluster of dividing cells at the root and stem apices or tips.

mesophyll   The area of leaves between the upper and lower epidermis; the large, thin-walled cell parenchyma.

metamorphosis   In biology, a series of changes where an insect passes from an egg to an adult.

microclimate   Environmental conditions in the immediate vicinity of plants or planting groups such as a golf green; also referred to as microenvironment.

micronutrient   Elements needed in only small (usually less than 100 mg/kg) amounts for plant growth (e.g., boron, chlorine, copper, iron, manganese, and zinc).

midrib   The main or central vein or rib of a leaf or leaflet.

midvein   The primary vein.

milliequivalent   One one-thousandth of an equivalent. One equivalent is one gram hydrogen in one liter of water, while one milliequivalent is 0.001 gram (or one milligram) hydrogen in one liter of water.

mineralization   Conversion of an organic form of an element to an inorganic form (e.g., conversion of organic nitrogen to ammonium nitrogen by microbial decomposition).

mitochondrion (plural mitochondria)   A double-membrane-bounded organelle in eukaryotic cells containing the enzymes of the Krebs cycle and the electron-transport chain.

mixture   In turf, seed combination of two or more turfgrass species.

mold   Any profuse or woolly fungus growth on damp or decaying matter or on plant tissue.

mole   In chemistry, the number of particles in one mole of any substance; always equal to Avogadro's number: 6.022×10^{23}.

molecular weight   The sum of relative weights of atoms in a molecule, with carbon atoms being the reference of 12.

molecule   Smallest possible unit of a compound, consisting of two or more atoms.

monocotyledon, monocot   Grass and grasslike plants in which embryos (seedlings) have one cotyledon (seed leaf), parallel-veined leaves, inconspicuous flowers, flower parts in multiples of threes, and no secondary growth.

monoecious   Situation of the staminate (male) and the pistillate (female) flowers being in separate inflorescences but occurring on the same plant, such as corn.

mosaic   Disease symptoms composed of mixed green, light-green, and yellow patches.

moss   Small, threadlike, branched primitive plants often growing in shaded, wet turf areas.

mottle   Irregular pattern of indistinct light and dark areas; often used to characterize disease symptoms.

mower   Machine used to uniformly cut the upper shoot growth of turfgrasses.

mowing frequency   Time (usually in days) between mowing events.

muck   *See* peat.

muck soil   Soil containing 20 to 50 percent of well-decomposed organic matter.

mulch   Layer of plant residues, leaves, sand, plastic, or paper on the soil surface to level the soil surface and protect it from the effects of raindrops, freezing, evaporation, and so forth.

mutation   Changes in genetic material that produce new characteristics; often artificially induced by exposure to radioactive radiation or certain chemicals.

mycelium   Cottony strands of individual hyphae that forms the body of a fungus.

mycoplasmas   *See* phytoplasmas.

mycorrhiza   A symbiotic association of a fungus with plant roots.

N

native   In biology, indigenous species of plants or animals to a specific region.

naturalized species   Introduced species that has adapted to a specific region.

necrosis   Plant death, usually accompanied by darkening or discoloration.

nematicide   Nematode-controlling compound.

nematode   Microscopic, nonsegmented wormlike animals that may parasitize plants or animals.

nitrification   Microbial oxidation of ammonium nitrogen to nitrites and eventually to nitrates.

node   The point or level of a stem at which one or more leaves and roots are attached.

non-point-source pollution   Contamination from a general area and not from a specific site.

noxious plants   Weedy plants that are usually difficult to control or eradicate.

nursery   In turf, designated area of turf often maintained similar to a golf green used to repair or replace damaged grass.

O

obligate parasite   A parasite that requires a living organism on which to grow and multiply.

off-site mixing   Soil and amendment mixing away from the planting site.

opposite   An arrangement of paired leaves attached oppositely from each other at the same node.

oral toxicity   Degree of toxicity of a compound when ingested.

order   In biology, a category of classification between the rank of class and family; classes contain one or more orders, and orders compose one or more families.

organic fertilizer   Fertilizer derived from natural organic materials.

organic matter   Residual decomposition of plant or animal content in soil.

osmosis   Diffusion of water, or any solvent, from a region of greater water potential to one of lesser water potential across a selectively permeable membrane.

osmotic (solute) potential   Change in chemical potential (or free energy) of water produced by solutes being added to it; carries a negative (minus) sign; also called solute potential.

ovary   Lower part of the pistil containing the ovules or, later, the seed.

overseeding   Planting or seeding onto an existing turf; performed primarily to provide a temporary turf cover for green color.

oxidation   Loss of an electron by an atom or molecule; the atom or molecule that loses the electron is referred to as being oxidized. This is called oxidation since oxygen, which strongly attracts electrons, is often the electron acceptor.

oxidation-reduction reactions (or redox)   The passing of electrons from one atom or molecule to another during chemical reactions.

oxidative phosphorylation   The formation of ATP from ADP and inorganic phosphate.

P

palea   Uppermost (inner) of the two bracts enclosing the flower of a grass floret; this bract is enclosed by the largest lower bract (lemma) and is located on the side opposite the embryo.

palmate   A type of leaf where leaflets or lobes originate from a common point, and diverge like the fingers from the palm of the hand.

panicle   An inflorescence composed of several branches and sub-branches.

parasite   An organism that obtains its food from another.

particle-size distribution   Fractions of various soil separates in a soil sample.

parts per million (ppm)   Parts by weight of a compound in one million parts of the final mixture; ppm = mg/L.

pathogen   Any organism capable of causing disease by obtaining nutrition from its diseased host.

pathogenicity   Ability to cause disease.

peat   Partially decomposed organic matter accumulating under wet conditions. *Peat* refers to partially decomposed deposits while *muck* includes highly decomposed materials.

peat moss   Dried peat from various plants that is slow to decompose.

pedicel   The stalk of a simple flower or spikelet.

perched water table   Saturated zone of fine-textured soil over an underlying coarser-textured soil. Water in the saturated zone will not move into the coarse-textured soil interface until sufficient water potential builds to overcome the attraction between water and the fine-textured soil.

percolation rate   Downward movement of water through soil, especially saturated or near-saturated soil.

percolation test   Rate of water percolation in a soil profile.

perennial   A plant that normally lives for more than two years.

perfect flower   Flower with both functional pistils (female) and stamens (male); bisexual.

perfect fungus   A fungus that produces sexual spores.

pericarp   The wall of a matured ovary when it becomes a fruit.

perlite   A light, expanded soil amendment from firing volcanic rock that resists weathering but may be fragile and is used to increase soil porosity and available soil water.

permanent wilting point   Soil water content at which plants wilt and do not recover; often considered to be the soil water content at −1.5 MPa (−15 bars) water potential.

pesticide   Compound designed to kill pests or render them harmless.

petal   An inner floral leaf that makes up a flower's corolla, which is generally colored or white.

petiole   The stalk or stem of a leaf.

pH   Degree of acidity or alkalinity; defined as the negative logarithm of hydrogen ion activity. A scale of 0 to 14 is used where 7 is neutral, <7 is increasingly acidic, and >7 is increasingly basic (or alkaline).

phenolics   Compounds with a hydroxyl group (−OH) attached to an aromatic ring (a ring of six carbons containing three double bonds); includes flavonoids, lignins, salicylic acid, and tannins.

phloem   Food-conducting tissue of plants.

photorespiration   Consumption of oxygen and release of carbon dioxide when the enzyme Rubisco binds oxygen instead of carbon dioxide.

photosynthesis   Process of converting water and carbon dioxide by chlorophyll into sugars, starches, and oxygen, using energy from sunlight.

phototropism   Plant growth response to light.

phytochrome   Bluish photoreversible protein pigment responsible for the photoperiodic control of flowering and seed germination.

phytoplasmas   Microorganisms that lack an organized and bounded nucleus (like bacteria) but also lack a true cell wall or the ability to form one (unlike bacteria); formally called *mycoplasmas*.

phytotoxicity   Plant injury from a chemical.

pistil   Female flower composed of stigma, style, and ovary, and formed from one or more carpels.

pith   The central soft tissue of a stem.

plant growth regulator (PGR)   Applied substance that controls or modifies plant growth.

plugging   Vegetative propagation of turf using plugs or small sod pieces.

point-source pollution   Pollution from a known, identifiable source such as a spill, smokestack, or discharge from a pipe.

poling   In turf, the process of using a long pole to mechanically break-up dew on plants, clipping clumps, or earthworm castings.

polyacrylamide gels   A synthetic polymer used as a soil amendment due to its ability to hold water.

polyploid   Containing more than two complete sets of chromosomes.

pore space (soil porosity; void space)   Pore portion of soil bulk volume occupied by air or water.

porosity   Ratio percentage of pores (or voids) to total volume of solids.

postemergence (POST)   Weed control after seedling emergence.

preemergence (PRE)   Weed control before seedling emergence.

pressure potential   Pressure that develops in cell walls due to its contents; also called turgor potential.

preventative   Fungicides applied prior to anticipated disease incidence.

primary root   The first root of the plant; the taproot.

primary rough   Rough area immediately adjacent to the intermediate rough (if present) or fairway where errant balls often land and that is maintained between the levels of the fairway and more distant secondary rough.

prokaryote   Simple organism without nuclear material enclosed in a nuclear membrane such as actinomycetes, bacteria, and cyanobacteria.

prostrate   Parallel to or lying flat on the ground.

protoplasm   Living substance in plant or animal cells.

pubescent   Covered with hairs.

puffiness   Spongelike characteristic of turf, usually from excessive thatch, causing inferior smoothness and scalping.

pure live seed (PLS)   Percentage of germinable pure seed in a seed lot. Mathematically, it is the percent germination multiplied by the percent pure seed, which is then divided by 100.

R

raceme   An elongated inflorescence with each flower on individual stalks.

reduction (redox)   Gain of an electron by an atom or molecule.

reel mower   Mower with a vertically mounted rotating reel (or blade) that cuts against a stationary bed knife.

registered seed   A class of certified seed produced from foundation seed and planted to produce certified (or blue-tag) seed. It is identified by a purple tag.

relative humidity (RH)   Ratio (expressed as a percentage) of water vapor in the atmosphere to the greatest possible quantity at the same temperature.

remediation   Correcting, restoring, or eliminating a contaminated or polluted soil.

renovation   To renew; make over; repair.

residual sodium carbonate (RSC)   Measurement of irrigation water to determine whether sodium in it will cause soil structure problems from the potential precipitation of calcium and magnesium ions.

resistance   Ability of an organism to overcome the effect of a normally phytotoxic material or pathogen.

respiration   Intracellular process in which molecules are oxidized with the release of energy.

restricted-use pesticide   A pesticide that can be purchased and used only by certified applicators to avoid adverse health or environmental effects.

rhizome   A creeping, horizontal underground stem, producing shoots above ground and roots below; distinguished from a root by the presence of nodes, buds, or scalelike leaves; may originate from the main stem or from tillers.

rhizosphere   Soil immediately adjacent to plant roots containing microorganisms that may differ from those in the general bulk soil.

ribonucleic acid (RNA)   Type of nucleic acid formed on chromosomal DNA and involved in protein synthesis.

rippling   Wave or washboard turf pattern from mower misadjustment, excessive mower speed, or too slow cutting frequency for the cutting height.

riprap   Placing broken rock, cobbles, or boulders on slopes to prevent soil erosion.

roguing   In turf, hand removing of undesirable plants.

rolled   Cylindrical arrangement of the youngest leaf in the bud shoot.

rolling   In golf, use of a mechanical roller on greens to smooth the playing surface or increase ball roll.

root   Subterranean portion of a plant used for anchorage, aeration, and absorption.

rosette   Circular cluster of leaves usually appressed to or located near the ground level.

rotary mower   A mower with a horizontal, rapidly rotating impact blade.

rough   In golf, the area surrounding fairways maintained with taller grass. Consists of intermediate rough (if present), primary rough, and secondary rough.

row sprigging   Planting turf sprigs in rows or furrows.

RSC   *See* residual sodium carbonate.

rudimentary   Small, often incompletely developed.

runner   A slender stolon (or horizontal stem).

rust   In turf, orange- or rust-colored disease, caused by one of the Uredinales (rust fungi).

S

saline-sodic soil   Soil with enough soluble salts (>4 dS/m) and exchangeable sodium (>15%) to impair its productivity.

saline soil   Soil with enough soluble salts (>4 dS/m) to impair its productivity.

salt   Compound containing positive ions from a base and negative ions from an acid, or that results from direct combination of metal and nonmetal (e.g., NaCl breaks up into Na^+ and Cl^- in water).

sand   A soil textural class consisting of particles between 0.05 and 2.0 millimeters in diameter.

saprophyte   Organism feeding on dead or decaying organic matter.

SAR   *See* sodium adsorption ratio.

saturate   Completely soak.

scald   In turf, turfgrass collapse when exposed to conditions of standing water and intense light.

scalping   In turf, excessive low mowing of plant leaf tissue, leaving brown stems, clippings, and exposed soil.

scum   In turf, a thin, slippery layer of algae on the turf surface, usually from excessive moisture and insufficient light and drainage that impedes healthy turf growth.

scutellum   A shield-shaped organ of grass embryos.

secondary rough   Rough farthest away from the fairway, normally maintained at the tallest heights.

seed   A ripened ovule.

seedbed   Soil preparation that supports seed germination and seedling growth.

seedhead   A collection of flowers clustered upon a main stem; refers as used here to the inflorescence of the grasses, sedges, and rushes.

seeding   To sow (plant) with seeds.

seedling   A young plant.

selective herbicide   A chemical that controls one plant species within another.

semiarid turfgrass   Turfgrass adapted to low-rainfall, semiarid regions; includes buffalograss, bluegrama, wheatgrass, and sideoats grama.

seminal root   Root arising from the base of the hypocotyl.

sepal   A part of a flower that is usually petal-like in appearance and green in color.

serrate   A type of leaf margin with sharp teeth pointing forward; saw-toothed.

sessile   Without a petiole, stem, or stalk; usually refers to a leaf being attached directly on the axis or stem of a plant.

sewage sludge   Settled sewage solids removed by screening, sedimentation, chemical precipitation, or bacterial digestion.

shattering   Turf cultivation method involving fragmentation of a rigid or brittle soil mass, usually by a vibrating tine or mole device.

sheath   The lower portion of a leaf that encircles the stem.

shoot   In botany, a general term for the aboveground portion of a plant.

short-day plants   Plants that initiate flowering best under short-day (long-night) regimes.

sign   In biology, visible pathogen or its parts or products on a host plant.

silt   A soil textural class consisting of fine particles between 0.05 and 0.002 millimeters in diameter.

simple   A type of leaf consisting of a blade not divided into individual leaflets; unbranched.

slag   A byproduct of smelting, containing mostly silicates that may be suitable as a nutrient source.

slicing   A turf cultivation procedure where vertically positioned blades rotate into the turf, providing a slicing or cutting action of stolons, rhizomes, and thatch.

slime molds   Fungi in the class Myxomycetes; also, superficial diseases caused by these fungi on low-lying plants.

slit drain   A narrow trench backfilled with a porous medium, such as sand or gravel, used to intercept surface or lateral subsurface drainage water; also called *French drain.*

slit seeding   The process of using vertically mounted knives or blades to cut slits in the turf, followed by seeding and rolling to increase seed-to-soil contact with minimum surface disruption.

slow-release (water-insoluble) fertilizer   Fertilizer source designed to control its nutrient release rate.

smooth   Lacking hairs, divisions, or teeth; not rough to the touch.

smut   Black, smooty-colored disease caused by the smut fungi (Ustilaginales).

sod   Vegetative planting material consisting of turfgrass strips with or without adhering soil.

sod strength   Ability of sod to resist tearing during harvesting and handling.

sodic soil   A nonsaline soil with sufficient sodium (exchangeable sodium percentage of ≥15 or sodium adsorption ratio of ≥13), a pH from 8.5 to 10, and dispersed soil colloids to reduce permeability.

sodium adsorption ratio (SAR)   Relative hazard of irrigation water from its sodium content relative to its amount of calcium and magnesium, measured as millimoles of charge per liter (mmol/L).

soil   Upper layer of earth surface used as the natural medium for plant growth.

soil conditioner   Any material added to a soil to improve its physical properties.

soil mix   Prepared mixture of soil or sand plus amendments used as a growth medium.

soil modification   Artificial altering of soil by adding soil amendments to improve physical conditions of turf soils.

soil test   Chemical, physical, or microbiological property of a soil.

soil texture   Relative soil coarseness or fineness as determined by its proportions of sand, silt, and clay.

solute   A molecule dissolved in a solution.

solute potential   *See* osmotic potential.

species   A group of individuals having certain distinctive characteristics in common.

spike   In plants, an unbranched inflorescence with the spikelets sessile (stalkless) on a rachis.

spikelet   The basic individual unit of the spike of grasses and some sedges; composed of one or more flowers and their subtending bracts (two glumes and one or more florets).

spiking   A turf cultivation procedure where solid tines or spoons penetrate into the turf and soil surface.

sprig   A single turfgrass unit containing viable stolons, rhizomes, or tillers and roots, used for establishment.

sprigging   Vegetative establishment by placing stolons, rhizomes, or tillers (with roots) into furrows.

spring green-up   Initial growth of green shoots in spring.

stalk   Any slender supporting structure such as a petiole for a leaf, a peduncle for an inflorescence, or a pedicel for a flower.

stamen   The male or pollen-bearing organ of a flowering plant consisting of the filament (stalk) and the anther.

starch   Complex insoluble principal food storage substance of plants consisting of glucose units forming polysaccharides.

stem   Plant organ for support, leaf production, food storage, and limited food production.

sterile   Without seeds or pollen.

stigma   Upper feathery part of the female flower pistil that receives pollen.

stimpmeter   Device used on golf greens to measure ball roll distance and putting surface uniformity.

stipule   Bract-like appendages at the base of some leaves.

Stokes' law   Equation used to determine soil texture from the settling rates of suspended sands, silts, and clay based on the diameter of the particle and viscosity of the suspension medium.

stolon   A creeping, aboveground stem that roots at the nodes.

stolonize   Vegetative establishment method of broadcasting stolons over a prepared soil and covering with topdressing or press rolling.

stomate (plural: stomata) A small porelike opening in the leaf or stem epidermis through which gas exchange occurs.

strain Descendants of an isolated organism; biotype; race.

stroma Soluble environment of chloroplasts.

style The stalk that connects the stigma to the ovary in flowers.

subgrade Soil elevation beneath the final grade that allows subsequent placement of topsoil to achieve the final grade.

subsoil Soil below the plow layer.

subspecies Subdivision of a species.

succulent Soft and fleshy.

sucker A plant shoot that arises from an adventitious bud on a root.

summer annual A plant that germinates in spring, grows and flowers in summer, and sets seed in fall, after which it dies.

summer dormancy Cessation of growth of perennial plants due to heat and/or moisture stress.

surfactant A material that improves the emulsifying, dispersing, spreading, or wettting properties of liquids.

swing joint Piping configuration that flexes to protect irrigation heads and lines from traffic.

symptom Visual reactions by a plant indicating disease presence.

syringing In turf, the light application of moisture to reduce surface temperatures, prevent wilt, and remove dew, frost, and exudates.

systemic Compounds that enter and move (translocate) throughout plants.

T

taproot A single enlarged vertical main root lacking major divisions.

tee In golf, the area on each hole where play begins.

tee-marker A movable device that indicates where golf play begins on each hole.

terminal bud Bud located at the end or apex of a stem or branch.

texture In turf, blade leaf width and arrangement.

thatch Brown- to black-colored layer of dead leaves, stems, rhizomes, crowns, and stolons between the green vegetation and soil surface.

thermal stratification Layering in bodies of water due to temperature differences. *Epilimnion* is an upper layer of warm water while *hypolimnion* is a lower layer of cold or cooler water. *Thermocline* is the dividing line between the two layers.

three-ranked Diverging from the stem in three directions, as in the sedge family.

thylakoid Sac-like membranous structures in chloroplasts that contain chlorophyll and stack to form grana.

tiller Grass shoot, usually erect, originating intravaginally (grows upward within the enclosing leaf sheath) from axillary buds in the axis of a leaf or in the unelongated crown portion of a stem.

tipburn Leaf-tip necrosis from desiccation, mower, temperature, or pesticide damage.

toothed Sawteeth-like projections (or "teeth") on the margins of leaves.

topdressing In turf, addition of a thin layer of soil, sand, or fertilizer following plant establishment.

topsoil Uppermost layer of soil.

total dissolved salts (TDS) Sum of all dissolved solids in a water or wastewater, normally reported as parts per million (ppm).

transition zone In turf, the area or zone between warm (subtropical) and cool (temperate) regions where both warm-season and cool-season turf species grow but is not optimal for either.

transpiration Water vapor loss from plants, primarily through leaf stomata.

trifoliate A type of compound leaf composed of three leaflets.

triploid Having three complete chromosome sets per cell ($3n$).

tuber Thickened storage portion of a rhizome or stolon (stem), bearing nodes and buds.

tufted In compact clusters, forming clumps.

turf Uniform ground covering of mowed vegetation, usually a turfgrass.

turfgrass Grass species or cultivar maintained as a uniform mowed vegetation.

turgor pressure Cell pressure from the movement of water into it.

two-ranked In two vertical rows on opposite sides of a stem or axis, as in the grass family.

U

ubiquitous Occurring everywhere.

V

variety A distinguishing, stable subdivision of a plant species.

vein Ribs of a leaf; one of the vascular bundles of a leaf.

verdure Green plant tissue remaining following mowing.

vernalization Flowering induction from cold treatment or exposure.

vernation Arrangement of the youngest leaf in the bud shoot; either rolled or folded.

vertebrate An organism with a backbone or spinal column.

vertical mowing Slicing turf with a series of vertically mounted blades rotating on a shaft, usually to reduce thatch; also called *verticutting*.

virus Infectious microscopic agents consisting of a protein sheath surrounding a nucleic acid core that is totally dependent on living cells (obligate parasite).

W

warm-season grass C_4 grass with optimum growth between temperatures of 80 and 95°F (27 to 35°C).

washboard effect   *See* rippling.

waste area   Large nonturfed area not routinely raked that is not a hazard.

water hammer   Shock waves in pipelines from water surges.

water potential   The potential (or gradient) energy of water measured as the sum of matric, osmotic, and pressure potential; it is a negative value, and as the value is more negative, lower water potential occurs.

water table   Top level of permanent groundwater zone.

weed   A plant growing out of place or where it is not wanted.

wetland   Land area that floods for part of the year, supports vegetation adapted to wet conditions (called *hydrophytes*), has unique soil conditions that differ from adjacent uplands, and forms a transition zone between aquatic and terrestrial systems; generally includes swamps, marshes, bogs, and similar areas.

wetting agent   Substance that reduces surface tension and causes liquids to make better contact with treated surfaces.

wet wilt   Turf wilting in the presence of water when evaporation exceeds root water uptake.

white grub   C-shaped, whitish larvae of insects in the family Scarabaeidae.

whorl   In botany, a cluster of leaves around a stem.

wilt   Plant collapse usually when evapotranspiration exceeds water uptake by roots.

winter annual   A plant that germinates in late summer, grows vegetatively during winter, and flowers and sets seed in late spring to early summer, after which it dies.

winter desiccation   Plant death from drying during winter dormancy.

winter feeding (or fertilization)   Late autumn application of fertilizer to cool-season grasses to maintain green color without adverse effects.

winter kill   Injury to plants during winter; most often from desiccation plus low temperatures.

witches' broom   An abnormal brush- or broom-like growth of weak, tightly clustered plant shoots.

woody   Consisting or composed of wood or wood-like tissue.

X

xanthophyll   A yellow chloroplast-located pigment that is a member of the carotenoids.

xerophytes   Plants that grow in extremely dry habitats.

xylem   Water-conducting tissue of a plant's vascular system.

Z

zeatin   A natural cytokinin plant hormone isolated from maize.

zeolite   A mined soil mineral used as a soil amendment to improve water- and nutrient-holding capacity. It is also used in water softening by replacing calcium ions with sodium.

zygote   A fertilized egg.

INDEX

chlorinated organics, 613
chlorinated synthetics, 613
chlorine, 309, 396
chloronicotinyls/neonicotinoids, 613
chlorophyll, 8, 10, 64
Chlorophyllum, 575–577
chloropolasts, 61, 62, 69
chlorosis, 286
chlorsulfuron (Telar 75DG), 710
choker layer, alternatives to, 230
C horizon, 98
citric acid cycle, 72–73
clay
    CEC value, 101–102
    modifications during construction, 203–205
    types of, 128
clay loams, types of, 128
cleistothecia, 582
climatic zones, 18–20, 50
clubhouse, site selection for, 186
coefficient of uniformity (irrigation system), 311
cohesion (water in soil), 135–136, 358
cold water insoluble nitrogen (CWIN), 294
cold water soluble nitrogen (CWSN), 294
coleoptile, 8
coleorhiza, 8
collar region of grasses, 10
    construction, 248–249
    construction of, 248–249
Colletotrichum graminicola (Ces.) Wils, 560, 564, 568
Colletotrichum graminicola (Wes.) Wils, 568
colloidal phosphate, 241, 242
colloids, 98
colonial bentgrass (*Agrostis tenius*), 16, 37–40, 46
color of turfgrass, 6, 286, 360, 669
combing, greens and, 460
common name, 717
    of herbicides, 701–703
    of plant growth regulators (PGRs), 707–708
composts, 241
concrete sand, 129
contact fungicides, 556–557
cool arid zone, 19
cool humid zone, 18–19, 50
cool-season grasses, 37–51, 685–686
copper, 98–99, 309
copper spot, 573–574
coring/core aerification. *See* aerification
corn gluten meal, 676–677
CoRoN (fertilizer), 314
corrugated pipe drains, 157–158
creeping bentgrass (*Agrostis palustris*), 16, 37–39, 46
crested wheatgrass (*Agropyron cristatum*), 16, 46, 56–57
crop coefficient, 364
crop oils, 725
cross-resistance (fungicide), 558
crown hydration, 75–76
crowns, 7, 8–9, 11
culm, 9, 11
cultivars (CULTivated VARieties), 5, 20–57
    bermudagrass, 20–26
    zoysiagrass, 31
    See also names of specific turfgrasses
curative/eradicants, chemical control
    practices, 555

curvularia blight (*Curvalaria geniculata*), 597
cuticle, 10
cutworms, 620–621
cyanobacteria, 593
Cynodon. See bermudagrass (*Cynodon*)
cytokinesis, 93
cytokinins (growth hormone), 91, 92, 93

D

dagger nematodes, 655
Dallisgrass (*Paspalum dilatum*), herbicide control, 694
Darcy's equation, 812–813
Darcy's Law, 135, 137, 812–813
day-neutral plants, 17
dazomet, 672
dead spot, 597–598
degradation, 747–748
denitrification, 176, 285
density, organic matter and, 237
density of turfgrass, 6
desalination, 404
desiccation
    from heat exposure/stress, 87
    for low-temperatures, 77
design uniformity (irrigation system), 311
diaphragm pumps, 780–782
dicots (dicotyledonous plants), 6–8, 664
diflocculation, 108
Digitaria dactyloides (blue couch), 37
dihydropteroate (DHP) synthase inhibitors, 670
dilutions, of pesticde formulations, 778–779
Diodia virginiana (Virginia buttonweed), herbicide control, 698
direct low-temperature exposure/"chilling" injury, 76–77
disease. *See* turfgrass diseases
dispersion, 108
distillation, 404
distribution uniformity (DU), of irrigation systems, 367, 369–370
dithiopyr (Dimension), 689
dollar spot, 574–575
dolomite, 115
dolomitic limestone, 115
double cutting, bermudagrass and, 527–528
downy mildew, 597
drainage
    design during construction, 192–193
    gravel size in, 149–150
    greens construction and, 216–217, 222–230
    methods of, 140–162
    multiple layered systems, 155–156
    rate calculation, 153–155
    retention facilities for, 193
    subsurface, 144–162, 194–195
    sump and pump for, 195
    surface, 141–144, 194
    turfgrass maintenance and, 80
drains
    depth of, 144
    French, 159–160, 197
    interceptor, 142–144
    line patterns of, 161, 196
    line spacing, 150–152, 195, 222
    line trenches, 161–162, 196, 224–225
    line types, 157–161, 195, 223–224
    pipe sizing, 144, 156

Drechslera, 579–581
drift, and pesticide applications, 745–746
drop-type (gravity) spreader calibration, 783–784
drought resistance, 366
dry spots, 436–437
dune sand, 129

E

earthworms, 648
ectoparasites, 649
edaphic (fairy ring), 576
effective calcium carbonate (ECC), 117–118
effluent wastewater
    characteristics of, 412–420
    EPA guidelines, 413–414
    heavy metal concentrations, 417
    irrigation system design, 419
    for irrigation use, 409–420
    nutrient content, 415–416
    primary treatment, 410–411
    secondary treatment, 411
    storage ponds, 417–418
    sulfur concentrations, 416
    tertiary treatment, 411, 412
    total suspended solid (TSS), 412
E horizon, 98
electrical conductivity (EC), 383
electrical conductivity (ECe), 387
electrical conductivity (ECw), 381–383, 385
electrodialysis, 405, 406
electron transport chain, 65, 67, 72, 73
elemental sulfur, 121–123
Eleusine indica (goosegrass), herbicide control, 694
Emergency Planning and Community Right-to-Know Act (EPCRA), 735
emulsifiers, 724
endangered species protection, 752–753
endoparasites, 649
endophytes, insect control and, 604
endosperm, 8
enhanced biodegradation, 176
enhanced microbial degradation, insect control and, 612
environmental factors
    air quality/atmosphere and pesticide use, 744–746
    erosion control during construction and, 188
    in golf course property selection, 185
    and grass leaf appearance, 10
    pesticides and nutrients and, 743–753
    for pesticide storage, 728–729
    for turfgrass maintenance, 352
    water quality and pesticide use, 748–751
environmental protection, 743–769
    of endangered species, 752–753
    golf course construction, 188, 755–756
    golf course design, 753–755
    and golf course management, 756–769
    golf course management summary checklist, 765–769
    of groundwater, 751–752
environmental stresses, 73–94
epidermis, 10
equipment manager, 805
equipment operator, 807–808
equivalent weight, 104–107
Eragrostis (lovegrass), 56

property selection, in golf course construction, 182–186
protoporphyrinogen oxidase (Protox) inhibitors, 670
protozoa, 173
pseudothecia, 598
psychrophilic, 591
Puccinella distans (weeping alkaligrass), 49, 57
Puccinia graminis, 586
pumice, as soil amendment, 241, 242
pupation (insects), 600
pure live seed (PLS), 256
Pyriculariagrisea (Cke.) Sacc., 578–579
pyruvate, 72
Pythium aphanidermatum (Edson) Fitzpatrick, 582–584
Pythium aristosporum Vanterpool, 584–585
Pythium arrhenomanes Drechs, 582–584
pythium blight, 582–584
Pythium myriotylum Drechs, 582–584
Pythium ultimum Trow, 582–584

Q

quantum, 63
quicklime, 115

R

racemes (seedhead), 14, 17
radicle, 8
rapid blight, 598
ratings of golf courses, 4
ratios (element), 520
reactive layer coating, 293
reactive oxygen species, 66
reclaimed water. *See* effluent wastewater
red fescue (*F. rubra* L.), 16, 42, 43, 46, 472
redox potential, 165–166
red thread, 585–586
reduction, 165–166
reel mowers, 429–431
registered seed, 255
regulatory issues, fertigation and, 317
relative humidity, 354, 365
reproduction, turfgrass disease cycle, 549
residual sodium carbonate (RSC), 388–389
respiration, 59, 60, 72–73
restricted-use pesticides, 718, 719–720
retention curve, 134
reverse osmosis, 405
Rhizoctonia cerealis Van der Hoeven, 572–573
rhizoctonia leaf and sheath spot, 571–572
Rhizoctonia oryzae Ryker & Gooch, 571–572
Rhizoctonia solani Kuhn, 570–571
Rhizoctonia zeae Voorhees, 571–572
rhizomes, 7, 8, 11
rimsulfuron (TranXit), 689
ring nematodes, 652–653
riparian zones, 762–763
river sand, 129
roller pumps, 780–782
rolling
    bentgrass/*Poa annua* greens, 502
    greens, for putting speed, 461–462
root cap, 12
root growth, and mowing height, 426
root-knot nematodes, 653–654
roots/root systems of grasses, 8, 12–14

depth of and water potential, 359–360
factors influencing, 13
life expectancy, 12
root-to-shoot ratio, 14
root-to-shoot ratio, 14
rootzone installation, in greens, 243–248
rootzone mix. *See* soil
rotary (centrifugal) spreader calibration, 784–786
rotary mowers, 431–433
rough grading, in course construction, 190–191
roughs
    bermudagrass, 22–24
    common seed mixtures for, 50
    fertilization program for, 324–325
    mowing height recommendations, 425
    typical size of, 3
    zyosiagrass, 31–32
roughstalk bluegrass (*Poa trivialis*), 16, 696
row planting, 265
RSC. *See* residual sodium carbonate (RSC)
Rubisco (RuBP carboxylase/oxygenase), 66, 69
rushes, 664–665
rust, 586
ryegrass (*Lolium*), 5
    annual (*L. multiflorum*), 16, 45, 471–472
    intermediate (*L. hybridum*), 472
    perennial (*L. perenne*), 16, 42, 46, 48, 471

S

saline-sodic soils, 386–387
saline soils, 380, 383, 386–387
salinity, 89–91, 380–388, 397, 496–497
salt index, 298
salts. *See* salinity
salt tolerance, 89–91, 398
sand
    in bunkers, 249–250
    CEC value, 100–101
    classes of, 128
    in greens construction, 230–231
    shape and composition of, 230–233
sandbur/sandspur (*Cenchrus* sp.), herbicide control, 696
sand dune grasses, 57
sandy soil, modifications during construction, 203
SAR. *See* sodium adsorption ratio (SAR)
saturated, 133
saturated hydraulic conductivity, 137
sawdust, 240
scalding, 87
scalping (mowing), 428
schlerenchyma cells (leaf), 63
Sclerophthora macrospora (Sacc.)Thirum, 597
sclerotia, 547
    in turfgrass disease cycle, 550
Sclerotinia homoeocarpa F. T. Bennett, 574–575
Sclerotium rolfsii Sacc., 587–588
scouts
    insect detection techniques, 539–542
    pest control, 536, 602
scutellum, 8
seashore paspalum (*Paspalum vaginatum* Swartz.), 34–37
    advantages of, 35
    characteristics of, 47
    disadvantages of, 35–37
    morphology, 15

range of use in U.S., 35
seaweed extract, 94
secondary grass roots, 8, 12
secondary nutrients (turfgrass), 279–281, 303–306
sedentary parasites, 649
sedges, 664–665
    broomsedge (*Andropogon virginicus* L.), 55–56
    characteristics of, 665
    herbicide control, 698–700
seed, 8
    certified, 255
    quality in overseeding, 475
seedbed preparation, during construction, 203–206
seed calculation, examples of, 276
seed germination (turfgrass), 254
seedhead (inflorescence), 11, 14–17
seedhead production, 705
seeding, 255–262
    germination and establishment of, 269
    methods, 261–262
    rates and times for, 258–261, 475
seed purity (turfgrass), 254, 255–256
seep, 143
seminal grass roots, 9, 12
sethoxydim (Vantage 1.0 L; Poast 1.5 L), 711
shade
    and grass leaf growth, 11
    greens turfgrasses and, 217
    and mowing height, 426
shade tolerance, 79–80
sheath (leaf), 7, 9
sheep fescue (*F. ovina* L.), 42, 43, 472
shell marl, 116
shoes, nonmetal spiked golf, 509–510
shoot development. *See* tillering
short-day plants, 17
side oats grama (*Bouteloua curtipendula*), 55, 56
silt, classes of, 128
Sisyrinchium rosulatum (annual blue-eyed grass), herbicide control, 693
slags, 116
slaked lime, 115
slicing (soil cultivation), 500–501, 521–522
slime mold, 587
slit drains, 158
slopes
    drainage, 142, 196
    in greens construction, 225–226, 244–245
slurry fertilizers, 312
smoothness of turfgrass, 6
smutgrass (*Sporobolus indicus*), herbicide control, 696
soap flush, insect detection and, 601
sodding, 266–269
sodic soils, 386–387, 388
sodium (Na)
    as a toxic ion, 394
    in cation exchange, 98–99
sodium adsorption ratio (SAR), 384–386, 415
sodium hazards, 383–388
    adjusted SAR, 385–386
    assessing the problem, 384–386
    excess sodium with soil amendments, 399
    exchangeable sodium percentage (ESP), 386–387
    irrigation water quality and, 382

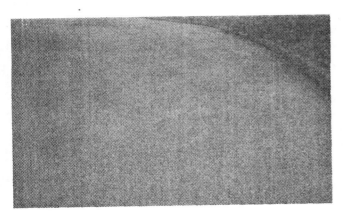

PLATE 22-69 Rapid blight (*Labyrinthula* spp.) initial symptoms include small yellow spots that enlarge quickly to one foot (0.3 m) in diameter. This disease is primarily on overseeded ryegrass or roughstalk bluegrass irrigated with water high in salts, pH, and/or bicarbonates.

PLATE 22-70 Spots of rapid blight (*Labyrinthula* spp.) appear roughly circular, with chlorotic turf in the center of patches, surrounded with a darker water-soaked appearance in the grass bordering the affected patches. No association with mycelium of true fungi has been observed.

PLATE 24-1 Nematode damage to a golf green reveals thinning, chlorotic patches of grass, especially in areas of stress such as the mower clean-up lap along the green's perimeter.

PLATE 24-2 Sting nematode damage (right) may occur on a bermudagrass fairway.

PLATE 24-3 Extensive spurge (*Chamaesyce* spp.) occurs in a fairway with high populations of sting nematodes. Spurge and other indicator weeds often invade areas with high nematodes.

PLATE 24-4 Root-knot nematode damage suffered by a bermudagrass green.

PLATE 24–5 Nematode and drought damage suffered by a golf green.

PLATE 25–1 Weeds disrupt the uniformity and function of turfgrass. They also host other pests, and certain ones can be irritants to humans. Shown is nutsedge in turf.

PLATE 25–2 Most turf weeds are either grasses, broadleaves, or sedges. Weed identification is extremely important prior to implementing control strategies. Shown is white clover, a persistent perennial weed in many turfgrass situations.

PLATE 25–3 Annual bluegrass (*Poa annua*) is a prolific seedhead producer, even when mowed at greens height, which disrupts the playing surface and reduces the turf's aesthetic value. *Poa annua* is currently the worst golf course weed in the United States due to: (1) its prolific seed production; (2) its ability to thrive in a wide array of growing conditions and mowing heights; (3) its occurrence of annual and perennial biotypes; and (4) its herbicide-resistant biotypes.

PLATE 25–4 Applying liquid charcoal can help "deactivate" certain herbicides and other misapplied organic chemicals.

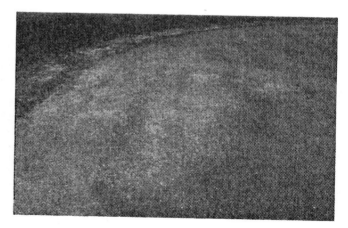

PLATE 25–5 Plant growth regulators (PGR) selectively retard the growth of one plant species within another. Shown is the use of a PGR to selectively retard bermudagrass encroachment into a creeping bentgrass green.